CRIME

IN THE UNITED STATES | 2003

Uniform Crime Reports

Printed Annually
Federal Bureau of Investigation
U.S. Department of Justice
Washington, D.C. 20535

Advisory:

Criminal Justice Information Systems Committee,

International Association of Chiefs of Police;

Criminal Justice Information Services Committee,

National Sheriffs' Association;

Criminal Justice Information Services Advisory Policy Board

For sale by Superintendent of Documents

U.S. Government Printing Office, Mail Stop: SSOP, Washington, D.C. 20402-9328

In the 1929 Foreword to *Uniform Crime Reporting: A Complete Manual for the Police*, the International Association of Chiefs of Police's Committee on Uniform Crime Reports stated, "The urgent need for national crime statistics in the United States is so well recognized as to require no debate."

That need is as great today as it was 75 years ago. Police executives, governmental officials, and others maintain an "unflagging interest in reliable compilations dealing with crime and criminals."

The Uniform Crime Reporting (UCR) Program was created by law enforcement for law enforcement, to meet the need for crime statistics used in operational planning and policymaking. Police departments and sheriff's offices rely on the data to help them support staffing decisions, allocate funding and resources, gauge the effectiveness of specific law enforcement programs, and support legislative and judicial mandates. Many local and state agencies use UCR data to support their requests to secure federal grant monies, to design new crime-fighting initiatives, or to craft anti-crime legislation.

UCR data has also become a staple for researchers and criminologists, news and information services, academics, and others seeking a better understanding of crime in the United States. Today's UCR data consumers may range from a renowned criminologist whose research will be widely quoted in the media to the president of a small-town PTA who is preparing documentation on juvenile crime to help obtain funding for after-school programs.

Initiated by the International Association of Chiefs of Police and assigned to the FBI to manage in 1930, the UCR Program has changed a great deal over the years. In order to meet the critical assignment of amassing pertinent crime statistics, the FBI is constantly reconciling the need to change and improve with the need to protect the integrity of the long-running data series upon which law enforcement and the public have come to rely. This year's *Crime in the United States* reflects some of these well-considered changes. As outlined in the Recent Developments segment of Section I, we have suspended the Crime Index and further refined the Metropolitan Statistical Area concept as part of our efforts to keep the Program vital and relevant to all of its users.

While there have been many such changes since its creation, the fundamentals of the UCR Program have remained constant. First, the UCR Program has never lost sight of its purpose: to collect accurate and pertinent crime data for the daily use of law enforcement, as well as the government and citizens of this nation. Second, the Program has always gathered its data at the grassroots level. It is the law enforcement officers who are in a position to know what crimes have been committed, the results of investigations, and the facts concerning persons arrested for these offenses. This is the source from which the UCR gathers its information.

These fundamentals, coupled with the flexibility to adapt to the needs of its users, make the UCR Program a vital part of the FBI's efforts to support our partners in law enforcement. We continue striving to improve *Crime in the United States*, and we hope that the 2003 edition will help law enforcement leaders around the country make the best possible decisions to secure safety and prosperity in their communities.

Robert S. Mueller, III
Director

Data users are cautioned against comparing crime trends presented in this report and those estimated by the National Crime Victimization Survey (NCVS), administered by the Bureau of Justice Statistics. Because of differences in methodology and crime coverage, the two programs examine the Nation's crime problem from somewhat different perspectives, and their results are not strictly comparable. The definitional and procedural differences can account for many of the apparent discrepancies in results from the two programs.

The national Uniform Crime Reporting (UCR) Program would like to hear from you.

The staff at the national UCR Program are continually striving to improve the publications. We would appreciate it if the primary user of this publication would complete the evaluation form at the end of this book and either mail it to us at the indicated address or fax it: (304) 625-5394.

Crime Factors

Each year when *Crime in the United States* is published, many entities—news media, tourism agencies, and other groups with an interest in crime in our Nation—use reported figures to compile rankings of cities and counties. These rankings, however, are merely a quick choice made by the data user; they provide no insight into the many variables that mold the crime in a particular town, city, county, state, or region. Consequently, these rankings lead to simplistic and/or incomplete analyses that often create misleading perceptions adversely affecting cities and counties, along with their residents. To assess criminality and law enforcement's response from jurisdiction to jurisdiction, one must consider many variables, some of which, while having significant impact on crime, are not readily measurable nor applicable pervasively among all locales. Geographic and demographic factors specific to each jurisdiction must be considered and applied if one is going to make an accurate and complete assessment of crime in that jurisdiction. Several sources of information are available that may assist the responsible researcher in exploring the many variables that affect crime in a particular locale. The U.S. Census Bureau data, for example, can be used to better understand the makeup of a locale's population. The transience of the population, its racial and ethnic makeup, its composition by age and gender, educational levels, and prevalent family structures are all key factors in assessing and comprehending the crime issue.

Local chambers of commerce, planning offices, or similar entities provide information regarding the economic and cultural makeup of cities and counties. Understanding a jurisdiction's industrial/economic base; its dependence upon neighboring jurisdictions; its transportation system; its economic dependence on nonresidents (such as tourists and convention attendees); its proximity to military installations, correctional facilities, etc., all contribute to accurately gauging and interpreting the crime known to and reported by law enforcement.

The strength (personnel and other resources) and the aggressiveness of a jurisdiction's law enforcement agency are also key factors. Although information pertaining to the number of sworn and civilian law enforcement employees can be found in this publication, it cannot alone be used as an assessment of the emphasis that a community places on enforcing the law. For example, one city may report more crime than a comparable one, not because there is more crime, but rather because its law enforcement agency through proactive efforts identifies more offenses. Attitudes of the citizens toward crime and their crime reporting practices, especially concerning more minor offenses, have an impact on the volume of crimes known to police.

It is incumbent upon all data users to become as well educated as possible about how to understand and quantify the nature and extent of crime in the United States and in any of the more than 17,000 jurisdictions represented by law enforcement contributors to this Program. Valid assessments are possible only with careful study and analysis of the various unique conditions affecting each local law enforcement jurisdiction.

Historically, the causes and origins of crime have been the subjects of investigation by many disciplines. Some factors that are known to affect the volume and type of crime occurring from place to place are:

- Population density and degree of urbanization.

- Variations in composition of the population, particularly youth concentration.

- Stability of population with respect to residents' mobility, commuting patterns, and transient factors.

- Modes of transportation and highway system.

- Economic conditions, including median income, poverty level, and job availability.

- Cultural factors and educational, recreational, and religious characteristics.

- Family conditions with respect to divorce and family cohesiveness.

- Climate.

- Effective strength of law enforcement agencies.

- Administrative and investigative emphases of law enforcement.

- Policies of other components of the criminal justice system (i.e., prosecutory, judicial, correctional, and probational).

- Citizens' attitudes toward crime.

- Crime reporting practices of the citizenry.

Crime in the United States provides a nationwide view of crime based on statistics contributed by local, state, tribal, and federal law enforcement agencies. Population size is the only correlate of crime presented in this publication. Although many of the listed factors equally affect the crime of a particular area, the UCR Program makes no attempt to relate them to the data presented. ***The reader is, therefore, cautioned against comparing statistical data of individual reporting units from cities, counties, metropolitan areas, states, or colleges and universities solely on the basis of their population coverage or student enrollment.*** Until data users examine all the variables that affect crime in a town, city, county, state, region, or college or university, they can make no meaningful comparisons.

Contents

Tables—Continued

Tables—Continued

Tables—Continued

Tables—Continued

SECTION I

The Uniform Crime Reporting Program is a nationwide, cooperative statistical effort of more than 17,000 city, county, and state law enforcement agencies voluntarily reporting data on crimes brought to their attention. During 2003, law enforcement agencies active in the UCR Program represented 93.0 percent of the total population. The coverage amounted to 94.9 percent of the United States population in Metropolitan Statistical Areas (MSAs), 84.8 percent of the population in cities outside metropolitan areas, and 82.8 percent in nonmetropolitan counties.

Since 1930, the FBI has administered the Uniform Crime Reporting Program and continued to assess and monitor the nature and type of crime in the Nation. The Program's primary objective is to generate reliable information for use in law enforcement administration, operation, and management; however, its data have over the years become one of the country's leading social indicators. The American public looks to the Uniform Crime Reports for information on fluctuations in the level of crime, and criminologists, sociologists, legislators, municipal planners, the media, and other students of criminal justice use the statistics for varied research and planning purposes.

Historical Background

Recognizing a need for national crime statistics, the International Association of Chiefs of Police (IACP) formed the Committee on Uniform Crime Records in the 1920s to develop a system of uniform crime statistics. Establishing offenses known to law enforcement as the appropriate measure, the Committee evaluated various crimes on the basis of their seriousness, frequency of occurrence, pervasiveness in all geographic areas of the country, and likelihood of being reported to law enforcement. After studying state criminal codes and making an evaluation of the recordkeeping practices in use, the Committee completed a plan for crime reporting that became the foundation of the UCR Program in 1929.

Seven main offense classifications, known as Part I crimes, were chosen to gauge the state of crime in the Nation. These seven offense classifications that eventually became known as the Crime Index included the violent crimes of murder and nonnegligent manslaughter, forcible rape, robbery, and aggravated assault, and the property crimes of burglary, larceny-theft, and motor vehicle theft. By congressional mandate, arson was added as the eighth Index offense category in 1979. (See Recent Developments at the end of this Summary for information on the suspension of the Crime Index.)

During the early planning of the Program, it was recognized that the differences among criminal codes precluded a mere aggregation of state statistics to arrive at a national total. Further, because of the variances in punishment for the same offenses in different state codes, no distinction between felony and misdemeanor crimes was possible. To avoid these problems and provide nationwide uniformity in crime reporting, standardized offense definitions by which law enforcement agencies were to submit data without regard for local statutes were formulated. The definitions used by the Program are set forth in Appendix II of this publication.

In January 1930, 400 cities representing 20 million inhabitants in 43 states began participating in the UCR Program. Congress enacted Title 28, Section 534, of the United States Code authorizing the Attorney General to gather crime information that same year. The Attorney General, in turn, designated the FBI to serve as the national clearinghouse for the crime data collected. Since that time, data based on uniform classifications and procedures for reporting have been obtained from the Nation's law enforcement agencies every year.

Advisory Groups

Providing vital links between local law enforcement and the FBI in the conduct of the UCR Program are the Criminal Justice Information Systems Committees of the IACP and the National Sheriffs' Association (NSA). The IACP, as it has since the Program began, represents the thousands of police departments nationwide. The NSA encourages sheriffs throughout the country to participate fully in the Program. Both committees serve in advisory capacities concerning the UCR Program's operation.

To function in an advisory capacity concerning UCR policy and to provide suggestions on UCR data usage, a Data Providers' Advisory Policy Board (APB) was established in August 1988. The Board operated until 1993 when a new Board, designed to address all FBI criminal justice information services, was approved. The Board functions in an advisory capacity concerning UCR policy and data collection and use. The UCR Subcommittee of the Board ensures continuing emphasis on UCR-related issues.

The Association of State Uniform Crime Reporting Programs (ASUCRP) and committees focus on UCR within individual state law enforcement associations and are also active in promoting interest in the UCR Program. These organizations foster widespread and more intelligent use of uniform crime statistics and lend assistance to contributors when needed.

Redesign of UCR

Although UCR data collection had originally been conceived as a tool for law enforcement administration, by the 1980s, the data were widely used by other entities involved in various forms of social planning. Recognizing the need for more detailed crime statistics, law enforcement called for a thorough evaluative study that would modernize the UCR Program. The FBI fully concurred with the need for an updated Program and lent its complete support, formulating a comprehensive three-phase redesign effort. The Bureau of Justice Statistics (BJS), the Department of Justice agency responsible for funding criminal justice information projects, agreed to underwrite the first two phases. Conducted by an independent contractor, these phases were structured to determine what, if any, changes should be made to the current Program. The third phase would involve implementation of the changes identified. Abt Associates Inc. of Cambridge, Massachusetts, overseen by the FBI, BJS, and a Steering Committee comprised of highly qualified individuals representing a myriad of disciplines, commenced the first phase in 1982.

During the first phase, the historical evolution of the UCR Program was examined. All aspects of the Program, including the objectives and intended user audience, data items, reporting mechanisms, quality control issues, publications and user services, and relationships with other criminal justice data systems, were studied.

Early in 1984, a conference on the future of UCR, held in Elkridge, Maryland, launched the second phase of the study that examined the potential of UCR and concluded with a set of recommended changes. Attendees at this conference reviewed work conducted during the first phase and discussed the recommendations that should be considered during phase two.

Findings from the evaluation's first phase and input on alternatives for the future were also major topics of discussion at the seventh National UCR Conference in July 1984. A survey of law enforcement agencies overlapped phases one and two.

Phase two ended in early 1985 with the production of a draft, *Blueprint for the Future of the Uniform Crime Reporting Program*. The study's Steering Committee reviewed the draft report at a March 1985 meeting and made various recommendations for revision. The Committee members, however, endorsed the report's concepts.

In April 1985, the phase two recommendations were presented at the eighth National UCR Conference. Various considerations for the final report were set forth, and the overall concept for the revised Program was unanimously approved. The joint IACP/NSA Committee on UCR also issued a resolution endorsing the *Blueprint*.

The final report, the *Blueprint for the Future of the Uniform Crime Reporting Program*, was released in the summer of 1985. It specifically outlined recommendations for an expanded, improved UCR Program to meet future informational needs. There were three recommended areas of enhancement to the UCR Program. First, offenses and arrests would be reported using an incident-based system. Second, data would be collected on two levels. Agencies in level one would report important details about those offenses comprising the current Crime Index, their victims, and arrestees. Law enforcement agencies covering populations of over 100,000 and a sampling of smaller agencies that would collect expanded detail on all significant offenses would be included in level two. The third proposal involved introducing a quality assurance program.

To begin implementation, the FBI awarded a contract to develop new offense definitions and data elements for the redesigned system. The work involved (a) revising the definitions of certain Index offenses, (b) identifying additional significant offenses to be reported, (c) refining definitions for both, and (d) developing data elements (incident details) for all UCR offenses in order to fulfill the requirements of incident-based reporting versus the current summary system.

Concurrent with the preparation of the data elements, the FBI studied the various state systems to select an experimental site for implementing the redesigned Program. In view of its long-standing incident-based Program and well-established staff dedicated solely to UCR, the South Carolina Law Enforcement Division (SLED) was chosen. SLED agreed to adapt its existing system to meet the requirements of the redesigned Program and collect data on both offenses and arrests relating to the newly defined offenses.

To assist SLED with the pilot project, offense definitions and data elements developed under the private contract were put at the staff's disposal. Also, FBI automated data processing personnel developed Automated Data

Capture Specifications for use in adapting the state's data processing procedures to incorporate the revised system. The BJS supplied funding to facilitate software revisions needed by the state. SLED completed its testing of the new Program in late 1987.

Following the completion of the pilot project conducted by SLED, the FBI produced a draft of guidelines for an enhanced UCR Program. Law enforcement executives from around the country were then invited to a conference in Orange Beach, Alabama, where the guidelines were presented for final review.

During the conference, three overall recommendations were passed without dissent: first, that there be established a new, incident-based national crime reporting system; second, that the FBI manage this Program; and third, that an Advisory Policy Board composed of law enforcement executives be formed to assist in directing and implementing the new Program.

Information about the redesigned UCR Program, called the National Incident-Based Reporting System, or NIBRS, is contained in three documents. *Data Collection Guidelines* contains a system overview and descriptions of the offenses, offense codes, reports, data elements, and data values used in the system. *Data Submission Specifications* is for the use of state and local systems personnel who are responsible for preparing magnetic media for submission to the FBI. *Error Message Manual* contains designations of mandatory and optional data elements, data element edits, and error messages.

A NIBRS edition of the *UCR Handbook* was published to assist law enforcement agency data contributors implementing NIBRS within their departments. This document is geared toward familiarizing local and state law enforcement personnel with the definitions, policies, and procedures of NIBRS. It does not contain the technical coding and data transmission requirements presented in the other three NIBRS publications.

NIBRS collects data on each single incident and arrest within 22 crime categories. For each offense known to police within these categories, incident, victim, property, offender, and arrestee information are gathered when available. The goal of the redesign is to modernize crime information by collecting data presently maintained in law enforcement records; the enhanced UCR Program is, therefore, a by-product of current records systems. The integrity of UCR's long-running statistical series will, of course, be maintained.

It became apparent during the development of the prototype system that the level one and level two reporting proposed in the *Blueprint* might not be the most practical approach. Many state and local law enforcement administrators indicated that the collection of data on all pertinent offenses could be handled with more ease than could the extraction of selected ones. Although "Limited" participation, equivalent to the *Blueprint's* level one, remains an option, most reporting jurisdictions, upon implementation, go immediately to "Full" participation, meeting all NIBRS' data submission requirements.

Implementation of NIBRS is occurring at a pace commensurate with the resources, abilities, and limitations of the contributing law enforcement agencies. The FBI was able to accept NIBRS data as of January 1989, and to date, the following 25 state Programs have been certified for NIBRS participation: Arkansas, Colorado, Connecticut, Delaware, Idaho, Iowa, Kansas, Kentucky, Louisiana, Maine, Massachusetts, Michigan, Nebraska, New Hampshire, North Dakota, Ohio, South Carolina, South Dakota, Tennessee, Texas, Utah, Vermont, Virginia, West Virginia, and Wisconsin. Among those that submit NIBRS data, eight states (Delaware, Idaho, Iowa, South Carolina, Tennessee, Virginia, West Virginia, and Vermont) submit all their data via NIBRS.

Twelve state Programs are in various stages of testing NIBRS. Eight other state agencies, as well as agencies in the District of Columbia, are in various stages of planning and development.

Recent Developments

Suspension of the Crime Index—In June 2004, the CJIS APB approved discontinuing the use of the Crime Index in the UCR Program and its publications and directed that the FBI publish a violent crime total and a property crime total until a more viable index is developed. The Crime Index was first published in *Crime in the United States* in 1960. However, in recent years the Crime Index has not been a true indicator of the degree of criminality. The Crime Index was simply the title used for an aggregation of the seven main offense classifications, known as Part I crimes, for which data has been collected since the Program's implementation. The Crime Index was driven upward by the offense with the highest number, in this case larceny-theft, creating a bias against a jurisdiction with a high number of larceny-thefts, but a low number of other serious crimes such as murder and forcible rape. Currently, larceny-theft makes up nearly 60 percent of reported crime, and thus the sheer volume of those offenses overshadow more serious, but less frequently committed offenses. The CJIS Division staff have been studying the appropriateness and usefulness of the Crime Index for several years and have brought the matter before many advisory groups including the UCR Subcommittee of the CJIS Advisory Board, the ASUCRP, and a meeting of leading criminologists and sociologists hosted by the Bureau of Justice Statistics. The consensus was that the Crime Index no longer served its original purpose, that the UCR Program should suspend its use, and that a more robust index should be developed.

Creation of New Statistical Compilation Areas—The UCR Program began publishing data aggregated into metropolitan areas in 1958. The Office of Management and Budget (OMB) criteria for metropolitan areas undergoes minor revisions with each decennial Census. Prior to the 2000 Census, the qualifying standards for a Metropolitan Statistical Area (MSA) included a combination of commuting data, population density data, and some indication as to major industry for the county to be considered metropolitan. Following the 2000 Census, the OMB bases its metropolitan designation solely on the journey-to-work information collected in the decennial Census. The OMB's current definition of an MSA is "a Core Based Statistical Area associated with at least one urbanized area that has a population of at least 50,000. The Metropolitan Statistical Area comprises the central county or counties containing the core, plus adjacent outlying counties having a high degree of social and economic integration with the central county as measured through commuting." (Fed. Reg. 65(249): 82238). Based on the revised standards for defining MSAs, the UCR Program now refers to suburban counties as metropolitan counties, rural counties as nonmetropolitan counties, and central cities as principal cities. The Program will continue to use the current designations for suburban areas and cities outside of metropolitan areas. In addition, this publication now includes Metropolitan Division, subdivisions of an MSA that consist of "a core with a population of at least 2.5 million. A Metropolitan Division consists of one or more main/secondary counties that represent an employment center or centers, plus adjacent counties associated with the main county or counties thought commuting ties," (Fed. Reg. 65(249): 82238).

Quality Assurance Review—Effective October 1, 2003, the CJIS Audit Unit included the Quality Assurance Reviews (QARs) in the triennial audit of all systems managed by the FBI's CJIS Division. As approved on by the CJIS Advisory Policy Board, each state Program is subject to a QAR every three years. Agencies interested in participating in a QAR should contact their state's UCR Program manager for more details.

NIBRS—The detailed, accurate, and meaningful data produced by NIBRS benefit local agencies. Armed with comprehensive crime data, local agencies can better make their case to acquire and effectively allocate the resources needed to fight crime. Currently, 5,271 law enforcement agencies contribute NIBRS data to the national UCR Program. The data submitted by these agencies represent 20 percent of the U.S. population and 16 percent of the crime statistics collected by the UCR Program.

CRIME CLOCK

Every 22.8 seconds	One Violent Crime

Every 31.8 minutes	One Murder
Every 5.6 minutes	One Forcible Rape
Every 1.3 minutes	One Robbery
Every 36.8 seconds	One Aggravated Assault

Every 3.0 seconds	One Property Crime

Every 14.6 seconds	One Burglary
Every 4.5 seconds	One Larceny-theft
Every 25.0 seconds	One Motor Vehicle Theft

The Crime Clock should be viewed with care. The most aggregate representation of UCR data, it conveys the annual reported crime experience by showing a relative frequency of occurrence of Part I offenses. It should not be taken to imply a regularity in the commission of crime. The Crime Clock represents the annual ratio of crime to fixed time intervals.

SECTION II

Violent Crime

Definition

Violent crime is composed of four offenses: murder and nonnegligent manslaughter, forcible rape, robbery, and aggravated assault. According to the Uniform Crime Reporting (UCR) Program's definition, violent crimes involve force or threat of force.

Trend

Year	Number of offenses	Rate per 100,000 inhabitants
2002	1,423,677	494.4
2003	1,381,259	475.0
Percent change	-3.0	-3.9

National Volume, Trends, and Rates

An estimated 1,381,259 violent crimes were committed in the Nation in 2003. This represented a decrease of 3.0 percent from the violent crime figure from 2002. An analysis of 5- and 10-year trend data showed that the 2003 volume fell 3.1 percent when compared to violent crime data from 1999, and it dropped 25.6 percent from the estimate 10 years ago in 1994. (See Table 1, national estimates.)

As in previous years, in 2003, aggravated assault was the offense that made up the largest portion of violent crime at 62.1 percent. Robbery accounted for 29.9 percent of violent crime, and forcible rape made up 6.8 percent. Murder was the least often committed violent offense, comprising an estimated 1.2 percent of violent crime. (Based on Table 1, national estimates.)

The violent crime rate per 100,000 inhabitants (475.0) declined 3.9 percent in 2003 when compared to the previous year's rate. A comparison between violent crime rates in 2003 and 1999 (a five-year trend) disclosed a 9.2-percent drop in the rate. In 2003, there was a 33.4-percent drop in the violent crime rate per 100,000 persons in comparison to figures from 1994 (a 10-year trend). (See Table 1, national estimates.)

Figure 2.2

Violent Crime
Percent Change from 1999

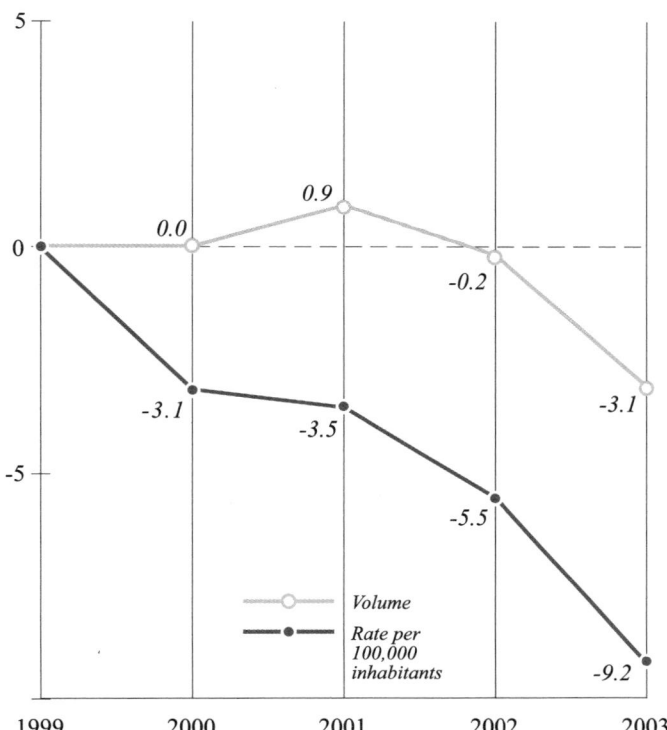

Regional Offense Trends and Rates

The UCR Program separates the United States into four regions: the Northeast, the Midwest, the South, and the West. A map of the United States outlining the regions is included in Appendix III of this book. A breakdown of offense trends and rates by region showed the following:

The Northeast

The Northeast accounted for 18.7 percent of the U.S. population in 2003. An estimated 15.8 percent of the Nation's violent crime occurred in this region. The estimated 218,106 violent crimes in the Northeast represented a 3.5-percent decline from the 2002 estimate. The violent crime rate in this region was 400.9 violent crimes per 100,000 inhabitants. This 2003 figure represented a 3.9-percent drop when compared to the figure from the previous year. Within the violent crime category, the number of murders rose 4.6 percent and that of robbery increased by 0.3 percent over figures from the previous year. The number of forcible rapes and aggravated assaults declined 2.6 percent and 6.0 percent, respectively. (See Tables 3 and 4, regional estimates.)

The Midwest

In 2003, 18.8 percent of the Nation's violent crime occurred in the Midwest, which was home to 22.5 percent of the Nation's population. The Midwest experienced an estimated 259,925 violent crimes, which is a 5.2-percent decline when compared to the 2002 figure. The violent crime rate in 2003 was 397.4 offenses per 100,000 inhabitants, a 5.7-percent decrease from the previous year's rate. All offenses within the violent crime category showed a decrease in volume in 2003; robbery presented the largest decline, 5.7 percent, followed closely by aggravated assault with a 5.4-percent drop. Forcible rape offenses fell 3.2 percent, and those of murder decreased 2.7 percent. (See Tables 3 and 4, regional estimates.)

The South

The South, with an estimated 35.9 percent of the 2003 population, was the region in which the most people lived.

It contributed the largest percent of the Nation's violent crime, 41.6. An estimated 574,226 violent crimes occurred in the South in 2003, a 2.6-percent decline in volume when compared to the 2002 estimate. In 2003, the violent crime rate was an estimated 549.3 offenses per 100,000 inhabitants, a 3.9-percent drop compared to the previous year's figure. Within the violent crime category, murder presented the lone rise in volume, up 3.0 percent from 2002 data. A comparison of 2002 and 2003 data showed the South experienced a 3.6 percent decrease in aggravated assault, a 1.6-percent decline in forcible rape, and a 0.9-percent decrease in robbery. (See Tables 3 and 4, regional estimates.)

The West

The West had 22.9 percent of the U.S. population in 2003, and 23.8 percent of violent crime occurred there. The West experienced an estimated 329,002 violent crimes, which represented a 1.4-percent decline when compared to the 2002 estimate. The violent crime rate was an estimated 495.0 violent offenses per 100,000 individuals, down 2.8 percent from the figure calculated in the previous year. Within the violent crime category, murder presented the only rise in volume, up 1.4 percent between 2002 and 2003. Robbery decreased by 1.6 percent. Aggravated assault and forcible rape offenses each declined from the previous year's calculations, 1.4 percent and 0.5 percent, respectively. (See Tables 3 and 4, regional estimates.)

Community Types

The UCR Program aggregates data by three community types: Metropolitan Statistical Areas (MSAs), cities outside metropolitan areas, and nonmetropolitan counties. MSAs are areas that include a principal city or urbanized area with at least 50,000 inhabitants and the county

that contains the principal city and other adjacent counties that have, as defined by the U.S. Census Bureau, a high degree of economic and social integration with the principal city and county as measured through commuting. In 2003, an estimated 82.8 percent of the U.S. population lived in an MSA. An estimated 1,244,205 violent crime offenses were committed in this community type. This figure represented 90.1 percent of the estimated total of violent crime. MSAs experienced a violent crime rate of 516.8 per 100,000 inhabitants in 2003. (Based on Table 2, community type estimates.)

Almost 7 percent (6.8) of the Nation's population lived in cities outside MSAs (mostly incorporated areas) in 2003. Violent crimes in this community type accounted for 5.5 percent of the estimated total number of violent offenses. In 2003, an estimated 76,043 violent crimes were committed in cities outside MSAs, which translated to a rate of 385.0 violent crimes per 100,000 inhabitants. (Based on Table 2, community type estimates.)

In 2003, an estimated 10.4 percent of the U.S. population resided in nonmetropolitan counties, which are composed of unincorporated areas. There were an estimated 61,011 violent crimes in these counties, representing 4.4 percent of the violent crime total in the Nation. Nonmetropolitan counties had a violent crime rate of 201.5 violent offenses per 100,000 persons. (Based on Table 2, community type estimates.)

Population Groups: Trends and Rates

The UCR Program organizes the agencies that contribute data by population groups. There are 6 population groups that contain cities aggregated by size, as well as a group for metropolitan coun-

Table 2.1

Violent Crime by Month
Percent Distribution, 1999-2003

Month	1999	2000	2001	2002	2003
January	8.2	7.9	7.7	7.9	7.8
February	7.1	7.2	6.7	6.8	6.5
March	7.9	8.1	7.9	7.9	8.2
April	8.1	8.1	8.1	8.1	8.3
May	8.8	8.9	8.7	8.7	8.9
June	8.5	8.6	8.7	8.8	8.8
July	9.3	9.3	9.3	9.3	9.2
August	9.1	9.1	8.9	9.3	9.2
September	8.4	8.6	8.7	9.2	8.6
October	8.6	8.7	9.0	8.6	8.8
November	8.0	7.8	8.2	7.7	7.9
December	8.0	7.7	8.1	7.7	7.7

ties and one for nonmetropolitan counties. (Appendix III of this book further delineates UCR area definitions.)

Collectively, the Nation's cities reported a 3.9-percent drop in violent crime in 2003 when compared to the previous year's data. (See Table 12.) All agencies labeled city, jointly experienced a violent crime rate of 597.0 per 100,000 inhabitants. (See Table 16.) Cities with 250,000 or more in population reported a 5.8-percent drop in violent crime. Within this population group comprised of the largest U.S. cities, the subcategory of cities with 1 million and over in population had the largest decline in violent crime, 6.5 percent. Violent crime decreased 3.7 percent in nonmetropolitan counties and 1.0 percent in metropolitan counties. (See Table 12.)

The population group with the largest U.S. cities, those with more than 250,000 in population, reported a violent crime rate of 967.5 violent offenses per 100,000 inhabitants. Within this group, the highest violent crime rate per 100,000 inhabitants, 980.0, was reported by law enforcement in those cities with 1 million or more in population. The lowest violent crime rate for city population groups (321.3 per 100,000 persons) was in cities with a population range of 10,000 to 24,999. Metropolitan counties experienced a violent crime rate of 345.8 per 100,000 inhabitants, and nonmetropolitan counties recorded a rate of 219.5 per 100,000 persons. (See Table 16.)

In 2003, the percentage of murders in the Nation's largest cities, those with 250,000 or more inhabitants, remained virtually unchanged from the 2002 number (+0.1 percent). However, within this population group, law enforcement in cities within the population subcategory of 500,000 to 999,999 inhabitants reported the largest decline in the occurrence of murder, 1.0 percent. Conversely, the Nation's smallest cities,

those with fewer than 10,000 inhabitants, experienced the largest increase in murder, 20.0 percent. (See Table 12.)

Weapons Distribution

The UCR Program collects information about the weapons used in the violent crimes murder, robbery, and aggravated assault. In 2003, most of these violent crimes, 30.7 percent, were committed with personal weapons (hands, fists, feet, etc.). Firearms were the weapon of choice in 26.9 percent of these offenses. Knives or cutting instruments accounted for 15.2 percent of the weapons used in these three violent crimes, and other weapons were employed in 27.3 percent of these offenses. (Based on Tables 2.10 and 19.)

Clearances

Law enforcement agencies reporting offenses to the national UCR Program can clear these offenses by either arrest or by exceptional means. When clearing an offense by arrest, an offender must be arrested, charged with the commission of an offense, and turned over to the court for prosecution. When a factor beyond law enforcement's control prevents the agency from placing formal charges against the known offender, the agency can clear the offense exceptionally.

In 2003, law enforcement cleared 46.5 percent of all violent crimes in the United States by arrest or exceptional means. In the violent crime category, 62.4 percent of murders were cleared, making it the violent offense most often cleared. Additionally, 55.9 percent of aggravated assaults, 44.0 percent of forcible rapes, and 26.3 percent of robberies were cleared. (See Table 25.)

Within population groups, law enforcement in cities collectively cleared 44.7 percent of violent crimes, with law enforcement in the smallest cities (under

10,000 in population) reporting the highest percentage of offenses cleared, 57.6 percent. Agencies in nonmetropolitan counties cleared 59.9 percent of violent crimes, and those in metropolitan counties cleared 51.6 percent. (See Table 25.)

Regionally, law enforcement in the Northeast cleared the highest percentage of violent crimes at 49.8 percent. Those in the West cleared 47.2 percent; those in the South 45.7 percent; and the agencies in the Midwest cleared 44.8 percent of their violent crimes. (See Table 26.)

Clearances and Juveniles

Both nationwide and in U.S. cities overall, 12.2 percent of violent crime clearances involved only juveniles (persons under the age of 18). The highest percentage of violent crime clearances (14.9) involving juveniles was in cities with populations between 25,000 and 49,999. Law enforcement agencies in metropolitan counties reported that 12.7 percent of their violent crime clearances involved juveniles, and nonmetropolitan counties recorded 9.8 percent of their clearances with only juvenile involvement. (See Table 28.)

Arrests

Law enforcement made an estimated 597,026 arrests for violent crime in the United States in 2003. This accounted for an estimated 4.4 percent of all arrests and 27.1 percent of Part I offense arrests. Within the violent crime category, there were an estimated 13,190 arrests for murder, accounting for 2.2 percent of all violent crime arrests. Forcible rape accounted for 4.4 percent of violent crime arrests with 26,350 arrests estimated. There were an estimated 107,553 arrests for robbery, which represented 18.0 percent of the violent crime arrest total. With an estimated 449,933 arrests, aggravated assault accounted for

75.4 percent of arrests, the most of any violent crime. (Based on Table 29.)

Within the Nation's regions, law enforcement agencies in the West had the highest arrest rate for violent crime with 276.4 arrests per 100,000 inhabitants. Law enforcement in the South reported a rate of 190.4 violent crime arrests per 100,000 persons. Agencies in the Northeast and the Midwest had violent crime arrest rates of 166.5 and 165.8 per 100,000 persons, respectively. (See Table 30.)

Within all population groups, cities overall had a violent crime arrest rate of 231.8 per 100,000 individuals. Among city groups, those with a population of 250,000 and over had the highest violent crime arrest rate of 332.9 per 100,000. The lowest rate among cities was experienced by those with a population range of 10,000 to 24,999—154.2 violent crime arrests per 100,000 inhabitants. (See Table 31.)

In 2003, the number of arrests for violent crime decreased 2.3 percent in comparison with that in 2002. The number of arrests of adults declined 2.7 percent from 2002 to 2003; the number of juvenile arrests remained virtually unchanged (+0.1 percent). (See Table 36.) When compared to the 1994 figure, the number of arrests for violent crime decreased 15.9 percent in 2003. In this same 10-year period, the number of arrests of juveniles dropped 32.5 percent, and the number of adults arrested fell by 12.1 percent. (See Table 32.)

Arrestees

During 2003, 15.5 percent of arrestees for violent crimes were under the age of 18; 28.7 percent were under the age of 21, and 44.3 percent were under the age of 25. Juveniles under the age of 15 made up 5.1 percent of violent crime arrestees. (See Table 41.)

The gender of 82.2 percent of those persons arrested for violent crimes was male. By violent offense, males accounted for 98.7 percent of forcible rape arrestees, 89.7 percent of murder arrestees, 89.6 percent of robbery arrestees, and 79.3 percent of aggravated assault arrests. (See Table 42.)

By race, whites accounted for 60.5 percent of violent crime arrestees and blacks, 37.2 percent. The remainder of arrestees were of other races (American Indian or Alaskan Native and Asian or Pacific Islander). The race of arrestees for the violent offense of murder was nearly evenly divided between white and black individuals, 49.1 percent and 48.5 percent, respectively. The remaining murder arrestees were of other races. (See Table 43.)

Murder

Definition

Murder and nonnegligent manslaughter, as defined in the Uniform Crime Reporting (UCR) Program, is the willful (nonnegligent) killing of one human being by another.

The classification of this offense is based solely on police investigation as opposed to the determination of a court, medical examiner, coroner, jury, or other judicial body. The UCR Program does not include the following situations in the count for this offense classification: deaths caused by negligence, suicide, or accident; justifiable homicides; and attempts to murder or assaults to murder, which are scored as aggravated assaults.

Trend

Year	Number of offenses	Rate per 100,000 inhabitants
2002	16,229	5.6
2003	16,503	5.7
Percent change	+1.7	+0.7

National Volume, Trends, and Rates

There were 16,503 criminal homicides in the United States during 2003. This figure represented a 1.7-percent increase over the 2002 estimate and a 6.3-percent rise from the 1999 figure. Measured against the 1994 total, however, the 2003 estimate

Figure 2.3

Murder
Percent Change from 1999

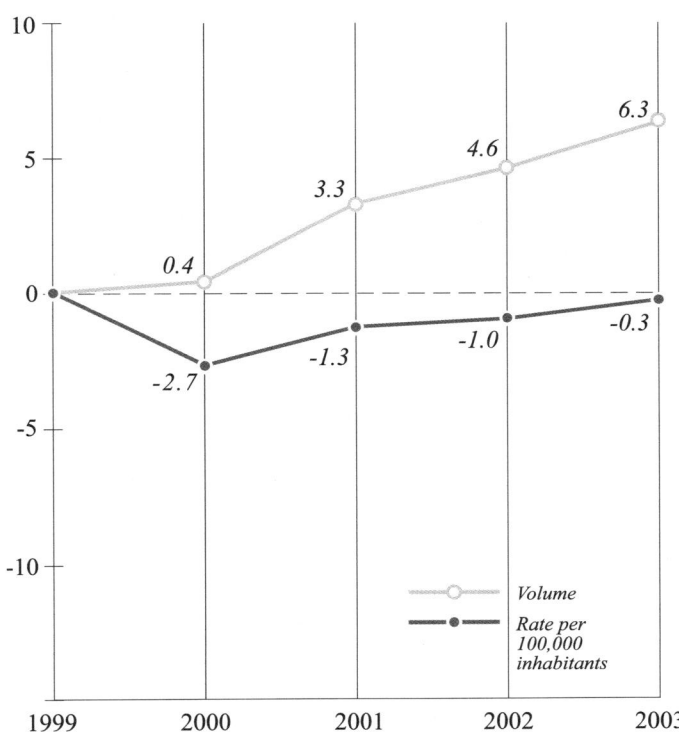

reflected a 29.3-percent decrease in the number of murders. (See Table 1, national estimates.)

For 2003, the UCR Program estimated the murder rate at 5.7 offenses per 100,000 U.S. inhabitants, an increase of 0.7 percent compared to the prior year's rate. The murder rate for 2003 decreased only slightly (-0.3 percent) from the 1999 rate. However, the 2003 murder rate was 36.7 percent lower than the rate recorded for 1994. (See Table 1, national estimates.)

Regional Offense Trends and Rates

The UCR Program divides the United States into four regions: the Northeast, the Midwest, the South, and the West. (Appendix III provides a map delineating the regions.) The following paragraphs provide the murder breakdowns by region for 2003:

The Northeast

An estimated 2,311 murders occurred in the Northeast during 2003. That figure represented an increase of 4.6 percent over the 2002 approximation. The murder rate was 4.2 offenses per 100,000 inhabitants, which was a 4.2-percent increase over the 2002 rate. Nearly 19 percent (18.7) of the Nation's population were living in the Northeast during 2003, and 14.0 percent of the total murders occurred in those states. (See Tables 3 and 4, regional estimates.)

The Midwest

The Midwest Region was the only area of the country to reflect a decrease in the number of murders when comparing 2002 and 2003 data. The 3,221 murders in the Midwest represented a 2.7-percent decrease from the region's murder total in 2002. The 2003 murder rate per 100,000 population was 4.9, a decrease of 3.1 percent from the previous year's rate. With 22.5 percent of the U.S. population, the Midwest accounted for 19.5 percent of the country's murders during 2003. (See Tables 3 and 4, regional estimates.)

Table 2.2

Murder by Month
Percent Distribution, 1999-2003

Month	1999	2000	2001[1]	2002	2003
January	8.8	8.4	7.9	8.2	7.7
February	7.1	7.3	6.2	6.8	6.9
March	7.6	7.6	7.1	7.8	8.0
April	7.7	7.7	7.9	7.7	8.2
May	8.3	8.5	8.3	8.0	8.6
June	8.1	8.5	8.5	8.1	8.3
July	9.1	9.3	9.5	9.7	9.3
August	9.1	9.4	9.0	9.2	9.1
September	8.7	8.3	8.6	9.7	8.7
October	8.4	8.7	9.3	8.4	8.5
November	8.2	7.7	8.5	7.9	7.8
December	8.8	8.7	9.2	8.6	9.0

[1] The murder and nonnegligent homicides that occurred as a result of the events of September 11, 2001, are not included.

Table 2.3

Murder Victims
by Race and Sex, 2003

		Sex		
Race	Total	Male	Female	Unknown
White	6,913	4,986	1,927	0
Black	6,887	5,771	1,113	3
Other race	408	277	131	0
Unknown race	200	133	44	23
Total	14,408	11,167	3,215	26

The South

The Southern states, the Nation's most populous region, made up 35.9 percent of the Nation's population and accounted for 43.6 percent of the murders in the United States in 2003. The estimated 7,197 offenses reflected a 3.0-percent increase in the number of murders during 2003 compared to the previous year's volume. The murder rate in the South was 6.9 murders per 100,000 persons, an increase of 1.7 percent over the 2002 murder rate. (See Tables 3 and 4, regional estimates.)

The West

During 2003, the West had an estimated 3,774 murders. This figure reflected an increase of 1.4 percent compared to the prior year's figure. With 22.9 percent of the national population, the West also accounted for 22.9 percent of the Nation's murders. The murder rate calculated for the Western States in 2003, 5.7 murders for every 100,000 persons, was unchanged from the 2002 rate. (See Tables 3 and 4, regional estimates.)

Community Types

The UCR Program estimates the number of criminal offenses for three community types: Metropolitan Statistical Areas (MSAs), cities outside of MSAs, and nonmetropolitan counties. During 2003, MSAs accounted for 82.8 percent of the Nation's population and 89.1 percent of the Nation's murders. The murder rate for MSAs was 6.1 offenses per 100,000 persons. Cities lying outside MSAs (mostly incorporated areas) accounted for 6.8 percent of the national population and 4.5 percent of the murder offenses in 2003. Based upon reported offenses, the UCR Program estimated a rate of 3.8 homicides for each 100,000 inhabitants for these community types. Nonmetropolitan counties, comprised of mostly unincorporated areas, accounted

for approximately 10.4 percent of the Nation's population and 6.4 percent of its homicides. These community types had a rate of 3.5 murder offenses per 100,000 inhabitants. (See Table 2, community type estimates.)

Population Groups: Trends and Rates

The UCR Program presents crime statistics by population groups, which include cities, metropolitan counties, and nonmetropolitan counties. Collectively, the Nation's cities experienced a 2.7-percent increase in the number of murders in 2003 compared to the 2002 number. Those cities with 250,000 or more in population and those with populations within the 50,000 to 99,999 range showed virtually no change in the number of murders from the previous year's number (+ 0.1 percent and - 0.1 percent, respectively). However, a comparison of the data from 2002 and 2003 showed increases in the number of murders in all other population groups labeled city. Cities with 100,000 to 249,999 inhabitants experienced an increase in murders of 6.8 percent, those with 25,000 to 49,999 populations had an increase of 5.5 percent, and those with populations of 10,000 to 24,999 showed a rise of 8.5 percent. The 2-year trend data indicated that the number of murders in cities with fewer than 10,000 inhabitants increased 20.0 percent from 2002 to 2003. The Nation's metropolitan counties and nonmetropolitan counties, however, experienced decreases in the number of murders—3.3 percent and 2.3 percent, respectively—when comparing data from 2003 and 2002. (See Table 12.)

U.S. cities collectively had a murder rate of 7.1 murders per 100,000 inhabitants for 2003. The highest rate was 13.2 in cities with 250,000 or more inhabitants. The lowest rate was computed for cities with populations of 10,000

Table 2.4

Murder Victims
by Age, Sex, and Race, 2003

Age	Total	Sex			Race			
		Male	Female	Unknown	White	Black	Other	Unknown
Total	**14,408**	**11,167**	**3,215**	**26**	**6,913**	**6,887**	**408**	**200**
Percent distribution[1]	100.0	77.5	22.3	0.2	48.0	47.8	2.8	1.4
Under 18[2]	1,333	905	424	4	660	617	40	16
Under 22[2]	3,445	2,724	716	5	1,556	1,749	100	40
18 and over[2]	12,811	10,083	2,721	7	6,133	6,189	358	131
Infant (under 1)	225	131	91	3	139	73	7	6
1 to 4	307	164	142	1	165	131	6	5
5 to 8	82	41	41	0	44	34	3	1
9 to 12	69	36	33	0	33	34	1	1
13 to 16	369	293	76	0	150	202	14	3
17 to 19	1,283	1,113	169	1	549	689	34	11
20 to 24	2,855	2,432	420	3	1,165	1,585	74	31
25 to 29	2,148	1,826	322	0	839	1,234	54	21
30 to 34	1,594	1,249	344	1	692	842	43	17
35 to 39	1,286	973	313	0	636	605	36	9
40 to 44	1,114	783	330	1	589	484	32	9
45 to 49	951	694	256	1	552	362	26	11
50 to 54	630	463	167	0	382	226	19	3
55 to 59	365	256	109	0	236	113	12	4
60 to 64	226	160	66	0	148	57	16	5
65 to 69	164	113	51	0	122	32	8	2
70 to 74	153	90	63	0	105	42	4	2
75 and over	323	171	152	0	247	61	9	6
Unknown	264	179	70	15	120	81	10	53

[1] Because of rounding, the percentages may not add to 100.0.
[2] Does not include unknown ages.

Table 2.5

Murder Offenders
by Age, Sex, and Race, 2003

Age	Total	Sex			Race			
		Male	Female	Unknown	White	Black	Other	Unknown
Total	**16,043**	**10,218**	**1,123**	**4,702**	**5,132**	**5,729**	**308**	**4,874**
Percent distribution[1]	100.0	63.7	7.0	29.3	32.0	35.7	1.9	30.4
Under 18[2]	813	726	86	1	351	433	21	8
Under 22[2]	3,327	3,049	275	3	1,366	1,832	95	34
18 and over[2]	9,396	8,387	997	12	4,489	4,542	280	85
Infant (under 1)	0	0	0	0	0	0	0	0
1 to 4	0	0	0	0	0	0	0	0
5 to 8	1	1	0	0	1	0	0	0
9 to 12	12	9	2	1	7	4	0	1
13 to 16	432	381	51	0	185	229	13	5
17 to 19	1,585	1,470	114	1	625	889	49	22
20 to 24	2,780	2,538	240	2	1,147	1,542	76	15
25 to 29	1,641	1,483	157	1	696	885	45	15
30 to 34	1,054	921	129	4	533	480	30	11
35 to 39	800	672	128	0	431	340	23	6
40 to 44	713	598	113	2	448	235	23	7
45 to 49	471	407	63	1	266	185	17	3
50 to 54	277	242	34	1	174	91	9	3
55 to 59	166	141	25	0	114	43	7	2
60 to 64	94	87	7	0	71	19	3	1
65 to 69	66	60	6	0	48	16	1	1
70 to 74	44	43	1	0	33	9	2	0
75 and over	73	60	13	0	61	8	3	1
Unknown	5,834	1,105	40	4,689	292	754	7	4,781

[1] Because of rounding, the percentages may not add to 100.0.
[2] Does not include unknown ages.

to 24,999—2.7 murders per 100,000 inhabitants. Metropolitan counties had a rate of 4.0 murders, and nonmetropolitan counties had a rate of 3.4 murders per 100,000 inhabitants. (See Table 16.)

Supplementary Homicide Reports

During 2003, law enforcement agencies contributing data to the UCR Program submitted Supplementary Homicide Reports (SHRs) for 14,408 homicides. The SHR supplies data on the age, sex, and race of both the victim and the offender; the type of weapon used; the relationship of the victim to the offender; and the circumstance surrounding the incident.

Table 2.6

Murder Victim/Offender Relationship
by Age, 2003
[Single victim/single offender]

Age of victim	Total	Age of offender		
		Under 18	18 and over	Unknown
Total	7,024	346	6,089	589
Under 18	728	111	589	28
18 and over	6,199	231	5,424	544
Unknown	97	4	76	17

NOTE: This table is based upon incidents where some information about the offender is known by law enforcement. It excludes incidents reported with a value of "unknown offender."

Victims

Based on 2003 SHR data (where age, sex, or race were known for the victims), 90.6 percent of murder victims were adults. Males accounted for 77.6 percent of murder victims. Just over 8 percent (8.2 percent) of male victims and 13.5 percent of female victims were under the age of 18. By race, 48.7 percent of murder victims were white, 48.5 percent were black, and the remainder were of other races (American Indian, Alaskan Native, Asian, or Pacific Islander). (Based on Table 2.4.)

Offenders

A review of the SHR data for known murder offenders showed that 90.1 percent were identified as male and 92.0 were over 18 years of age. A breakdown of murder offenders for whom race was known showed that 51.3 percent were black, 45.9 percent were white, and 2.8 percent were of other races. (Based on Table 2.5.)

Data from single victim/single offender incidents indicated that 92.4 percent of black victims were slain by black offenders, and 84.7 percent of white victims were murdered by white offenders. (Based on Table 2.7.)

Weapons

Of the homicides for which the weapon type was specified on the 2003 SHR, 70.9 percent involved a firearm. Breaking down those incidents further indicated that 79.9 percent of all incidents in which a firearm was used involved handguns; 4.0 percent, rifles; 4.7 percent, shotguns; and 11.4 percent, other type or unknown firearms. Offenders used knives or cutting instruments in 13.4 percent of the murders, personal weapons (hands, fists, feet, etc.) in 7.0 percent, and blunt objects in 4.8 percent of the incidents. Other weapon types (poison, arson, narcotics, etc.) accounted for approximately 4.0 percent of murder weapons. (Based on Table 2.9.)

Victim/Offender Relationships

The relationship of the victim to the offender was unknown for 44.5 percent of the homicides reported on the SHR for 2003. An analysis of the 55.5 percent of the victims for whom the relationships to their offenders were known revealed that 77.6 percent knew their assailants and that 22.4 percent were slain by strangers. Among the incidents in which the victims knew their assailants, 70.9 percent were acquainted with their

Table 2.7

Murder Victim/Offender Relationship
by Race and Sex, 2003
[Single victim/single offender]

Race of victim	Total	Race of offender				Sex of offender		
		White	Black	Other	Unknown	Male	Female	Unknown
White victims	3,603	3,017	501	44	41	3,199	363	41
Black victims	3,147	226	2,864	8	49	2,793	305	49
Other race victims	199	47	26	122	4	179	16	4
Unknown race	75	33	21	2	19	49	7	19

Sex of victim	Total	Race of offender				Sex of offender		
		White	Black	Other	Unknown	Male	Female	Unknown
Male victims	4,987	2,163	2,642	111	71	4,417	499	71
Female victims	1,962	1,127	749	63	23	1,754	185	23
Unknown sex	75	33	21	2	19	49	7	19

NOTE: This table is based upon incidents where some information about the offender is known by law enforcement. It excludes incidents reported with a value of "unknown offender."

Table 2.8

Murder, Types of Weapons Used
Percent Distribution by Region, 2003

Region	Total all weapons[1]	Firearms	Knives or cutting instruments	Unknown or other dangerous weapons	Personal weapons (hands, fists, feet, etc.)[2]
Total	**100.0**	**66.9**	**12.6**	**13.9**	**6.6**
Northeast	100.0	61.9	16.8	14.1	7.2
Midwest	100.0	68.1	10.9	14.9	6.2
South	100.0	67.7	12.3	13.7	6.4
West	100.0	67.8	12.0	13.5	6.7

[1] Because of rounding, the percentages may not add to 100.0.
[2] Pushed is included in personal weapons.

Table 2.9

Murder Victims
by Weapon 1999-2003

Weapons	1999	2000	2001[1]	2002	2003
Total	**13,011**	**13,230**	**14,061**	**14,263**	**14,408**
Total firearms:	8,480	8,661	8,890	9,528	9,638
Handguns	6,658	6,778	6,931	7,294	7,701
Rifles	400	411	386	488	390
Shotguns	531	485	511	486	452
Other guns	92	53	59	75	75
Firearms, type not stated	799	934	1,003	1,185	1,020
Knives or cutting instruments	1,712	1,782	1,831	1,776	1,816
Blunt objects (clubs, hammers, etc.)	756	617	680	681	651
Personal weapons (hands, fists, feet, etc.)[2]	885	927	961	954	946
Poison	11	8	12	23	9
Explosives	0	9	4	11	4
Fire	133	134	109	103	163
Narcotics	26	20	37	48	41
Drowning	28	15	23	20	17
Strangulation	190	166	153	145	184
Asphyxiation	106	92	116	100	128
Other weapons or weapons not stated	684	799	1,245	874	811

[1] The murder and nonnegligent homicides that occurred as a result of the events of September 11, 2001, are not included.
[2] Pushed is included in personal weapons.

Table 2.10

Murder Victims by Age
by Weapon, 2003

Age	Total murder victims	Firearms	Knives or cutting instruments	Blunt objects (clubs, hammers, etc.)	Personal weapons (hands, fists, feet, etc.)[1]	Poison	Explosives	Fire	Narcotics	Strangulation	Asphyxiation	Other weapon or weapon not stated[2]
Total	**14,408**	**9,638**	**1,816**	**651**	**946**	**9**	**4**	**163**	**41**	**184**	**128**	**828**
Percent distribution[3]	100.0	66.9	12.6	4.5	6.6	0.1	*	1.1	0.3	1.3	0.9	5.7
Under 18[4]	1,333	599	97	57	315	3	0	43	15	15	41	148
Under 22[4]	3,445	2,330	282	86	371	3	0	56	17	36	50	214
18 and over[4]	12,811	8,901	1,694	583	611	6	4	112	26	168	79	627
Infant (under 1)	225	10	6	12	120	0	0	3	4	5	20	45
1 to 4	307	32	12	22	153	2	0	12	3	4	10	57
5 to 8	82	24	10	8	14	0	0	9	0	1	4	12
9 to 12	69	32	3	6	8	0	0	10	1	0	2	7
13 to 16	369	276	42	7	14	0	0	5	3	3	3	16
17 to 19	1,283	1,037	111	19	35	1	0	10	6	13	8	43
20 to 24	2,855	2,340	273	43	69	0	0	10	2	21	5	92
25 to 29	2,148	1,706	216	51	59	0	3	10	3	20	12	68
30 to 34	1,594	1,165	216	43	54	0	0	6	3	23	14	70
35 to 39	1,286	845	201	50	71	1	0	15	2	20	9	72
40 to 44	1,114	665	192	89	61	0	0	10	4	18	5	70
45 to 49	951	540	165	79	66	1	0	9	3	16	6	66
50 to 54	630	330	125	53	64	1	0	11	1	10	5	30
55 to 59	365	189	57	35	36	0	0	7	1	5	2	33
60 to 64	226	106	39	26	19	0	0	6	0	5	3	22
65 to 69	164	55	33	32	22	0	0	4	1	2	0	15
70 to 74	153	59	36	20	7	0	0	6	1	4	2	18
75 and over	323	89	54	45	54	3	1	12	3	13	10	39
Unknown	264	138	25	11	20	0	0	8	0	1	8	53

[1] Pushed is included in personal weapons.
[2] Includes drowning.
[3] Because of rounding, the percentages may not add to 100.0.
[4] Does not include unknown ages.
* Less than one-tenth of 1 percent.

Table 2.11

Murder Circumstances by Relationship,[1] 2003

Circumstances	Total murder victims	Husband	Wife	Mother	Father	Son	Daughter	Brother	Sister	Other family	Acquaintance	Friend	Boyfriend	Girlfriend	Neighbor	Employee	Employer	Stranger	Unknown
Total	**14,408**	**123**	**573**	**105**	**129**	**268**	**193**	**87**	**27**	**299**	**3,294**	**339**	**160**	**464**	**112**	**13**	**19**	**1,795**	**6,408**
Felony type total:	2,359	1	16	9	9	14	10	5	3	30	606	43	7	22	28	2	3	571	980
Rape	43	0	0	0	0	0	1	0	1	3	12	0	0	2	0	0	0	10	13
Robbery	1,056	0	0	2	2	0	0	2	0	6	196	17	0	0	0	2	2	387	435
Burglary	93	0	1	1	0	0	0	0	1	2	23	2	1	2	1	0	0	33	26
Larceny-theft	22	0	0	0	1	0	0	0	0	1	4	0	0	1	1	0	0	10	3
Motor vehicle theft	30	0	1	0	0	0	0	0	0	1	8	2	0	1	0	0	0	5	12
Arson	77	1	0	2	1	3	0	0	1	3	13	0	0	1	16	0	0	3	33
Prostitution and commercialized vice	16	0	0	0	0	0	0	0	0	0	2	0	0	0	0	0	0	6	8
Other sex offenses	10	0	0	0	0	0	0	0	0	0	5	0	0	0	1	0	0	1	3
Narcotic drug laws	666	0	3	1	1	1	0	0	0	5	258	17	1	3	0	0	0	69	307
Gambling	6	0	0	0	0	0	0	0	0	0	4	0	0	0	0	0	0	0	2
Other—not specified	340	0	10	3	4	10	9	3	0	9	81	5	5	12	4	0	0	47	138
Suspected felony type	88	0	2	0	0	0	0	0	0	0	4	0	0	0	0	0	0	6	76
Other than felony type total:	7,070	109	484	76	101	224	153	68	17	229	2,165	243	136	380	70	10	11	937	1,657
Romantic triangle	98	2	4	0	0	0	0	1	0	2	48	2	5	7	3	0	0	13	11
Child killed by babysitter	29	0	0	0	0	0	2	0	0	2	20	3	0	0	0	0	0	0	2
Brawl due to influence of alcohol	128	2	2	1	1	2	0	1	1	4	59	10	0	4	1	0	0	24	16
Brawl due to influence of narcotics	53	0	1	1	1	0	0	0	0	4	22	7	0	4	0	0	0	7	6
Argument over money or property	220	2	5	2	1	2	0	4	0	10	114	10	1	5	2	0	1	12	49
Other arguments	3,806	79	324	45	68	47	22	48	7	145	1,284	162	98	291	49	2	5	496	634
Gangland killings	115	0	0	0	0	0	0	0	0	0	41	1	0	0	0	0	0	33	40
Juvenile gang killings	819	0	0	0	0	0	0	0	0	2	143	5	0	0	0	0	0	132	537
Institutional killings	13	0	0	0	0	0	0	0	0	0	10	0	0	0	0	0	0	2	1
Sniper attack	2	0	0	0	0	0	0	0	0	0	0	0	0	0	0	0	0	2	0
Other—not specified	1,787	24	148	27	30	173	129	14	9	60	424	43	32	69	15	8	5	216	361
Unknown	4,891	13	71	20	19	30	30	14	7	40	519	53	17	62	14	1	5	281	3,695

[1] Relationship is that of victim to offender.

NOTE: The relationship categories of husband and wife include both common-law and ex-spouses. The categories of mother, father, sister, brother, son, and daughter include stepparents, stepchildren, and stepsiblings. The category of acquaintance includes homosexual relationships and the composite category of other known to victim.

Figure 2.4

Murder by Relationship[1]

Percent Distribution,[2] Volume by Known Relationship, 2003

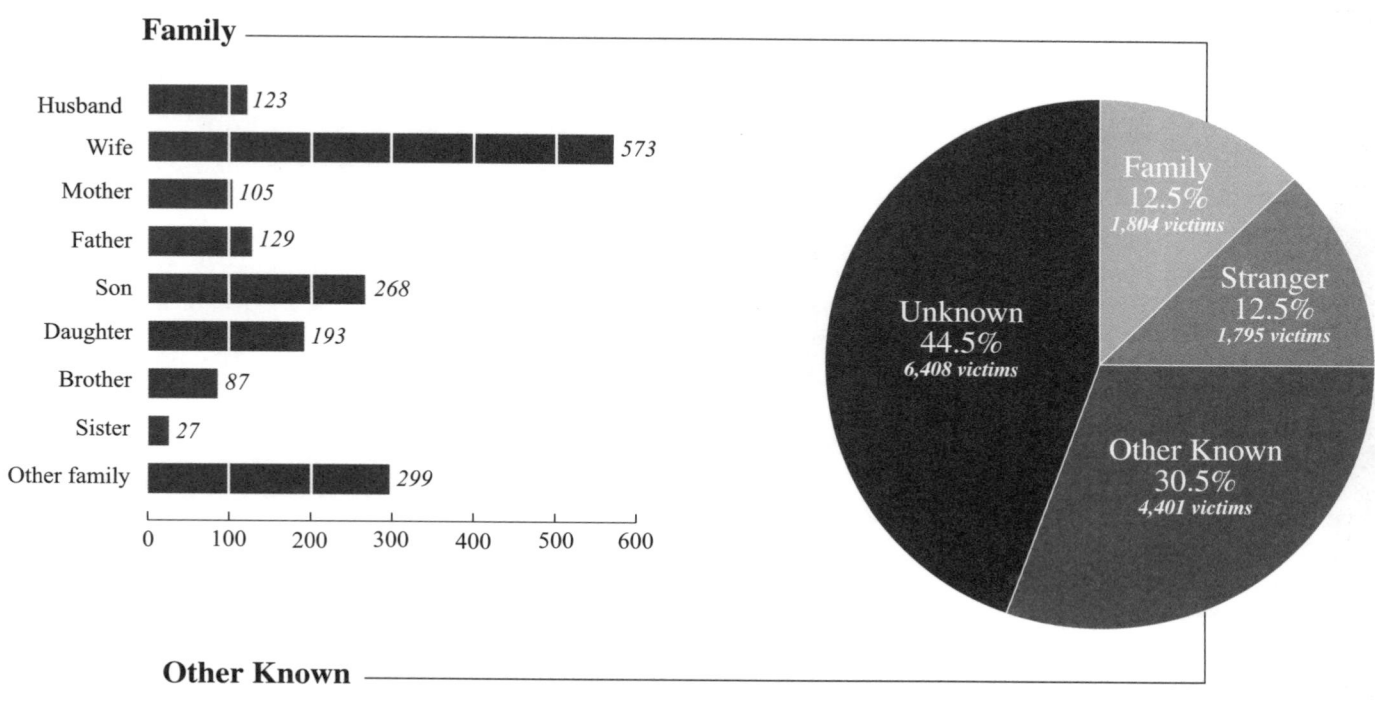

Family

Husband	123
Wife	573
Mother	105
Father	129
Son	268
Daughter	193
Brother	87
Sister	27
Other family	299

0   100   200   300   400   500   600

Pie chart:
- Unknown 44.5% — 6,408 victims
- Family 12.5% — 1,804 victims
- Stranger 12.5% — 1,795 victims
- Other Known 30.5% — 4,401 victims

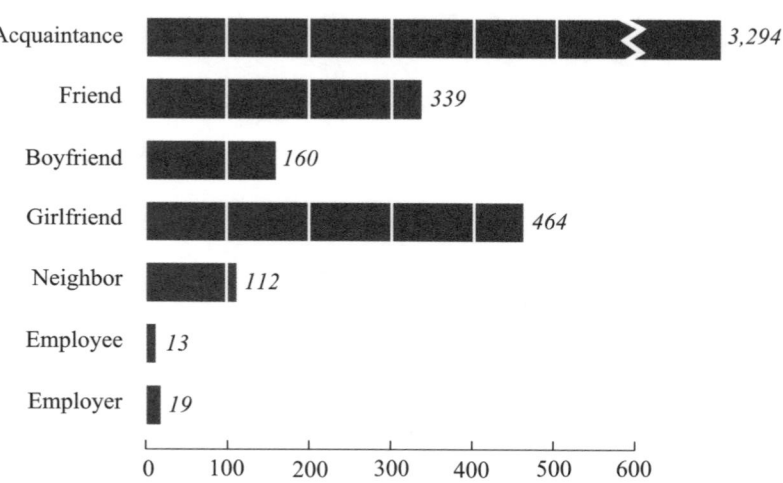

Other Known

Acquaintance	3,294
Friend	339
Boyfriend	160
Girlfriend	464
Neighbor	112
Employee	13
Employer	19

0   100   200   300   400   500   600

[1] Relationship is that of victim to offender.

[2] Due to rounding, the percentages may not add to 100.0.

Figures are based on 14,408 murder victims for whom Supplementary Homicide Report data were received.

Table 2.12

Murder Circumstances
by Weapon, 2003

Circumstances	Total murder victims	Total firearms	Handguns	Rifles	Shotguns	Other guns or type not stated	Knives or cutting instruments	Blunt objects (clubs, hammers, etc.)	Personal weapons (hands, fists, feet, etc.)	Poison	Pushed or thrown out window	Explosives	Fire	Narcotics	Drowning	Strangulation	Asphyxiation	Other
Total	**14,408**	**9,638**	**7,701**	**390**	**452**	**1,095**	**1,816**	**651**	**944**	**9**	**2**	**4**	**163**	**41**	**17**	**184**	**128**	**811**
Felony type total:	2,359	1,680	1,402	53	75	150	182	123	113	2	0	2	82	14	2	36	22	101
Rape	43	4	3	0	0	1	10	5	11	0	0	0	0	0	0	6	2	5
Robbery	1,056	790	681	24	26	59	84	77	52	0	0	0	0	0	0	7	10	36
Burglary	93	55	42	4	5	4	19	6	6	1	0	0	0	0	0	0	0	6
Larceny-theft	22	17	9	5	1	2	1	1	1	0	0	0	0	0	0	2	0	1
Motor vehicle theft	30	12	7	1	1	3	4	5	1	0	0	0	0	0	0	0	1	7
Arson	77	6	6	0	0	0	0	0	2	0	0	0	62	0	0	1	2	4
Prostitution and commercialized vice	16	4	4	0	0	0	1	0	1	0	0	0	0	0	1	9	0	0
Other sex offenses	10	2	2	0	0	0	1	2	2	0	0	0	0	0	0	2	1	0
Narcotic drug laws	666	571	485	11	28	47	36	17	8	0	0	0	2	14	0	4	1	13
Gambling	6	5	4	0	0	1	1	0	0	0	0	0	0	0	0	0	0	0
Other—not specified	340	214	159	8	14	33	25	10	30	1	0	2	18	0	1	5	5	29
Suspected felony type	88	76	65	2	3	6	5	2	0	0	0	0	1	0	0	2	0	2
Other than felony type total:	7,070	4,446	3,601	248	263	334	1,146	313	631	4	2	1	38	19	11	71	77	311
Romantic triangle	98	61	50	3	5	3	26	2	5	0	0	0	0	0	0	0	1	3
Child killed by babysitter	29	0	0	0	0	0	1	4	15	0	0	0	0	1	0	0	2	6
Brawl due to influence of alcohol	128	57	46	8	1	2	34	12	16	0	0	0	1	0	0	0	2	6
Brawl due to influence of narcotics	53	33	24	4	2	3	11	1	1	0	0	0	0	2	0	0	0	4
Argument over money or property	220	156	131	7	10	8	26	14	16	0	0	0	0	0	0	6	0	2
Other arguments	3,806	2,321	1,884	112	152	173	821	177	267	2	1	0	20	1	2	46	21	127
Gangland killings	115	105	81	6	4	14	6	1	2	0	0	0	0	0	0	0	1	0
Juvenile gang killings	819	797	727	31	10	29	17	2	1	0	0	0	0	0	0	0	0	2
Institutional killings	13	1	1	0	0	0	1	3	6	0	0	0	0	0	0	0	0	2
Sniper attack	2	2	0	2	0	0	0	0	0	0	0	0	0	0	0	0	0	0
Other—not specified	1,787	913	657	75	79	102	203	97	302	2	1	1	17	15	9	19	49	159
Unknown	4,891	3,436	2,633	87	111	605	483	213	200	3	0	1	42	8	4	75	29	397

murderers, and 29.1 percent were related to them. Husbands and boyfriends
killed 32.3 percent of female victims,
and wives and girlfriends murdered 2.5
percent of male victims. (Based on
Table 2.11.)

Circumstances

The circumstance was unknown for 33.9
percent of the homicides reported on
the SHR for 2003. The supplemental
data indicated that 16.4 percent of the
homicides for which circumstances were
known involved the commission of another felony such as robbery or narcotic
drug laws. Investigators suspected that
another 0.6 percent of homicides likely
resulted from a felonious activity. Investigators cited arguments as the cause
of 28.6 percent of the killings. Other
types of circumstances, such as juvenile
gang killings, sniper attacks, and brawls
involving alcohol or drugs, were docu-
mented in 20.4 percent of the murders.
(Based on Table 2.13.)

Clearances

In the UCR Program, law enforcement
clearances occur by arrest or, in certain
specific circumstances, by exceptional
means, i.e., when elements beyond the
control of law enforcement prevent the
placing of formal charges against the offender. (Section III provides more information regarding clearances.) Typically,
the crime of murder has the highest
percentage of clearances. During 2003,
law enforcement cleared 62.4 percent
of murders reported nationwide. (See
Table 25.) Of the total clearances for
murder, 5.2 percent involved only juvenile offenders. (See Table 28.)

During 2003, law enforcement in
the Nation's cities collectively cleared
61.9 percent of reported murders.
Among the city population groupings,
those with populations of 10,000 to
24,999 had the highest percentages of

Table 2.13

Murder Circumstances, 1999-2003

Circumstances	1999	2000	2001[1]	2002	2003
Total	**13,011**	**13,230**	**14,061**	**14,263**	**14,408**
Felony type total:	2,215	2,229	2,364	2,340	2,359
Rape	47	58	61	44	43
Robbery	1,057	1,077	1,080	1,111	1,056
Burglary	81	76	80	97	93
Larceny-theft	14	23	17	16	22
Motor vehicle theft	12	25	22	15	30
Arson	66	81	71	59	77
Prostitution and commercialized vice	8	6	5	8	16
Other sex offenses	19	10	7	8	10
Narcotic drug laws	581	589	575	664	666
Gambling	17	12	3	5	6
Other—not specified	313	272	443	313	340
Suspected felony type	65	60	72	66	88
Other than felony type total:	6,880	6,871	7,073	7,185	7,070
Romantic triangle	137	122	118	129	98
Child killed by babysitter	34	30	37	39	29
Brawl due to influence of alcohol	203	188	152	149	128
Brawl due to influence of narcotics	127	99	118	85	53
Argument over money or property	213	206	198	203	220
Other arguments	3,471	3,589	3,618	3,577	3,806
Gangland killings	122	65	76	75	115
Juvenile gang killings	580	653	862	911	819
Institutional killings	13	10	8	12	13
Sniper attack	5	8	7	10	2
Other—not specified	1,975	1,901	1,879	1,995	1,787
Unknown	3,851	4,070	4,552	4,672	4,891

[1] The murder and nonnegligent homicides that occurred as a result of the events of September 11, 2001, are not included.

Table 2.14

Murder Circumstances
by Victim Sex, 2003

Circumstances	Total murder victims	Male	Female	Unknown
Total	**14,408**	**11,167**	**3,215**	**26**
Felony type total:	2,359	1,924	431	4
Rape	43	0	43	0
Robbery	1,056	908	145	3
Burglary	93	75	18	0
Larceny-theft	22	18	4	0
Motor vehicle theft	30	19	11	0
Arson	77	37	40	0
Prostitution and commercialized vice	16	3	13	0
Other sex offenses	10	4	6	0
Narcotic drug laws	666	611	54	1
Gambling	6	6	0	0
Other—not specified	340	243	97	0
Suspected felony type	88	71	17	0
Other than felony type total:	7,070	5,241	1,825	4
Romantic triangle	98	81	17	0
Child killed by babysitter	29	17	12	0
Brawl due to influence of alcohol	128	109	19	0
Brawl due to influence of narcotics	53	40	13	0
Argument over money or property	220	186	34	0
Other arguments	3,806	2,772	1,033	1
Gangland killings	115	111	4	0
Juvenile gang killings	819	782	37	0
Institutional killings	13	13	0	0
Sniper attack	2	1	1	0
Other—not specified	1,787	1,129	655	3
Unknown	4,891	3,931	942	18

Table 2.15

Justifiable Homicide
by Weapon, Law Enforcement,[1] 1999-2003

Year	Total	Total firearms	Handguns	Rifles	Shotguns	Firearms, type not stated	Knives or cutting instruments	Other dangerous weapons	Personal weapons
1999	308	305	274	11	15	5	0	1	2
2000	309	308	274	14	13	7	0	1	0
2001	378	375	318	25	11	21	0	3	0
2002	341	338	296	19	7	16	0	3	0
2003	370	363	316	16	9	22	0	2	5

[1] The killing of a felon by a law enforcement officer in the line of duty.

Table 2.16

Justifiable Homicide
by Weapon, Private Citizen,[1] 1999-2003

Year	Total	Total firearms	Handguns	Rifles	Shotguns	Firearms, type not stated	Knives or cutting instruments	Other dangerous weapons	Personal weapons
1999	192	158	137	5	10	6	18	9	7
2000	164	138	123	4	7	4	15	8	3
2001	222	183	143	10	13	17	26	6	7
2002	233	189	158	11	13	7	26	9	9
2003	246	203	163	6	20	14	22	13	8

[1] The killing of a felon, during the commission of a felony, by a private citizen.

clearances for murder, 71.8 percent. Law enforcement agencies in metropolitan counties cleared 60.0 percent, and those in nonmetropolitan counties cleared 76.3 percent of reported murders. (See Tables 25.)

Arrests

The UCR Program estimates the number of arrests nationwide for all Part I and Part II offenses; these data are presented in Table 29. All other tabular presentations are based upon data from agencies that submitted reports for all 12 months of the year.

Total Arrests

Nationwide, there were an estimated 13,190 arrests for murder during 2003. (See Table 29.) Adults, defined by the UCR Program as individuals 18 years of age and older, accounted for 91.4 percent of murder arrestees. (Based on Table 38.) Overall, 48.9 percent of those arrested for murder were under the age of 25, and 8.6 percent were under the age of 18. (See Table 41.)

Arrest Rates

Based upon 2003 arrest data and population figures, nationwide, the arrest rate for murder was 4.5 arrests per 100,000 inhabitants. By region, the South had

the highest murder arrest rate at 5.6 arrests; the West followed with 4.4 arrests, the Midwest with 4.2 arrests, and the Northeast with 3.1 murder arrests per 100,000 inhabitants. (See Table 30.)

Among the population groups in 2003, the Nation's cities collectively had a murder arrest rate of 4.8 per 100,000 persons. Law enforcement in the largest cities, those with more than 250,000 inhabitants, had the highest rate of arrests for murder, 9.4 for every 100,000 in population. Law enforcement in cities with 10,000 to 24,999 residents had the lowest rate, 2.1 murder arrests per 100,000 individuals. Metropolitan and nonmetropolitan counties both had a murder arrest rate of 3.8 for every 100,000 inhabitants. (See Table 31.)

Arrest Trends

A comparison of 2003 data to those of 2002 indicated an overall 6.6-percent drop in arrests for murder. The number of juveniles arrested for murder declined 10.0 percent, and the number of adults decreased 6.2 percent. By gender, the number of males arrested for murder decreased 5.9 percent and the number of females decreased 11.4 percent. (See Tables 36 and 37.)

The 5-year trend data showed that the number of arrests for murder in 2003

dropped 5.1 percent compared to the 1999 number. Arrests of juveniles fell 18.3 percent, and arrests of adults decreased 3.6 percent. An analysis of gender data for 1999 and 2003 showed that arrests of males for murder declined 4.3 percent over the time period, and arrests of females fell 11.5 percent. (See Tables 34 and 35.)

A review of the 10-year trend data showed 36.2 percent fewer arrests for murder in 2003 than in 1994. Arrests of juveniles were 67.6 percent lower and arrests of adults were 29.6 percent lower than the 1994 figure. The 10-year trend also revealed that arrests of males for murder were down 36.9 percent, and arrests of females for murder were down 30.1 percent from the 1993 figure. (See Tables 32 and 33.)

Arrest Distribution by Age, Sex, and Race

Based upon arrest data for 2003, males comprised 89.7 percent of all murder arrestees. (See Table 42.) By race, whites accounted for 49.1 percent of the murder arrestees, and blacks made up 48.5 percent of the total murder arrestees. Other races accounted for the remainder of persons arrested for murder. (See Table 43.)

Justifiable Homicide

The UCR Program defines justifiable homicide as the killing of a felon by a peace officer in the line of duty or the killing of a felon, during the commission of a felony, by a private citizen. Because these willful killings are determined through law enforcement investigation to be justifiable, or excusable, they are tabulated separately from the murder and nonnegligent manslaughter classification.

During 2003, contributing law enforcement agencies provided supplemental data for 616 justifiable homicides. According to those data, law enforcement officers justifiably killed 370 felons, and private citizens justifiably killed 246 felons. Tables 2.15 and 2.16 provide additional information about justifiable homicides.

Information regarding the UCR Program's statistical methodology and table construction can be found in Appendix I.

Forcible Rape

Definition

Forcible rape, as defined in the Uniform Crime Reporting (UCR) Program, is the carnal knowledge of a female forcibly and against her will. Assaults or attempts to commit rape by force or threat of force are also included; however, statutory rape (without force) and other sex offenses are excluded.

Trend

Year	Number of offenses	Rate per 100,000 inhabitants
2002	95,235	33.1
2003	93,433	32.1
Percent change	-1.9	-2.8

Offense Methodology

The UCR Program counts one offense per victim when a female of any age is forcibly raped or upon whom an assault to rape or attempt to rape is made. Additionally, the Program classifies all sex offenses (except forcible rape) as Part II offenses and, as such, collects only arrest data, which are presented in aggregated totals. (See Appendix II.) Consequently, statutory rapes of female victims where no force is used and the victim is under the age of consent are included in sex offenses. Sexual attacks on males are classified as assaults or sex offenses depending on the nature of the crime and the extent of injury.

Figure 2.5

Forcible Rape
Percent Change from 1999

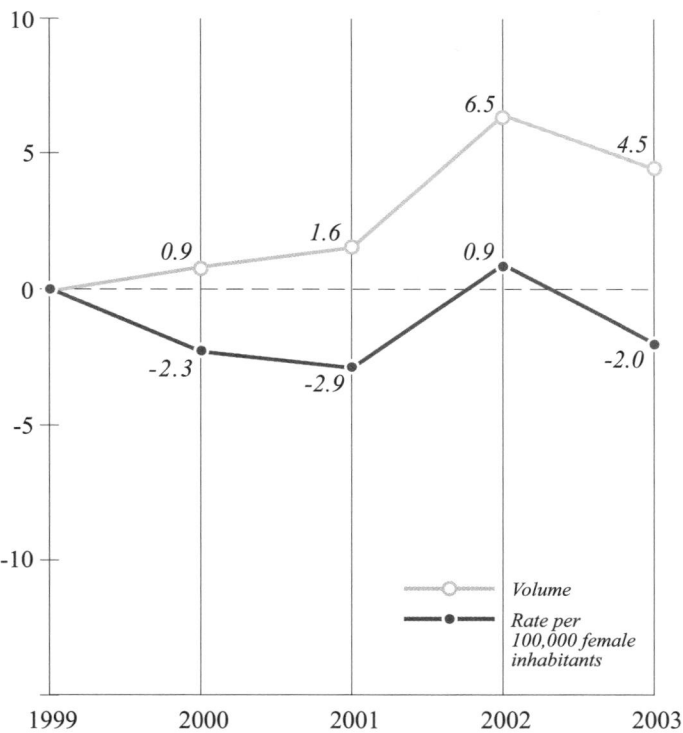

National Volume, Trends, and Rate

Based on law enforcement reports, an estimated 93,433 forcible rape offenses occurred nationwide in 2003. This figure was 1.9 percent lower than the 95,235 forcible rapes estimated for 2002. Five- and 10-year trend comparisons revealed that the 2003 volume was 4.5 percent above the estimated 89,411 offenses in 1999 but 8.6 percent below the 102,216 forcible rapes recorded in 1994. (See Table 1, national estimates.) Of the total number of forcible rapes estimated for 2003, rapes by force accounted for 91.0 percent. The remainder was attempts. (Based on Table 19.)

Throughout this publication, the UCR Program calculated forcible rape rates (including those listed above and those in subsequent tables) using estimates of the total U.S. population. Within this narrative, however, the forcible rape rates were based on the U.S. Census Bureau's 2003 estimate of the Nation's female population. According to those calculations, 63.2 forcible rapes occurred per 100,000 females in 2003, a 2.7-percent decrease from the 2002 rate of 65.0. The 2003 rate of forcible rape declined 1.4 percent from the 1999 rate of 64.1 (the 5-year trend) and fell 17.9 percent from the 1994 estimate of 77.0 forcible rapes per 100,000 females (the 10-year trend).

Regional Offense Trends and Rates

For data analyses, the UCR Program divides the United States into four regions: the Northeast, the Midwest, the South, and the West. (A map delineating these regions is published in Appendix III.) Overall, the rate of forcible rape declined in all four regions from 2002 to 2003. Regional tabulations of forcible rape data (based on Tables 3 and 4, regional estimates) revealed the following:

The Northeast

Law enforcement agencies in the Northeast reported an estimated 12,511 forcible rape offenses—13.4 percent of the forcible rape total—in 2003. In that region, which accounted for 18.7 percent of the total U.S. population, 45.3 forcible rapes occurred per 100,000 female inhabitants. The rate of forcible rape for 2003 was a 2.9-percent decrease from the 46.6 rapes per 100,000 females in 2002.

The Midwest

In 2003, an estimated 23,404 forcible rape offenses occurred in the Midwest, where 22.5 percent of the Nation's population resided. Forcible rape offenses in that region comprised 25.0 percent of the national forcible rape volume.

Females were victims of forcible rape in the Midwest at a rate of 70.4 offenses per 100,000 female inhabitants in 2003, a 3.5-percent decline from the 2002 rate of 73.0 forcible rapes per 100,000 female population.

The South

Based on law enforcement reports from the South, an estimated 35,133 forcible rape offenses were committed in that region in 2003. The South, which comprised 35.9 percent of total U.S. population, had 37.6 percent of the forcible rape offenses that occurred nationwide. The rate of forcible rape in the South was 66.1 offenses per 100,000 females in 2003, a 2.7-percent decrease from the 68.0 rapes per 100,000 female inhabitants in 2002.

The West

In 2003, law enforcement agencies in the West reported an estimated 22,385 forcible rape offenses, which equated to 24.0 percent of all forcible rapes nationwide. In that region, where 22.9 percent of the Nation's population resided, forcible rapes were committed at a rate of 66.3 per 100,000 females in 2003, a 1.9-percent decline from the 2002 rate of 67.5.

Community Types

The UCR Program aggregates data for three community types: Metropolitan Statistical Areas (MSAs), cities outside metropolitan areas, and nonmetropolitan counties. (Appendix III further explains the composition of these community types.) In 2003, the rate of forcible rape among MSAs was 64.5 offenses per 100,000 females. The highest forcible rape rate, recorded for cities outside metropolitan areas, was estimated at 75.1 rapes per 100,000 female inhabitants. Lastly, nonmetropolitan counties had 45.7 forcible rapes per 100,000

female population. (Based on Table 2, community types estimates.)

Clearances

Clearances occur either by arrest or by exceptional means, i.e., when elements beyond the control of law enforcement prevent the placing of formal charges against the offender. (Section III provides more information regarding clearances.) During 2003, law enforcement cleared 44.0 percent of forcible rapes that were reported in the United States. By population grouping, agencies in cities (collectively) cleared 43.4 percent of all rape offenses. The percentage of forcible rape offenses cleared in the Nation's largest cities, those with 1 million and more inhabitants, was 48.5 percent. Law enforcement agencies in metropolitan counties cleared 45.4 percent of the reported forcible rapes in their communities, and agencies in nonmetropolitan counties cleared 46.8 percent. (See Table 25.)

Law enforcement agencies in the Northeast cleared 48.5 percent of the forcible rape offenses brought to their attention in 2003, the highest clearance percentage among law enforcement in all four regions. Agencies in the South cleared 46.8 percent of forcible rape offenses, and those in the West cleared 41.9 percent of the region's forcible rape offenses. Law enforcement in the Midwest cleared 38.5 percent of forcible rape offenses by arrest or exceptional means. (See Table 26.)

Clearances and Juveniles

When an offender under the age of 18 is cited to appear in juvenile court or before other juvenile authorities, the UCR Program records the incident as a clearance by arrest even though a physical arrest may not have occurred. In addition, according to Program definitions,

---

Table 2.17

Forcible Rape by Month
Percent Distribution, 1999-2003

Month	1999	2000	2001	2002	2003
January	8.1	8.0	7.7	7.6	7.9
February	7.3	7.5	7.1	7.0	6.8
March	8.2	8.5	8.4	7.8	8.3
April	8.2	8.0	8.3	8.6	8.1
May	8.6	9.0	8.8	9.0	9.0
June	8.8	9.1	8.7	9.0	8.7
July	9.6	9.5	9.7	9.6	9.5
August	9.5	9.3	9.4	9.5	9.6
September	8.3	8.4	8.6	9.1	8.9
October	8.3	8.3	8.5	8.4	8.4
November	7.9	7.5	7.6	7.4	7.7
December	7.2	6.9	7.2	6.9	7.1

clearances involving both adult and juvenile offenders are classified as adult clearances. Therefore, the following clearance data do not necessarily depict the full extent to which juveniles were offenders of forcible rape.

Nationwide, the clearance of rape offenses involving juveniles only accounted for 11.5 percent of total forcible rape clearances in 2003. Law enforcement agencies in cities (collectively) reported that 10.6 percent of all forcible rape clearances involved only juveniles. Among the Nation's cities, the highest percentage of forcible rape clearances involving only juveniles, 13.4 percent, was in cities with populations of 25,000 to 49,999. Forcible rape clearances involving only juveniles comprised 7.2 percent, the lowest percentage, of forcible rape clearances in cities with populations of 250,000 and over. Clearances of offenders under the age of 18 made up 13.6 percent of all forcible rape clearances in metropolitan counties and 16.0 percent of those in nonmetropolitan counties. (See Table 28.)

Arrests

Law enforcement agencies nationwide made an estimated 26,350 arrests for forcible rape in 2003. (See Table 29.) The national rate of arrests for forcible rape was 9.0 arrests per 100,000 U.S. inhabitants. In cities, collectively, law enforcement made 9.4 arrests per 100,000 in population. Agencies in metropolitan counties and nonmetropolitan counties recorded 7.8 arrests and 8.9 arrests per 100,000 persons of their respective populations. (See Table 31.)

Based on the data of those arrested for forcible rape, 45.9 percent were under 25 years old, and 30.9 percent were under 21 years old. Further, the data showed that 16.1 percent of forcible rape arrestees were under the age of 18, and 6.0 percent were under 15 years old. (See Table 41.) Adults, defined by the UCR Program as individuals 18 years of age and older, accounted for 83.9 percent of forcible rape arrestees. (See Table 38.)

Race distributions for adults and juveniles arrested for forcible rape were similar for 2003. Of those adults arrested for the offense, 64.1 percent were white, 33.3 percent were black, and 2.6 percent were other races. (See Table 43.) Among juvenile arrestees, 64.1 percent were white, 33.4 percent were black, and 2.5 percent were other races. (See Table 43.)

Arrest Trends

When compared to the arrest volume recorded for 2002, the number of arrests for forcible rape decreased 5.1 percent overall in 2003. The 2-year trend (2002 and 2003) showed that arrests of adults for the offense declined 4.3 percent and those of juveniles decreased 9.0 percent. (See Table 36.) Five-year trend data (from 1999 and 2003) revealed a 5.0-percent decrease in the number of persons arrested for forcible rape in 2003, with the number of arrests for forcible rape involving adult arrestees down 3.8 percent and that involving juvenile arrestees down 10.5 percent. (See Table 34.) Ten-year trend data (those from 1994 and 2003) indicated a 22.3-percent drop in the number of persons arrested for forcible rape; forcible rape arrests of adults and juveniles decreased 21.8 percent and 24.7 percent, respectively. (See Table 32.)

Robbery

Definition

The Uniform Crime Reporting (UCR) Program defines robbery as the taking or attempted taking of anything of value from the care, custody, or control of a person or persons by force or threat of force or violence and/or putting the victim in fear.

Trend

Year	Number of offenses	Rate per 100,000 inhabitants
2002	420,806	146.1
2003	413,402	142.2
Percent change	-1.8	-2.7

National Volume, Trends, and Rates

There were an estimated 413,402 robberies in the Nation in 2003, a 1.8-percent decrease from the 2002 estimate. Five- and 10-year trend data indicated that the number of robberies in 2003 rose 1.0 percent when compared to 1999 data; the number of robberies in 2003 fell 33.2 percent from the 1994 figure. (See Table 1, national estimates.) Robbery accounted for 29.9 percent of all violent crimes in 2003. (Based on Table 1, national estimates.)

National trend data also showed that in 2003 robbery offenses occurred at a

rate of 142.2 offenses per 100,000 inhabitants, a 2.7-percent decrease from the 2002 estimate, a 5.3-percent decline from the 1999 data, and a 40.2-percent drop from the 1994 rate. (See Table 1, national estimates.)

Regional Offense Trends and Rates

The UCR Program divides the United States into four regions: the Northeast, the Midwest, the South, and the West. (Geographic region breakdowns can be found in Appendix III.) Data collected by the UCR Program and aggregated by region concerning robbery reflected the following:

The Northeast

The Northeast was home to 18.7 percent of the Nation's population in 2003; 19.6 percent of the Nation's robberies were reported in that region. Law enforcement in the region reported a 0.3-percent increase in the volume of robberies in 2003 when compared to the volume of robberies reported in 2002. In 2003, an estimated 148.7 robberies per 100,000 inhabitants were committed in the Northeast, a 0.2-percent decline from the 2002 rate. (See Tables 3 and 4, regional estimates.)

The Midwest

The Midwest had 22.5 percent of the

Figure 2.6

Robbery
Percent Change from 1999

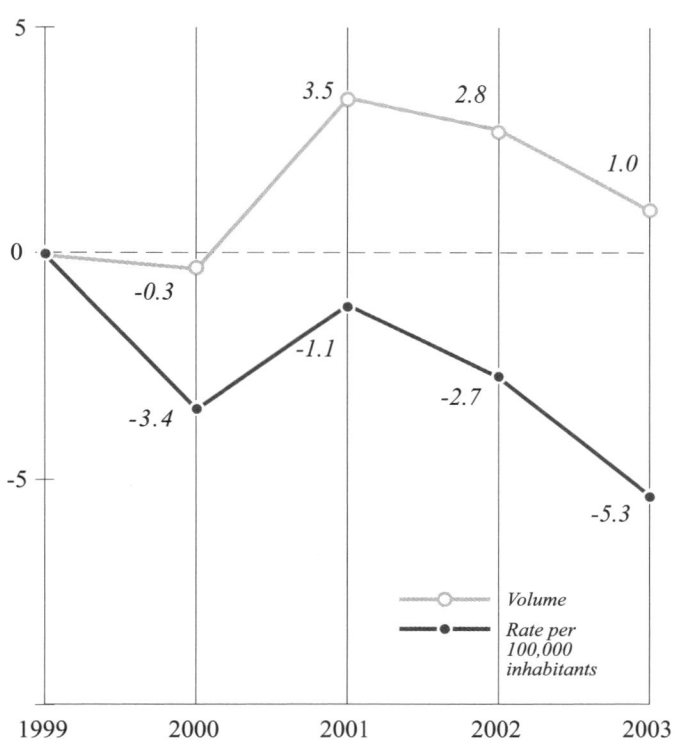

Nation's population. Law enforcement in the Midwest Region reported 5.7 percent fewer robberies in 2003 from the 2002 volume. The number of robberies in the Midwest accounted for 18.8 percent all robberies in the Nation in 2003. The rate of robberies in the Midwest, 118.5 per 100,000 inhabitants, declined 6.1 percent from the 2002 rate. The Midwest Region had the lowest volume of robberies and the lowest rate of robberies per 100,000 inhabitants of the four regions in 2003. (See Tables 3 and 4, regional estimates.)

The South

Nearly 36 percent (35.9) of the Nation's population resided in the South in 2003, and law enforcement agencies in the region reported an estimated 38.9 percent of the country's robberies. The South had the highest volume, 160,675 estimated offenses, and rate, 153.7 per 100,000 population, of the four geographic regions. The number of robberies reported in the South declined 0.9 percent from the 2002 number, and the rate of robberies per 100,000 inhabitants declined 2.1 percent from the 2002 figure. (See Tables 3 and 4, regional estimates.)

The West

The West accounted for 22.9 percent of the Nation's total population and 22.8 percent of the country's robberies in 2003. The region had a 1.6-percent decrease in robberies from the 2002 estimate, and a rate of 141.9 robberies per 100,000 in population, a 3.1-percent decline from the 2002 rate. (See Tables 3 and 4, regional estimates.)

Community Types

The UCR Program aggregates data by three community types: Metropolitan Statistical Areas (MSAs), cities outside metropolitan statistical areas, and non-metropolitan counties. (Additional in-depth information regarding community types is located in Appendix III.) Nearly 83 percent (82.8) of the Nation's population lived in MSAs in 2003. Residents of cities outside MSAs accounted for 6.8 percent of the country's population, and 10.4 percent of the population lived in nonmetropolitan counties. (Based on Table 2, community type estimates.) The Nation's MSAs had a rate of 164.8 robberies per 100,000 inhabitants in 2003. Cities outside MSAs had a rate of 60.0 robberies per 100,000 inhabitants, and nonmetropolitan counties had a rate of 15.8 robberies per 100,000 in population. (See Table 2, community type estimates.)

Population Groups: Trends and Rates

The UCR Program aggregates crime statistics by population groups. (An explanation of these groupings can be found in Appendix III.) The Nation's cities collectively reported a 2.2-percent decrease in the number of robberies in 2003. Among population groups with the label *city*, cities with populations of 250,000 or more had the largest decrease, 3.1 percent, in robberies from the 2002 figure. Cities with 10,000 to 24,999 inhabitants had the largest increase, 1.3 percent, in the volume of robberies reported to law enforcement. Metropolitan counties had a 0.6-percent increase in robberies; the number of robberies reported in nonmetropolitan counties remained virtually unchanged (+0.1 percent) from the 2002 number. Additional data for population groups are provided in Table 12.

In terms of the rate of robberies, the country's cities collectively had a rate of 201.1 robbery offenses per 100,000 inhabitants. Of the population groups, the Nation's largest cities, those with 250,000 or more inhabitants, had the highest rate at 379.7 robbery offenses per 100,000 inhabitants, and the Nation's smallest cities, those with less

Table 2.18

Robbery by Month
Percent Distribution, 1999-2003

Month	1999	2000	2001	2002	2003
January	8.9	8.6	8.3	8.8	8.6
February	7.3	7.1	6.5	6.7	6.5
March	7.7	7.7	7.6	7.6	8.0
April	7.6	7.5	7.4	7.4	8.0
May	8.1	8.1	8.1	8.0	8.4
June	8.1	7.9	8.0	7.9	8.2
July	8.7	8.7	8.7	8.8	8.8
August	8.8	9.0	8.7	8.9	8.7
September	8.3	8.5	8.5	8.8	8.4
October	8.8	9.1	9.7	9.1	9.0
November	8.6	8.7	9.2	8.6	8.4
December	9.2	9.0	9.4	9.2	9.1

Table 2.19

Robbery
Percent Distribution by Region, 2003

Type	United States total	Northeast	Midwest	South	West
Total[1]	100.0	100.0	100.0	100.0	100.0
Street/highway	43.4	56.9	47.1	37.0	43.1
Commercial house	14.6	9.6	11.5	15.4	17.6
Gas or service station	2.7	3.8	3.4	2.4	2.4
Convenience store	6.2	6.0	5.0	7.4	5.2
Residence	13.7	9.3	12.1	18.7	9.9
Bank	2.3	2.6	2.2	1.9	2.7
Miscellaneous	17.0	11.8	18.7	17.1	19.1

[1] Because of rounding, the percentages may not add to 100.0.

Figure 2.7

Robbery Categories
Percent Change from 1999

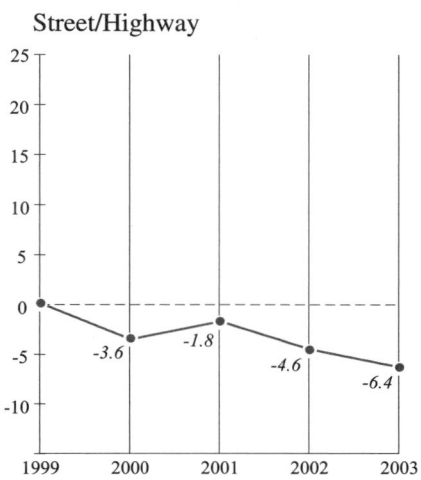

Street/Highway

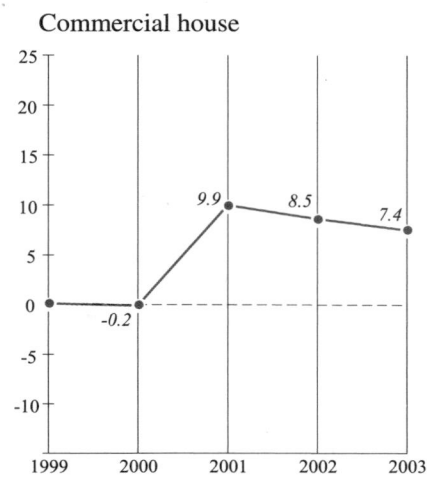

Commercial house

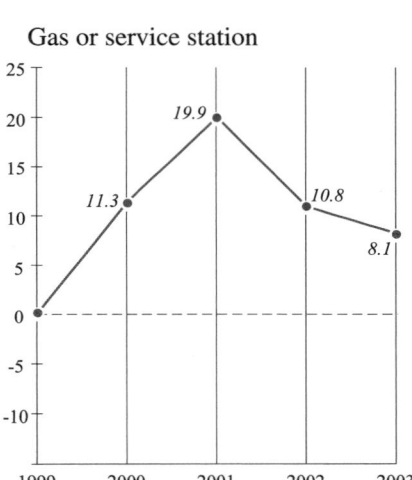

Gas or service station

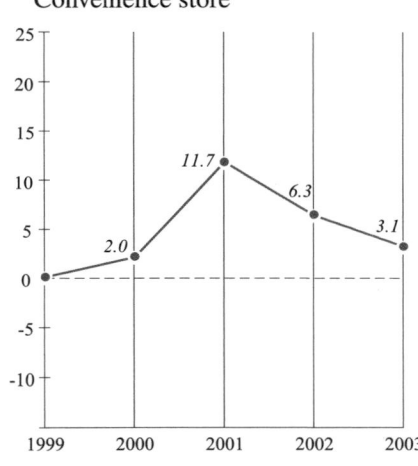

Convenience store

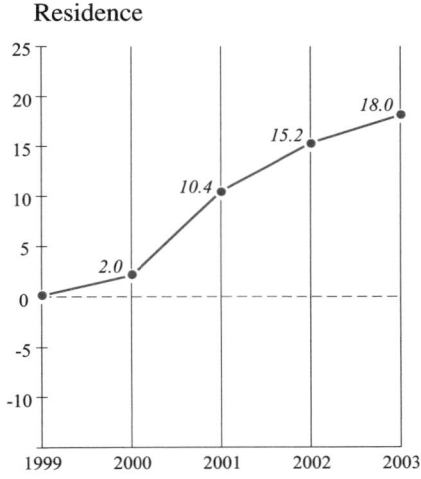

Residence

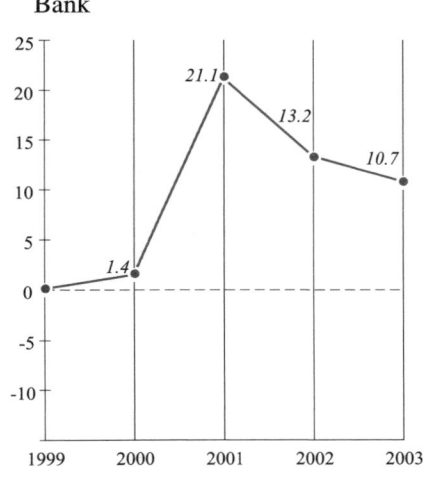

Bank

than 10,000 inhabitants, had the lowest rate at 55.2 per 100,000 population. Law enforcement personnel in metropolitan counties reported 72.3 robberies per 100,000 inhabitants, and those in nonmetropolitan counties reported a rate of 16.7 offenses per 100,000 population. Robbery rates for each of the population groups are furnished in Table 16.

Offense Analysis

Supplemental data concerning robberies reported by law enforcement personnel to the national UCR Program during 2003 indicated the following:

Robbery by Weapon

An examination of information collected about weapons used in the commission of a robbery showed that firearms were again the weapon of choice. During 2003, offenders used firearms in 41.8 percent of all reported robberies. Strong-arm tactics such as hands, fists, and feet were used in 39.9 percent of robberies, and knives or other cutting instruments were used in 8.9 percent of robberies. Other weapons were employed in 9.4 percent of the robberies

reported in 2003. (See Tables 2.21 and 19.) Table 21 provides a state-by-state breakdown of the weapons used in robberies.

Loss by Dollar Value

Robbery offenders took an estimated $514 million from their victims in 2003. (Based on Tables 1 and 23.) Nationally, the average monetary value of property stolen during a robbery was $1,244. (See Table 23.) Banks lost an average of $4,767 per robbery, and commercial houses (such as supermarkets, department stores, restaurants, taverns, finance companies, hotels, and motels) lost an average of $1,778 per robbery. The estimated value of losses from robberies of residences was $1,472 per robbery. Losses to victims of robberies on streets or highways averaged $898, and to victims of robberies of convenience stores, $813. Owners of gas/service stations lost an average of $690 per robbery. Robberies that occurred at unspecified locations (denoted as miscellaneous) cost victims an average of $1,258 per incident. (See Table 23.)

Robbery Trends by Location

The only type of location for which law enforcement reported an increase in the number of robberies in 2003 when compared to 2002 data were residences at 2.4 percent. Among the types of locations, the location type with the largest decrease, 3.0 percent, was convenience stores. The remaining location types and their decreases were gas/service stations, 2.4 percent; banks, 2.2 percent; street/highway, 1.9 percent; and commercial houses, 1.0 percent. Collectively, the number of robberies at miscellaneous locations decreased 2.5 percent. (See Table 23.)

Percent Distribution

In 2003, 43.4 percent of all robberies occurred on streets or highways; 14.6 percent of all robberies happened in commercial houses. Robberies in residences accounted for 13.7 percent of robberies, and robberies of convenience stores made up 6.2 percent of the Nation's reported robberies. Robberies of gas/service stations accounted for 2.7 percent of the Nation's robberies, and robberies of banks comprised 2.3

Table 2.20

Robbery
Percent Distribution by Population Group, 2003

Type	Group I (58 cities, 250,000 and over; population 37,217,317)	Group II (146 cities, 100,000 to 249,999; population 21,875,380)	Group III (353 cities, 50,000 to 99,999; population 24,412,026)	Group IV (684 cities, 25,000 to 49,999; population 23,742,865)	Group V (1,512 cities, 10,000 to 24,999; population 23,834,682)	Group VI (5,925 cities, under 10,000; population 19,204,778)	County agencies (3,302 agencies; population 74,231,706)
Total[1]	100.0	100.0	100.0	100.0	100.0	100.0	100.0
Street/highway	51.7	43.6	42.2	33.4	28.6	25.4	31.2
Commercial house	12.3	16.6	15.3	16.5	17.5	14.9	17.9
Gas or service station	1.7	2.8	3.3	4.2	4.8	4.4	3.7
Convenience store	4.5	6.6	7.0	8.6	8.5	10.1	7.9
Residence	12.6	13.1	12.0	12.7	14.6	14.3	19.5
Bank	1.5	2.5	2.7	3.6	3.9	3.6	2.7
Miscellaneous	15.6	14.8	17.5	21.1	22.1	27.3	17.0

[1] Because of rounding, the percentages may not add to 100.0.

percent of all robberies in 2003. Seventeen percent of robberies occurred at miscellaneous venues. (See Table 23.)

Clearances

The UCR Program considers an offense to be cleared by arrest or solved for crime reporting purposes when at least one person is arrested, charged with the commission of the offense, and turned over to the court for prosecution. A clearance by exceptional means can be recorded when the offender has been identified and located and there is enough evidence to support an arrest but conditions beyond law enforcement's control prevent the agency from bringing charges. Section III of this publication provides additional information regarding clearances.

Nationally, law enforcement agencies cleared 26.3 percent of robberies; in the Nation's cities collectively in 2003, law enforcement personnel cleared 25.7 percent of robberies by arrest or exceptional means. Among population groups labeled *city*, cities with less than 10,000 inhabitants had the highest percentage of robberies cleared at 33.6 percent; cities with populations of 250,000 and over had the lowest percentage of clearances at 23.0 percent. Law enforcement in metropolitan counties cleared 29.0 percent of reported robberies, and those in nonmetropolitan counties cleared 43.1 percent of robberies. (See Table 25.)

Clearances and Juveniles

When an offender under the age of 18 is cited to appear in juvenile court or before other juvenile authorities, the UCR Program considers the incident as cleared by arrest even though a physical arrest may not have occurred. Also, the UCR Program considers clearances involving both juvenile and adult offenders as adult clearances. Throughout the Nation, 14.1 percent of robbery

clearances involved only juveniles. In 2003, juveniles (persons under the age of 18) accounted for 14.2 percent of robbery clearances in the Nation's cities collectively. An analysis of the data by population group showed that law enforcement in cities with populations of 50,000 to 99,999 inhabitants reported the highest percentage of clearances of robberies involving only juveniles at 15.6 percent; those in cities with populations of 250,000 or greater reported the lowest percentage at 13.1 percent. In the country's metropolitan counties, 13.8 percent of robbery clearances involved juveniles only, and in the nonmetropolitan counties, 8.6 percent of robbery clearances involved juveniles only. (See Table 28.)

Arrests

Table 29 in this book provides the estimated number of arrests in the Nation for the 29 offenses for which the UCR Program collects arrest data. The remaining tables in Section IV of this publication contain actual arrest data for those agencies that provided 12 months of arrest data to the national UCR Program.

Total Arrests

In 2003, law enforcement agencies throughout the Nation reported an estimated 107,553 arrests for robbery, which comprised 18.0 percent of all arrests for violent crime. (Based on Table 29.)

Arrest Trends

An examination of the number of arrests for robbery in the Nation showed that the volume of robbery arrests in 2003 remained virtually unchanged when compared to the number of arrests in 2002. Throughout the Nation, the number of arrests of adults for robbery decreased 0.8 percent, but the number of arrests of juveniles for robbery rose 2.5 percent

when compared to the 2002 figure. (See Table 36.) The number of males arrested for robbery in 2003 was virtually unchanged (-0.2 percent), but the number of females arrested for robbery rose 1.6 percent when compared to the 2002 figure. (See Table 37.)

The 5-year trend for arrest data for robbery showed that the number of arrests for robbery showed little change (+0.2 percent) when the 2003 data were compared to those from 1999. The number of juveniles arrested for robbery decreased 7.6 percent from the 1999 figure, but the number of adults arrested for robbery increased 3.0 percent. (See Table 34.) The number of males arrested for robbery in 2003 declined 0.4 percent from the 1999 figure; however, the number of females arrested for robbery rose 5.8 percent. (See Table 35.)

The 10-year trend data for robbery arrests showed that the number of robbery arrests in 2003 declined 25.0 percent from the 1994 number. An examination of that trend data by age showed that the number of arrests of juveniles for robbery dropped 43.1 percent and the number of arrests of adults fell 16.9 percent. (See Table 32.) By gender, a comparison of data regarding arrestees for robbery indicated that the number of males arrested for robbery in 2003 was 26.2 percent less than in 1994, and the number of females arrested for robbery was 12.4 percent less. (See Table 33.)

Arrest Rates

Nationally, the robbery arrest rate in 2003 was 37.1 arrests per 100,000 inhabitants. In those population groups labeled as *city*, the rate of robbery arrests in cities collectively was 45.6 arrests per 100,000 inhabitants. Cities with populations of 250,000 or more inhabitants had the highest rate at 76.1 arrests per 100,000 inhabitants, and cities with less than 10,000 in population had the lowest rate at 19.5 arrests per 100,000 citizens. Law enforcement agencies in metropolitan counties recorded 22.9 robbery arrests per 100,000 inhabitants, and those in nonmetropolitan counties recorded 9.1 arrests for robbery per 100,000 in population. (See Table 31.)

By region, law enforcement agencies in the Northeast reported 41.6 arrests for robbery per 100,000 population; those in the West, 39.6; in the South, 37.9; and in the Midwest, 28.5 arrests for robbery per 100,000 inhabitants. (See Table 30.)

Distribution by Age, Sex, and Race

An analysis of arrest data by age showed that adults comprised 76.3 percent of all persons arrested for robbery in the Nation in 2003. (Based on Table 38.) A gender breakdown of the data showed that the majority (89.6 percent) of robbery arrestees were male. (See Table 42.) By race, 54.4 percent of robbery arrestees were black, 43.9 percent were white, and the remainder were of other races. (See Table 43.) Further breakdowns of robbery arrestees by age and sex are presented in Tables 39 and 40.

Table 2.21

Robbery, Types of Weapons Used
Percent Distribution by Region, 2003

| Region | Total all weapons[1] | Armed | | | |
		Firearms	Knives or cutting instruments	Other weapons	Strongarm
Total	**100.0**	**41.8**	**8.9**	**9.4**	**39.9**
Northeast	100.0	35.0	11.2	8.6	45.2
Midwest	100.0	43.4	6.3	10.0	40.3
South	100.0	47.9	8.0	9.6	34.6
West	100.0	35.3	10.3	9.5	44.9

[1] Because of rounding, the percentages may not add to 100.0.

Aggravated Assault

Definition

According to the Uniform Crime Reporting (UCR) Program, an aggravated assault is an unlawful attack by one person upon another for the purpose of inflicting severe or aggravated bodily injury. This type of assault is usually accompanied by the use of weapon or by means likely to produce death or great bodily harm. Attempts involving the display or threat of a gun, knife, or other weapon are included because serious personal injury would likely result if the assault were completed.

Trend

Year	Number of offenses	Rate per 100,000 inhabitants
2002	891,407	309.5
2003	857,921	295.0
Percent change	-3.8	-4.7

National Volume, Trends, and Rates

Nationally, 2003 marked the tenth consecutive decline in the volume of aggravated assaults. The estimated total, 857,921 offenses, represents a 3.8-percent decline from the 2002 figure. The 2003 estimate was 5.9 percent lower than the 1999 volume and 22.9 percent below the volume recorded for 1994. Likewise, the rate of aggravated assaults, 295.0 per 100,000 persons, decreased 4.7 percent from the previous year's rate. Five- and 10-year trend data revealed that the 2003 rate was 11.8 percent lower than the 1999 rate and 31.0 percent lower than the 1994 estimate. (See Table 1, national estimates.)

Regional Offense Trends and Rates

The UCR Program divides the United States into four regions: the Northeast, the Midwest, the South, and the West. (A map delineating the regions can be found in Appendix III.) The offense of aggravated assault declined in both volume and rate per 100,000 persons in all four regions when comparing 2003 to 2002 estimates.

The Northeast

In 2003, the Northeast Region, which had the smallest proportion of the U.S. population (18.7 percent) also had the smallest proportion of aggravated assaults, 14.3 percent of the total. (See Table 3, regional estimates.) States in the Northeast collectively had a 6.0-percent decline—the largest decline among the regions—in the number of aggravated assaults from 2002. These states also

Figure 2.8

Aggravated Assault
Percent Change from 1999

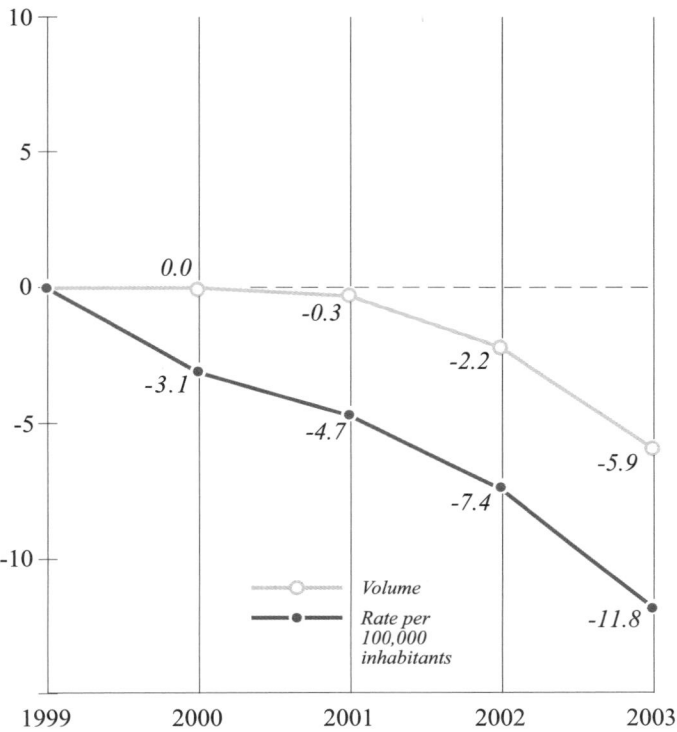

showed the largest decline in the rate of aggravated assaults: the 225.0 offenses per 100,000 persons was a 6.4-percent drop from the previous year's rate. (See Table 4, regional, divisional, state estimates.)

The Midwest

Accounting for 22.5 percent of the national population, the Midwest had approximately 18.2 percent of the aggravated assaults in 2003. (See Table 3, regional estimates.) Compared to 2002 data, the region had a 5.4-percent decline in the number of aggravated assaults. The 2003 rate of 238.1 offenses per 100,000 persons was a 5.8-percent decrease from the 2002 rate. (See Table 4, regional, divisional, state estimates.)

The South

In 2003, the South, the Nation's most populous region (35.9 percent of the population), accounted for an estimated 43.3 percent of the aggravated assaults in the United States. (See Table 3, regional estimates.) The number of aggravated assault offenses dropped 3.6 percent from the prior year's estimate. The South had a rate of 355.1 aggravated assaults per 100,000 inhabitants, which represented a 4.8-percent decline from the 2002 rate. (See Table 4, regional, divisional, state estimates.)

The West

Comprising 22.9 percent of the population, the West accounted for a 24.3 percent of the aggravated assaults in the Nation in 2003. (See Table 3, regional estimates.) By volume, the number of offenses estimated for the Western States was 1.4 percent lower than the 2002 estimate. The region had a rate of 313.8 aggravated assaults per 100,000 people. That rate was a decrease of 2.8 percent from the 2002 rate. (See Table 4, regional, divisional, state estimates.)

Community Types

The UCR Program classifies communities as Metropolitan Statistical Areas (MSAs), metropolitan counties, and nonmetropolitan counties. MSAs are those community types made up of a principal city of at least 50,000 inhabitants, the county containing that city, and adjacent areas with strong economic or cultural ties to the principal city as measured through commuting. Metropolitan counties are composed of mostly incorporated areas, and nonmetropolitan counties are mostly unincorporated.

MSAs, which accounted for 82.8 percent of the Nation's population and had 87.9 percent of the aggravated assaults in 2003, had a rate of 313.1 aggravated assaults per 100,000 inhabitants. Cities outside metropolitan areas, with 6.8 percent of the population and 6.5 percent of aggravated assaults, had a rate of 283.0 aggravated assaults per 100,000 inhabitants. Nonmetropolitan counties, accounting for 10.4 percent of the national population and 5.6 percent of aggravated assaults, had a rate of 159.0 aggravated assaults per 100,000 persons. (Based on Table 2, community type estimates.)

Population Groups: Trends and Rates

In order to establish a 2-year trend, the UCR Program reviewed data from all agencies that submitted aggravated assault data for at least 6 common months in both 2002 and 2003. Collectively, cities had a 5.1-percent decline in the number of aggravated assaults in 2003, and the Nation's largest cities, those with populations of 250,000 and over, showed an 8.0-percent drop from the previous year's data. Nonmetropolitan counties experienced a decrease of 4.2 percent. Metropolitan counties recorded a decrease of 1.3 percent. (See Table 12.)

The UCR Program calculated offense rates for the population groups by reviewing reports from all agencies that provided 12 months of data. Based upon that review, the Nation's cities collectively had an aggravated assault rate of 352.7 per 100,000 inhabitants.

Table 2.22

Aggravated Assault by Month
Percent Distribution, 1999-2003

Month	1999	2000	2001	2002	2003
January	7.9	7.5	7.5	7.5	7.5
February	7.0	7.2	6.7	6.7	6.4
March	8.0	8.3	8.1	8.0	8.3
April	8.3	8.4	8.5	8.4	8.5
May	9.1	9.3	9.0	9.0	9.2
June	8.8	8.9	8.9	9.2	9.1
July	9.5	9.5	9.6	9.6	9.4
August	9.2	9.1	9.0	9.4	9.4
September	8.5	8.6	8.8	9.4	8.7
October	8.6	8.6	8.7	8.4	8.7
November	7.7	7.3	7.7	7.3	7.7
December	7.5	7.2	7.5	7.1	7.1

Table 2.23

Aggravated Assault, Types of Weapons Used
Percent Distribution by Region, 2003

Region	Total all weapons[1]	Firearms	Knives or cutting instruments	Other weapons (clubs, blunt objects, etc.)	Personal weapons
Total	**100.0**	**19.1**	**18.2**	**35.9**	**26.9**
Northeast	100.0	14.8	19.6	34.0	31.6
Midwest	100.0	18.0	16.7	34.9	30.3
South	100.0	21.0	19.9	38.2	20.9
West	100.0	18.2	15.5	33.3	33.0

[1] Because of rounding, the percentages may not add to 100.0.

Among the Nation's population groups labeled city, those with populations of 250,000 and over had the highest aggravated assault rate of 533.2 offenses per 100,000 persons. Within that population group, those cities with 500,000 to 999,999 had the highest rate, 537.4 per 100,000 individuals. Cities with populations from 10,000 to 24,999 had the lowest rate of aggravated assaults, 212.9 per 100,000 inhabitants; the Nation's smallest cities, those with fewer than 10,000 in population, had a rate of 249.1. Collectively, agencies in metropolitan counties recorded a rate of 242.8 aggravated assaults per 100,000 in population, and those in nonmetropolitan counties recorded a rate of 175.1. (See Table 16.)

Offense Analysis

By weapon type, personal weapons, such as hands, fists, and feet, were used in 26.9 percent of the aggravated assaults, firearms in 19.1 percent, and knives or other cutting instruments in 18.2 percent. Other weapon types were used in 35.9 percent of the aggravated assaults in 2003. (Based on Table 19.)

A breakdown of the aggravated assault rates per 100,000 persons by type of weapon revealed the following: For every 100,000 individuals, there were 80.9 attacks using personal weapons (hands, fists, feet, etc.), 57.5 attacks using a firearm, 54.8 attacks with a knife or cutting instrument, and 108.1 attacks using another weapon (blunt instrument, club, etc.). (See Table 19.)

Clearances

Nationwide in 2002, law enforcement agencies cleared 55.9 percent of reported aggravated assaults. Collectively, cities cleared 54.6 percent of aggravated assaults. Law enforcement agencies in the Nation's largest cities, those with populations of 250,000 and over, cleared

50.6 percent of the aggravated assaults that came to their attention. Agencies in the smallest cities (those with fewer than 10,000 in population) showed the highest percentage of clearances for the offense of aggravated assault—64.5 percent. Agencies serving metropolitan counties cleared 58.8 percent, and those in nonmetropolitan counties cleared 62.9 percent of the reported aggravated assaults in their jurisdictions. (See Table 25.)

Law enforcement agencies nationwide cleared 63.9 percent of the aggravated assaults involving personal weapons such as hands, fists, or feet and 61.4 percent of the aggravated assaults involving knives or cutting instruments. In addition, agencies cleared 39.7 percent of the aggravated assaults that involved firearms and 55.6 percent of those that involved other weapon types. (See Table 27.)

Law enforcement in the Northeastern states cleared the highest percentage of aggravated assaults, 61.9 percent. Law enforcement in the Western states cleared 57.1 percent of aggravated assaults, followed by agencies in the Southern states with 54.2 percent, and those in the Midwestern states with 53.8 percent. (See Table 26.)

Clearances and Juveniles

When an offender under the age of 18 is arrested or cited to appear in juvenile court or before other juvenile authorities, the UCR Program considers that incident as a clearance by arrest. However, according to Program definitions, clearances involving both adult and juvenile offenders are classified as adult clearances.

Of all aggravated assault clearances reported nationally in 2003, 11.9 percent involved only juveniles, defined by the UCR Program as persons under the age of 18. In the Nation's cities,

collectively, 12.0 percent of clearances for aggravated assault involved only juveniles. In metropolitan counties, 12.6 percent of aggravated assault clearances involved only persons under the age of 18; in nonmetropolitan counties, 9.4 percent of aggravated assault clearances involved only juveniles. (See Table 28.)

Arrests

In 2003, the UCR Program estimated arrests for aggravated assault at 449,933. Arrests for aggravated assault comprised an estimated 75.4 percent of all violent crime arrests and 3.3 percent of all arrests. (Based on Table 29, which presents the estimated number of arrests for the Nation.)

Arrest Trends

Nationally, aggravated assault arrests declined 2.5 percent from the previous year's figure. (See Table 36.) The 5- and 10-year trend data showed declines in arrests for this offense of 4.6 percent and 12.3 percent, respectively. (See Tables 32 and 34.)

Arrest Distribution by Age, Sex, and Race

Of those persons arrested for aggravated assault in 2003, 86.3 percent were adults. (Based on Table 38.) A review of the total arrests for this offense indicated that 39.9 percent of arrestees were under the age of 25, approximately 25 percent (24.8) were under the age of 21, and 5.0 percent were under the age of 15. (See Table 41.) The number of adult arrests for aggravated assault declined 2.9 percent when compared to the number in 2002, 3.8 percent when compared to that in 1999, and 9.8 percent compared to the 1994 figure. The number of juveniles arrested for aggravated assault in 2003 showed virtually no change from the previous year's rate (+ 0.1 percent). However, the number of juveniles arrested for aggravated assault declined 9.1 percent from the 1999 total and 25.8 percent from the 1994 number. (See Tables 32, 34, and 36.)

Persons arrested for aggravated assault during 2003 were overwhelmingly male—79.3 percent. (See Table 42.) Of the males arrested for this offense, 86.8 percent were adults. Of juvenile males arrested for aggravated assault, 35.5 percent were under the age of 15. (Based on Table 39.) A review of the data concerning females arrested for aggravated assault demonstrated that 84.4 percent were adults. Of the female juveniles arrested for aggravated assault in 2003, 38.5 percent were under the age of 15. (Based on Table 40.)

When distributed by race, the data showed that 64.7 percent of all persons arrested for aggravated assault were white and 33.0 percent were black. The two other racial groups, Asian or Pacific Islanders and American Indians or Alaskan Natives, accounted for 1.2 percent and 1.1 percent of arrestees, respectively. (See Table 43.)

Property Crime

Definition

In the Uniform Crime Reporting (UCR) Program, property crime includes the offenses of burglary, larceny-theft, motor vehicle theft, and arson. The object of the theft-type offenses is the taking of money or property, but there is no force or threat of force against the victims. The property crime category includes arson because the offense involves the destruction of property; however, arson victims may be subjected to force. Because of limited participation and varying collection procedures by local agencies, only limited data are available for arson. Arson statistics are included in trend, clearance, and arrest tables throughout *Crime in the United States*, but they are not included in any estimated volume data. The arson section in this report provides more information on that offense.

Trend

Year	Number of offenses[1]	Rate per 100,000 inhabitants[1]
2002	10,455,277	3,630.6
2003	10,435,523	3,588.4
Percent change	-0.2	-1.2

[1]Does not include arson. See Offense Tabulations.

Figure 2.9

Property Crime
Percent Change from 1999

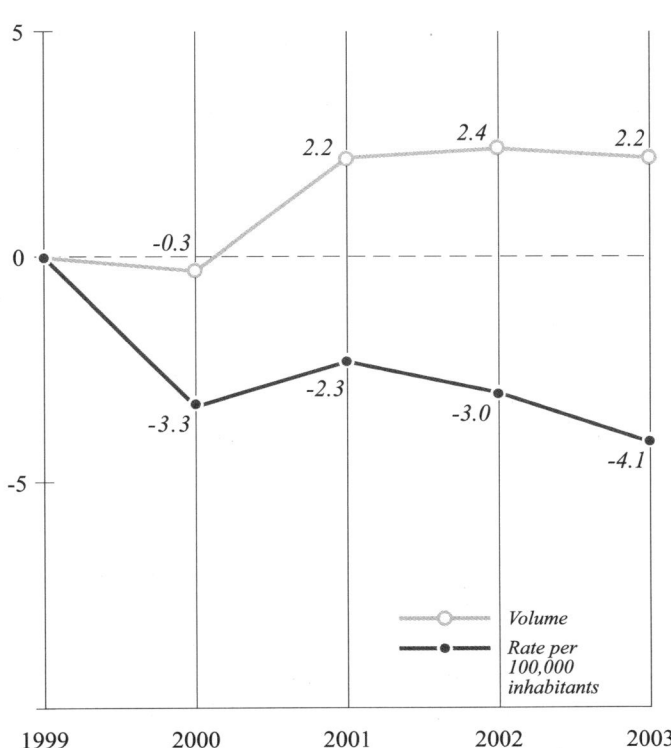

National Volume, Trends, and Rates

Volume

In 2003, law enforcement agencies reported an estimated 10,435,523 property crimes. The figure was 0.2 percent lower than the 2002 estimate. Further trend analyses of 5- and 10-year volumes for property crime indicated that the 2003 figure was 2.2 percent higher than the 1999 number and 14.0 percent lower than the number in 1994. (See Table 1, national estimates.)

Among individual property crimes in 2003, burglary offenses rose 0.1 percent, and motor vehicle theft increased 1.1 percent when compared to the 2002 estimates. Larceny-theft decreased 0.5 percent. (See Table 1, national estimates.)

Rate

The Nation's rate of property crime offenses in 2003 was measured at 3,588.4 offenses per 100,000 inhabitants. The 2003 rate decreased 1.2 percent compared to the previous year's rate. When measured against the rates from 5 and 10 years ago, property crime rates declined 4.1 percent from the 1999 rate and fell 23.0 percent from the 1994 rate. (See Table 1, national estimates.)

Regional Offense Trends and Rates

The UCR Program divides the United States into four regions for data analyses: the Northeast, the Midwest, the South, and the West. (Appendix III provides more information on UCR area definitions.) An examination of 2003 data showed the following information regarding the Nation's four regions.

The Northeast

Property crimes reported by law enforcement agencies in the Northeast accounted for an estimated 12.6 percent of property crimes nationwide. (See Table 3, regional estimates.) Compared to the 2002 volume, property crime decreased 2.3 percent in the Northeast in 2003. The rate of property crime offenses in the Northeast—2,410.1 per 100,000 inhabitants—also showed a decline, 2.7 percent from the previous year's rate. (See Table 4, regional, divisional, state estimates.)

The Midwest

Property crimes reported by the Midwest's law enforcement agencies were estimated at 21.1 percent of the Nation's property crime total. (See Table 3, regional estimates.) The region's volume showed a 2.3-percent decrease from the 2002 volume. When compared to the 2002 rate, the Midwest's property crime rate, 3,369.5 property crimes per 100,000 inhabitants, declined 2.7 percent. (See Table 4, regional, divisional, state estimates.)

The South

Law enforcement agencies in the South had an estimated 41.2 percent of the property crimes nationwide. (See Table 3, regional estimates.) A comparison to the previous year's volume showed that property crime reported for 2003 increased 0.3 percent in the South. The 2003 rate of 4,115.6 property crimes per 100,000 population in the South was a 1.0-percent decrease from the 2002 rate. (See Table 4, regional, divisional, state estimates.)

The West

Law enforcement agencies in the West had an estimated 25.1 percent of the Nation's property crime. (See Table 3, regional estimates.) The volume of property crime offenses in the West increased 2.0 percent from the volume reported for 2002. The West's property crime rate of 3,939.3 offenses per 100,000 population was 0.5 percent above the rate for the previous year. (See Table 4, regional, divisional, state estimates.)

Community Types

When presenting crime data, the UCR Program designates three types of communities: Metropolitan Statistical Areas (MSAs), cities outside of MSAs, and nonmetropolitan counties. In 2003, MSAs, which accounted for an estimated 82.8 percent of the Nation's population, had an estimated property crime rate of 3,783.0 offenses per 100,000 persons. Cities outside MSAs, with 6.8 percent of the population, had a rate of 4,147.5 property offenses per 100,000 inhabitants. Nonmetropolitan counties, making up 10.4 percent of the overall population, had a rate of 1,677.1 property crimes per 100,000 in population. (See Table 2, community type estimates.) For more information on UCR area definitions, see Appendix III.

Population Groups: Trends and Rates

The UCR Program aggregates crime statistics by population groups; an explanation of these groupings can be found in Appendix III. Among population groups in 2003, property crime decreased 0.3 percent in the Nation's cities collectively. Changes from the 2002 percentage for city groupings ranged from a 1.2-percent increase in property crime in the Nation's smallest cities, those with populations less than 10,000 inhabitants, to a 1.2-percent decrease in the Nation's largest cities, those with 250,000 and over in population. (See Table 12.)

In terms of reported property crime, the Nation's cities collectively had a property crime rate of 4,342.8 per 100,000 population. Nonmetropolitan counties had a property crime rate of 1,808.2 per 100,000 people, and metropolitan counties experienced a rate of 2,650.9 property crime offenses per 100,000 inhabitants. (See Table 16.)

Offense Analysis

In 2003, the estimated dollar loss attributable to property crimes (excluding arson) was nearly $17 billion. This figure represented an increase of 2.1 percent from the 2002 estimated dollar loss

Table 2.24

Property Crime by Month
Percent Distribution, 1999-2003

Month	1999	2000	2001	2002	2003
January	8.0	7.8	7.8	8.3	8.0
February	7.2	7.3	6.8	7.0	6.7
March	8.0	8.2	7.8	7.8	8.0
April	7.9	7.9	7.9	8.0	8.2
May	8.3	8.6	8.5	8.5	8.6
June	8.6	8.6	8.5	8.4	8.5
July	9.1	9.1	9.1	9.2	9.1
August	9.2	9.2	9.1	9.0	8.9
September	8.5	8.5	8.5	8.6	8.7
October	8.7	8.8	9.2	8.8	8.8
November	8.2	8.1	8.5	8.1	8.1
December	8.4	8.0	8.5	8.3	8.3

for property crime. (Based on Table 1, which provides national estimates, and Table 23, which includes data from law enforcement agencies submitting at least 6 months of complete offense reports for 2003.)

Among the individual property crimes, the 2003 estimated dollar losses were $3.5 billion for burglary, $4.9 billion for larceny-theft, and $8.6 billion for motor vehicle theft. (Based on Tables 1 and 23.) Arson (which is excluded from the estimated property crime tabulations because of limited coverage and participation) had an average dollar loss of $11,942 for the 64,043 offenses for which monetary values were reported. (See Table 2.31.)

Clearances

In the UCR Program, law enforcement can clear offenses either by arrest or by exceptional means, i.e., when elements beyond the control of law enforcement prevent the placing of formal charges against the offender. (Section III provides more information regarding clearances.) During 2003, law enforcement nationwide cleared 16.4 percent of reported property crimes. (See Table 25.)

By region in 2003, law enforcement in the Northeast cleared 20.1 percent of property crimes; law enforcement in the South cleared 16.6 percent, followed by the Midwest with 16.5 percent, and the West with 14.4 percent of reported property crime. (See Table 26.)

Law enforcement in the Nation's cities collectively cleared 16.3 percent of property crimes in 2003. In nonmetropolitan counties, law enforcement cleared 17.8 percent of property crimes and in metropolitan counties, 16.2 percent. (See Table 25.)

Among the population groups labeled city, law enforcement in cities with populations of 10,000 to 24,999 had the greatest percentage of property crimes cleared, 20.7 percent. Law enforcement in the nation's largest cities, those with populations of over 250,000 inhabitants, cleared the lowest percentage of property crimes during 2003, 12.8 percent. (See Table 25.)

Clearances and Juveniles

For UCR purposes, when an offender under the age of 18 is cited to appear before juvenile authorities, the incident is cleared by arrest, even though a physical arrest may not have occurred. Additionally, clearances involving both adult and juvenile offenders are classified as adult clearances.

In 2003, clearances involving only juveniles (persons under the age of 18) comprised 19.3 percent of all property crime clearances. By offense breakdown, this age group accounted for 16.8 percent of burglary clearances, 20.2 percent of larceny-theft clearances, and 17.3 percent of motor vehicle theft clearances.

In the Nation's cities during 2003, juvenile clearances accounted for 20.1 percent of all property crime clearances. In nonmetropolitan counties, 15.7 percent of the clearances involved juveniles only and in the metropolitan counties, 16.7 percent. (See Table 28.)

Arrests

Total Arrests

Table 29 in this publication provides the estimated number of arrests in the Nation for the 29 offenses for which the UCR Program collects arrest data. The remaining tables in Section IV of this publication contain actual arrest data for those agencies that provided 12 months of arrest data to the national Program.

Law enforcement agencies made an estimated 1.6 million arrests during 2003 for property crime offenses (in-cluding arson). Property crime arrests accounted for an estimated 11.8 percent of all arrests. Of the estimated arrests for property crimes, arrests for larceny-theft offenses comprised the largest percentage, 71.3 percent. (Additional arrest breakdowns can be found in Table 29.)

Arrest Rates

In 2003, the national property crime arrest rate was 558.4 per 100,000 inhabitants. Among the regions, the South had the highest arrest rate for property crimes with 604.0 arrests per 100,000 persons. The West had the second highest rate for property crime arrests with 582.2, followed by the Midwest with 562.1, and the Northeast with 438.4 property crime arrests per 100,000 inhabitants. (See Table 30.)

Collectively, the Nation's cities recorded an overall property crime arrest rate of 661.1 arrests per 100,000 inhabitants. Among those population groups labeled as city, the rate of arrests per 100,000 residents ranged from a low of 604.6 in cities with populations under 10,000 to a high of 711.5 in cities with 50,000 to 99,999 in population. The Nation's metropolitan counties had an arrest rate of 361.6 property crime arrests per 100,000 people, and nonmetropolitan counties experienced 277.0 property crime arrests per 100,000 residents. (See Table 31.)

Arrest Trends

A comparison of the volume of property crime arrests from 2003 to 2002 showed a 0.7-percent increase in the overall category. Property crime arrests increased for burglary by 2.2 percent, for motor vehicle theft by 0.8 percent, and for larceny-theft by 0.5 percent. Arson arrests declined by 5.8 percent. Arrests of adults for property crime in 2003 were up 2.3 percent when compared to the 2002 figure, but arrests of juveniles declined 2.9 percent when compared to the previous years' arrests. (See Table 36.)

An analysis of 5-year and 10-year trend data revealed a nationwide decline in the number of arrests for property crimes from the 1999 and 1994 levels. Property crime arrests in 2003 were 3.3 percent less than in 1999 and 23.4 percent fewer than in 1994. Tables 32 and 34 provide more information regarding trend data.

Distribution by Age, Sex, and Race

Tables 38-43 in Section IV of this report include information on the age, sex, and race of persons arrested for property crimes. In 2003, a total of 71.1 percent of persons arrested for property crime were adults (persons 18 years and older). Of the adults arrested for property crime offenses, 40.1 percent were 18 to 24 years of age. By gender, 69.2 percent of all persons arrested for property crime were male. By race, 68.2 percent of all persons arrested for property crime were white, 29.1 percent were black, and 2.6 percent were of other races. (See Tables 38, 42, and 43.)

Information regarding the UCR Program's statistical methodology and table construction can be found in Appendix I.

Burglary

Definition

Burglary is defined in the Uniform Crime Reporting (UCR) Program as the unlawful entry of a structure to commit a felony or a theft. The use of force to gain entry is not required to classify an offense as a burglary. Burglary in the UCR Program is categorized into three subclassifications: forcible entry, unlawful entry where no force is used, and attempted forcible entry.

Trend

Year	Number of offenses	Rate per 100,000 inhabitants
2002	2,151,252	747.0
2003	2,153,464	740.5
Percent change	+0.1	-0.9

National Volume, Trends, and Rates

In 2003, burglary offenses in the Nation were estimated at 2,153,464; this number remained virtually unchanged (+0.1 percent) when compared to the 2002 estimate. Burglary offenses accounted for 20.6 percent of all property crimes. Five- and 10-year trends showed that the burglary volume increased 2.5 percent when compared to the 1999 estimate, but fell 20.6 percent when compared to 1994 estimate. (See Table 1, national estimates.)

Figure 2.10

Burglary
Percent Change from 1999

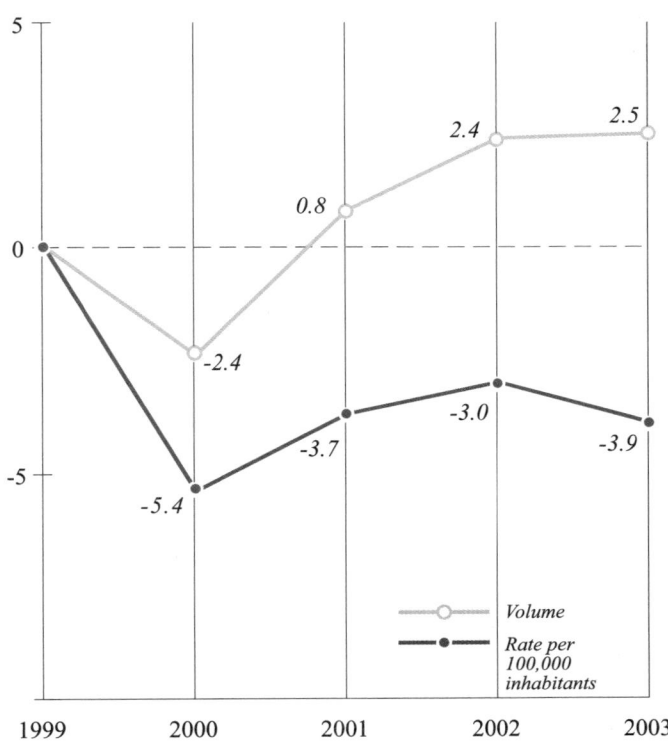

The estimated burglary rate in 2003 was 740.5 offenses per 100,000 inhabitants. Two-, 5-, and 10-year trend data showed that the 2003 rate was a 0.9-percent decrease when compared to the estimated burglary rate in 2002, a 3.9-percent decrease from the 1999 rate, and a 28.9-percent decrease from the 1994 rate. (See Table 1, national estimates.)

Regional Offense Trends and Rates

The UCR Program divides the United States into four regions: the Northeast, the Midwest, the South, and the West. (See Appendix III.) In 2003, data collected regarding the Nation's four regions reflected the following:

The Northeast

The Northeast, comprising 18.7 percent of the U.S. population, had an estimated 11.3 percent of the burglaries nationwide. A comparison with 2002 data showed that in 2003 the Northeast experienced a 2.2-percent decrease in the estimated volume of burglaries. The rate of 446.3 burglaries per 100,000 persons was a 2.6-percent decrease from the 2002 rate. (See Tables 3 and 4, regional estimates.)

The Midwest

The Midwest, accounting for 22.5 percent of the country's population, had an estimated 20.1 percent of all burglaries. In 2003, the region experienced a 3.2-percent decrease in the estimated volume of burglaries from the 2002 estimate. The 2003 rate of an estimated 661.3 burglaries per 100,000 inhabitants was a 3.6-percent decrease from the 2002 estimate. (See Tables 3 and 4, regional estimates.)

The South

In 2003, the South, the Nation's largest region having 35.9 percent of the U.S. population, experienced an estimated 45.1 percent of the Nation's burglaries—a 0.8-percent increase from the 2002 estimate. The estimated rate of 928.5 burglaries per 100,000 inhabitants was a 0.5-percent decrease when compared to the 2002 rate. (See Table 3 and 4, regional estimates.)

The West

With 22.9 percent of the Nation's population, the West had an estimated 23.6 percent of all burglaries. When compared to the 2002 estimated volume, the region experienced a 2.9-percent increase in 2003. This was the only region that showed an increase in the burglary rate with an estimated 763.6 burglaries per 100,000 persons, up 1.4 percent from the 2002 rate. (See Tables 3 and 4, regional estimates.)

Community Types

Metropolitan Statistical Areas (MSAs), which made up approximately 82.8 percent of the total U.S. population, accounted for an estimated 84.7 percent of the Nation's burglaries. MSAs had a burglary rate estimated at 757.7 burglaries per 100,000 persons in 2003. Cities outside of MSAs, which comprised approximately 6.8 percent of the Nation's population, accounted for 7.5 percent of the burglaries, and these communities had a rate of 815.8 burglaries per 100,000 in population. Nonmetropolitan areas, which comprised approximately 10.4 percent of the U.S. population, accounted for an estimated 7.8 percent of the country's burglaries. These areas had a rate of 554.9 burglaries per 100,000 inhabitants. (See Table 2, community type estimates.)

Population Groups: Trends and Rates

An examination of the data by population group showed that, collectively, those cities with populations under 10,000 experienced the largest year-to-year increase, 1.5 percent, in reported burglaries from 2002 to 2003. Those cities with populations of 250,000 and over had the largest decrease, 0.4 percent, from the 2002 volume. The Nation's cities collectively saw a 0.2-percent increase in the number of burglaries reported in 2003 when compared to the number of burglaries reported in 2002. Metropolitan counties had an increase of 0.2 percent, and nonmetropolitan counties had a decrease in burglaries of 0.7 percent when compared to the 2002 numbers. (See Table 12.)

In 2003, the Nation's cities collectively had a rate of 829.5 burglaries per 100,000 persons. Those cities with populations 250,000 and over had the highest rate among all population groups at 979.6 burglaries per 100,000 inhabitants. Cities with populations of 10,000 to 24,999 had the lowest burglary rate among the Nation's cities, 645.9 offenses per 100,000 persons. Metropolitan counties had a rate of 637.9 burglaries per 100,000 in population, and nonmetropolitan counties had a rate of 584.5 burglaries per 100,000 persons. (See Table 16.)

Offense Analysis

Among those agencies that reported burglary statistics for all 12 months of 2003, the data showed that forcible entry burglaries accounted for 62.4 percent of the burglary offenses, unlawful entry comprised 31.2 percent, and attempted forcible entry accounted for approximately 6.3 percent. (Based on Table 19.)

The majority of burglaries, 65.8 percent, were residential, and the remaining 34.2 percent were of nonresidences, such as stores and offices. The data also showed that most residential burglaries, 62.0 percent, occurred during daytime hours, and most nonresidential burglaries, 58.4 percent, occurred at night. The time of occurrence was unknown for 25.3 percent of burglaries. (Based on Table 23.)

Losses due to burglaries totaled an estimated $3.5 billion in 2003, with an average value of $1,626 per offense. The losses in residential burglaries averaged $1,600 per offense, and in nonresidential burglaries $1,676 per offense. (Based on Tables 1 and 23.)

Table 2.25

Burglary by Month
Percent Distribution, 1999-2003

Month	1999	2000	2001	2002	2003
January	8.3	8.1	7.9	8.5	8.1
February	7.2	7.2	6.6	6.9	6.4
March	7.9	8.0	7.6	7.7	7.8
April	7.7	7.8	7.7	7.8	8.1
May	8.2	8.5	8.3	8.5	8.6
June	8.4	8.4	8.2	8.2	8.4
July	9.0	9.2	9.1	9.1	9.1
August	9.1	9.2	9.1	9.0	8.9
September	8.7	8.6	8.6	8.7	8.8
October	8.6	8.7	9.3	8.8	8.9
November	8.4	8.3	8.9	8.2	8.2
December	8.5	8.1	8.8	8.5	8.5

Figure 2.11

Burglary
Percent Change from 1999

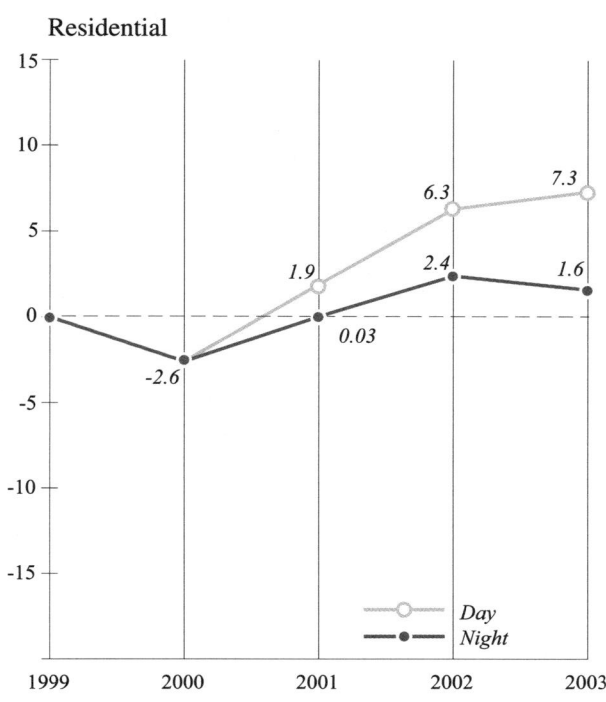

Residential

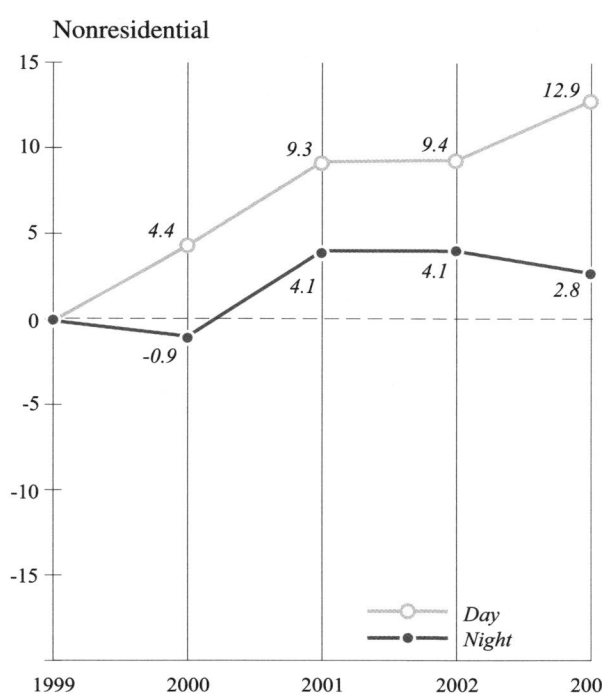

Nonresidential

Clearances

The UCR Program considers an offense to be cleared by arrest or "solved" when at least one person is arrested, charged with the commission of the offense, and turned over to the court for prosecution. A clearance by exceptional means can be recorded when the offender has been identified and located and there is enough evidence to support an arrest, but conditions beyond law enforcement's control prevent an agency from bringing charges. (More information about clearances is available in Section III of this publication.)

In 2003, law enforcement cleared 13.1 percent of reported burglaries by arrest or exceptional means. Agencies in cities overall cleared 12.5 percent of burglaries. Within population groups labeled as city, those cities with under 10,000 in population showed 16.5 per-

cent of reported burglaries as cleared, the highest percentage of clearances among the Nation's cities. Law enforcement in the Nation's largest cities, those cities with populations 250,000 and over, cleared the lowest percentage of burglaries, 11.0 percent. In nonmetropolitan counties, law enforcement cleared 16.3 percent of reported burglary offenses, and in metropolitan counties, they cleared 13.8 percent. (See Table 25.)

Regionally, law enforcement agencies in the Northeast cleared 17.3 percent of the burglaries brought to their attention. Those in the South cleared 13.1 percent of reported burglaries; in the Midwest, 12.1 percent; and in the West, 11.8 percent. (See Table 26.)

Burglaries involving unlawful entry without use of force were cleared by arrest or exceptional means in 14.1 percent of the reported cases during 2003.

Approximately 12.4 percent of forcible entry burglaries and 11.0 percent of attempted forcible entry burglaries were cleared. (See Table 27.)

Clearances and Juveniles

The UCR Program considers an incident involving only offenders under the age of 18 to be cleared by arrest when an offender is cited to appear in juvenile court or before other juvenile authorities, even though a physical arrest may not have occurred. Clearances involving both adult and juvenile offenders are classified as adult clearances. Therefore, clearances involving juveniles who may be participating in a burglary with an adult were not included in these figures.

In 2003, only persons under 18 years of age were involved in 16.8 percent of the burglaries cleared by arrest or exceptional means. A review of the data by city population group showed that cities with populations under 10,000 had the highest percentage of clearances involving only juveniles at 20.3 percent. Cities with populations of 250,000 and over had the lowest percentage of cleared offenses involving juveniles only at 13.3 percent. Nonmetropolitan county agencies reported that 16.2 percent of the burglary clearances in their jurisdictions were of juveniles, and metropolitan county agencies reported 17.0 percent of their burglary clearances involved juveniles only. (See Table 28.)

Arrests

The estimated number of burglary arrests for 2003 was 290,956. Burglary arrests accounted for an estimated 18.1 percent of the arrests for property crimes. (Based on Table 29.) The remaining tables in Section IV of this publication provide actual arrest totals for agencies that submitted 12 months of arrest data to the UCR Program.

In 2003, law enforcement agencies in the West reported 122.0 burglary arrests per 100,000 inhabitants. Agencies in the South reported an arrest rate of 107.5, the Midwest a rate of 79.9, and law enforcement in the Northeast, a rate of 78.1 burglary arrests per 100,000 in population. (See Table 30.)

Law enforcement in the Nation's cities collectively reported a rate of 106.3 arrests for burglary per 100,000 inhabitants. Those in cities with populations of 25,000 to 49,999 reported the fewest arrests for burglaries per 100,000 inhabitants, 89.4. Law enforcements in cities with 100,000 to 249,999 inhabitants reported the highest number of arrests per 100,000 population, 125.5. Those in metropolitan and non-metropolitan counties reported rates of 85.5 and 92.3 arrests for burglary per 100,000 inhabitants, respectively. (See Table 31.)

Five- and 10-year trend data showed that burglary arrests overall declined 0.3 percent from burglary arrest totals in 1999 and 23.5 percent from the 1994 number. Additionally, in 2003, arrests of adults for burglary increased 7.1 percent when measured against the number of adults arrested for burglary in 1999 but declined 13.8 percent when compared to 1994 arrest data; arrests of juveniles declined 14.7 percent from the 1999 figure and 39.8 percent from the 1994 figure. (See Tables 32 and 34.)

When compared to 2002 data, overall arrests for burglaries in 2003 increased 2.2 percent. Arrests of adults increased 3.8 percent; however, arrests of juveniles declined 1.2 percent. (See Table 36.)

In 2003, males accounted for 86.3 percent of burglary arrestees. (See Table 42.) Of the male arrestees, 29.9 percent were juveniles (under 18 years of age). (Based on Table 39.) Of the female arrestees, 25.2 percent were juveniles. (Based on Table 40.)

By race, 70.5 percent of all burglary arrestees in 2003 were white, 27.5 percent were black, and 2.0 percent were of other races. Of those adults arrested for burglary, 70.2 percent were white, 28.0 percent were black, and 1.8 percent were of other races. Of burglary arrestees under 18 years of age, 71.4 percent were white, 26.1 percent were black, and 2.5 percent were of other races. (See Table 43.)

Larceny-theft

Definition

Larceny-theft is defined as the unlawful taking, carrying, leading, or riding away of property from the possession or constructive possession of another. It includes crimes such as shoplifting, pocket-picking, purse-snatching, thefts from motor vehicles, thefts of motor vehicle parts and accessories, bicycle thefts, etc., in which no use of force, violence, or fraud occurs. In the Uniform Crime Reporting (UCR) Program, this crime category does not include embezzlement, confidence games, forgery, and worthless checks. Motor vehicle theft is also excluded from this category inasmuch as it is a separate offense.

Trend

Year	Number of offenses	Rate per 100,000 inhabitants
2002	7,057,379	2,450.7
2003	7,021,588	2,414.5
Percent change	-0.5	-1.5

National Volume, Trends, and Rates

In 2003, there were more than 7 million estimated larceny-thefts in the Nation, which cost victims an estimated $4.9 billion in losses. (Based on Table 1, which includes national estimates, and Table 23, which includes data from those agencies supplying at least 6 months of complete offense reports.)

Larceny-theft offenses in the United States accounted for 67.3 percent of the estimated total property crimes, i.e., burglary, larceny-theft, and motor vehicle theft. When 2003 data were compared to 2002 data, the estimated number of larceny-thefts in the Nation decreased 0.5 percent. Five- and 10-year trends showed that the estimated volume of larceny-thefts in the Nation increased 0.9 percent from the 1999 estimate but decreased 10.9 percent when compared to the 1994 estimate. (See Table 1, national estimates.)

The rate of larceny-thefts in the Nation for 2003 was an estimated 2,414.5 offenses per 100,000 inhabitants, a 1.5-percent decrease from the 2002 rate. The 2003 estimated rate reflected a 5.3-percent decrease from the 1999 rate and a 20.2-percent drop from the 1994 rate. (See Table 1, national estimates.)

Figure 2.12

Larceny-theft
Percent Change from 1999

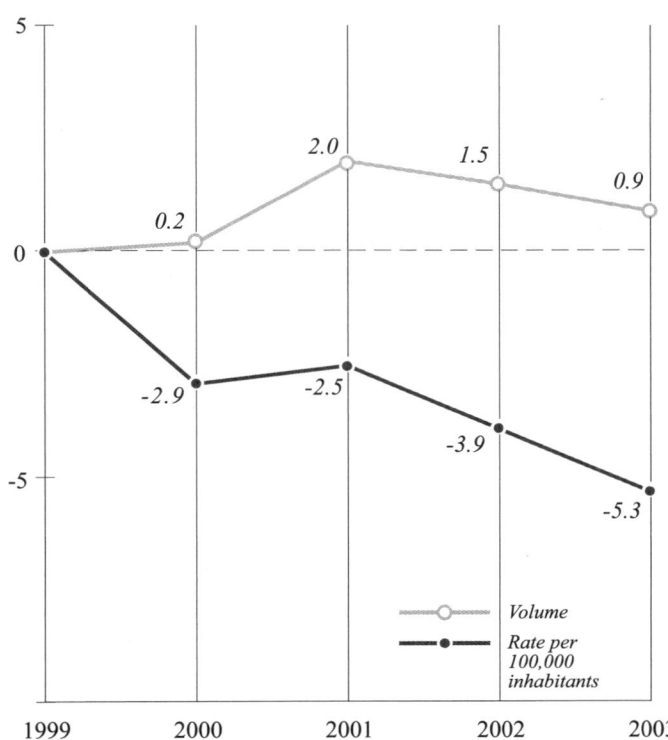

Regional Offense Trends and Rates

The UCR Program divides the Nation into four regions: the Northeast, the Midwest, the South, and the West. (See Appendix III for a map delineating the regions.) By region, larceny-theft data for 2003 reflected the following:

The Northeast

The Northeast accounted for 18.7 percent of the Nation's total estimated population and an estimated 13.0 percent of the country's larceny-theft offenses. The estimated volume of larceny-theft offenses occurring in the region during 2003 declined 2.1 percent from the 2002 estimate. Among the regions, the Northeast had the lowest rate of larceny-theft offenses per 100,000 inhabitants, estimated at 1,673.0; this was a decline of 2.5 percent from the 2002 rate. (See Tables 3 and 4, regional estimates.)

The Midwest

With 22.5 percent of the Nation's population, the Midwestern states accounted for 21.9 percent of the Nation's larceny-thefts in 2003. Those data reflected a 2.3-percent decrease in the volume of larceny-theft offenses when compared to the 2002 estimate. The Midwest had an estimated 2,351.2 larceny-theft offenses per 100,000 in population, which was a 2.8-percent decline from 2002 data. (See Tables 3 and 4, regional estimates.)

The South

The Nation's most populous region, the South, with 35.9 percent of the U.S. population, had 41.3 percent of the Nation's larceny-theft offenses in 2003. From 2002 to 2003, the number of larceny-theft offenses increased slightly, 0.3 percent, but the rate—2,771.0 per 100,000 population—decreased 1.0 percent. (See Tables 3 and 4, regional estimates.)

The West

Nearly twenty-three percent (22.9) of the Nation's population resided in the West in 2003, and this region accounted for an estimated 23.9 percent of the total larceny-thefts during that year. Despite a 0.8-percent increase in the estimated number of larceny-thefts during 2003, the West recorded a 0.7-percent decline in the rate when compared to 2002 estimate—2,522.9 larcenies per 100,000 inhabitants. (See Tables 3 and 4, regional estimates.)

Community Types

The UCR Program compiles data for three community types: Metropolitan Statistical Areas (MSAs), cities outside metropolitan areas, and nonmetropolitan counties. (Additional information regarding community types is located in Appendix III.) Nearly 83 percent (82.8) of the Nation's estimated population resided an MSAs in 2003, 6.8 percent lived in cities outside MSAs, and 10.4 percent of the population lived in nonmetropolitan counties. (Based on Table 2, community type estimates.) The Nation's MSAs had a rate estimated at 2,534.3 larceny-theft offenses per 100,000 inhabitants during 2003. Cities outside MSAs had a rate of 3,132.2, and nonmetropolitan counties had a rate of 993.6 larceny-thefts per 100,000 inhabitants. (See Table 2, community type estimates.)

Population Groups: Trends and Rates

The UCR Program aggregates crime statistics into population groups. A list of these groups is located in Appendix III. Collectively, the Nation's cities had a 0.6-percent decrease in the number of larceny-thefts in 2003 when compared to the 2002 figure. The largest decline, 1.4

Table 2.26

Larceny-theft by Month
Percent Distribution, 1999-2003

Month	1999	2000	2001	2002	2003
January	7.8	7.6	7.7	8.1	7.9
February	7.2	7.3	6.8	7.0	6.8
March	8.0	8.2	7.8	7.8	8.1
April	8.0	7.9	8.0	8.1	8.3
May	8.4	8.6	8.6	8.6	8.7
June	8.7	8.8	8.6	8.5	8.6
July	9.1	9.2	9.1	9.2	9.1
August	9.2	9.2	9.1	9.1	9.0
September	8.5	8.5	8.4	8.6	8.6
October	8.7	8.8	9.1	8.9	8.8
November	8.1	8.0	8.3	8.0	8.0
December	8.3	7.9	8.4	8.1	8.2

Table 2.27

Larceny-theft
Percent Distribution by Region, 2003

Type	United States total	Northeast	Midwest	South	West
Total[1]	100.0	100.0	100.0	100.0	100.0
Pocket-picking	0.5	0.9	0.4	0.4	0.4
Purse-snatching	0.6	1.2	0.5	0.5	0.6
Shoplifting	14.4	15.4	13.6	14.0	15.1
From motor vehicles (except accessories)	26.4	21.1	23.2	25.0	33.0
Motor vehicle accessories	11.1	9.1	11.0	11.7	11.3
Bicycles	3.9	5.2	4.3	3.1	4.1
From buildings	12.4	16.1	14.2	10.6	12.0
From coin-operated machines	0.7	0.7	0.7	0.9	0.7
All others	30.0	30.4	32.1	33.8	23.0

[1] Because of rounding, the percentages may not add to 100.0.

Figure 2.13

Larceny-theft Categories
Percent Change from 1999

Pocket-picking

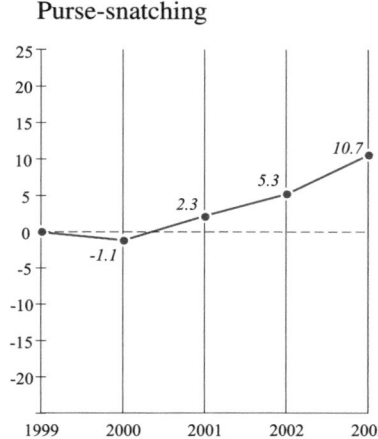

Purse-snatching

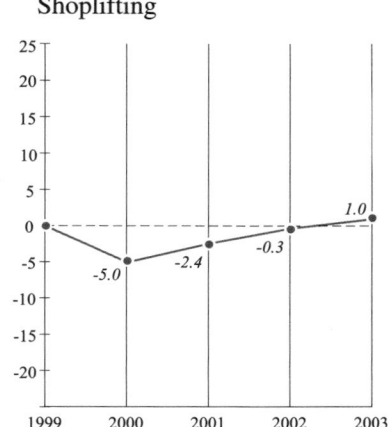

Shoplifting

From motor vehicles (except accessories)

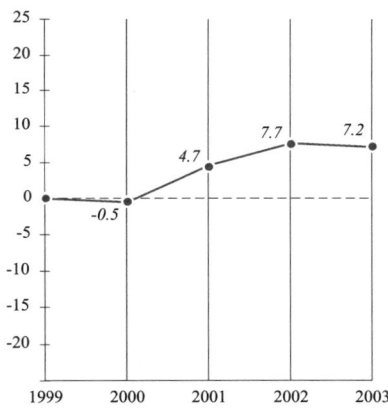

Motor vehicle accessories

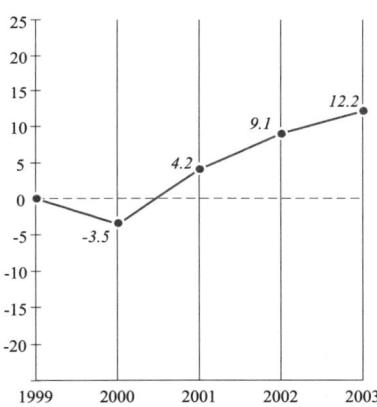

Bicycles

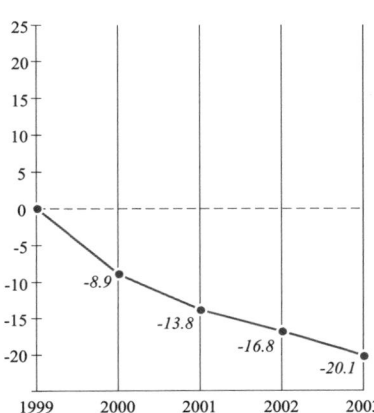

From buildings

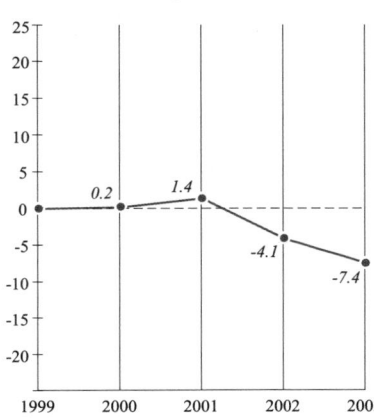

From coin-operated machines

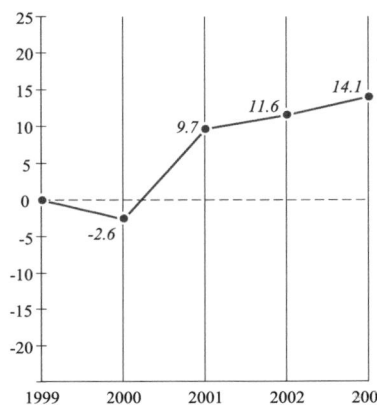

percent, occurred in the Nation's largest cities, those with 250,000 or more inhabitants. The Nation's smallest cities, those with under 10,000 inhabitants, had a 1.1-percent increase in larceny-thefts when comparing 2003 to 2002 data. Metropolitan counties showed a 0.5-percent decline in larcenies between 2003 and 2002. Over the same time frame, nonmetropolitan counties experienced a 1.2-percent increase in the number of larceny-thefts. (See Table 12.)

An examination of the rate of larceny-theft by population group indicated that the Nation's cities, collectively, had 2,951.7 larcenies per 100,000 inhabitants in 2003. Of the city population groups, those cities with 100,000 to 249,999 inhabitants had the highest rate, 3,297.7 reported larceny-thefts per 100,000 inhabitants. Cities with populations of 10,000 to 24,999 inhabitants had the lowest rate, 2,583.4 larceny-thefts per 100,000 population. Metropolitan counties had a rate of 1,689.6 larceny-

thefts per 100,000 population, and nonmetropolitan counties had a rate of 1,084.1 per 100,000 inhabitants. (See Table 16.)

Offense Analysis

Distribution

A breakdown of larceny-theft offenses showed that thefts from motor vehicles accounted for 26.4 percent of reported larceny-thefts in the Nation during 2003. Shoplifting accounted for 14.4 percent of larceny-thefts, and thefts from buildings made up 12.4 percent of the larceny-theft total. The theft of motor vehicle parts and accessories comprised 11.1 percent of larcenies, and the theft of bicycles accounted for 3.9 percent of larceny-thefts. Thefts from coin-operated machines, purse-snatchings, pocket-pickings, and other miscellaneous types of larceny-thefts comprised the remainder. (See Table 23.)

Loss by Dollar Value

Larceny-theft offenses cost an estimated $4.9 billion in lost property in 2003. (Based on Table 1, which includes national estimates, and Table 23, which includes data from those agencies supplying at least 6 months of complete offense reports.) The average value of property stolen per offense, $698, remained virtually unchanged from the 2002 average value of $699. (See Table 23.)

In 2003, the larceny-theft category with the highest average loss, $1,030, was thefts from buildings. For thefts from motor vehicles, the average value loss was $680, and for thefts of motor vehicle parts and accessories, the average loss was $442. Purse-snatchings had an average value loss of $367; pocket-pickings, $294; and thefts of bicycles, $247. Thefts from coin-operated machines had an average loss of $262.

Figure 2.14

Larceny-theft
Percent Distribution,[1] 2003

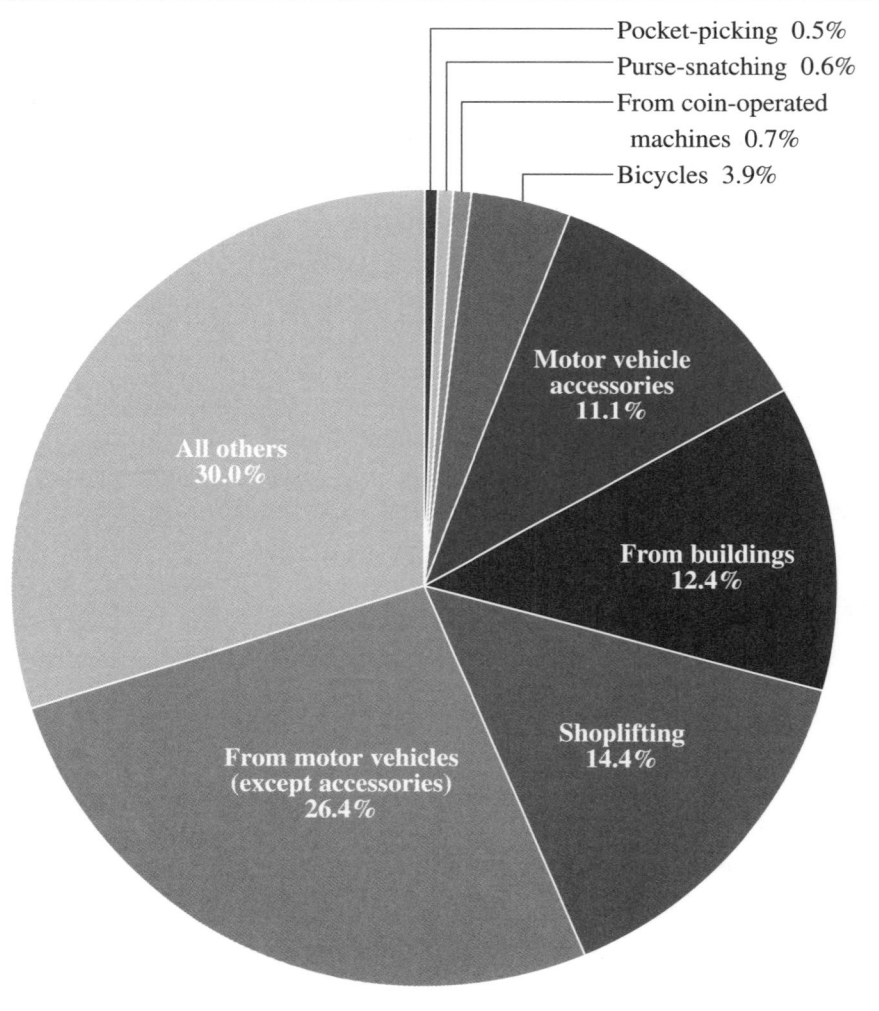

Pocket-picking 0.5%
Purse-snatching 0.6%
From coin-operated machines 0.7%
Bicycles 3.9%
Motor vehicle accessories 11.1%
From buildings 12.4%
Shoplifting 14.4%
From motor vehicles (except accessories) 26.4%
All others 30.0%

[1] Due to rounding, the percentages may not add to 100.0.

The larceny-theft category with the lowest average dollar value was shoplifting at $163. (See Table 23.)

An examination of larceny-theft offenses by monetary value indicated that incidents in which the stolen property was valued at over $200 accounted for 39.3 percent of all reported larceny-thefts. Property valued at under $50 made up 38.1 percent of the reported larceny-theft offenses, and property valued from $50 to $200 made up 22.6 percent of the larcenies. (See Table 23.)

Clearances

In the UCR Program, law enforcement agencies may clear an offense either by the arrest of an individual or by exceptional means, i.e., when elements beyond the control of law enforcement preclude the agency from placing formal charges against the offender. (Section III of this publication provides additional information regarding clearances.) Nationwide, law enforcement cleared 18.0 percent of all reported larceny-theft offenses in 2003.

The Nation's cities, collectively, cleared 18.1 percent of larceny-theft offenses. Cities with 10,000 to 24,999 in population cleared the highest percentage of larceny-thefts, 22.2 percent. The Nation's largest cities, those with populations of 250,000 or more inhabitants, had the lowest percentage of larcenies cleared at 14.2 percent. Law enforcement agencies in metropolitan counties cleared 17.4 percent of larcenies, and agencies in nonmetropolitan counties cleared 17.5 percent of larceny-theft offenses. (See Table 25.)

An examination of larceny-theft clearances by region showed that law enforcement agencies in the Northeast cleared 21.9 percent of the larceny-theft offenses brought to their attention. Law enforcement agencies in the Midwest cleared 18.1 percent of larceny-theft offenses, those in the South cleared 18.0 percent, and agencies in the West cleared 16.1 percent of reported larceny-thefts. (See Table 26.)

In the UCR Program, a juvenile clearance is counted when an offender under the age of 18 is cited to appear in juvenile court or before other juvenile authorities even though a physical arrest may not have occurred. Clearances involving both adult and juvenile offenders are considered adult clearances and are not counted in the juvenile figures. For 2003, slightly more than 20 percent (20.2) of the larceny-theft clearances in the Nation involved only juveniles. Twenty-one percent of larceny-theft clearances in the Nation's cities, collectively, involved only juveniles. Of all city population groups, cities with populations in the 50,000 to 99,999 range had 23.6 percent of the larceny-theft clearances involve only juveniles—the highest percentage. Law enforcement personnel in cities with populations of 250,000 or more inhabitants cleared 17.0 percent of the larceny-thefts that involved only juveniles—the lowest percentage. Law enforcement agencies in the Nation's metropolitan counties reported that 16.8 percent of larceny-theft clearances involved only juveniles; those in nonmetropolitan counties reported that 15.0 percent of larceny-theft clearances involved only juveniles. (See Table 28.)

Arrests

Table 29 provides the estimated number of arrests for the Nation for the 29 offenses for which the UCR Program collects arrest data. The remaining tables in Section IV of this publication contain actual arrest data for those agencies that furnished 12 months of arrest data to the national UCR Program.

Law enforcement agencies in the Nation made an estimated 1,145,074 arrests for larceny-theft in 2003, the highest arrest total of all reported property offenses. Arrests for larceny-theft comprised an estimated 71.3 percent of arrests for all property crime offenses. (Based on Table 29.) Nationally in 2003, law enforcement reported a rate of 400.4 larceny-theft arrests per 100,000 inhabitants. A review of larceny-theft arrests by region showed that in 2003 the South had the highest rate, 449.6 arrests per 100,000 inhabitants. Law enforcement agencies in the Midwest made 424.7 arrests for larceny-theft per 100,000 inhabitants; the West, 377.1; and the Northeast, 323.8. (See Table 30).

The Nation's cities collectively had a rate of 489.9 larceny-theft arrests per 100,000 inhabitants. By city population groups, those cities with 50,000 to 99,999 inhabitants had the highest arrest rate for larceny-theft, 546.5 per 100,000 inhabitants; cities with 250,000 or more inhabitants had the lowest arrest rate, 452.0. The Nation's metropolitan counties had a rate of 231.3 larceny-theft arrests; nonmetropolitan counties had a rate of 150.6 larceny-theft arrests per 100,000 in population. (See Table 31.)

When compared to 2002 figures, the number of larceny-theft arrests during 2003 increased 0.5 percent nationally. The number of arrests of juveniles for larceny-theft in 2003 decreased 3.2 percent from the 2002 figure, and the number of arrests of adults for larceny-theft increased 2.0 percent. (See Table 36.)

The number of arrests of males for larceny-theft in 2003 remained virtually unchanged (+0.1 percent) from the 2002 data; the number of arrests of females for larceny-theft increased 1.1 percent. (See Table 37.)

Of those persons arrested for larceny-theft in the Nation in 2003, 28.4 percent were juveniles. Slightly more than 30 percent (30.2) of all females arrested for larceny-theft in 2003 were under the age of 18. (Based on Tables 38 and 40.) A breakdown of arrest data by gender showed that 62.9 percent of larceny-theft arrestees were male. (See Table 42.) By race, 68.5 percent of larceny-theft arrestees were white, 28.8 percent were black, and the remainder were of other races. Of the juveniles arrested for larceny-theft in 2003, 69.8 percent were white, 26.7 percent were black, and 3.5 percent were of other races. (See Table 43.)

Motor Vehicle Theft

Definition

The Uniform Crime Reporting (UCR) Program defines motor vehicle theft as the theft or attempted theft of a motor vehicle. This offense includes the stealing of automobiles, trucks, buses, motorcycles, motorscooters, snowmobiles, etc. The taking of a motor vehicle for temporary use by persons having lawful access is excluded from this definition.

Trend

Year	Number of offenses	Rate per 100,000 inhabitants
2002	1,246,646	432.9
2003	1,260,471	433.4
Percent change	+1.1	+0.1

National Volume, Trends, and Rates

In 2003, there were an estimated 1,260,471 motor vehicle thefts in the United States. This number represented a 1.1-percent increase in volume when compared to the 2002 estimate and a 9.4-percent increase over the 1999 estimate. The estimated number of motor vehicle thefts in 2003 was a decrease of 18.1 percent when compared to the 1994 estimate. (See Table 1, national estimates.)

The rate of motor vehicle thefts in the Nation in 2003 was an estimated 433.4 offenses per 100,000 inhabitants, which represented virtually no change (+0.1 percent) over the 2002 rate. The estimated rate of motor vehicle thefts per 100,000 inhabitants increased 2.6 percent when compared to the 1999 rate but decreased 26.7 percent from the 1994 rate. (See Table 1.)

Regional Offense Trends and Rates

As shown in Appendix III, the UCR Program divides the Nation into four regions: the Northeast, the Midwest, the South, and the West. An examination of motor vehicle theft data by region indicated the following:

The Northeast

The Northeast Region, which comprised 18.7 percent of the Nation's population, accounted for an estimated 12.5 percent of all motor vehicle thefts. (See Table 3, regional estimates.) The 2003 estimate was a 3.0-percent decrease from the 2002 estimate. In 2003, the rate of stolen vehicles in the Northeast was an estimated 290.7 offenses per 100,000 inhabitants, a 3.5-percent decrease from the previous year's estimate. (See Table 4, regional, divisional, state estimates.)

Figure 2.15

Motor Vehicle Theft
Percent Change from 1999

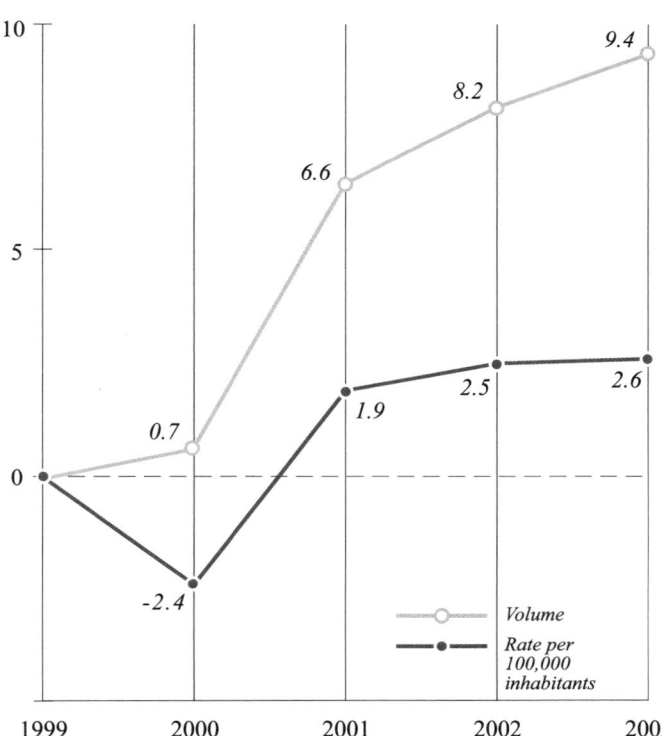

The Midwest

In 2003, 22.5 percent of the U.S. population resided in the Midwest. The region accounted for an estimated 18.5 percent of all motor vehicle thefts in the Nation. (See Table 3, regional estimates.) The estimated number of motor vehicle thefts in the region showed a slight decline, 0.3 percent, from the previous year's estimate. The Midwest had an estimated rate of 356.9 motor vehicle thefts per 100,000 inhabitants, which was a 0.7-percent decline from the 2002 estimate. (See Table 4, regional, divisional, state estimates.)

The South

The Nation's most populous region, the South, accounted for 35.9 percent of the Nation's inhabitants and had an estimated 34.5 percent of the Nation's motor vehicle thefts. (See Table 3,

Table 2.28

Motor Vehicle Theft by Month
Percent Distribution, 1999-2003

Month	1999	2000	2001	2002	2003
January	8.5	8.1	8.1	8.6	8.3
February	7.3	7.4	6.9	7.2	7.0
March	7.9	8.0	7.7	8.0	8.0
April	7.7	7.6	7.6	7.8	8.1
May	8.0	8.2	8.0	8.1	8.3
June	8.2	8.3	8.2	8.1	8.3
July	8.8	8.9	9.0	9.0	8.8
August	9.0	9.1	8.9	8.8	8.8
September	8.5	8.5	8.5	8.6	8.6
October	8.8	8.7	9.3	8.8	8.7
November	8.5	8.5	8.9	8.4	8.3
December	8.8	8.6	9.0	8.6	8.7

Table 2.29

Motor Vehicle Theft
Percent Distribution by Region, 2003

Region	Total[1]	Autos	Trucks and buses	Other vehicles
Total	**100.0**	**73.3**	**18.5**	**8.2**
Northeast	100.0	88.8	5.0	6.1
Midwest	100.0	76.9	15.1	8.1
South	100.0	68.0	21.2	10.8
West	100.0	72.3	21.2	6.5

[1] Because of rounding, the percentages may not add to 100.0.

regional estimates.) The 2003 estimate of motor vehicle thefts in the region was a 0.9-percent decrease from the 2002 estimate. In 2003, the region had a rate of 416.1 motor vehicle thefts per 100,000 in population, which was a 2.2-percent decrease from the 2002 estimated rate. (See Table 4, regional, divisional, state estimates.)

The West

The Western Region, with 22.9 percent of the Nation's population, had an estimated 34.4 percent of the motor vehicle theft offenses. (See Table 3, regional estimates.) The West was the only region with an increase in the estimated number of motor vehicle thefts, 5.7 percent over the 2002 estimate. The region had the highest estimated rate, 652.8 motor vehicle thefts per 100,000 inhabitants, among the regions and the only increase, 4.2 percent, in the estimate from 2002 to 2003. (See Table 4, regional, divisional, state estimates.)

Community Types

The UCR Program defines three community types: Metropolitan Statistical Areas (MSAs), cities outside metropolitan areas, and nonmetropolitan counties. Additional information regarding community types is presented in Appendix III.

In 2003, the estimated motor vehicle theft rate per 100,000 inhabitants was 491.0 in MSAs, 199.5 in cities outside MSAs, and 128.6 in nonmetropolitan counties. (See Table 2, community type estimates.)

Population Groups: Trends and Rates

In the UCR Program, cities are grouped according to population size and counties are classified as either metropolitan or nonmetropolitan. (Additional information about population groups is located in Appendix III.) In 2003, the Nation's cities collectively had a 0.5-percent increase in the number of motor vehicle thefts reported. Among city groups, those with populations of 100,000 to 249,999 inhabitants had the largest year-to-year increase in motor vehicle thefts, 3.7 percent, from the previous year's total. Those agencies in cities with populations of 250,000 and over, collectively, had the only decrease in motor vehicle thefts, 1.2 percent lower than the 2002 total. (See Table 12.)

Both metropolitan and nonmetropolitan counties had increases in the number of motor vehicle theft offenses when comparing 2002 to 2003 data—a 4.0-percent increase in metropolitan counties and a 2.3-percent increase in nonmetropolitan counties. (See Table 12.)

Cities overall had a rate of 561.6 motor vehicle thefts per 100,000 inhabitants in 2003. The Nation's largest cities, cities with populations of 250,000 and over, had the highest rate among city population groups at 910.9, and the Nation's smallest cities, those with fewer than 10,000 inhabitants, had the lowest rate among the city groups at 230.0 motor vehicle thefts per 100,000 in population. Metropolitan counties had a rate of 323.5 motor vehicle theft offenses per 100,000 inhabitants. In nonmetropolitan counties, the rate was 139.5. (See Table 16.)

Offense Analysis

In 2003, automobiles were stolen at a rate of 341.9 cars per 100,000 inhabitants. Trucks and buses (commercial vehicles) were stolen at a rate of 86.2 vehicles per 100,000 in population. Other types of vehicles were stolen at a rate of 38.3 vehicles per 100,000 people. (See Table 19.)

In the Nation, 73.3 percent of stolen vehicles were automobiles. In the Northeast, 88.8 percent of the vehicles stolen were automobiles. In the Midwest, 76.9 percent of the vehicles stolen were automobiles, in the West, 72.3 percent, and in the South, 68.0 percent of the motor vehicles reported stolen were automobiles. (See Table 2.29.)

The average value of motor vehicles reported stolen in 2003 was $6,797. The estimated total value of all motor vehicles reported stolen in 2003 was $8.6 billion. (Based on Tables 1 and 23.)

Clearances

The UCR Program considers an offense to be cleared by arrest or solved when at least one person is arrested, charged with the commission of the offense, and turned over to the court for prosecution. A clearance by exceptional means can be recorded when the offender has been identified and located and there is enough evidence to support an arrest, but conditions beyond law enforcement's control prevent an agency from bringing charges. (More information about clearances is available in Section III of this publication.)

Law enforcement agencies cleared 13.1 percent of reported motor vehicle thefts by arrest or exceptional means in 2003. In the Nation's cities overall, law enforcement cleared 12.3 percent of motor vehicle thefts. Of all the city population groupings, the Nation's smallest cities, those with populations under 10,000 persons, had the highest percentage of clearances, 24.2 percent; the Nation's largest cities, those with 250,000 or more inhabitants, had the lowest percentage of clearances, 10.1 percent. Law enforcement in nonmetro-

politan counties cleared 27.1 percent of motor vehicle thefts by arrest or exceptional means, and those in metropolitan counties cleared 14.7 percent. (See Table 25.)

By region, law enforcement agencies in the South had the highest clearance rate, 14.9 percent. Agencies in the Midwest cleared 14.6 percent of the motor vehicle theft offenses reported in that region and those in the Northeast cleared 14.4 percent. The West's law enforcement agencies cleared 10.4 percent of the motor vehicle thefts brought to their attention. (See Table 26.)

Clearances and Juveniles

The UCR Program also considers an incident cleared by arrest if an offender under the age of 18 is physically arrested or if the individual is cited to appear before juvenile authorities. According to UCR guidelines, any clearance that involves both adult and juvenile offenders is listed as an adult clearance. Clearances involving only juveniles (those under age 18) accounted for 17.3 percent of all reported motor vehicle theft clearances. In cities overall, 17.8 percent of motor vehicle theft clearances involved only juveniles. Among the city population groups, those cities with populations of 250,000 and over inhabitants had the highest percentage of clearances involving only juveniles at 18.9 percent. Cities with populations of 100,000 to 249,999 had the lowest percentage of clearances involving juveniles at 15.7 percent. Law enforcement officials in nonmetropolitan counties reported 17.6 percent of clearances involved only juveniles; metropolitan county law enforcement agencies reported 15.3 percent of motor vehicle theft clearances involved only juveniles. (See Table 28.)

Arrests

In 2003, there were an estimated 152,934 arrests for motor vehicle theft in the United States. (See Table 29.) Table 29 provides estimated arrest data for the Nation, however, the remaining tables in Section IV of this publication furnish actual arrest totals based on agencies that submitted 12 months of arrest data to the UCR Program.

Two- and 5-year trend data showed that the number of motor vehicle theft arrests in the Nation was 0.8 percent higher than in 2002 and 5.5 percent higher than the number of motor vehicle theft arrests in 1999. However, the 10-year trend data showed the number of motor vehicle theft arrests during 2003 was 26.5 percent lower than for 1994. (See Tables 32, 34, and 36.)

In the Nation, the rate of motor vehicle theft arrests was 52.1 per 100,000 inhabitants. Among the four geographic regions, the West had the highest arrest rate for motor vehicle theft at 77.3 per 100,000 inhabitants, followed by the Midwest, 52.1; the South, 41.2; and the Northeast, 31.4. (See Table 30.)

In cities overall, law enforcement reported a rate of 59.3 motor vehicle thefts per 100,000 persons. By city population groups, the Nation's largest cities, those with 250,000 inhabitants or greater, had the highest arrest rate for motor vehicle theft at 111.5 per 100,000 in population. Cities with populations of 10,000 to 24,999 had the lowest arrest rate for motor vehicle theft at 32.4 per 100,000 in population. Law enforcement agencies in metropolitan counties reported a motor vehicle theft arrest rate of 39.5 per 100,000 inhabitants; nonmetropolitan law enforcement agencies reported a rate of 29.5. (See Table 31.)

By age, 62.3 percent of those persons arrested for motor vehicle thefts in 2003 were under the age of 25, and 29.1 percent were under the age of 18. Adults comprised 70.9 percent of motor vehicle theft arrestees. (See Tables 38 and 41.)

In 2003, 83.4 percent of arrestees for motor vehicle theft were male. Arrests of male juveniles decreased 3.3 percent from the 2002 number. Arrests of females increased 1.9 percent from 2002 to 2003; however, arrests of female juveniles from 2002 to 2003 declined 5.3 percent. (See Tables 37 and 42.)

By race, 61.3 percent of arrestees for motor vehicle theft were white, 35.9 percent were black, and the remainder were of other races. Whites accounted for 56.1 percent of juveniles arrested for motor vehicle theft, and blacks comprised 40.3 percent of juveniles arrested for motor vehicle theft. (See Table 43.)

Figure 2.16

Regional Crime Rates 2003
Violent and Property Crimes per 100,000 Inhabitants

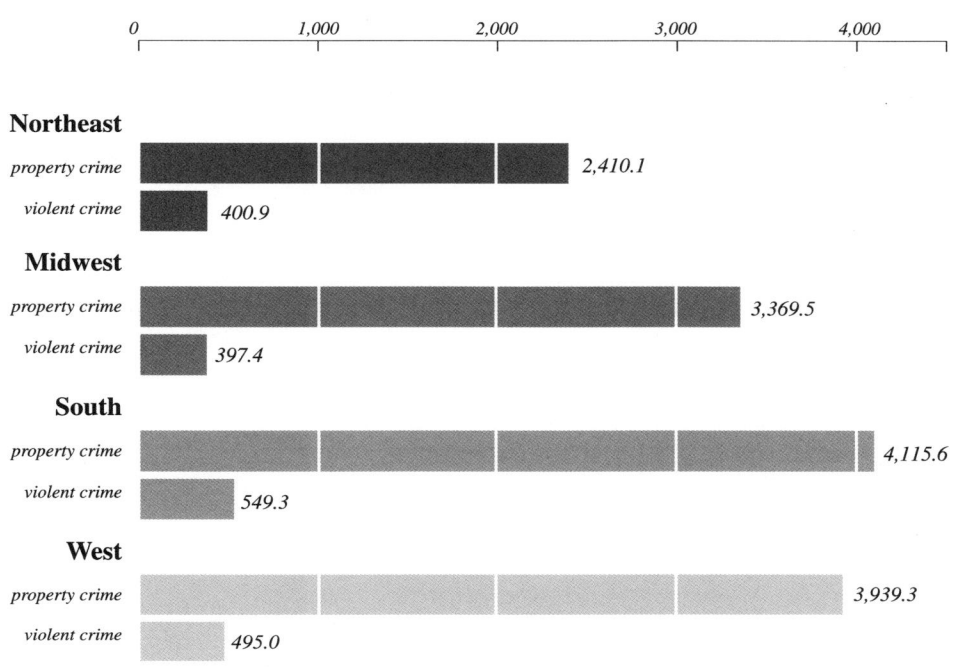

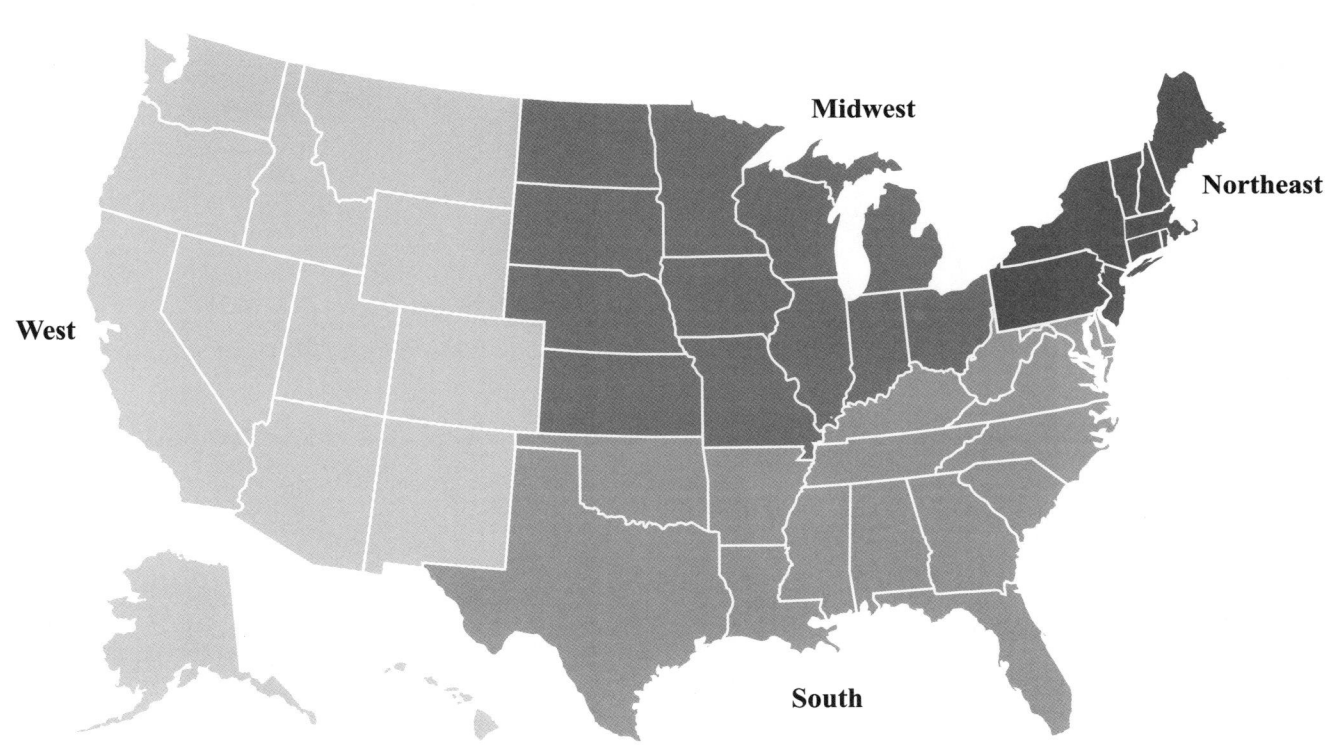

Arson

Definition

The Uniform Crime Reporting (UCR) Program defines arson as any willful or malicious burning or attempt to burn, with or without intent to defraud, a dwelling house, public building, motor vehicle or aircraft, personal property of another, etc.

Offense Methodology

According to the UCR Program's data collection guidelines, only fires determined through investigation to have been willfully or maliciously set are classified as arsons. Fires of suspicious or unknown origins are excluded from this classification.

Due to the limited reporting of arson offenses by law enforcement, certain UCR data presentations are not possible. Because the UCR Program does not estimate for arson offenses, it does not include them in Tables 1-7, which all contain offense estimations. The UCR Program does, however, present the total number of arsons reported by individual law enforcement agencies in Tables 8-11 in this report. Though arson is not included in national rate calculations, the UCR Program computes arson rates separately (based on the data of those agencies for which 12 months of complete data were submitted) and publishes them in Table 2.30. Tables 12-15 in this report provide 2-year arson trend data. Clearance data for arson are published in Table 2.31 and Tables 25-28. Additional information regarding the specific composition of each table is provided in the Table Methodology section of Appendix I.

National Coverage

In 2003, 12,776 law enforcement agencies provided to the UCR Program 1 to 12 months of arson data, which included 71,319 offenses. Of the 12,776 agencies, 12,738 submitted additional information (such as the structure type and the estimated value of property damage) for 64,043 arsons. (See Table 2.31.) Of those agencies submitting supplemental information, 9,790 agencies covering 72.0 percent of the population provided 12 months of complete data. (See Table 2.30.)

Population Groups: Trends and Rates

Trends

The UCR Program aggregates data by various population groups, which include cities, metropolitan counties, and nonmetropolitan counties. (See Appendix III.) A comparison of 2003 data to those from 2002 showed that the number of arson offenses was down 6.3 percent nationwide. The 2-year trend also showed that cities, collectively, experienced a 6.8-percent decline in the number of arsons within their boundaries. Among the population groups labeled city, the Nation's smallest cities, those with 10,000 or fewer inhabitants, had the most significant decrease, 11.8 percent, in their arson offenses. The largest cities, those with 250,000 or more inhabitants, had a 9.1-percent decline in their arson offenses from 2002 to 2003. Law enforcement agencies in metropolitan counties recorded a 6.1-percent decline in the number of arsons from the 2002 level, and nonmetropolitan county law enforcement agencies recorded a 0.6-percent decrease in their number of reported arsons. (See Table 12.)

Rates

Based on 12 months of complete data, 9,790 law enforcement agencies in the Nation measured arson at a rate of 30.4 offenses per 100,000 in population in 2003. Collectively, cities had a rate of 33.6 arsons per 100,000 inhabitants. Among city population groupings, the country's largest cities, those with populations of 250,000 and over, experienced the greatest frequency in reported arson offenses at 52.8 offenses per 100,000 persons. Arson offenses occurred in metropolitan counties at a rate of 25.8 offenses per 100,000 inhabitants, and

Table 2.30

Arson Rate
by Population Group, 2003
[9,790 agencies; 2003 estimated population 209,483,192; rate per 100,000 inhabitants]

Population group	Rate
Total	**30.4**
Total cities	33.6
Group I (cities 250,000 and over)	52.8
(cities 1,000,000 and over)	48.8
(cities 500,000 to 999,999)	52.7
(cities 250,000 to 499,999)	58.1
Group II (cities 100,000 to 249,999)	34.5
Group III (cities 50,000 to 99,999)	28.0
Group IV (cities 25,000 to 49,999)	23.4
Group V (cities 10,000 to 24,999)	20.4
Group VI (cities under 10,000)	22.3
Metropolitan counties	25.8
Nonmetropolitan counties	17.7
Suburban area[1]	23.4

[1] Suburban area includes law enforcement agencies in cities with less than 50,000 inhabitants and county law enforcement agencies that are within a Metropolitan Statistical Area (see Appendix III). Suburban area excludes all metropolitan agencies associated with a principal city. The agencies associated with suburban areas also appear in other groups within this table.

Table 2.31

Arson
by Type of Property, 2003

[12,738 agencies; 2003 estimated population 226, 463,194]

Property classification	Number of offenses	Percent distribution[1]	Percent not in use	Average damage	Total clearances	Percent of offenses cleared[2]	Percent of clearances under 18
Total	**64,043**	**100.0**		**$11,942**	**10,683**	**16.7**	**40.9**
Total structure:	26,994	42.1	18.5	21,276	5,929	22.0	40.2
Single occupancy residential	12,071	18.8	20.7	19,062	2,645	21.9	30.3
Other residential	4,399	6.9	13.1	23,977	940	21.4	31.5
Storage	1,865	2.9	19.9	16,794	309	16.6	49.2
Industrial/manufacturing	287	0.4	20.9	136,644	69	24.0	34.8
Other commercial	2,760	4.3	14.3	33,557	450	16.3	26.4
Community/public	3,073	4.8	14.1	11,061	1,014	33.0	73.4
Other structure	2,539	4.0	26.0	16,366	502	19.8	49.0
Total mobile:	21,310	33.3		6,381	1,475	6.9	21.2
Motor vehicles	20,292	31.7		6,234	1,318	6.5	20.6
Other mobile	1,018	1.6		9,292	157	15.4	26.1
Other	15,739	24.6		3,467	3,279	20.8	51.2

[1] Because of rounding, the percentages may not add to 100.0.

[2] Includes offenses cleared by arrest or exceptional means.

they happened in nonmetropolitan counties at a rate of 17.7 arsons per 100,000 in population. (See Table 2.30.)

Offense Analysis

Supplemental arson data submitted by law enforcement agencies throughout the country revealed the following information about the types of fires reported and the resulting monetary losses.

Type

The UCR Program collects arson data according to the type of property burned: structure (residential, commercial, industrial, etc.), mobile (motor vehicles, trailers, etc.), and other (crops, timber, etc.). (See Table 2.31.)

In 2003, structural arson accounted for 42.1 percent of reported arson. Among these types of fires, residential properties were the target in 61.0 percent of the offenses. Of residential property targets, 73.3 percent were single-occupancy dwellings. Nearly 19 percent

(18.5) of all structure arsons were abandoned or unused properties at the time of the fire. Mobile property arson made up 33.3 percent of the total arson reported in 2003. The majority of mobile property arson, 95.2 percent, was of motor vehicles. Other types of property comprised the remaining 24.6 percent of properties targeted by arsonists. (See Table 2.31.)

A comparison of arson property data for 2002 and 2003 showed that the number of structural arsons declined 3.9 percent, and arson incidents involving mobile property decreased 6.8 percent. Arsons of other types of property in 2003 also decreased, down 7.3 percent from the 2002 number. (See Table 15.)

Dollar Loss

The average dollar loss for property damaged or destroyed by arson in 2003 was $11,942 per offense. Overall, structural losses averaged $21,276. Arsons of industrial and manufacturing structures resulted in the highest average dollar

loss during 2003, $136,644 per offense. Residential structure losses averaged $19,062 for single-occupancy dwellings, and losses in other residential-type dwellings averaged $23,977 per offense. Mobile property losses averaged $6,381 per arson offense, and other property types, averaged losses of $3,467. (See Table 2.31.)

Clearances

In the UCR Program, law enforcement clears offenses when an officer arrests an offender or when elements beyond the control of law enforcement prevent the placing of formal charges against the offender, i.e., exceptional means. (Section III provides more information regarding clearances.)

In 2003, law enforcement cleared 16.7 percent of the arson offenses reported in the United States. With the highest clearance percentage among the Nation's regions, law enforcement in the Northeast cleared 20.7 percent of reported arson. Law enforcement agencies in the Midwest cleared 16.1 percent, and those in the South cleared 18.9 percent. The percentage of arson offenses cleared in the West was 13.5 percent. (See Table 26.)

Data aggregations by population group showed that law enforcement agencies in cities, collectively, cleared 16.5 percent of arson offenses reported within their jurisdictions. Among city population groupings, agencies in the Nation's smallest cities, those with populations of 10,000 and under, cleared 27.6 percent of their reported arson offenses; this was the highest percentage of clearances for arson among cities, as well as for all population groups. Law enforcement agencies serving the Nation's largest cities, those with populations of 250,000 and over, cleared 10.9 percent of reported arson, the lowest clearance percentage among city population groups. Law enforcement in metropolitan counties throughout the Nation cleared 16.0 percent of reported arson offenses, and nonmetropolitan county law enforcement cleared 23.5 percent of the reported arson during 2003. (See Table 25.)

Based on supplemental arson data for 2003 (from 12,738 agencies regarding structural property and mobile property arson), law enforcement cleared 22.0 percent of structural property arson nationwide. Additionally, agencies cleared 6.9 percent of mobile property arson. (See Table 2.31.)

An analysis of clearances by population group further revealed that law enforcement agencies in cities with populations under 10,000 cleared the highest percentages of reported structural and mobile property arson offenses during 2003. These agencies cleared 31.6 percent of structural property arson and 17.8 percent of mobile property ar-

son. Cities with populations of 10,000 to 24,999 cleared the greatest proportion of arson offenses for other property types of arson, 28.4 percent. (See Table 27.)

Clearances and Juveniles

The UCR Program lists any clearance involving both adults (those aged 18 and over) and juveniles (persons under age 18) as an adult clearance. In addition, if an offender under the age of 18 is cited to appear before juvenile authorities, the UCR Program considers that incident as cleared by arrest even though a physical arrest may not have occurred.

Clearances involving only juveniles comprised 41.3 percent of total arsons cleared nationwide during 2003. Of all offenses collected by the UCR Program, arson was the offense with the greatest degree of juvenile involvement. Clearances involving only juvenile offenders accounted for 44.2 percent of all arsons clearances in cities collectively. In the Nation's largest cities, those with populations of 250,000 and greater, clearances involving juveniles only comprised 38.7 percent of all arson clearances. Clearances of offenders under the age of 18 accounted for approximately 48.0 percent of the arson clearances in cities with populations of 24,999 inhabitants or less. In the country's metropolitan and nonmetropolitan counties, clearances involving juveniles only comprised 37.1 percent and 24.6 percent, respectively, of the total number of arsons cleared. (See Table 28.)

An examination of clearance data for the different types of arson showed that clearances involving juveniles only accounted for 40.2 percent of the clearances that involved structure arson. Of these, 73.4 percent of the clearances for community/public structure arson involved juveniles only. Clearances involving mobile property arsons had the

least juvenile-only involvement, 21.2 percent. (See Table 2.31.)

Arrests

Total Arrests and Rates

In 2003 law enforcement personnel arrested an estimated 16,163 people for committing arson offenses. (See Table 29.) Based on the 9,790 agencies that submitted 12 months of complete arrest data for arson, the national arrest rate for the offense was 5.6 arrests per 100,000 inhabitants. Among the Nation's geographic regions, the West had the highest arson arrest rate, 5.8 arrests per 100,000 persons. Law enforcement agencies in the South made 5.6 arson arrests per 100,000 persons, and the Midwest and the Northeast arrested 5.5 and 5.1 persons per 100,000, respectively. (See Table 30.)

By population group, law enforcement in the Nation's cities made 5.8 arson arrests for every 100,000 inhabitants. Within city population groupings, those with 10,000 or fewer inhabitants had the highest arson arrest rate, 7.0. Law enforcement agencies in metropolitan counties arrested 5.4 persons for arson per 100,000 population, and those in nonmetropolitan counties arrested 4.6 arson suspects per every 100,000 in population. (See Table 31.)

Arrest Trends

Nationwide, the number of arrests for arson in 2003 declined 5.8 percent from the number of arrests recorded for 2002. Arrests of adults for arson decreased 8.3 percent, and arrests of juveniles declined 3.5 percent from the previous year's number. (See Table 36.) By gender, the number of males arrested for arson was down 6.1 percent from the 2002 figure, and the number of females arrested for arson decreased 4.1 percent. (See Table 37.)

Five-year arrest trends for the Nation showed that the number of arson arrests for 2003 declined 7.9 percent when compared to 1999 arrest data. Law enforcement agencies reported a 3.6-percent decrease in the number of adults arrested for arson and an 11.6-percent drop in the number of juveniles arrested for arson for the period. (See Table 34.) Overall, the number of males and the number of females arrested for arson declined 8.6 percent and 3.6 percent, respectively. (See Table 35.)

A 10-year comparison of arson arrest data indicated that there were 28.5 percent fewer arson arrests in 2003 than in 1994. According to trend data for those years, the number of adults arrested for arson was down 17.7 percent, and the number of juveniles arrested for the offense decreased 36.2 percent. (See Table 32.) By sex, there were 29.3 percent fewer arrests of males for arson in 2003 than in 1994. Arrests of females for the offense also declined by 23.7 percent for the same years. (See Table 33.)

Distribution by Age, Sex, and Race

Data regarding the age, sex, and race of persons arrested for arson in 2003 indicated that juveniles accounted for 50.8 percent of all arrestees for arson; 31.2 percent of all arson arrestees were of juveniles under the age of 15. (See Table 41.) Males comprised 84.4 percent of the total of arson arrestees. (See Table 42.) By race, 77.5 percent of all individuals arrested for arson were reported as being white, 20.9 percent of arson arrestees were black, and 1.6 percent were persons of other races. (See Table 43.)

Hate Crime

Definition

A hate crime, also known as a bias crime, is a criminal offense committed against a person, property, or society that is motivated, in whole or in part, by the offender's bias against a race, religion, disability, sexual orientation, or ethnicity/national origin.

Background

In response to mounting national concern over crimes motivated by bias, Congress enacted on April 23, 1990, the Hate Crime Statistics Act of 1990. This law required the Attorney General to collect data "about crimes that manifest evidence of prejudice based on race, religion, sexual orientation, or ethnicity." The Attorney General delegated the responsibilities of developing the procedures for implementing, collecting, and managing hate crime data to the Director of the FBI, who in turn assigned the tasks to the Uniform Crime Reporting (UCR) Program. In September 1994, Congress passed the Violent Crime Control and Law Enforcement Act, which amended the Hate Crime Statistics Act to include both physical and mental disabilities as potential bias factors, and collection of this data began in January 1997. Lastly, the Church Arson Prevention Act of 1996 mandated that hate crime data collection become a permanent part of the UCR Program.

Those who developed the guidelines for hate crime data collection recognized that hate crimes are not separate, distinct crimes; instead, they are traditional offenses motivated by the offender's bias. After much consideration, the developers decided that hate crime data could be derived by capturing the additional element of bias in those offenses already being reported to the UCR Program. Attaching the collection of hate crime statistics to the established UCR data collection procedures, they concluded, would fulfill the directives of the Hate Crime Statistics Act without placing an undue additional reporting burden on law enforcement and, in time, would develop a substantial body of data about the nature and frequency of bias crimes occurring throughout the Nation. As a result, the law enforcement agencies that participate in the national

Figure 2.17

Bias-motivated Offenses
Percent Distribution,[1] 2003

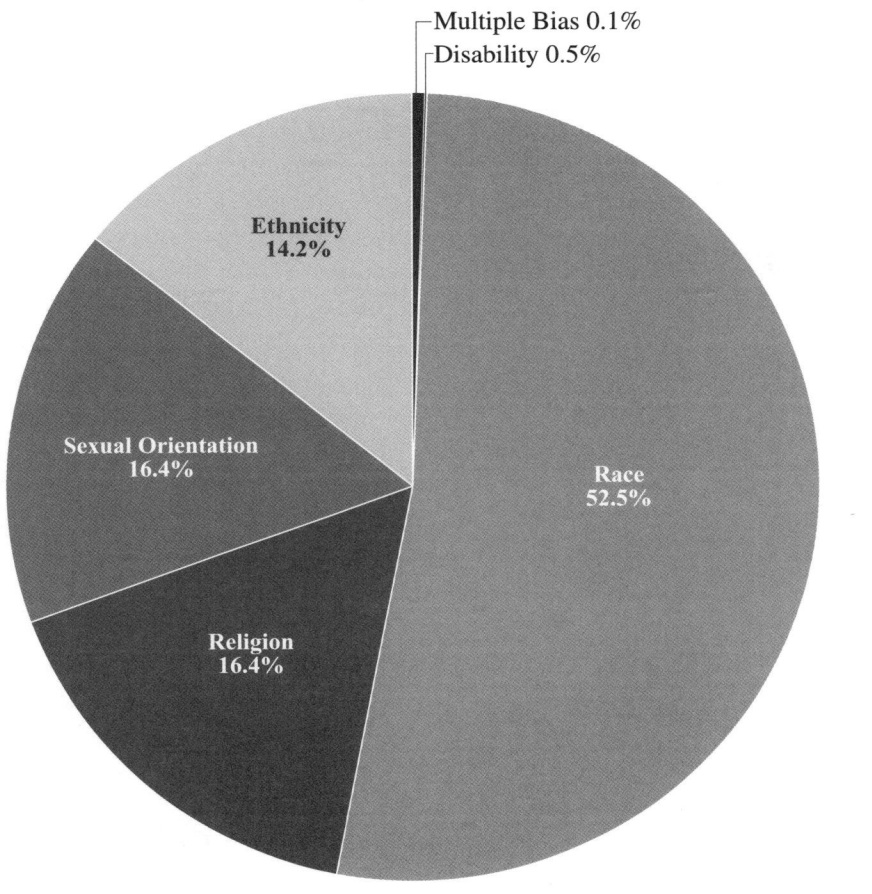

- Multiple Bias 0.1%
- Disability 0.5%
- Ethnicity 14.2%
- Sexual Orientation 16.4%
- Religion 16.4%
- Race 52.5%

[1] Due to rounding, the percentages may not add to 100.0.

Table 2.32

Incidents, Offenses, Victims, and Known Offenders
by Bias Motivation, 2003

Bias motivation	Incidents	Offenses	Victims[1]	Known offenders[2]
Total	**7,489**	**8,715**	**9,100**	**6,934**
Single-Bias Incidents	7,485	8,706	9,091	6,927
Race:	3,844	4,574	4,754	3,886
Anti-White	830	969	1,006	1,019
Anti-Black	2,548	3,032	3,150	2,456
Anti-American Indian/Alaskan Native	76	83	85	80
Anti-Asian/Pacific Islander	231	277	289	196
Anti-Multiple Races, Group	159	213	224	135
Religion:	1,343	1,426	1,489	574
Anti-Jewish	927	987	1,025	332
Anti-Catholic	76	78	80	32
Anti-Protestant	49	50	54	20
Anti-Islamic	149	155	171	94
Anti-Other Religion	109	118	120	69
Anti-Multiple Religions, Group	24	25	26	17
Anti-Atheism/Agnosticism/etc.	9	13	13	10
Sexual Orientation:	1,239	1,430	1,479	1,313
Anti-Male Homosexual	783	881	910	863
Anti-Female Homosexual	187	220	230	167
Anti-Homosexual	247	305	314	257
Anti-Heterosexual	14	15	15	10
Anti-Bisexual	8	9	10	16
Ethnicity/National Origin:	1,026	1,236	1,326	1,119
Anti-Hispanic	426	529	595	577
Anti-Other Ethnicity/National Origin	600	707	731	542
Disability:	33	40	43	35
Anti-Physical	24	30	32	24
Anti-Mental	9	10	11	11
Multiple-Bias Incidents[3]	4	9	9	7

[1] The term *victim* may refer to a person, business, institution, or society as a whole.
[2] The term *known offender* does not imply that the identity of the suspect is known, but only that an attribute of the suspect is identified, which distinguishes him/her from an unknown offender.
[3] A multiple-bias incident occurs only when two or more offense types are committed in a single incident. In a situation where there is more than one offense type, the agency can indicate a different bias motivation for each offense type. In the case of a single offense type, only one bias motivation can be indicated.

Table 2.33

Incidents, Offenses, Victims, and Known Offenders
by Offense Type, 2003

Offense type	Incidents[1]	Offenses	Victims[2]	Known offenders[3]
Total	**7,489**	**8,715**	**9,100**	**6,934**
Crimes against persons:	4,511	5,517	5,517	5,543
Murder and nonnegligent manslaughter	13	14	14	19
Forcible rape	5	5	5	7
Aggravated assault	706	920	920	1,234
Simple assault	1,523	1,809	1,809	2,234
Intimidation	2,252	2,744	2,744	2,025
Other[4]	12	25	25	24
Crimes against property:	3,139	3,139	3,524	1,558
Robbery	107	107	152	255
Burglary	164	164	190	92
Larceny-theft	173	173	187	105
Motor vehicle theft	15	15	15	11
Arson	34	34	44	24
Destruction/damage/vandalism	2,618	2,618	2,899	1,042
Other[4]	28	28	37	29
Crimes against society[4]	59	59	59	92

[1] The actual number of incidents is 7,489. However, the column figures will not add to the total because incidents may include more than one offense type, and these are counted in each appropriate offense type category.
[2] The term *victim* may refer to a person, business, institution, or society as a whole.
[3] The term *known offender* does not imply that the identity of the suspect is known, but only that an attribute of the suspect is identified, which distinguishes him/her from an unknown offender. The actual number of known offenders is 6,934. However, the column figures will not add to the total because some offenders are responsible for more than one offense type, and they are, therefore, counted more than once in this table.
[4] Includes additional offenses collected in NIBRS.

hate crime program collect details about an offender's bias motivation associated with the following offense types: murder and nonnegligent manslaughter, forcible rape, aggravated assault, simple assault, intimidation, robbery, burglary, larceny-theft, motor vehicle theft, arson, and destruction/damage/vandalism of property. (The law enforcement agencies participating in the UCR Program's National Incident-Based Reporting System also collect additional offenses for crimes against persons and crimes against property, which the Program publishes as "Other." In addition, these agencies collect hate crime data for another category called "Crimes Against Society.")

An abstract based on the information received from law enforcement agencies that provided 1 to 12 months of hate crime reports during 2003 follows.

Participation

A total of 11,909 law enforcement agencies participated in the hate crime program during 2003, a 1.4 percent decrease from the 12,073 agencies that participated in 2002. Of the agencies that participated in 2003, 1,967 (16.5 percent) reported 7,489 hate crime incidents to the FBI. (See Table 2.35.) The number of incidents reported to the FBI in 2003 was 27 more than the number reported during 2002.

Law Enforcement Reports

The UCR Program data collection guidelines stipulate that a hate crime may involve multiple offenses, victims, and offenders within one incident. Accordingly, the 7,489 hate crime incidents reported to the FBI in 2003 involved 8,715 separate offenses, 9,100 victims, and 6,934 known offenders. (See Table 2.32.) (The term *known offender* does not imply that the identity of the suspect is known but only that an attribute of the suspect has been identified, distinguishing him or her from an unknown offender.)

Incidents

Of the 7,485 single-bias incidents reported in 2003, 51.4 percent were motivated by racial bias, 17.9 percent were driven by prejudice against a particular religion, 16.6 percent involved a sexual-orientation bias, 13.7 percent resulted from a bias against an ethnicity or national origin, and 0.4 percent of the incidents were motivated by a disability bias. (Based on Table 2.32.)

In addition to single-bias incidents, hate crime data collection guidelines permit the identification of multiple-bias incidents. These are incidents in which two or more types of offenses were committed as a result of two or more bias motivations. Four of the 7,489 incidents reported in 2003 met that criterion. (See Table 2.32.)

Offenses

According to the UCR definition, a victim of an offense motivated by a bias may be a person, a business, an institution, or society as a whole. When aggregating the number of hate crime offenses committed against individuals, the UCR Program counts one offense for each victim. The offense types of murder, forcible rape, aggravated assault, simple assault, and intimidation are crimes against persons. When counting crimes against property, the UCR Program allots one offense for each distinct incident regardless of the number of victims. Robbery, burglary, larceny-theft, motor vehicle theft, arson, and destruction/damage/vandalism comprise the offense types that the Program considers to be crimes against property.

During 2003, a total of 5,517 (63.3 percent) reported hate crime offenses were crimes against persons, and 3,139 (36.0 percent) were crimes against property. Fifty-nine crimes against society (0.7 percent) were reported in 2003. Intimidation continued to be the most frequently reported hate crime and accounted for 49.7 percent of all crimes against persons and 31.5 percent of all hate crime offenses. Destruction/damage/vandalism of property was the

Table 2.34

Race of Known Offender, 2003[1]

Known offender's race

Total	**6,934**
White	4,317
Black	1,286
American Indian/Alaskan Native	61
Asian/Pacific Islander	93
Multiple Races, Group[2]	436
Unknown Race	741

[1] The term *known offender* does not imply that the identity of the suspect is known, but only that an attribute of the suspect is identified, which distinguishes him/her from an unknown offender.

[2] The term *multiple races, group* is used to describe a group of offenders comprised of individuals of varying races.

Table 2.35

Agency Hate Crime Reporting by State, 2003

Participating state	Number of participating agencies	Population covered	Agencies submitting incident reports	Total number of incidents reported
Total	**11,909**	**240,906,049**	**1,967**	**7,489**
Alabama	36	234,120	1	1
Alaska	1	271,085	1	13
Arizona	89	5,411,197	26	246
Arkansas	128	1,166,678	40	170
California	727	35,484,453	235	1,472
Colorado	185	4,153,634	35	82
Connecticut	95	3,165,048	52	134
Delaware	53	817,491	6	17
District of Columbia	2	563,384	2	31
Florida	489	16,973,420	86	231
Georgia	82	1,617,487	7	23
Idaho	119	1,357,404	12	20
Illinois	73	5,140,241	61	208
Indiana	139	3,086,471	19	48
Iowa	221	2,870,482	27	38
Kansas	341	2,379,824	19	49
Kentucky	435	3,750,474	42	81
Louisiana	140	3,422,474	7	7
Maine	149	1,305,728	25	77
Maryland	149	5,508,909	31	248
Massachusetts	247	5,208,869	97	403
Michigan	610	8,784,731	162	427
Minnesota	327	5,028,715	60	215
Mississippi	57	825,576	1	1
Missouri	183	2,881,465	21	54
Montana	82	853,039	5	5
Nebraska	202	1,368,604	16	46
Nevada	35	2,241,154	9	97
New Hampshire	125	832,285	29	36
New Jersey	555	8,638,396	236	594
New Mexico	47	1,161,022	2	11
New York	520	19,162,447	61	602
North Carolina	461	8,337,322	22	77
North Dakota	65	549,642	8	18
Ohio	387	8,511,723	64	231
Oklahoma	298	3,511,532	23	38
Oregon	1	545,271	1	95
Pennsylvania	828	11,043,680	31	115
Rhode Island	48	1,076,164	10	45
South Carolina	419	4,144,591	33	54
South Dakota	114	503,221	6	10
Tennessee	456	5,841,748	62	161
Texas	983	22,101,481	84	294
Utah	57	1,775,428	21	59
Vermont	59	569,065	11	27
Virginia	393	7,312,051	66	280
Washington	253	6,071,292	56	222
West Virginia	392	1,712,606	16	33
Wisconsin	16	1,337,978	16	31
Wyoming	36	294,947	4	12

most frequently reported crime against property in 2003, comprising 83.4 percent of those offenses. Additionally, destruction/damage/vandalism accounted for 30.0 of all hate crime offenses. (Based on Table 2.33.)

Victims

A total of 9,100 individuals, businesses, institutions, or society as a whole were victims of hate crimes in 2003. Approximately 52.3 percent of all single-bias hate crime victims were targets of racial prejudice. Of these victims, 66.3 percent were attacked because of an anti-black bias motivation, and 21.2 percent were attacked because of an anti-white bias motivation. Of the total victims of single-bias hate crimes, 16.4 were targets because of the offender's bias toward a particular religion. Of these, 68.8 percent were targeted because of an anti-Jewish bias motivation, and 11.5 percent were victims of anti-Islamic bias. Additionally, 16.3 percent of total single-bias hate crime victims were attacked because of the offender's prejudice against sexual-orientation; among these victims, 61.5 percent were victims of an anti-male homosexual bias motivation. Approximately 14.6 percent of hate crime victims in single-bias incidents were targets of a bias against ethnicity or national origin. Of these, 44.9 percent were victims of anti-Hispanic sentiment. Of the victims of single-bias motivations, 43 victims were attacked because of the offenders' biases against a disability. Nine victims were attacked in 2003 as a result of their attackers' multiple biases. (Based on Table 2.32.)

Offenders

In 2003, there were 6,934 known offenders who committed crimes motivated by their perceived biases. The majority of these known hate crime offenders, 62.3 percent, were white; 18.5 percent were black; 6.3 were identified as groups of offenders with individuals of more than one race; and 2.2 percent of known offenders were of other races. The races of 10.7 percent of offenders were not determined. (Based on Table 2.34.) More detailed information concerning the characteristics of hate crime can be found in the UCR Program's annual publication *Hate Crime Statistics*.

Offense Tabulations

The tables in Section II—Offenses Reported—organize crime data in many ways. First, the data are categorized for the Nation as a whole, then by geographic divisions; individual states; Metropolitan Statistical Areas (MSAs); and cities, towns, and counties. The data are presented as crime volume and/or crime rate (occurrence per 100,000 U.S. inhabitants).

The exact number of crimes occurring within the United States is unknown. The UCR Program estimates the level of criminal activity based upon the number of offenses that are known to law enforcement and, using these estimates, computes crime rates for each 100,000 population segment. The Program uses current, permanent population counts in computing crimes rates. The reader should be aware that all communities are affected to some degree by seasonal or transient population changes, and the Program's crime rates do not account for these short-term variations. In addition, the reader should remember that many factors influence the amount and type of crime occurring from place to place, and shifting variables may cause crime to vary from time to time within the same place. Other factors contributing to the level of crime in a given area are discussed in Crime Factors (page v).

One tool that law enforcement administrators can use in analyzing the volume of local crime and the performance of the law enforcement agencies is national data. That analysis, however, should not end with a comparison based solely on data presented in this publica-tion. A true assessment of a community's crime problem or the effectiveness of law enforcement operations can be made only by including all the factors that shape local crime.

Brief Description of the Tables

An in-depth discussion of table construction methodology can be found in Appendix I. The following summarizes the contents of the tables contained in Section II–Offenses Reported.

Table 1 is a 20-year table that sets forth national estimates of volume and rate per 100,000 inhabitants for the Part I offenses. Table 2 shows estimates of crime volume and rates for 2003 for the Nation as a whole and for the Nation disaggregated by community type: MSAs, nonmetropolitan counties, and cities and towns outside metropolitan areas. Definitions of these community types can be found in Appendix III.

Data showing the regional distribution of estimated Part I crimes along with proportional population estimates are provided in Table 3. A map of the United States illustrating the regions and divisions employed by the UCR Program appears in Appendix III.

Table 4 offers a 2-year trend in the volume and rate estimates by region, geographic division, and state. The estimated volume and rate of Part I offenses for each state by community type is shown in Table 5, and for individual MSAs in Table 6. Table 7 provides breakdowns for the offenses of robbery (by location), burglary (by time of day), and larceny-theft (by type) over the past 5 years.

Offenses known to police for cities over 10,000 in population are presented in Table 8, and Table 9 shows the number of offenses occurring on college and university campuses as reported to the UCR Program by college and university law enforcement agencies. The UCR Program does not assign population to educational institutions, but does provide student enrollment information when available.

Offenses reported by metropolitan and nonmetropolitan county law enforcement agencies are presented in Table 10. Table 11 provides offenses reported by state law enforcement agencies, including state police, and federal agencies. Tables 12–19 supply crime trends for volumes and rates by population groupings. The UCR Program's definition of the population groups can be found in Appendix III.

Data concerning weapons used in the violent crimes of murder, robbery, and aggravated assault are presented in Tables 20–22. Tables 23 and 24 provide an analysis of the value of property lost through the crimes of robbery, burglary, motor vehicle theft, and larceny-theft, and offer breakdowns by type and value of property stolen and recovered.

Note

Because the UCR Program does not estimate for arson, arson offenses are not included in the tables containing offense estimates. However, arson offenses reported by individual law enforcement agencies are displayed in Tables 8–11. Two-year arson trends are shown in Tables 12–15.

Table 1

Crime in the United States
by Volume and Rate, 1984-2003

Population[1]	Violent crime	Murder and non-negligent man-slaughter	Forcible rape	Robbery	Aggravated assault	Property crime	Burglary	Larceny-theft	Motor vehicle theft
				Violent crime				*Property crime*	
					Number of Offenses				
Population by year:									
1984-235,824,902	1,273,282	18,692	84,233	485,008	685,349	10,608,473	2,984,434	6,591,874	1,032,165
1985-237,923,795	1,327,767	18,976	87,671	497,874	723,246	11,102,590	3,073,348	6,926,380	1,102,862
1986-240,132,887	1,489,169	20,613	91,459	542,775	834,322	11,722,700	3,241,410	7,257,153	1,224,137
1987-242,288,918	1,483,999	20,096	91,111	517,704	855,088	12,024,709	3,236,184	7,499,851	1,288,674
1988-244,498,982	1,566,221	20,675	92,486	542,968	910,092	12,356,865	3,218,077	7,705,872	1,432,916
1989-246,819,230	1,646,037	21,500	94,504	578,326	951,707	12,605,412	3,168,170	7,872,442	1,564,800
1990-249,464,396	1,820,127	23,438	102,555	639,271	1,054,863	12,655,486	3,073,909	7,945,670	1,635,907
1991-252,153,092	1,911,767	24,703	106,593	687,732	1,092,739	12,961,116	3,157,150	8,142,228	1,661,738
1992-255,029,699	1,932,274	23,760	109,062	672,478	1,126,974	12,505,917	2,979,884	7,915,199	1,610,834
1993-257,782,608	1,926,017	24,526	106,014	659,870	1,135,607	12,218,777	2,834,808	7,820,909	1,563,060
1994-260,327,021	1,857,670	23,326	102,216	618,949	1,113,179	12,131,873	2,712,774	7,879,812	1,539,287
1995-262,803,276	1,798,792	21,606	97,470	580,509	1,099,207	12,063,935	2,593,784	7,997,710	1,472,441
1996-265,228,572	1,688,540	19,645	96,252	535,594	1,037,049	11,805,323	2,506,400	7,904,685	1,394,238
1997-267,783,607	1,636,096	18,208	96,153	498,534	1,023,201	11,558,475	2,460,526	7,743,760	1,354,189
1998-270,248,003	1,533,887	16,974	93,144	447,186	976,583	10,951,827	2,332,735	7,376,311	1,242,781
1999-272,690,813	1,426,044	15,522	89,411	409,371	911,740	10,208,334	2,100,739	6,955,520	1,152,075
2000-281,421,906	1,425,486	15,586	90,178	408,016	911,706	10,182,584	2,050,992	6,971,590	1,160,002
2001-285,317,559[2]	1,439,480	16,037	90,863	423,557	909,023	10,437,189	2,116,531	7,092,267	1,228,391
2002-287,973,924[3]	1,423,677	16,229	95,235	420,806	891,407	10,455,277	2,151,252	7,057,379	1,246,646
2003-290,809,777	1,381,259	16,503	93,433	413,402	857,921	10,435,523	2,153,464	7,021,588	1,260,471
Percent change, number of offenses:									
2003/2002	-3.0	+1.7	-1.9	-1.8	-3.8	-0.2	+0.1	-0.5	+1.1
2003/1999	-3.1	+6.3	+4.5	+1.0	-5.9	+2.2	+2.5	+0.9	+9.4
2003/1994	-25.6	-29.3	-8.6	-33.2	-22.9	-14.0	-20.6	-10.9	-18.1
					Rate per 100,000 Inhabitants				
Year:									
1984	539.9	7.9	35.7	205.7	290.6	4,498.5	1,265.5	2,795.2	437.7
1985	558.1	8.0	36.8	209.3	304.0	4,666.4	1,291.7	2,911.2	463.5
1986	620.1	8.6	38.1	226.0	347.4	4,881.8	1,349.8	3,022.1	509.8
1987	612.5	8.3	37.6	213.7	352.9	4,963.0	1,335.7	3,095.4	531.9
1988	640.6	8.5	37.8	222.1	372.2	5,054.0	1,316.2	3,151.7	586.1
1989	666.9	8.7	38.3	234.3	385.6	5,107.1	1,283.6	3,189.6	634.0
1990	729.6	9.4	41.1	256.3	422.9	5,073.1	1,232.2	3,185.1	655.8
1991	758.2	9.8	42.3	272.7	433.4	5,140.2	1,252.1	3,229.1	659.0
1992	757.7	9.3	42.8	263.7	441.9	4,903.7	1,168.4	3,103.6	631.6
1993	747.1	9.5	41.1	256.0	440.5	4,740.0	1,099.7	3,033.9	606.3
1994	713.6	9.0	39.3	237.8	427.6	4,660.2	1,042.1	3,026.9	591.3
1995	684.5	8.2	37.1	220.9	418.3	4,590.5	987.0	3,043.2	560.3
1996	636.6	7.4	36.3	201.9	391.0	4,451.0	945.0	2,980.3	525.7
1997	611.0	6.8	35.9	186.2	382.1	4,316.3	918.8	2,891.8	505.7
1998	567.6	6.3	34.5	165.5	361.4	4,052.5	863.2	2,729.5	459.9
1999	523.0	5.7	32.8	150.1	334.3	3,743.6	770.4	2,550.7	422.5
2000	506.5	5.5	32.0	145.0	324.0	3,618.3	728.8	2,477.3	412.2
2001[2]	504.5	5.6	31.8	148.5	318.6	3,658.1	741.8	2,485.7	430.5
2002[3]	494.4	5.6	33.1	146.1	309.5	3,630.6	747.0	2,450.7	432.9
2003	475.0	5.7	32.1	142.2	295.0	3,588.4	740.5	2,414.5	433.4
Percent change, rate per 100,000 inhabitants:									
2003/2002	-3.9	+0.7	-2.8	-2.7	-4.7	-1.2	-0.9	-1.5	+0.1
2003/1999	-9.2	-0.3	-2.0	-5.3	-11.8	-4.1	-3.9	-5.3	+2.6
2003/1994	-33.4	-36.7	-18.2	-40.2	-31.0	-23.0	-28.9	-20.2	-26.7

[1] Populations are U.S. Census Bureau provisional estimates as of July 1 for each year except 1990 and 2000 which are decennial census counts.

[2] The murder and nonnegligent homicides that occurred as a result of the events of September 11, 2001, are not included in this table.

[3] The 2002 crime figures have been adjusted.

NOTE: Although arson data are included in the trend and clearance tables, sufficient data are not available to estimate totals for this offense.

Table 2

Crime in the United States
by Community Type, 2003

Area	Population[1]	Violent crime	Murder and non-negligent man-slaughter	Forcible rape	Robbery	Aggravated assault	Property crime	Burglary	Larceny-theft	Motor vehicle theft
				Violent crime				*Property crime*		
United States Total	**290,809,777**	**1,381,259**	**16,503**	**93,433**	**413,402**	**857,921**	**10,435,523**	**2,153,464**	**7,021,588**	**1,260,471**
Rate per 100,000 inhabitants		475.0	5.7	32.1	142.2	295.0	3,588.4	740.5	2,414.5	433.4
Metropolitan Statistical Area	**240,773,811**									
Area actually reporting[2]	94.9%	1,205,651	14,392	74,165	388,990	728,104	8,764,006	1,758,136	5,851,689	1,154,181
Estimated total	100.0%	1,244,205	14,706	78,862	396,779	753,858	9,108,399	1,824,281	6,102,000	1,182,118
Rate per 100,000 inhabitants		516.8	6.1	32.8	164.8	313.1	3,783.0	757.7	2,534.3	491.0
Cities outside metropolitan areas	**19,753,338**									
Area actually reporting[2]	84.8%	66,773	645	6,457	10,209	49,462	705,302	139,166	531,471	34,665
Estimated total	100.0%	76,043	748	7,540	11,848	55,907	819,267	161,144	618,709	39,414
Rate per 100,000 inhabitants		385.0	3.8	38.2	60.0	283.0	4,147.5	815.8	3,132.2	199.5
Nonmetropolitan Counties	**30,282,628**									
Area actually reporting[2]	82.8%	54,544	843	5,826	4,229	43,646	446,470	146,827	265,269	34,374
Estimated total	100.0%	61,011	1,049	7,031	4,775	48,156	507,857	168,039	300,879	38,939
Rate per 100,000 inhabitants		201.5	3.5	23.2	15.8	159.0	1,677.1	554.9	993.6	128.6

[1] Populations are U.S. Census Bureau provisional estimates as of July 1, 2003.
[2] The percentage reported under "Area actually reporting" is based upon the population covered by agencies providing 3 months or more of crime reports to the FBI.
NOTE: Although arson data are included in the trend and clearance tables, sufficient data are not available to estimate totals for this offense.

Table 3

Crime in the United States
Offense and Population Distribution by Region, 2003

Region	Population	Violent crime	Murder and non-negligent man-slaughter	Forcible rape	Robbery	Aggravated assault	Property crime	Burglary	Larceny-theft	Motor vehicle theft
				Violent crime				*Property crime*		
United States Total[1]	**100.0**	**100.0**	**100.0**	**100.0**	**100.0**	**100.0**	**100.0**	**100.0**	**100.0**	**100.0**
Northeast	18.7	15.8	14.0	13.4	19.6	14.3	12.6	11.3	13.0	12.5
Midwest	22.5	18.8	19.5	25.0	18.8	18.2	21.1	20.1	21.9	18.5
South	35.9	41.6	43.6	37.6	38.9	43.3	41.2	45.1	41.3	34.5
West	22.9	23.8	22.9	24.0	22.8	24.3	25.1	23.6	23.9	34.4

[1] Because of rounding, the percentages may not add to 100.0.
NOTE: Although arson data are included in the trend and clearance tables, sufficient data are not available to estimate totals for this offense.

Table 4

Crime in the United States
by Region, Geographic Division, and State, 2002-2003

| Area | Year | Population[1] | Violent crime | | Violent crime | | | | | | | |
| | | | | | Murder and non-negligent manslaughter | | Forcible rape | | Robbery | | Aggravated assault | |
			Number	Rate per 100,000	Number	Rate per 100,000	Number	Rate per 100,000	Number	Rate per 100,000	Number	Rate per 100,000
United States Total[2, 3, 4]	**2002**	**287,973,924**	**1,423,677**	**494.4**	**16,229**	**5.6**	**95,235**	**33.1**	**420,806**	**146.1**	**891,407**	**309.5**
	2003	**290,809,777**	**1,381,259**	**475.0**	**16,503**	**5.7**	**93,433**	**32.1**	**413,402**	**142.2**	**857,921**	**295.0**
Percent change			-3.0	-3.9	+1.7	+0.7	-1.9	-2.8	-1.8	-2.7	-3.8	-4.7
Northeast[2]	**2002**	**54,172,792**	**225,965**	**417.1**	**2,209**	**4.1**	**12,842**	**23.7**	**80,685**	**148.9**	**130,229**	**240.4**
	2003	**54,399,446**	**218,106**	**400.9**	**2,311**	**4.2**	**12,511**	**23.0**	**80,892**	**148.7**	**122,392**	**225.0**
Percent change			-3.5	-3.9	+4.6	+4.2	-2.6	-3.0	+0.3	-0.2	-6.0	-6.4
New England[2]	2002	14,134,420	49,105	347.4	337	2.4	3,861	27.3	12,914	91.4	31,993	226.3
	2003	14,205,480	48,026	338.1	319	2.2	3,857	27.2	13,788	97.1	30,062	211.6
Percent change			-2.2	-2.7	-5.3	-5.8	-0.1	-0.6	+6.8	+6.2	-6.0	-6.5
Connecticut[2]	2002	3,458,587	10,807	312.5	84	2.4	740	21.4	4,069	117.6	5,914	171.0
	2003	3,483,372	10,736	308.2	104	3.0	652	18.7	4,146	119.0	5,834	167.5
Percent change			-0.7	-1.4	+23.8	+22.9	-11.9	-12.5	+1.9	+1.2	-1.4	-2.1
Maine	2002	1,294,894	1,396	107.8	14	1.1	377	29.1	270	20.9	735	56.8
	2003	1,305,728	1,422	108.9	16	1.2	354	27.1	289	22.1	763	58.4
Percent change			+1.9	+1.0	+14.3	+13.3	-6.1	-6.9	+7.0	+6.1	+3.8	+2.9
Massachusetts	2002	6,421,800	31,137	484.9	173	2.7	1,777	27.7	7,169	111.6	22,018	342.9
	2003	6,433,422	30,196	469.4	142	2.2	1,798	27.9	7,985	124.1	20,271	315.1
Percent change			-3.0	-3.2	-17.9	-18.1	+1.2	+1.0	+11.4	+11.2	-7.9	-8.1
New Hampshire	2002	1,274,405	2,056	161.3	12	0.9	446	35.0	413	32.4	1,185	93.0
	2003	1,287,687	1,916	148.8	18	1.4	427	33.2	478	37.1	993	77.1
Percent change			-6.8	-7.8	+50.0	+48.5	-4.3	-5.2	+15.7	+14.5	-16.2	-17.1
Rhode Island	2002	1,068,326	3,051	285.6	41	3.8	395	37.0	916	85.7	1,699	159.0
	2003	1,076,164	3,074	285.6	25	2.3	505	46.9	830	77.1	1,714	159.3
Percent change			+0.8	*	-39.0	-39.5	+27.8	+26.9	-9.4	-10.0	+0.9	+0.1
Vermont	2002	616,408	658	106.7	13	2.1	126	20.4	77	12.5	442	71.7
	2003	619,107	682	110.2	14	2.3	121	19.5	60	9.7	487	78.7
Percent change			+3.6	+3.2	+7.7	+7.2	-4.0	-4.4	-22.1	-22.4	+10.2	+9.7
Middle Atlantic[2]	2002	40,038,372	176,860	441.7	1,872	4.7	8,981	22.4	67,771	169.3	98,236	245.4
	2003	40,193,966	170,080	423.1	1,992	5.0	8,654	21.5	67,104	167.0	92,330	229.7
Percent change			-3.8	-4.2	+6.4	+6.0	-3.6	-4.0	-1.0	-1.4	-6.0	-6.4
New Jersey[2]	2002	8,575,252	32,252	376.1	339	4.0	1,365	15.9	13,955	162.7	16,593	193.5
	2003	8,638,396	31,599	365.8	407	4.7	1,325	15.3	13,366	154.7	16,501	191.0
Percent change			-2.0	-2.7	+20.1	+19.2	-2.9	-3.6	-4.2	-4.9	-0.6	-1.3
New York	2002	19,134,293	95,030	496.6	909	4.8	3,885	20.3	36,653	191.6	53,583	280.0
	2003	19,190,115	89,265	465.2	934	4.9	3,773	19.7	35,758	186.3	48,800	254.3
Percent change			-6.1	-6.3	+2.8	+2.5	-2.9	-3.2	-2.4	-2.7	-8.9	-9.2
Pennsylvania	2002	12,328,827	49,578	402.1	624	5.1	3,731	30.3	17,163	139.2	28,060	227.6
	2003	12,365,455	49,216	398.0	651	5.3	3,556	28.8	17,980	145.4	27,029	218.6
Percent change			-0.7	-1.0	+4.3	+4.0	-4.7	-5.0	+4.8	+4.4	-3.7	-4.0
Midwest[2, 3]	**2002**	**65,098,828**	**274,308**	**421.4**	**3,310**	**5.1**	**24,181**	**37.1**	**82,186**	**126.2**	**164,631**	**252.9**
	2003	**65,406,134**	**259,925**	**397.4**	**3,221**	**4.9**	**23,404**	**35.8**	**77,537**	**118.5**	**155,763**	**238.1**
Percent change			**-5.2**	**-5.7**	**-2.7**	**-3.1**	**-3.2**	**-3.7**	**-5.7**	**-6.1**	**-5.4**	**-5.8**
East North Central[2, 3]	2002	45,634,972	204,432	448.0	2,681	5.9	17,623	38.6	66,357	145.4	117,771	258.1
	2003	45,837,269	194,034	423.3	2,557	5.6	17,123	37.4	62,744	136.9	111,610	243.5
Percent change			-5.1	-5.5	-4.6	-5.0	-2.8	-3.3	-5.4	-5.9	-5.2	-5.6
Illinois[2, 3]	2002	12,586,447	75,759	601.9	961	7.6	4,370	34.7	25,314	201.1	45,114	358.4
	2003	12,653,544	70,456	556.8	896	7.1	4,167	32.9	23,809	188.2	41,584	328.6
Percent change			-7.0	-7.5	-6.8	-7.3	-4.6	-5.2	-5.9	-6.4	-7.8	-8.3

See footnotes at end of table.

| Property crime | | Property crime | | | | | |
| Property crime | | Burglary | | Larceny-theft | | Motor vehicle theft | |
Number	Rate per 100,000	Number	Rate per 100,000	Number	Rate per 100,000	Number	Rate per 100,000
10,455,277	3,630.6	2,151,252	747.0	7,057,379	2,450.7	1,246,646	432.9
10,435,523	3,588.4	2,153,464	740.5	7,021,588	2,414.5	1,260,471	433.4
-0.2	-1.2	+0.1	-0.9	-0.5	-1.5	+1.1	+0.1
1,341,372	2,476.1	248,270	458.3	929,978	1,716.7	163,124	301.1
1,311,085	2,410.1	242,809	446.3	910,111	1,673.0	158,165	290.7
-2.3	-2.7	-2.2	-2.6	-2.1	-2.5	-3.0	-3.5
370,698	2,622.7	72,061	509.8	251,451	1,779.0	47,186	333.8
359,197	2,528.6	69,944	492.4	244,315	1,719.9	44,938	316.3
-3.1	-3.6	-2.9	-3.4	-2.8	-3.3	-4.8	-5.2
93,426	2,701.3	17,111	494.7	64,735	1,871.7	11,580	334.8
90,801	2,606.7	15,609	448.1	64,166	1,842.1	11,026	316.5
-2.8	-3.5	-8.8	-9.4	-0.9	-1.6	-4.8	-5.5
32,985	2,547.3	6,965	537.9	24,591	1,899.1	1,429	110.4
32,078	2,456.7	6,579	503.9	24,043	1,841.3	1,456	111.5
-2.7	-3.6	-5.5	-6.3	-2.2	-3.0	+1.9	+1.0
167,753	2,612.2	33,243	517.7	107,922	1,680.6	26,588	414.0
164,018	2,549.5	34,722	539.7	103,790	1,613.3	25,506	396.5
-2.2	-2.4	+4.4	+4.3	-3.8	-4.0	-4.1	-4.2
26,250	2,059.8	4,838	379.6	19,468	1,527.6	1,944	152.5
26,448	2,053.9	4,552	353.5	19,979	1,551.5	1,917	148.9
+0.8	-0.3	-5.9	-6.9	+2.6	+1.6	-1.4	-2.4
35,342	3,308.2	6,415	600.5	24,051	2,251.3	4,876	456.4
32,231	2,995.0	5,524	513.3	22,320	2,074.0	4,387	407.7
-8.8	-9.5	-13.9	-14.5	-7.2	-7.9	-10.0	-10.7
14,942	2,424.0	3,489	566.0	10,684	1,733.3	769	124.8
13,621	2,200.1	2,958	477.8	10,017	1,618.0	646	104.3
-8.8	-9.2	-15.2	-15.6	-6.2	-6.7	-16.0	-16.4
970,674	2,424.4	176,209	440.1	678,527	1,694.7	115,938	289.6
951,888	2,368.2	172,865	430.1	665,796	1,656.5	113,227	281.7
-1.9	-2.3	-1.9	-2.3	-1.9	-2.3	-2.3	-2.7
227,715	2,655.5	43,899	511.9	148,061	1,726.6	35,755	417.0
219,799	2,544.4	43,453	503.0	141,778	1,641.3	34,568	400.2
-3.5	-4.2	-1.0	-1.7	-4.2	-4.9	-3.3	-4.0
442,091	2,310.5	76,700	400.9	318,025	1,662.1	47,366	247.5
431,448	2,248.3	75,493	393.4	310,738	1,619.3	45,217	235.6
-2.4	-2.7	-1.6	-1.9	-2.3	-2.6	-4.5	-4.8
300,868	2,440.4	55,610	451.1	212,441	1,723.1	32,817	266.2
300,641	2,431.3	53,919	436.0	213,280	1,724.8	33,442	270.4
-0.1	-0.4	-3.0	-3.3	+0.4	+0.1	+1.9	+1.6
2,255,352	3,464.5	446,788	686.3	1,574,516	2,418.7	234,048	359.5
2,203,834	3,369.5	432,545	661.3	1,537,833	2,351.2	233,456	356.9
-2.3	-2.7	-3.2	-3.6	-2.3	-2.8	-0.3	-0.7
1,568,229	3,436.5	322,105	705.8	1,075,077	2,355.8	171,047	374.8
1,528,047	3,333.6	309,622	675.5	1,048,841	2,288.2	169,584	370.0
-2.6	-3.0	-3.9	-4.3	-2.4	-2.9	-0.9	-1.3
430,479	3,420.2	81,440	647.0	304,227	2,417.1	44,812	356.0
415,593	3,284.4	78,288	618.7	295,541	2,335.6	41,764	330.1
-3.5	-4.0	-3.9	-4.4	-2.9	-3.4	-6.8	-7.3

Table 4

Crime in the United States
by Region, Geographic Division, and State, 2002-2003—Continued

Area	Year	Population[1]	Violent crime		Murder and non-negligent manslaughter		Forcible rape		Robbery		Aggravated assault	
			Number	Rate per 100,000	Number	Rate per 100,000	Number	Rate per 100,000	Number	Rate per 100,000	Number	Rate per 100,000
Indiana	2002	6,156,913	22,001	357.3	362	5.9	1,843	29.9	6,612	107.4	13,184	214.1
	2003	6,195,643	21,856	352.8	341	5.5	1,720	27.8	6,403	103.3	13,392	216.2
Percent change			-0.7	-1.3	-5.8	-6.4	-6.7	-7.3	-3.2	-3.8	+1.6	+0.9
Michigan	2002	10,043,221	54,306	540.7	678	6.8	5,364	53.4	11,847	118.0	36,417	362.6
	2003	10,079,985	51,524	511.2	617	6.1	5,451	54.1	11,257	111.7	34,199	339.3
Percent change			-5.1	-5.5	-9.0	-9.3	+1.6	+1.3	-5.0	-5.3	-6.1	-6.4
Ohio	2002	11,408,699	40,128	351.7	526	4.6	4,809	42.2	17,871	156.6	16,922	148.3
	2003	11,435,798	38,103	333.2	522	4.6	4,587	40.1	16,889	147.7	16,105	140.8
Percent change			-5.0	-5.3	-0.8	-1.0	-4.6	-4.8	-5.5	-5.7	-4.8	-5.1
Wisconsin	2002	5,439,692	12,238	225.0	154	2.8	1,237	22.7	4,713	86.6	6,134	112.8
	2003	5,472,299	12,095	221.0	181	3.3	1,198	21.9	4,386	80.1	6,330	115.7
Percent change			-1.2	-1.8	+17.5	+16.8	-3.2	-3.7	-6.9	-7.5	+3.2	+2.6
West North Central	2002	19,463,856	69,876	359.0	629	3.2	6,558	33.7	15,829	81.3	46,860	240.8
	2003	19,568,865	65,891	336.7	664	3.4	6,281	32.1	14,793	75.6	44,153	225.6
Percent change			-5.7	-6.2	+5.6	+5.0	-4.2	-4.7	-6.5	-7.0	-5.8	-6.3
Iowa	2002	2,935,840	8,388	285.7	44	1.5	797	27.1	1,169	39.8	6,378	217.2
	2003	2,944,062	8,020	272.4	47	1.6	762	25.9	1,123	38.1	6,088	206.8
Percent change			-4.4	-4.7	+6.8	+6.5	-4.4	-4.7	-3.9	-4.2	-4.5	-4.8
Kansas	2002	2,711,769	10,229	377.2	78	2.9	1,035	38.2	2,165	79.8	6,951	256.3
	2003	2,723,507	10,771	395.5	123	4.5	1,042	38.3	2,246	82.5	7,360	270.2
Percent change			+5.3	+4.8	+57.7	+57.0	+0.7	+0.2	+3.7	+3.3	+5.9	+5.4
Minnesota	2002	5,024,791	13,428	267.2	112	2.2	2,273	45.2	3,937	78.4	7,106	141.4
	2003	5,059,375	13,288	262.6	128	2.5	2,083	41.2	3,904	77.2	7,173	141.8
Percent change			-1.0	-1.7	+14.3	+13.5	-8.4	-9.0	-0.8	-1.5	+0.9	+0.3
Missouri	2002	5,669,544	30,557	539.0	331	5.8	1,465	25.8	7,024	123.9	21,737	383.4
	2003	5,704,484	26,968	472.8	288	5.0	1,394	24.4	6,203	108.7	19,083	334.5
Percent change			-11.7	-12.3	-13.0	-13.5	-4.8	-5.4	-11.7	-12.2	-12.2	-12.7
Nebraska	2002	1,727,564	5,428	314.2	48	2.8	464	26.9	1,359	78.7	3,557	205.9
	2003	1,739,291	5,026	289.0	56	3.2	495	28.5	1,162	66.8	3,313	190.5
Percent change			-7.4	-8.0	+16.7	+15.9	+6.7	+6.0	-14.5	-15.1	-6.9	-7.5
North Dakota	2002	633,911	496	78.2	5	0.8	163	25.7	58	9.1	270	42.6
	2003	633,837	493	77.8	12	1.9	151	23.8	51	8.0	279	44.0
Percent change			-0.6	-0.6	+140.0	+140.0	-7.4	-7.4	-12.1	-12.1	+3.3	+3.3
South Dakota	2002	760,437	1,350	177.5	11	1.4	361	47.5	117	15.4	861	113.2
	2003	764,309	1,325	173.4	10	1.3	354	46.3	104	13.6	857	112.1
Percent change			-1.9	-2.3	-9.1	-9.6	-1.9	-2.4	-11.1	-11.6	-0.5	-1.0
South[2, 3, 4]	**2002**	**103,197,968**	**589,769**	**571.5**	**6,989**	**6.8**	**35,705**	**34.6**	**162,070**	**157.0**	**385,005**	**373.1**
	2003	**104,538,348**	**574,226**	**549.3**	**7,197**	**6.9**	**35,133**	**33.6**	**160,675**	**153.7**	**371,221**	**355.1**
Percent change			**-2.6**	**-3.9**	**+3.0**	**+1.7**	**-1.6**	**-2.9**	**-0.9**	**-2.1**	**-3.6**	**-4.8**
South Atlantic[4]	2002	53,563,636	322,521	602.1	3,611	6.7	17,173	32.1	90,015	168.1	211,722	395.3
	2003	54,344,651	313,109	576.2	3,663	6.7	16,996	31.3	89,511	164.7	202,939	373.4
Percent change			-2.9	-4.3	+1.4	*	-1.0	-2.5	-0.6	-2.0	-4.1	-5.5
Delaware	2002	805,945	4,836	600.0	26	3.2	358	44.4	1,154	143.2	3,298	409.2
	2003	817,491	5,379	658.0	24	2.9	353	43.2	1,389	169.9	3,613	442.0
Percent change			+11.2	+9.7	-7.7	-9.0	-1.4	-2.8	+20.4	+18.7	+9.6	+8.0
District of Columbia[4]	2002	569,157	9,322	1,637.9	264	46.4	262	46.0	3,834	673.6	4,962	871.8
	2003	563,384	9,060	1,608.1	249	44.2	274	48.6	3,941	699.5	4,596	815.8
Percent change			-2.8	-1.8	-5.7	-4.7	+4.6	+5.7	+2.8	+3.8	-7.4	-6.4

See footnotes at end of table.

Property crime		Property crime					
		Burglary		Larceny-theft		Motor vehicle theft	
Number	Rate per 100,000	Number	Rate per 100,000	Number	Rate per 100,000	Number	Rate per 100,000
208,965	3,394.0	42,605	692.0	146,073	2,372.5	20,287	329.5
208,034	3,357.7	41,581	671.1	145,685	2,351.4	20,768	335.2
-0.4	-1.1	-2.4	-3.0	-0.3	-0.9	+2.4	+1.7
335,060	3,336.2	70,970	706.6	214,367	2,134.4	49,723	495.1
330,356	3,277.3	68,260	677.2	208,360	2,067.1	53,736	533.1
-1.4	-1.8	-3.8	-4.2	-2.8	-3.2	+8.1	+7.7
428,976	3,760.1	99,164	869.2	287,045	2,516.0	42,767	374.9
416,317	3,640.5	94,931	830.1	280,390	2,451.9	40,996	358.5
-3.0	-3.2	-4.3	-4.5	-2.3	-2.5	-4.1	-4.4
164,749	3,028.6	27,926	513.4	123,365	2,267.9	13,458	247.4
157,747	2,882.6	26,562	485.4	118,865	2,172.1	12,320	225.1
-4.3	-4.8	-4.9	-5.5	-3.6	-4.2	-8.5	-9.0
687,123	3,530.3	124,683	640.6	499,439	2,566.0	63,001	323.7
675,787	3,453.4	122,923	628.2	488,992	2,498.8	63,872	326.4
-1.6	-2.2	-1.4	-1.9	-2.1	-2.6	+1.4	+0.8
92,877	3,163.6	18,643	635.0	68,411	2,330.2	5,823	198.3
87,178	2,961.1	17,546	596.0	64,031	2,174.9	5,601	190.2
-6.1	-6.4	-5.9	-6.1	-6.4	-6.7	-3.8	-4.1
100,768	3,716.0	19,679	725.7	73,877	2,724.3	7,212	266.0
108,777	3,994.0	21,887	803.6	79,113	2,904.8	7,777	285.6
+7.9	+7.5	+11.2	+10.7	+7.1	+6.6	+7.8	+7.4
164,026	3,264.3	28,034	557.9	122,150	2,430.9	13,842	275.5
157,691	3,116.8	27,696	547.4	116,236	2,297.4	13,759	272.0
-3.9	-4.5	-1.2	-1.9	-4.8	-5.5	-0.6	-1.3
230,520	4,065.9	42,721	753.5	159,921	2,820.7	27,878	491.7
229,004	4,014.5	40,908	717.1	159,437	2,794.9	28,659	502.4
-0.7	-1.3	-4.2	-4.8	-0.3	-0.9	+2.8	+2.2
68,178	3,946.5	10,329	597.9	51,440	2,977.6	6,409	371.0
64,552	3,711.4	10,072	579.1	48,356	2,780.2	6,124	352.1
-5.3	-6.0	-2.5	-3.1	-6.0	-6.6	-4.4	-5.1
14,762	2,328.7	2,243	353.8	11,501	1,814.3	1,018	160.6
13,286	2,096.1	1,941	306.2	10,267	1,619.8	1,078	170.1
-10.0	-10.0	-13.5	-13.5	-10.7	-10.7	+5.9	+5.9
15,992	2,103.0	3,034	399.0	12,139	1,596.3	819	107.7
15,299	2,001.7	2,873	375.9	11,552	1,511.4	874	114.4
-4.3	-4.8	-5.3	-5.8	-4.8	-5.3	+6.7	+6.2
4,291,126	**4,158.1**	**962,840**	**933.0**	**2,889,223**	**2,799.7**	**439,063**	**425.5**
4,302,332	**4,115.6**	**970,607**	**928.5**	**2,896,775**	**2,771.0**	**434,950**	**416.1**
+0.3	**-1.0**	**+0.8**	**-0.5**	**+0.3**	**-1.0**	**-0.9**	**-2.2**
2,190,742	4,090.0	486,178	907.7	1,467,227	2,739.2	237,337	443.1
2,184,736	4,020.1	482,249	887.4	1,464,273	2,694.4	238,214	438.3
-0.3	-1.7	-0.8	-2.2	-0.2	-1.6	+0.4	-1.1
26,967	3,346.0	5,355	664.4	18,555	2,302.3	3,057	379.3
27,667	3,384.4	5,966	729.8	18,821	2,302.3	2,880	352.3
+2.6	+1.1	+11.4	+9.8	+1.4	*	-5.8	-7.1
36,477	6,409.0	5,170	908.4	21,708	3,814.1	9,599	1,686.5
32,678	5,800.3	4,671	829.1	18,104	3,213.4	9,903	1,757.8
-10.4	-9.5	-9.7	-8.7	-16.6	-15.7	+3.2	+4.2

Table 4

Crime in the United States
by Region, Geographic Division, and State, 2002-2003—Continued

Area	Year	Population[1]	Violent crime Number	Violent crime Rate per 100,000	Murder and non-negligent manslaughter Number	Murder and non-negligent manslaughter Rate per 100,000	Forcible rape Number	Forcible rape Rate per 100,000	Robbery Number	Robbery Rate per 100,000	Aggravated assault Number	Aggravated assault Rate per 100,000
Florida	2002	16,691,701	128,721	771.2	911	5.5	6,753	40.5	32,581	195.2	88,476	530.1
	2003	17,019,068	124,280	730.2	924	5.4	6,727	39.5	31,523	185.2	85,106	500.1
Percent change			-3.5	-5.3	+1.4	-0.5	-0.4	-2.3	-3.2	-5.1	-3.8	-5.7
Georgia	2002	8,544,005	39,271	459.6	606	7.1	2,108	24.7	13,432	157.2	23,125	270.7
	2003	8,684,715	39,422	453.9	656	7.6	2,233	25.7	14,055	161.8	22,478	258.8
Percent change			+0.4	-1.2	+8.3	+6.5	+5.9	+4.2	+4.6	+2.9	-2.8	-4.4
Maryland	2002	5,450,525	42,015	770.8	513	9.4	1,370	25.1	13,417	246.2	26,715	490.1
	2003	5,508,909	38,778	703.9	525	9.5	1,358	24.7	13,302	241.5	23,593	428.3
Percent change			-7.7	-8.7	+2.3	+1.3	-0.9	-1.9	-0.9	-1.9	-11.7	-12.6
North Carolina	2002	8,305,820	39,118	471.0	548	6.6	2,196	26.4	12,205	146.9	24,169	291.0
	2003	8,407,248	38,246	454.9	509	6.1	2,139	25.4	12,229	145.5	23,369	278.0
Percent change			-2.2	-3.4	-7.1	-8.2	-2.6	-3.8	+0.2	-1.0	-3.3	-4.5
South Carolina	2002	4,103,770	33,761	822.7	298	7.3	1,959	47.7	5,774	140.7	25,730	627.0
	2003	4,147,152	32,908	793.5	300	7.2	1,843	44.4	5,670	136.7	25,095	605.1
Percent change			-2.5	-3.5	+0.7	-0.4	-5.9	-6.9	-1.8	-2.8	-2.5	-3.5
Virginia	2002	7,287,829	21,256	291.7	388	5.3	1,839	25.2	6,961	95.5	12,068	165.6
	2003	7,386,330	20,375	275.8	413	5.6	1,773	24.0	6,672	90.3	11,517	155.9
Percent change			-4.1	-5.4	+6.4	+5.0	-3.6	-4.9	-4.2	-5.4	-4.6	-5.8
West Virginia	2002	1,804,884	4,221	233.9	57	3.2	328	18.2	657	36.4	3,179	176.1
	2003	1,810,354	4,661	257.5	63	3.5	296	16.4	730	40.3	3,572	197.3
Percent change			+10.4	+10.1	+10.5	+10.2	-9.8	-10.0	+11.1	+10.8	+12.4	+12.0
East South Central[2,3]	2002	17,225,247	82,452	478.7	1,178	6.8	6,168	35.8	21,862	126.9	53,244	309.1
	2003	17,341,608	79,665	459.4	1,150	6.6	5,872	33.9	21,625	124.7	51,018	294.2
Percent change			-3.4	-4.0	-2.4	-3.0	-4.8	-5.4	-1.1	-1.7	-4.2	-4.8
Alabama	2002	4,478,896	19,931	445.0	303	6.8	1,664	37.2	5,962	133.1	12,002	268.0
	2003	4,500,752	19,331	429.5	299	6.6	1,656	36.8	6,038	134.2	11,338	251.9
Percent change			-3.0	-3.5	-1.3	-1.8	-0.5	-1.0	+1.3	+0.8	-5.5	-6.0
Kentucky[2,3]	2002	4,089,822	11,101	271.4	191	4.7	1,087	26.6	3,131	76.6	6,692	163.6
	2003	4,117,827	10,777	261.7	188	4.6	1,054	25.6	3,196	77.6	6,339	153.9
Percent change			-2.9	-3.6	-1.6	-2.2	-3.0	-3.7	+2.1	+1.4	-5.3	-5.9
Mississippi	2002	2,866,733	9,858	343.9	264	9.2	1,127	39.3	3,356	117.1	5,111	178.3
	2003	2,881,281	9,380	325.5	268	9.3	1,077	37.4	3,019	104.8	5,016	174.1
Percent change			-4.8	-5.3	+1.5	+1.0	-4.4	-4.9	-10.0	-10.5	-1.9	-2.4
Tennessee	2002	5,789,796	41,562	717.8	420	7.3	2,290	39.6	9,413	162.6	29,439	508.5
	2003	5,841,748	40,177	687.8	395	6.8	2,085	35.7	9,372	160.4	28,325	484.9
Percent change			-3.3	-4.2	-6.0	-6.8	-9.0	-9.8	-0.4	-1.3	-3.8	-4.6
West South Central	2002	32,409,085	184,796	570.2	2,200	6.8	12,364	38.1	50,193	154.9	120,039	370.4
	2003	32,852,089	181,452	552.3	2,384	7.3	12,265	37.3	49,539	150.8	117,264	356.9
Percent change			-1.8	-3.1	+8.4	+6.9	-0.8	-2.1	-1.3	-2.6	-2.3	-3.6
Arkansas	2002	2,706,268	11,501	425.0	142	5.2	754	27.9	2,524	93.3	8,081	298.6
	2003	2,725,714	12,431	456.1	174	6.4	903	33.1	2,228	81.7	9,126	334.8
Percent change			+8.1	+7.3	+22.5	+21.7	+19.8	+18.9	-11.7	-12.4	+12.9	+12.1
Louisiana	2002	4,476,192	29,690	663.3	593	13.2	1,529	34.2	7,123	159.1	20,445	456.7
	2003	4,496,334	29,062	646.3	586	13.0	1,849	41.1	7,069	157.2	19,558	435.0
Percent change			-2.1	-2.6	-1.2	-1.6	+20.9	+20.4	-0.8	-1.2	-4.3	-4.8
Oklahoma	2002	3,489,700	17,587	504.0	163	4.7	1,573	45.1	2,966	85.0	12,885	369.2
	2003	3,511,532	17,758	505.7	206	5.9	1,501	42.7	3,224	91.8	12,827	365.3
Percent change			+1.0	+0.3	+26.4	+25.6	-4.6	-5.2	+8.7	+8.0	-0.5	-1.1

See footnotes at end of table.

		Property crime					
		Burglary		Larceny-theft		Motor vehicle theft	
Property crime							
Number	Rate per 100,000	Number	Rate per 100,000	Number	Rate per 100,000	Number	Rate per 100,000
777,236	4,656.4	177,242	1,061.9	511,478	3,064.3	88,516	530.3
757,696	4,452.0	170,644	1,002.7	505,489	2,970.1	81,563	479.2
-2.5	-4.4	-3.7	-5.6	-1.2	-3.1	-7.9	-9.6
346,559	4,056.2	73,932	865.3	234,591	2,745.7	38,036	445.2
369,501	4,254.6	78,961	909.2	247,169	2,846.0	43,371	499.4
+6.6	+4.9	+6.8	+5.1	+5.4	+3.7	+14.0	+12.2
217,105	3,983.2	39,765	729.6	143,320	2,629.5	34,020	624.2
209,418	3,801.4	38,641	701.4	134,372	2,439.2	36,405	660.8
-3.5	-4.6	-2.8	-3.9	-6.2	-7.2	+7.0	+5.9
353,708	4,258.6	99,535	1,198.4	229,307	2,760.8	24,866	299.4
359,660	4,278.0	100,687	1,197.6	232,081	2,760.5	26,892	319.9
+1.7	+0.5	+1.2	-0.1	+1.2	*	+8.1	+6.8
183,808	4,479.0	43,745	1,066.0	123,196	3,002.0	16,867	411.0
185,671	4,477.1	43,582	1,050.9	126,327	3,046.1	15,762	380.1
+1.0	*	-0.4	-1.4	+2.5	+1.5	-6.6	-7.5
207,783	2,851.1	31,757	435.8	157,548	2,161.8	18,478	253.5
199,731	2,704.1	28,919	391.5	152,898	2,070.0	17,914	242.5
-3.9	-5.2	-8.9	-10.2	-3.0	-4.2	-3.1	-4.3
41,099	2,277.1	9,677	536.2	27,524	1,525.0	3,898	216.0
42,714	2,359.4	10,178	562.2	29,012	1,602.6	3,524	194.7
+3.9	+3.6	+5.2	+4.9	+5.4	+5.1	-9.6	-9.9
647,973	3,761.8	160,310	930.7	428,388	2,487.0	59,275	344.1
655,687	3,781.0	163,947	945.4	432,058	2,491.5	59,682	344.2
+1.2	+0.5	+2.3	+1.6	+0.9	+0.2	+0.7	*
180,400	4,027.8	42,578	950.6	123,932	2,767.0	13,890	310.1
182,241	4,049.1	43,245	960.8	124,039	2,756.0	14,957	332.3
+1.0	+0.5	+1.6	+1.1	+0.1	-0.4	+7.7	+7.2
108,590	2,655.1	26,891	657.5	72,378	1,769.7	9,321	227.9
110,418	2,681.5	27,656	671.6	73,396	1,782.4	9,366	227.5
+1.7	+1.0	+2.8	+2.1	+1.4	+0.7	+0.5	-0.2
109,584	3,822.6	29,593	1,032.3	70,468	2,458.1	9,523	332.2
107,195	3,720.4	29,839	1,035.6	68,407	2,374.2	8,949	310.6
-2.2	-2.7	+0.8	+0.3	-2.9	-3.4	-6.0	-6.5
249,399	4,307.6	61,248	1,057.9	161,610	2,791.3	26,541	458.4
255,833	4,379.4	63,207	1,082.0	166,216	2,845.3	26,410	452.1
+2.6	+1.7	+3.2	+2.3	+2.9	+1.9	-0.5	-1.4
1,452,411	4,481.5	316,352	976.1	993,608	3,065.8	142,451	439.5
1,461,909	4,450.0	324,411	987.5	1,000,444	3,045.3	137,054	417.2
+0.7	-0.7	+2.5	+1.2	+0.7	-0.7	-3.8	-5.1
101,171	3,738.4	23,229	858.3	71,129	2,628.3	6,813	251.7
98,710	3,621.4	24,903	913.6	67,797	2,487.3	6,010	220.5
-2.4	-3.1	+7.2	+6.4	-4.7	-5.4	-11.8	-12.4
198,838	4,442.1	45,350	1,013.1	133,302	2,978.0	20,186	451.0
195,569	4,349.5	44,877	998.1	130,810	2,909.3	19,882	442.2
-1.6	-2.1	-1.0	-1.5	-1.9	-2.3	-1.5	-1.9
148,128	4,244.7	35,171	1,007.9	100,185	2,870.9	12,772	366.0
151,208	4,306.0	34,846	992.3	103,404	2,944.7	12,958	369.0
+2.1	+1.4	-0.9	-1.5	+3.2	+2.6	+1.5	+0.8

Table 4

Crime in the United States

by Region, Geographic Division, and State, 2002-2003—Continued

Area	Year	Population[1]	Violent crime		Murder and non-negligent manslaughter		Forcible rape		Robbery		Aggravated assault	
			Number	Rate per 100,000	Number	Rate per 100,000	Number	Rate per 100,000	Number	Rate per 100,000	Number	Rate per 100,000
Texas	2002	21,736,925	126,018	579.7	1,302	6.0	8,508	39.1	37,580	172.9	78,628	361.7
	2003	22,118,509	122,201	552.5	1,418	6.4	8,012	36.2	37,018	167.4	75,753	342.5
Percent change			-3.0	-4.7	+8.9	+7.0	-5.8	-7.5	-1.5	-3.2	-3.7	-5.3
West	**2002**	**65,504,336**	**333,635**	**509.3**	**3,721**	**5.7**	**22,507**	**34.4**	**95,865**	**146.3**	**211,542**	**322.9**
	2003	**66,465,849**	**329,002**	**495.0**	**3,774**	**5.7**	**22,385**	**33.7**	**94,298**	**141.9**	**208,545**	**313.8**
Percent change			**-1.4**	**-2.8**	**+1.4**	*****	**-0.5**	**-2.0**	**-1.6**	**-3.1**	**-1.4**	**-2.8**
Mountain	2002	19,032,790	87,096	457.6	1,013	5.3	7,454	39.2	20,659	108.5	57,970	304.6
	2003	19,383,929	84,405	435.4	1,054	5.4	7,342	37.9	20,347	105.0	55,662	287.2
Percent change			-3.1	-4.8	+4.0	+2.2	-1.5	-3.3	-1.5	-3.3	-4.0	-5.7
Arizona	2002	5,441,125	30,171	554.5	387	7.1	1,608	29.6	8,000	147.0	20,176	370.8
	2003	5,580,811	28,638	513.2	441	7.9	1,856	33.3	7,619	136.5	18,722	335.5
Percent change			-5.1	-7.5	+14.0	+11.1	+15.4	+12.5	-4.8	-7.1	-7.2	-9.5
Colorado	2002	4,501,051	15,882	352.9	179	4.0	2,066	45.9	3,579	79.5	10,058	223.5
	2003	4,550,688	15,706	345.1	177	3.9	1,893	41.6	3,735	82.1	9,901	217.6
Percent change			-1.1	-2.2	-1.1	-2.2	-8.4	-9.4	+4.4	+3.2	-1.6	-2.6
Idaho	2002	1,343,124	3,419	254.6	36	2.7	497	37.0	240	17.9	2,646	197.0
	2003	1,366,332	3,316	242.7	25	1.8	508	37.2	244	17.9	2,539	185.8
Percent change			-3.0	-4.7	-30.6	-31.7	+2.2	+0.5	+1.7	-0.1	-4.0	-5.7
Montana	2002	910,372	3,197	351.2	16	1.8	237	26.0	283	31.1	2,661	292.3
	2003	917,621	3,351	365.2	30	3.3	246	26.8	298	32.5	2,777	302.6
Percent change			+4.8	+4.0	+87.5	+86.0	+3.8	+3.0	+5.3	+4.5	+4.4	+3.5
Nevada	2002	2,167,455	13,856	639.3	181	8.4	928	42.8	5,118	236.1	7,629	352.0
	2003	2,241,154	13,765	614.2	197	8.8	874	39.0	5,162	230.3	7,532	336.1
Percent change			-0.7	-3.9	+8.8	+5.3	-5.8	-8.9	+0.9	-2.5	-1.3	-4.5
New Mexico	2002	1,852,044	13,719	740.7	152	8.2	1,027	55.5	2,206	119.1	10,334	558.0
	2003	1,874,614	12,470	665.2	112	6.0	937	50.0	1,950	104.0	9,471	505.2
Percent change			-9.1	-10.2	-26.3	-27.2	-8.8	-9.9	-11.6	-12.7	-8.4	-9.5
Utah	2002	2,318,789	5,488	236.7	47	2.0	943	40.7	1,140	49.2	3,358	144.8
	2003	2,351,467	5,845	248.6	58	2.5	892	37.9	1,255	53.4	3,640	154.8
Percent change			+6.5	+5.0	+23.4	+21.7	-5.4	-6.7	+10.1	+8.6	+8.4	+6.9
Wyoming	2002	498,830	1,364	273.4	15	3.0	148	29.7	93	18.6	1,108	222.1
	2003	501,242	1,314	262.1	14	2.8	136	27.1	84	16.8	1,080	215.5
Percent change			-3.7	-4.1	-6.7	-7.1	-8.1	-8.6	-9.7	-10.1	-2.5	-3.0
Pacific	2002	46,471,546	246,539	530.5	2,708	5.8	15,053	32.4	75,206	161.8	153,572	330.5
	2003	47,081,920	244,597	519.5	2,720	5.8	15,043	32.0	73,951	157.1	152,883	324.7
Percent change			-0.8	-2.1	+0.4	-0.9	-0.1	-1.4	-1.7	-2.9	-0.4	-1.7
Alaska	2002	641,482	3,627	565.4	33	5.1	511	79.7	489	76.2	2,594	404.4
	2003	648,818	3,850	593.4	39	6.0	600	92.5	444	68.4	2,767	426.5
Percent change			+6.1	+4.9	+18.2	+16.8	+17.4	+16.1	-9.2	-10.2	+6.7	+5.5
California	2002	35,001,986	208,388	595.4	2,395	6.8	10,198	29.1	64,968	185.6	130,827	373.8
	2003	35,484,453	205,551	579.3	2,407	6.8	9,994	28.2	63,770	179.7	129,380	364.6
Percent change			-1.4	-2.7	+0.5	-0.9	-2.0	-3.3	-1.8	-3.2	-1.1	-2.5
Hawaii	2002	1,240,663	3,262	262.9	24	1.9	372	30.0	1,210	97.5	1,656	133.5
	2003	1,257,608	3,400	270.4	22	1.7	367	29.2	1,168	92.9	1,843	146.5
Percent change			+4.2	+2.8	-8.3	-9.6	-1.3	-2.7	-3.5	-4.8	+11.3	+9.8
Oregon	2002	3,520,355	10,298	292.5	72	2.0	1,238	35.2	2,742	77.9	6,246	177.4
	2003	3,559,596	10,520	295.5	68	1.9	1,218	34.2	2,851	80.1	6,383	179.3
Percent change			+2.2	+1.0	-5.6	-6.6	-1.6	-2.7	+4.0	+2.8	+2.2	+1.1

See footnotes at end of table.

	Property crime		Property crime Burglary		Larceny-theft		Motor vehicle theft	
Number	Rate per 100,000	Number	Rate per 100,000	Number	Rate per 100,000	Number	Rate per 100,000
1,004,274	4,620.1	212,602	978.1	688,992	3,169.7	102,680	472.4
1,016,422	4,595.3	219,785	993.7	698,433	3,157.7	98,204	444.0
+1.2	-0.5	+3.4	+1.6	+1.4	-0.4	-4.4	-6.0
2,567,427	**3,919.5**	**493,354**	**753.2**	**1,663,662**	**2,539.8**	**410,411**	**626.5**
2,618,272	**3,939.3**	**507,503**	**763.6**	**1,676,869**	**2,522.9**	**433,900**	**652.8**
+2.0	**+0.5**	**+2.9**	**+1.4**	**+0.8**	**-0.7**	**+5.7**	**+4.2**
844,737	4,438.3	157,652	828.3	568,436	2,986.6	118,649	623.4
851,265	4,391.6	163,071	841.3	567,327	2,926.8	120,867	623.5
+0.8	-1.1	+3.4	+1.6	-0.2	-2.0	+1.9	*
318,296	5,849.8	59,087	1,085.9	201,541	3,704.0	57,668	1,059.9
314,335	5,632.4	58,613	1,050.3	198,725	3,560.9	56,997	1,021.3
-1.2	-3.7	-0.8	-3.3	-1.4	-3.9	-1.2	-3.6
180,054	4,000.3	31,678	703.8	125,193	2,781.4	23,183	515.1
179,340	3,940.9	32,370	711.3	124,271	2,730.8	22,699	498.8
-0.4	-1.5	+2.2	+1.1	-0.7	-1.8	-2.1	-3.2
39,128	2,913.2	7,441	554.0	29,060	2,163.6	2,627	195.6
39,742	2,908.7	7,791	570.2	29,342	2,147.5	2,609	190.9
+1.6	-0.2	+4.7	+2.9	+1.0	-0.7	-0.7	-2.4
28,751	3,158.2	3,289	361.3	23,679	2,601.0	1,783	195.9
28,428	3,098.0	3,722	405.6	22,800	2,484.7	1,906	207.7
-1.1	-1.9	+13.2	+12.3	-3.7	-4.5	+6.9	+6.1
83,896	3,870.7	18,951	874.3	47,459	2,189.6	17,486	806.8
96,109	4,288.4	21,977	980.6	53,294	2,378.0	20,838	929.8
+14.6	+10.8	+16.0	+12.2	+12.3	+8.6	+19.2	+15.3
80,477	4,345.3	19,634	1,060.1	53,406	2,883.6	7,437	401.6
77,301	4,123.6	19,218	1,025.2	50,827	2,711.3	7,256	387.1
-3.9	-5.1	-2.1	-3.3	-4.8	-6.0	-2.4	-3.6
97,641	4,210.9	15,124	652.2	74,795	3,225.6	7,722	333.0
99,362	4,225.5	16,769	713.1	74,829	3,182.2	7,764	330.2
+1.8	+0.3	+10.9	+9.3	*	-1.3	+0.5	-0.9
16,494	3,306.5	2,448	490.7	13,303	2,666.8	743	148.9
16,648	3,321.3	2,611	520.9	13,239	2,641.2	798	159.2
+0.9	+0.4	+6.7	+6.1	-0.5	-1.0	+7.4	+6.9
1,722,690	3,707.0	335,702	722.4	1,095,226	2,356.8	291,762	627.8
1,767,007	3,753.0	344,432	731.6	1,109,542	2,356.6	313,033	664.9
+2.6	+1.2	+2.6	+1.3	+1.3	*	+7.3	+5.9
24,118	3,759.7	3,908	609.2	17,739	2,765.3	2,471	385.2
24,280	3,742.2	3,855	594.2	17,977	2,770.7	2,448	377.3
+0.7	-0.5	-1.4	-2.5	+1.3	+0.2	-0.9	-2.1
1,176,484	3,361.2	238,428	681.2	715,692	2,044.7	222,364	635.3
1,215,086	3,424.3	242,274	682.8	731,486	2,061.4	241,326	680.1
+3.3	+1.9	+1.6	+0.2	+2.2	+0.8	+8.5	+7.1
71,976	5,801.4	12,722	1,025.4	49,344	3,977.2	9,910	798.8
65,867	5,237.5	11,409	907.2	44,807	3,562.9	9,651	767.4
-8.5	-9.7	-10.3	-11.5	-9.2	-10.4	-2.6	-3.9
161,145	4,577.5	25,696	729.9	118,925	3,378.2	16,524	469.4
170,230	4,782.3	28,626	804.2	122,615	3,444.6	18,989	533.5
+5.6	+4.5	+11.4	+10.2	+3.1	+2.0	+14.9	+13.7

Table 4

Crime in the United States

by Region, Geographic Division, and State, 2002-2003—Continued

Area	Year	Population[1]	Violent crime		Murder and non-negligent manslaughter		Forcible rape		Robbery		Aggravated assault	
			Number	Rate per 100,000	Number	Rate per 100,000	Number	Rate per 100,000	Number	Rate per 100,000	Number	Rate per 100,000
Washington	2002	6,067,060	20,964	345.5	184	3.0	2,734	45.1	5,797	95.5	12,249	201.9
	2003	6,131,445	21,276	347.0	184	3.0	2,864	46.7	5,718	93.3	12,510	204.0
Percent change			+1.5	+0.4	0.0	-1.1	+4.8	+3.7	-1.4	-2.4	+2.1	+1.1
Puerto Rico	2002	3,859,523	13,471	349.0	774	20.1	241	6.2	8,978	232.6	3,478	90.1
	2003	3,878,532	11,885	306.4	779	20.1	204	5.3	7,737	199.5	3,165	81.6
Percent change			-11.8	-12.2	+0.6	+0.2	-15.4	-15.8	-13.8	-14.2	-9.0	-9.4

[1] Populations are U.S. Census Bureau provisional estimates as of July 1, 2003, and July 1, 2002.

[2] The 2002 crime figures have been adjusted.

[3] Limited data for 2003 were available for Illinois and Kentucky. See Offense Estimation, Appendix I, for details.

[4] Includes offenses reported by the Zoological Police and the Metro Transit Police.

* Less than one-tenth of 1 percent.

NOTE: Although arson data are included in the trend and clearance tables, sufficient data are not available to estimate totals for this offense.

| Property crime | | Property crime | | | | | |
| | | Burglary | | Larceny-theft | | Motor vehicle theft | |
Number	Rate per 100,000	Number	Rate per 100,000	Number	Rate per 100,000	Number	Rate per 100,000
288,967	4,762.9	54,948	905.7	193,526	3,189.8	40,493	667.4
291,544	4,754.9	58,268	950.3	192,657	3,142.1	40,619	662.5
+0.9	-0.2	+6.0	+4.9	-0.4	-1.5	+0.3	-0.7
77,312	2,003.1	24,737	640.9	39,640	1,027.1	12,935	335.1
69,895	1,802.1	20,857	537.8	36,827	949.5	12,211	314.8
-9.6	-10.0	-15.7	-16.1	-7.1	-7.6	-5.6	-6.1

Table 5

Crime in the United States
by State, 2003

Area	Population	Violent crime	Murder and non-negligent man-slaughter	Forcible rape	Robbery	Aggravated assault	Property crime	Burglary	Larceny-theft	Motor vehicle theft
				Violent crime					Property crime	
ALABAMA										
Metropolitan Statistical Area	3,179,196									
Area actually reporting	95.2%	14,871	242	1,197	5,305	8,127	139,325	33,305	93,858	12,162
Estimated total	100.0%	15,364	247	1,240	5,441	8,436	144,477	34,489	97,441	12,547
Cities outside metropolitan areas	557,794									
Area actually reporting	92.9%	2,698	30	245	477	1,946	26,129	5,004	19,687	1,438
Estimated total	100.0%	2,881	32	263	507	2,079	27,863	5,339	20,993	1,531
Nonmetropolitan counties	763,762									
Area actually reporting	79.7%	866	16	122	72	656	7,894	2,724	4,469	701
Estimated total	100.0%	1,086	20	153	90	823	9,901	3,417	5,605	879
State Total	**4,500,752**	**19,331**	**299**	**1,656**	**6,038**	**11,338**	**182,241**	**43,245**	**124,039**	**14,957**
Rate per 100,000 inhabitants		429.5	6.6	36.8	134.2	251.9	4,049.1	960.8	2,756.0	332.3
ALASKA										
Metropolitan Statistical Area	315,592									
Area actually reporting	100.0%	2,222	21	291	389	1,521	14,707	1,798	11,488	1,421
Cities outside metropolitan areas	122,843									
Area actually reporting	93.4%	689	3	122	30	534	4,421	522	3,471	428
Estimated total	100.0%	738	3	131	32	572	4,733	559	3,716	458
Nonmetropolitan counties	210,383									
Area actually reporting	100.0%	890	15	178	23	674	4,840	1,498	2,773	569
State Total	**648,818**	**3,850**	**39**	**600**	**444**	**2,767**	**24,280**	**3,855**	**17,977**	**2,448**
Rate per 100,000 inhabitants		593.4	6.0	92.5	68.4	426.5	3,742.2	594.2	2,770.7	377.3
ARIZONA										
Metropolitan Statistical Area	4,958,626									
Area actually reporting	98.4%	25,898	415	1,719	7,393	16,371	288,776	52,742	181,499	54,535
Estimated total	100.0%	26,208	416	1,745	7,460	16,587	292,974	53,653	184,112	55,209
Cities outside metropolitan areas	302,704									
Area actually reporting	98.8%	1,177	13	68	123	973	14,582	2,663	10,828	1,091
Estimated total	100.0%	1,192	13	69	125	985	14,765	2,696	10,964	1,105
Nonmetropolitan counties	319,481									
Area actually reporting	100.0%	1,238	12	42	34	1,150	6,596	2,264	3,649	683
State Total	**5,580,811**	**28,638**	**441**	**1,856**	**7,619**	**18,722**	**314,335**	**58,613**	**198,725**	**56,997**
Rate per 100,000 inhabitants		513.2	7.9	33.3	136.5	335.5	5,632.4	1,050.3	3,560.9	1,021.3
ARKANSAS										
Metropolitan Statistical Area	1,566,369									
Area actually reporting	92.8%	8,199	115	651	1,804	5,629	71,247	15,972	50,710	4,565
Estimated total	100.0%	8,486	117	680	1,830	5,859	74,132	16,800	52,599	4,733
Cities outside metropolitan areas	456,839									
Area actually reporting	86.1%	2,429	25	108	288	2,008	14,204	4,166	9,417	621
Estimated total	100.0%	2,822	29	125	335	2,333	16,501	4,840	10,940	721
Nonmetropolitan counties	702,506									
Area actually reporting	79.6%	894	22	78	50	744	6,431	2,598	3,390	443
Estimated total	100.0%	1,123	28	98	63	934	8,077	3,263	4,258	556
State Total	**2,725,714**	**12,431**	**174**	**903**	**2,228**	**9,126**	**98,710**	**24,903**	**67,797**	**6,010**
Rate per 100,000 inhabitants		456.1	6.4	33.1	81.7	334.8	3,621.4	913.6	2,487.3	220.5
CALIFORNIA										
Metropolitan Statistical Area	34,663,398									
Area actually reporting	100.0%	202,433	2,369	9,695	63,482	126,887	1,191,157	235,397	716,933	238,827
Cities outside metropolitan areas	263,004									
Area actually reporting	100.0%	1,397	7	152	180	1,058	12,364	2,960	8,383	1,021
Nonmetropolitan counties	558,051									
Area actually reporting	100.0%	1,721	31	147	108	1,435	11,565	3,917	6,170	1,478
State Total	**35,484,453**	**205,551**	**2,407**	**9,994**	**63,770**	**129,380**	**1,215,086**	**242,274**	**731,486**	**241,326**
Rate per 100,000 inhabitants		579.3	6.8	28.2	179.7	364.6	3,424.3	682.8	2,061.4	680.1

See footnotes at end of table.

Table 5

Crime in the United States
by State, 2003—Continued

Area	Population	Violent crime	Murder and non-negligent man-slaughter	Forcible rape	Robbery	Aggravated assault	Property crime	Burglary	Larceny-theft	Motor vehicle theft
COLORADO										
Metropolitan Statistical Area	3,900,941									
Area actually reporting	95.4%	13,767	160	1,638	3,562	8,407	154,403	28,339	105,124	20,940
Estimated total	100.0%	14,276	164	1,699	3,669	8,744	162,012	29,524	110,630	21,858
Cities outside metropolitan areas	295,314									
Area actually reporting	87.4%	863	9	135	52	667	11,047	1,648	8,923	476
Estimated total	100.0%	986	10	154	59	763	12,635	1,885	10,206	544
Nonmetropolitan counties	354,433									
Area actually reporting	94.5%	420	3	38	7	372	4,435	908	3,246	281
Estimated total	100.0%	444	3	40	7	394	4,693	961	3,435	297
State Total	**4,550,688**	**15,706**	**177**	**1,893**	**3,735**	**9,901**	**179,340**	**32,370**	**124,271**	**22,699**
Rate per 100,000 inhabitants		345.1	3.9	41.6	82.1	217.6	3,940.9	711.3	2,730.8	498.8
CONNECTICUT										
Metropolitan Statistical Area	2,813,777									
Area actually reporting	100.0%	9,359	101	570	4,002	4,686	81,477	13,071	58,074	10,332
Cities outside metropolitan areas	157,399									
Area actually reporting	100.0%	300	0	26	66	208	3,307	640	2,445	222
Nonmetropolitan counties	512,196									
Area actually reporting	100.0%	1,077	3	56	78	940	6,017	1,898	3,647	472
State Total	**3,483,372**	**10,736**	**104**	**652**	**4,146**	**5,834**	**90,801**	**15,609**	**64,166**	**11,026**
Rate per 100,000 inhabitants		308.2	3.0	18.7	119.0	167.5	2,606.7	448.1	1,842.1	316.5
DELAWARE										
Metropolitan Statistical Area	651,493									
Area actually reporting	100.0%	4,430	19	278	1,272	2,861	22,802	4,662	15,478	2,662
Cities outside metropolitan areas	38,608									
Area actually reporting	100.0%	340	0	24	72	244	2,051	427	1,567	57
Nonmetropolitan counties	127,390									
Area actually reporting	100.0%	609	5	51	45	508	2,814	877	1,776	161
State Total	**817,491**	**5,379**	**24**	**353**	**1,389**	**3,613**	**27,667**	**5,966**	**18,821**	**2,880**
Rate per 100,000 inhabitants		658.0	2.9	43.2	169.9	442.0	3,384.4	729.8	2,302.3	352.3
DISTRICT OF COLUMBIA[1]										
Metropolitan Statistical Area	563,384									
Area actually reporting	100.0%	9,060	249	274	3,941	4,596	32,678	4,671	18,104	9,903
Cities outside metropolitan areas	None									
Nonmetropolitan counties	None									
Total	**563,384**	**9,060**	**249**	**274**	**3,941**	**4,596**	**32,678**	**4,671**	**18,104**	**9,903**
Rate per 100,000 inhabitants		1,608.1	44.2	48.6	699.5	815.8	5,800.3	829.1	3,213.4	1,757.8
FLORIDA										
Metropolitan Statistical Area	15,959,074									
Area actually reporting	99.9%	118,630	872	6,335	30,844	80,579	725,538	161,346	484,816	79,376
Estimated total	100.0%	118,659	872	6,337	30,852	80,598	725,762	161,392	484,973	79,397
Cities outside metropolitan areas	196,937									
Area actually reporting	99.2%	1,746	11	81	327	1,327	11,687	2,634	8,333	720
Estimated total	100.0%	1,761	11	82	330	1,338	11,780	2,655	8,399	726
Nonmetropolitan counties	863,057									
Area actually reporting	100.0%	3,860	41	308	341	3,170	20,154	6,597	12,117	1,440
State Total	**17,019,068**	**124,280**	**924**	**6,727**	**31,523**	**85,106**	**757,696**	**170,644**	**505,489**	**81,563**
Rate per 100,000 inhabitants		730.2	5.4	39.5	185.2	500.1	4,452.0	1,002.7	2,970.1	479.2

See footnotes at end of table.

Table 5

Crime in the United States

by State, 2003—Continued

Area	Population	Violent crime	Murder and non-negligent man-slaughter	Forcible rape	Robbery	Aggravated assault	Property crime	Burglary	Larceny-theft	Motor vehicle theft
				Violent crime				Property crime		
GEORGIA										
Metropolitan Statistical Area	6,964,510									
Area actually reporting	97.1%	31,989	563	1,828	12,668	16,930	302,922	63,860	199,987	39,075
Estimated total	100.0%	32,721	573	1,876	12,936	17,336	311,054	65,516	205,459	40,079
Cities outside metropolitan areas	642,357									
Area actually reporting	85.1%	3,511	44	201	746	2,520	30,512	5,917	23,222	1,373
Estimated total	100.0%	4,127	52	236	877	2,962	35,857	6,954	27,289	1,614
Nonmetropolitan counties	1,077,848									
Area actually reporting	87.4%	2,251	27	106	212	1,906	19,750	5,675	12,608	1,467
Estimated total	100.0%	2,574	31	121	242	2,180	22,590	6,491	14,421	1,678
State Total	**8,684,715**	**39,422**	**656**	**2,233**	**14,055**	**22,478**	**369,501**	**78,961**	**247,169**	**43,371**
Rate per 100,000 inhabitants		453.9	7.6	25.7	161.8	258.8	4,254.6	909.2	2,846.0	499.4
HAWAII										
Metropolitan Statistical Area	905,301									
Area actually reporting	100.0%	2,606	15	266	989	1,336	48,306	7,967	32,086	8,253
Cities outside metropolitan areas	None									
Nonmetropolitan counties	352,307									
Area actually reporting	100.0%	794	7	101	179	507	17,561	3,442	12,721	1,398
State Total	**1,257,608**	**3,400**	**22**	**367**	**1,168**	**1,843**	**65,867**	**11,409**	**44,807**	**9,651**
Rate per 100,000 inhabitants		270.4	1.7	29.2	92.9	146.5	5,237.5	907.2	3,562.9	767.4
IDAHO										
Metropolitan Statistical Area	864,948									
Area actually reporting	99.0%	2,354	17	402	195	1,740	28,531	5,308	21,332	1,891
Estimated total	100.0%	2,370	17	405	195	1,753	28,715	5,352	21,460	1,903
Cities outside metropolitan areas	212,578									
Area actually reporting	97.7%	491	0	52	37	402	7,067	1,419	5,279	369
Estimated total	100.0%	502	0	53	38	411	7,233	1,452	5,403	378
Nonmetropolitan counties	288,806									
Area actually reporting	98.4%	437	8	49	11	369	3,733	971	2,439	323
Estimated total	100.0%	444	8	50	11	375	3,794	987	2,479	328
State Total	**1,366,332**	**3,316**	**25**	**508**	**244**	**2,539**	**39,742**	**7,791**	**29,342**	**2,609**
Rate per 100,000 inhabitants		242.7	1.8	37.2	17.9	185.8	2,908.7	570.2	2,147.5	190.9
ILLINOIS[2]										
State Total	**12,653,544**	**70,456**	**896**	**4,167**	**23,809**	**41,584**	**415,593**	**78,288**	**295,541**	**41,764**
Rate per 100,000 inhabitants		556.8	7.1	32.9	188.2	328.6	3,284.4	618.7	2,335.6	330.1
INDIANA										
Metropolitan Statistical Area	4,790,924									
Area actually reporting	91.2%	18,489	312	1,371	5,839	10,967	165,549	32,915	114,774	17,860
Estimated total	100.0%	19,314	317	1,437	5,991	11,569	174,579	34,672	121,187	18,720
Cities outside metropolitan areas	507,223									
Area actually reporting	86.8%	978	8	104	223	643	18,672	3,211	14,493	968
Estimated total	100.0%	1,126	9	120	257	740	21,499	3,697	16,687	1,115
Nonmetropolitan counties	897,496									
Area actually reporting	59.4%	841	9	97	92	643	7,101	1,908	4,639	554
Estimated total	100.0%	1,416	15	163	155	1,083	11,956	3,212	7,811	933
State Total	**6,195,643**	**21,856**	**341**	**1,720**	**6,403**	**13,392**	**208,034**	**41,581**	**145,685**	**20,768**
Rate per 100,000 inhabitants		352.8	5.5	27.8	103.3	216.2	3,357.7	671.1	2,351.4	335.2

See footnotes at end of table.

Table 5

Crime in the United States
by State, 2003—Continued

Area	Population	Violent crime	Murder and non-negligent man-slaughter	Forcible rape	Robbery	Aggravated assault	Property crime	Burglary	Larceny-theft	Motor vehicle theft
IOWA										
Metropolitan Statistical Area	1,592,457									
Area actually reporting	98.6%	5,734	37	577	1,005	4,115	61,238	11,192	45,787	4,259
Estimated total	100.0%	5,778	37	582	1,010	4,149	61,890	11,303	46,303	4,284
Cities outside metropolitan areas	594,558									
Area actually reporting	91.0%	1,622	5	137	95	1,385	18,059	3,860	13,376	823
Estimated total	100.0%	1,783	5	151	104	1,523	19,852	4,243	14,704	905
Nonmetropolitan counties	757,047									
Area actually reporting	99.3%	456	5	29	9	413	5,398	1,986	3,003	409
Estimated total	100.0%	459	5	29	9	416	5,436	2,000	3,024	412
State Total	**2,944,062**	**8,020**	**47**	**762**	**1,123**	**6,088**	**87,178**	**17,546**	**64,031**	**5,601**
Rate per 100,000 inhabitants		272.4	1.6	25.9	38.1	206.8	2,961.1	596.0	2,174.9	190.2
KANSAS										
Metropolitan Statistical Area	1,691,995									
Area actually reporting	96.7%	7,559	79	659	1,969	4,852	72,431	14,104	52,314	6,013
Estimated total	100.0%	7,737	80	677	2,007	4,973	74,483	14,468	53,837	6,178
Cities outside metropolitan areas	605,937									
Area actually reporting	95.5%	2,110	34	248	199	1,629	25,391	5,046	19,315	1,030
Estimated total	100.0%	2,210	36	260	208	1,706	26,598	5,286	20,233	1,079
Nonmetropolitan counties	425,575									
Area actually reporting	97.3%	802	7	102	30	663	7,491	2,076	4,909	506
Estimated total	100.0%	824	7	105	31	681	7,696	2,133	5,043	520
State Total	**2,723,507**	**10,771**	**123**	**1,042**	**2,246**	**7,360**	**108,777**	**21,887**	**79,113**	**7,777**
Rate per 100,000 inhabitants		395.5	4.5	38.3	82.5	270.2	3,994.0	803.6	2,904.8	285.6
KENTUCKY[2]										
State Total	**4,117,827**	**10,777**	**188**	**1,054**	**3,196**	**6,339**	**110,418**	**27,656**	**73,396**	**9,366**
Rate per 100,000 inhabitants		261.7	4.6	25.6	77.6	153.9	2,681.5	671.6	1,782.4	227.5
LOUISIANA										
Metropolitan Statistical Area	3,368,338									
Area actually reporting	97.9%	22,398	495	1,514	6,254	14,135	155,065	34,164	103,087	17,814
Estimated total	100.0%	22,799	497	1,537	6,333	14,432	158,822	34,822	105,952	18,048
Cities outside metropolitan areas	420,432									
Area actually reporting	74.7%	2,389	26	125	367	1,871	16,728	4,234	11,772	722
Estimated total	100.0%	3,197	35	167	491	2,504	22,389	5,667	15,756	966
Nonmetropolitan counties	707,564									
Area actually reporting	88.5%	2,713	48	128	217	2,320	12,703	3,882	8,053	768
Estimated total	100.0%	3,066	54	145	245	2,622	14,358	4,388	9,102	868
State Total	**4,496,334**	**29,062**	**586**	**1,849**	**7,069**	**19,558**	**195,569**	**44,877**	**130,810**	**19,882**
Rate per 100,000 inhabitants		646.3	13.0	41.1	157.2	435.0	4,349.5	998.1	2,909.3	442.2
MAINE										
Metropolitan Statistical Area	757,912									
Area actually reporting	100.0%	874	10	224	243	397	19,985	3,763	15,329	893
Cities outside metropolitan areas	276,145									
Area actually reporting	100.0%	397	3	99	38	257	8,322	1,547	6,441	334
Nonmetropolitan counties	271,671									
Area actually reporting	100.0%	151	3	31	8	109	3,771	1,269	2,273	229
State Total	**1,305,728**	**1,422**	**16**	**354**	**289**	**763**	**32,078**	**6,579**	**24,043**	**1,456**
Rate per 100,000 inhabitants		108.9	1.2	27.1	22.1	58.4	2,456.7	503.9	1,841.3	111.5

See footnotes at end of table.

Table 5

Crime in the United States
by State, 2003—Continued

Area	Population	Violent crime	Murder and non-negligent man-slaughter	Forcible rape	Robbery	Aggravated assault	Property crime	Burglary	Larceny-theft	Motor vehicle theft
MARYLAND										
Metropolitan Statistical Area	5,223,096									
Area actually reporting	100.0%	37,461	520	1,276	13,147	22,518	201,714	37,049	128,701	35,964
Cities outside metropolitan areas	73,338									
Area actually reporting	100.0%	632	2	40	92	498	4,063	642	3,241	180
Nonmetropolitan counties	212,475									
Area actually reporting	100.0%	685	3	42	63	577	3,641	950	2,430	261
State Total	**5,508,909**	**38,778**	**525**	**1,358**	**13,302**	**23,593**	**209,418**	**38,641**	**134,372**	**36,405**
Rate per 100,000 inhabitants		703.9	9.5	24.7	241.5	428.3	3,801.4	701.4	2,439.2	660.8
MASSACHUSETTS										
Metropolitan Statistical Area	6,400,207									
Area actually reporting	97.0%	29,564	142	1,760	7,887	19,775	159,700	33,851	100,813	25,036
Estimated total	100.0%	30,122	142	1,795	7,982	20,203	163,170	34,621	103,067	25,482
Cities outside metropolitan areas	32,237									
Area actually reporting	87.1%	56	0	3	3	50	739	88	630	21
Estimated total	100.0%	74	0	3	3	68	848	101	723	24
Nonmetropolitan counties	978									
Area actually reporting	100.0%	0	0	0	0	0	0	0	0	0
State Total	**6,433,422**	**30,196**	**142**	**1,798**	**7,985**	**20,271**	**164,018**	**34,722**	**103,790**	**25,506**
Rate per 100,000 inhabitants		469.4	2.2	27.9	124.1	315.1	2,549.5	539.7	1,613.3	396.5
MICHIGAN										
Metropolitan Statistical Area	8,213,764									
Area actually reporting	99.4%	47,359	591	4,254	11,074	31,440	286,422	57,943	177,145	51,334
Estimated total	100.0%	47,498	591	4,271	11,104	31,532	288,034	58,213	178,297	51,524
Cities outside metropolitan areas	643,814									
Area actually reporting	91.9%	1,414	4	339	82	989	18,855	2,706	15,409	740
Estimated total	100.0%	1,511	4	363	88	1,056	20,251	2,905	16,549	797
Nonmetropolitan counties	1,222,407									
Area actually reporting	97.5%	2,452	21	797	63	1,571	21,528	6,966	13,182	1,380
Estimated total	100.0%	2,515	22	817	65	1,611	22,071	7,142	13,514	1,415
State Total	**10,079,985**	**51,524**	**617**	**5,451**	**11,257**	**34,199**	**330,356**	**68,260**	**208,360**	**53,736**
Rate per 100,000 inhabitants		511.2	6.1	54.1	111.7	339.3	3,277.3	677.2	2,067.1	533.1
MINNESOTA										
Metropolitan Statistical Area	3,654,803									
Area actually reporting	94.3%	11,001	102	1,487	3,690	5,722	117,187	19,488	86,591	11,108
Estimated total	100.0%	11,315	105	1,545	3,757	5,908	123,606	20,347	91,724	11,535
Cities outside metropolitan areas	548,339									
Area actually reporting	99.5%	1,080	9	276	102	693	19,661	2,797	15,861	1,003
Estimated total	100.0%	1,086	9	277	103	697	19,760	2,811	15,941	1,008
Nonmetropolitan counties	856,233									
Area actually reporting	100.0%	887	14	261	44	568	14,325	4,538	8,571	1,216
State Total	**5,059,375**	**13,288**	**128**	**2,083**	**3,904**	**7,173**	**157,691**	**27,696**	**116,236**	**13,759**
Rate per 100,000 inhabitants		262.6	2.5	41.2	77.2	141.8	3,116.8	547.4	2,297.4	272.0
MISSISSIPPI										
Metropolitan Statistical Area	1,228,282									
Area actually reporting	81.6%	3,999	93	497	1,820	1,589	50,539	13,344	31,500	5,695
Estimated total	100.0%	4,505	105	555	1,952	1,893	57,394	15,164	35,868	6,362
Cities outside metropolitan areas	604,143									
Area actually reporting	78.8%	2,131	56	258	657	1,160	27,283	6,348	19,745	1,190
Estimated total	100.0%	2,706	71	328	834	1,473	34,644	8,061	25,072	1,511
Nonmetropolitan counties	1,048,856									
Area actually reporting	41.3%	895	38	80	96	681	6,256	2,730	3,082	444
Estimated total	100.0%	2,169	92	194	233	1,650	15,157	6,614	7,467	1,076
State Total	**2,881,281**	**9,380**	**268**	**1,077**	**3,019**	**5,016**	**107,195**	**29,839**	**68,407**	**8,949**
Rate per 100,000 inhabitants		325.5	9.3	37.4	104.8	174.1	3,720.4	1,035.6	2,374.2	310.6

See footnotes at end of table.

Table 5

Crime in the United States
by State, 2003—Continued

Area	Population	Violent crime	Murder and non-negligent man-slaughter	Forcible rape	Robbery	Aggravated assault	Property crime	Burglary	Larceny-theft	Motor vehicle theft
				Violent crime				**Property crime**		
MISSOURI										
Metropolitan Statistical Area	4,161,628									
Area actually reporting	99.9%	22,469	240	1,091	5,898	15,240	190,529	31,803	132,006	26,720
Estimated total	100.0%	22,478	240	1,092	5,900	15,246	190,642	31,820	132,091	26,731
Cities outside metropolitan areas	667,620									
Area actually reporting	100.0%	2,450	25	186	229	2,010	25,748	4,557	20,198	993
Nonmetropolitan counties	875,236									
Area actually reporting	100.0%	2,040	23	116	74	1,827	12,614	4,531	7,148	935
State Total	**5,704,484**	**26,968**	**288**	**1,394**	**6,203**	**19,083**	**229,004**	**40,908**	**159,437**	**28,659**
Rate per 100,000 inhabitants		472.8	5.0	24.4	108.7	334.5	4,014.5	717.1	2,794.9	502.4
MONTANA										
Metropolitan Statistical Area	321,651									
Area actually reporting	87.9%	957	12	59	220	666	13,144	1,606	10,666	872
Estimated total	100.0%	1,033	13	63	224	733	13,939	1,698	11,309	932
Cities outside metropolitan areas	180,244									
Area actually reporting	70.2%	650	4	56	31	559	5,458	554	4,607	297
Estimated total	100.0%	927	6	80	44	797	7,777	789	6,565	423
Nonmetropolitan counties	415,726									
Area actually reporting	70.0%	974	8	72	21	873	4,700	865	3,449	386
Estimated total	100.0%	1,391	11	103	30	1,247	6,712	1,235	4,926	551
State Total	**917,621**	**3,351**	**30**	**246**	**298**	**2,777**	**28,428**	**3,722**	**22,800**	**1,906**
Rate per 100,000 inhabitants		365.2	3.3	26.8	32.5	302.6	3,098.0	405.6	2,484.7	207.7
NEBRASKA										
Metropolitan Statistical Area	972,426									
Area actually reporting	98.1%	4,071	43	323	1,081	2,624	45,104	6,669	33,198	5,237
Estimated total	100.0%	4,091	43	325	1,083	2,640	45,395	6,730	33,403	5,262
Cities outside metropolitan areas	395,801									
Area actually reporting	89.3%	588	7	106	60	415	13,075	1,849	10,693	533
Estimated total	100.0%	659	8	119	67	465	14,640	2,070	11,973	597
Nonmetropolitan counties	371,064									
Area actually reporting	91.6%	253	5	47	11	190	4,136	1,165	2,728	243
Estimated total	100.0%	276	5	51	12	208	4,517	1,272	2,980	265
State Total	**1,739,291**	**5,026**	**56**	**495**	**1,162**	**3,313**	**64,552**	**10,072**	**48,356**	**6,124**
Rate per 100,000 inhabitants		289.0	3.2	28.5	66.8	190.5	3,711.4	579.1	2,780.2	352.1
NEVADA										
Metropolitan Statistical Area	2,002,686									
Area actually reporting	100.0%	13,117	193	813	5,094	7,017	90,426	20,215	49,780	20,431
Cities outside metropolitan areas	43,757									
Area actually reporting	100.0%	116	1	10	25	80	1,597	348	1,157	92
Nonmetropolitan counties	194,711									
Area actually reporting	100.0%	532	3	51	43	435	4,086	1,414	2,357	315
State Total	**2,241,154**	**13,765**	**197**	**874**	**5,162**	**7,532**	**96,109**	**21,977**	**53,294**	**20,838**
Rate per 100,000 inhabitants		614.2	8.8	39.0	230.3	336.1	4,288.4	980.6	2,378.0	929.8
NEW HAMPSHIRE										
Metropolitan Statistical Area	804,274									
Area actually reporting	85.3%	1,262	12	236	387	627	14,907	2,459	11,153	1,295
Estimated total	100.0%	1,393	13	271	411	698	16,871	2,734	12,704	1,433
Cities outside metropolitan areas	426,204									
Area actually reporting	66.1%	315	3	90	43	179	6,109	1,121	4,687	301
Estimated total	100.0%	477	5	136	65	271	9,242	1,696	7,091	455
Nonmetropolitan counties	57,209									
Area actually reporting	81.9%	38	0	16	2	20	275	100	151	24
Estimated total	100.0%	46	0	20	2	24	335	122	184	29
State Total	**1,287,687**	**1,916**	**18**	**427**	**478**	**993**	**26,448**	**4,552**	**19,979**	**1,917**
Rate per 100,000 inhabitants		148.8	1.4	33.2	37.1	77.1	2,053.9	353.5	1,551.5	148.9

See footnotes at end of table.

Table 5

Crime in the United States
by State, 2003—Continued

Area	Population	Violent crime	Murder and non-negligent man-slaughter	Forcible rape	Robbery	Aggravated assault	Property crime	Burglary	Larceny-theft	Motor vehicle theft
NEW JERSEY										
Metropolitan Statistical Area	8,638,396									
Area actually reporting	100.0%	31,599	407	1,325	13,366	16,501	219,799	43,453	141,778	34,568
Cities outside metropolitan areas	None									
Nonmetropolitan counties	None									
State Total	**8,638,396**	**31,599**	**407**	**1,325**	**13,366**	**16,501**	**219,799**	**43,453**	**141,778**	**34,568**
Rate per 100,000 inhabitants		365.8	4.7	15.3	154.7	191.0	2,544.4	503.0	1,641.3	400.2
NEW MEXICO										
Metropolitan Statistical Area	1,200,062									
Area actually reporting	88.0%	7,758	75	614	1,493	5,576	49,668	11,777	32,206	5,685
Estimated total	100.0%	8,454	79	672	1,565	6,138	52,717	12,715	33,993	6,009
Cities outside metropolitan areas	397,362									
Area actually reporting	91.3%	3,105	21	163	315	2,606	18,983	4,465	13,593	925
Estimated total	100.0%	3,402	23	179	345	2,855	20,794	4,891	14,890	1,013
Nonmetropolitan counties	277,190									
Area actually reporting	70.5%	433	7	61	28	337	2,673	1,137	1,371	165
Estimated total	100.0%	614	10	86	40	478	3,790	1,612	1,944	234
State Total	**1,874,614**	**12,470**	**112**	**937**	**1,950**	**9,471**	**77,301**	**19,218**	**50,827**	**7,256**
Rate per 100,000 inhabitants		665.2	6.0	50.0	104.0	505.2	4,123.6	1,025.2	2,711.3	387.1
NEW YORK										
Metropolitan Statistical Area	17,630,414									
Area actually reporting	99.3%	85,641	909	3,244	35,348	46,140	397,171	67,795	285,262	44,114
Estimated total	100.0%	85,872	909	3,255	35,427	46,281	399,777	68,176	287,311	44,290
Cities outside metropolitan areas	582,644									
Area actually reporting	90.0%	1,328	6	184	208	930	15,573	2,564	12,627	382
Estimated total	100.0%	1,475	7	204	231	1,033	17,297	2,848	14,025	424
Nonmetropolitan counties	977,057									
Area actually reporting	93.0%	1,783	17	292	93	1,381	13,362	4,154	8,740	468
Estimated total	100.0%	1,918	18	314	100	1,486	14,374	4,469	9,402	503
State Total	**19,190,115**	**89,265**	**934**	**3,773**	**35,758**	**48,800**	**431,448**	**75,493**	**310,738**	**45,217**
Rate per 100,000 inhabitants		465.2	4.9	19.7	186.3	254.3	2,248.3	393.4	1,619.3	235.6
NORTH CAROLINA										
Metropolitan Statistical Area	5,765,063									
Area actually reporting	98.0%	28,614	320	1,503	9,879	16,912	259,950	68,549	170,223	21,178
Estimated total	100.0%	28,934	323	1,524	9,958	17,129	263,927	69,699	172,827	21,401
Cities outside metropolitan areas	815,560									
Area actually reporting	92.5%	4,885	66	279	1,485	3,055	49,166	12,119	34,784	2,263
Estimated total	100.0%	5,271	71	302	1,602	3,296	53,080	13,082	37,560	2,438
Nonmetropolitan counties	1,826,625									
Area actually reporting	97.5%	3,939	112	305	652	2,870	41,574	17,453	21,145	2,976
Estimated total	100.0%	4,041	115	313	669	2,944	42,653	17,906	21,694	3,053
State Total	**8,407,248**	**38,246**	**509**	**2,139**	**12,229**	**23,369**	**359,660**	**100,687**	**232,081**	**26,892**
Rate per 100,000 inhabitants		454.9	6.1	25.4	145.5	278.0	4,278.0	1,197.6	2,760.5	319.9
NORTH DAKOTA										
Metropolitan Statistical Area	286,263									
Area actually reporting	99.5%	253	3	73	28	149	7,382	1,039	5,825	518
Estimated total	100.0%	254	3	73	28	150	7,432	1,047	5,864	521
Cities outside metropolitan areas	141,733									
Area actually reporting	84.0%	140	6	51	16	67	3,527	424	2,804	299
Estimated total	100.0%	167	7	61	19	80	4,201	505	3,340	356
Nonmetropolitan counties	205,841									
Area actually reporting	81.6%	59	2	14	3	40	1,348	317	867	164
Estimated total	100.0%	72	2	17	4	49	1,653	389	1,063	201
State Total	**633,837**	**493**	**12**	**151**	**51**	**279**	**13,286**	**1,941**	**10,267**	**1,078**
Rate per 100,000 inhabitants		77.8	1.9	23.8	8.0	44.0	2,096.1	306.2	1,619.8	170.1

See footnotes at end of table.

Table 5

Crime in the United States
by State, 2003—Continued

Area	Population	Violent crime	Violent crime — Murder and non-negligent man-slaughter	Violent crime — Forcible rape	Violent crime — Robbery	Violent crime — Aggravated assault	Property crime	Property crime — Burglary	Property crime — Larceny-theft	Property crime — Motor vehicle theft
OHIO										
Metropolitan Statistical Area	9,211,400									
Area actually reporting	90.2%	33,940	443	3,829	15,781	13,887	335,607	77,844	221,267	36,496
Estimated total	100.0%	35,357	454	4,051	16,274	14,578	360,292	82,495	239,706	38,091
Cities outside metropolitan areas	834,409									
Area actually reporting	69.6%	1,261	24	241	354	642	26,246	4,677	20,544	1,025
Estimated total	100.0%	1,810	34	346	508	922	37,688	6,716	29,500	1,472
Nonmetropolitan counties	1,389,989									
Area actually reporting	70.9%	664	24	135	76	429	12,999	4,055	7,928	1,016
Estimated total	100.0%	936	34	190	107	605	18,337	5,720	11,184	1,433
State Total	**11,435,798**	**38,103**	**522**	**4,587**	**16,889**	**16,105**	**416,317**	**94,931**	**280,390**	**40,996**
Rate per 100,000 inhabitants		333.2	4.6	40.1	147.7	140.8	3,640.5	830.1	2,451.9	358.5
OKLAHOMA										
Metropolitan Statistical Area	2,212,103									
Area actually reporting	100.0%	13,093	154	995	2,808	9,136	113,012	24,122	78,534	10,356
Cities outside metropolitan areas	696,232									
Area actually reporting	100.0%	3,222	29	364	373	2,456	29,735	7,394	20,615	1,726
Nonmetropolitan counties	603,197									
Area actually reporting	100.0%	1,443	23	142	43	1,235	8,461	3,330	4,255	876
State Total	**3,511,532**	**17,758**	**206**	**1,501**	**3,224**	**12,827**	**151,208**	**34,846**	**103,404**	**12,958**
Rate per 100,000 inhabitants		505.7	5.9	42.7	91.8	365.3	4,306.0	992.3	2,944.7	369.0
OREGON										
Metropolitan Statistical Area	2,740,172									
Area actually reporting	99.0%	9,033	54	981	2,575	5,423	139,022	22,234	100,182	16,606
Estimated total	100.0%	9,075	54	987	2,584	5,450	139,928	22,406	100,810	16,712
Cities outside metropolitan areas	371,581									
Area actually reporting	98.2%	956	5	134	212	605	20,455	3,489	15,542	1,424
Estimated total	100.0%	973	5	136	216	616	20,835	3,554	15,831	1,450
Nonmetropolitan counties	447,843									
Area actually reporting	90.4%	427	8	86	46	287	8,559	2,410	5,401	748
Estimated total	100.0%	472	9	95	51	317	9,467	2,666	5,974	827
State Total	**3,559,596**	**10,520**	**68**	**1,218**	**2,851**	**6,383**	**170,230**	**28,626**	**122,615**	**18,989**
Rate per 100,000 inhabitants		295.5	1.9	34.2	80.1	179.3	4,782.3	804.2	3,444.6	533.5
PENNSYLVANIA										
Metropolitan Statistical Area	10,391,620									
Area actually reporting	91.3%	43,421	606	2,848	16,917	23,050	245,380	43,022	172,494	29,864
Estimated total	100.0%	45,463	622	2,996	17,441	24,404	264,583	45,786	187,517	31,280
Cities outside metropolitan areas	867,466									
Area actually reporting	73.9%	1,763	9	173	274	1,307	15,180	2,352	12,068	760
Estimated total	100.0%	2,386	12	234	371	1,769	20,543	3,183	16,331	1,029
Nonmetropolitan counties	1,106,369									
Area actually reporting	100.0%	1,367	17	326	168	856	15,515	4,950	9,432	1,133
State Total	**12,365,455**	**49,216**	**651**	**3,556**	**17,980**	**27,029**	**300,641**	**53,919**	**213,280**	**33,442**
Rate per 100,000 inhabitants		398.0	5.3	28.8	145.4	218.6	2,431.3	436.0	1,724.8	270.4
PUERTO RICO										
Metropolitan Statistical Area	3,683,868									
Area actually reporting	100.0%	11,614	756	200	7,636	3,022	68,252	19,969	36,220	12,063
Cities outside metropolitan areas	194,664									
Area actually reporting	100.0%	271	23	4	101	143	1,643	888	607	148
Total	**3,878,532**	**11,885**	**779**	**204**	**7,737**	**3,165**	**69,895**	**20,857**	**36,827**	**12,211**
Rate per 100,000 inhabitants		306.4	20.1	5.3	199.5	81.6	1,802.1	537.8	949.5	314.8

See footnotes at end of table.

Table 5

Crime in the United States
by State, 2003—Continued

Area	Population	Violent crime	Murder and non-negligent man-slaughter	Forcible rape	Robbery	Aggravated assault	Property crime	Burglary	Larceny-theft	Motor vehicle theft
RHODE ISLAND										
Metropolitan Statistical Area	1,076,164									
Area actually reporting	100.0%	3,050	23	491	828	1,708	32,184	5,521	22,285	4,378
Cities outside metropolitan areas	None									
Nonmetropolitan counties	None									
Area actually reporting	100.0%	24	2	14	2	6	47	3	35	9
State Total	**1,076,164**	**3,074**	**25**	**505**	**830**	**1,714**	**32,231**	**5,524**	**22,320**	**4,387**
Rate per 100,000 inhabitants		285.6	2.3	46.9	77.1	159.3	2,995.0	513.3	2,074.0	407.7
SOUTH CAROLINA										
Metropolitan Statistical Area	3,112,033									
Area actually reporting	99.9%	24,873	223	1,445	4,581	18,624	143,710	32,333	98,452	12,925
Estimated total	100.0%	24,880	223	1,445	4,582	18,630	143,772	32,343	98,500	12,929
Cities outside metropolitan areas	265,266									
Area actually reporting	99.5%	3,275	27	114	518	2,616	16,812	3,547	12,461	804
Estimated total	100.0%	3,292	27	115	521	2,629	16,896	3,565	12,523	808
Nonmetropolitan counties	769,853									
Area actually reporting	100.0%	4,736	50	283	567	3,836	25,003	7,674	15,304	2,025
State Total	**4,147,152**	**32,908**	**300**	**1,843**	**5,670**	**25,095**	**185,671**	**43,582**	**126,327**	**15,762**
Rate per 100,000 inhabitants		793.5	7.2	44.4	136.7	605.1	4,477.1	1,050.9	3,046.1	380.1
SOUTH DAKOTA										
Metropolitan Statistical Area	324,249									
Area actually reporting	97.1%	846	6	240	81	519	8,996	1,562	6,910	524
Estimated total	100.0%	864	6	247	81	530	9,185	1,593	7,057	535
Cities outside metropolitan areas	201,164									
Area actually reporting	91.1%	267	1	64	10	192	4,343	759	3,372	212
Estimated total	100.0%	293	1	70	11	211	4,770	834	3,703	233
Nonmetropolitan counties	238,896									
Area actually reporting	83.8%	140	2	31	10	97	1,127	374	664	89
Estimated total	100.0%	168	3	37	12	116	1,344	446	792	106
State Total	**764,309**	**1,325**	**10**	**354**	**104**	**857**	**15,299**	**2,873**	**11,552**	**874**
Rate per 100,000 inhabitants		173.4	1.3	46.3	13.6	112.1	2,001.7	375.9	1,511.4	114.4
TENNESSEE										
Metropolitan Statistical Area	4,237,335									
Area actually reporting	100.0%	33,347	337	1,770	8,796	22,444	205,209	48,498	134,118	22,593
Cities outside metropolitan areas	578,487									
Area actually reporting	100.0%	3,576	29	172	461	2,914	29,700	6,595	21,328	1,777
Nonmetropolitan counties	1,025,926									
Area actually reporting	100.0%	3,254	29	143	115	2,967	20,924	8,114	10,770	2,040
State Total	**5,841,748**	**40,177**	**395**	**2,085**	**9,372**	**28,325**	**255,833**	**63,207**	**166,216**	**26,410**
Rate per 100,000 inhabitants		687.8	6.8	35.7	160.4	484.9	4,379.4	1,082.0	2,845.3	452.1
TEXAS										
Metropolitan Statistical Area	19,139,661									
Area actually reporting	99.9%	112,887	1,287	7,172	36,079	68,349	933,337	196,088	643,619	93,630
Estimated total	100.0%	112,910	1,287	7,174	36,085	68,364	933,649	196,149	643,847	93,653
Cities outside metropolitan areas	1,373,327									
Area actually reporting	99.3%	5,889	62	554	769	4,504	55,776	12,868	40,288	2,620
Estimated total	100.0%	5,918	62	556	770	4,530	56,063	12,937	40,497	2,629
Nonmetropolitan counties	1,605,521									
Area actually reporting	100.0%	3,373	69	282	163	2,859	26,710	10,699	14,089	1,922
State Total	**22,118,509**	**122,201**	**1,418**	**8,012**	**37,018**	**75,753**	**1,016,422**	**219,785**	**698,433**	**98,204**
Rate per 100,000 inhabitants		552.5	6.4	36.2	167.4	342.5	4,595.3	993.7	3,157.7	444.0

See footnotes at end of table.

Table 5

Crime in the United States

by State, 2003—Continued

Area	Population	Violent crime	Violent crime — Murder and non-negligent man-slaughter	Violent crime — Forcible rape	Violent crime — Robbery	Violent crime — Aggravated assault	Property crime	Property crime — Burglary	Property crime — Larceny-theft	Property crime — Motor vehicle theft
UTAH										
Metropolitan Statistical Area	2,078,616									
Area actually reporting	98.1%	5,317	52	785	1,212	3,268	90,781	15,082	68,451	7,248
Estimated total	100.0%	5,401	53	802	1,223	3,323	92,168	15,325	69,488	7,355
Cities outside metropolitan areas	128,198									
Area actually reporting	91.9%	226	3	50	16	157	4,173	719	3,237	217
Estimated total	100.0%	245	3	54	17	171	4,539	782	3,521	236
Nonmetropolitan counties	144,653									
Area actually reporting	94.3%	188	2	34	14	138	2,504	624	1,717	163
Estimated total	100.0%	199	2	36	15	146	2,655	662	1,820	173
State Total	**2,351,467**	**5,845**	**58**	**892**	**1,255**	**3,640**	**99,362**	**16,769**	**74,829**	**7,764**
Rate per 100,000 inhabitants		248.6	2.5	37.9	53.4	154.8	4,225.5	713.1	3,182.2	330.2
VERMONT										
Metropolitan Statistical Area	203,769									
Area actually reporting	96.4%	344	4	55	34	251	5,334	1,153	3,944	237
Estimated total	100.0%	352	4	55	35	258	5,521	1,189	4,089	243
Cities outside metropolitan areas	197,181									
Area actually reporting	100.0%	225	1	46	19	159	5,215	792	4,227	196
Nonmetropolitan counties	218,157									
Area actually reporting	100.0%	105	9	20	6	70	2,885	977	1,701	207
State Total	**619,107**	**682**	**14**	**121**	**60**	**487**	**13,621**	**2,958**	**10,017**	**646**
Rate per 100,000 inhabitants		110.2	2.3	19.5	9.7	78.7	2,200.1	477.8	1,618.0	104.3
VIRGINIA										
Metropolitan Statistical Area	6,295,851									
Area actually reporting	99.2%	18,115	373	1,498	6,306	9,938	177,667	24,735	136,521	16,411
Estimated total	100.0%	18,324	375	1,516	6,363	10,070	179,518	24,986	137,964	16,568
Cities outside metropolitan areas	265,881									
Area actually reporting	96.6%	754	5	79	149	521	8,099	979	6,684	436
Estimated total	100.0%	780	5	82	154	539	8,383	1,013	6,919	451
Nonmetropolitan counties	824,598									
Area actually reporting	97.6%	1,240	32	171	151	886	11,543	2,849	7,821	873
Estimated total	100.0%	1,271	33	175	155	908	11,830	2,920	8,015	895
State Total	**7,386,330**	**20,375**	**413**	**1,773**	**6,672**	**11,517**	**199,731**	**28,919**	**152,898**	**17,914**
Rate per 100,000 inhabitants		275.8	5.6	24.0	90.3	155.9	2,704.1	391.5	2,070.0	242.5
WASHINGTON										
Metropolitan Statistical Area	5,366,728									
Area actually reporting	99.9%	19,625	167	2,461	5,518	11,479	261,672	51,146	171,859	38,667
Estimated total	100.0%	19,643	167	2,464	5,523	11,489	261,989	51,198	172,079	38,712
Cities outside metropolitan areas	323,537									
Area actually reporting	95.7%	841	3	215	130	493	17,777	3,231	13,575	971
Estimated total	100.0%	879	3	225	136	515	18,570	3,375	14,181	1,014
Nonmetropolitan counties	441,180									
Area actually reporting	88.2%	664	12	154	52	446	9,683	3,257	5,639	787
Estimated total	100.0%	754	14	175	59	506	10,985	3,695	6,397	893
State Total	**6,131,445**	**21,276**	**184**	**2,864**	**5,718**	**12,510**	**291,544**	**58,268**	**192,657**	**40,619**
Rate per 100,000 inhabitants		347.0	3.0	46.7	93.3	204.0	4,754.9	950.3	3,142.1	662.5
WEST VIRGINIA										
Metropolitan Statistical Area	989,502									
Area actually reporting	91.7%	2,866	29	182	563	2,092	26,729	6,141	18,295	2,293
Estimated total	100.0%	3,041	30	187	586	2,238	28,672	6,488	19,768	2,416
Cities outside metropolitan areas	226,821									
Area actually reporting	82.3%	473	3	32	58	380	4,198	830	3,167	201
Estimated total	100.0%	575	4	39	70	462	5,100	1,008	3,848	244
Nonmetropolitan counties	594,031									
Area actually reporting	86.1%	900	25	60	64	751	7,702	2,310	4,648	744
Estimated total	100.0%	1,045	29	70	74	872	8,942	2,682	5,396	864
State Total	**1,810,354**	**4,661**	**63**	**296**	**730**	**3,572**	**42,714**	**10,178**	**29,012**	**3,524**
Rate per 100,000 inhabitants		257.5	3.5	16.4	40.3	197.3	2,359.4	562.2	1,602.6	194.7

See footnotes at end of table.

Table 5

Crime in the United States
by State, 2003—Continued

Area	Population	Violent crime	Violent crime Murder and non-negligent man-slaughter	Violent crime Forcible rape	Violent crime Robbery	Violent crime Aggravated assault	Property crime	Property crime Burglary	Property crime Larceny-theft	Property crime Motor vehicle theft
WISCONSIN										
Metropolitan Statistical Area	3,955,013									
Area actually reporting	97.2%	10,340	159	937	4,248	4,996	124,460	19,927	93,776	10,757
Estimated total	100.0%	10,432	160	952	4,266	5,054	126,387	20,270	95,261	10,856
Cities outside metropolitan areas	610,884									
Area actually reporting	99.0%	980	4	144	86	746	19,669	2,523	16,437	709
Estimated total	100.0%	989	4	145	87	753	19,862	2,548	16,598	716
Nonmetropolitan counties	906,402									
Area actually reporting	100.0%	674	17	101	33	523	11,498	3,744	7,006	748
State Total	**5,472,299**	**12,095**	**181**	**1,198**	**4,386**	**6,330**	**157,747**	**26,562**	**118,865**	**12,320**
Rate per 100,000 inhabitants		221.0	3.3	21.9	80.1	115.7	2,882.6	485.4	2,172.1	225.1
WYOMING										
Metropolitan Statistical Area	150,994									
Area actually reporting	100.0%	338	6	51	46	235	6,529	1,052	5,106	371
Cities outside metropolitan areas	208,513									
Area actually reporting	97.5%	612	4	59	29	520	7,666	1,039	6,319	308
Estimated total	100.0%	627	4	60	30	533	7,859	1,065	6,478	316
Nonmetropolitan counties	141,735									
Area actually reporting	95.8%	335	4	24	8	299	2,164	473	1,585	106
Estimated total	100.0%	349	4	25	8	312	2,260	494	1,655	111
State Total	**501,242**	**1,314**	**14**	**136**	**84**	**1,080**	**16,648**	**2,611**	**13,239**	**798**
Rate per 100,000 inhabitants		262.1	2.8	27.1	16.8	215.5	3,321.3	520.9	2,641.2	159.2

[1] Includes offenses reported by the Zoological Police and the Metro Transit Police.

[2] Limited data for 2003 were available for Illinois and Kentucky. See Offense Estimation, Appendix I, for details.

NOTE: Although arson data are included in the trend and clearance tables, sufficient data are not available to estimate totals for this offense.

Table 6

Crime in the United States
by Metropolitan Statistical Area, 2003

Metropolitan Statistical Area	Population	Violent crime	Murder and non-negligent man-slaughter	Forcible rape	Robbery	Aggravated assault	Property crime	Burglary	Larceny-theft	Motor vehicle theft
Abilene, TX M.S.A.	**161,159**									
(Includes Callahan, Jones, and Taylor Counties.)										
City of Abilene	117,016	517	6	71	129	311	6,107	1,814	3,991	302
Total area actually reporting	100.0%	599	7	77	137	378	6,790	2,083	4,360	347
Rate per 100,000 inhabitants		371.7	4.3	47.8	85.0	234.6	4,213.2	1,292.5	2,705.4	215.3
Akron, OH M.S.A.	**701,158**									
(Includes Portage and Summit Counties.)										
City of Akron	214,622	1,288	16	206	623	443	12,172	3,177	7,779	1,216
Total area actually reporting	83.0%	1,778	19	321	778	660	22,655	4,868	16,030	1,757
Estimated total	100.0%	1,921	20	350	827	724	25,429	5,479	17,992	1,958
Rate per 100,000 inhabitants		274.0	2.9	49.9	117.9	103.3	3,626.7	781.4	2,566.0	279.3
Albany, GA M.S.A.	**162,243**									
(Includes Baker, Dougherty, Lee, Terrell, and Worth Counties.)										
City of Albany	77,434	537	6	37	261	233	4,648	1,280	2,967	401
Total area actually reporting	99.5%	706	7	50	292	357	6,414	1,727	4,188	499
Estimated total	100.0%	711	7	50	294	360	6,462	1,735	4,223	504
Rate per 100,000 inhabitants		438.2	4.3	30.8	181.2	221.9	3,982.9	1,069.4	2,602.9	310.6
Albuquerque, NM M.S.A.	**761,936**									
(Includes Bernalillo, Sandoval, Torrance, and Valencia Counties.)										
City of Albuquerque	468,764	4,439	51	263	1,080	3,045	29,294	5,543	19,663	4,088
Total area actually reporting	93.2%	5,950	61	363	1,231	4,295	36,124	7,308	23,905	4,911
Estimated total	100.0%	6,212	62	385	1,256	4,509	37,354	7,655	24,664	5,035
Rate per 100,000 inhabitants		815.3	8.1	50.5	164.8	591.8	4,902.5	1,004.7	3,237.0	660.8
Alexandria, LA M.S.A.	**146,057**									
(Includes Grant and Rapides Parishes.)										
City of Alexandria	45,996	970	8	13	194	755	4,491	1,275	3,013	203
Total area actually reporting	94.0%	1,347	10	29	216	1,092	7,395	2,217	4,784	394
Estimated total	100.0%	1,401	10	32	227	1,132	7,910	2,303	5,183	424
Rate per 100,000 inhabitants		959.2	6.8	21.9	155.4	775.0	5,415.7	1,576.8	3,548.6	290.3
Allentown-Bethlehem-Easton, PA-NJ M.S.A.	**760,286**									
(Includes Warren County, NJ and Carbon, Lehigh, and Northampton Counties, PA.)										
City of:										
Allentown, PA	106,366	641	12	51	359	219	5,654	1,111	3,851	692
Bethlehem, PA	71,926	190	1	20	94	75	1,965	337	1,460	168
Total area actually reporting	88.5%	1,701	16	166	617	902	17,434	2,951	13,093	1,390
Estimated total	100.0%	1,899	18	180	668	1,033	19,296	3,219	14,550	1,527
Rate per 100,000 inhabitants		249.8	2.4	23.7	87.9	135.9	2,538.0	423.4	1,913.8	200.8
Altoona, PA M.S.A.	**128,155**									
(Includes Blair County.)										
City of Altoona	48,609	156	1	24	68	63	1,420	357	983	80
Total area actually reporting	86.5%	241	2	34	93	112	2,421	583	1,706	132
Estimated total	100.0%	280	2	37	103	138	2,788	636	1,993	159
Rate per 100,000 inhabitants		218.5	1.6	28.9	80.4	107.7	2,175.5	496.3	1,555.1	124.1
Amarillo, TX M.S.A.	**235,243**									
(Includes Armstrong, Carson, Potter, and Randall Counties.)										
City of Amarillo	179,762	1,501	17	97	378	1,009	11,604	2,203	8,501	900
Total area actually reporting	100.0%	1,612	17	113	389	1,093	12,613	2,464	9,176	973
Rate per 100,000 inhabitants		685.2	7.2	48.0	165.4	464.6	5,361.7	1,047.4	3,900.6	413.6
Ames, IA M.S.A.	**80,850**									
(Includes Story County.)										
City of Ames	51,040	279	0	25	7	247	1,738	215	1,437	86
Total area actually reporting	100.0%	328	0	30	7	291	2,508	368	2,017	123
Rate per 100,000 inhabitants		405.7	0.0	37.1	8.7	359.9	3,102.0	455.2	2,494.7	152.1
Anchorage, AK M.S.A.	**282,940**									
(Includes Anchorage Municipality and Matanuska-Susitna Borough.)										
City of Anchorage	271,085	1,744	17	244	340	1,143	11,706	1,418	9,091	1,197
Total area actually reporting	100.0%	1,921	17	249	347	1,308	12,869	1,508	10,086	1,275
Rate per 100,000 inhabitants		678.9	6.0	88.0	122.6	462.3	4,548.3	533.0	3,564.7	450.6

See footnotes at end of table.

Table 6

Crime in the United States
by Metropolitan Statistical Area, 2003—Continued

Metropolitan Statistical Area	Population	Violent crime	Violent crime				Property crime	Property crime		
		Violent crime	Murder and non-negligent man-slaughter	Forcible rape	Robbery	Aggravated assault	Property crime	Burglary	Larceny-theft	Motor vehicle theft
Anderson, SC M.S.A.	**172,238**									
(Includes Anderson County.)										
City of Anderson	25,940	210	2	8	60	140	1,592	273	1,211	108
Total area actually reporting	100.0%	1,168	9	62	167	930	8,257	2,093	5,519	645
Rate per 100,000 inhabitants		678.1	5.2	36.0	97.0	540.0	4,793.9	1,215.2	3,204.3	374.5
Ann Arbor, MI M.S.A.[1]	**335,334**									
(Includes Washtenaw County.)										
City of Ann Arbor[1]	115,552	327	1	24	99	203	3,405	771	2,409	225
Total area actually reporting	100.0%	1,007	8	143	230	626	10,972	2,243	7,661	1,068
Rate per 100,000 inhabitants		300.3	2.4	42.6	68.6	186.7	3,272.0	668.9	2,284.6	318.5
Anniston-Oxford, AL M.S.A.	**111,970**									
(Includes Calhoun County.)										
City of:										
Anniston	23,868	502	2	28	155	317	3,164	937	2,011	216
Oxford	12,841	105	1	3	28	73	1,120	193	850	77
Total area actually reporting	100.0%	728	4	47	214	463	6,131	1,607	4,148	376
Rate per 100,000 inhabitants		650.2	3.6	42.0	191.1	413.5	5,475.6	1,435.2	3,704.6	335.8
Appleton, WI M.S.A.	**209,705**									
(Includes Calumet and Outagamie Counties.)										
City of Appleton	71,037	139	0	17	21	101	1,737	247	1,417	73
Total area actually reporting	100.0%	194	2	30	33	129	4,093	516	3,415	162
Rate per 100,000 inhabitants		92.5	1.0	14.3	15.7	61.5	1,951.8	246.1	1,628.5	77.3
Asheville, NC M.S.A.	**382,525**									
(Includes Buncombe, Haywood, Henderson, and Madison Counties.)										
City of Asheville	69,917	456	8	26	221	201	5,003	960	3,541	502
Total area actually reporting	99.7%	1,111	12	78	318	703	11,912	2,975	7,925	1,012
Estimated total	100.0%	1,116	12	78	320	706	11,984	2,991	7,977	1,016
Rate per 100,000 inhabitants		291.7	3.1	20.4	83.7	184.6	3,132.9	781.9	2,085.4	265.6
Athens-Clarke County, GA M.S.A.	**173,523**									
(Includes Clarke, Madison, Oconee, and Oglethorpe Counties.)										
City of Athens-Clarke County	104,313	387	9	52	139	187	6,084	1,076	4,612	396
Total area actually reporting	99.7%	528	11	60	156	301	8,098	1,444	6,118	536
Estimated total	100.0%	531	11	60	157	303	8,127	1,449	6,139	539
Rate per 100,000 inhabitants		306.0	6.3	34.6	90.5	174.6	4,683.5	835.0	3,537.9	310.6
Atlanta-Sandy Springs-Marietta, GA M.S.A.[1]	**4,595,081**									
(Includes Barrow, Bartow, Butts, Carroll, Cherokee, Clayton, Cobb, Coweta, Dawson, DeKalb, Douglas, Fayette, Forsyth, Fulton, Gwinnett, Haralson, Heard, Henry, Jasper, Lamar, Meriwether, Newton, Paulding, Pickens, Pike, Rockdale, Spalding, and Walton Counties.)										
City of:										
Atlanta	431,043	8,491	149	281	3,701	4,360	38,231	8,065	22,931	7,235
Marietta	62,921	324	5	15	156	148	2,754	568	1,852	334
Total area actually reporting	96.1%	22,938	389	1,171	9,685	11,693	191,624	41,004	121,041	29,579
Estimated total	100.0%	23,551	399	1,212	9,913	12,027	198,505	42,456	125,592	30,457
Rate per 100,000 inhabitants		512.5	8.7	26.4	215.7	261.7	4,319.9	923.9	2,733.2	662.8
Atlantic City, NJ M.S.A.	**260,875**									
(Includes Atlantic County.)										
City of Atlantic City	40,397	600	5	23	276	296	4,854	596	4,094	164
Total area actually reporting	100.0%	1,254	17	63	483	691	11,081	1,888	8,699	494
Rate per 100,000 inhabitants		480.7	6.5	24.1	185.1	264.9	4,247.6	723.7	3,334.5	189.4
Auburn-Opelika, AL M.S.A.	**118,498**									
(Includes Lee County.)										
City of:										
Auburn	45,533	146	1	22	50	73	1,972	546	1,347	79
Opelika	23,671	370	5	18	59	288	1,475	311	1,153	11
Total area actually reporting	100.0%	616	7	53	127	429	5,051	1,299	3,553	199
Rate per 100,000 inhabitants		519.8	5.9	44.7	107.2	362.0	4,262.5	1,096.2	2,998.4	167.9

See footnotes at end of table.

Table 6

Crime in the United States
by Metropolitan Statistical Area, 2003—Continued

Metropolitan Statistical Area	Population	Violent crime	Murder and non-negligent man-slaughter	Forcible rape	Robbery	Aggravated assault	Property crime	Burglary	Larceny-theft	Motor vehicle theft
Augusta-Richmond County, GA-SC M.S.A.	513,730									
(Includes Burke, Columbia, McDuffie, and Richmond Counties, GA and Aiken and Edgefield Counties, SC.)										
Total area actually reporting	99.5%	1,988	46	262	618	1,062	20,776	4,326	14,644	1,806
Estimated total	100.0%	2,002	46	263	622	1,071	20,919	4,349	14,750	1,820
Rate per 100,000 inhabitants		389.7	9.0	51.2	121.1	208.5	4,072.0	846.6	2,871.2	354.3
Bakersfield, CA M.S.A.[1]	701,341									
(Includes Kern County.)										
City of Bakersfield[1]	263,707	1,514	24	41	439	1,010	14,102	2,693	9,415	1,994
Total area actually reporting	100.0%	3,742	46	203	784	2,709	29,383	7,189	17,743	4,451
Rate per 100,000 inhabitants		533.5	6.6	28.9	111.8	386.3	4,189.5	1,025.0	2,529.9	634.6
Baltimore-Towson, MD M.S.A.	2,626,193									
(Includes Anne Arundel, Baltimore, Carroll, Harford, Howard, and Queen Anne's Counties and Baltimore City.)										
City of Baltimore	644,554	11,183	270	204	4,339	6,370	37,470	7,789	22,824	6,857
Total area actually reporting	100.0%	23,190	341	652	7,255	14,942	100,269	19,339	67,926	13,004
Rate per 100,000 inhabitants		883.0	13.0	24.8	276.3	569.0	3,818.0	736.4	2,586.5	495.2
Bangor, ME M.S.A.	147,286									
(Includes Penobscot County.)										
City of Bangor	31,815	43	2	4	19	18	1,746	209	1,495	42
Total area actually reporting	100.0%	108	3	15	29	61	4,443	845	3,445	153
Rate per 100,000 inhabitants		73.3	2.0	10.2	19.7	41.4	3,016.6	573.7	2,339.0	103.9
Barnstable Town, MA M.S.A.	228,777									
(Includes Barnstable County.)										
City of Barnstable	48,898	332	1	41	27	263	1,148	391	665	92
Total area actually reporting	97.5%	1,128	2	93	57	976	5,247	1,654	3,317	276
Estimated total	100.0%	1,146	2	94	60	990	5,364	1,680	3,393	291
Rate per 100,000 inhabitants		500.9	0.9	41.1	26.2	432.7	2,344.6	734.3	1,483.1	127.2
Baton Rouge, LA M.S.A.	719,006									
(Includes Ascension, East Baton Rouge, East Feliciana, Iberville, Livingston, Pointe Coupee, St. Helena, West Baton Rouge, and West Feliciana Parishes.)										
City of Baton Rouge	226,391	2,839	41	117	1,039	1,642	15,897	3,887	10,403	1,607
Total area actually reporting	96.2%	5,122	60	248	1,382	3,432	36,542	7,944	25,818	2,780
Estimated total	100.0%	5,260	61	256	1,409	3,534	37,788	8,183	26,738	2,867
Rate per 100,000 inhabitants		731.6	8.5	35.6	196.0	491.5	5,255.6	1,138.1	3,718.7	398.7
Battle Creek, MI M.S.A.	138,782									
(Includes Calhoun County.)										
City of Battle Creek	53,808	691	2	69	122	498	3,766	791	2,745	230
Total area actually reporting	100.0%	1,052	3	146	169	734	6,898	1,550	4,883	465
Rate per 100,000 inhabitants		758.0	2.2	105.2	121.8	528.9	4,970.4	1,116.9	3,518.5	335.1
Bay City, MI M.S.A.	109,994									
(Includes Bay County.)										
City of Bay City	35,949	192	2	21	43	126	1,258	321	831	106
Total area actually reporting	100.0%	316	3	67	61	185	3,151	759	2,166	226
Rate per 100,000 inhabitants		287.3	2.7	60.9	55.5	168.2	2,864.7	690.0	1,969.2	205.5
Beaumont-Port Arthur, TX M.S.A.	388,186									
(Includes Hardin, Jefferson, and Orange Counties.)										
City of:										
Beaumont	114,626	1,051	6	85	331	629	8,829	1,726	6,613	490
Port Arthur	57,769	437	9	20	175	233	2,793	1,055	1,445	293
Total area actually reporting	100.0%	2,119	23	158	625	1,313	18,764	4,655	12,786	1,323
Rate per 100,000 inhabitants		545.9	5.9	40.7	161.0	338.2	4,833.8	1,199.2	3,293.8	340.8
Bellingham, WA M.S.A.	176,156									
(Includes Whatcom County.)										
City of Bellingham	71,205	181	1	30	60	90	5,138	790	4,080	268
Total area actually reporting	100.0%	423	3	108	83	229	8,695	1,951	6,238	506
Rate per 100,000 inhabitants		240.1	1.7	61.3	47.1	130.0	4,936.0	1,107.5	3,541.2	287.2
Bend, OR M.S.A.	126,613									
(Includes Deschutes County.)										
City of Bend	57,626	161	0	16	33	112	3,468	597	2,636	235
Total area actually reporting	100.0%	203	0	27	42	134	5,434	1,041	3,993	400
Rate per 100,000 inhabitants		160.3	0.0	21.3	33.2	105.8	4,291.8	822.2	3,153.7	315.9

See footnotes at end of table.

Table 6

Crime in the United States
by Metropolitan Statistical Area, 2003—Continued

Metropolitan Statistical Area	Population	Violent crime	Murder and non-negligent man-slaughter	Forcible rape	Robbery	Aggravated assault	Property crime	Burglary	Larceny-theft	Motor vehicle theft
				Violent crime				Property crime		
Billings, MT M.S.A.	**142,566**									
(Includes Carbon and Yellowstone Counties.)										
City of Billings	92,834	230	3	19	66	142	4,959	577	4,048	334
Total area actually reporting	100.0%	333	3	23	73	234	6,160	736	5,005	419
Rate per 100,000 inhabitants		233.6	2.1	16.1	51.2	164.1	4,320.8	516.3	3,510.7	293.9
Binghamton, NY M.S.A.	**252,525**									
(Includes Broome and Tioga Counties.)										
City of Binghamton	46,815	182	3	10	77	92	1,947	213	1,683	51
Total area actually reporting	100.0%	427	4	55	125	243	6,046	809	5,070	167
Rate per 100,000 inhabitants		169.1	1.6	21.8	49.5	96.2	2,394.2	320.4	2,007.7	66.1
Birmingham-Hoover, AL M.S.A.	**1,071,569**									
(Includes Bibb, Blount, Chilton, Jefferson, St. Clair, Shelby, and Walker Counties.)										
City of:										
Birmingham	240,176	3,347	85	204	1,352	1,706	19,574	4,831	11,934	2,809
Hoover	64,469	242	0	18	113	111	1,920	310	1,480	130
Total area actually reporting	92.4%	5,686	109	398	2,097	3,082	42,292	9,939	27,673	4,680
Estimated total	100.0%	5,997	112	424	2,191	3,270	45,621	10,619	30,085	4,917
Rate per 100,000 inhabitants		559.6	10.5	39.6	204.5	305.2	4,257.4	991.0	2,807.6	458.9
Bismarck, ND M.S.A.	**96,307**									
(Includes Burleigh and Morton Counties.)										
City of Bismarck	56,210	26	2	1	5	18	1,282	122	1,070	90
Total area actually reporting	100.0%	63	3	12	5	43	1,910	213	1,555	142
Rate per 100,000 inhabitants		65.4	3.1	12.5	5.2	44.6	1,983.2	221.2	1,614.6	147.4
Bloomington, IN M.S.A.	**177,976**									
(Includes Greene, Monroe, and Owen Counties.)										
City of Bloomington	70,403	69	0	15	27	27	2,485	441	1,930	114
Total area actually reporting	82.6%	225	5	28	36	156	4,120	825	3,107	188
Estimated total	100.0%	285	5	33	47	200	4,781	954	3,576	251
Rate per 100,000 inhabitants		160.1	2.8	18.5	26.4	112.4	2,686.3	536.0	2,009.3	141.0
Boise City-Nampa, ID M.S.A.	**507,451**									
(Includes Ada, Boise, Canyon, Gem, and Owyhee Counties.)										
City of:										
Boise	193,414	632	3	108	78	443	8,122	1,422	6,223	477
Nampa	61,391	245	3	70	18	154	2,544	456	1,830	258
Total area actually reporting	98.6%	1,446	13	256	137	1,040	17,409	3,286	12,864	1,259
Estimated total	100.0%	1,458	13	258	137	1,050	17,546	3,322	12,956	1,268
Rate per 100,000 inhabitants		287.3	2.6	50.8	27.0	206.9	3,457.7	654.6	2,553.2	249.9
Boston-Cambridge-Quincy, MA-NH M.S.A.	**4,453,436**									
(Includes the Metropolitan Divisions of Boston-Quincy, MA, Cambridge-Newton-Framingham, MA, and Essex County, MA and Rockingham County-Strafford County, NH.)										
City of:										
Boston, MA	589,795	7,173	39	262	2,759	4,113	27,876	4,344	17,069	6,463
Cambridge, MA	101,896	513	3	7	229	274	3,450	651	2,389	410
Quincy, MA	89,265	316	1	15	97	203	1,530	334	1,041	155
Newton, MA	83,953	99	0	5	23	71	916	145	739	32
Framingham, MA	66,885	173	1	17	36	119	1,530	305	1,038	187
Waltham, MA	59,125	100	2	11	20	67	815	116	601	98
Total area actually reporting	96.4%	19,463	84	986	5,460	12,933	103,069	18,733	67,441	16,895
Estimated total	100.0%	19,853	86	1,031	5,538	13,198	106,193	19,268	69,669	17,256
Rate per 100,000 inhabitants		445.8	1.9	23.2	124.4	296.4	2,384.5	432.7	1,564.4	387.5
Boston-Quincy, MA M.D.	**1,833,760**									
(Includes Norfolk, Plymouth, and Suffolk Counties.)										
Total area actually reporting	95.6%	12,411	58	506	3,908	7,939	52,199	8,841	33,483	9,875
Estimated total	100.0%	12,680	59	521	3,962	8,138	53,842	9,168	34,553	10,121
Rate per 100,000 inhabitants		691.5	3.2	28.4	216.1	443.8	2,936.2	500.0	1,884.3	551.9
Cambridge-Newton-Framingham, MA M.D.	**1,475,450**									
(Includes Middlesex County.)										
Total area actually reporting	99.8%	3,718	11	210	922	2,575	27,875	5,688	18,750	3,437
Estimated total	100.0%	3,728	11	211	924	2,582	27,935	5,700	18,789	3,446
Rate per 100,000 inhabitants		252.7	0.7	14.3	62.6	175.0	1,893.3	386.3	1,273.4	233.6

See footnotes at end of table.

Table 6

Crime in the United States

by Metropolitan Statistical Area, 2003—Continued

Metropolitan Statistical Area	Population	Violent crime	Murder and non-negligent man-slaughter	Forcible rape	Robbery	Aggravated assault	Property crime	Burglary	Larceny-theft	Motor vehicle theft
Essex County, MA M.D.	**736,249**									
(Includes Essex County.)										
Total area actually reporting	99.5%	2,888	11	142	541	2,194	16,871	3,374	10,348	3,149
Estimated total	100.0%	2,899	11	143	543	2,202	16,938	3,387	10,392	3,159
Rate per 100,000 inhabitants		393.8	1.5	19.4	73.8	299.1	2,300.6	460.0	1,411.5	429.1
Rockingham County-Strafford County, NH M.D.	**407,977**									
(Includes Rockingham and Strafford Counties.)										
Total area actually reporting	81.8%	446	4	128	89	225	6,124	830	4,860	434
Estimated total	100.0%	546	5	157	109	275	7,477	1,013	5,934	530
Rate per 100,000 inhabitants		133.8	1.2	38.5	26.7	67.4	1,832.7	248.3	1,454.5	129.9
Boulder, CO M.S.A.	**281,932**									
(Includes Boulder County.)										
City of Boulder	95,089	214	0	52	37	125	3,930	549	3,184	197
Total area actually reporting	99.5%	848	4	111	89	644	9,201	1,520	7,108	573
Estimated total	100.0%	852	4	111	90	647	9,262	1,529	7,153	580
Rate per 100,000 inhabitants		302.2	1.4	39.4	31.9	229.5	3,285.2	542.3	2,537.1	205.7
Bremerton-Silverdale, WA M.S.A.	**238,604**									
(Includes Kitsap County.)										
City of Bremerton	36,680	416	3	66	65	282	2,010	453	1,383	174
Total area actually reporting	100.0%	993	6	175	104	708	7,033	1,735	4,715	583
Rate per 100,000 inhabitants		416.2	2.5	73.3	43.6	296.7	2,947.6	727.1	1,976.1	244.3
Bridgeport-Stamford-Norwalk, CT M.S.A.	**883,882**									
(Includes Fairfield County.)										
City of:										
Bridgeport	141,030	1,365	15	49	439	862	6,401	1,243	3,954	1,204
Stamford	120,642	271	2	11	135	123	2,167	319	1,595	253
Norwalk	84,683	355	1	13	156	185	2,470	373	1,750	347
Danbury	77,425	118	0	16	56	46	1,722	213	1,352	157
Stratford	50,503	114	2	8	73	31	1,822	314	1,290	218
Total area actually reporting	100.0%	2,429	22	122	927	1,358	19,681	3,304	13,806	2,571
Rate per 100,000 inhabitants		274.8	2.5	13.8	104.9	153.6	2,226.7	373.8	1,562.0	290.9
Brownsville-Harlingen, TX M.S.A.	**359,058**									
(Includes Cameron County.)										
City of:										
Brownsville	152,764	757	8	42	164	543	9,590	1,024	8,121	445
Harlingen	60,307	324	2	13	53	256	4,260	911	3,171	178
Total area actually reporting	100.0%	1,597	12	114	270	1,201	20,015	3,407	15,712	896
Rate per 100,000 inhabitants		444.8	3.3	31.7	75.2	334.5	5,574.3	948.9	4,375.9	249.5
Brunswick, GA M.S.A.[1]	**96,630**									
(Includes Brantley, Glynn, and McIntosh Counties.)										
City of Brunswick	15,825	133	0	16	85	32	1,627	361	1,179	87
Total area actually reporting	100.0%		2	35	146		6,609	1,111	5,244	254
Rate per 100,000 inhabitants			2.1	36.2	151.1		6,839.5	1,149.7	5,426.9	262.9
Burlington, NC M.S.A.	**137,316**									
(Includes Alamance County.)										
City of Burlington	46,498	264	3	12	89	160	3,197	638	2,402	157
Total area actually reporting	98.6%	485	6	22	126	331	5,540	1,364	3,911	265
Estimated total	100.0%	494	6	23	129	336	5,651	1,389	3,992	270
Rate per 100,000 inhabitants		359.8	4.4	16.7	93.9	244.7	4,115.3	1,011.5	2,907.2	196.6
Cape Coral-Fort Myers, FL M.S.A.	**484,345**									
(Includes Lee County.)										
City of:										
Cape Coral	114,966	312	1	11	33	267	3,763	1,044	2,544	175
Fort Myers	50,874	965	12	29	275	649	3,410	667	2,130	613
Total area actually reporting	100.0%	2,597	27	129	651	1,790	17,373	4,702	10,715	1,956
Rate per 100,000 inhabitants		536.2	5.6	26.6	134.4	369.6	3,586.9	970.8	2,212.3	403.8
Carson City, NV M.S.A.	**56,002**									
(Includes Carson City.)										
Total area actually reporting	100.0%	265	0	1	24	240	1,807	430	1,214	163
Rate per 100,000 inhabitants		473.2	0.0	1.8	42.9	428.6	3,226.7	767.8	2,167.8	291.1

See footnotes at end of table.

Table 6

Crime in the United States
by Metropolitan Statistical Area, 2003—Continued

Metropolitan Statistical Area	Population	Violent crime	Violent crime Murder and non-negligent man-slaughter	Forcible rape	Robbery	Aggravated assault	Property crime	Burglary	Larceny-theft	Motor vehicle theft
Casper, WY M.S.A.	**67,679**									
(Includes Natrona County.)										
City of Casper	50,279	125	4	15	15	91	2,768	464	2,141	163
Total area actually reporting	100.0%	157	5	16	17	119	3,521	676	2,619	226
Rate per 100,000 inhabitants		232.0	7.4	23.6	25.1	175.8	5,202.5	998.8	3,869.7	333.9
Cedar Rapids, IA M.S.A.	**242,086**									
(Includes Benton, Jones, and Linn Counties.)										
City of Cedar Rapids	122,819	387	4	46	100	237	6,456	1,110	5,046	300
Total area actually reporting	96.1%	488	4	58	107	319	7,732	1,450	5,902	380
Estimated total	100.0%	506	4	60	109	333	8,002	1,496	6,116	390
Rate per 100,000 inhabitants		209.0	1.7	24.8	45.0	137.6	3,305.4	618.0	2,526.4	161.1
Charleston-North Charleston, SC M.S.A.	**568,142**									
(Includes Berkeley, Charleston, and Dorchester Counties.)										
City of:										
Charleston	99,756	879	15	33	245	586	5,022	888	3,572	562
North Charleston	81,476	1,336	12	96	417	811	6,754	1,374	4,428	952
Total area actually reporting	100.0%	4,626	52	286	1,016	3,272	24,812	5,325	16,668	2,819
Rate per 100,000 inhabitants		814.2	9.2	50.3	178.8	575.9	4,367.2	937.3	2,933.8	496.2
Charlottesville, VA M.S.A.	**181,201**									
(Includes Albemarle, Fluvanna, Greene, and Nelson Counties and Charlottesville City.)										
City of Charlottesville	44,391	303	1	20	71	211	1,572	195	1,229	148
Total area actually reporting	100.0%	498	10	71	96	321	4,083	528	3,265	290
Rate per 100,000 inhabitants		274.8	5.5	39.2	53.0	177.2	2,253.3	291.4	1,801.9	160.0
Chattanooga, TN-GA M.S.A.	**487,287**									
(Includes Catoosa, Dade, and Walker Counties, GA and Hamilton, Marion, and Sequatchie Counties, TN.)										
City of Chattanooga, TN	156,596	1,973	19	89	464	1,401	13,087	2,357	9,306	1,424
Total area actually reporting	100.0%	2,918	31	146	574	2,167	22,494	4,374	15,929	2,191
Rate per 100,000 inhabitants		598.8	6.4	30.0	117.8	444.7	4,616.2	897.6	3,268.9	449.6
Cheyenne, WY M.S.A.	**83,315**									
(Includes Laramie County.)										
City of Cheyenne	53,931	110	0	23	24	63	2,465	258	2,095	112
Total area actually reporting	100.0%	181	1	35	29	116	3,008	376	2,487	145
Rate per 100,000 inhabitants		217.2	1.2	42.0	34.8	139.2	3,610.4	451.3	2,985.1	174.0
Chico, CA M.S.A.	**211,398**									
(Includes Butte County.)										
City of Chico	66,595	265	1	47	63	154	2,622	818	1,378	426
Total area actually reporting	100.0%	741	9	104	129	499	8,221	2,538	4,403	1,280
Rate per 100,000 inhabitants		350.5	4.3	49.2	61.0	236.0	3,888.9	1,200.6	2,082.8	605.5
Cincinnati-Middletown, OH-KY-IN M.S.A.	**2,045,569**									
(Includes Dearborn, Franklin, and Ohio Counties, IN; Boone, Bracken, Campbell, Gallatin, Grant, Kenton, and Pendleton Counties, KY; and Brown, Butler, Clermont, Hamilton, and Warren Counties, OH.)										
City of:										
Cincinnati, OH	324,297	3,643	71	307	2,184	1,081	24,167	5,922	14,796	3,449
Middletown, OH	51,250	166	0	23	64	79	3,421	700	2,562	159
Total area actually reporting	80.1%	6,476	90	761	3,046	2,579	66,018	13,331	46,594	6,093
Estimated total	100.0%	7,838	105	949	3,460	3,324	84,576	16,900	60,724	6,952
Rate per 100,000 inhabitants		383.2	5.1	46.4	169.1	162.5	4,134.6	826.2	2,968.6	339.9
Clarksville, TN-KY M.S.A.	**236,561**									
(Includes Christian and Trigg Counties, KY and Montgomery and Stewart Counties, TN.)										
City of Clarksville, TN	106,710	636	2	45	102	487	5,444	1,058	4,167	219
Total area actually reporting	76.7%	934	6	75	171	682	8,137	1,876	5,903	358
Estimated total	100.0%	1,067	7	100	195	765	9,492	2,179	6,886	427
Rate per 100,000 inhabitants		451.0	3.0	42.3	82.4	323.4	4,012.5	921.1	2,910.9	180.5
Cleveland, TN M.S.A.	**106,631**									
(Includes Bradley and Polk Counties.)										
City of Cleveland	37,667	310	3	10	30	267	2,099	452	1,518	129
Total area actually reporting	100.0%	545	6	24	36	479	3,498	893	2,342	263
Rate per 100,000 inhabitants		511.1	5.6	22.5	33.8	449.2	3,280.5	837.5	2,196.4	246.6

See footnotes at end of table.

Table 6

Crime in the United States

by Metropolitan Statistical Area, 2003—Continued

Metropolitan Statistical Area	Population	Violent crime	Murder and non-negligent man-slaughter	Forcible rape	Robbery	Aggravated assault	Property crime	Burglary	Larceny-theft	Motor vehicle theft
Coeur d'Alene, ID M.S.A.	**116,095**									
(Includes Kootenai County.)										
City of Coeur d'Alene	36,940	203	1	28	16	158	2,021	354	1,552	115
Total area actually reporting	100.0%	383	1	65	26	291	4,085	919	2,922	244
Rate per 100,000 inhabitants		329.9	0.9	56.0	22.4	250.7	3,518.7	791.6	2,516.9	210.2
College Station-Bryan, TX M.S.A.	**191,955**									
(Includes Brazos, Burleson, and Robertson Counties.)										
City of:										
College Station	71,647	164	2	40	17	105	2,762	384	2,276	102
Bryan	67,706	611	2	81	85	443	4,110	971	2,963	176
Total area actually reporting	100.0%	958	7	143	115	693	8,589	1,816	6,431	342
Rate per 100,000 inhabitants		499.1	3.6	74.5	59.9	361.0	4,474.5	946.1	3,350.3	178.2
Colorado Springs, CO M.S.A.	**570,942**									
(Includes El Paso and Teller Counties.)										
City of Colorado Springs	374,818	1,730	16	242	421	1,051	18,517	3,360	13,338	1,819
Total area actually reporting	99.7%	2,005	21	262	448	1,274	22,147	4,151	15,867	2,129
Estimated total	100.0%	2,010	21	263	449	1,277	22,223	4,163	15,922	2,138
Rate per 100,000 inhabitants		352.0	3.7	46.1	78.6	223.7	3,892.3	729.1	2,788.7	374.5
Columbia, MO M.S.A.	**150,337**									
(Includes Boone and Howard Counties.)										
City of Columbia	87,470	422	2	17	84	319	3,266	459	2,632	175
Total area actually reporting	100.0%	527	3	23	103	398	4,919	725	3,930	264
Rate per 100,000 inhabitants		350.5	2.0	15.3	68.5	264.7	3,272.0	482.2	2,614.1	175.6
Columbia, SC M.S.A.	**670,693**									
(Includes Calhoun, Fairfield, Kershaw, Lexington, Richland, and Saluda Counties.)										
City of Columbia	118,536	1,342	15	58	461	808	8,127	1,395	5,907	825
Total area actually reporting	100.0%	5,759	40	293	1,224	4,202	32,085	6,316	22,697	3,072
Rate per 100,000 inhabitants		858.7	6.0	43.7	182.5	626.5	4,783.9	941.7	3,384.1	458.0
Columbus, GA-AL M.S.A.	**286,686**									
(Includes Russell County, AL and Chattahoochee, Harris, Marion, and Muscogee Counties, GA.)										
City of Columbus, GA	188,116	837	19	22	331	465	12,978	2,204	9,555	1,219
Total area actually reporting	91.1%	1,009	22	40	379	568	14,672	2,626	10,670	1,376
Estimated total	100.0%	1,073	23	46	393	611	15,294	2,806	11,056	1,432
Rate per 100,000 inhabitants		374.3	8.0	16.0	137.1	213.1	5,334.8	978.8	3,856.5	499.5
Columbus, IN M.S.A.	**72,061**									
(Includes Bartholomew County.)										
City of Columbus	39,000	74	2	10	8	54	1,981	174	1,733	74
Total area actually reporting	99.6%	99	3	11	9	76	2,295	206	2,006	83
Estimated total	100.0%	100	3	11	9	77	2,307	208	2,015	84
Rate per 100,000 inhabitants		138.8	4.2	15.3	12.5	106.9	3,201.5	288.6	2,796.2	116.6
Columbus, OH M.S.A.	**1,662,005**									
(Includes Delaware, Fairfield, Franklin, Licking, Madison, Morrow, Pickaway, and Union Counties.)										
City of Columbus	726,151	6,215	109	615	3,332	2,159	56,338	14,650	33,343	8,345
Total area actually reporting	91.9%	7,526	131	848	3,904	2,643	83,015	20,747	52,149	10,119
Estimated total	100.0%	7,729	133	881	3,974	2,741	86,597	21,440	54,802	10,355
Rate per 100,000 inhabitants		465.0	8.0	53.0	239.1	164.9	5,210.4	1,290.0	3,297.3	623.0
Corpus Christi, TX M.S.A.	**411,414**									
(Includes Aransas, Nueces, and San Patricio Counties.)										
City of Corpus Christi	282,850	2,462	21	228	592	1,621	20,101	3,757	15,064	1,280
Total area actually reporting	100.0%	2,801	25	273	648	1,855	25,585	5,149	18,932	1,504
Rate per 100,000 inhabitants		680.8	6.1	66.4	157.5	450.9	6,218.8	1,251.5	4,601.7	365.6
Cumberland, MD-WV M.S.A.	**102,107**									
(Includes Allegany County, MD and Mineral County, WV.)										
City of Cumberland, MD	21,278	164	1	15	27	121	1,205	266	896	43
Total area actually reporting	99.3%	320	2	23	43	252	2,751	700	1,930	121
Estimated total	100.0%	321	2	23	43	253	2,770	703	1,945	122
Rate per 100,000 inhabitants		314.4	2.0	22.5	42.1	247.8	2,712.8	688.5	1,904.9	119.5

See footnotes at end of table.

Table 6

Crime in the United States
by Metropolitan Statistical Area, 2003—Continued

Metropolitan Statistical Area	Population	Violent crime	Murder and non-negligent man-slaughter	Forcible rape	Robbery	Aggravated assault	Property crime	Burglary	Larceny-theft	Motor vehicle theft
Dallas-Fort Worth-Arlington, TX M.S.A.	**5,569,323**									
(Includes the Metropolitan Divisions of Dallas-Plano-Irving and Fort Worth-Arlington.)										
City of:										
Dallas	1,230,302	16,865	226	601	7,963	8,075	97,900	21,927	58,554	17,419
Fort Worth	576,339	3,751	57	243	1,462	1,989	37,529	8,788	25,092	3,649
Arlington	355,385	1,863	9	167	598	1,089	19,921	3,606	14,656	1,659
Plano	241,793	709	5	48	134	522	9,453	1,527	7,254	672
Irving	199,168	873	7	75	258	533	10,007	1,515	7,254	1,238
Carrollton	116,897	238	2	15	77	144	4,039	808	2,742	489
Richardson	98,463	241	1	16	101	123	3,619	698	2,593	328
Denton	91,754	367	3	67	63	234	3,501	673	2,598	230
McKinney	74,217	161	0	42	36	83	2,017	477	1,408	132
Total area actually reporting	99.9%	32,406	384	1,931	12,401	17,690	283,191	60,557	187,930	34,704
Estimated total	100.0%	32,413	384	1,932	12,403	17,694	283,281	60,575	187,994	34,712
Rate per 100,000 inhabitants		582.0	6.9	34.7	222.7	317.7	5,086.5	1,087.7	3,375.5	623.3
Dallas-Plano-Irving, TX M.D.	**3,729,921**									
(Includes Collin, Dallas, Delta, Denton, Ellis, Hunt, Kaufman, and Rockwall Counties.)										
Total area actually reporting	99.9%	24,364	296	1,253	9,894	12,921	194,170	41,624	125,632	26,914
Estimated total	100.0%	24,371	296	1,254	9,896	12,925	194,260	41,642	125,696	26,922
Rate per 100,000 inhabitants		653.4	7.9	33.6	265.3	346.5	5,208.2	1,116.4	3,369.9	721.8
Fort Worth-Arlington, TX M.D.	**1,839,402**									
(Includes Johnson, Parker, Tarrant, and Wise Counties.)										
Total area actually reporting	100.0%	8,042	88	678	2,507	4,769	89,021	18,933	62,298	7,790
Rate per 100,000 inhabitants		437.2	4.8	36.9	136.3	259.3	4,839.7	1,029.3	3,386.9	423.5
Dalton, GA M.S.A.	**127,406**									
(Includes Murray and Whitfield Counties.)										
City of Dalton	30,329	195	0	4	42	149	1,840	285	1,426	129
Total area actually reporting	98.3%	442	4	16	62	360	5,174	1,130	3,577	467
Estimated total	100.0%	454	4	17	66	367	5,296	1,150	3,667	479
Rate per 100,000 inhabitants		356.3	3.1	13.3	51.8	288.1	4,156.8	902.6	2,878.2	376.0
Danville, VA M.S.A.	**110,733**									
(Includes Pittsylvania County and Danville City.)										
City of Danville	48,202	296	5	20	77	194	2,214	313	1,763	138
Total area actually reporting	100.0%	394	10	36	88	260	2,747	524	2,003	220
Rate per 100,000 inhabitants		355.8	9.0	32.5	79.5	234.8	2,480.7	473.2	1,808.9	198.7
Dayton, OH M.S.A.	**847,787**									
(Includes Greene, Miami, Montgomery, and Preble Counties.)										
City of Dayton	162,876	1,654	28	173	951	502	13,230	3,814	6,874	2,542
Total area actually reporting	92.5%	2,621	40	421	1,347	813	33,802	7,594	21,973	4,235
Estimated total	100.0%	2,736	41	437	1,387	871	35,705	7,923	23,431	4,351
Rate per 100,000 inhabitants		322.7	4.8	51.5	163.6	102.7	4,211.6	934.6	2,763.8	513.2
Decatur, AL M.S.A.	**146,845**									
(Includes Lawrence and Morgan Counties.)										
City of Decatur	54,112	221	4	11	117	89	3,957	780	3,001	176
Total area actually reporting	98.5%	286	5	15	133	133	5,470	1,232	3,983	255
Estimated total	100.0%	295	5	16	136	138	5,569	1,251	4,056	262
Rate per 100,000 inhabitants		200.9	3.4	10.9	92.6	94.0	3,792.4	851.9	2,762.1	178.4
Deltona-Daytona Beach-Ormond Beach, FL M.S.A.	**467,845**									
(Includes Volusia County.)										
City of:										
Daytona Beach	65,788	1,214	5	81	420	708	6,141	1,567	3,651	923
Ormond Beach	37,883	110	1	6	33	70	1,217	428	714	75
Total area actually reporting	100.0%	3,103	18	223	725	2,137	19,336	5,149	12,089	2,098
Rate per 100,000 inhabitants		663.3	3.8	47.7	155.0	456.8	4,133.0	1,100.6	2,584.0	448.4

See footnotes at end of table.

Table 6

Crime in the United States
by Metropolitan Statistical Area, 2003—Continued

Metropolitan Statistical Area	Population	Violent crime	Murder and non-negligent man-slaughter	Forcible rape	Robbery	Aggravated assault	Property crime	Burglary	Larceny-theft	Motor vehicle theft
Denver-Aurora, CO M.S.A.	**2,302,921**									
(Includes Adams, Arapahoe, Broomfield, Clear Creek, Denver, Douglas, Elbert, Gilpin, Jefferson, and Park Counties.)										
City of:										
Denver	565,905	3,531	63	304	1,421	1,743	29,064	7,097	14,839	7,128
Aurora	288,830	1,691	18	213	571	889	15,253	2,329	10,272	2,652
Total area actually reporting	93.3%	8,561	119	961	2,676	4,805	94,136	17,535	60,331	16,270
Estimated total	100.0%	8,993	123	1,013	2,766	5,091	100,575	18,542	64,986	17,047
Rate per 100,000 inhabitants		390.5	5.3	44.0	120.1	221.1	4,367.3	805.2	2,821.9	740.2
Des Moines, IA M.S.A.	**498,493**									
(Includes Dallas, Guthrie, Madison, Polk, and Warren Counties.)										
City of Des Moines	198,568	699	8	92	284	315	12,115	1,527	9,692	896
Total area actually reporting	98.0%	1,242	12	143	339	748	19,465	3,002	15,144	1,319
Estimated total	100.0%	1,261	12	145	341	763	19,752	3,051	15,371	1,330
Rate per 100,000 inhabitants		253.0	2.4	29.1	68.4	153.1	3,962.3	612.0	3,083.5	266.8
Detroit-Warren-Livonia, MI M.S.A.[1]	**4,497,319**									
(Includes the Metropolitan Divisions of Detroit-Livonia-Dearborn and Warren-Farmington Hills-Troy.)										
City of:										
Detroit	927,766	18,724	366	814	5,817	11,727	64,809	14,100	25,353	25,356
Warren[1]	138,077	790	3	80	188	519		763	2,301	
Livonia	100,636	185	0	13	56	116	2,506	389	1,846	271
Dearborn	98,121	1,099	0	13	144	942	5,098	525	3,257	1,316
Farmington Hills	81,666	146	0	18	26	102	1,751	355	1,236	160
Troy	81,150	100	1	11	28	60	2,024	292	1,573	159
Southfield	78,088	1,072	2	34	139	897	4,379	754	2,499	1,126
Pontiac	66,331	912	8	73	156	675	2,356	796	1,151	409
Taylor	66,087	267	2	40	58	167	3,115	466	2,095	554
Total area actually reporting	99.4%	30,165	449	1,973	8,114	19,629		30,685	89,611	
Estimated total	100.0%	30,229	449	1,980	8,130	19,670		30,803	90,089	
Rate per 100,000 inhabitants		672.2	10.0	44.0	180.8	437.4		684.9	2,003.2	
Detroit-Livonia-Dearborn, MI M.D.[1]	**2,051,552**									
(Includes Wayne County.)										
Total area actually reporting	99.0%	23,027	400	1,133	6,805	14,689	102,070	20,346	48,938	32,786
Estimated total	100.0%	23,079	400	1,139	6,818	14,722	102,647	20,442	49,329	32,876
Rate per 100,000 inhabitants		1,125.0	19.5	55.5	332.3	717.6	5,003.4	996.4	2,404.5	1,602.5
Warren-Farmington Hills-Troy, MI M.D.[1]	**2,445,767**									
(Includes Lapeer, Livingston, Macomb, Oakland, and St. Clair Counties.)										
Total area actually reporting	99.8%	7,138	49	840	1,309	4,940		10,339	40,673	
Estimated total	100.0%	7,149	49	841	1,312	4,947		10,361	40,760	
Rate per 100,000 inhabitants		292.3	2.0	34.4	53.6	202.3		423.6	1,666.6	
Dothan, AL M.S.A.	**132,022**									
(Includes Geneva, Henry, and Houston Counties.)										
City of Dothan	58,433	251	4	38	109	100	2,970	680	2,139	151
Total area actually reporting	95.9%	377	10	50	116	201	4,074	1,007	2,825	242
Estimated total	100.0%	399	10	52	123	214	4,316	1,054	3,003	259
Rate per 100,000 inhabitants		302.2	7.6	39.4	93.2	162.1	3,269.2	798.4	2,274.6	196.2
Dover, DE M.S.A.	**132,710**									
(Includes Kent County.)										
City of Dover	32,989	239	1	24	47	167	1,917	166	1,647	104
Total area actually reporting	100.0%	983	5	82	111	785	4,563	864	3,435	264
Rate per 100,000 inhabitants		740.7	3.8	61.8	83.6	591.5	3,438.3	651.0	2,588.4	198.9
Dubuque, IA M.S.A.	**89,609**									
(Includes Dubuque County.)										
City of Dubuque	57,173	235	2	17	15	201	1,814	398	1,319	97
Total area actually reporting	100.0%	272	2	23	15	232	2,089	473	1,485	131
Rate per 100,000 inhabitants		303.5	2.2	25.7	16.7	258.9	2,331.2	527.8	1,657.2	146.2

See footnotes at end of table.

Table 6

Crime in the United States

by Metropolitan Statistical Area, 2003—Continued

Metropolitan Statistical Area	Population	Violent crime	Murder and non-negligent man-slaughter	Forcible rape	Robbery	Aggravated assault	Property crime	Burglary	Larceny-theft	Motor vehicle theft
Duluth, MN-WI M.S.A.	**278,385**									
(Includes Carlton and St. Louis Counties, MN and Douglas County, WI.)										
City of Duluth, MN	87,102	290	4	53	83	150	4,794	773	3,640	381
Total area actually reporting	100.0%	604	9	134	107	354	10,066	2,157	7,193	716
Rate per 100,000 inhabitants		217.0	3.2	48.1	38.4	127.2	3,615.9	774.8	2,583.8	257.2
Durham, NC M.S.A.	**449,820**									
(Includes Chatham, Durham, Orange, and Person Counties.)										
City of Durham	197,965	1,663	22	76	883	682	13,621	3,528	9,027	1,066
Total area actually reporting	100.0%	2,462	25	116	1,129	1,192	23,752	6,092	16,121	1,539
Rate per 100,000 inhabitants		547.3	5.6	25.8	251.0	265.0	5,280.3	1,354.3	3,583.9	342.1
El Centro, CA M.S.A.	**147,782**									
(Includes Imperial County.)										
City of El Centro	38,079	325	0	7	52	266	1,675	584	893	198
Total area actually reporting	100.0%	773	12	21	136	604	5,269	1,839	2,587	843
Rate per 100,000 inhabitants		523.1	8.1	14.2	92.0	408.7	3,565.4	1,244.4	1,750.6	570.4
Elkhart-Goshen, IN M.S.A.	**187,572**									
(Includes Elkhart County.)										
City of:										
Elkhart	52,090	187	6	25	136	20	4,203	872	3,022	309
Goshen	29,859	124	0	1	9	114	1,336	154	1,131	51
Total area actually reporting	100.0%	387	8	40	166	173	7,783	1,519	5,634	630
Rate per 100,000 inhabitants		206.3	4.3	21.3	88.5	92.2	4,149.3	809.8	3,003.6	335.9
El Paso, TX M.S.A.	**708,407**									
(Includes El Paso County.)										
City of El Paso	586,392	3,502	21	219	581	2,681	21,780	2,185	17,735	1,860
Total area actually reporting	100.0%	3,920	21	263	638	2,998	24,786	2,689	19,983	2,114
Rate per 100,000 inhabitants		553.4	3.0	37.1	90.1	423.2	3,498.8	379.6	2,820.8	298.4
Erie, PA M.S.A.	**281,060**									
(Includes Erie County.)										
City of Erie	102,373	447	3	70	191	183	3,134	725	2,284	125
Total area actually reporting	98.2%	682	6	116	226	334	6,240	1,456	4,499	285
Estimated total	100.0%	694	6	117	229	342	6,350	1,472	4,585	293
Rate per 100,000 inhabitants		246.9	2.1	41.6	81.5	121.7	2,259.3	523.7	1,631.3	104.2
Eugene-Springfield, OR M.S.A.	**330,199**									
(Includes Lane County.)										
City of:										
Eugene	141,913	478	2	53	176	247	8,904	1,424	6,591	889
Springfield	54,619	158	0	16	41	101	4,274	639	3,038	597
Total area actually reporting	100.0%	867	5	111	252	499	16,581	3,064	11,657	1,860
Rate per 100,000 inhabitants		262.6	1.5	33.6	76.3	151.1	5,021.5	927.9	3,530.3	563.3
Fairbanks, AK M.S.A.	**32,652**									
(Includes Fairbanks North Star Borough.)										
City of Fairbanks	31,021	289	4	42	42	201	1,561	271	1,158	132
Total area actually reporting	100.0%	301	4	42	42	213	1,838	290	1,402	146
Rate per 100,000 inhabitants		921.8	12.3	128.6	128.6	652.3	5,629.1	888.2	4,293.8	447.1
Fargo, ND-MN M.S.A.	**177,421**									
(Includes Clay County, MN and Cass County, ND.)										
City of Fargo, ND	91,165	77	0	41	11	25	2,283	335	1,759	189
Total area actually reporting	100.0%	177	2	62	24	89	4,402	703	3,387	312
Rate per 100,000 inhabitants		99.8	1.1	34.9	13.5	50.2	2,481.1	396.2	1,909.0	175.9
Farmington, NM M.S.A.	**121,636**									
(Includes San Juan County.)										
City of Farmington	40,991	434	3	53	24	354	1,493	389	974	130
Total area actually reporting	100.0%	688	4	85	39	560	3,130	746	2,161	223
Rate per 100,000 inhabitants		565.6	3.3	69.9	32.1	460.4	2,573.3	613.3	1,776.6	183.3
Fayetteville, NC M.S.A.	**342,912**									
(Includes Cumberland and Hoke Counties.)										
City of Fayetteville	125,587	1,230	13	33	492	692	9,652	2,035	6,939	678
Total area actually reporting	100.0%	2,369	23	85	769	1,492	19,062	5,388	12,495	1,179
Rate per 100,000 inhabitants		690.8	6.7	24.8	224.3	435.1	5,558.9	1,571.2	3,643.8	343.8

See footnotes at end of table.

Table 6

Crime in the United States
by Metropolitan Statistical Area, 2003—Continued

Metropolitan Statistical Area	Population	Violent crime	Murder and non-negligent man-slaughter	Forcible rape	Robbery	Aggravated assault	Property crime	Burglary	Larceny-theft	Motor vehicle theft
Fayetteville-Springdale-Rogers, AR-MO M.S.A.[1]	**370,164**									
(Includes Benton, Madison, and Washington Counties, AR and McDonald County, MO.)										
City of:										
Fayetteville, AR	61,082	251	0	36	36	179	2,895	292	2,464	139
Springdale, AR	51,235	160	0	32	19	109	2,055	281	1,639	135
Rogers, AR	41,785	68	0	30	7	31	1,858	192	1,603	63
Bentonville, AR	24,225	39	1	22	3	13	782	121	630	31
Total area actually reporting	100.0%	891	7	178	78	628	10,225	1,730	7,910	585
Rate per 100,000 inhabitants		240.7	1.9	48.1	21.1	169.7	2,762.3	467.4	2,136.9	158.0
Flagstaff, AZ M.S.A.	**123,037**									
(Includes Coconino County.)										
City of Flagstaff	56,430	401	1	44	45	311	4,614	643	3,770	201
Total area actually reporting	100.0%	635	2	74	56	503	6,587	1,061	5,230	296
Rate per 100,000 inhabitants		516.1	1.6	60.1	45.5	408.8	5,353.7	862.3	4,250.8	240.6
Flint, MI M.S.A.	**442,720**									
(Includes Genesee County.)										
City of Flint	122,121	1,484	28	124	338	994	6,714	2,063	3,353	1,298
Total area actually reporting	99.9%	2,471	37	289	558	1,587	17,175	4,428	10,416	2,331
Estimated total	100.0%	2,472	37	289	558	1,588	17,186	4,430	10,424	2,332
Rate per 100,000 inhabitants		558.4	8.4	65.3	126.0	358.7	3,881.9	1,000.6	2,354.5	526.7
Florence-Muscle Shoals, AL M.S.A.	**142,417**									
(Includes Colbert and Lauderdale Counties.)										
City of:										
Florence	35,928	166	0	15	42	109	1,601	304	1,241	56
Muscle Shoals	12,271	43	0	4	9	30	665	112	532	21
Total area actually reporting	99.1%	379	5	30	70	274	4,319	950	3,199	170
Estimated total	100.0%	384	5	30	72	277	4,373	960	3,239	174
Rate per 100,000 inhabitants		269.6	3.5	21.1	50.6	194.5	3,070.6	674.1	2,274.3	122.2
Florence, SC M.S.A.	**197,067**									
(Includes Darlington and Florence Counties.)										
City of Florence	30,311	478	6	21	155	296	3,749	611	2,892	246
Total area actually reporting	100.0%	2,059	22	92	347	1,598	12,119	2,988	8,369	762
Rate per 100,000 inhabitants		1,044.8	11.2	46.7	176.1	810.9	6,149.7	1,516.2	4,246.8	386.7
Fond du Lac, WI M.S.A.	**98,368**									
(Includes Fond du Lac County.)										
City of Fond du Lac	42,537	46	0	10	7	29	1,332	177	1,106	49
Total area actually reporting	100.0%	73	0	18	8	47	2,095	331	1,666	98
Rate per 100,000 inhabitants		74.2	0.0	18.3	8.1	47.8	2,129.8	336.5	1,693.6	99.6
Fort Smith, AR-OK M.S.A.[1]	**279,891**									
(Includes Crawford, Franklin, and Sebastian Counties, AR and Le Flore and Sequoyah Counties, OK.)										
City of Fort Smith, AR	81,989	804	12	74	135	583	7,173	1,111	5,764	298
Total area actually reporting	95.9%	1,329	20	108	153	1,048	10,222	2,197	7,557	468
Estimated total	100.0%	1,354	20	111	155	1,068	10,396	2,256	7,658	482
Rate per 100,000 inhabitants		483.8	7.1	39.7	55.4	381.6	3,714.3	806.0	2,736.1	172.2
Fort Walton Beach-Crestview-Destin, FL M.S.A.	**178,924**									
(Includes Okaloosa County.)										
City of:										
Fort Walton Beach	20,466	122	0	16	19	87	772	116	598	58
Crestview	15,634	60	0	3	15	42	581	124	439	18
Total area actually reporting	100.0%	603	3	52	118	430	4,880	940	3,646	294
Rate per 100,000 inhabitants		337.0	1.7	29.1	65.9	240.3	2,727.4	525.4	2,037.7	164.3
Fort Wayne, IN M.S.A.	**399,002**									
(Includes Allen, Wells, and Whitley Counties.)										
City of Fort Wayne	211,317	772	19	118	354	281	11,113	2,188	8,145	780
Total area actually reporting	92.5%	913	19	144	385	365	13,719	2,685	10,048	986
Estimated total	100.0%	971	19	149	396	407	14,343	2,808	10,490	1,045
Rate per 100,000 inhabitants		243.4	4.8	37.3	99.2	102.0	3,594.7	703.8	2,629.1	261.9
Fresno, CA M.S.A.[1]	**843,389**									
(Includes Fresno County.)										
City of Fresno	449,898	3,505	37	164	1,215	2,089	27,196	3,927	17,608	5,661
Total area actually reporting	100.0%	5,055	61	270	1,505	3,219	42,465	7,148	26,932	8,385
Rate per 100,000 inhabitants		599.4	7.2	32.0	178.4	381.7	5,035.0	847.5	3,193.3	994.2

See footnotes at end of table.

Table 6

Crime in the United States

by Metropolitan Statistical Area, 2003—Continued

Metropolitan Statistical Area	Population	Violent crime	Murder and non-negligent man-slaughter	Forcible rape	Robbery	Aggravated assault	Property crime	Burglary	Larceny-theft	Motor vehicle theft
				Violent crime					*Property crime*	
Gainesville, FL M.S.A.	**241,311**									
(Includes Alachua and Gilchrist Counties.)										
City of Gainesville	96,919	1,004	5	55	197	747	5,049	1,208	3,370	471
Total area actually reporting	100.0%	2,068	7	115	308	1,638	10,608	2,662	7,047	899
Rate per 100,000 inhabitants		857.0	2.9	47.7	127.6	678.8	4,396.0	1,103.1	2,920.3	372.5
Gainesville, GA M.S.A.	**154,447**									
(Includes Hall County.)										
City of Gainesville	28,374	177	1	8	50	118	2,069	286	1,660	123
Total area actually reporting	99.9%	417	7	31	79	300	5,353	1,049	3,748	556
Estimated total	100.0%	417	7	31	79	300	5,361	1,050	3,754	557
Rate per 100,000 inhabitants		270.0	4.5	20.1	51.2	194.2	3,471.1	679.8	2,430.6	360.6
Glens Falls, NY M.S.A.	**125,314**									
(Includes Warren and Washington Counties.)										
City of Glens Falls	14,218	35	0	1	6	28	367	59	299	9
Total area actually reporting	100.0%	319	1	36	18	264	2,335	451	1,832	52
Rate per 100,000 inhabitants		254.6	0.8	28.7	14.4	210.7	1,863.3	359.9	1,461.9	41.5
Goldsboro, NC M.S.A.	**114,136**									
(Includes Wayne County.)										
City of Goldsboro	38,881	390	5	9	99	277	2,577	608	1,823	146
Total area actually reporting	99.8%	585	10	9	148	418	4,910	1,479	3,139	292
Estimated total	100.0%	586	10	9	148	419	4,924	1,482	3,149	293
Rate per 100,000 inhabitants		513.4	8.8	7.9	129.7	367.1	4,314.2	1,298.5	2,759.0	256.7
Grand Forks, ND-MN M.S.A.	**96,253**									
(Includes Polk County, MN and Grand Forks County, ND.)										
City of Grand Forks, ND	48,525	68	0	13	9	46	1,989	255	1,618	116
Total area actually reporting	98.5%	130	1	26	11	92	3,098	466	2,452	180
Estimated total	100.0%	131	1	26	11	93	3,148	474	2,491	183
Rate per 100,000 inhabitants		136.1	1.0	27.0	11.4	96.6	3,270.5	492.5	2,588.0	190.1
Grand Junction, CO M.S.A.	**122,608**									
(Includes Mesa County.)										
City of Grand Junction	43,593	233	0	34	17	182	3,236	513	2,561	162
Total area actually reporting	94.2%	324	1	35	32	256	4,694	845	3,571	278
Estimated total	100.0%	345	1	37	37	270	5,010	893	3,801	316
Rate per 100,000 inhabitants		281.4	0.8	30.2	30.2	220.2	4,086.2	728.3	3,100.1	257.7
Grand Rapids-Wyoming, MI M.S.A.[1]	**760,075**									
(Includes Barry, Ionia, Kent, and Newaygo Counties.)										
City of:										
Grand Rapids[1]	197,173	2,070	11	68	533	1,458	9,326	2,048	6,569	709
Wyoming	70,535	331	0	51	70	210	2,189	628	1,347	214
Total area actually reporting	99.5%	3,436	22	396	708	2,310	23,853	5,264	17,124	1,465
Estimated total	100.0%	3,446	22	397	710	2,317	23,973	5,284	17,210	1,479
Rate per 100,000 inhabitants		453.4	2.9	52.2	93.4	304.8	3,154.0	695.2	2,264.3	194.6
Great Falls, MT M.S.A.	**80,102**									
(Includes Cascade County.)										
City of Great Falls	56,549	293	5	13	58	217	4,056	376	3,534	146
Total area actually reporting	100.0%	334	6	15	59	254	4,525	398	3,955	172
Rate per 100,000 inhabitants		417.0	7.5	18.7	73.7	317.1	5,649.0	496.9	4,937.5	214.7
Greeley, CO M.S.A.	**207,022**									
(Includes Weld County.)										
City of Greeley	82,919	279	2	49	52	176	5,329	689	4,255	385
Total area actually reporting	92.2%	523	3	83	75	362	8,262	1,323	6,204	735
Estimated total	100.0%	570	3	89	85	393	8,979	1,432	6,725	822
Rate per 100,000 inhabitants		275.3	1.4	43.0	41.1	189.8	4,337.2	691.7	3,248.4	397.1
Greensboro-High Point, NC M.S.A.	**664,819**									
(Includes Guilford, Randolph, and Rockingham Counties.)										
City of:										
Greensboro	230,606	1,547	36	97	697	717	13,758	3,255	9,455	1,048
High Point	90,275	774	8	34	260	472	5,824	1,563	3,712	549
Total area actually reporting	99.4%	3,071	56	175	1,176	1,664	31,755	7,917	21,556	2,282
Estimated total	100.0%	3,087	56	176	1,181	1,674	31,977	7,966	21,718	2,293
Rate per 100,000 inhabitants		464.3	8.4	26.5	177.6	251.8	4,809.9	1,198.2	3,266.8	344.9

See footnotes at end of table.

Table 6

Crime in the United States
by Metropolitan Statistical Area, 2003—Continued

Metropolitan Statistical Area	Population	Violent crime	Murder and non-negligent man-slaughter	Forcible rape	Robbery	Aggravated assault	Property crime	Burglary	Larceny-theft	Motor vehicle theft
Greenville, NC M.S.A.	**158,296**									
(Includes Greene and Pitt Counties.)										
City of Greenville	66,183	596	4	10	253	329	4,662	1,348	3,097	217
Total area actually reporting	100.0%	1,019	6	44	332	637	8,378	2,633	5,353	392
Rate per 100,000 inhabitants		643.7	3.8	27.8	209.7	402.4	5,292.6	1,663.3	3,381.6	247.6
Greenville, SC M.S.A.	**580,535**									
(Includes Greenville, Laurens, and Pickens Counties.)										
City of Greenville	56,728	571	2	33	106	430	4,264	781	3,192	291
Total area actually reporting	100.0%	3,520	35	213	500	2,772	21,373	5,319	14,502	1,552
Rate per 100,000 inhabitants		606.3	6.0	36.7	86.1	477.5	3,681.6	916.2	2,498.0	267.3
Hanford-Corcoran, CA M.S.A.	**136,460**									
(Includes Kings County.)										
City of:										
Hanford	44,815	162	1	15	38	108	1,614	251	1,172	191
Corcoran	21,149	31	0	2	9	20	273	94	164	15
Total area actually reporting	100.0%	434	5	35	83	311	3,483	725	2,239	519
Rate per 100,000 inhabitants		318.0	3.7	25.6	60.8	227.9	2,552.4	531.3	1,640.8	380.3
Harrisburg-Carlisle, PA M.S.A.	**515,819**									
(Includes Cumberland, Dauphin, and Perry Counties.)										
City of:										
Harrisburg	48,659	687	6	29	375	277	2,395	543	1,698	154
Carlisle	18,080	53	0	13	28	12	500	58	423	19
Total area actually reporting	93.1%	1,432	13	138	587	694	10,878	2,077	8,228	573
Estimated total	100.0%	1,513	14	144	608	747	11,629	2,185	8,816	628
Rate per 100,000 inhabitants		293.3	2.7	27.9	117.9	144.8	2,254.5	423.6	1,709.1	121.7
Harrisonburg, VA M.S.A.	**110,950**									
(Includes Rockingham County and Harrisonburg City.)										
City of Harrisonburg	41,429	106	0	13	23	70	1,179	183	927	69
Total area actually reporting	100.0%	160	0	33	25	102	1,879	348	1,412	119
Rate per 100,000 inhabitants		144.2	0.0	29.7	22.5	91.9	1,693.6	313.7	1,272.6	107.3
Hinesville-Fort Stewart, GA M.S.A.	**73,563**									
(Includes Liberty and Long Counties.)										
City of:										
Hinesville	30,985	168	4	9	63	92	1,846	302	1,471	73
Total area actually reporting	96.4%	254	4	14	85	151	2,664	522	2,028	114
Estimated total	100.0%	269	4	15	90	160	2,812	546	2,137	129
Rate per 100,000 inhabitants		365.7	5.4	20.4	122.3	217.5	3,822.6	742.2	2,905.0	175.4
Holland-Grand Haven, MI M.S.A.	**246,636**									
(Includes Ottawa County.)										
City of:										
Holland	27,438	91	0	21	4	66	916	134	750	32
Grand Haven	10,962	36	0	15	2	19	433	76	332	25
Total area actually reporting	97.1%	447	1	164	20	262	4,778	925	3,602	251
Estimated total	100.0%	466	1	166	24	275	4,999	962	3,760	277
Rate per 100,000 inhabitants		188.9	0.4	67.3	9.7	111.5	2,026.9	390.0	1,524.5	112.3
Honolulu, HI M.S.A.	**905,301**									
(Includes Honolulu County.)										
City of Honolulu	905,301	2,606	15	266	989	1,336	48,306	7,967	32,086	8,253
Total area actually reporting	100.0%	2,606	15	266	989	1,336	48,306	7,967	32,086	8,253
Rate per 100,000 inhabitants		287.9	1.7	29.4	109.2	147.6	5,335.9	880.0	3,544.2	911.6
Houma-Bayou Cane-Thibodaux, LA M.S.A.	**197,462**									
(Includes Lafourche and Terrebonne Parishes.)										
City of:										
Houma	32,228	356	2	25	61	268	1,764	280	1,382	102
Thibodaux	14,558	93	0	8	13	72	636	150	471	15
Total area actually reporting	98.7%	968	7	87	144	730	7,790	1,677	5,679	434
Estimated total	100.0%	984	7	88	147	742	7,945	1,703	5,799	443
Rate per 100,000 inhabitants		498.3	3.5	44.6	74.4	375.8	4,023.6	862.4	2,936.8	224.3

See footnotes at end of table.

Table 6

Crime in the United States
by Metropolitan Statistical Area, 2003—Continued

Metropolitan Statistical Area	Population	Violent crime	Murder and non-negligent man-slaughter	Forcible rape	Robbery	Aggravated assault	Property crime	Burglary	Larceny-theft	Motor vehicle theft
Houston-Baytown-Sugar Land, TX M.S.A.	**5,063,922**									
(Includes Austin, Brazoria, Chambers, Fort Bend, Galveston, Harris, Liberty, Montgomery, San Jacinto, and Waller Counties.)										
City of:										
Houston	2,041,081	23,988	278	768	10,985	11,957	120,005	26,522	72,032	21,451
Baytown	68,407	264	5	31	75	153	2,925	590	2,103	232
Sugar Land	69,666	154	5	10	42	97	1,675	262	1,311	102
Galveston	57,566	479	8	85	183	203	3,417	636	2,410	371
Total area actually reporting	99.9%	37,396	407	1,811	14,450	20,728	220,696	50,479	139,040	31,177
Estimated total	100.0%	37,397	407	1,811	14,450	20,729	220,718	50,483	139,056	31,179
Rate per 100,000 inhabitants		738.5	8.0	35.8	285.4	409.3	4,358.6	996.9	2,746.0	615.7
Huntsville, AL M.S.A.	**354,865**									
(Includes Limestone and Madison Counties.)										
City of Huntsville	163,052	988	19	84	316	569	9,388	1,740	6,774	874
Total area actually reporting	100.0%	1,255	22	120	372	741	14,035	2,924	9,882	1,229
Rate per 100,000 inhabitants		353.7	6.2	33.8	104.8	208.8	3,955.0	824.0	2,784.7	346.3
Idaho Falls, ID M.S.A.	**106,934**									
(Includes Bonneville and Jefferson Counties.)										
City of Idaho Falls	52,056	148	2	22	12	112	1,941	244	1,553	144
Total area actually reporting	100.0%	242	2	47	16	177	2,894	462	2,228	204
Rate per 100,000 inhabitants		226.3	1.9	44.0	15.0	165.5	2,706.3	432.0	2,083.5	190.8
Indianapolis, IN M.S.A.	**1,584,030**									
(Includes Boone, Brown, Hamilton, Hancock, Hendricks, Johnson, Marion, Morgan, Putnam, and Shelby Counties.)										
City of Indianapolis	800,167	7,069	107	420	2,828	3,714	45,386	10,062	27,891	7,433
Total area actually reporting	91.9%	8,408	116	501	3,047	4,744	59,286	12,298	38,564	8,424
Estimated total	100.0%	8,685	119	522	3,103	4,941	62,374	12,866	40,797	8,711
Rate per 100,000 inhabitants		548.3	7.5	33.0	195.9	311.9	3,937.7	812.2	2,575.5	549.9
Iowa City, IA M.S.A.	**135,742**									
(Includes Johnson and Washington Counties.)										
City of Iowa City	63,975	368	0	28	47	293	2,031	343	1,606	82
Total area actually reporting	100.0%	535	1	62	58	414	3,601	677	2,779	145
Rate per 100,000 inhabitants		394.1	0.7	45.7	42.7	305.0	2,652.8	498.7	2,047.3	106.8
Jackson, MI M.S.A.	**161,445**									
(Includes Jackson County.)										
City of Jackson	35,618	196	5	39	63	89	2,077	363	1,573	141
Total area actually reporting	100.0%	532	10	102	93	327	4,925	1,026	3,564	335
Rate per 100,000 inhabitants		329.5	6.2	63.2	57.6	202.5	3,050.6	635.5	2,207.6	207.5
Jackson, MS M.S.A.	**507,181**									
(Includes Copiah, Hinds, Madison, Rankin, and Simpson Counties.)										
City of Jackson	181,479	1,648	45	179	962	462	15,496	4,369	8,323	2,804
Total area actually reporting	79.7%	1,987	58	230	1,044	655	20,997	5,900	11,834	3,263
Estimated total	100.0%	2,247	63	262	1,127	795	24,864	6,792	14,491	3,581
Rate per 100,000 inhabitants		443.0	12.4	51.7	222.2	156.7	4,902.4	1,339.2	2,857.2	706.1
Jackson, TN M.S.A.	**110,128**									
(Includes Chester and Madison Counties.)										
City of Jackson	61,100	691	2	35	198	456	4,329	980	2,964	385
Total area actually reporting	100.0%	863	2	56	212	593	5,573	1,358	3,724	491
Rate per 100,000 inhabitants		783.6	1.8	50.8	192.5	538.5	5,060.5	1,233.1	3,381.5	445.8
Jacksonville, FL M.S.A.	**1,199,156**									
(Includes Baker, Clay, Duval, Nassau, and St. Johns Counties.)										
City of Jacksonville	776,417	6,729	92	213	2,344	4,080	43,791	8,910	30,043	4,838
Total area actually reporting	100.0%	9,051	107	290	2,602	6,052	54,724	11,334	37,737	5,653
Rate per 100,000 inhabitants		754.8	8.9	24.2	217.0	504.7	4,563.5	945.2	3,147.0	471.4
Janesville, WI M.S.A.	**154,973**									
(Includes Rock County.)										
City of Janesville	61,269	148	0	20	38	90	3,251	566	2,583	102
Total area actually reporting	100.0%	350	3	42	99	206	6,058	1,132	4,662	264
Rate per 100,000 inhabitants		225.8	1.9	27.1	63.9	132.9	3,909.1	730.4	3,008.3	170.4

See footnotes at end of table.

Table 6

Crime in the United States
by Metropolitan Statistical Area, 2003—Continued

Metropolitan Statistical Area	Population	Violent crime	Murder and non-negligent man-slaughter	Forcible rape	Robbery	Aggravated assault	Property crime	Burglary	Larceny-theft	Motor vehicle theft
Jefferson City, MO M.S.A.	**142,965**									
(Includes Callaway, Cole, Moniteau, and Osage Counties.)										
City of Jefferson City	39,299	276	3	27	21	225	1,326	190	1,064	72
Total area actually reporting	100.0%	444	5	43	43	353	2,937	621	2,147	169
Rate per 100,000 inhabitants		310.6	3.5	30.1	30.1	246.9	2,054.3	434.4	1,501.8	118.2
Johnson City, TN M.S.A.	**184,912**									
(Includes Carter, Unicoi, and Washington Counties.)										
City of Johnson City	57,202	395	1	11	86	297	3,811	546	3,033	232
Total area actually reporting	100.0%	737	4	28	109	596	7,134	1,449	5,172	513
Rate per 100,000 inhabitants		398.6	2.2	15.1	58.9	322.3	3,858.1	783.6	2,797.0	277.4
Jonesboro, AR M.S.A.	**110,107**									
(Includes Craighead and Poinsett Counties.)										
City of Jonesboro	57,216	332	4	12	107	209	3,377	875	2,359	143
Total area actually reporting	100.0%	423	4	18	122	279	4,572	1,497	2,882	193
Rate per 100,000 inhabitants		384.2	3.6	16.3	110.8	253.4	4,152.3	1,359.6	2,617.5	175.3
Joplin, MO M.S.A.	**161,104**									
(Includes Jasper and Newton Counties.)										
City of Joplin	46,447	191	5	29	48	109	3,679	641	2,803	235
Total area actually reporting	100.0%	518	9	64	67	378	6,725	1,334	4,939	452
Rate per 100,000 inhabitants		321.5	5.6	39.7	41.6	234.6	4,174.3	828.0	3,065.7	280.6
Kennewick-Richland-Pasco, WA M.S.A.	**205,201**									
(Includes Benton and Franklin Counties.)										
City of:										
Kennewick	58,545	208	3	23	32	150	2,731	495	2,090	146
Richland	41,923	82	0	14	9	59	1,242	242	947	53
Pasco	35,784	105	0	20	20	65	1,513	237	1,160	116
Total area actually reporting	100.0%	518	5	68	67	378	6,830	1,382	5,053	395
Rate per 100,000 inhabitants		252.4	2.4	33.1	32.7	184.2	3,328.4	673.5	2,462.5	192.5
Killeen-Temple-Fort Hood, TX M.S.A.	**343,264**									
(Includes Bell, Coryell, and Lampasas Counties.)										
City of:										
Killeen	94,148	788	6	76	186	520	5,585	1,812	3,502	271
Temple	55,293	170	5	1	48	116	2,725	677	1,862	186
Total area actually reporting	100.0%	1,376	17	149	287	923	12,662	3,697	8,271	694
Rate per 100,000 inhabitants		400.9	5.0	43.4	83.6	268.9	3,688.7	1,077.0	2,409.5	202.2
Kingsport-Bristol-Bristol, TN-VA M.S.A.	**302,188**									
(Includes Hawkins and Sullivan Counties, TN and Scott and Washington Counties and Bristol City, VA.)										
City of:										
Kingsport, TN	44,702	387	2	40	63	282	3,015	477	2,377	161
Bristol, TN	25,080	109	1	11	14	83	1,285	206	1,006	73
Bristol, VA	17,336	89	0	4	4	81	654	84	547	23
Total area actually reporting	99.3%	1,177	13	121	113	930	9,979	2,130	7,219	630
Estimated total	100.0%	1,187	13	122	116	936	10,059	2,141	7,281	637
Rate per 100,000 inhabitants		392.8	4.3	40.4	38.4	309.7	3,328.7	708.5	2,409.4	210.8
Kingston, NY M.S.A.	**180,292**									
(Includes Ulster County.)										
City of Kingston	23,387	118	1	7	62	48	1,124	176	873	75
Total area actually reporting	91.8%	569	5	36	106	422	3,348	649	2,491	208
Estimated total	100.0%	596	5	37	115	439	3,657	694	2,734	229
Rate per 100,000 inhabitants		330.6	2.8	20.5	63.8	243.5	2,028.4	384.9	1,516.4	127.0
Knoxville, TN M.S.A.	**634,806**									
(Includes Anderson, Blount, Knox, Loudon, and Union Counties.)										
City of Knoxville	174,993	1,692	18	81	443	1,150	11,081	2,432	7,231	1,418
Total area actually reporting	100.0%	3,264	35	233	645	2,351	25,230	5,824	16,964	2,442
Rate per 100,000 inhabitants		514.2	5.5	36.7	101.6	370.3	3,974.4	917.4	2,672.3	384.7

See footnotes at end of table.

Table 6

Crime in the United States
by Metropolitan Statistical Area, 2003—Continued

Metropolitan Statistical Area	Population	Violent crime	Murder and non-negligent man-slaughter	Forcible rape	Robbery	Aggravated assault	Property crime	Burglary	Larceny-theft	Motor vehicle theft
Kokomo, IN M.S.A.	**101,974**									
(Includes Howard and Tipton Counties.)										
City of Kokomo	46,229	194	2	17	66	109	3,029	551	2,339	139
Total area actually reporting	88.9%	285	3	22	73	187	3,894	758	2,937	199
Estimated total	100.0%	302	3	24	75	200	4,062	798	3,047	217
Rate per 100,000 inhabitants		296.2	2.9	23.5	73.5	196.1	3,983.4	782.6	2,988.0	212.8
La Crosse, WI-MN M.S.A.	**128,769**									
(Includes Houston County, MN and La Crosse County, WI.)										
City of La Crosse, WI	51,502	104	3	15	18	68	1,695	216	1,417	62
Total area actually reporting	100.0%	179	5	23	22	129	3,050	386	2,546	118
Rate per 100,000 inhabitants		139.0	3.9	17.9	17.1	100.2	2,368.6	299.8	1,977.2	91.6
Lafayette, IN M.S.A.	**182,512**									
(Includes Benton, Carroll, and Tippecanoe Counties.)										
City of Lafayette	60,954	243	1	30	64	148	3,205	603	2,459	143
Total area actually reporting	85.1%	339	2	52	80	205	5,344	957	4,157	230
Estimated total	100.0%	385	2	56	87	240	5,824	1,061	4,485	278
Rate per 100,000 inhabitants		210.9	1.1	30.7	47.7	131.5	3,191.0	581.3	2,457.4	152.3
Lafayette, LA M.S.A.	**243,294**									
(Includes Lafayette and St. Martin Parishes.)										
City of Lafayette	111,612	1,251	7	325	166	753	6,624	1,197	4,955	472
Total area actually reporting	91.2%	1,568	9	361	207	991	8,865	1,800	6,439	626
Estimated total	100.0%	1,701	10	369	233	1,089	10,123	2,010	7,413	700
Rate per 100,000 inhabitants		699.2	4.1	151.7	95.8	447.6	4,160.8	826.2	3,046.9	287.7
Lake Charles, LA M.S.A.	**193,577**									
(Includes Calcasieu and Cameron Parishes.)										
City of Lake Charles	70,942	524	6	43	139	336	4,163	1,678	2,288	197
Total area actually reporting	96.6%	993	13	103	222	655	9,649	2,865	6,260	524
Estimated total	100.0%	1,033	13	105	230	685	10,038	2,930	6,561	547
Rate per 100,000 inhabitants		533.6	6.7	54.2	118.8	353.9	5,185.5	1,513.6	3,389.3	282.6
Lakeland, FL M.S.A.	**507,850**									
(Includes Polk County.)										
City of Lakeland	87,752	516	5	39	215	257	5,165	954	3,844	367
Total area actually reporting	99.4%	2,755	22	176	611	1,946	22,867	5,837	15,221	1,809
Estimated total	100.0%	2,773	22	177	616	1,958	23,004	5,865	15,317	1,822
Rate per 100,000 inhabitants		546.0	4.3	34.9	121.3	385.5	4,529.7	1,154.9	3,016.0	358.8
Lancaster, PA M.S.A.	**479,739**									
(Includes Lancaster County.)										
City of Lancaster	55,765	557	8	37	245	267	3,033	563	2,152	318
Total area actually reporting	90.1%	994	9	91	368	526	10,318	1,915	7,573	830
Estimated total	100.0%	1,102	10	99	396	597	11,331	2,061	8,365	905
Rate per 100,000 inhabitants		229.7	2.1	20.6	82.5	124.4	2,361.9	429.6	1,743.7	188.6
Lansing-East Lansing, MI M.S.A.	**454,953**									
(Includes Clinton, Eaton, and Ingham Counties.)										
City of:										
Lansing	118,937	1,220	8	164	208	840	5,149	1,016	3,677	456
East Lansing	46,408	229	4	18	31	176	1,369	257	1,040	72
Total area actually reporting	99.2%	2,053	17	333	334	1,369	14,221	2,803	10,442	976
Estimated total	100.0%	2,062	17	334	336	1,375	14,333	2,822	10,522	989
Rate per 100,000 inhabitants		453.2	3.7	73.4	73.9	302.2	3,150.4	620.3	2,312.8	217.4
Laredo, TX M.S.A.	**210,839**									
(Includes Webb County.)										
City of Laredo	194,516	1,317	29	55	257	976	13,573	1,975	10,619	979
Total area actually reporting	100.0%	1,372	31	61	263	1,017	14,052	2,161	10,882	1,009
Rate per 100,000 inhabitants		650.7	14.7	28.9	124.7	482.4	6,664.8	1,025.0	5,161.3	478.6
Las Vegas-Paradise, NV M.S.A.	**1,569,549**									
(Includes Clark County.)										
City of Las Vegas Metropolitan Police Department	1,189,388	9,158	141	511	3,955	4,551	57,552	12,782	30,052	14,718
Total area actually reporting	100.0%	10,901	172	668	4,441	5,620	71,581	16,392	37,117	18,072
Rate per 100,000 inhabitants		694.5	11.0	42.6	282.9	358.1	4,560.6	1,044.4	2,364.8	1,151.4

See footnotes at end of table.

Table 6

Crime in the United States
by Metropolitan Statistical Area, 2003—Continued

Metropolitan Statistical Area	Population	Violent crime	Murder and non-negligent man-slaughter	Forcible rape	Robbery	Aggravated assault	Property crime	Burglary	Larceny-theft	Motor vehicle theft
Lawrence, KS M.S.A.	**102,603**									
(Includes Douglas County.)										
City of Lawrence	81,833	365	3	37	59	266	4,205	810	3,222	173
Total area actually reporting	100.0%	423	4	44	61	314	5,053	1,036	3,815	202
Rate per 100,000 inhabitants		412.3	3.9	42.9	59.5	306.0	4,924.8	1,009.7	3,718.2	196.9
Lawton, OK M.S.A.	**113,992**									
(Includes Comanche County.)										
City of Lawton	91,799	693	5	37	113	538	5,015	1,285	3,485	245
Total area actually reporting	100.0%	773	5	41	115	612	5,409	1,393	3,725	291
Rate per 100,000 inhabitants		678.1	4.4	36.0	100.9	536.9	4,745.1	1,222.0	3,267.8	255.3
Lebanon, PA M.S.A.	**121,497**									
(Includes Lebanon County.)										
City of Lebanon	24,072	180	2	15	63	100	938	209	653	76
Total area actually reporting	86.6%	322	2	31	82	207	2,402	429	1,830	143
Estimated total	100.0%	358	2	34	91	231	2,749	479	2,101	169
Rate per 100,000 inhabitants		294.7	1.6	28.0	74.9	190.1	2,262.6	394.2	1,729.3	139.1
Lewiston, ID-WA M.S.A.	**58,466**									
(Includes Nez Perce County, ID and Asotin County, WA.)										
City of Lewiston, ID	31,060	39	0	2	6	31	1,309	269	978	62
Total area actually reporting	98.1%	94	0	9	10	75	2,197	460	1,618	119
Estimated total	100.0%	98	0	10	10	78	2,244	468	1,654	122
Rate per 100,000 inhabitants		167.6	0.0	17.1	17.1	133.4	3,838.1	800.5	2,829.0	208.7
Lewiston-Auburn, ME M.S.A.	**105,717**									
(Includes Androscoggin County.)										
City of:										
Lewiston	35,958	79	2	36	29	12	1,330	235	1,035	60
Auburn	23,343	17	0	2	9	6	769	105	628	36
Total area actually reporting	100.0%	128	4	49	40	35	2,928	494	2,301	133
Rate per 100,000 inhabitants		121.1	3.8	46.4	37.8	33.1	2,769.7	467.3	2,176.6	125.8
Lima, OH M.S.A.	**108,258**									
(Includes Allen County.)										
City of Lima	40,872	423	2	70	108	243	2,380	637	1,599	144
Total area actually reporting	96.6%	485	2	86	124	273	3,980	848	2,941	191
Estimated total	100.0%	491	2	87	126	276	4,091	867	3,026	198
Rate per 100,000 inhabitants		453.5	1.8	80.4	116.4	254.9	3,778.9	800.9	2,795.2	182.9
Lincoln, NE M.S.A.	**275,781**									
(Includes Lancaster and Seward Counties.)										
City of Lincoln	233,721	1,114	5	94	153	862	13,487	1,959	11,049	479
Total area actually reporting	100.0%	1,141	5	100	157	879	14,586	2,207	11,861	518
Rate per 100,000 inhabitants		413.7	1.8	36.3	56.9	318.7	5,289.0	800.3	4,300.9	187.8
Little Rock-North Little Rock, AR M.S.A.[1]	**626,440**									
(Includes Faulkner, Grant, Lonoke, Perry, Pulaski, and Saline Counties.)										
City of:										
Little Rock	185,117	2,858	44	129	896	1,789	18,600	4,442	12,743	1,415
North Little Rock	60,353	516	8	41	163	304	5,270	809	3,986	475
Total area actually reporting	97.0%	4,403	63	272	1,168	2,900	35,773	8,054	25,100	2,619
Estimated total	100.0%	4,461	63	277	1,175	2,946	36,517	8,247	25,616	2,654
Rate per 100,000 inhabitants		712.1	10.1	44.2	187.6	470.3	5,829.3	1,316.5	4,089.1	423.7
Longview, TX M.S.A.	**200,362**									
(Includes Gregg, Rusk, and Upshur Counties.)										
City of Longview	73,852	488	4	71	161	252	5,020	1,036	3,536	448
Total area actually reporting	99.4%	1,000	7	124	201	668	9,649	2,133	6,729	787
Estimated total	100.0%	1,003	7	124	202	670	9,699	2,143	6,765	791
Rate per 100,000 inhabitants		500.6	3.5	61.9	100.8	334.4	4,840.7	1,069.6	3,376.4	394.8
Longview, WA M.S.A.	**95,487**									
(Includes Cowlitz County.)										
City of Longview	35,829	200	1	12	37	150	3,840	910	2,511	419
Total area actually reporting	100.0%	386	4	45	61	276	6,598	1,547	4,289	762
Rate per 100,000 inhabitants		404.2	4.2	47.1	63.9	289.0	6,909.8	1,620.1	4,491.7	798.0

See footnotes at end of table.

Table 6

Crime in the United States
by Metropolitan Statistical Area, 2003—Continued

Metropolitan Statistical Area	Population	Violent crime	Murder and non-negligent man-slaughter	Forcible rape	Robbery	Aggravated assault	Property crime	Burglary	Larceny-theft	Motor vehicle theft
Los Angeles-Long Beach-Santa Ana, CA M.S.A.	**12,878,801**									
(Includes the Metropolitan Divisions of Los Angeles-Long Beach-Glendale and Santa Ana-Anaheim-Irvine.)										
City of:										
Los Angeles	3,838,838	48,824	515	1,226	16,577	30,506	135,781	25,115	77,111	33,555
Long Beach	477,368	3,579	49	136	1,411	1,983	14,823	3,003	8,072	3,748
Santa Ana	347,016	1,788	17	76	739	956	9,728	1,110	5,932	2,686
Anaheim	336,132	1,319	9	76	410	824	10,446	1,971	6,708	1,767
Glendale	201,522	363	6	18	146	193	3,876	800	2,283	793
Pomona	155,166	1,217	17	49	422	729	5,459	914	2,905	1,640
Irvine	163,823	144	2	18	51	73	3,310	816	2,238	256
Torrance	143,101	402	2	23	216	161	4,292	785	2,753	754
Pasadena	141,178	700	4	38	265	393	4,586	849	3,206	531
Orange	132,987	262	1	10	97	154	3,376	440	2,423	513
Fullerton	130,194	363	5	37	120	201	4,599	784	3,222	593
Costa Mesa	111,281	304	1	42	112	149	3,586	516	2,665	405
Burbank	103,993	283	3	15	69	196	2,694	500	1,728	466
Compton	96,562	1,549	43	41	444	1,021	2,340	548	991	801
Carson	93,904	731	12	15	207	497	2,685	509	1,453	723
Santa Monica	87,710	555	2	21	242	290	3,943	761	2,716	466
Newport Beach	78,915	115	0	16	27	72	2,526	666	1,671	189
Tustin	69,357	265	1	11	55	198	1,895	328	1,316	251
Montebello	64,274	248	4	17	88	139	2,007	237	1,138	632
Monterey Park	62,471	167	1	6	99	61	1,380	272	654	454
Gardena	60,283	527	3	17	269	238	1,683	396	850	437
Paramount	57,082	430	10	14	182	224	2,083	331	1,060	692
Fountain Valley	56,136	108	0	9	43	56	1,449	254	1,037	158
Arcadia	55,480	137	2	5	55	75	1,540	383	987	170
Cerritos	53,172	199	2	7	97	93	1,972	328	1,261	383
Total area actually reporting	100.0%	92,890	1,118	3,083	31,586	57,103	380,455	73,250	220,688	86,517
Rate per 100,000 inhabitants		721.3	8.7	23.9	245.3	443.4	2,954.1	568.8	1,713.6	671.8
Los Angeles-Long Beach-Glendale, CA M.D.	**9,909,465**									
(Includes Los Angeles County.)										
Total area actually reporting	100.0%	84,671	1,054	2,586	28,962	52,069	307,294	60,277	171,781	75,236
Rate per 100,000 inhabitants		854.4	10.6	26.1	292.3	525.4	3,101.0	608.3	1,733.5	759.2
Santa Ana-Anaheim-Irvine, CA M.D.	**2,969,336**									
(Includes Orange County.)										
Total area actually reporting	100.0%	8,219	64	497	2,624	5,034	73,161	12,973	48,907	11,281
Rate per 100,000 inhabitants		276.8	2.2	16.7	88.4	169.5	2,463.9	436.9	1,647.1	379.9
Lubbock, TX M.S.A.	**258,395**									
(Includes Crosby and Lubbock Counties.)										
City of Lubbock	206,882	2,395	14	101	311	1,969	13,246	2,829	9,726	691
Total area actually reporting	100.0%	2,528	18	117	315	2,078	14,892	3,259	10,849	784
Rate per 100,000 inhabitants		978.3	7.0	45.3	121.9	804.2	5,763.3	1,261.2	4,198.6	303.4
Lynchburg, VA M.S.A.	**232,783**									
(Includes Amherst, Appomattox, Bedford, and Campbell Counties and Bedford and Lynchburg Cities.)										
City of Lynchburg	65,438	267	6	25	72	164	2,395	411	1,822	162
Total area actually reporting	100.0%	480	8	59	95	318	4,524	765	3,456	303
Rate per 100,000 inhabitants		206.2	3.4	25.3	40.8	136.6	1,943.4	328.6	1,484.6	130.2
Macon, GA M.S.A.	**228,316**									
(Includes Bibb, Crawford, Jones, Monroe, and Twiggs Counties.)										
City of Macon	97,255	647	18	46	229	354	9,072	1,881	6,181	1,010
Total area actually reporting	97.1%	793	21	73	254	445	13,508	2,986	9,063	1,459
Estimated total	100.0%	828	21	75	266	466	13,877	3,046	9,335	1,496
Rate per 100,000 inhabitants		362.7	9.2	32.8	116.5	204.1	6,078.0	1,334.1	4,088.6	655.2
Madera, CA M.S.A.	**131,632**									
(Includes Madera County.)										
City of Madera	46,699	478	2	30	145	301	1,923	471	1,054	398
Total area actually reporting	100.0%	864	7	50	170	637	4,158	1,227	2,090	841
Rate per 100,000 inhabitants		656.4	5.3	38.0	129.1	483.9	3,158.8	932.1	1,587.8	638.9

See footnotes at end of table.

Table 6

Crime in the United States
by Metropolitan Statistical Area, 2003—Continued

Metropolitan Statistical Area	Population	Violent crime	Murder and non-negligent man-slaughter	Forcible rape	Robbery	Aggravated assault	Property crime	Burglary	Larceny-theft	Motor vehicle theft
Madison, WI M.S.A.	**522,573**									
(Includes Columbia, Dane, and Iowa Counties.)										
City of Madison	216,441	774	8	63	278	425	7,905	1,605	5,671	629
Total area actually reporting	84.0%	1,100	15	124	355	606	14,089	2,282	10,929	878
Estimated total	100.0%	1,162	16	134	364	648	15,324	2,537	11,841	946
Rate per 100,000 inhabitants		222.4	3.1	25.6	69.7	124.0	2,932.4	485.5	2,265.9	181.0
Mansfield, OH M.S.A.	**128,167**									
(Includes Richland County.)										
City of Mansfield	50,812	162	7	22	100	33	3,482	822	2,507	153
Total area actually reporting	100.0%	210	7	40	113	50	5,886	1,361	4,287	238
Rate per 100,000 inhabitants		163.8	5.5	31.2	88.2	39.0	4,592.4	1,061.9	3,344.9	185.7
McAllen-Edinburg-Pharr, TX M.S.A.	**624,027**									
(Includes Hidalgo County.)										
City of:										
McAllen	115,647	512	6	29	145	332	8,542	902	6,985	655
Edinburg	53,584	265	6	17	44	198	6,639	765	5,617	257
Pharr	52,075	332	5	10	76	241	3,083	664	2,329	90
Mission	52,232	58	0	2	17	39	3,697	761	2,568	368
Total area actually reporting	99.8%	2,832	51	185	562	2,034	36,537	7,336	26,808	2,393
Estimated total	100.0%	2,836	51	185	563	2,037	36,597	7,348	26,852	2,397
Rate per 100,000 inhabitants		454.5	8.2	29.6	90.2	326.4	5,864.7	1,177.5	4,303.0	384.1
Medford, OR M.S.A.	**188,446**									
(Includes Jackson County.)										
City of Medford	65,352	299	4	29	35	231	4,235	484	3,494	257
Total area actually reporting	99.8%	603	5	56	66	476	7,882	1,133	6,285	464
Estimated total	100.0%	603	5	56	66	476	7,902	1,136	6,300	466
Rate per 100,000 inhabitants		320.0	2.7	29.7	35.0	252.6	4,193.2	602.8	3,343.1	247.3
Memphis, TN-MS-AR M.S.A.	**1,239,073**									
(Includes Crittenden County, AR; DeSoto, Marshall, Tate, and Tunica Counties, MS; and Fayette, Shelby, and Tipton Counties, TN.)										
City of Memphis	653,858	10,297	126	438	4,297	5,436	55,475	16,900	30,049	8,526
Total area actually reporting	94.4%	12,207	150	570	4,683	6,804	72,920	21,047	41,635	10,238
Estimated total	100.0%	12,376	152	586	4,710	6,928	75,068	21,652	43,008	10,408
Rate per 100,000 inhabitants		998.8	12.3	47.3	380.1	559.1	6,058.4	1,747.4	3,471.0	840.0
Merced, CA M.S.A.	**227,763**									
(Includes Merced County.)										
City of Merced	68,941	636	7	29	168	432	4,716	882	3,182	652
Total area actually reporting	100.0%	1,603	16	76	285	1,226	9,930	2,624	5,780	1,526
Rate per 100,000 inhabitants		703.8	7.0	33.4	125.1	538.3	4,359.8	1,152.1	2,537.7	670.0
Miami-Fort Lauderdale-Miami Beach, FL M.S.A.	**5,327,879**									
(Includes the Metropolitan Divisions of Fort Lauderdale-Pompano Beach-Deerfield Beach, Miami-Miami Beach-Kendall, and West Palm Beach-Boca Raton-Boynton Beach.)										
City of:										
Miami	381,651	7,157	74	107	2,928	4,048	26,370	5,878	15,404	5,088
Fort Lauderdale	161,090	1,352	18	49	640	645	9,736	2,320	6,281	1,135
Miami Beach	91,215	1,172	6	72	507	587	9,438	1,414	6,840	1,184
Pompano Beach	88,748	707	3	24	207	473	3,061	592	2,091	378
West Palm Beach	88,101	1,161	14	64	538	545	8,718	1,474	5,977	1,267
Boca Raton	78,828	175	1	10	46	118	2,522	597	1,722	203
Deerfield Beach	66,836	359	1	27	97	234	1,695	314	1,127	254
Boynton Beach	64,849	678	1	5	185	487	4,881	848	3,558	475
Delray Beach	63,412	521	1	15	125	380	4,036	683	2,952	401
Total area actually reporting	100.0%	43,323	333	1,892	14,068	27,030	267,997	51,614	180,811	35,572
Rate per 100,000 inhabitants		813.1	6.3	35.5	264.0	507.3	5,030.1	968.8	3,393.7	667.7
Fort Lauderdale-Pompano Beach-Deerfield Beach, FL M.D.	**1,740,402**									
(Includes Broward County.)										
Total area actually reporting	100.0%	9,115	67	477	2,877	5,694	60,495	11,726	41,282	7,487
Rate per 100,000 inhabitants		523.7	3.8	27.4	165.3	327.2	3,475.9	673.8	2,372.0	430.2
Miami-Miami Beach-Kendall, FL M.D.	**2,375,298**									
(Includes Miami-Dade County.)										
Total area actually reporting	100.0%	25,544	205	941	8,559	15,839	143,488	25,811	97,027	20,650
Rate per 100,000 inhabitants		1,075.4	8.6	39.6	360.3	666.8	6,040.8	1,086.6	4,084.8	869.4

See footnotes at end of table.

Table 6

Crime in the United States
by Metropolitan Statistical Area, 2003—Continued

Metropolitan Statistical Area	Population	Violent crime	Murder and non-negligent man-slaughter	Forcible rape	Robbery	Aggravated assault	Property crime	Burglary	Larceny-theft	Motor vehicle theft
West Palm Beach-Boca Raton-Boynton Beach, FL M.D.	**1,212,179**									
(Includes Palm Beach County.)										
Total area actually reporting	100.0%	8,664	61	474	2,632	5,497	64,014	14,077	42,502	7,435
Rate per 100,000 inhabitants		714.7	5.0	39.1	217.1	453.5	5,280.9	1,161.3	3,506.2	613.4
Michigan City-La Porte, IN M.S.A.	**111,040**									
(Includes La Porte County.)										
City of:										
Michigan City	32,757	150	1	18	72	59	2,071	364	1,538	169
La Porte	21,419	60	0	5	7	48	1,142	123	953	66
Total area actually reporting	98.7%	275	3	27	88	157	4,356	742	3,291	323
Estimated total	100.0%	279	3	27	89	160	4,413	751	3,334	328
Rate per 100,000 inhabitants		251.3	2.7	24.3	80.2	144.1	3,974.2	676.3	3,002.5	295.4
Midland, TX M.S.A.	**119,498**									
(Includes Midland County.)										
City of Midland	97,319	510	2	39	74	395	4,037	941	2,925	171
Total area actually reporting	100.0%	566	2	41	75	448	4,699	1,118	3,363	218
Rate per 100,000 inhabitants		473.6	1.7	34.3	62.8	374.9	3,932.3	935.6	2,814.3	182.4
Milwaukee-Waukesha-West Allis, WI M.S.A.	**1,521,148**									
(Includes Milwaukee, Ozaukee, Washington, and Waukesha Counties.)										
City of:										
Milwaukee	594,269	5,289	109	246	2,868	2,066	37,798	6,041	25,526	6,231
Waukesha	66,564	96	1	16	20	59	1,313	350	908	55
West Allis	60,985	166	3	16	84	63	2,386	402	1,781	203
Total area actually reporting	98.5%	6,309	119	403	3,234	2,553	59,044	9,044	42,766	7,234
Estimated total	100.0%	6,335	119	407	3,242	2,567	59,655	9,122	43,272	7,261
Rate per 100,000 inhabitants		416.5	7.8	26.8	213.1	168.8	3,921.7	599.7	2,844.7	477.3
Minneapolis-St. Paul-Bloomington, MN-WI M.S.A.	**3,078,535**									
(Includes Anoka, Carver, Chisago, Dakota, Hennepin, Isanti, Ramsey, Scott, Sherburne, Washington, and Wright Counties, MN and Pierce and St. Croix Counties, WI.)										
City of:										
Minneapolis, MN	378,602	4,517	46	384	2,192	1,895	20,405	4,482	12,404	3,519
St. Paul, MN	286,281	2,178	20	217	638	1,303	13,540	3,074	8,376	2,090
Bloomington, MN	84,756	149	1	24	52	72	3,569	332	2,988	249
Plymouth, MN	67,836	67	0	17	11	39	1,792	391	1,338	63
Eagan, MN	64,553	65	0	16	24	25	1,529	211	1,238	80
Eden Prairie, MN	57,794	48	0	14	1	33	1,367	189	1,132	46
Minnetonka, MN	51,524	42	1	16	6	19	1,241	280	917	44
Total area actually reporting	93.3%	9,767	88	1,171	3,505	5,003	99,949	16,378	73,602	9,969
Estimated total	100.0%	10,078	91	1,229	3,571	5,187	106,292	17,227	78,675	10,390
Rate per 100,000 inhabitants		327.4	3.0	39.9	116.0	168.5	3,452.7	559.6	2,555.6	337.5
Mobile, AL M.S.A.	**401,433**									
(Includes Mobile County.)										
City of Mobile[2]	251,345	1,300	24	113	739	424	16,151	3,976	10,855	1,320
Total area actually reporting	99.1%	2,224	34	180	1,006	1,004	22,911	6,116	14,882	1,913
Estimated total	100.0%	2,239	34	181	1,011	1,013	23,077	6,148	15,004	1,925
Rate per 100,000 inhabitants		557.8	8.5	45.1	251.8	252.3	5,748.7	1,531.5	3,737.6	479.5
Modesto, CA M.S.A.	**487,502**									
(Includes Stanislaus County.)										
City of Modesto	205,691	1,409	17	73	380	939	12,600	1,743	8,463	2,394
Total area actually reporting	100.0%	3,110	27	170	724	2,189	26,964	4,872	16,641	5,451
Rate per 100,000 inhabitants		637.9	5.5	34.9	148.5	449.0	5,531.1	999.4	3,413.5	1,118.1
Monroe, MI M.S.A.	**149,692**									
(Includes Monroe County.)										
City of Monroe	22,094	90	1	16	18	55	738	147	561	30
Total area actually reporting	98.9%	372	2	79	53	238	3,885	874	2,704	307
Estimated total	100.0%	377	2	80	54	241	3,934	882	2,739	313
Rate per 100,000 inhabitants		251.9	1.3	53.4	36.1	161.0	2,628.1	589.2	1,829.8	209.1

See footnotes at end of table.

Table 6

Crime in the United States
by Metropolitan Statistical Area, 2003—Continued

Metropolitan Statistical Area	Population	Violent crime	Murder and non-negligent man-slaughter	Forcible rape	Robbery	Aggravated assault	Property crime	Burglary	Larceny-theft	Motor vehicle theft
			Violent crime					*Property crime*		
Montgomery, AL M.S.A.	**352,344**									
(Includes Autauga, Elmore, Lowndes, and Montgomery Counties.)										
City of Montgomery	202,064	1,307	18	115	658	516	16,125	4,092	10,268	1,765
Total area actually reporting	100.0%	1,798	29	189	778	802	21,078	5,309	13,666	2,103
Rate per 100,000 inhabitants		510.3	8.2	53.6	220.8	227.6	5,982.2	1,506.8	3,878.6	596.9
Morristown, TN M.S.A.	**126,496**									
(Includes Grainger, Hamblen, and Jefferson Counties.)										
City of Morristown	25,330	181	1	16	28	136	1,874	206	1,511	157
Total area actually reporting	100.0%	532	9	44	59	420	4,657	960	3,283	414
Rate per 100,000 inhabitants		420.6	7.1	34.8	46.6	332.0	3,681.5	758.9	2,595.3	327.3
Mount Vernon-Anacortes, WA M.S.A.	**108,006**									
(Includes Skagit County.)										
City of:										
Mount Vernon	27,488	75	0	22	22	31	2,350	293	1,948	109
Anacortes	15,359	11	0	2	2	7	487	97	365	25
Total area actually reporting	100.0%	227	1	74	47	105	6,944	1,367	5,153	424
Rate per 100,000 inhabitants		210.2	0.9	68.5	43.5	97.2	6,429.3	1,265.7	4,771.0	392.6
Muncie, IN M.S.A.	**118,899**									
(Includes Delaware County.)										
City of Muncie	67,594	291	1	56	68	166	3,018	545	2,255	218
Total area actually reporting	100.0%	370	1	94	73	202	4,121	742	3,078	301
Rate per 100,000 inhabitants		311.2	0.8	79.1	61.4	169.9	3,466.0	624.1	2,588.8	253.2
Muskegon-Norton Shores, MI M.S.A.	**172,270**									
(Includes Muskegon County.)										
City of:										
Muskegon	39,547	332	1	52	48	231	2,631	478	1,937	216
Norton Shores	23,152	53	0	8	13	32	1,028	102	870	56
Total area actually reporting	100.0%	851	4	110	121	616	8,253	1,312	6,274	667
Rate per 100,000 inhabitants		494.0	2.3	63.9	70.2	357.6	4,790.7	761.6	3,642.0	387.2
Myrtle Beach-Conway-North Myrtle Beach, SC M.S.A.	**208,044**									
(Includes Horry County.)										
City of:										
Myrtle Beach	24,764	608	4	63	195	346	4,835	773	3,547	515
Conway	12,137	148	1	9	27	111	1,388	224	1,081	83
North Myrtle Beach	12,135	68	0	13	18	37	1,387	234	1,060	93
Total area actually reporting	100.0%	1,893	13	167	367	1,346	15,478	2,989	11,047	1,442
Rate per 100,000 inhabitants		909.9	6.2	80.3	176.4	647.0	7,439.8	1,436.7	5,309.9	693.1
Napa, CA M.S.A.	**131,635**									
(Includes Napa County.)										
City of Napa	75,819	306	0	26	48	232	2,450	308	1,969	173
Total area actually reporting	100.0%	380	2	39	51	288	3,623	581	2,670	372
Rate per 100,000 inhabitants		288.7	1.5	29.6	38.7	218.8	2,752.3	441.4	2,028.3	282.6
Naples-Marco Island, FL M.S.A.	**281,756**									
(Includes Collier County.)										
City of:										
Naples	21,549	54	0	4	13	37	1,084	183	866	35
Marco Island	15,469	11	0	0	3	8	263	38	216	9
Total area actually reporting	100.0%	1,433	10	105	236	1,082	7,806	1,974	5,372	460
Rate per 100,000 inhabitants		508.6	3.5	37.3	83.8	384.0	2,770.5	700.6	1,906.6	163.3
Nashville-Davidson–Murfreesboro, TN M.S.A.	**1,363,472**									
(Includes Cannon, Cheatham, Davidson, Dickson, Hickman, Macon, Robertson, Rutherford, Smith, Sumner, Trousdale, Williamson, and Wilson Counties.)										
City of:										
Nashville	554,888	8,331	74	335	2,197	5,725	38,648	7,369	26,630	4,649
Murfreesboro	75,468	459	2	27	77	353	3,232	475	2,482	275
Total area actually reporting	100.0%	11,516	102	578	2,525	8,311	61,081	11,789	42,922	6,370
Rate per 100,000 inhabitants		844.6	7.5	42.4	185.2	609.5	4,479.8	864.6	3,148.0	467.2

See footnotes at end of table.

Table 6

Crime in the United States

by Metropolitan Statistical Area, 2003—Continued

Metropolitan Statistical Area	Population	Violent crime	Murder and non-negligent man-slaughter	Forcible rape	Robbery	Aggravated assault	Property crime	Burglary	Larceny-theft	Motor vehicle theft
New Orleans-Metairie-Kenner, LA M.S.A.	**1,319,270**									
(Includes Jefferson, Orleans, Plaquemines, St. Bernard, St. Charles, St. John the Baptist, and St. Tammany Parishes.)										
City of:										
New Orleans	475,128	4,596	274	213	2,071	2,038	24,477	4,879	12,726	6,872
Kenner	70,717	291	4	17	69	201	2,801	362	2,119	320
Total area actually reporting	99.8%	8,700	336	451	3,150	4,763	56,882	11,209	35,106	10,567
Estimated total	100.0%	8,712	336	452	3,152	4,772	57,003	11,229	35,200	10,574
Rate per 100,000 inhabitants		660.4	25.5	34.3	238.9	361.7	4,320.8	851.2	2,668.1	801.5
New York-Northern New Jersey-Long Island, NY-NJ-PA M.S.A.	**18,659,493**									
(Includes the Metropolitan Divisions of Edison, NJ; Nassau-Suffolk County, NY; Newark-Union, NJ-PA; and New York-Wayne-White Plains, NY-NJ.)										
City of:										
New York, NY	8,098,066	59,448	597	1,609	25,989	31,253	176,767	28,293	124,846	23,628
Newark, NJ	278,551	2,731	81	85	1,304	1,261	13,861	2,281	5,562	6,018
Edison Township, NJ	100,484	285	1	11	115	158	2,633	465	1,755	413
Wayne Township, NJ	55,241	39	0	2	8	29	1,480	105	1,204	171
White Plains, NY	55,488	221	2	9	81	129	1,669	134	1,452	83
Union Township, NJ	55,849	161	1	9	89	62	2,022	349	1,281	392
Total area actually reporting	99.7%	90,041	966	2,807	39,104	47,164	403,542	69,262	274,626	59,654
Estimated total	100.0%	90,184	967	2,812	39,160	47,245	404,619	69,429	275,427	59,763
Rate per 100,000 inhabitants		483.3	5.2	15.1	209.9	253.2	2,168.4	372.1	1,476.1	320.3
Edison, NJ M.D.	**2,264,946**									
(Includes Middlesex, Monmouth, Ocean, and Somerset Counties.)										
Total area actually reporting	100.0%	4,426	38	224	1,432	2,732	45,758	8,782	33,317	3,659
Rate per 100,000 inhabitants		195.4	1.7	9.9	63.2	120.6	2,020.3	387.7	1,471.0	161.5
Nassau-Suffolk, NY M.D.	**2,808,315**									
(Includes Nassau and Suffolk Counties.)										
Total area actually reporting	99.2%	5,486	57	256	2,134	3,039	51,397	8,166	37,565	5,666
Estimated total	100.0%	5,542	57	258	2,157	3,070	51,813	8,232	37,872	5,709
Rate per 100,000 inhabitants		197.3	2.0	9.2	76.8	109.3	1,845.0	293.1	1,348.6	203.3
Newark-Union, NJ-PA M.D.	**2,144,145**									
(Includes Essex, Hunterdon, Morris, Sussex, and Union Counties, NJ and Pike County, PA.)										
Total area actually reporting	99.6%	9,619	176	345	4,675	4,423	60,404	11,657	32,236	16,511
Estimated total	100.0%	9,637	176	346	4,680	4,435	60,559	11,678	32,356	16,525
Rate per 100,000 inhabitants		449.5	8.2	16.1	218.3	206.8	2,824.4	544.6	1,509.0	770.7
New York-Wayne-White Plains, NY-NJ M.D.	**11,442,087**									
(Includes Bergen, Hudson, and Passaic Counties, NJ and Bronx, Kings, New York, Putnam, Queens, Richmond, Rockland, and Westchester Counties, NY.)										
Total area actually reporting	99.8%	70,510	695	1,982	30,863	36,970	245,983	40,657	171,508	33,818
Estimated total	100.0%	70,579	696	1,984	30,891	37,008	246,489	40,737	171,882	33,870
Rate per 100,000 inhabitants		616.8	6.1	17.3	270.0	323.4	2,154.2	356.0	1,502.2	296.0
Niles-Benton Harbor, MI M.S.A.	**162,762**									
(Includes Berrien County.)										
City of:										
Niles	12,009	74	0	17	8	49	729	132	543	54
Benton Harbor	11,084	321	2	14	28	277	674	239	344	91
Total area actually reporting	99.6%	779	5	113	76	585	5,047	1,081	3,618	348
Estimated total	100.0%	780	5	113	76	586	5,065	1,084	3,631	350
Rate per 100,000 inhabitants		479.2	3.1	69.4	46.7	360.0	3,111.9	666.0	2,230.9	215.0
Ocala, FL M.S.A.	**277,542**									
(Includes Marion County.)										
City of Ocala	47,790	645	2	39	165	439	3,674	926	2,520	228
Total area actually reporting	100.0%	2,023	10	161	254	1,598	8,720	2,513	5,619	588
Rate per 100,000 inhabitants		728.9	3.6	58.0	91.5	575.8	3,141.9	905.4	2,024.6	211.9

See footnotes at end of table.

Table 6

Crime in the United States

by Metropolitan Statistical Area, 2003—Continued

Metropolitan Statistical Area	Population	Violent crime	Murder and non-negligent man-slaughter	Forcible rape	Robbery	Aggravated assault	Property crime	Burglary	Larceny-theft	Motor vehicle theft
Ocean City, NJ M.S.A.	**102,584**									
(Includes Cape May County.)										
City of Ocean City	15,603	23	0	2	9	12	875	162	706	7
Total area actually reporting	100.0%	338	2	21	70	245	4,180	936	3,100	144
Rate per 100,000 inhabitants		329.5	1.9	20.5	68.2	238.8	4,074.7	912.4	3,021.9	140.4
Odessa, TX M.S.A.	**124,214**									
(Includes Ector County.)										
City of Odessa	92,375	588	3	12	65	508	4,639	826	3,608	205
Total area actually reporting	100.0%	721	6	19	76	620	6,171	1,082	4,804	285
Rate per 100,000 inhabitants		580.4	4.8	15.3	61.2	499.1	4,968.0	871.1	3,867.5	229.4
Oklahoma City, OK M.S.A.	**1,126,991**									
(Includes Canadian, Cleveland, Grady,										
Lincoln, Logan, McClain, and Oklahoma										
Counties.)										
City of Oklahoma City	521,681	4,642	49	365	1,381	2,847	47,595	8,300	35,367	3,928
Total area actually reporting	100.0%	6,353	67	547	1,662	4,077	66,331	12,813	48,299	5,219
Rate per 100,000 inhabitants		563.7	5.9	48.5	147.5	361.8	5,885.7	1,136.9	4,285.7	463.1
Olympia, WA M.S.A.	**219,880**									
(Includes Thurston County.)										
City of Olympia	43,967	145	0	38	32	75	2,189	303	1,724	162
Total area actually reporting	100.0%	578	4	108	91	375	7,443	1,658	5,191	594
Rate per 100,000 inhabitants		262.9	1.8	49.1	41.4	170.5	3,385.0	754.0	2,360.8	270.1
Omaha-Council Bluffs, NE-IA M.S.A.	**788,655**									
(Includes Harrison, Mills, and Pottawattamie										
Counties, IA and Cass, Douglas, Sarpy,										
Saunders, and Washington Counties, NE.)										
City of:										
Omaha, NE	401,692	2,627	35	179	896	1,517	24,512	3,449	16,869	4,194
Council Bluffs, IA	58,786	497	5	71	78	343	6,138	1,005	4,271	862
Total area actually reporting	97.3%	3,496	43	304	1,001	2,148	37,543	5,743	26,057	5,743
Estimated total	100.0%	3,523	43	307	1,004	2,169	37,929	5,820	26,337	5,772
Rate per 100,000 inhabitants		446.7	5.5	38.9	127.3	275.0	4,809.3	738.0	3,339.5	731.9
Orlando, FL M.S.A.	**1,784,264**									
(Includes Lake, Orange, Osceola, and										
Seminole Counties.)										
City of Orlando	197,268	3,322	21	136	849	2,316	17,024	3,593	11,511	1,920
Total area actually reporting	100.0%	13,540	90	745	3,034	9,671	80,987	19,872	52,769	8,346
Rate per 100,000 inhabitants		758.9	5.0	41.8	170.0	542.0	4,539.0	1,113.7	2,957.5	467.8
Oshkosh-Neenah, WI M.S.A.	**159,306**									
(Includes Winnebago County.)										
City of:										
Oshkosh	63,827	122	0	8	23	91	2,286	324	1,888	74
Neenah	24,615	18	0	4	3	11	493	70	409	14
Total area actually reporting	100.0%	202	2	26	29	145	4,153	636	3,387	130
Rate per 100,000 inhabitants		126.8	1.3	16.3	18.2	91.0	2,606.9	399.2	2,126.1	81.6
Owensboro, KY M.S.A.	**110,986**									
(Includes Daviess, Hancock, and McLean										
Counties.)										
City of Owensboro	54,506	172	0	7	53	112	2,687	537	2,049	101
Total area actually reporting	83.1%	232	1	7	59	165	3,239	716	2,397	126
Estimated total	100.0%	279	1	16	68	194	3,748	828	2,769	151
Rate per 100,000 inhabitants		251.4	0.9	14.4	61.3	174.8	3,377.0	746.0	2,494.9	136.1
Oxnard-Thousand Oaks-Ventura, CA M.S.A.	**792,144**									
(Includes Ventura County.)										
City of:										
Oxnard	179,851	808	22	37	352	397	4,719	975	3,156	588
Thousand Oaks	123,987	201	1	12	38	150	1,785	332	1,311	142
Ventura	104,706	261	3	21	96	141	3,968	764	2,855	349
Camarillo	60,068	98	1	10	15	72	1,071	224	772	75
Total area actually reporting	100.0%	2,029	42	129	645	1,213	16,369	3,479	11,170	1,720
Rate per 100,000 inhabitants		256.1	5.3	16.3	81.4	153.1	2,066.4	439.2	1,410.1	217.1

See footnotes at end of table.

Table 6

Crime in the United States

by Metropolitan Statistical Area, 2003—Continued

Metropolitan Statistical Area	Population	Violent crime	Murder and non-negligent man-slaughter	Forcible rape	Robbery	Aggravated assault	Property crime	Burglary	Larceny-theft	Motor vehicle theft
				Violent crime				Property crime		
Palm Bay-Melbourne-Titusville, FL M.S.A.	**504,647**									
(Includes Brevard County.)										
City of:										
Palm Bay	84,558	576	8	72	64	432	3,199	890	2,130	179
Melbourne	75,155	593	4	31	122	436	3,628	881	2,490	257
Titusville	41,879	356	2	19	70	265	1,726	548	937	241
Total area actually reporting	100.0%	3,544	22	265	539	2,718	18,182	4,798	12,060	1,324
Rate per 100,000 inhabitants		702.3	4.4	52.5	106.8	538.6	3,602.9	950.8	2,389.8	262.4
Panama City-Lynn Haven, FL M.S.A.	**154,681**									
(Includes Bay County.)										
City of:										
Panama City	37,393	378	1	34	87	256	2,818	490	2,173	155
Lynn Haven	13,508	45	1	1	7	36	477	119	331	27
Total area actually reporting	100.0%	1,179	7	120	215	837	8,711	1,855	6,406	450
Rate per 100,000 inhabitants		762.2	4.5	77.6	139.0	541.1	5,631.6	1,199.2	4,141.4	290.9
Pascagoula, MS M.S.A.	**153,562**									
(Includes George and Jackson Counties.)										
City of Pascagoula	26,076	136	1	46	72	17	1,947	696	1,114	137
Total area actually reporting	88.7%	435	4	89	161	181	5,967	2,043	3,397	527
Estimated total	100.0%	470	5	93	168	204	6,382	2,173	3,633	576
Rate per 100,000 inhabitants		306.1	3.3	60.6	109.4	132.8	4,156.0	1,415.1	2,365.8	375.1
Pensacola-Ferry Pass-Brent, FL M.S.A.	**432,254**									
(Includes Escambia and Santa Rosa Counties.)										
City of Pensacola	56,251	375	4	41	83	247	2,625	600	1,919	106
Total area actually reporting	100.0%	2,233	12	193	417	1,611	14,759	3,856	10,060	843
Rate per 100,000 inhabitants		516.6	2.8	44.6	96.5	372.7	3,414.4	892.1	2,327.3	195.0
Philadelphia-Camden-Wilmington, PA-NJ-DE-MD M.S.A.	**5,775,734**									
(Includes the Metropolitan Divisions of Camden, NJ; Philadelphia, PA; and Wilmington, DE-MD-NJ.)										
City of:										
Philadelphia, PA	1,495,903	20,620	348	1,004	9,617	9,651	62,454	10,656	37,864	13,934
Camden, NJ	80,132	1,925	41	56	856	972	5,279	1,459	2,671	1,149
Wilmington, DE	73,411	1,088	7	37	416	628	3,823	869	2,192	762
Total area actually reporting	98.3%	34,958	478	1,916	14,152	18,412	161,859	29,034	108,835	23,990
Estimated total	100.0%	35,200	480	1,933	14,218	18,569	163,834	29,305	110,358	24,171
Rate per 100,000 inhabitants		609.4	8.3	33.5	246.2	321.5	2,836.6	507.4	1,910.7	418.5
Camden, NJ M.D.	**1,218,662**									
(Includes Burlington, Camden, and Gloucester Counties.)										
Total area actually reporting	100.0%	4,838	68	276	1,848	2,646	32,991	7,104	22,525	3,362
Rate per 100,000 inhabitants		397.0	5.6	22.6	151.6	217.1	2,707.1	582.9	1,848.3	275.9
Philadelphia, PA M.D.	**3,882,315**									
(Includes Bucks, Chester, Delaware, Montgomery, and Philadelphia Counties.)										
Total area actually reporting	97.5%	26,031	391	1,418	11,054	13,168	106,444	17,003	71,517	17,924
Estimated total	100.0%	26,273	393	1,435	11,120	13,325	108,419	17,274	73,040	18,105
Rate per 100,000 inhabitants		676.7	10.1	37.0	286.4	343.2	2,792.6	444.9	1,881.4	466.3
Wilmington, DE-MD-NJ M.D.	**674,757**									
(Includes New Castle County, DE; Cecil County, MD; and Salem County, NJ.)										
Total area actually reporting	100.0%	4,089	19	222	1,250	2,598	22,424	4,927	14,793	2,704
Rate per 100,000 inhabitants		606.0	2.8	32.9	185.3	385.0	3,323.3	730.2	2,192.3	400.7
Phoenix-Mesa-Scottsdale, AZ M.S.A.[1]	**3,579,924**									
(Includes Maricopa and Pinal Counties.)										
City of:										
Phoenix	1,403,228	9,722	241	526	3,676	5,279	97,823	17,104	55,068	25,651
Mesa	436,569	2,346	14	116	431	1,785	26,127	4,112	17,452	4,563
Scottsdale	220,697	493	7	62	163	261	9,475	2,315	5,659	1,501
Tempe	163,143	1,013	7	74	299	633	14,887	2,430	9,756	2,701
Total area actually reporting	98.5%	17,926	328	1,146	5,536	10,916	206,736	39,755	122,399	44,582
Estimated total	100.0%	18,132	329	1,163	5,581	11,059	209,519	40,359	124,131	45,029
Rate per 100,000 inhabitants		506.5	9.2	32.5	155.9	308.9	5,852.6	1,127.4	3,467.4	1,257.8

See footnotes at end of table.

Table 6

Crime in the United States
by Metropolitan Statistical Area, 2003—Continued

Metropolitan Statistical Area	Population	Violent crime	Murder and non-negligent man-slaughter	Forcible rape	Robbery	Aggravated assault	Property crime	Burglary	Larceny-theft	Motor vehicle theft
				Violent crime				*Property crime*		
Pine Bluff, AR M.S.A.[1]	**106,774**									
(Includes Cleveland, Jefferson, and Lincoln Counties.)										
City of Pine Bluff	54,482	578	16	44	150	368	4,530	1,198	2,930	402
Total area actually reporting	100.0%	703	18	52	163	470	5,271	1,596	3,245	430
Rate per 100,000 inhabitants		658.4	16.9	48.7	152.7	440.2	4,936.6	1,494.7	3,039.1	402.7
Pittsburgh, PA M.S.A.	**2,424,149**									
(Includes Allegheny, Armstrong, Beaver, Butler, Fayette, Washington, and Westmoreland Counties.)										
City of Pittsburgh	335,302	3,559	67	136	1,635	1,721	16,435	3,180	10,610	2,645
Total area actually reporting	86.8%	7,991	110	470	2,740	4,671	51,558	9,625	36,524	5,409
Estimated total	100.0%	8,715	116	522	2,926	5,151	58,368	10,605	41,852	5,911
Rate per 100,000 inhabitants		359.5	4.8	21.5	120.7	212.5	2,407.8	437.5	1,726.5	243.8
Pittsfield, MA M.S.A.	**133,579**									
(Includes Berkshire County.)										
City of Pittsfield	45,062	197	3	13	15	166	711	109	441	161
Total area actually reporting	86.7%	422	4	43	30	345	2,193	573	1,368	252
Estimated total	100.0%	445	4	44	33	364	2,363	615	1,475	273
Rate per 100,000 inhabitants		333.1	3.0	32.9	24.7	272.5	1,769.0	460.4	1,104.2	204.4
Pocatello, ID M.S.A.	**84,746**									
(Includes Bannock and Power Counties.)										
City of Pocatello	52,205	138	1	19	8	110	1,752	204	1,464	84
Total area actually reporting	100.0%	229	1	28	10	190	2,654	342	2,201	111
Rate per 100,000 inhabitants		270.2	1.2	33.0	11.8	224.2	3,131.7	403.6	2,597.2	131.0
Portland-South Portland-Biddeford, ME M.S.A.	**504,909**									
(Includes Cumberland, Sagadahoc, and York Counties.)										
City of:										
Portland	64,438	242	1	51	101	89	3,036	676	2,191	169
South Portland	23,457	43	0	11	9	23	1,214	108	1,065	41
Biddeford	21,874	63	0	18	17	28	877	110	734	33
Total area actually reporting	100.0%	638	3	160	174	301	12,614	2,424	9,583	607
Rate per 100,000 inhabitants		126.4	0.6	31.7	34.5	59.6	2,498.3	480.1	1,898.0	120.2
Portland-Vancouver-Beaverton, OR-WA M.S.A.[1]	**2,037,963**									
(Includes Clackamas, Columbia, Multnomah, Washington, and Yamhill Counties, OR and Clark and Skamania Counties, WA.)										
City of:										
Portland, OR	545,271	4,436	27	310	1,367	2,732	41,951	6,484	29,599	5,868
Vancouver, WA[1]	151,353	642	2	128	164	348	8,723	1,283	6,244	1,196
Beaverton, OR	80,631	163	2	24	55	82	3,398	471	2,516	411
Hillsboro, OR	76,766	182	0	30	70	82	3,622	444	2,810	368
Total area actually reporting	98.7%	7,317	40	852	2,169	4,256	100,245	15,837	71,713	12,695
Estimated total	100.0%	7,357	40	858	2,177	4,282	101,086	15,999	72,293	12,794
Rate per 100,000 inhabitants		361.0	2.0	42.1	106.8	210.1	4,960.1	785.0	3,547.3	627.8
Port St. Lucie-Fort Pierce, FL M.S.A.	**343,818**									
(Includes Martin and St. Lucie Counties.)										
City of:										
Port St. Lucie	100,342	281	1	17	30	233	2,699	683	1,906	110
Fort Pierce	38,684	830	15	57	249	509	3,448	1,043	2,132	273
Total area actually reporting	100.0%	2,063	21	128	456	1,458	12,482	3,334	8,331	817
Rate per 100,000 inhabitants		600.0	6.1	37.2	132.6	424.1	3,630.4	969.7	2,423.1	237.6
Poughkeepsie-Newburgh-Middletown, NY M.S.A.	**645,621**									
(Includes Dutchess and Orange Counties.)										
City of:										
Poughkeepsie	30,124	348	2	26	131	189	1,162	257	822	83
Newburgh	28,430	260	2	26	57	175	1,047	316	624	107
Middletown	25,819	84	2	11	38	33	656	94	527	35
Total area actually reporting	96.2%	1,539	11	130	384	1,014	11,758	2,100	9,007	651
Estimated total	100.0%	1,585	11	132	400	1,042	12,272	2,175	9,411	686
Rate per 100,000 inhabitants		245.5	1.7	20.4	62.0	161.4	1,900.8	336.9	1,457.7	106.3

See footnotes at end of table.

Table 6

Crime in the United States
by Metropolitan Statistical Area, 2003—Continued

Metropolitan Statistical Area	Population	Violent crime	Violent crime Murder and non-negligent man-slaughter	Violent crime Forcible rape	Violent crime Robbery	Violent crime Aggravated assault	Property crime	Property crime Burglary	Property crime Larceny-theft	Property crime Motor vehicle theft
Prescott, AZ M.S.A.	**183,138**									
(Includes Yavapai County.)										
City of Prescott	37,127	159	1	7	24	127	2,146	413	1,627	106
Total area actually reporting	95.2%	683	6	37	48	592	6,603	1,508	4,606	489
Estimated total	100.0%	717	6	40	55	616	7,065	1,608	4,894	563
Rate per 100,000 inhabitants		391.5	3.3	21.8	30.0	336.4	3,857.7	878.0	2,672.3	307.4
Providence-New Bedford-Fall River, RI-MA M.S.A.	**1,620,073**									
(Includes Bristol County, MA and Bristol, Kent, Newport, Providence, and Washington Counties, RI.)										
City of:										
Providence, RI	176,960	1,395	18	133	515	729	11,083	1,682	6,756	2,645
New Bedford, MA	94,170	679	11	104	234	330	2,666	945	1,187	534
Fall River, MA	92,741	1,067	3	77	270	717	3,477	1,260	1,664	553
Warwick, RI	87,563	129	0	36	27	66	2,558	341	2,038	179
Cranston, RI	81,601	159	0	35	43	81	2,340	436	1,649	255
Total area actually reporting	99.6%	5,843	40	744	1,483	3,576	46,104	9,405	30,455	6,244
Estimated total	100.0%	5,864	40	745	1,487	3,592	46,231	9,433	30,538	6,260
Rate per 100,000 inhabitants		362.0	2.5	46.0	91.8	221.7	2,853.6	582.3	1,885.0	386.4
Provo-Orem, UT M.S.A.	**402,411**									
(Includes Juab and Utah Counties.)										
City of:										
Provo	106,769	114	0	36	16	62	3,512	841	2,492	179
Orem	84,934	68	2	18	18	30	3,503	372	2,932	199
Total area actually reporting	99.1%	364	3	104	50	207	13,508	2,568	10,234	706
Estimated total	100.0%	372	3	106	51	212	13,638	2,591	10,331	716
Rate per 100,000 inhabitants		92.4	0.7	26.3	12.7	52.7	3,389.1	643.9	2,567.3	177.9
Pueblo, CO M.S.A.	**148,319**									
(Includes Pueblo County.)										
City of Pueblo	104,424	817	6	38	175	598	5,571	1,241	3,928	402
Total area actually reporting	100.0%	857	7	39	182	629	6,920	1,565	4,906	449
Rate per 100,000 inhabitants		577.8	4.7	26.3	122.7	424.1	4,665.6	1,055.2	3,307.7	302.7
Punta Gorda, FL M.S.A.	**151,399**									
(Includes Charlotte County.)										
City of Punta Gorda	16,303	30	0	3	4	23	419	141	253	25
Total area actually reporting	100.0%	429	4	27	51	347	4,534	1,259	3,027	248
Rate per 100,000 inhabitants		283.4	2.6	17.8	33.7	229.2	2,994.7	831.6	1,999.4	163.8
Racine, WI M.S.A.	**192,104**									
(Includes Racine County.)										
City of Racine	81,173	317	3	22	205	87	4,290	836	3,055	399
Total area actually reporting	100.0%	377	5	30	231	111	6,545	1,134	4,898	513
Rate per 100,000 inhabitants		196.2	2.6	15.6	120.2	57.8	3,407.0	590.3	2,549.7	267.0
Raleigh-Cary, NC M.S.A.	**868,120**									
(Includes Franklin, Johnston, and Wake Counties.)										
City of:										
Raleigh	310,157	2,004	14	81	748	1,161	14,771	3,327	10,186	1,258
Cary	99,067	109	0	17	36	56	2,244	397	1,717	130
Total area actually reporting	99.1%	3,171	30	165	1,078	1,898	30,131	7,320	20,538	2,273
Estimated total	100.0%	3,205	30	167	1,089	1,919	30,576	7,419	20,862	2,295
Rate per 100,000 inhabitants		369.2	3.5	19.2	125.4	221.1	3,522.1	854.6	2,403.1	264.4
Rapid City, SD M.S.A.	**115,820**									
(Includes Meade and Pennington Counties.)										
City of Rapid City	60,519	242	0	67	35	140	2,712	409	2,167	136
Total area actually reporting	100.0%	400	3	126	39	232	4,408	609	3,581	218
Rate per 100,000 inhabitants		345.4	2.6	108.8	33.7	200.3	3,805.9	525.8	3,091.9	188.2
Reading, PA M.S.A.	**383,049**									
(Includes Berks County.)										
City of Reading	80,692	946	16	56	434	440	4,643	1,140	2,458	1,045
Total area actually reporting	93.7%	1,272	19	86	518	649	9,602	1,828	6,319	1,455
Estimated total	100.0%	1,326	19	90	532	685	10,111	1,901	6,717	1,493
Rate per 100,000 inhabitants		346.2	5.0	23.5	138.9	178.8	2,639.6	496.3	1,753.6	389.8

See footnotes at end of table.

Table 6

Crime in the United States
by Metropolitan Statistical Area, 2003—Continued

Metropolitan Statistical Area	Population	Violent crime	Murder and non-negligent man-slaughter	Forcible rape	Robbery	Aggravated assault	Property crime	Burglary	Larceny-theft	Motor vehicle theft
Redding, CA M.S.A.	**173,601**									
(Includes Shasta County.)										
City of Redding	86,559	393	2	67	88	236	3,156	779	2,039	338
Total area actually reporting	100.0%	765	5	110	111	539	5,084	1,454	2,987	643
Rate per 100,000 inhabitants		440.7	2.9	63.4	63.9	310.5	2,928.6	837.6	1,720.6	370.4
Reno-Sparks, NV M.S.A.	**377,135**									
(Includes Storey and Washoe Counties.)										
City of:										
Reno	196,171	1,255	11	89	493	662	11,231	1,976	7,708	1,547
Sparks	76,025	358	3	44	102	209	3,756	828	2,482	446
Total area actually reporting	100.0%	1,951	21	144	629	1,157	17,038	3,393	11,449	2,196
Rate per 100,000 inhabitants		517.3	5.6	38.2	166.8	306.8	4,517.7	899.7	3,035.8	582.3
Richmond, VA M.S.A.[1]	**1,140,589**									
(Includes Amelia, Caroline, Charles City, Chesterfield, Cumberland, Dinwiddie, Goochland, Hanover, Henrico, King and Queen, King William, Louisa, New Kent, Powhatan, Prince George, and Sussex Counties, and Colonial Heights, Hopewell, Petersburg, and Richmond Cities.)										
City of Richmond[1]	199,968	2,474	93	98	1,174	1,109		2,816		2,711
Total area actually reporting	99.2%	4,666	155	280	1,922	2,309		7,341		4,538
Estimated total	100.0%	4,687	155	282	1,928	2,322		7,372		4,557
Rate per 100,000 inhabitants		410.9	13.6	24.7	169.0	203.6		646.3		399.5
Riverside-San Bernardino-Ontario, CA M.S.A.	**3,552,063**									
(Includes Riverside and San Bernardino Counties.)										
City of:										
Riverside	277,103	1,916	24	102	573	1,217	12,891	2,194	8,098	2,599
San Bernardino	193,641	2,864	48	120	1,032	1,664	12,238	2,524	6,401	3,313
Ontario	166,796	904	11	47	323	523	7,472	1,019	4,331	2,122
Chino	70,695	243	2	15	88	138	2,366	459	1,387	520
Victorville	71,571	323	3	28	130	162	3,863	856	2,415	592
Redlands	67,449	379	2	17	94	266	2,767	531	1,733	503
Hemet	64,032	438	1	29	107	301	2,957	801	1,819	337
Temecula	74,567	222	1	22	38	161	2,026	414	1,314	298
Total area actually reporting	100.0%	19,335	258	1,035	5,375	12,667	131,091	30,311	73,672	27,108
Rate per 100,000 inhabitants		544.3	7.3	29.1	151.3	356.6	3,690.6	853.3	2,074.1	763.2
Rochester, MN M.S.A.	**170,754**									
(Includes Dodge, Olmsted, and Wabasha Counties.)										
City of Rochester	91,230	257	0	59	47	151	3,004	477	2,360	167
Total area actually reporting	100.0%	335	0	87	52	196	4,050	772	3,033	245
Rate per 100,000 inhabitants		196.2	0.0	51.0	30.5	114.8	2,371.8	452.1	1,776.2	143.5
Rochester, NY M.S.A.	**1,044,556**									
(Includes Livingston, Monroe, Ontario, Orleans, and Wayne Counties.)										
City of Rochester	217,527	2,034	58	86	1,166	724	15,708	2,497	9,773	3,438
Total area actually reporting	98.9%	3,034	66	210	1,467	1,291	35,033	5,464	24,918	4,651
Estimated total	100.0%	3,055	66	211	1,474	1,304	35,279	5,500	25,111	4,668
Rate per 100,000 inhabitants		292.5	6.3	20.2	141.1	124.8	3,377.4	526.5	2,404.0	446.9
Rocky Mount, NC M.S.A.	**145,804**									
(Includes Edgecombe and Nash Counties.)										
City of Rocky Mount	56,601	459	7	21	195	236	5,065	1,227	3,589	249
Total area actually reporting	100.0%	708	16	36	255	401	7,632	2,169	5,043	420
Rate per 100,000 inhabitants		485.6	11.0	24.7	174.9	275.0	5,234.4	1,487.6	3,458.8	288.1
Rome, GA M.S.A.	**93,952**									
(Includes Floyd County.)										
City of Rome	35,749	438	6	13	67	352	2,761	624	1,972	165
Total area actually reporting	100.0%	524	10	13	75	426	4,529	1,077	3,134	318
Rate per 100,000 inhabitants		557.7	10.6	13.8	79.8	453.4	4,820.5	1,146.3	3,335.7	338.5

See footnotes at end of table.

Table 6

Crime in the United States
by Metropolitan Statistical Area, 2003—Continued

Metropolitan Statistical Area	Population	Violent crime	Murder and non-negligent man-slaughter	Forcible rape	Robbery	Aggravated assault	Property crime	Burglary	Larceny-theft	Motor vehicle theft
				Violent crime				Property crime		
Sacramento–Arden-Arcade–Roseville, CA M.S.A.	**1,950,441**									
(Includes El Dorado, Placer, Sacramento, and Yolo Counties.)										
City of:										
Sacramento	439,811	3,420	43	187	1,630	1,560	28,266	5,606	15,374	7,286
Roseville	92,724	266	4	22	68	172	3,652	572	2,650	430
Folsom	61,899	119	0	16	24	79	1,638	360	1,131	147
Woodland	51,383	281	2	22	42	215	1,517	607	569	341
Total area actually reporting	100.0%	9,850	101	688	3,286	5,775	82,424	17,349	47,363	17,712
Rate per 100,000 inhabitants		505.0	5.2	35.3	168.5	296.1	4,225.9	889.5	2,428.3	908.1
Saginaw-Saginaw Township North, MI M.S.A.	**210,704**									
(Includes Saginaw County.)										
City of Saginaw	60,273	1,640	16	74	173	1,377	2,684	1,054	1,350	280
Total area actually reporting	100.0%	2,218	20	140	253	1,805	7,575	1,908	5,137	530
Rate per 100,000 inhabitants		1,052.7	9.5	66.4	120.1	856.7	3,595.1	905.5	2,438.0	251.5
Salem, OR M.S.A.	**361,681**									
(Includes Marion and Polk Counties.)										
City of Salem	142,501	514	5	75	180	254	11,563	1,575	8,417	1,571
Total area actually reporting	99.7%	886	8	124	236	518	21,808	3,325	15,466	3,017
Estimated total	100.0%	888	8	124	237	519	21,853	3,332	15,499	3,022
Rate per 100,000 inhabitants		245.5	2.2	34.3	65.5	143.5	6,042.1	921.3	4,285.3	835.5
Salinas, CA M.S.A.	**417,745**									
(Includes Monterey County.)										
City of Salinas	150,305	1,200	19	57	399	725	7,415	837	5,163	1,415
Total area actually reporting	100.0%	2,054	27	131	660	1,236	14,526	2,623	9,854	2,049
Rate per 100,000 inhabitants		491.7	6.5	31.4	158.0	295.9	3,477.2	627.9	2,358.9	490.5
Salisbury, MD M.S.A.	**112,914**									
(Includes Somerset and Wicomico Counties.)										
City of Salisbury	24,874	469	0	17	128	324	1,831	498	1,269	64
Total area actually reporting	100.0%	859	3	39	190	627	4,225	1,175	2,867	183
Rate per 100,000 inhabitants		760.8	2.7	34.5	168.3	555.3	3,741.8	1,040.6	2,539.1	162.1
Salt Lake City, UT M.S.A.	**1,012,356**									
(Includes Salt Lake, Summit, and Tooele Counties.)										
City of Salt Lake City	184,022	1,294	17	79	503	695	16,745	2,359	12,464	1,922
Total area actually reporting	99.8%	3,671	39	465	987	2,180	56,385	8,636	42,551	5,198
Estimated total	100.0%	3,676	39	466	988	2,183	56,463	8,649	42,610	5,204
Rate per 100,000 inhabitants		363.1	3.9	46.0	97.6	215.6	5,577.4	854.3	4,209.0	514.0
San Angelo, TX M.S.A.	**106,404**									
(Includes Irion and Tom Green Counties.)										
City of San Angelo	88,782	407	1	77	62	267	5,965	1,264	4,464	237
Total area actually reporting	100.0%	425	2	79	62	282	6,307	1,349	4,704	254
Rate per 100,000 inhabitants		399.4	1.9	74.2	58.3	265.0	5,927.4	1,267.8	4,420.9	238.7
San Antonio, TX M.S.A.	**1,814,397**									
(Includes Atascosa, Bandera, Bexar, Comal, Guadalupe, Kendall, Medina, and Wilson Counties.)										
City of San Antonio	1,212,789	7,252	85	537	2,060	4,570	83,000	14,619	62,179	6,202
Total area actually reporting	100.0%	8,800	114	751	2,270	5,665	103,709	19,106	77,329	7,274
Rate per 100,000 inhabitants		485.0	6.3	41.4	125.1	312.2	5,715.9	1,053.0	4,262.0	400.9
San Diego-Carlsbad-San Marcos, CA M.S.A.	**2,937,155**									
(Includes San Diego County.)										
City of:										
San Diego	1,272,746	7,366	65	406	1,626	5,269	46,382	8,076	25,739	12,567
Carlsbad	87,548	266	4	14	64	184	2,199	496	1,445	258
San Marcos	62,785	205	3	18	46	138	1,475	440	765	270
National City	56,124	546	9	33	155	349	2,740	337	1,407	996
Total area actually reporting	100.0%	14,007	130	856	3,375	9,646	96,636	18,893	54,278	23,465
Rate per 100,000 inhabitants		476.9	4.4	29.1	114.9	328.4	3,290.1	643.2	1,848.0	798.9
Sandusky, OH M.S.A.	**79,308**									
(Includes Erie County.)										
City of Sandusky	27,391	115	0	11	26	78	1,709	338	1,300	71
Total area actually reporting	99.5%	163	0	24	30	109	2,866	562	2,200	104
Estimated total	100.0%	163	0	24	30	109	2,877	564	2,208	105
Rate per 100,000 inhabitants		205.5	0.0	30.3	37.8	137.4	3,627.6	711.2	2,784.1	132.4

See footnotes at end of table.

Table 6

Crime in the United States
by Metropolitan Statistical Area, 2003—Continued

Metropolitan Statistical Area	Population	Violent crime	Murder and non-negligent man-slaughter	Forcible rape	Robbery	Aggravated assault	Property crime	Burglary	Larceny-theft	Motor vehicle theft
			Violent crime					*Property crime*		
San Francisco-Oakland-Fremont, CA M.S.A.	**4,223,349**									
(Includes the Metropolitan Divisions of Oakland-Fremont-Hayward and San Francisco-San Mateo-Redwood City.)										
City of:										
San Francisco	772,065	5,725	69	215	3,065	2,376	38,163	5,784	25,388	6,991
Oakland	407,003	5,613	109	268	2,474	2,762	22,630	4,568	12,551	5,511
Fremont	209,026	433	2	34	140	257	5,693	1,059	3,876	758
Hayward	144,215	600	8	41	257	294	5,125	847	2,647	1,631
Berkeley	104,727	926	6	16	402	502	8,695	1,245	6,217	1,233
San Mateo	92,900	341	1	28	95	217	2,756	294	2,208	254
San Leandro	81,455	578	3	26	292	257	4,040	748	2,453	839
Redwood City	75,234	367	2	17	61	287	2,190	383	1,590	217
Walnut Creek	66,031	106	0	8	18	80	2,635	434	1,938	263
Pleasanton	66,845	82	0	8	31	43	1,598	205	1,208	185
South San Francisco	60,584	135	2	17	56	60	1,481	321	891	269
San Rafael	56,879	208	0	25	66	117	2,010	327	1,233	450
Total area actually reporting	100.0%	22,710	302	1,149	9,762	11,497	171,400	28,867	108,900	33,633
Rate per 100,000 inhabitants		537.7	7.2	27.2	231.1	272.2	4,058.4	683.5	2,578.5	796.4
Oakland-Fremont-Hayward, CA M.D.	**2,490,526**									
(Includes Alameda and Contra Costa Counties.)										
Total area actually reporting	100.0%	14,291	213	715	5,889	7,474	107,816	18,736	65,865	23,215
Rate per 100,000 inhabitants		573.8	8.6	28.7	236.5	300.1	4,329.0	752.3	2,644.6	932.1
San Francisco-San Mateo-Redwood City, CA M.D.	**1,732,823**									
(Includes Marin, San Francisco, and San Mateo Counties.)										
Total area actually reporting	100.0%	8,419	89	434	3,873	4,023	63,584	10,131	43,035	10,418
Rate per 100,000 inhabitants		485.9	5.1	25.0	223.5	232.2	3,669.4	584.7	2,483.5	601.2
San Jose-Sunnyvale-Santa Clara, CA M.S.A.	**1,757,692**									
(Includes San Benito and Santa Clara Counties.)										
City of:										
San Jose	909,890	3,378	29	279	815	2,255	20,748	3,314	13,770	3,664
Sunnyvale	131,048	172	2	26	65	79	2,884	372	2,269	243
Santa Clara	102,936	253	7	25	48	173	3,006	420	2,244	342
Mountain View	70,781	291	1	6	42	242	1,837	209	1,489	139
Milpitas	64,368	200	3	23	38	136	2,203	301	1,663	239
Palo Alto	58,147	88	2	5	40	41	1,968	276	1,606	86
Cupertino	50,530	77	1	8	18	50	1,174	184	954	36
Total area actually reporting	100.0%	5,573	50	470	1,254	3,799	43,388	7,017	30,714	5,657
Rate per 100,000 inhabitants		317.1	2.8	26.7	71.3	216.1	2,468.5	399.2	1,747.4	321.8
San Luis Obispo-Paso Robles, CA M.S.A.	**256,067**									
(Includes San Luis Obispo County.)										
City of:										
San Luis Obispo	44,720	139	1	20	19	99	1,944	344	1,469	131
Paso Robles	26,635	122	3	13	14	92	933	376	483	74
Total area actually reporting	100.0%	638	7	79	61	491	7,015	1,642	4,879	494
Rate per 100,000 inhabitants		249.2	2.7	30.9	23.8	191.7	2,739.5	641.2	1,905.4	192.9
Santa Cruz-Watsonville, CA M.S.A.	**256,477**									
(Includes Santa Cruz County.)										
City of:										
Santa Cruz	54,401	510	4	48	112	346	3,121	523	2,420	178
Watsonville	47,133	329	3	23	99	204	2,049	331	1,569	149
Total area actually reporting	100.0%	1,268	13	102	264	889	9,865	1,814	7,356	695
Rate per 100,000 inhabitants		494.4	5.1	39.8	102.9	346.6	3,846.3	707.3	2,868.1	271.0
Santa Fe, NM M.S.A.	**135,943**									
(Includes Santa Fe County.)										
City of Santa Fe	65,814	387	9	40	104	234	4,671	2,301	2,137	233
Total area actually reporting	98.0%	657	9	79	120	449	5,685	2,808	2,583	294
Estimated total	100.0%	674	9	80	121	464	5,794	2,829	2,662	303
Rate per 100,000 inhabitants		495.8	6.6	58.8	89.0	341.3	4,262.1	2,081.0	1,958.2	222.9

See footnotes at end of table.

Table 6

Crime in the United States

by Metropolitan Statistical Area, 2003—Continued

Metropolitan Statistical Area	Population	Violent crime	Murder and non-negligent man-slaughter	Forcible rape	Robbery	Aggravated assault	Property crime	Burglary	Larceny-theft	Motor vehicle theft
Santa Rosa-Petaluma, CA M.S.A.	**473,300**									
(Includes Sonoma County.)										
City of:										
Santa Rosa	155,099	998	2	84	133	779	5,878	1,080	4,069	729
Petaluma	55,832	111	1	20	21	69	1,174	240	815	119
Total area actually reporting	100.0%	2,259	9	208	256	1,786	14,283	2,965	9,679	1,639
Rate per 100,000 inhabitants		477.3	1.9	43.9	54.1	377.4	3,017.7	626.5	2,045.0	346.3
Sarasota-Bradenton-Venice, FL M.S.A.	**631,487**									
(Includes Manatee and Sarasota Counties.)										
City of:										
Sarasota	54,297	566	5	31	199	331	3,987	903	2,826	258
Bradenton	52,304	455	7	29	162	257	3,320	894	2,073	353
Venice	18,941	37	0	1	5	31	528	78	436	14
Total area actually reporting	100.0%	3,940	28	197	885	2,830	28,215	6,839	19,477	1,899
Rate per 100,000 inhabitants		623.9	4.4	31.2	140.1	448.1	4,468.0	1,083.0	3,084.3	300.7
Savannah, GA M.S.A.	**304,146**									
(Includes Bryan, Chatham, and Effingham Counties.)										
City of Savannah	129,547	1,073	28	42	603	400	9,241	2,135	5,782	1,324
Total area actually reporting	98.4%	1,671	36	77	726	832	15,626	3,620	10,153	1,853
Estimated total	100.0%	1,695	36	78	734	847	15,894	3,664	10,350	1,880
Rate per 100,000 inhabitants		557.3	11.8	25.6	241.3	278.5	5,225.8	1,204.7	3,403.0	618.1
Scranton–Wilkes-Barre, PA M.S.A.	**554,517**									
(Includes Lackawanna, Luzerne, and Wyoming Counties.)										
City of:										
Scranton	74,896	263	2	37	92	132	2,260	528	1,547	185
Wilkes-Barre	42,124	148	2	15	92	39	2,119	406	1,579	134
Total area actually reporting	79.4%	1,165	25	117	312	711	10,979	2,130	8,062	787
Estimated total	100.0%	1,423	27	136	378	882	13,403	2,479	9,958	966
Rate per 100,000 inhabitants		256.6	4.9	24.5	68.2	159.1	2,417.1	447.1	1,795.8	174.2
Seattle-Tacoma-Bellevue, WA M.S.A.	**3,157,999**									
(Includes the Metropolitan Divisions of Seattle-Bellevue-Everett and Tacoma.)										
City of:										
Seattle	576,296	3,946	34	174	1,509	2,229	46,306	8,536	28,718	9,052
Tacoma	199,586	2,154	13	149	739	1,253	16,058	3,028	10,096	2,934
Bellevue	114,056	164	0	28	68	68	4,319	518	3,213	588
Everett	98,087	546	2	77	168	299	6,406	981	3,846	1,579
Kent	82,565	317	12	34	146	125	5,157	1,109	2,919	1,129
Renton	53,723	279	1	27	89	162	4,335	642	2,822	871
Total area actually reporting	100.0%	12,937	110	1,335	4,151	7,341	159,438	29,569	100,330	29,539
Rate per 100,000 inhabitants		409.7	3.5	42.3	131.4	232.5	5,048.7	936.3	3,177.0	935.4
Seattle-Bellevue-Everett, WA M.D.	**2,418,182**									
(Includes King and Snohomish Counties.)										
Total area actually reporting	100.0%	8,758	84	990	2,986	4,698	121,618	21,951	76,073	23,594
Rate per 100,000 inhabitants		362.2	3.5	40.9	123.5	194.3	5,029.3	907.7	3,145.9	975.7
Tacoma, WA M.D.	**739,817**									
(Includes Pierce County.)										
Total area actually reporting	100.0%	4,179	26	345	1,165	2,643	37,820	7,618	24,257	5,945
Rate per 100,000 inhabitants		564.9	3.5	46.6	157.5	357.3	5,112.1	1,029.7	3,278.8	803.6
Sheboygan, WI M.S.A.	**113,123**									
(Includes Sheboygan County.)										
City of Sheboygan	49,729	76	2	34	12	28	2,344	270	1,982	92
Total area actually reporting	100.0%	111	2	40	13	56	3,342	378	2,831	133
Rate per 100,000 inhabitants		98.1	1.8	35.4	11.5	49.5	2,954.3	334.1	2,502.6	117.6
Sherman-Denison, TX M.S.A.	**115,630**									
(Includes Grayson County.)										
City of:										
Sherman	36,344	168	1	2	33	132	2,056	386	1,598	72
Denison	23,529	90	1	1	21	67	1,241	237	928	76
Total area actually reporting	100.0%	339	3	18	59	259	4,590	1,008	3,337	245
Rate per 100,000 inhabitants		293.2	2.6	15.6	51.0	224.0	3,969.6	871.7	2,885.9	211.9

See footnotes at end of table.

Table 6

Crime in the United States

by Metropolitan Statistical Area, 2003—Continued

Metropolitan Statistical Area	Population	Violent crime	Murder and non-negligent man-slaughter	Forcible rape	Robbery	Aggravated assault	Property crime	Burglary	Larceny-theft	Motor vehicle theft
Shreveport-Bossier City, LA M.S.A.	379,039									
(Includes Bossier, Caddo, and De Soto Parishes.)										
City of:										
Shreveport	199,641	2,056	42	112	689	1,213	14,905	3,595	9,745	1,565
Bossier City	57,331	476	4	31	97	344	3,491	644	2,517	330
Total area actually reporting	100.0%	2,941	55	171	806	1,909	21,618	4,939	14,617	2,062
Rate per 100,000 inhabitants		775.9	14.5	45.1	212.6	503.6	5,703.4	1,303.0	3,856.3	544.0
Sioux City, IA-NE-SD M.S.A.	143,270									
(Includes Woodbury County, IA; Dakota and Dixon Counties, NE; and Union County SD.)										
City of Sioux City, IA	84,340	357	1	43	49	264	4,556	967	3,227	362
Total area actually reporting	99.4%	437	1	48	52	336	5,220	1,132	3,685	403
Estimated total	100.0%	438	1	48	52	337	5,231	1,134	3,693	404
Rate per 100,000 inhabitants		305.7	0.7	33.5	36.3	235.2	3,651.1	791.5	2,577.7	282.0
Sioux Falls, SD M.S.A.	195,488									
(Includes Lincoln, McCook, Minnehaha, and Turner Counties.)										
City of Sioux Falls	131,048	392	3	104	40	245	4,023	770	2,997	256
Total area actually reporting	95.6%	442	3	113	42	284	4,509	935	3,273	301
Estimated total	100.0%	459	3	120	42	294	4,687	964	3,412	311
Rate per 100,000 inhabitants		234.8	1.5	61.4	21.5	150.4	2,397.6	493.1	1,745.4	159.1
South Bend-Mishawaka, IN-MI M.S.A.	320,141									
(Includes St. Joseph County, IN and Cass County, MI.)										
City of:										
South Bend, IN	107,191	768	16	78	324	350	6,853	1,716	4,596	541
Mishawaka, IN	48,551	314	2	12	57	243	3,986	507	3,307	172
Total area actually reporting	97.3%	1,340	20	121	435	764	14,611	3,138	10,529	944
Estimated total	100.0%	1,363	20	124	440	779	14,880	3,183	10,721	976
Rate per 100,000 inhabitants		425.7	6.2	38.7	137.4	243.3	4,648.0	994.2	3,348.8	304.9
Spartanburg, SC M.S.A.	261,846									
(Includes Spartanburg County.)										
City of Spartanburg	39,448	821	6	31	185	599	3,777	754	2,679	344
Total area actually reporting	100.0%	1,963	21	115	385	1,442	11,271	2,679	7,583	1,009
Rate per 100,000 inhabitants		749.7	8.0	43.9	147.0	550.7	4,304.4	1,023.1	2,896.0	385.3
Spokane, WA M.S.A.	431,905									
(Includes Spokane County.)										
City of Spokane	198,325	1,161	13	84	354	710	15,906	3,053	11,260	1,593
Total area actually reporting	98.9%	1,638	16	141	458	1,023	23,718	4,668	16,805	2,245
Estimated total	100.0%	1,651	16	143	462	1,030	23,942	4,705	16,960	2,277
Rate per 100,000 inhabitants		382.3	3.7	33.1	107.0	238.5	5,543.3	1,089.4	3,926.8	527.2
Springfield, MA M.S.A.	677,488									
(Includes Franklin, Hampden, and Hampshire Counties.)										
City of Springfield	152,048	2,914	15	115	847	1,937	11,628	2,647	6,414	2,567
Total area actually reporting	94.4%	4,972	24	316	1,179	3,453	24,948	5,896	15,037	4,015
Estimated total	100.0%	5,063	23	321	1,194	3,525	25,512	6,024	15,400	4,088
Rate per 100,000 inhabitants		747.3	3.4	47.4	176.2	520.3	3,765.7	889.2	2,273.1	603.4
Springfield, MO M.S.A.	380,857									
(Includes Christian, Dallas, Greene, Polk, and Webster Counties.)										
City of Springfield	151,859	1,038	6	73	171	788	12,351	1,833	9,754	764
Total area actually reporting	100.0%	1,422	10	97	188	1,127	17,333	2,977	13,262	1,094
Rate per 100,000 inhabitants		373.4	2.6	25.5	49.4	295.9	4,551.1	781.7	3,482.1	287.2
Springfield, OH M.S.A.	143,598									
(Includes Clark County.)										
City of Springfield	64,214	558	5	74	285	194	6,253	1,573	4,022	658
Total area actually reporting	99.8%	643	8	89	318	228	8,687	2,189	5,688	810
Estimated total	100.0%	643	8	89	318	228	8,696	2,190	5,695	811
Rate per 100,000 inhabitants		447.8	5.6	62.0	221.5	158.8	6,055.8	1,525.1	3,965.9	564.8
State College, PA M.S.A.	138,865									
(Includes Centre County.)										
City of State College	51,741	48	0	17	8	23	1,029	108	902	19
Total area actually reporting	100.0%	215	1	37	18	159	2,853	362	2,421	70
Rate per 100,000 inhabitants		154.8	0.7	26.6	13.0	114.5	2,054.5	260.7	1,743.4	50.4

See footnotes at end of table.

Table 6

Crime in the United States
by Metropolitan Statistical Area, 2003—Continued

Metropolitan Statistical Area	Population	Violent crime	Murder and non-negligent man-slaughter	Forcible rape	Robbery	Aggravated assault	Property crime	Burglary	Larceny-theft	Motor vehicle theft
St. Joseph, MO-KS M.S.A.	**122,494**									
(Includes Doniphan County, KS and Andrew, Buchanan, and De Kalb Counties, MO.)										
City of St. Joseph, MO	73,559	167	1	16	68	82	4,907	924	3,729	254
Total area actually reporting	100.0%	248	1	27	72	148	5,863	1,201	4,342	320
Rate per 100,000 inhabitants		202.5	0.8	22.0	58.8	120.8	4,786.4	980.5	3,544.7	261.2
St. Louis, MO-IL M.S.A.	**2,744,792**									
(Includes Bond, Calhoun, Clinton, Jersey, Macoupin, Madison, Monroe, and St. Clair Counties, IL and Franklin, Jefferson, Lincoln, St. Charles, St. Louis, Warren, and Washington Counties and St. Louis City, MO.)										
City of:										
St. Louis, MO	340,256	6,325	73	75	2,303	3,874	40,310	5,889	23,747	10,674
St. Charles, MO	61,097	193	0	15	35	143	2,016	238	1,577	201
Total area actually reporting	75.2%	10,958	113	343	3,200	7,302	92,049	13,278	62,351	16,420
Estimated total	100.0%	13,058	152	343	3,842	8,721	107,088	16,093	73,525	17,470
Rate per 100,000 inhabitants		475.7	5.5	12.5	140.0	317.7	3,901.5	586.3	2,678.7	636.5
Stockton, CA M.S.A.	**620,747**									
(Includes San Joaquin County.)										
City of Stockton	265,593	3,625	37	155	1,208	2,225	18,779	3,125	11,791	3,863
Total area actually reporting	100.0%	5,381	58	211	1,546	3,566	35,400	6,441	22,140	6,819
Rate per 100,000 inhabitants		866.9	9.3	34.0	249.1	574.5	5,702.8	1,037.6	3,566.7	1,098.5
Sumter, SC M.S.A.	**106,222**									
(Includes Sumter County.)										
City of Sumter	39,765	722	5	26	168	523	3,014	793	1,931	290
Total area actually reporting	99.0%	1,247	12	46	230	959	5,679	1,812	3,257	610
Estimated total	100.0%	1,253	12	46	231	964	5,729	1,820	3,296	613
Rate per 100,000 inhabitants		1,179.6	11.3	43.3	217.5	907.5	5,393.4	1,713.4	3,102.9	577.1
Syracuse, NY M.S.A.	**654,609**									
(Includes Madison, Onondaga, and Oswego Counties.)										
City of Syracuse	145,411	1,383	17	44	477	845	7,773	1,975	4,612	1,186
Total area actually reporting	98.4%	1,992	25	108	622	1,237	17,843	3,940	12,449	1,454
Estimated total	100.0%	2,012	25	109	629	1,249	18,068	3,973	12,626	1,469
Rate per 100,000 inhabitants		307.4	3.8	16.7	96.1	190.8	2,760.1	606.9	1,928.8	224.4
Tallahassee, FL M.S.A.	**333,871**									
(Includes Gadsden, Jefferson, Leon, and Wakulla Counties.)										
City of Tallahassee	158,011	1,412	4	155	342	911	9,338	2,223	6,413	702
Total area actually reporting	99.4%	2,391	12	237	459	1,683	14,604	3,811	9,727	1,066
Estimated total	100.0%	2,402	12	238	462	1,690	14,691	3,829	9,788	1,074
Rate per 100,000 inhabitants		719.4	3.6	71.3	138.4	506.2	4,400.2	1,146.9	2,931.7	321.7
Tampa-St. Petersburg-Clearwater, FL M.S.A.	**2,535,878**									
(Includes Hernando, Hillsborough, Pasco, and Pinellas Counties.)										
City of:										
Tampa	320,908	5,733	41	222	1,769	3,701	28,449	6,390	16,715	5,344
St. Petersburg	253,095	4,054	22	106	1,198	2,728	16,431	3,852	10,583	1,996
Clearwater	110,296	1,162	4	53	253	852	5,572	1,055	4,037	480
Largo	71,943	342	4	30	60	248	2,754	517	2,051	186
Total area actually reporting	100.0%	21,904	134	1,217	5,136	15,417	124,471	28,062	81,575	14,834
Rate per 100,000 inhabitants		863.8	5.3	48.0	202.5	608.0	4,908.4	1,106.6	3,216.8	585.0
Toledo, OH M.S.A.	**660,354**									
(Includes Fulton, Lucas, Ottawa, and Wood Counties.)										
City of Toledo	309,499	3,182	21	152	1,354	1,655	23,159	5,664	14,383	3,112
Total area actually reporting	93.5%	3,512	22	194	1,459	1,837	32,695	7,060	22,050	3,585
Estimated total	100.0%	3,563	22	204	1,477	1,860	33,698	7,281	22,760	3,657
Rate per 100,000 inhabitants		539.6	3.3	30.9	223.7	281.7	5,103.0	1,102.6	3,446.6	553.8
Topeka, KS M.S.A.	**226,430**									
(Includes Jackson, Jefferson, Osage, Shawnee, and Wabaunsee Counties.)										
City of Topeka	122,446	728	16	52	298	362	9,208	1,518	7,183	507
Total area actually reporting	97.8%	975	18	77	310	570	11,346	2,040	8,634	672
Estimated total	100.0%	991	18	79	313	581	11,530	2,073	8,770	687
Rate per 100,000 inhabitants		437.7	7.9	34.9	138.2	256.6	5,092.1	915.5	3,873.2	303.4

See footnotes at end of table.

Table 6

Crime in the United States
by Metropolitan Statistical Area, 2003—Continued

Metropolitan Statistical Area	Population	Violent crime	Murder and non-negligent man-slaughter	Forcible rape	Robbery	Aggravated assault	Property crime	Burglary	Larceny-theft	Motor vehicle theft
Trenton-Ewing, NJ M.S.A.	**361,476**									
(Includes Mercer County.)										
City of:										
Trenton	86,130	1,518	13	36	645	824	4,677	1,073	2,514	1,090
Ewing Township	36,355	120	0	14	55	51	1,078	178	772	128
Total area actually reporting	100.0%	1,942	16	64	843	1,019	10,499	2,095	6,757	1,647
Rate per 100,000 inhabitants		537.2	4.4	17.7	233.2	281.9	2,904.5	579.6	1,869.3	455.6
Tucson, AZ M.S.A.	**901,305**									
(Includes Pima County.)										
City of Tucson	514,618	4,709	47	330	1,478	2,854	47,298	6,397	34,542	6,359
Total area actually reporting	100.0%	5,759	75	419	1,692	3,573	63,640	9,231	45,965	8,444
Rate per 100,000 inhabitants		639.0	8.3	46.5	187.7	396.4	7,060.9	1,024.2	5,099.8	936.9
Tulsa, OK M.S.A.	**882,386**									
(Includes Creek, Okmulgee, Osage, Pawnee, Rogers, Tulsa, and Wagoner Counties.)										
City of Tulsa	393,907	4,304	61	272	891	3,080	27,253	6,403	17,343	3,507
Total area actually reporting	100.0%	5,592	76	387	1,023	4,106	39,668	9,447	25,493	4,728
Rate per 100,000 inhabitants		633.7	8.6	43.9	115.9	465.3	4,495.5	1,070.6	2,889.1	535.8
Tuscaloosa, AL M.S.A.	**194,229**									
(Includes Greene, Hale, and Tuscaloosa Counties.)										
City of Tuscaloosa	79,400	555	7	50	222	276	5,063	999	3,809	255
Total area actually reporting	98.6%	1,021	9	77	268	667	8,692	1,893	6,208	591
Estimated total	100.0%	1,031	9	78	271	673	8,810	1,916	6,295	599
Rate per 100,000 inhabitants		530.8	4.6	40.2	139.5	346.5	4,535.9	986.5	3,241.0	308.4
Tyler, TX M.S.A.	**184,258**									
(Includes Smith County.)										
City of Tyler	88,383	717	8	40	147	522	5,280	994	4,019	267
Total area actually reporting	98.9%	1,210	15	87	175	933	7,749	1,758	5,523	468
Estimated total	100.0%	1,217	15	88	177	937	7,835	1,775	5,586	474
Rate per 100,000 inhabitants		660.5	8.1	47.8	96.1	508.5	4,252.2	963.3	3,031.6	257.2
Utica-Rome, NY M.S.A.	**299,215**									
(Includes Herkimer and Oneida Counties.)										
City of:										
Utica	60,049	409	7	43	186	173	2,280	744	1,392	144
Rome	34,768	51	0	5	23	23	746	200	504	42
Total area actually reporting	96.7%	950	9	112	235	594	6,907	1,705	4,893	309
Estimated total	100.0%	968	9	113	241	605	7,113	1,735	5,055	323
Rate per 100,000 inhabitants		323.5	3.0	37.8	80.5	202.2	2,377.2	579.9	1,689.4	107.9
Valdosta, GA M.S.A.	**121,843**									
(Includes Brooks, Echols, Lanier, and Lowndes Counties.)										
City of Valdosta	45,357	298	3	24	101	170	3,238	600	2,489	149
Total area actually reporting	100.0%	630	3	47	131	449	5,212	1,040	3,917	255
Rate per 100,000 inhabitants		517.1	2.5	38.6	107.5	368.5	4,277.6	853.6	3,214.8	209.3
Vallejo-Fairfield, CA M.S.A.	**415,385**									
(Includes Solano County.)										
City of:										
Vallejo	121,055	997	6	42	339	610	5,817	1,021	3,631	1,165
Fairfield	103,004	621	12	36	177	396	4,752	660	3,394	698
Total area actually reporting	100.0%	2,226	20	133	644	1,429	15,603	2,701	10,343	2,559
Rate per 100,000 inhabitants		535.9	4.8	32.0	155.0	344.0	3,756.3	650.2	2,490.0	616.1
Vero Beach, FL M.S.A.	**120,167**									
(Includes Indian River County.)										
City of Vero Beach	17,660	93	1	5	32	55	734	130	572	32
Total area actually reporting	100.0%	451	5	63	79	304	4,282	935	3,127	220
Rate per 100,000 inhabitants		375.3	4.2	52.4	65.7	253.0	3,563.4	778.1	2,602.2	183.1
Victoria, TX M.S.A.	**114,352**									
(Includes Calhoun, Goliad, and Victoria Counties.)										
City of Victoria	61,980	526	8	46	111	361	4,345	850	3,290	205
Total area actually reporting	100.0%	664	29	73	116	446	5,681	1,207	4,193	281
Rate per 100,000 inhabitants		580.7	25.4	63.8	101.4	390.0	4,968.0	1,055.5	3,666.7	245.7

See footnotes at end of table.

Table 6

Crime in the United States

by Metropolitan Statistical Area, 2003—Continued

Metropolitan Statistical Area	Population	Violent crime	Violent crime				Property crime	Property crime		
		Violent crime	Murder and non-negligent man-slaughter	Forcible rape	Robbery	Aggravated assault	Property crime	Burglary	Larceny-theft	Motor vehicle theft
Vineland-Millville-Bridgeton, NJ M.S.A.	**148,595**									
(Includes Cumberland County.)										
City of:										
Vineland	56,655	416	4	16	169	227	3,039	747	2,127	165
Millville	27,068	229	3	28	77	121	1,480	382	1,017	81
Bridgeton	22,780	385	6	21	125	233	1,032	320	613	99
Total area actually reporting	100.0%	1,148	17	67	377	687	6,327	1,695	4,167	465
Rate per 100,000 inhabitants		772.6	11.4	45.1	253.7	462.3	4,257.9	1,140.7	2,804.3	312.9
Virginia Beach-Norfolk-Newport News, VA-NC M.S.A.[1]	**1,633,403**									
(Includes Currituck County, NC and Gloucester, Isle of Wight, James City, Mathews, Surry, and York Counties and Chesapeake, Hampton, Newport News, Norfolk, Poquoson, Portsmouth, Suffolk, Virginia Beach, and Williamsburg Cities, VA.)										
City of:										
Virginia Beach, VA	439,454	928	24	119	408	377	14,564	2,138	11,621	805
Norfolk, VA	242,077	1,383	40	86	717	540	13,854	1,784	10,632	1,438
Newport News, VA[1]	182,565	1,253	27	94	389	743			5,489	980
Hampton, VA	147,777	599	10	56	246	287	5,115	896	3,659	560
Portsmouth, VA	101,060	901	18	43	403	437	5,002	1,179	3,323	500
Total area actually reporting	100.0%	7,104	130	560	2,646	3,768			45,727	5,289
Rate per 100,000 inhabitants		434.9	8.0	34.3	162.0	230.7			2,799.5	323.8
Visalia-Porterville, CA M.S.A.[1]	**385,777**									
(Includes Tulare County.)										
City of:										
Visalia	97,906	789	9	47	144	589	5,857	1,080	3,971	806
Porterville	41,742	237	1	12	54	170	2,068	430	1,272	366
Total area actually reporting	100.0%	2,566	30	130	381	2,025		4,041	10,999	
Rate per 100,000 inhabitants		665.2	7.8	33.7	98.8	524.9		1,047.5	2,851.1	
Waco, TX M.S.A.	**221,098**									
(Includes McLennan County.)										
City of Waco	117,549	809	14	40	215	540	8,773	2,176	5,990	607
Total area actually reporting	100.0%	1,191	18	83	238	852	12,392	3,085	8,490	817
Rate per 100,000 inhabitants		538.7	8.1	37.5	107.6	385.3	5,604.8	1,395.3	3,839.9	369.5
Warner Robins, GA M.S.A.	**118,465**									
(Includes Houston County.)										
City of Warner Robins	53,242	212	5	20	79	108	3,471	724	2,563	184
Total area actually reporting	100.0%	329	7	28	102	192	5,544	1,110	4,124	310
Rate per 100,000 inhabitants		277.7	5.9	23.6	86.1	162.1	4,679.9	937.0	3,481.2	261.7
Washington-Arlington-Alexandria, DC-VA-MD-WV M.S.A.	**5,067,631**									
(Includes the Metropolitan Divisions of Bethesda-Frederick-Gaithersburg, MD and Washington-Arlington-Alexandria, DC-VA-MD-WV.)										
City of:										
Washington, D.C.	563,384	8,839	248	273	3,836	4,482	31,581	4,670	17,362	9,549
Alexandria, VA	132,468	405	3	25	169	208	4,292	429	3,253	610
Frederick, MD	56,585	568	4	21	91	452	1,785	319	1,369	97
Total area actually reporting	99.2%	24,565	460	1,094	10,627	12,384	169,696	23,057	109,939	36,700
Estimated total	100.0%	24,683	461	1,105	10,665	12,452	171,043	23,181	111,015	36,847
Rate per 100,000 inhabitants		487.1	9.1	21.8	210.5	245.7	3,375.2	457.4	2,190.7	727.1
Bethesda-Frederick-Gaithersburg, MD M.D.	**1,129,694**									
(Includes Frederick and Montgomery Counties.)										
Total area actually reporting	100.0%	3,102	28	190	1,194	1,690	30,391	5,038	21,437	3,916
Rate per 100,000 inhabitants		274.6	2.5	16.8	105.7	149.6	2,690.2	446.0	1,897.6	346.6

See footnotes at end of table.

Table 6

Crime in the United States
by Metropolitan Statistical Area, 2003—Continued

Metropolitan Statistical Area	Population	Violent crime	Violent crime				Property crime	Property crime		
			Murder and non-negligent man-slaughter	Forcible rape	Robbery	Aggravated assault	Property crime	Burglary	Larceny-theft	Motor vehicle theft
Washington-Arlington-Alexandria, DC-VA-MD-WV M.D.	**3,937,937**									
(Includes District of Columbia, Calvert, Charles, and Prince George's Counties, MD; Arlington, Clarke, Fairfax, Fauquier, Loudoun, Prince William, Spotsylvania, Stafford, and Warren Counties and Alexandria, Fairfax, Falls Church, Fredericksburg, Manassas, and Manassas Park Cities, VA; and Jefferson County, WV.)										
Total area actually reporting	99.0%	21,463	432	904	9,433	10,694	139,305	18,019	88,502	32,784
Estimated total	100.0%	21,581	433	915	9,471	10,762	140,652	18,143	89,578	32,931
Rate per 100,000 inhabitants		548.0	11.0	23.2	240.5	273.3	3,571.7	460.7	2,274.7	836.3
Waterloo-Cedar Falls, IA M.S.A.	**163,497**									
(Includes Black Hawk, Bremer, and Grundy Counties.)										
City of:										
Waterloo	67,910	326	4	47	93	182	3,707	922	2,543	242
Cedar Falls	36,751	114	2	13	5	94	973	138	802	33
Total area actually reporting	100.0%	470	7	66	98	299	5,304	1,183	3,826	295
Rate per 100,000 inhabitants		287.5	4.3	40.4	59.9	182.9	3,244.1	723.6	2,340.1	180.4
Wausau, WI M.S.A.	**127,452**									
(Includes Marathon County.)										
City of Wausau	37,948	149	1	20	27	101	1,703	344	1,265	94
Total area actually reporting	100.0%	198	1	24	35	138	3,006	697	2,162	147
Rate per 100,000 inhabitants		155.4	0.8	18.8	27.5	108.3	2,358.5	546.9	1,696.3	115.3
Wenatchee, WA M.S.A.	**101,493**									
(Includes Chelan and Douglas Counties.)										
City of Wenatchee	28,559	104	0	28	22	54	1,809	365	1,361	83
Total area actually reporting	100.0%	190	4	59	33	94	4,155	831	3,149	175
Rate per 100,000 inhabitants		187.2	3.9	58.1	32.5	92.6	4,093.9	818.8	3,102.7	172.4
Wichita, KS M.S.A.[1]	**583,008**									
(Includes Butler, Harvey, Sedgwick, and Sumner Counties.)										
City of Wichita[1]	356,123	2,227	18	216	556	1,437	19,518	3,825	14,284	1,409
Total area actually reporting	98.7%	2,722	23	276	581	1,842	25,447	4,980	18,780	1,687
Estimated total	100.0%	2,746	23	278	586	1,859	25,735	5,031	18,994	1,710
Rate per 100,000 inhabitants		471.0	3.9	47.7	100.5	318.9	4,414.2	862.9	3,257.9	293.3
Wichita Falls, TX M.S.A.	**152,694**									
(Includes Archer, Clay, and Wichita Counties.)										
City of Wichita Falls	104,526	1,082	8	49	199	826	7,507	1,719	5,208	580
Total area actually reporting	100.0%	1,167	9	53	205	900	8,535	2,063	5,816	656
Rate per 100,000 inhabitants		764.3	5.9	34.7	134.3	589.4	5,589.6	1,351.1	3,808.9	429.6
Williamsport, PA M.S.A.	**119,293**									
(Includes Lycoming County.)										
City of Williamsport	30,158	116	0	11	61	44	1,418	298	1,048	72
Total area actually reporting	93.8%	193	1	27	75	90	2,650	581	1,926	143
Estimated total	100.0%	209	1	28	79	101	2,808	604	2,049	155
Rate per 100,000 inhabitants		175.2	0.8	23.5	66.2	84.7	2,353.9	506.3	1,717.6	129.9
Wilmington, NC M.S.A.	**290,018**									
(Includes Brunswick, New Hanover, and Pender Counties.)										
City of Wilmington	91,593	819	5	30	325	459	7,356	1,855	4,900	601
Total area actually reporting	98.6%	1,224	6	77	420	721	15,247	4,956	9,281	1,010
Estimated total	100.0%	1,240	6	78	425	731	15,468	5,005	9,442	1,021
Rate per 100,000 inhabitants		427.6	2.1	26.9	146.5	252.1	5,333.5	1,725.8	3,255.7	352.0
Winchester, VA-WV M.S.A.	**109,442**									
(Includes Frederick County and Winchester City, VA and Hampshire County, WV.)										
City of Winchester, VA	24,536	73	0	9	30	34	1,346	168	1,125	53
Total area actually reporting	99.8%	202	3	20	48	131	3,034	556	2,310	168
Estimated total	100.0%	202	3	20	48	131	3,039	557	2,314	168
Rate per 100,000 inhabitants		184.6	2.7	18.3	43.9	119.7	2,776.8	508.9	2,114.4	153.5

See footnotes at end of table.

Table 6

Crime in the United States

by Metropolitan Statistical Area, 2003—Continued

Metropolitan Statistical Area	Population	Violent crime	Murder and non-negligent man-slaughter	Forcible rape	Robbery	Aggravated assault	Property crime	Burglary	Larceny-theft	Motor vehicle theft
Winston-Salem, NC M.S.A.	**438,524**									
(Includes Davie, Forsyth, Stokes, and Yadkin Counties.)										
City of Winston-Salem	190,912	1,579	11	118	547	903	13,938	3,957	8,810	1,171
Total area actually reporting	99.2%	2,278	21	174	635	1,448	22,248	6,200	14,466	1,582
Estimated total	100.0%	2,293	21	175	640	1,457	22,447	6,244	14,611	1,592
Rate per 100,000 inhabitants		522.9	4.8	39.9	145.9	332.3	5,118.8	1,423.9	3,331.9	363.0
Worcester, MA M.S.A.	**770,995**									
(Includes Worcester County.)										
City of Worcester	175,115	1,536	7	59	411	1,059	7,637	1,548	4,637	1,452
Total area actually reporting	95.4%	3,131	15	197	595	2,324	16,447	3,941	10,340	2,166
Estimated total	100.0%	3,241	15	204	614	2,408	17,124	4,088	10,781	2,255
Rate per 100,000 inhabitants		420.4	1.9	26.5	79.6	312.3	2,221.0	530.2	1,398.3	292.5
Yakima, WA M.S.A.	**227,136**									
(Includes Yakima County.)										
City of Yakima	74,052	430	5	55	141	229	5,967	1,252	4,152	563
Total area actually reporting	99.2%	713	10	137	194	372	13,730	3,418	8,947	1,365
Estimated total	100.0%	718	10	138	195	375	13,823	3,433	9,012	1,378
Rate per 100,000 inhabitants		316.1	4.4	60.8	85.9	165.1	6,085.8	1,511.4	3,967.7	606.7
Youngstown-Warren-Boardman, OH-PA M.S.A.	**597,240**									
(Includes Mahoning and Trumbull Counties, OH and Mercer County, PA.)										
City of:										
Youngstown, OH	80,128	768	19	60	286	403	4,833	1,763	2,568	502
Warren, OH	47,285	368	6	32	153	177	2,441	715	1,444	282
Boardman, OH	41,718	74	1	3	49	21	2,351	319	1,796	236
Total area actually reporting	80.3%	1,643	29	140	591	883	15,989	4,159	10,301	1,529
Estimated total	100.0%	1,866	30	167	664	1,005	19,291	4,715	12,840	1,736
Rate per 100,000 inhabitants		312.4	5.0	28.0	111.2	168.3	3,230.0	789.5	2,149.9	290.7
Yuba City, CA M.S.A.	**146,439**									
(Includes Sutter and Yuba Counties.)										
City of Yuba City	47,708	201	0	28	46	127	1,969	358	1,409	202
Total area actually reporting	100.0%	676	8	71	113	484	5,614	1,454	3,288	872
Rate per 100,000 inhabitants		461.6	5.5	48.5	77.2	330.5	3,833.7	992.9	2,245.3	595.5
Yuma, AZ M.S.A.	**171,222**									
(Includes Yuma County.)										
City of Yuma	82,189	517	1	40	47	429	3,631	588	2,538	505
Total area actually reporting	89.4%	895	4	43	61	787	5,210	1,187	3,299	724
Estimated total	100.0%	965	4	49	76	836	6,163	1,394	3,892	877
Rate per 100,000 inhabitants		563.6	2.3	28.6	44.4	488.3	3,599.4	814.1	2,273.1	512.2
Aguadilla-Isabela-San Sebastian, Puerto Rico M.S.A.	**321,318**									
(Includes Aguada, Aguadilla, Anasco, Isabela, Lares, Moca, Rincon, and San Sebastian Municipios.)										
Total area actually reporting	100.0%	337	19	6	180	132	3,225	1,252	1,714	259
Rate per 100,000 inhabitants		104.9	5.9	1.9	56.0	41.1	1,003.7	389.6	533.4	80.6
Fajardo, Puerto Rico M.S.A.	**80,032**									
(Includes Ceiba, Fajardo, and Luquillo Municipios.)										
Total area actually reporting	100.0%	185	17	8	104	56	1,433	502	812	119
Rate per 100,000 inhabitants		231.2	21.2	10.0	129.9	70.0	1,790.5	627.2	1,014.6	148.7
Guayama, Puerto Rico M.S.A.	**84,565**									
(Includes Arroyo, Guayama, and Patillas Municipios.)										
Total area actually reporting	100.0%	177	18	2	84	73	676	405	191	80
Rate per 100,000 inhabitants		209.3	21.3	2.4	99.3	86.3	799.4	478.9	225.9	94.6
Mayaguez, Puerto Rico M.S.A.	**115,307**									
(Includes Hormigueros and Mayaguez Municipios.)										
Total area actually reporting	100.0%	198	10	8	109	71	3,229	830	2,242	157
Rate per 100,000 inhabitants		171.7	8.7	6.9	94.5	61.6	2,800.4	719.8	1,944.4	136.2

See footnotes at end of table.

Table 6

Crime in the United States
by Metropolitan Statistical Area, 2003—Continued

Metropolitan Statistical Area	Population	Violent crime	Violent crime				Property crime	Property crime		
			Murder and non-negligent man-slaughter	Forcible rape	Robbery	Aggravated assault	Property crime	Burglary	Larceny-theft	Motor vehicle theft
Ponce, Puerto Rico M.S.A.	**267,587**									
(Includes Juana Diaz, Ponce, and Villalba Municipios.)										
Total area actually reporting	100.0%	783	60	28	457	238	5,849	1,380	3,922	547
Rate per 100,000 inhabitants		292.6	22.4	10.5	170.8	88.9	2,185.8	515.7	1,465.7	204.4
San German-Cabo Rojo, Puerto Rico M.S.A.	**139,876**									
(Includes Cabo Rojo, Lajas, Sabana Grande, and San German Municipios.)										
Total area actually reporting	100.0%	112	6	4	62	40	1,208	407	753	48
Rate per 100,000 inhabitants		80.1	4.3	2.9	44.3	28.6	863.6	291.0	538.3	34.3
San Juan-Caguas-Guaynabo, Puerto Rico M.S.A.	**2,554,433**									
(Includes Aguas Buenas, Aibonito, Arecibo, Barceloneta, Barranquitas, Bayamon, Caguas, Camuy, Canovanas, Carolina, Catano, Cayey, Ciales, Cidra, Comerio, Corozal, Dorado, Florida, Guaynabo, Gurabo, Hatillo, Humacao, Juncos, Las Piedras, Loiza, Manati, Maunabo, Morovis, Naguabo, Naranjito, Orocovis, Quebradillas, Rio Grande, San Juan, San Lorenzo, Toa Alta, Toa Baja, Trujillo Alto, Vega Alta, Vega Baja, and Yabucoa Municipios.)										
Total area actually reporting	100.0%	9,569	616	133	6,495	2,325	51,137	14,595	25,771	10,771
Rate per 100,000 inhabitants		374.6	24.1	5.2	254.3	91.0	2,001.9	571.4	1,008.9	421.7
Yauco, Puerto Rico M.S.A.	**120,750**									
(Includes Guanica, Guayanilla, Penuelas, and Yauco Municipios.)										
Total area actually reporting	100.0%	253	10	11	145	87	1,495	598	815	82
Rate per 100,000 inhabitants		209.5	8.3	9.1	120.1	72.0	1,238.1	495.2	674.9	67.9

[1] Due to changes in reporting practices, annexations, and/or incomplete data, figures are not comparable to previous years' data.

[2] The population for the city of Mobile, Alabama, includes 55,864 inhabitants from the jurisdiction of the Mobile County Sheriff's Department.

NOTE: Although arson data are included in the trend and clearance tables, sufficient data are not available to estimate totals for this offense.

Due to rounding, the estimated totals of the individual Metropolitan Divisions may not add to the estimated totals of their Metropolitan Statistical Area.

Table 7

Offense Analysis
United States, 1999-2003

Classification	1999	2000	2001[1]	2002[2]	2003
Murder	**15,522**	**15,586**	**16,037**	**16,229**	**16,503**
Forcible rape	**89,411**	**90,178**	**90,863**	**95,235**	**93,433**
Robbery:					
Total[3]	**409,371**	**408,016**	**423,557**	**420,806**	**413,402**
Street/highway	197,770	187,688	187,571	180,058	179,296
Commercial house	55,678	56,714	61,152	61,312	60,493
Gas or service station	8,844	11,832	12,084	11,254	11,362
Convenience store	24,712	26,113	27,783	27,183	25,774
Residence	49,793	49,778	53,268	56,723	56,641
Bank	8,021	8,568	10,262	9,693	9,504
Miscellaneous	64,552	67,323	71,436	74,584	70,333
Burglary:					
Total[3]	**2,100,739**	**2,050,992**	**2,116,531**	**2,151,252**	**2,153,464**
Residence (dwelling):	1,394,868	1,337,247	1,380,472	1,415,561	1,417,522
Night	402,548	399,943	410,071	418,094	408,927
Day	612,429	617,349	642,264	673,781	668,334
Unknown	379,891	319,955	328,137	323,687	340,261
Nonresidence (store, office, etc.):	705,871	713,745	736,059	735,691	735,942
Night	296,303	299,445	310,596	312,516	309,990
Day	186,166	219,456	224,538	228,698	221,099
Unknown	223,402	194,844	200,925	194,477	204,853
Larceny-theft (except motor vehicle theft):					
Total[3]	**6,955,520**	**6,971,590**	**7,092,267**	**7,057,379**	**7,021,588**
By type:					
Pocket-picking	43,035	34,858	33,346	32,451	31,943
Purse-snatching	40,377	34,858	38,550	38,896	42,150
Shoplifting	1,002,576	962,079	978,802	986,296	1,012,513
From motor vehicles (except accessories)	1,788,630	1,756,841	1,832,934	1,866,922	1,856,240
Motor vehicle accessories	723,720	676,244	723,419	756,250	780,700
Bicycles	325,683	313,722	291,203	277,003	271,599
From buildings	946,419	913,278	943,631	883,847	867,977
From coin-operated machines	46,479	48,801	52,039	52,374	52,334
All others	2,038,602	2,230,909	2,198,344	2,163,340	2,106,132
By value:					
Over $200	2,692,746	2,711,949	2,792,231	2,796,465	2,759,703
$50 to $200	1,609,400	1,631,352	1,630,567	1,592,830	1,585,495
Under $50	2,653,374	2,628,289	2,669,469	2,668,084	2,676,390
Motor vehicle theft	**1,152,075**	**1,160,002**	**1,228,391**	**1,246,646**	**1,260,471**

[1] The murder and nonnegligent homicides that occurred as a result of the events of September 11, 2001, are not included in this table.

[2] The 2002 crime figures have been adjusted.

[3] Because of rounding, the number of offenses may not add to the total.

Table 8

Offenses Known to Law Enforcement
by City 10,000 and over in Population, 2003

City by state	Population	Violent crime	Murder and non-negligent man-slaughter	Forcible rape	Robbery	Aggravated assault	Property crime	Burglary	Larceny-theft	Motor vehicle theft	Arson[1]
ALABAMA											
Alabaster	24,956	23	0	2	3	18	202	23	160	19	0
Albertville[2]	17,658	54	1	9	8	36			517	69	
Alexander City	14,879	108	0	4	17	87	811	136	663	12	
Anniston	23,868	502	2	28	155	317	3,164	937	2,011	216	
Athens	19,612	12	0	0	7	5	668	97	546	25	0
Auburn	45,533	146	1	22	50	73	1,972	546	1,347	79	
Birmingham	240,176	3,347	85	204	1,352	1,706	19,574	4,831	11,934	2,809	175
Cullman	14,103	18	0	8	5	5	891	121	709	61	2
Daphne	17,285	19	0	3	6	10	459	74	363	22	
Decatur	54,112	221	4	11	117	89	3,957	780	3,001	176	
Dothan	59,185	239	4	38	110	87	2,917	670	2,100	147	
Enterprise	21,438	66	2	10	18	36	843	180	630	33	
Eufaula	13,812	57	1	6	34	16	544	65	454	25	
Fairfield	12,106	118	5	9	74	30	1,643	252	1,210	181	
Fairhope	13,520	23	0	3	4	16	494	120	340	34	
Florence	35,928	166	0	15	42	109	1,601	304	1,241	56	12
Fort Payne	13,123	31	0	2	3	26	428	81	343	4	
Gadsden[2]	38,087		6	21	78		3,155	580	2,312	263	
Gardendale	12,043	30	1	3	17	9	461	64	363	34	
Hartselle	12,213	6	0	0	2	4	318	39	267	12	
Helena	11,438	1	0	1	0	0	43	4	38	1	
Homewood	24,861	110	0	9	62	39	1,525	286	1,138	101	
Hoover	64,469	242	0	18	113	111	1,920	310	1,480	130	
Hueytown	15,462	70	2	0	40	28	479	112	325	42	
Huntsville	163,052	988	19	84	316	569	9,388	1,740	6,774	874	
Jasper	13,968	62	1	9	18	34	857	160	638	59	
Leeds	10,826	30	2	4	10	14	406	78	299	29	
Madison	32,438	52	1	8	15	28	1,064	166	843	55	
Millbrook	11,501	52	1	4	4	43	429	109	300	20	
Mobile[3]	251,345	1,300	24	113	739	424	16,151	3,976	10,855	1,320	
Montgomery	202,064	1,307	18	115	658	516	16,125	4,092	10,268	1,765	
Mountain Brook	20,215	12	0	1	5	6	404	59	329	16	
Muscle Shoals	12,271	43	0	4	9	30	665	112	532	21	
Northport	19,854	144	1	12	22	109	842	131	652	59	4
Opelika	23,671	370	5	18	59	288	1,475	311	1,153	11	
Oxford	15,260	125	1	4	33	87	1,331	229	1,011	91	
Ozark	15,024	70	0	7	6	57	587	101	437	49	2
Pelham	16,573	15	1	0	9	5	359	32	296	31	
Pell City	10,130	71	0	5	9	57	552	68	449	35	
Phenix City	28,593	127	2	16	44	65	1,232	321	797	114	
Prattville	25,949	100	1	18	28	53	1,308	206	1,044	58	
Prichard	28,290	481	6	30	187	258	2,543	824	1,354	365	
Saraland	12,454	24	0	0	11	13	583	89	474	20	
Scottsboro	14,858	13	1	3	6	3	716	159	530	27	
Selma	20,054	418	7	34	104	273	2,301	661	1,421	219	
Sylacauga	12,685	50	1	1	17	31	790	135	641	14	
Talladega	15,074	51	0	18	16	17	1,192	224	906	62	
Troy	13,877	75	1	1	23	50	1,069	169	837	63	
Trussville	13,903	34	0	1	12	21	709	66	614	29	0
Tuscaloosa	79,400	555	7	50	222	276	5,063	999	3,809	255	
Vestavia Hills	25,734	29	0	2	9	18	329	76	219	34	
ALASKA											
Anchorage	271,085	1,744	17	244	340	1,143	11,706	1,418	9,091	1,197	128
Fairbanks	31,021	289	4	42	42	201	1,561	271	1,158	132	13
Juneau	30,991	97	0	36	5	56	1,236	99	1,105	32	2
ARIZONA											
Apache Junction	34,763	98	1	12	13	72	1,880	432	1,235	213	16
Bullhead City	36,268	215	4	3	21	187	2,021	422	1,433	166	10
Camp Verde	10,006	58	0	3	1	54	436	73	311	52	0
Casa Grande	29,351	281	0	7	42	232	2,665	786	1,578	301	19

See footnotes at end of table.

Table 8

Offenses Known to Law Enforcement
by City 10,000 and over in Population, 2003—Continued

City by state	Population	Violent crime	Murder and non-negligent man-slaughter	Forcible rape	Robbery	Aggravated assault	Property crime	Burglary	Larceny-theft	Motor vehicle theft	Arson[1]
ARIZONA—Continued											
Chandler	206,620	624	5	58	131	430	10,332	1,819	7,006	1,507	54
Cottonwood	10,284	39	0	5	4	30	754	153	536	65	2
Douglas	16,816	44	0	6	4	34	741	120	542	79	10
El Mirage	13,557	123	4	8	21	90	819	272	391	156	6
Flagstaff	56,430	401	1	44	45	311	4,614	643	3,770	201	13
Gilbert	138,082	172	1	21	40	110	5,358	1,609	3,169	580	26
Glendale	235,819	1,270	14	96	463	697	13,642	2,593	7,459	3,590	93
Goodyear	28,367	72	1	8	6	57	1,333	677	474	182	4
Kingman	22,595	105	2	6	21	76	2,121	341	1,604	176	3
Lake Havasu City	47,465	103	2	9	10	82	1,881	263	1,476	142	7
Marana	18,495	58	0	5	3	50	1,043	182	732	129	3
Mesa	436,569	2,346	14	116	431	1,785	26,127	4,112	17,452	4,563	45
Nogales	21,765	63	0	3	4	56	716	149	422	145	2
Oro Valley	34,436	21	0	0	5	16	717	93	578	46	5
Paradise Valley	14,423	15	0	1	2	12	526	319	177	30	4
Payson	14,458	31	0	1	2	28	518	66	429	23	6
Peoria	126,048	368	2	50	59	257	5,736	1,026	3,563	1,147	15
Phoenix	1,403,228	9,722	241	526	3,676	5,279	97,823	17,104	55,068	25,651	436
Prescott	37,127	159	1	7	24	127	2,146	413	1,627	106	14
Prescott Valley	26,747	105	0	7	5	93	908	138	702	68	7
Scottsdale	220,697	493	7	62	163	261	9,475	2,315	5,659	1,501	57
Sedona	11,002	36	0	0	1	35	323	127	183	13	1
Sierra Vista	39,888	117	1	10	18	88	1,782	237	1,423	122	11
Tempe	163,143	1,013	7	74	299	633	14,887	2,430	9,756	2,701	48
Tucson	514,618	4,709	47	330	1,478	2,854	47,298	6,397	34,542	6,359	285
Yuma	82,189	517	1	40	47	429	3,631	588	2,538	505	36
ARKANSAS[2]											
Arkadelphia	11,107	35	0	2	5	28	161	79	76	6	1
Benton	23,411	105	1	5	8	91	1,504	395	1,019	90	3
Bentonville	24,225	39	1	22	3	13	782	121	630	31	0
Bryant	10,576	14	0	0	0	14	404	43	340	21	0
Camden	12,697	67	3	10	14	40	699	139	529	31	4
Conway	46,180	81	0	16	18	47	2,129	299	1,723	107	2
Fayetteville	61,082	251	0	36	36	179	2,895	292	2,464	139	6
Forrest City	14,582	293	1	4	25	263	954	167	748	39	1
Fort Smith	81,989	804	12	74	135	583	7,173	1,111	5,764	298	22
Hot Springs	36,566	392	3	18	80	291	4,391	915	3,246	230	17
Jacksonville	30,558	180	0	16	23	141	1,683	439	1,179	65	11
Jonesboro	57,216	332	4	12	107	209	3,377	875	2,359	143	7
Little Rock	185,117	2,858	44	129	896	1,789	18,600	4,442	12,743	1,415	120
Magnolia	10,756	145	1	0	16	128	465	128	324	13	4
Maumelle	12,089	9	1	0	3	5	111	80	30	1	0
Mountain Home	11,207	12	0	4	0	8	353	22	317	14	2
North Little Rock	60,353	516	8	41	163	304	5,270	809	3,986	475	25
Paragould	22,739	11	0	6	4	1	350	47	250	53	0
Pine Bluff	54,482	578	16	44	150	368	4,530	1,198	2,930	402	59
Rogers	41,785	68	0	30	7	31	1,858	192	1,603	63	8
Searcy	19,655	132	1	4	11	116	924	81	782	61	0
Sherwood	22,045	98	1	3	11	83	818	94	641	83	3
Siloam Springs	11,660	24	0	3	2	19	454	44	386	24	0
Springdale	51,235	160	0	32	19	109	2,055	281	1,639	135	12
Van Buren	19,891	63	0	5	6	52	873	265	567	41	0
CALIFORNIA											
Adelanto	19,067	87	1	4	29	53	525	246	177	102	13
Agoura Hills	21,932	60	0	4	9	47	309	75	209	25	6
Alameda	73,692	332	0	7	135	190	2,729	381	2,024	324	35
Albany	16,802	67	0	6	44	17	864	172	529	163	7
Alhambra	88,575	286	5	17	156	108	2,475	443	1,412	620	22
Aliso Viejo	41,022	43	0	1	4	38	483	98	327	58	14
American Canyon	12,279	10	0	1	1	8	347	90	191	66	0

See footnotes at end of table.

Table 8

Offenses Known to Law Enforcement
by City 10,000 and over in Population, 2003—Continued

City by state	Population	Violent crime	Murder and non-negligent man-slaughter	Forcible rape	Robbery	Aggravated assault	Property crime	Burglary	Larceny-theft	Motor vehicle theft	Arson[1]
CALIFORNIA—Continued											
Anaheim	336,132	1,319	9	76	410	824	10,446	1,971	6,708	1,767	43
Antioch	100,918	714	6	15	223	470	2,896	626	1,354	916	30
Apple Valley	58,533	204	4	5	78	117	2,125	529	1,268	328	14
Arcadia	55,480	137	2	5	55	75	1,540	383	987	170	10
Arcata	16,838	41	0	6	12	23	753	154	541	58	6
Arroyo Grande	16,461	27	0	3	3	21	379	79	278	22	3
Artesia	16,931	118	1	3	34	80	343	83	177	83	2
Arvin	13,797	64	1	3	12	48	670	155	441	74	26
Atascadero	27,194	66	1	8	4	53	846	182	602	62	10
Atwater	24,936	164	2	9	29	124	1,106	332	622	152	11
Auburn	12,678	39	2	2	2	33	320	72	215	33	2
Avenal	15,494	36	0	6	3	27	168	76	84	8	13
Azusa	46,809	177	3	11	74	89	1,469	343	873	253	5
Bakersfield[2]	263,707	1,514	24	41	439	1,010	14,102	2,693	9,415	1,994	173
Baldwin Park	78,645	283	5	12	87	179	1,673	288	757	628	10
Banning	25,858	194	2	10	26	156	630	311	206	113	0
Barstow	22,791	234	2	17	62	153	1,233	328	662	243	8
Beaumont	13,413	62	0	5	12	45	479	131	260	88	2
Bell	37,751	213	2	9	59	143	588	157	190	241	0
Bellflower	75,307	480	7	24	219	230	2,531	488	1,370	673	21
Bell Gardens	45,745	298	10	11	79	198	1,039	207	353	479	2
Belmont	25,076	38	1	4	8	25	509	131	330	48	0
Benicia	27,444	38	1	3	8	26	553	169	292	92	8
Berkeley	104,727	926	6	16	402	502	8,695	1,245	6,217	1,233	32
Beverly Hills	35,223	138	0	6	73	59	1,154	302	771	81	4
Blythe	21,600	164	1	6	20	137	705	222	457	26	17
Brawley	22,071	147	3	5	38	101	1,136	326	700	110	9
Brea	37,411	68	0	6	29	33	1,589	241	1,213	135	6
Brentwood	31,858	53	2	5	6	40	1,259	177	884	198	10
Buena Park	79,844	326	2	21	115	188	1,945	399	1,172	374	26
Burbank	103,993	283	3	15	69	196	2,694	500	1,728	466	19
Burlingame	28,064	62	0	10	18	34	1,026	111	813	102	13
Calabasas	20,906	31	0	2	4	25	332	76	225	31	2
Calexico	31,069	58	1	0	33	24	1,050	357	329	364	13
Camarillo	60,068	98	1	10	15	72	1,071	224	772	75	43
Campbell	37,867	60	0	9	26	25	1,030	166	783	81	25
Canyon Lake	10,754	25	0	1	1	23	140	31	85	24	0
Capitola	10,053	74	1	2	16	55	1,077	127	926	24	0
Carlsbad	87,548	266	4	14	64	184	2,199	496	1,445	258	13
Carpinteria	14,383	24	0	3	7	14	246	63	164	19	0
Carson	93,904	731	12	15	207	497	2,685	509	1,453	723	47
Cathedral City	46,781	224	2	16	48	158	1,785	556	849	380	0
Ceres	37,092	200	0	12	44	144	2,234	380	1,330	524	11
Cerritos	53,172	199	2	7	97	93	1,972	328	1,261	383	6
Chico	66,595	265	1	47	63	154	2,622	818	1,378	426	55
Chino	70,695	243	2	15	88	138	2,366	459	1,387	520	47
Chino Hills	73,053	73	1	2	20	50	1,093	247	673	173	13
Chowchilla	14,460	48	0	3	4	41	329	98	184	47	20
Chula Vista	195,954	776	7	48	249	472	7,106	1,004	3,954	2,148	43
Claremont	35,196	76	0	11	29	36	1,108	308	704	96	4
Clayton	11,153	6	0	0	0	6	159	20	130	9	4
Clearlake	14,118	86	1	3	12	70	890	359	433	98	10
Clovis	75,285	162	9	18	42	93	3,042	487	2,144	411	24
Coachella	27,463	173	3	8	35	127	945	201	542	202	5
Coalinga	16,219	35	0	1	1	33	408	114	270	24	2
Colton	50,356	220	4	18	90	108	2,320	456	1,306	558	14
Commerce	13,256	146	2	3	59	82	1,089	155	518	416	15
Compton	96,562	1,549	43	41	444	1,021	2,340	548	991	801	136
Concord	126,539	398	4	22	136	236	5,253	882	3,358	1,013	5
Corcoran	21,149	31	0	2	9	20	273	94	164	15	0
Corona	139,777	280	6	33	125	116	4,028	673	2,547	808	35
Coronado	24,112	35	0	5	3	27	600	104	424	72	11
Costa Mesa	111,281	304	1	42	112	149	3,586	516	2,665	405	14
Covina	48,523	205	1	16	95	93	2,043	425	1,302	316	8

See footnotes at end of table.

Table 8

Offenses Known to Law Enforcement

by City 10,000 and over in Population, 2003—Continued

City by state	Population	Violent crime	Violent crime Murder and non-negligent man-slaughter	Violent crime Forcible rape	Violent crime Robbery	Violent crime Aggravated assault	Property crime	Property crime Burglary	Property crime Larceny-theft	Property crime Motor vehicle theft	Arson[1]
CALIFORNIA—Continued											
Cudahy	25,428	158	2	6	46	104	520	88	223	209	6
Culver City	40,114	181	2	5	131	43	1,176	226	795	155	6
Cupertino	50,530	77	1	8	18	50	1,174	184	954	36	18
Cypress	47,745	74	1	9	27	37	1,051	191	748	112	6
Daly City	102,970	344	0	24	154	166	2,172	242	1,490	440	13
Dana Point	36,180	81	1	4	11	65	649	129	448	72	11
Danville	43,012	39	0	0	8	31	645	126	464	55	1
Davis	64,895	191	0	28	23	140	2,247	392	1,631	224	60
Delano	42,534	124	4	14	35	71	2,122	460	1,156	506	52
Desert Hot Springs	17,492	252	0	14	65	173	1,415	625	644	146	0
Diamond Bar	58,527	93	1	2	27	63	900	225	518	157	10
Dinuba	17,772	134	0	8	14	112	1,049	226	686	137	12
Dixon	16,432	44	0	1	7	36	653	118	480	55	17
Downey[2]	110,992	505	7	25	216	257	3,576	588	1,819	1,169	4
Duarte	22,304	93	0	8	35	50	449	95	282	72	2
Dublin	34,705	84	0	5	18	61	675	129	417	129	2
East Palo Alto	32,042	312	9	19	97	187	1,159	339	600	220	5
El Cajon	96,558	556	5	43	154	354	4,339	887	2,300	1,152	25
El Centro	38,079	325	0	7	52	266	1,675	584	893	198	4
El Cerrito	23,760	156	0	4	107	45	1,639	264	954	421	3
El Monte	121,176	730	3	24	217	486	3,192	651	1,586	955	24
El Segundo	16,557	43	0	1	27	15	679	146	431	102	0
Encinitas	60,423	150	0	10	40	100	1,377	329	804	244	7
Escondido	137,334	591	5	46	161	379	5,054	963	3,094	997	32
Eureka	26,137	186	1	25	59	101	2,043	421	1,352	270	34
Fairfield	103,004	621	12	36	177	396	4,752	660	3,394	698	41
Fillmore	15,076	70	2	3	7	58	218	56	133	29	2
Folsom	61,899	119	0	16	24	79	1,638	360	1,131	147	16
Fontana	145,114	897	18	51	263	565	3,547	745	1,405	1,397	38
Fortuna	10,813	28	0	3	7	18	543	83	430	30	5
Foster City	29,500	46	0	3	6	37	513	99	379	35	8
Fountain Valley	56,136	108	0	9	43	56	1,449	254	1,037	158	6
Fremont	209,026	433	2	34	140	257	5,693	1,059	3,876	758	12
Fresno	449,898	3,505	37	164	1,215	2,089	27,196	3,927	17,608	5,661	602
Fullerton	130,194	363	5	37	120	201	4,599	784	3,222	593	46
Galt	22,555	58	2	7	11	38	925	204	547	174	7
Gardena	60,283	527	3	17	269	238	1,683	396	850	437	3
Garden Grove	169,186	732	6	27	211	488	4,602	754	2,814	1,034	37
Gilroy	43,598	275	1	14	48	212	1,587	224	1,183	180	4
Glendale	201,522	363	6	18	146	193	3,876	800	2,283	793	50
Glendora	51,098	76	0	5	29	42	1,248	202	921	125	6
Goleta	28,926	40	0	6	7	27	446	91	314	41	8
Grand Terrace	12,194	23	0	2	9	12	335	63	205	67	3
Grass Valley	11,248	82	0	11	13	58	539	102	368	69	4
Greenfield	13,071	95	0	2	22	71	348	105	199	44	1
Grover Beach	13,214	36	0	3	5	28	334	66	249	19	2
Half Moon Bay	12,108	27	0	3	7	17	222	44	168	10	0
Hanford	44,815	162	1	15	38	108	1,614	251	1,172	191	12
Hawaiian Gardens	15,396	156	4	1	66	85	479	100	272	107	5
Hawthorne	86,836	694	12	30	294	358	2,362	747	1,034	581	9
Hayward	144,215	600	8	41	257	294	5,125	847	2,647	1,631	58
Healdsburg	11,217	38	0	2	12	24	376	136	213	27	0
Hemet	64,032	438	1	29	107	301	2,957	801	1,819	337	26
Hercules	20,444	38	0	0	20	18	552	75	317	160	4
Hermosa Beach	19,483	81	1	6	15	59	645	154	446	45	3
Hesperia	67,724	155	3	11	45	96	1,962	510	1,092	360	15
Highland	47,579	201	7	12	101	81	1,434	307	762	365	16
Hillsborough	10,815	7	0	0	0	7	62	21	37	4	0
Hollister	36,831	201	2	10	23	166	1,252	293	845	114	11
Huntington Beach	195,832	411	3	44	101	263	4,118	961	2,716	441	21
Huntington Park	63,637	544	8	19	320	197	2,908	239	1,416	1,253	18
Imperial Beach	27,521	144	0	8	34	102	855	236	438	181	11
Indio	54,790	443	9	20	100	314	2,823	827	1,397	599	1
Inglewood	116,165	1,091	32	56	581	422	3,273	801	1,242	1,230	14

See footnotes at end of table.

Table 8

Offenses Known to Law Enforcement
by City 10,000 and over in Population, 2003—Continued

City by state	Population	Violent crime	Murder and non-negligent man-slaughter	Forcible rape	Robbery	Aggravated assault	Property crime	Burglary	Larceny-theft	Motor vehicle theft	Arson[1]
CALIFORNIA—Continued											
Irvine	163,823	144	2	18	51	73	3,310	816	2,238	256	50
King City	11,401	42	0	0	10	32	516	143	330	43	0
Kingsburg	10,166	12	0	0	3	9	393	68	234	91	2
La Canada Flintridge	21,076	22	1	0	7	14	260	82	164	14	0
Lafayette	24,804	28	0	2	11	15	610	98	447	65	0
Laguna Beach	24,423	55	0	4	7	44	583	151	381	51	3
Laguna Hills	33,980	45	1	3	9	32	661	108	484	69	17
Laguna Niguel	63,719	78	0	1	23	54	957	165	728	64	12
Laguna Woods	16,687	8	0	0	3	5	94	13	70	11	0
La Habra	60,613	225	5	8	56	156	1,568	278	1,060	230	17
Lake Elsinore	32,200	229	0	7	38	184	1,166	230	714	222	2
Lake Forest	77,749	107	0	3	30	74	1,231	255	848	128	13
Lakewood	81,901	340	4	17	146	173	2,820	398	1,892	530	11
La Mesa	55,543	173	2	12	66	93	2,126	358	1,214	554	15
La Mirada	48,987	161	1	8	46	106	1,052	221	609	222	6
Lancaster	125,899	1,270	18	68	322	862	4,035	1,075	2,026	934	60
La Palma	15,939	29	0	1	8	20	297	80	179	38	1
La Puente	42,448	243	10	7	61	165	818	156	408	254	6
La Quinta	30,358	77	3	7	15	52	1,349	391	836	122	4
La Verne	33,054	75	1	7	23	44	788	159	559	70	6
Lawndale	32,728	192	2	9	81	100	611	182	248	181	7
Lemon Grove	25,320	145	1	4	50	90	830	232	361	237	3
Lemoore	21,297	75	1	5	15	54	672	106	482	84	4
Lincoln	19,882	47	0	7	7	33	567	154	350	63	6
Lindsay	10,634	108	1	3	15	89	468	150	267	51	6
Livermore	77,433	145	1	19	37	88	1,925	417	1,244	264	21
Livingston	11,364	63	0	4	10	49	349	139	158	52	7
Lodi	61,292	263	1	11	49	202	3,298	416	2,338	544	18
Loma Linda	20,021	44	0	1	17	26	823	143	482	198	5
Lomita	20,697	117	0	4	38	75	468	107	295	66	6
Lompoc	41,823	225	0	24	44	157	974	226	673	75	28
Long Beach	477,368	3,579	49	136	1,411	1,983	14,823	3,003	8,072	3,748	217
Los Alamitos	11,833	45	0	4	20	21	303	75	182	46	7
Los Altos	27,601	17	0	1	4	12	276	82	183	11	3
Los Angeles	3,838,838	48,824	515	1,226	16,577	30,506	135,781	25,115	77,111	33,555	2,072
Los Banos	29,835	216	0	12	21	183	901	233	563	105	4
Los Gatos	28,505	36	1	3	12	20	527	118	368	41	11
Lynwood	72,136	919	15	19	307	578	1,687	328	612	747	64
Madera	46,699	478	2	30	145	301	1,923	471	1,054	398	5
Malibu	13,223	50	0	5	8	37	350	77	232	41	5
Manhattan Beach	35,873	62	1	10	25	26	1,122	264	775	83	2
Manteca	57,501	195	2	6	60	127	2,702	415	1,787	500	33
Marina	21,368	84	0	7	38	39	467	147	306	14	5
Martinez	37,092	89	0	7	25	57	1,267	244	833	190	0
Marysville	12,651	116	1	11	25	79	681	132	450	99	0
Maywood	29,011	183	1	1	53	128	489	74	212	203	3
Menlo Park	30,595	66	0	6	27	33	841	182	600	59	2
Merced	68,941	636	7	29	168	432	4,716	882	3,182	652	51
Millbrae	20,530	30	1	1	14	14	318	69	210	39	2
Mill Valley	13,699	13	0	2	4	7	315	83	210	22	1
Milpitas	64,368	200	3	23	38	136	2,203	301	1,663	239	3
Mission Viejo	97,317	114	1	4	25	84	1,468	244	1,136	88	20
Modesto	205,691	1,409	17	73	380	939	12,600	1,743	8,463	2,394	112
Monrovia	38,245	106	2	9	38	57	1,011	198	642	171	8
Montclair	34,738	194	0	14	62	118	2,229	293	1,416	520	3
Montebello	64,274	248	4	17	88	139	2,007	237	1,138	632	21
Monterey	29,960	157	1	12	36	108	1,281	221	990	70	8
Monterey Park	62,471	167	1	6	99	61	1,380	272	654	454	5
Moorpark	34,940	40	0	3	7	30	323	54	239	30	2
Moraga	16,861	18	0	0	2	16	236	50	175	11	8
Moreno Valley[2]	152,355	810	4	67	271	468	5,674	1,481	3,214	979	22
Morgan Hill	34,146	63	0	7	18	38	1,102	198	806	98	14
Morro Bay	10,614	26	0	4	0	22	208	54	150	4	3
Mountain View	70,781	291	1	6	42	242	1,837	209	1,489	139	11

See footnotes at end of table.

Table 8

Offenses Known to Law Enforcement

by City 10,000 and over in Population, 2003—Continued

City by state	Population	Violent crime	Murder and non-negligent man-slaughter	Forcible rape	Robbery	Aggravated assault	Property crime	Burglary	Larceny-theft	Motor vehicle theft	Arson[1]
CALIFORNIA—Continued											
Murrieta	54,668	64	0	8	25	31	1,132	291	759	82	0
Napa	75,819	306	0	26	48	232	2,450	308	1,969	173	14
National City	56,124	546	9	33	155	349	2,740	337	1,407	996	13
Newark	43,786	183	1	18	53	111	2,063	324	1,478	261	9
Newport Beach	78,915	115	0	16	27	72	2,526	666	1,671	189	8
Norco	26,109	143	0	2	25	116	875	258	485	132	5
Norwalk	107,197	690	9	23	201	457	2,827	629	1,404	794	20
Novato	48,636	69	0	7	19	43	1,193	244	745	204	22
Oakdale	17,072	41	0	8	14	19	1,167	324	709	134	6
Oakland	407,003	5,613	109	268	2,474	2,762	22,630	4,568	12,551	5,511	334
Oakley	26,481	103	0	8	12	83	735	98	495	142	2
Oceanside	167,620	1,090	8	63	332	687	5,490	1,114	3,637	739	20
Ontario	166,796	904	11	47	323	523	7,472	1,019	4,331	2,122	123
Orange	132,987	262	1	10	97	154	3,376	440	2,423	513	26
Orinda	18,259	12	0	0	4	8	315	65	216	34	0
Oroville[2]	13,249	145	1	10	23	111	1,238	392	675	171	2
Oxnard	179,851	808	22	37	352	397	4,719	975	3,156	588	47
Pacifica	38,167	65	1	7	15	42	611	126	401	84	2
Pacific Grove	15,812	23	0	3	6	14	289	61	212	16	0
Palmdale	125,651	920	11	43	284	582	4,819	1,009	2,961	849	63
Palm Springs	44,993	390	5	29	90	266	3,356	924	2,039	393	25
Palo Alto	58,147	88	2	5	40	41	1,968	276	1,606	86	45
Palos Verdes Estates	13,894	1	0	0	0	1	136	45	84	7	0
Paradise	27,024	63	0	7	7	49	969	320	597	52	9
Paramount	57,082	430	10	14	182	224	2,083	331	1,060	692	34
Parlier	12,422	105	0	8	20	77	569	74	344	151	7
Pasadena	141,178	700	4	38	265	393	4,586	849	3,206	531	52
Paso Robles	26,635	122	3	13	14	92	933	376	483	74	9
Patterson	13,663	24	0	1	4	19	437	108	273	56	10
Perris	38,700	305	4	17	80	204	1,653	392	841	420	13
Petaluma	55,832	111	1	20	21	69	1,174	240	815	119	11
Pico Rivera	65,539	385	7	10	82	286	1,402	249	734	419	18
Piedmont	11,152	14	0	0	7	7	227	63	118	46	1
Pinole	19,643	79	2	5	30	42	1,319	151	844	324	3
Pittsburg	61,160	233	6	10	82	135	2,466	435	1,473	558	4
Placentia	48,299	127	1	6	36	84	1,010	280	612	118	5
Placerville	10,230	40	0	5	9	26	384	111	232	41	3
Pleasant Hill	33,889	134	0	8	52	74	1,919	371	1,299	249	16
Pleasanton	66,845	82	0	8	31	43	1,598	205	1,208	185	12
Pomona	155,166	1,217	17	49	422	729	5,459	914	2,905	1,640	30
Porterville	41,742	237	1	12	54	170	2,068	430	1,272	366	2
Port Hueneme	22,482	89	0	8	32	49	458	137	250	71	1
Poway	49,630	78	2	3	11	62	858	229	529	100	12
Rancho Cucamonga	145,219	308	4	19	128	157	4,181	832	2,602	747	30
Rancho Palos Verdes	42,568	46	0	1	8	37	474	162	276	36	0
Rancho Santa Margarita	48,666	34	0	1	6	27	476	78	355	43	4
Red Bluff	13,650	167	0	10	6	151	678	153	465	60	11
Redding	86,559	393	2	67	88	236	3,156	779	2,039	338	15
Redlands	67,449	379	2	17	94	266	2,767	531	1,733	503	29
Redondo Beach	66,483	195	1	8	69	117	1,775	441	1,128	206	2
Redwood City	75,234	367	2	17	61	287	2,190	383	1,590	217	17
Reedley	21,454	144	1	6	27	110	652	134	419	99	8
Rialto	97,630	973	11	43	268	651	2,914	603	1,318	993	28
Richmond	103,629	1,078	38	50	482	508	7,024	1,102	3,470	2,452	66
Ridgecrest	25,598	119	0	20	7	92	757	238	466	53	9
Ripon	11,590	30	1	0	2	27	360	61	262	37	0
Riverbank	17,825	54	0	4	13	37	800	225	438	137	14
Riverside	277,103	1,916	24	102	573	1,217	12,891	2,194	8,098	2,599	231
Rocklin	43,717	71	2	6	9	54	1,035	202	734	99	8
Rohnert Park	42,786	203	2	28	29	144	1,572	248	1,172	152	7
Rosemead	55,532	257	6	6	107	138	1,410	344	551	515	13
Roseville	92,724	266	4	22	68	172	3,652	572	2,650	430	10
Sacramento	439,811	3,420	43	187	1,630	1,560	28,266	5,606	15,374	7,286	401
Salinas	150,305	1,200	19	57	399	725	7,415	837	5,163	1,415	51

See footnotes at end of table.

Table 8

Offenses Known to Law Enforcement
by City 10,000 and over in Population, 2003—Continued

City by state	Population	Violent crime	Murder and non-negligent man-slaughter	Forcible rape	Robbery	Aggravated assault	Property crime	Burglary	Larceny-theft	Motor vehicle theft	Arson[1]
CALIFORNIA—Continued											
San Anselmo	12,381	23	0	3	2	18	264	66	181	17	0
San Bernardino	193,641	2,864	48	120	1,032	1,664	12,238	2,524	6,401	3,313	93
San Bruno	39,779	89	1	9	23	56	968	155	649	164	0
San Carlos	27,450	33	0	4	4	25	543	95	393	55	0
San Clemente	56,573	76	0	4	13	59	830	157	547	126	21
San Diego	1,272,746	7,366	65	406	1,626	5,269	46,382	8,076	25,739	12,567	238
San Dimas	36,252	118	0	4	33	81	863	195	565	103	3
San Fernando	24,429	146	3	6	54	83	624	102	316	206	4
San Francisco	772,065	5,725	69	215	3,065	2,376	38,163	5,784	25,388	6,991	260
San Gabriel	41,212	204	3	8	85	108	850	217	466	167	10
Sanger	20,037	91	1	5	19	66	763	113	510	140	4
San Jose	909,890	3,378	29	279	815	2,255	20,748	3,314	13,770	3,664	208
San Juan Capistrano	35,000	50	1	0	13	36	554	81	403	70	10
San Leandro	81,455	578	3	26	292	257	4,040	748	2,453	839	16
San Luis Obispo	44,720	139	1	20	19	99	1,944	344	1,469	131	41
San Marcos	62,785	205	3	18	46	138	1,475	440	765	270	12
San Marino	13,356	20	0	0	10	10	141	47	88	6	0
San Mateo	92,900	341	1	28	95	217	2,756	294	2,208	254	28
San Pablo	31,315	221	6	10	116	89	2,140	324	814	1,002	12
San Rafael	56,879	208	0	25	66	117	2,010	327	1,233	450	6
San Ramon	46,702	58	1	1	17	39	1,087	157	816	114	7
Santa Ana	347,016	1,788	17	76	739	956	9,728	1,110	5,932	2,686	121
Santa Barbara	90,320	562	1	37	78	446	3,166	634	2,341	191	43
Santa Clara	102,936	253	7	25	48	173	3,006	420	2,244	342	18
Santa Clarita	162,238	304	3	16	97	188	3,157	681	2,003	473	20
Santa Cruz	54,401	510	4	48	112	346	3,121	523	2,420	178	21
Santa Fe Springs	18,126	117	2	3	44	68	1,403	228	874	301	2
Santa Monica	87,710	555	2	21	242	290	3,943	761	2,716	466	48
Santa Paula	29,138	82	2	4	28	48	515	112	345	58	7
Santa Rosa	155,099	998	2	84	133	779	5,878	1,080	4,069	729	44
Santee	53,788	129	0	15	18	96	1,325	293	824	208	9
Saratoga	29,805	19	0	2	3	14	307	88	206	13	3
Scotts Valley	11,558	22	0	4	4	14	341	64	264	13	0
Seal Beach	24,784	61	1	5	17	38	397	84	277	36	1
Seaside	32,666	131	1	14	57	59	734	177	470	87	7
Selma	20,753	74	1	5	15	53	1,268	166	821	281	4
Shafter	13,551	54	1	2	4	47	490	102	322	66	12
Sierra Madre	10,992	13	0	1	0	12	116	44	64	8	0
Signal Hill	10,110	59	0	3	34	22	616	115	412	89	2
Simi Valley	117,785	164	2	16	45	101	1,882	466	1,211	205	22
Solana Beach	13,205	20	0	3	5	12	298	103	157	38	1
Soledad	23,686	35	1	6	12	16	288	127	115	46	2
South El Monte	21,902	130	2	8	45	75	726	155	352	219	8
South Gate	99,827	584	9	14	289	272	3,292	590	1,278	1,424	20
South Lake Tahoe	24,225	207	0	15	29	163	566	169	351	46	5
South Pasadena	25,101	54	0	8	29	17	630	149	383	98	24
South San Francisco	60,584	135	2	17	56	60	1,481	321	891	269	19
Stanton	38,356	118	1	11	36	70	890	164	514	212	18
Stockton	265,593	3,625	37	155	1,208	2,225	18,779	3,125	11,791	3,863	79
Suisun City	27,262	84	1	10	23	50	817	100	535	182	7
Sunnyvale	131,048	172	2	26	65	79	2,884	372	2,269	243	24
Susanville	17,897	72	0	6	2	64	348	98	241	9	3
Temecula	74,567	222	1	22	38	161	2,026	414	1,314	298	3
Temple City	35,990	65	1	3	17	44	478	156	250	72	1
Thousand Oaks	123,987	201	1	12	38	150	1,785	332	1,311	142	29
Torrance	143,101	402	2	23	216	161	4,292	785	2,753	754	29
Tracy	68,732	140	2	11	50	77	2,582	413	1,722	447	29
Truckee	14,783	48	0	4	3	41	276	66	192	18	5
Tulare	46,461	506	5	22	68	411	2,568	803	1,456	309	33
Turlock	62,294	384	4	26	83	271	4,052	751	2,358	943	21
Tustin	69,357	265	1	11	55	198	1,895	328	1,316	251	11
Twentynine Palms	29,492	91	2	15	11	63	554	203	298	53	5
Twin Cities	21,460	16	0	2	12	2	671	172	418	81	4
Ukiah	15,707	151	3	14	14	120	739	242	450	47	9

See footnotes at end of table.

Table 8

Offenses Known to Law Enforcement
by City 10,000 and over in Population, 2003—Continued

City by state	Population	Violent crime	Violent crime: Murder and non-negligent man-slaughter	Violent crime: Forcible rape	Violent crime: Robbery	Violent crime: Aggravated assault	Property crime	Property crime: Burglary	Property crime: Larceny-theft	Property crime: Motor vehicle theft	Arson[1]
CALIFORNIA—Continued											
Union City	70,612	269	1	19	117	132	2,692	441	1,714	537	32
Upland	71,728	249	3	12	105	129	2,901	465	1,943	493	5
Vacaville	94,555	272	0	24	71	177	2,152	313	1,590	249	32
Vallejo	121,055	997	6	42	339	610	5,817	1,021	3,631	1,165	55
Ventura	104,706	261	3	21	96	141	3,968	764	2,855	349	15
Victorville	71,571	323	3	28	130	162	3,863	856	2,415	592	15
Visalia	97,906	789	9	47	144	589	5,857	1,080	3,971	806	29
Vista	92,526	381	2	30	122	227	2,602	835	1,293	474	26
Walnut	31,096	56	0	1	19	36	475	146	251	78	7
Walnut Creek	66,031	106	0	8	18	80	2,635	434	1,938	263	16
Watsonville	47,133	329	3	23	99	204	2,049	331	1,569	149	9
West Covina	108,824	395	5	13	178	199	4,108	585	2,654	869	26
West Hollywood	37,055	342	3	10	170	159	1,626	330	1,030	266	7
Westminster	90,454	328	1	16	110	201	3,047	506	2,061	480	21
West Sacramento	36,927	477	3	20	99	355	1,499	512	622	365	49
Whittier	86,342	290	1	16	86	187	2,538	339	1,741	458	12
Woodland	51,383	281	2	22	42	215	1,517	607	569	341	39
Yorba Linda	61,706	61	0	9	13	39	814	160	588	66	14
Yuba City	47,708	201	0	28	46	127	1,969	358	1,409	202	14
Yucaipa	44,290	54	3	5	10	36	1,027	198	687	142	4
Yucca Valley	17,946	67	1	3	11	52	568	150	362	56	13
COLORADO											
Arvada	103,191	178	3	18	49	108	3,731	586	2,746	399	41
Aurora	288,830	1,691	18	213	571	889	15,253	2,329	10,272	2,652	110
Boulder	95,089	214	0	52	37	125	3,930	549	3,184	197	43
Canon City	15,845	32	0	0	1	31	572	85	450	37	14
Castle Rock	26,079	27	0	2	2	23	660	105	501	54	0
Centennial	100,421	185	1	31	22	131	2,346	417	1,716	213	45
Colorado Springs	374,818	1,730	16	242	421	1,051	18,517	3,360	13,338	1,819	191
Commerce City	24,161	177	2	17	35	123	2,160	358	1,427	375	15
Denver	565,905	3,531	63	304	1,421	1,743	29,064	7,097	14,839	7,128	228
Durango	14,773	38	0	4	4	30	930	103	775	52	7
Englewood	33,286	91	2	26	40	23	2,430	319	1,664	447	19
Evans	13,423	29	0	1	11	17	623	96	467	60	5
Federal Heights	12,228	29	1	2	14	12	968	120	677	171	1
Fort Collins	125,886	413	2	105	30	276	5,520	850	4,368	302	38
Fort Morgan	11,130	15	0	4	2	9	367	42	314	11	6
Fountain	15,851	19	1	0	3	15	339	31	285	23	0
Golden	17,536	46	0	2	8	36	628	102	474	52	12
Grand Junction	43,593	233	0	34	17	182	3,236	513	2,561	162	37
Greeley	82,919	279	2	49	52	176	5,329	689	4,255	385	35
Greenwood Village	12,827	41	0	5	14	22	816	147	608	61	4
Lafayette	24,042	240	0	4	4	232	647	100	501	46	28
Littleton	40,772	60	0	13	20	27	1,497	226	1,071	200	11
Montrose	13,919	33	1	7	5	20	739	132	582	25	3
Northglenn	33,982	114	0	14	21	79	1,992	249	1,438	305	7
Parker	32,664	25	0	0	8	17	710	141	524	45	13
Pueblo	104,424	817	6	38	175	598	5,571	1,241	3,928	402	65
Sterling	13,030	39	0	11	1	27	442	78	360	4	9
Thornton	94,540	396	5	37	56	298	4,891	603	3,654	634	43
Wheat Ridge	32,595	115	0	15	41	59	1,794	309	1,216	269	21
Windsor	12,637	2	0	1	1	0	53	23	24	6	1
CONNECTICUT											
Ansonia	18,863	25	0	2	10	13	364	40	275	49	1
Avon	16,454	9	1	0	5	3	198	37	153	8	0
Berlin	19,242	13	0	0	4	9	360	65	268	27	0
Bethel	18,571	7	0	2	0	5	184	44	134	6	2
Bloomfield	19,925	91	0	16	24	51	551	73	438	40	4
Branford	29,142	40	1	9	15	15	843	77	723	43	1
Bridgeport	141,030	1,365	15	49	439	862	6,401	1,243	3,954	1,204	

See footnotes at end of table.

Table 8

Offenses Known to Law Enforcement

by City 10,000 and over in Population, 2003—Continued

City by state	Population	Violent crime	Murder and non-negligent man-slaughter	Forcible rape	Robbery	Aggravated assault	Property crime	Burglary	Larceny-theft	Motor vehicle theft	Arson[1]
CONNECTICUT—Continued											
Bristol	60,941	142	2	9	66	65	1,755	333	1,292	130	8
Brookfield	16,028	26	0	0	1	25	178	26	141	11	0
Cheshire	29,288	12	0	2	3	7	292	63	198	31	2
Clinton	13,495	15	0	5	1	9	252	51	188	13	2
Coventry	12,053	5	0	0	1	4	136	42	82	12	2
Danbury	77,425	118	0	16	56	46	1,722	213	1,352	157	8
Darien	20,018	12	0	1	6	5	193	35	149	9	0
Derby	12,603	7	0	0	7	0	320	48	250	22	1
East Hampton	13,922	8	0	1	0	7	107	17	83	7	4
East Haven	28,752	44	0	7	17	20	638	74	480	84	5
Enfield	45,679	57	0	5	24	28	1,098	148	806	144	5
Fairfield	58,096	41	0	5	13	23	1,326	221	992	113	2
Farmington	24,349	15	0	1	11	3	689	86	572	31	5
Glastonbury	32,790	9	0	0	8	1	401	67	316	18	2
Granby	10,767	5	0	1	1	3	162	19	138	5	2
Groton	10,145	30	0	7	11	12	263	89	170	4	1
Groton Town	29,709	63	0	20	21	22	413	57	339	17	0
Guilford	22,013	23	0	5	2	16	363	40	309	14	4
Hartford	125,381	1,812	45	64	1,024	679	9,857	1,326	6,143	2,388	
Madison	18,669	1	0	0	0	1	152	22	124	6	0
Manchester	55,448	581	1	27	40	513	2,191	288	1,692	211	5
Meriden	59,063	127	2	8	60	57	2,283	504	1,633	146	0
Middletown	44,448	47	0	0	21	26	1,242	124	1,003	115	0
Milford	53,825	63	1	3	36	23	1,728	175	1,405	148	7
Monroe	19,680	2	0	0	0	2	222	34	154	34	0
Naugatuck	31,637	31	0	2	9	20	548	81	439	28	4
New Britain	72,062	275	0	8	122	145	2,891	587	1,977	327	1
New Canaan	19,864	8	0	1	3	4	99	10	83	6	2
New London	26,240	159	2	17	56	84	873	185	593	95	12
New Milford	28,144	17	0	8	5	4	300	82	195	23	2
Newtown	26,037	8	0	4	1	3	250	46	196	8	3
North Haven	23,615	7	0	0	4	3	455	54	356	45	1
Norwalk	84,683	355	1	13	156	185	2,470	373	1,750	347	7
Old Saybrook	10,554	2	0	0	0	2	281	17	258	6	0
Orange	13,471	6	0	0	5	1	339	36	286	17	2
Plainfield	15,116	37	0	3	3	31	148	31	103	14	0
Plainville	17,522	20	0	3	8	9	636	75	526	35	3
Ridgefield	24,213	0	0	0	0	0	74	13	60	1	0
Rocky Hill	18,426	24	1	2	2	19	356	43	286	27	2
Seymour	15,831	43	0	1	10	32	254	44	177	33	3
Shelton	39,102	29	0	6	12	11	401	96	223	82	1
Simsbury	23,576	3	0	0	1	2	220	26	187	7	0
Southington	41,214	34	0	3	10	21	901	162	653	86	3
South Windsor	25,010	13	0	1	4	8	348	65	256	27	0
Stamford	120,642	271	2	11	135	123	2,167	319	1,595	253	7
Stratford	50,503	114	2	8	73	31	1,822	314	1,290	218	5
Suffield	14,114	5	0	0	1	4	186	45	126	15	1
Torrington	35,891	139	0	5	12	122	1,114	202	838	74	4
Trumbull	35,087	25	1	3	16	5	821	79	695	47	6
Wallingford	44,116	36	0	5	16	15	792	138	598	56	5
Waterbury	108,596	481	5	50	234	192	6,396	1,082	4,347	967	
Watertown	22,246	10	0	0	4	6	356	38	306	12	0
West Hartford	61,771	133	1	4	93	35	1,858	291	1,414	153	13
West Haven	53,081	155	0	13	66	76	1,969	256	1,416	297	9
Weston	10,297	4	1	0	0	3	74	13	57	4	0
Westport	26,344	14	0	0	6	8	475	83	373	19	2
Wethersfield	26,564	39	0	4	16	19	585	83	434	68	2
Willimantic	16,184	63	0	9	39	15	675	128	500	47	5
Windsor	28,707	36	1	5	8	22	559	50	463	46	5
Windsor Locks	12,318	15	5	3	5	2	184	35	115	34	0
Wolcott	15,786	4	0	0	4	0	307	47	236	24	0

See footnotes at end of table.

Table 8

Offenses Known to Law Enforcement
by City 10,000 and over in Population, 2003—Continued

City by state	Population	Violent crime	Murder and non-negligent man-slaughter	Forcible rape	Robbery	Aggravated assault	Property crime	Burglary	Larceny-theft	Motor vehicle theft	Arson[1]
DELAWARE											
Dover	32,989	239	1	24	47	167	1,917	166	1,647	104	7
Newark	30,171	168	0	11	70	87	1,186	171	929	86	14
Wilmington	73,411	1,088	7	37	416	628	3,823	869	2,192	762	2
DISTRICT OF COLUMBIA											
Washington	563,384	8,839	248	273	3,836	4,482	31,581	4,670	17,362	9,549	
FLORIDA											
Altamonte Springs	41,726	149	4	16	46	83	1,773	291	1,290	192	5
Apopka	30,207	319	1	13	82	223	1,664	378	1,160	126	0
Atlantic Beach	13,799	65	0	3	16	46	491	108	358	25	1
Auburndale	11,897	69	0	3	31	35	844	194	621	29	1
Aventura	26,984	54	0	1	37	16	2,206	148	1,945	113	3
Bartow	15,738	123	0	15	31	77	1,540	371	1,067	102	2
Belle Glade	15,483	461	1	9	149	302	1,548	455	982	111	11
Boca Raton	78,828	175	1	10	46	118	2,522	597	1,722	203	3
Boynton Beach	64,849	678	1	5	185	487	4,881	848	3,558	475	3
Bradenton	52,304	455	7	29	162	257	3,320	894	2,073	353	0
Cape Coral	114,966	312	1	11	33	267	3,763	1,044	2,544	175	30
Casselberry	24,115	143	1	9	25	108	957	187	686	84	3
Clearwater	110,296	1,162	4	53	253	852	5,572	1,055	4,037	480	50
Clermont	10,325	84	0	5	24	55	448	160	266	22	3
Cocoa	16,703	442	1	41	92	308	1,302	365	851	86	4
Cocoa Beach	12,738	122	0	16	24	82	909	134	735	40	2
Coconut Creek	48,586	112	1	7	16	88	1,027	205	703	119	2
Cooper City	29,400	63	1	8	3	51	716	125	550	41	3
Coral Gables	43,411	158	3	3	68	84	2,644	440	1,975	229	2
Coral Springs	127,974	290	2	24	70	194	3,541	560	2,695	286	8
Crestview	15,634	60	0	3	15	42	581	124	439	18	2
Dania	28,580	204	1	15	49	139	934	215	549	170	2
Davie	81,315	355	4	13	94	244	3,263	580	2,326	357	28
Daytona Beach	65,788	1,214	5	81	420	708	6,141	1,567	3,651	923	25
Deerfield Beach	66,836	359	1	27	97	234	1,695	314	1,127	254	7
Deland	21,829	147	0	8	32	107	1,361	366	938	57	5
Delray Beach	63,412	521	1	15	125	380	4,036	683	2,952	401	13
Dunedin	37,335	81	0	10	21	50	994	206	737	51	8
Edgewater	20,098	62	0	3	6	53	704	167	493	44	2
Eustis	16,182	81	0	7	10	64	311	52	232	27	1
Fernandina Beach	11,223	21	0	4	6	11	372	73	274	25	0
Fort Lauderdale	161,090	1,352	18	49	640	645	9,736	2,320	6,281	1,135	38
Fort Myers	50,874	965	12	29	275	649	3,410	667	2,130	613	20
Fort Pierce	38,684	830	15	57	249	509	3,448	1,043	2,132	273	29
Fort Walton Beach	20,466	122	0	16	19	87	772	116	598	58	3
Gainesville	96,919	1,004	5	55	197	747	5,049	1,208	3,370	471	18
Greenacres City	30,996	233	0	12	41	180	1,529	297	1,077	155	2
Gulfport	12,798	77	1	3	33	40	631	170	389	72	2
Haines City	13,959	92	0	4	29	59	1,217	309	823	85	9
Hallandale	35,941	454	4	9	132	309	1,779	389	1,203	187	8
Hialeah	232,325	1,429	13	31	427	958	10,806	1,804	7,141	1,861	33
Hialeah Gardens	20,241	46	1	1	11	33	1,003	173	657	173	1
Holly Hill	12,792	127	0	7	46	74	1,073	321	631	121	3
Hollywood	145,834	944	4	46	412	482	7,976	1,289	5,670	1,017	43
Homestead	34,344	620	4	24	260	332	3,124	197	2,656	271	6
Jacksonville	776,417	6,729	92	213	2,344	4,080	43,791	8,910	30,043	4,838	283
Jacksonville Beach	21,636	144	0	4	44	96	1,221	175	942	104	3
Jupiter	44,179	166	0	7	33	126	1,492	328	1,094	70	4
Key Biscayne	10,663	11	0	0	6	5	386	45	328	13	4
Key West	25,736	152	2	7	69	74	1,879	384	1,336	159	0
Kissimmee	49,828	531	4	9	130	388	3,028	630	2,179	219	6
Lady Lake	12,765	28	0	1	0	27	232	51	167	14	0
Lake City	10,364	154	0	4	22	128	1,209	185	964	60	1
Lakeland	87,752	516	5	39	215	257	5,165	954	3,844	367	13

See footnotes at end of table.

Table 8

Offenses Known to Law Enforcement
by City 10,000 and over in Population, 2003—Continued

City by state	Population	Violent crime	Murder and non-negligent man-slaughter	Forcible rape	Robbery	Aggravated assault	Property crime	Burglary	Larceny-theft	Motor vehicle theft	Arson[1]
FLORIDA—Continued											
Lake Mary	12,877	29	1	5	3	20	242	50	179	13	1
Lake Wales	10,576	80	1	2	25	52	852	203	586	63	0
Lake Worth	36,226	500	5	22	284	189	2,887	697	1,896	294	8
Largo	71,943	342	4	30	60	248	2,754	517	2,051	186	7
Lauderdale Lakes	32,245	241	5	19	71	146	802	141	478	183	4
Lauderhill	59,898	493	4	24	134	331	2,120	495	1,245	380	21
Leesburg	16,779	222	0	3	59	160	1,143	385	691	67	5
Lighthouse Point	11,287	16	1	0	4	11	237	55	159	23	0
Longwood	13,946	309	2	4	12	291	656	207	429	20	1
Lynn Haven	13,508	45	1	1	7	36	477	119	331	27	6
Maitland	12,222	38	2	4	11	21	473	123	289	61	0
Marco Island	15,469	11	0	0	3	8	263	38	216	9	4
Margate	55,789	186	0	4	31	151	1,111	244	734	133	5
Melbourne	75,155	593	4	31	122	436	3,628	881	2,490	257	20
Miami	381,651	7,157	74	107	2,928	4,048	26,370	5,878	15,404	5,088	239
Miami Beach	91,215	1,172	6	72	507	587	9,438	1,414	6,840	1,184	5
Miami Lakes	23,287	91	1	3	16	71	1,023	170	699	154	1
Miami Shores	10,554	76	0	1	48	27	735	199	491	45	0
Miami Springs	13,995	80	0	2	43	35	634	131	456	47	0
Miramar	92,013	373	1	24	96	252	3,022	896	1,683	443	17
Mount Dora	10,137	100	0	6	16	78	529	116	384	29	5
Naples	21,549	54	0	4	13	37	1,084	183	866	35	3
New Port Richey	16,766	154	0	13	34	107	974	250	650	74	8
New Smyrna Beach	20,850	126	1	2	23	100	922	253	606	63	3
Niceville	12,292	18	0	4	1	13	143	27	107	9	0
North Lauderdale	33,836	224	0	16	32	176	637	133	422	82	2
North Miami	61,133	823	1	30	399	393	4,637	1,057	2,835	745	13
North Miami Beach	41,596	467	1	29	219	218	2,437	704	1,379	354	7
North Palm Beach	12,754	42	0	2	16	24	461	93	312	56	0
North Port	28,077	107	1	19	8	79	856	199	621	36	7
Oakland Park	32,063	279	2	15	83	179	1,229	273	745	211	6
Ocala	47,790	645	2	39	165	439	3,674	926	2,520	228	22
Ocoee	27,208	141	0	9	24	108	1,404	269	1,039	96	2
Oldsmar	12,958	35	0	2	3	30	599	121	441	37	2
Opa Locka	15,238	633	6	19	227	381	1,136	285	692	159	8
Orlando	197,268	3,322	21	136	849	2,316	17,024	3,593	11,511	1,920	48
Ormond Beach	37,883	110	1	6	33	70	1,217	428	714	75	1
Oviedo	28,102	106	0	8	5	93	690	139	524	27	11
Palatka	10,496	170	0	5	33	132	950	116	794	40	5
Palm Bay	84,558	576	8	72	64	432	3,199	890	2,130	179	19
Palm Beach Gardens	38,825	128	0	6	47	75	1,825	321	1,340	164	0
Palmetto	13,050	184	0	8	58	118	692	158	471	63	2
Palm Springs	13,404	62	0	4	27	31	783	133	538	112	5
Panama City	37,393	378	1	34	87	256	2,818	490	2,173	155	5
Parkland	17,899	13	0	1	2	10	340	93	229	18	0
Pembroke Pines	149,321	394	0	23	132	239	4,420	618	3,291	511	40
Pensacola	56,251	375	4	41	83	247	2,625	600	1,919	106	4
Pinellas Park	47,231	281	3	12	47	219	2,846	572	2,077	197	13
Plantation	86,371	237	3	7	109	118	3,764	549	2,881	334	9
Plant City	31,542	269	2	13	88	166	1,947	307	1,468	172	4
Pompano Beach	88,748	707	3	24	207	473	3,061	592	2,091	378	8
Port Orange	50,225	44	3	5	9	27	1,019	190	761	68	6
Port St. Lucie	100,342	281	1	17	30	233	2,699	683	1,906	110	14
Punta Gorda	16,303	30	0	3	4	23	419	141	253	25	1
Riviera Beach	31,013	636	10	28	233	365	3,350	1,049	1,726	575	15
Rockledge	22,070	44	0	2	10	32	748	155	559	34	1
Royal Palm Beach	25,957	132	0	11	30	91	1,709	550	1,055	104	4
Safety Harbor	17,690	27	0	3	1	23	386	114	246	26	3
Sanford	44,240	298	4	29	104	161	3,271	641	2,365	265	0
Sarasota	54,297	566	5	31	199	331	3,987	903	2,826	258	7
Satellite Beach	10,425	30	0	3	2	25	264	66	192	6	4
Sebastian	17,467	54	1	6	4	43	461	130	318	13	3
Seminole	16,969	58	0	3	18	37	600	113	451	36	1
South Daytona	13,494	53	0	2	17	34	682	261	357	64	3

See footnotes at end of table.

Table 8

Offenses Known to Law Enforcement
by City 10,000 and over in Population, 2003—Continued

City by state	Population	Violent crime	Murder and non-negligent man-slaughter	Forcible rape	Robbery	Aggravated assault	Property crime	Burglary	Larceny-theft	Motor vehicle theft	Arson[1]
FLORIDA—Continued											
South Miami	10,985	115	0	1	47	67	867	132	675	60	1
St. Augustine	12,011	113	1	3	21	88	837	84	721	32	1
St. Cloud	20,979	107	1	12	14	80	1,011	253	723	35	3
St. Pete Beach	10,171	48	0	4	12	32	532	107	402	23	0
St. Petersburg	253,095	4,054	22	106	1,198	2,728	16,431	3,852	10,583	1,996	87
Stuart	15,029	92	0	9	17	66	881	145	685	51	1
Sunny Isles Beach	15,750	62	0	4	25	33	657	132	458	67	3
Sunrise	90,098	424	1	23	145	255	3,762	513	2,857	392	3
Sweetwater	14,564	58	0	4	21	33	271	57	182	32	0
Tallahassee	158,011	1,412	4	155	342	911	9,338	2,223	6,413	702	27
Tamarac	58,521	183	2	9	71	101	883	165	581	137	5
Tampa	320,908	5,733	41	222	1,769	3,701	28,449	6,390	16,715	5,344	146
Tarpon Springs	22,338	136	0	6	16	114	705	143	486	76	3
Tavares	10,581	28	0	1	2	25	237	51	170	16	0
Temple Terrace	22,337	67	0	2	27	38	830	196	510	124	2
Titusville	41,879	356	2	19	70	265	1,726	548	937	241	9
Venice	18,941	37	0	1	5	31	528	78	436	14	3
Vero Beach	17,660	93	1	5	32	55	734	130	572	32	3
Village of Pinecrest	19,784	51	0	2	20	29	699	114	538	47	3
Wellington	44,349	106	0	14	22	70	1,511	288	1,109	114	6
West Melbourne	11,712	101	0	1	9	91	585	80	477	28	1
Weston	62,684	80	0	3	9	68	454	75	326	53	6
West Palm Beach	88,101	1,161	14	64	538	545	8,718	1,474	5,977	1,267	13
Wilton Manors	13,116	64	0	1	32	31	671	156	447	68	3
Winter Garden	18,591	110	1	8	19	82	681	214	405	62	1
Winter Haven	26,906	217	0	29	82	106	2,397	457	1,755	185	10
Winter Park	25,722	70	1	4	36	29	1,010	193	719	98	5
Winter Springs	31,853	73	0	7	5	61	550	123	397	30	1
Zephyrhills	11,471	48	1	2	5	40	716	160	501	55	2
GEORGIA											
Acworth	16,846	51	0	0	14	37	512	51	425	36	0
Albany	77,434	537	6	37	261	233	4,648	1,280	2,967	401	23
Alpharetta	36,258	113	1	6	25	81	1,521	192	1,197	132	
Americus	17,164	136	0	8	27	101	1,394	284	1,060	50	4
Athens-Clarke County	104,313	387	9	52	139	187	6,084	1,076	4,612	396	30
Atlanta	431,043	8,491	149	281	3,701	4,360	38,231	8,065	22,931	7,235	165
Bainbridge	12,071	68	3	11	24	30	970	178	769	23	0
Brunswick	15,825	133	0	16	85	32	1,627	361	1,179	87	0
Calhoun	11,885	47	0	5	18	24	1,035	166	817	52	
Canton	11,503	59	1	7	15	36	577	74	467	36	2
Carrollton	20,447	212	2	8	31	171	1,520	210	1,250	60	
Cartersville	17,419	90	5	3	28	54	1,385	302	940	143	
College Park	19,813	335	2	20	130	183	2,166	516	1,236	414	7
Columbus	188,116	837	19	22	331	465	12,978	2,204	9,555	1,219	40
Conyers	11,961	136	0	8	41	87	1,228	169	917	142	
Cordele	11,719	76	1	7	28	40	1,057	185	842	30	4
Covington	12,693	59	0	1	29	29	995	208	715	72	0
Dalton	30,329	195	0	4	42	149	1,840	285	1,426	129	
Decatur	18,436	51	1	8	18	24	697	149	473	75	
Doraville	10,204	77	0	3	38	36	455	81	315	59	0
Douglas	10,815	90	0	3	11	76	1,343	218	1,061	64	1
Douglasville	22,075	162	0	11	57	94	2,208	236	1,807	165	
Dublin	16,300	120	1	6	36	77	1,114	233	848	33	1
Duluth	23,119	31	1	2	8	20	403	104	261	38	0
East Point	38,417	305	6	11	177	111	2,805	787	1,514	504	
Fayetteville	13,118	15	0	0	6	9	594	25	543	26	2
Forest Park	21,625	196	1	9	113	73	1,718	269	1,223	226	
Gainesville	28,374	177	1	8	50	118	2,069	286	1,660	123	
Garden City	11,245	127	0	8	22	97	645	156	409	80	
Griffin	23,564	190	4	13	45	128	1,182	212	857	113	
Hinesville	30,985	168	4	9	63	92	1,846	302	1,471	73	
Kennesaw	25,183	23	1	0	7	15	591	89	455	47	

See footnotes at end of table.

Table 8

Offenses Known to Law Enforcement
by City 10,000 and over in Population, 2003—Continued

City by state	Population	Violent crime	Murder and non-negligent man-slaughter	Forcible rape	Robbery	Aggravated assault	Property crime	Burglary	Larceny-theft	Motor vehicle theft	Arson[1]
GEORGIA—Continued											
Kingsland	11,150	76	2	1	9	64	498	111	368	19	
LaGrange	26,808	166	3	19	52	92	2,244	294	1,838	112	
Lawrenceville	25,948	80	2	6	30	42	940	205	633	102	3
Macon	97,255	647	18	46	229	354	9,072	1,881	6,181	1,010	54
Marietta	62,921	324	5	15	156	148	2,754	568	1,852	334	0
McDonough	10,142	110	2	3	11	94	736	113	570	53	1
Milledgeville	19,035	33	0	4	8	21	741	150	574	17	
Monroe	11,935	56	0	4	13	39	448	93	324	31	2
Moultrie	14,586	140	2	9	51	78	1,601	360	1,140	101	
Newnan	19,646	68	1	3	22	42	894	127	705	62	9
Peachtree City	32,877	23	0	4	4	15	325	18	230	77	3
Perry	10,296	52	0	2	9	41	353	46	283	24	4
Riverdale	14,719	117	0	4	70	43	1,058	183	763	112	0
Rome	35,749	438	6	13	67	352	2,761	624	1,972	165	18
Savannah	129,547	1,073	28	42	603	400	9,241	2,135	5,782	1,324	15
Smyrna	46,342	192	2	15	96	79	2,142	368	1,490	284	4
Snellville	17,798	20	0	0	14	6	741	85	619	37	3
Statesboro	23,663	78	1	9	41	27	1,125	237	838	50	5
St. Marys	15,322	37	1	3	11	22	610	127	451	32	5
Suwanee	10,593	28	0	1	8	19	283	49	206	28	1
Thomasville	18,225	110	0	8	43	59	1,281	317	903	61	10
Tifton	16,104	128	1	6	39	82	1,386	234	1,104	48	1
Union City	12,639	83	0	1	35	47	916	180	574	162	0
Valdosta	45,357	298	3	24	101	170	3,238	600	2,489	149	
Warner Robins	53,329	212	5	20	79	108	3,477	725	2,568	184	11
Waycross	15,386	93	4	10	32	47	1,055	188	817	50	10
Winder	11,320	118	2	7	18	91	668	117	422	129	2
Woodstock	13,384	24	0	2	7	15	588	55	498	35	0
HAWAII											
Honolulu	905,301	2,606	15	266	989	1,336	48,306	7,967	32,086	8,253	389
IDAHO											
Blackfoot	10,750	26	0	3	4	19	408	58	334	16	2
Boise	193,414	632	3	108	78	443	8,122	1,422	6,223	477	105
Caldwell	30,020	141	0	19	11	111	1,959	322	1,464	173	14
Chubbuck	10,190	41	0	1	2	38	473	44	414	15	1
Coeur d'Alene	36,940	203	1	28	16	158	2,021	354	1,552	115	26
Garden City	11,191	81	0	12	8	61	659	105	478	76	4
Idaho Falls	52,056	148	2	22	12	112	1,941	244	1,553	144	8
Lewiston	31,060	39	0	2	6	31	1,309	269	978	62	2
Meridian	39,801	67	2	10	12	43	1,277	205	1,025	47	6
Moscow	22,081	8	0	2	2	4	670	71	579	20	1
Mountain Home	11,748	23	0	3	0	20	425	72	321	32	6
Nampa	61,391	245	3	70	18	154	2,544	456	1,830	258	14
Pocatello	52,205	138	1	19	8	110	1,752	204	1,464	84	13
Post Falls	19,090	44	0	12	5	27	678	120	526	32	5
Rexburg	17,888	9	0	1	0	8	240	35	196	9	0
Twin Falls	36,303	159	0	15	20	124	2,489	505	1,865	119	5
ILLINOIS[4, 5]											
Aurora	157,633		13		215	475	5,032	942	3,739	351	44
Chicago	2,898,374		598		17,302	19,784	144,622	25,064	96,779	22,779	947
Joliet	118,920		11		164	383	4,026	883	2,853	290	64
Naperville	135,958		0		23	61	2,471	291	2,096	84	16
Peoria	113,143		7		285	363	7,559	1,850	4,989	720	83
Rockford	151,703		12		500	732	12,055	2,996	7,895	1,164	
Springfield	112,304		7		324	1,158	9,041	2,112	6,522	407	71

See footnotes at end of table.

Table 8

Offenses Known to Law Enforcement
by City 10,000 and over in Population, 2003—Continued

City by state	Population	Violent crime	Murder and non-negligent man-slaughter	Forcible rape	Robbery	Aggravated assault	Property crime	Burglary	Larceny-theft	Motor vehicle theft	Arson[1]
INDIANA											
Auburn	12,350	17	0	2	3	12	488	67	402	19	0
Bedford	13,629	16	0	2	3	11	526	57	449	20	3
Beech Grove	14,713	42	0	3	17	22	544	127	352	65	5
Bloomington	70,403	69	0	15	27	27	2,485	441	1,930	114	17
Brownsburg	16,370	5	1	0	2	2	307	31	271	5	0
Carmel	41,121	12	0	3	7	2	757	115	612	30	2
Chesterton	10,981	17	0	3	2	12	318	49	250	19	0
Clarksville	21,434	60	0	17	30	13	1,820	182	1,504	134	3
Columbus	39,000	74	2	10	8	54	1,981	174	1,733	74	13
Connersville	15,168	25	0	5	2	18	989	136	824	29	2
Crawfordsville	15,421	18	0	2	10	6	805	129	658	18	1
Crown Point	20,613	23	0	0	5	18	378	53	290	35	6
Dyer	14,547	11	0	2	5	4	270	32	212	26	1
East Chicago	31,919	527	20	9	111	387	2,007	431	1,129	447	19
Elkhart	52,090	187	6	25	136	20	4,203	872	3,022	309	31
Evansville[2]	119,788	1,393	12	40	145	1,196	5,229	1,065	3,876	288	76
Fishers	44,705	54	0	4	3	47	591	80	486	25	1
Fort Wayne	211,317	772	19	118	354	281	11,113	2,188	8,145	780	114
Frankfort	16,692	50	0	8	10	32	997	157	795	45	4
Franklin	20,635	55	0	2	5	48	1,262	91	1,141	30	0
Gary	101,544	797	68	71	391	267	5,272	1,662	2,373	1,237	
Goshen	29,859	124	0	1	9	114	1,336	154	1,131	51	1
Greenfield	15,646	16	0	8	3	5	318	39	256	23	4
Greenwood	39,180	204	0	10	16	178	1,825	188	1,556	81	4
Griffith	17,211	33	0	7	15	11	656	56	512	88	6
Hammond	81,896	668	14	38	256	360	4,742	994	3,015	733	63
Highland	23,729	25	0	3	16	6	1,012	98	830	84	2
Huntington	17,408	20	0	5	3	12	524	61	448	15	1
Indianapolis	800,167	7,069	107	420	2,828	3,714	45,386	10,062	27,891	7,433	499
Jasper	12,761	6	0	1	0	5	148	17	115	16	0
Jeffersonville	27,987	85	0	12	36	37	1,273	322	783	168	0
Kokomo	46,229	194	2	17	66	109	3,029	551	2,339	139	4
Lafayette	60,954	243	1	30	64	148	3,205	603	2,459	143	8
La Porte	21,419	60	0	5	7	48	1,142	123	953	66	0
Lawrence	40,696	190	2	4	63	121	946	198	619	129	2
Logansport	19,582	17	0	6	4	7	750	124	579	47	2
Madison	12,198	26	0	0	2	24	384	113	244	27	0
Marion	30,835	186	4	13	70	99	1,820	382	1,352	86	3
Martinsville	11,646	26	0	2	2	22	703	50	628	25	5
Merrillville	31,127	53	1	2	23	27	1,105	91	833	181	1
Michigan City	32,757	150	1	18	72	59	2,071	364	1,538	169	19
Mishawaka	48,551	314	2	12	57	243	3,986	507	3,307	172	27
Mooresville	10,296	11	0	4	2	5	363	37	291	35	0
Muncie	67,594	290	0	56	68	166	3,018	545	2,255	218	17
Munster	22,004	46	0	0	8	38	553	48	459	46	2
New Albany	37,752	199	1	10	84	104	2,676	601	1,905	170	20
New Castle	19,107	18	0	8	7	3	1,881	368	1,427	86	4
New Haven	13,570	21	0	5	5	11	420	84	306	30	0
Noblesville	32,058	25	0	3	7	15	669	95	541	33	8
Plainfield	20,842	21	0	0	6	15	942	140	743	59	2
Plymouth	10,500	10	0	3	5	2	458	40	401	17	2
Portage	34,703	89	0	4	10	75	1,359	188	1,087	84	9
Richmond	38,698	200	1	26	65	108	1,626	411	1,041	174	74
Schererville	25,728	13	0	0	4	9	711	62	582	67	2
Seymour	18,506	87	2	2	9	74	1,168	82	1,026	60	6
South Bend	107,191	768	16	78	324	350	6,853	1,716	4,596	541	74
Speedway	12,980	51	0	7	37	7	420	61	292	67	1
Valparaiso[2]	28,352	89	0	4	7	78	1,027	66	923	38	2
Vincennes	18,354	24	0	6	9	9	1,265	304	869	92	4
Wabash	11,587	4	0	2	2	0	167	59	93	15	1
Warsaw	12,510	37	0	3	1	33	333	56	257	20	0
West Lafayette	29,254	30	0	8	2	20	624	109	490	25	1

See footnotes at end of table.

Table 8

Offenses Known to Law Enforcement
by City 10,000 and over in Population, 2003—Continued

City by state	Population	Violent crime	Murder and non-negligent man-slaughter	Forcible rape	Robbery	Aggravated assault	Property crime	Burglary	Larceny-theft	Motor vehicle theft	Arson[1]
IOWA											
Altoona	10,980	10	0	1	0	9	479	39	428	12	0
Ames	51,040	279	0	25	7	247	1,738	215	1,437	86	0
Ankeny	29,940	35	1	8	5	21	719	140	539	40	3
Bettendorf	31,625	135	0	3	8	124	808	153	635	20	11
Boone	12,834	9	0	0	1	8	371	49	305	17	6
Burlington	26,113	129	1	11	18	99	1,253	319	895	39	3
Carroll	10,019	8	0	0	2	6	218	32	169	17	0
Cedar Falls	36,751	114	2	13	5	94	973	138	802	33	8
Cedar Rapids	122,819	387	4	46	100	237	6,456	1,110	5,046	300	21
Clive	13,591	42	0	6	5	31	436	69	338	29	6
Coralville	16,531	18	0	10	4	4	725	60	646	19	10
Council Bluffs	58,786	497	5	71	78	343	6,138	1,005	4,271	862	31
Davenport	98,020	1,201	5	59	242	895	6,951	1,401	5,162	388	49
Des Moines	198,568	699	8	92	284	315	12,115	1,527	9,692	896	78
Dubuque	57,173	235	2	17	15	201	1,814	398	1,319	97	33
Fort Dodge	24,959	134	0	6	16	112	1,822	429	1,271	122	13
Fort Madison	11,033	17	0	3	0	14	482	97	363	22	3
Indianola	13,147	24	0	2	1	21	352	32	300	20	2
Iowa City	63,975	368	0	28	47	293	2,031	343	1,606	82	8
Keokuk	11,056	109	0	5	1	103	420	69	313	38	0
Marion	27,680	27	0	4	4	19	423	117	286	20	4
Marshalltown	26,167	192	0	1	9	182	1,399	329	985	85	6
Mason City	28,535	56	0	10	14	32	1,666	337	1,289	40	9
Muscatine	22,706	177	0	24	4	149	871	202	639	30	8
Newton	15,660	15	0	0	7	8	548	93	439	16	0
Oskaloosa	11,018	22	0	2	3	17	375	98	258	19	5
Ottumwa	24,756	207	0	8	5	194	1,236	235	936	65	10
Pella	10,244	30	0	0	1	29	188	40	141	7	4
Sioux City	84,340	357	1	43	49	264	4,556	967	3,227	362	36
Spencer	11,224	1	1	0	0	0	416	98	297	21	0
Storm Lake	10,109	30	0	8	4	18	373	65	296	12	4
Urbandale	31,229	72	0	4	11	57	890	199	665	26	7
Waterloo	67,910	326	4	47	93	182	3,707	922	2,543	242	33
West Des Moines	50,085	70	1	9	10	50	1,792	310	1,409	73	7
KANSAS											
Arkansas City	12,077	69	0	11	5	53	475	87	357	31	6
Atchison	10,134	26	0	1	3	22	350	99	238	13	1
Coffeyville	10,636	50	1	6	11	32	661	146	486	29	6
Derby	18,961	21	0	4	3	14	567	98	432	37	8
Dodge City	25,416	173	1	11	35	126	1,344	230	1,045	69	9
El Dorado	12,705	29	0	10	0	19	551	72	451	28	4
Emporia	26,814	80	0	19	8	53	1,567	216	1,289	62	17
Garden City	27,756	190	0	18	11	161	1,823	380	1,349	94	24
Gardner	10,731	54	0	9	1	44	438	77	339	22	8
Hays	19,964	23	1	2	3	17	724	196	500	28	1
Hutchinson	40,855	220	1	32	24	163	2,454	545	1,824	85	35
Junction City	17,803	136	1	11	19	105	1,475	198	1,234	43	10
Lawrence	81,833	365	3	37	59	266	4,205	810	3,222	173	8
Leavenworth	35,509	208	2	17	41	148	1,498	266	1,149	83	30
Liberal	20,138	83	0	9	9	65	1,157	276	824	57	8
McPherson	13,813	26	0	6	2	18	264	60	193	11	4
Merriam	10,874	53	0	9	15	29	831	124	615	92	8
Newton	17,963	55	0	9	2	44	679	109	552	18	8
Ottawa	12,012	33	0	5	3	25	552	94	435	23	5
Parsons	11,321	66	0	1	9	56	715	203	491	21	2
Pittsburg	19,140	156	8	21	12	115	1,732	334	1,328	70	17
Prairie Village	21,825	25	0	0	4	21	320	75	233	12	7
Salina	46,098	142	10	31	11	90	3,168	366	2,707	95	31
Shawnee	52,863	83	0	13	16	54	1,476	236	1,107	133	14
Topeka	122,446	728	16	52	298	362	9,208	1,518	7,183	507	
Wichita[2]	356,123	2,227	18	216	556	1,437	19,518	3,825	14,284	1,409	139

See footnotes at end of table.

Table 8

Offenses Known to Law Enforcement
by City 10,000 and over in Population, 2003—Continued

City by state	Population	Violent crime	Murder and non-negligent man-slaughter	Forcible rape	Robbery	Aggravated assault	Property crime	Burglary	Larceny-theft	Motor vehicle theft	Arson[1]
KENTUCKY[5]											
Ashland	21,733	122	0	11	19	92	1,143	182	913	48	6
Bowling Green	50,532	420	2	51	64	303	2,859	588	2,121	150	3
Florence	24,456	91	1	7	32	51	1,529	169	1,279	81	5
Hopkinsville	29,457	135	4	21	62	48	1,840	526	1,240	74	13
Lexington	265,224	1,242	18	122	518	584	11,565	2,694	8,129	742	41
Louisville Metro[6]	623,771	3,253	42	83	1,455	1,673	25,022	6,405	15,463	3,154	164
Madisonville	19,357	65	2	12	5	46	1,080	176	836	68	8
Murray	15,191	28	0	4	7	17	575	100	455	20	2
Owensboro	54,506	172	0	7	53	112	2,687	537	2,049	101	3
Paducah	25,733	230	5	22	38	165	1,745	279	1,326	140	4
Radcliff	22,112	92	0	19	23	50	749	179	550	20	
Richmond	28,264	63	1	8	22	32	1,526	237	1,203	86	4
LOUISIANA											
Alexandria	45,996	970	8	13	194	755	4,491	1,275	3,013	203	0
Baker	13,690	57	1	3	12	41	662	113	508	41	2
Baton Rouge	226,391	2,839	41	117	1,039	1,642	15,897	3,887	10,403	1,607	180
Bogalusa	13,104	144	2	7	39	96	980	317	619	44	1
Bossier City	57,331	476	4	31	97	344	3,491	644	2,517	330	22
Crowley	14,031	73	2	0	7	64	748	215	509	24	0
Eunice	11,444	57	0	1	6	50	561	227	281	53	0
Gretna	17,222	183	3	16	63	101	959	197	630	132	4
Houma	32,228	356	2	25	61	268	1,764	280	1,382	102	13
Jennings	10,818	77	0	3	12	62	462	131	316	15	7
Kenner	70,717	291	4	17	69	201	2,801	362	2,119	320	8
Lafayette	111,612	1,251	7	325	166	753	6,624	1,197	4,955	472	25
Lake Charles	70,942	524	6	43	139	336	4,163	1,678	2,288	197	31
Mandeville	11,395	20	0	0	7	13	467	62	384	21	4
Minden	13,286	37	2	2	7	26	322	74	229	19	0
Morgan City	12,293	74	0	11	15	48	701	108	552	41	0
Natchitoches	17,768	221	3	15	38	165	1,229	366	812	51	2
New Iberia	32,605	250	1	4	43	202	1,629	237	1,306	86	4
New Orleans	475,128	4,596	274	213	2,071	2,038	24,477	4,879	12,726	6,872	
Pineville	13,917	43	0	2	10	31	728	193	506	29	
Ruston	20,655	119	3	2	29	85	931	233	649	49	1
Shreveport	199,641	2,056	42	112	689	1,213	14,905	3,595	9,745	1,565	190
Slidell	26,547	163	0	12	49	102	1,990	227	1,610	153	0
Thibodaux	14,558	93	0	8	13	72	636	150	471	15	3
West Monroe	13,089	100	0	10	18	72	1,149	154	913	82	12
Westwego	10,615	55	0	4	18	33	315	55	225	35	2
MAINE											
Auburn	23,343	17	0	2	9	6	769	105	628	36	0
Augusta	18,712	32	0	16	3	13	1,105	201	876	28	10
Bangor	31,815	43	2	4	19	18	1,746	209	1,495	42	4
Biddeford	21,874	63	0	18	17	28	877	110	734	33	10
Brunswick	21,550	16	0	7	2	7	424	49	361	14	8
Falmouth	10,599	1	0	1	0	0	150	26	118	6	0
Gorham	14,747	8	0	2	1	5	278	73	193	12	2
Kennebunk	11,240	8	0	3	0	5	185	43	137	5	8
Lewiston	35,958	79	2	36	29	12	1,330	235	1,035	60	12
Portland	64,438	242	1	51	101	89	3,036	676	2,191	169	30
Saco	17,787	11	0	4	3	4	538	62	450	26	3
Sanford	21,738	42	1	17	12	12	568	88	453	27	13
Scarborough	18,421	15	0	4	2	9	328	58	258	12	0
South Portland	23,457	43	0	11	9	23	1,214	108	1,065	41	2
Waterville	15,765	15	0	3	5	7	552	85	451	16	2
Westbrook	16,243	22	0	1	4	17	479	96	363	20	4
Windham	15,326	8	0	0	5	3	389	93	272	24	5
York	13,431	5	0	2	1	2	239	40	195	4	2

See footnotes at end of table.

Table 8

Offenses Known to Law Enforcement
by City 10,000 and over in Population, 2003—Continued

City by state	Population	Violent crime	Murder and non-negligent man-slaughter	Forcible rape	Robbery	Aggravated assault	Property crime	Burglary	Larceny-theft	Motor vehicle theft	Arson[1]
MARYLAND											
Aberdeen	14,148	91	0	12	33	46	785	103	651	31	2
Annapolis	36,533	390	5	17	141	227	2,091	406	1,480	205	23
Baltimore	644,554	11,183	270	204	4,339	6,370	37,470	7,789	22,824	6,857	485
Baltimore City Sheriff		0	0	0	0	0	0	0	0	0	0
Bel Air	10,413	83	0	4	27	52	518	54	435	29	10
Cambridge	10,892	95	1	5	15	74	651	101	519	31	5
Cumberland	21,278	164	1	15	27	121	1,205	266	896	43	7
Easton	12,293	91	1	7	7	76	586	104	469	13	0
Elkton	13,216	126	0	5	21	100	841	163	633	45	22
Frederick	56,585	568	4	21	91	452	1,785	319	1,369	97	17
Greenbelt	22,211	139	3	11	79	46	1,493	142	952	399	0
Hagerstown	37,000	238	0	11	83	144	1,526	376	1,009	141	24
Havre de Grace	11,423	97	0	0	24	73	489	77	394	18	3
Hyattsville	15,262	103	2	3	71	27	799	110	492	197	0
Laurel	20,782	135	1	4	57	73	1,207	146	780	281	0
Ocean Pines	10,918	7	0	1	1	5	85	11	67	7	0
Salisbury	24,874	469	0	17	128	324	1,831	498	1,269	64	13
Takoma Park	17,852	106	2	9	67	28	779	156	447	176	0
Westminster	17,287	131	1	4	17	109	763	107	615	41	12
MASSACHUSETTS											
Abington	15,268	50	0	3	15	32	271	105	138	28	2
Acton	20,850	5	0	3	0	2	258	51	191	16	1
Acushnet	10,486	15	0	0	2	13	160	68	79 ·	13	1
Agawam	28,416	43	0	10	3	30	640	291	279	70	6
Amesbury	16,695	58	0	13	4	41	218	59	148	11	1
Amherst	34,447	111	0	16	16	79	388	187	151	50	5
Andover	31,846	9	0	2	1	6	443	60	348	35	2
Arlington	42,177	43	0	4	9	30	403	90	282	31	0
Ashland	15,405	15	1	4	1	9	69	26	40	3	1
Athol	11,478	48	0	6	2	40	152	66	77	9	0
Attleboro	43,202	139	1	13	21	104	743	158	483	102	
Auburn[7]	16,301		0	10	11		580	133	408	39	8
Barnstable	48,898	332	1	41	27	263	1,148	391	665	92	24
Bedford	12,658	0	0	0	0	0	28	4	23	1	0
Belchertown	13,524	33	0	11	1	21	140	52	70	18	0
Bellingham	15,606	38	0	0	2	36	275	61	192	22	0
Belmont	24,066	31	0	1	4	26	163	53	104	6	1
Beverly	40,270	87	0	6	5	76	573	98	443	32	1
Billerica	39,488	31	0	4	6	21	427	62	338	27	4
Boston	589,795	7,173	39	262	2,759	4,113	27,876	4,344	17,069	6,463	
Bourne[7]	19,389		0	8	3		685	313	326	46	6
Braintree	33,947	93	1	5	15	72	1,061	122	837	102	1
Brewster	10,372	3	0	0	0	3	106	32	69	5	0
Brockton[7]	95,519		10	44	231		4,077	665	2,327	1,085	23
Brookline	57,082	174	1	4	52	117	901	200	593	108	
Burlington	22,943	32	0	0	8	24	717	83	606	28	0
Cambridge	101,896	513	3	7	229	274	3,450	651	2,389	410	
Charlton	11,878	23	0	1	0	22	111	37	68	6	2
Chelmsford	34,027	59	0	3	11	45	612	69	518	25	3
Chelsea	34,944	576	0	26	158	392	1,282	337	520	425	16
Chicopee	54,881	400	1	28	74	297	1,997	502	1,199	296	10
Clinton	13,745	7	0	0	1	6	54	8	41	5	1
Concord	17,043	16	0	0	2	14	157	21	134	2	1
Danvers	25,468	50	0	4	19	27	845	71	714	60	4
Dartmouth	30,794	78	1	12	16	49	1,091	342	661	88	3
Dedham	23,398	32	0	1	10	21	416	31	313	72	1
Dennis	16,208	85	0	2	5	78	446	163	267	16	6
Dracut	28,853	61	0	4	7	50	405	78	223	104	1
East Bridgewater	13,513	6	0	0	1	5	111	14	94	3	1
Easthampton	16,194	57	0	8	2	47	246	97	131	18	5
East Longmeadow	14,518	27	0	2	8	17	317	57	235	25	4
Easton	22,718	8	0	1	2	5	161	41	111	9	0

See footnotes at end of table.

Table 8

Offenses Known to Law Enforcement
by City 10,000 and over in Population, 2003—Continued

City by state	Population	Violent crime	Murder and non-negligent man-slaughter	Forcible rape	Robbery	Aggravated assault	Property crime	Burglary	Larceny-theft	Motor vehicle theft	Arson[1]
MASSACHUSETTS—Continued											
Everett	37,805	135	0	8	54	73	1,101	183	681	237	1
Fairhaven	16,363	134	0	2	20	112	565	203	330	32	1
Fall River	92,741	1,067	3	77	270	717	3,477	1,260	1,664	553	
Falmouth	33,657	98	0	4	3	91	889	171	678	40	7
Fitchburg	39,762	243	3	27	60	153	1,102	285	719	98	6
Foxborough	16,415	39	0	5	3	31	162	55	95	12	0
Framingham	66,885	173	1	17	36	119	1,530	305	1,038	187	
Franklin	29,984	9	0	2	1	6	115	10	95	10	0
Gardner[7]	21,009		0	12	18		639	224	371	44	1
Gloucester	30,691	53	0	3	3	47	604	113	473	18	2
Greenfield[7]	18,021		1	18	19		484	175	270	39	6
Groton	10,024	5	0	1	1	3	100	27	73	0	0
Hanover	13,608	11	0	0	6	5	251	54	189	8	0
Harwich	12,812	29	0	0	1	28	249	79	160	10	1
Haverhill	59,686	326	1	41	49	235	1,683	711	648	324	
Hingham	20,239	17	0	0	6	11	366	59	292	15	2
Holbrook	10,887	28	0	6	12	10	168	54	102	12	0
Holden	16,151	15	1	0	1	13	84	9	72	3	4
Holliston	14,001	11	0	2	0	9	75	18	49	8	0
Holyoke	39,904	481	4	44	92	341	2,822	537	1,985	300	16
Hudson	18,352	8	0	2	0	6	236	21	188	27	2
Hull	11,357	64	0	7	5	52	90	32	45	13	2
Ipswich	13,282	12	0	0	0	12	177	38	130	9	1
Kingston	12,167	8	0	1	4	3	395	26	341	28	4
Lawrence	72,514	449	8	26	153	262	2,507	467	831	1,209	
Leicester	10,766	13	0	1	3	9	117	39	67	11	0
Leominster	41,932	59	0	9	26	24	1,104	184	829	91	4
Lexington	30,690	14	0	0	2	12	200	23	173	4	5
Lowell	104,995	866	2	45	146	673	3,079	626	1,737	716	
Ludlow	21,697	20	0	1	6	13	318	77	202	39	2
Lynn	89,669	1,111	1	9	205	896	2,925	467	1,717	741	
Lynnfield[7]	11,670		0	0	4		180	54	115	11	0
Malden[7]	56,204		0	17	82		1,587	552	799	236	0
Mansfield	22,847	53	0	3	9	41	153	49	80	24	2
Marblehead	20,500	13	0	1	2	10	233	35	188	10	0
Marlborough	38,177	71	1	7	3	60	740	159	513	68	0
Marshfield	24,837	31	0	1	6	24	214	17	179	18	0
Mashpee[7]	13,995		0	3	2		251	56	181	14	1
Maynard	10,455	6	0	1	1	4	20	1	16	3	0
Medfield	12,458	8	0	1	1	6	82	17	62	3	1
Medford	55,185	84	0	2	67	15	1,424	238	1,013	173	
Medway	12,899	2	0	0	1	1	56	11	45	0	0
Methuen	44,677	77	0	8	19	50	1,155	164	803	188	1
Middleboro	20,740	40	0	2	3	35	422	72	291	59	3
Milford	27,333	48	0	5	3	40	283	86	163	34	0
Milton	26,033	26	0	1	17	8	190	18	155	17	0
Nantucket[7]	10,425		0	1	0		451	35	405	11	0
Natick	32,412	27	0	6	8	13	682	84	559	39	0
Needham	29,223	7	0	0	2	5	221	36	180	5	2
New Bedford	94,170	679	11	104	234	330	2,666	945	1,187	534	
Newton	83,953	99	0	5	23	71	916	145	739	32	0
Norfolk	10,509	3	0	0	0	3	42	7	34	1	0
North Adams	14,443	75	0	12	9	54	535	224	277	34	3
Northampton	29,004	68	0	9	14	45	1,070	193	790	87	4
North Attleboro	27,850	36	0	2	12	22	787	70	674	43	9
Northborough	14,258	12	0	1	0	11	121	16	96	9	0
Northbridge	13,533	25	0	2	2	21	192	63	113	16	3
North Reading	14,011	12	0	1	2	9	91	32	59	0	1
Norton	18,583	13	0	2	0	11	188	48	126	14	0
Norwell	10,175	23	0	2	6	15	114	27	86	1	2
Norwood	28,869	52	0	3	11	38	448	60	313	75	1
Oxford	13,712	35	0	3	3	29	142	59	61	22	3
Palmer	12,719	42	0	4	3	35	249	62	147	40	2
Peabody	49,711	103	0	4	19	80	1,343	272	940	131	6

See footnotes at end of table.

Table 8

Offenses Known to Law Enforcement

by City 10,000 and over in Population, 2003—Continued

City by state	Population	Violent crime	Murder and non-negligent man-slaughter	Forcible rape	Robbery	Aggravated assault	Property crime	Burglary	Larceny-theft	Motor vehicle theft	Arson[1]
MASSACHUSETTS—Continued											
Pembroke	17,556	54	0	3	10	41	339	104	211	24	5
Pepperell	11,428	16	0	0	0	16	84	26	56	2	0
Pittsfield	45,062	197	3	13	15	166	711	109	441	161	
Plymouth	53,836	130	0	14	27	89	1,103	266	745	92	7
Quincy	89,265	316	1	15	97	203	1,530	334	1,041	155	
Randolph	31,071	140	0	10	25	105	629	63	485	81	3
Raynham	12,287	66	0	0	8	58	538	39	452	47	0
Reading	23,701	7	0	0	3	4	169	35	129	5	0
Rehoboth	10,730	6	0	0	0	6	118	40	61	17	0
Revere	47,538	316	1	18	72	225	1,742	301	1,110	331	14
Rockland	18,042	77	0	4	11	62	427	81	280	66	
Salem	42,186	98	0	8	17	73	959	135	717	107	0
Sandwich	20,810	94	0	18	0	76	338	107	213	18	3
Saugus[7]	26,438		0	7	31		1,232	256	825	151	1
Scituate	18,168	4	0	0	0	4	147	38	100	9	0
Seekonk	13,682	42	0	5	8	29	602	84	469	49	0
Sharon	17,551	16	0	0	1	15	75	12	56	7	2
Shrewsbury	32,780	34	0	2	11	21	533	110	394	29	1
Somerset	18,670	42	1	4	1	36	326	61	244	21	3
Somerville	76,989	258	0	11	98	149	1,807	378	908	521	
Southbridge	17,413	62	2	7	13	40	412	196	188	28	8
South Hadley	17,263	35	0	3	5	27	240	46	179	15	4
Spencer	11,940	46	0	2	0	44	165	46	107	12	2
Springfield	152,048	2,914	15	115	847	1,937	11,628	2,647	6,414	2,567	169
Stoneham	22,184	37	0	0	6	31	375	64	277	34	0
Stoughton	27,251	116	0	10	12	94	435	131	238	66	4
Sudbury	17,274	7	0	4	1	2	109	16	91	2	0
Swampscott	14,474	8	0	0	0	8	206	35	160	11	0
Swansea	16,192	44	0	3	8	33	298	49	213	36	1
Tewksbury	29,381	34	0	1	0	33	408	51	312	45	1
Tyngsboro	11,340	33	0	1	4	28	191	36	132	23	2
Uxbridge	11,774	12	0	1	0	11	108	40	57	11	3
Wakefield	24,839	20	0	3	6	11	247	42	179	26	0
Walpole	23,219	10	0	5	1	4	258	15	233	10	0
Waltham	59,125	100	2	11	20	67	815	116	601	98	2
Wareham[7]	20,953		0	13	6		691	235	386	70	0
Wayland	13,251	3	0	0	1	2	102	12	89	1	0
Webster	16,751	87	0	8	11	68	332	94	190	48	5
Wellesley	26,694	30	0	3	2	25	251	60	183	8	4
Westborough	18,559	29	0	8	4	17	299	62	221	16	3
Westfield	40,349	149	0	12	8	129	714	177	455	82	6
Westford	21,268	1	0	0	0	1	88	6	78	4	0
Westport	14,569	61	0	3	3	55	276	114	140	22	1
West Springfield	28,008	144	1	8	54	81	1,680	241	1,218	221	7
Westwood	14,193	15	0	0	5	10	155	15	136	4	1
Weymouth	54,802	187	0	10	38	139	837	142	591	104	
Wilbraham	13,738	18	1	2	1	14	240	39	180	21	0
Wilmington	21,648	24	0	4	2	18	383	47	306	30	
Winchester	21,111	9	0	0	4	5	209	28	171	10	1
Winthrop[7]	18,251		0	2	13		168	63	95	10	0
Woburn	38,036	96	0	6	27	63	868	91	681	96	4
Worcester	175,115	1,536	7	59	411	1,059	7,637	1,548	4,637	1,452	36
Wrentham	10,961	2	0	0	1	1	125	4	121	0	0
Yarmouth	25,258	167	0	14	14	139	650	247	380	23	
MICHIGAN											
Adrian	21,422	100	0	16	10	74	976	128	809	39	4
Allen Park	29,233	44	0	4	12	28	768	141	473	154	3
Alpena	11,104	35	0	13	1	21	370	62	295	13	1
Ann Arbor[2]	115,552	327	1	24	99	203	3,405	771	2,409	225	35
Auburn Hills	20,388	87	0	15	21	51	1,250	117	1,067	66	4
Battle Creek	53,808	691	2	69	122	498	3,766	791	2,745	230	35
Bay City	35,949	192	2	21	43	126	1,258	321	831	106	12

See footnotes at end of table.

Table 8

Offenses Known to Law Enforcement
by City 10,000 and over in Population, 2003—Continued

City by state	Population	Violent crime	Murder and non-negligent man-slaughter	Forcible rape	Robbery	Aggravated assault	Property crime	Burglary	Larceny-theft	Motor vehicle theft	Arson[1]
MICHIGAN—Continued											
Benton Harbor	11,084	321	2	14	28	277	674	239	344	91	19
Benton Township	16,259	90	0	17	16	57	901	120	721	60	5
Berkley	15,414	12	0	2	4	6	195	15	160	20	0
Beverly Hills	10,341	5	0	1	0	4	130	17	105	8	0
Birmingham	19,337	15	1	0	4	10	489	58	388	43	3
Blackman Township	24,158	57	1	8	10	38	728	108	589	31	1
Bloomfield Township	42,720	35	0	4	11	20	838	167	636	35	3
Bridgeport Township	11,609	50	0	4	17	29	303	71	213	19	5
Brownstown Township	25,486	75	0	13	12	50	713	163	461	89	6
Buena Vista Township	10,259	132	2	8	23	99	614	199	365	50	14
Burton	30,474	117	1	18	31	67	1,617	340	1,119	158	11
Cadillac	10,063	42	1	6	2	33	569	98	440	31	10
Canton Township	81,572	102	2	27	16	57	1,655	264	1,236	155	10
Chesterfield Township	40,490	28	1	3	5	19	699	118	522	59	3
Clawson	12,605	7	0	1	3	3	169	21	133	15	1
Clinton Township[2]	96,271	349	0	30	58	261	2,352	421	1,621	310	28
Coldwater	10,728	44	0	11	1	32	464	64	381	19	6
Davison Township	18,209	29	0	6	3	20	396	108	247	41	2
Dearborn	98,121	1,099	0	13	144	942	5,098	525	3,257	1,316	25
Dearborn Heights	58,218	156	3	12	63	78	1,622	276	962	384	5
Detroit[2]	927,766	18,724	366	814	5,817	11,727	64,809	14,100	25,353	25,356	1,744
Dewitt Township	12,911	25	0	4	5	16	240	54	158	28	0
East Grand Rapids	10,708	4	0	1	3	0	181	44	132	5	1
East Lansing	46,408	229	4	18	31	176	1,369	257	1,040	72	26
Eastpointe	33,966	168	1	22	65	80	1,363	176	810	377	9
Emmett Township	12,051	59	0	8	14	37	626	104	483	39	1
Farmington	10,297	20	0	1	2	17	239	36	184	19	0
Farmington Hills	81,666	146	0	18	26	102	1,751	355	1,236	160	16
Fenton	11,867	20	0	4	3	13	262	54	180	28	0
Ferndale	21,922	93	0	11	26	56	738	146	430	162	3
Flint[2]	122,121	1,484	28	124	338	994	6,714	2,063	3,353	1,298	98
Flint Township	33,586	187	1	18	65	103	2,416	414	1,779	223	10
Flushing Township	10,486	10	0	4	0	6	116	40	70	6	0
Fraser	15,354	28	0	3	8	17	401	55	298	48	3
Garden City	29,968	75	0	6	15	54	715	133	468	114	5
Genesee Township	24,664	108	2	9	22	75	678	213	372	93	9
Grand Blanc Township	32,794	69	0	9	8	52	704	179	454	71	3
Grand Haven	10,962	36	0	15	2	19	433	76	332	25	7
Grand Rapids[2]	197,173	2,070	11	68	533	1,458	9,326	2,048	6,569	709	89
Grandville	16,647	44	0	13	11	20	1,028	88	912	28	5
Green Oak Township	16,395	20	1	3	3	13	245	54	157	34	5
Grosse Ile Township	10,973	1	0	1	0	0	64	8	55	1	0
Grosse Pointe Park	12,388	15	0	0	8	7	398	30	241	127	1
Grosse Pointe Woods	16,985	8	0	0	3	5	254	30	193	31	0
Hamburg Township	21,710	16	0	2	1	13	225	53	162	10	0
Hamtramck	22,819	311	1	6	140	164	1,431	377	400	654	14
Harper Woods	14,175	61	0	8	38	15	1,572	82	1,055	435	7
Hazel Park	18,745	90	2	12	29	47	722	122	409	191	2
Holland	34,790	115	0	26	5	84	1,161	170	951	40	3
Huron Township	14,359	32	0	4	5	23	363	107	217	39	10
Inkster	29,983	362	7	13	65	277	909	326	364	219	20
Ionia	11,061	29	0	16	0	13	285	46	225	14	0
Jackson	35,618	196	5	39	63	89	2,077	363	1,573	141	33
Kalamazoo Township	21,907	86	1	12	30	43	859	180	578	101	4
Kentwood	46,453	137	0	18	20	99	1,545	284	1,207	54	11
Lansing	118,937	1,220	8	164	208	840	5,149	1,016	3,677	456	47
Leoni Township	13,590	38	1	3	5	29	358	101	243	14	0
Lincoln Park	39,776	144	0	10	43	91	1,656	320	1,034	302	1
Lincoln Township	14,149	21	0	2	2	17	221	38	172	11	0
Livonia	100,636	185	0	13	56	116	2,506	389	1,846	271	26
Madison Heights	30,788	80	0	7	38	35	1,436	199	938	299	15
Marquette	20,607	19	0	9	0	10	460	65	373	22	3
Melvindale	10,687	24	0	2	9	13	264	51	153	60	2
Meridian Township	39,512	75	1	15	9	50	1,305	213	1,041	51	15

See footnotes at end of table.

Table 8

Offenses Known to Law Enforcement
by City 10,000 and over in Population, 2003—Continued

City by state	Population	Violent crime	Murder and non-negligent man-slaughter	Forcible rape	Robbery	Aggravated assault	Property crime	Burglary	Larceny-theft	Motor vehicle theft	Arson[1]
MICHIGAN—Continued											
Midland	42,204	73	0	18	4	51	1,003	145	830	28	8
Milford	15,575	14	0	8	0	6	193	50	127	16	4
Monroe	22,094	90	1	16	18	55	738	147	561	30	6
Mount Clemens	17,411	64	0	3	24	37	696	116	499	81	4
Mount Morris Township	24,000	171	2	33	54	82	1,122	397	531	194	15
Mount Pleasant	26,094	53	0	9	4	40	690	101	555	34	3
Mundy Township	12,998	22	0	1	8	13	573	82	456	35	2
Muskegon	39,547	332	1	52	48	231	2,631	478	1,937	216	8
Muskegon Heights	11,892	256	0	10	44	202	1,194	246	735	213	17
Muskegon Township	18,126	60	0	14	6	40	1,039	107	872	60	5
Niles	12,009	74	0	17	8	49	729	132	543	54	3
Northville Township	22,898	16	0	2	0	14	593	92	451	50	2
Norton Shores	23,152	53	0	8	13	32	1,028	102	870	56	4
Novi	49,258	45	2	7	15	21	1,385	200	1,100	85	4
Oak Park	29,513	142	1	10	42	89	1,023	194	584	245	1
Owosso	15,524	46	0	12	2	32	546	90	429	27	6
Pittsfield Township	31,970	64	1	11	12	40	1,150	147	863	140	4
Plymouth Township	28,617	33	0	2	7	24	511	80	385	46	2
Pontiac	66,331	912	8	73	156	675	2,356	796	1,151	409	34
Portage	45,330	101	0	9	15	77	2,137	321	1,725	91	7
Port Huron	32,399	193	0	23	23	147	1,197	202	906	89	8
Redford Township	51,405	170	1	14	55	100	1,678	387	842	449	13
Riverview	13,240	14	0	1	3	10	281	32	224	25	1
Rochester	10,802	1	0	0	0	1	182	17	153	12	2
Romulus	23,665	133	0	15	32	86	1,315	282	743	290	16
Roseville	48,478	157	0	10	56	91	2,394	323	1,617	454	5
Royal Oak	59,394	103	0	9	42	52	1,508	275	1,078	155	5
Saginaw	60,273	1,640	16	74	173	1,377	2,684	1,054	1,350	280	88
Saginaw Township	40,127	91	0	5	12	74	1,121	133	940	48	6
Sault Ste. Marie	14,306	25	0	3	4	18	433	41	354	38	1
Shelby Township	67,097	78	0	7	7	64	978	156	741	81	2
Southfield	78,088	1,072	2	34	139	897	4,379	754	2,499	1,126	5
Southgate	30,488	82	0	5	15	62	1,457	175	1,057	225	8
South Lyon	10,695	12	0	3	0	9	178	31	139	8	1
St. Clair Shores	62,921	156	0	15	34	107	1,519	244	998	277	25
Sterling Heights	126,517	258	1	18	46	193	2,944	358	2,294	292	10
St. Joseph Township	10,068	12	0	0	3	9	156	37	109	10	0
Sturgis	11,153	47	1	12	0	34	470	89	359	22	1
Summit Township	21,876	38	0	5	8	25	298	64	209	25	0
Sumpter Township	12,020	34	0	9	0	25	261	67	157	37	0
Taylor	66,087	267	2	40	58	167	3,115	466	2,095	554	31
Thomas Township	12,558	30	0	2	1	27	412	41	363	8	0
Traverse City	14,511	43	0	12	5	26	512	51	439	22	3
Troy	81,150	100	1	11	28	60	2,024	292	1,573	159	5
Van Buren Township	25,717	18	0	2	5	11	646	95	443	108	1
Walker	23,108	51	3	12	12	24	1,090	138	909	43	4
Warren[2]	138,077	790	3	80	188	519		763	2,301		65
Waterford Township	73,865	163	1	40	28	94	1,563	306	1,094	163	14
Wayne	19,077	142	0	19	32	91	1,005	202	625	178	16
West Bloomfield Township	65,494	17	0	6	8	3	752	97	635	20	6
Westland	86,536	277	1	38	43	195	2,718	635	1,552	531	46
White Lake Township	28,880	23	0	10	2	11	593	103	451	39	4
Wixom	13,569	34	0	13	2	19	383	40	301	42	2
Woodhaven	12,802	38	0	5	6	27	418	38	352	28	2
Wyandotte	27,927	53	0	7	16	30	854	151	587	116	7
Wyoming	70,535	331	0	51	70	210	2,189	628	1,347	214	16
Ypsilanti	22,883	197	0	22	57	118	1,201	285	765	151	20
MINNESOTA											
Albert Lea	18,155	37	0	1	4	32	448	38	382	28	0
Anoka	18,081	41	0	17	9	15	685	101	537	47	7
Apple Valley	48,863	57	1	10	10	36	1,407	168	1,191	48	15
Austin	23,687	81	0	27	12	42	894	126	707	61	6

See footnotes at end of table.

Table 8

Offenses Known to Law Enforcement

by City 10,000 and over in Population, 2003—Continued

City by state	Population	Violent crime	Violent crime	Violent crime	Violent crime	Violent crime	Property crime	Property crime	Property crime	Property crime	Property crime
		Violent crime	Murder and non-negligent man-slaughter	Forcible rape	Robbery	Aggravated assault	Property crime	Burglary	Larceny-theft	Motor vehicle theft	Arson[1]
MINNESOTA—Continued											
Bemidji	12,472	44	2	8	4	30	996	55	884	57	3
Bloomington	84,756	149	1	24	52	72	3,569	332	2,988	249	19
Brainerd	13,417	66	0	24	4	38	952	155	740	57	32
Brooklyn Center	28,980	132	2	25	50	55	2,136	203	1,708	225	53
Brooklyn Park	68,666	266	2	40	68	156	3,007	591	2,094	322	28
Buffalo	11,747	29	0	8	2	19	496	45	429	22	0
Burnsville	60,507	88	1	23	28	36	1,863	183	1,559	121	13
Chaska	19,569	20	0	9	0	11	373	45	315	13	19
Cloquet	11,411	21	0	1	3	17	344	39	282	23	6
Cottage Grove	31,336	46	0	9	5	32	798	101	665	32	25
Crystal	22,702	50	0	6	15	29	846	120	691	35	9
Duluth	87,102	290	4	53	83	150	4,794	773	3,640	381	19
Eagan	64,553	65	0	16	24	25	1,529	211	1,238	80	7
Eden Prairie	57,794	48	0	14	1	33	1,367	189	1,132	46	14
Edina	47,486	30	0	5	15	10	1,061	164	867	30	1
Elk River	18,198	16	0	5	1	10	636	88	526	22	5
Fairmont	10,763	19	0	5	3	11	592	77	497	18	5
Faribault	21,509	65	0	19	4	42	834	170	627	37	12
Farmington	14,837	8	0	2	0	6	234	50	177	7	7
Fergus Falls	13,929	33	0	7	0	26	446	64	357	25	15
Forest Lake	15,217	11	0	4	0	7	485	47	380	58	3
Golden Valley	20,885	49	0	7	25	17	680	130	493	57	7
Hastings	19,244	22	0	9	2	11	560	61	466	33	9
Hibbing	17,109	11	0	4	1	6	315	84	195	36	1
Hutchinson	13,348	29	0	12	2	15	551	50	473	28	2
Inver Grove Heights	30,988	53	1	12	8	32	994	137	777	80	30
Lakeville	46,769	25	0	3	5	17	907	122	760	25	10
Mankato	33,420	62	0	23	14	25	1,788	273	1,441	74	4
Maple Grove	57,157	45	2	7	6	30	1,433	242	1,160	31	10
Maplewood	35,994	89	1	6	25	57	2,762	242	2,321	199	21
Marshall	12,786	29	1	9	5	14	481	67	399	15	4
Minneapolis	378,602	4,517	46	384	2,192	1,895	20,405	4,482	12,404	3,519	249
Minnetonka	51,524	42	1	16	6	19	1,241	280	917	44	13
Moorhead	32,839	54	1	15	9	29	1,056	134	875	47	11
Mounds View	12,823	28	0	4	6	18	703	46	621	36	3
New Brighton	22,231	17	0	1	10	6	762	113	606	43	10
New Hope	20,762	38	0	11	7	20	572	78	469	25	2
New Ulm	13,571	16	0	3	0	13	354	53	288	13	2
Northfield	17,961	17	0	4	1	12	513	68	403	42	0
North Mankato	12,148	5	0	4	1	0	235	5	217	13	5
North St. Paul	11,932	30	0	2	3	25	549	65	437	47	4
Oakdale	27,802	64	1	8	20	35	1,378	175	1,111	92	14
Orono	11,897	3	0	0	1	2	182	27	147	8	0
Owatonna	23,186	41	0	5	4	32	662	121	517	24	9
Plymouth	67,836	67	0	17	11	39	1,792	391	1,338	63	11
Prior Lake	18,266	17	0	3	3	11	555	78	439	38	5
Red Wing	16,162	48	0	13	7	28	697	96	542	59	2
Richfield	34,971	150	0	17	48	85	1,134	200	810	124	13
Robbinsdale	13,989	52	3	3	23	23	597	108	442	47	2
Rochester	91,230	257	0	59	47	151	3,004	477	2,360	167	47
Rosemount	16,390	16	0	2	2	12	447	63	366	18	3
Roseville	33,713	43	0	11	12	20	1,597	135	1,334	128	8
Sartell	11,123	7	0	0	0	7	192	30	145	17	0
Sauk Rapids	11,485	10	0	1	2	7	300	33	251	16	4
Savage	25,007	33	0	5	6	22	579	102	455	22	4
Shakopee	25,516	37	1	4	1	31	724	61	611	52	3
Shoreview	27,148	15	0	5	2	8	421	32	371	18	16
South Lake Minnetonka	12,397	16	1	3	0	12	173	26	133	14	7
South St. Paul	20,063	38	0	5	9	24	604	91	455	58	5
Stillwater	16,320	15	0	2	3	10	480	69	385	26	10
St. Louis Park	44,472	83	0	7	34	42	1,515	200	1,202	113	23
St. Paul	286,281	2,178	20	217	638	1,303	13,540	3,074	8,376	2,090	196
Vadnais Heights	13,327	9	0	2	2	5	286	23	230	33	5
White Bear Lake	24,658	17	0	3	3	11	816	140	615	61	5

See footnotes at end of table.

Table 8

Offenses Known to Law Enforcement
by City 10,000 and over in Population, 2003—Continued

City by state	Population	Violent crime	Murder and non-negligent man-slaughter	Forcible rape	Robbery	Aggravated assault	Property crime	Burglary	Larceny-theft	Motor vehicle theft	Arson[1]
MINNESOTA—Continued											
Willmar	18,224	48	0	10	6	32	785	124	634	27	2
Winona	26,747	25	0	3	9	13	750	138	575	37	7
Woodbury	49,551	33	0	8	7	18	1,109	116	952	41	4
Worthington	11,179	21	0	2	3	16	339	97	229	13	1
MISSISSIPPI											
Brandon	17,552	14	0	5	3	6	218	77	126	15	0
Cleveland	13,442	38	0	5	15	18	994	334	628	32	5
Columbus	25,336	73	4	13	22	34	1,622	273	1,276	73	1
Greenville	40,419	370	13	19	140	198	4,040	1,101	2,749	190	49
Greenwood	17,832	64	2	2	25	35	1,233	343	845	45	2
Grenada	14,753	89	5	10	17	57	699	182	475	42	6
Gulfport	72,751	270	11	48	147	64	5,737	1,181	4,091	465	24
Indianola	11,814	75	0	16	21	38	765	243	496	26	3
Jackson	181,479	1,648	45	179	962	462	15,496	4,369	8,323	2,804	59
Laurel	18,136	119	5	30	47	37	1,690	265	1,403	22	9
Long Beach	17,059	21	1	8	9	3	678	97	545	36	1
Madison	15,469	6	0	0	3	3	169	15	152	2	0
McComb	13,226	95	0	0	27	68	868	176	623	69	0
Meridian	39,649	195	8	27	94	66	1,823	573	1,138	112	27
Moss Point	15,527	143	2	14	61	66	1,197	601	495	101	
Natchez	17,923	57	2	10	18	27	1,220	186	1,011	23	3
Ocean Springs	17,363	26	0	10	8	8	757	146	562	49	1
Olive Branch	23,448	77	2	12	28	35	840	248	504	88	3
Oxford	12,528	29	0	3	13	13	286	71	199	16	1
Pascagoula	26,076	136	1	46	72	17	1,947	696	1,114	137	8
Pearl	22,717	67	0	25	10	32	754	316	387	51	4
Picayune	10,686	50	1	5	11	33	721	111	576	34	4
Ridgeland	20,761	40	3	1	21	15	947	75	813	59	1
Southaven	33,271	68	0	3	47	18	1,995	164	1,633	198	2
Starkville	22,277	55	0	3	18	34	1,170	232	897	41	1
Tupelo	35,091	90	1	19	32	38	1,966	379	1,446	141	4
Vicksburg	26,313	261	3	39	41	178	2,256	357	1,809	90	15
West Point	12,030	62	2	16	12	32	479	166	312	1	1
MISSOURI											
Arnold	20,074	32	1	2	6	23	1,198	66	1,098	34	1
Ballwin	31,441	15	0	2	4	9	330	53	254	23	7
Bellefontaine Neighbors	11,049	42	0	0	6	36	591	81	415	95	2
Belton	23,345	48	0	10	9	29	766	114	599	53	3
Berkeley	10,016	121	3	7	27	84	639	111	366	162	8
Blue Springs	49,729	87	1	18	28	40	2,078	337	1,594	147	8
Bridgeton	15,651	81	0	4	27	50	1,037	98	830	109	1
Cape Girardeau	35,866	82	1	13	37	31	2,025	284	1,681	60	6
Carthage	12,882	42	4	8	6	24	397	81	289	27	0
Chesterfield	47,391	45	1	3	5	36	917	149	749	19	7
Clayton	16,139	23	0	0	6	17	498	59	409	30	4
Columbia	87,470	422	2	17	84	319	3,266	459	2,632	175	20
Crestwood	11,941	14	0	0	8	6	700	19	645	36	4
Creve Coeur	16,857	14	0	0	3	11	312	48	225	39	2
Excelsior Springs	11,201	56	0	6	5	45	546	127	382	37	14
Farmington	14,164	108	0	2	7	99	499	42	438	19	3
Ferguson	22,256	108	1	11	46	50	1,399	192	895	312	1
Florissant	50,257	78	1	10	37	30	1,259	188	913	158	2
Fulton	12,839	52	2	5	9	36	337	44	276	17	3
Gladstone	26,929	46	0	3	17	26	812	174	542	96	16
Grandview	25,686	140	3	14	44	79	908	279	475	154	13
Hannibal	17,616	96	1	13	15	67	1,402	191	1,204	7	1
Hazelwood	26,188	121	2	8	23	88	902	161	600	141	0
Independence	113,663	757	2	43	107	605	8,364	1,328	6,080	956	47
Jackson	12,373	15	0	1	2	12	267	38	224	5	3
Jefferson City	39,299	276	3	27	21	225	1,326	190	1,064	72	12

See footnotes at end of table.

Table 8

Offenses Known to Law Enforcement
by City 10,000 and over in Population, 2003—Continued

City by state	Population	Violent crime	Murder and non-negligent man-slaughter	Forcible rape	Robbery	Aggravated assault	Property crime	Burglary	Larceny-theft	Motor vehicle theft	Arson[1]
MISSOURI—Continued											
Jennings	15,404	173	2	8	37	126	1,306	302	668	336	13
Joplin	46,447	191	5	29	48	109	3,679	641	2,803	235	19
Kansas City	445,965	6,151	82	308	1,890	3,871	35,469	6,896	22,973	5,600	478
Kennett	11,219	75	0	6	5	64	430	95	323	12	0
Kirksville	17,379	66	0	7	1	58	605	101	485	19	4
Kirkwood	27,579	45	0	5	8	32	841	80	721	40	9
Lake St. Louis	11,044	18	0	1	1	16	200	18	171	11	2
Lebanon	12,456	58	1	5	2	50	714	90	588	36	3
Lee's Summit	75,370	70	1	16	31	22	2,318	377	1,808	133	16
Liberty	27,687	89	0	3	8	78	577	89	443	45	4
Manchester	19,294	10	0	2	6	2	230	35	182	13	1
Marshall	12,157	2	0	1	1	0	260	64	188	8	4
Maryland Heights	25,927	30	2	2	14	12	1,124	159	881	84	3
Maryville	10,624	14	0	3	1	10	161	12	143	6	0
Mexico	11,073	21	1	4	4	12	241	54	178	9	0
Moberly	13,689	25	1	5	3	16	759	114	628	17	4
Neosho	10,657	56	0	1	2	53	556	94	441	21	0
Nixa	13,748	21	0	2	2	17	304	42	250	12	4
O'Fallon	60,014	68	0	5	13	50	1,638	180	1,413	45	2
Overland	16,699	54	0	4	22	28	912	154	698	60	0
Ozark	11,717	10	0	0	0	10	402	51	316	35	0
Poplar Bluff	16,688	77	1	10	20	46	1,104	194	863	47	8
Raymore	12,683	12	0	3	0	9	288	29	248	11	1
Raytown	30,229	76	1	9	19	47	1,133	281	740	112	5
Rolla	17,057	44	1	4	13	26	926	165	732	29	2
Sedalia	20,339	194	0	6	14	174	1,642	357	1,227	58	2
Sikeston	16,960	76	3	10	17	46	725	130	564	31	11
Springfield	151,859	1,038	6	73	171	788	12,351	1,833	9,754	764	74
St. Ann	13,608	110	2	4	19	85	957	63	787	107	3
St. Charles	61,097	193	0	15	35	143	2,016	238	1,577	201	18
St. Joseph	73,559	167	1	16	68	82	4,907	924	3,729	254	22
St. Louis	340,256	6,325	73	75	2,303	3,874	40,310	5,889	23,747	10,674	470
St. Peters	53,897	116	1	8	30	77	1,431	169	1,186	76	3
Town and Country	11,013	10	0	0	4	6	236	25	203	8	3
University City	38,064	174	4	14	83	73	2,310	265	1,730	315	7
Warrensburg	17,033	34	0	2	2	30	410	80	306	24	3
Washington	13,537	27	0	2	0	25	316	30	274	12	3
Webb City	10,208	13	0	4	2	7	296	51	228	17	4
Webster Groves	23,546	20	0	1	11	8	363	62	263	38	4
Wentzville	10,048	38	0	8	5	25	400	39	338	23	1
West Plains	10,896	32	1	3	2	26	721	140	559	22	3
MONTANA											
Billings	92,834	230	3	19	66	142	4,959	577	4,048	334	0
Bozeman	29,724	82	0	8	8	66	1,483	134	1,271	78	0
Great Falls	56,549	293	5	13	58	217	4,056	376	3,534	146	0
Kalispell	15,602	56	2	0	5	49	909	65	811	33	3
NEBRASKA											
Beatrice	12,880	25	0	6	4	15	563	78	470	15	4
Columbus	20,999	9	0	2	3	4	534	72	446	16	1
Fremont	25,335	32	0	3	7	22	968	136	782	50	3
Grand Island	43,261	134	3	19	16	96	2,756	349	2,317	90	0
Hastings	24,048	31	2	9	3	17	1,096	144	910	42	11
Kearney	28,073	80	0	5	6	69	1,089	184	855	50	10
La Vista	13,036	14	0	1	4	9	514	37	440	37	7
Lexington	10,177	23	0	10	3	10	400	93	281	26	0
Lincoln	233,721	1,114	5	94	153	862	13,487	1,959	11,049	479	9
Norfolk	24,324	38	1	21	5	11	1,107	130	944	33	3
Omaha	401,692	2,627	35	179	896	1,517	24,512	3,449	16,869	4,194	210
Scottsbluff	14,775	32	0	2	6	24	905	93	768	44	3
South Sioux City	12,039	5	0	1	2	2	221	33	172	16	0

See footnotes at end of table.

Table 8

Offenses Known to Law Enforcement

by City 10,000 and over in Population, 2003—Continued

City by state	Population	Violent crime	Murder and non-negligent man-slaughter	Forcible rape	Robbery	Aggravated assault	Property crime	Burglary	Larceny-theft	Motor vehicle theft	Arson[1]
NEVADA											
Boulder City	15,842	37	2	1	3	31	284	116	140	28	5
Elko	16,785	29	0	5	11	13	545	128	385	32	3
Henderson	212,571	429	10	104	103	212	5,689	1,441	2,884	1,364	46
Las Vegas Metropolitan Police Department	1,189,388	9,158	141	511	3,955	4,551	57,552	12,782	30,052	14,718	280
Mesquite	11,615	18	1	0	4	13	272	10	228	34	0
North Las Vegas	140,133	1,158	18	48	332	760	6,110	1,642	2,687	1,781	49
Reno	196,171	1,255	11	89	493	662	11,231	1,976	7,708	1,547	41
Sparks	76,025	358	3	44	102	209	3,756	828	2,482	446	
NEW HAMPSHIRE[2]											
Bedford	20,039	7	0	0	3	4	171	27	134	10	0
Berlin	10,310	27	1	10	1	15	174	35	133	6	2
Claremont	13,326	22	0	6	3	13	276	29	231	16	0
Derry	34,877	70	0	21	14	35	790	122	572	96	27
Dover	28,059	19	0	8	3	8	554	56	471	27	5
Exeter	14,468	14	0	5	2	7	212	20	180	12	2
Hampton	15,307	34	0	13	8	13	481	53	390	38	3
Hanover	11,233	1	0	0	1	0	96	20	70	6	2
Hooksett	12,556	11	0	4	5	2	377	50	316	11	7
Hudson	23,709	14	0	1	2	11	340	55	253	32	6
Keene	22,939	36	2	10	6	18	639	87	533	19	18
Laconia	17,117	31	0	7	6	18	654	94	525	35	5
Lebanon	12,915	4	0	0	0	4	182	23	154	5	1
Londonderry	24,459	23	0	2	8	13	297	48	214	35	6
Manchester	109,472	301	4	61	158	78	3,414	659	2,431	324	33
Merrimack	26,710	0	0	0	0	0	298	24	262	12	0
Milford	14,160	22	0	6	3	13	209	29	166	14	4
Pelham	11,788	9	0	1	2	6	221	54	144	23	0
Portsmouth	21,257	63	0	10	15	38	622	64	507	51	14
Rochester	29,641	75	1	40	12	22	789	85	682	22	1
Somersworth	11,874	21	0	1	11	9	493	35	441	17	6
Windham	11,969	9	0	1	0	8	200	67	115	18	3
NEW JERSEY											
Aberdeen Township	18,722	29	0	2	7	20	312	75	211	26	3
Asbury Park	16,889	377	2	7	182	186	913	261	562	90	2
Atlantic City	40,397	600	5	23	276	296	4,854	596	4,094	164	6
Barnegat Township	16,497	42	0	2	5	35	208	32	168	8	2
Bayonne	61,950	245	1	9	93	142	1,049	212	672	165	4
Beachwood	10,688	14	0	0	0	14	175	27	142	6	0
Belleville	36,066	133	1	11	42	79	1,045	230	503	312	2
Bellmawr	11,328	20	1	0	10	9	213	48	144	21	0
Bergenfield	26,362	26	0	0	12	14	290	42	230	18	1
Berkeley Heights Township	13,678	4	0	1	0	3	125	37	80	8	1
Berkeley Township	42,181	61	0	4	8	49	604	107	470	27	7
Bernards Township	25,605	6	0	1	3	2	165	54	104	7	6
Bloomfield	47,792	165	0	5	94	66	1,891	273	1,052	566	6
Bound Brook	10,252	9	0	2	5	2	284	64	209	11	3
Branchburg Township	14,950	5	0	2	2	1	113	16	91	6	0
Brick Township	78,269	91	0	0	14	77	1,296	250	999	47	3
Bridgeton	22,780	385	6	21	125	233	1,032	320	613	99	1
Bridgewater Township	44,377	19	0	0	8	11	659	92	516	51	0
Brigantine	12,675	15	0	0	1	14	184	66	107	11	0
Burlington Township	21,500	41	0	5	22	14	490	57	398	35	4
Camden	80,132	1,925	41	56	856	972	5,279	1,459	2,671	1,149	201
Carteret	21,761	75	0	11	21	43	411	96	247	68	1
Cedar Grove Township	12,397	8	0	0	0	8	242	31	190	21	0
Chatham Township	10,111	2	0	0	1	1	77	17	58	2	0
Cherry Hill Township	70,702	107	0	8	39	60	2,180	197	1,804	179	6
Cinnaminson Township	14,928	21	1	0	9	11	390	52	303	35	4
Clark Township	14,862	10	0	0	1	9	184	29	140	15	1

See footnotes at end of table.

Table 8

Offenses Known to Law Enforcement

by City 10,000 and over in Population, 2003—Continued

City by state	Population	Violent crime	Murder and non-negligent man-slaughter	Forcible rape	Robbery	Aggravated assault	Property crime	Burglary	Larceny-theft	Motor vehicle theft	Arson[1]
NEW JERSEY—Continued											
Cliffside Park	23,083	36	0	1	4	31	186	37	126	23	0
Clifton	80,072	197	0	11	84	102	2,068	329	1,355	384	4
Collingswood	14,341	43	0	8	17	18	407	80	291	36	2
Colts Neck Township	12,735	15	0	1	1	13	103	17	80	6	1
Cranford Township	22,927	19	0	7	3	9	299	46	235	18	0
Delran Township	16,161	23	0	0	10	13	385	65	296	24	0
Denville Township	15,991	11	0	0	2	9	189	37	147	5	0
Deptford Township	27,566	136	2	1	46	87	1,408	225	1,080	103	6
Dover	18,209	55	0	2	19	34	371	98	245	28	1
Dover Township	93,410	150	1	12	38	99	2,070	329	1,658	83	22
Dumont	17,631	14	0	1	2	11	194	29	157	8	0
East Brunswick Township	48,351	37	1	4	13	19	972	143	752	77	4
East Hanover Township	11,498	11	0	0	1	10	293	27	242	24	0
East Orange	70,141	1,394	22	30	647	695	4,757	1,059	1,930	1,768	78
East Windsor Township	26,658	29	1	3	9	16	420	81	311	28	2
Eatontown	14,165	31	0	1	10	20	559	54	489	16	1
Edison Township	100,484	285	1	11	115	158	2,633	465	1,755	413	11
Egg Harbor Township	33,569	111	1	13	30	67	1,086	245	793	48	16
Elizabeth	123,970	757	14	14	525	204	5,730	1,118	2,956	1,656	16
Elmwood Park	19,067	52	0	2	27	23	495	67	385	43	0
Englewood	26,305	68	1	6	27	34	525	121	344	60	7
Evesham Township	44,804	32	1	10	10	11	721	127	558	36	9
Ewing Township	36,355	120	0	14	55	51	1,078	178	772	128	2
Fair Lawn	31,808	32	1	2	9	20	401	68	313	20	0
Fairview	13,438	20	0	0	0	20	97	17	52	28	0
Florence Township	11,242	21	0	2	9	10	149	39	92	18	6
Florham Park	12,316	6	0	2	1	3	128	14	101	13	0
Fort Lee	37,170	8	0	1	7	0	513	101	365	47	2
Franklin Lakes	11,117	1	0	0	0	1	137	17	120	0	0
Franklin Township (Gloucester County)	15,898	33	1	0	7	25	319	112	174	33	4
Franklin Township (Somerset County)	55,970	85	0	7	49	29	986	269	621	96	8
Freehold	11,571	55	2	3	15	35	339	66	261	12	2
Freehold Township	33,519	49	0	5	17	27	908	70	808	30	5
Galloway Township	33,781	67	5	5	18	39	660	121	503	36	16
Garfield	29,932	55	1	0	27	27	604	92	372	140	2
Glassboro	19,157	87	2	8	32	45	731	153	549	29	4
Glen Rock	11,592	7	0	0	3	4	128	26	102	0	0
Gloucester City	11,521	29	1	2	13	13	312	58	223	31	1
Gloucester Township	66,056	197	0	23	48	126	1,564	390	1,063	111	20
Guttenberg	11,137	68	0	1	28	39	200	64	118	18	9
Hackensack	43,769	155	1	2	65	87	1,134	95	889	150	3
Hackettstown	10,820	14	0	1	3	10	151	17	126	8	0
Haddonfield	11,705	6	1	1	3	1	151	10	138	3	1
Haddon Township	14,776	21	0	2	8	11	354	70	258	26	2
Hamilton Township (Atlantic County)	22,091	62	1	4	19	38	863	114	706	43	9
Hamilton Township (Mercer County)	89,392	118	1	3	77	37	1,735	344	1,149	242	4
Hammonton	12,912	24	0	0	7	17	286	52	221	13	1
Hanover Township	12,990	12	0	1	6	5	145	53	81	11	3
Harrison	14,459	52	0	0	23	29	361	61	174	126	2
Hasbrouck Heights	11,712	10	0	0	5	5	145	18	111	16	0
Hawthorne	18,452	14	0	0	10	4	252	50	181	21	0
Hazlet Township	21,523	4	0	0	2	2	268	23	216	29	0
Highland Park	14,305	14	0	1	6	7	250	69	160	21	0
Hillsborough Township	37,918	19	0	3	5	11	420	92	312	16	4
Hillsdale	10,156	5	0	0	2	3	102	9	89	4	0
Hillside Township	22,116	103	3	6	55	39	890	230	430	230	1
Hoboken	39,728	140	1	2	62	75	1,493	375	855	263	1
Holmdel Township	16,671	10	0	0	3	7	261	24	227	10	0
Hopatcong	16,069	10	0	2	0	8	158	30	121	7	4
Hopewell Township	16,688	8	0	2	0	6	79	17	58	4	0
Howell Township	50,318	68	0	2	12	54	558	71	449	38	4
Irvington	60,855	1,497	27	45	766	659	3,613	898	1,266	1,449	23

See footnotes at end of table.

Table 8

Offenses Known to Law Enforcement

by City 10,000 and over in Population, 2003—Continued

City by state	Population	Violent crime	Murder and non-negligent man-slaughter	Forcible rape	Robbery	Aggravated assault	Property crime	Burglary	Larceny-theft	Motor vehicle theft	Arson[1]
NEW JERSEY—Continued											
Jackson Township	47,846	37	1	2	4	30	572	89	433	50	11
Jefferson Township	20,027	8	0	0	3	5	201	48	145	8	2
Jersey City	241,443	2,927	24	98	1,416	1,389	8,814	2,191	4,564	2,059	50
Keansburg	10,873	63	0	0	12	51	291	66	205	20	2
Kearny	40,526	97	1	4	46	46	1,209	232	770	207	8
Lacey Township	26,317	21	0	0	5	16	476	78	372	26	0
Lakewood Township	65,585	194	2	12	78	102	1,596	448	1,031	117	8
Lawrence Township	30,689	75	0	4	29	42	978	136	765	77	2
Lincoln Park	10,928	2	0	0	1	1	80	21	51	8	2
Linden	40,226	110	3	0	65	42	1,804	281	1,139	384	7
Lindenwold	17,491	115	3	9	49	54	712	264	375	73	5
Little Egg Harbor Township	17,794	27	0	2	1	24	388	64	308	16	4
Little Falls Township	12,002	23	0	3	4	16	402	82	276	44	1
Little Ferry	10,865	8	0	1	1	6	117	17	75	25	0
Livingston Township	27,871	29	0	3	6	20	528	66	411	51	2
Lodi	24,276	34	2	0	9	23	416	48	296	72	1
Long Branch	31,748	139	1	4	55	79	773	291	433	49	5
Lower Township	22,785	38	0	4	7	27	511	105	372	34	9
Lumberton Township	11,698	24	0	2	7	15	384	46	324	14	5
Lyndhurst Township	19,536	20	0	1	9	10	373	60	267	46	0
Madison	15,442	11	0	3	2	6	149	23	118	8	2
Mahwah Township	24,503	25	0	0	5	20	203	11	181	11	1
Manalapan Township	35,665	21	1	0	6	14	277	50	216	11	1
Manchester Township	41,663	25	0	0	5	20	367	73	280	14	3
Mantua Township	14,281	19	1	3	6	9	333	65	245	23	0
Manville	10,508	8	1	0	2	5	250	30	207	13	1
Maple Shade Township	19,262	52	0	10	17	25	421	78	273	70	2
Maplewood Township	23,944	84	1	5	46	32	693	99	439	155	0
Marlboro Township	38,539	15	1	1	6	7	374	71	287	16	4
Medford Township	23,176	12	0	0	2	10	335	71	238	26	5
Metuchen	13,316	16	0	1	4	11	249	66	167	16	0
Middlesex	14,052	15	0	0	4	11	183	20	149	14	1
Middle Township	16,810	91	1	6	18	66	588	158	388	42	8
Middletown Township	66,128	37	0	5	4	28	797	164	584	49	0
Millburn Township	19,904	30	1	2	22	5	715	77	527	111	1
Millville	27,068	229	3	28	77	121	1,480	382	1,017	81	16
Monroe Township (Gloucester County)	29,687	45	0	4	17	24	700	176	426	98	4
Monroe Township (Middlesex County)	30,483	16	0	0	2	14	241	32	201	8	1
Montclair	39,006	126	1	3	55	67	1,261	282	674	305	0
Montgomery Township	18,877	9	0	0	2	7	150	16	126	8	2
Montville Township	21,177	9	0	1	1	7	223	42	155	26	1
Moorestown Township	19,803	30	0	3	22	5	470	41	413	16	1
Morristown	18,936	125	1	5	57	62	666	128	495	43	2
Morris Township	21,459	16	0	4	0	12	175	30	138	7	0
Mount Holly Township	10,805	93	2	0	32	59	405	72	311	22	1
Mount Laurel Township	40,665	42	1	4	16	21	775	144	582	49	6
Mount Olive Township	25,146	11	0	1	1	9	305	47	245	13	5
Neptune Township	32,852	111	2	3	41	65	1,259	264	881	114	2
Newark	278,551	2,731	81	85	1,304	1,261	13,861	2,281	5,562	6,018	238
New Brunswick	49,674	336	8	15	188	125	2,383	535	1,549	299	11
New Milford	16,478	5	0	1	0	4	96	16	75	5	2
New Providence	12,112	3	0	0	0	3	127	28	93	6	0
North Arlington	15,305	24	0	2	7	15	165	26	124	15	1
North Bergen Township	59,364	135	2	8	73	52	1,298	221	781	296	12
North Brunswick Township	38,342	97	0	2	36	59	1,074	193	792	89	9
North Plainfield	21,308	65	0	11	32	22	546	131	342	73	6
Nutley Township	28,327	47	1	0	14	32	474	104	314	56	2
Oakland	13,356	10	0	1	1	8	135	15	116	4	1
Ocean City	15,603	23	0	2	9	12	875	162	706	7	2
Ocean Township (Monmouth County)	27,464	44	0	2	17	25	712	120	565	27	6
Old Bridge Township	63,415	74	2	3	23	46	1,017	212	658	147	8
Orange	33,028	406	2	8	234	162	2,130	425	943	762	9
Palisades Park	17,901	20	2	1	7	10	136	37	83	16	1
Paramus	26,422	96	0	6	38	52	2,038	112	1,722	204	10

See footnotes at end of table.

Table 8

Offenses Known to Law Enforcement
by City 10,000 and over in Population, 2003—Continued

City by state	Population	Violent crime	Murder and non-negligent man-slaughter	Forcible rape	Robbery	Aggravated assault	Property crime	Burglary	Larceny-theft	Motor vehicle theft	Arson[1]
NEW JERSEY—Continued											
Parsippany-Troy Hills Township	51,232	25	1	0	11	13	847	204	547	96	3
Passaic	68,828	770	4	2	355	409	2,087	323	1,190	574	11
Paterson	151,593	1,241	20	35	674	512	5,188	1,466	2,439	1,283	26
Pemberton Township	28,933	80	0	4	25	51	597	160	391	46	10
Pennsauken Township	35,983	213	1	14	119	79	1,194	261	710	223	11
Pennsville Township	13,194	27	0	2	4	21	320	32	279	9	1
Pequannock Township	14,221	5	0	0	0	5	225	22	175	28	4
Perth Amboy	48,413	232	1	3	89	139	1,380	281	863	236	3
Phillipsburg	15,330	34	0	3	16	15	248	64	161	23	2
Pine Hill	11,008	40	0	3	10	27	221	45	162	14	4
Piscataway Township	51,952	77	3	5	21	48	1,089	177	843	69	11
Plainfield	48,543	519	5	17	276	221	1,844	452	1,033	359	10
Plainsboro Township	21,105	13	0	1	3	9	185	37	135	13	2
Pleasantville	19,114	177	4	1	72	100	626	168	399	59	6
Point Pleasant	19,778	10	0	1	0	9	322	76	239	7	1
Pompton Lakes	10,958	12	0	2	0	10	150	26	113	11	0
Princeton	14,315	17	0	0	8	9	461	102	349	10	0
Princeton Township	16,683	4	0	1	1	2	157	35	119	3	3
Rahway	27,060	82	2	2	49	29	711	154	457	100	5
Ramsey	14,579	14	0	2	4	8	173	11	150	12	2
Randolph Township	25,607	16	0	0	1	15	262	37	218	7	2
Raritan Township	21,128	11	0	0	2	9	170	23	132	15	0
Readington Township	16,302	4	0	0	0	4	154	44	102	8	3
Red Bank	11,905	39	0	3	21	15	274	30	234	10	0
Ridgefield	10,990	10	0	0	1	9	73	19	33	21	1
Ridgefield Park	12,895	17	0	5	5	7	224	49	152	23	1
Ridgewood	25,016	10	0	2	5	3	255	53	199	3	0
Ringwood	12,696	5	1	0	1	3	87	27	57	3	0
River Edge	11,050	7	0	1	4	2	115	20	88	7	1
Rockaway Township	24,636	28	2	1	12	13	488	46	416	26	1
Roselle	21,660	56	0	3	34	19	508	151	272	85	0
Roselle Park	13,463	27	0	0	12	15	275	113	139	23	0
Roxbury Township	23,852	21	0	0	4	17	296	38	234	24	2
Rutherford	18,148	5	1	0	1	3	258	48	175	35	0
Saddle Brook Township	13,235	13	0	0	6	7	263	31	200	32	1
Sayreville	42,002	78	0	9	16	53	755	173	484	98	9
Scotch Plains Township	23,179	15	0	2	7	6	321	66	229	26	0
Secaucus	15,971	10	1	0	7	2	744	27	567	150	0
Somers Point	11,600	33	0	1	7	25	324	82	232	10	2
Somerville	12,530	30	1	1	9	19	310	61	236	13	1
South Brunswick Township	40,101	38	1	1	9	27	632	165	408	59	1
South Orange	17,082	66	0	3	36	27	596	85	292	219	0
South Plainfield	23,024	47	1	7	15	24	462	77	351	34	5
South River	15,918	38	0	1	13	24	209	79	113	17	2
Sparta Township	18,871	10	0	0	1	9	76	8	65	3	0
Springfield	14,836	17	0	2	10	5	345	37	220	88	2
Stafford Township	23,918	28	0	5	1	22	513	85	407	21	5
Summit	21,454	8	0	1	2	5	329	61	239	29	0
Teaneck Township	39,388	112	0	2	43	67	772	252	480	40	13
Tenafly	14,029	0	0	0	0	0	144	38	97	9	0
Tinton Falls	15,797	10	0	2	1	7	244	41	187	16	2
Totowa	10,066	11	0	1	6	4	339	37	269	33	0
Trenton	86,130	1,518	13	36	645	824	4,677	1,073	2,514	1,090	26
Union City	67,277	332	6	16	176	134	1,790	453	893	444	0
Union Township	55,849	161	1	9	89	62	2,022	349	1,281	392	2
Ventnor City	12,898	20	1	1	8	10	291	85	197	9	2
Vernon Township	25,377	10	0	1	0	9	250	38	202	10	1
Verona	13,582	9	0	1	1	7	182	50	108	24	0
Vineland	56,655	416	4	16	169	227	3,039	747	2,127	165	8
Voorhees Township	28,629	62	0	9	17	36	770	90	652	28	8
Wallington	11,618	12	0	1	5	6	168	24	121	23	0
Wall Township	26,193	31	0	1	6	24	415	91	311	13	1
Wanaque	10,426	10	0	0	0	10	133	27	97	9	0
Warren Township	15,300	3	0	0	2	1	136	23	110	3	0

See footnotes at end of table.

Table 8

Offenses Known to Law Enforcement
by City 10,000 and over in Population, 2003—Continued

City by state	Population	Violent crime	Murder and non-negligent man-slaughter	Forcible rape	Robbery	Aggravated assault	Property crime	Burglary	Larceny-theft	Motor vehicle theft	Arson[1]
NEW JERSEY—Continued											
Washington Township (Gloucester County)	49,687	64	0	3	36	25	1,224	445	704	75	9
Washington Township (Mercer County)	10,885	7	0	0	1	6	119	19	87	13	1
Washington Township (Morris County)	18,225	7	0	0	0	7	156	38	103	15	1
Waterford Township	10,686	26	0	4	1	21	149	32	110	7	3
Wayne Township	55,241	39	0	2	8	29	1,480	105	1,204	171	1
Weehawken Township	13,486	34	0	0	21	13	424	69	265	90	1
West Caldwell Township	11,289	2	0	0	2	0	140	16	115	9	1
West Deptford Township	19,849	31	0	2	13	16	488	76	383	29	5
Westfield	30,196	12	0	1	7	4	327	43	271	13	3
West Milford Township	27,765	19	0	7	2	10	422	125	285	12	3
West New York	47,146	137	1	0	59	77	936	267	461	208	2
West Orange	45,512	81	1	1	49	30	1,394	270	753	371	2
West Paterson	11,263	22	0	4	5	13	222	43	150	29	2
West Windsor Township	23,561	17	0	0	8	9	504	67	398	39	2
Westwood	11,078	20	0	0	5	15	95	14	77	4	0
Willingboro Township	33,220	151	2	5	60	84	728	205	449	74	5
Winslow Township	35,150	167	0	11	27	129	772	214	510	48	12
Woodbridge Township	100,982	348	4	17	72	255	3,275	643	2,259	373	31
Woodbury	10,497	49	1	5	18	25	485	77	374	34	2
Wyckoff Township	16,956	11	0	0	0	11	124	17	106	1	0
NEW MEXICO											
Alamogordo	35,477	93	1	4	8	80	927	135	758	34	0
Albuquerque	468,764	4,439	51	263	1,080	3,045	29,294	5,543	19,663	4,088	65
Carlsbad	25,462	155	1	4	10	140	1,310	268	982	60	
Deming	14,275	99	1	5	7	86	915	287	552	76	7
Farmington	40,991	434	3	53	24	354	1,493	389	974	130	13
Gallup	20,390	380	0	18	65	297	2,458	259	2,077	122	3
Hobbs	28,779	325	1	22	34	268	1,788	372	1,357	59	
Las Cruces	75,806	415	1	83	99	232	4,089	808	3,036	245	13
Las Vegas	14,373	185	5	11	16	153	835	203	569	63	10
Portales	11,215	37	0	1	5	31	547	110	419	18	1
Rio Rancho	57,211	193	1	31	12	149	1,353	283	968	102	2
Roswell	44,522	477	7	41	48	381	3,298	724	2,444	130	24
Santa Fe	65,814	387	9	40	104	234	4,671	2,301	2,137	233	25
Silver City	10,321	48	1	3	6	38	673	168	477	28	0
Sunland Park	13,738	22	0	0	3	19	192	44	140	8	0
NEW YORK											
Albany	93,938	1,160	8	33	383	736	4,990	1,302	3,274	414	44
Amherst Town	111,945	120	1	5	40	74	1,977	176	1,735	66	
Amsterdam	18,096	24	0	2	3	19	199	54	141	4	
Auburn	28,234	77	0	20	13	44	1,012	203	800	9	
Batavia	15,967	58	0	7	17	34	762	114	647	1	
Beacon	13,978	53	0	4	13	36	289	90	170	29	
Bedford Town	18,554	22	0	0	2	20	174	26	131	17	
Bethlehem Town	32,053	23	0	2	7	14	491	84	391	16	
Binghamton	46,815	182	3	10	77	92	1,947	213	1,683	51	
Blooming Grove Town	11,750	5	0	3	0	2	144	28	103	13	
Brighton Town	35,303	25	0	3	18	4	961	144	723	94	
Buffalo	288,187	3,701	63	203	1,625	1,810	15,862	4,154	9,180	2,528	
Camillus Town and Village	23,366	11	0	0	2	9	347	37	301	9	
Carmel Town	34,025	20	0	0	6	14	342	49	278	15	
Cheektowaga Town	83,006	159	1	19	63	76	2,909	366	2,323	220	
Cicero Town	26,734	9	0	0	1	8	567	101	436	30	
Clarkstown Town	79,143	133	0	2	43	88	2,050	202	1,758	90	
Clay Town	54,318	7	0	0	4	3	437	57	378	2	
Cohoes	15,359	54	0	1	4	49	192	58	114	20	
Colonie Town	76,211	48	0	12	22	14	2,746	371	2,272	103	

See footnotes at end of table.

Table 8

Offenses Known to Law Enforcement

by City 10,000 and over in Population, 2003—Continued

City by state	Population	Violent crime	Murder and non-negligent man-slaughter	Forcible rape	Robbery	Aggravated assault	Property crime	Burglary	Larceny-theft	Motor vehicle theft	Arson[1]
NEW YORK—Continued											
Corning	10,734	23	0	5	3	15	375	30	337	8	
Cortland	18,831	63	0	15	16	32	563	104	438	21	
Depew Village	16,374	19	0	3	7	9	346	49	268	29	
Dewitt Town	22,019	43	0	2	18	23	656	127	509	20	
Dobbs Ferry Village	10,975	8	0	0	5	3	111	16	84	11	
Dunkirk	12,863	44	1	1	15	27	391	55	330	6	
East Aurora-Aurora Town	13,978	6	0	1	2	3	162	20	137	5	
Eastchester Town	18,795	30	0	0	8	22	358	19	321	18	
East Fishkill Town	27,054	38	0	1	2	35	335	55	268	12	
East Greenbush Town	15,846	33	0	1	12	20	309	30	272	7	
East Hampton Town	18,442	8	0	1	1	6	438	94	325	19	
Endicott Village	12,908	40	0	5	3	32	522	72	436	14	
Evans Town	15,292	21	1	2	1	17	233	49	174	10	
Fallsburg Town	11,480	53	0	3	4	46	178	76	98	4	
Fishkill Town	18,780	16	0	3	2	11	306	31	258	17	
Floral Park Village	16,001	13	0	0	8	5	103	23	73	7	
Fredonia Village	10,668	18	0	2	4	12	273	18	249	6	
Freeport Village	44,053	182	1	12	76	93	969	150	614	205	
Fulton City	11,701	26	1	1	2	22	506	64	430	12	
Garden City Village	21,737	13	0	0	7	6	275	17	241	17	
Gates Town	29,221	37	0	1	31	5	1,213	128	950	135	
Geddes Town	10,891	8	1	0	3	4	244	35	202	7	
Geneva	13,580	28	0	3	2	23	375	21	346	8	
Glens Falls	14,218	35	0	1	6	28	367	59	299	9	
Gloversville	15,280	38	1	3	3	31	640	90	523	27	
Greece Town	94,667	74	2	15	42	15	2,296	298	1,815	183	
Greenburgh Town	43,546	51	0	0	28	23	1,009	111	824	74	
Guilderland Town	32,949	23	0	0	7	16	1,047	89	938	20	
Hamburg Town	44,191	20	0	1	8	11	649	96	525	28	
Harrison Town	24,993	10	0	3	0	7	342	38	297	7	
Haverstraw Town	24,624	102	0	3	11	88	307	57	240	10	
Haverstraw Village	10,170	73	0	0	15	58	197	37	143	17	
Hyde Park Town	21,056	9	0	3	3	3	101	13	83	5	
Irondequoit Town	52,378	91	0	5	65	21	2,060	295	1,558	207	
Jamestown	31,086	164	0	18	41	105	1,225	325	816	84	
Kenmore Village	16,127	23	0	1	14	8	272	57	188	27	
Kent Town	14,351	4	0	0	0	4	182	33	145	4	
Kingston	23,387	118	1	7	62	48	1,124	176	873	75	
Lancaster Town	22,422	11	0	1	6	4	299	26	255	18	
Lewiston Town and Village	16,192	14	0	2	2	10	187	37	136	14	
Lynbrook Village	19,967	16	0	2	7	7	239	51	148	40	
Mamaroneck Town	11,240	5	0	0	3	2	170	25	131	14	
Mamaroneck Village	18,865	28	0	0	14	14	262	35	208	19	
Manlius Town	24,991	19	0	0	10	9	385	72	306	7	
Massena Village	11,011	8	0	0	3	5	247	39	204	4	
Middletown	25,819	84	2	11	38	33	656	94	527	35	
Mount Kisco Village	10,081	39	0	0	12	27	239	32	200	7	
Mount Pleasant Town	26,443	28	1	1	6	20	245	32	198	15	
Mount Vernon	68,732	402	2	13	193	194	1,640	417	924	299	
Newburgh	28,430	260	2	26	57	175	1,047	316	624	107	
Newburgh Town	28,789	35	0	0	22	13	1,085	109	926	50	
New Rochelle	72,595	255	1	7	141	106	1,644	241	1,224	179	
New Windsor Town	23,846	76	0	2	8	66	513	77	398	38	
New York	8,098,066	59,448	597	1,609	25,989	31,253	176,767	28,293	124,846	23,628	
Niskayuna Town	20,794	12	1	0	6	5	375	51	309	15	
North Castle Town	11,421	7	0	2	1	4	144	26	110	8	
North Greenbush Town	11,046	17	0	3	2	12	160	18	137	5	
North Tonawanda	32,642	53	0	9	10	34	572	127	411	34	
Ogdensburg	12,060	7	0	3	1	3	482	84	378	20	
Ogden Town	18,920	8	0	1	5	2	397	78	303	16	
Olean	15,050	23	0	6	8	9	614	101	512	1	
Oneida	10,967	21	0	2	5	14	471	78	389	4	
Oneonta City	13,139	46	0	8	8	30	358	107	240	11	
Orangetown Town	35,813	31	2	0	13	16	507	77	414	16	

See footnotes at end of table.

Table 8

Offenses Known to Law Enforcement
by City 10,000 and over in Population, 2003—Continued

City by state	Population	Violent crime	Murder and non-negligent man-slaughter	Forcible rape	Robbery	Aggravated assault	Property crime	Burglary	Larceny-theft	Motor vehicle theft	Arson[1]
NEW YORK—Continued											
Orchard Park Town	27,817	11	0	0	1	10	461	51	386	24	
Ossining Village	24,179	102	0	6	32	64	340	41	255	44	
Oswego City	18,058	45	0	1	9	35	572	120	440	12	
Peekskill	23,116	69	1	1	28	39	272	49	199	24	
Plattekill Town	10,299	0	0	0	0	0	28	9	18	1	
Plattsburgh City	19,189	14	0	4	2	8	521	93	413	15	
Port Chester Village	27,997	91	0	4	48	39	782	109	617	56	
Port Washington	17,927	13	0	0	6	7	204	24	158	22	
Poughkeepsie	30,124	348	2	26	131	189	1,162	257	822	83	
Poughkeepsie Town	43,103	101	0	2	25	74	1,329	153	1,145	31	
Ramapo Town	72,980	92	1	6	25	60	748	162	562	24	
Rochester	217,527	2,034	58	86	1,166	724	15,708	2,497	9,773	3,438	319
Rockville Centre Village	24,615	25	0	1	15	9	305	67	209	29	
Rome	34,768	51	0	5	23	23	746	200	504	42	
Rotterdam Town	28,475	20	0	0	8	12	756	81	660	15	
Rye	15,118	1	0	0	0	1	230	20	206	4	
Saratoga Springs	27,060	37	0	4	6	27	643	93	522	28	
Saugerties Town	15,106	47	0	3	3	41	249	53	185	11	
Scarsdale Village	17,989	5	0	0	5	0	227	28	189	10	
Schodack Town	10,984	7	0	2	0	5	154	39	111	4	
Shawangunk Town	12,407	19	0	0	0	19	77	14	58	5	
Southport Town	11,025	4	0	0	1	3	20	5	15	0	
Stony Point Town	14,674	13	0	1	3	9	81	11	65	5	
Syracuse	145,411	1,383	17	44	477	845	7,773	1,975	4,612	1,186	
Tarrytown Village	11,466	22	0	0	5	17	139	30	99	10	
Tonawanda	15,875	36	0	4	6	26	289	36	237	16	
Tonawanda Town	60,774	74	0	3	29	42	1,129	133	897	99	
Troy	48,901	293	2	30	84	177	2,139	520	1,438	181	
Ulster Town	12,661	13	1	1	5	6	226	25	179	22	
Utica	60,049	409	7	43	186	173	2,280	744	1,392	144	
Vestal Town	27,076	12	0	0	2	10	560	53	499	8	
Wallkill Town	25,584	16	0	0	7	9	230	22	200	8	
Warwick Town	19,296	2	0	0	2	0	197	33	156	8	
Watertown	25,625	86	1	26	19	40	929	200	711	18	
Watervliet	10,091	25	2	0	5	18	220	49	151	20	
Webster Town and Village	39,385	14	1	4	5	4	614	103	472	39	
West Seneca Town	45,506	165	0	6	15	144	1,164	122	987	55	
White Plains	55,488	221	2	9	81	129	1,669	134	1,452	83	
Yonkers	197,569	879	13	25	454	387	3,789	816	2,185	788	36
NORTH CAROLINA											
Albemarle	15,614	90	1	4	19	66	975	281	648	46	15
Apex	24,940	84	0	6	8	70	420	96	301	23	1
Asheboro	22,844	48	0	1	33	14	2,086	484	1,489	113	1
Asheville	69,917	456	8	26	221	201	5,003	960	3,541	502	48
Boone	13,367	25	0	2	4	19	453	73	359	21	1
Burlington	46,498	264	3	12	89	160	3,197	638	2,402	157	11
Carrboro	17,075	77	0	8	33	36	990	173	758	59	0
Cary	99,067	109	0	17	36	56	2,244	397	1,717	130	5
Chapel Hill	52,177	207	0	10	84	113	2,341	515	1,728	98	13
Charlotte-Mecklenburg	668,003	7,194	66	306	2,688	4,134	44,534	11,066	26,628	6,840	300
Cornelius	14,231	30	0	2	9	19	195	87	106	2	2
Durham	197,965	1,663	22	76	883	682	13,621	3,528	9,027	1,066	55
Eden	15,888	69	2	1	28	38	1,137	282	783	72	2
Elizabeth City	17,436	151	2	7	51	91	1,008	271	691	46	5
Fayetteville	125,587	1,230	13	33	492	692	9,652	2,035	6,939	678	30
Garner	20,162	97	0	4	48	45	1,252	151	1,040	61	1
Goldsboro	38,881	390	5	9	99	277	2,577	608	1,823	146	4
Graham	13,380	63	0	5	11	47	656	164	459	33	2
Greensboro	230,606	1,547	36	97	697	717	13,758	3,255	9,455	1,048	91
Greenville	66,183	596	4	10	253	329	4,662	1,348	3,097	217	10
Havelock	23,213	40	0	2	8	30	462	74	367	21	0
Henderson	16,466	212	1	4	84	123	2,105	402	1,611	92	11

See footnotes at end of table.

Table 8

Offenses Known to Law Enforcement
by City 10,000 and over in Population, 2003—Continued

City by state	Population	Violent crime	Murder and non-negligent man-slaughter	Forcible rape	Robbery	Aggravated assault	Property crime	Burglary	Larceny-theft	Motor vehicle theft	Arson[1]
NORTH CAROLINA—Continued											
Hendersonville	10,797	96	2	5	22	67	939	124	766	49	0
Hickory	39,722	176	1	15	92	68	3,188	623	2,389	176	16
High Point	91,588	785	8	34	264	479	5,907	1,585	3,765	557	29
Holly Springs	11,944	9	0	1	1	7	150	44	102	4	0
Hope Mills	11,921	74	0	6	36	32	945	172	734	39	7
Huntersville	28,310	69	1	7	32	29	919	183	668	68	9
Jacksonville	67,613	149	2	19	19	109	767	151	573	43	3
Kannapolis	38,425	118	0	3	47	68	986	267	649	70	6
Kernersville	19,865	96	0	11	13	72	1,202	194	950	58	4
Kinston	23,481	260	5	12	64	179	2,233	487	1,676	70	8
Laurinburg	15,927	87	3	7	25	52	1,066	359	672	35	13
Lenoir	18,267	31	2	0	5	24	750	159	556	35	3
Lexington	20,354	165	0	7	53	105	1,360	457	838	65	4
Lincolnton	10,101	33	1	0	8	24	875	96	748	31	2
Lumberton	21,262	249	5	10	114	120	3,111	745	2,167	199	5
Matthews	23,853	48	0	4	17	27	962	228	677	57	12
Mooresville	19,509	37	0	6	14	17	776	117	644	15	3
Raleigh	310,157	2,004	14	81	748	1,161	14,771	3,327	10,186	1,258	75
Reidsville	15,027	89	4	7	33	45	924	206	680	38	4
Roanoke Rapids	16,771	99	0	6	36	57	1,011	224	739	48	1
Rocky Mount	56,601	459	7	21	195	236	5,065	1,227	3,589	249	22
Salisbury	26,721	206	1	16	72	117	1,706	322	1,280	104	10
Sanford	23,582	197	4	14	91	88	2,281	535	1,651	95	7
Shelby	19,803	250	6	14	56	174	1,727	428	1,217	82	6
Smithfield	12,056	131	1	1	34	95	1,117	185	863	69	0
Southern Pines	11,539	69	0	2	26	41	602	164	388	50	3
Statesville	24,096	244	2	14	86	142	1,855	296	1,483	76	5
Tarboro	10,744	56	0	4	13	39	552	139	396	17	0
Thomasville	21,795	128	0	5	42	81	1,265	267	917	81	6
Wake Forest	14,787	34	0	3	9	22	550	129	400	21	4
Wilmington	91,593	819	5	30	325	459	7,356	1,855	4,900	601	13
Wilson	46,039	245	2	18	87	138	2,424	552	1,688	184	7
Winston-Salem	190,912	1,579	11	118	547	903	13,938	3,957	8,810	1,171	
NORTH DAKOTA											
Bismarck	56,210	26	2	1	5	18	1,282	122	1,070	90	5
Dickinson	15,672	17	0	4	6	7	553	60	460	33	1
Fargo	91,165	77	0	41	11	25	2,283	335	1,759	189	11
Grand Forks	48,525	68	0	13	9	46	1,989	255	1,618	116	3
Jamestown	15,108	20	0	9	1	10	447	69	353	25	7
Mandan	16,762	19	0	5	0	14	403	37	333	33	7
Minot	35,602	57	1	26	6	24	1,150	126	913	111	7
West Fargo	15,794	17	0	2	3	12	451	114	308	29	5
Williston	12,371	16	1	11	0	4	269	27	189	53	1
OHIO											
Akron	214,622	1,288	16	206	623	443	12,172	3,177	7,779	1,216	92
Alliance	23,011	77	0	18	21	38	1,244	213	987	44	12
Amherst	11,733	8	0	0	2	6	205	34	171	0	2
Athens	21,572	9	1	6	2	0	644	72	545	27	0
Aurora	14,263	0	0	0	0	0	195	38	155	2	0
Avon	13,026	11	0	0	0	11	211	37	160	14	2
Avon Lake	19,155	13	0	4	1	8	174	28	137	9	0
Bainbridge Township	11,065	6	0	1	0	5	256	25	226	5	0
Barberton	27,698	64	0	19	23	22	1,175	177	933	65	6
Bay Village	15,894	0	0	0	0	0	2	0	0	2	0
Beavercreek	38,094	36	0	7	25	4	1,373	150	1,165	58	9
Bedford Heights	11,307	35	0	1	8	26	300	51	196	53	2
Bellefontaine	12,986	29	0	4	10	15	589	153	422	14	0
Berea	18,770	33	0	7	5	21	365	48	299	18	1
Bexley	12,866	38	0	3	32	3	492	146	328	18	3
Boardman	41,718	74	1	3	49	21	2,351	319	1,796	236	13

See footnotes at end of table.

Table 8

Offenses Known to Law Enforcement

by City 10,000 and over in Population, 2003—Continued

City by state	Population	Violent crime	Murder and non-negligent man-slaughter	Forcible rape	Robbery	Aggravated assault	Property crime	Burglary	Larceny-theft	Motor vehicle theft	Arson[1]
OHIO—Continued											
Bowling Green	29,520	42	0	5	11	26	849	143	676	30	4
Brecksville	13,565	6	0	0	1	5	99	17	74	8	0
Broadview Heights	16,364	14	0	1	1	12	116	15	82	19	1
Brookfield Township	10,023	6	0	1	1	4	257	57	189	11	5
Brooklyn	11,429	15	0	0	7	8	537	44	432	61	1
Brook Park	20,967	3	0	0	0	3	98	17	55	26	0
Cambridge	11,518	58	1	4	14	39	1,183	137	987	59	3
Celina	10,259	14	0	3	6	5	396	56	324	16	3
Centerville	23,101	25	0	2	10	13	581	109	446	26	4
Chillicothe	22,173	65	1	11	37	16	2,455	404	1,942	109	13
Cincinnati	324,297	3,643	71	307	2,184	1,081	24,167	5,922	14,796	3,449	243
Circleville	13,537	36	0	5	12	19	766	135	605	26	1
Cleveland	468,446	6,200	73	646	3,167	2,314	26,078	8,048	12,832	5,198	461
Cleveland Heights	49,797	13	0	0	13	0	711	101	520	90	0
Columbus	726,151	6,215	109	615	3,332	2,159	56,338	14,650	33,343	8,345	
Conneaut	12,338	20	0	1	1	18	430	75	340	15	3
Copley Township	13,943	12	0	2	8	2	371	42	294	35	0
Dayton	162,876	1,654	28	173	951	502	13,230	3,814	6,874	2,542	173
Delaware	26,503	65	0	32	16	17	918	204	677	37	23
Delhi Township	29,926	23	0	1	8	14	397	47	334	16	3
Dover	12,280	4	0	1	1	2	197	31	149	17	1
Dublin	32,848	11	0	3	4	4	773	174	566	33	4
East Cleveland	26,686	98	1	6	0	91	8	0	0	8	0
Eastlake	20,153	12	0	0	4	8	364	41	286	37	5
Englewood	12,406	37	0	8	17	12	606	69	502	35	3
Euclid	51,977	174	1	16	83	74	1,758	441	1,162	155	13
Fairborn	32,500	66	1	15	26	24	1,644	343	1,183	118	4
Fairfield	42,149	166	0	16	31	119	1,715	204	1,361	150	6
Fairview Park	17,328	0	0	0	0	0	20	4	9	7	0
Findlay	39,496	96	0	36	25	35	2,027	419	1,559	49	5
Forest Park	19,184	35	0	7	21	7	652	89	514	49	5
Franklin Township	14,855	9	0	3	2	4	223	87	125	11	5
Fremont	17,103	40	2	4	15	19	1,303	170	1,090	43	2
Gahanna	33,545	35	0	6	16	13	822	180	617	25	3
Galion	11,597	14	1	2	4	7	479	60	403	16	5
Garfield Heights	30,301	118	0	6	39	73	794	163	556	75	7
Genoa Township	11,971	2	0	0	1	1	191	50	140	1	0
Girard	10,780	13	1	0	7	5	534	86	401	47	1
Goshen Township	14,331	24	0	3	0	21	318	85	211	22	1
Greenville	13,163	89	0	13	4	72	543	109	416	18	3
Hamilton	60,167	488	4	72	144	268	4,361	1,019	2,931	411	4
Hilliard	25,384	15	0	7	5	3	712	136	545	31	15
Huber Heights	38,103	89	1	21	50	17	1,443	286	1,079	78	14
Hudson	22,988	5	0	2	2	1	233	45	176	12	0
Kent	27,777	70	0	14	17	39	802	159	601	42	57
Kettering	56,752	68	0	18	34	16	2,178	409	1,605	164	7
Lakewood	55,356	85	0	4	27	54	944	192	667	85	3
Lancaster	36,127	81	0	13	37	31	1,484	235	1,168	81	14
Lebanon	17,919	30	1	9	7	13	613	103	474	36	5
Liberty Township	12,564	22	0	5	13	4	494	103	321	70	5
Lima	40,872	423	2	70	108	243	2,380	637	1,599	144	27
Lorain	67,790	276	5	10	93	168	2,010	566	1,344	100	13
Lyndhurst	15,074	5	1	3	1	0	25	4	21	0	0
Madison Township	16,132	24	0	10	4	10	455	58	366	31	3
Mansfield	50,812	162	7	22	100	33	3,482	822	2,507	153	24
Marietta	14,137	31	0	17	4	10	385	85	291	9	1
Marion	37,155	77	1	18	29	29	2,019	549	1,412	58	9
Marysville	16,267	47	0	3	2	42	485	102	367	16	2
Mason	25,689	7	0	1	6	0	465	56	391	18	0
Mayfield Heights	19,145	12	0	0	3	9	255	22	224	9	0
Mentor	50,240	40	0	15	15	10	1,372	139	1,152	81	15
Miamisburg	19,814	53	0	7	24	22	1,144	216	816	112	11
Miami Township	37,266	43	0	4	6	33	901	103	761	37	2
Middletown	51,250	166	0	23	64	79	3,421	700	2,562	159	13

See footnotes at end of table.

Table 8

Offenses Known to Law Enforcement
by City 10,000 and over in Population, 2003—Continued

City by state	Population	Violent crime	Murder and non-negligent man-slaughter	Forcible rape	Robbery	Aggravated assault	Property crime	Burglary	Larceny-theft	Motor vehicle theft	Arson[1]
OHIO—Continued											
Monroe	10,749	89	0	14	9	66	576	91	465	20	0
Montgomery	10,024	5	0	0	0	5	243	23	208	12	3
New Philadelphia	17,343	9	0	1	5	3	156	15	135	6	4
North Canton	16,597	15	2	2	9	2	389	86	295	8	0
North Ridgeville	23,427	37	0	6	3	28	406	90	278	38	0
North Royalton	30,635	12	0	2	2	8	116	28	77	11	0
Norton	11,604	11	0	0	5	6	434	68	323	43	2
Norwalk	16,333	6	0	0	0	6	353	71	263	19	0
Norwood	21,012	127	0	14	79	34	1,424	206	1,095	123	0
Oregon	19,463	55	1	6	22	26	1,142	111	983	48	2
Parma	84,642	130	0	15	50	65	1,390	340	920	130	10
Parma Heights	21,410	31	0	4	12	15	455	79	340	36	4
Pataskala	10,568	11	0	2	4	5	263	71	181	11	2
Perrysburg	16,887	14	0	0	3	11	491	41	433	17	3
Perry Township	29,074	39	0	4	6	29	691	159	477	55	5
Pickerington	11,160	10	0	1	8	1	291	50	231	10	0
Pierce Township	12,533	16	0	6	3	7	334	85	229	20	0
Piqua	20,726	31	0	5	17	9	1,310	178	1,087	45	4
Portsmouth	20,465	208	6	31	70	101	2,567	620	1,780	167	2
Ravenna	11,607	39	0	4	9	26	709	50	628	31	0
Reading	11,026	43	0	2	14	27	463	76	334	53	4
Reynoldsburg	32,838	91	1	10	41	39	1,319	205	1,040	74	6
Richmond Heights	10,947	3	0	0	1	2	74	2	66	6	0
Riverside	23,479	72	0	11	37	24	1,039	301	566	172	6
Salem	12,334	6	0	2	0	4	77	19	55	3	0
Sandusky	27,391	115	0	11	26	78	1,709	338	1,300	71	2
Seven Hills	12,154	5	0	0	2	3	129	22	101	6	0
Shaker Heights	28,891	28	0	3	21	4	686	176	460	50	5
Sharonville	13,684	47	2	10	21	14	667	81	551	35	4
Solon	22,217	11	0	2	6	3	298	25	267	6	1
South Euclid	23,181	42	1	4	28	9	495	86	371	38	5
Springboro	14,188	7	0	2	2	3	264	52	200	12	0
Springdale	10,356	33	2	1	21	9	1,240	53	1,104	83	0
Springfield	64,214	558	5	74	285	194	6,253	1,573	4,022	658	23
Springfield Township (Hamilton County)	37,394	76	2	25	27	22	699	93	545	61	0
Springfield Township (Summit County)	15,529	27	0	7	13	7	757	159	559	39	6
Steubenville	19,713	132	1	7	31	93	932	125	747	60	0
Stow	33,956	23	0	11	8	4	727	116	594	17	6
Streetsboro	12,582	13	0	1	5	7	361	57	291	13	2
Struthers	11,469	7	0	0	4	3	294	48	219	27	3
Sylvania	19,004	10	0	0	7	3	276	38	226	12	3
Sylvania Township	25,867	20	0	1	7	12	779	78	646	55	1
Tallmadge	17,050	26	1	7	10	8	382	76	283	23	4
Tiffin	17,795	28	0	13	4	11	785	140	624	21	2
Toledo	309,499	3,182	21	152	1,354	1,655	23,159	5,664	14,383	3,112	434
Troy	22,057	37	1	21	10	5	789	125	636	28	4
Twinsburg	17,283	10	0	3	5	2	219	35	176	8	1
University Heights	13,951	41	0	2	11	28	256	19	231	6	0
Urbana	11,538	16	0	2	8	6	372	60	295	17	0
Vandalia	14,481	16	0	7	7	2	472	124	315	33	3
Van Wert	10,658	28	0	7	7	14	464	87	369	8	2
Vermilion	10,881	7	0	1	0	6	394	106	276	12	1
Wadsworth	19,095	15	0	9	4	2	350	61	273	16	2
Warren	47,285	368	6	32	153	177	2,441	715	1,444	282	86
Warrensville Heights	14,916	65	1	7	29	28	463	126	257	80	0
Washington Court House	13,275	23	0	5	11	7	670	171	478	21	1
West Carrollton	13,579	28	0	6	14	8	545	90	374	81	4
West Chester Township	53,862	77	2	11	35	29	1,633	285	1,253	95	10
Westerville	35,565	38	0	6	13	19	1,120	144	947	29	11
Westlake	32,201	0	0	0	0	0	27	2	11	14	0
Whitehall	18,875	157	3	14	112	28	1,660	353	1,170	137	23
Willoughby	22,611	44	0	4	12	28	477	79	363	35	4

See footnotes at end of table.

Table 8

Offenses Known to Law Enforcement
by City 10,000 and over in Population, 2003—Continued

City by state	Population	Violent crime	Murder and non-negligent man-slaughter	Forcible rape	Robbery	Aggravated assault	Property crime	Burglary	Larceny-theft	Motor vehicle theft	Arson[1]
OHIO—Continued											
Willowick	14,206	10	0	0	1	9	182	20	150	12	0
Worthington	13,860	18	0	5	10	3	388	51	318	19	1
Xenia	24,191	23	0	0	21	2	1,340	206	1,092	42	14
Youngstown	80,128	768	19	60	286	403	4,833	1,763	2,568	502	257
Zanesville[2]	25,479	110	5	19	51	35	1,928	350	1,494	84	28
OKLAHOMA											
Ada	15,933	135	1	14	13	107	899	228	622	49	5
Altus	20,674	78	1	20	18	39	1,235	516	687	32	7
Ardmore	24,061	241	0	20	44	177	1,953	398	1,464	91	9
Bartlesville	34,942	100	0	16	15	69	1,265	213	969	83	1
Bethany	20,344	71	1	9	19	42	850	150	614	86	9
Bixby	15,652	30	0	6	4	20	378	95	243	40	3
Broken Arrow	83,512	183	3	19	21	140	2,292	400	1,738	154	43
Chickasha	16,146	147	0	5	17	125	976	193	722	61	8
Choctaw	10,077	17	1	1	2	13	217	46	146	25	0
Claremore	16,664	64	0	10	4	50	730	125	540	65	4
Del City	22,294	94	1	1	28	64	899	289	515	95	10
Duncan	22,238	61	0	7	7	47	1,021	223	764	34	11
Durant	13,898	50	0	10	3	37	929	244	590	95	7
Edmond	70,900	97	0	13	23	61	1,708	317	1,310	81	18
Elk City	10,546	9	1	3	0	5	258	20	230	8	1
El Reno	16,228	71	1	4	12	54	467	101	333	33	5
Enid	46,768	201	1	35	24	141	2,780	550	2,126	104	5
Guthrie	10,038	53	0	4	4	45	396	86	294	16	5
Guymon	10,721	28	0	8	5	15	394	69	305	20	0
Jenks	11,011	3	0	0	0	3	116	40	69	7	0
Lawton	91,799	693	5	37	113	538	5,015	1,285	3,485	245	42
McAlester	17,742	56	1	5	8	42	827	213	541	73	6
Miami	13,631	74	0	7	5	62	752	161	572	19	6
Midwest City	54,781	152	0	22	44	86	2,072	494	1,436	142	4
Moore	43,962	127	4	12	40	71	1,807	395	1,259	153	7
Muskogee	38,797	242	6	22	64	150	1,933	722	1,056	155	17
Mustang	14,064	34	0	1	1	32	396	70	307	19	1
Norman	98,330	189	4	40	35	110	3,133	853	2,061	219	12
Oklahoma City	521,681	4,642	49	365	1,381	2,847	47,595	8,300	35,367	3,928	208
Okmulgee	12,938	65	0	5	17	43	631	178	421	32	3
Owasso	20,660	49	0	5	5	39	570	98	427	45	2
Ponca City	25,928	131	2	26	18	85	1,062	216	772	74	30
Sand Springs	17,734	42	0	7	8	27	797	133	514	150	2
Sapulpa	19,903	39	0	2	7	30	695	142	482	71	10
Shawnee	29,462	191	2	29	22	138	1,549	449	948	152	4
Stillwater	40,793	118	2	29	15	72	1,414	303	1,048	63	8
Tahlequah	15,089	46	0	12	6	28	759	195	507	57	4
The Village	10,169	75	1	3	8	63	477	69	381	27	2
Tulsa	393,907	4,304	61	272	891	3,080	27,253	6,403	17,343	3,507	281
Woodward	11,856	77	1	8	2	66	457	130	315	12	4
Yukon	21,229	18	0	2	3	13	612	99	487	26	4
OREGON											
Albany	42,646	77	0	10	34	33	4,044	518	3,178	348	13
Ashland	20,434	34	0	9	10	15	759	98	631	30	31
Beaverton	80,631	163	2	24	55	82	3,398	471	2,516	411	36
Bend	57,626	161	0	16	33	112	3,468	597	2,636	235	29
Canby	13,724	15	0	2	6	7	624	59	531	34	11
Central Point	13,967	4	0	0	2	2	670	96	538	36	7
Coos Bay	15,446	23	0	10	5	8	622	126	453	43	4
Cornelius	10,047	30	1	3	4	22	332	69	224	39	7
Dallas	13,004	52	0	5	3	44	392	61	290	41	2
Eugene	141,913	478	2	53	176	247	8,904	1,424	6,591	889	131
Forest Grove	18,926	23	0	6	6	11	952	210	674	68	7
Gladstone	12,004	19	1	4	3	11	671	87	505	79	0

See footnotes at end of table.

Table 8

Offenses Known to Law Enforcement
by City 10,000 and over in Population, 2003—Continued

City by state	Population	Violent crime	Murder and non-negligent man-slaughter	Forcible rape	Robbery	Aggravated assault	Property crime	Burglary	Larceny-theft	Motor vehicle theft	Arson[1]
OREGON—Continued											
Grants Pass	25,112	52	0	12	24	16	1,833	226	1,448	159	10
Gresham	95,730	481	0	67	154	260	6,061	955	3,941	1,165	18
Hermiston	13,719	11	3	4	4	0	837	172	601	64	4
Hillsboro	76,766	182	0	30	70	82	3,622	444	2,810	368	36
Keizer	33,865	54	1	4	9	40	1,412	221	1,048	143	6
Klamath Falls	19,524	75	0	8	31	36	789	174	551	64	9
La Grande	12,392	11	0	0	2	9	382	71	288	23	0
Lake Oswego	36,227	25	0	2	6	17	685	108	549	28	15
Lebanon	13,298	29	0	7	9	13	1,230	131	1,001	98	13
McMinnville[2]	28,302	28	0	9	6	13	581	104	421	56	15
Medford	65,352	299	4	29	35	231	4,235	484	3,494	257	52
Milwaukie	20,785	44	0	11	10	23	1,074	196	772	106	10
Newberg	19,469	21	0	2	4	15	603	75	492	36	3
Ontario	11,065	65	0	6	4	55	740	76	624	40	1
Oregon City	28,075	39	1	5	9	24	1,442	200	1,093	149	3
Pendleton	16,584	18	0	3	8	7	815	195	583	37	5
Portland	545,271	4,436	27	310	1,367	2,732	41,951	6,484	29,599	5,868	384
Redmond	16,196	21	0	9	3	9	1,063	211	776	76	8
Roseburg	20,173	62	0	8	32	22	1,179	172	917	90	21
Salem	142,501	514	5	75	180	254	11,563	1,575	8,417	1,571	42
Sherwood	13,652	4	0	2	0	2	251	25	221	5	2
Springfield	54,619	158	0	16	41	101	4,274	639	3,038	597	29
St. Helens	10,883	18	0	4	5	9	465	86	347	32	14
The Dalles	12,136	21	0	3	5	13	747	150	560	37	8
Tigard	45,640	94	1	20	31	42	2,262	295	1,788	179	9
Tualatin	24,135	57	0	15	19	23	1,088	139	850	99	2
West Linn	24,433	11	0	0	4	7	423	71	339	13	1
Wilsonville	14,942	18	0	5	4	9	628	77	487	64	3
Woodburn	21,438	32	0	4	9	19	1,388	161	894	333	10
PENNSYLVANIA											
Abington Township	56,252	52	1	6	23	22	1,039	165	809	65	3
Aliquippa	11,457	71	1	3	11	56	297	50	213	34	0
Allentown	106,366	641	12	51	359	219	5,654	1,111	3,851	692	54
Altoona	48,609	156	1	24	68	63	1,420	357	983	80	5
Aston Township	16,485	28	0	1	7	20	209	39	148	22	2
Bensalem Township	58,818	146	3	9	49	85	2,116	268	1,564	284	8
Berks-Lehigh Regional	22,083	11	0	2	2	7	211	34	156	21	2
Berwick	10,562	32	0	5	5	22	434	52	369	13	1
Bethel Park	33,217	25	0	1	9	15	321	46	257	18	1
Bethlehem	71,926	190	1	20	94	75	1,965	337	1,460	168	12
Bethlehem Township	22,081	25	0	1	5	19	366	28	322	16	0
Bloomsburg Town	12,469	18	0	3	3	12	368	56	297	15	0
Brecknock Township	11,343	1	0	0	0	1	35	8	22	5	2
Bristol	10,056	53	0	2	13	38	390	58	304	28	5
Buckingham Township	17,263	7	0	0	1	6	126	10	109	7	0
Butler	14,878	194	0	13	26	155	846	205	607	34	1
Butler Township (Butler County)	17,147	36	0	3	12	21	542	65	463	14	1
Caln Township	12,181	58	0	1	12	45	292	27	243	22	1
Carlisle	18,080	53	0	13	28	12	500	58	423	19	6
Center Township	11,569	28	1	0	3	24	342	29	303	10	2
Chambersburg	17,883	251	0	5	13	233	543	87	425	31	4
Cheltenham Township	37,027	116	1	8	71	36	1,060	227	667	166	0
Chippewa Township	10,866	7	0	1	3	3	316	44	255	17	3
Coatesville	11,142	118	2	4	45	67	395	64	286	45	3
Colonial Regional	17,667	48	0	0	2	46	385	39	336	10	0
Columbia	10,260	56	0	1	12	43	350	73	233	44	2
Cranberry Township	25,581	25	0	2	5	18	366	46	307	13	2
Darby	10,211	283	1	12	39	231	437	126	214	97	6
Derry Township (Dauphin County)	21,566	29	0	3	4	22	552	137	395	20	7
Doylestown Township	17,752	14	0	2	4	8	235	22	203	10	1
Dunmore	13,788	10	0	0	2	8	252	35	210	7	1
East Cocalico Township	10,183	2	0	0	1	1	186	19	156	11	1

See footnotes at end of table.

Table 8

Offenses Known to Law Enforcement

by City 10,000 and over in Population, 2003—Continued

City by state	Population	Violent crime	Murder and non-negligent man-slaughter	Forcible rape	Robbery	Aggravated assault	Property crime	Burglary	Larceny-theft	Motor vehicle theft	Arson[1]
PENNSYLVANIA—Continued											
East Hempfield Township	22,028	21	0	4	7	10	638	112	494	32	0
East Lampeter Township	13,923	24	0	3	18	3	821	62	729	30	1
East Norriton Township	13,596	7	0	0	3	4	336	22	291	23	5
Easton	26,203	158	1	18	54	85	1,138	226	824	88	12
East Pennsboro Township	18,783	19	1	4	8	6	360	71	264	25	2
Easttown Township	10,371	6	0	0	2	4	127	40	84	3	0
Elizabeth Township	13,678	27	0	0	3	24	118	11	96	11	0
Emmaus	11,278	42	0	5	2	35	332	43	284	5	1
Ephrata	13,149	25	0	4	2	19	302	63	221	18	1
Erie	102,373	447	3	70	191	183	3,134	725	2,284	125	33
Exeter Township (Berks County)	25,033	24	0	3	9	12	488	49	408	31	2
Fairview Township (York County)	14,725	42	0	1	5	36	353	62	283	8	0
Falls Township (Bucks County)	34,972	73	1	7	30	35	1,003	132	748	123	2
Ferguson Township	15,282	4	0	1	2	1	171	6	161	4	1
Franconia Township	12,044	10	0	1	0	9	75	12	59	4	1
Franklin Park	11,554	2	0	0	0	2	70	10	57	3	0
Greensburg	15,655	37	1	3	6	27	504	86	391	27	0
Hampden Township	24,885	14	0	1	9	4	391	55	323	13	1
Hampton Township	17,505	27	0	0	5	22	203	38	157	8	0
Hanover	14,748	19	0	3	7	9	560	60	486	14	3
Hanover Township (Luzerne County)	11,324	14	1	2	5	6	393	56	320	17	2
Harrisburg	48,659	687	6	29	375	277	2,395	543	1,698	154	26
Harrison Township	10,749	12	0	0	8	4	315	29	263	23	0
Hatfield Township	17,092	8	0	1	4	3	371	52	305	14	12
Haverford Township	48,380	22	0	1	13	8	609	66	506	37	1
Hazleton	22,808	31	1	2	13	15	482	102	301	79	0
Hermitage	16,402	18	0	1	12	5	583	36	540	7	2
Hilltown Township	12,343	37	0	6	1	30	208	19	183	6	1
Horsham Township	24,922	11	0	0	3	8	259	43	201	15	1
Indiana	14,859	28	0	6	1	21	321	38	272	11	3
Jeannette	10,482	37	0	2	5	30	274	37	212	25	3
Johnstown	27,870	179	2	25	42	110	1,113	298	739	76	17
Lancaster	55,765	557	8	37	245	267	3,033	563	2,152	318	44
Lancaster Township (Lancaster County)	14,118	26	0	3	12	11	409	77	273	59	7
Lansdale	16,169	17	0	6	3	8	359	57	277	25	8
Lansdowne	10,943	39	0	2	8	29	256	41	187	28	2
Lebanon	24,072	180	2	15	63	100	938	209	653	76	10
Lehigh Township (Northampton County)	10,113	2	0	0	0	2	122	17	97	8	0
Limerick Township	15,580	15	0	1	4	10	245	42	180	23	9
Logan Township	11,949	27	1	4	10	12	266	58	201	7	1
Lower Allen Township	17,431	24	0	3	13	8	396	53	338	5	1
Lower Burrell	12,585	18	0	1	3	14	187	41	141	5	0
Lower Gwynedd Township	10,848	12	0	0	0	12	185	25	157	3	0
Lower Makefield Township	33,026	15	0	1	2	12	403	80	304	19	0
Lower Merion Township	60,141	52	1	1	27	23	1,027	200	773	54	1
Lower Moreland Township	11,556	22	0	0	0	22	189	29	152	8	0
Lower Paxton Township	44,951	59	0	6	30	23	1,042	119	886	37	6
Lower Pottsgrove Township	11,713	19	0	1	5	13	219	32	178	9	1
Lower Providence Township	23,312	18	0	5	4	9	264	40	217	7	0
Lower Salford Township	13,679	8	0	2	1	5	94	9	80	5	0
Lower Saucon Township	10,384	7	0	0	0	7	112	8	101	3	0
Lower Southampton Township	19,342	29	0	2	9	18	341	28	281	32	0
Manheim Township	34,533	47	0	3	19	25	950	181	721	48	3
Manor Township	17,088	15	0	2	3	10	308	66	220	22	0
Marple Township	23,700	13	0	0	3	10	319	36	257	26	2
McCandless	28,843	10	0	1	4	5	353	26	318	9	0
Meadville	13,530	24	0	5	11	8	358	48	292	18	1
Middletown Township	45,866	48	0	5	22	21	1,272	145	1,046	81	13
Millcreek Township	52,721	43	2	3	15	23	871	206	630	35	0
Monroeville	29,023	114	1	7	30	76	913	96	719	98	3
Montgomery Township	23,321	8	0	0	5	3	531	18	502	11	0
Moon Township	22,808	11	0	0	9	2	396	58	321	17	0

See footnotes at end of table.

Table 8

Offenses Known to Law Enforcement
by City 10,000 and over in Population, 2003—Continued

City by state	Population	Violent crime	Murder and non-negligent man-slaughter	Forcible rape	Robbery	Aggravated assault	Property crime	Burglary	Larceny-theft	Motor vehicle theft	Arson[1]
PENNSYLVANIA—Continued											
Mount Lebanon	32,668	63	1	0	5	57	274	30	229	15	5
Muhlenberg Township	16,636	35	0	1	24	10	694	88	538	68	1
Munhall	12,041	12	0	0	6	6	148	34	95	19	0
Murrysville	19,089	5	0	0	4	1	204	30	165	9	0
Nanticoke	10,686	26	0	5	3	18	335	58	262	15	5
Nether Providence Township	13,448	23	0	2	1	20	128	10	114	4	0
New Britain Township	10,766	4	0	2	0	2	90	5	83	2	0
New Kensington	14,420	82	1	7	14	60	483	113	329	41	4
Newtown Township (Bucks County)	18,775	21	0	2	0	19	220	28	184	8	1
Newtown Township (Delaware County)	11,712	5	0	1	2	2	122	20	94	8	0
Norristown	31,388	344	4	33	157	150	1,677	324	1,161	192	9
Northampton Township	40,572	16	0	4	3	9	317	41	264	12	0
Northern Berks Regional	10,374	11	0	1	1	9	165	20	135	10	1
Northern York Regional	52,013	51	2	6	16	27	1,120	157	908	55	13
North Fayette Township	12,795	24	0	0	1	23	340	33	284	23	0
North Huntingdon Township	29,098	21	0	1	9	11	364	64	264	36	2
North Lebanon Township	10,680	13	0	1	2	10	380	36	336	8	0
North Strabane Township	10,719	29	2	3	1	23	250	24	210	16	1
North Versailles Township	10,996	61	0	0	15	46	238	27	195	16	1
Oil City	11,280	20	1	4	1	14	314	24	273	17	1
Patton Township	11,682	7	0	1	4	2	248	31	212	5	2
Penn Hills	46,849	162	5	12	73	72	1,179	226	780	173	7
Pennridge Regional	14,672	13	0	1	0	12	106	9	93	4	2
Penn Township (York County)	14,793	18	0	0	0	18	225	26	184	15	1
Peters Township	18,587	19	1	0	4	14	217	28	181	8	9
Philadelphia	1,495,903	20,620	348	1,004	9,617	9,651	62,454	10,656	37,864	13,934	
Phoenixville	14,821	47	0	7	4	36	343	14	320	9	0
Pine-Marshall-Bradford Woods	16,259	17	0	1	1	15	323	21	286	16	0
Pittsburgh	335,302	3,559	67	136	1,635	1,721	16,435	3,180	10,610	2,645	97
Plains Township	10,763	57	0	4	11	42	320	44	255	21	3
Plumstead Township	11,887	9	2	1	2	4	174	14	151	9	2
Plymouth Township (Montgomery County)	16,134	56	0	3	24	29	779	82	651	46	3
Pocono Township	10,291	17	0	2	6	9	285	36	225	24	0
Pottstown	21,878	222	1	26	50	145	1,122	175	853	94	14
Pottsville	15,204	43	0	4	6	33	303	43	240	20	4
Radnor Township	31,259	28	0	3	11	14	377	53	306	18	2
Reading	80,692	946	16	56	434	440	4,643	1,140	2,458	1,045	55
Richland Township (Bucks County)	10,903	20	0	2	5	13	251	18	222	11	1
Ridley Township	30,602	99	1	2	16	80	500	54	386	60	1
Robinson Township (Allegheny County)	13,623	16	0	3	4	9	398	38	338	22	1
Ross Township	32,311	24	0	0	11	13	904	72	790	42	9
Rostraver Township	11,725	9	0	3	3	3	491	39	440	12	1
Salisbury Township	13,574	42	0	4	4	34	375	33	327	15	5
Sandy Township	11,508	22	0	0	0	22	165	30	123	12	0
Scranton	74,896	263	2	37	92	132	2,260	528	1,547	185	10
Shaler Township	29,605	25	3	2	6	14	351	53	272	26	1
Sharon	15,900	83	1	7	13	62	482	105	343	34	3
Silver Spring Township	11,442	6	0	2	2	2	198	23	167	8	1
South Fayette Township	12,882	32	0	2	0	30	115	15	89	11	0
South Park Township	14,177	11	0	1	1	9	71	20	40	11	0
South Whitehall Township	18,246	60	0	1	5	54	621	71	534	16	0
Springettsbury Township	23,878	43	0	9	19	15	1,046	58	954	34	3
Springfield Township (Delaware County)	23,475	32	1	3	15	13	681	46	596	39	2
Springfield Township (Montgomery County)	19,629	18	0	0	7	11	205	34	156	15	0
Spring Garden Township	11,995	23	0	2	8	13	460	49	388	23	2
Spring Township (Berks County)	22,665	10	0	0	4	6	400	61	299	40	1
State College	51,741	48	0	17	8	23	1,029	108	902	19	4
St. Marys City	14,271	31	0	1	0	30	338	66	258	14	2
Stroud Area Regional	31,652	57	1	11	21	24	863	90	704	69	1

See footnotes at end of table.

Table 8

Offenses Known to Law Enforcement
by City 10,000 and over in Population, 2003—Continued

City by state	Population	Violent crime	Murder and non-negligent man-slaughter	Forcible rape	Robbery	Aggravated assault	Property crime	Burglary	Larceny-theft	Motor vehicle theft	Arson[1]
PENNSYLVANIA—Continued											
Sunbury	10,381	112	0	7	7	98	458	85	357	16	6
Susquehanna Township											
(Dauphin County)	22,324	51	0	1	31	19	640	85	526	29	1
Towamencin Township	17,862	18	3	1	2	12	194	38	146	10	3
Uniontown	12,242	67	0	6	30	31	584	120	398	66	0
Upper Allen Township	15,860	10	0	2	6	2	191	43	128	20	3
Upper Chichester Township	16,873	56	0	3	19	34	546	72	403	71	12
Upper Darby Township	81,141	169	4	5	108	52	1,285	131	916	238	0
Upper Dublin Township	26,616	50	0	2	4	44	278	51	207	20	0
Upper Gwynedd Township	14,431	26	0	0	4	22	140	31	105	4	3
Upper Moreland Township	25,145	22	0	0	8	14	391	54	305	32	6
Upper Providence Township											
(Delaware County)	11,020	5	0	0	2	3	51	12	35	4	0
Upper Providence Township											
(Montgomery County)	16,754	6	0	1	2	3	193	22	162	9	0
Upper Saucon Township	12,597	11	0	1	0	10	121	25	93	3	1
Upper Southampton Township	15,817	18	1	0	5	12	210	30	169	11	0
Upper St. Clair Township	19,898	2	1	0	1	0	95	10	76	9	0
Uwchlan Township	17,803	28	0	5	0	23	251	49	194	8	0
Warminster Township	31,385	51	0	12	17	22	534	73	432	29	3
Warrington Township	19,942	37	0	1	6	30	233	44	176	13	7
Warwick Township (Bucks County)	13,497	1	0	0	0	1	91	11	76	4	0
Warwick Township (Lancaster County)	16,551	5	0	1	1	3	106	26	77	3	0
Washington Township											
(Franklin County)	11,713	16	0	3	2	11	202	29	158	15	1
West Chester	17,881	117	0	20	48	49	627	126	425	76	9
West Goshen Township	20,934	41	0	4	11	26	580	47	501	32	0
West Hempfield Township	15,535	9	0	1	4	4	303	43	240	20	0
West Lampeter Township	13,675	5	0	1	4	0	169	12	148	9	1
West Manchester Township	17,264	40	0	1	15	24	776	61	686	29	6
West Mifflin	22,187	22	1	0	8	13	143	21	107	15	0
West Norriton Township	14,985	46	0	1	7	38	330	40	278	12	2
Westtown-East Goshen Township	30,817	32	0	1	3	28	351	55	274	22	1
West Whiteland Township	17,607	24	0	3	8	13	639	41	570	28	0
Whitehall	14,271	7	0	0	4	3	63	10	51	2	0
Whitehall Township	25,151	52	0	6	26	20	1,147	101	983	63	6
Whitpain Township	18,875	14	0	2	6	6	227	35	179	13	0
Wilkes-Barre	42,124	148	2	15	92	39	2,119	406	1,579	134	8
Wilkinsburg	18,820	209	6	12	81	110	761	228	346	187	11
Williamsport	30,158	116	0	11	61	44	1,418	298	1,048	72	9
Willistown Township	10,130	8	0	2	0	6	114	26	86	2	0
Yeadon	11,669	65	0	7	36	22	363	79	189	95	2
York Area Regional	45,911	80	1	7	17	55	706	96	561	49	7
RHODE ISLAND											
Barrington	17,087	15	0	7	2	6	264	53	206	5	6
Bristol	22,953	30	0	7	7	16	388	56	309	23	9
Burrillville	16,377	9	0	1	1	7	193	40	141	12	4
Central Falls	19,283	109	0	19	20	70	620	166	351	103	12
Coventry	34,873	33	0	4	3	26	438	97	310	31	21
Cranston	81,601	159	0	35	43	81	2,340	436	1,649	255	16
Cumberland	33,303	33	0	7	10	16	561	96	433	32	1
East Greenwich	13,427	5	0	1	0	4	149	24	120	5	1
East Providence	49,957	88	0	20	28	40	870	174	612	84	9
Glocester	10,345	5	0	0	0	5	66	15	47	4	3
Johnston	29,198	65	0	9	10	46	912	141	671	100	16
Lincoln	22,103	8	0	0	5	3	421	60	329	32	0
Middletown	17,503	18	0	1	2	15	384	73	306	5	2
Narragansett	16,910	15	0	3	1	11	364	51	305	8	1
Newport	26,471	114	1	24	13	76	1,320	293	953	74	22
North Kingstown	27,147	19	0	7	1	11	499	76	400	23	8
North Providence	33,438	61	0	5	8	48	553	109	383	61	13
North Smithfield	10,985	13	0	3	2	8	223	44	175	4	3

See footnotes at end of table.

Table 8

Offenses Known to Law Enforcement

by City 10,000 and over in Population, 2003—Continued

City by state	Population	Violent crime	Murder and non-negligent man-slaughter	Forcible rape	Robbery	Aggravated assault	Property crime	Burglary	Larceny-theft	Motor vehicle theft	Arson[1]
RHODE ISLAND—Continued											
Pawtucket	74,479	256	2	37	74	143	2,526	468	1,674	384	31
Portsmouth	17,565	17	0	4	2	11	262	62	186	14	1
Providence	176,960	1,395	18	133	515	729	11,083	1,682	6,756	2,645	
Scituate	10,760	6	0	0	0	6	104	32	66	6	5
Smithfield	21,265	6	0	1	0	5	308	41	256	11	10
South Kingstown	28,789	24	0	7	5	12	327	69	243	15	4
Tiverton	15,598	18	0	3	0	15	288	75	186	27	8
Warren	11,556	15	0	4	0	11	212	19	180	13	2
Warwick	87,563	129	0	36	27	66	2,558	341	2,038	179	36
Westerly	23,765	34	0	15	0	19	620	89	510	21	2
West Warwick	30,121	77	1	16	12	48	482	87	367	28	11
Woonsocket	44,143	183	0	48	29	106	1,320	307	919	94	24
SOUTH CAROLINA											
Aiken	26,300	75	0	8	29	38	1,141	146	933	62	2
Anderson	25,940	210	2	8	60	140	1,592	273	1,211	108	0
Beaufort	12,601	159	1	9	44	105	847	161	639	47	3
Cayce	12,509	115	1	11	18	85	861	104	677	80	4
Charleston	99,756	879	15	33	245	586	5,022	888	3,572	562	7
Clemson	12,083	22	0	2	2	18	369	70	268	31	1
Columbia	118,536	1,342	15	58	461	808	8,127	1,395	5,907	825	15
Conway	12,137	148	1	9	27	111	1,388	224	1,081	83	5
Easley	18,558	92	4	7	14	67	901	138	725	38	3
Florence	30,311	478	6	21	155	296	3,749	611	2,892	246	18
Forest Acres	10,512	83	1	2	27	53	818	101	670	47	3
Gaffney	13,049	122	1	12	25	84	931	157	724	50	3
Goose Creek	30,473	95	2	18	15	60	730	139	547	44	7
Greenville	56,728	571	2	33	106	430	4,264	781	3,192	291	13
Greenwood	22,397	397	2	16	46	333	1,503	320	1,130	53	5
Greer	18,924	105	6	12	27	60	702	107	535	60	5
Hanahan	12,968	61	2	8	16	35	531	92	353	86	4
Irmo	11,174	68	0	3	12	53	320	44	257	19	1
Lexington	10,458	19	0	1	5	13	551	37	491	23	2
Mauldin	16,990	65	0	9	8	48	501	71	401	29	2
Mount Pleasant	53,613	94	1	6	24	63	1,395	162	1,153	80	1
Myrtle Beach	24,764	608	4	63	195	346	4,835	773	3,547	515	10
Newberry	10,790	76	0	4	9	63	544	64	475	5	3
North Augusta	18,247	51	1	2	19	29	779	137	589	53	2
North Charleston	81,476	1,336	12	96	417	811	6,754	1,374	4,428	952	49
North Myrtle Beach	12,135	68	0	13	18	37	1,387	234	1,060	93	6
Orangeburg	12,706	129	2	5	62	60	1,122	285	760	77	2
Rock Hill	55,137	818	4	39	135	640	3,077	623	2,206	248	18
Simpsonville	14,843	63	1	3	2	57	683	91	572	20	2
Spartanburg	39,448	821	6	31	185	599	3,777	754	2,679	344	21
Summerville	30,291	128	2	5	22	99	1,230	181	969	80	5
Sumter	39,765	722	5	26	168	523	3,014	793	1,931	290	15
West Columbia	13,073	330	1	10	51	268	1,203	179	945	79	5
SOUTH DAKOTA											
Aberdeen	24,416	38	1	15	0	22	514	106	379	29	4
Brookings	18,783	7	0	3	1	3	409	55	336	18	0
Mitchell	14,688	15	0	5	0	10	433	76	340	17	4
Pierre	14,072	25	0	9	0	16	492	47	428	17	6
Rapid City	60,519	242	0	67	35	140	2,712	409	2,167	136	6
Sioux Falls	131,048	392	3	104	40	245	4,023	770	2,997	256	35
Vermillion	10,108	15	0	3	1	11	316	57	253	6	2
Watertown	20,277	35	0	2	1	32	578	110	430	38	2
Yankton	13,497	32	0	14	2	16	348	36	303	9	0

See footnotes at end of table.

Table 8

Offenses Known to Law Enforcement
by City 10,000 and over in Population, 2003—Continued

City by state	Population	Violent crime	Murder and non-negligent man-slaughter	Forcible rape	Robbery	Aggravated assault	Property crime	Burglary	Larceny-theft	Motor vehicle theft	Arson[1]
TENNESSEE											
Athens	13,567	190	1	4	23	162	1,116	207	847	62	5
Bartlett	42,190	106	2	6	27	71	1,347	193	1,060	94	4
Brentwood	27,969	28	0	2	8	18	470	67	390	13	3
Bristol	25,080	109	1	11	14	83	1,285	206	1,006	73	9
Brownsville	10,789	149	1	6	11	131	512	152	335	25	2
Chattanooga	156,596	1,973	19	89	464	1,401	13,087	2,357	9,306	1,424	62
Clarksville	106,710	636	2	45	102	487	5,444	1,058	4,167	219	30
Cleveland	37,667	310	3	10	30	267	2,099	452	1,518	129	6
Collierville	34,430	75	1	6	7	61	617	101	462	54	3
Columbia	33,321	325	1	8	69	247	1,980	448	1,425	107	10
Cookeville	26,100	67	0	8	22	37	1,196	211	893	92	1
Dickson	12,420	75	0	7	17	51	778	117	609	52	2
Dyersburg	17,360	166	1	14	18	133	1,183	205	919	59	7
East Ridge	20,370	120	1	7	22	90	1,233	230	912	91	7
Elizabethton	13,233	56	0	2	6	48	827	125	635	67	9
Franklin	45,521	78	0	10	13	55	945	92	802	51	3
Gallatin	24,833	156	1	10	20	125	1,265	156	1,035	74	8
Germantown	37,937	41	1	4	13	23	967	186	729	52	3
Goodlettsville	14,204	83	0	6	25	52	818	111	621	86	4
Greeneville	15,284	61	2	9	11	39	910	127	722	61	3
Hendersonville	42,540	122	0	0	7	115	955	157	746	52	6
Jackson	61,100	691	2	35	198	456	4,329	980	2,964	385	13
Johnson City	57,202	395	1	11	86	297	3,811	546	3,033	232	11
Kingsport	44,702	387	2	40	63	282	3,015	477	2,377	161	20
Knoxville	174,993	1,692	18	81	443	1,150	11,081	2,432	7,231	1,418	137
La Vergne	21,671	159	1	12	8	138	603	150	386	67	6
Lawrenceburg	10,884	163	3	4	4	152	788	153	595	40	9
Lebanon	21,013	163	3	11	17	132	1,267	209	965	93	2
Lewisburg	10,827	47	2	2	11	32	434	101	314	19	0
Martin	10,277	43	0	4	9	30	272	47	217	8	1
Maryville	24,291	79	2	20	16	41	681	122	514	45	5
McMinnville	13,040	63	2	6	10	45	769	151	562	56	3
Memphis	653,858	10,297	126	438	4,297	5,436	55,475	16,900	30,049	8,526	287
Millington	10,462	84	0	5	17	62	588	108	437	43	3
Morristown	25,330	181	1	16	28	136	1,874	206	1,511	157	5
Mount Juliet	15,584	44	3	2	4	35	553	69	462	22	3
Murfreesboro	75,468	459	2	27	77	353	3,232	475	2,482	275	11
Nashville	554,888	8,331	74	335	2,197	5,725	38,648	7,369	26,630	4,649	127
Oak Ridge	27,437	163	1	18	41	103	1,672	337	1,211	124	4
Red Bank	12,239	66	0	6	10	50	483	135	316	32	2
Sevierville	13,541	63	1	5	14	43	1,031	168	771	92	1
Shelbyville	17,316	104	0	5	21	78	584	153	384	47	7
Smyrna	29,047	147	0	14	20	113	1,151	204	872	75	12
Soddy-Daisy	11,972	51	0	4	3	44	321	67	236	18	1
Springfield	15,097	171	2	12	30	127	723	76	591	56	3
Spring Hill	10,362	19	1	1	1	16	126	22	100	4	3
Tullahoma	18,444	66	1	2	11	52	1,014	208	766	40	2
Union City	10,853	71	2	2	14	53	841	122	690	29	5
TEXAS											
Abilene	117,016	517	6	71	129	311	6,107	1,814	3,991	302	27
Addison	14,336	81	2	5	20	54	1,009	152	740	117	4
Alamo	15,759	41	1	0	13	27	973	86	818	69	7
Alice	19,401	334	0	8	7	319	1,810	300	1,441	69	22
Allen	58,106	60	3	7	12	38	1,377	338	983	56	4
Alvin	22,367	50	0	2	12	36	947	180	722	45	3
Amarillo	179,762	1,501	17	97	378	1,009	11,604	2,203	8,501	900	62
Angleton	18,826	57	1	5	10	41	484	114	334	36	0
Arlington	355,385	1,863	9	167	598	1,089	19,921	3,606	14,656	1,659	42
Athens	11,898	97	1	0	14	82	616	156	423	37	0
Austin	682,319	3,153	27	226	1,251	1,649	42,270	7,240	32,259	2,771	140
Azle	10,123	32	0	4	4	24	357	65	274	18	1
Balch Springs	19,783	128	2	13	37	76	1,325	314	841	170	1

See footnotes at end of table.

Table 8

Offenses Known to Law Enforcement

by City 10,000 and over in Population, 2003—Continued

City by state	Population	Violent crime	Violent crime Murder and non-negligent man-slaughter	Violent crime Forcible rape	Violent crime Robbery	Violent crime Aggravated assault	Property crime	Property crime Burglary	Property crime Larceny-theft	Property crime Motor vehicle theft	Arson[1]
TEXAS—Continued											
Bay City	18,737	136	0	1	44	91	1,164	243	899	22	1
Baytown	68,407	264	5	31	75	153	2,925	590	2,103	232	15
Beaumont	114,626	1,051	6	85	331	629	8,829	1,726	6,613	490	59
Bedford	49,130	139	0	28	39	72	1,950	325	1,443	182	11
Beeville	13,164	52	0	6	3	43	393	100	279	14	0
Bellaire	16,999	39	1	4	26	8	399	133	247	19	0
Belton	14,848	27	1	0	10	16	522	143	346	33	3
Benbrook	20,973	31	0	3	12	16	506	128	333	45	2
Big Spring	25,184	85	1	19	20	45	1,125	391	693	41	1
Bonham	10,201	50	1	5	2	42	417	90	302	25	1
Borger	13,922	57	1	10	2	44	746	107	604	35	2
Brenham	13,779	80	3	10	7	60	589	136	418	35	0
Brownsville	152,764	757	8	42	164	543	9,590	1,024	8,121	445	21
Brownwood	19,390	121	0	23	14	84	1,434	309	1,001	124	1
Bryan	67,706	611	2	81	85	443	4,110	971	2,963	176	21
Burkburnett	10,946	7	0	0	1	6	204	80	122	2	5
Burleson	24,195	47	0	7	10	30	1,203	172	964	67	6
Canyon	13,182	16	0	2	4	10	146	20	117	9	2
Carrollton	116,897	238	2	15	77	144	4,039	808	2,742	489	51
Cedar Hill	37,848	118	0	8	30	80	1,265	360	810	95	2
Cedar Park	38,351	54	1	12	4	37	638	91	524	23	2
Cleburne	27,919	138	4	20	11	103	1,724	292	1,322	110	4
Clute	10,864	69	1	10	7	51	397	79	288	30	2
College Station	71,647	164	2	40	17	105	2,762	384	2,276	102	1
Colleyville	21,413	10	0	0	1	9	332	60	261	11	1
Conroe	39,672	387	0	26	126	235	2,905	521	2,202	182	7
Converse	12,125	23	0	10	6	7	304	67	214	23	5
Coppell	40,073	21	0	2	4	15	954	170	709	75	1
Copperas Cove	30,059	152	2	11	11	128	959	270	643	46	8
Corinth	15,157	9	0	0	3	6	195	30	149	16	0
Corpus Christi	282,850	2,462	21	228	592	1,621	20,101	3,757	15,064	1,280	140
Corsicana	25,579	69	1	11	24	33	1,452	316	1,049	87	7
Dallas	1,230,302	16,865	226	601	7,963	8,075	97,900	21,927	58,554	17,419	1,301
Deer Park	29,443	60	0	2	11	47	573	145	400	28	2
Del Rio	35,149	165	1	2	14	148	1,072	181	823	68	0
Denison	23,529	90	1	1	21	67	1,241	237	928	76	1
Denton	91,754	367	3	67	63	234	3,501	673	2,598	230	21
DeSoto	40,053	135	2	14	36	83	1,943	485	1,277	181	5
Dickinson	17,943	58	2	4	17	35	440	117	276	47	2
Donna	15,719	88	2	13	13	60	1,150	263	808	79	4
Dumas	14,023	63	0	7	11	45	513	88	412	13	7
Duncanville	36,766	163	0	14	55	94	1,738	356	1,164	218	6
Eagle Pass	23,871	37	0	0	3	34	819	103	657	59	0
Edinburg	53,584	265	6	17	44	198	6,639	765	5,617	257	43
El Campo	11,058	54	0	6	7	41	491	131	339	21	1
El Paso	586,392	3,502	21	219	581	2,681	21,780	2,185	17,735	1,860	117
Ennis	18,161	66	1	8	23	34	984	167	786	31	3
Euless	49,217	125	0	11	28	86	1,719	327	1,276	116	7
Farmers Branch	27,881	65	0	5	35	25	1,348	247	869	232	0
Flower Mound	59,554	46	0	7	2	37	873	179	667	27	3
Forest Hill	13,429	124	1	9	33	81	458	124	275	59	2
Fort Worth	576,339	3,751	57	243	1,462	1,989	37,529	8,788	25,092	3,649	243
Freeport	13,001	54	0	15	14	25	485	173	283	29	1
Friendswood	31,987	72	0	12	7	53	513	120	362	31	4
Frisco	48,393	58	0	14	14	30	1,764	409	1,256	99	7
Gainesville	16,178	88	1	11	33	43	948	248	622	78	1
Galena Park	10,753	33	0	5	7	21	293	76	181	36	2
Galveston	57,566	479	8	85	183	203	3,417	636	2,410	371	8
Garland	223,061	735	7	44	362	322	10,102	2,197	6,848	1,057	
Gatesville	15,431	38	0	2	1	35	173	67	103	3	0
Georgetown	33,763	30	1	5	5	19	651	84	510	57	1
Grand Prairie	137,407	495	4	49	153	289	6,764	1,368	4,242	1,154	27
Grapevine	46,543	120	1	5	22	92	1,611	199	1,235	177	5
Greenville	24,885	309	1	8	68	232	2,048	467	1,433	148	4

See footnotes at end of table.

Table 8

Offenses Known to Law Enforcement
by City 10,000 and over in Population, 2003—Continued

City by state	Population	Violent crime	Violent crime — Murder and non-negligent man-slaughter	Violent crime — Forcible rape	Violent crime — Robbery	Violent crime — Aggravated assault	Property crime	Property crime — Burglary	Property crime — Larceny-theft	Property crime — Motor vehicle theft	Arson[1]
TEXAS—Continued											
Groves	15,654	25	1	0	17	7	621	167	409	45	0
Haltom City	40,509	178	1	16	41	120	2,103	539	1,340	224	16
Harker Heights	18,336	52	0	16	18	18	748	221	499	28	2
Harlingen	60,307	324	2	13	53	256	4,260	911	3,171	178	15
Henderson	11,323	189	0	12	10	167	785	139	609	37	1
Hereford	14,647	69	0	3	6	60	672	136	512	24	3
Hewitt	12,130	14	0	0	0	14	247	78	164	5	0
Highland Village	13,737	6	0	1	1	4	133	57	74	2	2
Houston	2,041,081	23,988	278	768	10,985	11,957	120,005	26,522	72,032	21,451	1,553
Humble	15,078	123	2	16	57	48	1,648	148	1,305	195	5
Huntsville	36,286	158	0	16	21	121	1,230	257	925	48	4
Hurst	37,381	173	2	18	35	118	2,423	357	1,930	136	3
Irving	199,168	873	7	75	258	533	10,007	1,515	7,254	1,238	56
Jacinto City	10,543	19	0	0	10	9	469	89	318	62	0
Jacksonville	14,252	96	3	11	12	70	757	218	504	35	1
Katy	12,623	89	0	2	10	77	684	76	590	18	1
Keller	33,433	25	0	6	3	16	516	76	426	14	2
Kerrville	21,418	40	1	6	10	23	700	106	571	23	1
Kilgore	11,655	59	0	14	7	38	1,070	153	860	57	0
Killeen	94,148	788	6	76	186	520	5,585	1,812	3,502	271	23
Kingsville	25,566	156	0	25	19	112	1,498	240	1,218	40	5
Lake Jackson	27,373	32	1	6	5	20	857	140	691	26	3
La Marque	13,942	89	3	20	28	38	800	240	491	69	4
Lancaster	27,503	131	0	6	36	89	1,313	562	557	194	6
La Porte	33,730	70	1	9	12	48	651	196	405	50	9
Laredo	194,516	1,317	29	55	257	976	13,573	1,975	10,619	979	92
League City	52,196	55	1	7	25	22	1,466	337	1,051	78	2
Leander	11,842	19	0	0	1	18	122	29	81	12	4
Levelland	13,133	80	3	8	5	64	478	126	334	18	4
Lewisville	85,265	171	3	15	49	104	3,995	611	2,952	432	10
Lockhart	12,968	69	0	4	5	60	331	57	256	18	0
Longview	75,486	500	4	73	165	258	5,133	1,059	3,616	458	49
Lubbock	206,882	2,395	14	101	311	1,969	13,246	2,829	9,726	691	54
Lufkin	33,257	200	1	21	39	139	2,168	483	1,596	89	5
Mansfield	32,122	74	6	8	13	47	925	251	627	47	5
Marshall	24,350	128	5	16	40	67	1,320	271	970	79	2
McAllen	115,647	512	6	29	145	332	8,542	902	6,985	655	67
McKinney	74,217	161	0	42	36	83	2,017	477	1,408	132	36
Memorial Villages	11,915	7	0	0	7	0	203	70	128	5	0
Mercedes	14,370	96	0	10	5	81	555	169	360	26	7
Mesquite	130,778	463	1	8	148	306	6,391	855	4,774	762	28
Midland	97,319	510	2	39	74	395	4,037	941	2,925	171	
Mineral Wells	17,232	39	1	16	6	16	685	150	498	37	2
Mission	52,232	58	0	2	17	39	3,697	761	2,568	368	0
Missouri City	60,106	146	1	19	63	63	1,239	317	832	90	20
Mount Pleasant	14,394	73	0	0	21	52	812	190	570	52	6
Nacogdoches	30,760	119	1	8	22	88	1,211	233	931	47	0
Nederland	17,300	32	0	5	6	21	796	188	576	32	0
New Braunfels	41,880	156	0	28	24	104	2,669	386	2,197	86	11
North Richland Hills	60,106	197	1	27	38	131	2,681	521	2,008	152	0
Odessa	92,375	588	3	12	65	508	4,639	826	3,608	205	39
Orange	18,481	189	1	14	45	129	1,155	261	811	83	7
Palestine	18,007	74	0	0	18	56	969	267	647	55	3
Pampa	17,581	140	3	14	15	108	1,416	399	981	36	1
Paris	26,620	343	1	51	41	250	2,530	428	2,008	94	6
Pasadena	147,289	578	5	51	153	369	5,975	1,269	4,068	638	68
Pearland	45,232	65	1	20	14	30	1,242	253	912	77	10
Pflugerville	23,431	26	0	10	3	13	466	62	382	22	2
Pharr	52,075	332	5	10	76	241	3,083	664	2,329	90	13
Plainview	22,257	96	2	9	14	71	1,388	298	1,064	26	7
Plano	241,793	709	5	48	134	522	9,453	1,527	7,254	672	21
Port Arthur	57,769	437	9	20	175	233	2,793	1,055	1,445	293	30
Portland	15,662	31	0	11	4	16	467	83	363	21	0
Port Lavaca	12,125	21	1	3	4	13	451	116	315	20	1

See footnotes at end of table.

Table 8

Offenses Known to Law Enforcement
by City 10,000 and over in Population, 2003—Continued

City by state	Population	Violent crime	Murder and non-negligent man-slaughter	Forcible rape	Robbery	Aggravated assault	Property crime	Burglary	Larceny-theft	Motor vehicle theft	Arson[1]
TEXAS—Continued											
Port Neches	13,545	31	0	7	6	18	649	160	452	37	1
Richardson	98,463	241	1	16	101	123	3,619	698	2,593	328	7
Richmond	12,047	54	0	5	15	34	492	83	382	27	6
Rio Grande City	12,799	58	0	0	10	48	250	70	123	57	1
Robstown	12,804	42	0	2	7	33	709	244	425	40	0
Rockwall	22,681	30	0	8	9	13	746	124	551	71	2
Roma	10,293	55	2	8	4	41	262	66	163	33	1
Rosenberg	27,558	144	2	24	31	87	890	182	647	61	13
Rowlett	50,684	54	2	10	3	39	1,065	228	779	58	5
Sachse	13,217	18	0	0	2	16	248	90	140	18	2
Saginaw	15,628	29	0	5	6	18	408	91	277	40	0
San Angelo	88,782	407	1	77	62	267	5,965	1,264	4,464	237	22
San Antonio	1,212,789	7,252	85	537	2,060	4,570	83,000	14,619	62,179	6,202	540
San Benito	24,442	60	0	8	18	34	2,217	358	1,797	62	2
San Marcos	42,249	127	1	14	31	81	1,609	267	1,243	99	2
Santa Fe	10,175	29	0	14	3	12	366	109	230	27	4
Schertz	21,085	28	1	11	5	11	409	66	332	11	0
Seabrook	10,335	18	0	2	5	11	262	77	170	15	4
Seagoville	11,266	56	2	6	14	34	674	153	416	105	1
Seguin	23,095	101	2	16	12	71	1,673	323	1,311	39	1
Sherman	36,344	168	1	2	33	132	2,056	386	1,598	72	7
Snyder	10,577	42	0	2	2	38	300	108	181	11	1
Socorro	28,399	66	0	8	14	44	477	84	323	70	3
South Houston	16,393	126	0	13	45	68	917	204	558	155	0
Southlake	24,137	10	0	2	5	3	473	89	364	20	0
Stafford	18,214	77	1	12	38	26	1,013	143	788	82	0
Stephenville	15,126	24	1	5	1	17	508	115	373	20	3
Sugar Land	69,666	154	5	10	42	97	1,675	262	1,311	102	2
Sulphur Springs	14,839	39	3	8	5	23	442	86	319	37	3
Sweetwater	11,107	37	1	4	7	25	402	168	216	18	0
Taylor	14,281	29	1	3	3	22	372	82	274	16	1
Temple	55,293	170	5	1	48	116	2,725	677	1,862	186	8
Terrell	15,382	172	1	15	33	123	1,169	240	778	151	4
Texarkana	35,752	409	6	27	68	308	2,993	645	2,135	213	14
Texas City	43,733	618	5	38	122	453	3,064	807	1,959	298	24
The Colony	32,759	25	0	6	8	11	911	188	672	51	13
Tyler	88,383	717	8	40	147	522	5,280	994	4,019	267	0
Universal City	15,307	33	0	0	13	20	385	55	305	25	4
University Park	24,187	24	0	1	10	13	581	94	464	23	0
Uvalde	15,415	57	0	9	6	42	829	222	573	34	8
Vernon	11,216	98	1	4	10	83	753	185	545	23	0
Victoria	61,980	526	8	46	111	361	4,345	850	3,290	205	2
Vidor	11,478	33	1	5	11	16	407	104	271	32	7
Waco	117,549	809	14	40	215	540	8,773	2,176	5,990	607	40
Watauga	23,739	53	1	3	11	38	569	116	426	27	3
Waxahachie	23,418	69	1	8	12	48	1,197	269	865	63	4
Weatherford	20,940	34	0	9	8	17	794	118	629	47	5
Weslaco	29,546	125	2	8	23	92	2,534	514	1,833	187	2
West University Place	15,140	12	0	1	9	2	254	77	168	9	0
White Settlement	15,390	31	0	1	11	19	767	176	519	72	10
Wichita Falls	104,526	1,082	8	49	199	826	7,507	1,719	5,208	580	61
Wylie	18,666	26	0	6	1	19	433	112	294	27	1
UTAH											
Alpine/Highland	17,728	10	0	4	0	6	261	79	165	17	0
American Fork	22,843	16	0	2	1	13	989	170	772	47	4
Bountiful	41,897	39	0	6	14	19	1,100	210	837	53	1
Brigham City	17,653	45	0	10	5	30	477	75	372	30	4
Cedar City	21,753	25	0	2	4	19	675	100	536	39	1
Centerville	14,913	9	0	3	0	6	410	82	313	15	13
Clinton	14,571	11	2	5	0	4	229	50	170	9	2
Farmington	13,151	6	0	1	0	5	250	38	200	12	5
Kaysville	21,278	14	0	5	0	9	470	33	398	39	4

See footnotes at end of table.

Table 8

Offenses Known to Law Enforcement
by City 10,000 and over in Population, 2003—Continued

City by state	Population	Violent crime	Violent crime	Violent crime	Violent crime	Violent crime	Property crime	Property crime	Property crime	Property crime	Arson[1]
		Violent crime	Murder and non-negligent manslaughter	Forcible rape	Robbery	Aggravated assault	Property crime	Burglary	Larceny-theft	Motor vehicle theft	Arson[1]
UTAH—Continued											
Layton	60,977	172	2	35	26	109	2,192	333	1,710	149	14
Lehi	22,173	13	0	3	1	9	576	202	330	44	3
Logan	43,574	39	0	11	1	27	1,059	176	832	51	3
Midvale	27,733	87	0	12	28	47	1,850	205	1,452	193	2
Murray	35,588	140	0	29	49	62	3,823	564	2,970	289	6
North Ogden	16,055	10	0	4	1	5	252	38	207	7	0
Ogden	79,836	392	2	49	93	248	4,788	915	3,473	400	2
Orem	84,934	68	2	18	18	30	3,503	372	2,932	199	2
Provo	106,769	114	0	36	16	62	3,512	841	2,492	179	18
Roy	35,529	69	0	13	9	47	912	130	739	43	7
Salt Lake City	184,022	1,294	17	79	503	695	16,745	2,359	12,464	1,922	68
Sandy	90,601	174	0	36	43	95	3,208	563	2,461	184	9
South Jordan	32,300	27	0	4	2	21	797	194	558	45	6
South Ogden	14,923	14	0	5	3	6	500	108	372	20	1
South Salt Lake	22,234	191	0	29	54	108	2,073	298	1,483	292	4
Spanish Fork	22,754	10	0	5	2	3	999	179	796	24	2
Springville	21,872	29	0	11	3	15	975	177	750	48	5
Syracuse	12,612	21	0	10	0	11	206	42	152	12	5
West Jordan	74,470	157	0	18	31	108	3,232	415	2,620	197	11
West Valley	112,945	468	8	59	135	266	6,925	1,121	5,064	740	28
VERMONT											
Bennington	15,984	32	0	6	2	24	403	75	302	26	3
Brattleboro	12,035	20	0	6	4	10	402	59	330	13	0
Burlington	39,627	140	3	20	14	103	1,413	260	1,107	46	4
Colchester	17,237	27	0	0	2	25	380	68	301	11	1
Essex	18,973	13	0	2	1	10	491	89	389	13	0
Hartford	10,502	9	0	1	2	6	177	32	136	9	1
Rutland	17,168	36	0	3	7	26	784	133	624	27	4
VIRGINIA											
Alexandria	132,468	405	3	25	169	208	4,292	429	3,253	610	21
Blacksburg	40,618	60	0	6	7	47	714	107	575	32	3
Bristol	17,336	89	0	4	4	81	654	84	547	23	5
Charlottesville	44,391	303	1	20	71	211	1,572	195	1,229	148	12
Colonial Heights	17,280	51	1	4	18	28	848	78	743	27	9
Danville	48,202	296	5	20	77	194	2,214	313	1,763	138	14
Falls Church	10,795	13	0	1	4	8	348	37	269	42	6
Front Royal	14,071	32	0	6	12	14	517	46	440	31	4
Hampton	147,777	599	10	56	246	287	5,115	896	3,659	560	40
Harrisonburg	41,429	106	0	13	23	70	1,179	183	927	69	13
Herndon	22,280	50	0	3	14	33	560	30	494	36	0
Hopewell	22,812	150	2	16	32	100	1,119	321	708	90	10
Leesburg	31,986	105	1	15	16	73	925	79	784	62	5
Lynchburg	65,438	267	6	25	72	164	2,395	411	1,822	162	13
Manassas	37,762	138	4	19	27	88	1,152	115	903	134	12
Manassas Park	11,048	20	1	1	3	15	247	17	184	46	2
Martinsville	15,457	58	0	6	14	38	621	118	475	28	2
Newport News[2]	182,565	1,253	27	94	389	743			5,489	980	85
Norfolk	242,077	1,383	40	86	717	540	13,854	1,784	10,632	1,438	22
Petersburg	33,536	289	9	22	89	169	2,296	574	1,505	217	18
Poquoson	11,835	3	0	0	0	3	180	20	154	6	2
Portsmouth	101,060	901	18	43	403	437	5,002	1,179	3,323	500	16
Richmond[2]	199,968	2,474	93	98	1,174	1,109		2,816		2,711	86
Salem	25,152	34	1	6	10	17	670	65	568	37	5
Staunton	23,936	42	1	6	7	28	852	81	718	53	5
Suffolk	70,856	399	2	38	110	249	2,538	408	1,971	159	34
Virginia Beach	439,454	928	24	119	408	377	14,564	2,138	11,621	805	188
Waynesboro	20,390	97	2	3	8	84	655	70	548	37	7
Williamsburg	11,842	25	0	6	9	10	322	24	285	13	1
Winchester	24,536	73	0	9	30	34	1,346	168	1,125	53	6

See footnotes at end of table.

Table 8

Offenses Known to Law Enforcement
by City 10,000 and over in Population, 2003—Continued

City by state	Population	Violent crime	Murder and non-negligent man-slaughter	Forcible rape	Robbery	Aggravated assault	Property crime	Burglary	Larceny-theft	Motor vehicle theft	Arson[1]
WASHINGTON											
Aberdeen	16,438	51	1	12	13	25	1,707	244	1,376	87	4
Anacortes	15,359	11	0	2	2	7	487	97	365	25	1
Arlington	13,504	28	0	0	11	17	786	115	565	106	4
Auburn	44,586	296	1	80	69	146	3,485	594	2,075	816	43
Bainbridge Island	21,522	7	0	2	1	4	295	67	212	16	3
Battle Ground	10,002	17	0	3	2	12	524	104	393	27	5
Bellevue	114,056	164	0	28	68	68	4,319	518	3,213	588	55
Bellingham	71,205	181	1	30	60	90	5,138	790	4,080	268	43
Bonney Lake	12,524	39	0	3	11	25	641	97	472	72	6
Bothell	31,022	31	0	3	5	23	800	116	520	164	5
Bremerton	36,680	416	3	66	65	282	2,010	453	1,383	174	11
Burien	31,772	196	0	24	74	98	1,924	368	1,107	449	10
Camas	14,101	16	0	8	1	7	552	85	425	42	4
Centralia	15,065	70	0	12	17	41	1,166	184	858	124	11
Covington	14,555	31	0	6	7	18	525	109	327	89	13
Des Moines	29,630	109	0	15	27	67	1,030	206	530	294	1
Edmonds	40,426	37	0	8	14	15	1,184	241	805	138	16
Ellensburg	15,929	28	0	14	2	12	1,146	213	903	30	6
Enumclaw	11,126	22	0	4	0	18	398	36	289	73	7
Everett	98,087	546	2	77	168	299	6,406	981	3,846	1,579	21
Federal Way	83,020	297	2	50	125	120	5,021	672	3,145	1,204	14
Issaquah	13,305	22	0	3	15	4	832	116	603	113	7
Kelso	11,908	83	3	22	10	48	1,196	185	867	144	7
Kenmore	19,204	31	0	10	10	11	440	101	270	69	2
Kennewick	58,545	208	3	23	32	150	2,731	495	2,090	146	26
Kent	82,565	317	12	34	146	125	5,157	1,109	2,919	1,129	54
Kirkland	46,003	70	1	15	41	13	1,728	264	1,227	237	20
Lacey	32,752	92	0	28	21	43	1,498	272	1,127	99	11
Lake Forest Park	12,833	9	0	0	1	8	283	56	191	36	0
Lakewood	59,373	423	4	48	124	247	4,021	874	2,706	441	12
Longview	35,829	200	1	12	37	150	3,840	910	2,511	419	21
Lynnwood	34,257	68	3	4	35	26	2,528	256	1,954	318	9
Maple Valley	14,257	22	0	6	2	14	454	98	271	85	2
Marysville	28,045	65	0	9	16	40	964	146	611	207	20
Mercer Island	22,543	16	0	2	10	4	371	62	277	32	3
Mill Creek	12,683	23	0	2	4	17	422	56	306	60	9
Monroe	14,682	27	1	5	5	16	391	56	274	61	1
Moses Lake	16,140	63	0	22	17	24	1,331	228	1,055	48	8
Mountlake Terrace	21,028	31	0	8	8	15	849	97	628	124	4
Mount Vernon	27,488	75	0	22	22	31	2,350	293	1,948	109	22
Mukilteo	19,146	19	1	1	4	13	538	88	350	100	4
Oak Harbor	20,785	38	0	16	4	18	626	137	457	32	7
Olympia	43,967	145	0	38	32	75	2,189	303	1,724	162	8
Pasco	35,784	105	0	20	20	65	1,513	237	1,160	116	6
Port Angeles	18,615	46	0	8	7	31	846	154	648	44	8
Pullman	25,186	36	0	16	4	16	532	111	407	14	2
Puyallup	35,765	106	0	15	35	56	2,622	297	1,919	406	11
Redmond	46,402	90	2	22	16	50	1,853	227	1,438	188	6
Renton	53,723	279	1	27	89	162	4,335	642	2,822	871	20
Richland	41,923	82	0	14	9	59	1,242	242	947	53	7
Sammamish	34,237	13	0	1	3	9	492	113	345	34	8
SeaTac	25,493	118	1	15	41	61	1,564	323	787	454	8
Seattle	576,296	3,946	34	174	1,509	2,229	46,306	8,536	28,718	9,052	205
Shoreline	53,334	129	1	15	48	65	2,193	324	1,544	325	21
Spokane	198,325	1,161	13	84	354	710	15,906	3,053	11,260	1,593	83
Sunnyside	14,166	34	0	4	12	18	1,284	223	955	106	13
Tacoma	199,586	2,154	13	149	739	1,253	16,058	3,028	10,096	2,934	112
Tukwila	17,334	200	1	23	87	89	2,939	296	2,102	541	15
Tumwater	13,239	49	0	10	10	29	452	98	309	45	6
University Place	30,923	126	1	13	31	81	981	217	648	116	5
Vancouver[2]	151,353	642	2	128	164	348	8,723	1,283	6,244	1,196	33
Walla Walla	30,125	122	0	30	19	73	1,729	319	1,335	75	28
Wenatchee	28,559	104	0	28	22	54	1,809	365	1,361	83	15
Yakima	74,052	430	5	55	141	229	5,967	1,252	4,152	563	70

See footnotes at end of table.

Table 8

Offenses Known to Law Enforcement
by City 10,000 and over in Population, 2003—Continued

City by state	Population	Violent crime	Murder and non-negligent man-slaughter	Forcible rape	Robbery	Aggravated assault	Property crime	Burglary	Larceny-theft	Motor vehicle theft	Arson[1]
WEST VIRGINIA											
Bluefield	11,243	49	0	1	6	42	376	100	251	25	5
Huntington	50,145	286	4	37	134	111	3,722	1,085	2,333	304	22
Vienna	10,906	9	0	2	1	6	220	12	203	5	2
WISCONSIN											
Appleton	71,037	139	0	17	21	101	1,737	247	1,417	73	
Ashwaubenon	17,456	17	0	6	3	8	735	40	662	33	
Baraboo	10,715	22	0	4	2	16	488	45	426	17	
Beaver Dam	15,058	14	0	0	3	11	577	65	500	12	
Beloit	35,882	127	3	13	56	55	1,781	314	1,353	114	
Brookfield	39,736	29	1	2	17	9	1,261	164	1,069	28	
Brown Deer	12,167	16	0	2	7	7	614	26	567	21	
Burlington	10,600	8	0	2	2	4	422	32	373	17	
Caledonia	24,020	12	0	3	5	4	334	70	238	26	
Cedarburg	11,194	1	0	1	0	0	128	18	110	0	
Chippewa Falls	12,807	22	0	3	1	18	315	37	257	21	
Cudahy	18,547	40	2	3	11	24	538	86	419	33	
De Pere	21,759	21	0	14	1	6	287	49	227	11	
Everest	14,772	13	0	1	3	9	344	67	261	16	
Fitchburg	21,441	60	0	16	21	23	580	82	449	49	
Fond du Lac	42,537	46	0	10	7	29	1,332	177	1,106	49	
Fort Atkinson	11,887	7	0	0	0	7	278	14	255	9	
Fox Valley	17,115	1	0	1	0	0	406	54	339	13	
Franklin	31,747	37	0	10	9	18	669	97	541	31	
Germantown	18,846	12	0	6	4	2	381	55	319	7	
Glendale	13,391	19	0	0	14	5	794	35	720	39	
Grafton	11,222	3	0	0	0	3	191	20	166	5	
Grand Chute[2]	19,275	15	0	3	6	6	778	52	708	18	
Greendale	14,373	7	0	0	3	4	406	27	361	18	
Greenfield	36,090	43	0	9	27	7	1,303	195	1,041	67	
Hartford	11,574	6	0	0	2	4	372	16	341	15	
Janesville	61,269	148	0	20	38	90	3,251	566	2,583	102	
Kaukauna	13,887	8	1	1	2	4	228	14	201	13	
Kenosha	93,042	163	0	23	64	76	2,674	468	2,002	204	
La Crosse	51,502	104	3	15	18	68	1,695	216	1,417	62	
Madison	216,441	774	8	63	278	425	7,905	1,605	5,671	629	119
Manitowoc	34,383	42	0	8	6	28	1,093	176	888	29	
Marinette	11,625	19	0	4	3	12	479	59	406	14	
Marshfield	18,712	9	0	8	0	1	497	60	415	22	
Menasha	16,506	27	1	2	0	24	515	95	407	13	
Menomonee Falls	33,499	11	0	0	5	6	528	79	415	34	
Menomonie	15,103	12	0	3	1	8	496	101	359	36	
Mequon	23,394	15	0	0	4	11	241	64	174	3	
Merrill	10,201	10	0	3	1	6	376	44	316	16	
Middleton	16,316	9	0	3	4	2	545	53	472	20	
Milwaukee	594,269	5,289	109	246	2,868	2,066	37,798	6,041	25,526	6,231	341
Monroe	10,752	12	0	4	1	7	218	18	191	9	
Mount Pleasant	24,309	20	0	3	11	6	617	87	502	28	
Neenah	24,615	18	0	4	3	11	493	70	409	14	
New Berlin	38,870	16	1	3	3	9	540	124	402	14	
Oak Creek	30,731	24	0	11	8	5	918	125	742	51	
Oconomowoc	12,942	9	0	3	1	5	130	29	97	4	
Oshkosh	63,827	122	0	8	23	91	2,286	324	1,888	74	
Pewaukee Township	12,563	5	0	1	0	4	135	26	100	9	
Pleasant Prairie	17,533	69	0	10	2	57	337	33	294	10	
Plover	10,848	19	0	2	2	15	199	30	159	10	
Port Washington	10,578	4	0	2	0	2	210	20	183	7	
Racine	81,173	317	3	22	205	87	4,290	836	3,055	399	
River Falls	12,709	7	0	0	3	4	538	51	464	23	
Sheboygan	49,729	76	2	34	12	28	2,344	270	1,982	92	
Shorewood	13,620	17	0	3	13	1	418	48	358	12	
South Milwaukee	21,561	34	0	9	10	15	600	94	479	27	
Stevens Point	24,507	46	0	10	3	33	832	103	696	33	

See footnotes at end of table.

Table 8

Offenses Known to Law Enforcement

by City 10,000 and over in Population, 2003—Continued

City by state	Population	Violent crime	Murder and non-negligent man-slaughter	Forcible rape	Robbery	Aggravated assault	Property crime	Burglary	Larceny-theft	Motor vehicle theft	Arson[1]
WISCONSIN—Continued											
Stoughton	12,649	5	0	0	1	4	302	42	251	9	
Sun Prairie	22,660	27	0	6	5	16	819	63	732	24	
Superior	27,368	74	2	11	12	49	1,477	280	1,129	68	
Town of Menasha	15,975	11	1	6	2	2	236	48	182	6	
Two Rivers	12,428	9	1	0	3	5	220	40	173	7	
Watertown	22,495	48	0	7	6	35	838	149	660	29	
Waukesha	66,564	96	1	16	20	59	1,313	350	908	55	
Waupun	10,424	12	0	1	0	11	220	56	161	3	
Wausau	37,948	149	1	20	27	101	1,703	344	1,265	94	
Wauwatosa	46,980	133	0	10	72	51	1,976	303	1,565	108	
West Allis	60,985	166	3	16	84	63	2,386	402	1,781	203	
West Bend	28,834	22	0	4	4	14	848	51	773	24	
Whitefish Bay	14,060	13	0	2	7	4	183	24	151	8	
Whitewater	13,989	25	0	3	2	20	345	26	311	8	
Wisconsin Rapids	18,318	11	0	3	1	7	866	155	685	26	
WYOMING											
Casper	50,279	125	4	15	15	91	2,768	464	2,141	163	21
Cheyenne	53,931	110	0	23	24	63	2,465	258	2,095	112	6
Evanston	11,506	8	0	2	1	5	551	43	489	19	0
Gillette	21,238	48	0	5	2	41	1,114	93	983	38	10
Green River	11,687	38	0	0	3	35	374	54	312	8	0
Laramie[2]	27,022	51	1	4	3	43	946	139	761	46	5
Rock Springs	18,558	126	1	10	10	105	701	104	549	48	4
Sheridan	16,027	28	0	3	1	24	509	54	432	23	0

[1] If the FBI does not receive 12 months of arson data from either the agency or the state, no arson will be shown.

[2] Due to changes in reporting practices, annexations, and/or incomplete data, figures are not comparable to previous years' data.

[3] The population for the city of Mobile, Alabama, includes 55,864 inhabitants from the jurisdiction of the Mobile County Sheriff's Department.

[4] Forcible rape figures furnished by the state Uniform Crime Reporting (UCR) Program administered by the Illinois State Police were not in accordance with national UCR guidelines; therefore, the figures were excluded from the forcible rape and violent crime categories.

[5] Limited data for 2003 were available for Illinois and Kentucky.

[6] Louisville Metro, Kentucky, is a city-county government that includes the Louisville and Jefferson County Police Departments.

[7] Aggravated assault figures furnished by these agencies were not in accordance with national UCR guidelines; therefore, the figures were excluded from the aggravated assault and violent crime categories.

Table 9

Offenses Known to Law Enforcement
by University and College, 2003

University/College by state	Student enrollment[1]	Violent crime	Murder and non-negligent man-slaughter	Forcible rape	Robbery	Aggravated assault	Property crime	Burglary	Larceny-theft	Motor vehicle theft	Arson[2]
ALABAMA											
Alabama State University	5,590	30	0	0	24	6	266	38	222	6	
Auburn University:											
Main Campus	22,469	3	0	0	1	2	301	37	258	6	
Montgomery	4,982	0	0	0	0	0	59	1	57	1	
Jacksonville State University	8,336	1	0	0	1	0	102	19	83	0	
Talladega College	540	0	0	0	0	0	10	0	10	0	
Troy State University	13,660	1	0	0	1	0	120	19	100	1	1
University of Alabama:											
Huntsville	6,754	3	0	0	2	1	85	6	77	2	
Tuscaloosa	19,130	11	0	4	1	6	423	14	400	9	
University of Montevallo	2,935	0	0	0	0	0	4	0	4	0	
University of North Alabama	5,522	1	0	1	0	0	59	0	59	0	
University of South Alabama	12,122	2	0	1	0	1	152	23	121	8	0
ALASKA											
University of Alaska:											
Anchorage	15,040	7	0	3	0	4	143	2	136	5	0
Fairbanks	7,142	10	0	0	0	10	114	10	99	5	1
ARIZONA											
Arizona State University,											
Main Campus	45,693	38	0	7	1	30	1,437	156	1,167	114	6
Central Arizona College	5,328	1	0	1	0	0	41	8	28	5	0
Northern Arizona University	19,728	26	0	7	1	18	484	61	416	7	7
Pima Community College	28,176	1	0	0	0	1	210	9	183	18	0
University of Arizona	35,747	23	0	6	4	13	1,233	82	1,103	48	5
Yavapai College	8,162	3	0	0	0	3	42	5	36	1	0
ARKANSAS[3]											
Arkansas State University	10,568	1	0	1	0	0	116	63	53	0	0
Southern Arkansas University	3,127	0	0	0	0	0	29	1	28	0	0
University of Arkansas:											
Fayetteville	15,752	2	0	1	0	1	231	45	182	4	0
Medical Sciences	1,936	1	0	0	0	1	229	8	220	1	0
University of Central Arkansas	8,486	6	0	1	0	5	88	38	50	0	3
CALIFORNIA											
Allan Hancock College	12,548	0	0	0	0	0	43	15	26	2	0
California State Polytechnic University:											
Pomona	19,041	4	0	1	3	0	322	40	252	30	0
San Luis Obispo	18,079	3	0	3	0	0	197	22	163	12	1
California State University:											
Bakersfield	7,050	1	0	0	0	1	66	14	50	2	0
Channel Islands[4]		0	0	0	0	0	15	2	12	1	4
Chico	16,704	9	0	3	2	4	262	33	221	8	2
Dominguez Hills	12,871	6	0	0	2	4	99	10	74	15	0
Fresno	20,007	5	0	0	0	5	412	30	342	40	1
Fullerton	30,357	1	0	0	1	0	163	15	128	20	0
Hayward	13,240	2	0	0	0	2	135	39	88	8	0
Long Beach	33,259	7	0	3	1	3	322	14	252	56	1
Los Angeles	20,675	7	0	1	3	3	284	38	229	17	1
Monterey Bay	3,020	8	0	2	2	4	160	38	121	1	1
Northridge	31,448	17	0	4	9	4	387	61	298	28	1
Sacramento	26,923	6	0	0	1	5	383	48	295	40	1
San Bernardino	15,985	8	0	2	0	6	147	46	93	8	1
San Jose[4]		4	0	2	1	1	391	26	358	7	4
San Marcos	6,496	1	0	0	0	1	32	6	25	1	0
Stanislaus	7,534	0	0	0	0	0	61	10	46	5	1
College of the Sequoias	11,447	3	0	0	0	3	79	24	44	11	1
Contra Costa Community College	7,432	15	0	1	5	9	263	22	208	33	0

See footnotes at end of table.

Table 9

Offenses Known to Law Enforcement
by University and College, 2003—Continued

University/College by state	Student enrollment[1]	Violent crime	Violent crime				Property crime	Property crime			
			Murder and non-negligent man-slaughter	Forcible rape	Robbery	Aggravated assault	Property crime	Burglary	Larceny-theft	Motor vehicle theft	Arson[2]
CALIFORNIA—Continued											
Cuesta College	9,823	0	0	0	0	0	82	4	78	0	0
El Camino College	24,917	1	0	0	0	1	214	3	193	18	0
Foothill-De Anza College	39,037	2	0	0	0	2	180	49	123	8	0
Fresno Community College	19,888	1	0	1	0	0	221	8	187	26	0
Humboldt State University	7,382	5	0	2	1	2	209	18	188	3	9
Marin Community College	8,475	0	0	0	0	0	40	0	36	4	0
Pasadena Community College	26,227	3	0	0	0	3	346	5	326	15	1
Reedley College	10,535	0	0	0	0	0	34	3	30	1	0
Riverside Community College	33,053	6	0	3	0	3	158	26	121	11	0
San Bernardino Community College	12,731	2	0	1	0	1	73	5	50	18	0
San Diego State University	34,171	32	0	7	7	18	663	32	471	160	4
San Francisco State University	26,866	12	0	4	4	4	365	92	248	25	0
San Jose/Evergreen Community College	21,140	3	0	0	0	3	116	13	96	7	6
Santa Rosa Junior College	26,984	3	0	0	1	2	95	9	83	3	0
Solano Community College	10,703	0	0	0	0	0	76	2	70	4	0
Sonoma State University	7,590	6	0	2	0	4	175	28	141	6	2
University of California:											
Berkeley	32,128	32	0	4	12	16	1,104	91	967	46	6
Davis	27,292	4	0	1	2	1	725	65	645	15	5
Hastings College of Law	1,252	2	0	0	2	0	18	1	17	0	0
Irvine	21,885	5	0	1	3	1	596	57	488	51	8
Lawrence-Livermore Laboratory[4]		0	0	0	0	0	13	0	13	0	0
Los Angeles	37,494	32	0	10	9	13	1,271	264	946	61	0
Medical Center, Sacramento[4]		11	0	1	3	7	226	25	176	25	0
Riverside	14,429	6	0	0	1	5	485	78	369	38	10
San Diego	21,558	7	0	1	3	3	567	63	450	54	2
San Francisco	3,574	4	0	0	3	1	509	49	448	12	0
Santa Barbara	20,373	9	0	4	1	4	420	58	358	4	3
Santa Cruz	13,170	6	0	2	1	3	242	55	186	1	3
West Valley-Mission College	21,133	0	0	0	0	0	123	10	104	9	0
COLORADO											
Arapahoe Community College	7,268	0	0	0	0	0	42	1	37	4	0
Auraria Higher Education Center[4]		6	0	0	1	5	234	7	218	9	1
Colorado School of Mines	3,705	0	0	0	0	0	19	3	15	1	0
Colorado State University	28,103	16	0	4	3	9	389	39	340	10	3
Fort Lewis College	4,429	4	0	2	0	2	94	24	69	1	1
Pikes Peak Community College	9,772	1	0	0	0	1	34	3	30	1	0
University of Colorado:											
Boulder	30,063	19	0	5	3	11	660	115	534	11	12
Colorado Springs	7,980	2	0	2	0	0	63	1	60	2	0
Health Sciences Center	2,523	5	0	1	2	2	143	18	124	1	0
Health Sciences Center, Fitzsimons Campus[4]		0	0	0	0	0	61	1	59	1	0
University of Northern Colorado	12,301	5	0	1	1	3	313	16	293	4	1
CONNECTICUT											
Central Connecticut State University	12,368	2	0	1	0	1	72	16	55	1	0
Eastern Connecticut State University	5,337	0	0	0	0	0	94	11	81	2	0
Southern Connecticut State University	12,254	3	0	2	1	0	93	9	82	2	0
University of Connecticut:											
Health Center[4]		0	0	0	0	0	36	1	30	5	0
Storrs, Avery Point, and Hartford[4]		12	0	5	2	5	321	83	232	6	4
Western Connecticut State University	5,918	2	0	1	0	1	50	8	42	0	0
Yale University	11,136	6	0	1	5	0	417	69	343	5	0
DELAWARE											
University of Delaware	20,949	26	0	4	8	14	448	46	395	7	2

See footnotes at end of table.

Table 9

Offenses Known to Law Enforcement
by University and College, 2003—Continued

University/College by state	Student enrollment[1]	Violent crime	Violent crime — Murder and non-negligent man-slaughter	Violent crime — Forcible rape	Violent crime — Robbery	Violent crime — Aggravated assault	Property crime	Property crime — Burglary	Property crime — Larceny-theft	Property crime — Motor vehicle theft	Arson[2]
FLORIDA											
Florida A&M University	12,316	23	0	2	10	11	529	57	455	17	1
Florida Atlantic University	23,345	7	0	1	2	4	304	68	219	17	1
Florida Gulf Coast University	4,214	6	0	1	0	5	36	1	33	2	0
Florida International University	31,727	5	0	1	3	1	551	150	369	32	1
Florida State University:[4]											
Panama City[4]		0	0	0	0	0	8	0	8	0	0
Tallahassee	34,982	23	0	4	9	10	745	68	656	21	0
New College of Florida	629	0	0	0	0	0	38	2	34	2	0
Pensacola Junior College	10,678	7	0	0	1	6	52	7	41	4	0
Santa Fe Community College	13,224	2	0	0	1	1	44	0	42	2	0
Tallahassee Community College	11,146	4	0	0	0	4	69	1	66	2	0
University of Central Florida	35,850	25	0	9	5	11	443	82	337	24	0
University of Florida	46,515	22	0	6	7	9	688	55	593	40	1
University of North Florida	12,992	2	0	1	0	1	136	24	108	4	1
University of South Florida:											
St. Petersburg[4]		0	0	0	0	0	38	1	34	3	0
Tampa	37,221	18	0	1	6	11	751	353	357	41	0
University of West Florida	9,052	6	0	0	0	6	110	10	95	5	3
GEORGIA											
Abraham Baldwin Agricultural College	2,855	0	0	0	0	0	50	8	42	0	0
Albany State University	3,456	0	0	0	0	0	61	4	57	0	0
Armstrong Atlantic State University	5,747	0	0	0	0	0	59	1	56	2	0
Augusta State University	5,382	0	0	0	0	0	32	2	30	0	0
Berry College	2,038	0	0	0	0	0	66	11	54	1	0
Clayton College and State University	4,674	4	0	1	1	2	58	8	43	7	0
Coastal Georgia Community College	2,210	0	0	0	0	0	19	2	16	1	
Dalton State College	3,641	0	0	0	0	0	12	2	10	0	0
Georgia College and State University	5,079	2	0	2	0	0	60	2	58	0	0
Georgia Institute of Technology	15,575	10	0	1	9	0	1,097	76	931	90	0
Georgia Perimeter College	15,372	5	0	0	1	4	134	1	115	18	0
Georgia Southern University	14,371	0	0	0	0	0	156	2	152	2	
Georgia Southwestern State University	2,535	2	0	0	0	2	44	5	39	0	0
Georgia State University	25,743	15	0	1	12	2	488	16	461	11	
Gordon College	3,074	0	0	0	0	0	8	2	5	1	0
Medical College of Georgia	1,939	1	0	0	0	1	148	8	133	7	0
Mercer University	7,315	1	0	0	0	1	69	1	65	3	0
Middle Georgia College	2,163	0	0	0	0	0	20	0	20	0	
Morehouse College	2,729	5	0	1	4	0	118	0	115	3	0
Morris-Brown College	2,874	2	0	0	0	2	104	45	45	14	0
North Georgia College	3,858	0	0	0	0	0	38	6	32	0	0
Piedmont College	1,728	0	0	0	0	0	0	0	0	0	0
Savannah State University	2,269	14	0	1	5	8	136	10	117	9	0
Southern Polytechnic State University	3,552	2	0	0	0	2	83	12	64	7	0
South Georgia College	1,325	0	0	0	0	0	19	5	14	0	0
University of Georgia	32,317	9	0	0	6	3	570	18	543	9	2
Valdosta State University	9,230	0	0	0	0	0	187	7	180	0	0
Young Harris College	594	0	0	0	0	0	0	0	0	0	0
ILLINOIS[5]											
INDIANA											
Ball State University	18,965	17	0	3	2	12	406	71	329	6	2
Indiana State University	11,321	9	0	4	2	3	292	67	219	6	0
Indiana University:											
Bloomington	37,963	13	0	3	2	8	678	74	600	4	1
Gary	4,639	1	0	0	1	0	42	0	40	2	0
Indianapolis[4]		3	0	0	0	3	533	5	511	17	0
New Albany	6,557	0	0	0	0	0	47	0	47	0	0
Marian College	1,260	0	0	0	0	0	12	0	11	1	0
Purdue University	39,882	10	0	3	5	2	590	33	551	6	0

See footnotes at end of table.

Table 9

Offenses Known to Law Enforcement

by University and College, 2003—Continued

University/College by state	Student enrollment[1]	Violent crime	Murder and non-negligent man-slaughter	Forcible rape	Robbery	Aggravated assault	Property crime	Burglary	Larceny-theft	Motor vehicle theft	Arson[2]
IOWA										
Iowa State University	27,823	11	0	4	0	7	367	41	323	3	2
University of Iowa	28,768	9	0	5	2	2	282	57	219	6	0
University of Northern Iowa	14,410	2	0	1	0	1	160	20	139	1	1
KANSAS										
Emporia State University	5,823	0	0	0	0	0	86	6	77	3	1
Fort Hays State University	5,626	0	0	0	0	0	37	12	25	0	1
Kansas State University	22,396	7	0	0	1	6	208	20	188	0	0
Pittsburg State University	6,723	1	0	0	0	1	75	17	57	1	1
University of Kansas:										
Main Campus	25,782	5	0	1	0	4	350	86	259	5	0
Medical Center	2,408	3	0	0	2	1	185	9	167	9	0
Wichita State University	14,854	7	0	2	4	1	158	14	140	4	1
KENTUCKY[5]										
University of Kentucky	23,901	8	0	2	3	3	817	95	698	24	9
LOUISIANA										
Delgado Community College	13,404	0	0	0	0	0	68	6	57	5	0
Grambling State University	4,500	8	0	1	5	2	114	51	62	1	0
Louisiana State University:										
Baton Rouge[4]		14	0	2	1	11	547	85	440	22	0
Eunice	2,717	0	0	0	0	0	0	0	0	0	0
Health Sciences Center, New Orleans	2,638	0	0	0	0	0	52	0	51	1	0
Health Sciences Center, Shreveport[4]		3	0	0	0	3	153	1	145	7	1
Shreveport	4,113	0	0	0	0	0	19	1	18	0	0
Louisiana Tech University	10,694	4	0	0	2	2	114	16	95	3	1
McNeese State University	7,780	6	0	0	2	4	150	26	122	2	1
Nicholls State University	7,188	1	0	0	0	1	22	1	21	0	0
Northwestern State University	9,415	5	0	0	1	4	133	74	50	9	0
Southeastern Louisiana University	14,506	8	0	2	2	4	217	60	148	9	0
Southern University and A&M College:										
Baton Rouge	9,035	11	0	0	5	6	146	15	128	3	0
New Orleans	3,741	0	0	0	0	0	55	13	33	9	0
Shreveport	1,444	0	0	0	0	0	15	0	15	0	0
Tulane University	11,825	9	0	1	4	4	291	41	238	12	2
University of Louisiana:										
Lafayette	15,489	13	0	0	1	12	170	75	93	2	0
Monroe	8,762	4	0	0	2	2	191	22	167	2	0
University of New Orleans	17,014	1	0	0	1	0	170	6	154	10	0
MAINE										
University of Maine:										
Farmington	2,435	0	0	0	0	0	12	0	12	0	0
Orono	10,698	1	0	0	0	1	244	39	204	1	23
University of Southern Maine	10,966	5	0	3	0	2	108	10	96	2	0
MARYLAND										
Bowie State University	5,181	19	0	0	2	17	76	12	63	1	0
Coppin State College	4,032	11	0	2	3	6	49	4	39	6	0
Frostburg State University	5,283	6	0	0	0	6	118	45	73	0	0
Morgan State University	6,498	19	0	2	17	0	150	44	101	5	0
Salisbury University	6,682	2	0	0	1	1	157	7	150	0	0
St. Mary's College	1,688	2	0	1	0	1	62	10	50	2	0
Towson University	16,980	4	0	0	1	3	224	42	179	3	1
University of Baltimore	4,639	0	0	0	0	0	102	4	95	3	0
University of Maryland:										
Baltimore City	5,476	12	0	0	4	8	173	13	158	2	0
Baltimore County	11,237	0	0	0	0	0	226	11	196	19	0
College Park	34,160	36	0	6	12	18	817	154	589	74	2
Eastern Shore	3,295	11	0	1	1	9	136	32	102	2	0

See footnotes at end of table.

Table 9

Offenses Known to Law Enforcement
by University and College, 2003—Continued

University/College by state	Student enrollment[1]	Violent crime	Violent crime — Murder and non-negligent man-slaughter	Violent crime — Forcible rape	Violent crime — Robbery	Violent crime — Aggravated assault	Property crime	Property crime — Burglary	Property crime — Larceny-theft	Property crime — Motor vehicle theft	Arson[2]
MASSACHUSETTS											
Boston University	27,756	29	0	2	6	21	592	95	490	7	
Brandeis University	4,882	3	0	2	0	1	115	45	69	1	0
Bristol Community College	6,132	0	0	0	0	0	22	0	20	2	0
Emerson College	4,339	6	0	2	1	3	75	13	62	0	0
Fitchburg State College	5,024	4	0	1	0	3	134	14	120	0	0
Framingham State College	5,903	5	0	1	0	4	28	8	20	0	0
Harvard University	24,474	10	0	2	2	6	738	530	202	6	
Holyoke Community College	5,998	3	0	0	0	3	44	2	42	0	0
Lasell College	894	1	0	0	0	1	23	8	15	0	0
Massachusetts College of Art	2,250	0	0	0	0	0	75	4	71	0	1
Massachusetts College of Liberal Arts	1,613	9	0	0	1	8	30	2	28	0	0
Massachusetts Institute of Technology	10,197	12	0	7	2	3	689	101	578	10	
Massasoit Community College	6,906	2	0	0	0	2	39	2	37	0	0
Mount Holyoke College	2,038	1	0	0	0	1	96	9	86	1	0
Northeastern University	23,422	20	1	3	9	7	551	26	521	4	2
North Shore Community College	6,100	1	0	0	0	1	14	0	13	1	0
Quinsigamond Community College	6,197	0	0	0	0	0	29	0	29	0	0
Springfield College	5,007	15	0	0	2	13	130	33	94	3	0
Tufts University:											
Medford	9,082	8	0	2	2	4	188	35	149	4	0
Suffolk[4]		0	0	0	0	0	48	1	47	0	0
Worcester[4]		0	0	0	0	0	17	0	17	0	0
University of Massachusetts:											
Dartmouth	7,460	11	0	1	0	10	235	13	218	4	0
Harbor Campus, Boston	13,348	1	0	0	0	1	115	4	111	0	4
Medical Center, Worcester	686	8	0	0	0	8	138	4	133	1	0
Wentworth Institute of Technology	3,273	4	0	0	3	1	72	1	71	0	
Westfield State College	5,153	1	0	1	0	0	50	21	28	1	1
MICHIGAN											
Central Michigan University	27,797	9	0	6	2	1	238	6	230	2	3
Delta College	9,764	0	0	0	0	0	40	0	38	2	0
Eastern Michigan University	24,287	11	0	4	2	5	544	49	475	20	5
Ferris State University	10,930	4	0	2	0	2	212	5	202	5	2
Grand Rapids Community College	13,483	0	0	0	0	0	148	1	147	0	1
Grand Valley State University	19,762	8	0	4	0	4	138	4	133	1	0
Lansing Community College	17,358	1	0	0	1	0	130	1	129	0	0
Macomb Community College	21,818	0	0	0	0	0	56	2	52	2	0
Michigan State University	44,227	31	0	3	10	18	1,064	116	924	24	3
Michigan Technological University	6,603	0	0	0	0	0	111	2	109	0	0
Mott Community College	9,019	1	0	0	0	1	79	2	70	7	2
Northern Michigan University	8,577	2	0	0	1	1	150	3	145	2	0
Oakland Community College	23,503	0	0	0	0	0	71	0	66	5	0
Oakland University	15,875	3	0	0	1	2	126	4	122	0	1
Saginaw Valley State University	8,936	3	0	3	0	0	105	5	100	0	0
University of Michigan:											
Ann Arbor	38,248	18	0	4	4	10	1,293	65	1,212	16	7
Dearborn	8,144	0	0	0	0	0	79	0	69	10	0
Flint	6,397	0	0	0	0	0	108	2	104	2	0
Western Michigan University	28,931	5	0	1	0	4	336	25	305	6	3
MINNESOTA											
University of Minnesota:											
Duluth	9,380	2	0	1	0	1	91	6	85	0	0
Twin Cities	46,597	9	0	2	5	2	841	77	749	15	25
MISSISSIPPI											
Coahoma Community College	1,318	1	0	0	0	1	22	17	4	1	0
Hinds Community College	9,534	2	0	0	2	0	79	15	62	2	0
Itawamba Community College	3,803	1	0	0	1	0	40	35	5	0	0
Jackson State University	7,098	6	0	0	3	3	231	44	181	6	0

See footnotes at end of table.

Table 9

Offenses Known to Law Enforcement

by University and College, 2003—Continued

University/College by state	Student enrollment[1]	Violent crime	Violent crime	Violent crime	Violent crime	Violent crime	Property crime	Property crime	Property crime	Property crime	Arson[2]
			Murder and non-negligent man-slaughter	Forcible rape	Robbery	Aggravated assault		Burglary	Larceny-theft	Motor vehicle theft	
MISSISSIPPI—Continued											
Mississippi State University	16,878	4	0	0	1	3	251	27	220	4	0
University of Mississippi:											
Medical Center	1,658	3	0	0	1	2	178	3	168	7	0
Oxford	12,626	2	0	2	0	0	152	10	140	2	0
MISSOURI											
Central Missouri State University	10,822	4	0	1	1	2	121	33	88	0	0
Lincoln University	3,332	1	0	0	0	1	74	16	58	0	0
Mineral Area College	2,878	3	0	1	1	1	12	9	3	0	0
Missouri Western State College	5,102	16	0	1	0	15	134	47	85	2	0
Northwest Missouri State University	6,625	5	0	2	0	3	41	5	36	0	0
Southeast Missouri State University	9,348	0	0	0	0	0	87	8	79	0	0
St. Louis Community College,											
Meramec	12,296	0	0	0	0	0	18	0	17	1	0
Truman State University	6,005	3	0	2	0	1	63	10	53	0	0
University of Missouri:											
Columbia	23,667	14	0	0	2	12	438	33	404	1	0
Kansas City	12,969	2	0	0	1	1	168	42	113	13	0
Rolla	4,883	0	0	0	0	0	63	15	48	0	0
St. Louis	14,993	4	0	0	1	3	177	31	135	11	4
Washington University	12,187	2	0	0	2	0	279	17	259	3	1
NEBRASKA											
University of Nebraska:											
Kearney	6,426	0	0	0	0	0	73	22	51	0	0
Lincoln	22,764	3	0	2	0	1	360	87	271	2	0
NEVADA											
Truckee Meadows Community College	9,697	0	0	0	0	0	17	5	12	0	0
University of Nevada:											
Las Vegas	23,313	13	0	4	3	6	491	132	268	91	1
Reno	14,316	11	0	7	1	3	189	26	153	10	1
NEW JERSEY											
Brookdale Community College	11,876	1	0	0	0	1	27	0	27	0	0
Essex County College	9,539	2	0	0	1	1	75	0	70	5	0
Kean University of New Jersey	12,094	0	0	0	0	0	144	14	118	12	0
Middlesex County College	10,802	0	0	0	0	0	70	2	64	4	0
Monmouth University	5,753	2	0	0	0	2	86	7	73	6	3
Montclair State University	13,855	12	0	5	0	7	191	34	140	17	1
New Jersey Institute of Technology	8,862	15	0	2	9	4	184	12	125	47	0
Richard Stockton College	6,459	2	0	0	0	2	74	13	60	1	0
Rowan University	9,788	7	0	1	2	4	181	21	160	0	0
Rutgers University:											
Camden	5,097	7	0	0	3	4	118	39	75	4	0
Newark	9,602	8	0	0	8	0	254	16	210	28	0
New Brunswick	35,650	24	0	5	11	8	815	154	637	24	5
The College of New Jersey	6,846	7	0	4	0	3	140	13	123	4	1
University of Medicine and Dentistry:											
Camden[4]		0	0	0	0	0	13	0	13	0	0
Newark	4,660	35	0	0	15	20	480	13	408	59	0
Piscataway[4]		4	0	0	1	3	61	0	61	0	0
William Paterson University	10,466	4	0	3	1	0	131	37	89	5	0
NEW MEXICO											
Eastern New Mexico University	3,556	3	0	1	0	2	65	43	21	1	0
New Mexico State University	15,224	22	0	4	1	17	432	51	377	4	0
University of New Mexico	23,753	27	0	6	6	15	891	43	789	59	3

See footnotes at end of table.

Table 9

Offenses Known to Law Enforcement
by University and College, 2003—Continued

University/College by state	Student enrollment[1]	Violent crime	Murder and non-negligent man-slaughter	Forcible rape	Robbery	Aggravated assault	Property crime	Burglary	Larceny-theft	Motor vehicle theft	Arson[2]
NEW YORK											
Cornell University[4]		13	0	0	2	11	468	67	400	1	
Ithaca College	6,483	1	0	1	0	0	130	2	128	0	
Rensselaer Polytechnic Institute	8,084	1	0	1	0	0	115	18	97	0	
State University of New York:											
Buffalo	25,838	18	0	1	12	5	585	140	434	11	
Downstate Medical Center[4]		2	0	0	0	2	86	2	84	0	
Stony Brook	20,855	12	0	2	5	5	695	43	638	14	
Upstate Medical Center[4]		1	0	0	1	0	206	2	203	1	
State University of New York Agricultural and Technical College:											
Alfred	3,041	5	0	3	1	1	127	18	108	1	
Canton	2,223	6	0	4	1	1	105	4	100	1	
Cobleskill	2,452	4	0	3	0	1	116	17	99	0	
Farmingdale	5,449	1	0	0	1	0	63	6	55	2	
Morrisville	3,130	5	0	2	2	1	109	14	95	0	
State University of New York College:											
Buffalo	11,743	6	1	1	0	4	148	21	126	1	
Cortland	7,705	0	0	0	0	0	86	6	79	1	
Fredonia	5,305	3	0	1	2	0	119	14	105	0	
Geneseo	5,649	2	0	0	1	1	131	5	126	0	
New Paltz	7,838	0	0	0	0	0	84	0	83	1	
Old Westbury	3,077	1	0	0	1	0	29	4	25	0	
Oswego	8,407	2	0	2	0	0	146	16	130	0	
Plattsburgh	6,236	2	0	1	0	1	97	11	86	0	
Potsdam	4,325	2	0	1	0	1	96	4	92	0	
Purchase	4,018	1	0	1	0	0	120	13	107	0	
United States Merchant Marine Academy	850	0	0	0	0	0	17	13	3	1	0
NORTH CAROLINA											
Appalachian State University	13,762	2	0	0	0	2	167	11	154	2	1
Davidson College	1,673	0	0	0	0	0	57	9	46	2	0
Duke University	11,926	13	0	1	5	7	850	41	796	13	0
East Carolina University	19,412	13	0	2	9	2	316	22	290	4	0
Elon University	4,341	1	0	1	0	0	95	24	71	0	0
North Carolina Agricultural and Technical State University	8,319	27	0	4	7	16	424	35	375	14	3
North Carolina School of the Arts	789	1	0	0	1	0	49	1	48	0	0
North Carolina State University, Raleigh	29,286	11	0	1	3	7	509	56	448	5	1
University of North Carolina:											
Asheville	3,293	0	0	0	0	0	38	3	35	0	0
Chapel Hill	25,494	8	0	1	4	3	479	28	441	10	1
Charlotte	18,308	3	0	1	2	0	252	31	207	14	2
Greensboro	13,775	6	0	1	0	5	236	29	198	9	1
Wilmington	10,799	4	0	2	1	1	269	54	210	5	0
Wake Forest University	6,271	2	0	1	1	0	131	28	103	0	1
Western Carolina University	6,863	7	0	1	1	5	185	38	142	5	3
Winston-Salem State University	2,992	4	0	0	0	4	131	20	106	5	2
NORTH DAKOTA											
North Dakota State College of Science	2,292	0	0	0	0	0	36	2	34	0	0
North Dakota State University	10,534	1	0	1	0	0	136	23	113	0	1
University of North Dakota	11,764	5	0	0	0	5	263	15	242	6	1
OHIO											
Bowling Green State University	18,739	3	0	2	1	0	266	8	255	3	2
Cleveland State University	15,701	8	0	2	4	2	260	7	239	14	0
Columbus State Community College	19,642	5	0	0	0	5	272	6	263	3	0
Cuyahoga Community College	20,496	1	0	1	0	0	101	2	97	2	0
Kent State University	22,828	2	0	0	0	2	281	8	271	2	1

See footnotes at end of table.

Table 9

Offenses Known to Law Enforcement

by University and College, 2003—Continued

University/College by state	Student enrollment[1]	Violent crime	Murder and non-negligent man-slaughter	Forcible rape	Robbery	Aggravated assault	Property crime	Burglary	Larceny-theft	Motor vehicle theft	Arson[2]
OHIO—Continued											
Lakeland Community College	8,253	2	0	0	0	2	9	0	9	0	0
Marietta College	1,270	2	0	1	1	0	30	5	25	0	0
Miami University	16,311	3	0	3	0	0	248	37	210	1	4
Ohio State University	48,477	19	0	3	11	5	1,426	316	1,077	33	4
Ohio University	20,288	4	0	0	1	3	216	25	188	3	3
Sinclair Community College	19,770	1	0	0	1	0	130	0	129	1	0
University of Cincinnati	27,289	13	0	3	8	2	831	136	691	4	0
University of Toledo	20,313	5	0	1	2	2	388	61	315	12	3
Wright State University	13,829	7	0	5	1	1	302	7	287	8	1
Youngstown State University	12,243	1	0	1	0	0	177	4	170	3	0
OKLAHOMA											
Cameron University	5,329	0	0	0	0	0	16	0	16	0	0
East Central University	4,189	0	0	0	0	0	27	14	13	0	0
Murray State College	1,891	0	0	0	0	0	9	6	2	1	0
Northeastern Oklahoma A&M College	1,808	3	0	0	0	3	23	11	12	0	0
Northeastern State College	8,534	5	0	2	1	2	132	12	119	1	0
Oklahoma State University:											
Main Campus	22,008	3	0	3	0	0	246	53	191	2	1
Okmulgee	2,365	2	0	2	0	0	43	2	41	0	0
Tulsa[4]		0	0	0	0	0	22	0	16	6	0
Rogers State University	2,872	0	0	0	0	0	17	4	13	0	0
Seminole State College	1,961	0	0	0	0	0	27	5	22	0	0
Southeastern Oklahoma State University	3,890	0	0	0	0	0	41	6	32	3	0
Southwestern Oklahoma State University	4,854	0	0	0	0	0	20	8	12	0	1
Tulsa Community College	16,741	0	0	0	0	0	47	0	47	0	0
University of Central Oklahoma	14,660	3	0	1	1	1	78	8	69	1	2
University of Oklahoma:											
Health Sciences Center	2,862	22	0	1	1	20	228	58	159	11	0
Norman	25,104	7	0	1	5	1	304	48	250	6	5
PENNSYLVANIA											
Bloomsburg University	7,914	1	0	1	0	0	65	2	62	1	1
California University	5,948	1	0	0	1	0	37	0	37	0	0
Cheyney University	1,514	15	0	2	0	13	44	2	42	0	5
Clarion University	6,271	1	0	0	0	1	60	20	40	0	0
East Stroudsburg University	5,996	3	0	1	2	0	115	0	114	1	2
Edinboro University	7,498	2	0	0	0	2	80	0	79	1	0
Elizabethtown College	1,902	1	0	0	0	1	19	0	19	0	0
Indiana University	13,457	19	0	4	1	14	110	6	104	0	0
Kutztown University	8,268	1	0	1	0	0	106	9	94	3	0
Lehigh University	6,479	7	0	1	4	2	108	3	104	1	0
Mansfield University	3,303	0	0	0	0	0	32	5	27	0	1
Millersville University	7,556	2	0	1	0	1	107	6	101	0	0
Moravian College	1,924	2	0	1	1	0	31	0	30	1	0
Pennsylvania State University:											
Altoona	3,823	1	0	0	0	1	34	2	32	0	0
Beaver	759	0	0	0	0	0	13	2	11	0	1
Behrend	3,708	2	0	2	0	0	31	7	24	0	1
Berks	2,329	0	0	0	0	0	35	9	23	3	0
Harrisburg	3,239	0	0	0	0	0	16	5	11	0	0
McKeesport	951	1	0	0	0	1	0	0	0	0	0
Mont Alto	1,164	0	0	0	0	0	10	0	10	0	0
University Park	40,828	8	0	1	2	5	581	38	539	4	3
Shippensburg University	7,193	6	0	5	0	1	55	4	49	2	0
Slippery Rock University	7,197	0	0	0	0	0	74	2	70	2	0
University of Pittsburgh:											
Bradford	1,467	0	0	0	0	0	17	1	16	0	0
Pittsburgh	26,710	13	0	3	7	3	569	39	521	9	3
West Chester University	12,244	6	0	1	0	5	108	0	102	6	0

See footnotes at end of table.

Table 9

Offenses Known to Law Enforcement
by University and College, 2003—Continued

University/College by state	Student enrollment[1]	Violent crime	Murder and non-negligent man-slaughter	Forcible rape	Robbery	Aggravated assault	Property crime	Burglary	Larceny-theft	Motor vehicle theft	Arson[2]
RHODE ISLAND											
Brown University	7,774	5	0	1	1	3	223	49	174	0	0
University of Rhode Island	14,264	4	0	0	2	2	266	34	224	8	4
SOUTH CAROLINA											
Benedict College	2,938	12	0	0	6	6	266	78	183	5	0
Clemson University	17,101	2	0	1	1	0	117	11	101	5	0
Coastal Carolina University	4,965	3	0	0	0	3	111	19	92	0	0
College of Charleston	11,617	6	0	3	3	0	188	21	160	7	3
Columbia College	1,476	2	0	0	2	0	26	2	23	1	0
Denmark Technical College	1,401	0	0	0	0	0	3	2	0	1	0
Erskine College	948	0	0	0	0	0	9	4	4	1	0
Francis Marion University	3,513	1	0	0	0	1	77	5	71	1	0
Lander University	2,710	1	0	1	0	0	41	6	35	0	0
Medical University of South Carolina	2,297	5	0	0	1	4	236	4	226	6	0
Midlands Technical College	9,874	0	0	0	0	0	98	3	95	0	0
South Carolina State University	4,467	4	0	0	3	1	179	42	136	1	0
The Citadel	4,001	0	0	0	0	0	24	0	23	1	0
Trident Technical College	10,461	0	0	0	0	0	53	12	41	0	0
University of South Carolina:											
Aiken	3,282	1	0	1	0	0	13	2	11	0	0
Columbia	23,000	17	0	3	4	10	601	26	550	25	1
Spartanburg	3,993	1	0	1	0	0	45	5	40	0	0
Winthrop University	6,306	13	0	0	4	9	142	40	97	5	0
SOUTH DAKOTA											
South Dakota State University	9,260	1	0	0	0	1	8	0	8	0	0
TENNESSEE											
Austin Peay State University	7,033	1	0	1	0	0	73	3	70	0	0
Chattanooga State Technical Community College	8,607	0	0	0	0	0	17	1	16	0	0
Cleveland State Community College	3,177	0	0	0	0	0	0	0	0	0	0
Dyersburg State Community College	2,284	15	0	0	0	15	2	0	2	0	0
East Tennessee State University	11,331	3	0	2	0	1	144	20	121	3	2
Jackson State Community College	3,926	0	0	0	0	0	18	1	16	1	0
Middle Tennessee State University	20,073	11	0	0	5	6	233	31	197	5	2
Southwest Tennessee Community College	12,736	1	0	0	1	0	120	3	100	17	0
Tennessee State University	8,664	8	0	0	3	5	273	7	217	49	3
Tennessee Technological University	8,653	3	0	0	0	3	188	69	117	2	1
University of Memphis	20,332	6	0	2	4	0	309	50	225	34	0
University of Tennessee:											
Chattanooga	8,485	3	0	1	1	1	208	56	144	8	0
Knoxville	26,033	8	0	2	1	5	543	20	507	16	0
Martin	5,954	3	0	0	1	2	79	5	74	0	0
Memphis[4]		3	0	0	3	0	180	20	147	13	0
Vanderbilt University	10,338	31	0	5	8	18	761	87	657	17	3
Volunteer State Community College	6,822	0	0	0	0	0	22	1	21	0	0
Walters State Community College	5,995	0	0	0	0	0	6	0	6	0	0
TEXAS											
Alamo Community College District[4]		8	0	0	4	4	347	2	332	13	0
Alvin Community College	3,671	0	0	0	0	0	11	0	11	0	0
Amarillo College	8,757	0	0	0	0	0	91	9	77	5	0
Angelo State University	6,266	1	0	1	0	0	65	9	56	0	0
Austin College	1,261	0	0	0	0	0	40	4	34	2	0
Baylor Health Care System[4]		7	0	1	3	3	442	15	416	11	0
Baylor University, Waco	14,221	3	0	0	0	3	240	48	187	5	0
Central Texas College	15,473	1	0	0	0	1	37	1	36	0	0
College of the Mainland	3,346	0	0	0	0	0	22	6	14	2	0

See footnotes at end of table.

Table 9

Offenses Known to Law Enforcement
by University and College, 2003—Continued

University/College by state	Student enrollment[1]	Violent crime	Murder and non-negligent man-slaughter	Forcible rape	Robbery	Aggravated assault	Property crime	Burglary	Larceny-theft	Motor vehicle theft	Arson[2]
TEXAS—Continued											
Eastfield College	9,002	0	0	0	0	0	55	3	46	6	0
El Paso Community College	20,063	2	0	0	0	2	96	2	89	5	0
Grayson County College	3,471	0	0	0	0	0	17	5	12	0	0
Hardin-Simmons University	2,276	0	0	0	0	0	31	12	17	2	0
Houston Baptist University	2,829	0	0	0	0	0	15	3	12	0	0
Lamar University, Beaumont	11,214	4	0	2	2	0	187	22	158	7	0
Laredo Community College	7,493	1	0	1	0	0	24	7	16	1	0
McLennan Community College	6,133	0	0	0	0	0	49	2	46	1	0
Midwestern State University	5,969	1	0	1	0	0	52	8	43	1	0
Mountain View College	6,055	0	0	0	0	0	70	1	56	13	0
North Lake College	8,200	1	0	0	1	0	42	0	39	3	0
Paris Junior College	3,290	0	0	0	0	0	36	6	30	0	1
Prairie View A&M University	6,747	15	0	2	1	12	245	57	170	18	4
Rice University	4,367	3	0	0	2	1	150	1	148	1	1
Richland College	13,313	1	0	0	0	1	103	3	96	4	0
Southern Methodist University	10,266	6	0	2	3	1	222	19	195	8	1
South Plains College	8,267	0	0	0	0	0	16	3	13	0	0
Southwestern University	1,320	1	0	1	0	0	27	4	23	0	0
Stephen F. Austin State University	11,569	2	0	0	1	1	164	26	137	1	0
St. Mary's University	4,135	9	0	3	0	6	74	16	56	2	0
Sul Ross State University	2,798	1	0	1	0	0	26	2	24	0	0
Tarleton State University	8,027	0	0	0	0	0	58	8	50	0	0
Texas A&M International University	3,373	3	0	0	0	3	21	1	19	1	0
Texas A&M University:											
College Station	44,618	6	0	1	2	3	639	68	566	5	0
Commerce	7,988	6	0	2	2	2	110	23	86	1	2
Corpus Christi	7,369	1	0	0	0	1	64	5	59	0	1
Galveston	1,366	0	0	0	0	0	22	2	19	1	1
Kingsville	6,148	3	0	0	1	2	111	17	92	2	0
Texas Christian University	8,054	0	0	0	0	0	271	16	246	9	0
Texas Southern University	8,119	13	0	1	3	9	276	58	192	26	4
Texas State Technical College:											
Harlingen	3,846	2	0	1	0	1	51	2	49	0	0
Waco	4,068	15	0	1	0	14	162	66	91	5	0
Texas State University, San Marcos[4]		4	0	2	1	1	265	35	223	7	0
Texas Technological University, Lubbock	25,573	4	0	0	0	4	499	16	480	3	2
Texas Woman's University	7,928	1	0	0	0	1	66	7	54	5	0
Trinity University	2,589	3	0	1	0	2	161	13	125	23	0
Tyler Junior College	8,546	2	0	0	0	2	103	17	85	1	0
University of Houston:											
Central Campus	33,007	22	0	3	15	4	555	14	507	34	0
Clearlake	7,738	1	0	0	0	1	39	3	35	1	0
Downtown Campus	9,704	2	0	0	0	2	80	3	74	3	0
University of Mary Hardin-Baylor	2,624	0	0	0	0	0	44	4	38	2	0
University of North Texas:											
Denton	27,858	11	0	0	0	11	287	41	236	10	0
Health Science Center	821	0	0	0	0	0	14	0	14	0	0
University of Texas:											
Austin	50,616	4	0	1	2	1	598	53	535	10	1
Brownsville	9,373	1	0	0	0	1	143	1	125	17	0
Dallas	12,454	6	0	4	0	2	162	9	151	2	0
El Paso	16,220	3	0	0	0	3	221	4	212	5	1
Health Science Center, San Antonio	2,665	0	0	0	0	0	58	3	55	0	0
Health Science Center, Tyler[4]		0	0	0	0	0	20	0	20	0	0
Houston[4]		4	0	0	0	4	303	5	292	6	0
Medical Branch	1,927	1	0	0	0	1	186	2	182	2	0
Pan American	13,640	1	0	0	0	1	132	6	125	1	0
Permian Basin	2,409	0	0	0	0	0	32	6	26	0	0
San Antonio	19,881	4	0	2	0	2	150	42	106	2	0
Southwestern Medical School	1,554	1	0	0	0	1	235	4	218	13	0
Tyler	3,728	4	0	0	0	4	38	0	38	0	1
West Texas A&M University	6,675	4	0	2	0	2	77	19	58	0	0

See footnotes at end of table.

Table 9

Offenses Known to Law Enforcement
by University and College, 2003—Continued

University/College by state	Student enrollment[1]	Violent crime	Murder and non-negligent man-slaughter	Forcible rape	Robbery	Aggravated assault	Property crime	Burglary	Larceny-theft	Motor vehicle theft	Arson[2]
UTAH											
Brigham Young University	32,771	3	0	0	0	3	382	8	367	7	1
College of Eastern Utah	2,746	3	0	3	0	0	17	1	16	0	0
Southern Utah University	6,095	0	0	0	0	0	46	4	40	2	1
University of Utah	27,668	6	0	0	1	5	496	21	448	27	1
Utah State University	23,001	2	0	2	0	0	167	26	140	1	0
Utah Valley State College	22,609	1	0	0	0	1	106	6	99	1	0
Weber State University	16,873	3	0	0	0	3	136	30	106	0	0
VIRGINIA											
Christopher Newport University	5,388	2	0	2	0	0	115	5	110	0	0
College of William and Mary	7,489	2	0	1	1	0	186	4	182	0	0
George Mason University	24,897	11	0	4	1	6	342	19	296	27	3
Hampton University	5,787	2	0	0	2	0	150	36	114	0	0
James Madison University	15,562	4	0	1	0	3	205	9	192	4	1
Longwood College	4,114	1	0	0	0	1	44	0	44	0	0
Norfolk State University	6,721	21	1	2	14	4	187	69	104	14	4
Northern Virginia Community College	38,159	1	0	0	1	0	155	0	148	7	0
Radford University	9,142	7	0	3	0	4	66	0	63	3	0
Thomas Nelson Community College	7,885	0	0	0	0	0	28	0	26	2	0
University of Richmond	4,369	6	0	2	0	4	108	9	96	3	2
University of Virginia	22,739	4	0	0	2	2	243	6	234	3	0
Virginia Commonwealth University	25,001	26	0	2	7	17	482	8	463	11	3
Virginia State University	4,638	10	0	0	6	4	106	2	100	4	0
WASHINGTON											
Central Washington University	8,826	8	0	4	0	4	166	28	135	3	3
Eastern Washington University	8,932	2	0	1	0	1	112	21	91	0	0
Evergreen State College	4,227	1	0	0	0	1	80	1	73	6	0
University of Washington	37,412	8	0	2	3	3	888	74	759	55	4
Washington State University:											
Pullman	21,073	7	0	2	0	5	293	66	221	6	7
Vancouver[4]		0	0	0	0	0	15	0	14	1	0
Western Washington University	12,409	2	0	2	0	0	189	12	173	4	0
WEST VIRGINIA											
Concord College	3,072	3	0	0	0	3	27	2	25	0	0
Fairmont State College	6,724	0	0	0	0	0	58	11	47	0	1
Marshall University	16,036	2	0	0	1	1	108	12	94	2	3
West Liberty State College	2,633	1	0	0	0	1	48	2	45	1	0
West Virginia State College	4,835	2	0	0	1	1	18	5	13	0	0
West Virginia Tech	2,374	0	0	0	0	0	8	1	7	0	0
West Virginia University	22,774	1	0	0	0	1	243	2	240	1	0
WISCONSIN											
University of Wisconsin:											
Eau Claire	10,802	0	0	0	0	0	101	0	99	2	
Green Bay	5,851	2	0	2	0	0	81	1	80	0	
La Crosse	9,650	0	0	0	0	0	55	3	51	1	
Madison	40,922	13	0	5	6	2	416	32	359	25	
Milwaukee	24,216	5	0	1	0	4	263	14	248	1	
Oshkosh	11,033	3	0	2	1	0	105	13	90	2	
Parkside	4,964	1	0	1	0	0	57	1	56	0	
Platteville	5,600	2	0	0	0	2	83	4	79	0	
Stevens Point	8,832	0	0	0	0	0	93	4	88	1	
Stout	8,052	2	0	0	0	2	125	39	80	6	
Superior	2,842	4	0	3	0	1	48	12	34	2	
Whitewater	10,549	7	0	4	0	3	120	26	91	3	

See footnotes at end of table.

Table 9

Offenses Known to Law Enforcement
by University and College, 2003—Continued

University/College by state	Student enrollment[1]	Violent crime	Violent crime				Property crime	Property crime			
			Murder and non-negligent man-slaughter	Forcible rape	Robbery	Aggravated assault	Property crime	Burglary	Larceny-theft	Motor vehicle theft	Arson[2]
WYOMING											
Sheridan College	2,729	0	0	0	0	0	12	3	9	0	0
University of Wyoming	12,366	0	0	0	0	0	222	17	203	2	0

[1] The student enrollment figures provided by the United States Department of Education are for the 2001 school year, the most recent available. The enrollment figures include full-time and part-time students. See Appendix I for details.

[2] If the FBI does not receive 12 months of arson data from either the agency or the state, no arson will be shown.

[3] Due to changes in reporting practices, annexations, and/or incomplete data, figures are not comparable to previous years' data.

[4] Student enrollment figures were not available.

[5] Limited data for 2003 were available for Illinois and Kentucky.

NOTE: Caution should be exercised in making any intercampus comparisons or ranking schools, as university/college crime statistics are affected by a variety of factors. These include demographic characteristics of the surrounding community, ratio of male to female students, number of on-campus residents, accessibility of outside visitors, size of enrollment, etc.

Table 10

Offenses Known to Law Enforcement

by Metropolitan and Nonmetropolitan Counties,[1] 2003

[The data shown in this table do not reflect county totals but are the number of offenses reported by the sheriff's office or county police department.]

County by state	Violent crime	Violent crime	Violent crime	Violent crime	Violent crime	Property crime	Property crime	Property crime	Property crime	Arson[2]
	Violent crime	Murder and non-negligent man-slaughter	Forcible rape	Robbery	Aggravated assault	Property crime	Burglary	Larceny-theft	Motor vehicle theft	
ALABAMA										
Metropolitan Counties										
Autauga	62	2	12	7	41	375	114	212	49	
Blount	26	1	8	5	12	817	221	509	87	
Calhoun	23	1	4	8	10	532	164	346	22	
Chilton	378	3	19	4	352	420	145	260	15	
Colbert	95	2	1	7	85	316	121	165	30	
Elmore	33	1	14	11	7	697	248	419	30	
Geneva	25	2	2	0	21	169	62	89	18	
Greene	35	0	0	2	33	163	73	81	9	
Hale	43	0	0	2	41	161	57	83	21	
Henry	29	3	3	3	20	144	45	84	15	
Houston	18	1	4	2	11	386	128	227	31	
Jefferson	393	4	34	157	198	4,537	1,336	2,773	428	
Lauderdale	31	2	3	3	23	604	193	383	28	
Lawrence	26	1	3	3	19	459	138	283	38	
Lee	88	1	12	14	61	1,210	381	735	94	
Limestone	31	1	4	1	25	398	135	209	54	
Lowndes	40	3	7	16	14	266	142	73	51	
Madison	155	1	20	29	105	2,095	653	1,236	206	
Mobile	301	4	29	45	223	2,456	910	1,407	139	6
Montgomery	93	3	11	18	61	784	219	477	88	
Morgan	21	0	1	9	11	482	222	238	22	
Shelby	83	1	19	29	34	740	268	390	82	
St. Clair	45	1	13	7	24	444	115	301	28	
Tuscaloosa	215	0	10	19	186	1,898	591	1,088	219	
Walker	56	0	3	17	36	1,379	545	701	133	
Nonmetropolitan Counties										
Baldwin	71	0	39	3	29	699	259	440	0	
Cullman	124	2	16	11	95	1,808	566	1,091	151	
Jackson	49	2	12	1	34	693	250	326	117	
Marshall	44	1	7	2	34	368	133	190	45	
Talladega	69	0	5	12	52	558	157	345	56	
ARIZONA										
Metropolitan Counties										
Coconino	111	1	8	7	95	733	206	477	50	6
Maricopa	611	25	50	81	455	6,884	2,063	3,653	1,168	20
Pima	799	28	77	174	520	12,345	2,352	8,235	1,758	132
Pinal[3]	203	5	33	36	129	2,985	718	1,732	535	14
Yavapai	285	5	14	12	254	1,969	587	1,210	172	1
Yuma	356	3	3	12	338	1,353	547	611	195	0
Nonmetropolitan Counties										
Apache	71	1	1	1	68	264	88	169	7	3
Cochise	677	4	25	13	635	1,290	366	711	213	18
Gila	122	0	5	0	117	703	330	315	58	2
Mohave	190	6	0	10	174	2,704	893	1,539	272	27
Navajo	72	0	9	4	59	646	360	242	44	4
ARKANSAS[3]										
Metropolitan Counties										
Benton	60	2	13	4	41	261	66	163	32	5
Cleveland	6	0	0	2	4	177	96	67	14	20
Craighead	51	0	1	7	43	451	139	273	39	6
Faulkner	155	2	5	1	147	617	181	385	51	1
Grant	3	0	2	1	0	30	16	13	1	1
Jefferson	85	2	8	9	66	287	215	69	3	10
Lonoke	32	0	6	0	26	320	138	174	8	2
Miller	63	1	9	4	49	316	90	201	25	10

See footnotes at end of table.

Table 10

Offenses Known to Law Enforcement

by Metropolitan and Nonmetropolitan Counties,[1] 2003—Continued

[The data shown in this table do not reflect county totals but are the number of offenses reported by the sheriff's office or county police department.]

County by state	Violent crime	Murder and non-negligent man-slaughter	Forcible rape	Robbery	Aggravated assault	Property crime	Burglary	Larceny-theft	Motor vehicle theft	Arson[2]
ARKANSAS[3]—Continued										
Metropolitan Counties—Continued										
Poinsett	8	0	0	2	6	120	101	14	5	5
Pulaski	182	4	24	32	122	2,016	343	1,482	191	13
Sebastian	48	1	5	2	40	200	154	44	2	2
Nonmetropolitan Counties										
Baxter	46	0	7	0	39	366	73	265	28	1
Independence	28	0	2	1	25	1,078	363	671	44	1
Pope	38	0	7	3	28	372	132	228	12	0
CALIFORNIA										
Metropolitan Counties										
Alameda	513	8	49	182	274	3,366	760	1,827	779	52
Contra Costa	554	9	31	115	399	3,710	914	2,788	8	23
El Dorado	233	2	24	23	184	2,227	729	1,478	20	13
Fresno[3]	771	11	59	141	560	6,185	1,774	3,306	1,105	387
Imperial	224	8	7	9	200	750	249	482	19	27
Kern	1,809	15	119	283	1,392	10,532	3,400	5,546	1,586	257
Kings	103	3	7	16	77	493	196	291	6	3
Los Angeles	7,971	144	225	1,756	5,846	20,591	4,921	9,463	6,207	539
Madera	338	5	17	21	295	1,457	658	778	21	7
Marin	211	0	5	33	173	1,126	263	862	1	5
Merced	466	7	20	49	390	1,997	941	1,029	27	9
Monterey	222	5	27	62	128	2,257	656	1,583	18	31
Napa	37	2	10	1	24	427	138	277	12	4
Orange	210	3	9	38	160	1,612	323	1,042	247	26
Placer	152	2	21	20	109	1,999	691	1,231	77	20
Riverside	2,374	29	85	304	1,956	12,492	3,135	6,673	2,684	72
Sacramento	4,069	38	295	1,262	2,474	25,379	6,484	17,670	1,225	305
San Benito	45	0	5	4	36	330	174	147	9	2
San Bernardino	1,136	32	57	229	818	7,575	2,463	3,387	1,725	125
San Diego	1,272	17	84	221	950	8,876	2,621	4,389	1,866	50
San Joaquin	926	15	21	156	734	5,009	1,486	3,271	252	27
San Luis Obispo	156	1	20	10	125	1,352	438	910	4	16
San Mateo	78	2	10	44	22	1,684	201	1,268	215	17
Santa Barbara	215	1	37	34	143	1,697	535	1,151	11	20
Santa Clara	352	1	42	39	270	2,059	475	1,354	230	5
Santa Cruz	325	5	22	32	266	2,549	712	1,821	16	21
Shasta	298	2	26	15	255	1,325	566	698	61	42
Solano	162	0	16	18	128	547	274	250	23	35
Stanislaus	925	6	41	181	697	4,562	1,157	2,568	837	322
Sutter	125	3	9	6	107	899	346	508	45	2
Tulare[3]	630	11	33	68	518		1,045	2,066		594
Ventura	194	9	15	21	149	1,098	313	650	135	23
Yolo	75	1	9	6	59	371	136	230	5	12
Yuba	230	3	23	36	168	1,511	614	888	9	29
Nonmetropolitan Counties										
Calaveras	207	2	14	10	181	613	229	379	5	10
Humboldt	104	7	13	10	74	1,121	335	778	8	11
Lake	231	0	9	19	203	909	389	511	9	3
Mendocino	262	6	14	17	225	901	387	503	11	10
Nevada	124	2	12	5	105	987	344	625	18	7
Tehama	104	0	5	6	93	742	303	439	0	30
Tuolumne	204	4	13	13	174	1,169	540	619	10	9
COLORADO										
Metropolitan Counties										
Adams	432	8	36	53	335	4,313	958	2,482	873	50
Arapahoe	264	2	35	28	199	1,832	462	1,126	244	24

See footnotes at end of table.

Table 10

Offenses Known to Law Enforcement

by Metropolitan and Nonmetropolitan Counties,[1] 2003—Continued

[The data shown in this table do not reflect county totals but are the number of offenses reported by the sheriff's office or county police department.]

County by state	Violent crime	Murder and non-negligent man-slaughter	Forcible rape	Robbery	Aggravated assault	Property crime	Burglary	Larceny-theft	Motor vehicle theft	Arson[2]
COLORADO—Continued										
Metropolitan Counties—Continued										
Boulder	108	0	16	0	92	938	199	690	49	11
Broomfield	32	0	4	7	21	1,626	158	1,373	95	10
Clear Creek	9	0	4	0	5	99	19	73	7	0
Douglas	176	3	56	19	98	3,010	540	2,236	234	27
Gilpin	11	0	0	0	11	58	17	38	3	1
Jefferson	331	3	36	43	249	3,520	654	2,523	343	40
Larimer	109	0	26	9	74	1,534	325	1,105	104	28
Mesa	87	1	1	15	70	1,424	325	984	115	27
Park	5	0	2	0	3	81	37	41	3	0
Pueblo	40	1	1	7	31	1,349	324	978	47	2
Teller	1	0	0	0	1	97	33	55	9	0
Weld	131	1	25	7	98	1,218	343	652	223	22
Nonmetropolitan Counties										
Eagle	30	0	6	2	22	580	58	517	5	7
Fremont	25	0	1	2	22	193	32	154	7	2
La Plata	16	0	3	0	13	311	92	194	25	0
DELAWARE										
Metropolitan Counties										
New Castle County Police Department	1,312	6	124	262	920	6,667	1,882	3,784	1,001	13
FLORIDA										
Metropolitan Counties										
Alachua	861	2	50	88	721	3,871	1,160	2,409	302	24
Baker	99	0	1	10	88	427	89	296	42	8
Bay	475	2	61	56	356	3,543	596	2,728	219	0
Brevard	1,245	7	79	142	1,017	5,457	1,582	3,449	426	44
Broward	831	7	71	164	589	2,218	522	1,342	354	12
Charlotte	398	4	24	47	323	4,115	1,118	2,774	223	4
Clay	431	3	37	61	330	2,774	605	1,955	214	23
Collier	1,367	10	101	220	1,036	6,451	1,751	4,285	415	40
Escambia	1,493	8	111	305	1,069	9,545	2,546	6,378	621	27
Gadsden	152	4	13	24	111	615	230	334	51	3
Gilchrist	78	0	0	3	75	294	81	200	13	0
Hernando	884	5	69	60	750	4,471	1,240	2,933	298	53
Hillsborough	5,515	29	313	1,077	4,096	31,976	6,677	21,417	3,882	172
Indian River	290	3	52	39	196	2,979	642	2,172	165	10
Jefferson	64	0	7	2	55	134	32	85	17	6
Lake	681	1	37	33	610	3,326	1,246	1,784	296	15
Lee	1,310	14	88	342	866	9,961	2,964	5,838	1,159	131
Leon	411	2	29	43	337	1,737	783	773	181	23
Manatee	1,775	8	62	338	1,367	9,887	2,511	6,652	724	44
Marion	1,340	8	116	79	1,137	4,762	1,540	2,882	340	10
Martin	456	4	18	105	329	3,201	730	2,294	177	10
Miami-Dade	11,583	95	588	3,019	7,881	67,939	11,565	46,719	9,655	194
Nassau	791	4	15	15	757	1,018	440	473	105	0
Okaloosa	393	3	27	82	281	3,288	653	2,432	203	5
Orange	5,143	38	294	1,339	3,472	30,505	7,336	19,258	3,911	0
Osceola	666	1	68	93	504	4,794	1,928	2,513	353	11
Palm Beach	2,931	24	225	678	2,004	21,778	5,074	13,782	2,922	138
Pasco	1,400	15	160	167	1,058	10,266	2,699	6,748	819	51
Pinellas	1,138	7	167	154	810	8,512	2,139	5,698	675	34
Polk	1,546	16	73	182	1,275	9,953	3,086	5,983	884	0
Santa Rosa	297	0	36	23	238	1,915	595	1,229	91	7
Sarasota	798	7	46	111	634	8,453	2,002	6,016	435	11
Seminole	599	7	38	79	475	3,785	890	2,629	266	6
St. Johns	459	3	6	52	398	2,472	587	1,705	180	4
St. Lucie	399	1	27	55	316	2,189	710	1,275	204	21

See footnotes at end of table.

Table 10

Offenses Known to Law Enforcement

by Metropolitan and Nonmetropolitan Counties,[1] 2003—Continued

[The data shown in this table do not reflect county totals but are the number of offenses reported by the sheriff's office or county police department.]

County by state	Violent crime	Murder and non-negligent man-slaughter	Forcible rape	Robbery	Aggravated assault	Property crime	Burglary	Larceny-theft	Motor vehicle theft	Arson[2]
FLORIDA—Continued										
Metropolitan Counties—Continued										
Volusia	1,052	8	104	115	825	4,918	1,324	3,012	582	42
Wakulla	123	0	16	5	102	566	172	348	46	14
Nonmetropolitan Counties										
Citrus	358	2	41	13	302	2,018	480	1,413	125	5
Columbia	261	1	21	20	219	1,416	539	753	124	14
DeSoto	132	1	7	16	108	882	457	394	31	1
Flagler	162	2	6	26	128	1,123	273	779	71	2
Hendry	176	8	11	30	127	717	200	451	66	3
Highlands	149	1	30	16	102	1,614	633	869	112	3
Jackson	138	3	3	11	121	649	195	423	31	0
Levy	171	2	29	6	134	809	276	470	63	14
Monroe	267	3	24	27	213	2,324	401	1,774	149	11
Okeechobee	203	1	14	24	164	687	303	338	46	7
Putnam	628	3	29	52	544	1,813	774	857	182	12
Sumter	159	4	14	19	122	802	230	510	62	1
Suwannee	99	1	6	9	83	643	202	376	65	2
Walton	107	1	3	6	97	863	240	570	53	5
GEORGIA										
Metropolitan Counties										
Augusta-Richmond	1,039	31	154	448	406	11,240	2,234	7,853	1,153	
Bartow	72	0	1	14	57	1,954	545	1,122	287	0
Bibb	96	2	22	19	53	2,784	692	1,779	313	
Brantley	25	1	3	1	20	433	147	254	32	1
Brooks	77	0	0	1	76	221	72	128	21	2
Bryan	26	0	1	6	19	533	81	442	10	0
Burke	163	1	0	3	159	446	138	289	19	0
Butts	45	2	5	11	27	582	109	387	86	0
Catoosa	40	2	2	11	25	1,051	236	700	115	
Chatham County Police Department	184	8	11	65	100	2,754	723	1,777	254	4
Chattahoochee	7	0	2	0	5	48	25	20	3	3
Clayton County Police Department	949	20	70	455	404	8,620	2,443	4,531	1,646	31
Cobb County Police Department	1,053	24	105	383	541	12,283	2,745	7,918	1,620	78
Columbia	63	3	19	12	29	1,846	278	1,487	81	8
Coweta	47	0	3	16	28	1,219	346	687	186	9
Crawford	13	0	1	0	12	369	117	226	26	
Dade	11	0	2	2	7	152	49	88	15	
Dawson	25	1	1	3	20	424	80	293	51	3
DeKalb	2	0	0	1	1	1	0	1	0	0
DeKalb County Police Department[3]	3,175	80	159	1,974	962	34,547	7,548	19,733	7,266	148
Dougherty County Police Department	29	1	6	14	8	361	102	231	28	1
Douglas	149	4	8	26	111	1,877	381	1,269	227	1
Effingham	64	0	4	6	54	586	202	308	76	
Fayette	33	4	1	13	15	519	81	399	39	2
Floyd County Police Department	76	4	0	8	64	1,676	438	1,094	144	
Forsyth	246	3	20	10	213	2,308	515	1,577	216	
Fulton	25	0	2	3	20	46	4	39	3	0
Fulton County Police Department	782	11	42	472	257	8,009	1,846	4,968	1,195	28
Glynn County Police Department[3]		1	16	59		4,266	534	3,624	108	6
Gwinnett County Police Department	1,398	33	149	624	592	15,901	4,071	9,710	2,120	113
Hall	228	6	23	27	172	3,133	740	1,968	425	7
Haralson	32	0	4	1	27	522	171	242	109	
Jones	19	1	2	1	15	576	112	403	61	
Lee	43	0	6	8	29	537	104	401	32	0
Liberty	56	0	5	17	34	654	140	482	32	
Long	30	0	0	5	25	164	80	75	9	3
Lowndes	95	0	16	14	65	1,118	262	788	68	
Madison	50	1	0	6	43	608	176	361	71	6
Marion	8	0	0	0	8	6	4	2	0	0

See footnotes at end of table.

Table 10

Offenses Known to Law Enforcement

by Metropolitan and Nonmetropolitan Counties,[1] 2003—Continued

[The data shown in this table do not reflect county totals but are the number of offenses reported by the sheriff's office or county police department.]

County by state	Violent crime	Murder and non-negligent man-slaughter	Forcible rape	Robbery	Aggravated assault	Property crime	Burglary	Larceny-theft	Motor vehicle theft	Arson[2]
		Violent crime				*Property crime*				
GEORGIA—Continued										
Metropolitan Counties—Continued										
McDuffie	39	1	3	3	32	404	85	284	35	0
McIntosh	18	0	0	0	18	225	63	144	18	
Meriwether	35	0	2	4	29	389	116	201	72	1
Monroe	10	0	2	3	5	361	128	196	37	0
Murray	53	1	0	0	52	651	244	357	50	0
Newton	63	4	4	19	36	1,269	385	706	178	7
Oconee	18	0	1	4	13	415	78	308	29	0
Oglethorpe	58	1	6	0	51	285	70	186	29	0
Paulding	203	1	12	8	182	2,030	488	1,251	291	5
Pickens	13	0	0	0	13	452	163	230	59	0
Pike	12	0	0	2	10	174	48	94	32	1
Rockdale	184	0	18	33	133	2,267	517	1,545	205	8
Spalding	142	1	11	26	104	1,225	299	787	139	0
Terrell	22	0	0	3	19	104	35	58	11	0
Walker	23	1	2	7	13	811	239	514	58	35
Walton	26	0	0	8	18	762	224	424	114	2
Whitfield	160	3	11	18	128	2,326	563	1,494	269	11
Worth	13	0	1	1	11	153	50	88	15	0
Nonmetropolitan Counties										
Baldwin	67	0	2	11	54	614	163	422	29	
Bulloch	42	0	1	12	29	594	153	407	34	
Habersham	31	1	6	2	22	426	131	251	44	1
Jackson	42	1	3	6	32	819	238	502	79	
Laurens	81	2	7	5	67	603	189	364	50	4
Troup	12	1	0	5	6	1,141	151	935	55	0
HAWAII										
Nonmetropolitan Counties										
Hawaii Police Department	295	6	48	77	164	6,838	1,437	4,924	477	48
Kauai Police Department	188	0	29	20	139	2,855	660	2,036	159	8
Maui Police Department	311	1	24	82	204	7,868	1,345	5,761	762	64
IDAHO										
Metropolitan Counties										
Ada	109	2	14	3	90	1,633	382	1,166	85	14
Bannock	37	0	5	0	32	246	64	177	5	5
Bonneville	73	0	23	3	47	767	186	524	57	6
Canyon	98	1	12	5	80	828	299	417	112	7
Franklin	0	0	0	0	0	30	1	29	0	0
Gem	4	0	0	1	3	28	14	12	2	4
Jefferson	19	0	1	1	17	121	25	93	3	0
Kootenai	122	0	21	5	96	1,170	397	695	78	17
Nez Perce	9	0	1	0	8	85	19	59	7	0
Owyhee	22	0	6	0	16	120	24	84	12	0
Power	7	0	1	0	6	57	7	46	4	1
Nonmetropolitan Counties										
Bingham	17	0	3	1	13	280	71	182	27	0
Bonner	58	4	11	5	38	470	89	334	47	5
ILLINOIS[4]										
INDIANA										
Metropolitan Counties										
Allen	72	0	18	21	33	1,717	324	1,256	137	5
Bartholomew	19	1	1	1	16	297	29	263	5	0
Brown	3	1	0	1	1	71	33	38	0	0

See footnotes at end of table.

Table 10

Offenses Known to Law Enforcement
by Metropolitan and Nonmetropolitan Counties,[1] 2003—Continued
[The data shown in this table do not reflect county totals but are the number of offenses reported by the sheriff's office or county police department.]

County by state	Violent crime	Violent crime — Murder and non-negligent man-slaughter	Violent crime — Forcible rape	Violent crime — Robbery	Violent crime — Aggravated assault	Property crime	Property crime — Burglary	Property crime — Larceny-theft	Property crime — Motor vehicle theft	Arson[2]
INDIANA—Continued										
Metropolitan Counties—Continued										
Clark	72	1	7	6	58	451	240	163	48	0
Clay	17	1	1	1	14	155	41	99	15	0
Dearborn	46	1	0	0	45	115	101	10	4	1
Delaware	55	0	34	1	20	673	122	475	76	0
Elkhart	48	2	12	14	20	1,961	472	1,243	246	18
Floyd	28	0	0	1	27	648	136	462	50	0
Franklin	10	0	1	0	9	211	80	115	16	2
Gibson	7	2	4	0	1	2	0	0	2	0
Greene	20	0	2	1	17	242	75	152	15	1
Hamilton	16	2	1	4	9	528	188	288	52	8
Hancock	12	0	2	4	6	270	81	178	11	2
Harrison	42	0	4	3	35	896	400	436	60	3
Hendricks	139	1	4	12	122	858	261	517	80	5
Howard	61	0	2	7	52	640	142	447	51	1
Johnson	29	0	1	1	27	500	99	374	27	1
Lake	48	0	6	13	29	641	128	390	123	2
La Porte	50	2	2	9	37	850	218	586	46	1
Madison	14	2	5	3	4	342	93	212	37	1
Monroe	93	2	2	5	84	601	216	347	38	6
Newton	6	0	1	2	3	165	52	106	7	0
Porter	38	0	5	5	28	1,189	172	924	93	1
Putnam	191	0	11	4	176	349	159	158	32	4
Shelby	51	0	1	3	47	343	92	214	37	3
St. Joseph	87	1	13	30	43	2,114	474	1,519	121	24
Tippecanoe	31	1	9	4	17	831	207	581	43	12
Vanderburgh	192	0	6	7	179	1,025	110	860	55	6
Warrick	126	0	2	10	114	535	114	413	8	6
Wells	5	0	0	1	4	137	38	79	20	1
Nonmetropolitan Counties										
Grant	8	1	1	4	2	419	112	279	28	4
Henry	8	1	2	1	4	770	223	510	37	1
Kosciusko	19	0	5	5	9	701	152	518	31	7
Lagrange	34	0	0	3	31	213	67	136	10	1
Lawrence	8	0	1	0	7	213	65	137	11	4
Steuben	17	1	5	2	9	617	156	430	31	0
Wayne	6	1	1	0	4	143	46	87	10	2
IOWA										
Metropolitan Counties										
Benton	2	0	0	0	2	36	15	18	3	0
Black Hawk	2	0	0	0	2	2	0	1	1	0
Bremer	8	0	0	0	8	53	16	35	2	0
Dallas	3	0	1	0	2	159	63	83	13	4
Dubuque	37	0	6	0	31	208	60	115	33	2
Grundy	0	0	0	0	0	81	27	53	1	0
Guthrie	0	0	0	0	0	50	15	34	1	0
Harrison	4	0	0	0	4	168	59	90	19	4
Johnson	77	0	4	3	70	326	109	190	27	0
Jones	6	0	2	0	4	64	11	48	5	0
Linn	42	0	4	1	37	413	141	228	44	10
Madison	5	0	0	0	5	75	24	43	8	3
Mills	29	0	2	1	26	249	70	119	60	7
Polk	180	1	11	13	155	1,114	283	692	139	5
Pottawattamie	29	0	10	0	19	646	219	334	93	1
Scott	55	0	5	2	48	253	53	171	29	2
Story	13	0	1	0	12	178	62	100	16	1
Warren	18	1	2	1	14	340	122	194	24	3
Washington	22	0	6	0	16	85	54	27	4	0
Woodbury	50	0	1	1	48	157	51	97	9	1

See footnotes at end of table.

Table 10

Offenses Known to Law Enforcement
by Metropolitan and Nonmetropolitan Counties,[1] 2003—Continued
[The data shown in this table do not reflect county totals but are the number of offenses reported by the sheriff's office or county police department.]

County by state	Violent crime	Murder and non-negligent man-slaughter	Forcible rape	Robbery	Aggravated assault	Property crime	Burglary	Larceny-theft	Motor vehicle theft	Arson[2]
KANSAS										
Metropolitan Counties										
Butler	41	1	3	0	37	380	118	233	29	5
Doniphan	4	0	0	0	4	45	12	22	11	1
Douglas	32	1	3	0	28	226	89	123	14	3
Franklin	30	0	2	2	26	202	70	112	20	7
Harvey	3	0	0	0	3	118	27	84	7	2
Jackson	34	0	2	1	31	124	45	68	11	4
Jefferson	29	0	6	0	23	382	93	260	29	5
Leavenworth	30	0	2	3	25	247	94	118	35	22
Linn	21	0	1	0	20	133	51	68	14	11
Miami	30	0	5	0	25	265	104	138	23	17
Osage	27	0	2	1	24	177	73	86	18	6
Sedgwick	188	1	12	10	165	956	274	629	53	7
Shawnee	85	1	11	9	64	920	221	616	83	12
Sumner	7	2	2	0	3	110	36	69	5	4
Wabaunsee	13	0	1	0	12	121	23	92	6	3
Wyandotte	5	0	0	1	4	4	1	1	2	0
Nonmetropolitan Counties										
Riley County Police Department	185	1	29	13	142	1,732	273	1,389	70	22
KENTUCKY[4]										
Metropolitan Counties										
Boone	155	0	34	15	106	1,215	281	852	82	6
Campbell County Police Department	40	0	23	1	16	193	51	122	20	4
Daviess	60	1	0	6	53	552	179	348	25	1
Woodford	0	0	0	0	0	23	7	16	0	0
LOUISIANA										
Metropolitan Counties										
Ascension	349	7	26	34	282	2,752	611	1,873	268	9
Bossier	58	0	8	0	50	685	119	546	20	3
Caddo	165	7	15	11	132	1,370	332	954	84	0
Calcasieu	267	7	49	59	152	3,616	842	2,550	224	15
Cameron	45	0	2	1	42	242	39	179	24	0
De Soto	136	1	1	2	132	433	157	253	23	0
East Baton Rouge	638	6	55	196	381	10,353	1,678	8,109	566	23
Grant	34	1	1	0	32	458	123	303	32	1
Iberville	188	1	2	1	184	430	72	347	11	2
Jefferson	2,304	41	131	692	1,440	17,065	3,382	11,470	2,213	174
Lafayette	204	2	27	28	147	1,492	484	878	130	18
Lafourche	173	2	25	24	122	1,897	305	1,489	103	10
Livingston	304	1	18	14	271	1,147	744	368	35	3
Ouachita	301	1	33	22	245	2,391	826	1,481	84	6
Plaquemines	82	1	6	13	62	439	142	238	59	0
Pointe Coupee	64	0	2	2	60	290	70	176	44	2
Rapides	299	1	13	12	273	1,713	622	962	129	0
St. Bernard	181	3	3	30	145	1,547	296	1,056	195	1
St. Charles	279	3	13	37	226	1,566	435	1,030	101	7
St. Helena	51	1	1	2	47	139	39	82	18	0
St. John the Baptist	89	3	1	36	49	1,045	189	741	115	9
St. Tammany	372	4	29	39	300	2,863	765	1,832	266	34
Terrebonne	342	3	29	46	264	3,421	928	2,279	214	12
Union	10	1	0	0	9	157	38	112	7	0
West Baton Rouge	90	1	3	22	64	767	57	669	41	1
West Feliciana	35	0	0	1	34	108	13	93	2	0
Nonmetropolitan Counties										
Acadia	23	2	3	10	8	637	126	495	16	1
St. Landry	172	2	6	14	150	1,032	337	613	82	3

See footnotes at end of table.

Table 10

Offenses Known to Law Enforcement
by Metropolitan and Nonmetropolitan Counties,[1] 2003—Continued

[The data shown in this table do not reflect county totals but are the number of offenses reported by the sheriff's office or county police department.]

County by state	Violent crime	Murder and non-negligent man-slaughter	Forcible rape	Robbery	Aggravated assault	Property crime	Burglary	Larceny-theft	Motor vehicle theft	Arson[2]
LOUISIANA—Continued										
Nonmetropolitan Counties—Continued										
Tangipahoa	702	6	20	59	617	2,717	1,066	1,545	106	9
Vermilion	38	1	1	2	34	275	47	210	18	0
Washington	53	3	6	12	32	339	112	193	34	1
MAINE										
Metropolitan Counties										
Androscoggin	1	0	0	0	1	324	66	237	21	3
Cumberland	27	0	9	2	16	690	254	392	44	3
Penobscot	11	0	2	0	9	601	210	368	23	1
Sagadahoc	4	0	0	0	4	204	73	119	12	2
York	15	0	0	0	15	386	156	182	48	2
Nonmetropolitan Counties										
Aroostook	2	0	0	0	2	107	38	61	8	0
Hancock	6	0	0	1	5	243	76	153	14	0
Kennebec	11	0	4	1	6	461	134	306	21	0
Somerset	21	0	4	0	17	296	153	121	22	1
Waldo	29	0	3	1	25	335	95	216	24	0
MARYLAND										
Metropolitan Counties										
Allegany	11	0	1	1	9	143	42	94	7	0
Anne Arundel	0	0	0	0	0	0	0	0	0	0
Anne Arundel County Police Department	3,097	19	76	610	2,392	15,573	2,698	11,647	1,228	137
Baltimore	0	0	0	0	0	0	0	0	0	0
Baltimore County Police Department	6,170	31	211	1,609	4,319	27,670	5,372	18,986	3,312	314
Calvert	201	2	7	15	177	1,072	250	753	69	0
Carroll	24	0	0	1	23	126	33	88	5	0
Cecil	61	0	2	6	53	651	210	382	59	0
Charles	742	3	38	148	553	4,099	690	2,842	567	0
Frederick	168	1	8	13	146	1,220	243	890	87	2
Harford	530	5	25	109	391	2,833	710	1,939	184	0
Howard	0	0	0	0	0	0	0	0	0	0
Howard County Police Department	543	7	46	222	268	6,959	1,157	5,122	680	72
Montgomery	10	0	4	0	6	0	0	0	0	0
Montgomery County Police Department	2,115	21	134	1,004	956	25,458	4,094	17,875	3,489	201
Prince George's	0	0	0	0	0	0	0	0	0	0
Prince George's County Police Department	6,917	116	245	3,553	3,003	44,675	7,331	22,007	15,337	464
Queen Anne's	144	0	5	12	127	621	136	460	25	2
Somerset	0	0	0	0	0	13	4	9	0	0
Washington	147	1	4	18	124	1,055	229	735	91	0
Wicomico	143	1	12	23	107	874	301	529	44	2
Nonmetropolitan Counties										
Garrett	27	0	3	0	24	284	58	221	5	0
St. Mary's	241	1	6	33	201	1,514	366	1,054	94	15
MICHIGAN										
Metropolitan Counties										
Barry	43	0	12	1	30	220	68	136	16	1
Bay	29	1	12	5	11	763	162	542	59	5
Berrien	106	1	14	8	83	684	179	457	48	1
Calhoun	53	0	6	2	45	433	153	235	45	2
Cass	53	0	13	9	31	927	308	557	62	9
Clinton	9	0	0	0	9	311	97	188	26	4
Eaton	129	2	28	26	73	1,688	350	1,236	102	5
Genesee	63	1	15	10	37	683	150	470	63	2
Ingham	144	0	61	16	67	932	351	490	91	6

See footnotes at end of table.

Table 10

Offenses Known to Law Enforcement

by Metropolitan and Nonmetropolitan Counties,[1] 2003—Continued

[The data shown in this table do not reflect county totals but are the number of offenses reported by the sheriff's office or county police department.]

County by state	Violent crime	Murder and non-negligent man-slaughter	Forcible rape	Robbery	Aggravated assault	Property crime	Burglary	Larceny-theft	Motor vehicle theft	Arson[2]
MICHIGAN—Continued										
Metropolitan Counties—Continued										
Ionia	40	0	11	0	29	382	109	247	26	1
Jackson	69	1	21	4	43	624	161	396	67	8
Kalamazoo	218	0	48	26	144	2,387	635	1,530	222	29
Kent	348	3	70	43	232	4,499	1,046	3,220	233	37
Lapeer	55	1	16	4	34	488	111	352	25	4
Livingston	60	0	12	5	43	834	190	561	83	9
Macomb	251	5	83	13	150	1,998	337	1,507	154	23
Monroe	223	1	47	28	147	2,658	620	1,824	214	59
Muskegon	111	1	21	6	83	1,567	250	1,237	80	25
Newaygo	80	0	27	2	51	436	198	222	16	3
Oakland	540	2	66	62	410	4,761	801	3,585	375	68
Ottawa	281	1	114	13	153	2,906	653	2,079	174	25
Saginaw	127	1	21	15	90	902	188	649	65	7
St. Clair	158	2	33	19	104	1,736	478	1,102	156	23
Van Buren	53	1	11	4	37	657	203	399	55	5
Washtenaw	307	6	61	51	189	2,422	726	1,269	427	21
Wayne[3]	90	4	2	24	60	241	42	131	68	1
Nonmetropolitan Counties										
Allegan	110	1	35	2	72	595	184	361	50	1
Branch	28	0	2	0	26	220	53	164	3	4
Clare	43	0	5	0	38	853	364	434	55	17
Grand Traverse	86	0	27	6	53	1,123	189	888	46	9
Hillsdale	34	0	10	0	24	279	88	179	12	1
Isabella	41	0	9	3	29	475	168	273	34	9
Lenawee	34	0	12	2	20	474	164	290	20	1
Mecosta	36	0	10	3	23	716	223	445	48	10
Midland	59	0	22	0	37	489	142	324	23	6
Montcalm	70	0	29	3	38	555	210	301	44	14
Sanilac	27	2	7	0	18	262	87	159	16	1
Shiawassee	81	1	16	5	59	483	110	339	34	4
St. Joseph	39	1	13	1	24	418	135	263	20	7
Tuscola	28	0	6	0	22	298	107	170	21	2
MINNESOTA										
Metropolitan Counties										
Carlton	31	1	16	1	13	345	84	229	32	1
Carver	50	0	9	3	38	829	117	650	62	5
Clay	9	1	2	1	5	112	35	67	10	0
Dakota	15	0	0	2	13	222	82	117	23	2
Dodge	23	0	12	0	11	242	73	152	17	0
Hennepin	25	1	12	1	11	142	26	103	13	1
Houston	9	0	2	0	7	125	21	95	9	5
Isanti	22	0	8	0	14	266	66	155	45	2
Olmsted	34	0	10	4	20	433	149	244	40	6
Ramsey	17	0	4	0	13	323	29	271	23	4
Sherburne	48	0	6	3	39	602	95	454	53	5
St. Louis	83	1	25	1	56	977	452	443	82	5
Wabasha	4	0	0	0	4	83	23	57	3	0
Washington	73	0	7	3	63	1,152	191	866	95	3
Wright	60	0	14	5	41	2,037	241	1,674	122	10
Nonmetropolitan Counties										
Beltrami	40	0	13	3	24	536	172	307	57	8
Cass	119	4	76	4	35	1,235	313	806	116	2
Crow Wing	22	0	5	1	16	851	295	496	60	5
Itasca	24	0	2	2	20	572	257	278	37	6
Otter Tail	38	0	11	1	26	568	188	326	54	2

See footnotes at end of table.

Table 10

Offenses Known to Law Enforcement
by Metropolitan and Nonmetropolitan Counties,[1] 2003—Continued

[The data shown in this table do not reflect county totals but are the number of offenses reported by the sheriff's office or county police department.]

County by state	Violent crime	Violent crime — Murder and non-negligent man-slaughter	Violent crime — Forcible rape	Violent crime — Robbery	Violent crime — Aggravated assault	Property crime	Property crime — Burglary	Property crime — Larceny-theft	Property crime — Motor vehicle theft	Arson[2]
MISSISSIPPI										
Metropolitan Counties										
Harrison	53	4	13	20	16	1,783	423	1,273	87	15
Hinds	48	3	5	17	23	925	380	417	128	10
Jackson	125	1	19	17	88	1,998	589	1,175	234	0
Lamar	31	3	11	4	13	625	183	376	66	2
Madison	93	4	8	9	72	477	152	247	78	4
Rankin	35	2	4	6	23	866	331	465	70	6
Stone	16	0	3	1	12	164	53	100	11	0
Tate	114	0	0	0	114	363	176	144	43	4
Tunica	65	2	9	45	9	681	138	323	220	0
Nonmetropolitan Counties										
Lauderdale	39	6	6	9	18	493	256	208	29	1
Lowndes	79	0	21	7	51	582	180	371	31	5
Panola	130	1	4	7	118	363	194	152	17	4
Pearl River	28	1	9	15	3	761	321	370	70	4
MISSOURI										
Metropolitan Counties										
Andrew	4	0	0	2	2	148	37	103	8	0
Boone	66	1	6	15	44	871	168	627	76	2
Buchanan	11	0	3	0	8	267	81	158	28	6
Caldwell	3	0	0	0	3	43	22	17	4	0
Callaway	26	0	2	8	16	494	127	329	38	2
Cass	83	1	8	5	69	446	114	251	81	5
Christian	64	2	6	0	56	519	176	293	50	4
Clay	36	0	3	0	33	169	62	94	13	1
Clinton	39	0	2	1	36	92	34	49	9	2
Cole	44	0	7	5	32	342	103	223	16	3
Dallas	1	0	0	0	1	103	53	44	6	0
De Kalb	17	0	2	0	15	60	20	33	7	1
Franklin	69	0	5	6	58	1,089	267	731	91	4
Greene	24	1	4	4	15	1,401	346	963	92	0
Howard	3	0	0	0	3	39	19	19	1	1
Jackson	79	0	2	9	68	637	210	359	68	3
Jasper	13	0	8	3	2	493	165	275	53	0
Jefferson	385	2	25	8	350	3,034	458	2,212	364	10
Lafayette	40	0	3	3	34	133	71	57	5	0
Lincoln	47	1	0	0	46	242	77	123	42	6
McDonald	54	0	4	4	46	351	149	158	44	6
Moniteau	16	0	1	0	15	60	30	29	1	2
Newton	151	0	4	4	143	886	210	603	73	13
Osage	7	0	0	0	7	116	60	41	15	1
Platte	32	0	1	1	30	371	82	260	29	9
Polk	53	0	6	1	46	362	116	203	43	1
Ray	21	0	2	1	18	151	48	82	21	0
St. Charles	211	1	8	11	191	1,371	319	969	83	26
St. Louis County Police Department	898	5	39	185	669	10,464	1,670	7,332	1,462	107
Warren	41	0	3	0	38	190	68	105	17	0
Washington	27	0	3	0	24	150	50	75	25	2
Webster	78	0	1	3	74	295	122	145	28	1
Nonmetropolitan Counties										
Camden	26	1	2	1	22	564	166	366	32	4
Johnson	31	0	3	1	27	298	116	153	29	0
Pulaski	40	0	3	2	35	200	71	114	15	0
Taney	114	3	6	3	102	598	198	375	25	3

See footnotes at end of table.

Table 10

Offenses Known to Law Enforcement

by Metropolitan and Nonmetropolitan Counties,[1] 2003—Continued

[The data shown in this table do not reflect county totals but are the number of offenses reported by the sheriff's office or county police department.]

County by state	Violent crime	Murder and non-negligent man-slaughter	Forcible rape	Robbery	Aggravated assault	Property crime	Burglary	Larceny-theft	Motor vehicle theft	Arson[2]
MONTANA										
Metropolitan Counties										
Carbon	7	0	0	0	7	46	3	42	1	0
Cascade	41	1	2	1	37	469	22	421	26	0
Yellowstone	75	0	4	6	65	779	125	583	71	3
Nonmetropolitan Counties										
Lewis and Clark	46	1	6	0	39	316	66	228	22	0
Ravalli	64	0	8	0	56	141	32	93	16	1
NEBRASKA										
Metropolitan Counties										
Dakota	4	0	0	0	4	66	21	39	6	0
Dixon	1	0	1	0	0	61	28	30	3	0
Douglas	140	1	4	13	122	1,358	211	1,029	118	1
Lancaster	11	0	2	2	7	502	113	366	23	2
Saunders	2	2	0	0	0	154	43	89	22	4
Seward	4	0	1	0	3	76	26	47	3	0
Washington	6	0	1	0	5	103	34	63	6	1
NEVADA										
Metropolitan Counties										
Carson City	265	0	1	24	240	1,807	430	1,214	163	15
Storey	5	0	0	5	0	48	7	38	3	2
Washoe	313	7	4	23	279	1,488	495	810	183	6
Nonmetropolitan Counties										
Douglas	74	0	0	9	65	1,064	269	736	59	4
Lyon	94	1	11	6	76	762	229	462	71	8
Nye	100	0	2	14	84	1,177	534	579	64	7
NEW JERSEY										
Metropolitan Counties										
Essex County Police Department	85	3	11	33	38	141	13	102	26	3
NEW MEXICO										
Metropolitan Counties										
Bernalillo	822	9	48	116	649	2,954	924	1,588	442	63
Sandoval	39	0	0	1	38	161	95	58	8	0
San Juan	152	1	23	13	115	1,080	235	774	71	3
Santa Fe	270	0	39	16	215	1,014	507	446	61	
Nonmetropolitan Counties										
McKinley	100	0	8	4	88	334	100	209	25	7
NEW YORK										
Metropolitan Counties										
Albany	29	0	0	0	29	123	30	87	6	
Broome	63	0	14	15	34	1,132	148	944	40	
Chemung	44	0	1	2	41	336	70	249	17	
Dutchess	72	1	4	6	61	917	239	633	45	
Erie	70	1	10	10	49	1,072	216	797	59	
Herkimer	5	0	0	0	5	0	0	0	0	
Madison	18	0	5	1	12	153	42	103	8	
Monroe	252	4	28	70	150	5,329	772	4,234	323	18
Nassau	1,790	13	86	774	917	16,046	2,567	11,702	1,777	

See footnotes at end of table.

Table 10

Offenses Known to Law Enforcement
by Metropolitan and Nonmetropolitan Counties,[1] 2003—Continued

[The data shown in this table do not reflect county totals but are the number of offenses reported by the sheriff's office or county police department.]

County by state	Violent crime	Murder and non-negligent man-slaughter	Forcible rape	Robbery	Aggravated assault	Property crime	Burglary	Larceny-theft	Motor vehicle theft	Arson[2]
NEW YORK—Continued										
Metropolitan Counties—Continued										
Oneida	106	2	40	3	61	634	166	435	33	
Onondaga	198	3	20	55	120	2,217	423	1,734	60	23
Ontario	51	0	7	12	32	1,073	236	787	50	
Orange	13	0	1	0	12	5	0	5	0	
Orleans	15	0	3	3	9	161	43	98	20	
Oswego	33	2	10	2	19	353	134	192	27	
Putnam	45	0	5	10	30	404	93	289	22	
Rensselaer	51	0	1	1	49	521	113	394	14	
Rockland	3	0	0	0	3	57	1	53	3	
Saratoga	29	1	5	4	19	755	155	568	32	5
Schenectady	8	0	0	0	8	1	0	1	0	
Schoharie	4	0	0	1	3	111	33	75	3	
Suffolk	232	0	1	1	230	35	11	18	6	
Suffolk County Police Department	2,401	31	112	958	1,300	26,883	4,091	19,959	2,833	
Tioga	11	1	2	2	6	221	68	139	14	
Tompkins	15	1	3	4	7	513	102	390	21	
Ulster	38	1	4	0	33	161	41	115	5	
Warren	71	0	9	3	59	947	172	752	23	
Washington	99	0	1	2	96	215	73	141	1	
Westchester Public Safety	50	0	2	4	44	270	32	224	14	
Nonmetropolitan Counties										
Allegany	2	0	0	1	1	13	0	12	1	
Cattaraugus	46	1	8	1	36	414	151	238	25	
Cayuga	24	0	4	1	19	339	67	262	10	
Chautauqua	60	1	3	4	52	958	215	715	28	
Chenango	66	0	3	0	63	425	109	310	6	
Columbia	9	0	0	3	6	314	75	229	10	
Cortland	11	0	3	2	6	312	53	257	2	
Delaware	18	0	2	2	14	85	38	47	0	
Essex	0	0	0	0	0	1	0	1	0	
Franklin	0	0	0	0	0	0	0	0	0	
Fulton	20	0	4	0	16	390	102	267	21	
Genesee	50	1	12	2	35	583	139	409	35	
Greene	13	0	0	0	13	22	9	9	4	
Jefferson	43	0	16	3	24	415	88	318	9	
Steuben	4	0	0	2	2	304	100	190	14	
St. Lawrence	40	0	6	6	28	390	109	263	18	
Sullivan	42	0	3	4	35	580	133	414	33	
Wyoming	54	0	4	4	46	425	225	187	13	
NORTH CAROLINA										
Metropolitan Counties										
Alexander	37	2	7	4	24	720	297	358	65	7
Anson	39	5	0	15	19	419	183	199	37	5
Cabarrus	43	2	6	8	27	827	351	451	25	6
Caldwell	86	1	2	6	77	1,144	417	655	72	8
Catawba	117	5	8	17	87	1,915	745	1,078	92	14
Chatham	99	0	8	18	73	1,152	434	638	80	6
Cumberland	788	5	23	147	613	6,275	2,314	3,628	333	82
Currituck	50	0	7	3	40	637	191	424	22	4
Durham	97	0	1	16	80	944	208	679	57	1
Edgecombe	72	1	6	21	44	759	310	404	45	4
Forsyth	301	6	22	46	227	3,908	1,107	2,625	176	37
Franklin	36	1	2	13	20	921	437	436	48	2
Gaston County Police Department	211	6	19	28	158	1,767	690	898	179	26
Greene	75	0	5	11	59	647	279	335	33	3
Guilford	254	1	15	54	184	2,267	714	1,360	193	29
Haywood	86	1	6	7	72	804	245	497	62	10
Henderson	80	1	18	10	51	1,278	509	684	85	4

See footnotes at end of table.

Table 10

Offenses Known to Law Enforcement
by Metropolitan and Nonmetropolitan Counties,[1] 2003—Continued

[The data shown in this table do not reflect county totals but are the number of offenses reported by the sheriff's office or county police department.]

County by state	Violent crime	Murder and non-negligent man-slaughter	Forcible rape	Robbery	Aggravated assault	Property crime	Burglary	Larceny-theft	Motor vehicle theft	Arson[2]
NORTH CAROLINA—Continued										
Metropolitan Counties—Continued										
Hoke	172	4	12	36	120	1,220	533	611	76	14
Johnston	189	3	10	38	138	2,367	750	1,407	210	16
Madison	12	0	1	0	11	128	56	58	14	1
Nash	61	7	0	14	40	822	324	426	72	10
New Hanover	169	0	16	44	109	2,571	828	1,639	104	13
Orange	44	3	3	32	6	886	386	436	64	2
Pender	50	1	2	12	35	726	293	367	66	2
Person	85	0	3	3	79	465	228	230	7	0
Pitt	246	2	24	29	191	1,846	678	1,068	100	6
Rockingham	89	1	4	18	66	1,479	453	984	42	0
Stokes	160	1	10	6	143	994	381	547	66	15
Wake	168	7	24	38	99	2,699	974	1,510	215	20
Wayne	157	5	0	39	113	1,951	772	1,066	113	3
Yadkin	37	2	6	1	28	534	187	299	48	6
Nonmetropolitan Counties										
Beaufort	95	2	8	16	69	907	399	475	33	6
Bladen	207	5	8	17	177	961	436	469	56	10
Carteret	44	0	7	6	31	549	189	314	46	4
Cleveland[3]		0	20	34		1,833	623	1,109	101	3
Craven	111	0	12	15	84	1,524	483	949	92	2
Davidson	63	3	0	19	41	1,868	35	1,649	184	8
Granville	45	1	7	11	26	762	367	341	54	4
Halifax	94	7	14	28	45	995	488	427	80	12
Harnett	296	8	7	38	243	2,606	1,184	1,207	215	17
Iredell	187	2	16	22	147	1,708	605	984	119	11
Lee	28	1	9	10	8	624	293	273	58	15
Lenoir	96	0	3	14	79	882	367	478	37	5
Macon	16	1	0	2	13	521	211	274	36	3
McDowell	39	1	4	11	23	576	271	260	45	10
Rowan	119	5	10	15	89	1,325	411	811	103	30
Rutherford	83	2	11	14	56	1,060	450	496	114	22
Vance	92	2	2	34	54	1,315	656	593	66	5
Watauga	37	2	3	1	31	586	279	269	38	4
Wilson	65	2	6	15	42	841	367	421	53	0
NORTH DAKOTA										
Metropolitan Counties										
Burleigh	11	0	2	0	9	126	41	71	14	2
Cass	14	0	1	0	13	233	55	154	24	0
Grand Forks	5	0	2	0	3	89	20	59	10	0
Morton	7	1	4	0	2	93	11	77	5	0
OHIO										
Metropolitan Counties										
Allen	49	0	16	14	19	1,385	175	1,169	41	3
Belmont	29	0	10	4	15	409	101	264	44	6
Brown	16	0	6	4	6	515	145	331	39	7
Butler	86	0	12	10	64	1,109	330	700	79	21
Carroll	5	0	1	1	3	276	95	164	17	2
Clark	74	3	15	26	30	2,104	574	1,385	145	11
Clermont	85	0	63	5	17	1,652	451	1,097	104	38
Delaware	46	1	19	9	17	1,227	451	664	112	6
Erie	35	0	9	4	22	397	136	238	23	2
Fairfield	25	0	10	8	7	1,123	394	641	88	17
Franklin	274	13	43	121	97	4,100	912	2,624	564	30
Fulton	10	0	2	1	7	370	87	243	40	4
Greene	15	2	10	0	3	515	131	350	34	0
Hamilton	272	1	44	160	67	7,628	1,075	6,147	406	75

See footnotes at end of table.

Table 10

Offenses Known to Law Enforcement

by Metropolitan and Nonmetropolitan Counties,[1] 2003—Continued

[The data shown in this table do not reflect county totals but are the number of offenses reported by the sheriff's office or county police department.]

County by state	Violent crime	Violent crime	Violent crime	Violent crime	Violent crime	Property crime	Property crime	Property crime	Property crime	Property crime
	Violent crime	Murder and non-negligent man-slaughter	Forcible rape	Robbery	Aggravated assault	Property crime	Burglary	Larceny-theft	Motor vehicle theft	Arson[2]
OHIO—Continued										
Metropolitan Counties—Continued										
Jefferson	54	1	3	18	32	315	76	209	30	4
Lake	22	0	1	9	12	685	99	551	35	6
Lawrence	17	0	0	0	17	199	61	118	20	3
Licking	26	0	4	4	18	765	178	524	63	9
Lorain	55	0	17	13	25	1,061	544	469	48	30
Mahoning	21	0	11	1	9	223	86	120	17	2
Morrow	7	0	1	1	5	407	195	161	51	0
Pickaway	30	0	6	6	18	736	360	338	38	16
Preble	38	0	11	3	24	425	149	251	25	2
Richland	30	0	10	7	13	1,294	405	829	60	7
Stark	120	2	18	63	37	3,011	860	1,937	214	32
Summit	58	0	18	25	15	1,248	277	899	72	3
Trumbull	21	0	2	5	14	530	201	285	44	2
Warren	19	2	1	12	4	1,310	312	935	63	6
Washington	24	1	18	2	3	519	169	313	37	14
Wood	17	0	4	1	12	651	167	448	36	4
Nonmetropolitan Counties										
Athens	14	0	2	4	8	43	32	2	9	1
Auglaize	4	0	1	0	3	86	33	48	5	0
Coshocton	1	0	0	0	1	605	54	525	26	0
Darke	28	4	9	1	14	321	123	183	15	3
Gallia	53	3	8	11	31	860	366	434	60	10
Highland	29	0	0	0	29	362	169	173	20	1
Huron	12	0	1	1	10	372	134	212	26	1
Logan	46	1	4	1	40	351	101	220	30	1
Marion	22	0	2	12	8	1,114	246	817	51	3
Muskingum	23	0	11	9	3	1,347	373	860	114	3
Perry	13	0	5	0	8	392	131	211	50	3
Putnam	6	2	1	0	3	156	53	100	3	4
Shelby	5	0	0	2	3	175	40	126	9	0
Wayne	30	0	7	3	20	612	225	366	21	9
Williams	9	0	5	0	4	342	114	218	10	4
OKLAHOMA										
Metropolitan Counties										
Canadian	14	1	1	0	12	99	36	44	19	7
Cleveland	53	0	17	1	35	268	125	123	20	7
Comanche	79	0	3	2	74	358	104	209	45	5
Creek	112	2	7	6	97	677	265	349	63	11
Grady	58	1	7	0	50	318	102	193	23	0
Le Flore	47	2	1	1	43	126	57	51	18	1
Lincoln	63	1	4	0	58	217	90	99	28	4
Logan	29	0	3	0	26	264	126	133	5	3
McClain	41	0	8	0	33	184	78	78	28	3
Oklahoma	39	1	0	3	35	245	118	106	21	0
Okmulgee	14	0	2	1	11	195	67	99	29	2
Osage	41	3	0	15	23	354	161	152	41	5
Pawnee	68	1	5	0	62	230	85	124	21	3
Rogers	8	0	0	1	7	394	142	209	43	0
Sequoyah	61	2	1	0	58	239	113	115	11	2
Tulsa	252	3	18	20	211	1,423	325	954	144	18
Wagoner	42	2	7	0	33	417	154	183	80	6
Nonmetropolitan Counties										
Cherokee	101	2	8	1	90	271	110	133	28	3
Delaware	86	1	6	0	79	375	177	162	36	7
Mayes	35	1	0	3	31	331	127	168	36	0
Pottawatomie	55	2	9	6	38	466	182	236	48	14

See footnotes at end of table.

Table 10

Offenses Known to Law Enforcement
by Metropolitan and Nonmetropolitan Counties,[1] 2003—Continued

[The data shown in this table do not reflect county totals but are the number of offenses reported by the sheriff's office or county police department.]

County by state	Violent crime	Murder and non-negligent man-slaughter	Forcible rape	Robbery	Aggravated assault	Property crime	Burglary	Larceny-theft	Motor vehicle theft	Arson[2]
OREGON										
Metropolitan Counties										
Clackamas	258	3	51	97	107	7,565	1,208	5,446	911	21
Deschutes	21	0	2	6	13	900	233	579	88	7
Jackson	244	1	16	10	217	1,481	336	1,043	102	11
Lane	162	1	24	20	117	1,743	618	909	216	6
Marion	158	2	16	27	113	4,768	938	3,070	760	9
Multnomah	52	0	8	10	34	1,091	136	840	115	1
Polk	28	0	7	1	20	424	117	252	55	1
Washington	187	0	40	43	104	4,929	959	3,461	509	24
Yamhill	54	0	9	5	40	442	131	247	64	6
Nonmetropolitan Counties										
Douglas	30	2	7	3	18	1,355	335	916	104	5
Josephine	43	3	13	15	12	945	236	563	146	3
Klamath	82	0	20	8	54	1,058	308	680	70	12
Linn	16	2	3	9	2	1,699	450	1,108	141	11
PENNSYLVANIA										
Metropolitan Counties										
Allegheny	11	0	0	1	10	2	0	0	2	0
Allegheny County Police Department	153	0	38	72	43	563	239	304	20	74
Beaver	11	0	0	0	11	4	1	3	0	1
Centre	0	0	0	0	0	1	0	1	0	0
Cumberland	0	0	0	0	0	1	0	1	0	0
Lancaster	2	0	0	0	2	0	0	0	0	0
York	6	0	0	0	6	0	0	0	0	0
SOUTH CAROLINA										
Metropolitan Counties										
Aiken	360	5	62	69	224	2,735	874	1,567	294	10
Anderson	864	3	50	98	713	5,900	1,609	3,804	487	31
Berkeley	552	9	46	82	415	2,592	795	1,483	314	12
Calhoun	98	0	2	6	90	304	81	189	34	1
Charleston	993	6	36	123	828	3,441	947	2,034	460	25
Darlington	598	6	26	36	530	2,293	876	1,239	178	14
Dorchester	362	0	25	42	295	1,544	517	861	166	12
Edgefield	33	0	5	4	24	351	90	237	24	0
Fairfield	258	1	10	11	236	911	157	710	44	12
Florence	603	6	30	99	468	3,431	961	2,229	241	6
Greenville	1,781	18	97	274	1,392	9,535	2,777	5,953	805	50
Horry	0	0	0	0	0	5	0	5	0	0
Horry County Police Department	1,019	8	81	111	819	7,300	1,659	4,924	717	14
Kershaw	187	1	9	12	165	1,126	346	652	128	11
Laurens	357	2	10	26	319	1,674	524	1,033	117	8
Lexington	741	11	46	134	550	4,609	1,325	2,734	550	12
Pickens	125	1	29	25	70	1,091	456	520	115	2
Richland	2,040	9	123	426	1,482	10,128	2,075	6,963	1,090	26
Saluda	73	0	3	3	67	168	60	100	8	2
Spartanburg	1,010	12	73	174	751	6,537	1,721	4,223	593	10
Sumter	525	7	20	62	436	2,665	1,019	1,326	320	33
York	955	4	42	47	862	2,978	672	2,064	242	24
Nonmetropolitan Counties										
Beaufort	806	3	53	150	600	4,762	1,360	3,070	332	29
Cherokee	207	2	12	20	173	1,522	366	1,064	92	4
Chester	156	1	9	25	121	995	253	684	58	4
Chesterfield	177	2	5	21	149	828	305	461	62	12
Clarendon	129	2	7	16	104	253	110	119	24	3
Colleton	342	5	9	39	289	1,066	319	629	118	29
Georgetown	247	0	17	23	207	1,336	387	849	100	10

See footnotes at end of table.

Table 10

Offenses Known to Law Enforcement
by Metropolitan and Nonmetropolitan Counties,[1] 2003—Continued

[The data shown in this table do not reflect county totals but are the number of offenses reported by the sheriff's office or county police department.]

County by state	Violent crime	Violent crime — Murder and non-negligent man-slaughter	Violent crime — Forcible rape	Violent crime — Robbery	Violent crime — Aggravated assault	Property crime	Property crime — Burglary	Property crime — Larceny-theft	Property crime — Motor vehicle theft	Arson[2]
SOUTH CAROLINA—Continued										
Nonmetropolitan Counties—Continued										
Greenwood	294	2	17	11	264	1,502	295	1,094	113	7
Lancaster	233	2	25	24	182	1,890	628	1,172	90	14
Oconee	248	4	22	16	206	1,477	514	841	122	9
Orangeburg	620	14	20	94	492	3,143	1,028	1,769	346	6
Williamsburg	118	2	2	25	89	400	190	143	67	5
SOUTH DAKOTA										
Metropolitan Counties										
McCook	4	0	0	0	4	36	3	29	4	0
Meade	56	2	21	0	33	206	57	129	20	0
Minnehaha	27	0	9	1	17	269	113	126	30	2
Pennington	80	1	36	2	41	1,210	102	1,071	37	4
Turner	5	0	0	0	5	39	12	25	2	0
Union	2	0	1	0	1	23	7	14	2	0
TENNESSEE										
Metropolitan Counties										
Anderson	111	2	6	12	91	1,011	374	555	82	10
Blount	311	4	53	5	249	1,595	521	906	168	13
Bradley	206	2	13	6	185	1,124	334	680	110	8
Cannon	30	0	0	3	27	118	50	48	20	0
Carter	102	3	4	2	93	764	263	421	80	20
Cheatham	79	0	6	4	69	467	117	286	64	2
Chester	13	0	1	2	10	141	58	68	15	0
Dickson	119	2	33	3	81	613	165	388	60	11
Fayette	98	0	3	13	82	660	265	328	67	4
Grainger	51	1	3	2	45	278	71	192	15	1
Hamblen	117	5	3	12	97	711	240	410	61	11
Hamilton	352	5	16	21	310	1,934	507	1,278	149	6
Hartsville-Trousdale	22	0	0	3	19	155	81	69	5	0
Hawkins	67	3	6	4	54	843	308	466	69	3
Hickman	92	4	4	7	77	481	160	298	23	17
Jefferson	105	0	11	4	90	834	277	454	103	12
Knox	603	6	32	83	482	5,893	1,496	4,009	388	43
Loudon	65	0	2	6	57	481	107	337	37	3
Macon	38	1	2	2	33	117	22	85	10	4
Madison	126	0	19	9	98	880	287	509	84	10
Montgomery	136	0	3	7	126	619	187	386	46	4
Robertson	88	2	13	2	71	452	131	264	57	3
Rutherford	197	0	20	5	172	1,112	342	658	112	12
Sequatchie	38	0	4	0	34	159	45	85	29	2
Shelby	338	5	33	60	240	3,162	1,132	1,723	307	17
Shelby County Police Department	0	0	0	0	0	51	3	45	3	0
Smith	46	2	1	0	43	101	33	50	18	4
Sullivan	349	3	35	17	294	1,888	596	1,139	153	32
Sumner	139	1	14	7	117	679	206	413	60	8
Tipton	184	3	10	6	165	749	299	369	81	5
Unicoi	19	0	0	2	17	204	46	145	13	3
Union	35	0	3	1	31	302	125	151	26	7
Washington	145	0	8	9	128	1,013	387	520	106	14
Williamson	52	1	4	8	39	631	139	444	48	4
Wilson	162	0	3	2	157	1,011	375	536	100	5
Nonmetropolitan Counties										
Campbell	137	1	4	1	131	671	242	380	49	4
Claiborne	114	0	4	4	106	542	229	272	41	13
Cocke	87	2	3	6	76	762	378	254	130	8
Cumberland	72	1	1	3	67	842	327	436	79	4
Greene	237	1	7	12	217	1,220	511	582	127	7

See footnotes at end of table.

Table 10

Offenses Known to Law Enforcement

by Metropolitan and Nonmetropolitan Counties,[1] 2003—Continued

[The data shown in this table do not reflect county totals but are the number of offenses reported by the sheriff's office or county police department.]

County by state	Violent crime	Violent crime				Property crime	Property crime			
	Violent crime	Murder and non-negligent man-slaughter	Forcible rape	Robbery	Aggravated assault	Property crime	Burglary	Larceny-theft	Motor vehicle theft	Arson[2]
TENNESSEE—Continued										
Nonmetropolitan Counties—Continued										
Lawrence	126	0	4	1	121	653	326	292	35	3
Maury	119	4	15	2	98	723	194	467	62	7
McMinn	128	2	6	8	112	803	296	415	92	2
Monroe	222	2	4	6	210	716	218	416	82	32
Putnam	70	1	6	7	56	693	137	498	58	1
Roane	91	0	1	7	83	904	337	475	92	10
Sevier	75	1	15	2	57	1,456	592	759	105	1
Warren	41	1	0	4	36	444	139	236	69	3
TEXAS										
Metropolitan Counties										
Aransas	32	0	0	2	30	663	205	440	18	1
Archer	8	0	0	1	7	87	33	51	3	0
Armstrong	3	0	2	0	1	39	13	21	5	0
Atascosa	25	2	0	3	20	331	152	158	21	3
Austin	35	0	9	0	26	189	60	104	25	0
Bandera	14	1	4	1	8	491	144	331	16	5
Bastrop	196	4	3	12	177	1,180	624	483	73	7
Bell	59	2	27	5	25	887	291	522	74	6
Bexar	478	12	52	48	366	5,140	1,419	3,343	378	134
Bowie	103	1	6	5	91	572	173	326	73	2
Brazoria	104	4	20	21	59	1,511	633	750	128	5
Brazos	36	2	8	3	23	434	142	264	28	4
Burleson	39	0	6	2	31	134	77	50	7	3
Caldwell	49	1	3	3	42	194	91	98	5	1
Calhoun	14	0	0	0	14	196	44	144	8	7
Callahan	6	0	1	1	4	57	28	25	4	1
Cameron	301	1	35	20	245	1,735	726	864	145	26
Carson	6	0	0	0	6	0	0	0	0	0
Chambers	72	0	1	5	66	506	185	296	25	9
Clay	12	0	2	1	9	219	71	128	20	3
Collin	91	4	17	4	66	718	239	398	81	2
Comal	129	0	21	3	105	859	289	525	45	5
Coryell	21	0	1	1	19	122	41	66	15	5
Crosby	13	0	0	0	13	27	14	8	5	0
Dallas	91	0	5	6	80	383	152	204	27	9
Delta	21	0	0	1	20	136	51	78	7	2
Denton	74	2	15	3	54	786	245	436	105	19
Ector	139	3	7	12	117	1,196	260	854	82	5
Ellis	111	0	13	13	85	1,315	537	665	113	8
El Paso	262	0	34	30	198	1,348	336	857	155	11
Fort Bend	587	12	38	70	467	3,205	1,113	1,840	252	57
Galveston	162	1	25	25	111	937	314	507	116	11
Goliad	4	0	0	0	4	63	18	44	1	0
Grayson	44	1	11	1	31	933	307	555	71	4
Gregg	73	1	9	11	52	823	206	546	71	6
Guadalupe	78	2	10	2	64	967	312	590	65	1
Hardin	30	0	2	2	26	408	164	188	56	3
Harris	6,569	47	344	1,807	4,371	37,393	9,455	23,292	4,646	543
Hays	75	1	7	6	61	1,017	305	598	114	0
Hidalgo	1,117	25	93	192	807	6,371	2,429	3,442	500	
Hunt	72	4	1	11	56	975	404	484	87	3
Irion	1	0	0	0	1	15	7	8	0	0
Jefferson	41	0	7	4	30	550	190	298	62	3
Johnson	126	1	2	4	119	1,407	476	747	184	22
Jones	13	0	0	5	8	72	43	24	5	0
Kaufman	314	2	17	13	282	1,320	475	695	150	19
Kendall	25	0	1	1	23	139	42	91	6	0
Lampasas	2	1	0	0	1	84	42	32	10	0
Liberty	86	4	1	11	70	1,068	407	513	148	16

See footnotes at end of table.

Table 10

Offenses Known to Law Enforcement

by Metropolitan and Nonmetropolitan Counties,[1] 2003—Continued

[The data shown in this table do not reflect county totals but are the number of offenses reported by the sheriff's office or county police department.]

County by state	Violent crime	Murder and non-negligent man-slaughter	Forcible rape	Robbery	Aggravated assault	Property crime	Burglary	Larceny-theft	Motor vehicle theft	Arson[2]
TEXAS—Continued										
Metropolitan Counties—Continued										
Lubbock	83	2	13	3	65	807	323	413	71	5
McLennan	95	1	29	5	60	848	324	428	96	9
Medina	52	4	10	3	35	356	150	178	28	0
Midland	49	0	2	0	47	550	150	355	45	1
Montgomery	850	5	59	137	649	6,999	1,808	4,658	533	39
Nueces	55	1	10	11	33	341	152	162	27	0
Orange	150	4	6	9	131	900	306	471	123	4
Parker	57	0	5	1	51	1,075	433	543	99	0
Potter	35	0	3	4	28	250	63	175	12	2
Randall	45	0	6	3	36	372	131	200	41	2
Robertson	20	0	0	0	20	110	63	40	7	1
Rockwall	60	0	3	1	56	279	101	140	38	1
Rusk	121	2	13	4	102	717	259	389	69	7
San Jacinto	54	2	4	5	43	589	272	284	33	6
San Patricio	32	3	0	2	27	349	98	226	25	2
Smith	461	7	39	25	390	1,863	646	1,042	175	42
Tarrant	129	0	29	22	78	973	330	567	76	1
Taylor	12	0	0	0	12	133	60	59	14	0
Tom Green	16	1	1	0	14	262	69	176	17	4
Travis	415	7	49	24	335	4,051	1,203	2,578	270	24
Upshur	43	0	2	1	40	432	191	188	53	4
Victoria	97	20	24	1	52	598	172	381	45	4
Waller	33	1	6	5	21	300	120	138	42	1
Webb	48	2	5	6	35	346	168	150	28	2
Wichita	26	1	1	2	22	179	83	80	16	5
Williamson	209	2	36	12	159	2,005	478	1,420	107	16
Wilson	39	0	4	1	34	238	95	119	24	1
Wise	147	0	17	3	127	498	198	290	10	0
Nonmetropolitan Counties										
Anderson	65	1	8	1	55	539	249	262	28	0
Angelina	233	2	6	10	215	872	411	391	70	0
Cherokee	88	0	12	0	76	458	204	213	41	4
Harrison	90	2	1	8	79	911	416	440	55	6
Henderson	225	3	17	5	200	1,417	663	605	149	5
Hood	60	0	1	2	57	927	282	576	69	5
Jasper	59	0	5	1	53	424	144	272	8	0
Maverick	99	2	3	5	89	567	178	365	24	3
Nacogdoches	71	1	3	3	64	491	207	250	34	2
Polk	37	2	2	2	31	756	308	381	67	5
Starr	83	9	8	7	59	452	228	181	43	2
Van Zandt	136	4	0	8	124	982	426	438	118	7
Walker	68	0	8	4	56	494	183	262	49	0
Wood	43	0	5	0	38	525	200	324	1	7
UTAH										
Metropolitan Counties										
Davis	21	1	7	0	13	170	45	109	16	2
Morgan	4	0	1	0	3	72	17	48	7	0
Salt Lake	820	12	162	122	524	13,772	2,247	10,409	1,116	39
Summit	16	1	9	3	3	643	97	521	25	0
Tooele	12	0	1	1	10	239	57	175	7	4
Utah	49	1	9	2	37	509	211	263	35	8
Washington	66	0	6	1	59	468	99	334	35	1
Weber	37	1	5	4	27	1,183	221	892	70	5

See footnotes at end of table.

Table 10

Offenses Known to Law Enforcement

by Metropolitan and Nonmetropolitan Counties,[1] 2003—Continued

[The data shown in this table do not reflect county totals but are the number of offenses reported by the sheriff's office or county police department.]

County by state	Violent crime	Murder and non-negligent man-slaughter	Forcible rape	Robbery	Aggravated assault	Property crime	Burglary	Larceny-theft	Motor vehicle theft	Arson[2]
VERMONT										
Metropolitan Counties										
Chittenden	0	0	0	0	0	0	0	0	0	0
Franklin	9	0	0	0	9	38	15	23	0	0
Grand Isle	1	0	0	0	1	40	15	24	1	0
VIRGINIA										
Metropolitan Counties										
Albemarle County Police Department	129	5	35	18	71	1,783	247	1,448	88	14
Amelia	5	1	1	1	2	121	31	83	7	1
Amherst	23	1	8	5	9	338	53	255	30	5
Appomattox	9	0	5	2	2	145	31	108	6	1
Arlington County Police Department	441	3	30	206	202	4,810	373	3,842	595	8
Bedford	47	0	6	3	38	692	118	525	49	8
Botetourt	36	2	8	3	23	321	55	251	15	1
Charles City	9	0	0	2	7	36	16	17	3	0
Chesterfield County Police Department	537	12	53	192	280	7,638	1,352	5,839	447	83
Clarke	36	1	2	0	33	182	17	149	16	0
Craig	3	0	0	0	3	11	6	5	0	0
Cumberland	13	0	3	0	10	64	20	42	2	2
Dinwiddie	12	2	3	3	4	597	53	526	18	2
Fairfax County Police Department	643	6	54	351	232	16,585	457	14,684	1,444	119
Fauquier	76	1	12	12	51	667	109	513	45	21
Fluvanna	26	0	8	3	15	203	36	153	14	3
Franklin	56	1	11	9	35	498	79	369	50	1
Frederick	72	2	10	15	45	1,314	245	994	75	6
Giles	20	0	0	0	20	4	3	1	0	0
Gloucester	36	0	8	1	27	465	34	409	22	12
Greene	16	4	3	0	9	80	12	60	8	3
Hanover	48	1	6	13	28	1,104	87	937	80	12
Henrico County Police Department	651	20	32	330	269	10,379	1,554	8,092	733	117
James City County Police Department	77	1	18	19	39	964	141	745	78	6
King William	6	1	2	0	3	54	13	37	4	0
Loudoun	216	0	23	39	154	3,065	335	2,548	182	51
Mathews	2	0	0	0	2	88	19	61	8	1
Montgomery	32	0	8	3	21	542	152	350	40	5
Nelson	16	0	5	1	10	187	31	131	25	0
New Kent	16	0	0	1	15	196	26	165	5	1
Powhatan	9	0	1	3	5	217	40	155	22	1
Prince George County Police Department	43	1	6	14	22	472	68	386	18	4
Prince William County Police Department	539	9	31	197	302	7,220	965	5,476	779	80
Pulaski	31	0	5	4	22	449	75	366	8	4
Roanoke County Police Department	201	1	13	16	171	1,229	247	885	97	15
Rockingham	31	0	15	1	15	352	126	207	19	1
Scott	32	2	4	2	24	343	117	206	20	3
Spotsylvania	168	3	20	23	122	1,964	203	1,675	86	10
Stafford	134	6	28	28	72	1,723	206	1,370	147	18
Surry	14	0	2	1	11	92	29	62	1	0
Sussex	18	0	2	3	13	157	32	115	10	0
Warren	12	0	7	3	2	258	40	197	21	4
Washington	57	2	14	1	40	935	149	733	53	4
York	70	0	11	16	43	1,043	132	868	43	19
Nonmetropolitan Counties										
Accomack	56	1	12	20	23	415	89	282	44	0
Augusta	59	3	16	4	36	889	164	673	52	3
Buchanan	45	2	4	5	34	613	209	352	52	7
Carroll	46	1	2	3	40	409	145	228	36	5
Halifax	32	4	5	7	16	375	97	264	14	3
Henry	219	5	21	37	156	1,545	334	1,112	99	10
Tazewell	51	2	9	4	36	674	203	430	41	5
Wise	81	2	11	0	68	400	125	243	32	7

See footnotes at end of table.

Table 10

Offenses Known to Law Enforcement
by Metropolitan and Nonmetropolitan Counties,[1] 2003—Continued

[The data shown in this table do not reflect county totals but are the number of offenses reported by the sheriff's office or county police department.]

County by state	Violent crime	Murder and non-negligent man-slaughter	Forcible rape	Robbery	Aggravated assault	Property crime	Burglary	Larceny-theft	Motor vehicle theft	Arson[2]
WASHINGTON										
Metropolitan Counties										
Asotin	17	0	2	1	14	279	66	200	13	2
Benton	86	1	7	6	72	755	249	462	44	11
Chelan	37	4	15	7	11	940	163	748	29	2
Clark	264	2	60	55	147	5,571	1,205	3,683	683	43
Cowlitz	75	0	8	10	57	1,119	376	593	150	9
Douglas	35	0	9	1	25	596	194	368	34	3
Franklin	9	1	1	0	7	189	70	100	19	1
King	713	15	111	203	384	9,515	2,489	5,147	1,879	245
Kitsap	476	3	85	34	354	3,997	1,082	2,547	368	25
Pierce	1,130	7	86	185	852	10,826	2,587	6,596	1,643	60
Skagit	94	1	35	12	46	2,001	652	1,191	158	15
Skamania	15	0	4	0	11	339	66	255	18	1
Snohomish	614	5	156	93	360	6,958	1,863	3,537	1,558	86
Spokane[3]	309	3	30	72	204	4,866	1,120	3,347	399	37
Thurston	279	4	30	24	221	2,841	900	1,693	248	27
Whatcom	152	1	58	11	82	1,819	811	825	183	14
Yakima	112	4	38	16	54	2,995	1,269	1,361	365	65
Nonmetropolitan Counties										
Clallam	50	0	9	2	39	853	245	562	46	10
Grant	71	1	12	5	53	1,247	414	717	116	13
Grays Harbor	40	0	3	4	33	514	208	259	47	9
Lewis	68	0	12	6	50	912	333	496	83	3
Mason	108	2	29	13	64	1,702	604	912	186	11
Stevens	68	6	12	3	47	683	235	395	53	2
WEST VIRGINIA										
Metropolitan Counties										
Boone	7	0	0	0	7	58	18	33	7	2
Cabell	12	1	0	9	2	918	88	780	50	2
Clay	2	0	0	0	2	5	1	4	0	0
Hampshire	25	0	0	0	25	86	52	29	5	2
Hancock	10	0	0	2	8	85	32	39	14	0
Mineral	11	1	0	3	7	52	23	26	3	4
Monongalia	49	1	1	15	32	487	111	337	39	3
Morgan	15	0	3	1	11	113	28	73	12	1
Ohio	38	0	0	3	35	84	32	41	11	0
Pleasants	0	0	0	0	0	1	1	0	0	0
Preston	12	0	0	0	12	91	34	48	9	2
Putnam	64	0	8	3	53	831	227	542	62	10
Wood	244	0	6	2	236	479	135	304	40	13
Nonmetropolitan Counties										
Fayette	53	2	5	2	44	338	134	180	24	0
Logan	2	0	0	0	2	48	12	29	7	1
Marion	11	0	3	1	7	189	42	128	19	2
Mercer	124	2	4	17	101	823	349	412	62	20
WISCONSIN										
Metropolitan Counties										
Brown	59	0	8	6	45	1,410	282	1,046	82	
Calumet	4	0	1	0	3	164	27	128	9	
Chippewa	17	0	7	0	10	320	72	213	35	
Columbia	13	1	2	1	9	298	71	205	22	
Douglas	7	0	3	0	4	280	131	131	18	
Eau Claire	10	0	5	0	5	311	71	226	14	
Fond du Lac	14	0	2	0	12	381	102	252	27	
Kenosha	43	1	6	5	31	723	147	528	48	
Kewaunee	6	0	3	1	2	312	15	293	4	

See footnotes at end of table.

Table 10

Offenses Known to Law Enforcement

by Metropolitan and Nonmetropolitan Counties,[1] 2003—Continued

[The data shown in this table do not reflect county totals but are the number of offenses reported by the sheriff's office or county police department.]

County by state	Violent crime	Violent crime — Murder and non-negligent man-slaughter	Violent crime — Forcible rape	Violent crime — Robbery	Violent crime — Aggravated assault	Property crime	Property crime — Burglary	Property crime — Larceny-theft	Property crime — Motor vehicle theft	Arson[2]
WISCONSIN—Continued										
Metropolitan Counties—Continued										
La Crosse	9	1	1	0	7	175	37	129	9	
Marathon	31	0	0	5	26	652	236	388	28	
Oconto	20	0	0	3	17	480	238	208	34	
Outagamie	12	1	3	3	5	441	81	334	26	
Ozaukee	14	0	7	1	6	233	34	188	11	
Pierce	12	0	2	1	9	261	91	151	19	
Racine	13	2	0	6	5	695	87	575	33	
Rock	46	0	8	3	35	479	160	296	23	
Sheboygan	29	0	4	1	24	606	92	483	31	
St. Croix	25	0	4	0	21	471	140	293	38	
Washington	26	0	8	4	14	579	98	447	34	
Waukesha	51	0	3	1	47	683	94	552	37	
Winnebago	17	0	4	0	13	383	75	291	17	
Nonmetropolitan Counties										
Barron	60	0	5	2	53	443	148	269	26	
Clark	10	2	2	2	4	168	49	102	17	
Dodge	23	0	5	3	15	286	108	158	20	
Dunn	18	0	6	2	10	253	85	155	13	
Grant	51	1	1	1	48	180	74	85	21	
Jefferson	32	0	10	0	22	297	55	225	17	
Manitowoc	20	1	8	0	11	313	73	209	31	
Polk	15	0	7	0	8	321	162	136	23	
Portage	10	1	4	0	5	341	97	226	18	
Sauk	18	0	1	2	15	706	124	556	26	
Shawano	15	1	4	2	8	566	189	357	20	
Walworth	18	3	5	3	7	368	87	252	29	
Waupaca	8	1	1	4	2	400	127	242	31	
Wood	4	0	0	0	4	292	85	180	27	
WYOMING										
Metropolitan Counties										
Laramie	68	1	11	5	51	505	113	361	31	1
Natrona	12	0	0	2	10	492	161	282	49	2

[1] Data provided for nonmetropolitan counties are inclusive of only those counties that are 25,000 and over in population.

[2] If the FBI does not receive 12 months of arson data from either the agency or the state, no arson will be shown.

[3] Due to changes in reporting practices, annexations, and/or incomplete data, figures are not comparable to previous years' data.

[4] Limited data for 2003 were available for Illinois and Kentucky.

NOTE: Tables 10 and 11 have been restructured. See Appendix I, Table Methodology.

Table 11

Offenses Known to Law Enforcement
by State Agency by State, 2003
by Federal Agency, 2003

State agency by state	Violent crime	Murder and non-negligent man-slaughter	Forcible rape	Robbery	Aggravated assault	Property crime	Burglary	Larceny-theft	Motor vehicle theft	Arson[1]
ALABAMA										
Alabama Department of Mental Health	1	0	0	0	1	0	0	0	0	
ALASKA										
Alaska State Troopers	890	15	178	23	674	4,840	1,498	2,773	569	67
ARIZONA										
Arizona Department of Public Safety	6	0	0	0	6	11	0	10	1	0
Arizona State Capitol	1	0	0	0	1	54	13	32	9	0
CALIFORNIA										
Agnews Developmental Center	0	0	0	0	0	0	0	0	0	0
Atascadero State Hospital	22	0	0	0	22	2	0	2	0	0
California State Fair	32	0	0	4	28	110	4	102	4	0
Department of Parks and Recreation:										
Angeles	0	0	0	0	0	9	0	9	0	0
Bay Area	0	0	0	0	0	6	0	6	0	3
Calaveras County	0	0	0	0	0	9	1	8	0	1
Capital	0	0	0	0	0	8	6	2	0	1
Channel Coast	2	0	0	0	2	55	7	48	0	0
Colorado	0	0	0	0	0	18	6	12	0	0
Four Rivers District	0	0	0	0	0	28	16	10	2	0
Gold Fields District	2	0	0	0	2	158	11	145	2	5
Hollister Hills	0	0	0	0	0	2	0	1	1	0
Hungry Valley	1	0	0	0	1	6	0	2	4	1
Inland Empire	0	0	0	0	0	16	0	16	0	0
Marin County	1	0	0	0	1	15	8	7	0	0
Mendocino Headquarters	0	0	0	0	0	65	1	63	1	0
Monterey County	1	0	1	0	0	40	16	23	1	0
North Coast Redwoods	2	0	0	0	2	44	8	36	0	0
Northern Buttes	2	0	2	0	0	20	5	15	0	0
Oceano Dunes	0	0	0	0	0	34	0	25	9	0
Octillo Wells	2	0	0	1	1	7	0	0	7	2
Orange Coast	1	0	0	1	0	70	19	46	5	0
Russian River	1	0	0	0	1	77	1	72	4	0
San Diego Coast	8	0	0	0	8	92	33	55	4	0
San Joaquin	0	0	0	0	0	4	2	2	0	0
San Luis Obispo Coast	6	0	0	0	6	72	2	68	2	2
San Simeon	0	0	0	0	0	8	0	8	0	0
Santa Cruz Mountains	1	0	1	0	0	57	2	55	0	0
Sierra	0	0	0	0	0	8	3	5	0	0
Silverado	0	0	0	0	0	50	0	48	2	1
Twin Cities	0	0	0	0	0	2	0	1	1	0
Fairview Developmental Center	14	0	0	0	14	15	0	15	0	1
Highway Patrol:										
Alameda County	0	0	0	0	0	255	0	23	232	0
Alpine County	0	0	0	0	0	2	0	0	2	0
Amador County	0	0	0	0	0	75	0	0	75	0
Butte County	1	0	1	0	0	653	0	101	552	0
Calaveras County	0	0	0	0	0	145	0	28	117	0
Colusa County	0	0	0	0	0	30	0	1	29	0
Contra Costa County	0	0	0	0	0	1,247	4	69	1,174	0
Del Norte County	0	0	0	0	0	95	0	0	95	0
El Dorado County	1	0	0	0	1	411	0	72	339	0
Fresno County	0	0	0	0	0	154	3	5	146	0
Glenn County	0	0	0	0	0	52	0	0	52	0
Humboldt County	1	0	0	1	0	251	0	15	236	0
Imperial County	0	0	0	0	0	138	0	14	124	0
Inyo County	0	0	0	0	0	30	0	8	22	0
Kern County	0	0	0	0	0	155	0	27	128	0
Kings County	0	0	0	0	0	239	0	25	214	0

See footnotes at end of table.

Table 11

Offenses Known to Law Enforcement
by State Agency by State, 2003—Continued
by Federal Agency, 2003

State agency by state	Violent crime	Murder and non-negligent man-slaughter	Forcible rape	Robbery	Aggravated assault	Property crime	Burglary	Larceny-theft	Motor vehicle theft	Arson[1]
CALIFORNIA—Continued										
Highway Patrol—Continued:										
Lake County	0	0	0	0	0	95	0	27	68	0
Lassen County	1	0	1	0	0	49	0	4	45	0
Los Angeles County	50	0	1	3	46	499	16	110	373	0
Madera County	0	0	0	0	0	449	0	74	375	0
Marin County	0	0	0	0	0	142	0	0	142	0
Mariposa County	0	0	0	0	0	30	0	9	21	0
Mendocino County	5	0	0	0	5	94	1	23	70	0
Merced County	2	0	0	0	2	603	0	95	508	2
Modoc County	0	0	0	0	0	11	0	5	6	0
Mono County	0	0	0	0	0	3	0	1	2	0
Monterey County	0	0	0	0	0	252	0	2	250	0
Napa County	0	0	0	0	0	102	0	0	102	0
Nevada County	0	0	0	0	0	104	0	16	88	0
Orange County	18	0	0	3	15	53	6	16	31	0
Placer County	0	0	0	0	0	273	1	11	261	0
Plumas County	0	0	0	0	0	47	0	8	39	0
Riverside County	22	0	0	0	22	62	17	8	37	0
Sacramento County	6	0	0	1	5	7,081	7	706	6,368	0
San Benito County	0	0	0	0	0	36	0	0	36	0
San Bernardino County	3	0	0	1	2	294	4	3	287	0
San Diego County	11	0	0	0	11	133	2	53	78	0
San Francisco County	2	0	0	1	1	120	1	14	105	0
San Joaquin County	0	0	0	0	0	1,651	1	514	1,136	0
San Luis Obispo County	6	0	0	0	6	196	0	61	135	0
San Mateo County	0	0	0	0	0	34	0	16	18	0
Santa Barbara County	2	0	0	0	2	127	0	24	103	0
Santa Clara County	1	0	0	0	1	66	0	13	53	0
Santa Cruz County	0	0	0	0	0	429	0	115	314	0
Shasta County	1	0	0	0	1	251	0	45	206	0
Sierra County	0	0	0	0	0	0	0	0	0	0
Siskiyou County	0	0	0	0	0	22	0	1	21	0
Solano County	0	0	0	0	0	82	6	0	76	0
Stanislaus County	1	0	0	1	0	374	0	43	331	0
Sutter County	0	0	0	0	0	79	0	3	76	0
Tehama County	0	0	0	0	0	116	0	7	109	0
Trinity County	0	0	0	0	0	41	0	0	41	0
Tulare County	7	0	0	0	7	1,330	0	384	946	0
Tuolumne County	0	0	0	0	0	267	0	29	238	0
Ventura County	0	0	0	0	0	46	0	20	26	0
Yolo County	0	0	0	0	0	59	0	6	53	0
Yuba County	0	0	0	0	0	438	0	1	437	1
Lanterman State Hospital	0	0	0	0	0	3	0	3	0	0
Napa State Hospital	11	0	0	0	11	9	0	9	0	0
Porterville Developmental Center	27	0	0	2	25	24	2	21	1	1
Sonoma Developmental Center	0	0	0	0	0	25	0	25	0	0
COLORADO										
Colorado Mental Health Institute	0	0	0	0	0	0	0	0	0	0
Colorado State Patrol	11	0	0	0	11	60	1	18	41	1
CONNECTICUT										
State Capitol Police	0	0	0	0	0	4	0	4	0	0
DELAWARE										
Alcoholic Beverage Commission	0	0	0	0	0	0	0	0	0	0
Fish and Wildlife	4	0	0	0	4	9	0	9	0	0
Office of Narcotics and Dangerous Drugs	0	0	0	0	0	28	0	28	0	0
Park Rangers	8	0	0	0	8	46	2	44	0	0
River and Bay Authority	3	0	0	2	1	12	2	6	4	0

See footnotes at end of table.

Table 11

Offenses Known to Law Enforcement
by State Agency by State, 2003—Continued
by Federal Agency, 2003

State agency by state	Violent crime	Violent crime Murder and non-negligent man-slaughter	Violent crime Forcible rape	Violent crime Robbery	Violent crime Aggravated assault	Property crime	Property crime Burglary	Property crime Larceny-theft	Property crime Motor vehicle theft	Arson[1]
DELAWARE—Continued										
State Capitol Police	4	0	0	1	3	33	3	26	4	0
State Fire Marshal	29	0	0	0	29	19	18	1	0	299
State Police:										
Kent County	554	3	50	36	465	1,737	558	1,056	123	2
New Castle County	764	1	18	376	369	5,521	723	4,314	484	2
Sussex County	609	5	51	45	508	2,814	877	1,776	161	9
DISTRICT OF COLUMBIA										
Metro Transit Police	220	1	1	105	113	1,072	0	718	354	0
National Zoological Park	1	0	0	0	1	25	1	24	0	0
FLORIDA										
Capitol Police	2	0	0	0	2	22	5	17	0	0
Department of Environmental Protection, Division of Law Enforcement:										
Alachua County	0	0	0	0	0	1	1	0	0	0
Bay County	0	0	0	0	0	7	6	1	0	0
Brevard County	0	0	0	0	0	3	1	2	0	0
Broward County	0	0	0	0	0	9	2	7	0	0
Charlotte County	0	0	0	0	0	0	0	0	0	0
Citrus County	0	0	0	0	0	0	0	0	0	0
Collier County	0	0	0	0	0	7	2	5	0	0
Columbia County	0	0	0	0	0	0	0	0	0	0
Dixie County	0	0	0	0	0	0	0	0	0	0
Duval County	0	0	0	0	0	5	2	3	0	0
Escambia County	0	0	0	0	0	1	1	0	0	0
Flagler County	0	0	0	0	0	1	1	0	0	0
Franklin County	0	0	0	0	0	0	0	0	0	0
Gadsden County	0	0	0	0	0	0	0	0	0	0
Gilchrist County	0	0	0	0	0	0	0	0	0	0
Gulf County	0	0	0	0	0	1	1	0	0	0
Hamilton County	0	0	0	0	0	0	0	0	0	0
Highlands County	0	0	0	0	0	0	0	0	0	0
Hillsborough County	0	0	0	0	0	1	0	1	0	0
Indian River County	0	0	0	0	0	8	2	6	0	0
Jackson County	0	0	0	0	0	0	0	0	0	0
Lafayette County	0	0	0	0	0	1	1	0	0	0
Lake County	0	0	0	0	0	0	0	0	0	0
Lee County	0	0	0	0	0	7	4	3	0	0
Leon County	0	0	0	0	0	1	1	0	0	0
Levy County	0	0	0	0	0	0	0	0	0	0
Madison County	0	0	0	0	0	0	0	0	0	0
Manatee County	0	0	0	0	0	1	1	0	0	0
Marion County	0	0	0	0	0	1	0	1	0	0
Martin County	0	0	0	0	0	6	4	2	0	0
Miami-Dade County	0	0	0	0	0	7	1	6	0	0
Monroe County	0	0	0	0	0	12	5	7	0	0
Nassau County	0	0	0	0	0	1	1	0	0	0
Okaloosa County	0	0	0	0	0	0	0	0	0	0
Okeechobee County	0	0	0	0	0	1	1	0	0	0
Orange County	0	0	0	0	0	1	1	0	0	0
Osceola County	0	0	0	0	0	0	0	0	0	0
Palm Beach County	0	0	0	0	0	1	1	0	0	0
Pasco County	0	0	0	0	0	0	0	0	0	0
Pinellas County	0	0	0	0	0	1	0	1	0	0
Polk County	0	0	0	0	0	0	0	0	0	0
Santa Rosa County	1	0	0	0	1	1	1	0	0	0
Sarasota County	0	0	0	0	0	4	2	2	0	0
Seminole County	0	0	0	0	0	1	1	0	0	0
St. Johns County	0	0	0	0	0	5	3	2	0	0
St. Lucie County	0	0	0	0	0	6	5	1	0	0

See footnotes at end of table.

Table 11

Offenses Known to Law Enforcement

by State Agency by State, 2003—Continued
by Federal Agency, 2003

State agency by state	Violent crime	Murder and non-negligent man-slaughter	Forcible rape	Robbery	Aggravated assault	Property crime	Burglary	Larceny-theft	Motor vehicle theft	Arson[1]
FLORIDA—Continued										
Department of Environmental Protection,										
Division of Law Enforcement—Continued:										
Sumter County	0	0	0	0	0	2	2	0	0	0
Suwannee County	0	0	0	0	0	1	1	0	0	0
Volusia County	0	0	0	0	0	4	3	1	0	0
Wakulla County	0	0	0	0	0	1	1	0	0	0
Walton County	0	0	0	0	0	0	0	0	0	0
Department of Insurance:										
Broward County	0	0	0	0	0	0	0	0	0	0
Duval County	0	0	0	0	0	0	0	0	0	0
Escambia County	0	0	0	0	0	0	0	0	0	0
Hillsborough County	0	0	0	0	0	0	0	0	0	0
Lee County	0	0	0	0	0	0	0	0	0	0
Miami-Dade County	0	0	0	0	0	0	0	0	0	0
Orange County	0	0	0	0	0	0	0	0	0	0
Palm Beach County	0	0	0	0	0	0	0	0	0	0
Department of Law Enforcement:										
Duval County, Jacksonville	1	1	0	0	0	0	0	0	0	0
Escambia County, Pensacola	0	0	0	0	0	0	0	0	0	0
Hillsborough County, Tampa	1	0	0	0	1	0	0	0	0	0
Leon County, Tallahassee	6	2	3	0	1	2	0	0	2	0
Orange County, Orlando	0	0	0	0	0	0	0	0	0	0
Florida Game Commission:										
Alachua County	0	0	0	0	0	0	0	0	0	0
Baker County	0	0	0	0	0	0	0	0	0	0
Bay County	0	0	0	0	0	0	0	0	0	0
Bradford County	0	0	0	0	0	0	0	0	0	0
Brevard County	0	0	0	0	0	0	0	0	0	0
Broward County	0	0	0	0	0	0	0	0	0	0
Calhoun County	0	0	0	0	0	0	0	0	0	0
Charlotte County	0	0	0	0	0	0	0	0	0	0
Citrus County	0	0	0	0	0	0	0	0	0	0
Clay County	0	0	0	0	0	0	0	0	0	0
Collier County	0	0	0	0	0	0	0	0	0	0
Columbia County	0	0	0	0	0	0	0	0	0	0
DeSoto County	0	0	0	0	0	0	0	0	0	0
Dixie County	0	0	0	0	0	0	0	0	0	0
Duval County	0	0	0	0	0	0	0	0	0	0
Escambia County	0	0	0	0	0	0	0	0	0	0
Flagler County	0	0	0	0	0	0	0	0	0	0
Franklin County	0	0	0	0	0	0	0	0	0	0
Gadsden County	0	0	0	0	0	0	0	0	0	0
Gilchrist County	0	0	0	0	0	0	0	0	0	0
Glades County	0	0	0	0	0	0	0	0	0	0
Gulf County	0	0	0	0	0	0	0	0	0	0
Hamilton County	0	0	0	0	0	0	0	0	0	0
Hardee County	0	0	0	0	0	0	0	0	0	0
Hendry County	0	0	0	0	0	0	0	0	0	0
Hernando County	0	0	0	0	0	0	0	0	0	0
Highlands County	0	0	0	0	0	0	0	0	0	0
Hillsborough County	0	0	0	0	0	0	0	0	0	0
Holmes County	0	0	0	0	0	0	0	0	0	0
Indian River County	0	0	0	0	0	0	0	0	0	0
Jackson County	0	0	0	0	0	0	0	0	0	0
Jefferson County	0	0	0	0	0	0	0	0	0	0
Lafayette County	0	0	0	0	0	0	0	0	0	0
Lake County	0	0	0	0	0	0	0	0	0	0
Lee County	0	0	0	0	0	0	0	0	0	0
Leon County	0	0	0	0	0	0	0	0	0	0
Levy County	0	0	0	0	0	0	0	0	0	0
Liberty County	0	0	0	0	0	0	0	0	0	0
Madison County	0	0	0	0	0	0	0	0	0	0
Manatee County	0	0	0	0	0	0	0	0	0	0

See footnotes at end of table.

Table 11

Offenses Known to Law Enforcement
by State Agency by State, 2003—Continued
by Federal Agency, 2003

State agency by state	Violent crime	Murder and non-negligent man-slaughter	Forcible rape	Robbery	Aggravated assault	Property crime	Burglary	Larceny-theft	Motor vehicle theft	Arson[1]
FLORIDA—Continued										
Florida Game Commission—Continued:										
Marion County	0	0	0	0	0	0	0	0	0	0
Martin County	0	0	0	0	0	0	0	0	0	0
Miami-Dade County	0	0	0	0	0	0	0	0	0	0
Monroe County	0	0	0	0	0	0	0	0	0	0
Nassau County	0	0	0	0	0	0	0	0	0	0
Okaloosa County	0	0	0	0	0	0	0	0	0	0
Okeechobee County	0	0	0	0	0	0	0	0	0	0
Orange County	0	0	0	0	0	0	0	0	0	0
Osceola County	0	0	0	0	0	0	0	0	0	0
Palm Beach County	0	0	0	0	0	0	0	0	0	0
Pasco County	0	0	0	0	0	0	0	0	0	0
Pinellas County	0	0	0	0	0	0	0	0	0	0
Polk County	0	0	0	0	0	0	0	0	0	0
Putnam County	0	0	0	0	0	0	0	0	0	0
Santa Rosa County	0	0	0	0	0	0	0	0	0	0
Sarasota County	0	0	0	0	0	0	0	0	0	0
Seminole County	0	0	0	0	0	0	0	0	0	0
St. Johns County	0	0	0	0	0	0	0	0	0	0
St. Lucie County	0	0	0	0	0	0	0	0	0	0
Sumter County	0	0	0	0	0	0	0	0	0	0
Suwannee County	0	0	0	0	0	0	0	0	0	0
Taylor County	0	0	0	0	0	0	0	0	0	0
Union County	0	0	0	0	0	0	0	0	0	0
Volusia County	0	0	0	0	0	0	0	0	0	0
Wakulla County	0	0	0	0	0	0	0	0	0	0
Walton County	0	0	0	0	0	0	0	0	0	0
Washington County	0	0	0	0	0	0	0	0	0	0
Highway Patrol:										
Alachua County	1	0	0	0	1	0	0	0	0	0
Baker County	0	0	0	0	0	0	0	0	0	0
Bay County	0	0	0	0	0	0	0	0	0	0
Bradford County	0	0	0	0	0	0	0	0	0	0
Brevard County	1	0	0	0	1	1	0	1	0	0
Broward County	58	0	0	0	58	76	0	32	44	0
Calhoun County	0	0	0	0	0	0	0	0	0	0
Charlotte County	1	0	0	0	1	0	0	0	0	0
Citrus County	0	0	0	0	0	0	0	0	0	0
Clay County	0	0	0	0	0	1	0	0	1	0
Collier County	1	0	0	0	1	1	0	0	1	0
Columbia County	2	0	0	0	2	1	0	1	0	0
DeSoto County	0	0	0	0	0	0	0	0	0	0
Dixie County	0	0	0	0	0	0	0	0	0	0
Duval County	12	0	0	0	12	6	0	4	2	0
Escambia County	6	0	0	0	6	2	0	2	0	0
Flagler County	0	0	0	0	0	0	0	0	0	0
Franklin County	0	0	0	0	0	0	0	0	0	0
Gadsden County	1	0	0	0	1	1	0	0	1	0
Gilchrist County	0	0	0	0	0	0	0	0	0	0
Glades County	0	0	0	0	0	0	0	0	0	0
Gulf County	1	0	1	0	0	2	0	0	2	0
Hamilton County	0	0	0	0	0	1	0	1	0	0
Hardee County	0	0	0	0	0	0	0	0	0	0
Hendry County	0	0	0	0	0	0	0	0	0	0
Hernando County	1	0	0	0	1	2	0	0	2	0
Highlands County	0	0	0	0	0	0	0	0	0	0
Hillsborough County	6	0	0	0	6	1	0	1	0	0
Holmes County	1	0	0	0	1	1	0	1	0	0
Indian River County	2	0	0	0	2	0	0	0	0	0
Jackson County	1	0	0	0	1	0	0	0	0	0
Jefferson County	0	0	0	0	0	0	0	0	0	0
Lafayette County	0	0	0	0	0	0	0	0	0	0
Lake County	0	0	0	0	0	1	0	1	0	0

See footnotes at end of table.

Table 11

Offenses Known to Law Enforcement
by State Agency by State, 2003—Continued
by Federal Agency, 2003

	Violent crime					Property crime				
State agency by state	Violent crime	Murder and non-negligent man-slaughter	Forcible rape	Robbery	Aggravated assault	Property crime	Burglary	Larceny-theft	Motor vehicle theft	Arson[1]
FLORIDA—Continued										
Highway Patrol—Continued:										
Lee County	2	0	0	0	2	2	0	2	0	0
Leon County	1	0	0	0	1	3	0	1	2	0
Levy County	0	0	0	0	0	0	0	0	0	0
Liberty County	0	0	0	0	0	0	0	0	0	0
Madison County	0	0	0	0	0	0	0	0	0	0
Manatee County	5	0	0	1	4	1	0	1	0	0
Marion County	1	0	0	0	1	0	0	0	0	0
Martin County	1	0	0	0	1	0	0	0	0	0
Miami-Dade County	44	0	0	1	43	41	0	13	28	0
Monroe County	2	0	0	1	1	0	0	0	0	0
Nassau County	1	0	0	0	1	0	0	0	0	0
Okaloosa County	0	0	0	0	0	0	0	0	0	0
Okeechobee County	1	0	0	0	1	1	0	1	0	0
Orange County	11	0	0	0	11	5	0	3	2	0
Osceola County	4	0	0	1	3	6	0	6	0	0
Palm Beach County	39	0	1	1	37	31	0	25	6	0
Pasco County	3	0	0	0	3	0	0	0	0	0
Pinellas County	4	0	0	0	4	0	0	0	0	0
Polk County	5	0	0	0	5	0	0	0	0	0
Putnam County	0	0	0	0	0	0	0	0	0	0
Santa Rosa County	2	0	0	0	2	0	0	0	0	0
Sarasota County	4	0	0	0	4	1	0	0	1	0
Seminole County	1	0	0	0	1	1	0	0	1	0
St. Johns County	1	0	0	0	1	0	0	0	0	0
St. Lucie County	3	0	0	0	3	5	0	5	0	0
Sumter County	2	0	0	0	2	2	0	2	0	0
Suwannee County	2	0	0	0	2	0	0	0	0	0
Taylor County	0	0	0	0	0	0	0	0	0	0
Union County	0	0	0	0	0	0	0	0	0	0
Volusia County	1	0	0	0	1	0	0	0	0	0
Wakulla County	0	0	0	0	0	0	0	0	0	0
Walton County	0	0	0	0	0	0	0	0	0	0
Washington County	0	0	0	0	0	1	0	1	0	0
State Treasurer's Office, Division of Insurance Fraud	0	0	0	0	0	0	0	0	0	0
GEORGIA										
Capitol Police	1	0	0	1	0	77	1	74	2	0
Georgia Department of Public Safety	4	0	0	0	4	0	0	0	0	0
Georgia Public Safety Training Center	0	0	0	0	0	0	0	0	0	0
Georgia World Congress	10	0	1	3	6	426	27	388	11	0
Ports Authority, Savannah	0	0	0	0	0	9	0	3	6	0
IDAHO										
Alcohol Beverage Control	0	0	0	0	0	0	0	0	0	0
Bureau of Narcotics:										
Region 1	0	0	0	0	0	0	0	0	0	0
Region 2	0	0	0	0	0	0	0	0	0	0
Region 3	2	0	1	0	1	0	0	0	0	0
Region 4	0	0	0	0	0	0	0	0	0	0
Region 5	0	0	0	0	0	0	0	0	0	0
Region 6	0	0	0	0	0	0	0	0	0	0
State Police:										
Boise	3	0	0	0	3	1	0	1	0	0
Coeur d'Alene	1	0	0	0	1	1	0	0	1	0
Idaho Falls	0	0	0	0	0	2	0	2	0	0
Lewiston	0	0	0	0	0	0	0	0	0	0
Pocatello	0	0	0	0	0	0	0	0	0	0
Twin Falls	0	0	0	0	0	0	0	0	0	0

See footnotes at end of table.

Table 11

Offenses Known to Law Enforcement
by State Agency by State, 2003—Continued
by Federal Agency, 2003

State agency by state	Violent crime	Violent crime — Murder and non-negligent man-slaughter	Violent crime — Forcible rape	Violent crime — Robbery	Violent crime — Aggravated assault	Property crime	Property crime — Burglary	Property crime — Larceny-theft	Property crime — Motor vehicle theft	Arson[1]
ILLINOIS[2]										
INDIANA										
Northern Indiana Commuter Transportation District	2	0	0	0	2	83	0	58	25	0
State Police:										
Adams County	6	0	0	2	4	8	1	4	3	0
Allen County	16	0	3	2	11	50	5	35	10	0
Bartholomew County	6	0	0	0	6	17	3	10	4	0
Benton County	2	0	0	0	2	3	1	2	0	0
Blackford County	0	0	0	0	0	1	0	1	0	0
Boone County	2	0	0	1	1	14	2	5	7	0
Brown County	1	0	0	0	1	7	1	5	1	0
Carroll County	6	0	1	1	4	8	0	7	1	0
Cass County	28	0	1	0	27	28	6	20	2	1
Clark County	15	0	2	1	12	77	11	42	24	0
Clay County	7	0	0	5	2	25	5	14	6	0
Clinton County	3	0	1	0	2	15	1	12	2	0
Crawford County	10	0	4	2	4	26	10	13	3	1
Daviess County	5	1	0	0	4	15	4	8	3	0
Dearborn County	22	0	2	1	19	80	9	50	21	1
Decatur County	4	0	1	0	3	20	2	15	3	0
De Kalb County	9	0	0	0	9	17	2	8	7	0
Delaware County	7	0	1	2	4	24	4	19	1	0
Dubois County	11	0	2	3	6	33	5	25	3	0
Elkhart County	22	0	0	4	18	68	11	41	16	1
Fayette County	3	0	1	1	1	21	11	9	1	0
Floyd County	4	0	0	1	3	28	5	15	8	1
Fountain County	2	0	0	1	1	7	2	5	0	0
Franklin County	15	0	0	2	13	45	8	34	3	0
Fulton County	1	0	0	0	1	9	7	2	0	0
Gibson County	5	0	1	1	3	18	2	8	8	0
Grant County	3	0	0	2	1	6	1	5	0	0
Greene County	15	2	1	0	12	37	9	20	8	2
Hamilton County	12	0	0	0	12	12	2	7	3	0
Hancock County	3	0	0	1	2	7	1	5	1	0
Harrison County	15	0	3	4	8	62	18	25	19	0
Hendricks County	16	0	1	2	13	29	3	20	6	0
Henry County	6	0	0	2	4	18	1	15	2	0
Howard County	0	0	0	0	0	18	7	8	3	0
Huntington County	1	0	0	0	1	10	1	6	3	0
Jackson County	18	0	2	3	13	115	36	68	11	3
Jasper County	1	0	0	0	1	16	0	10	6	0
Jay County	2	0	1	0	1	9	4	5	0	0
Jefferson County	7	0	1	0	6	32	14	14	4	0
Jennings County	6	0	2	0	4	27	6	18	3	0
Johnson County	6	0	1	0	5	11	0	4	7	0
Knox County	5	0	0	1	4	29	4	21	4	0
Kosciusko County	9	0	0	2	7	24	2	19	3	0
Lagrange County	4	0	0	1	3	32	10	19	3	1
Lake County	49	2	1	2	44	402	2	97	303	0
La Porte County	9	0	2	0	7	50	3	35	12	0
Lawrence County	8	0	3	1	4	11	4	5	2	0
Madison County	19	0	0	2	17	34	6	22	6	1
Marion County	60	0	5	5	50	275	1	196	78	1
Marshall County	9	0	3	1	5	39	9	25	5	0
Martin County	11	0	3	2	6	9	2	5	2	0
Miami County	11	1	0	0	10	38	6	27	5	1
Monroe County	11	0	3	1	7	68	8	53	7	0
Montgomery County	7	0	0	2	5	9	1	7	1	0
Morgan County	11	1	0	1	9	53	8	38	7	0
Newton County	1	0	0	0	1	13	4	7	2	0
Noble County	14	0	1	2	11	37	6	30	1	0
Ohio County	2	0	0	1	1	9	0	9	0	0
Orange County	17	0	6	2	9	35	6	27	2	0

See footnotes at end of table.

Table 11

Offenses Known to Law Enforcement
by State Agency by State, 2003—Continued
by Federal Agency, 2003

State agency by state	Violent crime	Murder and non-negligent man-slaughter	Forcible rape	Robbery	Aggravated assault	Property crime	Burglary	Larceny-theft	Motor vehicle theft	Arson[1]
		Violent crime					*Property crime*			
INDIANA—Continued										
State Police—Continued:										
Owen County	4	1	2	0	1	9	2	5	2	0
Parke County	9	0	1	1	7	16	3	11	2	0
Perry County	11	0	0	2	9	47	22	20	5	0
Pike County	9	0	4	0	5	15	1	14	0	0
Porter County	7	0	0	0	7	24	0	21	3	0
Posey County	13	0	2	2	9	23	5	15	3	2
Pulaski County	3	0	0	0	3	3	2	1	0	1
Putnam County	14	0	2	4	8	30	4	22	4	0
Randolph County	2	0	0	1	1	6	0	5	1	0
Ripley County	14	0	1	1	12	108	23	75	10	1
Rush County	1	0	0	1	0	11	2	8	1	0
Scott County	15	0	3	2	10	34	8	22	4	1
Shelby County	6	0	0	2	4	19	2	14	3	0
Spencer County	12	0	1	4	7	27	7	17	3	0
Starke County	2	0	0	2	0	7	0	4	3	1
Steuben County	18	0	1	4	13	31	7	20	4	1
St. Joseph County	18	0	1	2	15	73	17	43	13	0
Sullivan County	13	0	2	2	9	22	5	15	2	0
Switzerland County	8	0	2	1	5	18	3	11	4	1
Tippecanoe County	16	0	1	4	11	54	1	43	10	0
Tipton County	2	0	1	0	1	12	7	4	1	0
Union County	2	0	0	1	1	7	0	7	0	0
Vanderburgh County	11	0	4	1	6	41	1	30	10	0
Vermillion County	5	0	0	0	5	12	3	8	1	0
Vigo County	43	0	1	12	30	134	25	78	31	0
Wabash County	1	0	1	0	0	14	4	9	1	0
Warren County	0	0	0	0	0	2	0	2	0	0
Warrick County	7	0	0	2	5	22	5	17	0	0
Washington County	6	0	2	0	4	12	3	9	0	0
Wayne County	7	0	1	1	5	33	4	22	7	0
Wells County	4	0	0	0	4	3	0	2	1	0
White County	10	0	0	3	7	33	7	20	6	0
Whitley County	6	0	0	2	4	12	1	10	1	1
KANSAS										
Kansas Alcoholic Beverage Control	0	0	0	0	0	0	0	0	0	0
Kansas Bureau of Investigation	13	1	1	0	11	6	1	5	0	0
Kansas Department of Wildlife and Parks	2	0	1	0	1	57	5	52	0	1
Kansas Highway Patrol	33	0	0	1	32	141	6	92	43	0
Kansas Lottery Security Division	0	0	0	0	0	0	0	0	0	0
Securities Office, Investigation Section	0	0	0	0	0	0	0	0	0	0
KENTUCKY[2]										
LOUISIANA										
Tensas Basin Levee	0	0	0	0	0	0	0	0	0	0
MAINE										
Drug Enforcement Agency:										
Androscoggin County	0	0	0	0	0	0	0	0	0	0
Aroostook County	0	0	0	0	0	0	0	0	0	0
Cumberland County	0	0	0	0	0	0	0	0	0	0
Franklin County	0	0	0	0	0	0	0	0	0	0
Hancock County	0	0	0	0	0	0	0	0	0	0
Kennebec County	0	0	0	0	0	0	0	0	0	0
Knox County	0	0	0	0	0	0	0	0	0	0
Lincoln County	0	0	0	0	0	0	0	0	0	0
Oxford County	0	0	0	0	0	0	0	0	0	0
Penobscot County	0	0	0	0	0	0	0	0	0	0

See footnotes at end of table.

Table 11

Offenses Known to Law Enforcement

by State Agency by State, 2003—Continued
by Federal Agency, 2003

State agency by state	Violent crime	Murder and non-negligent man-slaughter	Forcible rape	Robbery	Aggravated assault	Property crime	Burglary	Larceny-theft	Motor vehicle theft	Arson[1]
MAINE—Continued										
Drug Enforcement Agency—Continued:										
Piscataquis County	0	0	0	0	0	0	0	0	0	0
Sagadahoc County	0	0	0	0	0	0	0	0	0	0
Somerset County	0	0	0	0	0	0	0	0	0	0
Waldo County	0	0	0	0	0	0	0	0	0	0
Washington County	0	0	0	0	0	0	0	0	0	0
York County	0	0	0	0	0	0	0	0	0	0
State Police:										
Androscoggin County	6	1	2	0	3	122	36	77	9	0
Aroostook County	8	1	4	0	3	223	96	112	15	1
Cumberland County	6	1	1	1	3	78	18	48	12	0
Franklin County	2	0	0	0	2	55	15	36	4	1
Hancock County	1	0	1	0	0	189	76	110	3	0
Kennebec County	8	0	1	0	7	240	58	159	23	0
Knox County	3	0	0	0	3	59	9	43	7	0
Lincoln County	0	0	0	0	0	7	1	5	1	0
Oxford County	3	0	2	0	1	121	46	63	12	0
Penobscot County	12	1	3	0	8	299	99	181	19	0
Piscataquis County	2	1	0	0	1	16	5	10	1	0
Sagadahoc County	1	0	0	1	0	3	1	2	0	0
Somerset County	1	1	0	0	0	146	33	106	7	0
Waldo County	1	0	1	0	0	43	17	24	2	1
Washington County	2	0	0	0	2	193	68	115	10	0
York County	6	0	0	0	6	77	35	39	3	0
MARYLAND										
Comptroller of the Treasury, Field Enforcement Division	0	0	0	0	0	0	0	0	0	0
Department of Public Safety and Correctional Services, Internal Investigations Unit	151	2	0	0	149	0	0	0	0	0
General Services:										
Annapolis, Anne Arundel County	0	0	0	0	0	19	0	19	0	
Baltimore City	2	0	0	1	1	92	1	90	1	0
Maryland State Police Statewide	5	0	1	0	4	2	0	0	2	0
Natural Resources Police	0	0	0	0	0	131	0	131	0	19
Rosewood	4	0	0	0	4	10	0	10	0	0
Springfield Hospital	0	0	0	0	0	17	11	6	0	0
State Police:										
Allegany County	71	0	6	1	64	579	141	408	30	4
Anne Arundel County	16	0	0	2	14	99	3	88	8	0
Baltimore City	0	0	0	0	0	0	0	0	0	0
Baltimore County	31	0	0	1	30	37	0	30	7	0
Calvert County	119	1	2	1	115	329	86	229	14	10
Caroline County	20	0	5	0	15	99	27	54	18	11
Carroll County	205	1	37	20	147	1,372	325	967	80	7
Cecil County	251	4	8	23	216	1,020	336	600	84	16
Charles County	19	1	0	0	18	37	2	30	5	39
Dorchester County	8	0	1	2	5	74	23	38	13	1
Frederick County	78	0	11	12	55	765	123	594	48	13
Garrett County	16	0	4	1	11	173	47	111	15	5
Harford County	155	0	5	55	95	644	138	438	68	36
Howard County	6	0	0	3	3	29	1	26	2	0
Kent County	6	0	0	0	6	25	9	12	4	2
Montgomery County	7	0	0	0	7	20	3	11	6	0
Prince George's County	46	0	0	0	46	160	1	107	52	0
Queen Anne's County	21	0	1	3	17	161	36	117	8	10
Somerset County	72	2	2	5	63	289	124	137	28	2
St. Mary's County	78	0	7	5	66	297	81	185	31	25
Talbot County	8	1	2	0	5	103	24	70	9	6
Washington County	84	0	8	6	70	360	59	265	36	19
Wicomico County	53	0	2	13	38	274	90	158	26	16
Worcester County	27	0	1	3	23	248	74	161	13	14

See footnotes at end of table.

Table 11

Offenses Known to Law Enforcement
by State Agency by State, 2003—Continued
by Federal Agency, 2003

State agency by state	Violent crime	Murder and non-negligent man-slaughter	Forcible rape	Robbery	Aggravated assault	Property crime	Burglary	Larceny-theft	Motor vehicle theft	Arson[1]
MARYLAND—Continued										
State Fire Marshal	0	0	0	0	0	0	0	0	0	0
Transit Administration	0	0	0	0	0	0	0	0	0	0
Transportation Authority	21	0	0	0	21	452	1	297	154	0
MASSACHUSETTS										
State Police:										
Barnstable County	3	0	0	1	2	2	0	2	0	0
Bristol County	8	0	0	1	7	5	0	4	1	0
Dukes County	0	0	0	0	0	0	0	0	0	0
Norfolk County	4	0	0	0	4	4	0	3	1	0
Plymouth County	11	0	0	2	9	9	0	5	4	0
MICHIGAN										
State Police:										
Alcona County	6	0	2	1	3	27	9	17	1	0
Alger County	10	0	1	0	9	121	46	64	11	4
Allegan County	43	0	17	2	24	402	125	245	32	4
Alpena County	33	3	7	0	23	251	71	165	15	1
Antrim County	8	0	5	0	3	20	6	12	2	1
Arenac County	14	0	4	0	10	62	24	38	0	3
Baraga County	9	0	2	0	7	43	13	26	4	0
Barry County	48	1	13	0	34	414	167	215	32	10
Bay County	79	0	33	9	37	519	170	308	41	6
Benzie County	13	0	7	0	6	51	15	32	4	0
Berrien County	69	2	34	2	31	390	124	234	32	6
Branch County	47	0	19	0	28	231	75	128	28	2
Calhoun County	45	0	19	2	24	287	115	154	18	1
Cass County	21	1	4	3	13	93	24	59	10	12
Charlevoix County	8	0	6	0	2	13	6	7	0	2
Cheboygan County	23	0	6	1	16	187	75	95	17	2
Chippewa County	35	1	3	1	30	158	68	83	7	2
Clare County	27	0	7	1	19	94	42	43	9	1
Clinton County	7	0	4	0	3	51	23	24	4	0
Crawford County	5	0	1	1	3	23	9	12	2	1
Delta County	24	0	13	0	11	117	29	70	18	3
Dickinson County	2	0	1	0	1	46	21	20	5	1
Eaton County	3	0	1	0	2	24	6	14	4	0
Emmet County	14	0	6	1	7	170	62	105	3	3
Genesee County	69	1	27	2	39	393	131	227	35	11
Gladwin County	32	0	5	0	27	137	69	53	15	4
Gogebic County	18	0	10	0	8	31	15	14	2	0
Grand Traverse County	27	0	13	0	14	252	38	198	16	3
Gratiot County	40	0	11	1	28	141	43	90	8	2
Hillsdale County	40	0	14	1	25	218	74	125	19	3
Houghton County	14	0	5	0	9	135	32	93	10	4
Huron County	7	0	5	0	2	49	15	29	5	0
Ingham County	9	0	7	0	2	62	4	57	1	1
Ionia County	42	0	17	0	25	257	90	156	11	3
Iosco County	38	0	10	1	27	192	76	107	9	4
Iron County	14	1	7	0	6	58	21	32	5	0
Isabella County	38	1	14	4	19	369	120	223	26	3
Jackson County	93	0	18	2	73	392	112	250	30	4
Kalamazoo County	10	0	4	1	5	24	4	18	2	2
Kalkaska County	20	0	10	0	10	91	39	43	9	0
Kent County	19	1	8	0	10	50	3	44	3	11
Lake County	21	0	10	0	11	28	7	15	6	3
Lapeer County	39	1	14	3	21	170	62	93	15	6
Leelanau County	1	0	1	0	0	15	5	10	0	1
Lenawee County	26	0	9	1	16	167	66	87	14	5
Livingston County	85	0	14	9	62	681	162	450	69	2
Luce County	13	0	1	0	12	71	23	44	4	1

See footnotes at end of table.

Table 11

Offenses Known to Law Enforcement
by State Agency by State, 2003—Continued
by Federal Agency, 2003

State agency by state	Violent crime	Violent crime	Violent crime	Violent crime	Violent crime	Property crime	Property crime	Property crime	Property crime	
	Violent crime	Murder and non-negligent man-slaughter	Forcible rape	Robbery	Aggravated assault	Property crime	Burglary	Larceny-theft	Motor vehicle theft	Arson[1]
MICHIGAN—Continued										
State Police—Continued:										
Mackinac County	8	0	2	0	6	124	49	69	6	2
Macomb County	22	1	9	1	11	51	17	28	6	6
Manistee County	16	0	4	2	10	224	92	123	9	5
Marquette County	29	0	5	0	24	251	97	131	23	5
Mason County	10	0	9	0	1	61	12	47	2	0
Mecosta County	19	0	13	0	6	84	23	56	5	2
Menominee County	13	0	6	0	7	135	68	57	10	0
Midland County	2	0	0	0	2	12	4	8	0	0
Missaukee County	5	0	1	0	4	38	16	20	2	2
Monroe County	33	0	14	4	15	241	64	145	32	7
Montcalm County	64	0	34	3	27	550	276	240	34	10
Montmorency County	8	0	3	1	4	42	20	19	3	0
Muskegon County	24	1	4	0	19	265	89	159	17	5
Newaygo County	49	1	27	0	21	363	97	241	25	6
Oakland County	53	3	16	3	31	263	67	165	31	2
Oceana County	16	0	11	2	3	196	65	113	18	2
Ogemaw County	12	0	6	0	6	203	78	108	17	7
Ontonagon County	5	0	4	0	1	39	14	22	3	3
Osceola County	23	0	14	0	9	148	58	73	17	3
Oscoda County	8	0	5	0	3	23	11	10	2	0
Otsego County	39	1	12	1	25	263	116	123	24	1
Ottawa County	27	0	10	1	16	168	36	125	7	2
Presque Isle County	7	0	7	0	0	24	13	10	1	1
Roscommon County	27	0	7	0	20	266	89	153	24	3
Saginaw County	97	1	20	9	67	382	111	241	30	8
Sanilac County	28	0	5	0	23	183	96	68	19	1
Schoolcraft County	22	0	3	0	19	115	38	71	6	3
Shiawassee County	33	0	12	2	19	260	58	183	19	2
St. Clair County	26	0	7	1	18	193	76	91	26	10
St. Joseph County	58	1	19	0	38	334	103	189	42	13
Tuscola County	46	2	22	0	22	178	57	104	17	3
Van Buren County	107	1	17	2	87	618	223	340	55	13
Washtenaw County	43	0	11	2	30	230	97	101	32	5
Wayne County	109	12	16	19	62	160	22	111	27	4
Wexford County	22	0	11	0	11	250	62	178	10	1
MINNESOTA										
Capitol Security, St. Paul	0	0	0	0	0	37	0	37	0	0
Minnesota State Patrol	1	0	0	0	1	1	0	0	1	0
State Patrol:										
Brainerd	1	0	0	0	1	2	0	0	2	0
Detroit Lakes	0	0	0	0	0	0	0	0	0	0
Duluth	0	0	0	0	0	0	0	0	0	0
Golden Valley	0	0	0	0	0	0	0	0	0	0
Mankato	0	0	0	0	0	1	0	0	1	0
Marshall	0	0	0	0	0	1	0	0	1	0
Oakdale	0	0	0	0	0	0	0	0	0	0
Rochester	1	0	0	0	1	0	0	0	0	0
St. Cloud	0	0	0	0	0	0	0	0	0	0
Thief River Falls	0	0	0	0	0	0	0	0	0	0
Virginia	0	0	0	0	0	0	0	0	0	0
NEBRASKA										
Nebraska State Patrol	11	0	0	0	11	0	0	0	0	0
State Patrol:										
Adams County	1	0	0	0	1	0	0	0	0	0
Antelope County	0	0	0	0	0	1	1	0	0	0
Arthur County	0	0	0	0	0	0	0	0	0	0
Banner County	0	0	0	0	0	0	0	0	0	0
Blaine County	0	0	0	0	0	0	0	0	0	0

See footnotes at end of table.

Table 11

Offenses Known to Law Enforcement
by State Agency by State, 2003—Continued
by Federal Agency, 2003

State agency by state	Violent crime	Violent crime	Violent crime	Violent crime	Violent crime	Property crime	Property crime	Property crime	Property crime	Property crime
	Violent crime	Murder and non-negligent man-slaughter	Forcible rape	Robbery	Aggravated assault	Property crime	Burglary	Larceny-theft	Motor vehicle theft	Arson[1]
NEBRASKA—Continued										
State Patrol—Continued:										
Boone County	0	0	0	0	0	0	0	0	0	0
Box Butte County	0	0	0	0	0	1	0	1	0	0
Boyd County	0	0	0	0	0	0	0	0	0	0
Brown County	0	0	0	0	0	0	0	0	0	0
Buffalo County	1	0	1	0	0	3	1	2	0	0
Burt County	0	0	0	0	0	0	0	0	0	0
Butler County	0	0	0	0	0	0	0	0	0	0
Cass County	1	0	0	0	1	8	1	0	7	0
Cedar County	2	0	1	0	1	0	0	0	0	0
Chase County	2	0	0	0	2	0	0	0	0	0
Cherry County	1	0	0	0	1	1	1	0	0	0
Cheyenne County	0	0	0	0	0	1	0	1	0	0
Clay County	0	0	0	0	0	0	0	0	0	0
Colfax County	2	0	0	0	2	0	0	0	0	0
Cuming County	0	0	0	0	0	0	0	0	0	0
Custer County	2	0	1	0	1	0	0	0	0	0
Dakota County	0	0	0	0	0	0	0	0	0	0
Dawes County	4	0	4	0	0	2	1	1	0	0
Dawson County	3	0	0	0	3	1	0	1	0	0
Deuel County	0	0	0	0	0	0	0	0	0	0
Dixon County	0	0	0	0	0	0	0	0	0	0
Dodge County	0	0	0	0	0	2	2	0	0	0
Douglas County	4	0	0	0	4	2	1	0	1	0
Dundy County	0	0	0	0	0	0	0	0	0	0
Fillmore County	0	0	0	0	0	2	1	1	0	0
Franklin County	0	0	0	0	0	0	0	0	0	0
Frontier County	0	0	0	0	0	0	0	0	0	0
Furnas County	0	0	0	0	0	0	0	0	0	0
Gage County	0	0	0	0	0	0	0	0	0	0
Garden County	1	0	0	0	1	0	0	0	0	0
Garfield County	0	0	0	0	0	0	0	0	0	0
Gosper County	0	0	0	0	0	0	0	0	0	0
Grant County	0	0	0	0	0	0	0	0	0	0
Greeley County	1	0	1	0	0	0	0	0	0	0
Hall County	6	0	1	0	5	1	1	0	0	0
Hamilton County	0	0	0	0	0	0	0	0	0	0
Harlan County	1	0	0	0	1	2	1	1	0	0
Hayes County	0	0	0	0	0	0	0	0	0	0
Hitchcock County	0	0	0	0	0	0	0	0	0	0
Holt County	1	0	0	0	1	0	0	0	0	0
Hooker County	0	0	0	0	0	0	0	0	0	0
Howard County	0	0	0	0	0	2	1	1	0	0
Jefferson County	0	0	0	0	0	0	0	0	0	0
Johnson County	3	0	0	0	3	0	0	0	0	0
Kearney County	0	0	0	0	0	0	0	0	0	0
Keith County	0	0	0	0	0	0	0	0	0	0
Keya Paha County	0	0	0	0	0	0	0	0	0	0
Kimball County	1	0	0	0	1	0	0	0	0	0
Knox County	0	0	0	0	0	0	0	0	0	0
Lancaster County	7	0	0	2	5	1	1	0	0	0
Lincoln County	4	0	0	1	3	2	1	0	1	0
Logan County	0	0	0	0	0	0	0	0	0	0
Loup County	0	0	0	0	0	0	0	0	0	0
Madison County	5	0	1	0	4	10	6	2	2	0
McPherson County	0	0	0	0	0	0	0	0	0	0
Merrick County	1	0	0	0	1	1	0	0	1	0
Morrill County	0	0	0	0	0	0	0	0	0	0
Nance County	0	0	0	0	0	0	0	0	0	0
Nemaha County	1	0	0	0	1	0	0	0	0	0
Nuckolls County	0	0	0	0	0	0	0	0	0	0
Otoe County	0	0	0	0	0	0	0	0	0	0
Pawnee County	0	0	0	0	0	0	0	0	0	0

See footnotes at end of table.

Table 11

Offenses Known to Law Enforcement
by State Agency by State, 2003—Continued
by Federal Agency, 2003

State agency by state	Violent crime	Violent crime — Murder and non-negligent man-slaughter	Violent crime — Forcible rape	Violent crime — Robbery	Violent crime — Aggravated assault	Property crime	Property crime — Burglary	Property crime — Larceny-theft	Property crime — Motor vehicle theft	Arson[1]
NEBRASKA—Continued										
State Patrol—Continued:										
Perkins County	0	0	0	0	0	0	0	0	0	0
Phelps County	0	0	0	0	0	0	0	0	0	0
Pierce County	2	0	0	0	2	5	3	1	1	0
Platte County	0	0	0	0	0	1	1	0	0	0
Polk County	0	0	0	0	0	0	0	0	0	0
Red Willow County	0	0	0	0	0	1	0	0	1	0
Richardson County	0	0	0	0	0	0	0	0	0	0
Rock County	0	0	0	0	0	0	0	0	0	0
Saline County	0	0	0	0	0	0	0	0	0	0
Sarpy County	0	0	0	0	0	2	0	0	2	0
Saunders County	0	0	0	0	0	0	0	0	0	0
Scotts Bluff County	1	0	1	0	0	3	0	2	1	0
Seward County	0	0	0	0	0	0	0	0	0	0
Sheridan County	0	0	0	0	0	0	0	0	0	0
Sherman County	2	0	2	0	0	0	0	0	0	0
Sioux County	0	0	0	0	0	1	0	1	0	0
Stanton County	0	0	0	0	0	0	0	0	0	0
Thayer County	0	0	0	0	0	0	0	0	0	0
Thomas County	0	0	0	0	0	0	0	0	0	0
Thurston County	3	0	1	0	2	0	0	0	0	0
Valley County	0	0	0	0	0	0	0	0	0	0
Washington County	1	0	0	0	1	0	0	0	0	0
Wayne County	1	0	0	0	1	2	0	1	1	0
Webster County	1	0	0	0	1	0	0	0	0	0
Wheeler County	0	0	0	0	0	0	0	0	0	0
York County	0	0	0	0	0	1	1	0	0	0
NEW HAMPSHIRE[3]										
Liquor Commission	2	0	0	1	1	4	3	1	0	0
State Police:										
Belknap County	2	0	0	1	1	4	3	1	0	0
Carroll County	6	0	1	0	5	74	19	53	2	0
Cheshire County	3	0	2	0	1	32	13	15	4	0
Hillsborough County	3	0	0	0	3	7	6	1	0	1
Merrimack County	5	0	3	0	2	78	33	33	12	0
Rockingham County	3	0	2	0	1	4	0	3	1	0
Sullivan County	5	0	1	0	4	20	9	8	3	0
NEW JERSEY										
Hunterdon Developmental Center	0	0	0	0	0	12	0	12	0	0
Port Authority of New York and New Jersey[4]	47	0	0	18	29	729	19	668	42	1
NEW YORK										
Port Authority of New York and New Jersey[5]	158	0	1	41	116	1,265	22	1,216	27	
State Park:										
Allegany County	0	0	0	0	0	0	0	0	0	
Broome County	1	0	0	0	1	15	1	13	1	
Cattaraugus County	0	0	0	0	0	12	0	12	0	
Cayuga County	1	0	0	0	1	2	0	2	0	
Chautauqua County	0	0	0	0	0	0	0	0	0	
Chenango County	0	0	0	0	0	0	0	0	0	
Columbia County	1	0	0	0	1	5	0	5	0	
Cortland County	0	0	0	0	0	0	0	0	0	
Delaware County	0	0	0	0	0	0	0	0	0	
Dutchess County	0	0	0	0	0	9	2	7	0	
Erie County	0	0	0	0	0	12	0	12	0	
Genesee County	0	0	0	0	0	1	0	1	0	
Herkimer County	0	0	0	0	0	0	0	0	0	
Livingston County	0	0	0	0	0	10	6	4	0	

See footnotes at end of table.

Table 11

Offenses Known to Law Enforcement
by State Agency by State, 2003—Continued
by Federal Agency, 2003

State agency by state	Violent crime	Murder and non-negligent man-slaughter	Forcible rape	Robbery	Aggravated assault	Property crime	Burglary	Larceny-theft	Motor vehicle theft	Arson[1]
NEW YORK—Continued										
State Park—Continued:										
Madison County	0	0	0	0	0	0	0	0	0	
Monroe County	1	0	0	0	1	6	0	6	0	
Niagara County	1	0	0	1	0	22	0	22	0	
Oneida County	0	0	0	0	0	10	1	9	0	
Onondaga County	0	0	0	0	0	15	0	15	0	
Ontario County	0	0	0	0	0	2	0	2	0	
Orange County	0	0	0	0	0	4	2	2	0	
Orleans County	1	0	0	0	1	1	1	0	0	
Oswego County	0	0	0	0	0	11	2	9	0	
Otsego County	0	0	0	0	0	3	0	3	0	
Putnam County	1	0	0	0	1	7	0	7	0	
Rockland County	0	0	0	0	0	28	2	26	0	
Schuyler County	0	0	0	0	0	6	1	5	0	
Seneca County	0	0	0	0	0	20	4	16	0	
Steuben County	0	0	0	0	0	0	0	0	0	
Sullivan County	0	0	0	0	0	0	0	0	0	
Tioga County	0	0	0	0	0	0	0	0	0	
Tompkins County	1	0	0	0	1	10	1	9	0	
Ulster County	0	0	0	0	0	2	0	2	0	
Wayne County	0	0	0	0	0	0	0	0	0	
Westchester County	1	0	0	0	1	26	0	26	0	
Wyoming County	0	0	0	0	0	3	0	3	0	
Yates County	0	0	0	0	0	0	0	0	0	
State Police:										
Albany County	22	0	0	1	21	242	22	208	12	
Allegany County	40	1	7	1	31	283	115	152	16	
Broome County	69	0	15	12	42	710	122	568	20	
Cattaraugus County	39	1	5	2	31	332	124	205	3	
Cayuga County	82	1	8	4	69	226	67	154	5	
Chautauqua County	18	0	4	0	14	155	29	116	10	
Chemung County	47	1	9	0	37	297	32	251	14	
Chenango County	25	0	6	1	18	172	61	111	0	
Clinton County	146	0	25	3	118	802	321	454	27	
Columbia County	33	0	7	5	21	321	61	246	14	
Cortland County	20	0	1	1	18	230	27	197	6	
Delaware County	48	1	4	1	42	383	150	226	7	
Dutchess County	111	2	15	8	86	619	174	412	33	
Erie County	64	2	5	1	56	561	98	441	22	
Essex County	38	0	10	0	28	351	164	176	11	
Franklin County	121	2	11	4	104	335	144	174	17	
Fulton County	18	0	3	0	15	102	24	77	1	
Genesee County	1	0	1	0	0	71	12	55	4	
Greene County	93	1	11	5	76	237	127	97	13	
Herkimer County	29	0	2	2	25	306	130	167	9	
Jefferson County	57	0	18	4	35	412	114	289	9	
Lewis County	15	0	2	1	12	93	64	29	0	
Livingston County	20	0	3	0	17	88	22	64	2	
Madison County	19	0	6	2	11	240	91	137	12	
Monroe County	27	0	0	0	27	23	1	22	0	
Montgomery County	14	0	1	1	12	87	15	70	2	
Nassau County	9	1	0	0	8	12	0	9	3	
New York County	1	0	0	1	0	72	0	72	0	
Niagara County	13	0	3	2	8	190	29	152	9	
Oneida County	80	0	6	2	72	573	184	367	22	
Onondaga County	52	1	5	7	39	717	182	525	10	
Ontario County	16	0	3	1	12	232	37	186	9	
Orange County	156	2	22	35	97	870	153	655	62	
Orleans County	16	0	2	0	14	53	14	39	0	
Oswego County	29	0	6	4	19	689	214	462	13	
Otsego County	71	0	8	2	61	479	148	326	5	
Putnam County	9	0	1	2	6	145	24	116	5	
Rensselaer County	91	0	12	2	77	442	141	289	12	

See footnotes at end of table.

Table 11

Offenses Known to Law Enforcement

by State Agency by State, 2003—Continued
by Federal Agency, 2003

State agency by state	Violent crime	Violent crime Murder and non-negligent man-slaughter	Violent crime Forcible rape	Violent crime Robbery	Violent crime Aggravated assault	Property crime	Property crime Burglary	Property crime Larceny-theft	Property crime Motor vehicle theft	Arson[1]
NEW YORK—Continued										
State Police—Continued:										
Rockland County	18	0	3	3	12	46	3	28	15	
Saratoga County	71	0	7	8	56	518	134	363	21	
Schenectady County	12	0	3	0	9	57	14	40	3	
Schoharie County	17	0	7	0	10	157	55	94	8	
Schuyler County	4	0	1	1	2	38	15	20	3	
Seneca County	14	0	5	0	9	91	26	65	0	
Steuben County	73	1	26	8	38	322	85	220	17	
St. Lawrence County	100	1	24	1	74	398	183	204	11	
Suffolk County	22	1	4	2	15	49	17	28	4	
Sullivan County	140	5	24	10	101	531	214	283	34	
Tioga County	5	0	3	0	2	121	41	75	5	
Tompkins County	48	0	2	0	46	264	30	223	11	
Ulster County	197	2	12	7	176	534	158	340	36	
Warren County	26	1	14	1	10	127	12	113	2	
Washington County	19	0	2	1	16	142	50	89	3	
Wayne County	37	1	8	4	24	444	104	327	13	
Westchester County	89	1	10	17	61	432	72	330	30	
Wyoming County	15	0	2	0	13	84	18	62	4	
Yates County	4	0	2	0	2	32	11	19	2	
NORTH CAROLINA										
Department of Human Resources	0	0	0	0	0	13	1	12	0	0
Division of Alcohol Law Enforcement	0	0	0	0	0	0	0	0	0	0
North Carolina Highway Patrol	0	0	0	0	0	0	0	0	0	0
State Capitol Police	3	0	0	1	2	89	15	72	2	0
OHIO										
Ohio State Highway Patrol	165	6	30	7	122	470	25	348	97	18
OKLAHOMA										
Capitol Park Police	1	0	0	0	1	44	5	35	4	1
PENNSYLVANIA										
Bureau of Narcotics:										
Adams County	0	0	0	0	0	0	0	0	0	0
Allegheny County	0	0	0	0	0	0	0	0	0	0
Bedford County	0	0	0	0	0	0	0	0	0	0
Blair County	0	0	0	0	0	0	0	0	0	0
Bradford County	0	0	0	0	0	0	0	0	0	0
Cambria County	0	0	0	0	0	0	0	0	0	0
Cameron County	0	0	0	0	0	0	0	0	0	0
Centre County	0	0	0	0	0	0	0	0	0	0
Chester County	0	0	0	0	0	0	0	0	0	0
Clearfield County	0	0	0	0	0	0	0	0	0	0
Clinton County	0	0	0	0	0	0	0	0	0	0
Columbia County	0	0	0	0	0	0	0	0	0	0
Crawford County	0	0	0	0	0	0	0	0	0	0
Cumberland County	0	0	0	0	0	0	0	0	0	0
Dauphin County	0	0	0	0	0	1	0	1	0	0
Delaware County	0	0	0	0	0	0	0	0	0	0
Elk County	0	0	0	0	0	0	0	0	0	0
Erie County	0	0	0	0	0	0	0	0	0	0
Fayette County	0	0	0	0	0	0	0	0	0	0
Forest County	0	0	0	0	0	0	0	0	0	0
Franklin County	0	0	0	0	0	0	0	0	0	0
Fulton County	0	0	0	0	0	0	0	0	0	0
Greene County	0	0	0	0	0	0	0	0	0	0
Huntingdon County	0	0	0	0	0	0	0	0	0	0

See footnotes at end of table.

Table 11

Offenses Known to Law Enforcement

by State Agency by State, 2003—Continued
by Federal Agency, 2003

State agency by state	Violent crime	Violent crime Murder and non-negligent man-slaughter	Violent crime Forcible rape	Violent crime Robbery	Violent crime Aggravated assault	Property crime	Property crime Burglary	Property crime Larceny-theft	Property crime Motor vehicle theft	Arson[1]
PENNSYLVANIA—Continued										
Bureau of Narcotics—Continued:										
Juniata County	0	0	0	0	0	0	0	0	0	0
Lackawanna County	0	0	0	0	0	0	0	0	0	0
Lancaster County	0	0	0	0	0	0	0	0	0	0
Lebanon County	0	0	0	0	0	1	0	1	0	0
Luzerne County	0	0	0	0	0	0	0	0	0	0
Lycoming County	0	0	0	0	0	0	0	0	0	0
McKean County	0	0	0	0	0	0	0	0	0	0
Mifflin County	0	0	0	0	0	0	0	0	0	0
Montour County	0	0	0	0	0	0	0	0	0	0
Northumberland County	0	0	0	0	0	0	0	0	0	0
Perry County	0	0	0	0	0	0	0	0	0	0
Philadelphia County	0	0	0	0	0	0	0	0	0	0
Pike County	0	0	0	0	0	0	0	0	0	0
Potter County	0	0	0	0	0	0	0	0	0	0
Snyder County	0	0	0	0	0	0	0	0	0	0
Somerset County	0	0	0	0	0	0	0	0	0	0
Sullivan County	0	0	0	0	0	0	0	0	0	0
Susquehanna County	0	0	0	0	0	0	0	0	0	0
Tioga County	0	0	0	0	0	0	0	0	0	0
Union County	0	0	0	0	0	0	0	0	0	0
Venango County	0	0	0	0	0	0	0	0	0	0
Warren County	0	0	0	0	0	0	0	0	0	0
Washington County	0	0	0	0	0	0	0	0	0	0
Wayne County	0	0	0	0	0	0	0	0	0	0
Westmoreland County	0	0	0	0	0	0	0	0	0	0
Wyoming County	0	0	0	0	0	0	0	0	0	0
York County	0	0	0	0	0	0	0	0	0	1
Department of Environmental Resources	1	0	0	0	1	10	0	9	1	0
State Capitol Police	5	0	0	1	4	95	2	91	2	0
State Park Police:										
Presque Isle	0	0	0	0	0	31	0	31	0	0
Pymatuning	0	0	0	0	0	39	3	36	0	1
State Police:										
Adams County	49	1	22	5	21	541	140	359	42	6
Allegheny County	60	1	2	2	55	38	5	29	4	0
Armstrong County	52	0	14	7	31	444	148	252	44	8
Beaver County	11	0	1	4	6	191	48	125	18	6
Bedford County	51	0	8	8	35	575	179	362	34	17
Berks County	94	0	9	7	78	563	167	337	59	17
Blair County	30	0	3	6	21	328	104	194	30	3
Bradford County	35	1	18	1	15	519	220	246	53	23
Bucks County	32	0	4	3	25	267	60	178	29	14
Butler County	51	0	16	14	21	716	205	468	43	11
Cambria County	67	0	5	5	57	303	113	143	47	8
Cameron County	4	0	2	0	2	106	40	59	7	1
Carbon County	24	0	9	3	12	358	112	226	20	4
Centre County	133	1	11	2	119	624	167	421	36	10
Chester County	124	1	19	21	83	1,094	321	688	85	35
Clarion County	33	0	11	5	17	456	133	306	17	3
Clearfield County	47	1	8	3	35	589	188	341	60	24
Clinton County	25	2	6	6	11	433	103	316	14	5
Columbia County	20	0	5	4	11	292	107	172	13	2
Crawford County	32	0	16	3	13	807	386	367	54	5
Cumberland County	111	2	13	7	89	636	150	440	46	12
Delaware County	86	1	10	19	56	873	187	619	67	15
Elizabethville	65	1	17	9	38	735	192	491	52	9
Elk County	20	0	10	1	9	221	96	108	17	5
Erie County	95	1	30	16	48	1,552	443	1,008	101	16
Fayette County	199	2	29	52	116	2,005	604	1,137	264	117
Forest County	8	0	3	0	5	165	100	60	5	0
Franklin County	130	1	34	24	71	1,162	264	811	87	12
Fulton County	37	0	6	4	27	182	69	108	5	2

See footnotes at end of table.

Table 11

Offenses Known to Law Enforcement
by State Agency by State, 2003—Continued
by Federal Agency, 2003

State agency by state	Violent crime	Murder and non-negligent man-slaughter	Forcible rape	Robbery	Aggravated assault	Property crime	Burglary	Larceny-theft	Motor vehicle theft	Arson[1]
PENNSYLVANIA—Continued										
State Police—Continued:										
Greene County	29	0	5	9	15	398	130	241	27	7
Huntingdon County	54	0	13	0	41	372	141	216	15	5
Indiana County	53	0	16	12	25	799	188	539	72	24
Jefferson County	33	1	4	3	25	292	125	146	21	14
Juniata County	22	1	7	3	11	253	145	99	9	6
Lackawanna County	35	2	4	4	25	233	80	127	26	31
Lancaster County	99	1	16	14	68	853	283	508	62	18
Lawrence County	62	0	6	12	44	718	201	454	63	108
Lebanon County	36	0	2	4	30	435	108	296	31	4
Lehigh County	97	2	17	16	62	998	237	699	62	19
Luzerne County	124	10	21	10	83	920	232	623	65	76
Lycoming County	46	0	14	10	22	771	231	494	46	7
McKean County	17	0	8	0	9	152	63	69	20	5
Mercer County	42	0	7	6	29	483	143	286	54	10
Mifflin County	11	2	0	4	5	197	89	99	9	2
Monroe County	106	0	20	23	63	1,137	343	673	121	22
Montour County	4	0	1	0	3	117	33	78	6	0
Northampton County	27	0	6	2	19	280	84	167	29	7
Northumberland County	32	0	6	2	24	393	100	268	25	3
Perry County	58	1	16	8	33	610	196	378	36	6
Philadelphia County	0	0	0	0	0	3	0	3	0	0
Pike County	49	1	12	3	33	575	288	251	36	16
Potter County	22	0	6	0	16	177	70	90	17	3
Schuylkill County	142	2	16	9	115	842	178	589	75	19
Skippack County	81	1	6	17	57	468	115	321	32	8
Snyder County	11	0	3	2	6	379	80	286	13	2
Somerset County	77	3	12	8	54	636	232	358	46	26
Sullivan County	14	0	4	1	9	139	65	68	6	4
Susquehanna County	43	0	13	5	25	486	139	297	50	12
Tioga County	15	0	5	2	8	359	83	252	24	6
Union County	20	0	7	0	13	273	78	185	10	2
Venango County	43	0	8	4	31	437	119	286	32	8
Warren County	22	2	6	1	13	284	116	149	19	7
Washington County	83	0	18	21	44	737	212	456	69	25
Wayne County	35	0	10	4	21	559	198	316	45	13
Westmoreland County	231	0	21	61	149	2,365	534	1,628	203	42
Wyoming County	29	0	6	3	20	348	91	224	33	8
York County	175	2	10	9	154	555	142	365	48	23
RHODE ISLAND										
Department of Environmental Management	0	0	0	0	0	19	2	14	3	0
Rhode Island State Police Headquarters	24	2	14	2	6	47	3	35	9	1
State Police:										
Chepachet	3	1	1	0	1	32	1	27	4	0
Hope Valley	22	0	11	1	10	128	28	92	8	0
Lincoln Woods	12	0	4	0	8	87	3	66	18	0
Portsmouth	3	0	1	0	2	17	0	14	3	0
Wickford	10	0	7	1	2	37	3	31	3	0
SOUTH CAROLINA										
Alcohol Beverage Control:										
Bamberg County	0	0	0	0	0	0	0	0	0	0
Edgefield County	0	0	0	0	0	0	0	0	0	0
Bureau of Protective Services	2	0	0	1	1	39	2	33	4	0
Department of Mental Health	15	0	0	0	15	27	0	26	1	0
Department of Natural Resources:										
Anderson County	0	0	0	0	0	0	0	0	0	0
Beaufort County	0	0	0	0	0	0	0	0	0	0
Berkeley County	0	0	0	0	0	0	0	0	0	0
Chesterfield County	0	0	0	0	0	0	0	0	0	0

See footnotes at end of table.

Table 11

Offenses Known to Law Enforcement

by State Agency by State, 2003—Continued
by Federal Agency, 2003

State agency by state	Violent crime	Murder and non-negligent man-slaughter	Forcible rape	Robbery	Aggravated assault	Property crime	Burglary	Larceny-theft	Motor vehicle theft	Arson[1]
			Violent crime				Property crime			
SOUTH CAROLINA—Continued										
Department of Natural Resources—Continued:										
Colleton County	0	0	0	0	0	0	0	0	0	0
Marion County	0	0	0	0	0	0	0	0	0	0
Richland County	0	0	0	0	0	0	0	0	0	0
Employment Security Commission	0	0	0	0	0	1	0	0	1	0
Highway Patrol:										
Abbeville County	0	0	0	0	0	0	0	0	0	0
Aiken County	0	0	0	0	0	0	0	0	0	0
Allendale County	0	0	0	0	0	0	0	0	0	0
Anderson County	0	0	0	0	0	0	0	0	0	0
Bamberg County	0	0	0	0	0	0	0	0	0	0
Barnwell County	0	0	0	0	0	0	0	0	0	0
Beaufort County	0	0	0	0	0	0	0	0	0	0
Berkeley County	0	0	0	0	0	0	0	0	0	0
Calhoun County	0	0	0	0	0	0	0	0	0	0
Charleston County	0	0	0	0	0	0	0	0	0	0
Cherokee County	0	0	0	0	0	0	0	0	0	0
Chester County	0	0	0	0	0	0	0	0	0	0
Chesterfield County	0	0	0	0	0	0	0	0	0	0
Clarendon County	0	0	0	0	0	0	0	0	0	0
Colleton County	0	0	0	0	0	0	0	0	0	0
Darlington County	0	0	0	0	0	0	0	0	0	0
Dillon County	0	0	0	0	0	0	0	0	0	0
Dorchester County	0	0	0	0	0	0	0	0	0	0
Edgefield County	0	0	0	0	0	0	0	0	0	0
Fairfield County	0	0	0	0	0	0	0	0	0	0
Florence County	0	0	0	0	0	0	0	0	0	0
Georgetown County	0	0	0	0	0	0	0	0	0	0
Greenville County	0	0	0	0	0	0	0	0	0	0
Greenwood County	0	0	0	0	0	0	0	0	0	0
Hampton County	0	0	0	0	0	0	0	0	0	0
Horry County	0	0	0	0	0	1	0	1	0	0
Jasper County	0	0	0	0	0	0	0	0	0	0
Kershaw County	0	0	0	0	0	0	0	0	0	0
Lancaster County	0	0	0	0	0	0	0	0	0	0
Laurens County	0	0	0	0	0	0	0	0	0	0
Lee County	0	0	0	0	0	0	0	0	0	0
Lexington County	0	0	0	0	0	0	0	0	0	0
Marion County	0	0	0	0	0	0	0	0	0	0
Marlboro County	0	0	0	0	0	0	0	0	0	0
McCormick County	0	0	0	0	0	0	0	0	0	0
Newberry County	0	0	0	0	0	0	0	0	0	0
Oconee County	0	0	0	0	0	0	0	0	0	0
Orangeburg County	0	0	0	0	0	0	0	0	0	0
Pickens County	0	0	0	0	0	0	0	0	0	0
Richland County	0	0	0	0	0	0	0	0	0	0
Saluda County	0	0	0	0	0	0	0	0	0	0
Spartanburg County	0	0	0	0	0	0	0	0	0	0
Sumter County	0	0	0	0	0	0	0	0	0	0
Union County	0	0	0	0	0	0	0	0	0	0
Williamsburg County	0	0	0	0	0	0	0	0	0	0
York County	0	0	0	0	0	0	0	0	0	0
License and Vehicle Enforcement Division	2	0	0	0	2	5	0	5	0	0
State Museum	0	0	0	0	0	1	0	1	0	0
State Transport Police:										
Aiken County	0	0	0	0	0	0	0	0	0	0
Greenville County	0	0	0	0	0	0	0	0	0	0
United States Department of Energy, Savannah River Plant	0	0	0	0	0	50	0	50	0	0
SOUTH DAKOTA										
Division of Criminal Investigation	38	1	14	3	20	55	24	22	9	2

See footnotes at end of table.

Table 11

Offenses Known to Law Enforcement

by State Agency by State, 2003—Continued
by Federal Agency, 2003

State agency by state	Violent crime	Violent crime Murder and non-negligent man-slaughter	Forcible rape	Robbery	Aggravated assault	Property crime	Burglary	Larceny-theft	Motor vehicle theft	Arson[1]
TENNESSEE										
Alcoholic Beverage Commission	0	0	0	0	0	0	0	0	0	0
Department of Safety	43	0	0	0	43	4	1	3	0	1
State Fire Marshal	0	0	0	0	0	1	1	0	0	46
State Park Rangers:										
Bicentennial Capitol Mall	1	0	0	0	1	0	0	0	0	0
Big Hill Pond	0	0	0	0	0	0	0	0	0	0
Big Ridge	0	0	0	0	0	0	0	0	0	0
Bledsoe Creek	0	0	0	0	0	0	0	0	0	0
Booker T. Washington	0	0	0	0	0	0	0	0	0	0
Burgess Falls Natural Area	0	0	0	0	0	0	0	0	0	0
Cedars of Lebanon	0	0	0	0	0	4	1	3	0	0
Chickasaw	0	0	0	0	0	2	1	1	0	0
Cove Lake	0	0	0	0	0	3	0	2	1	0
Cumberland Mountain	0	0	0	0	0	0	0	0	0	0
David Crockett	0	0	0	0	0	3	0	3	0	0
David Crockett Birthplace	0	0	0	0	0	1	1	0	0	0
Dunbar Cave Natural Area	0	0	0	0	0	0	0	0	0	0
Edgar Evins	0	0	0	0	0	0	0	0	0	0
Fall Creek Falls	0	0	0	0	0	3	0	3	0	0
Fort Loudon State Historic Area	0	0	0	0	0	0	0	0	0	0
Fort Pillow State Historic Park	0	0	0	0	0	0	0	0	0	0
Frozen Head Natural Area	0	0	0	0	0	0	0	0	0	0
Harrison Bay	0	0	0	0	0	12	0	12	0	0
Henry Horton	0	0	0	0	0	1	0	1	0	0
Hiwassee/Ocoee Rivers	0	0	0	0	0	6	1	5	0	0
Indian Mountain	0	0	0	0	0	0	0	0	0	0
Johnsonville State Historic Area	0	0	0	0	0	0	0	0	0	0
Long Hunter	0	0	0	0	0	7	0	7	0	0
Meeman-Shelby Forest	1	0	1	0	0	10	0	10	0	0
Montgomery Bell	0	0	0	0	0	6	0	6	0	0
Mousetail Landing	0	0	0	0	0	2	0	2	0	0
Natchez Trace	1	0	0	0	1	2	1	1	0	0
Nathan Bedford Forrest	0	0	0	0	0	1	1	0	0	0
Norris Dam	0	0	0	0	0	2	0	2	0	0
Old Stone Fort State Archaeological Area	0	0	0	0	0	0	0	0	0	0
Panther Creek	0	0	0	0	0	0	0	0	0	0
Paris Landing	0	0	0	0	0	3	0	3	0	0
Pickett	0	0	0	0	0	0	0	0	0	0
Pickwick Landing	1	0	0	0	1	12	2	8	2	1
Pinson Mounds State Archaeological Area	0	0	0	0	0	0	0	0	0	0
Radnor Lake Natural Area	0	0	0	0	0	2	0	2	0	0
Red Clay State Historic Park	0	0	0	0	0	1	1	0	0	0
Reelfoot Lake	0	0	0	0	0	1	0	1	0	0
Roan Mountain	0	0	0	0	0	0	0	0	0	0
Rock Island	0	0	0	0	0	4	0	4	0	0
Sgt. Alvin C. York	0	0	0	0	0	0	0	0	0	0
South Cumberland Recreation Area	0	0	0	0	0	0	0	0	0	0
Standing Stone	0	0	0	0	0	0	0	0	0	0
Sycamore Shoals State Historic Area	0	0	0	0	0	0	0	0	0	0
T.O. Fuller	0	0	0	0	0	1	0	0	1	0
Tim's Ford	0	0	0	0	0	0	0	0	0	0
Warrior's Path	0	0	0	0	0	2	1	1	0	0
Tennessee Bureau of Investigation	7	1	3	0	3	6	2	4	0	0
Tennessee Department of Revenue	0	0	0	0	0	0	0	0	0	0
Wildlife Resources Agency:										
Region 1	0	0	0	0	0	0	0	0	0	0
Region 2	0	0	0	0	0	0	0	0	0	0
Region 3	0	0	0	0	0	0	0	0	0	0
Region 4	0	0	0	0	0	0	0	0	0	0

See footnotes at end of table.

Table 11

Offenses Known to Law Enforcement

by State Agency by State, 2003—Continued
by Federal Agency, 2003

State agency by state	Violent crime	Murder and non-negligent man-slaughter	Forcible rape	Robbery	Aggravated assault	Property crime	Burglary	Larceny-theft	Motor vehicle theft	Arson[1]
			Violent crime					*Property crime*		
UTAH										
Parks and Recreation	4	0	0	0	4	43	7	31	5	0
Wildlife Resources	0	0	0	0	0	0	0	0	0	0
VERMONT										
State Police:										
Bethel	0	0	0	0	0	186	76	104	6	1
Bradford	7	2	1	2	2	202	80	112	10	1
Brattleboro	8	0	1	0	7	107	51	42	14	2
Middlebury	5	0	3	0	2	207	58	132	17	1
Middlesex	6	0	0	0	6	281	113	153	15	5
Rockingham	11	0	1	1	9	232	82	130	20	2
Rutland	13	1	1	0	11	546	137	373	36	5
Shaftsbury	7	1	1	0	5	172	72	94	6	4
St. Albans	46	0	12	6	28	860	301	462	97	9
St. Johnsbury	26	5	4	2	15	414	155	225	34	3
Williston	42	1	17	2	22	388	96	276	16	16
Vermont State Police	0	0	0	0	0	0	0	0	0	0
Vermont State Police Headquarters, Bureau of Criminal Investigations	0	0	0	0	0	1	0	0	1	0
VIRGINIA										
Alcoholic Beverage Control Commission	4	0	0	2	2	40	7	33	0	0
Southside Virginia Training Center	8	0	3	0	5	39	0	38	1	0
State Police:										
Accomack County	2	0	1	0	1	23	4	16	3	0
Albemarle County	4	0	0	1	3	3	0	1	2	0
Alleghany County	1	0	1	0	0	4	0	3	1	0
Appomattox County	1	0	0	0	1	4	0	4	0	0
Arlington County	1	0	0	0	1	1	0	1	0	0
Augusta County	4	0	1	0	3	44	2	27	15	0
Bath County	0	0	0	0	0	4	1	3	0	0
Bedford County	4	0	0	0	4	9	0	6	3	0
Bland County	2	0	0	2	0	11	0	11	0	0
Botetourt County	3	0	0	0	3	22	0	15	7	0
Brunswick County	1	0	0	0	1	3	0	3	0	0
Buchanan County	3	0	1	0	2	43	3	33	7	0
Buckingham County	0	0	0	0	0	8	1	5	2	0
Campbell County	3	0	0	0	3	13	0	10	3	0
Caroline County	3	1	0	1	1	34	0	21	13	2
Carroll County	0	0	0	0	0	12	0	12	0	0
Charlotte County	0	0	0	0	0	1	0	1	0	0
Chesapeake	1	0	0	0	1	3	0	2	1	0
Chesterfield County	7	0	0	0	7	12	0	6	6	0
Craig County	0	0	0	0	0	3	1	2	0	0
Culpeper County	4	0	1	0	3	8	2	4	2	0
Cumberland County	1	0	0	0	1	1	0	0	1	0
Dickenson County	1	0	1	0	0	7	1	0	6	0
Dinwiddie County	0	0	0	0	0	4	0	3	1	0
Essex County	0	0	0	0	0	4	1	2	1	0
Fairfax County	23	0	0	1	22	21	1	14	6	1
Fauquier County	1	1	0	0	0	16	2	11	3	0
Floyd County	3	0	0	1	2	3	0	2	1	0
Fluvanna County	0	0	0	0	0	4	0	3	1	0
Franklin County	1	0	0	0	1	6	0	2	4	0
Frederick County	5	0	0	0	5	23	1	17	5	0
Fredericksburg	2	0	0	0	2	6	0	4	2	0
Giles County	2	0	0	0	2	6	0	5	1	0
Gloucester County	0	0	0	0	0	8	0	6	2	0
Grayson County	0	0	0	0	0	4	0	4	0	0
Greensville County	2	0	0	0	2	0	0	0	0	0
Halifax County	1	0	0	1	0	13	3	6	4	0

See footnotes at end of table.

Table 11

Offenses Known to Law Enforcement
by State Agency by State, 2003—Continued
by Federal Agency, 2003

State agency by state	Violent crime	Murder and non-negligent man-slaughter	Forcible rape	Robbery	Aggravated assault	Property crime	Burglary	Larceny-theft	Motor vehicle theft	Arson[1]
VIRGINIA—Continued										
State Police—Continued:										
Hampton	8	0	0	0	8	4	0	3	1	0
Hanover County	2	0	0	0	2	8	0	7	1	0
Harrisonburg	1	0	0	0	1	4	0	3	1	0
Henrico County	3	1	0	0	2	16	0	14	2	0
Henry County	11	0	0	0	11	19	0	9	10	0
Isle of Wight County	1	0	0	0	1	3	0	1	2	0
James City County	2	0	0	0	2	4	0	4	0	0
Lee County	0	0	0	0	0	7	0	2	5	6
Loudoun County	2	0	0	1	1	17	1	12	4	0
Louisa County	3	0	1	0	2	7	0	7	0	0
Lunenburg County	5	0	5	0	0	1	0	1	0	0
Madison County	2	1	0	0	1	1	0	1	0	0
Mecklenburg County	2	0	0	0	2	7	0	4	3	0
Montgomery County	5	1	0	1	3	7	0	3	4	0
New Kent County	0	0	0	0	0	6	0	3	3	0
Newport News	6	0	0	0	6	3	0	1	2	0
Norfolk	16	0	0	0	16	3	0	1	2	0
Northampton County	0	0	0	0	0	11	0	11	0	0
Northumberland County	0	0	0	0	0	1	0	1	0	0
Nottoway County	0	0	0	0	0	0	0	0	0	0
Orange County	0	0	0	0	0	3	0	2	1	0
Page County	3	0	0	0	3	5	0	5	0	0
Patrick County	0	0	0	0	0	2	0	1	1	1
Petersburg	1	0	0	0	1	2	0	1	1	0
Pittsylvania County	6	2	1	0	3	61	1	16	44	3
Portsmouth	2	0	0	0	2	1	0	0	1	0
Powhatan County	3	0	0	0	3	1	0	1	0	0
Prince Edward County	2	0	0	0	2	0	0	0	0	0
Prince George County	1	0	0	0	1	2	0	1	1	0
Prince William County	7	0	1	1	5	21	0	18	3	0
Pulaski County	0	0	0	0	0	3	0	3	0	0
Richmond City	3	0	2	0	1	10	1	6	3	0
Richmond County	1	0	0	0	1	2	0	1	1	0
Roanoke City	2	0	0	1	1	9	0	8	1	0
Roanoke County	4	0	0	0	4	9	0	5	4	0
Rockbridge County	2	0	0	0	2	52	0	48	4	0
Rockingham County	7	0	0	1	6	28	1	10	17	0
Russell County	0	0	0	0	0	18	0	14	4	1
Scott County	1	0	0	0	1	9	0	4	5	2
Shenandoah County	7	0	0	0	7	16	5	8	3	0
Smyth County	0	0	0	0	0	9	0	5	4	0
Southampton County	0	0	0	0	0	6	0	3	3	0
Spotsylvania County	15	0	0	0	15	22	0	15	7	0
Stafford County	6	0	0	0	6	11	0	8	3	1
Surry County	0	0	0	0	0	1	0	1	0	0
Sussex County	4	0	0	0	4	6	0	5	1	0
Tazewell County	1	1	0	0	0	18	2	14	2	0
Virginia Beach	11	0	0	0	11	0	0	0	0	0
Warren County	3	0	0	0	3	5	0	3	2	0
Washington County	6	0	0	0	6	11	2	6	3	3
Westmoreland County	1	0	0	0	1	1	0	1	0	0
Winchester	1	0	0	1	0	4	0	4	0	1
Wise County	0	0	0	0	0	8	1	5	2	0
Wythe County	1	0	0	1	0	95	3	87	5	0
York County	0	0	0	0	0	1	0	0	1	0
Virginia State Capitol	4	1	0	1	2	84	4	78	2	0
WEST VIRGINIA										
Department of Natural Resources:										
Barbour County	0	0	0	0	0	0	0	0	0	0
Berkeley County	0	0	0	0	0	0	0	0	0	0

See footnotes at end of table.

Table 11

Offenses Known to Law Enforcement

by State Agency by State, 2003—Continued
by Federal Agency, 2003

State agency by state	Violent crime	Murder and non-negligent man-slaughter	Forcible rape	Robbery	Aggravated assault	Property crime	Burglary	Larceny-theft	Motor vehicle theft	Arson[1]
			Violent crime					*Property crime*		

WEST VIRGINIA—Continued

Department of Natural Resources—Continued:

State agency by state	Violent crime	Murder and non-negligent man-slaughter	Forcible rape	Robbery	Aggravated assault	Property crime	Burglary	Larceny-theft	Motor vehicle theft	Arson[1]
Boone County	0	0	0	0	0	0	0	0	0	0
Brooke County	0	0	0	0	0	0	0	0	0	0
Cabell County	0	0	0	0	0	0	0	0	0	0
Calhoun County	0	0	0	0	0	0	0	0	0	0
Doddridge County	0	0	0	0	0	0	0	0	0	0
Gilmer County	0	0	0	0	0	0	0	0	0	0
Grant County	0	0	0	0	0	0	0	0	0	0
Greenbrier County	0	0	0	0	0	1	1	0	0	1
Hampshire County	0	0	0	0	0	0	0	0	0	0
Hancock County	0	0	0	0	0	0	0	0	0	0
Hardy County	0	0	0	0	0	0	0	0	0	0
Harrison County	0	0	0	0	0	0	0	0	0	0
Jackson County	0	0	0	0	0	0	0	0	0	0
Jefferson County	0	0	0	0	0	0	0	0	0	0
Kanawha County	0	0	0	0	0	0	0	0	0	0
Logan County	0	0	0	0	0	0	0	0	0	0
Marion County	0	0	0	0	0	0	0	0	0	0
Marshall County	0	0	0	0	0	0	0	0	0	0
Mason County	0	0	0	0	0	0	0	0	0	0
Mineral County	0	0	0	0	0	0	0	0	0	0
Mingo County	0	0	0	0	0	0	0	0	0	0
Monongalia County	0	0	0	0	0	0	0	0	0	0
Monroe County	0	0	0	0	0	0	0	0	0	0
Morgan County	0	0	0	0	0	0	0	0	0	0
Nicholas County	0	0	0	0	0	0	0	0	0	0
Ohio County	0	0	0	0	0	0	0	0	0	0
Preston County	0	0	0	0	0	0	0	0	0	0
Putnam County	0	0	0	0	0	0	0	0	0	0
Roane County	0	0	0	0	0	0	0	0	0	0
Tucker County	0	0	0	0	0	0	0	0	0	0
Wayne County	0	0	0	0	0	0	0	0	0	0
Webster County	0	0	0	0	0	0	0	0	0	0
Wetzel County	0	0	0	0	0	0	0	0	0	0
Wirt County	0	0	0	0	0	0	0	0	0	0
Wood County	0	0	0	0	0	0	0	0	0	0
State Fire Marshal:										
Boone County	0	0	0	0	0	0	0	0	0	14
Braxton County	0	0	0	0	0	0	0	0	0	6
Brooke County	0	0	0	0	0	0	0	0	0	1
Cabell County	0	0	0	0	0	0	0	0	0	8
Calhoun County	0	0	0	0	0	0	0	0	0	1
Clay County	0	0	0	0	0	0	0	0	0	3
Fayette County	0	0	0	0	0	0	0	0	0	10
Gilmer County	0	0	0	0	0	0	0	0	0	2
Grant County	0	0	0	0	0	0	0	0	0	2
Hampshire County	0	0	0	0	0	0	0	0	0	8
Hancock County	0	0	0	0	0	0	0	0	0	7
Hardy County	0	0	0	0	0	0	0	0	0	3
Harrison County	0	0	0	0	0	0	0	0	0	5
Jackson County	0	0	0	0	0	0	0	0	0	6
Jefferson County	0	0	0	0	0	0	0	0	0	1
Kanawha County	0	0	0	0	0	0	0	0	0	9
Lincoln County	0	0	0	0	0	0	0	0	0	2
Logan County	0	0	0	0	0	0	0	0	0	3
Marion County	0	0	0	0	0	0	0	0	0	4
Mason County	0	0	0	0	0	0	0	0	0	4
McDowell County	0	0	0	0	0	0	0	0	0	6
Mercer County	0	0	0	0	0	0	0	0	0	1
Mineral County	0	0	0	0	0	0	0	0	0	5
Mingo County	0	0	0	0	0	0	0	0	0	12
Monongalia County	0	0	0	0	0	0	0	0	0	15
Monroe County	0	0	0	0	0	0	0	0	0	1

See footnotes at end of table.

Table 11

Offenses Known to Law Enforcement
by State Agency by State, 2003—Continued
by Federal Agency, 2003

State agency by state	Violent crime	Murder and non-negligent man-slaughter	Forcible rape	Robbery	Aggravated assault	Property crime	Burglary	Larceny-theft	Motor vehicle theft	Arson[1]
WEST VIRGINIA—Continued										
State Fire Marshal—Continued:										
Nicholas County	0	0	0	0	0	0	0	0	0	5
Ohio County	0	0	0	0	0	0	0	0	0	4
Preston County	0	0	0	0	0	0	0	0	0	4
Putnam County	0	0	0	0	0	0	0	0	0	3
Raleigh County	0	0	0	0	0	0	0	0	0	12
Randolph County	0	0	0	0	0	0	0	0	0	2
Ritchie County	0	0	0	0	0	0	0	0	0	2
Tucker County	0	0	0	0	0	0	0	0	0	1
Upshur County	0	0	0	0	0	0	0	0	0	4
Wayne County	0	0	0	0	0	0	0	0	0	9
Webster County	0	0	0	0	0	0	0	0	0	1
Wetzel County	0	0	0	0	0	0	0	0	0	1
Wirt County	0	0	0	0	0	0	0	0	0	2
Wood County	0	0	0	0	0	0	0	0	0	3
Wyoming County	0	0	0	0	0	0	0	0	0	12
State Police:										
Beckley	15	0	0	0	15	286	56	195	35	0
Berkeley Springs	6	0	0	0	6	114	41	60	13	1
Bridgeport	27	2	6	1	18	194	16	166	12	1
Buckeye	8	0	0	1	7	62	23	33	6	1
Buckhannon	13	2	3	0	8	103	32	63	8	3
Clay	10	1	0	1	8	62	26	21	15	3
Danville	14	0	0	1	13	157	27	119	11	1
Elizabeth	7	0	0	0	7	54	17	30	7	0
Elkins	24	1	3	1	19	323	67	235	21	3
Franklin	7	0	2	1	4	35	8	22	5	1
Gauley Bridge	1	0	0	0	1	44	13	27	4	1
Gilbert	19	0	0	1	18	95	25	53	17	0
Glenville	3	0	0	0	3	22	11	9	2	1
Grafton	4	0	0	0	4	23	9	14	0	0
Grantsville	6	2	0	1	3	45	13	31	1	0
Hamlin	50	0	0	3	47	378	117	197	64	8
Harrisville	13	0	0	0	13	75	14	50	11	1
Hinton	1	0	0	0	1	52	24	21	7	1
Hundred	3	0	0	0	3	36	13	20	3	0
Huntington	8	0	0	1	7	481	69	386	26	0
Kearneysville	28	1	1	6	20	347	73	233	41	1
Keyser	22	0	0	2	20	229	75	139	15	2
Kingwood	8	0	1	2	5	89	22	53	14	1
Lewisburg	15	1	0	2	12	103	16	82	5	1
Logan	105	0	2	12	91	754	167	477	110	11
Martinsburg	91	2	1	12	76	769	199	471	99	3
Moorefield	4	0	0	0	4	94	30	55	9	0
Morgantown	22	0	5	1	16	497	131	297	69	6
Moundsville	3	0	0	0	3	33	6	26	1	0
New Cumberland	2	0	0	0	2	7	3	4	0	0
Oak Hill	4	0	1	0	3	131	40	80	11	0
Paden City	3	0	0	0	3	29	5	23	1	0
Parkersburg	3	0	0	0	3	168	37	110	21	2
Parsons	2	0	0	0	2	33	5	27	1	0
Philippi	10	0	2	0	8	66	18	45	3	2
Point Pleasant	7	0	3	0	4	78	13	48	17	0
Princeton	36	1	0	7	28	554	131	381	42	3
Quincy	13	0	0	1	12	241	53	156	32	4
Rainelle	5	0	0	0	5	46	12	31	3	0
Ripley	9	1	4	0	4	65	17	40	8	0
Romney	20	1	1	1	17	181	81	83	17	3
South Charleston	17	0	1	0	16	937	82	801	54	2
Spencer	8	0	0	0	8	27	8	17	2	0
Summersville	6	0	0	1	5	73	26	37	10	2
Sutton	9	0	0	2	7	80	8	58	14	1
Teays Valley	10	0	1	1	8	125	22	91	12	0

See footnotes at end of table.

Table 11

Offenses Known to Law Enforcement
by State Agency by State, 2003—Continued
by Federal Agency, 2003

State agency by state	Violent crime	Murder and non-negligent man-slaughter	Forcible rape	Robbery	Aggravated assault	Property crime	Burglary	Larceny-theft	Motor vehicle theft	Arson[1]
WEST VIRGINIA—Continued										
State Police—Continued:										
Union	13	0	1	2	10	111	42	65	4	0
Upperglade	16	0	1	0	15	114	37	68	9	1
Wayne	56	0	0	4	52	436	150	226	60	3
Welch	13	0	1	2	10	88	39	37	12	1
Wellsburg	7	0	0	0	7	17	3	11	3	0
Weston	8	1	0	1	6	69	2	57	10	1
West Union	10	0	3	0	7	31	11	16	4	1
Wheeling	8	0	1	1	6	56	8	44	4	1
Whitesville	4	0	0	0	4	45	15	29	1	1
Williamson	7	0	0	0	7	170	46	93	31	2
Winfield	7	0	0	0	7	57	5	44	8	0
State Police, Bureau of Criminal Investigation:										
Beckley	0	0	0	0	0	0	0	0	0	0
Buckhannon	0	0	0	0	0	0	0	0	0	0
Charleston	0	0	0	0	0	0	0	0	0	0
Fairmont	0	0	0	0	0	0	0	0	0	0
State Police, Parkway Authority:										
Fayette County	0	0	0	0	0	4	0	4	0	0
Kanawha County	1	0	0	0	1	2	0	0	2	0
Mercer County	0	0	0	0	0	0	0	0	0	0
Raleigh County	0	0	0	0	0	4	0	4	0	0
WISCONSIN										
Capitol Police	0	0	0	0	0	187	3	184	0	
U.S. TERRITORIES										
American Samoa	125	3	19	1	102	317	196	110	11	0
FEDERAL AGENCIES										
National Institutes of Health	3	0	0	0	3	191	10	181	0	0
United States Department of the Interior:										
Bureau of Indian Affairs	10,217	148	613	258	9,198	17,400	4,690	9,769	2,941	1,029
Bureau of Land Management	14	3	0	0	11	690	16	631	43	86
Bureau of Reclamation	0	0	0	0	0	6	0	4	2	0
Fish and Wildlife Service	17	3	2	3	9	391	107	223	61	116
National Park Service	367	8	48	65	246	3,795	468	3,192	135	89

[1] If the FBI does not receive 12 months of arson data from either the agency or the state, no arson will be shown.
[2] Limited data for 2003 were available for Illinois and Kentucky.
[3] Due to changes in reporting practices, annexations, and/or incomplete data, figures are not comparable to previous years' data.
[4] Figures reported are the number of crimes occurring in New Jersey.
[5] Figures reported are the number of crimes occurring in New York.
NOTE: Tables 10 and 11 have been restructured. See Appendix I, Table Methodology.

Table 12

Crime Trends
by Population Group, 2002-2003
[2003 estimated population]

Population group	Violent crime	Murder and non-negligent man-slaughter	Forcible rape[1]	Robbery	Aggravated assault	Property crime	Burglary	Larceny-theft	Motor vehicle theft	Arson
TOTAL ALL AGENCIES:										
12,492 agencies;										
population 252,996,723										
2002	**1,305,648**	**14,907**	**82,457**	**394,046**	**814,238**	**9,356,387**	**1,913,066**	**6,283,249**	**1,160,072**	**72,773**
2003	**1,261,249**	**15,126**	**81,010**	**386,588**	**778,525**	**9,341,264**	**1,915,886**	**6,252,220**	**1,173,158**	**68,168**
Percent change	**-3.4**	**+1.5**	**-1.8**	**-1.9**	**-4.4**	**-0.2**	**+0.1**	**-0.5**	**+1.1**	**-6.3**
TOTAL CITIES: 8,835 cities;										
population 170,426,855										
2002	**1,047,075**	**11,671**	**60,640**	**347,430**	**627,334**	**7,374,784**	**1,399,809**	**5,030,672**	**944,303**	**53,985**
2003	**1,006,706**	**11,990**	**59,831**	**339,703**	**595,182**	**7,354,091**	**1,402,911**	**5,001,975**	**949,205**	**50,331**
Percent change	**-3.9**	**+2.7**	**-1.3**	**-2.2**	**-5.1**	**-0.3**	**+0.2**	**-0.6**	**+0.5**	**-6.8**
GROUP I										
68 cities, 250,000 and over;										
population 51,730,815										
2002	533,494	6,843	21,474	203,701	301,476	2,674,115	508,509	1,685,981	479,625	23,587
2003	502,307	6,853	20,636	197,333	277,485	2,642,504	506,464	1,662,304	473,736	21,449
Percent change	-5.8	+0.1	-3.9	-3.1	-8.0	-1.2	-0.4	-1.4	-1.2	-9.1
10 cities, 1,000,000 and over;										
population 24,680,715										
2002	257,755	3,090	7,385	102,672	144,608	1,030,727	188,526	645,634	196,567	7,904
2003	240,927	3,094	7,188	99,750	130,895	1,022,286	190,158	640,224	191,904	7,367
Percent change	-6.5	+0.1	-2.7	-2.8	-9.5	-0.8	+0.9	-0.8	-2.4	-6.8
21 cities, 500,000 to 999,999;										
population 13,929,178										
2002	141,583	1,955	7,071	49,717	82,840	846,416	163,156	540,894	142,366	7,715
2003	134,207	1,935	6,442	49,292	76,538	848,378	163,343	538,770	146,265	6,733
Percent change	-5.2	-1.0	-8.9	-0.9	-7.6	+0.2	+0.1	-0.4	+2.7	-12.7
37 cities, 250,000 to 499,999;										
population 13,120,922										
2002	134,156	1,798	7,018	51,312	74,028	796,972	156,827	499,453	140,692	7,968
2003	127,173	1,824	7,006	48,291	70,052	771,840	152,963	483,310	135,567	7,349
Percent change	-5.2	+1.4	-0.2	-5.9	-5.4	-3.2	-2.5	-3.2	-3.6	-7.8
GROUP II										
165 cities, 100,000 to 249,999;										
population 24,549,216										
2002	151,293	1,805	9,738	52,209	87,541	1,211,527	237,239	815,059	159,229	8,978
2003	148,070	1,927	9,616	51,176	85,351	1,211,495	238,632	807,682	165,181	8,208
Percent change	-2.1	+6.8	-1.3	-2.0	-2.5	*	+0.6	-0.9	+3.7	-8.6
GROUP III										
375 cities, 50,000 to 99,999;										
population 26,025,870										
2002	125,591	1,194	9,310	38,318	76,769	1,050,002	204,337	725,319	120,346	6,783
2003	125,010	1,193	9,161	37,656	77,000	1,045,056	203,889	719,184	121,983	6,758
Percent change	-0.5	-0.1	-1.6	-1.7	+0.3	-0.5	-0.2	-0.8	+1.4	-0.4
GROUP IV										
698 cities, 25,000 to 49,999;										
population 24,299,730										
2002	90,128	758	7,542	23,911	57,917	873,952	164,932	629,457	79,563	5,564
2003	88,291	800	7,686	23,911	55,894	877,347	166,126	630,482	80,739	5,365
Percent change	-2.0	+5.5	+1.9	0.0	-3.5	+0.4	+0.7	+0.2	+1.5	-3.6

See footnotes at end of table.

Table 12

Crime Trends

by Population Group, 2002-2003—Continued
[2003 estimated population]

| | | Violent crime | | | | | Property crime | | | |
Population group	Violent crime	Murder and non-negligent man-slaughter	Forcible rape[1]	Robbery	Aggravated assault	Property crime	Burglary	Larceny-theft	Motor vehicle theft	Arson
GROUP V										
1,543 cities, 10,000 to 24,999; population 24,398,402										
2002	79,099	597	7,085	18,194	53,223	836,487	153,840	621,367	61,280	4,604
2003	77,817	648	7,008	18,439	51,722	840,021	154,925	622,529	62,567	4,611
Percent change	-1.6	+8.5	-1.1	+1.3	-2.8	+0.4	+0.7	+0.2	+2.1	+0.2
GROUP VI										
5,986 cities, under 10,000; population 19,422,822										
2002	67,470	474	5,491	11,097	50,408	728,701	130,952	553,489	44,260	4,469
2003	65,211	569	5,724	11,188	47,730	737,668	132,875	559,794	44,999	3,940
Percent change	-3.3	+20.0	+4.2	+0.8	-5.3	+1.2	+1.5	+1.1	+1.7	-11.8
METROPOLITAN COUNTIES										
1,529 agencies; population 59,972,708										
2002	208,017	2,465	16,392	42,889	146,271	1,581,763	381,137	1,015,094	185,532	15,169
2003	205,840	2,383	15,893	43,154	144,410	1,584,873	381,832	1,010,014	193,027	14,238
Percent change	-1.0	-3.3	-3.0	+0.6	-1.3	+0.2	+0.2	-0.5	+4.0	-6.1
NONMETROPOLITAN COUNTIES[2]										
2,128 agencies; population 22,597,160										
2002	50,556	771	5,425	3,727	40,633	399,840	132,120	237,483	30,237	3,619
2003	48,703	753	5,286	3,731	38,933	402,300	131,143	240,231	30,926	3,599
Percent change	-3.7	-2.3	-2.6	+0.1	-4.2	+0.6	-0.7	+1.2	+2.3	-0.6
SUBURBAN AREA[3]										
6,661 agencies; population 108,182,452										
2002	352,427	3,540	28,115	79,103	241,669	3,132,492	657,177	2,153,317	321,998	24,727
2003	347,990	3,571	27,880	79,891	236,648	3,148,355	662,089	2,152,943	333,323	23,316
Percent change	-1.3	+0.9	-0.8	+1.0	-2.1	+0.5	+0.7	*	+3.5	-5.7

[1] Forcible rape figures furnished by the state Uniform Crime Reporting (UCR) Program administered by the Illinois State Police were not in accorda

therefore, the figures were excluded from the forcible rape and violent crime categories.

[2] Includes state police agencies that report aggregately for the entire state.

[3] Suburban area includes law enforcement agencies in cities with less than 50,000 inhabitants and county law enforcement agencies that are within a Metropolitan Statistical Area (see Appendix III). Suburban area excludes all metropolitan agencies associated with a principal city. The agencies associated with suburban areas also appear in other groups within this table.

*Less than one-tenth of 1 percent.

Table 13

Crime Trends
by Suburban and Nonsuburban Cities[1] by Population Group, 2002-2003
[2003 estimated population]

Population group	Violent crime	Murder and non-negligent man-slaughter	Forcible rape	Robbery	Aggravated assault	Property crime	Burglary	Larceny-theft	Motor vehicle theft	Arson
Suburban cities										
TOTAL SUBURBAN CITIES:										
5,132 cities;										
population 48,209,744										
2002	144,410	1,075	11,723	36,214	95,398	1,550,729	276,040	1,138,223	136,466	9,558
2003	142,150	1,188	11,987	36,737	92,238	1,563,482	280,257	1,142,929	140,296	9,078
Percent change	-1.6	+10.5	+2.3	+1.4	-3.3	+0.8	+1.5	+0.4	+2.8	-5.0
GROUP IV										
525 cities, 25,000 to 49,999;										
population 18,120,147										
2002	54,246	428	4,334	15,625	33,859	553,379	102,785	391,911	58,683	3,536
2003	53,735	478	4,418	15,666	33,173	556,421	103,168	392,550	60,703	3,443
Percent change	-0.9	+11.7	+1.9	+0.3	-2.0	+0.5	+0.4	+0.2	+3.4	-2.6
GROUP V										
1,151 cities, 10,000 to 24,999;										
population 18,308,820										
2002	51,524	388	4,314	12,819	34,003	539,921	96,915	396,375	46,631	3,073
2003	51,015	387	4,364	13,076	33,188	542,690	98,267	396,594	47,829	3,145
Percent change	-1.0	-0.3	+1.2	+2.0	-2.4	+0.5	+1.4	+0.1	+2.6	+2.3
GROUP VI										
3,456 cities, under 10,000;										
population 11,780,777										
2002	38,640	259	3,075	7,770	27,536	457,429	76,340	349,937	31,152	2,949
2003	37,400	323	3,205	7,995	25,877	464,371	78,822	353,785	31,764	2,490
Percent change	-3.2	+24.7	+4.2	+2.9	-6.0	+1.5	+3.3	+1.1	+2.0	-15.6
Nonsuburban cities										
TOTAL NONSUBURBAN CITIES:										
3,095 cities;										
population 19,911,210										
2002	92,287	754	8,395	16,988	66,150	888,411	173,684	666,090	48,637	5,079
2003	89,169	829	8,431	16,801	63,108	891,554	173,669	669,876	48,009	4,838
Percent change	-3.4	+9.9	+0.4	-1.1	-4.6	+0.4	*	+0.6	-1.3	-4.7
GROUP IV										
173 cities, 25,000 to 49,999;										
population 6,179,583										
2002	35,882	330	3,208	8,286	24,058	320,573	62,147	237,546	20,880	2,028
2003	34,556	322	3,268	8,245	22,721	320,926	62,958	237,932	20,036	1,922
Percent change	-3.7	-2.4	+1.9	-0.5	-5.6	+0.1	+1.3	+0.2	-4.0	-5.2
GROUP V										
392 cities, 10,000 to 24,999;										
population 6,089,582										
2002	27,575	209	2,771	5,375	19,220	296,566	56,925	224,992	14,649	1,531
2003	26,802	261	2,644	5,363	18,534	297,331	56,658	225,935	14,738	1,466
Percent change	-2.8	+24.9	-4.6	-0.2	-3.6	+0.3	-0.5	+0.4	+0.6	-4.2
GROUP VI										
2,530 cities, under 10,000;										
population 7,642,045										
2002	28,830	215	2,416	3,327	22,872	271,272	54,612	203,552	13,108	1,520
2003	27,811	246	2,519	3,193	21,853	273,297	54,053	206,009	13,235	1,450
Percent change	-3.5	+14.4	+4.3	-4.0	-4.5	+0.7	-1.0	+1.2	+1.0	-4.6

[1] Suburban includes law enforcement agencies in cities with less than 50,000 inhabitants that are within a Metropolitan Statistical Area (see Appendix III). Suburban excludes all metropolitan agencies associated with a principal city. Nonsuburban includes law enforcement agencies in cities with less than 50,000 inhabitants that are not associated with a Metropolitan Statistical Area.
*Less than one-tenth of 1 percent.

Table 14

Crime Trends
by Metropolitan and Nonmetropolitan Counties[1] by Population Group, 2002-2003
[2003 estimated population]

Population group	Violent crime	Murder and non-negligent man-slaughter	Forcible rape	Robbery	Aggravated assault	Property crime	Burglary	Larceny-theft	Motor vehicle theft	Arson
METROPOLITAN COUNTIES										
100,000 and over										
134 counties; population 35,752,492										
2002	143,376	1,599	9,761	35,685	96,331	1,048,012	233,946	684,701	129,365	10,244
2003	143,279	1,614	9,608	35,957	96,100	1,048,133	235,195	679,991	132,947	9,611
Percent change	-0.1	+0.9	-1.6	+0.8	-0.2	*	+0.5	-0.7	+2.8	-6.2
25,000 to 99,999										
396 counties; population 20,216,576										
2002	46,401	594	5,002	5,129	35,676	400,658	115,120	252,362	33,176	3,292
2003	45,031	560	4,705	4,890	34,876	400,805	114,875	252,063	33,867	3,056
Percent change	-3.0	-5.7	-5.9	-4.7	-2.2	*	-0.2	-0.1	+2.1	-7.2
Under 25,000										
999 counties; population 4,003,640										
2002	18,240	272	1,629	2,075	14,264	133,093	32,071	78,031	22,991	1,633
2003	17,530	209	1,580	2,307	13,434	135,935	31,762	77,960	26,213	1,571
Percent change	-3.9	-23.2	-3.0	+11.2	-5.8	+2.1	-1.0	-0.1	+14.0	-3.8
NONMETROPOLITAN COUNTIES										
25,000 and over										
253 counties; population 9,869,471										
2002	22,127	310	2,231	2,024	17,562	179,029	61,097	105,240	12,692	1,471
2003	21,104	335	2,063	1,953	16,753	180,228	60,559	106,776	12,893	1,525
Percent change	-4.6	+8.1	-7.5	-3.5	-4.6	+0.7	-0.9	+1.5	+1.6	+3.7
10,000 to 24,999										
489 counties; population 7,867,149										
2002	15,239	269	1,414	891	12,665	117,217	40,152	68,465	8,600	995
2003	14,649	235	1,436	928	12,050	118,029	40,214	69,021	8,794	880
Percent change	-3.9	-12.6	+1.6	+4.2	-4.9	+0.7	+0.2	+0.8	+2.3	-11.6
Under 10,000										
1,234 counties; population 3,714,776										
2002	9,661	134	1,403	430	7,694	68,293	21,740	40,848	5,705	908
2003	9,009	127	1,321	398	7,163	66,573	21,519	39,030	6,024	900
Percent change	-6.7	-5.2	-5.8	-7.4	-6.9	-2.5	-1.0	-4.5	+5.6	-0.9

[1] Metropolitan counties include sheriffs and county law enforcement agencies associated with a Metropolitan Statistical Area (see Appendix III). Nonmetropolitan counties include sheriffs and county law enforcement agencies that are not associated with a Metropolitan Statistical Area. The offenses from state police agencies are not included in this table.
*Less than one-tenth of 1 percent.

Table 15

Crime Trends
Breakdown of Offenses Known by Population Group, 2002–2003
[2003 estimated population]

Population group	Forcible rape		Robbery				Aggravated assault				Burglary			Motor vehicle theft			Arson		
	Rape by force	Assault to rape-attempts	Firearm	Knife or cutting instrument	Other weapon	Strong-arm	Firearm	Knife or cutting instrument	Other weapon	Hands, fists, feet, etc.	Forcible entry	Unlawful entry	Attempted forcible entry	Autos	Trucks and buses	Other vehicles	Structure	Mobile	Other
TOTAL ALL AGENCIES: 12,433 agencies; population 236,435,640																			
2002	71,249	7,066	139,245	29,362	31,176	132,955	136,866	131,163	261,459	200,356	1,126,642	549,067	117,365	787,120	201,290	82,953	27,075	22,422	17,093
2003	70,100	6,926	137,023	29,234	30,990	130,914	134,222	128,353	252,415	188,801	1,123,373	560,962	114,202	799,367	200,805	89,616	26,023	20,890	15,843
Percent change	-1.6	-2.0	-1.6	-0.4	-0.6	-1.5	-1.9	-2.1	-3.5	-5.8	-0.3	+2.2	-2.7	+1.6	-0.2	+8.0	-3.9	-6.8	-7.3
TOTAL CITIES: 8,796 cities; population 155,448,122																			
2002	51,448	5,524	118,687	25,641	26,189	116,585	106,355	102,315	193,269	143,887	808,738	394,506	88,019	647,594	159,480	53,536	20,074	15,686	12,467
2003	50,865	5,415	116,323	25,404	25,991	114,548	104,183	99,662	185,151	135,119	807,772	403,552	85,739	655,502	157,589	58,214	19,286	14,454	11,622
Percent change	-1.1	-2.0	-2.0	-0.9	-0.8	-1.7	-2.0	-2.6	-4.2	-6.1	-0.1	+2.3	-2.6	+1.2	-1.2	+8.7	-3.9	-7.9	-6.8
GROUP I																			
62 cities, 250,000 and over; population 39,173,593																			
2002	16,746	2,200	66,397	12,853	12,297	58,160	57,484	43,471	83,460	45,663	297,722	110,671	24,448	297,236	95,583	20,918	7,455	7,967	3,736
2003	16,054	2,055	64,712	12,655	12,474	56,293	55,252	41,637	78,605	40,962	296,737	113,330	23,719	295,502	94,099	23,942	7,098	7,389	3,166
Percent change	-4.1	-6.6	-2.5	-1.5	+1.4	-3.2	-3.9	-4.2	-5.8	-10.3	-0.3	+2.4	-3.0	-0.6	-1.6	+14.5	-4.8	-7.3	-15.3
8 cities, 1,000,000 and over; population 13,684,275																			
2002	4,870	826	25,949	5,544	4,508	20,910	22,239	15,111	25,348	22,734	91,761	34,490	6,621	97,763	38,496	8,029	2,258	3,423	1,201
2003	4,703	876	25,562	5,670	4,465	20,762	21,109	14,534	24,193	20,022	93,610	36,110	7,081	99,213	37,745	8,539	2,194	3,160	1,066
Percent change	-3.4	+6.1	-1.5	+2.3	-1.0	-0.7	-5.1	-3.8	-4.6	-11.9	+2.0	+4.7	+6.9	+1.5	-2.0	+6.4	-2.8	-7.7	-11.2
20 cities, 500,000 to 999,999; population 13,284,624																			
2002	6,133	760	20,491	3,755	4,212	16,545	18,651	14,912	29,942	10,691	108,735	36,183	9,479	97,258	30,862	7,690	2,180	1,602	1,115
2003	5,608	630	20,597	3,706	4,605	16,045	18,193	14,390	28,252	9,333	108,335	38,267	8,952	97,796	31,848	9,764	2,203	1,487	787
Percent change	-8.6	-17.1	+0.5	-1.3	+9.3	-3.0	-2.5	-3.5	-5.6	-12.7	-0.4	+5.8	-5.6	+0.6	+3.2	+27.0	+1.1	-7.2	-29.4
34 cities, 250,000 to 499,999; population 12,204,694																			
2002	5,743	614	19,957	3,554	3,577	20,705	16,594	13,448	28,170	12,238	97,226	39,998	8,348	102,215	26,225	5,199	3,017	2,942	1,420
2003	5,743	549	18,553	3,279	3,404	19,486	15,950	12,713	26,160	11,607	94,792	38,953	7,686	98,493	24,506	5,639	2,701	2,742	1,313
Percent change	0.0	-10.6	-7.0	-7.7	-4.8	-5.9	-3.9	-5.5	-7.1	-5.2	-2.5	-2.6	-7.9	-3.6	-6.6	+8.5	-10.5	-6.8	-7.5

See footnotes at end of table.

Table 15

Crime Trends

Breakdown of Offenses Known
by Population Group, 2002-2003—Continued
[2003 estimated population]

Population group	Forcible rape — Rape by force	Forcible rape — Assault to rape-attempts	Robbery — Firearm	Robbery — Knife or cutting instrument	Robbery — Other weapon	Robbery — Strong-arm	Aggravated assault — Firearm	Aggravated assault — Knife or cutting instrument	Aggravated assault — Other weapon	Aggravated assault — Hands, fists, feet, etc.	Burglary — Forcible entry	Burglary — Unlawful entry	Burglary — Attempted forcible entry	Motor vehicle theft — Autos	Motor vehicle theft — Trucks and buses	Motor vehicle theft — Other vehicles	Arson — Structure	Arson — Mobile	Arson — Other
GROUP II																			
153 cities, 100,000 to 249,999; population 22,689,730																			
2002	8,132	814	19,145	4,329	4,623	18,609	15,552	15,754	31,720	16,270	136,077	59,701	14,752	112,525	24,789	7,831	3,369	2,747	2,065
2003	7,855	1,052	18,951	4,327	4,378	18,056	15,610	15,680	30,501	15,070	134,752	62,222	14,265	117,768	24,656	8,308	3,207	2,374	1,887
Percent change	-3.4	+29.2	-1.0	*	-5.3	-3.0	+0.4	-0.5	-3.8	-7.4	-1.0	+4.2	-3.3	+4.7	-0.5	+6.1	-4.8	-13.6	-8.6
GROUP III																			
371 cities, 50,000 to 99,999; population 25,735,258																			
2002	8,362	718	14,054	3,606	3,659	16,538	12,679	14,547	28,134	19,997	120,125	65,635	15,479	94,762	15,363	7,516	2,873	1,940	1,812
2003	8,210	724	13,666	3,483	3,594	16,470	12,855	14,747	28,176	20,057	118,750	66,547	15,380	96,137	15,391	8,051	2,792	1,842	1,987
Percent change	-1.8	+0.8	-2.8	-3.4	-1.8	-0.4	+1.4	+1.4	+0.1	+0.3	-1.1	+1.4	-0.6	+1.5	+0.2	+7.1	-2.8	-5.1	+9.7
GROUP IV																			
694 cities, 25,000 to 49,999; population 24,134,633																			
2002	6,854	604	8,231	2,316	2,559	10,481	8,147	10,889	19,194	19,359	93,693	56,057	13,051	62,677	10,032	6,122	2,193	1,321	1,888
2003	7,094	541	8,386	2,261	2,483	10,505	8,052	10,681	18,558	18,336	94,971	57,071	12,350	64,297	9,535	6,352	2,221	1,231	1,773
Percent change	+3.5	-10.4	+1.9	-2.4	-3.0	+0.2	-1.2	-1.9	-3.3	-5.3	+1.4	+1.8	-5.4	+2.6	-5.0	+3.8	+1.3	-6.8	-6.1
GROUP V																			
1,540 cities, 10,000 to 24,999; population 24,341,351																			
2002	6,480	591	6,827	1,540	1,956	7,836	6,762	9,499	17,196	19,742	88,317	53,887	10,996	47,749	7,696	5,666	2,136	928	1,440
2003	6,426	559	6,546	1,663	1,835	8,354	6,940	9,442	16,387	18,930	88,678	54,641	11,011	48,287	7,908	6,193	2,043	955	1,542
Percent change	-0.8	-5.4	-4.1	+8.0	-6.2	+6.6	+2.6	-0.6	-4.7	-4.1	+0.4	+1.4	+0.1	+1.1	+2.8	+9.3	-4.4	+2.9	+7.1
GROUP VI																			
5,976 cities, under 10,000; population 19,373,557																			
2002	4,874	597	4,033	997	1,095	4,961	5,731	8,155	13,565	22,856	72,804	48,555	9,293	32,645	6,017	5,483	2,048	783	1,526
2003	5,226	484	4,062	1,015	1,227	4,870	5,474	7,475	12,924	21,764	73,884	49,741	9,014	33,511	6,000	5,368	1,925	663	1,267
Percent change	+7.2	-18.9	+0.7	+1.8	+12.1	-1.8	-4.5	-8.3	-4.7	-4.8	+1.5	+2.4	-3.0	+2.7	-0.3	-2.1	-6.0	-15.3	-17.0

See footnotes at end of table.

Table 15

Crime Trends
Breakdown of Offenses Known by Population Group, 2002-2003—Continued
[2003 estimated population]

Population group	Forcible rape		Robbery				Aggravated assault				Burglary			Motor vehicle theft			Arson		
	Rape by force	Assault to rape-attempts	Firearm	Knife or cutting instrument	Other weapon	Strong-arm	Firearm	Knife or cutting instrument	Other weapon	Hands, fists, feet, etc.	Forcible entry	Unlawful entry	Attempted forcible entry	Autos	Trucks and buses	Other vehicles	Structure	Mobile	Other
METROPOLITAN COUNTIES																			
1,516 agencies; population 58,526,401																			
2002	14,740	1,208	18,965	3,410	4,540	15,016	23,417	23,010	56,430	40,744	232,523	115,255	22,722	121,829	36,393	22,431	5,140	5,860	3,792
2003	14,351	1,135	19,176	3,502	4,513	14,997	23,452	22,978	55,716	38,838	232,530	116,739	22,031	125,927	37,514	24,303	4,960	5,522	3,374
Percent change	-2.6	-6.0	+1.1	+2.7	-0.6	-0.1	+0.1	-0.1	-1.3	-4.7	*	+1.3	-3.0	+3.4	+3.1	+8.3	-3.5	-5.8	-11.0
NONMETROPOLITAN COUNTIES																			
2,121 agencies; population 22,461,117																			
2002	5,061	334	1,593	311	447	1,354	7,094	5,838	11,760	15,725	85,381	39,306	6,624	17,697	5,417	6,986	1,861	876	834
2003	4,884	376	1,524	328	486	1,369	6,587	5,713	11,548	14,844	83,071	40,671	6,432	17,938	5,702	7,099	1,777	914	847
Percent change	-3.5	+12.6	-4.3	+5.5	+8.7	+1.1	-7.1	-2.1	-1.8	-5.6	-2.7	+3.5	-2.9	+1.4	+5.3	+1.6	-4.5	+4.3	+1.6
SUBURBAN AREA[1]																			
6,642 agencies; population 106,629,964																			
2002	25,359	2,300	32,261	6,633	8,338	30,856	34,597	38,881	87,057	78,368	385,720	215,660	44,659	229,248	53,347	34,290	9,093	7,896	7,193
2003	25,378	2,077	32,493	6,869	8,301	31,203	34,806	38,580	84,918	74,815	387,840	219,852	43,409	236,968	54,199	36,612	8,797	7,501	6,509
Percent change	+0.1	-9.7	+0.7	+3.6	-0.4	+1.1	+0.6	-0.8	-2.5	-4.5	+0.5	+1.9	-2.8	+3.4	+1.6	+6.8	-3.3	-5.0	-9.5

[1] Suburban area includes law enforcement agencies in cities with less than 50,000 inhabitants and county law enforcement agencies that are within a Metropolitan Statistical Area (see Appendix III). Suburban area excludes all metropolitan agencies associated with a principal city. The agencies associated with suburban areas also appear in other groups within this table.

*Less than one-tenth of 1 percent.

Table 16

Rate: Number of Crimes per 100,000 Inhabitants
by Population Group, 2003
[2003 estimated population]

Population group	Violent crime	Murder and non-negligent man-slaughter	Forcible rape[1]	Robbery	Aggravated assault	Property crime	Burglary	Larceny-theft	Motor vehicle theft
		Violent crime				Property crime			
TOTAL ALL AGENCIES:									
12,062 agencies;									
population 249,150,621									
Number of offenses known	1,257,813	15,044	81,885	385,310	775,574	9,275,118	1,900,771	6,206,646	1,167,701
Rate	504.8	6.0	32.9	154.6	311.3	3,722.7	762.9	2,491.1	468.7
TOTAL CITIES: 8,608 cities;									
population 168,597,746									
Number of offenses known	1,006,527	11,947	60,844	339,097	594,639	7,321,803	1,398,467	4,976,461	946,875
Rate	597.0	7.1	36.1	201.1	352.7	4,342.8	829.5	2,951.7	561.6
GROUP I									
69 cities, 250,000 and over;									
population 52,354,586									
Number of offenses known	506,516	6,895	21,675	198,788	279,158	2,667,526	512,869	1,677,767	476,890
Rate	967.5	13.2	41.4	379.7	533.2	5,095.1	979.6	3,204.6	910.9
10 cities, 1,000,000 and over;									
population 24,680,715									
Number of offenses known	241,883	3,094	8,144	99,750	130,895	1,022,286	190,158	640,224	191,904
Rate	980.0	12.5	33.0	404.2	530.4	4,142.0	770.5	2,594.0	777.5
22 cities, 500,000 to 999,999;									
population 14,552,949									
Number of offenses known	137,460	1,977	6,525	50,747	78,211	873,400	169,748	554,233	149,419
Rate	944.6	13.6	44.8	348.7	537.4	6,001.5	1,166.4	3,808.4	1,026.7
37 cities, 250,000 to 499,999;									
population 13,120,922									
Number of offenses known	127,173	1,824	7,006	48,291	70,052	771,840	152,963	483,310	135,567
Rate	969.2	13.9	53.4	368.0	533.9	5,882.5	1,165.8	3,683.5	1,033.2
GROUP II									
163 cities, 100,000 to 249,999;									
population 24,301,959									
Number of offenses known	149,752	1,923	9,840	51,000	86,989	1,202,702	237,168	801,401	164,133
Rate	616.2	7.9	40.5	209.9	358.0	4,949.0	975.9	3,297.7	675.4
GROUP III									
367 cities, 50,000 to 99,999;									
population 25,518,121									
Number of offenses known	123,182	1,174	9,074	37,093	75,841	1,028,823	201,066	707,116	120,641
Rate	482.7	4.6	35.6	145.4	297.2	4,031.7	787.9	2,771.0	472.8
GROUP IV									
679 cities, 25,000 to 49,999;									
population 23,607,380									
Number of offenses known	86,523	785	7,589	23,463	54,686	861,991	162,387	620,181	79,423
Rate	366.5	3.3	32.1	99.4	231.6	3,651.4	687.9	2,627.1	336.4
GROUP V									
1,520 cities, 10,000 to 24,999;									
population 24,022,656									
Number of offenses known	77,180	647	6,998	18,388	51,147	838,332	155,162	620,597	62,573
Rate	321.3	2.7	29.1	76.5	212.9	3,489.8	645.9	2,583.4	260.5

See footnotes at end of table.

Table 16

Rate: Number of Crimes per 100,000 Inhabitants

by Population Group, 2003—Continued

[2003 estimated population]

Population group	Violent crime	Violent crime				Property crime	Property crime		
	Violent crime	Murder and non-negligent man-slaughter	Forcible rape[1]	Robbery	Aggravated assault	Property crime	Burglary	Larceny-theft	Motor vehicle theft
GROUP VI									
5,810 cities, under 10,000; population 18,793,044									
Number of offenses known	63,374	523	5,668	10,365	46,818	722,429	129,815	549,399	43,215
Rate	337.2	2.8	30.2	55.2	249.1	3,844.1	690.8	2,923.4	230.0
METROPOLITAN COUNTIES									
1,426 agencies; population 58,949,265									
Number of offenses known	203,858	2,369	15,771	42,607	143,111	1,562,687	376,021	995,980	190,686
Rate	345.8	4.0	26.8	72.3	242.8	2,650.9	637.9	1,689.6	323.5
NONMETROPOLITAN COUNTIES[2]									
2,028 agencies; population 21,603,610									
Number of offenses known	47,428	728	5,270	3,606	37,824	390,628	126,283	234,205	30,140
Rate	219.5	3.4	24.4	16.7	175.1	1,808.2	584.5	1,084.1	139.5
SUBURBAN AREA[3]									
6,439 agencies; population 105,867,123									
Number of offenses known	342,693	3,511	27,619	78,240	233,323	3,098,628	651,701	2,118,878	328,049
Rate	323.7	3.3	26.1	73.9	220.4	2,926.9	615.6	2,001.5	309.9

[1] Forcible rape figures furnished by the state Uniform Crime Reporting (UCR) Program administered by the Illinois State Police were not in accorda
 therefore, the figures were estimated for inclusion in the forcible rape and violent crime categories. See Appendix I for details.

[2] Includes state police agencies that report aggregately for the entire state.

[3] Suburban area includes law enforcement agencies in cities with less than 50,000 inhabitants and county law enforcement agencies that are within a Metropolitan Statistical Area
 (see Appendix III). Suburban area excludes all metropolitan agencies associated with a principal city. The agencies associated with suburban areas also appear in other groups within
 this table.

Table 17

Rate: Number of Crimes per 100,000 Inhabitants
by Suburban and Nonsuburban Cities[1] by Population Group, 2003
[2003 estimated population]

Population group	Violent crime	Murder and non-negligent man-slaughter	Forcible rape	Robbery	Aggravated assault	Property crime	Burglary	Larceny-theft	Motor vehicle theft
Suburban cities									
TOTAL SUBURBAN CITIES:									
5,013 cities;									
population 46,917,858									
Number of offenses known	138,835	1,142	11,848	35,633	90,212	1,535,941	275,680	1,122,898	137,363
Rate	295.9	2.4	25.3	75.9	192.3	3,273.7	587.6	2,393.3	292.8
GROUP IV									
509 cities, 25,000 to 49,999;									
population 17,546,364									
Number of offenses known	52,456	466	4,350	15,375	32,265	544,137	100,933	383,661	59,543
Rate	299.0	2.7	24.8	87.6	183.9	3,101.1	575.2	2,186.6	339.3
GROUP V									
1,130 cities, 10,000 to 24,999;									
population 17,955,105									
Number of offenses known	50,351	388	4,332	13,016	32,615	539,663	98,253	393,721	47,689
Rate	280.4	2.2	24.1	72.5	181.6	3,005.6	547.2	2,192.8	265.6
GROUP VI									
3,374 cities, under 10,000;									
population 11,416,389									
Number of offenses known	36,028	288	3,166	7,242	25,332	452,141	76,494	345,516	30,131
Rate	315.6	2.5	27.7	63.4	221.9	3,960.5	670.0	3,026.5	263.9
Nonsuburban cities									
TOTAL NONSUBURBAN CITIES:									
2,996 cities;									
population 19,505,222									
Number of offenses known	88,242	813	8,407	16,583	62,439	886,811	171,684	667,279	47,848
Rate	452.4	4.2	43.1	85.0	320.1	4,546.5	880.2	3,421.0	245.3
GROUP IV									
170 cities, 25,000 to 49,999;									
population 6,061,016									
Number of offenses known	34,067	319	3,239	8,088	22,421	317,854	61,454	236,520	19,880
Rate	562.1	5.3	53.4	133.4	369.9	5,244.2	1,013.9	3,902.3	328.0
GROUP V									
390 cities, 10,000 to 24,999;									
population 6,067,551									
Number of offenses known	26,829	259	2,666	5,372	18,532	298,669	56,909	226,876	14,884
Rate	442.2	4.3	43.9	88.5	305.4	4,922.4	937.9	3,739.2	245.3
GROUP VI									
2,436 cities, under 10,000;									
population 7,376,655									
Number of offenses known	27,346	235	2,502	3,123	21,486	270,288	53,321	203,883	13,084
Rate	370.7	3.2	33.9	42.3	291.3	3,664.1	722.8	2,763.9	177.4

[1] Suburban includes law enforcement agencies in cities with less than 50,000 inhabitants that are within a Metropolitan Statistical Area (see Appendix III). Suburban excludes all metropolitan agencies associated with a principal city. Nonsuburban includes law enforcement agencies in cities with less than 50,000 inhabitants that are not associated with a Metropolitan Statistical Area.

Table 18

Rate: Number of Crimes per 100,000 Inhabitants
by Metropolitan and Nonmetropolitan Counties[1] by Population Group, 2003
[2003 estimated population]

Population group	Violent crime	Violent crime Murder and non-negligent man-slaughter	Violent crime Forcible rape	Violent crime Robbery	Violent crime Aggravated assault	Property crime	Property crime Burglary	Property crime Larceny-theft	Property crime Motor vehicle theft
METROPOLITAN COUNTIES									
100,000 and over									
133 counties;									
population 35,644,050									
Number of offenses known	143,612	1,616	9,601	35,973	96,422	1,047,940	234,979	680,107	132,854
Rate	402.9	4.5	26.9	100.9	270.5	2,940.0	659.2	1,908.1	372.7
25,000 to 99,999									
378 counties;									
population 19,432,410									
Number of offenses known	44,136	546	4,615	4,736	34,239	388,878	111,379	244,530	32,969
Rate	227.1	2.8	23.7	24.4	176.2	2,001.2	573.2	1,258.4	169.7
Under 25,000									
915 counties;									
population 3,872,805									
Number of offenses known	16,110	207	1,555	1,898	12,450	125,869	29,663	71,343	24,863
Rate	416.0	5.3	40.2	49.0	321.5	3,250.1	765.9	1,842.2	642.0
NONMETROPOLITAN COUNTIES									
25,000 and over									
242 counties;									
population 9,395,038									
Number of offenses known	20,251	312	2,047	1,870	16,022	171,834	57,193	102,400	12,241
Rate	215.5	3.3	21.8	19.9	170.5	1,829.0	608.8	1,089.9	130.3
10,000 to 24,999									
467 counties;									
population 7,542,141									
Number of offenses known	14,246	229	1,408	891	11,718	115,476	39,100	67,770	8,606
Rate	188.9	3.0	18.7	11.8	155.4	1,531.1	518.4	898.6	114.1
Under 10,000									
1,168 counties;									
population 3,520,667									
Number of offenses known	8,999	131	1,351	394	7,123	66,009	21,178	38,783	6,048
Rate	255.6	3.7	38.4	11.2	202.3	1,874.9	601.5	1,101.6	171.8

[1] Metropolitan counties include sheriffs and county law enforcement agencies associated with a Metropolitan Statistical Area (see Appendix III). Nonmetropolitan counties include sheriffs and county law enforcement agencies that are not associated with a Metropolitan Statistical Area. The offenses from state police agencies are not included in this table.

Table 19

Rate: Number of Crimes per 100,000 Inhabitants
Breakdown of Offenses Known
by Population Group, 2003
[2003 estimated population]

Population group	Forcible rape: Rape by force	Forcible rape: Assault to rape-attempts	Robbery: Firearm	Robbery: Knife or cutting instrument	Robbery: Other weapon	Robbery: Strong-arm	Aggravated assault: Firearm	Aggravated assault: Knife or cutting instrument	Aggravated assault: Other weapon	Aggravated assault: Hands, fists, feet, etc.	Burglary: Forcible entry	Burglary: Unlawful entry	Burglary: Attempted forcible entry	Motor vehicle theft: Autos	Motor vehicle theft: Trucks and buses	Motor vehicle theft: Other vehicles
TOTAL ALL AGENCIES: 12,011 agencies; population 232,648,552 Number of offenses known	69,810	6,898	136,626	29,076	30,887	130,371	133,836	127,592	251,504	188,310	1,114,635	557,572	113,060	795,416	200,494	89,013
Rate	30.0	3.0	58.7	12.5	13.3	56.0	57.5	54.8	108.1	80.9	479.1	239.7	48.6	341.9	86.2	38.3
TOTAL CITIES: 8,570 cities; population 153,527,154 Number of offenses known	50,663	5,389	116,147	25,322	26,029	114,186	104,066	99,218	184,650	135,365	805,989	401,603	85,167	653,094	157,798	58,121
Rate	33.0	3.5	75.7	16.5	17.0	74.4	67.8	64.6	120.3	88.2	525.0	261.6	55.5	425.4	102.8	37.9
GROUP I																
63 cities, 250,000 and over; population 39,797,364 Number of offenses known	16,131	2,061	65,362	12,749	12,753	56,725	55,424	41,790	79,135	41,780	301,598	114,560	24,033	297,999	94,642	24,056
Rate	40.5	5.2	164.2	32.0	32.0	142.5	139.3	105.0	198.8	105.0	757.8	287.9	60.4	748.8	237.8	60.4
8 cities, 1,000,000 and over; population 13,684,275 Number of offenses known	4,703	876	25,562	5,670	4,465	20,762	21,109	14,534	24,193	20,022	93,610	36,110	7,081	99,213	37,745	8,539
Rate	34.4	6.4	186.8	41.4	32.6	151.7	154.3	106.2	176.8	146.3	684.1	263.9	51.7	725.0	275.8	62.4
21 cities, 500,000 to 999,999; population 13,908,395 Number of offenses known	5,685	636	21,247	3,800	4,884	16,477	18,365	14,543	28,782	10,151	113,196	39,497	9,266	100,293	32,391	9,878
Rate	40.9	4.6	152.8	27.3	35.1	118.5	132.0	104.6	206.9	73.0	813.9	284.0	66.6	721.1	232.9	71.0
34 cities, 250,000 to 499,999; population 12,204,694 Number of offenses known	5,743	549	18,553	3,279	3,404	19,486	15,950	12,713	26,160	11,607	94,792	38,953	7,686	98,493	24,506	5,639
Rate	47.1	4.5	152.0	26.9	27.9	159.7	130.7	104.2	214.3	95.1	776.7	319.2	63.0	807.0	200.8	46.2
GROUP II																
150 cities, 100,000 to 249,999; population 22,297,062 Number of offenses known	7,749	1,048	18,899	4,293	4,349	17,928	15,838	15,649	30,544	16,281	133,800	61,444	14,091	116,440	24,714	8,317
Rate	34.8	4.7	84.8	19.3	19.5	80.4	71.0	70.2	137.0	73.0	600.1	275.6	63.2	522.2	110.8	37.3
GROUP III																
362 cities, 50,000 to 99,999; population 25,171,305 Number of offenses known	8,132	719	13,426	3,430	3,543	16,184	12,616	14,416	27,634	19,835	116,642	65,893	15,141	94,785	15,383	7,957
Rate	32.3	2.9	53.3	13.6	14.1	64.3	50.1	57.3	109.8	78.8	463.4	261.8	60.2	376.6	61.1	31.6

See footnotes at end of table.

Table 19

Rate: Number of Crimes per 100,000 Inhabitants
Breakdown of Offenses Known
by Population Group, 2003—Continued
[2003 estimated population]

Population group	Forcible rape		Robbery				Aggravated assault				Burglary			Motor vehicle theft		
	Rape by force	Assault to rape-attempts	Firearm	Knife or cutting instrument	Other weapon	Strong-arm	Firearm	Knife or cutting instrument	Other weapon	Hands, fists, feet, etc.	Forcible entry	Unlawful entry	Attempted forcible entry	Autos	Trucks and buses	Other vehicles
GROUP IV																
677 cities, 25,000 to 49,999; population 23,517,164																
Number of offenses known	7,043	527	8,249	2,243	2,437	10,381	7,880	10,536	18,302	17,770	93,162	55,893	12,130	63,473	9,416	6,254
Rate	29.9	2.2	35.1	9.5	10.4	44.1	33.5	44.8	77.8	75.6	396.1	237.7	51.6	269.9	40.0	26.6
GROUP V																
1,519 cities, 10,000 to 24,999; population 24,003,549																
Number of offenses known	6,433	557	6,532	1,656	1,861	8,332	6,989	9,433	16,299	18,423	89,300	54,468	11,026	48,395	7,923	6,169
Rate	26.8	2.3	27.2	6.9	7.8	34.7	29.1	39.3	67.9	76.8	372.0	226.9	45.9	201.6	33.0	25.7
GROUP VI																
5,799 cities, under 10,000; population 18,740,710																
Number of offenses known	5,175	477	3,679	951	1,086	4,636	5,319	7,394	12,736	21,276	71,487	49,345	8,746	32,002	5,720	5,368
Rate	27.6	2.5	19.6	5.1	5.8	24.7	28.4	39.5	68.0	113.5	381.5	263.3	46.7	170.8	30.5	28.6
METROPOLITAN COUNTIES																
1,417 agencies; population 57,632,624																
Number of offenses known	14,275	1,130	19,007	3,439	4,384	14,865	23,392	22,854	55,587	38,550	229,130	116,047	21,775	124,720	37,192	24,020
Rate	24.8	2.0	33.0	6.0	7.6	25.8	40.6	39.7	96.5	66.9	397.6	201.4	37.8	216.4	64.5	41.7
NONMETROPOLITAN COUNTIES																
2,024 agencies; population 21,488,774																
Number of offenses known	4,872	379	1,472	315	474	1,320	6,378	5,520	11,267	14,395	79,516	39,922	6,118	17,602	5,504	6,872
Rate	22.7	1.8	6.9	1.5	2.2	6.1	29.7	25.7	52.4	67.0	370.0	185.8	28.5	81.9	25.6	32.0
SUBURBAN AREA[1]																
6,425 agencies; population 104,479,176																
Number of offenses known	25,194	2,054	31,845	6,724	8,016	30,718	34,506	38,261	84,389	73,356	381,811	217,822	42,765	233,527	53,406	36,189
Rate	24.1	2.0	30.5	6.4	7.7	29.4	33.0	36.6	80.8	70.2	365.4	208.5	40.9	223.5	51.1	34.6

[1] Suburban area includes law enforcement agencies in cities with less than 50,000 inhabitants and county law enforcement agencies that are within a Metropolitan Statistical Area (see Appendix III). Suburban area excludes all metropolitan agencies associated with a principal city. The agencies associated with suburban areas also appear in other groups within this table.

Table 20

Murder
by State, 2003
Type of Weapon

State	Total murders[1]	Total firearms	Handguns	Rifles	Shotguns	Firearms (type unknown)	Knives or cutting instruments	Other weapons	Hands, fists, feet, etc.[2]
Alabama	292	207	185	0	22	0	28	33	24
Alaska	39	24	21	2	0	1	6	8	1
Arizona	439	311	275	14	15	7	43	53	32
Arkansas	154	103	68	11	10	14	23	21	7
California	2,407	1,727	1,558	64	53	52	261	281	138
Colorado	158	92	66	2	2	22	31	23	12
Connecticut	78	31	23	0	1	7	14	27	6
Delaware	24	16	10	0	1	5	2	6	0
District of Columbia[3]	1	0	0	0	0	0	1	0	0
Florida[3]									
Georgia	625	435	382	9	23	21	82	68	40
Hawaii	22	8	4	2	2	0	1	5	8
Idaho	25	13	10	2	0	1	2	4	6
Illinois[3]	594	483	438	5	8	32	52	35	24
Indiana	322	244	153	12	7	72	25	42	11
Iowa	47	21	13	1	2	5	7	12	7
Kansas	91	62	38	4	5	15	5	14	10
Kentucky[3]	79	54	22	1	2	29	9	14	2
Louisiana	573	454	382	39	21	12	50	46	23
Maine	16	8	2	0	3	3	3	1	4
Maryland	524	370	345	5	13	7	75	49	30
Massachusetts	140	73	51	0	0	22	32	32	3
Michigan	615	432	324	20	18	70	69	88	26
Minnesota	121	72	60	6	6	0	16	24	9
Mississippi	186	128	99	1	14	14	27	18	13
Missouri	288	183	83	7	7	86	37	59	9
Montana	21	15	6	4	0	5	3	3	0
Nebraska	19	5	3	1	0	1	5	7	2
Nevada	193	119	97	3	3	16	26	37	11
New Hampshire	11	4	0	0	4	0	1	3	3
New Jersey	405	240	218	4	9	9	83	43	39
New Mexico	100	51	43	3	1	4	12	18	19
New York	878	545	490	13	10	32	150	105	78
North Carolina	492	316	225	16	35	40	59	78	39
North Dakota	9	8	6	0	1	1	0	0	1
Ohio	473	245	195	3	11	36	68	101	59
Oklahoma	206	129	98	9	6	16	28	28	21
Oregon	66	34	18	2	0	14	8	19	5
Pennsylvania	629	432	371	9	12	40	80	93	24
Rhode Island	25	18	11	0	0	7	1	4	2
South Carolina	293	199	142	5	12	40	34	38	22
South Dakota	9	4	4	0	0	0	5	0	0
Tennessee	395	258	185	8	16	49	48	69	20
Texas	1,417	891	643	75	58	115	189	233	104
Utah	53	34	24	1	1	8	10	8	1
Vermont	14	8	5	0	1	2	4	2	0
Virginia	409	280	128	6	16	130	39	73	17
Washington	182	85	66	10	8	1	41	41	15
West Virginia	54	34	22	2	5	5	8	9	3
Wisconsin	181	126	85	7	7	27	12	30	13
Wyoming	14	7	4	2	1	0	1	3	3

[1] Total number of murders for which supplemental homicide data were received.

[2] Pushed is included in hands, fists, feet, etc.

[3] Limited or no supplemental homicide data were received. The murder for the District of Columbia was reported by the Metro Transit Police.

Table 21

Robbery
by State, 2003
Type of Weapon

State	Total robberies[1]	Firearms	Knives or cutting instruments	Other weapons	Strong-arm	Agency count	Population
Alabama	2,779	1,482	189	187	921	302	3,298,257
Alaska	442	135	39	43	225	31	632,621
Arizona	7,490	3,616	848	696	2,330	87	5,406,362
Arkansas	1,916	1,031	124	137	624	119	1,823,659
California	63,496	22,122	6,442	5,618	29,314	718	35,044,194
Colorado	3,255	1,036	339	730	1,150	163	3,394,519
Connecticut	3,043	1,104	332	259	1,348	76	2,338,057
Delaware	1,380	606	122	114	538	41	807,466
District of Columbia	3,941	1,850	220	285	1,586	3	563,384
Florida	31,512	12,288	2,214	3,430	13,580	596	17,012,655
Georgia	12,530	7,044	726	1,152	3,608	349	6,720,872
Hawaii	1,168	153	108	67	840	4	1,257,608
Idaho	242	78	30	35	99	112	1,341,105
Illinois[2]							
Indiana	5,906	2,927	388	453	2,138	269	4,917,075
Iowa	1,104	244	142	160	558	189	2,650,558
Kansas	364	108	24	115	117	229	1,321,692
Kentucky[2]	2,336	1,064	161	391	720	25	1,379,691
Louisiana	6,611	4,006	349	456	1,800	149	3,892,033
Maine	289	54	45	33	157	163	1,300,474
Maryland	8,963	4,523	850	499	3,091	148	4,864,355
Massachusetts	7,324	2,130	1,441	870	2,883	291	5,770,923
Michigan	10,929	5,143	665	1,277	3,844	561	9,630,438
Minnesota	909	292	75	258	284	261	3,642,880
Mississippi	2,064	1,176	133	198	557	98	1,548,999
Missouri	6,200	2,743	415	487	2,555	576	5,650,366
Montana	170	40	22	35	73	66	582,506
Nebraska	1,144	554	102	72	416	215	1,489,255
Nevada	5,153	2,092	515	412	2,134	34	2,196,620
New Hampshire	301	93	37	37	134	117	887,385
New Jersey	13,264	4,331	1,488	1,000	6,445	494	8,374,199
New Mexico	1,620	706	224	137	553	35	1,231,648
New York	8,319	2,648	870	970	3,831	514	9,606,134
North Carolina	11,092	5,909	860	1,096	3,227	333	6,694,134
North Dakota	46	10	5	8	23	55	504,086
Ohio	11,826	4,101	579	1,183	5,963	334	6,817,310
Oklahoma	3,224	1,416	324	207	1,277	298	3,511,532
Oregon	2,602	702	296	228	1,376	140	3,201,784
Pennsylvania	16,856	6,952	1,291	1,056	7,557	764	10,592,964
Rhode Island	830	276	112	106	336	48	1,076,164
South Carolina	5,021	2,511	401	479	1,630	298	3,628,858
South Dakota	100	24	10	10	56	123	673,184
Tennessee	9,354	5,356	659	1,046	2,293	443	5,738,034
Texas	36,958	16,661	3,745	3,432	13,120	969	21,978,733
Utah	1,218	424	108	174	512	98	2,057,602
Vermont	38	14	7	6	11	54	478,344
Virginia	4,431	2,174	351	602	1,304	251	5,319,103
Washington	4,620	1,216	474	467	2,463	235	5,370,779
West Virginia	144	54	15	25	50	260	726,434
Wisconsin	4,269	2,414	271	272	1,312	332	5,037,985
Wyoming	83	24	13	14	32	60	487,191

[1] The number of robberies for which breakdowns by type of weapon were received for 12 months of 2003.

[2] Limited or no robbery by type of weapon data for 2003 were received.

Table 22

Aggravated Assault
by State, 2003
Type of Weapon

State	Total aggravated assaults[1]	Firearms	Knives or cutting instruments	Other weapons	Personal weapons	Agency count	Population
Alabama	7,479	1,782	1,088	1,663	2,946	302	3,298,257
Alaska	2,709	495	636	686	892	31	632,621
Arizona	18,136	4,895	2,688	5,447	5,106	87	5,406,362
Arkansas	6,761	1,510	1,031	2,004	2,216	119	1,823,659
California	128,092	22,290	18,000	42,546	45,256	718	35,044,194
Colorado	8,188	1,531	1,773	2,748	2,136	163	3,394,519
Connecticut	3,824	373	743	1,371	1,337	76	2,338,057
Delaware	3,581	617	824	1,742	398	41	807,466
District of Columbia	4,596	904	1,275	1,891	526	3	563,384
Florida	85,076	12,862	15,286	39,652	17,276	596	17,012,655
Georgia	18,203	4,808	3,538	5,845	4,012	349	6,720,872
Hawaii	1,843	186	299	594	764	4	1,257,608
Idaho	2,500	460	588	1,003	449	112	1,341,105
Illinois[2]							
Indiana	11,407	1,415	1,246	2,979	5,767	269	4,917,075
Iowa	5,812	445	918	1,520	2,929	189	2,650,558
Kansas	3,012	488	532	1,568	424	229	1,321,692
Kentucky[2]	3,462	491	396	1,250	1,325	25	1,379,691
Louisiana	16,975	4,704	3,393	5,157	3,721	149	3,892,033
Maine	762	30	124	212	396	163	1,300,474
Maryland	17,223	2,381	3,519	7,587	3,736	148	4,864,355
Massachusetts	19,838	1,856	4,150	9,901	3,931	291	5,770,923
Michigan	33,103	7,219	6,333	13,959	5,592	561	9,630,438
Minnesota	3,266	376	781	1,080	1,029	261	3,642,880
Mississippi	2,562	689	515	608	750	98	1,548,999
Missouri	19,035	3,829	2,613	6,194	6,399	576	5,650,366
Montana	1,695	300	212	483	700	66	582,506
Nebraska	3,143	471	636	1,448	588	215	1,489,255
Nevada	7,467	1,586	1,653	2,967	1,261	34	2,196,620
New Hampshire	552	87	178	133	154	117	887,385
New Jersey	16,032	2,527	3,551	4,870	5,084	494	8,374,199
New Mexico	6,746	1,434	1,174	2,195	1,943	35	1,231,648
New York	14,562	1,696	3,123	4,241	5,502	514	9,606,134
North Carolina	19,887	5,586	4,022	6,024	4,255	333	6,694,134
North Dakota	230	9	45	66	110	55	504,086
Ohio	10,975	2,041	2,050	3,552	3,332	334	6,817,310
Oklahoma	12,827	2,071	2,065	4,815	3,876	298	3,511,532
Oregon	5,965	725	991	2,282	1,967	140	3,201,784
Pennsylvania	23,582	5,068	3,626	6,115	8,773	764	10,592,964
Rhode Island	1,714	358	382	650	324	48	1,076,164
South Carolina	22,418	5,000	4,641	6,846	5,931	298	3,628,858
South Dakota	776	114	220	198	244	123	673,184
Tennessee	28,021	8,799	5,917	10,440	2,865	443	5,738,034
Texas	75,584	16,352	16,767	28,419	14,046	969	21,978,733
Utah	3,253	546	701	1,077	929	98	2,057,602
Vermont	345	55	63	81	146	54	478,344
Virginia	6,799	1,125	1,407	2,216	2,051	251	5,319,103
Washington	9,955	1,365	1,825	3,462	3,303	235	5,370,779
West Virginia	1,399	360	181	284	574	260	726,434
Wisconsin	5,581	930	746	1,097	2,808	332	5,037,985
Wyoming	1,050	105	158	340	447	60	487,191

[1] The number of aggravated assaults for which breakdowns by type of weapon were received for 12 months of 2003.

[2] Limited or no aggravated assault by type of weapon data for 2003 were received.

Table 23

Offense Analysis
Number and Percent Change, 2002-2003
[11,980 agencies; 2003 estimated population 224,518,754]

Classification	Number of offenses 2003	Percent change over 2002	Percent distribution[1]	Average value
Murder	12,165	+0.8	–	
Forcible rape	71,833	-1.5	–	
Robbery:				
Total	**302,360**	**-1.4**	**100.0**	**$1,244**
Street/highway	131,136	-1.9	43.4	898
Commercial house	44,244	-1.0	14.6	1,778
Gas or service station	8,310	-2.4	2.7	690
Convenience store	18,851	-3.0	6.2	813
Residence	41,427	+2.4	13.7	1,472
Bank	6,951	-2.2	2.3	4,767
Miscellaneous	51,441	-2.5	17.0	1,258
Burglary:				
Total	**1,646,613**	**+0.5**	**100.0**	**1,626**
Residence (dwelling):	1,083,886	+0.5	65.8	1,600
Night	312,680	-0.8	19.0	1,305
Day	511,031	+1.0	31.0	1,700
Unknown	260,175	+1.1	15.8	1,758
Nonresidence (store, office, etc.):	562,727	+0.5	34.2	1,676
Night	237,029	-1.2	14.4	1,460
Day	169,060	+3.2	10.3	1,659
Unknown	156,638	+0.1	9.5	2,019
Larceny-theft (except motor vehicle theft):				
Total	**5,418,092**	**-0.2**	**100.0**	**698**
By type:				
Pocket-picking	24,648	-1.9	0.5	294
Purse-snatching	32,524	+5.1	0.6	367
Shoplifting	781,289	+1.3	14.4	163
From motor vehicles (except accessories)	1,432,337	-0.5	26.4	680
Motor vehicle accessories	602,414	+2.8	11.1	442
Bicycles	209,575	-3.9	3.9	247
From buildings	669,760	-3.5	12.4	1,030
From coin-operated machines	40,383	+2.2	0.7	262
All others	1,625,162	+0.1	30.0	1,012
By value:				
Over $200	2,129,479	-1.7	39.3	1,693
$50 to $200	1,223,421	-0.9	22.6	112
Under $50	2,065,192	+1.8	38.1	21
Motor vehicle theft	903,625	+6.7	–	6,797

[1] Because of rounding, the percentages may not add to 100.0.

Table 24

Property Stolen and Recovered
by Type and Value, 2003
[11,894 agencies; 2003 estimated population 223,958,172]

Type of property	Value of property		Percent recovered
	Stolen	Recovered	
Total	**$13,181,852,218**	**$4,509,149,255**	**34.2**
Currency, notes, etc.	947,441,557	37,190,984	3.9
Jewelry and precious metals	1,037,755,787	46,176,125	4.4
Clothing and furs	211,047,574	31,310,441	14.8
Locally stolen motor vehicles	6,438,458,427	4,049,658,523	62.9
Office equipment	456,024,692	21,420,579	4.7
Televisions, radios, stereos, etc.	902,706,861	41,569,206	4.6
Firearms	97,375,307	7,546,973	7.8
Household goods	214,767,746	9,810,482	4.6
Consumable goods	105,129,364	9,939,291	9.5
Livestock	16,071,308	2,064,282	12.8
Miscellaneous	2,755,073,595	252,462,369	9.2

SECTION III

Offenses Cleared

Law enforcement agencies reporting offenses to the national UCR Program can clear these offenses in one of two ways: by arrest or by exceptional means. However, the administrative closing or "clearing" of a case by a local law enforcement agency does not necessarily mean that the agency can clear an offense for UCR purposes. To clear an offense within the Program's guidelines, the reporting agency must adhere to certain criteria.

Cleared by Arrest

In the UCR Program, when a law enforcement agency reports that an offense is cleared, or solved by arrest, all of the following conditions have been met. At least one person was:

- Arrested.
- Charged with the commission of an offense.
- Turned over to the court for prosecution.

The UCR Program counts clearances by the number of offenses that are solved, not by the number of persons arrested. The arrest of one person may clear several crimes. Conversely, the arrest of many persons may clear only one offense. In addition, the clearances that an agency recorded in a particular calendar year such as 2003 may include offenses that occurred in previous years.

Cleared by Exceptional Means

When elements beyond law enforcement's control prevent the agency from placing formal charges against the offender, the agency can clear the offense exceptionally. There are four UCR Program requirements that law enforcement must meet in order to clear an offense

by exceptional means. The agency must have:

- Identified the offender.
- Gathered enough evidence to support an arrest, make a charge, and turn over the offender to the court for prosecution.
- Identified the offender's exact location so that the suspect could be taken into custody immediately.
- Encountered a circumstance outside the control of law enforcement that prohibits the agency from arresting, charging, and prosecuting the offender.

Examples of exceptional clearances include, but are not limited to, the death of the offender (suicide, justifiably killed by law enforcement officers or private citizens, etc.); the victim's refusal to cooperate with the prosecution after having identified the offender; or the denial of extradition because the offender committed a crime in another jurisdiction and is being prosecuted for that offense. In the UCR Program, the recovery of property does not clear an offense.

2003 National Clearances

Nationwide, law enforcement agencies cleared 46.5 percent of violent crimes (murder, forcible rape, robbery, and aggravated assault) and 16.4 percent of property crimes (burglary, larceny-theft, and motor vehicle theft). Additionally, law enforcement cleared 16.7 percent of reported arson offenses.

Continuing a long-term trend, in 2003 law enforcement cleared a higher percentage of violent crimes than property crimes. Violent crimes often

undergo a more vigorous investigative effort than crimes against property, and they more often involve victims and/or witnesses who are able to identify the perpetrators. A further breakdown of the violent crime clearances for 2003 revealed that the Nation's law enforcement agencies cleared 62.4 percent of murders, 55.9 percent of aggravated assaults, 44.0 percent of forcible rapes, and 26.3 percent of robberies. A review of the clearances for property crimes indicated that law enforcement cleared 18.0 percent of larceny-thefts and 13.1 percent of both burglaries and motor vehicle thefts. (See Table 25.)

2003 Regional Clearances

An examination of the 2003 clearance data for the four regions of the country showed that law enforcement agencies in the Northeast cleared the highest percentage of violent crimes in 2003—49.8 percent. Agencies in the West followed with a 47.2 clearance percentage for violent crimes. Law enforcement in the South and the Midwest cleared 45.7 percent and 44.8 percent, respectively, of their violent crimes. Clearance data for property crime reflected that agencies in the Northeast cleared 20.1 percent of those crimes, and law enforcement in the South and Midwest cleared 16.6 percent and 16.5 percent, respectively. Agencies in the West cleared 14.4 percent of their property crimes. (See Table 26.)

2003 Clearances by Population Group

When presenting crime data, the UCR Program uses eight population group designations for aggregating data for the Nation's cities, metropolitan counties, and nonmetropolitan counties.

Figure 3.1

Crimes Cleared by Arrest
Percent of crimes cleared by arrest, 2003

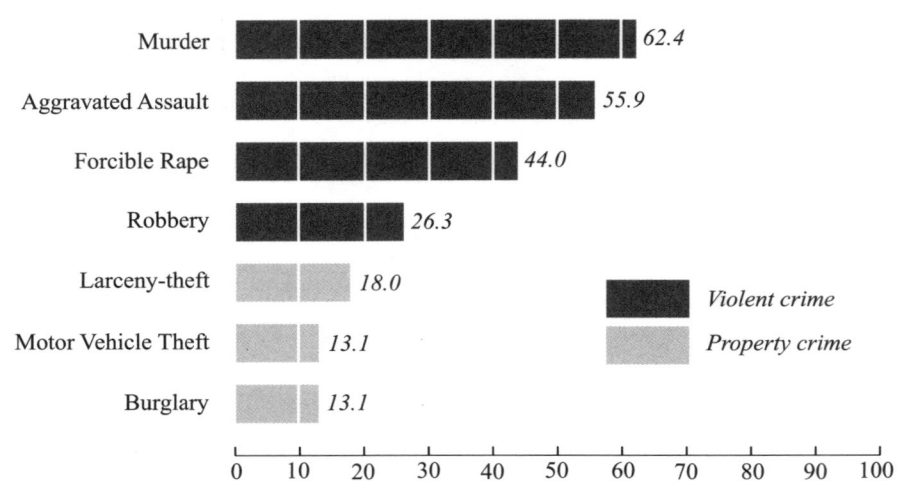

(Appendix III furnishes a breakdown of these classifications.) Clearance data for 2003 revealed that law enforcement agencies in the Nation's cities cleared 44.7 percent of all reported violent crimes. Agencies in cities collectively cleared 61.9 percent of murders, 54.6 percent of aggravated assaults, 43.4 percent of forcible rapes, and 25.7 percent of robberies. Law enforcement in cities with populations ranging from 10,000 to 24,999 cleared the greatest percentage of murders—71.8 percent. Cities with 100,000 to 249,999 inhabitants cleared the lowest percentage of murders—58.7 percent.

In 2003, agencies in metropolitan counties cleared 51.6 percent of their violent crimes. Of those crimes, 60.0 percent of murders were cleared, 58.8 percent of aggravated assaults were cleared, 45.4 percent of forcible rapes, and 29.0 percent of robberies were cleared.

Law enforcement in nonmetropolitan counties cleared 59.9 percent of reported violent crimes. Within that category, agencies in those counties cleared 76.3 percent of murders, 62.9 percent of aggravated assaults, 46.8 percent of

forcible rapes, and 43.1 percent of robberies.

An examination of data for property crime clearances reflected that agencies in the Nation's cities cleared 16.3 percent of those crimes in 2003. Of the property crimes cleared, law enforcement in cities collectively most often solved larceny-theft offenses, clearing 18.1 percent of those crimes. Similarly, agencies in metropolitan counties cleared 16.2 percent of their total property crimes, and they most often cleared larceny-theft offenses, reporting a 17.4 clearance percentage for that category. Data for nonmetropolitan counties reflected that law enforcement cleared 17.8 percent of their total property crimes, and the highest percentage of their clearances for that category—27.1 percent—was for motor vehicle theft. (See Table 25.)

Clearances Involving Only Persons Under 18 Years of Age

When an offender under the age of 18 is cited to appear in juvenile court or before other juvenile authorities, the UCR Program considers that incident to be

cleared by arrest although a physical arrest may not have occurred. In addition, according to Program definitions, clearances involving both adult and juvenile offenders are classified as adult clearances. Therefore, because the juvenile clearance percentages in this publication include only those clearances in which there were no adults involved, these figures should not be used to present a definitive picture of juvenile involvement in crime.

Of the violent crime clearances that were reported in the Nation's cities in 2003, 12.2 percent involved only juveniles. In addition, 19.3 percent of property crime clearances involved only juveniles. Nationally, murder clearances showed the lowest percentage of involvement by juveniles only—5.2 percent, and arson clearances showed the highest percentage—41.3 percent.

Upon consideration of clearance data broken down by population group, 12.2 percent of the violent crime clearances in cities collectively involved juveniles only, which mirrored the national clearance percentage for violent crimes. Of the city groups, cities with populations ranging from 25,000 to 49,999 reported the largest percentage of violent crime clearances that involved juveniles only—14.9 percent. During 2003, 12.7 percent of violent crime clearances in metropolitan counties and 9.8 percent of the violent crime clearances in nonmetropolitan counties involved juveniles only.

Property crime data for the Nation's cities for 2003 showed that 20.1 percent of the clearances for those offenses involved juveniles only. In metropolitan counties, 16.7 percent of the property crime clearances involved juveniles only; and in nonmetropolitan counties, 15.7 percent of property crime clearances involved juveniles only. (See Table 28.)

Table 25

Percent of Offenses Cleared by Arrest or Exceptional Means
by Population Group, 2003
[2003 estimated population]

Population group	Violent crime	Murder and non-negligent man-slaughter	Forcible rape	Robbery	Aggravated assault	Property crime	Burglary	Larceny-theft	Motor vehicle theft	Arson[1]
				Violent crime				*Property crime*		
TOTAL ALL AGENCIES:										
12,781 agencies;										
population 236,223,505										
Offenses known	**1,126,180**	**13,373**	**76,714**	**328,951**	**707,142**	**8,728,536**	**1,793,829**	**5,850,494**	**1,084,213**	**65,414**
Percent cleared by arrest	**46.5**	**62.4**	**44.0**	**26.3**	**55.9**	**16.4**	**13.1**	**18.0**	**13.1**	**16.7**
TOTAL CITIES: 9,050 cities;										
population 156,449,643										
Offenses known	**882,189**	**10,387**	**56,395**	**284,361**	**531,046**	**6,829,725**	**1,303,202**	**4,655,542**	**870,981**	**48,102**
Percent cleared by arrest	**44.7**	**61.9**	**43.4**	**25.7**	**54.6**	**16.3**	**12.5**	**18.1**	**12.3**	**16.5**
GROUP I										
62 cities, 250,000 and over;										
population 38,800,523										
Offenses known	390,601	5,498	17,617	146,873	220,613	2,216,153	429,385	1,378,410	408,358	19,460
Percent cleared by arrest	40.2	60.1	47.8	23.0	50.6	12.8	11.0	14.2	10.1	10.9
8 cities, 1,000,000 and over;										
population 13,684,275										
Offenses known	143,795	1,899	5,579	56,459	79,858	700,897	136,801	418,599	145,497	6,420
Percent cleared by arrest	41.6	56.4	48.5	24.1	53.1	12.7	11.3	14.2	9.5	9.3
20 cities, 500,000 to 999,999;										
population 13,023,877										
Offenses known	131,601	1,920	6,176	48,303	75,202	800,072	155,376	506,684	138,012	6,344
Percent cleared by arrest	38.6	64.9	47.7	21.9	47.9	11.9	10.4	12.9	10.0	13.2
34 cities, 250,000 to 499,999;										
population 12,092,371										
Offenses known	115,205	1,679	5,862	42,111	65,553	715,184	137,208	453,127	124,849	6,696
Percent cleared by arrest	40.3	58.8	47.3	22.8	50.5	13.9	11.5	15.5	11.0	10.1
GROUP II										
158 cities, 100,000 to 249,999;										
population 23,578,375										
Offenses known	141,997	1,736	9,414	48,035	82,812	1,146,915	222,807	765,303	158,805	7,885
Percent cleared by arrest	43.1	58.7	40.0	26.1	53.0	15.3	11.6	17.1	11.2	15.4
GROUP III										
374 cities, 50,000 to 99,999;										
population 25,886,988										
Offenses known	123,611	1,185	9,172	37,310	75,944	1,038,809	202,977	716,893	118,939	6,746
Percent cleared by arrest	46.0	63.2	40.4	27.8	55.4	17.2	12.1	19.6	11.5	18.1
GROUP IV										
693 cities, 25,000 to 49,999;										
population 24,075,976										
Offenses known	84,801	753	7,529	22,856	53,663	855,299	160,746	616,551	78,002	5,300
Percent cleared by arrest	49.0	66.4	40.2	30.7	57.8	18.7	12.7	20.8	14.7	19.3
GROUP V										
1,545 cities, 10,000 to 24,999;										
population 24,374,785										
Offenses known	75,908	641	6,897	18,084	50,286	833,892	153,275	619,076	61,541	4,637
Percent cleared by arrest	52.4	71.8	42.6	31.9	61.0	20.7	15.0	22.2	19.1	26.4

See footnotes at end of table.

Table 25

Percent of Offenses Cleared by Arrest or Exceptional Means
by Population Group, 2003—Continued
[2003 estimated population]

Population group	Violent crime	Murder and non-negligent man-slaughter	Forcible rape	Robbery	Aggravated assault	Property crime	Burglary	Larceny-theft	Motor vehicle theft	Arson[1]
GROUP VI										
6,218 cities, under 10,000; population 19,732,996										
Offenses known	65,271	574	5,766	11,203	47,728	738,657	134,012	559,309	45,336	4,074
Percent cleared by arrest	57.6	69.3	45.3	33.6	64.5	19.7	16.5	20.0	24.2	27.6
METROPOLITAN COUNTIES										
1,537 agencies; population 57,457,449										
Offenses known	198,030	2,260	15,163	41,342	139,265	1,517,290	364,856	968,497	183,937	13,767
Percent cleared by arrest	51.6	60.0	45.4	29.0	58.8	16.2	13.8	17.4	14.7	16.0
NONMETROPOLITAN COUNTIES										
2,194 agencies; population 22,316,413										
Offenses known	45,961	726	5,156	3,248	36,831	381,521	125,771	226,455	29,295	3,545
Percent cleared by arrest	59.9	76.3	46.8	43.1	62.9	17.8	16.3	17.5	27.1	23.5
SUBURBAN AREA[2]										
6,777 agencies; population 105,694,902										
Offenses known	338,098	3,434	27,034	77,599	230,031	3,069,739	642,917	2,104,718	322,104	22,911
Percent cleared by arrest	51.4	62.4	44.3	29.4	59.6	17.4	13.8	18.9	15.2	18.8

[1] Because arson is reported to the FBI separately from other offenses, the number of agency reports used in arson clearance rates is less than those used in compiling other offense clearance rates.

[2] Suburban area includes law enforcement agencies in cities with less than 50,000 inhabitants and county law enforcement agencies that are within a Metropolitan Statistical Area (see Appendix III). Suburban area excludes all metropolitan agencies associated with a principal city. The agencies associated with suburban areas also appear in other groups within this table.

Table 26

Percent of Offenses Cleared by Arrest or Exceptional Means
by Geographic Region and Division, 2003
[2003 estimated population]

Geographic region/division	Violent crime	Violent crime	Violent crime	Violent crime	Violent crime	Property crime	Property crime	Property crime	Property crime	Property crime
	Violent crime	Murder and non-negligent man-slaughter	Forcible rape	Robbery	Aggravated assault	Property crime	Burglary	Larceny-theft	Motor vehicle theft	Arson[1]
TOTAL ALL AGENCIES:										
12,781 agencies;										
population 236,223,505										
Offenses known	1,126,180	13,373	76,714	328,951	707,142	8,728,536	1,793,829	5,850,494	1,084,213	65,414
Percent cleared by arrest	46.5	62.4	44.0	26.3	55.9	16.4	13.1	18.0	13.1	16.7
NEW ENGLAND										
741 agencies;										
population 11,682,176										
Offenses known	39,977	267	3,233	11,550	24,927	299,786	57,436	205,062	37,288	1,892
Percent cleared by arrest	47.7	61.8	40.1	26.7	58.3	15.4	12.8	16.8	11.6	16.1
MIDDLE ATLANTIC										
1,966 agencies;										
population 30,177,502										
Offenses known	104,790	1,352	6,615	39,799	57,024	723,637	136,259	501,242	86,136	5,597
Percent cleared by arrest	50.6	68.6	52.6	31.2	63.5	22.0	19.1	23.9	15.7	22.3
NORTHEAST										
2,707 agencies;										
population 41,859,678										
Offenses known	**144,767**	**1,619**	**9,848**	**51,349**	**81,951**	**1,023,423**	**193,695**	**706,304**	**123,424**	**7,489**
Percent cleared by arrest	**49.8**	**67.5**	**48.5**	**30.2**	**61.9**	**20.1**	**17.3**	**21.9**	**14.4**	**20.7**
EAST NORTH CENTRAL										
1,574 agencies;										
population 26,650,577										
Offenses known	100,910	1,330	10,349	29,653	59,578	894,348	180,790	609,681	103,877	8,810
Percent cleared by arrest	40.6	56.1	35.6	23.2	49.8	15.4	11.5	17.0	12.8	14.2
WEST NORTH CENTRAL										
1,751 agencies;										
population 17,178,081										
Offenses known	53,592	532	5,147	10,525	37,388	578,156	103,611	421,553	52,992	4,727
Percent cleared by arrest	52.7	80.5	44.3	28.9	60.2	18.4	13.1	19.6	18.3	19.7
MIDWEST										
3,325 agencies;										
population 43,828,658										
Offenses known	**154,502**	**1,862**	**15,496**	**40,178**	**96,966**	**1,472,504**	**284,401**	**1,031,234**	**156,869**	**13,537**
Percent cleared by arrest	**44.8**	**63.1**	**38.5**	**24.7**	**53.8**	**16.5**	**12.1**	**18.1**	**14.6**	**16.1**
SOUTH ATLANTIC										
2,575 agencies;										
population 47,020,232										
Offenses known	280,673	3,255	14,794	82,024	180,600	1,931,194	423,924	1,292,004	215,266	10,762
Percent cleared by arrest	46.8	61.7	49.9	25.8	55.8	17.4	14.9	18.6	15.2	20.1

See footnotes at end of table.

Table 26

Percent of Offenses Cleared by Arrest or Exceptional Means
by Geographic Region and Division, 2003—Continued
[2003 estimated population]

Geographic region/division	Violent crime	Violent crime	Violent crime	Violent crime	Violent crime	Property crime	Property crime	Property crime	Property crime	Property crime
	Violent crime	Murder and non-negligent man-slaughter	Forcible rape	Robbery	Aggravated assault	Property crime	Burglary	Larceny-theft	Motor vehicle theft	Arson[1]
EAST SOUTH CENTRAL										
881 agencies;										
population 11,884,622										
Offenses known	65,626	803	4,495	17,348	42,980	515,909	125,552	343,043	47,314	2,288
Percent cleared by arrest	41.5	70.7	38.7	22.2	49.0	16.0	11.0	18.0	15.0	19.6
WEST SOUTH CENTRAL										
1,436 agencies;										
population 29,495,670										
Offenses known	165,455	2,178	11,160	46,649	105,468	1,335,007	292,835	912,624	129,548	9,827
Percent cleared by arrest	45.4	66.1	46.1	25.5	53.7	15.7	11.5	17.2	14.3	17.4
SOUTH										
4,892 agencies;										
population 88,400,524										
Offenses known	**511,754**	**6,236**	**30,449**	**146,021**	**329,048**	**3,782,110**	**842,311**	**2,547,671**	**392,128**	**22,877**
Percent cleared by arrest	**45.7**	**64.4**	**46.8**	**25.3**	**54.2**	**16.6**	**13.1**	**18.0**	**14.9**	**18.9**
MOUNTAIN										
736 agencies;										
population 17,715,023										
Offenses known	78,465	1,002	6,792	19,673	50,998	797,873	151,525	530,527	115,821	4,614
Percent cleared by arrest	43.7	53.1	36.6	23.4	52.3	15.0	11.5	16.6	12.3	19.2
PACIFIC										
1,121 agencies;										
population 44,419,622										
Offenses known	236,692	2,654	14,129	71,730	148,179	1,652,626	321,897	1,034,758	295,971	16,897
Percent cleared by arrest	48.4	57.5	44.4	27.4	58.7	14.0	12.0	15.9	9.7	11.9
WEST										
1,857 agencies;										
population 62,134,645										
Offenses known	**315,157**	**3,656**	**20,921**	**91,403**	**199,177**	**2,450,499**	**473,422**	**1,565,285**	**411,792**	**21,511**
Percent cleared by arrest	**47.2**	**56.3**	**41.9**	**26.5**	**57.1**	**14.4**	**11.8**	**16.1**	**10.4**	**13.5**

[1] Because arson is reported to the FBI separately from other offenses, the number of agency reports used in arson clearance rates is less than those used in compiling other offense clearance rates.

Table 27

Percent of Offenses Cleared by Arrest or Exceptional Means

Breakdown of Offenses Known
by Population Group, 2003
[2003 estimated population]

Population group	Forcible rape		Robbery				Aggravated assault				Burglary			Motor vehicle theft			Arson[1]		
	Rape by force	Assault to rape-attempts	Firearm	Knife or cutting instrument	Other weapon	Strong-arm	Firearm	Knife or cutting instrument	Other weapon	Hands, fists, feet, etc.	Forcible entry	Unlawful entry	Attempted forcible entry	Autos	Trucks and buses	Other vehicles	Structure	Mobile	Other
TOTAL ALL AGENCIES: 12,168 agencies; population 217,009,079																			
Offenses known	62,519	6,480	122,222	26,646	27,243	114,257	119,472	110,806	209,843	169,722	995,600	499,820	101,276	728,978	179,309	76,315	25,091	20,538	15,142
Percent cleared by arrest	**43.2**	**43.7**	**20.9**	**27.9**	**27.8**	**30.8**	**39.7**	**61.4**	**55.6**	**63.9**	**12.4**	**14.1**	**11.0**	**13.3**	**11.0**	**12.1**	**21.5**	**6.8**	**20.9**
TOTAL CITIES: 8,712 cities; population 146,707,339																			
Offenses known	47,207	5,177	106,304	23,636	23,619	102,392	96,561	90,004	163,525	125,901	738,357	371,073	78,084	609,876	145,332	51,486	19,135	14,523	11,382
Percent cleared by arrest	**42.9**	**43.6**	**20.7**	**27.4**	**27.1**	**30.4**	**37.2**	**60.4**	**54.2**	**64.6**	**11.9**	**13.7**	**10.5**	**12.6**	**10.5**	**11.3**	**20.9**	**6.2**	**21.5**
GROUP I																			
57 cities, 250,000 and over; population 36,423,898																			
Offenses known	14,749	2,016	59,968	11,915	11,465	50,947	52,180	38,230	71,257	38,019	269,594	105,310	21,662	274,588	88,425	21,222	7,462	7,703	2,984
Percent cleared by arrest	**47.2**	**50.3**	**18.6**	**24.7**	**24.0**	**28.0**	**32.7**	**58.2**	**52.0**	**65.2**	**10.4**	**12.1**	**9.7**	**10.8**	**8.3**	**8.5**	**15.0**	**3.6**	**18.5**
8 cities, 1,000,000 and over; population 13,684,275																			
Offenses known	4,703	876	25,562	5,670	4,465	20,762	21,109	14,534	24,193	20,022	93,610	36,110	7,081	99,213	37,745	8,539	2,194	3,160	1,066
Percent cleared by arrest	**48.2**	**50.1**	**18.8**	**25.2**	**26.1**	**29.9**	**31.3**	**57.1**	**52.2**	**74.4**	**10.9**	**12.6**	**10.1**	**11.1**	**6.0**	**6.3**	**14.8**	**1.9**	**19.8**
18 cities, 500,000 to 999,999; population 11,602,906																			
Offenses known	5,149	610	19,214	3,466	4,300	14,640	16,761	13,300	26,341	8,350	95,979	34,770	7,928	89,702	28,960	7,655	2,841	2,062	646
Percent cleared by arrest	**47.3**	**51.1**	**16.8**	**24.4**	**22.0**	**26.7**	**33.0**	**56.2**	**50.3**	**52.1**	**9.3**	**10.3**	**9.4**	**10.0**	**10.0**	**4.6**	**17.5**	**4.9**	**20.6**
31 cities, 250,000 to 499,999; population 11,136,717																			
Offenses known	4,897	530	15,192	2,779	2,700	15,545	14,310	10,396	20,723	9,647	80,005	34,430	6,653	85,673	21,720	5,028	2,427	2,481	1,272
Percent cleared by arrest	**46.3**	**49.8**	**20.6**	**24.0**	**23.7**	**26.8**	**34.3**	**62.4**	**54.0**	**57.5**	**11.0**	**13.3**	**9.5**	**11.1**	**10.2**	**18.2**	**12.4**	**4.7**	**16.3**
GROUP II																			
144 cities, 100,000 to 249,999; population 21,373,745																			
Offenses known	7,412	1,015	17,828	4,100	4,121	16,643	15,208	14,637	27,401	15,405	125,942	57,398	12,790	112,364	23,019	7,525	3,081	2,301	1,899
Percent cleared by arrest	**39.9**	**31.1**	**21.7**	**26.4**	**27.3**	**29.8**	**37.9**	**60.1**	**52.3**	**62.6**	**11.2**	**12.7**	**11.3**	**11.0**	**10.6**	**10.1**	**19.0**	**5.6**	**19.5**

See footnotes at end of table.

Table 27

Percent of Offenses Cleared by Arrest or Exceptional Means

Breakdown of Offenses Known
by Population Group, 2003—Continued
[2003 estimated population]

Population group	Forcible rape		Robbery				Aggravated assault				Burglary			Motor vehicle theft			Arson[1]		
	Rape by force	Assault to rape-attempts	Firearm	Knife or cutting instrument	Other weapon	Strong-arm	Firearm	Knife or cutting instrument	Other weapon	Hands, fists, feet, etc.	Forcible entry	Unlawful entry	Attempted forcible entry	Autos	Trucks and buses	Other vehicles	Structure	Mobile	Other
GROUP III																			
344 cities, 50,000 to 99,999; population 23,733,013																			
Offenses known	7,520	675	11,945	3,166	3,161	14,164	11,426	12,845	23,501	18,441	106,668	60,272	13,899	87,085	13,174	6,692	2,616	1,741	1,954
Percent cleared by arrest	39.5	43.4	21.8	30.5	29.2	31.7	38.3	60.3	55.1	62.2	11.3	13.4	9.7	11.1	11.5	11.4	21.9	7.6	20.5
GROUP IV																			
655 cities, 25,000 to 49,999; population 22,708,306																			
Offenses known	6,455	488	6,996	2,022	2,080	8,734	6,510	9,091	15,656	16,193	83,672	51,119	11,130	57,961	8,091	5,599	2,080	1,186	1,747
Percent cleared by arrest	39.3	39.5	25.7	31.0	31.8	34.3	44.4	61.1	56.3	61.8	12.0	13.8	9.9	14.3	15.5	12.4	24.2	9.3	20.3
GROUP V																			
1,475 cities, 10,000 to 24,999; population 23,301,899																			
Offenses known	6,030	510	5,738	1,514	1,668	7,422	6,208	8,396	14,081	16,814	82,230	49,638	10,018	45,427	6,968	5,440	1,949	914	1,538
Percent cleared by arrest	42.5	42.0	26.8	35.4	33.6	36.0	49.0	64.8	59.4	65.5	14.9	15.9	11.6	19.3	18.6	16.1	30.4	14.8	28.4
GROUP VI																			
6,037 cities, under 10,000; population 19,166,478																			
Offenses known	5,041	473	3,829	919	1,124	4,482	5,029	6,805	11,629	21,029	70,251	47,336	8,585	32,451	5,655	5,008	1,947	678	1,260
Percent cleared by arrest	44.8	47.4	27.1	35.1	33.5	38.4	56.5	67.0	60.5	68.4	16.7	16.6	12.4	25.1	23.7	18.4	31.6	17.8	26.4
METROPOLITAN COUNTIES																			
1,368 agencies; population 48,896,786																			
Offenses known	10,820	964	14,716	2,760	3,238	10,812	17,260	16,176	36,712	30,249	181,155	92,034	17,251	102,710	28,989	18,449	4,219	5,164	2,957
Percent cleared by arrest	43.2	42.8	20.4	30.2	31.5	33.3	45.9	65.0	60.3	61.4	12.6	14.7	11.0	14.9	11.4	12.1	23.2	6.9	17.6

See footnotes at end of table.

Table 27

Percent of Offenses Cleared by Arrest or Exceptional Means
Breakdown of Offenses Known
by Population Group, 2003—Continued
[2003 estimated population]

Population group	Forcible rape		Robbery				Aggravated assault				Burglary			Motor vehicle theft			Arson[1]		
	Rape by force	Assault to rape-attempts	Firearm	Knife or cutting instrument	Other weapon	Strong-arm	Firearm	Knife or cutting instrument	Other weapon	Hands, fists, feet, etc.	Forcible entry	Unlawful entry	Attempted forcible entry	Autos	Trucks and buses	Other vehicles	Structure	Mobile	Other
NONMETROPOLITAN COUNTIES																			
2,088 agencies; population 21,404,954																			
Offenses known	4,492	339	1,202	250	386	1,053	5,651	4,626	9,606	13,572	76,088	36,713	5,941	16,392	4,988	6,380	1,737	851	803
Percent cleared by arrest	46.5	47.8	39.2	49.6	43.8	48.4	61.9	69.4	62.5	63.6	16.2	16.2	18.3	30.8	25.5	17.9	25.0	15.4	24.4
SUBURBAN AREA[2]																			
6,381 agencies; population 94,684,897																			
Offenses known	20,911	1,826	26,236	5,762	6,534	24,672	26,911	29,549	61,233	62,422	320,406	184,901	36,507	205,106	43,505	29,421	7,877	7,080	6,025
Percent cleared by arrest	42.8	42.9	22.0	30.9	31.3	34.0	46.6	64.7	59.7	63.7	13.0	14.8	10.7	15.2	13.0	12.8	25.3	8.4	20.8

[1] Because arson is reported to the FBI separately from other offenses, the number of agency reports used in arson clearance rates is less than those used in compiling other offense clearance rates. Agencies must report arson clearances by detailed property classification as specified on the *Monthly Return of Arson Offenses Known to Law Enforcement* to be included in this table; therefore, clearances in this table may differ from other clearance tables.

[2] Suburban area includes law enforcement agencies in cities with less than 50,000 inhabitants and county law enforcement agencies that are within a Metropolitan Statistical Area (see Appendix III). Suburban area excludes all metropolitan agencies associated with a principal city. The agencies associated with suburban areas also appear in other groups within this table.

Table 28

Number of Offenses Cleared by Arrest or Exceptional Means
Percent of Clearances Involving Persons Under 18 Years of Age
by Population Group, 2003
[2003 estimated population]

Population group	Violent crime	Violent crime	Violent crime	Violent crime	Violent crime	Property crime	Property crime	Property crime	Property crime	Property crime
	Violent crime	Murder and non-negligent man-slaughter	Forcible rape	Robbery	Aggravated assault	Property crime	Burglary	Larceny-theft	Motor vehicle theft	Arson[1]
TOTAL ALL AGENCIES: **11,814 agencies;** **population 209,050,305**										
Total clearances	435,481	7,074	28,735	72,278	327,394	1,215,611	195,744	898,948	120,919	9,744
Percent under 18	12.2	5.2	11.5	14.1	11.9	19.3	16.8	20.2	17.3	41.3
TOTAL CITIES: 8,525 cities; **population 140,970,503**										
Total clearances	339,526	5,500	21,569	62,963	249,494	975,395	140,819	740,728	93,848	7,113
Percent under 18	12.2	5.3	10.6	14.2	12.0	20.1	16.8	21.0	17.8	44.2
GROUP I										
54 cities, 250,000 and over; population 34,515,076										
Total clearances	135,898	2,714	7,622	29,536	96,026	248,822	40,747	170,797	37,278	1,791
Percent under 18	10.0	6.1	7.2	13.1	9.3	16.7	13.3	17.0	18.9	38.7
8 cities, 1,000,000 and over; population 13,684,275										
Total clearances	59,797	1,071	2,707	13,604	42,415	88,831	15,461	59,575	13,795	596
Percent under 18	9.0	7.0	8.3	12.9	7.8	15.5	11.9	16.3	16.3	40.8
15 cities, 500,000 to 999,999; population 9,694,084										
Total clearances	35,936	737	2,386	7,328	25,485	69,200	11,270	47,121	10,809	564
Percent under 18	9.9	4.1	7.0	12.1	9.7	15.5	11.9	14.9	21.7	30.9
31 cities, 250,000 to 499,999; population 11,136,717										
Total clearances	40,165	906	2,529	8,604	28,126	90,791	14,016	64,101	12,674	631
Percent under 18	11.5	6.6	6.2	14.2	11.3	18.8	16.0	19.3	19.2	43.9
GROUP II										
136 cities, 100,000 to 249,999; population 20,204,537										
Total clearances	50,408	886	2,968	10,372	36,182	143,625	21,148	108,009	14,468	1,031
Percent under 18	12.2	4.9	10.1	15.3	11.7	19.8	15.5	21.2	15.7	41.6
GROUP III										
332 cities, 50,000 to 99,999; population 22,994,251										
Total clearances	48,445	660	3,189	8,722	35,874	154,329	20,907	121,870	11,552	1,106
Percent under 18	13.6	5.6	12.6	15.6	13.3	22.5	18.0	23.6	18.6	45.8
GROUP IV										
642 cities, 25,000 to 49,999; population 22,275,240										
Total clearances	36,151	442	2,702	6,028	26,979	141,804	17,821	113,942	10,041	967
Percent under 18	14.9	4.1	13.4	15.5	15.1	22.4	19.0	23.4	17.4	46.0

See footnotes at end of table.

Table 28

Number of Offenses Cleared by Arrest or Exceptional Means
Percent of Clearances Involving Persons Under 18 Years of Age
by Population Group, 2003—Continued
[2003 estimated population]

Population group	Violent crime	Murder and non-negligent man-slaughter	Forcible rape	Robbery	Aggravated assault	Property crime	Burglary	Larceny-theft	Motor vehicle theft	Arson[1]
			Violent crime					*Property crime*		
GROUP V										
1,402 cities, 10,000 to 24,999; population 22,166,613										
Total clearances	34,399	419	2,656	4,989	26,335	153,132	20,077	122,778	10,277	1,146
Percent under 18	14.0	3.6	13.2	14.2	14.2	21.2	18.8	21.9	17.3	48.3
GROUP VI										
5,959 cities, under 10,000; population 18,814,786										
Total clearances	34,225	379	2,432	3,316	28,098	133,683	20,119	103,332	10,232	1,072
Percent under 18	14.6	4.0	13.3	15.2	14.7	20.1	20.3	20.4	16.5	48.5
METROPOLITAN COUNTIES										
1,292 agencies; population 47,528,319										
Total clearances	71,476	1,075	4,977	8,131	57,293	180,004	36,704	123,273	20,027	1,860
Percent under 18	12.7	4.8	13.6	13.8	12.6	16.7	17.0	16.8	15.3	37.1
NONMETROPOLITAN COUNTIES										
1,997 agencies; population 20,551,483										
Total clearances	24,479	499	2,189	1,184	20,607	60,212	18,221	34,947	7,044	771
Percent under 18	9.8	4.2	16.0	8.6	9.4	15.7	16.2	15.0	17.6	24.6
SUBURBAN AREA[2]										
6,182 agencies; population 91,824,179										
Total clearances	132,743	1,780	9,494	17,272	104,197	433,692	69,988	324,498	39,206	3,828
Percent under 18	14.1	4.7	13.8	15.2	14.1	19.1	18.3	19.6	16.0	45.0

[1] Because arson is reported to the FBI separately from other offenses, the number of agency reports used in arson clearance rates is less than those used in compiling other offense clearance rates.
[2] Suburban area includes law enforcement agencies in cities with less than 50,000 inhabitants and county law enforcement agencies that are within a Metropolitan Statistical Area (see Appendix III). Suburban area excludes all metropolitan agencies associated with a principal city. The agencies associated with suburban areas also appear in other groups within this table.

SECTION IV

Persons Arrested

Arrests are often viewed, correctly or not, as a key measure of law enforcement's effectiveness in fighting crime. However, law enforcement practices with regard to arrests can differ significantly between two locales and even within a specific agency over time and with changes in administration. The pursuit of arrests for certain offenses such as disorderly conduct, vagrancy, and other violations sometimes thought of as "nuisance" crimes can vary widely from agency to agency. On the other hand, the arrest standard for crimes such as murder, forcible rape, and robbery is more likely to be consistent among law enforcement in all locales.

In the Uniform Crime Reporting (UCR) Program, one arrest is counted for each separate instance in which an individual is arrested, cited, or summoned for criminal acts in Part I and Part II crimes. (See Appendix II for additional information concerning Part I and Part II crimes.) One person may be arrested multiple times during the year; as a result, the arrest figures in this section should not be viewed as a total number of individuals arrested. Rather, this section provides the number of arrest occurrences that were reported by law enforcement.

National Volume, Trends, and Rates

In 2003, law enforcement in the United States made an estimated 13.6 million arrests for crime committed (excluding traffic offenses.) Law enforcement made 1.6 million arrests for property crimes that occurred in 2003, which represented 11.8 percent of the total arrests. An estimated 597,026 arrests for violent crimes made up 4.4 percent of the total arrests. Drug abuse violations accounted for nearly 1.7 million arrests, the most arrests for any offense type. (Based on Table 29.)

The number of arrests remained virtually unchanged (+0.2 percent) in 2003 when compared to arrest figures from the previous year. Arrests for violent crime decreased 2.3 percent and those for property crime increased 0.7 percent from 2002 data. Drug abuse violation arrests rose 5.2 percent in the 2-year period. (See Table 36.) The 5-year trend (comparing 2003 data with those from 1999) indicated a 3.4-percent drop in the number of arrests. (See Table 34.) A comparison of the 2003 arrest data to those of 1994 (the 10-year trend) showed a 2.8-percent decline in arrests. (See Table 32.)

The Nation as a whole had a total arrest rate of 4,695.1 arrests per 100,000 inhabitants. There were 558.4 arrests for property crimes per 100,000 persons and 205.3 arrests for violent crimes per 100,000 persons. Drug abuse and alcohol-related arrests were measured at a rate of 1,470.1 arrests per 100,000 inhabitants. (Based on Table 30.)

By Age, Sex, and Race

In 2003, adults (those over the age of 18) made up 83.7 percent of total arrestees. (See Table 38.) Persons under the age of 25 made up 46.3 percent of all arrestees, and nearly a third of arrestees (30.9 percent) were under 21 years of age. (See Table 41.)

A comparison of 2003 and 2002 data indicated that the number of arrests of juveniles for all offenses decreased 0.4 percent. The number of arrests of juveniles for violent crimes in 2003 remained virtually unchanged (+1.0 percent) from the 2002 number, but the number of arrests of juveniles for drug abuse violations rose 3.7 percent. (See Table 36.)

By gender, 76.8 percent of arrestees in the United States in 2003 were male. Males made up 82.2 percent of violent crime and 69.2 percent of prop-erty crime arrestees. (See Table 42.)

A comparison of 2003 arrest data to the 2002 figures revealed that the number of arrests of females increased 1.9 percent, and the number of arrests of males decreased 0.4 percent. (See Table 37.) The 5-year trend (comparing 2003 data to those of 1999) showed a 2.8-percent rise in the number of arrests of females and a 5.2-percent drop in the number of arrests of males. (See Table 35.) In 2003, the number of arrests of females was 12.3 percent higher, but the number of arrests of males was 6.7 percent fewer than in 1994 (the 10-year trend). (See Table 33.)

By race, 70.6 percent of arrestees in 2003 were white, 27.0 percent were black, and the remaining 2.5 percent were of other races (two categories defined by UCR: American Indian or Alaskan Native and Asian or Pacific Islander). Whites accounted for 60.5 percent of the individuals arrested for violent crimes. Blacks made up 37.2 percent of violent crime arrestees, and the remainder of the arrestees were of other races. With regard to property crime arrestees, 68.2 percent were white, 29.1 percent were black, and the remainder of the arrestees were of other races.

The offense with the greatest number of white arrestees was driving under the influence (877,810). The offense with the highest number of black arrestees was drug abuse violations (381,006). (See Table 43.)

Regional Arrest Rates

The United States is partitioned into four regions by the UCR Program: the Northeast, the Midwest, the South, and the West. (See Appendix III for more information concerning the UCR regions and divisions of the country.) In 2003, data collected within the four regions of the Nation indicated the following:

The Northeast

In the Northeast, law enforcement agencies had an overall arrest rate of 3,768.0 per 100,000 in population. The arrest rate for violent crime was 166.5 arrests per 100,000 in population. Property crime arrests in the region were calculated at a rate of 438.4 arrests per 100,000 individuals. (See Table 30.)

The Midwest

Law enforcement had a rate of 4,808.6 arrests per 100,000 inhabitants in the Midwest. The arrest rate for violent crime was 165.8 arrests per 100,000 in population. For property crimes, the region had a rate of 562.1 arrests per 100,000 persons. (See Table 30.)

The South

The South, the U.S. region with the most population, had a rate of 5,255.9 arrests per 100,000 inhabitants. This region had a violent crime rate of 190.4 arrests per 100,000 people, and property crime arrests were recorded at a rate of 604.0 arrests per 100,000 individuals. (See Table 30.)

The West

In the West, arrests were recorded at a rate of 4,584.0 arrests for every 100,000

persons. The violent crime rate in this region was 276.4 arrests per 100,000 in population. The property crime arrest rate in the West was 582.2 arrests per 100,000 inhabitants. (See Table 30.)

Population Groups: Trends and Rates

The national UCR Program aggregates crime data into population groups—a list of which is furnished in Appendix III. Law enforcement in cities as a group, in 2003, reported 5,109.3 arrests per 100,000 persons. Among the city population groups, the Nation's smallest cities, those with less than 10,000 inhabitants, recorded the highest arrest rate per 100,000 persons at 6,273.3. Law enforcement in cities with 25,000 to 49,999 in population recorded the lowest rate at 4,423.1 arrests per 100,000 inhabitants. The arrest rate for metropolitan counties was 3,731.0 per 100,000 in population, and the arrest rate for nonmetropolitan counties was 3,961.2 per 100,000 persons. (See Table 31.)

Overall, law enforcement in the Nation's cities reported that adults accounted for 82.2 percent of all arrestees, and juveniles comprised 17.8 percent of persons arrested. Juveniles accounted for 16.3 percent of arrestees for violent crimes and 29.7 percent of arrestees for property crimes. (See Table 46.) Of all persons arrested in cities during 2003, nearly half (47.9 percent) were under the age of 25. (See Table 47.)

A comparison of the number of 2003 arrests for all offenses reported to law enforcement in U.S. cities to the 2002 figure showed virtually no change (+0.2 percent) in the number of arrests. Property crime arrests increased 0.7 percent; however, violent crime arrests declined 2.5 percent. In the combined city population groups, arrests for drug abuse violations increased 5.1 percent. Total arrests of juveniles in U.S. cities decreased 0.3 percent in 2003 from the 2002 number. (See Table 44.) Law enforcement in metropolitan counties reported a 1.0-percent increase in total arrests, and those in nonmetropolitan

Table 4.1

Arrests for Drug Abuse Violations
by Region, 2003

Drug abuse violations	United States total	Northeast	Midwest	South	West
Total[1]	**100.0**	**100.0**	**100.0**	**100.0**	**100.0**
Sale/Manufacturing:	19.4	25.7	19.2	20.1	15.9
Heroin or cocaine and their derivatives	8.8	17.1	4.8	9.8	5.8
Marijuana	5.5	6.4	7.7	5.3	4.2
Synthetic or manufactured drugs	1.5	1.0	1.4	2.8	0.7
Other dangerous nonnarcotic drugs	3.6	1.2	5.2	2.3	5.2
Possession:	80.6	74.3	80.8	79.9	84.1
Heroin or cocaine and their derivatives	21.5	24.3	11.4	22.3	23.8
Marijuana	39.5	42.3	51.7	46.3	26.2
Synthetic or manufactured drugs	3.1	1.8	3.1	4.3	2.6
Other dangerous nonnarcotic drugs	16.6	5.7	14.7	6.9	31.5

[1] Because of rounding, the percentages may not add to 100.0.

counties had a decrease of 2.1 percent in arrests. A comparison of 2003 and 2002 arrest data indicates that in metropolitan counties, arrests of juveniles increased 1.1 percent, and in nonmetropolitan counties, arrests of juveniles dropped 5.5 percent. (See Tables 50 and 56.)

By race, 68.2 percent of arrestees in the Nation's cities, collectively, were white, 29.3 percent were black, and 2.5 percent were of other races. (See Table 49.) In the Nation's metropolitan counties, law enforcement reported that 75.1 percent of arrestees were white, 23.6 percent were black, and the remainder of arrestees were of other races; in nonmetropolitan counties, 82.8 percent of arrestees were white, 12.5 percent of arrestees were black, and the remainder of arrestees were of other races. (See Tables 55 and 61.)

Table 29

Estimated Number of Arrests
United States, 2003

Total[1]	**13,639,479**	Stolen property; buying, receiving, possessing	126,775
		Vandalism	273,431
Murder and nonnegligent manslaughter	13,190	Weapons; carrying, possessing, etc.	167,972
Forcible rape	26,350	Prostitution and commercialized vice	75,190
Robbery	107,553	Sex offenses (except forcible rape and prostitution)	91,546
Aggravated assault	449,933	Drug abuse violations	1,678,192
Burglary	290,956	Gambling	10,954
Larceny-theft	1,145,074	Offenses against the family and children	136,034
Motor vehicle theft	152,934	Driving under the influence	1,448,148
Arson	16,163	Liquor laws	612,079
		Drunkenness	548,616
Violent crime[2]	597,026	Disorderly conduct	639,371
Property crime[2]	1,605,127	Vagrancy	28,948
		All other offenses	3,665,543
Other assaults	1,246,698	Suspicion	7,163
Forgery and counterfeiting	111,823	Curfew and loitering law violations	136,461
Fraud	299,138	Runaways	123,581
Embezzlement	16,826		

[1] Does not include suspicion.

[2] Violent crimes are offenses of murder, forcible rape, robbery, and aggravated assault. Property crimes are offenses of burglary, larceny-theft, motor vehicle theft, and arson.

Table 30

Number and Rate of Arrests

by Geographic Region, 2003

[Rate: Number of arrests per 100,000 inhabitants]

Offense charged	United States total (10,843 agencies; population 204,034,545)	Northeast (2,450 agencies; population 37,522,549)	Midwest (2,920 agencies; population 43,412,431)	South (3,814 agencies; population 64,793,077)	West (1,659 agencies; population 58,306,488)
TOTAL[1]	9,579,611	1,413,866	2,087,525	3,405,479	2,672,741
Rate	4,695.1	3,768.0	4,808.6	5,255.9	4,584.0
Murder and nonnegligent manslaughter	9,119	1,145	1,837	3,597	2,540
Rate	4.5	3.1	4.2	5.6	4.4
Forcible rape	18,446	3,244	4,369	6,072	4,761
Rate	9.0	8.6	10.1	9.4	8.2
Robbery	75,667	15,612	12,365	24,573	23,117
Rate	37.1	41.6	28.5	37.9	39.6
Aggravated assault	315,732	42,480	53,387	89,108	130,757
Rate	154.7	113.2	123.0	137.5	224.3
Burglary	204,761	29,295	34,670	69,664	71,132
Rate	100.4	78.1	79.9	107.5	122.0
Larceny-theft	817,048	121,506	184,359	291,337	219,846
Rate	400.4	323.8	424.7	449.6	377.1
Motor vehicle theft	106,221	11,782	22,625	26,716	45,098
Rate	52.1	31.4	52.1	41.2	77.3
Arson	11,330	1,899	2,386	3,660	3,385
Rate	5.6	5.1	5.5	5.6	5.8
Violent crime[2]	418,964	62,481	71,958	123,350	161,175
Rate	205.3	166.5	165.8	190.4	276.4
Property crime[2]	1,139,360	164,482	244,040	391,377	339,461
Rate	558.4	438.4	562.1	604.0	582.2
Other assaults	877,105	141,202	184,689	351,956	199,258
Rate	429.9	376.3	425.4	543.2	341.7
Forgery and counterfeiting	79,188	11,391	13,430	31,874	22,493
Rate	38.8	30.4	30.9	49.2	38.6
Fraud	208,469	34,207	36,067	118,513	19,682
Rate	102.2	91.2	83.1	182.9	33.8
Embezzlement	11,986	1,047	2,036	6,168	2,735
Rate	5.9	2.8	4.7	9.5	4.7
Stolen property; buying, receiving, possessing	89,560	17,846	21,267	22,832	27,615
Rate	43.9	47.6	49.0	35.2	47.4
Vandalism	193,083	40,932	45,701	45,612	60,838
Rate	94.6	109.1	105.3	70.4	104.3
Weapons; carrying, possessing, etc.	117,844	15,591	23,311	39,478	39,464
Rate	57.8	41.6	53.7	60.9	67.7
Prostitution and commercialized vice	51,686	7,575	11,732	13,842	18,537
Rate	25.3	20.2	27.0	21.4	31.8
Sex offenses (except forcible rape and prostitution)	63,759	10,616	14,283	16,021	22,839
Rate	31.2	28.3	32.9	24.7	39.2
Drug abuse violations	1,172,222	175,322	235,444	377,572	383,884
Rate	574.5	467.2	542.3	582.7	658.4
Gambling	7,414	720	3,414	2,519	761
Rate	3.6	1.9	7.9	3.9	1.3
Offenses against the family and children	94,488	22,796	30,344	30,015	11,333
Rate	46.3	60.8	69.9	46.3	19.4
Driving under the influence	1,005,777	121,327	239,406	311,815	333,229
Rate	492.9	323.3	551.5	481.2	571.5
Liquor laws	431,912	53,844	165,260	93,313	119,495
Rate	211.7	143.5	380.7	144.0	204.9
Drunkenness	389,626	29,851	33,921	220,058	105,796
Rate	191.0	79.6	78.1	339.6	181.4
Disorderly conduct	453,645	112,955	138,895	130,403	71,392
Rate	222.3	301.0	319.9	201.3	122.4
Vagrancy	20,052	4,906	1,601	5,879	7,666
Rate	9.8	13.1	3.7	9.1	13.1
All other offenses (except traffic)	2,571,023	344,648	537,555	1,020,355	668,465
Rate	1,260.1	918.5	1,238.3	1,574.8	1,146.5
Suspicion	1,812	201	504	971	136
Rate	0.9	0.5	1.2	1.5	0.2
Curfew and loitering law violations	95,052	31,569	14,062	20,999	28,422
Rate	46.6	84.1	32.4	32.4	48.7
Runaways	87,396	8,558	19,109	31,528	28,201
Rate	42.8	22.8	44.0	48.7	48.4

[1] Does not include suspicion.

[2] Violent crimes are offenses of murder, forcible rape, robbery, and aggravated assault. Property crimes are offenses of burglary, larceny-theft, motor vehicle theft, and arson.

Table 31

Number and Rate of Arrests

by Population Group, 2003

[Rate: Number of arrests per 100,000 inhabitants]

Offense charged	Total (10,843 agencies; population 204,034,545)	Total cities (7,898 cities; population 139,498,658)	Cities Group I (50 cities, 250,000 and over; population 35,303,730)	Group II (135 cities, 100,000 to 249,999; population 20,341,032)	Group III (323 cities, 50,000 to 99,999; population 22,274,208)	Group IV (618 cities, 25,000 to 49,999; population 21,486,840)	Group V (1,412 cities, 10,000 to 24,999; population 22,385,366)	Group VI (5,360 cities, under 10,000; population 17,707,482)	Counties Metropolitan counties[1] (1,158 agencies; population 45,269,822)	Nonmetropolitan counties (1,787 agencies; population 19,266,065)	Suburban area[2] (5,889 agencies; population 92,793,659)
TOTAL[3]	9,579,611	7,127,426	1,900,698	976,023	1,100,984	950,389	1,088,487	1,110,845	1,689,021	763,164	3,890,249
Rate	4,695.1	5,109.3	5,383.8	4,798.3	4,942.9	4,423.1	4,862.5	6,273.3	3,731.0	3,961.2	4,192.4
Murder and nonnegligent manslaughter	9,119	6,671	3,308	1,146	837	483	465	432	1,719	729	2,625
Rate	4.5	4.8	9.4	5.6	3.8	2.2	2.1	2.4	3.8	3.8	2.8
Forcible rape	18,446	13,181	4,098	1,933	1,970	1,653	1,834	1,693	3,547	1,718	7,059
Rate	9.0	9.4	11.6	9.5	8.8	7.7	8.2	9.6	7.8	8.9	7.6
Robbery	75,667	63,564	26,851	11,052	9,563	6,701	5,936	3,461	10,347	1,756	23,065
Rate	37.1	45.6	76.1	54.3	42.9	31.2	26.5	19.5	22.9	9.1	24.9
Aggravated assault	315,732	239,941	83,271	41,005	37,052	28,068	26,292	24,253	57,201	18,590	114,343
Rate	154.7	172.0	235.9	201.6	166.3	130.6	117.5	137.0	126.4	96.5	123.2
Burglary	204,761	148,277	37,864	25,518	25,796	19,215	20,926	18,958	38,700	17,784	79,648
Rate	100.4	106.3	107.3	125.5	115.8	89.4	93.5	107.1	85.5	92.3	85.8
Larceny-theft	817,048	683,335	159,573	104,674	121,725	105,772	111,358	80,233	104,698	29,015	313,334
Rate	400.4	489.9	452.0	514.6	546.5	492.3	497.5	453.1	231.3	150.6	337.7
Motor vehicle theft	106,221	82,656	39,362	12,621	9,758	7,037	7,257	6,621	17,883	5,682	33,187
Rate	52.1	59.3	111.5	62.0	43.8	32.8	32.4	37.4	39.5	29.5	35.8
Arson	11,330	8,024	2,022	1,065	1,203	1,197	1,298	1,239	2,427	879	5,141
Rate	5.6	5.8	5.7	5.2	5.4	5.6	5.8	7.0	5.4	4.6	5.5
Violent crime[4]	418,964	323,357	117,528	55,136	49,422	36,905	34,527	29,839	72,814	22,793	147,092
Rate	205.3	231.8	332.9	271.1	221.9	171.8	154.2	168.5	160.8	118.3	158.5
Property crime[4]	1,139,360	922,292	238,821	143,878	158,482	133,221	140,839	107,051	163,708	53,360	431,310
Rate	558.4	661.1	676.5	707.3	711.5	620.0	629.2	604.6	361.6	277.0	464.8
Other assaults	877,105	652,391	171,940	98,076	98,756	90,104	97,046	96,469	161,436	63,278	350,603
Rate	429.9	467.7	487.0	482.2	443.4	419.3	433.5	544.8	356.6	328.4	377.8
Forgery and counterfeiting	79,188	59,999	12,787	8,912	10,575	9,195	10,067	8,463	13,709	5,480	32,240
Rate	38.8	43.0	36.2	43.8	47.5	42.8	45.0	47.8	30.3	28.4	34.7
Fraud	208,469	125,024	14,925	12,361	19,826	17,523	29,653	30,736	52,366	31,079	103,458
Rate	102.2	89.6	42.3	60.8	89.0	81.6	132.5	173.6	115.7	161.3	111.5
Embezzlement	11,986	8,946	1,620	1,644	1,979	1,352	1,382	969	2,318	722	4,744
Rate	5.9	6.4	4.6	8.1	8.9	6.3	6.2	5.5	5.1	3.7	5.1
Stolen property; buying, receiving, possessing	89,560	68,992	19,579	10,698	12,186	10,019	9,342	7,168	15,452	5,116	36,034
Rate	43.9	49.5	55.5	52.6	54.7	46.6	41.7	40.5	34.1	26.6	38.8
Vandalism	193,083	149,393	35,451	21,504	23,122	20,925	24,545	23,846	30,170	13,520	77,313
Rate	94.6	107.1	100.4	105.7	103.8	97.4	109.6	134.7	66.6	70.2	83.3
Weapons; carrying, possessing, etc.	117,844	91,520	31,960	14,362	13,588	10,707	10,370	10,533	19,532	6,792	43,191
Rate	57.8	65.6	90.5	70.6	61.0	49.8	46.3	59.5	43.1	35.3	46.5
Prostitution and commercialized vice	51,686	48,590	33,985	7,388	4,086	2,046	743	342	2,985	111	5,762
Rate	25.3	34.8	96.3	36.3	18.3	9.5	3.3	1.9	6.6	0.6	6.2
Sex offenses (except forcible rape and prostitution)	63,759	45,823	17,002	6,364	6,714	5,406	5,065	5,272	12,515	5,421	23,885
Rate	31.2	32.8	48.2	31.3	30.1	25.2	22.6	29.8	27.6	28.1	25.7

See footnotes at end of table.

Table 31

Number and Rate of Arrests

by Population Group, 2003—Continued

[Rate: Number of arrests per 100,000 inhabitants]

Offense charged	Total (10,843 agencies; population 204,034,545)	Total cities (7,898 cities; population 139,498,658)	Cities						Counties		
			Group I (50 cities, 250,000 and over; population 35,303,730)	Group II (135 cities, 100,000 to 249,999; population 20,341,032)	Group III (323 cities, 50,000 to 99,999; population 22,274,208)	Group IV (618 cities, 25,000 to 49,999; population 21,486,840)	Group V (1,412 cities, 10,000 to 24,999; population 22,385,366)	Group VI (5,360 cities, under 10,000; population 17,707,482)	Metropolitan counties[1] (1,158 agencies; population 45,269,822)	Nonmetropolitan counties (1,787 agencies; population 19,266,065)	Suburban area[2] (5,889 agencies; population 92,793,659)
Drug abuse violations	1,172,222	883,969	321,408	131,496	126,174	99,695	101,359	103,837	199,921	88,332	425,193
Rate	574.5	633.7	910.4	646.5	566.5	464.0	452.8	586.4	441.6	458.5	458.2
Gambling	7,414	6,085	4,426	348	423	165	365	358	717	612	1,296
Rate	3.6	4.4	12.5	1.7	1.9	0.8	1.6	2.0	1.6	3.2	1.4
Offenses against the family and children	94,488	45,440	5,887	6,321	8,355	7,931	9,342	7,604	36,120	12,928	53,431
Rate	46.3	32.6	16.7	31.1	37.5	36.9	41.7	42.9	79.8	67.1	57.6
Driving under the influence	1,005,777	613,904	120,525	67,893	85,523	90,926	115,883	133,154	238,681	153,192	478,094
Rate	492.9	440.1	341.4	333.8	384.0	423.2	517.7	752.0	527.2	795.1	515.2
Liquor laws	431,912	342,832	46,764	38,407	47,323	46,906	64,899	98,533	51,533	37,547	185,562
Rate	211.7	245.8	132.5	188.8	212.5	218.3	289.9	556.4	113.8	194.9	200.0
Drunkenness	389,626	329,648	75,828	48,702	53,043	43,770	52,423	55,882	40,255	19,723	138,143
Rate	191.0	236.3	214.8	239.4	238.1	203.7	234.2	315.6	88.9	102.4	148.9
Disorderly conduct	453,645	389,254	81,353	44,834	59,798	51,825	69,914	81,530	42,992	21,399	183,845
Rate	222.3	279.0	230.4	220.4	268.5	241.2	312.3	460.4	95.0	111.1	198.1
Vagrancy	20,052	17,518	9,192	1,847	2,429	946	884	2,220	2,185	349	5,289
Rate	9.8	12.6	26.0	9.1	10.9	4.4	3.9	12.5	4.8	1.8	5.7
All other offenses (except traffic)	2,571,023	1,848,925	478,602	238,412	294,869	253,580	290,172	293,290	507,655	214,443	1,107,854
Rate	1,260.1	1,325.4	1,355.7	1,172.1	1,323.8	1,180.2	1,296.3	1,656.3	1,121.4	1,113.1	1,193.9
Suspicion[3]	1,812	1,105	34	159	65	155	426	266	562	145	1,139
Rate	0.9	0.8	0.1	0.8	0.3	0.7	1.9	1.5	1.2	0.8	1.2
Curfew and loitering law violations	95,052	90,168	45,773	6,738	12,138	7,668	9,931	7,920	3,727	1,157	21,428
Rate	46.6	64.6	129.7	33.1	54.5	35.7	44.4	44.7	8.2	6.0	23.1
Runaways	87,396	63,356	15,342	10,702	12,173	9,574	9,736	5,829	18,230	5,810	34,482
Rate	42.8	45.4	43.5	52.6	54.7	44.6	43.5	32.9	40.3	30.2	37.2

[1] Includes only metropolitan county law enforcement agencies.
[2] Suburban area includes law enforcement agencies in cities with less than 50,000 inhabitants and county law enforcement agencies that are within a Metropolitan Statistical Area (see Appendix III). Suburban area excludes all metropolitan agencies associated with a principal city. The agencies associated with suburban areas also appear in other groups within this table.
[3] Does not include suspicion.
[4] Violent crimes are offenses of murder, forcible rape, robbery, and aggravated assault. Property crimes are offenses of burglary, larceny-theft, motor vehicle theft, and arson.

Table 32

Ten-Year Arrest Trends
Totals, 1994-2003
[7,592 agencies; 2003 estimated population 166,154,387; 1994 estimated population 149,051,209]

	Number of persons arrested								
	Total all ages			Under 18 years of age			18 years of age and over		
Offense charged	1994	2003	Percent change	1994	2003	Percent change	1994	2003	Percent change
TOTAL[1]	8,013,794	7,787,587	-2.8	1,564,349	1,289,876	-17.5	6,449,445	6,497,711	+0.7
Murder and nonnegligent manslaughter	10,999	7,015	-36.2	1,913	619	-67.6	9,086	6,396	-29.6
Forcible rape	19,125	14,863	-22.3	3,207	2,415	-24.7	15,918	12,448	-21.8
Robbery	83,369	62,547	-25.0	25,732	14,645	-43.1	57,637	47,902	-16.9
Aggravated assault	305,983	268,339	-12.3	47,488	35,221	-25.8	258,495	233,118	-9.8
Burglary	226,221	173,061	-23.5	84,494	50,903	-39.8	141,727	122,158	-13.8
Larceny-theft	884,239	682,312	-22.8	305,834	198,223	-35.2	578,405	484,089	-16.3
Motor vehicle theft	116,587	85,738	-26.5	50,996	24,371	-52.2	65,591	61,367	-6.4
Arson	12,450	8,898	-28.5	7,266	4,633	-36.2	5,184	4,265	-17.7
Violent crime[2]	419,476	352,764	-15.9	78,340	52,900	-32.5	341,136	299,864	-12.1
Property crime[2]	1,239,497	950,009	-23.4	448,590	278,130	-38.0	790,907	671,879	-15.0
Other assaults	678,846	699,287	+3.0	123,184	135,908	+10.3	555,662	563,379	+1.4
Forgery and counterfeiting	65,092	66,057	+1.5	5,355	2,856	-46.7	59,737	63,201	+5.8
Fraud	192,869	160,646	-16.7	6,075	4,336	-28.6	186,794	156,310	-16.3
Embezzlement	8,875	10,548	+18.9	632	729	+15.3	8,243	9,819	+19.1
Stolen property; buying, receiving, possessing	95,002	75,145	-20.9	27,077	14,602	-46.1	67,925	60,543	-10.9
Vandalism	196,056	161,052	-17.9	95,252	63,723	-33.1	100,804	97,329	-3.4
Weapons; carrying, possessing, etc.	150,470	96,063	-36.2	38,134	22,573	-40.8	112,336	73,490	-34.6
Prostitution and commercialized vice	46,850	38,577	-17.7	608	797	+31.1	46,242	37,780	-18.3
Sex offenses (except forcible rape and prostitution)	59,632	53,815	-9.8	10,765	10,950	+1.7	48,867	42,865	-12.3
Drug abuse violations	750,359	918,543	+22.4	89,520	106,293	+18.7	660,839	812,250	+22.9
Gambling	6,544	3,306	-49.5	778	320	-58.9	5,766	2,986	-48.2
Offenses against the family and children	69,149	76,462	+10.6	3,172	3,768	+18.8	65,977	72,694	+10.2
Driving under the influence	848,136	798,046	-5.9	8,617	11,495	+33.4	839,519	786,551	-6.3
Liquor laws	306,418	355,512	+16.0	77,061	79,994	+3.8	229,357	275,518	+20.1
Drunkenness	443,190	328,576	-25.9	11,477	10,176	-11.3	431,713	318,400	-26.2
Disorderly conduct	394,468	350,070	-11.3	94,875	106,874	+12.6	299,593	243,196	-18.8
Vagrancy	14,136	16,377	+15.9	2,775	1,397	-49.7	11,361	14,980	+31.9
All other offenses (except traffic)	1,813,187	2,115,810	+16.7	226,520	221,133	-2.4	1,586,667	1,894,677	+19.4
Suspicion	6,976	1,052	-84.9	1,355	318	-76.5	5,621	734	-86.9
Curfew and loitering law violations	86,860	86,249	-0.7	86,860	86,249	-0.7	–	–	–
Runaways	128,682	74,673	-42.0	128,682	74,673	-42.0	–	–	–

[1] Does not include suspicion.

[2] Violent crimes are offenses of murder, forcible rape, robbery, and aggravated assault. Property crimes are offenses of burglary, larceny-theft, motor vehicle theft, and arson.

Table 33

Ten-Year Arrest Trends
by Sex, 1994-2003
[7,592 agencies; 2003 estimated population 166,154,387; 1994 estimated population 149,051,209]

| | Male | | | | | | Female | | | | | |
| | Total | | | Under 18 | | | Total | | | Under 18 | | |
Offense charged	1994	2003	Percent change	1994	2003	Percent change	1994	2003	Percent change	1994	2003	Percent change
TOTAL[1]	6,384,846	5,958,949	-6.7	1,173,624	910,981	-22.4	1,628,948	1,828,638	+12.3	390,725	378,895	-3.0
Murder and nonnegligent manslaughter	9,931	6,268	-36.9	1,798	560	-68.9	1,068	747	-30.1	115	59	-48.7
Forcible rape	18,910	14,651	-22.5	3,137	2,366	-24.6	215	212	-1.4	70	49	-30.0
Robbery	75,729	55,851	-26.2	23,510	13,262	-43.6	7,640	6,696	-12.4	2,222	1,383	-37.8
Aggravated assault	257,370	212,913	-17.3	39,028	26,923	-31.0	48,613	55,426	+14.0	8,460	8,298	-1.9
Burglary	200,801	148,373	-26.1	76,003	44,700	-41.2	25,420	24,688	-2.9	8,491	6,203	-26.9
Larceny-theft	587,473	425,990	-27.5	209,100	119,520	-42.8	296,766	256,322	-13.6	96,734	78,703	-18.6
Motor vehicle theft	101,422	71,364	-29.6	43,381	20,114	-53.6	15,165	14,374	-5.2	7,615	4,257	-44.1
Arson	10,679	7,547	-29.3	6,388	4,089	-36.0	1,771	1,351	-23.7	878	544	-38.0
Violent crime[2]	361,940	289,683	-20.0	67,473	43,111	-36.1	57,536	63,081	+9.6	10,867	9,789	-9.9
Property crime[2]	900,375	653,274	-27.4	334,872	188,423	-43.7	339,122	296,735	-12.5	113,718	89,707	-21.1
Other assaults	549,316	528,194	-3.8	90,771	91,865	+1.2	129,530	171,093	+32.1	32,413	44,043	+35.9
Forgery and counterfeiting	40,983	39,420	-3.8	3,384	1,813	-46.4	24,109	26,637	+10.5	1,971	1,043	-47.1
Fraud	109,546	86,978	-20.6	3,981	2,817	-29.2	83,323	73,668	-11.6	2,094	1,519	-27.5
Embezzlement	5,149	5,256	+2.1	401	433	+8.0	3,726	5,292	+42.0	231	296	+28.1
Stolen property; buying, receiving, possessing	82,015	61,339	-25.2	23,964	12,400	-48.3	12,987	13,806	+6.3	3,113	2,202	-29.3
Vandalism	170,987	134,674	-21.2	85,417	54,957	-35.7	25,069	26,378	+5.2	9,835	8,766	-10.9
Weapons; carrying, possessing, etc.	138,622	88,251	-36.3	35,145	20,230	-42.4	11,848	7,812	-34.1	2,989	2,343	-21.6
Prostitution and commercialized vice	18,501	14,489	-21.7	305	232	-23.9	28,349	24,088	-15.0	303	565	+86.5
Sex offenses (except forcible rape and prostitution)	54,705	49,054	-10.3	9,945	9,916	-0.3	4,927	4,761	-3.4	820	1,034	+26.1
Drug abuse violations	621,938	745,452	+19.9	77,691	87,805	+13.0	128,421	173,091	+34.8	11,829	18,488	+56.3
Gambling	5,687	2,765	-51.4	731	306	-58.1	857	541	-36.9	47	14	-70.2
Offenses against the family and children	56,848	59,095	+4.0	2,076	2,330	+12.2	12,301	17,367	+41.2	1,096	1,438	+31.2
Driving under the influence	728,079	652,694	-10.4	7,366	9,200	+24.9	120,057	145,352	+21.1	1,251	2,295	+83.5
Liquor laws	242,837	263,033	+8.3	54,499	51,646	-5.2	63,581	92,479	+45.5	22,562	28,348	+25.6
Drunkenness	391,194	281,214	-28.1	9,600	7,841	-18.3	51,996	47,362	-8.9	1,877	2,335	+24.4
Disorderly conduct	308,177	260,122	-15.6	72,096	73,573	+2.0	86,291	89,948	+4.2	22,779	33,301	+46.2
Vagrancy	10,839	12,734	+17.5	2,218	1,044	-52.9	3,297	3,643	+10.5	557	353	-36.6
All other offenses (except traffic)	1,469,827	1,640,339	+11.6	174,408	160,150	-8.2	343,360	475,471	+38.5	52,112	60,983	+17.0
Suspicion	5,895	848	-85.6	1,104	241	-78.2	1,081	204	-81.1	251	77	-69.3
Curfew and loitering law violations	62,087	60,165	-3.1	62,087	60,165	-3.1	24,773	26,084	+5.3	24,773	26,084	+5.3
Runaways	55,194	30,724	-44.3	55,194	30,724	-44.3	73,488	43,949	-40.2	73,488	43,949	-40.2

[1] Does not include suspicion.

[2] Violent crimes are offenses of murder, forcible rape, robbery, and aggravated assault. Property crimes are offenses of burglary, larceny-theft, motor vehicle theft, and arson.

Table 34

Five-Year Arrest Trends
Totals, 1999-2003

[7,925 agencies; 2003 estimated population 163,898,254; 1999 estimated population 154,626,351]

Offense charged	Number of persons arrested								
	Total all ages			Under 18 years of age			18 years of age and over		
	1999	2003	Percent change	1999	2003	Percent change	1999	2003	Percent change
TOTAL[1]	7,877,446	7,606,247	-3.4	1,389,989	1,241,719	-10.7	6,487,457	6,364,528	-1.9
Murder and nonnegligent manslaughter	7,375	7,000	-5.1	756	618	-18.3	6,619	6,382	-3.6
Forcible rape	15,886	15,098	-5.0	2,695	2,411	-10.5	13,191	12,687	-3.8
Robbery	61,987	62,110	+0.2	16,350	15,112	-7.6	45,637	46,998	+3.0
Aggravated assault	272,164	259,751	-4.6	39,027	35,476	-9.1	233,137	224,275	-3.8
Burglary	170,484	169,896	-0.3	58,335	49,735	-14.7	112,149	120,161	+7.1
Larceny-theft	695,449	660,743	-5.0	221,239	189,080	-14.5	474,210	471,663	-0.5
Motor vehicle theft	81,647	86,120	+5.5	29,006	24,578	-15.3	52,641	61,542	+16.9
Arson	9,667	8,899	-7.9	5,285	4,673	-11.6	4,382	4,226	-3.6
Violent crime[2]	357,412	343,959	-3.8	58,828	53,617	-8.9	298,584	290,342	-2.8
Property crime[2]	957,247	925,658	-3.3	313,865	268,066	-14.6	643,382	657,592	+2.2
Other assaults	723,591	712,227	-1.6	133,511	140,838	+5.5	590,080	571,389	-3.2
Forgery and counterfeiting	61,162	63,312	+3.5	4,090	2,627	-35.8	57,072	60,685	+6.3
Fraud	197,304	170,575	-13.5	7,427	4,706	-36.6	189,877	165,869	-12.6
Embezzlement	10,773	10,704	-0.6	1,047	734	-29.9	9,726	9,970	+2.5
Stolen property; buying, receiving, possessing	65,937	69,180	+4.9	16,441	13,284	-19.2	49,496	55,896	+12.9
Vandalism	161,570	155,502	-3.8	69,559	62,137	-10.7	92,011	93,365	+1.5
Weapons; carrying, possessing, etc.	95,654	94,449	-1.3	24,216	22,705	-6.2	71,438	71,744	+0.4
Prostitution and commercialized vice	43,529	39,121	-10.1	634	777	+22.6	42,895	38,344	-10.6
Sex offenses (except forcible rape and prostitution)	51,843	50,193	-3.2	9,531	9,855	+3.4	42,312	40,338	-4.7
Drug abuse violations	876,090	936,297	+6.9	113,143	109,413	-3.3	762,947	826,884	+8.4
Gambling	5,512	5,589	+1.4	682	998	+46.3	4,830	4,591	-4.9
Offenses against the family and children	81,590	76,544	-6.2	4,993	3,802	-23.9	76,597	72,742	-5.0
Driving under the influence	840,984	799,612	-4.9	12,504	11,412	-8.7	828,480	788,200	-4.9
Liquor laws	376,878	324,081	-14.0	94,178	73,440	-22.0	282,700	250,641	-11.3
Drunkenness	387,798	328,154	-15.4	12,705	10,318	-18.8	375,093	317,836	-15.3
Disorderly conduct	356,616	319,557	-10.4	97,763	97,643	-0.1	258,853	221,914	-14.3
Vagrancy	13,461	13,246	-1.6	1,333	1,063	-20.3	12,128	12,183	+0.5
All other offenses (except traffic)	2,032,967	2,020,705	-0.6	234,011	206,702	-11.7	1,798,956	1,814,003	+0.8
Suspicion	4,177	1,031	-75.3	1,078	281	-73.9	3,099	750	-75.8
Curfew and loitering law violations	93,497	77,031	-17.6	93,497	77,031	-17.6	–	–	–
Runaways	86,031	70,551	-18.0	86,031	70,551	-18.0	–	–	–

[1] Does not include suspicion.

[2] Violent crimes are offenses of murder, forcible rape, robbery, and aggravated assault. Property crimes are offenses of burglary, larceny-theft, motor vehicle theft, and arson.

Table 35

Five-Year Arrest Trends

by Sex, 1999-2003

[7,925 agencies; 2003 estimated population 163,898,254; 1999 estimated population 154,626,351]

| | Male | | | | | | Female | | | | | |
| | Total | | | Under 18 | | | Total | | | Under 18 | | |
Offense charged	1999	2003	Percent change	1999	2003	Percent change	1999	2003	Percent change	1999	2003	Percent change
TOTAL[1]	6,159,807	5,841,305	-5.2	1,014,735	883,812	-12.9	1,717,639	1,764,942	+2.8	375,254	357,907	-4.6
Murder and nonnegligent manslaughter	6,556	6,275	-4.3	695	560	-19.4	819	725	-11.5	61	58	-4.9
Forcible rape	15,701	14,903	-5.1	2,647	2,373	-10.4	185	195	+5.4	48	38	-20.8
Robbery	55,861	55,626	-0.4	14,954	13,735	-8.2	6,126	6,484	+5.8	1,396	1,377	-1.4
Aggravated assault	219,507	206,947	-5.7	30,562	27,342	-10.5	52,657	52,804	+0.3	8,465	8,134	-3.9
Burglary	148,123	145,642	-1.7	51,586	43,656	-15.4	22,361	24,254	+8.5	6,749	6,079	-9.9
Larceny-theft	447,812	414,271	-7.5	142,757	114,591	-19.7	247,637	246,472	-0.5	78,482	74,489	-5.1
Motor vehicle theft	68,968	71,656	+3.9	24,267	20,467	-15.7	12,679	14,464	+14.1	4,739	4,111	-13.3
Arson	8,320	7,601	-8.6	4,688	4,148	-11.5	1,347	1,298	-3.6	597	525	-12.1
Violent crime[2]	297,625	283,751	-4.7	48,858	44,010	-9.9	59,787	60,208	+0.7	9,970	9,607	-3.6
Property crime[2]	673,223	639,170	-5.1	223,298	182,862	-18.1	284,024	286,488	+0.9	90,567	85,204	-5.9
Other assaults	559,403	538,314	-3.8	93,390	95,319	+2.1	164,188	173,913	+5.9	40,121	45,519	+13.5
Forgery and counterfeiting	37,719	37,826	+0.3	2,614	1,654	-36.7	23,443	25,486	+8.7	1,476	973	-34.1
Fraud	112,513	94,936	-15.6	5,347	3,152	-41.1	84,791	75,639	-10.8	2,080	1,554	-25.3
Embezzlement	5,538	5,350	-3.4	561	427	-23.9	5,235	5,354	+2.3	486	307	-36.8
Stolen property; buying, receiving, possessing	55,595	57,063	+2.6	14,288	11,537	-19.3	10,342	12,117	+17.2	2,153	1,747	-18.9
Vandalism	137,200	130,029	-5.2	61,187	53,554	-12.5	24,370	25,473	+4.5	8,372	8,583	+2.5
Weapons; carrying, possessing, etc.	88,266	86,963	-1.5	21,991	20,273	-7.8	7,388	7,486	+1.3	2,225	2,432	+9.3
Prostitution and commercialized vice	18,328	14,093	-23.1	299	235	-21.4	25,201	25,028	-0.7	335	542	+61.8
Sex offenses (except forcible rape and prostitution)	48,255	46,221	-4.2	8,829	9,039	+2.4	3,588	3,972	+10.7	702	816	+16.2
Drug abuse violations	720,685	762,906	+5.9	96,734	91,173	-5.7	155,405	173,391	+11.6	16,409	18,240	+11.2
Gambling	4,951	5,098	+3.0	653	974	+49.2	561	491	-12.5	29	24	-17.2
Offenses against the family and children	63,944	59,181	-7.4	3,179	2,331	-26.7	17,646	17,363	-1.6	1,814	1,471	-18.9
Driving under the influence	706,444	655,402	-7.2	10,353	9,113	-12.0	134,540	144,210	+7.2	2,151	2,299	+6.9
Liquor laws	292,059	241,846	-17.2	64,719	48,052	-25.8	84,819	82,235	-3.0	29,459	25,388	-13.8
Drunkenness	337,584	280,717	-16.8	10,203	7,974	-21.8	50,214	47,437	-5.5	2,502	2,344	-6.3
Disorderly conduct	274,515	240,337	-12.5	70,793	67,656	-4.4	82,101	79,220	-3.5	26,970	29,987	+11.2
Vagrancy	10,989	10,115	-8.0	1,097	813	-25.9	2,472	3,131	+26.7	236	250	+5.9
All other offenses (except traffic)	1,614,149	1,569,110	-2.8	175,520	150,787	-14.1	418,818	451,595	+7.8	58,491	55,915	-4.4
Suspicion	3,283	825	-74.9	838	220	-73.7	894	206	-77.0	240	61	-74.6
Curfew and loitering law violations	65,622	54,037	-17.7	65,622	54,037	-17.7	27,875	22,994	-17.5	27,875	22,994	-17.5
Runaways	35,200	28,840	-18.1	35,200	28,840	-18.1	50,831	41,711	-17.9	50,831	41,711	-17.9

[1] Does not include suspicion.

[2] Violent crimes are offenses of murder, forcible rape, robbery, and aggravated assault. Property crimes are offenses of burglary, larceny-theft, motor vehicle theft, and arson.

Table 36

Current Year Over Previous Year Arrest Trends

Totals, 2002-2003

[9,556 agencies; 2003 estimated population 180,434,745; 2002 estimated population 178,840,390]

	Number of persons arrested											
	Total all ages			Under 15 years of age			Under 18 years of age			18 years of age and over		
Offense charged	2002	2003	Percent change	2002	2003	Percent change	2002	2003	Percent change	2002	2003	Percent change
TOTAL[1]	8,411,718	8,424,570	+0.2	435,544	439,173	+0.8	1,375,467	1,370,377	-0.4	7,036,251	7,054,193	+0.3
Murder and nonnegligent manslaughter	7,712	7,206	-6.6	65	63	-3.1	660	594	-10.0	7,052	6,612	-6.2
Forcible rape	16,934	16,064	-5.1	1,074	970	-9.7	2,877	2,618	-9.0	14,057	13,446	-4.3
Robbery	60,920	60,899	*	3,072	3,321	+8.1	13,447	13,788	+2.5	47,473	47,111	-0.8
Aggravated assault	277,238	270,365	-2.5	13,073	13,048	-0.2	36,443	36,468	+0.1	240,795	233,897	-2.9
Burglary	178,095	182,094	+2.2	19,597	18,809	-4.0	54,414	53,750	-1.2	123,681	128,344	+3.8
Larceny-theft	728,334	731,736	+0.5	84,102	80,708	-4.0	219,921	212,960	-3.2	508,413	518,776	+2.0
Motor vehicle theft	82,268	82,962	+0.8	6,363	5,982	-6.0	24,784	23,872	-3.7	57,484	59,090	+2.8
Arson	10,557	9,943	-5.8	3,439	3,187	-7.3	5,361	5,176	-3.5	5,196	4,767	-8.3
Violent crime[2]	362,804	354,534	-2.3	17,284	17,402	+0.7	53,427	53,468	+0.1	309,377	301,066	-2.7
Property crime[2]	999,254	1,006,735	+0.7	113,501	108,686	-4.2	304,480	295,758	-2.9	694,774	710,977	+2.3
Other assaults	780,465	773,320	-0.9	61,299	64,286	+4.9	143,435	150,085	+4.6	637,030	623,235	-2.2
Forgery and counterfeiting	73,635	71,090	-3.5	416	394	-5.3	3,313	3,053	-7.8	70,322	68,037	-3.2
Fraud	191,804	189,966	-1.0	1,032	889	-13.9	5,610	5,132	-8.5	186,194	184,834	-0.7
Embezzlement	12,203	11,269	-7.7	88	51	-42.0	957	795	-16.9	11,246	10,474	-6.9
Stolen property; buying, receiving, possessing	82,558	83,436	+1.1	4,505	4,446	-1.3	17,025	16,205	-4.8	65,533	67,231	+2.6
Vandalism	172,788	174,223	+0.8	29,101	30,246	+3.9	67,094	68,739	+2.5	105,694	105,484	-0.2
Weapons; carrying, possessing, etc.	96,529	98,829	+2.4	6,991	8,269	+18.3	20,299	22,525	+11.0	76,230	76,304	+0.1
Prostitution and commercialized vice	36,040	35,457	-1.6	102	92	-9.8	631	702	+11.3	35,409	34,755	-1.8
Sex offenses (except forcible rape and prostitution)	56,243	54,024	-3.9	6,152	5,871	-4.6	11,809	11,442	-3.1	44,434	42,582	-4.2
Drug abuse violations	904,346	951,027	+5.2	18,279	19,995	+9.4	109,891	113,935	+3.7	794,455	837,092	+5.4
Gambling	4,162	3,715	-10.7	74	61	-17.6	350	353	+0.9	3,812	3,362	-11.8
Offenses against the family and children	86,216	80,299	-6.9	2,172	1,562	-28.1	5,494	4,467	-18.7	80,722	75,832	-6.1
Driving under the influence	913,638	899,949	-1.5	377	288	-23.6	13,898	13,295	-4.3	899,740	886,654	-1.5
Liquor laws	414,265	400,501	-3.3	9,210	8,730	-5.2	96,363	90,917	-5.7	317,902	309,584	-2.6
Drunkenness	380,763	368,085	-3.3	1,526	1,497	-1.9	12,451	11,695	-6.1	368,312	356,390	-3.2
Disorderly conduct	400,923	404,194	+0.8	48,966	52,444	+7.1	118,186	125,183	+5.9	282,737	279,011	-1.3
Vagrancy	12,825	16,466	+28.4	359	328	-8.6	1,253	1,360	+8.5	11,572	15,106	+30.5
All other offenses (except traffic)	2,284,629	2,308,406	+1.0	66,221	67,410	+1.8	243,873	242,223	-0.7	2,040,756	2,066,183	+1.2
Suspicion	2,617	1,216	-53.5	226	98	-56.6	764	360	-52.9	1,853	856	-53.8
Curfew and loitering law violations	60,778	56,053	-7.8	16,897	16,230	-3.9	60,778	56,053	-7.8	–	–	–
Runaways	84,850	82,992	-2.2	30,992	29,996	-3.2	84,850	82,992	-2.2	–	–	–

[1] Does not include suspicion.

[2] Violent crimes are offenses of murder, forcible rape, robbery, and aggravated assault. Property crimes are offenses of burglary, larceny-theft, motor vehicle theft, and arson.

*Less than one-tenth of 1 percent.

Table 37

Current Year Over Previous Year Arrest Trends
by Sex, 2002-2003

[9,556 agencies; 2003 estimated population 180,434,745; 2002 estimated population 178,840,390]

| | Male | | | | | | Female | | | | | |
| | Total | | | Under 18 | | | Total | | | Under 18 | | |
Offense charged	2002	2003	Percent change	2002	2003	Percent change	2002	2003	Percent change	2002	2003	Percent change
TOTAL[1]	6,465,604	6,440,910	-0.4	969,951	964,760	-0.5	1,946,114	1,983,660	+1.9	405,516	405,617	*
Murder and nonnegligent manslaughter	6,834	6,428	-5.9	586	535	-8.7	878	778	-11.4	74	59	-20.3
Forcible rape	16,694	15,839	-5.1	2,775	2,567	-7.5	240	225	-6.3	102	51	-50.0
Robbery	54,533	54,407	-0.2	12,249	12,554	+2.5	6,387	6,492	+1.6	1,198	1,234	+3.0
Aggravated assault	221,079	214,238	-3.1	27,912	27,944	+0.1	56,159	56,127	-0.1	8,531	8,524	-0.1
Burglary	154,329	156,741	+1.6	48,153	47,319	-1.7	23,766	25,353	+6.7	6,261	6,431	+2.7
Larceny-theft	456,433	456,767	+0.1	133,083	128,631	-3.3	271,901	274,969	+1.1	86,838	84,329	-2.9
Motor vehicle theft	68,317	68,745	+0.6	20,206	19,538	-3.3	13,951	14,217	+1.9	4,578	4,334	-5.3
Arson	8,997	8,447	-6.1	4,759	4,570	-4.0	1,560	1,496	-4.1	602	606	+0.7
Violent crime[2]	299,140	290,912	-2.8	43,522	43,600	+0.2	63,664	63,622	-0.1	9,905	9,868	-0.4
Property crime[2]	688,076	690,700	+0.4	206,201	200,058	-3.0	311,178	316,035	+1.6	98,279	95,700	-2.6
Other assaults	593,091	585,007	-1.4	97,566	101,468	+4.0	187,374	188,313	+0.5	45,869	48,617	+6.0
Forgery and counterfeiting	43,956	42,220	-3.9	2,139	1,965	-8.1	29,679	28,870	-2.7	1,174	1,088	-7.3
Fraud	106,900	104,993	-1.8	3,761	3,396	-9.7	84,904	84,973	+0.1	1,849	1,736	-6.1
Embezzlement	6,147	5,616	-8.6	567	473	-16.6	6,056	5,653	-6.7	390	322	-17.4
Stolen property; buying, receiving, possessing	67,510	68,079	+0.8	14,210	13,770	-3.1	15,048	15,357	+2.1	2,815	2,435	-13.5
Vandalism	144,246	145,404	+0.8	57,932	59,116	+2.0	28,542	28,819	+1.0	9,162	9,623	+5.0
Weapons; carrying, possessing, etc.	88,738	90,845	+2.4	18,228	20,281	+11.3	7,791	7,984	+2.5	2,071	2,244	+8.4
Prostitution and commercialized vice	14,208	13,265	-6.6	238	208	-12.6	21,832	22,192	+1.6	393	494	+25.7
Sex offenses (except forcible rape and prostitution)	52,262	50,126	-4.1	10,812	10,427	-3.6	3,981	3,898	-2.1	997	1,015	+1.8
Drug abuse violations	736,804	772,013	+4.8	91,076	93,823	+3.0	167,542	179,014	+6.8	18,815	20,112	+6.9
Gambling	3,529	3,059	-13.3	332	335	+0.9	633	656	+3.6	18	18	0.0
Offenses against the family and children	65,500	60,903	-7.0	3,309	2,764	-16.5	20,716	19,396	-6.4	2,185	1,703	-22.1
Driving under the influence	753,489	735,755	-2.4	11,234	10,603	-5.6	160,149	164,194	+2.5	2,664	2,692	+1.1
Liquor laws	310,395	295,997	-4.6	63,634	58,935	-7.4	103,870	104,504	+0.6	32,729	31,982	-2.3
Drunkenness	327,127	314,840	-3.8	9,748	9,015	-7.5	53,636	53,245	-0.7	2,703	2,680	-0.9
Disorderly conduct	299,876	300,573	+0.2	82,295	86,244	+4.8	101,047	103,621	+2.5	35,891	38,939	+8.5
Vagrancy	10,370	12,877	+24.2	990	1,031	+4.1	2,455	3,589	+46.2	263	329	+25.1
All other offenses (except traffic)	1,779,152	1,785,571	+0.4	177,069	175,093	-1.1	505,477	522,835	+3.4	66,804	67,130	+0.5
Suspicion	2,040	969	-52.5	556	274	-50.7	577	247	-57.2	208	86	-58.7
Curfew and loitering law violations	41,000	37,907	-7.5	41,000	37,907	-7.5	19,778	18,146	-8.3	19,778	18,146	-8.3
Runaways	34,088	34,248	+0.5	34,088	34,248	+0.5	50,762	48,744	-4.0	50,762	48,744	-4.0

[1] Does not include suspicion.

[2] Violent crimes are offenses of murder, forcible rape, robbery, and aggravated assault. Property crimes are offenses of burglary, larceny-theft, motor vehicle theft, and arson.

* Less than one-tenth of 1 percent.

Table 38

Arrests
by Age, 2003
[10,843 agencies; 2003 estimated population 204,034,545]

Offense charged	Total all ages	Ages under 15	Ages under 18	Ages 18 and over	Under 10	10-12	13-14	15	16	17	18	19	20	21
TOTAL	**9,581,423**	**497,975**	**1,563,149**	**8,018,274**	**18,177**	**115,088**	**364,710**	**299,866**	**361,152**	**404,156**	**467,190**	**474,982**	**454,196**	**412,171**
Percent distribution[1]	100.0	5.2	16.3	83.7	0.2	1.2	3.8	3.1	3.8	4.2	4.9	5.0	4.7	4.3
Murder and nonnegligent manslaughter	9,119	88	783	8,336	1	11	76	130	223	342	527	595	550	553
Forcible rape	18,446	1,108	2,966	15,480	28	266	814	522	570	766	953	915	871	782
Robbery	75,667	4,507	17,900	57,767	91	822	3,594	3,555	4,583	5,255	6,193	5,345	4,519	3,910
Aggravated assault	315,732	15,629	43,150	272,582	582	4,125	10,922	7,863	9,257	10,401	11,406	11,658	11,941	12,618
Burglary	204,761	21,219	59,870	144,891	1,035	5,330	14,854	11,616	13,025	14,010	15,471	12,894	10,221	8,825
Larceny-theft	817,048	88,145	232,322	584,726	2,966	23,462	61,717	43,859	49,643	50,675	49,444	40,655	34,062	28,198
Motor vehicle theft	106,221	7,731	30,874	75,347	58	877	6,796	7,300	8,059	7,784	7,514	6,514	5,266	4,731
Arson	11,330	3,532	5,757	5,573	365	1,146	2,021	968	718	539	465	400	336	281
Violent crime[2]	418,964	21,332	64,799	354,165	702	5,224	15,406	12,070	14,633	16,764	19,079	18,513	17,881	17,863
Percent distribution[1]	100.0	5.1	15.5	84.5	0.2	1.2	3.7	2.9	3.5	4.0	4.6	4.4	4.3	4.3
Property crime[2]	1,139,360	120,627	328,823	810,537	4,424	30,815	85,388	63,743	71,445	73,008	72,894	60,463	49,885	42,035
Percent distribution[1]	100.0	10.6	28.9	71.1	0.4	2.7	7.5	5.6	6.3	6.4	6.4	5.3	4.4	3.7
Other assaults	877,105	72,692	170,168	706,937	2,820	19,972	49,900	32,219	33,212	32,045	29,040	28,194	29,414	31,677
Forgery and counterfeiting	79,188	424	3,328	75,860	25	55	344	451	861	1,592	3,084	3,807	4,165	3,782
Fraud	208,469	1,026	5,642	202,827	80	172	774	848	1,414	2,354	4,993	7,224	8,046	8,420
Embezzlement	11,986	53	826	11,160	5	6	42	46	247	480	753	811	674	658
Stolen property; buying, receiving, possessing	89,560	4,692	17,184	72,376	112	947	3,633	3,284	4,147	5,061	6,239	5,610	4,897	4,279
Vandalism	193,083	33,310	76,042	117,041	2,347	9,815	21,148	13,173	14,723	14,836	13,116	10,110	8,224	7,955
Weapons; carrying, possessing, etc.	117,844	9,965	27,492	90,352	391	2,537	7,037	5,062	5,793	6,672	7,472	7,059	6,338	6,120
Prostitution and commercialized vice	51,686	133	972	50,714	7	7	119	157	243	439	1,311	1,676	1,597	1,645
Sex offenses (except forcible rape and prostitution)	63,759	6,531	12,747	51,012	420	1,873	4,238	2,197	2,010	2,009	2,385	2,389	2,250	2,120
Drug abuse violations	1,172,222	23,608	137,658	1,034,564	324	2,862	20,422	24,126	36,762	53,162	74,175	73,303	67,534	60,702
Gambling	7,414	172	1,151	6,263	4	21	147	244	285	450	519	543	463	366
Offenses against the family and children	94,488	1,718	4,859	89,629	137	412	1,169	863	1,079	1,199	1,861	1,887	2,233	2,712
Driving under the influence	1,005,777	324	14,570	991,207	123	13	188	601	3,546	10,099	24,611	32,158	37,167	49,975
Liquor laws	431,912	9,294	96,592	335,320	147	658	8,489	14,708	27,439	45,151	73,343	75,795	63,852	12,359
Drunkenness	389,626	1,609	12,529	377,097	72	114	1,423	1,938	2,957	6,025	11,572	12,629	13,153	17,990
Disorderly conduct	453,645	56,205	136,970	316,675	1,446	14,334	40,425	27,799	27,559	25,407	22,072	19,129	17,950	21,121
Vagrancy	20,052	396	1,594	18,458	10	81	305	340	365	493	611	617	579	528
All other offenses (except traffic)	2,571,023	74,370	266,365	2,304,658	3,242	14,918	56,210	52,397	64,436	75,162	97,972	112,970	117,801	119,794
Suspicion	1,812	102	390	1,422	6	22	74	76	100	112	88	95	93	70
Curfew and loitering law violations	95,052	27,719	95,052	–	529	5,099	22,091	21,372	26,023	19,938	–	–	–	–
Runaways	87,396	31,673	87,396	–	804	5,131	25,738	22,152	21,873	11,698	–	–	–	–

[1] Because of rounding, the percentages may not add to 100.0.

[2] Violent crimes are offenses of murder, forcible rape, robbery, and aggravated assault. Property crimes are offenses of burglary, larceny-theft, motor vehicle theft, and arson.

Table 38

Arrests

by Age, 2003—Continued

[10,843 agencies; 2003 estimated population 204,034,545]

Offense charged	22	23	24	25-29	30-34	35-39	40-44	45-49	50-54	55-59	60-64	65 and over
TOTAL	**384,543**	**357,246**	**318,416**	**1,202,370**	**1,025,775**	**959,689**	**861,848**	**556,418**	**288,439**	**135,478**	**63,173**	**56,340**
Percent distribution[1]	**4.0**	**3.7**	**3.3**	**12.5**	**10.7**	**10.0**	**9.0**	**5.8**	**3.0**	**1.4**	**0.7**	**0.6**
Murder and nonnegligent manslaughter	521	492	437	1,530	948	739	551	370	229	128	72	94
Forcible rape	746	631	606	2,287	2,181	1,955	1,538	942	486	295	140	152
Robbery	3,451	2,965	2,586	8,509	6,737	5,841	4,254	2,151	829	281	109	87
Aggravated assault	12,367	11,902	10,956	44,797	38,573	35,843	31,311	19,569	10,177	4,812	2,291	2,361
Burglary	7,557	6,744	5,715	20,217	17,712	15,853	12,486	6,826	2,775	961	358	276
Larceny-theft	25,438	22,766	19,916	76,528	72,310	71,556	62,550	41,330	20,983	9,769	4,526	4,695
Motor vehicle theft	4,242	3,688	3,370	12,151	10,032	8,010	5,440	2,739	1,038	377	129	106
Arson	246	202	189	692	636	633	610	412	221	131	56	63
Violent crime[2]	17,085	15,990	14,585	57,123	48,439	44,378	37,654	23,032	11,721	5,516	2,612	2,694
Percent distribution[1]	4.1	3.8	3.5	13.6	11.6	10.6	9.0	5.5	2.8	1.3	0.6	0.6
Property crime[2]	37,483	33,400	29,190	109,588	100,690	96,052	81,086	51,307	25,017	11,238	5,069	5,140
Percent distribution[1]	3.3	2.9	2.6	9.6	8.8	8.4	7.1	4.5	2.2	1.0	0.4	0.5
Other assaults	31,496	30,726	28,529	115,419	103,382	96,664	83,595	51,165	24,832	11,686	5,665	5,453
Forgery and counterfeiting	3,588	3,522	3,260	13,755	11,893	10,092	7,660	4,239	1,869	706	262	176
Fraud	8,613	8,344	7,880	34,952	33,168	29,232	23,239	14,238	7,386	3,762	1,756	1,574
Embezzlement	558	547	433	1,685	1,535	1,268	1,003	618	365	152	63	37
Stolen property; buying, receiving, possessing	3,808	3,436	2,933	11,209	9,644	8,110	6,272	3,441	1,488	566	251	193
Vandalism	6,631	5,767	5,020	16,782	12,817	11,284	9,354	5,290	2,490	1,121	519	561
Weapons; carrying, possessing, etc.	5,514	5,130	4,496	14,718	9,817	7,618	6,455	4,436	2,515	1,282	715	667
Prostitution and commercialized vice	1,765	1,677	1,493	7,295	8,733	9,185	7,252	3,883	1,735	758	324	385
Sex offenses (except forcible rape and prostitution)	1,895	1,726	1,577	6,425	6,502	6,733	5,998	4,165	2,660	1,737	1,071	1,379
Drug abuse violations	55,760	51,337	45,181	159,273	125,029	114,648	102,297	61,639	28,207	10,013	3,461	2,005
Gambling	342	352	235	818	521	466	437	361	277	239	160	164
Offenses against the family and children	2,880	3,079	3,129	14,991	16,355	15,350	12,600	7,202	3,067	1,282	556	445
Driving under the influence	49,077	47,081	42,062	158,223	129,312	118,176	116,343	83,651	50,209	27,568	13,809	11,785
Liquor laws	8,670	6,499	5,003	16,778	13,880	14,768	16,184	12,720	8,061	3,960	1,985	1,463
Drunkenness	16,168	14,817	12,859	48,477	43,863	48,065	53,371	40,153	23,362	11,384	5,399	3,835
Disorderly conduct	18,432	15,887	13,333	46,204	35,019	34,097	31,779	21,015	10,639	5,261	2,463	2,274
Vagrancy	525	534	460	1,959	2,168	2,774	2,942	2,397	1,369	594	244	157
All other offenses (except traffic)	114,170	107,329	96,697	366,487	312,824	290,573	256,193	161,389	81,115	36,632	16,767	15,945
Suspicion	83	66	61	209	184	156	134	77	55	21	22	8
Curfew and loitering law violations	–	–	–	–	–	–	–	–	–	–	–	–
Runaways	–	–	–	–	–	–	–	–	–	–	–	–

Table 39

Arrests

Males, by Age, 2003

[10,843 agencies; 2003 estimated population 204,034,545]

Offense charged	Total all ages	Ages under 15	Ages under 18	Ages 18 and over	Under 10	10-12	13-14	15	16	17	18	19	20	21
TOTAL	**7,355,693**	**342,741**	**1,109,865**	**6,245,828**	**14,878**	**84,736**	**243,127**	**204,037**	**257,779**	**305,308**	**367,498**	**374,591**	**358,753**	**328,892**
Percent distribution[1]	**100.0**	**4.7**	**15.1**	**84.9**	**0.2**	**1.2**	**3.3**	**2.8**	**3.5**	**4.2**	**5.0**	**5.1**	**4.9**	**4.5**
Murder and nonnegligent manslaughter	8,178	78	710	7,468	1	9	68	119	202	311	488	557	509	512
Forcible rape	18,199	1,073	2,907	15,292	25	255	793	515	561	758	941	904	858	775
Robbery	67,818	4,052	16,315	51,503	81	749	3,222	3,200	4,223	4,840	5,711	4,896	4,113	3,570
Aggravated assault	250,240	11,703	32,963	217,277	512	3,230	7,961	5,871	7,146	8,243	9,206	9,412	9,636	10,152
Burglary	176,718	18,435	52,812	123,906	900	4,625	12,910	10,264	11,613	12,500	14,002	11,399	8,947	7,685
Larceny-theft	514,090	54,075	140,865	373,225	2,243	15,353	36,479	25,844	29,574	31,372	32,048	26,493	21,877	18,029
Motor vehicle theft	88,541	6,166	25,652	62,889	53	708	5,405	5,958	6,791	6,737	6,530	5,623	4,504	4,024
Arson	9,565	3,087	5,043	4,522	335	1,030	1,722	845	617	494	417	361	291	248
Violent crime[2]	344,435	16,906	52,895	291,540	619	4,243	12,044	9,705	12,132	14,152	16,346	15,769	15,116	15,009
Percent distribution[1]	100.0	4.9	15.4	84.6	0.2	1.2	3.5	2.8	3.5	4.1	4.7	4.6	4.4	4.4
Property crime[2]	788,914	81,763	224,372	564,542	3,531	21,716	56,516	42,911	48,595	51,103	52,997	43,876	35,619	29,986
Percent distribution[1]	100.0	10.4	28.4	71.6	0.4	2.8	7.2	5.4	6.2	6.5	6.7	5.6	4.5	3.8
Other assaults	664,991	49,403	114,905	550,086	2,372	14,649	32,382	20,789	22,305	22,408	20,976	20,876	21,999	24,104
Forgery and counterfeiting	47,246	299	2,147	45,099	18	42	239	278	579	991	1,942	2,360	2,486	2,240
Fraud	115,459	681	3,775	111,684	39	117	525	562	940	1,592	2,966	4,139	4,560	4,777
Embezzlement	6,011	36	495	5,516	5	4	27	35	145	279	383	409	345	316
Stolen property; buying, receiving, possessing	73,216	3,856	14,623	58,593	96	772	2,988	2,786	3,546	4,435	5,325	4,737	4,069	3,573
Vandalism	161,413	28,461	65,554	95,859	2,125	8,448	17,888	11,336	12,821	12,936	11,487	8,714	6,985	6,672
Weapons; carrying, possessing, etc.	108,192	8,630	24,449	83,743	360	2,224	6,046	4,450	5,207	6,162	7,087	6,679	5,972	5,767
Prostitution and commercialized vice	18,522	41	304	18,218	5	4	32	38	78	147	284	369	454	568
Sex offenses (except forcible rape and prostitution)	58,344	5,897	11,559	46,785	359	1,710	3,828	1,979	1,829	1,854	2,151	2,133	2,036	1,911
Drug abuse violations	957,239	18,327	114,987	842,252	257	2,173	15,897	19,842	31,134	45,684	63,663	62,798	57,564	51,527
Gambling	6,609	167	1,124	5,485	4	18	145	240	279	438	502	509	420	351
Offenses against the family and children	72,789	1,026	2,970	69,819	99	267	660	508	634	802	1,383	1,363	1,551	1,949
Driving under the influence	822,963	235	11,623	811,340	100	7	128	457	2,750	8,181	20,136	26,462	30,880	40,604
Liquor laws	320,490	4,804	62,799	257,691	116	356	4,332	8,498	17,967	31,530	53,009	56,035	47,993	10,118
Drunkenness	333,071	1,004	9,622	323,449	63	78	863	1,363	2,283	4,972	9,845	10,856	11,561	15,850
Disorderly conduct	339,743	37,671	94,496	245,247	1,190	10,446	26,035	18,448	19,395	18,982	17,203	14,972	14,015	16,955
Vagrancy	15,747	289	1,190	14,557	9	56	224	253	285	363	510	547	475	426
All other offenses (except traffic)	1,996,512	51,791	193,421	1,803,091	2,557	11,122	38,112	36,477	46,915	58,238	79,233	90,905	94,570	96,131
Suspicion	1,529	77	297	1,232	5	17	55	60	74	86	70	83	83	58
Curfew and loitering law violations	66,206	18,522	66,206	–	415	3,633	14,474	14,389	18,584	14,711	–	–	–	–
Runaways	36,052	12,855	36,052	–	534	2,634	9,687	8,633	9,302	5,262	–	–	–	–

[1] Because of rounding, the percentages may not add to 100.0.

[2] Violent crimes are offenses of murder, forcible rape, robbery, and aggravated assault. Property crimes are offenses of burglary, larceny-theft, motor vehicle theft, and arson.

Table 39

Arrests
Males, by Age, 2003—Continued
[10,843 agencies; 2003 estimated population 204,034,545]

Offense charged	22	23	24	25-29	30-34	35-39	40-44	45-49	50-54	55-59	60-64	65 and over
TOTAL	**306,129**	**283,371**	**251,810**	**941,482**	**778,111**	**716,566**	**654,115**	**437,413**	**234,982**	**112,457**	**53,100**	**46,558**
Percent distribution[1]	**4.2**	**3.9**	**3.4**	**12.8**	**10.6**	**9.7**	**8.9**	**5.9**	**3.2**	**1.5**	**0.7**	**0.6**
Murder and nonnegligent manslaughter	475	447	404	1,387	832	627	461	319	195	105	67	83
Forcible rape	736	623	603	2,261	2,153	1,929	1,518	933	482	290	140	146
Robbery	3,144	2,669	2,307	7,531	5,859	4,997	3,675	1,869	725	257	99	81
Aggravated assault	9,924	9,526	8,753	35,780	30,242	27,686	24,576	15,707	8,472	4,124	1,980	2,101
Burglary	6,595	5,810	4,832	17,071	14,684	13,089	10,391	5,794	2,322	780	286	219
Larceny-theft	16,118	14,185	12,393	46,927	45,148	46,003	41,150	27,314	13,947	6,078	2,748	2,767
Motor vehicle theft	3,549	3,122	2,788	10,019	8,047	6,445	4,488	2,305	895	338	114	98
Arson	207	169	158	554	495	475	467	315	169	103	44	49
Violent crime[2]	14,279	13,265	12,067	46,959	39,086	35,239	30,230	18,828	9,874	4,776	2,286	2,411
Percent distribution[1]	4.1	3.9	3.5	13.6	11.3	10.2	8.8	5.5	2.9	1.4	0.7	0.7
Property crime[2]	26,469	23,286	20,171	74,571	68,374	66,012	56,496	35,728	17,333	7,299	3,192	3,133
Percent distribution[1]	3.4	3.0	2.6	9.5	8.7	8.4	7.2	4.5	2.2	0.9	0.4	0.4
Other assaults	24,361	23,774	22,197	90,587	80,509	74,592	65,562	41,098	20,369	9,709	4,767	4,606
Forgery and counterfeiting	2,152	2,166	1,892	7,998	6,699	5,918	4,547	2,580	1,316	469	193	141
Fraud	4,670	4,597	4,263	18,103	17,236	15,846	13,311	8,429	4,481	2,265	1,070	971
Embezzlement	278	283	219	840	702	643	508	282	173	83	29	23
Stolen property; buying, receiving, possessing	3,078	2,790	2,364	8,864	7,511	6,321	4,988	2,845	1,233	497	225	173
Vandalism	5,521	4,748	4,087	13,530	10,097	8,635	7,296	4,257	1,982	934	449	465
Weapons; carrying, possessing, etc.	5,218	4,824	4,218	13,756	8,924	6,767	5,718	3,991	2,317	1,201	675	629
Prostitution and commercialized vice	664	637	576	2,868	2,871	2,678	2,353	1,559	1,080	606	289	362
Sex offenses (except forcible rape and prostitution)	1,704	1,548	1,434	5,860	5,866	6,128	5,448	3,919	2,535	1,695	1,052	1,365
Drug abuse violations	47,301	43,267	37,963	132,164	97,833	85,815	76,919	48,524	23,377	8,673	3,074	1,790
Gambling	322	326	221	746	457	370	336	268	214	185	127	131
Offenses against the family and children	2,072	2,251	2,324	11,331	12,700	11,989	10,293	6,025	2,654	1,096	479	359
Driving under the influence	40,286	39,072	35,125	133,364	106,569	93,522	90,438	66,897	41,893	23,661	12,016	10,415
Liquor laws	7,212	5,356	4,164	13,848	11,047	11,782	12,972	10,648	6,958	3,486	1,773	1,290
Drunkenness	14,116	13,029	11,346	42,622	37,118	39,414	43,817	34,220	20,675	10,359	5,034	3,587
Disorderly conduct	14,708	12,644	10,573	36,033	26,141	24,898	23,789	16,476	8,645	4,301	2,045	1,849
Vagrancy	393	416	359	1,464	1,496	2,073	2,322	2,008	1,186	525	215	142
All other offenses (except traffic)	91,252	85,032	76,197	285,793	236,719	217,793	196,654	128,758	66,637	30,619	14,089	12,709
Suspicion	73	60	50	181	156	131	118	73	50	18	21	7
Curfew and loitering law violations	–	–	–	–	–	–	–	–	–	–	–	–
Runaways	–	–	–	–	–	–	–	–	–	–	–	–

Table 40

Arrests

Females, by Age, 2003

[10,843 agencies; 2003 estimated population 204,034,545]

Offense charged	Total all ages	Ages under 15	Ages under 18	Ages 18 and over	Under 10	10-12	13-14	15	16	17	18	19	20	21
TOTAL	**2,225,730**	**155,234**	**453,284**	**1,772,446**	**3,299**	**30,352**	**121,583**	**95,829**	**103,373**	**98,848**	**99,692**	**100,391**	**95,443**	**83,279**
Percent distribution[1]	**100.0**	**7.0**	**20.4**	**79.6**	**0.1**	**1.4**	**5.5**	**4.3**	**4.6**	**4.4**	**4.5**	**4.5**	**4.3**	**3.7**
Murder and nonnegligent manslaughter	941	10	73	868	0	2	8	11	21	31	39	38	41	41
Forcible rape	247	35	59	188	3	11	21	7	9	8	12	11	13	7
Robbery	7,849	455	1,585	6,264	10	73	372	355	360	415	482	449	406	340
Aggravated assault	65,492	3,926	10,187	55,305	70	895	2,961	1,992	2,111	2,158	2,200	2,246	2,305	2,466
Burglary	28,043	2,784	7,058	20,985	135	705	1,944	1,352	1,412	1,510	1,469	1,495	1,274	1,140
Larceny-theft	302,958	34,070	91,457	211,501	723	8,109	25,238	18,015	20,069	19,303	17,396	14,162	12,185	10,169
Motor vehicle theft	17,680	1,565	5,222	12,458	5	169	1,391	1,342	1,268	1,047	984	891	762	707
Arson	1,765	445	714	1,051	30	116	299	123	101	45	48	39	45	33
Violent crime[2]	74,529	4,426	11,904	62,625	83	981	3,362	2,365	2,501	2,612	2,733	2,744	2,765	2,854
Percent distribution[1]	100.0	5.9	16.0	84.0	0.1	1.3	4.5	3.2	3.4	3.5	3.7	3.7	3.7	3.8
Property crime[2]	350,446	38,864	104,451	245,995	893	9,099	28,872	20,832	22,850	21,905	19,897	16,587	14,266	12,049
Percent distribution[1]	100.0	11.1	29.8	70.2	0.3	2.6	8.2	5.9	6.5	6.3	5.7	4.7	4.1	3.4
Other assaults	212,114	23,289	55,263	156,851	448	5,323	17,518	11,430	10,907	9,637	8,064	7,318	7,415	7,573
Forgery and counterfeiting	31,942	125	1,181	30,761	7	13	105	173	282	601	1,142	1,447	1,679	1,542
Fraud	93,010	345	1,867	91,143	41	55	249	286	474	762	2,027	3,085	3,486	3,643
Embezzlement	5,975	17	331	5,644	0	2	15	11	102	201	370	402	329	342
Stolen property; buying, receiving, possessing	16,344	836	2,561	13,783	16	175	645	498	601	626	914	873	828	706
Vandalism	31,670	4,849	10,488	21,182	222	1,367	3,260	1,837	1,902	1,900	1,629	1,396	1,239	1,283
Weapons; carrying, possessing, etc.	9,652	1,335	3,043	6,609	31	313	991	612	586	510	385	380	366	353
Prostitution and commercialized vice	33,164	92	668	32,496	2	3	87	119	165	292	1,027	1,307	1,143	1,077
Sex offenses (except forcible rape and prostitution)	5,415	634	1,188	4,227	61	163	410	218	181	155	234	256	214	209
Drug abuse violations	214,983	5,281	22,671	192,312	67	689	4,525	4,284	5,628	7,478	10,512	10,505	9,970	9,175
Gambling	805	5	27	778	0	3	2	4	6	12	17	34	43	15
Offenses against the family and children	21,699	692	1,889	19,810	38	145	509	355	445	397	478	524	682	763
Driving under the influence	182,814	89	2,947	179,867	23	6	60	144	796	1,918	4,475	5,696	6,287	9,371
Liquor laws	111,422	4,490	33,793	77,629	31	302	4,157	6,210	9,472	13,621	20,334	19,760	15,859	2,241
Drunkenness	56,555	605	2,907	53,648	9	36	560	575	674	1,053	1,727	1,773	1,592	2,140
Disorderly conduct	113,902	18,534	42,474	71,428	256	3,888	14,390	9,351	8,164	6,425	4,869	4,157	3,935	4,166
Vagrancy	4,305	107	404	3,901	1	25	81	87	80	130	101	70	104	102
All other offenses (except traffic)	574,511	22,579	72,944	501,567	685	3,796	18,098	15,920	17,521	16,924	18,739	22,065	23,231	23,663
Suspicion	283	25	93	190	1	5	19	16	26	26	18	12	10	12
Curfew and loitering law violations	28,846	9,197	28,846	–	114	1,466	7,617	6,983	7,439	5,227	–	–	–	–
Runaways	51,344	18,818	51,344	–	270	2,497	16,051	13,519	12,571	6,436	–	–	–	–

[1] Because of rounding, the percentages may not add to 100.0.

[2] Violent crimes are offenses of murder, forcible rape, robbery, and aggravated assault. Property crimes are offenses of burglary, larceny-theft, motor vehicle theft, and arson.

Table 40

Arrests
Females, by Age, 2003—Continued
[10,843 agencies; 2003 estimated population 204,034,545]

Offense charged	22	23	24	25-29	30-34	35-39	40-44	45-49	50-54	55-59	60-64	65 and over
TOTAL	**78,414**	**73,875**	**66,606**	**260,888**	**247,664**	**243,123**	**207,733**	**119,005**	**53,457**	**23,021**	**10,073**	**9,782**
Percent distribution[1]	**3.5**	**3.3**	**3.0**	**11.7**	**11.1**	**10.9**	**9.3**	**5.3**	**2.4**	**1.0**	**0.5**	**0.4**
Murder and nonnegligent manslaughter	46	45	33	143	116	112	90	51	34	23	5	11
Forcible rape	10	8	3	26	28	26	20	9	4	5	0	6
Robbery	307	296	279	978	878	844	579	282	104	24	10	6
Aggravated assault	2,443	2,376	2,203	9,017	8,331	8,157	6,735	3,862	1,705	688	311	260
Burglary	962	934	883	3,146	3,028	2,764	2,095	1,032	453	181	72	57
Larceny-theft	9,320	8,581	7,523	29,601	27,162	25,553	21,400	14,016	7,036	3,691	1,778	1,928
Motor vehicle theft	693	566	582	2,132	1,985	1,565	952	434	143	39	15	8
Arson	39	33	31	138	141	158	143	97	52	28	12	14
Violent crime[2]	2,806	2,725	2,518	10,164	9,353	9,139	7,424	4,204	1,847	740	326	283
Percent distribution[1]	3.8	3.7	3.4	13.6	12.5	12.3	10.0	5.6	2.5	1.0	0.4	0.4
Property crime[2]	11,014	10,114	9,019	35,017	32,316	30,040	24,590	15,579	7,684	3,939	1,877	2,007
Percent distribution[1]	3.1	2.9	2.6	10.0	9.2	8.6	7.0	4.4	2.2	1.1	0.5	0.6
Other assaults	7,135	6,952	6,332	24,832	22,873	22,072	18,033	10,067	4,463	1,977	898	847
Forgery and counterfeiting	1,436	1,356	1,368	5,757	5,194	4,174	3,113	1,659	553	237	69	35
Fraud	3,943	3,747	3,617	16,849	15,932	13,386	9,928	5,809	2,905	1,497	686	603
Embezzlement	280	264	214	845	833	625	495	336	192	69	34	14
Stolen property; buying, receiving, possessing	730	646	569	2,345	2,133	1,789	1,284	596	255	69	26	20
Vandalism	1,110	1,019	933	3,252	2,720	2,649	2,058	1,033	508	187	70	96
Weapons; carrying, possessing, etc.	296	306	278	962	893	851	737	445	198	81	40	38
Prostitution and commercialized vice	1,101	1,040	917	4,427	5,862	6,507	4,899	2,324	655	152	35	23
Sex offenses (except forcible rape and prostitution)	191	178	143	565	636	605	550	246	125	42	19	14
Drug abuse violations	8,459	8,070	7,218	27,109	27,196	28,833	25,378	13,115	4,830	1,340	387	215
Gambling	20	26	14	72	64	96	101	93	63	54	33	33
Offenses against the family and children	808	828	805	3,660	3,655	3,361	2,307	1,177	413	186	77	86
Driving under the influence	8,791	8,009	6,937	24,859	22,743	24,654	25,905	16,754	8,316	3,907	1,793	1,370
Liquor laws	1,458	1,143	839	2,930	2,833	2,986	3,212	2,072	1,103	474	212	173
Drunkenness	2,052	1,788	1,513	5,855	6,745	8,651	9,554	5,933	2,687	1,025	365	248
Disorderly conduct	3,724	3,243	2,760	10,171	8,878	9,199	7,990	4,539	1,994	960	418	425
Vagrancy	132	118	101	495	672	701	620	389	183	69	29	15
All other offenses (except traffic)	22,918	22,297	20,500	80,694	76,105	72,780	59,539	32,631	14,478	6,013	2,678	3,236
Suspicion	10	6	11	28	28	25	16	4	5	3	1	1
Curfew and loitering law violations	–	–	–	–	–	–	–	–	–	–	–	–
Runaways	–	–	–	–	–	–	–	–	–	–	–	–

Table 41

Arrests
of Persons Under 15, 18, 21, and 25 Years of Age, 2003
[10,843 agencies; 2003 estimated population 204,034,545]

Offense charged	Total all ages	Number of persons arrested				Percent of total all ages			
		Under 15	Under 18	Under 21	Under 25	Under 15	Under 18	Under 21	Under 25
TOTAL	**9,581,423**	**497,975**	**1,563,149**	**2,959,517**	**4,431,893**	**5.2**	**16.3**	**30.9**	**46.3**
Murder and nonnegligent manslaughter	9,119	88	783	2,455	4,458	1.0	8.6	26.9	48.9
Forcible rape	18,446	1,108	2,966	5,705	8,470	6.0	16.1	30.9	45.9
Robbery	75,667	4,507	17,900	33,957	46,869	6.0	23.7	44.9	61.9
Aggravated assault	315,732	15,629	43,150	78,155	125,998	5.0	13.7	24.8	39.9
Burglary	204,761	21,219	59,870	98,456	127,297	10.4	29.2	48.1	62.2
Larceny-theft	817,048	88,145	232,322	356,483	452,801	10.8	28.4	43.6	55.4
Motor vehicle theft	106,221	7,731	30,874	50,168	66,199	7.3	29.1	47.2	62.3
Arson	11,330	3,532	5,757	6,958	7,876	31.2	50.8	61.4	69.5
Violent crime[1]	418,964	21,332	64,799	120,272	185,795	5.1	15.5	28.7	44.3
Property crime[1]	1,139,360	120,627	328,823	512,065	654,173	10.6	28.9	44.9	57.4
Other assaults	877,105	72,692	170,168	256,816	379,244	8.3	19.4	29.3	43.2
Forgery and counterfeiting	79,188	424	3,328	14,384	28,536	0.5	4.2	18.2	36.0
Fraud	208,469	1,026	5,642	25,905	59,162	0.5	2.7	12.4	28.4
Embezzlement	11,986	53	826	3,064	5,260	0.4	6.9	25.6	43.9
Stolen property; buying, receiving, possessing	89,560	4,692	17,184	33,930	48,386	5.2	19.2	37.9	54.0
Vandalism	193,083	33,310	76,042	107,492	132,865	17.3	39.4	55.7	68.8
Weapons; carrying, possessing, etc.	117,844	9,965	27,492	48,361	69,621	8.5	23.3	41.0	59.1
Prostitution and commercialized vice	51,686	133	972	5,556	12,136	0.3	1.9	10.7	23.5
Sex offenses (except forcible rape and prostitution)	63,759	6,531	12,747	19,771	27,089	10.2	20.0	31.0	42.5
Drug abuse violations	1,172,222	23,608	137,658	352,670	565,650	2.0	11.7	30.1	48.3
Gambling	7,414	172	1,151	2,676	3,971	2.3	15.5	36.1	53.6
Offenses against the family and children	94,488	1,718	4,859	10,840	22,640	1.8	5.1	11.5	24.0
Driving under the influence	1,005,777	324	14,570	108,506	296,701	*	1.4	10.8	29.5
Liquor laws	431,912	9,294	96,592	309,582	342,113	2.2	22.4	71.7	79.2
Drunkenness	389,626	1,609	12,529	49,883	111,717	0.4	3.2	12.8	28.7
Disorderly conduct	453,645	56,205	136,970	196,121	264,894	12.4	30.2	43.2	58.4
Vagrancy	20,052	396	1,594	3,401	5,448	2.0	7.9	17.0	27.2
All other offenses (except traffic)	2,571,023	74,370	266,365	595,108	1,033,098	2.9	10.4	23.1	40.2
Suspicion	1,812	102	390	666	946	5.6	21.5	36.8	52.2
Curfew and loitering law violations	95,052	27,719	95,052	95,052	95,052	29.2	100.0	100.0	100.0
Runaways	87,396	31,673	87,396	87,396	87,396	36.2	100.0	100.0	100.0

[1] Violent crimes are offenses of murder, forcible rape, robbery, and aggravated assault. Property crimes are offenses of burglary, larceny-theft, motor vehicle theft, and arson.
* Less than one-tenth of 1 percent.

Table 42

Arrests

by Sex, 2003

[10,843 agencies; 2003 estimated population 204,034,545]

Offense charged	Number of persons arrested			Percent male	Percent female	Percent distribution[1]		
	Total	Male	Female			Total	Male	Female
TOTAL	**9,581,423**	**7,355,693**	**2,225,730**	**76.8**	**23.2**	**100.0**	**100.0**	**100.0**
Murder and nonnegligent manslaughter	9,119	8,178	941	89.7	10.3	0.1	0.1	*
Forcible rape	18,446	18,199	247	98.7	1.3	0.2	0.2	*
Robbery	75,667	67,818	7,849	89.6	10.4	0.8	0.9	0.4
Aggravated assault	315,732	250,240	65,492	79.3	20.7	3.3	3.4	2.9
Burglary	204,761	176,718	28,043	86.3	13.7	2.1	2.4	1.3
Larceny-theft	817,048	514,090	302,958	62.9	37.1	8.5	7.0	13.6
Motor vehicle theft	106,221	88,541	17,680	83.4	16.6	1.1	1.2	0.8
Arson	11,330	9,565	1,765	84.4	15.6	0.1	0.1	0.1
Violent crime[2]	418,964	344,435	74,529	82.2	17.8	4.4	4.7	3.3
Property crime[2]	1,139,360	788,914	350,446	69.2	30.8	11.9	10.7	15.7
Other assaults	877,105	664,991	212,114	75.8	24.2	9.2	9.0	9.5
Forgery and counterfeiting	79,188	47,246	31,942	59.7	40.3	0.8	0.6	1.4
Fraud	208,469	115,459	93,010	55.4	44.6	2.2	1.6	4.2
Embezzlement	11,986	6,011	5,975	50.2	49.8	0.1	0.1	0.3
Stolen property; buying, receiving, possessing	89,560	73,216	16,344	81.8	18.2	0.9	1.0	0.7
Vandalism	193,083	161,413	31,670	83.6	16.4	2.0	2.2	1.4
Weapons; carrying, possessing, etc.	117,844	108,192	9,652	91.8	8.2	1.2	1.5	0.4
Prostitution and commercialized vice	51,686	18,522	33,164	35.8	64.2	0.5	0.3	1.5
Sex offenses (except forcible rape and prostitution)	63,759	58,344	5,415	91.5	8.5	0.7	0.8	0.2
Drug abuse violations	1,172,222	957,239	214,983	81.7	18.3	12.2	13.0	9.7
Gambling	7,414	6,609	805	89.1	10.9	0.1	0.1	*
Offenses against the family and children	94,488	72,789	21,699	77.0	23.0	1.0	1.0	1.0
Driving under the influence	1,005,777	822,963	182,814	81.8	18.2	10.5	11.2	8.2
Liquor laws	431,912	320,490	111,422	74.2	25.8	4.5	4.4	5.0
Drunkenness	389,626	333,071	56,555	85.5	14.5	4.1	4.5	2.5
Disorderly conduct	453,645	339,743	113,902	74.9	25.1	4.7	4.6	5.1
Vagrancy	20,052	15,747	4,305	78.5	21.5	0.2	0.2	0.2
All other offenses (except traffic)	2,571,023	1,996,512	574,511	77.7	22.3	26.8	27.1	25.8
Suspicion	1,812	1,529	283	84.4	15.6	*	*	*
Curfew and loitering law violations	95,052	66,206	28,846	69.7	30.3	1.0	0.9	1.3
Runaways	87,396	36,052	51,344	41.3	58.7	0.9	0.5	2.3

[1] Because of rounding, the percentages may not add to 100.0.

[2] Violent crimes are offenses of murder, forcible rape, robbery, and aggravated assault. Property crimes are offenses of burglary, larceny-theft, motor vehicle theft, and arson.

* Less than one-tenth of 1 percent.

Table 43

Arrests

by Race, 2003

[10,839 agencies; 2003 estimated population 203,489,015]

Offense charged	Total arrests					Percent distribution[1]				
	Total	White	Black	American Indian or Alaskan Native	Asian or Pacific Islander	Total	White	Black	American Indian or Alaskan Native	Asian or Pacific Islander
TOTAL	**9,529,469**	**6,723,093**	**2,570,770**	**125,438**	**110,168**	**100.0**	**70.6**	**27.0**	**1.3**	**1.2**
Murder and nonnegligent manslaughter	9,063	4,454	4,395	101	113	100.0	49.1	48.5	1.1	1.2
Forcible rape	18,355	11,766	6,114	245	230	100.0	64.1	33.3	1.3	1.3
Robbery	75,387	33,070	40,993	460	864	100.0	43.9	54.4	0.6	1.1
Aggravated assault	314,045	203,076	103,697	3,492	3,780	100.0	64.7	33.0	1.1	1.2
Burglary	204,035	143,889	56,050	1,995	2,101	100.0	70.5	27.5	1.0	1.0
Larceny-theft	812,542	556,215	233,806	10,177	12,344	100.0	68.5	28.8	1.3	1.5
Motor vehicle theft	105,902	64,910	38,012	1,076	1,904	100.0	61.3	35.9	1.0	1.8
Arson	11,287	8,743	2,357	104	83	100.0	77.5	20.9	0.9	0.7
Violent crime[2]	416,850	252,366	155,199	4,298	4,987	100.0	60.5	37.2	1.0	1.2
Property crime[2]	1,133,766	773,757	330,225	13,352	16,432	100.0	68.2	29.1	1.2	1.4
Other assaults	872,924	573,478	277,928	11,403	10,115	100.0	65.7	31.8	1.3	1.2
Forgery and counterfeiting	78,883	54,701	22,770	445	967	100.0	69.3	28.9	0.6	1.2
Fraud	207,511	142,858	62,107	1,196	1,350	100.0	68.8	29.9	0.6	0.7
Embezzlement	11,901	8,124	3,548	64	165	100.0	68.3	29.8	0.5	1.4
Stolen property; buying, receiving, possessing	88,985	53,932	33,493	649	911	100.0	60.6	37.6	0.7	1.0
Vandalism	192,406	146,640	40,886	2,664	2,216	100.0	76.2	21.2	1.4	1.2
Weapons; carrying, possessing, etc.	117,327	72,849	42,334	827	1,317	100.0	62.1	36.1	0.7	1.1
Prostitution and commercialized vice	51,356	29,776	20,204	250	1,126	100.0	58.0	39.3	0.5	2.2
Sex offenses (except forcible rape and prostitution)	63,573	46,839	15,204	663	867	100.0	73.7	23.9	1.0	1.4
Drug abuse violations	1,168,013	770,430	381,006	7,453	9,124	100.0	66.0	32.6	0.6	0.8
Gambling	7,394	1,964	5,153	15	262	100.0	26.6	69.7	0.2	3.5
Offenses against the family and children	94,189	63,311	28,587	1,201	1,090	100.0	67.2	30.4	1.3	1.2
Driving under the influence	998,035	877,810	96,211	14,163	9,851	100.0	88.0	9.6	1.4	1.0
Liquor laws	429,298	374,751	38,381	11,924	4,242	100.0	87.3	8.9	2.8	1.0
Drunkenness	388,582	326,605	49,725	10,047	2,205	100.0	84.1	12.8	2.6	0.6
Disorderly conduct	451,736	304,789	136,643	6,852	3,452	100.0	67.5	30.2	1.5	0.8
Vagrancy	20,041	11,199	8,346	353	143	100.0	55.9	41.6	1.8	0.7
All other offenses (except traffic)	2,552,922	1,707,425	776,135	35,375	33,987	100.0	66.9	30.4	1.4	1.3
Suspicion	1,791	1,156	609	11	15	100.0	64.5	34.0	0.6	0.8
Curfew and loitering law violations	94,855	64,418	28,469	746	1,222	100.0	67.9	30.0	0.8	1.3
Runaways	87,131	63,915	17,607	1,487	4,122	100.0	73.4	20.2	1.7	4.7

See footnotes at end of table.

Table 43

Arrests

by Race, 2003—Continued

[10,839 agencies; 2003 estimated population 203,489,015]

Offense charged	Arrests under 18					Percent distribution[1]				
	Total	White	Black	American Indian or Alaskan Native	Asian or Pacific Islander	Total	White	Black	American Indian or Alaskan Native	Asian or Pacific Islander
TOTAL	**1,555,801**	**1,098,012**	**413,236**	**19,917**	**24,636**	**100.0**	**70.6**	**26.6**	**1.3**	**1.6**
Murder and nonnegligent manslaughter	779	381	375	10	13	100.0	48.9	48.1	1.3	1.7
Forcible rape	2,958	1,895	988	48	27	100.0	64.1	33.4	1.6	0.9
Robbery	17,849	6,278	11,208	86	277	100.0	35.2	62.8	0.5	1.6
Aggravated assault	42,897	25,458	16,441	438	560	100.0	59.3	38.3	1.0	1.3
Burglary	59,657	42,586	15,581	709	781	100.0	71.4	26.1	1.2	1.3
Larceny-theft	230,876	161,082	61,715	3,424	4,655	100.0	69.8	26.7	1.5	2.0
Motor vehicle theft	30,785	17,281	12,417	431	656	100.0	56.1	40.3	1.4	2.1
Arson	5,734	4,663	969	54	48	100.0	81.3	16.9	0.9	0.8
Violent crime[2]	64,483	34,012	29,012	582	877	100.0	52.7	45.0	0.9	1.4
Property crime[2]	327,052	225,612	90,682	4,618	6,140	100.0	69.0	27.7	1.4	1.9
Other assaults	169,469	103,996	61,519	1,838	2,116	100.0	61.4	36.3	1.1	1.2
Forgery and counterfeiting	3,316	2,559	679	28	50	100.0	77.2	20.5	0.8	1.5
Fraud	5,616	3,725	1,774	34	83	100.0	66.3	31.6	0.6	1.5
Embezzlement	815	554	243	3	15	100.0	68.0	29.8	0.4	1.8
Stolen property; buying, receiving, possessing	17,075	9,756	6,928	163	228	100.0	57.1	40.6	1.0	1.3
Vandalism	75,753	60,654	13,319	930	850	100.0	80.1	17.6	1.2	1.1
Weapons; carrying, possessing, etc.	27,328	18,041	8,653	181	453	100.0	66.0	31.7	0.7	1.7
Prostitution and commercialized vice	966	492	456	4	14	100.0	50.9	47.2	0.4	1.4
Sex offenses (except forcible rape and prostitution)	12,692	9,067	3,359	89	177	100.0	71.4	26.5	0.7	1.4
Drug abuse violations	137,052	98,849	35,638	1,225	1,340	100.0	72.1	26.0	0.9	1.0
Gambling	1,151	133	994	3	21	100.0	11.6	86.4	0.3	1.8
Offenses against the family and children	4,850	3,719	971	81	79	100.0	76.7	20.0	1.7	1.6
Driving under the influence	14,447	13,530	539	245	133	100.0	93.7	3.7	1.7	0.9
Liquor laws	95,970	88,146	4,031	2,733	1,060	100.0	91.8	4.2	2.8	1.1
Drunkenness	12,504	11,091	1,046	263	104	100.0	88.7	8.4	2.1	0.8
Disorderly conduct	136,322	87,308	46,272	1,474	1,268	100.0	64.0	33.9	1.1	0.9
Vagrancy	1,594	984	594	8	8	100.0	61.7	37.3	0.5	0.5
All other offenses (except traffic)	264,970	197,193	60,322	3,179	4,276	100.0	74.4	22.8	1.2	1.6
Suspicion	390	258	129	3	0	100.0	66.2	33.1	0.8	0.0
Curfew and loitering law violations	94,855	64,418	28,469	746	1,222	100.0	67.9	30.0	0.8	1.3
Runaways	87,131	63,915	17,607	1,487	4,122	100.0	73.4	20.2	1.7	4.7

See footnotes at end of table.

Table 43

Arrests

by Race, 2003—Continued

[10,839 agencies; 2003 estimated population 203,489,015]

Offense charged	Arrests 18 and over					Percent distribution[1]				
	Total	White	Black	American Indian or Alaskan Native	Asian or Pacific Islander	Total	White	Black	American Indian or Alaskan Native	Asian or Pacific Islander
TOTAL	**7,973,668**	**5,625,081**	**2,157,534**	**105,521**	**85,532**	**100.0**	**70.5**	**27.1**	**1.3**	**1.1**
Murder and nonnegligent manslaughter	8,284	4,073	4,020	91	100	100.0	49.2	48.5	1.1	1.2
Forcible rape	15,397	9,871	5,126	197	203	100.0	64.1	33.3	1.3	1.3
Robbery	57,538	26,792	29,785	374	587	100.0	46.6	51.8	0.7	1.0
Aggravated assault	271,148	177,618	87,256	3,054	3,220	100.0	65.5	32.2	1.1	1.2
Burglary	144,378	101,303	40,469	1,286	1,320	100.0	70.2	28.0	0.9	0.9
Larceny-theft	581,666	395,133	172,091	6,753	7,689	100.0	67.9	29.6	1.2	1.3
Motor vehicle theft	75,117	47,629	25,595	645	1,248	100.0	63.4	34.1	0.9	1.7
Arson	5,553	4,080	1,388	50	35	100.0	73.5	25.0	0.9	0.6
Violent crime[2]	352,367	218,354	126,187	3,716	4,110	100.0	62.0	35.8	1.1	1.2
Property crime[2]	806,714	548,145	239,543	8,734	10,292	100.0	67.9	29.7	1.1	1.3
Other assaults	703,455	469,482	216,409	9,565	7,999	100.0	66.7	30.8	1.4	1.1
Forgery and counterfeiting	75,567	52,142	22,091	417	917	100.0	69.0	29.2	0.6	1.2
Fraud	201,895	139,133	60,333	1,162	1,267	100.0	68.9	29.9	0.6	0.6
Embezzlement	11,086	7,570	3,305	61	150	100.0	68.3	29.8	0.6	1.4
Stolen property; buying, receiving, possessing	71,910	44,176	26,565	486	683	100.0	61.4	36.9	0.7	0.9
Vandalism	116,653	85,986	27,567	1,734	1,366	100.0	73.7	23.6	1.5	1.2
Weapons; carrying, possessing, etc.	89,999	54,808	33,681	646	864	100.0	60.9	37.4	0.7	1.0
Prostitution and commercialized vice	50,390	29,284	19,748	246	1,112	100.0	58.1	39.2	0.5	2.2
Sex offenses (except forcible rape and prostitution)	50,881	37,772	11,845	574	690	100.0	74.2	23.3	1.1	1.4
Drug abuse violations	1,030,961	671,581	345,368	6,228	7,784	100.0	65.1	33.5	0.6	0.8
Gambling	6,243	1,831	4,159	12	241	100.0	29.3	66.6	0.2	3.9
Offenses against the family and children	89,339	59,592	27,616	1,120	1,011	100.0	66.7	30.9	1.3	1.1
Driving under the influence	983,588	864,280	95,672	13,918	9,718	100.0	87.9	9.7	1.4	1.0
Liquor laws	333,328	286,605	34,350	9,191	3,182	100.0	86.0	10.3	2.8	1.0
Drunkenness	376,078	315,514	48,679	9,784	2,101	100.0	83.9	12.9	2.6	0.6
Disorderly conduct	315,414	217,481	90,371	5,378	2,184	100.0	69.0	28.7	1.7	0.7
Vagrancy	18,447	10,215	7,752	345	135	100.0	55.4	42.0	1.9	0.7
All other offenses (except traffic)	2,287,952	1,510,232	715,813	32,196	29,711	100.0	66.0	31.3	1.4	1.3
Suspicion	1,401	898	480	8	15	100.0	64.1	34.3	0.6	1.1
Curfew and loitering law violations	–	–	–	–	–	–	–	–	–	–
Runaways	–	–	–	–	–	–	–	–	–	–

[1] Because of rounding, the percentages may not add to 100.0.

[2] Violent crimes are offenses of murder, forcible rape, robbery, and aggravated assault. Property crimes are offenses of burglary, larceny-theft, motor vehicle theft, and arson.

Table 44

Arrest Trends

City, 2002-2003

[6,914 agencies; 2003 estimated population 121,103,160; 2002 estimated population 120,079,143]

| | Number of persons arrested | | | | | | | | |
| | Total all ages | | | Under 18 years of age | | | 18 years of age and over | | |
Offense charged	2002	2003	Percent change	2002	2003	Percent change	2002	2003	Percent change
TOTAL[1]	6,167,649	6,179,223	+0.2	1,095,242	1,092,096	-0.3	5,072,407	5,087,127	+0.3
Murder and nonnegligent manslaughter	5,418	5,076	-6.3	517	443	-14.3	4,901	4,633	-5.5
Forcible rape	11,674	11,158	-4.4	2,076	1,805	-13.1	9,598	9,353	-2.6
Robbery	50,371	49,983	-0.8	11,426	11,637	+1.8	38,945	38,346	-1.5
Aggravated assault	206,927	201,338	-2.7	28,168	28,217	+0.2	178,759	173,121	-3.2
Burglary	126,998	130,009	+2.4	39,728	38,844	-2.2	87,270	91,165	+4.5
Larceny-theft	604,420	607,017	+0.4	189,219	183,208	-3.2	415,201	423,809	+2.1
Motor vehicle theft	61,084	61,568	+0.8	18,807	18,100	-3.8	42,277	43,468	+2.8
Arson	7,258	6,961	-4.1	4,020	3,910	-2.7	3,238	3,051	-5.8
Violent crime[2]	274,390	267,555	-2.5	42,187	42,102	-0.2	232,203	225,453	-2.9
Property crime[2]	799,760	805,555	+0.7	251,774	244,062	-3.1	547,986	561,493	+2.5
Other assaults	569,320	562,874	-1.1	108,410	112,986	+4.2	460,910	449,888	-2.4
Forgery and counterfeiting	56,026	54,234	-3.2	2,603	2,403	-7.7	53,423	51,831	-3.0
Fraud	111,831	113,669	+1.6	4,406	4,016	-8.9	107,425	109,653	+2.1
Embezzlement	9,212	8,410	-8.7	772	617	-20.1	8,440	7,793	-7.7
Stolen property; buying, receiving, possessing	64,935	65,175	+0.4	14,321	13,619	-4.9	50,614	51,556	+1.9
Vandalism	132,346	132,970	+0.5	52,345	53,290	+1.8	80,001	79,680	-0.4
Weapons; carrying, possessing, etc.	73,689	75,513	+2.5	16,380	18,221	+11.2	57,309	57,292	*
Prostitution and commercialized vice	33,435	32,614	-2.5	565	638	+12.9	32,870	31,976	-2.7
Sex offenses (except forcible rape and prostitution)	39,253	37,703	-3.9	8,300	8,030	-3.3	30,953	29,673	-4.1
Drug abuse violations	661,531	695,560	+5.1	85,666	88,024	+2.8	575,865	607,536	+5.5
Gambling	2,790	2,515	-9.9	316	286	-9.5	2,474	2,229	-9.9
Offenses against the family and children	45,789	42,084	-8.1	4,020	3,233	-19.6	41,769	38,851	-7.0
Driving under the influence	555,515	549,073	-1.2	9,235	8,927	-3.3	546,280	540,146	-1.1
Liquor laws	324,913	316,696	-2.5	72,034	69,094	-4.1	252,879	247,602	-2.1
Drunkenness	319,655	310,441	-2.9	10,607	10,016	-5.6	309,048	300,425	-2.8
Disorderly conduct	341,613	344,948	+1.0	101,622	107,651	+5.9	239,991	237,297	-1.1
Vagrancy	10,912	14,353	+31.5	1,051	1,199	+14.1	9,861	13,154	+33.4
All other offenses (except traffic)	1,623,937	1,635,649	+0.7	191,831	192,050	+0.1	1,432,106	1,443,599	+0.8
Suspicion	1,788	1,016	-43.2	675	314	-53.5	1,113	702	-36.9
Curfew and loitering law violations	55,268	51,303	-7.2	55,268	51,303	-7.2	–	–	–
Runaways	61,529	60,329	-2.0	61,529	60,329	-2.0	–	–	–

[1] Does not include suspicion.

[2] Violent crimes are offenses of murder, forcible rape, robbery, and aggravated assault. Property crimes are offenses of burglary, larceny-theft, motor vehicle theft, and arson.

* Less than one-tenth of 1 percent.

Table 45

Arrest Trends

City
by Sex, 2002-2003
[6,914 agencies; 2003 estimated population 121,103,160; 2002 estimated population 120,079,143]

| | Male | | | | | | Female | | | | | |
| | Total | | | Under 18 | | | Total | | | Under 18 | | |
Offense charged	2002	2003	Percent change	2002	2003	Percent change	2002	2003	Percent change	2002	2003	Percent change
TOTAL[1]	**4,712,043**	**4,694,775**	**-0.4**	**768,130**	**765,445**	**-0.3**	**1,455,606**	**1,484,448**	**+2.0**	**327,112**	**326,651**	**-0.1**
Murder and nonnegligent manslaughter	4,832	4,575	-5.3	463	404	-12.7	586	501	-14.5	54	39	-27.8
Forcible rape	11,507	11,027	-4.2	1,990	1,772	-11.0	167	131	-21.6	86	33	-61.6
Robbery	44,995	44,630	-0.8	10,398	10,580	+1.8	5,376	5,353	-0.4	1,028	1,057	+2.8
Aggravated assault	163,754	158,439	-3.2	21,438	21,512	+0.3	43,173	42,899	-0.6	6,730	6,705	-0.4
Burglary	109,262	111,121	+1.7	34,808	33,907	-2.6	17,736	18,888	+6.5	4,920	4,937	+0.3
Larceny-theft	373,571	373,685	*	112,627	109,116	-3.1	230,849	233,332	+1.1	76,592	74,092	-3.3
Motor vehicle theft	50,541	50,896	+0.7	15,305	14,770	-3.5	10,543	10,672	+1.2	3,502	3,330	-4.9
Arson	6,180	5,897	-4.6	3,572	3,460	-3.1	1,078	1,064	-1.3	448	450	+0.4
Violent crime[2]	225,088	218,671	-2.9	34,289	34,268	-0.1	49,302	48,884	-0.8	7,898	7,834	-0.8
Property crime[2]	539,554	541,599	+0.4	166,312	161,253	-3.0	260,206	263,956	+1.4	85,462	82,809	-3.1
Other assaults	431,874	425,095	-1.6	73,293	76,005	+3.7	137,446	137,779	+0.2	35,117	36,981	+5.3
Forgery and counterfeiting	33,279	32,013	-3.8	1,667	1,513	-9.2	22,747	22,221	-2.3	936	890	-4.9
Fraud	65,024	64,799	-0.3	2,980	2,631	-11.7	46,807	48,870	+4.4	1,426	1,385	-2.9
Embezzlement	4,572	4,165	-8.9	457	370	-19.0	4,640	4,245	-8.5	315	247	-21.6
Stolen property; buying, receiving, possessing	52,924	52,990	+0.1	11,919	11,575	-2.9	12,011	12,185	+1.4	2,402	2,044	-14.9
Vandalism	109,987	110,414	+0.4	45,090	45,673	+1.3	22,359	22,556	+0.9	7,255	7,617	+5.0
Weapons; carrying, possessing, etc.	67,808	69,440	+2.4	14,765	16,442	+11.4	5,881	6,073	+3.3	1,615	1,779	+10.2
Prostitution and commercialized vice	12,919	12,002	-7.1	199	169	-15.1	20,516	20,612	+0.5	366	469	+28.1
Sex offenses (except forcible rape and prostitution)	36,179	34,688	-4.1	7,571	7,288	-3.7	3,074	3,015	-1.9	729	742	+1.8
Drug abuse violations	539,977	566,025	+4.8	71,167	72,615	+2.0	121,554	129,535	+6.6	14,499	15,409	+6.3
Gambling	2,405	2,100	-12.7	302	273	-9.6	385	415	+7.8	14	13	-7.1
Offenses against the family and children	32,041	29,390	-8.3	2,421	1,955	-19.2	13,748	12,694	-7.7	1,599	1,278	-20.1
Driving under the influence	453,668	444,341	-2.1	7,467	7,145	-4.3	101,847	104,732	+2.8	1,768	1,782	+0.8
Liquor laws	243,383	234,408	-3.7	47,539	45,122	-5.1	81,530	82,288	+0.9	24,495	23,972	-2.1
Drunkenness	275,486	266,175	-3.4	8,324	7,742	-7.0	44,169	44,266	+0.2	2,283	2,274	-0.4
Disorderly conduct	255,596	256,624	+0.4	70,794	74,219	+4.8	86,017	88,324	+2.7	30,828	33,432	+8.4
Vagrancy	8,898	11,185	+25.7	839	905	+7.9	2,014	3,168	+57.3	212	294	+38.7
All other offenses (except traffic)	1,259,618	1,259,102	*	138,972	138,733	-0.2	364,319	376,547	+3.4	52,859	53,317	+0.9
Suspicion	1,398	808	-42.2	500	235	-53.0	390	208	-46.7	175	79	-54.9
Curfew and loitering law violations	37,442	34,792	-7.1	37,442	34,792	-7.1	17,826	16,511	-7.4	17,826	16,511	-7.4
Runaways	24,321	24,757	+1.8	24,321	24,757	+1.8	37,208	35,572	-4.4	37,208	35,572	-4.4

[1] Does not include suspicion.

[2] Violent crimes are offenses of murder, forcible rape, robbery, and aggravated assault. Property crimes are offenses of burglary, larceny-theft, motor vehicle theft, and arson.

* Less than one-tenth of 1 percent.

Table 46

Arrests

City

by Age, 2003

[7,898 agencies; 2003 estimated population 139,498,658]

Offense charged	Total all ages	Ages under 15	Ages under 18	Ages 18 and over	Under 10	10-12	13-14	15	16	17	18	19	20	21
TOTAL	**7,128,531**	**411,405**	**1,266,104**	**5,862,427**	**14,471**	**95,424**	**301,510**	**245,779**	**290,477**	**318,443**	**355,396**	**361,476**	**340,834**	**307,672**
Percent distribution[1]	100.0	5.8	17.8	82.2	0.2	1.3	4.2	3.4	4.1	4.5	5.0	5.1	4.8	4.3
Murder and nonnegligent manslaughter	6,671	70	617	6,054	1	6	63	110	169	268	399	467	423	436
Forcible rape	13,181	809	2,122	11,059	19	198	592	372	415	526	654	636	610	542
Robbery	63,564	4,025	15,583	47,981	83	750	3,192	3,127	3,978	4,453	4,989	4,432	3,739	3,200
Aggravated assault	239,941	12,575	34,355	205,586	452	3,379	8,744	6,307	7,378	8,095	8,663	8,980	9,179	9,774
Burglary	148,277	16,171	44,025	104,252	763	4,046	11,362	8,712	9,374	9,768	10,421	8,862	7,064	6,186
Larceny-theft	683,335	77,378	200,941	482,394	2,641	20,719	54,018	38,248	42,544	42,771	40,973	33,484	27,840	23,098
Motor vehicle theft	82,656	6,255	24,649	58,007	49	712	5,494	5,872	6,429	6,093	5,843	5,047	4,020	3,708
Arson	8,024	2,761	4,361	3,663	296	901	1,564	723	510	367	290	257	221	175
Violent crime[2]	323,357	17,479	52,677	270,680	555	4,333	12,591	9,916	11,940	13,342	14,705	14,515	13,951	13,952
Percent distribution[1]	100.0	5.4	16.3	83.7	0.2	1.3	3.9	3.1	3.7	4.1	4.5	4.5	4.3	4.3
Property crime[2]	922,292	102,565	273,976	648,316	3,749	26,378	72,438	53,555	58,857	58,999	57,527	47,650	39,145	33,167
Percent distribution[1]	100.0	11.1	29.7	70.3	0.4	2.9	7.9	5.8	6.4	6.4	6.2	5.2	4.2	3.6
Other assaults	652,391	56,867	130,888	521,503	2,146	15,703	39,018	24,892	25,044	24,085	21,684	21,422	22,260	24,296
Forgery and counterfeiting	59,999	324	2,628	57,371	22	38	264	352	719	1,233	2,444	2,958	3,236	2,877
Fraud	125,024	850	4,454	120,570	71	136	643	671	1,105	1,828	3,644	4,879	5,293	5,315
Embezzlement	8,946	47	645	8,301	5	4	38	41	176	381	597	666	529	526
Stolen property; buying, receiving, possessing	68,992	4,050	14,306	54,686	98	831	3,121	2,755	3,362	4,139	4,825	4,362	3,723	3,247
Vandalism	149,393	26,886	59,701	89,692	1,820	7,930	17,136	10,498	11,216	11,101	9,909	7,622	6,238	6,216
Weapons; carrying, possessing, etc.	91,520	8,282	22,702	68,818	301	2,092	5,889	4,197	4,783	5,440	5,908	5,681	5,068	4,850
Prostitution and commercialized vice	48,590	121	900	47,690	5	6	110	142	219	418	1,250	1,605	1,526	1,558
Sex offenses (except forcible rape and prostitution)	45,823	4,748	9,063	36,760	287	1,384	3,077	1,533	1,400	1,382	1,587	1,669	1,536	1,488
Drug abuse violations	883,969	19,237	109,873	774,096	226	2,292	16,719	19,889	29,678	41,069	56,015	55,056	49,991	45,065
Gambling	6,085	142	1,066	5,019	3	8	131	228	270	426	468	466	395	326
Offenses against the family and children	45,440	1,230	3,453	41,987	89	314	827	618	764	841	1,172	1,224	1,345	1,609
Driving under the influence	613,904	222	9,649	604,255	93	10	119	417	2,362	6,648	15,740	20,784	23,395	31,859
Liquor laws	342,832	7,457	73,461	269,371	103	528	6,826	11,352	20,900	33,752	56,657	60,135	51,067	9,986
Drunkenness	329,648	1,381	10,760	318,888	56	95	1,230	1,678	2,554	5,147	9,564	10,491	10,930	15,340
Disorderly conduct	389,254	48,833	118,448	270,806	1,171	12,389	35,273	24,098	23,585	21,932	18,800	16,610	15,639	18,756
Vagrancy	17,518	353	1,410	16,108	7	77	269	312	327	418	505	527	471	444
All other offenses (except traffic)	1,848,925	60,376	212,191	1,636,734	2,528	12,037	45,811	42,218	51,226	58,371	72,339	83,094	85,033	86,756
Suspicion	1,105	91	329	776	6	20	65	60	76	102	56	60	63	39
Curfew and loitering law violations	90,168	26,416	90,168	–	502	4,912	21,002	20,294	24,504	18,954	–	–	–	–
Runaways	63,356	23,448	63,356	–	628	3,907	18,913	16,063	15,410	8,435	–	–	–	–

See footnotes at end of table.

Table 46

Arrests
City
by Age, 2003—Continued
[7,898 agencies; 2003 estimated population 139,498,658]

Offense charged	22	23	24	25-29	30-34	35-39	40-44	45-49	50-54	55-59	60-64	65 and over
TOTAL	**284,888**	**263,082**	**233,026**	**872,507**	**733,885**	**688,585**	**621,802**	**405,595**	**210,594**	**97,575**	**45,052**	**40,458**
Percent distribution[1]	**4.0**	**3.7**	**3.3**	**12.2**	**10.3**	**9.7**	**8.7**	**5.7**	**3.0**	**1.4**	**0.6**	**0.6**
Murder and nonnegligent												
manslaughter	396	364	344	1,143	673	490	356	243	137	74	50	59
Forcible rape	551	468	439	1,706	1,584	1,398	1,098	684	331	187	86	85
Robbery	2,818	2,417	2,096	7,063	5,673	4,916	3,650	1,853	733	238	93	71
Aggravated assault	9,597	9,287	8,458	34,266	29,045	26,542	23,036	14,454	7,492	3,499	1,632	1,682
Burglary	5,226	4,692	4,050	14,501	12,995	11,975	9,552	5,330	2,198	725	277	198
Larceny-theft	20,756	18,534	16,178	62,314	58,944	59,022	52,290	34,875	17,945	8,297	3,783	4,061
Motor vehicle theft	3,276	2,850	2,569	9,306	7,691	6,217	4,180	2,103	767	270	94	66
Arson	170	137	137	431	403	433	414	282	148	94	37	34
Violent crime[2]	13,362	12,536	11,337	44,178	36,975	33,346	28,140	17,234	8,693	3,998	1,861	1,897
Percent distribution[1]	4.1	3.9	3.5	13.7	11.4	10.3	8.7	5.3	2.7	1.2	0.6	0.6
Property crime[2]	29,428	26,213	22,934	86,552	80,033	77,647	66,436	42,590	21,058	9,386	4,191	4,359
Percent distribution[1]	3.2	2.8	2.5	9.4	8.7	8.4	7.2	4.6	2.3	1.0	0.5	0.5
Other assaults	24,086	23,375	21,500	87,622	75,916	69,562	59,621	36,755	17,756	8,101	3,831	3,716
Forgery and counterfeiting	2,644	2,706	2,487	10,327	8,831	7,561	5,829	3,191	1,441	526	190	123
Fraud	5,326	5,073	4,727	20,293	19,087	16,744	13,726	8,278	4,226	2,112	968	879
Embezzlement	423	419	342	1,251	1,127	903	687	435	242	95	40	19
Stolen property; buying,												
receiving, possessing	2,930	2,595	2,228	8,359	7,186	6,088	4,734	2,604	1,106	410	170	119
Vandalism	5,206	4,513	3,962	13,105	9,782	8,589	7,117	4,029	1,878	798	356	372
Weapons; carrying,												
possessing, etc.	4,308	4,015	3,554	11,457	7,341	5,438	4,501	3,137	1,763	882	451	464
Prostitution and												
commercialized vice	1,699	1,594	1,414	6,901	8,203	8,622	6,802	3,608	1,584	682	295	347
Sex offenses (except forcible												
rape and prostitution)	1,351	1,273	1,153	4,695	4,774	4,950	4,424	3,110	1,885	1,220	711	934
Drug abuse violations	41,264	38,105	33,432	118,010	93,184	86,147	77,426	46,917	21,641	7,681	2,632	1,530
Gambling	292	307	200	669	393	336	302	261	198	152	126	128
Offenses against the family												
and children	1,681	1,693	1,624	7,235	6,920	6,567	5,337	3,119	1,347	564	288	262
Driving under the influence	31,141	29,722	26,381	97,796	78,081	70,548	68,866	49,190	29,489	16,170	8,123	6,970
Liquor laws	7,056	5,190	3,973	13,461	11,318	12,254	13,702	11,107	7,024	3,450	1,732	1,259
Drunkenness	13,757	12,629	10,924	41,078	36,840	40,545	45,119	34,177	19,869	9,729	4,620	3,276
Disorderly conduct	16,215	13,877	11,630	39,823	29,436	28,533	26,613	17,734	8,907	4,365	2,035	1,833
Vagrancy	437	452	389	1,652	1,849	2,433	2,631	2,159	1,257	538	223	141
All other offenses												
(except traffic)	82,234	76,759	68,806	257,923	216,524	201,691	179,721	115,917	59,201	26,705	12,205	11,826
Suspicion	48	36	29	120	85	81	68	43	29	11	4	4
Curfew and loitering law												
violations	–	–	–	–	–	–	–	–	–	–	–	–
Runaways	–	–	–	–	–	–	–	–	–	–	–	–

[1] Because of rounding, the percentages may not add to 100.0.

[2] Violent crimes are offenses of murder, forcible rape, robbery, and aggravated assault. Property crimes are offenses of burglary, larceny-theft, motor vehicle theft, and arson.

Table 47

Arrests

City

of Persons Under 15, 18, 21, and 25 Years of Age, 2003

[7,898 agencies; 2003 estimated population 139,498,658]

Offense charged	Total all ages	Number of persons arrested				Percent of total all ages			
		Under 15	Under 18	Under 21	Under 25	Under 15	Under 18	Under 21	Under 25
TOTAL	**7,128,531**	**411,405**	**1,266,104**	**2,323,810**	**3,412,478**	**5.8**	**17.8**	**32.6**	**47.9**
Murder and nonnegligent manslaughter	6,671	70	617	1,906	3,446	1.0	9.2	28.6	51.7
Forcible rape	13,181	809	2,122	4,022	6,022	6.1	16.1	30.5	45.7
Robbery	63,564	4,025	15,583	28,743	39,274	6.3	24.5	45.2	61.8
Aggravated assault	239,941	12,575	34,355	61,177	98,293	5.2	14.3	25.5	41.0
Burglary	148,277	16,171	44,025	70,372	90,526	10.9	29.7	47.5	61.1
Larceny-theft	683,335	77,378	200,941	303,238	381,804	11.3	29.4	44.4	55.9
Motor vehicle theft	82,656	6,255	24,649	39,559	51,962	7.6	29.8	47.9	62.9
Arson	8,024	2,761	4,361	5,129	5,748	34.4	54.3	63.9	71.6
Violent crime[1]	323,357	17,479	52,677	95,848	147,035	5.4	16.3	29.6	45.5
Property crime[1]	922,292	102,565	273,976	418,298	530,040	11.1	29.7	45.4	57.5
Other assaults	652,391	56,867	130,888	196,254	289,511	8.7	20.1	30.1	44.4
Forgery and counterfeiting	59,999	324	2,628	11,266	21,980	0.5	4.4	18.8	36.6
Fraud	125,024	850	4,454	18,270	38,711	0.7	3.6	14.6	31.0
Embezzlement	8,946	47	645	2,437	4,147	0.5	7.2	27.2	46.4
Stolen property; buying, receiving, possessing	68,992	4,050	14,306	27,216	38,216	5.9	20.7	39.4	55.4
Vandalism	149,393	26,886	59,701	83,470	103,367	18.0	40.0	55.9	69.2
Weapons; carrying, possessing, etc.	91,520	8,282	22,702	39,359	56,086	9.0	24.8	43.0	61.3
Prostitution and commercialized vice	48,590	121	900	5,281	11,546	0.2	1.9	10.9	23.8
Sex offenses (except forcible rape and prostitution)	45,823	4,748	9,063	13,855	19,120	10.4	19.8	30.2	41.7
Drug abuse violations	883,969	19,237	109,873	270,935	428,801	2.2	12.4	30.6	48.5
Gambling	6,085	142	1,066	2,395	3,520	2.3	17.5	39.4	57.8
Offenses against the family and children	45,440	1,230	3,453	7,194	13,801	2.7	7.6	15.8	30.4
Driving under the influence	613,904	222	9,649	69,568	188,671	*	1.6	11.3	30.7
Liquor laws	342,832	7,457	73,461	241,320	267,525	2.2	21.4	70.4	78.0
Drunkenness	329,648	1,381	10,760	41,745	94,395	0.4	3.3	12.7	28.6
Disorderly conduct	389,254	48,833	118,448	169,497	229,975	12.5	30.4	43.5	59.1
Vagrancy	17,518	353	1,410	2,913	4,635	2.0	8.0	16.6	26.5
All other offenses (except traffic)	1,848,925	60,376	212,191	452,657	767,212	3.3	11.5	24.5	41.5
Suspicion	1,105	91	329	508	660	8.2	29.8	46.0	59.7
Curfew and loitering law violations	90,168	26,416	90,168	90,168	90,168	29.3	100.0	100.0	100.0
Runaways	63,356	23,448	63,356	63,356	63,356	37.0	100.0	100.0	100.0

[1] Violent crimes are offenses of murder, forcible rape, robbery, and aggravated assault. Property crimes are offenses of burglary, larceny-theft, motor vehicle theft, and arson.

* Less than one-tenth of 1 percent.

Table 48

Arrests

City

by Sex, 2003

[7,898 agencies; 2003 estimated population 139,498,658]

Offense charged	Number of persons arrested			Percent male	Percent female	Percent distribution[1]		
	Total	Male	Female			Total	Male	Female
TOTAL	**7,128,531**	**5,444,900**	**1,683,631**	**76.4**	**23.6**	**100.0**	**100.0**	**100.0**
Murder and nonnegligent manslaughter	6,671	6,037	634	90.5	9.5	0.1	0.1	*
Forcible rape	13,181	13,035	146	98.9	1.1	0.2	0.2	*
Robbery	63,564	56,988	6,576	89.7	10.3	0.9	1.0	0.4
Aggravated assault	239,941	188,847	51,094	78.7	21.3	3.4	3.5	3.0
Burglary	148,277	127,219	21,058	85.8	14.2	2.1	2.3	1.3
Larceny-theft	683,335	424,612	258,723	62.1	37.9	9.6	7.8	15.4
Motor vehicle theft	82,656	68,880	13,776	83.3	16.7	1.2	1.3	0.8
Arson	8,024	6,762	1,262	84.3	15.7	0.1	0.1	0.1
Violent crime[2]	323,357	264,907	58,450	81.9	18.1	4.5	4.9	3.5
Property crime[2]	922,292	627,473	294,819	68.0	32.0	12.9	11.5	17.5
Other assaults	652,391	494,019	158,372	75.7	24.3	9.2	9.1	9.4
Forgery and counterfeiting	59,999	35,579	24,420	59.3	40.7	0.8	0.7	1.5
Fraud	125,024	71,539	53,485	57.2	42.8	1.8	1.3	3.2
Embezzlement	8,946	4,434	4,512	49.6	50.4	0.1	0.1	0.3
Stolen property; buying, receiving, possessing	68,992	56,159	12,833	81.4	18.6	1.0	1.0	0.8
Vandalism	149,393	124,358	25,035	83.2	16.8	2.1	2.3	1.5
Weapons; carrying, possessing, etc.	91,520	83,973	7,547	91.8	8.2	1.3	1.5	0.4
Prostitution and commercialized vice	48,590	17,142	31,448	35.3	64.7	0.7	0.3	1.9
Sex offenses (except forcible rape and prostitution)	45,823	41,432	4,391	90.4	9.6	0.6	0.8	0.3
Drug abuse violations	883,969	724,263	159,706	81.9	18.1	12.4	13.3	9.5
Gambling	6,085	5,560	525	91.4	8.6	0.1	0.1	*
Offenses against the family and children	45,440	31,624	13,816	69.6	30.4	0.6	0.6	0.8
Driving under the influence	613,904	498,523	115,381	81.2	18.8	8.6	9.2	6.9
Liquor laws	342,832	254,923	87,909	74.4	25.6	4.8	4.7	5.2
Drunkenness	329,648	282,482	47,166	85.7	14.3	4.6	5.2	2.8
Disorderly conduct	389,254	292,032	97,222	75.0	25.0	5.5	5.4	5.8
Vagrancy	17,518	13,725	3,793	78.3	21.7	0.2	0.3	0.2
All other offenses (except traffic)	1,848,925	1,430,931	417,994	77.4	22.6	25.9	26.3	24.8
Suspicion	1,105	885	220	80.1	19.9	*	*	*
Curfew and loitering law violations	90,168	62,996	27,172	69.9	30.1	1.3	1.2	1.6
Runaways	63,356	25,941	37,415	40.9	59.1	0.9	0.5	2.2

[1] Because of rounding, the percentages may not add to 100.0.

[2] Violent crimes are offenses of murder, forcible rape, robbery, and aggravated assault. Property crimes are offenses of burglary, larceny-theft, motor vehicle theft, and arson.

*Less than one-tenth of 1 percent.

Table 49

Arrests

City
by Race, 2003
[7,894 agencies; 2003 estimated population 138,953,128]

Offense charged	Total arrests					Percent distribution[1]				
	Total	White	Black	American Indian or Alaskan Native	Asian or Pacific Islander	Total	White	Black	American Indian or Alaskan Native	Asian or Pacific Islander
TOTAL	**7,081,879**	**4,826,952**	**2,078,041**	**92,253**	**84,633**	**100.0**	**68.2**	**29.3**	**1.3**	**1.2**
Murder and nonnegligent manslaughter	6,619	2,815	3,664	49	91	100.0	42.5	55.4	0.7	1.4
Forcible rape	13,105	7,699	5,074	141	191	100.0	58.7	38.7	1.1	1.5
Robbery	63,284	27,116	35,072	362	734	100.0	42.8	55.4	0.6	1.2
Aggravated assault	238,411	147,112	85,864	2,309	3,126	100.0	61.7	36.0	1.0	1.3
Burglary	147,633	99,228	45,498	1,279	1,628	100.0	67.2	30.8	0.9	1.1
Larceny-theft	679,004	460,710	198,485	9,191	10,618	100.0	67.9	29.2	1.4	1.6
Motor vehicle theft	82,374	47,254	32,826	780	1,514	100.0	57.4	39.8	0.9	1.8
Arson	7,988	5,965	1,885	71	67	100.0	74.7	23.6	0.9	0.8
Violent crime[2]	321,419	184,742	129,674	2,861	4,142	100.0	57.5	40.3	0.9	1.3
Property crime[2]	916,999	613,157	278,694	11,321	13,827	100.0	66.9	30.4	1.2	1.5
Other assaults	648,572	406,489	225,709	8,579	7,795	100.0	62.7	34.8	1.3	1.2
Forgery and counterfeiting	59,727	40,585	18,034	319	789	100.0	68.0	30.2	0.5	1.3
Fraud	124,230	79,487	43,096	642	1,005	100.0	64.0	34.7	0.5	0.8
Embezzlement	8,865	5,976	2,718	45	126	100.0	67.4	30.7	0.5	1.4
Stolen property; buying, receiving, possessing	68,455	39,022	28,201	453	779	100.0	57.0	41.2	0.7	1.1
Vandalism	148,791	110,644	34,389	2,023	1,735	100.0	74.4	23.1	1.4	1.2
Weapons; carrying, possessing, etc.	91,032	53,856	35,571	530	1,075	100.0	59.2	39.1	0.6	1.2
Prostitution and commercialized vice	48,263	27,576	19,556	236	895	100.0	57.1	40.5	0.5	1.9
Sex offenses (except forcible rape and prostitution)	45,689	32,019	12,518	420	732	100.0	70.1	27.4	0.9	1.6
Drug abuse violations	880,261	545,837	322,735	4,786	6,903	100.0	62.0	36.7	0.5	0.8
Gambling	6,067	1,190	4,749	7	121	100.0	19.6	78.3	0.1	2.0
Offenses against the family and children	45,200	31,077	12,296	884	943	100.0	68.8	27.2	2.0	2.1
Driving under the influence	607,178	532,242	60,239	8,313	6,384	100.0	87.7	9.9	1.4	1.1
Liquor laws	340,683	293,350	33,680	10,159	3,494	100.0	86.1	9.9	3.0	1.0
Drunkenness	328,687	273,139	44,891	8,723	1,934	100.0	83.1	13.7	2.7	0.6
Disorderly conduct	387,399	256,971	121,863	5,552	3,013	100.0	66.3	31.5	1.4	0.8
Vagrancy	17,509	9,469	7,570	336	134	100.0	54.1	43.2	1.9	0.8
All other offenses (except traffic)	1,832,665	1,183,728	600,143	24,201	24,593	100.0	64.6	32.7	1.3	1.3
Suspicion	1,096	713	361	11	11	100.0	65.1	32.9	1.0	1.0
Curfew and loitering law violations	89,974	60,729	27,710	666	869	100.0	67.5	30.8	0.7	1.0
Runaways	63,118	44,954	13,644	1,186	3,334	100.0	71.2	21.6	1.9	5.3

See footnotes at end of table.

Table 49

Arrests

City

by Race, 2003—Continued

[7,894 agencies; 2003 estimated population 138,953,128]

Offense charged	Arrests under 18					Percent distribution[1]				
	Total	White	Black	American Indian or Alaskan Native	Asian or Pacific Islander	Total	White	Black	American Indian or Alaskan Native	Asian or Pacific Islander
TOTAL	**1,259,313**	**874,121**	**349,137**	**15,617**	**20,438**	**100.0**	**69.4**	**27.7**	**1.2**	**1.6**
Murder and nonnegligent manslaughter	614	283	317	3	11	100.0	46.1	51.6	0.5	1.8
Forcible rape	2,115	1,247	826	17	25	100.0	59.0	39.1	0.8	1.2
Robbery	15,532	5,434	9,778	72	248	100.0	35.0	63.0	0.5	1.6
Aggravated assault	34,123	19,395	13,957	290	481	100.0	56.8	40.9	0.8	1.4
Burglary	43,837	30,163	12,606	466	602	100.0	68.8	28.8	1.1	1.4
Larceny-theft	199,539	139,169	53,083	3,178	4,109	100.0	69.7	26.6	1.6	2.1
Motor vehicle theft	24,568	12,938	10,783	314	533	100.0	52.7	43.9	1.3	2.2
Arson	4,342	3,482	781	38	41	100.0	80.2	18.0	0.9	0.9
Violent crime[2]	52,384	26,359	24,878	382	765	100.0	50.3	47.5	0.7	1.5
Property crime[2]	272,286	185,752	77,253	3,996	5,285	100.0	68.2	28.4	1.5	1.9
Other assaults	130,237	78,412	48,696	1,379	1,750	100.0	60.2	37.4	1.1	1.3
Forgery and counterfeiting	2,616	1,990	565	21	40	100.0	76.1	21.6	0.8	1.5
Fraud	4,433	2,805	1,527	29	72	100.0	63.3	34.4	0.7	1.6
Embezzlement	635	449	174	3	9	100.0	70.7	27.4	0.5	1.4
Stolen property; buying, receiving, possessing	14,206	7,760	6,115	132	199	100.0	54.6	43.0	0.9	1.4
Vandalism	59,445	46,991	11,081	694	679	100.0	79.0	18.6	1.2	1.1
Weapons; carrying, possessing, etc.	22,541	14,691	7,327	129	394	100.0	65.2	32.5	0.6	1.7
Prostitution and commercialized vice	894	440	436	4	14	100.0	49.2	48.8	0.4	1.6
Sex offenses (except forcible rape and prostitution)	9,021	6,132	2,691	47	151	100.0	68.0	29.8	0.5	1.7
Drug abuse violations	109,296	76,145	31,267	885	999	100.0	69.7	28.6	0.8	0.9
Gambling	1,066	97	956	0	13	100.0	9.1	89.7	0.0	1.2
Offenses against the family and children	3,444	2,557	741	72	74	100.0	74.2	21.5	2.1	2.1
Driving under the influence	9,542	8,903	391	167	81	100.0	93.3	4.1	1.8	0.8
Liquor laws	72,940	66,510	3,442	2,137	851	100.0	91.2	4.7	2.9	1.2
Drunkenness	10,735	9,472	946	221	96	100.0	88.2	8.8	2.1	0.9
Disorderly conduct	117,817	75,411	40,131	1,138	1,137	100.0	64.0	34.1	1.0	1.0
Vagrancy	1,410	869	526	7	8	100.0	61.6	37.3	0.5	0.6
All other offenses (except traffic)	210,944	156,472	48,535	2,319	3,618	100.0	74.2	23.0	1.1	1.7
Suspicion	329	221	105	3	0	100.0	67.2	31.9	0.9	0.0
Curfew and loitering law violations	89,974	60,729	27,710	666	869	100.0	67.5	30.8	0.7	1.0
Runaways	63,118	44,954	13,644	1,186	3,334	100.0	71.2	21.6	1.9	5.3

See footnotes at end of table.

Table 49

Arrests

City
by Race, 2003—Continued
[7,894 agencies; 2003 estimated population 138,953,128]

Offense charged	Arrests 18 and over					Percent distribution[1]				
	Total	White	Black	American Indian or Alaskan Native	Asian or Pacific Islander	Total	White	Black	American Indian or Alaskan Native	Asian or Pacific Islander
TOTAL	**5,822,566**	**3,952,831**	**1,728,904**	**76,636**	**64,195**	**100.0**	**67.9**	**29.7**	**1.3**	**1.1**
Murder and nonnegligent manslaughter	6,005	2,532	3,347	46	80	100.0	42.2	55.7	0.8	1.3
Forcible rape	10,990	6,452	4,248	124	166	100.0	58.7	38.7	1.1	1.5
Robbery	47,752	21,682	25,294	290	486	100.0	45.4	53.0	0.6	1.0
Aggravated assault	204,288	127,717	71,907	2,019	2,645	100.0	62.5	35.2	1.0	1.3
Burglary	103,796	69,065	32,892	813	1,026	100.0	66.5	31.7	0.8	1.0
Larceny-theft	479,465	321,541	145,402	6,013	6,509	100.0	67.1	30.3	1.3	1.4
Motor vehicle theft	57,806	34,316	22,043	466	981	100.0	59.4	38.1	0.8	1.7
Arson	3,646	2,483	1,104	33	26	100.0	68.1	30.3	0.9	0.7
Violent crime[2]	269,035	158,383	104,796	2,479	3,377	100.0	58.9	39.0	0.9	1.3
Property crime[2]	644,713	427,405	201,441	7,325	8,542	100.0	66.3	31.2	1.1	1.3
Other assaults	518,335	328,077	177,013	7,200	6,045	100.0	63.3	34.2	1.4	1.2
Forgery and counterfeiting	57,111	38,595	17,469	298	749	100.0	67.6	30.6	0.5	1.3
Fraud	119,797	76,682	41,569	613	933	100.0	64.0	34.7	0.5	0.8
Embezzlement	8,230	5,527	2,544	42	117	100.0	67.2	30.9	0.5	1.4
Stolen property; buying, receiving, possessing	54,249	31,262	22,086	321	580	100.0	57.6	40.7	0.6	1.1
Vandalism	89,346	63,653	23,308	1,329	1,056	100.0	71.2	26.1	1.5	1.2
Weapons; carrying, possessing, etc.	68,491	39,165	28,244	401	681	100.0	57.2	41.2	0.6	1.0
Prostitution and commercialized vice	47,369	27,136	19,120	232	881	100.0	57.3	40.4	0.5	1.9
Sex offenses (except forcible rape and prostitution)	36,668	25,887	9,827	373	581	100.0	70.6	26.8	1.0	1.6
Drug abuse violations	770,965	469,692	291,468	3,901	5,904	100.0	60.9	37.8	0.5	0.8
Gambling	5,001	1,093	3,793	7	108	100.0	21.9	75.8	0.1	2.2
Offenses against the family and children	41,756	28,520	11,555	812	869	100.0	68.3	27.7	1.9	2.1
Driving under the influence	597,636	523,339	59,848	8,146	6,303	100.0	87.6	10.0	1.4	1.1
Liquor laws	267,743	226,840	30,238	8,022	2,643	100.0	84.7	11.3	3.0	1.0
Drunkenness	317,952	263,667	43,945	8,502	1,838	100.0	82.9	13.8	2.7	0.6
Disorderly conduct	269,582	181,560	81,732	4,414	1,876	100.0	67.3	30.3	1.6	0.7
Vagrancy	16,099	8,600	7,044	329	126	100.0	53.4	43.8	2.0	0.8
All other offenses (except traffic)	1,621,721	1,027,256	551,608	21,882	20,975	100.0	63.3	34.0	1.3	1.3
Suspicion	767	492	256	8	11	100.0	64.1	33.4	1.0	1.4
Curfew and loitering law violations	–	–	–	–	–	–	–	–	–	–
Runaways	–	–	–	–	–	–	–	–	–	–

[1] Because of rounding, the percentages may not add to 100.0.
[2] Violent crimes are offenses of murder, forcible rape, robbery, and aggravated assault. Property crimes are offenses of burglary, larceny-theft, motor vehicle theft, and arson.

Table 50

Arrest Trends
Metropolitan Counties, 2002-2003
[1,046 agencies; 2003 estimated population 42,015,453; 2002 estimated population 41,347,805]

| | Number of persons arrested | | | | | | | | |
| | Total all ages | | | Under 18 years of age | | | 18 years of age and over | | |
Offense charged	2002	2003	Percent change	2002	2003	Percent change	2002	2003	Percent change
TOTAL[1]	**1,550,107**	**1,566,304**	**+1.0**	**205,018**	**207,239**	**+1.1**	**1,345,089**	**1,359,065**	**+1.0**
Murder and nonnegligent manslaughter	1,666	1,479	-11.2	104	99	-4.8	1,562	1,380	-11.7
Forcible rape	3,538	3,307	-6.5	557	539	-3.2	2,981	2,768	-7.1
Robbery	9,001	9,338	+3.7	1,831	1,969	+7.5	7,170	7,369	+2.8
Aggravated assault	52,176	51,819	-0.7	6,496	6,547	+0.8	45,680	45,272	-0.9
Burglary	34,338	35,872	+4.5	10,013	10,453	+4.4	24,325	25,419	+4.5
Larceny-theft	96,760	98,303	+1.6	24,206	24,051	-0.6	72,554	74,252	+2.3
Motor vehicle theft	15,659	16,201	+3.5	4,223	4,237	+0.3	11,436	11,964	+4.6
Arson	2,399	2,201	-8.3	1,061	1,013	-4.5	1,338	1,188	-11.2
Violent crime[2]	66,381	65,943	-0.7	8,988	9,154	+1.8	57,393	56,789	-1.1
Property crime[2]	149,156	152,577	+2.3	39,503	39,754	+0.6	109,653	112,823	+2.9
Other assaults	151,641	152,595	+0.6	27,540	29,320	+6.5	124,101	123,275	-0.7
Forgery and counterfeiting	12,698	12,103	-4.7	491	457	-6.9	12,207	11,646	-4.6
Fraud	51,514	47,987	-6.8	818	775	-5.3	50,696	47,212	-6.9
Embezzlement	2,294	2,153	-6.1	161	148	-8.1	2,133	2,005	-6.0
Stolen property; buying, receiving, possessing	13,509	14,031	+3.9	2,167	2,003	-7.6	11,342	12,028	+6.0
Vandalism	28,276	28,681	+1.4	10,557	10,961	+3.8	17,719	17,720	*
Weapons; carrying, possessing, etc.	16,418	17,185	+4.7	3,183	3,586	+12.7	13,235	13,599	+2.8
Prostitution and commercialized vice	2,491	2,743	+10.1	55	55	0.0	2,436	2,688	+10.3
Sex offenses (except forcible rape and prostitution)	11,741	11,293	-3.8	2,351	2,281	-3.0	9,390	9,012	-4.0
Drug abuse violations	169,886	180,605	+6.3	17,943	19,720	+9.9	151,943	160,885	+5.9
Gambling	665	634	-4.7	28	50	+78.6	637	584	-8.3
Offenses against the family and children	28,804	26,489	-8.0	903	676	-25.1	27,901	25,813	-7.5
Driving under the influence	224,333	226,295	+0.9	2,581	2,575	-0.2	221,752	223,720	+0.9
Liquor laws	50,224	49,536	-1.4	13,982	13,253	-5.2	36,242	36,283	+0.1
Drunkenness	41,014	39,253	-4.3	1,339	1,233	-7.9	39,675	38,020	-4.2
Disorderly conduct	38,993	39,242	+0.6	11,963	12,906	+7.9	27,030	26,336	-2.6
Vagrancy	1,626	1,807	+11.1	162	143	-11.7	1,464	1,664	+13.7
All other offenses (except traffic)	466,151	474,378	+1.8	38,011	37,415	-1.6	428,140	436,963	+2.1
Suspicion	700	73	-89.6	69	24	-65.2	631	49	-92.2
Curfew and loitering law violations	4,527	3,655	-19.3	4,527	3,655	-19.3	–	–	–
Runaways	17,765	17,119	-3.6	17,765	17,119	-3.6	–	–	–

[1] Does not include suspicion.

[2] Violent crimes are offenses of murder, forcible rape, robbery, and aggravated assault. Property crimes are offenses of burglary, larceny-theft, motor vehicle theft, and arson.

* Less than one-tenth of 1 percent.

Table 51

Arrest Trends
Metropolitan Counties
by Sex, 2002-2003
[1,046 agencies; 2003 estimated population 42,015,453; 2002 estimated population 41,347,805]

| | Male | | | | | | Female | | | | | |
| | Total | | | Under 18 | | | Total | | | Under 18 | | |
Offense charged	2002	2003	Percent change	2002	2003	Percent change	2002	2003	Percent change	2002	2003	Percent change
TOTAL[1]	1,206,837	1,215,601	+0.7	147,243	148,258	+0.7	343,270	350,703	+2.2	57,775	58,981	+2.1
Murder and nonnegligent manslaughter	1,455	1,301	-10.6	89	89	0.0	211	178	-15.6	15	10	-33.3
Forcible rape	3,484	3,250	-6.7	543	533	-1.8	54	57	+5.6	14	6	-57.1
Robbery	8,144	8,391	+3.0	1,677	1,812	+8.1	857	947	+10.5	154	157	+1.9
Aggravated assault	42,253	41,739	-1.2	5,034	5,074	+0.8	9,923	10,080	+1.6	1,462	1,473	+0.8
Burglary	30,121	31,394	+4.2	9,040	9,430	+4.3	4,217	4,478	+6.2	973	1,023	+5.1
Larceny-theft	63,319	64,241	+1.5	15,661	15,362	-1.9	33,441	34,062	+1.9	8,545	8,689	+1.7
Motor vehicle theft	13,173	13,593	+3.2	3,494	3,537	+1.2	2,486	2,608	+4.9	729	700	-4.0
Arson	2,046	1,879	-8.2	932	884	-5.2	353	322	-8.8	129	129	0.0
Violent crime[2]	55,336	54,681	-1.2	7,343	7,508	+2.2	11,045	11,262	+2.0	1,645	1,646	+0.1
Property crime[2]	108,659	111,107	+2.3	29,127	29,213	+0.3	40,497	41,470	+2.4	10,376	10,541	+1.6
Other assaults	115,154	115,334	+0.2	19,040	20,082	+5.5	36,487	37,261	+2.1	8,500	9,238	+8.7
Forgery and counterfeiting	7,859	7,464	-5.0	346	321	-7.2	4,839	4,639	-4.1	145	136	-6.2
Fraud	27,020	25,598	-5.3	535	548	+2.4	24,494	22,389	-8.6	283	227	-19.8
Embezzlement	1,200	1,099	-8.4	95	88	-7.4	1,094	1,054	-3.7	66	60	-9.1
Stolen property; buying, receiving, possessing	11,138	11,563	+3.8	1,844	1,694	-8.1	2,371	2,468	+4.1	323	309	-4.3
Vandalism	23,901	24,233	+1.4	9,176	9,517	+3.7	4,375	4,448	+1.7	1,381	1,444	+4.6
Weapons; carrying, possessing, etc.	14,998	15,758	+5.1	2,793	3,200	+14.6	1,420	1,427	+0.5	390	386	-1.0
Prostitution and commercialized vice	1,218	1,207	-0.9	31	34	+9.7	1,273	1,536	+20.7	24	21	-12.5
Sex offenses (except forcible rape and prostitution)	11,110	10,671	-4.0	2,174	2,104	-3.2	631	622	-1.4	177	177	0.0
Drug abuse violations	137,688	145,968	+6.0	14,834	16,291	+9.8	32,198	34,637	+7.6	3,109	3,429	+10.3
Gambling	520	489	-6.0	24	47	+95.8	145	145	0.0	4	3	-25.0
Offenses against the family and children	24,044	22,018	-8.4	565	455	-19.5	4,760	4,471	-6.1	338	221	-34.6
Driving under the influence	187,141	187,347	+0.1	2,090	2,048	-2.0	37,192	38,948	+4.7	491	527	+7.3
Liquor laws	38,047	36,726	-3.5	9,356	8,505	-9.1	12,177	12,810	+5.2	4,626	4,748	+2.6
Drunkenness	34,615	33,149	-4.2	1,025	936	-8.7	6,399	6,104	-4.6	314	297	-5.4
Disorderly conduct	28,996	29,033	+0.1	8,292	8,855	+6.8	9,997	10,209	+2.1	3,671	4,051	+10.4
Vagrancy	1,241	1,432	+15.4	120	113	-5.8	385	375	-2.6	42	30	-28.6
All other offenses (except traffic)	366,445	371,154	+1.3	27,926	27,129	-2.9	99,706	103,224	+3.5	10,085	10,286	+2.0
Suspicion	530	54	-89.8	38	19	-50.0	170	19	-88.8	31	5	-83.9
Curfew and loitering law violations	2,976	2,447	-17.8	2,976	2,447	-17.8	1,551	1,208	-22.1	1,551	1,208	-22.1
Runaways	7,531	7,123	-5.4	7,531	7,123	-5.4	10,234	9,996	-2.3	10,234	9,996	-2.3

[1] Does not include suspicion.

[2] Violent crimes are offenses of murder, forcible rape, robbery, and aggravated assault. Property crimes are offenses of burglary, larceny-theft, motor vehicle theft, and arson.

Table 52

Arrests

Metropolitan Counties
by Age, 2003
[1,158 agencies; 2003 estimated population 45,269,822]

Offense charged	Total all ages	Ages under 15	Ages under 18	Ages 18 and over	Under 10	10-12	13-14	15	16	17	18	19	20	21
TOTAL	**1,689,583**	**66,679**	**220,711**	**1,468,872**	**2,603**	**15,237**	**48,839**	**41,289**	**51,914**	**60,829**	**75,616**	**76,403**	**76,258**	**71,677**
Percent distribution[1]	**100.0**	**3.9**	**13.1**	**86.9**	**0.2**	**0.9**	**2.9**	**2.4**	**3.1**	**3.6**	**4.5**	**4.5**	**4.5**	**4.2**
Murder and nonnegligent manslaughter	1,719	8	112	1,607	0	1	7	10	33	61	101	99	103	94
Forcible rape	3,547	195	560	2,987	4	52	139	98	118	149	196	194	181	164
Robbery	10,347	463	2,125	8,222	8	72	383	398	547	717	1,046	764	676	593
Aggravated assault	57,201	2,475	6,990	50,211	99	602	1,774	1,250	1,482	1,783	2,070	2,020	2,107	2,122
Burglary	38,700	3,561	11,058	27,642	161	892	2,508	2,116	2,533	2,848	3,303	2,648	2,045	1,778
Larceny-theft	104,698	8,721	25,333	79,365	248	2,165	6,308	4,608	5,677	6,327	6,395	5,461	4,764	3,957
Motor vehicle theft	17,883	1,024	4,582	13,301	4	109	911	1,082	1,180	1,296	1,286	1,114	970	779
Arson	2,427	617	1,123	1,304	52	185	380	201	168	137	120	102	82	65
Violent crime[2]	72,814	3,141	9,787	63,027	111	727	2,303	1,756	2,180	2,710	3,413	3,077	3,067	2,973
Percent distribution[1]	100.0	4.3	13.4	86.6	0.2	1.0	3.2	2.4	3.0	3.7	4.7	4.2	4.2	4.1
Property crime[2]	163,708	13,923	42,096	121,612	465	3,351	10,107	8,007	9,558	10,608	11,104	9,325	7,861	6,579
Percent distribution[1]	100.0	8.5	25.7	74.3	0.3	2.0	6.2	4.9	5.8	6.5	6.8	5.7	4.8	4.0
Other assaults	161,436	12,898	30,992	130,444	521	3,549	8,828	5,875	6,270	5,949	5,367	4,820	5,217	5,266
Forgery and counterfeiting	13,709	74	489	13,220	2	13	59	66	108	241	440	620	679	652
Fraud	52,366	127	827	51,539	4	24	99	126	215	359	809	1,468	1,691	1,979
Embezzlement	2,318	4	151	2,167	0	1	3	3	63	81	136	113	123	108
Stolen property; buying, receiving, possessing	15,452	517	2,196	13,256	12	96	409	418	576	685	1,033	899	869	783
Vandalism	30,170	4,560	11,554	18,616	344	1,334	2,882	1,959	2,443	2,592	2,128	1,695	1,284	1,169
Weapons; carrying, possessing, etc.	19,532	1,444	4,029	15,503	77	384	983	734	822	1,029	1,242	1,073	985	987
Prostitution and commercialized vice	2,985	11	63	2,922	2	1	8	14	21	17	56	62	67	85
Sex offenses (except forcible rape and prostitution)	12,515	1,238	2,490	10,025	70	364	804	450	386	416	526	495	481	440
Drug abuse violations	199,921	3,371	20,919	179,002	68	432	2,871	3,313	5,351	8,884	12,764	12,540	11,961	10,672
Gambling	717	25	65	652	1	9	15	6	15	19	39	39	38	18
Offenses against the family and children	36,120	318	830	35,290	42	69	207	146	174	192	440	434	626	768
Driving under the influence	238,681	61	2,699	235,982	18	2	41	100	646	1,892	5,102	6,796	8,210	11,265
Liquor laws	51,533	1,078	13,747	37,786	25	72	981	1,963	3,808	6,898	9,749	9,088	7,199	1,310
Drunkenness	40,255	170	1,274	38,981	5	13	152	194	293	617	1,348	1,463	1,500	1,784
Disorderly conduct	42,992	5,675	13,685	29,307	171	1,550	3,954	2,722	2,897	2,391	2,193	1,669	1,463	1,532
Vagrancy	2,185	36	165	2,020	3	4	29	25	36	68	90	80	96	77
All other offenses (except traffic)	507,655	10,684	40,663	466,992	513	2,158	8,013	7,933	9,972	12,074	17,616	20,618	22,815	23,206
Suspicion	562	8	33	529	0	1	7	4	14	7	21	29	26	24
Curfew and loitering law violations	3,727	1,003	3,727	–	13	142	848	817	1,155	752	–	–	–	–
Runaways	18,230	6,313	18,230	–	136	941	5,236	4,658	4,911	2,348	–	–	–	–

See footnotes at end of table.

Table 52

Arrests
Metropolitan Counties
by Age, 2003—Continued
[1,158 agencies; 2003 estimated population 45,269,822]

Offense charged	22	23	24	25-29	30-34	35-39	40-44	45-49	50-54	55-59	60-64	65 and over
TOTAL	**68,642**	**64,968**	**59,198**	**227,401**	**201,660**	**187,009**	**162,945**	**101,389**	**50,952**	**24,062**	**11,162**	**9,530**
Percent distribution[1]	**4.1**	**3.8**	**3.5**	**13.5**	**11.9**	**11.1**	**9.6**	**6.0**	**3.0**	**1.4**	**0.7**	**0.6**
Murder and nonnegligent manslaughter	91	88	70	266	176	162	129	85	65	36	18	24
Forcible rape	133	111	117	396	398	393	278	167	106	72	35	46
Robbery	512	467	398	1,178	895	778	513	259	81	34	13	15
Aggravated assault	2,091	1,984	1,868	7,975	7,150	7,025	6,218	3,783	1,932	926	460	480
Burglary	1,598	1,383	1,128	3,946	3,282	2,730	2,063	1,088	382	159	54	55
Larceny-theft	3,582	3,261	2,919	11,020	10,433	9,884	8,055	5,121	2,362	1,151	540	460
Motor vehicle theft	757	663	645	2,187	1,793	1,389	959	444	190	71	21	33
Arson	56	47	30	181	158	135	127	95	51	24	11	20
Violent crime[2]	2,827	2,650	2,453	9,815	8,619	8,358	7,138	4,294	2,184	1,068	526	565
Percent distribution[1]	3.9	3.6	3.4	13.5	11.8	11.5	9.8	5.9	3.0	1.5	0.7	0.8
Property crime[2]	5,993	5,354	4,722	17,334	15,666	14,138	11,204	6,748	2,985	1,405	626	568
Percent distribution[1]	3.7	3.3	2.9	10.6	9.6	8.6	6.8	4.1	1.8	0.9	0.4	0.3
Other assaults	5,379	5,331	5,122	19,402	19,341	19,091	16,637	10,038	4,813	2,361	1,158	1,101
Forgery and counterfeiting	638	563	541	2,412	2,206	1,846	1,310	781	315	133	52	32
Fraud	2,084	2,103	1,976	9,290	8,885	7,965	5,953	3,674	1,885	982	440	355
Embezzlement	104	95	66	336	316	269	220	139	82	36	13	11
Stolen property; buying, receiving, possessing	663	612	506	2,162	1,863	1,552	1,172	625	282	119	62	54
Vandalism	983	853	745	2,514	2,151	1,889	1,548	844	407	199	99	108
Weapons; carrying, possessing, etc.	915	832	708	2,372	1,719	1,506	1,292	858	493	240	164	117
Prostitution and commercialized vice	64	75	77	383	513	547	444	266	147	72	27	37
Sex offenses (except forcible rape and prostitution)	391	313	307	1,228	1,187	1,252	1,143	773	574	372	251	292
Drug abuse violations	9,844	9,082	8,070	28,392	22,006	19,900	17,081	9,937	4,372	1,533	549	299
Gambling	20	21	13	69	67	69	75	64	42	41	14	23
Offenses against the family and children	838	988	1,072	5,699	7,097	6,577	5,453	3,130	1,316	556	193	103
Driving under the influence	11,467	11,051	10,016	38,676	32,197	28,854	28,161	20,181	11,857	6,427	3,139	2,583
Liquor laws	880	741	563	1,867	1,461	1,489	1,439	908	599	278	132	83
Drunkenness	1,630	1,434	1,264	4,991	4,717	5,039	5,508	4,061	2,333	1,072	496	341
Disorderly conduct	1,408	1,307	1,112	4,167	3,575	3,462	3,252	2,043	1,104	518	246	256
Vagrancy	82	71	59	259	272	295	258	208	93	46	19	15
All other offenses (except traffic)	22,399	21,466	19,782	75,960	67,720	62,853	53,602	31,789	15,047	6,594	2,941	2,584
Suspicion	33	26	24	73	82	58	55	28	22	10	15	3
Curfew and loitering law violations	–	–	–	–	–	–	–	–	–	–	–	–
Runaways	–	–	–	–	–	–	–	–	–	–	–	–

[1] Because of rounding, the percentages may not add to 100.0.
[2] Violent crimes are offenses of murder, forcible rape, robbery, and aggravated assault. Property crimes are offenses of burglary, larceny-theft, motor vehicle theft, and arson.

Table 53

Arrests

Metropolitan Counties
of Persons Under 15, 18, 21, and 25 Years of Age, 2003
[1,158 agencies; 2003 estimated population 45,269,822]

Offense charged	Total all ages	Number of persons arrested				Percent of total all ages			
		Under 15	Under 18	Under 21	Under 25	Under 15	Under 18	Under 21	Under 25
TOTAL	**1,689,583**	**66,679**	**220,711**	**448,988**	**713,473**	**3.9**	**13.1**	**26.6**	**42.2**
Murder and nonnegligent manslaughter	1,719	8	112	415	758	0.5	6.5	24.1	44.1
Forcible rape	3,547	195	560	1,131	1,656	5.5	15.8	31.9	46.7
Robbery	10,347	463	2,125	4,611	6,581	4.5	20.5	44.6	63.6
Aggravated assault	57,201	2,475	6,990	13,187	21,252	4.3	12.2	23.1	37.2
Burglary	38,700	3,561	11,058	19,054	24,941	9.2	28.6	49.2	64.4
Larceny-theft	104,698	8,721	25,333	41,953	55,672	8.3	24.2	40.1	53.2
Motor vehicle theft	17,883	1,024	4,582	7,952	10,796	5.7	25.6	44.5	60.4
Arson	2,427	617	1,123	1,427	1,625	25.4	46.3	58.8	67.0
Violent crime[1]	72,814	3,141	9,787	19,344	30,247	4.3	13.4	26.6	41.5
Property crime[1]	163,708	13,923	42,096	70,386	93,034	8.5	25.7	43.0	56.8
Other assaults	161,436	12,898	30,992	46,396	67,494	8.0	19.2	28.7	41.8
Forgery and counterfeiting	13,709	74	489	2,228	4,622	0.5	3.6	16.3	33.7
Fraud	52,366	127	827	4,795	12,937	0.2	1.6	9.2	24.7
Embezzlement	2,318	4	151	523	896	0.2	6.5	22.6	38.7
Stolen property; buying, receiving, possessing	15,452	517	2,196	4,997	7,561	3.3	14.2	32.3	48.9
Vandalism	30,170	4,560	11,554	16,661	20,411	15.1	38.3	55.2	67.7
Weapons; carrying, possessing, etc.	19,532	1,444	4,029	7,329	10,771	7.4	20.6	37.5	55.1
Prostitution and commercialized vice	2,985	11	63	248	549	0.4	2.1	8.3	18.4
Sex offenses (except forcible rape and prostitution)	12,515	1,238	2,490	3,992	5,443	9.9	19.9	31.9	43.5
Drug abuse violations	199,921	3,371	20,919	58,184	95,852	1.7	10.5	29.1	47.9
Gambling	717	25	65	181	253	3.5	9.1	25.2	35.3
Offenses against the family and children	36,120	318	830	2,330	5,996	0.9	2.3	6.5	16.6
Driving under the influence	238,681	61	2,699	22,807	66,606	*	1.1	9.6	27.9
Liquor laws	51,533	1,078	13,747	39,783	43,277	2.1	26.7	77.2	84.0
Drunkenness	40,255	170	1,274	5,585	11,697	0.4	3.2	13.9	29.1
Disorderly conduct	42,992	5,675	13,685	19,010	24,369	13.2	31.8	44.2	56.7
Vagrancy	2,185	36	165	431	720	1.6	7.6	19.7	33.0
All other offenses (except traffic)	507,655	10,684	40,663	101,712	188,565	2.1	8.0	20.0	37.1
Suspicion	562	8	33	109	216	1.4	5.9	19.4	38.4
Curfew and loitering law violations	3,727	1,003	3,727	3,727	3,727	26.9	100.0	100.0	100.0
Runaways	18,230	6,313	18,230	18,230	18,230	34.6	100.0	100.0	100.0

[1] Violent crimes are offenses of murder, forcible rape, robbery, and aggravated assault. Property crimes are offenses of burglary, larceny-theft, motor vehicle theft, and arson.
* Less than one-tenth of 1 percent.

Table 54

Arrests

Metropolitan Counties
by Sex, 2003
[1,158 agencies; 2003 estimated population 45,269,822]

Offense charged	Number of persons arrested			Percent male	Percent female	Percent distribution[1]		
	Total	Male	Female			Total	Male	Female
TOTAL	**1,689,583**	**1,313,835**	**375,748**	**77.8**	**22.2**	**100.0**	**100.0**	**100.0**
Murder and nonnegligent manslaughter	1,719	1,519	200	88.4	11.6	0.1	0.1	0.1
Forcible rape	3,547	3,485	62	98.3	1.7	0.2	0.3	*
Robbery	10,347	9,286	1,061	89.7	10.3	0.6	0.7	0.3
Aggravated assault	57,201	46,191	11,010	80.8	19.2	3.4	3.5	2.9
Burglary	38,700	33,866	4,834	87.5	12.5	2.3	2.6	1.3
Larceny-theft	104,698	68,716	35,982	65.6	34.4	6.2	5.2	9.6
Motor vehicle theft	17,883	14,997	2,886	83.9	16.1	1.1	1.1	0.8
Arson	2,427	2,055	372	84.7	15.3	0.1	0.2	0.1
Violent crime[2]	72,814	60,481	12,333	83.1	16.9	4.3	4.6	3.3
Property crime[2]	163,708	119,634	44,074	73.1	26.9	9.7	9.1	11.7
Other assaults	161,436	122,180	39,256	75.7	24.3	9.6	9.3	10.4
Forgery and counterfeiting	13,709	8,483	5,226	61.9	38.1	0.8	0.6	1.4
Fraud	52,366	27,896	24,470	53.3	46.7	3.1	2.1	6.5
Embezzlement	2,318	1,216	1,102	52.5	47.5	0.1	0.1	0.3
Stolen property; buying, receiving, possessing	15,452	12,793	2,659	82.8	17.2	0.9	1.0	0.7
Vandalism	30,170	25,492	4,678	84.5	15.5	1.8	1.9	1.2
Weapons; carrying, possessing, etc.	19,532	17,949	1,583	91.9	8.1	1.2	1.4	0.4
Prostitution and commercialized vice	2,985	1,316	1,669	44.1	55.9	0.2	0.1	0.4
Sex offenses (except forcible rape and prostitution)	12,515	11,779	736	94.1	5.9	0.7	0.9	0.2
Drug abuse violations	199,921	161,937	37,984	81.0	19.0	11.8	12.3	10.1
Gambling	717	548	169	76.4	23.6	*	*	*
Offenses against the family and children	36,120	30,680	5,440	84.9	15.1	2.1	2.3	1.4
Driving under the influence	238,681	197,590	41,091	82.8	17.2	14.1	15.0	10.9
Liquor laws	51,533	38,240	13,293	74.2	25.8	3.1	2.9	3.5
Drunkenness	40,255	33,968	6,287	84.4	15.6	2.4	2.6	1.7
Disorderly conduct	42,992	31,757	11,235	73.9	26.1	2.5	2.4	3.0
Vagrancy	2,185	1,728	457	79.1	20.9	0.1	0.1	0.1
All other offenses (except traffic)	507,655	397,541	110,114	78.3	21.7	30.0	30.3	29.3
Suspicion	562	520	42	92.5	7.5	*	*	*
Curfew and loitering law violations	3,727	2,492	1,235	66.9	33.1	0.2	0.2	0.3
Runaways	18,230	7,615	10,615	41.8	58.2	1.1	0.6	2.8

[1] Because of rounding, the percentages may not add to 100.0.

[2] Violent crimes are offenses of murder, forcible rape, robbery, and aggravated assault. Property crimes are offenses of burglary, larceny-theft, motor vehicle theft, and arson.

* Less than one-tenth of 1 percent.

Table 55

Arrests

Metropolitan Counties
by Race, 2003
[1,158 agencies; 2003 estimated population 45,269,822]

Offense charged	Total arrests					Percent distribution[1]				
	Total	White	Black	American Indian or Alaskan Native	Asian or Pacific Islander	Total	White	Black	American Indian or Alaskan Native	Asian or Pacific Islander
TOTAL	**1,686,476**	**1,265,814**	**397,889**	**12,838**	**9,935**	**100.0**	**75.1**	**23.6**	**0.8**	**0.6**
Murder and nonnegligent manslaughter	1,718	1,137	542	18	21	100.0	66.2	31.5	1.0	1.2
Forcible rape	3,538	2,696	795	28	19	100.0	76.2	22.5	0.8	0.5
Robbery	10,347	4,952	5,297	58	40	100.0	47.9	51.2	0.6	0.4
Aggravated assault	57,080	41,478	14,720	457	425	100.0	72.7	25.8	0.8	0.7
Burglary	38,653	29,905	8,298	223	227	100.0	77.4	21.5	0.6	0.6
Larceny-theft	104,583	71,575	31,573	519	916	100.0	68.4	30.2	0.5	0.9
Motor vehicle theft	17,864	12,934	4,699	116	115	100.0	72.4	26.3	0.6	0.6
Arson	2,422	2,008	391	8	15	100.0	82.9	16.1	0.3	0.6
Violent crime[2]	72,683	50,263	21,354	561	505	100.0	69.2	29.4	0.8	0.7
Property crime[2]	163,522	116,422	44,961	866	1,273	100.0	71.2	27.5	0.5	0.8
Other assaults	161,202	115,785	43,238	1,156	1,023	100.0	71.8	26.8	0.7	0.6
Forgery and counterfeiting	13,689	9,677	3,846	65	101	100.0	70.7	28.1	0.5	0.7
Fraud	52,292	38,002	13,848	234	208	100.0	72.7	26.5	0.4	0.4
Embezzlement	2,317	1,553	727	13	24	100.0	67.0	31.4	0.6	1.0
Stolen property; buying, receiving, possessing	15,437	10,801	4,443	98	95	100.0	70.0	28.8	0.6	0.6
Vandalism	30,130	24,369	5,286	244	231	100.0	80.9	17.5	0.8	0.8
Weapons; carrying, possessing, etc.	19,520	13,489	5,765	116	150	100.0	69.1	29.5	0.6	0.8
Prostitution and commercialized vice	2,982	2,111	627	14	230	100.0	70.8	21.0	0.5	7.7
Sex offenses (except forcible rape and prostitution)	12,492	10,066	2,262	91	73	100.0	80.6	18.1	0.7	0.6
Drug abuse violations	199,646	151,917	45,763	1,005	961	100.0	76.1	22.9	0.5	0.5
Gambling	715	485	202	5	23	100.0	67.8	28.3	0.7	3.2
Offenses against the family and children	36,072	22,359	13,488	118	107	100.0	62.0	37.4	0.3	0.3
Driving under the influence	237,986	212,095	22,922	1,731	1,238	100.0	89.1	9.6	0.7	0.5
Liquor laws	51,263	46,699	3,555	664	345	100.0	91.1	6.9	1.3	0.7
Drunkenness	40,208	36,115	3,445	457	191	100.0	89.8	8.6	1.1	0.5
Disorderly conduct	42,965	30,875	11,497	368	225	100.0	71.9	26.8	0.9	0.5
Vagrancy	2,184	1,517	653	7	7	100.0	69.5	29.9	0.3	0.3
All other offenses (except traffic)	506,671	353,615	145,452	4,853	2,751	100.0	69.8	28.7	1.0	0.5
Suspicion	562	371	187	0	4	100.0	66.0	33.3	0.0	0.7
Curfew and loitering law violations	3,725	2,936	737	27	25	100.0	78.8	19.8	0.7	0.7
Runaways	18,213	14,292	3,631	145	145	100.0	78.5	19.9	0.8	0.8

See footnotes at end of table.

Table 55

Arrests

Metropolitan Counties
by Race, 2003—Continued
[1,158 agencies; 2003 estimated population 45,269,822]

| | Arrests under 18 | | | | | Percent distribution[1] | | | | |
Offense charged	Total	White	Black	American Indian or Alaskan Native	Asian or Pacific Islander	Total	White	Black	American Indian or Alaskan Native	Asian or Pacific Islander
TOTAL	**220,356**	**159,982**	**56,918**	**1,816**	**1,640**	**100.0**	**72.6**	**25.8**	**0.8**	**0.7**
Murder and nonnegligent manslaughter	112	62	46	2	2	100.0	55.4	41.1	1.8	1.8
Forcible rape	560	416	137	7	0	100.0	74.3	24.5	1.3	0.0
Robbery	2,125	761	1,346	10	8	100.0	35.8	63.3	0.5	0.4
Aggravated assault	6,971	4,689	2,174	61	47	100.0	67.3	31.2	0.9	0.7
Burglary	11,038	8,352	2,542	56	88	100.0	75.7	23.0	0.5	0.8
Larceny-theft	25,305	16,767	8,107	122	309	100.0	66.3	32.0	0.5	1.2
Motor vehicle theft	4,580	2,955	1,547	41	37	100.0	64.5	33.8	0.9	0.8
Arson	1,121	941	169	4	7	100.0	83.9	15.1	0.4	0.6
Violent crime[2]	9,768	5,928	3,703	80	57	100.0	60.7	37.9	0.8	0.6
Property crime[2]	42,044	29,015	12,365	223	441	100.0	69.0	29.4	0.5	1.0
Other assaults	30,956	19,210	11,355	235	156	100.0	62.1	36.7	0.8	0.5
Forgery and counterfeiting	489	376	105	0	8	100.0	76.9	21.5	0.0	1.6
Fraud	825	600	214	3	8	100.0	72.7	25.9	0.4	1.0
Embezzlement	151	81	67	0	3	100.0	53.6	44.4	0.0	2.0
Stolen property; buying, receiving, possessing	2,191	1,421	739	16	15	100.0	64.9	33.7	0.7	0.7
Vandalism	11,534	9,370	1,973	91	100	100.0	81.2	17.1	0.8	0.9
Weapons; carrying, possessing, etc.	4,028	2,757	1,193	31	47	100.0	68.4	29.6	0.8	1.2
Prostitution and commercialized vice	63	45	18	0	0	100.0	71.4	28.6	0.0	0.0
Sex offenses (except forcible rape and prostitution)	2,483	1,898	565	10	10	100.0	76.4	22.8	0.4	0.4
Drug abuse violations	20,898	16,821	3,799	154	124	100.0	80.5	18.2	0.7	0.6
Gambling	65	29	36	0	0	100.0	44.6	55.4	0.0	0.0
Offenses against the family and children	830	624	199	4	3	100.0	75.2	24.0	0.5	0.4
Driving under the influence	2,691	2,575	83	19	14	100.0	95.7	3.1	0.7	0.5
Liquor laws	13,686	12,922	459	209	96	100.0	94.4	3.4	1.5	0.7
Drunkenness	1,274	1,161	87	19	7	100.0	91.1	6.8	1.5	0.5
Disorderly conduct	13,675	8,317	5,150	131	77	100.0	60.8	37.7	1.0	0.6
Vagrancy	165	98	66	1	0	100.0	59.4	40.0	0.6	0.0
All other offenses (except traffic)	40,569	29,486	10,361	418	304	100.0	72.7	25.5	1.0	0.7
Suspicion	33	20	13	0	0	100.0	60.6	39.4	0.0	0.0
Curfew and loitering law violations	3,725	2,936	737	27	25	100.0	78.8	19.8	0.7	0.7
Runaways	18,213	14,292	3,631	145	145	100.0	78.5	19.9	0.8	0.8

See footnotes at end of table.

Table 55

Arrests
Metropolitan Counties
by Race, 2003—Continued
[1,158 agencies; 2003 estimated population 45,269,822]

| Offense charged | Arrests 18 and over | | | | | Percent distribution[1] | | | | |
	Total	White	Black	American Indian or Alaskan Native	Asian or Pacific Islander	Total	White	Black	American Indian or Alaskan Native	Asian or Pacific Islander
TOTAL	**1,466,120**	**1,105,832**	**340,971**	**11,022**	**8,295**	**100.0**	**75.4**	**23.3**	**0.8**	**0.6**
Murder and nonnegligent manslaughter	1,606	1,075	496	16	19	100.0	66.9	30.9	1.0	1.2
Forcible rape	2,978	2,280	658	21	19	100.0	76.6	22.1	0.7	0.6
Robbery	8,222	4,191	3,951	48	32	100.0	51.0	48.1	0.6	0.4
Aggravated assault	50,109	36,789	12,546	396	378	100.0	73.4	25.0	0.8	0.8
Burglary	27,615	21,553	5,756	167	139	100.0	78.0	20.8	0.6	0.5
Larceny-theft	79,278	54,808	23,466	397	607	100.0	69.1	29.6	0.5	0.8
Motor vehicle theft	13,284	9,979	3,152	75	78	100.0	75.1	23.7	0.6	0.6
Arson	1,301	1,067	222	4	8	100.0	82.0	17.1	0.3	0.6
Violent crime[2]	62,915	44,335	17,651	481	448	100.0	70.5	28.1	0.8	0.7
Property crime[2]	121,478	87,407	32,596	643	832	100.0	72.0	26.8	0.5	0.7
Other assaults	130,246	96,575	31,883	921	867	100.0	74.1	24.5	0.7	0.7
Forgery and counterfeiting	13,200	9,301	3,741	65	93	100.0	70.5	28.3	0.5	0.7
Fraud	51,467	37,402	13,634	231	200	100.0	72.7	26.5	0.4	0.4
Embezzlement	2,166	1,472	660	13	21	100.0	68.0	30.5	0.6	1.0
Stolen property; buying, receiving, possessing	13,246	9,380	3,704	82	80	100.0	70.8	28.0	0.6	0.6
Vandalism	18,596	14,999	3,313	153	131	100.0	80.7	17.8	0.8	0.7
Weapons; carrying, possessing, etc.	15,492	10,732	4,572	85	103	100.0	69.3	29.5	0.5	0.7
Prostitution and commercialized vice	2,919	2,066	609	14	230	100.0	70.8	20.9	0.5	7.9
Sex offenses (except forcible rape and prostitution)	10,009	8,168	1,697	81	63	100.0	81.6	17.0	0.8	0.6
Drug abuse violations	178,748	135,096	41,964	851	837	100.0	75.6	23.5	0.5	0.5
Gambling	650	456	166	5	23	100.0	70.2	25.5	0.8	3.5
Offenses against the family and children	35,242	21,735	13,289	114	104	100.0	61.7	37.7	0.3	0.3
Driving under the influence	235,295	209,520	22,839	1,712	1,224	100.0	89.0	9.7	0.7	0.5
Liquor laws	37,577	33,777	3,096	455	249	100.0	89.9	8.2	1.2	0.7
Drunkenness	38,934	34,954	3,358	438	184	100.0	89.8	8.6	1.1	0.5
Disorderly conduct	29,290	22,558	6,347	237	148	100.0	77.0	21.7	0.8	0.5
Vagrancy	2,019	1,419	587	6	7	100.0	70.3	29.1	0.3	0.3
All other offenses (except traffic)	466,102	324,129	135,091	4,435	2,447	100.0	69.5	29.0	1.0	0.5
Suspicion	529	351	174	0	4	100.0	66.4	32.9	0.0	0.8
Curfew and loitering law violations	–	–	–	–	–	–	–	–	–	–
Runaways	–	–	–	–	–	–	–	–	–	–

[1] Because of rounding, the percentages may not add to 100.0.

[2] Violent crimes are offenses of murder, forcible rape, robbery, and aggravated assault. Property crimes are offenses of burglary, larceny-theft, motor vehicle theft, and arson.

Table 56

Arrest Trends

Nonmetropolitan Counties, 2002-2003

[1,596 agencies; 2003 estimated population 17,316,132; 2002 estimated population 17,413,442]

	Number of persons arrested								
	Total all ages			Under 18 years of age			18 years of age and over		
Offense charged	2002	2003	Percent change	2002	2003	Percent change	2002	2003	Percent change
TOTAL[1]	693,962	679,043	-2.1	75,207	71,042	-5.5	618,755	608,001	-1.7
Murder and nonnegligent manslaughter	628	651	+3.7	39	52	+33.3	589	599	+1.7
Forcible rape	1,722	1,599	-7.1	244	274	+12.3	1,478	1,325	-10.4
Robbery	1,548	1,578	+1.9	190	182	-4.2	1,358	1,396	+2.8
Aggravated assault	18,135	17,208	-5.1	1,779	1,704	-4.2	16,356	15,504	-5.2
Burglary	16,759	16,213	-3.3	4,673	4,453	-4.7	12,086	11,760	-2.7
Larceny-theft	27,154	26,416	-2.7	6,496	5,701	-12.2	20,658	20,715	+0.3
Motor vehicle theft	5,525	5,193	-6.0	1,754	1,535	-12.5	3,771	3,658	-3.0
Arson	900	781	-13.2	280	253	-9.6	620	528	-14.8
Violent crime[2]	22,033	21,036	-4.5	2,252	2,212	-1.8	19,781	18,824	-4.8
Property crime[2]	50,338	48,603	-3.4	13,203	11,942	-9.6	37,135	36,661	-1.3
Other assaults	59,504	57,851	-2.8	7,485	7,779	+3.9	52,019	50,072	-3.7
Forgery and counterfeiting	4,911	4,753	-3.2	219	193	-11.9	4,692	4,560	-2.8
Fraud	28,459	28,310	-0.5	386	341	-11.7	28,073	27,969	-0.4
Embezzlement	697	706	+1.3	24	30	+25.0	673	676	+0.4
Stolen property; buying, receiving, possessing	4,114	4,230	+2.8	537	583	+8.6	3,577	3,647	+2.0
Vandalism	12,166	12,572	+3.3	4,192	4,488	+7.1	7,974	8,084	+1.4
Weapons; carrying, possessing, etc.	6,422	6,131	-4.5	736	718	-2.4	5,686	5,413	-4.8
Prostitution and commercialized vice	114	100	-12.3	11	9	-18.2	103	91	-11.7
Sex offenses (except forcible rape and prostitution)	5,249	5,028	-4.2	1,158	1,131	-2.3	4,091	3,897	-4.7
Drug abuse violations	72,929	74,862	+2.7	6,282	6,191	-1.4	66,647	68,671	+3.0
Gambling	707	566	-19.9	6	17	+183.3	701	549	-21.7
Offenses against the family and children	11,623	11,726	+0.9	571	558	-2.3	11,052	11,168	+1.0
Driving under the influence	133,790	124,581	-6.9	2,082	1,793	-13.9	131,708	122,788	-6.8
Liquor laws	39,128	34,269	-12.4	10,347	8,570	-17.2	28,781	25,699	-10.7
Drunkenness	20,094	18,391	-8.5	505	446	-11.7	19,589	17,945	-8.4
Disorderly conduct	20,317	20,004	-1.5	4,601	4,626	+0.5	15,716	15,378	-2.2
Vagrancy	287	306	+6.6	40	18	-55.0	247	288	+16.6
All other offenses (except traffic)	194,541	198,379	+2.0	14,031	12,758	-9.1	180,510	185,621	+2.8
Suspicion	129	127	-1.6	20	22	+10.0	109	105	-3.7
Curfew and loitering law violations	983	1,095	+11.4	983	1,095	+11.4	–	–	–
Runaways	5,556	5,544	-0.2	5,556	5,544	-0.2	–	–	–

[1] Does not include suspicion.

[2] Violent crimes are offenses of murder, forcible rape, robbery, and aggravated assault. Property crimes are offenses of burglary, larceny-theft, motor vehicle theft, and arson.

Table 57

Arrest Trends

Nonmetropolitan Counties
by Sex, 2002-2003
[1,596 agencies; 2003 estimated population 17,316,132; 2002 estimated population 17,413,442]

| | Male | | | | | | Female | | | | | |
| | Total | | | Under 18 | | | Total | | | Under 18 | | |
Offense charged	2002	2003	Percent change	2002	2003	Percent change	2002	2003	Percent change	2002	2003	Percent change
TOTAL[1]	**546,724**	**530,534**	**-3.0**	**54,578**	**51,057**	**-6.5**	**147,238**	**148,509**	**+0.9**	**20,629**	**19,985**	**-3.1**
Murder and nonnegligent manslaughter	547	552	+0.9	34	42	+23.5	81	99	+22.2	5	10	+100.0
Forcible rape	1,703	1,562	-8.3	242	262	+8.3	19	37	+94.7	2	12	+500.0
Robbery	1,394	1,386	-0.6	174	162	-6.9	154	192	+24.7	16	20	+25.0
Aggravated assault	15,072	14,060	-6.7	1,440	1,358	-5.7	3,063	3,148	+2.8	339	346	+2.1
Burglary	14,946	14,226	-4.8	4,305	3,982	-7.5	1,813	1,987	+9.6	368	471	+28.0
Larceny-theft	19,543	18,841	-3.6	4,795	4,153	-13.4	7,611	7,575	-0.5	1,701	1,548	-9.0
Motor vehicle theft	4,603	4,256	-7.5	1,407	1,231	-12.5	922	937	+1.6	347	304	-12.4
Arson	771	671	-13.0	255	226	-11.4	129	110	-14.7	25	27	+8.0
Violent crime[2]	18,716	17,560	-6.2	1,890	1,824	-3.5	3,317	3,476	+4.8	362	388	+7.2
Property crime[2]	39,863	37,994	-4.7	10,762	9,592	-10.9	10,475	10,609	+1.3	2,441	2,350	-3.7
Other assaults	46,063	44,578	-3.2	5,233	5,381	+2.8	13,441	13,273	-1.2	2,252	2,398	+6.5
Forgery and counterfeiting	2,818	2,743	-2.7	126	131	+4.0	2,093	2,010	-4.0	93	62	-33.3
Fraud	14,856	14,596	-1.8	246	217	-11.8	13,603	13,714	+0.8	140	124	-11.4
Embezzlement	375	352	-6.1	15	15	0.0	322	354	+9.9	9	15	+66.7
Stolen property; buying, receiving, possessing	3,448	3,526	+2.3	447	501	+12.1	666	704	+5.7	90	82	-8.9
Vandalism	10,358	10,757	+3.9	3,666	3,926	+7.1	1,808	1,815	+0.4	526	562	+6.8
Weapons; carrying, possessing, etc.	5,932	5,647	-4.8	670	639	-4.6	490	484	-1.2	66	79	+19.7
Prostitution and commercialized vice	71	56	-21.1	8	5	-37.5	43	44	+2.3	3	4	+33.3
Sex offenses (except forcible rape and prostitution)	4,973	4,767	-4.1	1,067	1,035	-3.0	276	261	-5.4	91	96	+5.5
Drug abuse violations	59,139	60,020	+1.5	5,075	4,917	-3.1	13,790	14,842	+7.6	1,207	1,274	+5.6
Gambling	604	470	-22.2	6	15	+150.0	103	96	-6.8	0	2	–
Offenses against the family and children	9,415	9,495	+0.8	323	354	+9.6	2,208	2,231	+1.0	248	204	-17.7
Driving under the influence	112,680	104,067	-7.6	1,677	1,410	-15.9	21,110	20,514	-2.8	405	383	-5.4
Liquor laws	28,965	24,863	-14.2	6,739	5,308	-21.2	10,163	9,406	-7.4	3,608	3,262	-9.6
Drunkenness	17,026	15,516	-8.9	399	337	-15.5	3,068	2,875	-6.3	106	109	+2.8
Disorderly conduct	15,284	14,916	-2.4	3,209	3,170	-1.2	5,033	5,088	+1.1	1,392	1,456	+4.6
Vagrancy	231	260	+12.6	31	13	-58.1	56	46	-17.9	9	5	-44.4
All other offenses (except traffic)	153,089	155,315	+1.5	10,171	9,231	-9.2	41,452	43,064	+3.9	3,860	3,527	-8.6
Suspicion	112	107	-4.5	18	20	+11.1	17	20	+17.6	2	2	0.0
Curfew and loitering law violations	582	668	+14.8	582	668	+14.8	401	427	+6.5	401	427	+6.5
Runaways	2,236	2,368	+5.9	2,236	2,368	+5.9	3,320	3,176	-4.3	3,320	3,176	-4.3

[1] Does not include suspicion.

[2] Violent crimes are offenses of murder, forcible rape, robbery, and aggravated assault. Property crimes are offenses of burglary, larceny-theft, motor vehicle theft, and arson.

Table 58

Arrests
Nonmetropolitan Counties
by Age, 2003
[1,787 agencies; 2003 estimated population 19,266,065]

Offense charged	Total all ages	Ages under 15	Ages under 18	Ages 18 and over	Under 10	10-12	13-14	15	16	17	18	19	20	21
TOTAL	763,309	19,891	76,334	686,975	1,103	4,427	14,361	12,798	18,761	24,884	36,178	37,103	37,104	32,822
Percent distribution[1]	100.0	2.6	10.0	90.0	0.1	0.6	1.9	1.7	2.5	3.3	4.7	4.9	4.9	4.3
Murder and nonnegligent manslaughter	729	10	54	675	0	4	6	10	21	13	27	29	24	23
Forcible rape	1,718	104	284	1,434	5	16	83	52	37	91	103	85	80	76
Robbery	1,756	19	192	1,564	0	0	19	30	58	85	158	149	104	117
Aggravated assault	18,590	579	1,805	16,785	31	144	404	306	397	523	673	658	655	722
Burglary	17,784	1,487	4,787	12,997	111	392	984	788	1,118	1,394	1,747	1,384	1,112	861
Larceny-theft	29,015	2,046	6,048	22,967	77	578	1,391	1,003	1,422	1,577	2,076	1,710	1,458	1,143
Motor vehicle theft	5,682	452	1,643	4,039	5	56	391	346	450	395	385	353	276	244
Arson	879	154	273	606	17	60	77	44	40	35	55	41	33	41
Violent crime[2]	22,793	712	2,335	20,458	36	164	512	398	513	712	961	921	863	938
Percent distribution[1]	100.0	3.1	10.2	89.8	0.2	0.7	2.2	1.7	2.3	3.1	4.2	4.0	3.8	4.1
Property crime[2]	53,360	4,139	12,751	40,609	210	1,086	2,843	2,181	3,030	3,401	4,263	3,488	2,879	2,289
Percent distribution[1]	100.0	7.8	23.9	76.1	0.4	2.0	5.3	4.1	5.7	6.4	8.0	6.5	5.4	4.3
Other assaults	63,278	2,927	8,288	54,990	153	720	2,054	1,452	1,898	2,011	1,989	1,952	1,937	2,115
Forgery and counterfeiting	5,480	26	211	5,269	1	4	21	33	34	118	200	229	250	253
Fraud	31,079	49	361	30,718	5	12	32	51	94	167	540	877	1,062	1,126
Embezzlement	722	2	30	692	0	1	1	2	8	18	20	32	22	24
Stolen property; buying, receiving, possessing	5,116	125	682	4,434	2	20	103	111	209	237	381	349	305	249
Vandalism	13,520	1,864	4,787	8,733	183	551	1,130	716	1,064	1,143	1,079	793	702	570
Weapons; carrying, possessing, etc.	6,792	239	761	6,031	13	61	165	131	188	203	322	305	285	283
Prostitution and commercialized vice	111	1	9	102	0	0	1	1	3	4	5	9	4	2
Sex offenses (except forcible rape and prostitution)	5,421	545	1,194	4,227	63	125	357	214	224	211	272	225	233	192
Drug abuse violations	88,332	1,000	6,866	81,466	30	138	832	924	1,733	3,209	5,396	5,707	5,582	4,965
Gambling	612	5	20	592	0	4	1	10	0	5	12	38	30	22
Offenses against the family and children	12,928	170	576	12,352	6	29	135	99	141	166	249	229	262	335
Driving under the influence	153,192	41	2,222	150,970	12	1	28	84	538	1,559	3,769	4,578	5,562	6,851
Liquor laws	37,547	759	9,384	28,163	19	58	682	1,393	2,731	4,501	6,937	6,572	5,586	1,063
Drunkenness	19,723	58	495	19,228	11	6	41	66	110	261	660	675	723	866
Disorderly conduct	21,399	1,697	4,837	16,562	104	395	1,198	979	1,077	1,084	1,079	850	848	833
Vagrancy	349	7	19	330	0	0	7	3	2	7	16	10	12	7
All other offenses (except traffic)	214,443	3,310	13,511	200,932	201	723	2,386	2,246	3,238	4,717	8,017	9,258	9,953	9,832
Suspicion	145	3	28	117	0	1	2	12	10	3	11	6	4	7
Curfew and loitering law violations	1,157	300	1,157	–	14	45	241	261	364	232	–	–	–	–
Runaways	5,810	1,912	5,810	–	40	283	1,589	1,431	1,552	915	–	–	–	–

See footnotes at end of table.

Table 58

Arrests
Nonmetropolitan Counties
by Age, 2003—Continued
[1,787 agencies; 2003 estimated population 19,266,065]

Offense charged	22	23	24	25-29	30-34	35-39	40-44	45-49	50-54	55-59	60-64	65 and over
TOTAL	**31,013**	**29,196**	**26,192**	**102,462**	**90,230**	**84,095**	**77,101**	**49,434**	**26,893**	**13,841**	**6,959**	**6,352**
Percent distribution[1]	**4.1**	**3.8**	**3.4**	**13.4**	**11.8**	**11.0**	**10.1**	**6.5**	**3.5**	**1.8**	**0.9**	**0.8**
Murder and nonnegligent manslaughter	34	40	23	121	99	87	66	42	27	18	4	11
Forcible rape	62	52	50	185	199	164	162	91	49	36	19	21
Robbery	121	81	92	268	169	147	91	39	15	9	3	1
Aggravated assault	679	631	630	2,556	2,378	2,276	2,057	1,332	753	387	199	199
Burglary	733	669	537	1,770	1,435	1,148	871	408	195	77	27	23
Larceny-theft	1,100	971	819	3,194	2,933	2,650	2,205	1,334	676	321	203	174
Motor vehicle theft	209	175	156	658	548	404	301	192	81	36	14	7
Arson	20	18	22	80	75	65	69	35	22	13	8	9
Violent crime[2]	896	804	795	3,130	2,845	2,674	2,376	1,504	844	450	225	232
Percent distribution[1]	3.9	3.5	3.5	13.7	12.5	11.7	10.4	6.6	3.7	2.0	1.0	1.0
Property crime[2]	2,062	1,833	1,534	5,702	4,991	4,267	3,446	1,969	974	447	252	213
Percent distribution[1]	3.9	3.4	2.9	10.7	9.4	8.0	6.5	3.7	1.8	0.8	0.5	0.4
Other assaults	2,031	2,020	1,907	8,395	8,125	8,011	7,337	4,372	2,263	1,224	676	636
Forgery and counterfeiting	306	253	232	1,016	856	685	521	267	113	47	20	21
Fraud	1,203	1,168	1,177	5,369	5,196	4,523	3,560	2,286	1,275	668	348	340
Embezzlement	31	33	25	98	92	96	96	44	41	21	10	7
Stolen property; buying, receiving, possessing	215	229	199	688	595	470	366	212	100	37	19	20
Vandalism	442	401	313	1,163	884	806	689	417	205	124	64	81
Weapons; carrying, possessing, etc.	291	283	234	889	757	674	662	441	259	160	100	86
Prostitution and commercialized vice	2	8	2	11	17	16	6	9	4	4	2	1
Sex offenses (except forcible rape and prostitution)	153	140	117	502	541	531	431	282	201	145	109	153
Drug abuse violations	4,652	4,150	3,679	12,871	9,839	8,601	7,790	4,785	2,194	799	280	176
Gambling	30	24	22	80	61	61	60	36	37	46	20	13
Offenses against the family and children	361	398	433	2,057	2,338	2,206	1,810	953	404	162	75	80
Driving under the influence	6,469	6,308	5,665	21,751	19,034	18,774	19,316	14,280	8,863	4,971	2,547	2,232
Liquor laws	734	568	467	1,450	1,101	1,025	1,043	705	438	232	121	121
Drunkenness	781	754	671	2,408	2,306	2,481	2,744	1,915	1,160	583	283	218
Disorderly conduct	809	703	591	2,214	2,008	2,102	1,914	1,238	628	378	182	185
Vagrancy	6	11	12	48	47	46	53	30	19	10	2	1
All other offenses (except traffic)	9,537	9,104	8,109	32,604	28,580	26,029	22,870	13,683	6,867	3,333	1,621	1,535
Suspicion	2	4	8	16	17	17	11	6	4	0	3	1
Curfew and loitering law violations	–	–	–	–	–	–	–	–	–	–	–	–
Runaways	–	–	–	–	–	–	–	–	–	–	–	–

[1] Because of rounding, the percentages may not add to 100.0.

[2] Violent crimes are offenses of murder, forcible rape, robbery, and aggravated assault. Property crimes are offenses of burglary, larceny-theft, motor vehicle theft, and arson.

Table 59

Arrests

Nonmetropolitan Counties
of Persons Under 15, 18, 21, and 25 Years of Age, 2003
[1,787 agencies; 2003 estimated population 19,266,065]

Offense charged	Total all ages	Number of persons arrested				Percent of total all ages			
		Under 15	Under 18	Under 21	Under 25	Under 15	Under 18	Under 21	Under 25
TOTAL	**763,309**	**19,891**	**76,334**	**186,719**	**305,942**	**2.6**	**10.0**	**24.5**	**40.1**
Murder and nonnegligent manslaughter	729	10	54	134	254	1.4	7.4	18.4	34.8
Forcible rape	1,718	104	284	552	792	6.1	16.5	32.1	46.1
Robbery	1,756	19	192	603	1,014	1.1	10.9	34.3	57.7
Aggravated assault	18,590	579	1,805	3,791	6,453	3.1	9.7	20.4	34.7
Burglary	17,784	1,487	4,787	9,030	11,830	8.4	26.9	50.8	66.5
Larceny-theft	29,015	2,046	6,048	11,292	15,325	7.1	20.8	38.9	52.8
Motor vehicle theft	5,682	452	1,643	2,657	3,441	8.0	28.9	46.8	60.6
Arson	879	154	273	402	503	17.5	31.1	45.7	57.2
Violent crime[1]	22,793	712	2,335	5,080	8,513	3.1	10.2	22.3	37.3
Property crime[1]	53,360	4,139	12,751	23,381	31,099	7.8	23.9	43.8	58.3
Other assaults	63,278	2,927	8,288	14,166	22,239	4.6	13.1	22.4	35.1
Forgery and counterfeiting	5,480	26	211	890	1,934	0.5	3.9	16.2	35.3
Fraud	31,079	49	361	2,840	7,514	0.2	1.2	9.1	24.2
Embezzlement	722	2	30	104	217	0.3	4.2	14.4	30.1
Stolen property; buying, receiving, possessing	5,116	125	682	1,717	2,609	2.4	13.3	33.6	51.0
Vandalism	13,520	1,864	4,787	7,361	9,087	13.8	35.4	54.4	67.2
Weapons; carrying, possessing, etc.	6,792	239	761	1,673	2,764	3.5	11.2	24.6	40.7
Prostitution and commercialized vice	111	1	9	27	41	0.9	8.1	24.3	36.9
Sex offenses (except forcible rape and prostitution)	5,421	545	1,194	1,924	2,526	10.1	22.0	35.5	46.6
Drug abuse violations	88,332	1,000	6,866	23,551	40,997	1.1	7.8	26.7	46.4
Gambling	612	5	20	100	198	0.8	3.3	16.3	32.4
Offenses against the family and children	12,928	170	576	1,316	2,843	1.3	4.5	10.2	22.0
Driving under the influence	153,192	41	2,222	16,131	41,424	*	1.5	10.5	27.0
Liquor laws	37,547	759	9,384	28,479	31,311	2.0	25.0	75.8	83.4
Drunkenness	19,723	58	495	2,553	5,625	0.3	2.5	12.9	28.5
Disorderly conduct	21,399	1,697	4,837	7,614	10,550	7.9	22.6	35.6	49.3
Vagrancy	349	7	19	57	93	2.0	5.4	16.3	26.6
All other offenses (except traffic)	214,443	3,310	13,511	40,739	77,321	1.5	6.3	19.0	36.1
Suspicion	145	3	28	49	70	2.1	19.3	33.8	48.3
Curfew and loitering law violations	1,157	300	1,157	1,157	1,157	25.9	100.0	100.0	100.0
Runaways	5,810	1,912	5,810	5,810	5,810	32.9	100.0	100.0	100.0

[1] Violent crimes are offenses of murder, forcible rape, robbery, and aggravated assault. Property crimes are offenses of burglary, larceny-theft, motor vehicle theft, and arson.

* Less than one-tenth of 1 percent.

Table 60

Arrests

Nonmetropolitan Counties
by Sex, 2003
[1,787 agencies; 2003 estimated population 19,266,065]

Offense charged	Number of persons arrested			Percent male	Percent female	Percent distribution[1]		
	Total	Male	Female			Total	Male	Female
TOTAL	**763,309**	**596,958**	**166,351**	**78.2**	**21.8**	**100.0**	**100.0**	**100.0**
Murder and nonnegligent manslaughter	729	622	107	85.3	14.7	0.1	0.1	0.1
Forcible rape	1,718	1,679	39	97.7	2.3	0.2	0.3	*
Robbery	1,756	1,544	212	87.9	12.1	0.2	0.3	0.1
Aggravated assault	18,590	15,202	3,388	81.8	18.2	2.4	2.5	2.0
Burglary	17,784	15,633	2,151	87.9	12.1	2.3	2.6	1.3
Larceny-theft	29,015	20,762	8,253	71.6	28.4	3.8	3.5	5.0
Motor vehicle theft	5,682	4,664	1,018	82.1	17.9	0.7	0.8	0.6
Arson	879	748	131	85.1	14.9	0.1	0.1	0.1
Violent crime[2]	22,793	19,047	3,746	83.6	16.4	3.0	3.2	2.3
Property crime[2]	53,360	41,807	11,553	78.3	21.7	7.0	7.0	6.9
Other assaults	63,278	48,792	14,486	77.1	22.9	8.3	8.2	8.7
Forgery and counterfeiting	5,480	3,184	2,296	58.1	41.9	0.7	0.5	1.4
Fraud	31,079	16,024	15,055	51.6	48.4	4.1	2.7	9.1
Embezzlement	722	361	361	50.0	50.0	0.1	0.1	0.2
Stolen property; buying, receiving, possessing	5,116	4,264	852	83.3	16.7	0.7	0.7	0.5
Vandalism	13,520	11,563	1,957	85.5	14.5	1.8	1.9	1.2
Weapons; carrying, possessing, etc.	6,792	6,270	522	92.3	7.7	0.9	1.1	0.3
Prostitution and commercialized vice	111	64	47	57.7	42.3	*	*	*
Sex offenses (except forcible rape and prostitution)	5,421	5,133	288	94.7	5.3	0.7	0.9	0.2
Drug abuse violations	88,332	71,039	17,293	80.4	19.6	11.6	11.9	10.4
Gambling	612	501	111	81.9	18.1	0.1	0.1	0.1
Offenses against the family and children	12,928	10,485	2,443	81.1	18.9	1.7	1.8	1.5
Driving under the influence	153,192	126,850	26,342	82.8	17.2	20.1	21.2	15.8
Liquor laws	37,547	27,327	10,220	72.8	27.2	4.9	4.6	6.1
Drunkenness	19,723	16,621	3,102	84.3	15.7	2.6	2.8	1.9
Disorderly conduct	21,399	15,954	5,445	74.6	25.4	2.8	2.7	3.3
Vagrancy	349	294	55	84.2	15.8	*	*	*
All other offenses (except traffic)	214,443	168,040	46,403	78.4	21.6	28.1	28.1	27.9
Suspicion	145	124	21	85.5	14.5	*	*	*
Curfew and loitering law violations	1,157	718	439	62.1	37.9	0.2	0.1	0.3
Runaways	5,810	2,496	3,314	43.0	57.0	0.8	0.4	2.0

[1] Because of rounding, the percentages may not add to 100.0.

[2] Violent crimes are offenses of murder, forcible rape, robbery, and aggravated assault. Property crimes are offenses of burglary, larceny-theft, motor vehicle theft, and arson.

* Less than one-tenth of 1 percent.

Table 61

Arrests
Nonmetropolitan Counties
by Race, 2003
[1,787 agencies; 2003 estimated population 19,266,065]

Offense charged	Total arrests					Percent distribution[1]				
	Total	White	Black	American Indian or Alaskan Native	Asian or Pacific Islander	Total	White	Black	American Indian or Alaskan Native	Asian or Pacific Islander
TOTAL	**761,114**	**630,327**	**94,840**	**20,347**	**15,600**	**100.0**	**82.8**	**12.5**	**2.7**	**2.0**
Murder and nonnegligent manslaughter	726	502	189	34	1	100.0	69.1	26.0	4.7	0.1
Forcible rape	1,712	1,371	245	76	20	100.0	80.1	14.3	4.4	1.2
Robbery	1,756	1,002	624	40	90	100.0	57.1	35.5	2.3	5.1
Aggravated assault	18,554	14,486	3,113	726	229	100.0	78.1	16.8	3.9	1.2
Burglary	17,749	14,756	2,254	493	246	100.0	83.1	12.7	2.8	1.4
Larceny-theft	28,955	23,930	3,748	467	810	100.0	82.6	12.9	1.6	2.8
Motor vehicle theft	5,664	4,722	487	180	275	100.0	83.4	8.6	3.2	4.9
Arson	877	770	81	25	1	100.0	87.8	9.2	2.9	0.1
Violent crime[2]	22,748	17,361	4,171	876	340	100.0	76.3	18.3	3.9	1.5
Property crime[2]	53,245	44,178	6,570	1,165	1,332	100.0	83.0	12.3	2.2	2.5
Other assaults	63,150	51,204	8,981	1,668	1,297	100.0	81.1	14.2	2.6	2.1
Forgery and counterfeiting	5,467	4,439	890	61	77	100.0	81.2	16.3	1.1	1.4
Fraud	30,989	25,369	5,163	320	137	100.0	81.9	16.7	1.0	0.4
Embezzlement	719	595	103	6	15	100.0	82.8	14.3	0.8	2.1
Stolen property; buying, receiving, possessing	5,093	4,109	849	98	37	100.0	80.7	16.7	1.9	0.7
Vandalism	13,485	11,627	1,211	397	250	100.0	86.2	9.0	2.9	1.9
Weapons; carrying, possessing, etc.	6,775	5,504	998	181	92	100.0	81.2	14.7	2.7	1.4
Prostitution and commercialized vice	111	89	21	0	1	100.0	80.2	18.9	0.0	0.9
Sex offenses (except forcible rape and prostitution)	5,392	4,754	424	152	62	100.0	88.2	7.9	2.8	1.1
Drug abuse violations	88,106	72,676	12,508	1,662	1,260	100.0	82.5	14.2	1.9	1.4
Gambling	612	289	202	3	118	100.0	47.2	33.0	0.5	19.3
Offenses against the family and children	12,917	9,875	2,803	199	40	100.0	76.4	21.7	1.5	0.3
Driving under the influence	152,871	133,473	13,050	4,119	2,229	100.0	87.3	8.5	2.7	1.5
Liquor laws	37,352	34,702	1,146	1,101	403	100.0	92.9	3.1	2.9	1.1
Drunkenness	19,687	17,351	1,389	867	80	100.0	88.1	7.1	4.4	0.4
Disorderly conduct	21,372	16,943	3,283	932	214	100.0	79.3	15.4	4.4	1.0
Vagrancy	348	213	123	10	2	100.0	61.2	35.3	2.9	0.6
All other offenses (except traffic)	213,586	170,082	30,540	6,321	6,643	100.0	79.6	14.3	3.0	3.1
Suspicion	133	72	61	0	0	100.0	54.1	45.9	0.0	0.0
Curfew and loitering law violations	1,156	753	22	53	328	100.0	65.1	1.9	4.6	28.4
Runaways	5,800	4,669	332	156	643	100.0	80.5	5.7	2.7	11.1

See footnotes at end of table.

Table 61

Arrests

Nonmetropolitan Counties
by Race, 2003—Continued
[1,787 agencies; 2003 estimated population 19,266,065]

Offense charged	Arrests under 18					Percent distribution[1]				
	Total	White	Black	American Indian or Alaskan Native	Asian or Pacific Islander	Total	White	Black	American Indian or Alaskan Native	Asian or Pacific Islander
TOTAL	**76,132**	**63,909**	**7,181**	**2,484**	**2,558**	**100.0**	**83.9**	**9.4**	**3.3**	**3.4**
Murder and nonnegligent manslaughter	53	36	12	5	0	100.0	67.9	22.6	9.4	0.0
Forcible rape	283	232	25	24	2	100.0	82.0	8.8	8.5	0.7
Robbery	192	83	84	4	21	100.0	43.2	43.8	2.1	10.9
Aggravated assault	1,803	1,374	310	87	32	100.0	76.2	17.2	4.8	1.8
Burglary	4,782	4,071	433	187	91	100.0	85.1	9.1	3.9	1.9
Larceny-theft	6,032	5,146	525	124	237	100.0	85.3	8.7	2.1	3.9
Motor vehicle theft	1,637	1,388	87	76	86	100.0	84.8	5.3	4.6	5.3
Arson	271	240	19	12	0	100.0	88.6	7.0	4.4	0.0
Violent crime[2]	2,331	1,725	431	120	55	100.0	74.0	18.5	5.1	2.4
Property crime[2]	12,722	10,845	1,064	399	414	100.0	85.2	8.4	3.1	3.3
Other assaults	8,276	6,374	1,468	224	210	100.0	77.0	17.7	2.7	2.5
Forgery and counterfeiting	211	193	9	7	2	100.0	91.5	4.3	3.3	0.9
Fraud	358	320	33	2	3	100.0	89.4	9.2	0.6	0.8
Embezzlement	29	24	2	0	3	100.0	82.8	6.9	0.0	10.3
Stolen property; buying, receiving, possessing	678	575	74	15	14	100.0	84.8	10.9	2.2	2.1
Vandalism	4,774	4,293	265	145	71	100.0	89.9	5.6	3.0	1.5
Weapons; carrying, possessing, etc.	759	593	133	21	12	100.0	78.1	17.5	2.8	1.6
Prostitution and commercialized vice	9	7	2	0	0	100.0	77.8	22.2	0.0	0.0
Sex offenses (except forcible rape and prostitution)	1,188	1,037	103	32	16	100.0	87.3	8.7	2.7	1.3
Drug abuse violations	6,858	5,883	572	186	217	100.0	85.8	8.3	2.7	3.2
Gambling	20	7	2	3	8	100.0	35.0	10.0	15.0	40.0
Offenses against the family and children	576	538	31	5	2	100.0	93.4	5.4	0.9	0.3
Driving under the influence	2,214	2,052	65	59	38	100.0	92.7	2.9	2.7	1.7
Liquor laws	9,344	8,714	130	387	113	100.0	93.3	1.4	4.1	1.2
Drunkenness	495	458	13	23	1	100.0	92.5	2.6	4.6	0.2
Disorderly conduct	4,830	3,580	991	205	54	100.0	74.1	20.5	4.2	1.1
Vagrancy	19	17	2	0	0	100.0	89.5	10.5	0.0	0.0
All other offenses (except traffic)	13,457	11,235	1,426	442	354	100.0	83.5	10.6	3.3	2.6
Suspicion	28	17	11	0	0	100.0	60.7	39.3	0.0	0.0
Curfew and loitering law violations	1,156	753	22	53	328	100.0	65.1	1.9	4.6	28.4
Runaways	5,800	4,669	332	156	643	100.0	80.5	5.7	2.7	11.1

See footnotes at end of table.

Table 61

Arrests
Nonmetropolitan Counties
by Race, 2003—Continued
[1,787 agencies; 2003 estimated population 19,266,065]

Offense charged	Arrests 18 and over					Percent distribution[1]				
	Total	White	Black	American Indian or Alaskan Native	Asian or Pacific Islander	Total	White	Black	American Indian or Alaskan Native	Asian or Pacific Islander
TOTAL	**684,982**	**566,418**	**87,659**	**17,863**	**13,042**	**100.0**	**82.7**	**12.8**	**2.6**	**1.9**
Murder and nonnegligent manslaughter	673	466	177	29	1	100.0	69.2	26.3	4.3	0.1
Forcible rape	1,429	1,139	220	52	18	100.0	79.7	15.4	3.6	1.3
Robbery	1,564	919	540	36	69	100.0	58.8	34.5	2.3	4.4
Aggravated assault	16,751	13,112	2,803	639	197	100.0	78.3	16.7	3.8	1.2
Burglary	12,967	10,685	1,821	306	155	100.0	82.4	14.0	2.4	1.2
Larceny-theft	22,923	18,784	3,223	343	573	100.0	81.9	14.1	1.5	2.5
Motor vehicle theft	4,027	3,334	400	104	189	100.0	82.8	9.9	2.6	4.7
Arson	606	530	62	13	1	100.0	87.5	10.2	2.1	0.2
Violent crime[2]	20,417	15,636	3,740	756	285	100.0	76.6	18.3	3.7	1.4
Property crime[2]	40,523	33,333	5,506	766	918	100.0	82.3	13.6	1.9	2.3
Other assaults	54,874	44,830	7,513	1,444	1,087	100.0	81.7	13.7	2.6	2.0
Forgery and counterfeiting	5,256	4,246	881	54	75	100.0	80.8	16.8	1.0	1.4
Fraud	30,631	25,049	5,130	318	134	100.0	81.8	16.7	1.0	0.4
Embezzlement	690	571	101	6	12	100.0	82.8	14.6	0.9	1.7
Stolen property; buying, receiving, possessing	4,415	3,534	775	83	23	100.0	80.0	17.6	1.9	0.5
Vandalism	8,711	7,334	946	252	179	100.0	84.2	10.9	2.9	2.1
Weapons; carrying, possessing, etc.	6,016	4,911	865	160	80	100.0	81.6	14.4	2.7	1.3
Prostitution and commercialized vice	102	82	19	0	1	100.0	80.4	18.6	0.0	1.0
Sex offenses (except forcible rape and prostitution)	4,204	3,717	321	120	46	100.0	88.4	7.6	2.9	1.1
Drug abuse violations	81,248	66,793	11,936	1,476	1,043	100.0	82.2	14.7	1.8	1.3
Gambling	592	282	200	0	110	100.0	47.6	33.8	0.0	18.6
Offenses against the family and children	12,341	9,337	2,772	194	38	100.0	75.7	22.5	1.6	0.3
Driving under the influence	150,657	131,421	12,985	4,060	2,191	100.0	87.2	8.6	2.7	1.5
Liquor laws	28,008	25,988	1,016	714	290	100.0	92.8	3.6	2.5	1.0
Drunkenness	19,192	16,893	1,376	844	79	100.0	88.0	7.2	4.4	0.4
Disorderly conduct	16,542	13,363	2,292	727	160	100.0	80.8	13.9	4.4	1.0
Vagrancy	329	196	121	10	2	100.0	59.6	36.8	3.0	0.6
All other offenses (except traffic)	200,129	158,847	29,114	5,879	6,289	100.0	79.4	14.5	2.9	3.1
Suspicion	105	55	50	0	0	100.0	52.4	47.6	0.0	0.0
Curfew and loitering law violations	–	–	–	–	–	–	–	–	–	–
Runaways	–	–	–	–	–	–	–	–	–	–

[1] Because of rounding, the percentages may not add to 100.0.
[2] Violent crimes are offenses of murder, forcible rape, robbery, and aggravated assault. Property crimes are offenses of burglary, larceny-theft, motor vehicle theft, and arson.

Table 62

Arrest Trends
Suburban Areas,[1] 2002-2003
[5,084 agencies; 2003 estimated population 82,838,763; 2002 estimated population 81,232,887]

| Offense charged | Number of persons arrested | | | | | | | | |
| | Total all ages | | | Under 18 years of age | | | 18 years of age and over | | |
	2002	2003	Percent change	2002	2003	Percent change	2002	2003	Percent change
TOTAL[2]	3,303,110	3,364,003	+1.8	554,739	556,392	+0.3	2,748,371	2,807,611	+2.2
Murder and nonnegligent manslaughter	2,379	2,150	-9.6	166	153	-7.8	2,213	1,997	-9.8
Forcible rape	6,395	6,119	-4.3	1,128	1,053	-6.6	5,267	5,066	-3.8
Robbery	18,415	19,368	+5.2	4,091	4,458	+9.0	14,324	14,910	+4.1
Aggravated assault	98,466	97,972	-0.5	14,181	14,415	+1.7	84,285	83,557	-0.9
Burglary	66,769	69,645	+4.3	20,958	21,373	+2.0	45,811	48,272	+5.4
Larceny-theft	264,719	264,974	+0.1	77,612	74,526	-4.0	187,107	190,448	+1.8
Motor vehicle theft	28,261	29,122	+3.0	8,373	8,347	-0.3	19,888	20,775	+4.5
Arson	4,631	4,442	-4.1	2,492	2,458	-1.4	2,139	1,984	-7.2
Violent crime[3]	125,655	125,609	*	19,566	20,079	+2.6	106,089	105,530	-0.5
Property crime[3]	364,380	368,183	+1.0	109,435	106,704	-2.5	254,945	261,479	+2.6
Other assaults	299,788	303,703	+1.3	60,619	64,291	+6.1	239,169	239,412	+0.1
Forgery and counterfeiting	27,795	27,010	-2.8	1,321	1,231	-6.8	26,474	25,779	-2.6
Fraud	89,909	90,574	+0.7	2,559	2,255	-11.9	87,350	88,319	+1.1
Embezzlement	4,336	4,177	-3.7	385	344	-10.6	3,951	3,833	-3.0
Stolen property; buying, receiving, possessing	29,948	31,283	+4.5	6,221	5,898	-5.2	23,727	25,385	+7.0
Vandalism	66,919	67,396	+0.7	28,454	28,814	+1.3	38,465	38,582	+0.3
Weapons; carrying, possessing, etc.	34,520	36,603	+6.0	7,959	9,242	+16.1	26,561	27,361	+3.0
Prostitution and commercialized vice	4,155	4,459	+7.3	95	117	+23.2	4,060	4,342	+6.9
Sex offenses (except forcible rape and prostitution)	21,201	20,506	-3.3	4,698	4,500	-4.2	16,503	16,006	-3.0
Drug abuse violations	341,373	367,486	+7.6	46,970	50,089	+6.6	294,403	317,397	+7.8
Gambling	1,174	1,158	-1.4	108	116	+7.4	1,066	1,042	-2.3
Offenses against the family and children	42,012	40,164	-4.4	2,198	1,920	-12.6	39,814	38,244	-3.9
Driving under the influence	427,047	428,394	+0.3	6,192	6,035	-2.5	420,855	422,359	+0.4
Liquor laws	166,304	163,827	-1.5	43,577	41,559	-4.6	122,727	122,268	-0.4
Drunkenness	121,323	119,678	-1.4	5,151	4,919	-4.5	116,172	114,759	-1.2
Disorderly conduct	152,193	155,664	+2.3	51,767	54,448	+5.2	100,426	101,216	+0.8
Vagrancy	4,462	4,549	+1.9	607	476	-21.6	3,855	4,073	+5.7
All other offenses (except traffic)	927,391	956,062	+3.1	105,632	105,837	+0.2	821,759	850,225	+3.5
Suspicion	1,533	572	-62.7	301	132	-56.1	1,232	440	-64.3
Curfew and loitering law violations	20,204	17,682	-12.5	20,204	17,682	-12.5	–	–	–
Runaways	31,021	29,836	-3.8	31,021	29,836	-3.8	–	–	–

[1] Suburban area includes law enforcement agencies in cities with less than 50,000 inhabitants and county law enforcement agencies that are within a Metropolitan Statistical Area (see Appendix III). Suburban area excludes all metropolitan agencies associated with a principal city.

[2] Does not include suspicion.

[3] Violent crimes are offenses of murder, forcible rape, robbery, and aggravated assault. Property crimes are offenses of burglary, larceny-theft, motor vehicle theft, and arson.

* Less than one-tenth of 1 percent.

Table 63

Arrest Trends
Suburban Areas[1]
by Sex, 2002-2003
[5,084 agencies; 2003 estimated population 82,838,763; 2002 estimated population 81,232,887]

| | Male | | | | | | Female | | | | | |
| | Total | | | Under 18 | | | Total | | | Under 18 | | |
Offense charged	2002	2003	Percent change	2002	2003	Percent change	2002	2003	Percent change	2002	2003	Percent change
TOTAL[2]	2,550,632	2,585,497	+1.4	398,566	399,561	+0.2	752,478	778,506	+3.5	156,173	156,831	+0.4
Murder and nonnegligent manslaughter	2,058	1,888	-8.3	140	139	-0.7	321	262	-18.4	26	14	-46.2
Forcible rape	6,319	6,032	-4.5	1,106	1,039	-6.1	76	87	+14.5	22	14	-36.4
Robbery	16,549	17,336	+4.8	3,762	4,102	+9.0	1,866	2,032	+8.9	329	356	+8.2
Aggravated assault	79,602	78,667	-1.2	11,002	11,231	+2.1	18,864	19,305	+2.3	3,179	3,184	+0.2
Burglary	58,493	60,646	+3.7	18,836	19,120	+1.5	8,276	8,999	+8.7	2,122	2,253	+6.2
Larceny-theft	168,204	167,859	-0.2	48,639	46,440	-4.5	96,515	97,115	+0.6	28,973	28,086	-3.1
Motor vehicle theft	23,658	24,256	+2.5	6,843	6,886	+0.6	4,603	4,866	+5.7	1,530	1,461	-4.5
Arson	4,014	3,853	-4.0	2,216	2,193	-1.0	617	589	-4.5	276	265	-4.0
Violent crime[3]	104,528	103,923	-0.6	16,010	16,511	+3.1	21,127	21,686	+2.6	3,556	3,568	+0.3
Property crime[3]	254,369	256,614	+0.9	76,534	74,639	-2.5	110,011	111,569	+1.4	32,901	32,065	-2.5
Other assaults	226,958	229,058	+0.9	41,952	44,212	+5.4	72,830	74,645	+2.5	18,667	20,079	+7.6
Forgery and counterfeiting	17,012	16,368	-3.8	909	852	-6.3	10,783	10,642	-1.3	412	379	-8.0
Fraud	50,082	50,274	+0.4	1,726	1,548	-10.3	39,827	40,300	+1.2	833	707	-15.1
Embezzlement	2,229	2,069	-7.2	230	216	-6.1	2,107	2,108	*	155	128	-17.4
Stolen property; buying, receiving, possessing	24,564	25,481	+3.7	5,277	4,956	-6.1	5,384	5,802	+7.8	944	942	-0.2
Vandalism	56,768	57,348	+1.0	24,755	25,191	+1.8	10,151	10,048	-1.0	3,699	3,623	-2.1
Weapons; carrying, possessing, etc.	31,536	33,602	+6.6	7,092	8,341	+17.6	2,984	3,001	+0.6	867	901	+3.9
Prostitution and commercialized vice	1,962	1,969	+0.4	56	63	+12.5	2,193	2,490	+13.5	39	54	+38.5
Sex offenses (except forcible rape and prostitution)	20,071	19,377	-3.5	4,320	4,128	-4.4	1,130	1,129	-0.1	378	372	-1.6
Drug abuse violations	278,159	298,150	+7.2	38,738	41,014	+5.9	63,214	69,336	+9.7	8,232	9,075	+10.2
Gambling	957	922	-3.7	99	106	+7.1	217	236	+8.8	9	10	+11.1
Offenses against the family and children	33,394	31,808	-4.7	1,350	1,254	-7.1	8,618	8,356	-3.0	848	666	-21.5
Driving under the influence	351,040	349,108	-0.6	5,007	4,831	-3.5	76,007	79,286	+4.3	1,185	1,204	+1.6
Liquor laws	123,795	120,084	-3.0	29,065	27,181	-6.5	42,509	43,743	+2.9	14,512	14,378	-0.9
Drunkenness	102,591	101,064	-1.5	3,987	3,748	-6.0	18,732	18,614	-0.6	1,164	1,171	+0.6
Disorderly conduct	114,765	117,176	+2.1	37,130	38,817	+4.5	37,428	38,488	+2.8	14,637	15,631	+6.8
Vagrancy	3,675	3,827	+4.1	465	371	-20.2	787	722	-8.3	142	105	-26.1
All other offenses (except traffic)	725,641	742,707	+2.4	77,328	77,014	-0.4	201,750	213,355	+5.8	28,304	28,823	+1.8
Suspicion	1,197	473	-60.5	213	104	-51.2	336	99	-70.5	88	28	-68.2
Curfew and loitering law violations	13,704	12,162	-11.3	13,704	12,162	-11.3	6,500	5,520	-15.1	6,500	5,520	-15.1
Runaways	12,832	12,406	-3.3	12,832	12,406	-3.3	18,189	17,430	-4.2	18,189	17,430	-4.2

[1] Suburban area includes law enforcement agencies in cities with less than 50,000 inhabitants and county law enforcement agencies that are within a Metropolitan Statistical Area (see Appendix III). Suburban area excludes all metropolitan agencies associated with a principal city.

[2] Does not include suspicion.

[3] Violent crimes are offenses of murder, forcible rape, robbery, and aggravated assault. Property crimes are offenses of burglary, larceny-theft, motor vehicle theft, and arson.

* Less than one-tenth of 1 percent.

Table 64

Arrests

Suburban Areas[1]
by Age, 2003
[5,889 agencies; 2003 estimated population 92,793,659]

Offense charged	Total all ages	Ages under 15	Ages under 18	Ages 18 and over	Under 10	10-12	13-14	15	16	17	18	19	20	21
TOTAL	**3,891,388**	**202,143**	**643,600**	**3,247,788**	**7,667**	**46,618**	**147,858**	**121,647**	**149,039**	**170,771**	**203,467**	**200,113**	**188,178**	**167,152**
Percent distribution[2]	**100.0**	**5.2**	**16.5**	**83.5**	**0.2**	**1.2**	**3.8**	**3.1**	**3.8**	**4.4**	**5.2**	**5.1**	**4.8**	**4.3**
Murder and nonnegligent manslaughter	2,625	15	185	2,440	0	1	14	22	55	93	146	157	155	155
Forcible rape	7,059	445	1,212	5,847	11	110	324	215	233	319	413	380	368	310
Robbery	23,065	1,259	5,260	17,805	34	231	994	1,005	1,345	1,651	2,076	1,635	1,437	1,255
Aggravated assault	114,343	6,076	16,799	97,544	243	1,564	4,269	3,029	3,575	4,119	4,470	4,256	4,253	4,415
Burglary	79,648	8,245	24,252	55,396	388	2,012	5,845	4,735	5,394	5,878	6,533	5,318	4,017	3,482
Larceny-theft	313,334	32,557	89,482	223,852	1,032	8,263	23,262	16,670	19,554	20,701	20,010	16,546	13,604	11,180
Motor vehicle theft	33,187	2,231	9,503	23,684	22	242	1,967	2,274	2,438	2,560	2,462	2,049	1,679	1,400
Arson	5,141	1,689	2,825	2,316	139	534	1,016	460	395	281	245	208	146	121
Violent crime[3]	147,092	7,795	23,456	123,636	288	1,906	5,601	4,271	5,208	6,182	7,105	6,428	6,213	6,135
Percent distribution[2]	100.0	5.3	15.9	84.1	0.2	1.3	3.8	2.9	3.5	4.2	4.8	4.4	4.2	4.2
Property crime[3]	431,310	44,722	126,062	305,248	1,581	11,051	32,090	24,139	27,781	29,420	29,250	24,121	19,446	16,183
Percent distribution[2]	100.0	10.4	29.2	70.8	0.4	2.6	7.4	5.6	6.4	6.8	6.8	5.6	4.5	3.8
Other assaults	350,603	31,423	73,249	277,354	1,240	8,774	21,409	13,776	14,427	13,623	12,139	11,127	11,448	11,937
Forgery and counterfeiting	32,240	186	1,429	30,811	16	25	145	203	389	651	1,248	1,558	1,780	1,572
Fraud	103,458	485	2,592	100,866	49	87	349	370	631	1,106	2,345	3,515	3,788	4,038
Embezzlement	4,744	26	376	4,368	2	2	22	22	139	189	288	284	247	242
Stolen property; buying, receiving, possessing	36,034	1,829	6,806	29,228	44	369	1,416	1,367	1,674	1,936	2,574	2,189	2,029	1,770
Vandalism	77,313	14,140	32,756	44,557	975	4,043	9,122	5,641	6,294	6,681	5,848	4,330	3,290	3,013
Weapons; carrying, possessing, etc.	43,191	4,142	10,869	32,322	192	1,088	2,862	2,028	2,144	2,555	2,872	2,550	2,257	2,151
Prostitution and commercialized vice	5,762	33	148	5,614	3	5	25	27	45	43	116	145	142	167
Sex offenses (except forcible rape and prostitution)	23,885	2,659	5,237	18,648	162	759	1,738	913	804	861	974	976	902	778
Drug abuse violations	425,193	9,778	56,504	368,689	164	1,210	8,404	9,513	14,785	22,428	31,692	29,511	26,465	22,958
Gambling	1,296	37	135	1,161	4	10	23	21	36	41	70	69	70	41
Offenses against the family and children	53,431	831	2,418	51,013	73	206	552	424	560	603	847	898	1,106	1,337
Driving under the influence	478,094	165	6,748	471,346	72	5	88	274	1,582	4,727	11,800	15,215	17,517	23,451
Liquor laws	185,562	4,165	47,052	138,510	71	270	3,824	6,982	13,273	22,632	36,210	35,349	27,874	4,817
Drunkenness	138,143	764	5,627	132,516	22	57	685	916	1,366	2,581	4,822	5,019	5,003	6,656
Disorderly conduct	183,845	25,751	62,362	121,483	675	6,740	18,336	12,469	12,750	11,392	9,821	7,907	7,073	7,926
Vagrancy	5,289	139	529	4,760	4	28	107	112	136	142	204	205	198	179
All other offenses (except traffic)	1,107,854	34,860	123,156	984,698	1,665	7,146	26,049	24,265	29,982	34,049	43,193	48,657	51,269	51,752
Suspicion	1,139	57	179	960	2	17	38	29	54	39	49	60	61	49
Curfew and loitering law violations	21,428	6,155	21,428	–	97	990	5,068	5,065	6,018	4,190	–	–	–	–
Runaways	34,482	12,001	34,482	–	266	1,830	9,905	8,820	8,961	4,700	–	–	–	–

See footnotes at end of table.

Table 64

Arrests

Suburban Areas[1]

by Age, 2003—Continued

[5,889 agencies; 2003 estimated population 92,793,659]

Offense charged	22	23	24	25-29	30-34	35-39	40-44	45-49	50-54	55-59	60-64	65 and over
TOTAL	**156,045**	**144,548**	**129,572**	**483,119**	**415,931**	**387,780**	**343,094**	**216,895**	**111,135**	**52,936**	**24,839**	**22,984**
Percent distribution[2]	**4.0**	**3.7**	**3.3**	**12.4**	**10.7**	**10.0**	**8.8**	**5.6**	**2.9**	**1.4**	**0.6**	**0.6**
Murder and nonnegligent manslaughter	140	125	110	409	279	248	187	123	88	46	30	42
Forcible rape	275	241	239	834	763	732	543	337	167	123	57	65
Robbery	1,088	937	816	2,570	2,003	1,740	1,225	643	228	89	33	30
Aggravated assault	4,379	4,064	3,805	15,573	13,653	13,084	11,595	6,981	3,603	1,720	847	846
Burglary	3,055	2,666	2,269	7,845	6,713	5,640	4,153	2,288	883	308	126	100
Larceny-theft	9,942	9,089	7,933	29,728	27,602	26,830	22,475	14,565	7,292	3,625	1,621	1,810
Motor vehicle theft	1,338	1,164	1,088	3,834	3,174	2,462	1,717	774	322	134	38	49
Arson	105	75	61	287	261	244	237	152	80	43	20	31
Violent crime[3]	5,882	5,367	4,970	19,386	16,698	15,804	13,550	8,084	4,086	1,978	967	983
Percent distribution[2]	4.0	3.6	3.4	13.2	11.4	10.7	9.2	5.5	2.8	1.3	0.7	0.7
Property crime[3]	14,440	12,994	11,351	41,694	37,750	35,176	28,582	17,779	8,577	4,110	1,805	1,990
Percent distribution[2]	3.3	3.0	2.6	9.7	8.8	8.2	6.6	4.1	2.0	1.0	0.4	0.5
Other assaults	11,890	11,522	10,788	42,501	40,500	39,272	33,970	20,805	10,046	4,736	2,351	2,322
Forgery and counterfeiting	1,458	1,395	1,318	5,549	4,890	4,048	3,023	1,730	756	299	120	67
Fraud	4,239	4,133	3,933	17,201	16,546	14,826	11,836	7,223	3,709	1,894	879	761
Embezzlement	207	192	152	685	659	509	402	246	157	60	20	18
Stolen property; buying, receiving, possessing	1,572	1,348	1,169	4,567	3,883	3,306	2,480	1,339	570	225	111	96
Vandalism	2,464	2,147	1,830	5,815	4,624	4,138	3,388	1,891	922	418	204	235
Weapons; carrying, possessing, etc.	1,861	1,693	1,499	4,898	3,353	2,904	2,509	1,713	980	512	316	254
Prostitution and commercialized vice	161	151	180	758	913	1,029	817	495	272	139	57	72
Sex offenses (except forcible rape and prostitution)	744	602	610	2,291	2,241	2,323	2,101	1,403	976	689	442	596
Drug abuse violations	20,601	18,649	16,306	56,117	42,976	38,500	33,060	19,140	8,330	2,832	970	582
Gambling	34	42	27	121	119	115	136	100	78	66	36	37
Offenses against the family and children	1,443	1,611	1,624	8,252	9,647	9,132	7,573	4,402	1,833	785	303	220
Driving under the influence	23,217	22,244	19,844	74,451	61,062	56,755	56,478	40,533	23,934	13,001	6,449	5,395
Liquor laws	3,313	2,418	1,856	5,823	4,550	4,500	4,672	3,223	1,962	999	503	441
Drunkenness	5,902	5,389	4,614	16,732	15,475	16,721	18,377	13,428	7,792	3,667	1,691	1,228
Disorderly conduct	6,925	5,931	4,937	17,269	13,092	12,940	12,138	7,699	3,943	1,896	971	1,015
Vagrancy	168	155	125	538	582	697	673	517	262	152	57	48
All other offenses (except traffic)	49,463	46,517	42,396	158,327	136,234	124,996	107,239	65,093	31,911	14,462	6,570	6,619
Suspicion	61	48	43	144	137	89	90	52	39	16	17	5
Curfew and loitering law violations	–	–	–	–	–	–	–	–	–	–	–	–
Runaways	–	–	–	–	–	–	–	–	–	–	–	–

[1] Suburban area includes law enforcement agencies in cities with less than 50,000 inhabitants and county law enforcement agencies that are within a Metropolitan Statistical Area (see Appendix III). Suburban area excludes all metropolitan agencies associated with a principal city.

[2] Because of rounding, the percentages may not add to 100.0.

[3] Violent crimes are offenses of murder, forcible rape, robbery, and aggravated assault. Property crimes are offenses of burglary, larceny-theft, motor vehicle theft, and arson.

Table 65

Arrests

Suburban Areas[1]
of Persons Under 15, 18, 21, and 25 Years of Age, 2003
[5,889 agencies; 2003 estimated population 92,793,659]

Offense charged	Total all ages	Number of persons arrested				Percent of total all ages			
		Under 15	Under 18	Under 21	Under 25	Under 15	Under 18	Under 21	Under 25
TOTAL	**3,891,388**	**202,143**	**643,600**	**1,235,358**	**1,832,675**	**5.2**	**16.5**	**31.7**	**47.1**
Murder and nonnegligent manslaughter	2,625	15	185	643	1,173	0.6	7.0	24.5	44.7
Forcible rape	7,059	445	1,212	2,373	3,438	6.3	17.2	33.6	48.7
Robbery	23,065	1,259	5,260	10,408	14,504	5.5	22.8	45.1	62.9
Aggravated assault	114,343	6,076	16,799	29,778	46,441	5.3	14.7	26.0	40.6
Burglary	79,648	8,245	24,252	40,120	51,592	10.4	30.4	50.4	64.8
Larceny-theft	313,334	32,557	89,482	139,642	177,786	10.4	28.6	44.6	56.7
Motor vehicle theft	33,187	2,231	9,503	15,693	20,683	6.7	28.6	47.3	62.3
Arson	5,141	1,689	2,825	3,424	3,786	32.9	55.0	66.6	73.6
Violent crime[2]	147,092	7,795	23,456	43,202	65,556	5.3	15.9	29.4	44.6
Property crime[2]	431,310	44,722	126,062	198,879	253,847	10.4	29.2	46.1	58.9
Other assaults	350,603	31,423	73,249	107,963	154,100	9.0	20.9	30.8	44.0
Forgery and counterfeiting	32,240	186	1,429	6,015	11,758	0.6	4.4	18.7	36.5
Fraud	103,458	485	2,592	12,240	28,583	0.5	2.5	11.8	27.6
Embezzlement	4,744	26	376	1,195	1,988	0.5	7.9	25.2	41.9
Stolen property; buying, receiving, possessing	36,034	1,829	6,806	13,598	19,457	5.1	18.9	37.7	54.0
Vandalism	77,313	14,140	32,756	46,224	55,678	18.3	42.4	59.8	72.0
Weapons; carrying, possessing, etc.	43,191	4,142	10,869	18,548	25,752	9.6	25.2	42.9	59.6
Prostitution and commercialized vice	5,762	33	148	551	1,210	0.6	2.6	9.6	21.0
Sex offenses (except forcible rape and prostitution)	23,885	2,659	5,237	8,089	10,823	11.1	21.9	33.9	45.3
Drug abuse violations	425,193	9,778	56,504	144,172	222,686	2.3	13.3	33.9	52.4
Gambling	1,296	37	135	344	488	2.9	10.4	26.5	37.7
Offenses against the family and children	53,431	831	2,418	5,269	11,284	1.6	4.5	9.9	21.1
Driving under the influence	478,094	165	6,748	51,280	140,036	*	1.4	10.7	29.3
Liquor laws	185,562	4,165	47,052	146,485	158,889	2.2	25.4	78.9	85.6
Drunkenness	138,143	764	5,627	20,471	43,032	0.6	4.1	14.8	31.2
Disorderly conduct	183,845	25,751	62,362	87,163	112,882	14.0	33.9	47.4	61.4
Vagrancy	5,289	139	529	1,136	1,763	2.6	10.0	21.5	33.3
All other offenses (except traffic)	1,107,854	34,860	123,156	266,275	456,403	3.1	11.1	24.0	41.2
Suspicion	1,139	57	179	349	550	5.0	15.7	30.6	48.3
Curfew and loitering law violations	21,428	6,155	21,428	21,428	21,428	28.7	100.0	100.0	100.0
Runaways	34,482	12,001	34,482	34,482	34,482	34.8	100.0	100.0	100.0

[1] Suburban area includes law enforcement agencies in cities with less than 50,000 inhabitants and county law enforcement agencies that are within a Metropolitan Statistical Area (see Appendix III). Suburban area excludes all metropolitan agencies associated with a principal city.

[2] Violent crimes are offenses of murder, forcible rape, robbery, and aggravated assault. Property crimes are offenses of burglary, larceny-theft, motor vehicle theft, and arson.

* Less than one-tenth of 1 percent.

Table 66

Arrests

Suburban Areas[1]

by Sex, 2003

[5,889 agencies; 2003 estimated population 92,793,659]

Offense charged	Number of persons arrested			Percent male	Percent female	Percent distribution[2]		
	Total	Male	Female			Total	Male	Female
TOTAL	**3,891,388**	**2,985,008**	**906,380**	**76.7**	**23.3**	**100.0**	**100.0**	**100.0**
Murder and nonnegligent manslaughter	2,625	2,318	307	88.3	11.7	0.1	0.1	*
Forcible rape	7,059	6,953	106	98.5	1.5	0.2	0.2	*
Robbery	23,065	20,635	2,430	89.5	10.5	0.6	0.7	0.3
Aggravated assault	114,343	91,624	22,719	80.1	19.9	2.9	3.1	2.5
Burglary	79,648	69,446	10,202	87.2	12.8	2.0	2.3	1.1
Larceny-theft	313,334	197,969	115,365	63.2	36.8	8.1	6.6	12.7
Motor vehicle theft	33,187	27,575	5,612	83.1	16.9	0.9	0.9	0.6
Arson	5,141	4,435	706	86.3	13.7	0.1	0.1	0.1
Violent crime[3]	147,092	121,530	25,562	82.6	17.4	3.8	4.1	2.8
Property crime[3]	431,310	299,425	131,885	69.4	30.6	11.1	10.0	14.6
Other assaults	350,603	264,182	86,421	75.4	24.6	9.0	8.9	9.5
Forgery and counterfeiting	32,240	19,503	12,737	60.5	39.5	0.8	0.7	1.4
Fraud	103,458	56,967	46,491	55.1	44.9	2.7	1.9	5.1
Embezzlement	4,744	2,350	2,394	49.5	50.5	0.1	0.1	0.3
Stolen property; buying, receiving, possessing	36,034	29,443	6,591	81.7	18.3	0.9	1.0	0.7
Vandalism	77,313	65,500	11,813	84.7	15.3	2.0	2.2	1.3
Weapons; carrying, possessing, etc.	43,191	39,615	3,576	91.7	8.3	1.1	1.3	0.4
Prostitution and commercialized vice	5,762	2,429	3,333	42.2	57.8	0.1	0.1	0.4
Sex offenses (except forcible rape and prostitution)	23,885	22,463	1,422	94.0	6.0	0.6	0.8	0.2
Drug abuse violations	425,193	345,098	80,095	81.2	18.8	10.9	11.6	8.8
Gambling	1,296	1,029	267	79.4	20.6	*	*	*
Offenses against the family and children	53,431	43,028	10,403	80.5	19.5	1.4	1.4	1.1
Driving under the influence	478,094	389,342	88,752	81.4	18.6	12.3	13.0	9.8
Liquor laws	185,562	136,105	49,457	73.3	26.7	4.8	4.6	5.5
Drunkenness	138,143	116,535	21,608	84.4	15.6	3.5	3.9	2.4
Disorderly conduct	183,845	137,728	46,117	74.9	25.1	4.7	4.6	5.1
Vagrancy	5,289	4,403	886	83.2	16.8	0.1	0.1	0.1
All other offenses (except traffic)	1,107,854	858,100	249,754	77.5	22.5	28.5	28.7	27.6
Suspicion	1,139	1,010	129	88.7	11.3	*	*	*
Curfew and loitering law violations	21,428	14,815	6,613	69.1	30.9	0.6	0.5	0.7
Runaways	34,482	14,408	20,074	41.8	58.2	0.9	0.5	2.2

[1] Suburban area includes law enforcement agencies in cities with less than 50,000 inhabitants and county law enforcement agencies that are within a Metropolitan Statistical Area (see Appendix III). Suburban area excludes all metropolitan agencies associated with a principal city.

[2] Because of rounding, the percentages may not add to 100.0.

[3] Violent crimes are offenses of murder, forcible rape, robbery, and aggravated assault. Property crimes are offenses of burglary, larceny-theft, motor vehicle theft, and arson.

* Less than one-tenth of 1 percent.

Table 67

Arrests

Suburban Areas[1]
by Race, 2003
[5,888 agencies; 2003 estimated population 92,790,194]

Offense charged	Total arrests					Percent distribution[2]				
	Total	White	Black	American Indian or Alaskan Native	Asian or Pacific Islander	Total	White	Black	American Indian or Alaskan Native	Asian or Pacific Islander
TOTAL	**3,882,202**	**2,967,553**	**853,774**	**31,984**	**28,891**	**100.0**	**76.4**	**22.0**	**0.8**	**0.7**
Murder and nonnegligent manslaughter	2,624	1,668	899	26	31	100.0	63.6	34.3	1.0	1.2
Forcible rape	7,038	5,223	1,703	55	57	100.0	74.2	24.2	0.8	0.8
Robbery	23,041	11,595	11,164	133	149	100.0	50.3	48.5	0.6	0.6
Aggravated assault	114,094	82,933	29,129	967	1,065	100.0	72.7	25.5	0.8	0.9
Burglary	79,526	61,315	17,147	481	583	100.0	77.1	21.6	0.6	0.7
Larceny-theft	312,271	222,212	84,138	2,456	3,465	100.0	71.2	26.9	0.8	1.1
Motor vehicle theft	33,141	23,851	8,716	242	332	100.0	72.0	26.3	0.7	1.0
Arson	5,129	4,321	741	31	36	100.0	84.2	14.4	0.6	0.7
Violent crime[3]	146,797	101,419	42,895	1,181	1,302	100.0	69.1	29.2	0.8	0.9
Property crime[3]	430,067	311,699	110,742	3,210	4,416	100.0	72.5	25.7	0.7	1.0
Other assaults	349,859	256,453	87,776	2,919	2,711	100.0	73.3	25.1	0.8	0.8
Forgery and counterfeiting	32,190	23,042	8,763	127	258	100.0	71.6	27.2	0.4	0.8
Fraud	103,138	71,276	30,932	410	520	100.0	69.1	30.0	0.4	0.5
Embezzlement	4,739	3,272	1,400	19	48	100.0	69.0	29.5	0.4	1.0
Stolen property; buying, receiving, possessing	35,993	24,475	10,962	220	336	100.0	68.0	30.5	0.6	0.9
Vandalism	77,122	63,413	12,499	557	653	100.0	82.2	16.2	0.7	0.8
Weapons; carrying, possessing, etc.	43,139	30,410	12,103	232	394	100.0	70.5	28.1	0.5	0.9
Prostitution and commercialized vice	5,756	4,044	1,379	23	310	100.0	70.3	24.0	0.4	5.4
Sex offenses (except forcible rape and prostitution)	23,827	19,197	4,259	150	221	100.0	80.6	17.9	0.6	0.9
Drug abuse violations	424,487	329,262	90,617	2,216	2,392	100.0	77.6	21.3	0.5	0.6
Gambling	1,293	799	444	8	42	100.0	61.8	34.3	0.6	3.2
Offenses against the family and children	53,289	35,577	17,127	335	250	100.0	66.8	32.1	0.6	0.5
Driving under the influence	476,616	427,929	41,485	3,889	3,313	100.0	89.8	8.7	0.8	0.7
Liquor laws	184,821	166,949	13,324	2,798	1,750	100.0	90.3	7.2	1.5	0.9
Drunkenness	137,875	122,799	12,875	1,541	660	100.0	89.1	9.3	1.1	0.5
Disorderly conduct	183,516	137,661	43,027	1,509	1,319	100.0	75.0	23.4	0.8	0.7
Vagrancy	5,284	3,376	1,832	24	52	100.0	63.9	34.7	0.5	1.0
All other offenses (except traffic)	1,105,394	789,177	298,675	10,117	7,425	100.0	71.4	27.0	0.9	0.7
Suspicion	1,137	776	346	3	12	100.0	68.2	30.4	0.3	1.1
Curfew and loitering law violations	21,405	17,367	3,761	108	169	100.0	81.1	17.6	0.5	0.8
Runaways	34,458	27,181	6,551	388	338	100.0	78.9	19.0	1.1	1.0

See footnotes at end of table.

Table 67

Arrests

Suburban Areas[1]
by Race, 2003—Continued
[5,888 agencies; 2003 estimated population 92,790,194]

Offense charged	Arrests under 18					Percent distribution[2]				
	Total	White	Black	American Indian or Alaskan Native	Asian or Pacific Islander	Total	White	Black	American Indian or Alaskan Native	Asian or Pacific Islander
TOTAL	**642,163**	**489,262**	**141,473**	**5,124**	**6,304**	**100.0**	**76.2**	**22.0**	**0.8**	**1.0**
Murder and nonnegligent manslaughter	185	105	76	2	2	100.0	56.8	41.1	1.1	1.1
Forcible rape	1,209	888	310	9	2	100.0	73.4	25.6	0.7	0.2
Robbery	5,251	2,132	3,051	28	40	100.0	40.6	58.1	0.5	0.8
Aggravated assault	16,741	11,289	5,160	131	161	100.0	67.4	30.8	0.8	1.0
Burglary	24,202	18,577	5,269	124	232	100.0	76.8	21.8	0.5	1.0
Larceny-theft	89,155	63,239	23,743	819	1,354	100.0	70.9	26.6	0.9	1.5
Motor vehicle theft	9,495	6,213	3,026	96	160	100.0	65.4	31.9	1.0	1.7
Arson	2,821	2,430	351	21	19	100.0	86.1	12.4	0.7	0.7
Violent crime[3]	23,386	14,414	8,597	170	205	100.0	61.6	36.8	0.7	0.9
Property crime[3]	125,673	90,459	32,389	1,060	1,765	100.0	72.0	25.8	0.8	1.4
Other assaults	73,131	49,291	22,851	506	483	100.0	67.4	31.2	0.7	0.7
Forgery and counterfeiting	1,428	1,162	239	2	25	100.0	81.4	16.7	0.1	1.8
Fraud	2,587	1,718	826	7	36	100.0	66.4	31.9	0.3	1.4
Embezzlement	375	247	122	1	5	100.0	65.9	32.5	0.3	1.3
Stolen property; buying, receiving, possessing	6,795	4,330	2,320	51	94	100.0	63.7	34.1	0.8	1.4
Vandalism	32,665	27,237	4,950	194	284	100.0	83.4	15.2	0.6	0.9
Weapons; carrying, possessing, etc.	10,856	7,831	2,807	63	155	100.0	72.1	25.9	0.6	1.4
Prostitution and commercialized vice	147	106	38	2	1	100.0	72.1	25.9	1.4	0.7
Sex offenses (except forcible rape and prostitution)	5,214	3,954	1,209	20	31	100.0	75.8	23.2	0.4	0.6
Drug abuse violations	56,397	47,257	8,341	384	415	100.0	83.8	14.8	0.7	0.7
Gambling	135	58	75	0	2	100.0	43.0	55.6	0.0	1.5
Offenses against the family and children	2,414	1,898	480	19	17	100.0	78.6	19.9	0.8	0.7
Driving under the influence	6,733	6,404	232	54	43	100.0	95.1	3.4	0.8	0.6
Liquor laws	46,892	43,883	1,797	718	494	100.0	93.6	3.8	1.5	1.1
Drunkenness	5,620	5,091	443	52	34	100.0	90.6	7.9	0.9	0.6
Disorderly conduct	62,281	43,592	17,688	411	590	100.0	70.0	28.4	0.7	0.9
Vagrancy	529	329	195	3	2	100.0	62.2	36.9	0.6	0.4
All other offenses (except traffic)	122,863	95,333	25,504	910	1,116	100.0	77.6	20.8	0.7	0.9
Suspicion	179	120	58	1	0	100.0	67.0	32.4	0.6	0.0
Curfew and loitering law violations	21,405	17,367	3,761	108	169	100.0	81.1	17.6	0.5	0.8
Runaways	34,458	27,181	6,551	388	338	100.0	78.9	19.0	1.1	1.0

See footnotes at end of table.

Table 67

Arrests

Suburban Areas[1]
by Race, 2003—Continued
[5,888 agencies; 2003 estimated population 92,790,194]

Offense charged	Arrests 18 and over					Percent distribution[2]				
	Total	White	Black	American Indian or Alaskan Native	Asian or Pacific Islander	Total	White	Black	American Indian or Alaskan Native	Asian or Pacific Islander
TOTAL	**3,240,039**	**2,478,291**	**712,301**	**26,860**	**22,587**	**100.0**	**76.5**	**22.0**	**0.8**	**0.7**
Murder and nonnegligent manslaughter	2,439	1,563	823	24	29	100.0	64.1	33.7	1.0	1.2
Forcible rape	5,829	4,335	1,393	46	55	100.0	74.4	23.9	0.8	0.9
Robbery	17,790	9,463	8,113	105	109	100.0	53.2	45.6	0.6	0.6
Aggravated assault	97,353	71,644	23,969	836	904	100.0	73.6	24.6	0.9	0.9
Burglary	55,324	42,738	11,878	357	351	100.0	77.3	21.5	0.6	0.6
Larceny-theft	223,116	158,973	60,395	1,637	2,111	100.0	71.3	27.1	0.7	0.9
Motor vehicle theft	23,646	17,638	5,690	146	172	100.0	74.6	24.1	0.6	0.7
Arson	2,308	1,891	390	10	17	100.0	81.9	16.9	0.4	0.7
Violent crime[3]	123,411	87,005	34,298	1,011	1,097	100.0	70.5	27.8	0.8	0.9
Property crime[3]	304,394	221,240	78,353	2,150	2,651	100.0	72.7	25.7	0.7	0.9
Other assaults	276,728	207,162	64,925	2,413	2,228	100.0	74.9	23.5	0.9	0.8
Forgery and counterfeiting	30,762	21,880	8,524	125	233	100.0	71.1	27.7	0.4	0.8
Fraud	100,551	69,558	30,106	403	484	100.0	69.2	29.9	0.4	0.5
Embezzlement	4,364	3,025	1,278	18	43	100.0	69.3	29.3	0.4	1.0
Stolen property; buying, receiving, possessing	29,198	20,145	8,642	169	242	100.0	69.0	29.6	0.6	0.8
Vandalism	44,457	36,176	7,549	363	369	100.0	81.4	17.0	0.8	0.8
Weapons; carrying, possessing, etc.	32,283	22,579	9,296	169	239	100.0	69.9	28.8	0.5	0.7
Prostitution and commercialized vice	5,609	3,938	1,341	21	309	100.0	70.2	23.9	0.4	5.5
Sex offenses (except forcible rape and prostitution)	18,613	15,243	3,050	130	190	100.0	81.9	16.4	0.7	1.0
Drug abuse violations	368,090	282,005	82,276	1,832	1,977	100.0	76.6	22.4	0.5	0.5
Gambling	1,158	741	369	8	40	100.0	64.0	31.9	0.7	3.5
Offenses against the family and children	50,875	33,679	16,647	316	233	100.0	66.2	32.7	0.6	0.5
Driving under the influence	469,883	421,525	41,253	3,835	3,270	100.0	89.7	8.8	0.8	0.7
Liquor laws	137,929	123,066	11,527	2,080	1,256	100.0	89.2	8.4	1.5	0.9
Drunkenness	132,255	117,708	12,432	1,489	626	100.0	89.0	9.4	1.1	0.5
Disorderly conduct	121,235	94,069	25,339	1,098	729	100.0	77.6	20.9	0.9	0.6
Vagrancy	4,755	3,047	1,637	21	50	100.0	64.1	34.4	0.4	1.1
All other offenses (except traffic)	982,531	693,844	273,171	9,207	6,309	100.0	70.6	27.8	0.9	0.6
Suspicion	958	656	288	2	12	100.0	68.5	30.1	0.2	1.3
Curfew and loitering law violations	–	–	–	–	–	–	–	–	–	–
Runaways	–	–	–	–	–	–	–	–	–	–

[1] Suburban area includes law enforcement agencies in cities with less than 50,000 inhabitants and county law enforcement agencies that are within a Metropolitan Statistical Area (see Appendix III). Suburban area excludes all metropolitan agencies associated with a principal city.

[2] Because of rounding, the percentages may not add to 100.0.

[3] Violent crimes are offenses of murder, forcible rape, robbery, and aggravated assault. Property crimes are offenses of burglary, larceny-theft, motor vehicle theft, and arson.

Table 68

Police Disposition
of Juvenile Offenders Taken into Custody, 2003
[2003 estimated population]

Population group	Total[1]	Handled within department and released	Referred to juvenile court jurisdiction	Referred to welfare agency	Referred to other police agency	Referred to criminal or adult court
TOTAL AGENCIES: 5,443 agencies; population 121,368,878						
Number	736,817	148,133	523,412	4,060	8,651	52,561
Percent[2]	100.0	20.1	71.0	0.6	1.2	7.1
TOTAL CITIES: 4,142 cities; population 86,263,336						
Number	623,265	132,025	439,151	3,069	6,962	42,058
Percent[2]	100.0	21.2	70.5	0.5	1.1	6.7
GROUP I						
30 cities, 250,000 and over; population 23,175,309						
Number	138,712	42,728	92,650	138	1,096	2,100
Percent[2]	100.0	30.8	66.8	0.1	0.8	1.5
GROUP II						
90 cities, 100,000 to 249,999; population 13,159,658						
Number	80,819	14,829	59,427	815	1,341	4,407
Percent[2]	100.0	18.3	73.5	1.0	1.7	5.5
GROUP III						
214 cities, 50,000 to 99,999; population 14,674,288						
Number	109,146	24,664	76,635	493	1,626	5,728
Percent[2]	100.0	22.6	70.2	0.5	1.5	5.2
GROUP IV						
367 cities, 25,000 to 49,999; population 12,899,668						
Number	94,018	18,246	68,018	510	1,115	6,129
Percent[2]	100.0	19.4	72.3	0.5	1.2	6.5
GROUP V						
820 cities, 10,000 to 24,999; population 13,045,230						
Number	107,368	16,825	76,889	652	789	12,213
Percent[2]	100.0	15.7	71.6	0.6	0.7	11.4
GROUP VI						
2,621 cities, under 10,000; population 9,309,183						
Number	93,202	14,733	65,532	461	995	11,481
Percent[2]	100.0	15.8	70.3	0.5	1.1	12.3
METROPOLITAN COUNTIES						
583 agencies; population 26,212,844						
Number	85,751	12,543	64,494	662	1,265	6,787
Percent[2]	100.0	14.6	75.2	0.8	1.5	7.9
NONMETROPOLITAN COUNTIES						
718 agencies; population 8,892,698						
Number	27,801	3,565	19,767	329	424	3,716
Percent[2]	100.0	12.8	71.1	1.2	1.5	13.4
SUBURBAN AREA[3]						
3,260 agencies; population 58,887,524						
Number	317,226	56,934	224,585	2,093	3,401	30,213
Percent[2]	100.0	17.9	70.8	0.7	1.1	9.5

[1] Includes all offenses except traffic and neglect cases.

[2] Because of rounding, the percentages may not add to 100.0.

[3] Suburban area includes law enforcement agencies in cities with less than 50,000 inhabitants and county law enforcement agencies that are within a Metropolitan Statistical Area (see Appendix III). Suburban area excludes all metropolitan agencies associated with a principal city. The agencies associated with suburban areas also appear in other groups within this table.

Table 69

Arrests
by State, 2003
[2003 estimated population]

State	Total all classes[1]	Violent crime[2]	Property crime[2]	Murder and non-negligent man-slaughter	Forcible rape	Robbery	Aggra-vated assault	Burglary	Larceny-theft	Motor vehicle theft	Arson	Other assaults	Forgery and counter-feiting	Fraud
ALABAMA: 309 agencies; population 4,079,102														
Under 18	13,018	584	3,541	24	24	199	337	572	2,747	202	20	2,180	36	55
Total all ages	208,757	6,492	20,100	311	386	1,563	4,232	3,059	15,621	1,306	114	28,388	2,394	10,974
ALASKA: 30 agencies; population 631,457														
Under 18	5,521	215	1,949	3	28	25	159	304	1,416	203	26	493	14	13
Total all ages	35,754	1,418	4,462	22	103	110	1,183	587	3,429	406	40	4,071	137	147
ARIZONA: 84 agencies; population 5,365,487														
Under 18	51,400	1,427	11,363	17	22	291	1,097	1,609	8,353	1,247	154	4,922	101	126
Total all ages	305,252	8,657	40,305	210	223	1,561	6,663	5,198	29,615	5,262	230	22,999	2,825	2,221
ARKANSAS:[4] 120 agencies; population 1,790,768														
Under 18	9,128	267	2,623	2	10	46	209	461	2,098	47	17	712	47	43
Total all ages	120,392	3,290	10,797	29	105	479	2,677	2,078	8,316	323	80	5,212	1,511	11,730
CALIFORNIA: 686 agencies; population 34,990,394														
Under 18	220,348	15,374	49,786	167	297	4,670	10,240	13,732	28,603	6,465	986	22,314	471	679
Total all ages	1,457,151	128,047	176,805	1,835	2,434	17,353	106,425	50,355	94,486	30,198	1,766	86,137	12,030	10,566
COLORADO: 157 agencies; population 3,238,375														
Under 18	37,332	850	7,535	8	53	175	614	802	5,654	906	173	2,776	69	83
Total all ages	195,911	5,314	24,375	94	411	788	4,021	2,483	19,235	2,372	285	17,990	1,282	1,450
CONNECTICUT: 78 agencies; population 2,269,425														
Under 18	15,231	743	3,449	3	38	216	486	559	2,581	260	49	2,422	25	40
Total all ages	87,176	3,692	12,502	57	164	991	2,480	1,732	10,017	650	103	11,673	528	1,055
DELAWARE: 42 agencies; population 813,337														
Under 18	6,592	541	1,439	0	27	148	366	298	1,028	84	29	1,436	9	110
Total all ages	34,912	2,470	4,860	15	117	477	1,861	890	3,735	177	58	7,114	505	1,934
DISTRICT OF COLUMBIA:[4,5] 2 agencies;														
Under 18	332	27	37	0	1	10	16	0	7	30	0	31	0	0
Total all ages	5,421	68	77	1	1	20	46	0	37	40	0	133	1	0
FLORIDA:[4,6] 596 agencies; population 17,012,655														
Under 18	122,706	9,514	38,642	44	325	1,804	7,341	9,091	25,526	3,763	262	18,043	199	570
Total all ages	974,805	52,752	130,353	701	2,251	9,096	40,704	26,503	90,952	12,331	567	94,188	5,381	14,123
GEORGIA: 273 agencies; population 4,729,207														
Under 18	36,061	1,479	7,833	58	36	449	936	1,329	5,645	734	125	4,653	138	422
Total all ages	265,932	11,837	32,120	417	425	2,396	8,599	5,163	24,347	2,269	341	22,076	4,507	11,154
HAWAII: 4 agencies; population 1,257,608														
Under 18	11,743	263	1,850	2	16	135	110	237	1,408	199	6	1,086	13	24
Total all ages	58,719	1,355	6,710	26	127	457	745	784	4,759	1,151	16	4,711	378	413
IDAHO: 106 agencies; population 1,285,541														
Under 18	16,117	257	3,460	4	18	17	218	395	2,808	178	79	1,361	44	52
Total all ages	73,523	1,292	7,572	24	110	106	1,052	1,025	6,004	426	117	6,803	401	734

See footnotes at end of table.

Embezzlement	Stolen property; buying, receiving, possessing	Vandalism	Weapons; carrying, possessing, etc.	Prostitution and commercialized vice	Sex offenses (except forcible rape and prostitution)	Drug abuse violations	Gambling	Offenses against the family and children	Driving under the influence	Liquor laws	Drunkenness[3]	Disorderly conduct	Vagrancy	All other offenses (except traffic)	Suspicion	Curfew and loitering law violations	Runaways
0	223	482	144	0	29	1,095	3	8	148	786	111	1,348	10	1,740	0	52	443
17	2,380	2,596	1,334	135	433	16,133	110	1,506	14,340	6,909	9,845	4,129	199	79,847	1	52	443
0	5	318	75	3	51	431	0	14	102	438	5	100	0	1,040	0	2	253
2	26	966	382	55	239	2,045	0	343	4,891	1,602	26	912	9	13,764	2	2	253
24	208	2,817	459	54	340	5,255	0	455	603	4,837	0	3,631	30	5,888	0	3,489	5,371
264	1,614	9,427	3,123	2,160	1,785	32,796	1	3,321	39,046	24,972	0	16,830	718	83,328	0	3,489	5,371
0	87	271	131	5	42	671	1	19	145	224	199	791	39	1,884	11	498	418
3	931	907	1,164	360	326	9,301	50	567	9,248	1,756	8,219	2,563	661	50,744	136	498	418
162	3,188	12,749	7,653	419	2,707	22,052	84	8	1,583	4,715	3,749	12,129	293	37,563	0	16,720	5,950
1,917	18,813	27,806	27,119	13,776	15,544	273,226	564	594	184,679	27,092	97,808	17,255	5,908	308,795	0	16,720	5,950
8	158	1,572	616	9	313	2,856	2	53	400	3,467	16	2,607	19	7,258	5	2,695	3,965
107	693	5,550	1,933	1,010	1,111	15,054	3	2,329	19,715	14,304	231	11,958	875	63,962	5	2,695	3,965
13	57	751	231	1	113	1,226	3	59	82	251	15	2,999	9	2,493	7	107	135
156	369	2,094	895	244	409	9,744	16	998	5,527	1,015	23	12,522	32	23,433	7	107	135
18	111	264	134	0	20	699	0	7	0	282	11	688	0	725	0	98	0
191	327	935	372	157	76	4,211	2	233	223	1,791	354	2,076	471	6,512	0	98	0
0	2	12	3	0	0	11	0	0	0	5	0	69	0	131	0	4	0
0	17	21	25	0	1	108	0	0	29	1,714	56	213	254	2,700	0	4	0
56	397	3,031	1,986	71	552	13,887	49		448	1,677				33,584			
1,007	3,978	8,238	6,760	7,529	4,137	136,804	699		56,976	34,223				417,657			
7	578	702	852	33	556	2,975	31	217	288	794	248	4,175	153	7,480	30	486	1,931
179	3,889	2,026	3,990	1,628	3,727	32,940	327	4,080	24,806	8,850	4,348	20,936	1,589	67,899	607	486	1,931
3	28	286	48	11	96	565	19	72	72	235	0	85	0	2,081	0	613	4,293
43	183	776	312	350	382	3,286	183	898	4,049	1,171	12	649	0	27,952	0	613	4,293
2	83	684	196	0	123	773	0	7	219	1,657	28	622	0	3,714	0	778	2,057
68	330	1,438	575	3	360	5,258	0	518	9,355	5,048	201	2,281	9	28,442	0	778	2,057

Table 69

Arrests
by State, 2003—Continued
[2003 estimated population]

State	Total all classes[1]	Violent crime[2]	Property crime[2]	Murder and non-negligent man-slaughter	Forcible rape	Robbery	Aggra-vated assault	Burglary	Larceny-theft	Motor vehicle theft	Arson	Other assaults	Forgery and counter-feiting	Fraud
ILLINOIS:[4] 1 agency; population 2,898,374														
Under 18	36,113	3,150	6,925	52	114	1,142	1,842	1,166	3,005	2,707	47	7,058	10	168
Total all ages	197,983	9,570	29,111	472	603	2,909	5,586	3,325	17,244	8,402	140	29,059	258	1,962
INDIANA: 160 agencies; population 4,568,601														
Under 18	33,746	1,716	6,590	14	32	196	1,474	760	5,220	526	84	2,400	26	56
Total all ages	208,042	10,610	22,657	204	209	1,440	8,757	3,293	17,358	1,826	180	11,373	1,187	1,871
IOWA: 190 agencies; population 2,662,631														
Under 18	21,176	741	6,199	0	25	85	631	821	5,011	295	72	2,410	56	62
Total all ages	116,510	3,993	15,051	31	126	353	3,483	2,191	12,048	685	127	10,118	869	1,658
KANSAS: 225 agencies; population 1,306,978														
Under 18	8,309	201	1,615	1	17	19	164	323	1,151	109	32	1,328	19	12
Total all ages	54,354	1,147	4,558	21	86	75	965	844	3,380	263	71	6,692	277	1,306
KENTUCKY:[4] 23 agencies; population 1,063,935														
Under 18	5,646	268	1,679	3	5	55	205	271	1,322	65	21	461	25	16
Total all ages	60,090	2,157	7,970	35	86	462	1,574	1,235	6,341	355	39	3,680	1,101	3,226
LOUISIANA: 139 agencies; population 3,281,940														
Under 18	35,285	1,403	7,274	15	79	253	1,056	1,536	5,379	304	55	5,361	34	28
Total all ages	219,924	9,938	28,803	265	444	1,400	7,829	5,565	21,859	1,210	169	27,821	1,466	2,793
MAINE: 163 agencies; population 1,300,474														
Under 18	9,238	112	2,694	0	19	16	77	453	2,055	143	43	1,101	30	27
Total all ages	55,320	814	7,332	5	94	127	588	1,257	5,628	371	76	7,261	333	1,060
MARYLAND: 149 agencies; population 5,508,909														
Under 18	51,325	3,255	12,564	41	62	1,184	1,968	2,648	7,310	2,245	361	9,300	56	81
Total all ages	324,414	12,215	38,204	324	431	3,500	7,960	7,340	24,907	5,308	649	38,816	1,177	3,455
MASSACHUSETTS: 278 agencies; population 4,488,437														
Under 18	14,694	1,290	2,457	4	42	194	1,050	509	1,705	193	50	1,856	26	32
Total all ages	98,390	6,930	11,669	34	291	793	5,812	2,065	8,819	680	105	12,712	528	1,045
MICHIGAN: 564 agencies; population 9,724,692														
Under 18	43,681	1,922	10,982	17	179	357	1,369	1,666	8,402	761	153	3,723	58	390
Total all ages	353,346	16,769	34,325	468	1,006	2,337	12,958	6,059	25,734	2,094	438	32,345	1,240	6,199
MINNESOTA: 302 agencies; population 4,217,436														
Under 18	40,941	867	9,140	10	121	141	595	1,034	7,434	532	140	3,183	133	179
Total all ages	155,088	3,377	22,362	71	567	406	2,333	2,706	18,216	1,216	224	13,053	1,586	3,812
MISSISSIPPI: 88 agencies; population 1,380,220														
Under 18	11,403	226	2,490	15	33	82	96	492	1,788	114	96	1,182	19	39
Total all ages	100,844	2,024	10,522	131	186	532	1,175	1,912	7,878	478	254	10,239	1,117	1,680
MISSOURI: 458 agencies; population 5,527,314														
Under 18	48,176	1,882	11,015	13	100	407	1,362	1,727	7,855	1,229	204	7,082	142	95
Total all ages	324,705	14,623	43,346	305	596	2,157	11,565	6,244	32,267	4,367	468	35,498	3,397	4,449

See footnotes at end of table.

Embezzlement	Stolen property; buying, receiving, possessing	Vandalism	Weapons; carrying, possessing, etc.	Prostitution and commercialized vice	Sex offenses (except forcible rape and prostitution)	Drug abuse violations	Gambling	Offenses against the family and children	Driving under the influence	Liquor laws	Drunkenness[3]	Disorderly conduct	Vagrancy	All other offenses (except traffic)	Suspicion	Curfew and loitering law violations	Runaways
0	0	1,516	1,278	69	136	8,203	690	9	54	362	0	3,040	0	3,445	0	0	0
0	0	4,401	4,824	5,522	2,118	55,793	2,662	397	5,967	1,018	0	20,126	0	25,195	0	0	0
0	1,138	1,254	151	11	217	2,366	2	421	279	3,108	468	2,720	22	5,996	36	1,349	3,420
19	4,512	2,401	1,481	1,190	1,317	20,323	177	1,924	28,501	12,502	16,055	8,158	175	56,614	226	1,349	3,420
17	80	1,629	132	2	91	1,204	0	3	309	2,413	242	1,528	0	2,835	0	742	481
172	220	3,274	579	246	269	10,244	9	606	12,645	12,908	7,927	5,073	27	29,399	0	742	481
2	56	487	38	0	55	697	0	6	250	1,184	1	406	0	962	0	0	990
38	301	1,427	228	19	176	5,315	0	165	10,723	4,910	243	1,946	0	13,893	0	0	990
0	216	217	65	0	37	688	1	1	61	190	176	434	0	814	0	132	165
70	1,031	868	502	85	261	8,896	13	1,125	5,379	1,129	5,607	2,601	3	14,089	0	132	165
1	426	1,432	242	8	268	2,253	24	204	162	561	73	5,042	73	6,886	59	1,585	1,886
28	2,367	4,383	1,541	546	1,283	23,602	131	1,945	11,152	5,019	4,190	15,204	314	73,827	100	1,585	1,886
2	70	586	37	0	43	812	5	9	160	999	19	204	0	2,028	0	106	194
34	306	1,659	254	12	250	5,048	26	344	7,294	3,431	79	1,570	0	17,913	0	106	194
63	36	2,516	1,440	34	343	7,953	79	52	298	1,387	0	2,352	21	8,141	15	561	778
400	245	4,596	4,013	2,371	1,295	54,531	402	2,669	23,558	6,234	4	6,469	170	122,187	64	561	778
4	234	652	136	11	78	1,617	2	118	131	931	296	1,112	2	3,262	32	29	386
52	959	2,090	595	630	420	9,397	13	1,839	8,582	3,192	6,250	5,286	11	25,626	149	29	386
94	958	1,686	616	17	344	3,771	11	7	846	5,720	38	1,327	28	8,059	33	1,234	1,817
1,282	5,619	4,228	4,584	1,336	1,376	33,020	111	4,650	48,382	27,098	716	9,867	292	116,823	33	1,234	1,817
0	413	2,094	500	1	247	2,844	6	12	785	6,363	0	3,359	9	8,723	0	0	2,083
2	1,434	4,069	1,128	84	946	13,040	22	443	24,851	22,930	0	9,603	62	30,201	0	0	2,083
17	81	246	116	1	20	875	25	191	155	308	195	1,805	0	2,639	11	483	279
546	723	999	685	102	282	10,697	423	3,195	11,120	2,596	6,025	7,162	87	29,795	63	483	279
17	370	3,200	554	20	523	4,333	12	184	690	1,992	43	2,542	76	7,721	0	2,185	3,498
121	2,636	9,606	4,227	1,394	3,226	42,131	323	5,701	36,826	10,451	2,166	14,737	642	83,522	0	2,185	3,498

Table 69

Arrests

by State, 2003—Continued

[2003 estimated population]

State	Total all classes[1]	Violent crime[2]	Property crime[2]	Murder and non-negligent man-slaughter	Forcible rape	Robbery	Aggra-vated assault	Burglary	Larceny-theft	Motor vehicle theft	Arson	Other assaults	Forgery and counter-feiting	Fraud
MONTANA: 64 agencies; population 546,626														
Under 18	5,292	128	1,379	1	4	21	102	104	1,153	99	23	356	7	9
Total all ages	18,855	769	3,167	10	26	80	653	247	2,683	212	25	1,926	64	145
NEBRASKA: 215 agencies; population 1,489,255														
Under 18	13,273	167	3,162	4	11	49	103	340	2,595	151	76	1,473	37	60
Total all ages	86,544	1,286	8,823	55	140	275	816	918	7,382	415	108	8,543	752	1,878
NEVADA:[4]														
NEW HAMPSHIRE:[4] 117 agencies; population 887,385														
Under 18	6,575	74	702	0	6	23	45	97	548	45	12	746	6	37
Total all ages	36,477	360	1,892	5	41	91	223	269	1,502	102	19	3,960	151	651
NEW JERSEY: 521 agencies; population 8,018,213														
Under 18	59,499	3,495	8,454	26	61	1,302	2,106	1,698	6,055	451	250	5,921	45	158
Total all ages	363,297	14,344	32,342	293	519	3,945	9,587	6,208	24,421	1,292	421	28,950	1,781	5,590
NEW MEXICO: 22 agencies; population 1,031,982														
Under 18	8,126	285	1,771	4	8	43	230	218	1,446	89	18	872	14	24
Total all ages	64,435	2,249	5,519	69	85	273	1,822	820	4,399	276	24	4,612	270	375
NEW YORK:[4] 440 agencies; population 8,561,046														
Under 18	45,172	2,464	11,372	26	96	838	1,504	2,501	7,908	738	225	4,195	284	393
Total all ages	297,442	12,818	42,567	226	709	3,150	8,733	7,199	32,390	2,574	404	26,343	4,357	11,272
NORTH CAROLINA: 329 agencies; population 6,614,261														
Under 18	45,130	2,276	11,615	43	68	701	1,464	2,580	8,189	716	130	7,510	132	431
Total all ages	432,569	19,411	54,500	591	726	4,154	13,940	13,671	38,247	2,231	351	49,865	3,806	32,764
NORTH DAKOTA: 57 agencies; population 535,956														
Under 18	6,516	27	1,119	0	9	6	12	111	887	106	15	360	18	20
Total all ages	25,585	176	2,292	3	35	21	117	238	1,835	201	18	1,391	191	1,027
OHIO: 326 agencies; population 5,657,483														
Under 18	44,836	975	7,943	7	118	301	549	1,502	5,828	441	172	5,029	70	65
Total all ages	236,081	5,277	27,987	114	451	1,678	3,034	4,658	21,737	1,235	357	21,951	1,749	2,447
OKLAHOMA: 298 agencies; population 3,511,532														
Under 18	24,678	869	6,357	16	51	120	682	1,077	4,761	399	120	1,557	41	98
Total all ages	166,495	6,047	18,109	159	365	678	4,845	3,227	13,307	1,277	298	10,215	1,121	3,317
OREGON: 144 agencies; population 3,252,321														
Under 18	26,649	538	6,205	3	35	123	377	932	4,629	414	230	1,815	109	67
Total all ages	115,141	3,118	21,284	95	261	783	1,979	2,890	15,898	2,171	325	10,758	1,754	1,200
PENNSYLVANIA: 751 agencies; population 10,443,061														
Under 18	103,922	4,658	14,150	39	233	1,613	2,773	2,703	8,860	2,278	309	8,495	134	379
Total all ages	421,100	21,903	50,739	504	1,244	6,207	13,948	9,587	34,704	5,776	672	43,206	3,404	11,994

See footnotes at end of table.

Embezzlement	Stolen property; buying, receiving, possessing	Vandalism	Weapons; carrying, possessing, etc.	Prostitution and commercialized vice	Sex offenses (except forcible rape and prostitution)	Drug abuse violations	Gambling	Offenses against the family and children	Driving under the influence	Liquor laws	Drunkenness[3]	Disorderly conduct	Vagrancy	All other offenses (except traffic)	Suspicion	Curfew and loitering law violations	Runaways
0	5	354	20	0	14	187	1	33	58	699	0	432	0	1,065	0	301	244
6	20	681	59	2	62	664	1	328	2,239	1,801	0	1,567	12	4,797	0	301	244
7	164	1,051	144	6	102	1,010	0	20	359	2,243	0	751	0	2,020	0	250	247
119	1,026	2,686	998	490	583	9,614	22	1,376	12,911	12,106	0	4,013	1	18,819	1	250	247
4	89	286	9	0	33	470	0	4	119	991	414	186	2	2,073	0	15	315
9	250	794	74	14	131	2,114	8	154	5,063	4,603	3,608	1,120	57	11,134	0	15	315
9	1,650	3,589	1,936	21	390	6,234	33	59	320	2,647	0	5,810	272	8,575	0	5,205	4,676
112	6,139	7,263	5,623	2,106	1,844	51,630	280	15,093	23,992	7,953	9	21,169	2,816	124,380	0	5,205	4,676
15	98	258	226	5	21	970	0	11	163	889	53	525	1	1,381	0	50	494
118	672	579	597	251	96	5,084	0	713	8,832	3,304	1,319	2,358	4	26,908	31	50	494
14	1,219	3,894	656	22	991	5,308	6	378	318	1,038	0	2,284	64	10,272	0	0	0
216	5,987	12,430	3,440	1,605	4,336	44,095	123	2,882	26,843	5,970	0	13,730	1,536	76,892	0	0	0
47	1,023	2,265	1,318	5	154	3,837	3	86	624	1,497	0	4,331	4	7,114	0	2	856
1,893	6,637	8,153	6,568	1,243	1,631	39,583	360	7,069	54,264	13,480	0	14,850	1,491	114,143	0	2	856
2	78	389	20	0	29	193	0	62	63	1,405	0	719	0	1,042	0	339	631
7	127	629	89	0	84	1,623	0	200	3,806	5,678	451	1,570	3	5,271	0	339	631
3	1,030	1,925	453	16	280	2,877	8	1,334	280	2,775	116	3,205	7	11,898	26	2,895	1,626
11	3,957	4,097	2,472	1,331	1,223	22,877	53	12,636	20,377	12,669	5,728	14,624	117	69,881	96	2,895	1,626
42	333	624	325	2	68	1,876	3	19	416	562	926	907	0	3,370	0	3,102	3,181
597	2,091	1,567	2,315	346	786	23,013	11	1,111	20,942	3,029	24,795	3,021	0	37,779	0	3,102	3,181
3	64	1,846	192	1	240	1,875	0	17	193	3,889	0	1,297	0	3,921	0	2,083	2,294
65	440	4,031	1,436	116	1,224	13,766	3	505	13,508	13,063	0	6,271	0	18,222	0	2,083	2,294
13	717	5,234	1,423	15	694	6,470	15	56	556	7,552	259	16,310	83	8,002	0	26,065	2,642
281	3,247	12,660	4,137	2,685	3,069	47,438	231	972	39,384	25,939	19,812	53,634	446	47,212	0	26,065	2,642

Table 69

Arrests

by State, 2003—Continued
[2003 estimated population]

State	Total all classes[1]	Violent crime[2]	Property crime[2]	Murder and non-negligent man-slaughter	Forcible rape	Robbery	Aggra-vated assault	Burglary	Larceny-theft	Motor vehicle theft	Arson	Other assaults	Forgery and counter-feiting	Fraud
RHODE ISLAND: 48 agencies; population 1,076,164														
Under 18	7,605	334	1,592	2	52	72	208	270	1,143	126	53	1,126	13	11
Total all ages	43,914	1,368	4,518	14	134	307	913	769	3,397	276	76	6,018	203	1,210
SOUTH CAROLINA:[4] 177 agencies; population 535,689														
Under 18	1,353	29	131	2	1	6	20	41	85	4	1	188	4	3
Total all ages	17,583	294	657	8	18	34	234	159	458	34	6	741	158	1,900
SOUTH DAKOTA: 120 agencies; population 658,233														
Under 18	7,832	86	1,388	2	13	1	70	186	1,142	49	11	411	11	11
Total all ages	35,298	510	3,038	8	59	28	415	430	2,482	103	23	2,653	138	1,056
TENNESSEE: 398 agencies; population 4,892,622														
Under 18	30,437	1,188	5,664	27	55	269	837	949	4,134	494	87	4,084	58	161
Total all ages	253,709	11,913	30,044	302	294	1,617	9,700	4,793	22,601	2,412	238	26,117	2,806	10,125
TEXAS: 945 agencies; population 20,875,272														
Under 18	169,176	4,795	33,152	77	338	1,198	3,182	5,881	24,695	2,184	392	20,501	320	426
Total all ages	982,963	30,433	116,101	811	2,189	6,371	21,062	17,862	89,257	8,192	790	92,840	8,267	16,120
UTAH: 94 agencies; population 1,690,633														
Under 18	23,684	483	5,606	2	54	37	390	389	4,836	282	99	1,796	49	58
Total all ages	98,509	1,640	14,477	48	158	313	1,121	1,350	12,362	617	148	8,109	968	904
VERMONT: 54 agencies; population 478,344														
Under 18	1,527	44	304	1	9	0	34	87	184	23	10	189	8	20
Total all ages	10,951	252	921	7	48	1	196	209	628	61	23	1,079	106	330
VIRGINIA: 260 agencies; population 5,526,389														
Under 18	27,931	652	5,198	11	47	201	393	992	3,727	334	145	4,163	79	89
Total all ages	213,059	4,866	20,818	190	305	1,108	3,263	3,018	16,355	1,181	264	26,915	2,008	7,184
WASHINGTON: 210 agencies; population 4,540,101														
Under 18	36,088	1,279	10,860	10	170	310	789	1,842	8,141	662	215	5,267	108	36
Total all ages	216,720	6,773	32,282	96	795	1,259	4,623	5,079	24,934	1,892	377	28,578	2,269	1,335
WEST VIRGINIA: 263 agencies; population 813,665														
Under 18	1,224	33	318	3	0	2	28	60	221	37	0	131	7	9
Total all ages	19,879	778	2,095	20	20	58	680	387	1,512	170	26	2,955	211	455
WISCONSIN: 302 agencies; population 4,165,478														
Under 18	79,901	898	13,696	5	129	176	588	1,644	10,938	969	145	2,719	174	233
Total all ages	294,493	4,620	30,490	85	491	686	3,358	3,764	24,676	1,818	232	12,013	1,786	8,402
WYOMING: 58 agencies; population 475,963														
Under 18	6,126	49	1,054	0	3	2	44	98	904	46	6	594	5	15
Total all ages	32,907	543	2,503	11	28	34	470	314	2,042	115	32	2,564	115	192

[1] Does not include traffic arrests.

[2] Violent crimes are offenses of murder, forcible rape, robbery, and aggravated assault. Property crimes are offenses of burglary, larceny-theft, motor vehicle theft, and arson.

[3] Drunkenness is not considered a crime in some states; therefore, the figures vary widely from state to state.

[4] See Arrest Data, Appendix I, for details.

[5] Includes arrests reported by the Zoological Police and the Metro Transit Police. These agencies have no population associated with them.

[6] The arrest category *all other offenses* also includes the arrest counts for offenses against the family and children, drunkenness, disorderly conduct, vagrancy, suspicion, curfew and loitering law violations, and runaways.

NOTE: Direct comparisons of arrest totals listed in this table made with prior years' issues should be made with caution as participation levels may vary. Additionally, some Part II offenses are not considered crimes in some states; therefore, figures may vary widely from state to state.

Embezzlement	Stolen property; buying, receiving, possessing	Vandalism	Weapons; carrying, possessing, etc.	Prostitution and commercialized vice	Sex offenses (except forcible rape and prostitution)	Drug abuse violations	Gambling	Offenses against the family and children	Driving under the influence	Liquor laws	Drunkenness[3]	Disorderly conduct	Vagrancy	All other offenses (except traffic)	Suspicion	Curfew and loitering law violations	Runaways
13	88	677	186	1	27	672	0	132	23	156	1	850	0	1,440	12	41	210
163	472	1,660	564	275	129	4,621	23	217	2,023	1,038	69	3,305	8	15,734	45	41	210
0	13	36	45	0	7	112	0	4	43	129	14	334	0	238	0	4	19
24	137	183	174	13	43	981	13	86	3,929	2,195	1,159	1,524	25	3,324	0	4	19
1	50	222	65	0	27	616	0	84	134	1,622	18	449	0	1,796	0	283	558
38	141	533	157	0	183	2,788	3	340	5,357	6,951	440	1,640	12	8,479	0	283	558
29	118	1,167	532	8	173	2,512	32	46	232	1,246	324	4,165	0	4,242	0	1,651	2,805
461	799	3,312	2,701	1,739	659	29,368	247	1,150	24,688	6,705	18,317	10,095	33	67,974	0	1,651	2,805
63	228	5,328	1,661	96	835	15,270	43	108	1,255	5,469	3,967	20,503	181	29,072	0	10,564	15,339
647	827	11,742	11,344	4,794	4,425	106,273	411	4,696	87,023	25,194	119,851	35,628	507	279,937	0	10,564	15,339
2	204	1,439	408	2	330	1,269	0	35	142	2,016	219	2,213	2	5,279	0	1,316	816
17	802	2,978	1,297	241	726	7,582	0	1,196	5,944	10,214	4,797	5,564	13	28,908	0	1,316	816
5	23	117	6	1	2	175	0	6	23	234	0	145	0	224	0	1	0
24	117	282	9	4	28	1,235	0	297	2,619	703	1	619	0	2,324	0	1	0
49	132	1,092	545	1	216	2,320	2	41	223	1,180	235	1,203	0	5,321	0	1,765	3,425
1,096	737	3,315	2,752	392	790	20,137	28	766	18,819	6,044	17,524	4,488	75	69,115	0	1,765	3,425
9	635	2,165	589	47	258	2,755	0	11	594	3,992	2	684	1	4,497	9	17	2,273
124	3,913	6,025	2,514	571	1,198	22,544	3	339	36,802	12,701	14	4,619	107	51,701	18	17	2,273
0	9	65	6	1	13	131	0	0	25	126	6	3	0	291	0	12	38
38	128	469	178	10	87	2,060	1	62	3,670	1,065	654	209	0	4,704	0	12	38
42	480	3,473	855	13	1,038	4,098	6	158	514	9,840	21	14,392	185	18,483	40	4,785	3,758
227	1,294	8,350	2,544	120	2,782	18,676	32	1,906	29,060	36,039	195	47,538	270	79,458	148	4,785	3,758
0	14	206	45	0	17	430	0	19	74	1,198	29	272	8	1,484	64	358	191
4	109	581	117	2	112	2,579	3	249	4,169	4,223	1,388	1,128	11	11,686	80	358	191

SECTION V

VIOLENCE AMONG FAMILY MEMBERS AND INTIMATE PARTNERS

INTRODUCTION

The phenomenon of violence among family members has been present in Western society throughout its history. It is a significant societal as well as an individual problem, but it has not always been considered a crime. History records instances of wife beating as early as the time of the Roman Empire. Further, the English common law as codified by jurist Sir William Blackstone in 1768 affirmed the right of a husband to physically chastise his wife as long as "the stick was no bigger than his thumb." This right was upheld by an appellate court in North Carolina as late as 1867.[1]

M. A. Straus and R. J. Gelles, who have authored several works about family violence, also categorized instances of child abuse throughout history. Some of the cases they examined date to biblical times. "Infanticide, mutilation, and other forms of violence were legal parental prerogatives from ancient Rome to colonial America."[2]

Child abuse was identified as a social problem by church and social workers in the last quarter of the nineteenth century. However, it was not until C. Henry Kemper published his 1962 study, "The Battered Child Syndrome"[3] that child abuse found its way onto the public agenda. Likewise, it was not until the 1970s that wife beating was recognized as a problem and that significant scholarly research on spousal abuse began. In their writings, Straus and Gelles (1988) and Straus (2000) listed some of the factors that led to the reformation in our society's view of family violence. Those factors included the social movements of the 1960s that undertook to aid oppressed groups; the growth in paid employment of married women; the re-emergence of the women's movement in the 1970s; the provision of shelters for battered women; public abhorrence of violence evidenced by the rising homicide and assault rates; violent political and social protests; assassinations; terrorist activity; the Vietnam War; the critical reassessment of the family; and changes in theoretical perspectives in sociology, family studies, and criminology.[4]

Measuring Domestic Violence

The subject of domestic violence is broad in scope and there are many ways to measure it. For example, the Department of Justice's National Crime Victimization Survey (NCVS) questions individuals regarding their victimization experiences. Investigators from other agencies examine hospital records and physicians' reports to determine the frequency of broken bones and use that information as evidence of child or spousal abuse.[5]

The present work investigates the problem of violence among intimate partners and other family members by examining the incidents reported to law enforcement who, in turn, submitted data to the Uniform Crime Reporting (UCR) Program. The years considered are 1996 through 2001. Although there are other studies of this criminal phenomenon from the vantage point of the victim or from a public health perspective, this study is confined to the experiences of victims in close relationships with their offenders. Some additional data presented in this report are from other sources and are tendered to underline the nature of the phenomenon. However, those data are presented only as background information.

Data from the UCR Program clearly demonstrate that violence among family members is a prevalent problem. For instance, the Program's 1996 Supplementary Homicide Report[6] (SHR) showed that 30 percent of all female victims of murder or nonnegligent manslaughter in the U.S. were killed by their husbands, ex-husbands, or boyfriends.[7] The 2000 SHR data indicated that of the 3,173 women homicide victims for which supplemental data were provided, 1,029 were killed by their husbands, former husbands, or boyfriends. Further, data from the UCR Program's National Incident-Based Reporting System (NIBRS) for 2001 showed that an estimated 38,614 women were beaten and/or sexually assaulted by family members.[8]

Intimate Partner and Spousal Abuse

Domestic violence takes many forms including intimate partner and spousal abuse, child abuse, and elder abuse. Regarding spousal abuse, data from the American Psychological Association (APA)[9] indicate that one-third of all adult women will be assaulted by a partner during adulthood. The Centers for Disease Control and Prevention reported that "nearly two-thirds of women who reported being raped, physically assaulted, or stalked since the age of 18 were victimized by a current or former husband, cohabiting partner, boyfriend, or date."[10] Further, one in three of these women were injured.[11]

Reports from the NCVS from 1992 to 1996 showed that, without adjusting for socioeconomic status, an average of 12 per 1,000 black women experienced violence by an intimate partner compared to an estimated 8 per 1,000 white women.[12]

In studies of visits to hospital emergency rooms in 1994, the Bureau of Justice Statistics reported that women accounted for nearly 40 percent of all the patients in need of treatment for violent victimizations. Thirty-six percent of these victims were attacked by their intimate partners.[13] Female victims were more likely than male victims to require medical attention, take time off work, and spend more days in bed.[14] Moreover, the National Research Council argues that the psychological costs for these victims are quite high and "can include depression, suicidal thoughts and attempts, lowered self-esteem, alcohol and other drug abuse, and post-traumatic stress disorder."[15]

According to Straus and Gelles, perpetrators of violence are more likely to have had a history of physical or sexual abuse themselves or were victims of threats of abuse. Furthermore, men who abuse their partners are more likely to abuse their children.[16]

Both victims and perpetrators of domestic violence are more likely to abuse alcohol. Statistics from the National Institute on Alcohol Abuse and Alcoholism show that more than 50 percent of male batterers and 20 percent of female victims are alcohol abusers.[17]

Surveys taken by the NCVS between 1992 and 1996 indicated that financial losses to women victims of non-lethal intimate violence amounted to more than $150 million per year. This amount was made up of medical costs (approximately 40 percent), property losses (about 44 percent), and the rest comprised lost pay.[18]

Child Abuse

Men are more likely to be the offenders in cases of physical and sexual abuse against children. Approximately 10 percent of all injuries to children under 7

years of age who are examined in emergency rooms come from abuse.[19]

More than 50 percent of murder victims under the age of 12 are killed by a parent. About 3.3 million children each year witness acts of violence by family members against their mothers or female caretakers. The APA estimates that 16 to 34 percent of girls and 10 to 20 percent of boys are sexually abused, most often by a family member or trusted family friend. The APA has for a long time indicated that children who experience violence are at greater risk of becoming adult abusers. The Association terms this the "cycle of violence."[20]

Children at risk for being abused include those who are unwanted, who have physical or mental disabilities, and whose parents are under stress (e.g., parents with more than four children, those who make less than $15,000 annually, those who abuse drugs, or young mothers who are isolated from others outside the family.)[21]

The U.S. Advisory Board on Child Abuse and Neglect reports that there are particular characteristics that are associated with child abusers. Usually, the offenders are in their mid-20s, do not have high school educations, live at or below the poverty level, suffer from depression, and may have difficulty coping with stressful situations.[22]

Elder Abuse

Elder abuse affects thousands of individuals each year, but according to the National Center on Elder Abuse,[23] the incidents are underreported. Few studies examine this topic; however, a 1997 study of case reports of various protective agencies by the National Center on Elder Abuse found that neglect is the most common form of elder maltreatment in domestic settings, and adult children are the most frequent abusers

of the elderly. From the data that were available, authors Tatara, Kuzmeskus, and Duckhorn (1997) found that cases of elder neglect increased substantially over the years 1990 to 1996, rising from 47 percent in 1990 to 55 percent in 1996.[24]

Also according to Tatara, Kuzmeskus, and Duckhorn, most elderly victims of abuse were female, but from 1990 to 1996, the gap between male and female victims narrowed somewhat, changing from 68.3 percent female/31.5 percent male in 1990 to 67.3 percent female/32.4 percent male in 1996.[25] Additionally, they found that nearly a third of the murders of victims 60 years of age or older were committed by a family member. Further, most elder abuse was committed by someone with whom the elderly victim lived. Because most caregivers for the elderly are women, they found that most of the neglect cases were committed by female family members. On the other hand, the most frequent offenders of physical abuse against the elderly were male family members.[26]

OBJECTIVES

This study examines violent crime incidents in which at least one of the offenders and one of the victims are related within the family. The crimes included in this analysis are murder and nonnegligent manslaughter, forcible rape, aggravated assault, simple assault, intimidation, forcible sodomy, sexual assault with an object, forcible fondling, and kidnapping/abduction.

The relationships included in this study fall into the categories of family members and intimate partners and include spouse, common-law spouse, parent, sibling, child, grandparent, grandchild, in-law, stepparent, stepchild, stepbrother or stepsister, boyfriend, girlfriend, ex-wife, ex-husband, and other family member.

The general objective of this study is to analyze the domestic violence data that are provided in the UCR Program's NIBRS data. It will show the types of crimes that are committed in domestic disputes (e.g., assaults, rapes, and sexual assaults). The relationships of the individuals involved (i.e., partner or ex-partner, parent, or other relationship) are examined. Further, variables such as the number and degree of injury in the cases, the weapons used, and the severity of the sustained injuries are included.

Study Question 1—Characteristics of the Incidents and Offenses

The level of analysis in this study question is the incident itself. In the NIBRS data that were used in this study, an incident includes all the family violence offenses within a single incident, whether the offense is against an intimate partner, a child, or an elder. Variables that describe the incident such as the number of incidents per year, the use of alcohol, and the violence involved (i.e., homicides, injuries, and types of weapons used) are addressed in question 1.

Study Question 2—Victims, Offenders, and Relationship Status

Question 2 concerns the victim and offender characteristics. The age, sex, and race of the victims and offenders are examined here. The incidents are broken down by the selected relationships of victim to offender (intimate partner, child/offspring, or elderly relative).

This question also concerns the relationships of the victims to the offenders. In this section, different crime categories are examined by types of incidents to show the similarities and differences between them.

DATA

The UCR's National Incident-Based Reporting System (NIBRS) data from 1996-2001

Data for this study came from the UCR Program's NIBRS database. The NIBRS, which is the redesigned, expanded version of the Program's original Summary system, was established in the 1980s, and a limited number of agencies began submitting data to the FBI via the NIBRS in January 1989. This database contains information on each single incident and arrest reported by the participating local, county, and state law enforcement agencies. The NIBRS collects data for 22 crime categories and includes information about each incident, the offenses committed within the incident, and details about the victim and offender. The data collected by this method provide a rich, disaggregated source of information that can be used to enhance law enforcement and crime research as well as assist officials in strategic and administrative decision-making.

METHODS

The years considered for this study are 1996 through 2001. Frequency distributions and cross tabulations are used to explore the data and to address the Study Questions.

For this report, relationships that fall into the spousal abuse category are defined as those in which the victim and offender were related as spouse, common-law spouse, ex-spouse, boyfriend, or girlfriend. Child abuse cases are defined as those in which at least one victim was below age 18. However, when relationships are considered in the data presented in this study, the term child can also mean the offspring (adult or juvenile) of a victim or offender. Footnotes are provided in the appropriate

tables to clarify how this classification applies. Elderly abuse cases are defined as those in which as least one victim was above age 65 and had a familial relationship to one of the offenders.

FINDINGS

Incident Characteristics

Number of Incidents and Offenses

Table 5.1 shows the total number of incidents reported to the UCR Program via the NIBRS for each year from 1996 through 2001. The number of incidents reflect violent and property crimes. As expected, the numbers steadily increased over the period as more jurisdictions began reporting data via the NIBRS. The total number of incidents over the period was 12,545,546, and of those, 2,929,070 (23.3 percent) contained at least one violent offense.

Table 5.2 presents the number of incidents reported each year containing at least one violent offense. During the timeframe of this study, simple assault was the most prevalent violent crime, present in 57.6 percent of the total violent incidents. Aggravated assault and intimidation followed comprising 16.1 percent and 15.5 percent, respectively.

Table 5.3 also shows the prevalence of the violent offenses examined in this study. The highest percentages

Table 5.1

Number of Incidents Reported in NIBRS, 1996-2001

	Total incidents	Incidents containing at least one violent crime	Percentage of total incidents containing at least one violent crime
1996	1,064,763	255,111	23.96
1997	1,426,978	330,167	23.14
1998	1,822,675	435,641	23.90
1999	2,157,326	530,751	24.60
2000	2,841,523	697,230	24.54
2001	3,232,281	680,170	21.04
TOTAL	**12,545,546**	**2,929,070**	**23.35**

Table 5.2

**Number of Incidents with a Violent Crime, NIBRS
by Crime Type, 1996-2001**

	1996	Percent of total	1997	Percent of total	1998	Percent of total	1999	Percent of total	2000	Percent of total	2001	Percent of total	Number of incidents	Percent of total
Murder/Nonnegligent Manslaughter	596	0.23	708	0.21	963	0.22	1,176	0.22	1,570	0.23	1,500	0.22	6,513	0.22
Negligent Manslaughter	67	0.03	60	0.02	105	0.02	115	0.02	146	0.02	112	0.02	605	0.02
Justifiable Homicide	18	0.01	20	0.01	14	*	25	*	40	0.01	50	0.01	167	0.01
Forcible Rape	4,957	1.94	6,868	2.08	10,213	2.34	11,408	2.15	14,310	2.05	14,531	2.14	62,287	2.13
Forcible Sodomy	1,335	0.52	1,743	0.53	2,661	0.61	3,159	0.60	3,395	0.49	3,231	0.48	15,524	0.53
Sexual Assault with an Object	741	0.29	1,079	0.33	1,447	0.33	1,648	0.31	2,165	0.31	1,759	0.26	8,839	0.30
Forcible Fondling	5,898	2.31	7,804	2.36	10,802	2.48	13,521	2.55	16,616	2.38	15,698	2.31	70,339	2.40
Incest	199	0.08	288	0.09	301	0.07	386	0.07	433	0.06	400	0.06	2,007	0.07
Statutory Rape	954	0.37	1,061	0.32	1,521	0.35	1,957	0.37	2,347	0.34	2,456	0.36	10,296	0.35
Robbery	11,809	4.63	14,719	4.46	19,735	4.53	22,973	4.33	34,577	4.96	36,521	5.37	140,334	4.79
Aggravated Assault	49,113	19.25	60,551	18.34	73,839	16.95	81,584	15.37	105,411	15.12	102,042	15.00	472,540	16.13
Simple Assault	144,141	56.50	187,857	56.90	251,316	57.69	308,361	58.10	407,021	58.38	387,315	56.94	1,686,011	57.56
Intimidation	35,283	13.83	47,409	14.36	62,724	14.40	84,438	15.91	109,199	15.66	114,555	16.84	453,608	15.49
TOTAL	**255,111**	**100.00**	**330,167**	**100.00**	**435,641**	**100.00**	**530,751**	**100.00**	**697,230**	**100.00**	**680,170**	**100.00**	**2,929,070**	**100.00**

Due to rounding, the percent of total may not add to 100.00 percent.

*Less than 1 one-hundreth of 1 percent.

of violent offenses for each year were for simple assault (57.6 percent average), aggravated assault (16.5 percent average), and intimidation (15.1 percent average). Each of the remaining crime categories reflected percentages less than 5.5 percent.

Relationships in Violent Offenses

Tables 5.4 and 5.5 show the relationships of the victims to the offenders in the violent offenses studied. Table 5.4 shows all relationship categories that were available and that applied to this study. Of the 3,031,884 violent offenses reported during the period, there were 3,534,254 offenses for which the UCR Program knew the relationships of victims to offenders. Of these, 1,551,143 were familial relationships, and the totals for each of these categories are provided in Table 5.5, broken down by year. The most prevalent relationship was boyfriend/girlfriend (29.6 percent) followed by spouse (24.4

percent). When spouse, common-law spouse, and ex-spouse were considered together, the percentage of the total rose to 32.4 percent.

Table 5.6 shows violent offenses by the type of abuse being studied. There were 873,732 offenses; 53 percent were spousal abuse; 719,752, or 44 percent, were child abuse; and 47,695, or 3 percent, were elder abuse. Simple assault was the most prevalent offense in all three relationship categories followed by aggravated assault and intimidation in the spousal abuse category.

In the case of child abuse, simple assault was the most prevalent offense, followed by the sum of the sexual assaults, then aggravated assault, and intimidation.

In the elderly abuse categories, simple assault comprised the largest offense total, followed by intimidation, robbery, and aggravated assault. Most sex offenses (i.e., forcible rape, forcible sodomy, sexual assault with an object, forcible fondling, incest, and statutory rape) fall in the cat-

egory of child abuse, comprising 122,644, or 17.0 percent, of those offenses.

Weapons

The weapons used in violent offenses in which there was a familial relationship are broken down by year in Table 5.7. For each year studied, the most prevalent weapon used were those categorized by the UCR as "personal" (i.e., hands, fists, or feet). Nearly 70 percent of violent offenses involving familial relationships were carried out using this type of weapon. Following personal weapons, no weapons (11.4 percent) and knives, handguns, and blunt objects, (between 3 and 4 percent) were used most often to carry out the most common offenses reported for the period.

Weapon use in offenses involving familial relationships broken down by the three types of relationships studied is presented in Table 5.8. Personal weapons were used most often in cases of spousal and child abuse, (78.4 percent and 73.3 percent, respectively). However, in the elderly abuse category,

Table 5.3

Number of Offenses, by Violent Crime, 1996-2001

	1996	Percent of total	1997	Percent of total	1998	Percent of total	1999	Percent of total	2000	Percent of total	2001	Percent of total	Number of offenses	Percent of all offenses
Murder/Nonnegligent Manslaughter	594	0.23	702	0.21	959	0.22	1,176	0.22	1,570	0.23	1,820	0.23	6,821	0.22
Negligent Manslaughter	67	0.03	59	0.02	104	0.02	114	0.02	146	0.02	138	0.02	628	0.02
Justifiable Homicide	18	0.01	20	0.01	14	*	25	*	40	0.01	58	0.01	175	0.01
Forcible Rape	4,929	1.93	6,821	2.07	10,171	2.34	11,373	2.14	14,302	2.05	16,204	2.07	63,800	2.10
Forcible Sodomy	1,327	0.52	1,728	0.52	2,639	0.61	3,152	0.59	3,392	0.49	3,819	0.49	16,057	0.53
Sexual Assault with an Object	737	0.29	1,073	0.33	1,440	0.33	1,634	0.31	2,163	0.31	2,163	0.28	9,210	0.30
Forcible Fondling	5,854	2.30	7,733	2.34	10,743	2.47	13,481	2.54	16,607	2.38	17,796	2.27	72,214	2.38
Incest	194	0.08	282	0.09	301	0.07	380	0.07	433	0.06	458	0.06	2,048	0.07
Statutory Rape	951	0.37	1,056	0.32	1,510	0.35	1,948	0.37	2,346	0.34	2,806	0.36	10,617	0.35
Robbery	11,805	4.63	14,709	4.46	19,718	4.53	22,969	4.33	34,572	4.96	42,855	5.46	146,628	4.84
Aggravated Assault	49,083	19.26	60,524	18.35	73,818	16.96	81,569	15.38	105,405	15.12	114,002	14.54	484,401	15.98
Simple Assault	144,061	56.52	187,785	56.93	251,158	57.70	308,269	58.11	407,006	58.38	454,558	57.97	1,752,837	57.81
Intimidation	35,263	13.83	47,385	14.36	62,685	14.40	84,412	15.91	109,191	15.66	127,512	16.26	466,448	15.38
TOTAL	**254,883**	**100.00**	**329,877**	**100.00**	**435,260**	**100.00**	**530,502**	**100.00**	**697,173**	**100.00**	**784,189**	**100.00**	**3,031,884**	**100.00**

Due to rounding, the percent of total may not add to 100.00 percent
*Less than 1 one-hundreth of 1 percent.

Table 5.4

Relationship of Victim to Offender, 1996-2001

Relationship to Victim	Year													
	1996		1997		1998		1999		2000		2001		Total	
	Number	Percent	Number	Percent	Number	Percent	Number	Percent	Number	Percent	Number	Percent	Number	Percent
Spouse	33,432	11.32	42,880	11.24	54,552	10.77	67,662	10.99	87,681	10.77	92,896	10.08	379,103	10.73
Common-Law Spouse	7,225	2.45	9,371	2.46	13,253	2.62	14,910	2.42	17,229	2.12	17,105	1.86	79,093	2.24
Parent	6,910	2.34	9,222	2.42	12,200	2.41	15,842	2.57	21,028	2.58	24,171	2.62	89,373	2.53
Sibling	7,505	2.54	9,605	2.52	12,815	2.53	16,177	2.63	21,206	2.60	24,588	2.67	91,896	2.60
Child	7,312	2.47	10,012	2.63	14,313	2.83	18,185	2.95	23,943	2.94	26,567	2.88	100,332	2.84
Grandparent	315	0.11	452	0.12	618	0.12	783	0.13	1,122	0.14	1,348	0.15	4,638	0.13
Grandchild	502	0.17	606	0.16	939	0.19	1,095	0.18	1,344	0.17	1,440	0.16	5,926	0.17
In-Law	2,346	0.79	2,854	0.75	3,595	0.71	4,450	0.72	5,389	0.66	6,001	0.65	24,635	0.70
Stepparent	1,165	0.39	1,485	0.39	2,258	0.45	3,000	0.49	3,804	0.47	4,345	0.47	16,057	0.45
Stepchild	1,920	0.65	2,413	0.63	3,464	0.68	4,300	0.70	5,509	0.68	6,037	0.66	23,643	0.67
Stepsibling	326	0.11	493	0.13	720	0.14	890	0.14	1,266	0.16	1,335	0.14	5,030	0.14
Other Family Member	5,784	1.96	7,313	1.92	10,947	2.16	14,336	2.33	19,112	2.35	22,435	2.43	79,927	2.26
Boyfriend/Girlfriend	35,805	12.12	48,650	12.76	62,133	12.27	77,247	12.55	108,280	13.30	126,556	13.73	458,671	12.98
Child of Boyfriend/Girlfriend	808	0.27	1,054	0.28	1,482	0.29	1,840	0.30	2,404	0.30	2,894	0.31	10,482	0.30
Ex-Spouse	3,879	1.31	4,922	1.29	6,213	1.23	7,911	1.29	10,055	1.24	11,659	1.27	44,639	1.26
Acquaintance	72,411	24.51	88,514	23.21	110,506	21.82	124,845	20.28	157,013	19.29	176,002	19.10	729,291	20.63
Friend	8,379	2.84	10,051	2.64	13,796	2.72	17,086	2.78	22,720	2.79	24,422	2.65	96,454	2.73
Neighbor	4,703	1.59	6,389	1.68	8,670	1.71	10,845	1.76	13,950	1.71	15,863	1.72	60,420	1.71
Babysittee (the baby)	346	0.12	455	0.12	595	0.12	665	0.11	742	0.09	778	0.08	3,581	0.10
Homosexual relationship	296	0.10	492	0.13	757	0.15	968	0.16	1,578	0.19	2,027	0.22	6,118	0.17
Employee	725	0.25	1,123	0.29	1,338	0.26	1,742	0.28	2,388	0.29	2,821	0.31	10,137	0.29
Employer	572	0.19	862	0.23	1,034	0.20	1,391	0.23	1,731	0.21	1,922	0.21	7,512	0.21
Stranger	36,725	12.43	44,114	11.57	53,302	10.53	60,622	9.85	83,666	10.28	95,169	10.33	373,598	10.57
Victim was Offender[1]	17,447	5.91	22,003	5.77	27,873	5.50	34,016	5.53	47,280	5.81	55,772	6.05	204,391	5.78
Otherwise Known	13,692	4.63	20,979	5.50	30,918	6.11	41,675	6.77	57,798	7.10	67,205	7.29	232,267	6.57
Unknown	24,920	8.43	35,092	9.20	58,134	11.48	72,986	11.86	95,850	11.77	110,058	11.94	397,040	11.23
TOTAL	**295,450**	**100.00**	**381,406**	**100.00**	**506,425**	**100.00**	**615,469**	**100.00**	**814,088**	**100.00**	**921,416**	**100.00**	**3,534,254**	**100.0**

[1]The category "Victim was Offender" is used in cases where all of the participants in an incident were victims and offenders of the same offense such as domestic disputes where both husband and wife are charged with assault, double murders, etc.
Due to rounding, the percent of total may not add to 100.00 percent.

Table 5.5

Relationship of Victim to Offender, Within Family Relationship, 1996-2001

Relationship to Victim	1996		1997		1998		1999		2000		2001		Total	
	Number	Percent	Number	Percent	Number	Percent	Number	Percent	Number	Percent	Number	Percent	Number	Percent
Spouse	33,432	26.38	42,880	25.86	54,552	24.97	67,662	24.90	87,681	24.27	92,896	22.82	379,103	24.44
Common-Law Spouse	7,225	5.70	9,371	5.65	13,253	6.07	14,910	5.49	17,229	4.77	17,105	4.20	79,093	5.10
Parent	6,910	5.45	9,222	5.56	12,200	5.58	15,842	5.83	21,028	5.82	24,171	5.94	89,373	5.76
Sibling	7,505	5.92	9,605	5.79	12,815	5.87	16,177	5.95	21,206	5.87	24,588	6.04	91,896	5.92
Child	7,312	5.77	10,012	6.04	14,313	6.55	18,185	6.69	23,943	6.63	26,567	6.53	100,332	6.47
Grandparent	315	0.25	452	0.27	618	0.28	783	0.29	1,122	0.31	1,348	0.33	4,638	0.30
Grandchild	502	0.40	606	0.37	939	0.43	1,095	0.40	1,344	0.37	1,440	0.35	5,926	0.38
In-Law	2,346	1.85	2,854	1.72	3,595	1.65	4,450	1.64	5,389	1.49	6,001	1.47	24,635	1.59
Stepparent	1,165	0.92	1,485	0.90	2,258	1.03	3,000	1.10	3,804	1.05	4,345	1.07	16,057	1.04
Stepchild	1,920	1.51	2,413	1.46	3,464	1.59	4,300	1.58	5,509	1.52	6,037	1.48	23,643	1.52
Stepsibling	326	0.26	493	0.30	720	0.33	890	0.33	1,266	0.35	1,335	0.33	5,030	0.32
Other Family Member	5,784	4.56	7,313	4.41	10,947	5.01	14,336	5.27	19,112	5.29	22,435	5.51	79,927	5.15
Boyfriend/Girlfriend	35,805	28.25	48,650	29.34	62,133	28.44	77,247	28.42	108,280	29.97	126,556	31.10	458,671	29.57
Child of Boyfriend/Girlfriend	808	0.64	1,054	0.64	1,482	0.68	1,840	0.68	2,404	0.67	2,894	0.71	10,482	0.68
Ex-Spouse	3,879	3.06	4,922	2.97	6,213	2.84	7,911	2.91	10,055	2.78	11,659	2.86	44,639	2.88
Victim was Offender[1]	9,744	7.69	12,318	7.43	15,868	7.26	19,239	7.08	27,397	7.58	32,634	8.02	117,200	7.56
Otherwise Known	393	0.31	572	0.34	1,226	0.56	1,943	0.71	2,301	0.64	2,506	0.62	8,941	0.58
Unknown	1,373	1.08	1,586	0.96	1,890	0.87	1,975	0.73	2,256	0.62	2,477	0.61	11,557	0.75
TOTAL	**126,744**	**100.00**	**165,808**	**100.00**	**218,486**	**100.00**	**271,785**	**100.00**	**361,326**	**100.00**	**406,994**	**100.00**	**1,551,143**	**100.00**

[1]The category "Victim was Offender" is used in cases where all of the participants in an incident were victims and offenders of the same offense such as domestic disputes where both husband and wife are charged with assault, double murders, etc.

Due to rounding, the percent of total may not add to 100.00 percent

Table 5.6

Violent Offenses, by Family Relationship, 1996-2001

	Spouse	Child	Elderly relative
Murder/Nonnegligent Manslaughter	1,226	1,061	444
Negligent Manslaughter	38	200	51
Justifiable Homicide	7	14	5
Forcible Rape	8,195	33,644	432
Forcible Sodomy	852	12,112	78
Sexual Assault with an Object	612	6,588	71
Forcible Fondling	1,920	57,941	363
Incest	88	1,789	5
Statutory Rape	2,765	10,570	3
Robbery	1,801	19,080	7,140
Aggravated Assault	115,769	102,675	6,919
Simple Assault	647,286	397,775	20,955
Intimidation	93,173	76,303	11,229
TOTAL	**873,732**	**719,752**	**47,695**

personal weapons constituted only 36.1 percent of the offenses involving weapons. Almost 44 percent of elder abuse offenses involved the use of a handgun.

Victims, Offenders, and Relationships

Substance Abuse

Table 5.9 shows the number of family violence incidents in which substance abuse was involved. The overwhelming majority of these situations involved alcohol, which was used in 99.8 percent of violent family incidents for which there was a substance abuse code.

Substance abuse in offenses involving the three domestic relationships studied is presented in Table 5.10. In all three relationships, more than 99 percent of the offenses involving abused substances involved alcohol.

Table 5.7

Use of Weapons in Violent Offenses, 1996-2001

	1996	Percent of total	1997	Percent of total	1998	Percent of total	1999	Percent of total	2000	Percent of total	2001	Percent of total	Total	Percent of total
Firearm (Type Unknown)	1,678	0.78	2,184	0.79	2,506	0.70	3,478	0.82	5,195	0.93	5,245	0.97	**20,286**	**0.86**
Handgun	9,330	4.36	10,808	3.92	13,214	3.68	15,165	3.58	22,821	4.08	24,791	4.60	**96,129**	**4.05**
Rifle	712	0.33	857	0.31	1,084	0.30	1,213	0.29	1,481	0.26	1,418	0.26	**6,765**	**0.29**
Shotgun	1,313	0.61	1,471	0.53	1,741	0.49	2,076	0.49	2,545	0.45	2,485	0.46	**11,631**	**0.49**
Other Firearm	384	0.18	507	0.18	757	0.21	681	0.16	969	0.17	965	0.18	**4,263**	**0.18**
Knife/Cutting Instrument	11,399	5.33	13,421	4.87	16,535	4.61	19,214	4.53	24,747	4.42	25,510	4.73	**110,826**	**4.67**
Blunt Object	11,128	5.20	12,222	4.43	13,676	3.81	14,582	3.44	19,813	3.54	19,841	3.68	**91,262**	**3.85**
Motor Vehicle	2,445	1.14	3,093	1.12	4,313	1.20	5,123	1.21	7,101	1.27	7,811	1.45	**29,886**	**1.26**
Personal Weapons (hands, fists, feet, etc.)	154,076	72.04	197,632	71.69	247,287	68.96	287,413	67.78	381,916	68.23	369,559	68.53	**1,637,883**	**69.07**
Poison	38	0.02	38	0.01	67	0.02	72	0.02	79	0.01	89	0.02	**383**	**0.02**
Explosives	42	0.02	37	0.01	72	0.02	104	0.02	132	0.02	125	0.02	**512**	**0.02**
Fire/Incendiary Device	117	0.05	145	0.05	147	0.04	205	0.05	275	0.05	293	0.05	**1,182**	**0.05**
Asphyxiation	21	0.01	34	0.01	59	0.02	111	0.03	133	0.02	100	0.02	**458**	**0.02**
Unknown Weapon	5,084	2.38	9,385	3.40	10,991	3.06	13,969	3.29	27,199	4.86	21,992	4.08	**88,620**	**3.74**
No Weapon	16,112	7.53	23,832	8.65	46,168	12.87	60,623	14.30	65,381	11.68	59,032	10.95	**271,148**	**11.43**
TOTAL	**213,879**	**100.00**	**275,666**	**100.00**	**358,617**	**100.00**	**424,029**	**100.00**	**559,787**	**100.00**	**539,256**	**100.00**	**2,371,234**	**100.00**

Due to rounding, the percent of total may not add to 100.00 percent.

Gender, Race, and Age

Victims of violent family crimes tend to be female. Table 5.11 presents the overall breakdown, indicating that 74.8 percent of the victims were female.

The races of the victims of violent crime are presented in Table 5.12. Over 70 percent of the victims were white; black victims accounted for a little more than 27 percent of all victims.

Age groups of victims of domestic violence are presented in Table 5.13. As we would expect, the 18 to 65 age group is the most prevalent, comprising 83.4 percent of the victims. The two juvenile groups follow. The elderly group is very small; the over-65 age group accounted for 1.1 percent of the violent crime victims in familial relationships.

Table 5.14 displays the number of events or confrontations by the age ranges of the victims and their offenders. The first part of the table contains the total number of all confrontations by all victims and offenders (broken down by age range). These data were reported to the UCR Program via the NIBRS from 1996–2001. Most of the confrontations

Table 5.8

Use of Weapons
Number of Offenses by Family Relationship, 1996-2001

	Spouse	Percent of total	Child	Percent of total	Elderly relative	Percent of total
Firearm (Type Unknown)	1,679	0.22	91	0.11	2,253	8.22
Handgun	8,997	1.18	450	0.57	11,989	43.72
Rifle	1,464	0.19	115	0.14	67	0.24
Shotgun	2,189	0.29	130	0.16	103	0.38
Other Firearm	202	0.03	29	0.04	7	0.03
Knife/Cutting Instrument	26,415	3.46	1,287	1.62	396	1.44
Blunt Object	17,721	2.32	2,078	2.62	593	2.16
Motor Vehicle	6,867	0.90	369	0.47	72	0.26
Personal Weapons (hands, fists, feet, etc.)	599,072	78.37	58,141	73.28	9,889	36.06
Poison	78	0.01	5	0.01	10	0.04
Explosives	22	*	2	*	1	*
Fire/Incendiary Device	331	0.04	73	0.09	19	0.07
Asphyxiation	200	0.03	37	0.05	8	0.03
Unknown Weapon	19,787	2.59	3,490	4.40	475	1.73
No Weapon	79,397	10.39	13,040	16.44	1,542	5.62
TOTAL	**764,421**	**100.00**	**79,337**	**100.00**	**27,424**	**100.00**

Due to rounding, the percent of total may not add to 100.00 percent.
*Less than 1 one-hundreth of 1 percent.

involved victims and offenders in the 18 to 65 age category.

The second part of the table shows the number of confrontations where a familial relationship exists between the victim and the offender. Again, the highest number of confrontations oc-

curred where both victims and offenders were in the 18 to 65 age group.

The third section of the table contains the number of confrontations that could be considered spousal abuse by the age groups of victims and by the age groups of offenders. As expected,

Table 5.9

Number of Family Violence Incidents Involving Substance Abuse, 1996-2001

Substance	1996	Percent of total	1997	Percent of total	1998	Percent of total	1999	Percent of total	2000	Percent of total	2001	Percent of total	Total	Percent of total
Alcohol	39,486	99.93	47,088	99.89	59,189	99.83	68,079	99.76	89,877	99.79	79,972	99.78	383,691	99.82
Drugs	27	0.07	52	0.11	100	0.17	163	0.24	188	0.21	173	0.22	703	0.18
TOTAL	**39,513**	**100.00**	**47,140**	**100.00**	**59,289**	**100.00**	**68,242**	**100.00**	**90,065**	**100.00**	**80,145**	**100.00**	**384,394**	**100.00**

Table 5.10

Number of Offenses Involving Substance Abuse by Family Relationship 1996-2001

Substance	Spouse	Percent of total	Child	Percent of total	Elderly relative	Percent of total
Alcohol	182,822	99.96	10,691	99.56	3,476	99.91
Drugs	77	0.04	47	0.44	3	0.09
TOTAL	**182,899**	**100.00**	**10,738**	**100.00**	**3,479**	**100.00**

the greatest number of confrontations involved victims and offenders in the 18-to 65-year-old group (891,514).

The number of confrontations between parent and child by the ages of the victims and the ages of offenders is shown in the fourth section of the table. Most of these confrontations occurred where the offenders were in the 18-to 65-year-old category.

Confrontations involving elderly victims are shown by the age groups of the victims and the age groups of their offenders in the final section of the table. Again, most of the confrontations involved offenders 18 to 65 years old (27,574).

Injuries

The types of injuries suffered by victims of domestic violence during the study period are presented in Table 5.15. Major injuries are defined as those in which the victims suffered broken bones, possible internal injuries, loss of teeth, severe lacerations, or unconsciousness. Major and minor injuries were nearly equal in number for every year except 1997 when the data showed a few more minor injuries than major. Overall, 49.3 percent of the injuries reported were major, and 46.0 percent were minor. No injuries were reported in 4.7 percent of the reported offenses.

The numbers and types of injuries by type of abuse (i.e., spousal, child, and elderly) are presented in Table 5.16. In the spousal abuse category, the most prevalent type of injuries were minor. In child and elderly abuse situations, a majority of the cases involved no reported injuries (50.0 percent in child abuse cases and 50.4 percent in elderly abuse situations). Nearly 47 percent of child abuse cases and 45.1 percent of elderly abuse cases involved minor injuries. In all three categories, less than 5 percent of the cases involved major injuries.

LIMITATIONS

There are several limitations to this study. The UCR Program's Summary data, which comprise approximately 80 to 85 percent of the Program's database, could not be used to develop an in-depth study of this type. Those data are submitted as summary counts for the seven Part I crimes—murder, rape, robbery, aggravated assault, burglary, larceny, and motor vehicle theft—and cannot be

Table 5.11

Victims of Violent Crime in Family Relationships by Gender, 1996-2001

Gender	Number	Percent of total
Female	1,041,498	74.82
Male	348,267	25.02
Unknown	2,156	0.15
TOTAL	**1,391,921**	**100.00**

Due to rounding, the percent of total may not add to 100.00 percent.

Table 5.12

Victims of Violent Crime in Family Relationships by Race, 1996-2001

Race	Number	Percent of total
Asian/Pacific Islander	6,676	0.48
Black	379,884	27.29
American Indian/ Alaskan Native	5,320	0.38
Unknown	22,707	1.63
White	977,334	70.21
TOTAL	**1,391,921**	**100.00**

Due to rounding, the percent of total may not add to 100.00 percent.

Table 5.13

Victims of Violent Crime in Family Relationships by Age, 1996-2001

Age	Number	Percent of total
0-11	92,865	6.67
12-17	122,948	8.83
18-65	1,160,300	83.36
66 and up	15,808	1.14
TOTAL	**1,391,921**	**100.00**

Table 5.14

Number of Confrontations Specific to Incidents involving Family Relationships by Age of Victim and Offender, 1996-2001

	Offender age 0-11	Offender age 12-17	Offender age 18-65	Offender age 66 and up	Offender all ages
All					
Victim age 0-11	69,911	60,730	163,449	2,892	**296,982**
Victim age 12-17	41,498	228,466	244,432	2,495	**516,891**
Victim age 18-65	202,189	192,708	2,095,617	18,335	**2,508,849**
Victim age 66 and up	5,513	2,936	27,574	5,576	**41,599**
Victim all ages	**319,111**	**484,840**	**2,531,072**	**29,298**	**3,364,321**
All Family Relationships					
Victim age 0-11	8,473	14,031	75,443	965	**98,912**
Victim age 12-17	2,915	30,951	98,374	807	**133,047**
Victim age 18-65	19,579	73,687	1,077,014	6,995	**1,177,275**
Victim age 66 and up	289	1,102	11,828	3,284	**16,503**
Victim all ages	**31,256**	**119,771**	**1,262,659**	**12,051**	**1,425,737**
Significant Other					
Victim age 0-11	1,707	196	12,180	84	**14,167**
Victim age 12-17	576	8,829	23,497	54	**32,956**
Victim age 18-65	11,821	8,548	891,514	4,037	**915,920**
Victim age 66 and up	46	22	2,422	2,658	**5,148**
Victim all ages	**14,150**	**17,595**	**929,613**	**6,833**	**968,191**
Parent–Child					
Victim age 0-11	1,877	2,278	52,831	734	**57,720**
Victim age 12-17	680	4,399	51,559	614	**57,252**
Victim age 18-65	564	1,464	29,631	1,683	**33,342**
Victim age 66 and up	12	5	86	28	**131**
Victim all ages	**3,133**	**8,146**	**134,107**	**3,059**	**148,445**
Elderly Relative					
Victim age 0-11	0	0	0	0	–
Victim age 12-17	0	0	0	0	–
Victim age 18-65	0	0	0	0	–
Victim age 66 and up	5,513	2,936	27,574	5,576	**41,599**

Table 5.15

Number and Type of Injuries in Violent Offenses, 1996-2001

	1996	Percent of total	1997	Percent of total	1998	Percent of total	1999	Percent of total	2000	Percent of total	2001	Percent of total	Number of injuries	Percent of total
Major	102,488	48.46	129,192	47.07	176,386	48.66	215,217	49.55	285,087	49.79	276,795	50.35	**1,185,165**	**49.28**
Minor	94,422	44.65	130,012	47.37	168,686	46.53	200,054	46.06	262,678	45.88	250,099	45.49	**1,105,951**	**45.98**
None	14,573	6.89	15,239	5.55	17,434	4.81	19,091	4.40	24,794	4.33	22,891	4.16	**114,022**	**4.74**
TOTAL	**211,483**	**100.00**	**274,443**	**100.00**	**362,506**	**100.00**	**434,362**	**100.00**	**572,559**	**100.00**	**549,785**	**100.00**	**2,405,138**	**100.00**

Due to rounding, the percent of total may not add to 100.00 percent.

Table 5.16

Number of Injuries in Violent Offenses by Victim Category, 1996-2001

	Spousal abuse	Percent of total	Child abuse	Percent of total	Elderly abuse	Percent of total
Major	24,769	3.17	2,546	3.01	648	4.54
Minor	425,267	54.37	39,714	46.94	6,436	45.07
None	332,142	42.46	42,344	50.05	7,195	50.39
TOTAL	**782,178**	**100.00**	**84,604**	**100.00**	**14,279**	**100.00**

disaggregated to study an incident. Further, the use of the Hierarchy Rule in the Summary system limits the reporting of data to the offenses that fall inside the "hierarchy" structure of Part I crimes as defined by the UCR Program. In multiple offense situations, this procedure requires the reporting agency to count only the highest offense on the hierarchy list and ignore all others. For example, if a man beat, raped, and murdered his wife, the only offense that would be reported to the UCR Program (if the law enforcement agency was not reporting data via the NIBRS) is murder—the highest crime in the hierarchy. The other offenses would simply be lost data.

NIBRS data are richer and more disaggregated than Summary data. However, NIBRS data are not as universally submitted as are Summary data. Over the decade of the nineties, more states became certified NIBRS participants and began submitting NIBRS data. The number of states submitting NIBRS data has grown from year to year. Even so, as of 2002, there were only 4,239 law enforcement agencies from 24 states using the NIBRS. This number represents 17 percent of the U.S. population and 18 percent of the crime statistics collected by the UCR Program. These data do not represent a scientific sample to reflect the national phenomenon. There are no cities participating in the NIBRS that have populations of 1 million or more inhabitants. There are only 11 cities or consolidated counties that contribute NIBRS data whose populations are 250,000 or more.

A regional analysis would be valuable in this study. Regional variances could indicate cultural differences that could be studied to determine the causes and effects of domestic violence. For this study, however, regional analysis may hide more than it shows. NIBRS data for the period 1996–2001 are available for 20 states and the District of Columbia. Many of these states joined the program some time in the late nineties; therefore, the data for some of these states are not complete for that period. This study may better have been conducted by examining states for a particular year for which each had NIBRS data available.

Even so, until more states contribute NIBRS data, regional analysis will be limited. For example, the West is defined by the UCR Program as Arizona, Colorado, Idaho, Montana, Nevada, New Mexico, Utah, Wyoming, Alaska, California, Hawaii, Oregon, and Washington. As of 2003, the only states from this region that were participating in the NIBRS program were Arizona, Colorado, Idaho, and Utah. The largest state in the region is California, which has the highest population and the highest number of crimes. In addition, it has many of the largest cities in the region. Its absence from regional statistics could present an inaccurate crime picture of the West.

With these limitations, NIBRS data may not represent the crime experience in the entire United States. Due to these limitations, the results of this study must be interpreted with caution and with the noted caveats.

SUMMARY AND CONCLUSIONS

The objective of depicting violence among family members and intimate partners as reported in the data collected by the FBI's UCR Program has been met. Even though the findings in this report cannot be generalized to the entire country, it has demonstrated the utility of NIBRS data for analyses of this type. Moreover, other crimes or crime categories can be examined at a more in-depth level using NIBRS data. The simple methods used here demonstrate that characteristics of incidents, offenses, victims, and offenders can be examined across data segments.

These findings are interesting and have significant implications for law- and policymakers. This study and other research concerning the demographic characteristics of the victims, offenders, and locations of domestic violence and information on prior criminal history and probationary status of offenders could be used to paint a fuller picture of the problem. This information could be valuable in enabling law enforcement policymakers, state legislatures, and Congress to develop better, more effective strategies for preventing spousal, child, and elderly abuse.

ENDNOTES

[1] Straus, M. A. and R. J. Gelles. (1988). "Violence in American Families: How Much is There and Why Does It Occur?" In E. W. Nunnally, C. S. Chilman, and F. M. Cox. Troubled Relationships. Families in Trouble Series, v. 3. Newbury Park, CA: Sage (1988), p. 141.

[2] Straus, M. A. (2000). "Family Violence." In E. G. Borgatta and M. L. Borgatta (eds), Encyclopedia of Sociology, Second Edition, v. 2. NY: Macmillan, pp. 981-987. Straus and Gelles. (1988), p. 142.

[3] Kemper, C. Henry. (1962). "The Battered Child Syndrome," Journal of the American Medical Association.

[4] Straus and Gelles. pp. 141-142.

[5] Abbott, J., R. Johnson, J. Kaziol-McLain. (1995). "Domestic Violence Against Women: Incidence and Prevalence in an Emergency Department Population." Journal of the American Medical Association. V. 272: 1763-1767.

[6] Supplementary Homicide Report. (2002). U.S. Department of Justice, Federal Bureau of Investigation.

[7] Crime in the United States. (1996). U.S. Department of Justice, Federal Bureau of Investigation.

[8] National Incident-Based Reporting System. (2002). U.S. Department of Justice, Federal Bureau of Investigation.

[9] American Psychological Association http://www.apa.org.

[10] Tjaden, P., N. Thoennes. (2000). Full Report of the Prevalence, Incidence, and Consequences of Intimate Partner Violence Against Women: Findings from the National Violence Against Women Survey. Report for grant 93-IJ-CX-0012, funded by the National Institute of Justice and the Centers for Disease Control and Prevention. Washington, D.C.: NIJ.

[11] Tjaden and Thoennes. (2000).

[12] Rand, M. R. (1997). Violence-Related Injuries Treated in Hospital Emergency Departments. Bureau of Justice Statistics, Special Report. Washington, D.C.: U.S. Department of Justice.

[13] Rand. (1997).

[14] Stets, J. E., M. A. Straus. (1990). "Gender Differences in Reporting Marital Violence and its Consequences." Straus, M. A. and R. J. Gelles, editors. Physical Violence in American Families: Risk Factors and Adaptations to Violence in 8,145 Families. New Brunswick, NJ: Transaction Publishers, (1990): pp. 151-165.

[15] National Research Council. (1996). Understanding Violence Against Women. Washington, D.C.: National Academy Press, 79-90.

[16] Straus, M. A. and R. J. Gelles, eds., (1990). Physical Violence in American Families: Risk Factors and Adaptations to Violence in 8,145 Families. New Brunswick, NJ: Transaction Books.

[17] Roizen, J. (1993). "Issues in the Epidemiology of Alcohol and Violence." In S. E. Martin, ed., Alcohol and Interpersonal Violence: Fostering Multidisciplinary Perspectives. Bethesda, MD: National Institute on Alcohol Abuse and Alcoholism. NIAAA Research Monograph No. 24, pp. 3-36.

[18] National Crime Victimization Survey, 1992-1996. U.S. Department of Justice, Bureau of Justice Statistics.

[19] APA Online Press Release, http://www.apa.org/releases/facts.html.

[20] APA Online Press Release, http://www.apa.org/releases/facts.html.

[21] APA Online Press Release, http://www.apa.org/releases/facts.html.

[22] U.S. Advisory Board on Child Abuse and Neglect. (1995). A Nation's Shame: Fatal Child Abuse and Neglect in the United States. Washington, D.C.: U.S. Department of Health and Human Services.

[23] Tatara, T., L. M. Kuzmeskus, and E. Duckhorn. (1997). "Trends in Elder Abuse in Domestic Settings," Elder Abuse Information Series No. 2. Report for grant 90-am-0660, funded by the National Center on Elder Abuse. Washington, D.C.: NCEA.

[24] Tatara, Kuzmeskus, and Duckhorn. (1997).

[25] Tatara, Kuzmeskus, and Duckhorn. (1997).

[26] Tatara, Kuzmeskus, and Duckhorn. (1997).

HOMICIDE AS A COMMUNITY PROBLEM IN THE UNITED STATES

The Importance of Homicide as a Community Problem in the United States

Within the realm of criminal justice, probably no offense is as studied as that of homicide. In the United States, most certainly no other offense is treated more seriously in the criminal justice system. The most severe punishments are reserved for those individuals found guilty of homicide, and no statute of limitations exists for homicide as is found in most other types of offenses. Homicide, or fear of homicide, garners an immediate reaction from communities. As such, law enforcement continually focuses efforts on the issues surrounding violent crime such as illegal gun or drug crime crackdowns. Ultimately, they hope to lessen the likelihood of homicide victimization and, as a result, fear within a community.

Patterns of Homicide

To understand the dynamics of any criminal offense, one would focus upon general patterns, and homicide is no exception. These patterns can be expressed in terms of temporal patterns (how homicide has changed over time), spatial patterns (how homicide changes over regions or locations), patterns in the inherent characteristics in terms of victims, offenders or other qualities of the homicide incident, or any combination of these qualities. To provide a thorough review of the studies conducted about homicide is beyond the scope and purpose of this paper. Suffice it to say, there have been numerous studies focusing on any one of the major themes listed above. However, in terms of recognizing patterns in the

homicide data, these studies traditionally limit themselves to analyzing only a few dimensions at one time. For example, age-specific rates for victims or offenders may be analyzed over time or space. Even though theoretically possible, difficulties in interpretation arise when traditional pattern analysis techniques, such as cross-tabulations or scatter plots, are used to analyze more than three dimensions at one time. To try to view large complex data sets such as can be found with homicide in order to recognize patterns requires a more sophisticated approach. Newer technologies have made these sophisticated pattern analysis techniques more accessible through both the availability of computing resources and the ease of use.

Pattern Recognition and Data Mining

The underlying goal of pattern recognition is, ultimately, data reduction. Instinctively, humans reduce the amount of information in the world by organizing its constituents into a series of conceptual types. This is accomplished through highlighting important characteristics that define the differences and disregarding the details that add little value. The details of criminal incidents are invaluable to law enforcement to achieve the goals of solving and reducing crime. However, making sense of those details is a challenge when the scope is broader than a single incident. In order to truly use the data, the analyst must first organize the data. This can be done in one of two ways: either conceptual classification or numerical classification.

Conceptual classification methods are often used to identify ideal or polar (extreme) types and are more likely to be drawn from a collective set of ex-

periences that represent the concepts rather than an actual set of cases. Numerical classification uses quantitative techniques to identify like cases that translate into classes. Numerical classification has been more readily used in biology and other sciences rather than in the social realm. However, that practice is beginning to change as the technology involved has become more accessible to a wider audience (Bailey 1994).

The amount of information available to law enforcement via their incident reports and external sources, such as medical examiners offices, drug laboratories, and other sources of intelligence, have placed new demands on already overstretched resources which have limited the time and attention that each law enforcement employee can spend on investigation and analysis. Law enforcement would benefit from the application of newer computer technologies in both hardware and software to help cut a clearer path through their data in order to help define problems in their communities. For these and many other reasons, the pattern recognition capabilities in data mining have become increasingly popular with law enforcement.

Crime analysts also can use pattern recognition techniques common to data mining to examine large criminal justice data sets. In the case of homicide, the Uniform Crime Reporting (UCR) Program through its Supplementary Homicide Report (SHR) collects information on the incident for the vast majority of reported homicides from state and local law enforcement. By using pattern recognition techniques, such as cluster analysis, with homicide incident information, the patterns that occur naturally within the data set can be used to provide a deeper understanding of the dynamics of homicide in the United States. This can aid more in-depth studies that focus on the underlying causes of or concurrent factors that contribute to homicide.

Objectives of the Study

By using incident-specific information available through the SHR, pattern recognition or data mining techniques can be applied to discern any patterns that exist in the homicide data. One methodology employed is cluster analysis. Cluster analysis uses a series of mathematical computations to identify groups that occur in data sets. These groups, or clusters, could be used to delve beneath the surface of the homicide rate so often quoted to reveal the nature of those rates and to explore them in a regional and temporal context. The objectives could be summarized by the following questions:

- What do the characteristics of homicide incidents reveal about the nature of homicide in the United States?
- How might the homicide data be decomposed to research it over time and space?
- How have the characteristics of homicide changed regionally since 1980?

Methodology

Data

The UCR Program defines murder and nonnegligent homicide as "the willful (nonnegligent) killing of one human being by another" (USDOJ 1984, p. 6). This definition does not include suicides, accidental deaths, assaults to murder, traffic fatalities, or attempted murders. Although justifiable homicides by law enforcement officers in the line of duty or private citizens during the commission of a felony are considered willful

killings, they have not been used in the calculation of published murder rates. Since 1962,[1] the FBI has collected information on homicide incidents that can be employed by a variety of users to explore the nature of homicides. This information, the Supplementary Homicide Report, is collected in addition to the official reports of crime used to calculate the national murder rate. The attributes collected on the form include the age, sex, and race of both victim and offender, weapons, relationship of victim to offender, circumstances of the homicide, as well as information on multiple victims and offenders. Additionally, law enforcement submits information on those incidents classified as justifiable homicide by UCR definitions via the SHR. It is included in this analysis.

The SHR data from 1980 through 2002 were recoded to express each incident in terms of 36 characteristics. These characteristics include the presence or absence of such things as juvenile offenders or victims, male victims or offenders, a firearm, or familial relationships between victims and offenders to name a few. More detail can be found on these characteristics in the Appendix of this study. These variables become the basis for the cluster analysis. For the remainder of the analysis, the homicide data are assigned to a county based upon the location and jurisdiction of the reporting agency. These county-level files form the basis of the geographic analysis. Because the incident-level homicide data can have fluctuations based upon the reporting history of the agencies involved as well as rare or extreme events, the data used for this study are the 3-year centered moving averages for each county. For example, the 3-year centered moving average representing levels of homicide for a county for 1982 is the average of the reports for 1981, 1982, and 1983. By using this

data smoothing technique, however, the first and last years in the series are lost. The final time series used in this study represent the years 1981 to 2001.

Cluster analysis of homicides incidents to determine types

The methodology of this study focuses on two primary areas: the use of cluster analysis to detect patterns inherent in the data set itself and the mapping of those homicides to a location with the help of geographic information system (GIS) technology.

As stated previously, a cluster analysis was performed on the recoded SHR data in order to discern any patterns inherent in the data. Cluster analysis allows for the data to drive the determination of types or groups rather than preconceived ideas of how homicides occur in the nation. It uses measurements of similarity based upon the characteristics of each homicide incident to allow "clustering" of types to be identified. Once the valid and reliable "types" of homicide are determined for each year, each reporting agency's types of homicide will be analyzed within each region to track their spatial movement and to see if they are related to one another or could be considered to be related to population movements. For a more thorough discussion of the technique, including the checks on the validity and reliability of the results, a Technical Note is available upon request from the FBI's Crime Analysis, Research and Development Unit, telephone (304) 625-3600.

GIS analysis of homicide incidents

In addition to cluster analysis, the homicide information was tracked through space with the aid of GIS technology. Initially, the location of the incident-level homicides is determined

Figure 5.1

Mean Center of Homicides Reported as Incident Data
1981-2001 (3-year centered moving average)

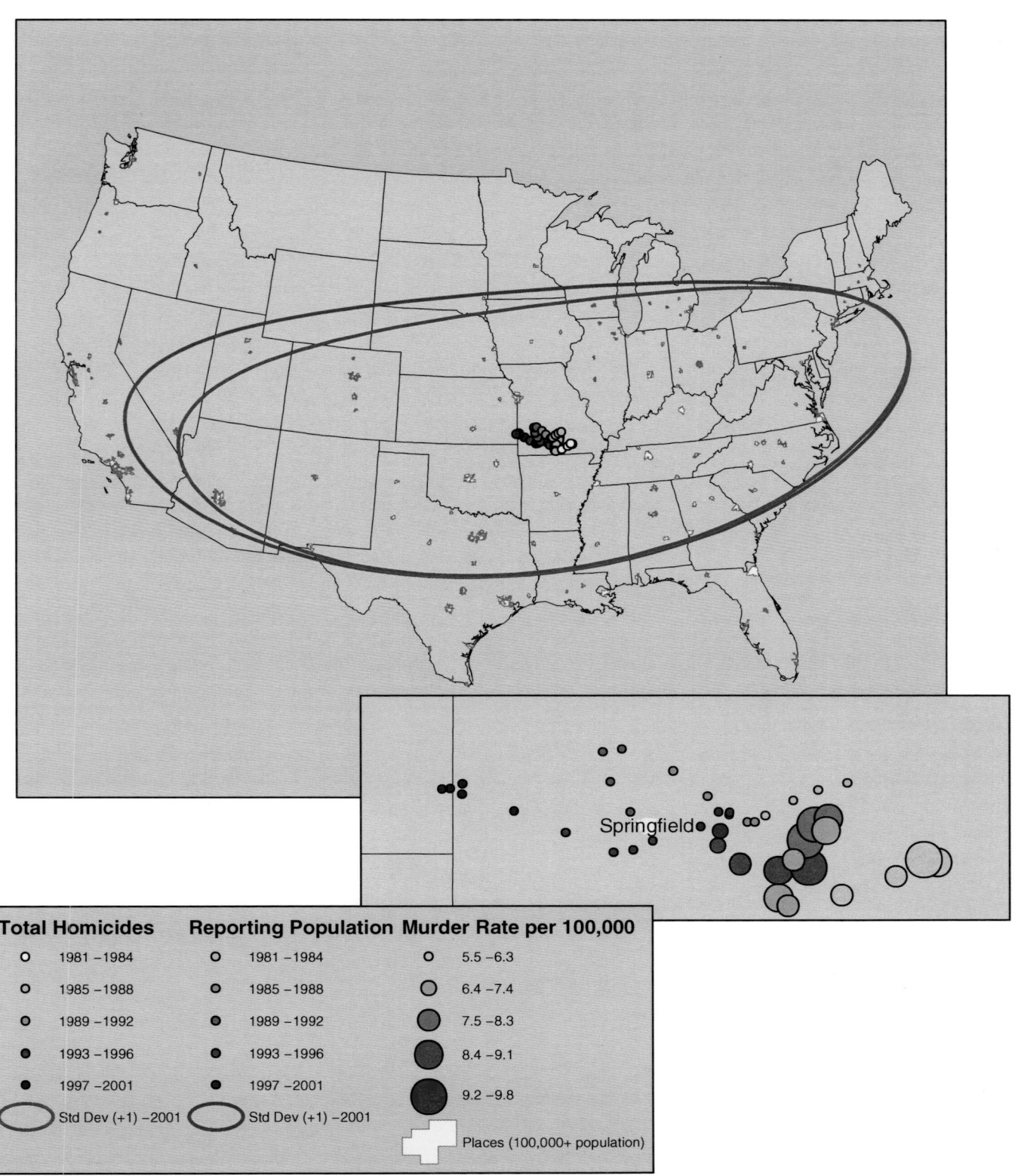

Total Homicides	Reporting Population	Murder Rate per 100,000
1981 –1984	1981 –1984	5.5 –6.3
1985 –1988	1985 –1988	6.4 –7.4
1989 –1992	1989 –1992	7.5 –8.3
1993 –1996	1993 –1996	8.4 –9.1
1997 –2001	1997 –2001	9.2 –9.8
Std Dev (+1) –2001	Std Dev (+1) –2001	Places (100,000+ population)

based upon the county in which the reporting agency resides. These incidents are spatially attributed to the point of the county centroid, which is the spatial center of the county. The mean center weighted by the number of reported homicides for each year, as well as by cluster type, is calculated for the Nation and each of the four regions. The mean center is the geographic equivalent to the average in a data set, and can be thought of as the "balancing point." Additionally, the standard deviation for the mean center is calculated for each year to indicate the dispersion of the data. This standard deviation is calculated for both the x- and y-dimension in space and is represented by an ellipse. For a more thorough discussion of the calculation of the weighted mean center and standard deviational ellipse, a Technical Note is available upon request from the FBI's Crime Analysis, Research and Development Unit, telephone (304) 625-3600.

Incidents of Homicide in the United States

Spatial trend of homicide incidents from 1981 to 2001 for the Nation

An examination of the calculated mean centers for the reports of incident-level homicide revealed that they appeared to be balanced near the geographic center of the United States. However, the standard deviational ellipse for the 2001 centered value indicated that the majority of the homicide incidents drifted to the east coast, and the reporting population was more geographically dispersed than the reports of homicide. This is primarily reflected in the northwest extant of the standard deviational ellipse. In other words, homicides were more concentrated than the reporting populations of the same counties for the same time period (2001). Additionally, there appears to be an urban bias to the homicide incidents

shown in this map. Approximately 66 percent of the Nation's homicides took place in an area that encompassed nearly 51 percent of the urban places with a population of 100,000 or more. (See Figure 5.1.)

The study period (1981-2001) began with a murder rate of approximately 9.8 murders per 100,000 inhabitants. However, the murder rate declined in subsequent years. The rate again rose to the same high in 1991 and then declined to the lowest point in 21 years by 2000 to 5.5 murders per 100,000 inhabitants (USDOJ 2003). Over time, the population covered by agencies reporting SHR data has shown a nearly true westerly progression from east to west. Interestingly, the Census Bureau reported the same momentum for the U.S. population. During the same time period, the incidence of homicide appears to have a western bias in its trend, and there is less movement for reported homicides. When the homicide rate is taken into consideration, there is a more easterly bias in higher crime rate years than the lower crime rate years in the latter part of the study period. This may be a reflection of a decline in the homicide rates in the East. (See Figure 5.1, Inset.)

Spatial trend of homicide incidents from 1981 to 2001 for each region

The UCR Program divides the United States into four geographic regions for data analyses: the Northeast, the Midwest, the South and the West. When the homicide data are analyzed by region, there appears to be strong evidence that the level of urbanity is tied to the incidence of homicide on a regional level, as well. Visually, the data show that urban areas are in a more geographically dispersed pattern in the Midwest and South. Although the West accounts for approximately 40 percent of the Nation's

populated places with 100,000 or more in population, they are almost all concentrated around San Francisco and Los Angeles. In the Northeast, these larger urban centers are almost all concentrated around the New York City and Boston areas. Additionally, the Northeast proportionally contributes only about 10 percent to the total number of the larger urban centers for the Nation. (See Figure 5.2.)

The regional dispersion of homicides in relation to reporting population nearly mimics the results of the national analysis. Except for the Northeast, homicides tend to be more concentrated than reporting population over time. With the exception of the South, most mean centers are also geographically close to major urban centers of the region (for example, New York City, Chicago/Detroit, and Los Angeles/San Francisco). The South shows a much wider dispersion of homicide, which may reflect the geographic pull of more widely dispersed urban centers (for example, New Orleans, Washington, D.C., Houston, and Atlanta). (See Figure 5.2.)

This urban pull is also reflected in the geographic progression of the mean centers through time. Although the reporting population of the Midwest appears to split the difference between Chicago and Detroit, there appears to be a bias towards Chicago in terms of the homicide reports. The reporting population in the Northeast appears to be geographically stagnant near New York City. However, the incidence of homicide drifts westerly during the study period. The reporting population mean center of the West has been moving in a southerly direction towards Los Angeles, but homicides show a southeasternly pull between Los Angeles and Las Vegas. Again, the South does not show a bias towards any particular urban area with the reporting population mov-

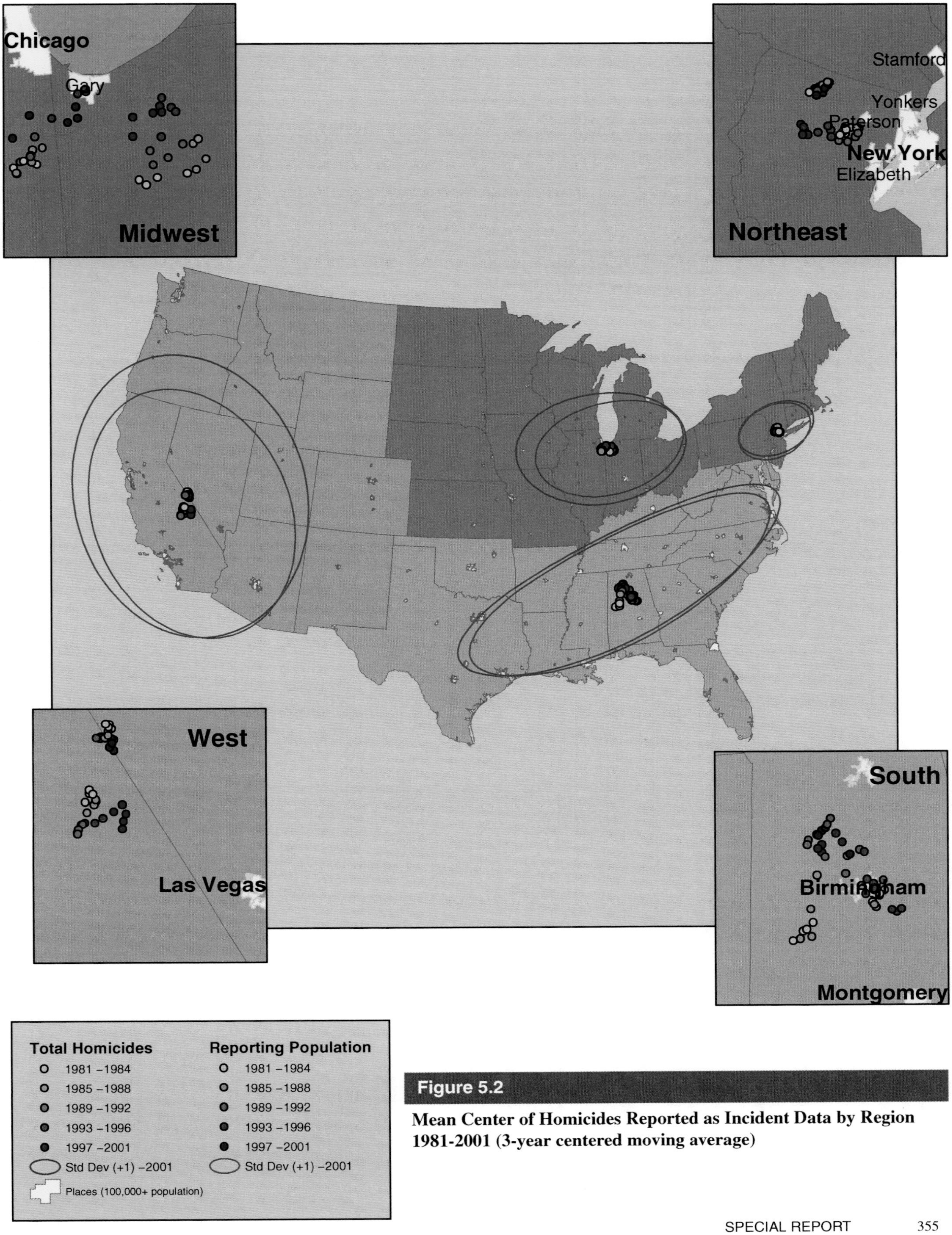

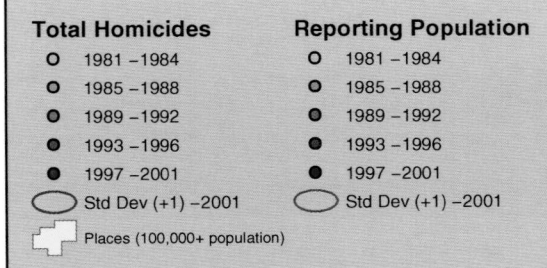

Chicago
Gary
Midwest

Stamford
Yonkers
Paterson
New York
Elizabeth
Northeast

West

Las Vegas

South
Birmingham
Montgomery

Total Homicides
- ○ 1981 –1984
- ○ 1985 –1988
- ○ 1989 –1992
- ◑ 1993 –1996
- ● 1997 –2001
- ⬭ Std Dev (+1) –2001

Reporting Population
- ○ 1981 –1984
- ○ 1985 –1988
- ◑ 1989 –1992
- ◑ 1993 –1996
- ● 1997 –2001
- ⬭ Std Dev (+1) –2001

⬜ Places (100,000+ population)

Figure 5.2

**Mean Center of Homicides Reported as Incident Data by Region
1981-2001 (3-year centered moving average)**

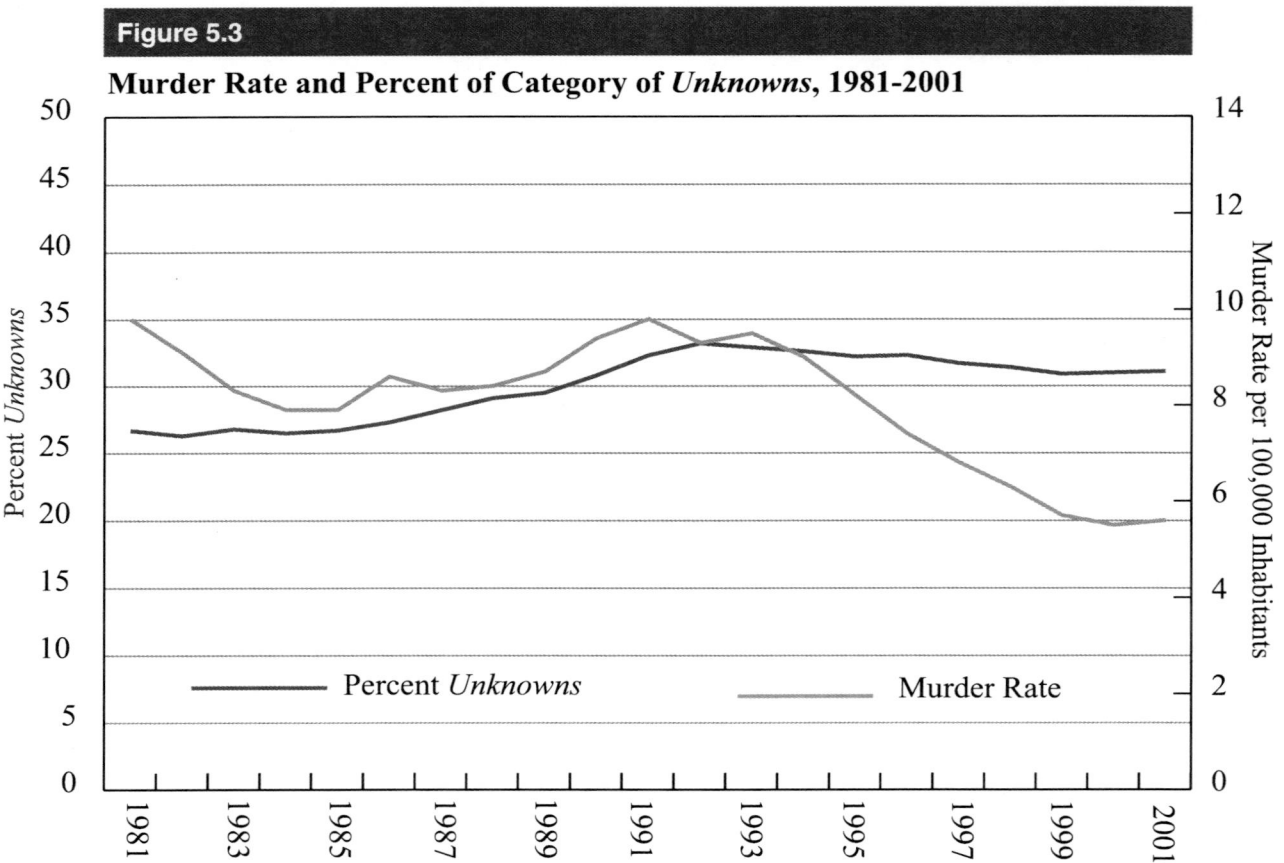

Figure 5.3

Murder Rate and Percent of Category of *Unknowns*, 1981-2001

Percent *Unknowns* ———— Murder Rate ————

ing towards the northwest and homicide incidents moving towards the northeast. In general, one does not see evidence that the incidence of homicide appears to be linearly related to the reporting population during the study period.

Characteristics of Detected Homicide Clusters

The results of the cluster analysis produced two highly robust types of homicide that can be tracked for the entire study period. The first robust cluster is comprised primarily of incidents that involve an unknown offender, and as such, much of the information about the offender and the circumstances surrounding the incident are reported as *unknown*. The remaining incidents are either clustered together as one *all other* type, or in some years, the remaining cases are divided based primarily on

the race of the offender. In those years, there are two remaining clusters: one with black offenders and one with white and all other race[2] offenders. Given the consistency (reliability) of the results from each year, the clusters produced by this analysis will form the basis of the remaining analyses.

The category *unknowns* accounts for approximately 30 percent of the 417,505 homicides reported through the SHR during the study period. These are the homicides in which little to nothing is known about the offender at the time of the incident report. There is a slight urban bias to these *unknowns*, and the victims are more likely to be black, male, and adult than the rest of the victims of the homicides. However, when the *unknowns* are compared to all other homicides, both groups appear to be very similar in terms of weapons used.

(See Table 5.17.) Over the length of the study period, there appears to be a slight increase in the proportion of *unknowns*. (See Figure 5.3.)

Regionally, the data reflected many of the same patterns concerning age and weapons associated with the two identified types of homicide. However, some striking differences are obscured by the national figures. In the West, one sees a significant increase in the proportion of white victims (65 and 70 percent, respectively for *unknowns* and *all other* homicides) when compared to the national figures (46 and 51 percent, respectively). Additionally, both the South and the West show a higher incidence of each type of homicide in suburban areas than do the remaining regions. In general, although many of the differences between the two types are subtle, the South also showed much more similarity

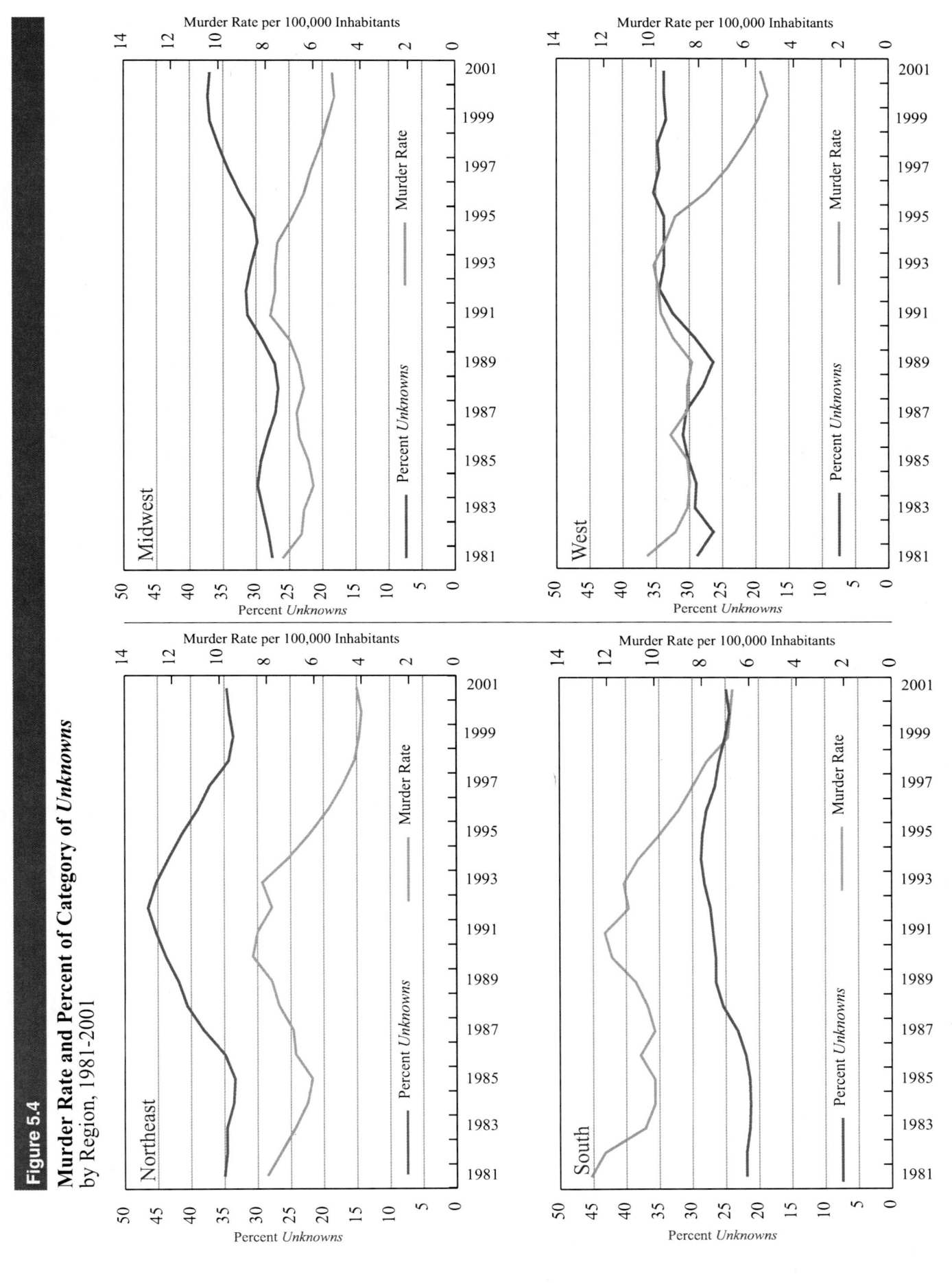

Figure 5.4

Murder Rate and Percent of Category of *Unknowns*
by Region, 1981-2001

between the *unknowns* and all other homicides than did the other regions. (See Table 5.17.) Since 1981, the proportion of *unknowns* on a regional level does not consistently track with fluctuations in the murder rate. In the Midwest, the South, and the West, the percent of *unknowns* either grew or remained stable during times of declining murder rate. It was only in the Northeast that the trends of the murder rate and percentage of *unknowns* appear to move in congruent directions (See Figure 5.4.)

Spatial Occurrence of Homicide Clusters

Spatial trend of homicide clusters from 1981 to 2001 for the Nation

Unknowns show a lot more geographic progression in a westerly direction during the study period than do all other homicides. In the early part of the study period, the mean center for *unknowns* appeared more to the east than the mean center for the remaining homicides. That bias is almost nonexistent by the end of the study period. For the entire study period, the unknown offender

homicides also show a more northern bias than other homicides. The standard deviational ellipse for the centered average value for 2001 (the most current data year in the study) shows a wider dispersion for the *unknowns* on the east-to-west axis. However, the remaining homicides are more dispersed on the north-to-south axis. This indicates a more concentrated band of *unknowns* that incorporates the effects of urban areas in the northern part of the Northeast (Boston/Connecticut) as well as in southern California. The *all others* seem to incorporate the effect of more southerly urban areas such as Atlanta, New Orleans, and Houston. (See Figure 5.5.)

Spatial trend of homicide clusters from 1981 to 2001 for each region

Within the Nation's four regions, the data reflected a similar pattern where each type of homicide has distinct mean centers. These differences for the two types reflect the influence of diverse communities even within the same region. All regions but the West showed the same spatial progression through time for the two types of homicide. In

all cases, this progression runs counter to the progression for the reporting population. Interestingly, *unknowns* show an almost true southerly progression in the West while *all other* homicides drift to the northeast. The standard deviational ellipse for the most recent data year (the centered average value for 2001) showed that the dispersion of *unknowns* was less than or equal to the remaining homicides in all regions but the South. (See Figure 5.6.)

Discussion and Conclusion

The differing rates of homicide amongst the regions, particularly in the South and West, have been noted in the past by law enforcement and researchers alike. However, instead of these differences in the levels of homicide being a result of global processes within a region, there appears to be evidence of more subtle processes that are connected to local urban centers. The regional incidence of homicide may be a reflection of the level of urbanity or change in urbanity rather than strictly the numbers of people that reside there. Since the patterns of

Table 5.17

Characteristics of detected homicide clusters
Percent of total

	Nation		Northeast		Midwest		South		West	
	Unknowns	All Other	Unknowns	All Other	Unknowns	All Other	Unknowns	All Other	Unknowns	All Other
MSA status	94.2	84.8	98.3	94.7	96.1	90.4	89.7	76.3	95.5	90.3
Suburban	18.1	21.7	8.3	17.1	11.1	15.0	22.8	24.8	25.8	24.0
Black Victim	50.6	45.9	53.1	49.2	67.8	57.8	56.2	51.5	27.7	23.4
White Victim	45.9	51.4	43.3	48.2	31.1	40.7	41.6	47.1	65.3	70.3
Female Victim	19.8	24.3	17.1	24.8	21.2	25.3	21.4	24.0	18.8	23.8
Male Victim	81.3	77.4	83.7	76.9	80.5	76.5	79.4	77.5	82.4	78.0
Juvenile Victim	7.0	10.7	6.7	11.8	7.4	12.6	5.8	8.7	8.6	12.0
Firearm Used	65.4	64.5	66.6	55.7	67.1	63.2	64.2	68.4	64.7	63.7
Other Serious Weapon Used	34.6	35.6	33.4	44.3	32.9	36.9	35.8	31.8	35.3	36.3

Figure 5.5

Mean Center of Homicide by Type
1981-2001 (3-year centered moving average)

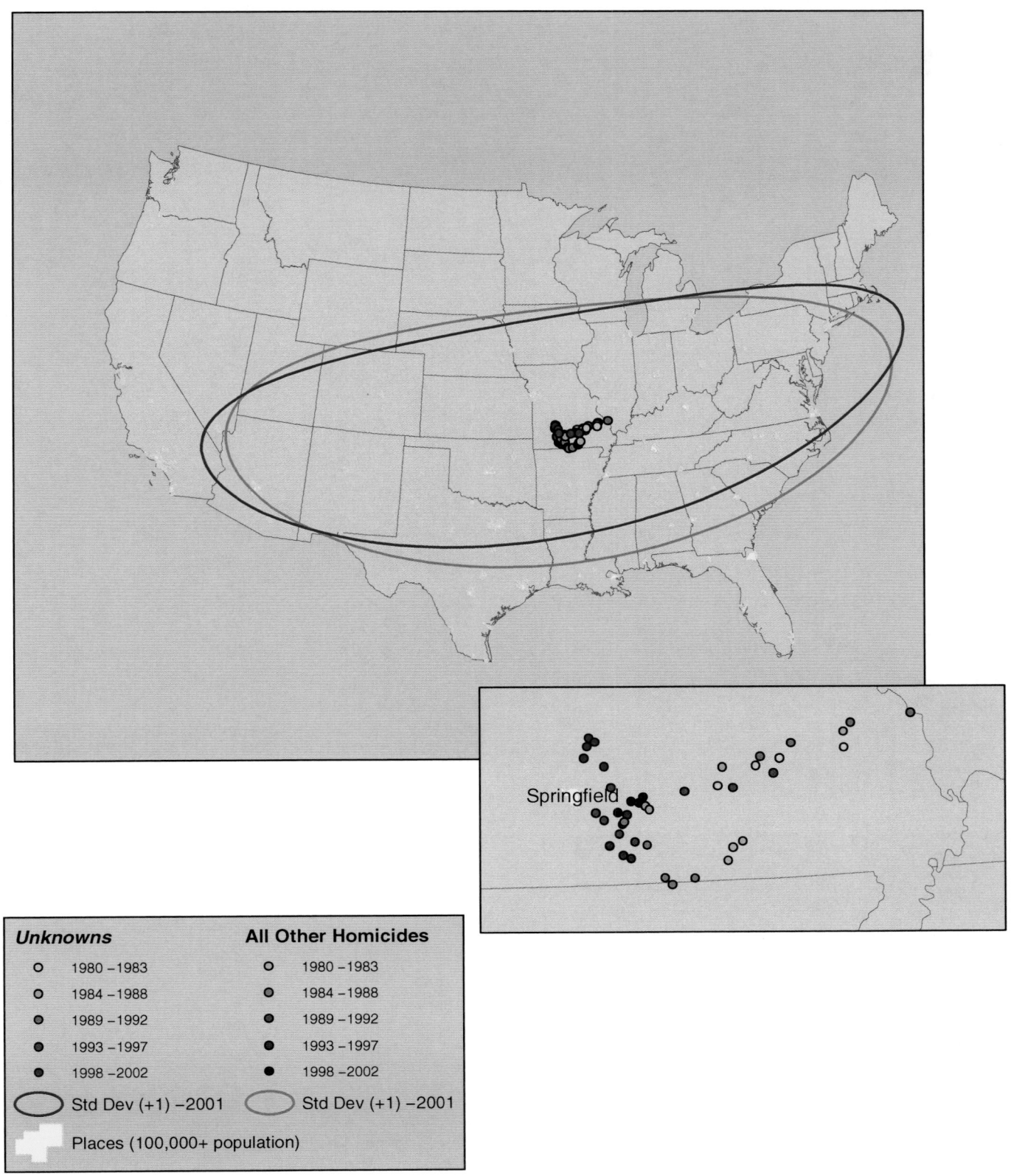

Unknowns

○	1980 –1983
○	1984 –1988
◐	1989 –1992
●	1993 –1997
●	1998 –2002
Std Dev (+1) –2001	
Places (100,000+ population)	

All Other Homicides

○	1980 –1983
○	1984 –1988
◐	1989 –1992
●	1993 –1997
●	1998 –2002
Std Dev (+1) –2001	

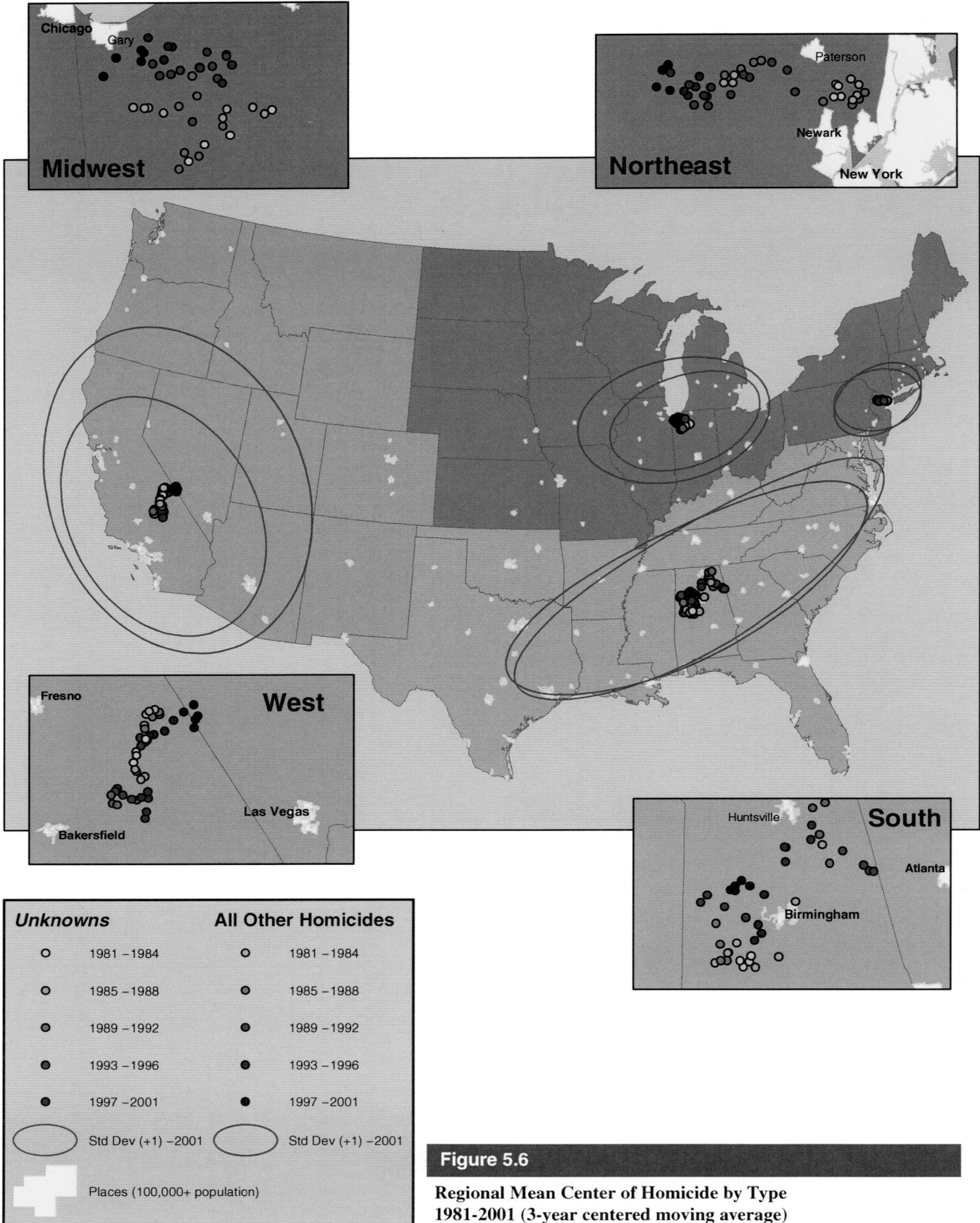

Midwest

Chicago
Gary

Northeast

Paterson
Newark
New York

West

Fresno
Bakersfield
Las Vegas

South

Huntsville
Atlanta
Birmingham

Unknowns		All Other Homicides	
○	1981 –1984	○	1981 –1984
○	1985 –1988	◒	1985 –1988
◉	1989 –1992	◉	1989 –1992
●	1993 –1996	●	1993 –1996
●	1997 –2001	●	1997 –2001
⬭	Std Dev (+1) –2001	⬭	Std Dev (+1) –2001
▨	Places (100,000+ population)		

Figure 5.6

**Regional Mean Center of Homicide by Type
1981-2001 (3-year centered moving average)**

growth and decline vary by region, this could be one explanation for the varying results in movement and types of homicide among regions.

The *unknowns* are difficult to draw too many conclusions about, since, by definition, little is known of the circumstances surrounding the homicide. However, it could easily be seen how these homicides may differ qualitatively from the remaining homicides that are often between people who know one another and in many cases are the result of arguments. The regional differences in the trends and proportions of these unknown homicides appear to be influenced by communities different from the remaining homicides. Again, this points to the dominance of communities different from those that drive the trends for the remaining homicides. The results of this analysis show that there is a definite need for further exploration of what is driving regional trends in homicide. The evidence seems to point to a complex interaction between regional differences in the underlying factors affecting homicide and the regional differences in the types of homicide itself.

References

Aldenderfer, Mark S. and Roger K. Blashfield. (1984). *Cluster Analysis.* Newbury Park, CA: Sage Publications.

Bailey, Kenneth D. (1994). *Typologies and Taxonomies: An Introduction to Classification Techniques.* Newbury Park, CA: Sage Publications.

Goldsmith, Victor, Philip G. McGuire, John H. Mollenkopf, Timothy A. Ross, eds. (2000). *Analyzing Crime Patterns: Frontiers of Practice.* Thousand Oaks, CA: Sage Publications, Inc.

Langworthy, Robert H. and Eric S. Jefferis. (2000). The Utility of Standard Deviation Ellipses for Evaluating Hot Spots. In Goldsmith, Victor, Philip G. McGuire, John H. Mollenkopf, Timothy A. Ross, (Eds.), *Analyzing Crime Patterns: Frontiers of Practice.* Thousand Oaks, CA: Sage Publications, Inc.

Levine, Ned. (May 2002). CrimeStatII: A Spatial Statistics Program for the analysis of Crime Incident Locations. Houston, TX: Ned Levine & Associations and Washington, D.C.: the National Institute of Justice.

McCue, Colleen, Emily S. Stone, and Teresa P. Gooch. (2003). "Data Mining and Value-Added Analysis," *Law Enforcement Bulletin.* November, p.1-5.

Romesburg, H. Charles. (1984). *Cluster Analysis for Researchers.* Belmont, CA: Lifetime Learning Publications.

SPSS. "The SPSS TwoStep Cluster Component," Technical Report downloaded from www.spss.com on April 1, 2004.

U.S. Department of Justice. Federal Bureau of Investigation (2003). *Crime in the United States, 2002.* Washington, D.C.

U.S. Department of Justice. Federal Bureau of Investigation (1984). *Uniform Crime Reporting Handbook.* Washington, D.C.

Endnotes

[1] Supplementary homicide information has been collected since the beginning of the UCR Program in the early 1930s. However, this information was not made available for general dissemination until 1962 and has gone through various revisions since that time. The data used for this analysis reflect the latest version of information collected which has remained the same since 1980.

[2] These race categories include *Asian and Other Pacific Islander* and *American Indian and Alaskan Native.*

Appendix

Variable	Description
MSA	MSA location
Suburban	Suburban location
Single Victim	Incident involved only a single victim
Single Offender	Incident involved only a single offender
Unknown Offender	Incident involved an unknown offender
Juvenile Victim	Victim under the age of 18 years old
Male Victim	Male victim involved
Female Victim	Female victim involved
Unknown Victim	Unknown victim involved
White Victim	White victim involved
Black Victim	Black victim involved
AIAN Victim	American Indian or Alaskan Native victim involved
AOPI Victim	Asian or Pacific Islander victim involved
Juvenile Offender	Offender under the age of 18 years old involved
Male Offender	Male offender involved
Female Offender	Female offender involved
Unknown Offender	Unknown offender involved
White Offender	White offender involved
Black Offender	Black offender involved
AIAN Offender	American Indian or Alaskan Native offender involved
AOPI Offender	Asian or Pacific Islander offender involved
Firearm used	Includes handgun, rifle, shotgun, other gun, and general firearm
Other Serious Weapon	Includes knife/cutting instrument, blunt object, personal weapons, poison, pushed/thrown out of window, explosives, fire, narcotics/drugs, drowning, strangulation, asphyxiation, and other
Intimate Relationship	Includes husband, wife, common-law husband, common-law wife, boyfriend, girlfriend, ex-husband, ex-wife, and homosexual relationship
Other Family Relationship	Includes mother, father, son, daughter, brother, sister, in-law, stepfather, stepmother, stepson, stepdaughter, and other family
Otherwise Known	Includes neighbor, acquaintance, employee, employer, friend, and otherwise known to victim
Not Known to Victim	Includes stranger.
Unknown Relationship	All instances where relationship of victim to offender cannot be determined.
Felony Type Circumstance - Violent	Includes rape and robbery
Felony Type Circumstance - Drug	Includes narcotic drug laws
Felony Type Circumstance - Other	Includes burglary, larceny, motor vehicle theft, arson, prostitution and commercialized vice, other sex offenses, abortion, gambling, and other–not specified
Other Circumstance - Arguments	Includes lover's triangle, brawl due to influence of alcohol, brawl due to influence of narcotics, argument over money or property, and other arguments.
Other Circumstance - Organized	Includes gangland killings, juvenile gang killings, and institutional killings.
Other Circumstance - Other	Includes child killed by babysitter, sniper attack, and other.
Suspected Felony	Circumstances indicate possible felony type murder, but sufficient facts to identify type of felony not available.
Justifiable Homicide	The intentional killing of a person without evil design and under such circumstance of necessity or duty as to render the act proper. Includes felons killed by either private citizen or police.

The preceding list reflects particular characteristics captured in a homicide incident reporting through the SHR. These characteristics were recoded to reflect whether or not that characteristic was present or not present. If the characteristic was present on the incident, that variable was coded as the value *1*. Otherwise, the variable was set to the value of *0*. The cluster analysis algorithm described in detail in the Technical Note used these values in its calculations. The Technical Note is available upon request from the Crime Analysis, Research and Development Unit, telephone (304) 625-3600.

SECTION VI

Law Enforcement Personnel

Law enforcement personnel provide many different services in many different settings including cities, colleges and universities, metropolitan (suburban) counties, nonmetropolitan (rural) counties, and states. Each of these settings has its own unique needs based on its demographic traits. For example, a small town situated between two larger cities may require more law enforcement personnel than a community of the same size that does not have an urban center nearby. A town with legal gambling establishments poses different law enforcement challenges than a locale with a large military base; a municipality that is the site of a small college has different needs than one comprised mostly of retirees.

Law enforcement personnel provide services in a variety of settings, and the services they provide vary from place to place. The responsibilities of state police and highway patrol agencies differ from one jurisdiction to another—ranging from traffic enforcement on state highways and interstate roads to responsibility for investigating violent crimes committed throughout the state. In some areas, the county sheriff's office may handle civil functions such as tax collections; they may be the enforcement authority for local and state courts; or they may administer jail facilities. In other areas, sheriff's deputies may be the sole provider of law enforcement in the county and are therefore responsible for providing all law enforcement services across a vast geographical area. Consequently, data users must consider these differences in service requirements and duties when attempting to compare law enforcement employee rates.

The information in the following tables are guidelines or averages; data

users should not consider these numbers as recommended staffing levels. Users must carefully study and analyze a myriad of conditions affecting service requirements before determining the appropriate personnel needs of a jurisdiction.

The following section includes Tables 70-73, which present the average rates of law enforcement personnel per 1,000 inhabitants collectively employed by agencies within population groups. Table 74 represents the percent of male and female officers and civilians by population group. (See Appendix III.) Table 75 provides the percent of total full-time civilian employees, and Table 76 furnishes the number of law enforcement employees working within state law enforcement agencies by state. Tables 78-81 list the number of law enforcement employees for cities, colleges and universities, and metropolitan and nonmetropolitan counties. Table 82 furnishes employee data for law enforcement agencies that serve the Nation's transit systems, parks and forests, schools and school districts, hospitals, etc. The jurisdictions of these entities usually overlap with the jurisdictions of local law enforcement; thus, no population is assigned to the agencies listed in Table 82.

Law Enforcement Rate

There were 3.5 full-time law enforcement employees, officers and civilians, for every 1,000 inhabitants in the Nation in 2003. (Based on Table 74.) A total of 14,072 city, county, and state police agencies employed 663,796 full-time officers and 285,146 civilians, who provided law enforcement services to more than 274 million inhabitants.

(See Table 74.)

Overall, cities in the Nation averaged 3.0 law enforcement employees per 1,000 inhabitants in 2003. Cities with less than 10,000 inhabitants had the highest average among city population groups, with 4.2 employees per 1,000 inhabitants; those cities with populations of 25,000 to 99,999 had the lowest average with 2.3 employees per 1,000 inhabitants. The Nation's largest cities, those with populations of 250,000 or more inhabitants, had 3.6 employees per 1,000 inhabitants. Metropolitan counties had 4.4 law enforcement employees per 1,000 inhabitants; nonmetropolitan counties had 4.6 employees per 1,000 inhabitants.

Of the Nation's four regions—the Northeast, the Midwest, the South, and the West—cities in the South had the highest law enforcement employee rate of 3.5 employees per 1,000 inhabitants. Northeastern cities had a rate of 3.2; Midwestern cities, 2.8; and Western cities, 2.4. (See Table 71.)

Sworn Personnel

The Nation's cities collectively had a rate of 2.3 sworn law enforcement officers per 1,000 inhabitants in 2003. Cities with populations of less than 10,000 inhabitants had the highest rate, 3.3, of sworn officers per 1,000 inhabitants, and cities with populations of 25,000 to 99,999 had the lowest rate, 1.8, of sworn officers per 1,000 inhabitants. Cities with a population of more than 250,000 inhabitants, the Nation's largest cities, had a rate of 2.7 sworn officers per 1,000 inhabitants. The Nation's metropolitan counties had a rate of 2.6 sworn officers per 1,000 inhabitants, and nonmetropolitan counties had a rate of 2.8 sworn officers for every 1,000 in population. (Based on Table 74.)

In terms of the number of sworn personnel by region, cities in the South had 2.7 sworn law enforcement officers per 1,000 inhabitants; the Northeast, 2.6; the Midwest, 2.2; and the West, 1.7. (See Table 71.)

The gender breakdown of sworn law enforcement officers was as follows: in the Nation, 88.6 percent male and 11.4 percent female; in cities collectively, 88.7 percent male and 11.3 percent female; in metropolitan counties, 86.7 percent male and 13.3 percent female; and in nonmetropolitan counties, 92.2 percent male and 7.8 percent female. (Based on Table 74.)

Civilian Employees

Thirty percent of the Nation's law enforcement workforce were civilian employees. In cities overall, 23.0 percent of law enforcement employees were civilians. Civilian employees made up 39.8 percent of the law enforcement workforce in metropolitan counties and 39.2 percent in nonmetropolitan counties. Females accounted for 62.5 percent of all civilian law enforcement employees. (Based on Table 74.)

Law Enforcement Officers Killed and Assaulted

Fifty-two law enforcement officers were feloniously slain in the line of duty in 2003, a decrease from the 56 officers who were killed in the line of duty in 2002. In addition, 80 officers were accidentally killed during the performance of their official duties in 2003, an increase from the 76 officers accidentally killed in 2002. The UCR publication *Law Enforcement Officers Killed and Assaulted* contains more extensive information on line-of-duty deaths as well as data on assaults on city, county, state, and federal officers.

Table 70

Full-time Law Enforcement Employees[1] as of October 31, 2003
Number and Rate per 1,000 Inhabitants
by Geographic Region and Division by Population Group
[2003 estimated population]

Geographic region/division	Total (10,658 cities; population 183,400,149)	Population group					
		Group I (71 cities, 250,000 and over; population 53,436,860)	Group II (168 cities, 100,000 to 249,999; population 25,195,766)	Group III (391 cities, 50,000 to 99,999; population 26,866,391)	Group IV (757 cities, 25,000 to 49,999; population 26,172,918)	Group V (1,774 cities, 10,000 to 24,999; population 28,090,979)	Group VI (7,497 cities, under 10,000; population 23,637,235)
TOTAL CITIES: 10,658 cities; population 183,400,149:							
Number of employees	**546,920**	**193,530**	**62,624**	**61,788**	**60,637**	**69,084**	**99,257**
Average number of employees per 1,000 inhabitants	**3.0**	**3.6**	**2.5**	**2.3**	**2.3**	**2.5**	**4.2**
New England: 761 cities; population 12,571,444:							
Number of employees	32,595	2,645	4,721	5,649	6,966	7,321	5,293
Average number of employees per 1,000 inhabitants	2.6	4.5	3.3	2.4	2.3	2.2	2.9
Middle Atlantic: 1,451 cities; population 29,301,193:							
Number of employees	102,361	53,552	5,154	8,245	11,164	12,165	12,081
Average number of employees per 1,000 inhabitants	3.5	5.1	3.2	2.6	2.5	2.2	3.1
NORTHEAST: 2,212 cities; population 41,872,637:							
Number of employees	**134,956**	**56,197**	**9,875**	**13,894**	**18,130**	**19,486**	**17,374**
Average number of employees per 1,000 inhabitants	**3.2**	**5.1**	**3.2**	**2.5**	**2.4**	**2.2**	**3.0**
East North Central: 2,014 cities; population 31,671,139:							
Number of employees	90,653	30,856	7,179	10,208	12,731	14,238	15,441
Average number of employees per 1,000 inhabitants	2.9	4.4	2.4	2.2	2.1	2.3	3.2
West North Central: 1,212 cities; population 12,739,419:							
Number of employees	31,522	7,486	3,273	3,790	3,739	5,025	8,209
Average number of employees per 1,000 inhabitants	2.5	3.4	2.2	1.8	1.9	2.2	3.1
MIDWEST: 3,226 cities; population 44,410,558:							
Number of employees	**122,175**	**38,342**	**10,452**	**13,998**	**16,470**	**19,263**	**23,650**
Average number of employees per 1,000 inhabitants	**2.8**	**4.1**	**2.4**	**2.1**	**2.1**	**2.3**	**3.2**
South Atlantic: 1,697 cities; population 21,131,333:							
Number of employees	85,343	20,756	12,164	11,023	8,069	10,956	22,375
Average number of employees per 1,000 inhabitants	4.0	4.3	3.0	3.2	3.1	3.4	7.3
East South Central: 959 cities; population 9,039,418:							
Number of employees	32,521	7,294	4,279	1,991	3,363	5,349	10,245
Average number of employees per 1,000 inhabitants	3.6	3.1	3.5	3.2	2.9	3.1	5.3
West South Central: 1,231 cities; population 22,073,165:							
Number of employees	63,777	23,100	7,796	7,041	4,914	7,132	13,794
Average number of employees per 1,000 inhabitants	2.9	2.8	2.4	2.3	2.4	2.7	5.0
SOUTH: 3,887 cities; population 52,243,916:							
Number of employees	**181,641**	**51,150**	**24,239**	**20,055**	**16,346**	**23,437**	**46,414**
Average number of employees per 1,000 inhabitants	**3.5**	**3.3**	**2.9**	**2.8**	**2.8**	**3.1**	**6.0**
Mountain: 562 cities; population 13,355,943:							
Number of employees	35,472	14,848	6,120	3,252	3,020	2,767	5,465
Average number of employees per 1,000 inhabitants	2.7	2.8	2.2	2.0	2.3	2.6	4.3
Pacific: 771 cities; population 31,517,095:							
Number of employees	72,676	32,993	11,938	10,589	6,671	4,131	6,354
Average number of employees per 1,000 inhabitants	2.3	2.7	1.8	1.8	1.9	2.0	4.8
WEST: 1,333 cities; population 44,873,038:							
Number of employees	**108,148**	**47,841**	**18,058**	**13,841**	**9,691**	**6,898**	**11,819**
Average number of employees per 1,000 inhabitants	**2.4**	**2.7**	**1.9**	**1.9**	**2.0**	**2.2**	**4.6**

Suburban Area:[2] 7,265 agencies; population 116,874,267:		County:[3] 3,414 agencies; population 90,704,265:	
Number of employees	432,107	Number of employees	402,022
Average number of employees per 1,000 inhabitants	3.7	Average number of employees per 1,000 inhabitants	4.4

[1] Full-time law enforcement employees include civilians.

[2] Suburban area includes law enforcement agencies in cities with less than 50,000 inhabitants and county law enforcement agencies that are within a Metropolitan Statistical Area (see Appendix III). Suburban area excludes all metropolitan agencies associated with a principal city. The agencies associated with suburban areas also appear in other groups within this table.

[3] County is a combination of both metropolitan and nonmetropolitan counties.

Table 71

Full-time Law Enforcement Officers as of October 31, 2003
Number and Rate per 1,000 Inhabitants
by Geographic Region and Division by Population Group
[2003 estimated population]

Geographic region/division	Total (10,658 cities; population 183,400,149)	Population group					
		Group I (71 cities, 250,000 and over; population 53,436,860)	Group II (168 cities, 100,000 to 249,999; population 25,195,766)	Group III (391 cities, 50,000 to 99,999; population 26,866,391)	Group IV (757 cities, 25,000 to 49,999; population 26,172,918)	Group V (1,774 cities, 10,000 to 24,999; population 28,090,979)	Group VI (7,497 cities, under 10,000; population 23,637,235)
TOTAL CITIES: 10,658 cities; population 183,400,149:							
Number of officers	421,074	146,274	47,188	47,523	47,536	54,983	77,570
Average number of officers per 1,000 inhabitants	2.3	2.7	1.9	1.8	1.8	2.0	3.3
New England: 761 cities; population 12,571,444:							
Number of officers	26,866	2,053	3,970	4,893	5,816	5,972	4,162
Average number of officers per 1,000 inhabitants	2.1	3.5	2.8	2.1	1.9	1.8	2.3
Middle Atlantic: 1,451 cities; population 29,301,193:							
Number of officers	80,070	38,639	4,288	6,815	9,369	10,348	10,611
Average number of officers per 1,000 inhabitants	2.7	3.7	2.7	2.2	2.1	1.9	2.7
NORTHEAST: 2,212 cities; population 41,872,637:							
Number of officers	106,936	40,692	8,258	11,708	15,185	16,320	14,773
Average number of officers per 1,000 inhabitants	2.6	3.7	2.7	2.1	2.0	1.8	2.6
East North Central: 2,014 cities; population 31,671,139:							
Number of officers	73,938	26,279	5,876	8,003	9,938	11,289	12,553
Average number of officers per 1,000 inhabitants	2.3	3.7	2.0	1.7	1.7	1.8	2.6
West North Central: 1,212 cities; population 12,739,419:							
Number of officers	24,657	5,454	2,560	3,006	2,905	4,005	6,727
Average number of officers per 1,000 inhabitants	1.9	2.5	1.7	1.4	1.5	1.7	2.5
MIDWEST: 3,226 cities; population 44,410,558:							
Number of officers	98,595	31,733	8,436	11,009	12,843	15,294	19,280
Average number of officers per 1,000 inhabitants	2.2	3.4	1.9	1.6	1.6	1.8	2.6
South Atlantic: 1,697 cities; population 21,131,333:							
Number of officers	65,095	15,662	9,106	8,345	6,201	8,622	17,159
Average number of officers per 1,000 inhabitants	3.1	3.3	2.3	2.4	2.4	2.7	5.6
East South Central: 959 cities; population 9,039,418:							
Number of officers	24,908	5,420	3,128	1,529	2,719	4,139	7,973
Average number of officers per 1,000 inhabitants	2.8	2.3	2.6	2.4	2.3	2.4	4.1
West South Central: 1,231 cities; population 22,073,165:							
Number of officers	48,548	18,448	5,798	5,324	3,703	5,450	9,825
Average number of officers per 1,000 inhabitants	2.2	2.2	1.8	1.7	1.8	2.1	3.5
SOUTH: 3,887 cities; population 52,243,916:							
Number of officers	138,551	39,530	18,032	15,198	12,623	18,211	34,957
Average number of officers per 1,000 inhabitants	2.7	2.6	2.1	2.1	2.2	2.4	4.5
Mountain: 562 cities; population 13,355,943:							
Number of officers	24,830	10,001	4,284	2,355	2,160	2,068	3,962
Average number of officers per 1,000 inhabitants	1.9	1.9	1.5	1.5	1.6	1.9	3.1
Pacific: 771 cities; population 31,517,095:							
Number of officers	52,162	24,318	8,178	7,253	4,725	3,090	4,598
Average number of officers per 1,000 inhabitants	1.7	2.0	1.3	1.3	1.3	1.5	3.4
WEST: 1,333 cities; population 44,873,038:							
Number of officers	76,992	34,319	12,462	9,608	6,885	5,158	8,560
Average number of officers per 1,000 inhabitants	1.7	2.0	1.3	1.3	1.4	1.6	3.3

Suburban Area:[1] 7,265 agencies; population 116,874,267:		**County:[2] 3,414 agencies; population 90,704,265:**	
Number of officers	288,522	Number of officers	242,722
Average number of officers per 1,000 inhabitants	2.5	Average number of officers per 1,000 inhabitants	2.7

[1] Suburban area includes law enforcement agencies in cities with less than 50,000 inhabitants and county law enforcement agencies that are within a Metropolitan Statistical Area (see Appendix III). Suburban area excludes all metropolitan agencies associated with a principal city. The agencies associated with suburban areas also appear in other groups within this table.

[2] County is a combination of both metropolitan and nonmetropolitan counties.

Table 72

Agencies with Full-time Law Enforcement Employees[1] as of October 31, 2003
Range in Rate per 1,000 Inhabitants
by Population Group
[2003 estimated population]

Rate range		Total cities[2] (9,770 cities; population 183,400,149)	Group I (71 cities, 250,000 and over; population 53,436,860)	Group II (168 cities, 100,000 to 249,999; population 25,195,766)	Group III (391 cities, 50,000 to 99,999; population 26,866,391)	Group IV (757 cities, 25,000 to 49,999; population 26,172,918)	Group V (1,774 cities, 10,000 to 24,999; population 28,090,979)	Group VI (6,609 cities, under 10,000; population 23,637,235)
.1-.5	Number	82	0	0	1	1	8	72
	Percent	0.8	0	0	0.3	0.1	0.5	1.1
.6-1.0	Number	383	0	0	3	9	47	324
	Percent	3.9	0	0	0.8	1.2	2.7	4.9
1.1-1.5	Number	980	0	12	38	87	163	680
	Percent	10.0	0	7.1	9.7	11.5	9.2	10.3
1.6-2.0	Number	1,835	7	49	136	201	369	1,073
	Percent	18.8	9.9	29.2	34.8	26.6	20.8	16.2
2.1-2.5	Number	1,933	19	42	108	229	484	1,051
	Percent	19.8	26.8	25.0	27.6	30.3	27.3	15.9
2.6-3.0	Number	1,469	18	29	53	122	332	915
	Percent	15.0	25.4	17.3	13.6	16.1	18.7	13.8
3.1-3.5	Number	908	8	20	23	63	177	617
	Percent	9.3	11.3	11.9	5.9	8.3	10.0	9.3
3.6-4.0	Number	635	2	11	12	21	94	495
	Percent	6.5	2.8	6.5	3.1	2.8	5.3	7.5
4.1-4.5	Number	431	7	2	9	15	51	347
	Percent	4.4	9.9	1.2	2.3	2.0	2.9	5.3
4.6-5.0	Number	286	3	3	6	6	21	247
	Percent	2.9	4.2	1.8	1.5	0.8	1.2	3.7
5.1 and over	Number	828	7	0	2	3	28	788
	Percent	8.5	9.9	0	0.5	0.4	1.6	11.9
Total cities	**Number**	**9,770**	**71**	**168**	**391**	**757**	**1,774**	**6,609**
Percent[3]	**Percent**	**100.0**	**100.0**	**100.0**	**100.0**	**100.0**	**100.0**	**100.0**

[1] Full-time law enforcement employees include civilians.

[2] The number of agencies used to compile these figures differs from the other Law Enforcement Employee tables because agencies with no resident population are excluded from this table. These agencies include those associated with universities and colleges (see Table 79) and other agencies (see Table 82), as well as some state agencies that have concurrent jurisdiction with other local law enforcement.

[3] Because of rounding, the percentages may not add to 100.0.

Table 73

Agencies with Full-time Law Enforcement Officers as of October 31, 2003
Range in Rate per 1,000 Inhabitants
by Population Group
[2003 estimated population]

Rate range		Total cities[1] (9,770 cities; population 183,400,149)	Group I (71 cities, 250,000 and over; population 53,436,860)	Group II (168 cities, 100,000 to 249,999; population 25,195,766)	Group III (391 cities, 50,000 to 99,999; population 26,866,391)	Group IV (757 cities, 25,000 to 49,999; population 26,172,918)	Group V (1,774 cities, 10,000 to 24,999; population 28,090,979)	Group VI (6,609 cities, under 10,000; population 23,637,235)
.1-.5	Number	88	0	0	1	1	8	78
	Percent	0.9	0	0	0.3	0.1	0.5	1.2
.6-1.0	Number	536	1	10	22	46	86	371
	Percent	5.5	1.4	6.0	5.6	6.1	4.8	5.6
1.1-1.5	Number	1,810	8	60	144	223	382	993
	Percent	18.5	11.3	35.7	36.8	29.5	21.5	15.0
1.6-2.0	Number	2,498	25	39	120	280	621	1,413
	Percent	25.6	35.2	23.2	30.7	37.0	35.0	21.4
2.1-2.5	Number	1,845	14	36	64	120	380	1,231
	Percent	18.9	19.7	21.4	16.4	15.9	21.4	18.6
2.6-3.0	Number	1,076	9	9	21	55	167	815
	Percent	11.0	12.7	5.4	5.4	7.3	9.4	12.3
3.1-3.5	Number	672	5	14	9	24	80	540
	Percent	6.9	7.0	8.3	2.3	3.2	4.5	8.2
3.6-4.0	Number	354	2	0	7	6	30	309
	Percent	3.6	2.8	0	1.8	0.8	1.7	4.7
4.1-4.5	Number	248	2	0	2	1	9	234
	Percent	2.5	2.8	0	0.5	0.1	0.5	3.5
4.6-5.0	Number	164	3	0	0	0	6	155
	Percent	1.7	4.2	0	0	0	0.3	2.3
5.1 and over	Number	479	2	0	1	1	5	470
	Percent	4.9	2.8	0	0.3	0.1	0.3	7.1
Total cities	**Number**	**9,770**	**71**	**168**	**391**	**757**	**1,774**	**6,609**
Percent[2]	**Percent**	**100.0**	**100.0**	**100.0**	**100.0**	**100.0**	**100.0**	**100.0**

[1] The number of agencies used to compile these figures differs from the other Law Enforcement Officer tables because agencies with no resident population are excluded from this table. These agencies include those associated with universities and colleges (see Table 79) and other agencies (see Table 82), as well as some state agencies that have concurrent jurisdiction with other local law enforcement.

[2] Because of rounding, the percentages may not add to 100.0.

Table 74

Full-time Law Enforcement Employees as of October 31, 2003
Percent Male and Female
by Population Group
[2003 estimated population]

Population group	Total	Percent law enforcement employees		Total	Percent officers		Total	Percent civilians	
		Male	Female		Male	Female		Male	Female
TOTAL AGENCIES: 14,072 agencies; population 274,104,414	**948,942**	**73.3**	**26.7**	**663,796**	**88.6**	**11.4**	**285,146**	**37.5**	**62.5**
TOTAL CITIES: 10,658 cities; population 183,400,149	**546,920**	**75.2**	**24.8**	**421,074**	**88.7**	**11.3**	**125,846**	**30.1**	**69.9**
GROUP I									
71 cities, 250,000 and over; population 53,436,860	193,530	71.0	29.0	146,274	83.6	16.4	47,256	31.9	68.1
10 cities, 1,000,000 and over; population 24,680,715	100,463	70.0	30.0	75,511	82.8	17.2	24,952	31.5	68.5
23 cities, 500,000 to 999,999; population 15,279,100	52,735	73.1	26.9	40,704	83.9	16.1	12,031	36.4	63.6
38 cities, 250,000 to 499,999; population 13,477,045	40,332	70.7	29.3	30,059	85.3	14.7	10,273	27.8	72.2
GROUP II									
168 cities, 100,000 to 249,999; population 25,195,766	62,624	73.4	26.6	47,188	89.0	11.0	15,436	25.8	74.2
GROUP III									
391 cities, 50,000 to 99,999; population 26,866,391	61,788	76.2	23.8	47,523	91.1	8.9	14,265	26.5	73.5
GROUP IV									
757 cities, 25,000 to 49,999; population 26,172,918	60,637	77.8	22.2	47,536	91.8	8.2	13,101	26.7	73.3
GROUP V									
1,774 cities, 10,000 to 24,999; population 28,090,979	69,084	79.3	20.7	54,983	92.9	7.1	14,101	26.6	73.4
GROUP VI									
7,497 cities, under 10,000; population 23,637,235	99,257	79.6	20.4	77,570	91.9	8.1	21,687	35.6	64.4
METROPOLITAN COUNTIES									
1,267 agencies; population 63,113,926	274,890	69.9	30.1	165,387	86.7	13.3	109,503	44.4	55.6
NONMETROPOLITAN COUNTIES									
2,147 agencies; population 27,590,339	127,132	72.3	27.7	77,335	92.2	7.8	49,797	41.4	58.6
SUBURBAN AREA[1]									
7,265 agencies; population 116,874,267	432,107	73.2	26.8	288,522	88.9	11.1	143,585	41.6	58.4

[1] Suburban area includes law enforcement agencies in cities with less than 50,000 inhabitants and county law enforcement agencies that are within a Metropolitan Statistical Area (see Appendix III). Suburban area excludes all metropolitan agencies associated with a principal city. The agencies associated with suburban areas also appear in other groups within this table.

Table 75

Full-time Civilian Law Enforcement Employees as of October 31, 2003
Percent of Total
by Population Group
[2003 estimated population]

Population group	Percent civilian employees	Population group	Percent civilian employees
TOTAL AGENCIES: 14,072 agencies; **population 274,104,414**	**30.0**	GROUP IV 757 cities, 25,000 to 49,999; population 26,172,918	21.6
TOTAL CITIES: 10,658 cities; **population 183,400,149**	**23.0**	GROUP V 1,774 cities, 10,000 to 24,999; population 28,090,979	20.4
GROUP I 71 cities, 250,000 and over; population 53,436,860	24.4	GROUP VI 7,497 cities, under 10,000; population 23,637,235	21.8
10 cities, 1,000,000 and over; population 24,680,715	24.8		
23 cities, 500,000 to 999,999; population 15,279,100	22.8	METROPOLITAN COUNTIES 1,267 agencies; population 63,113,926	39.8
38 cities, 250,000 to 499,999; population 13,477,045	25.5		
GROUP II 168 cities, 100,000 to 249,999; population 25,195,766	24.6	NONMETROPOLITAN COUNTIES 2,147 agencies; population 27,590,339	39.2
GROUP III 391 cities, 50,000 to 99,999; population 26,866,391	23.1	SUBURBAN AREA[1] 7,265 agencies; population 116,874,267	33.2

[1] Suburban area includes law enforcement agencies in cities with less than 50,000 inhabitants and county law enforcement agencies that are within a Metropolitan Statistical Area (see Appendix III). Suburban area excludes all metropolitan agencies associated with a principal city. The agencies associated with suburban areas also appear in other groups within this table.

Table 76

Full-time State Law Enforcement Employees as of October 31, 2003
by State

State	Total law enforcement employees	Total officers		Total civilians		State	Total law enforcement employees	Total officers		Total civilians	
		Male	Female	Male	Female			Male	Female	Male	Female
ALABAMA						**MARYLAND**					
Department of Public Safety	1,294	641	14	187	452	State Police	2,354	1,434	144	402	374
Other state agencies	226	176	8	6	36	Other state agencies	1,638	877	149	323	289
ALASKA						**MASSACHUSETTS**					
State Troopers	542	301	19	77	145	State Police	2,692	2,063	211	204	214
ARIZONA						**MICHIGAN**					
Department of Public Safety	1,971	1,016	79	324	552	State Police	2,675	1,585	225	364	501
Other state agencies	56	25	3	19	9	**MINNESOTA**					
CALIFORNIA						State Patrol	780	474	49	155	102
Highway Patrol	10,202	6,581	668	1,192	1,761	**MISSISSIPPI**					
Other state agencies	1,012	669	159	104	80	Highway Safety Patrol	813	502	9	95	207
COLORADO						Other state agencies	45	40	5	0	0
State Patrol	931	633	42	68	188	**MISSOURI**					
Other state agencies	56	13	3	25	15	State Highway Patrol	2,162	1,006	41	542	573
CONNECTICUT						Other state agencies	452	381	24	17	30
State Police	1,652	1,110	76	204	262	**MONTANA**					
Other state agencies	31	22	1	6	2	Highway Patrol	270	199	7	20	44
DELAWARE						Other state agencies	19	16	0	0	3
State Police	855	562	67	94	132	**NEBRASKA**					
Other state agencies	606	253	91	66	196	State Patrol	714	493	23	67	131
FLORIDA						**NEVADA**					
Highway Patrol	2,129	1,422	178	182	347	Highway Patrol	567	353	25	45	144
Other state agencies	2,295	1,210	149	339	597	**NEW HAMPSHIRE**					
GEORGIA						State Police	401	260	23	44	74
Department of Public Safety	1,275	839	27	196	213	Other state agencies	30	18	2	3	7
Other state agencies	1,552	585	64	336	567	**NEW JERSEY**					
IDAHO						State Police	4,000	2,582	100	606	712
State Police	329	238	13	14	64	Other state agencies	366	278	31	41	16
ILLINOIS						Port Authority of New York and New Jersey[1]	897	748	65	20	64
State Police	3,495	1,816	200	539	940	**NEW MEXICO**					
Other state agencies	388	274	32	31	51	State Police	728	554	24	51	99
INDIANA						**NEW YORK**					
State Police	1,870	1,128	66	276	400	State Police	5,403	4,093	356	391	563
Other state agencies	7	7	0	0	0	Port Authority of New York and New Jersey[2]	857	768	63	2	24
IOWA						**NORTH CAROLINA**					
Department of Public Safety	852	552	33	106	161	Highway Patrol	2,137	1,617	47	287	186
KANSAS						Other state agencies	1,130	671	121	96	242
Highway Patrol	799	507	19	103	170	**NORTH DAKOTA**					
Other state agencies	477	263	13	68	133	Highway Patrol	188	125	6	33	24
KENTUCKY						**OHIO**					
State Police	1,680	929	31	371	349	State Highway Patrol	2,600	1,349	137	521	593
Other state agencies	504	403	10	43	48	**OKLAHOMA**					
LOUISIANA						Department of Public Safety	1,410	813	19	255	323
State Police	1,671	976	36	247	412	Other state agencies	63	41	5	12	5
Other state agencies	3	2	0	0	1	**OREGON**					
MAINE						State Police	1,072	640	59	104	269
State Police	466	303	20	59	84						
Other state agencies	88	15	1	40	32						

Table 76

Full-time State Law Enforcement Employees as of October 31, 2003

by State—Continued

State	Total law enforcement employees	Total officers		Total civilians		State	Total law enforcement employees	Total officers		Total civilians	
		Male	Female	Male	Female			Male	Female	Male	Female
PENNSYLVANIA						**UTAH**					
State Police	5,773	4,012	177	713	871	Highway Patrol	467	420	10	8	29
Other state agencies	578	477	35	14	52	Other state agencies	150	88	4	9	49
RHODE ISLAND						**VERMONT**					
State Police	244	183	18	26	17	State Police	435	276	23	34	102
Other state agencies	40	27	5	5	3						
						VIRGINIA					
SOUTH CAROLINA						State Police	2,441	1,707	82	208	444
Highway Patrol	996	787	25	56	128	Other state agencies	529	350	43	52	84
Other state agencies	281	149	33	73	26						
						WASHINGTON					
SOUTH DAKOTA						State Patrol	2,192	999	82	536	575
Highway Patrol	224	145	2	56	21						
Other state agencies	134	37	3	35	59	**WEST VIRGINIA**					
						State Police	1,001	627	17	120	237
TENNESSEE						Other state agencies	177	162	1	0	14
Department of Safety	1,807	886	43	188	690						
Other state agencies	1,020	523	56	172	269	**WISCONSIN**					
						State Patrol	709	461	68	72	108
TEXAS						Other state agencies	294	234	21	16	23
Department of Public Safety	7,298	2,938	192	1,403	2,765						
						WYOMING					
						Highway Patrol	335	174	7	64	90

[1] Data reported are the number of law enforcement employees for the state of New Jersey.

[2] Data reported are the number of law enforcement employees for the state of New York.

NOTE: Caution should be used when comparing data from one state to that of another. The responsibilities of the various state police, highway patrol, and department of public safety agencies range from full law enforcement duties to only traffic patrol, which can impact both level of employment for agencies as well as the ratio of sworn officers to civilians employed. Any valid comparison must take these factors and the other identified crime factors (see page v) into consideration.

Table 77

Full-time Law Enforcement Employees as of October 31, 2003
by State
[2003 estimated population]

State	Total law enforcement employees	Total officers		Total civilians	
		Male	Female	Male	Female
ALABAMA 317 agencies; population 4,350,590	15,286	9,410	740	1,864	3,272
ALASKA 41 agencies; population 648,020	1,812	1,027	108	212	465
ARIZONA 97 agencies; population 5,489,285	18,855	9,830	1,173	3,300	4,552
ARKANSAS 206 agencies; population 2,702,925	7,705	4,596	529	996	1,584
CALIFORNIA 456 agencies; population 30,948,866	114,219	65,526	9,385	13,726	25,582
COLORADO 224 agencies; population 4,393,483	15,446	9,254	1,337	1,472	3,383
CONNECTICUT 101 agencies; population 3,483,372	9,609	7,183	675	658	1,093
DELAWARE 51 agencies; population 817,491	3,081	1,938	273	339	531
DISTRICT OF COLUMBIA 3 agencies; population 563,384	4,703	2,995	914	279	515
FLORIDA 501 agencies; population 16,516,256	68,748	36,278	5,859	10,156	16,455
GEORGIA 464 agencies; population 7,959,233	30,944	18,993	2,992	3,127	5,832
HAWAII 4 agencies; population 1,257,608	3,573	2,553	263	216	541
IDAHO 116 agencies; population 1,348,560	3,538	2,281	144	210	903
ILLINOIS 759 agencies; population 12,590,504	50,303	31,176	5,397	6,060	7,670
INDIANA 253 agencies; population 6,122,366	17,330	10,008	798	3,028	3,496
IOWA 233 agencies; population 2,944,062	7,497	4,658	345	901	1,593
KANSAS 349 agencies; population 2,699,012	10,158	6,330	573	1,246	2,009
KENTUCKY 374 agencies; population 4,075,332	10,084	7,185	585	859	1,455
LOUISIANA 220 agencies; population 4,306,455	21,337	13,403	2,922	1,428	3,584
MAINE 134 agencies; population 1,305,728	2,920	2,082	132	327	379
MARYLAND 124 agencies; population 5,338,977	19,290	12,740	2,048	1,669	2,833
MASSACHUSETTS 326 agencies; population 6,359,754	19,439	14,950	1,324	1,298	1,867
MICHIGAN 607 agencies; population 10,043,587	27,812	17,756	2,802	3,094	4,160
MINNESOTA 294 agencies; population 4,881,448	12,354	7,124	912	1,743	2,575
MISSISSIPPI 172 agencies; population 2,220,219	7,782	4,443	410	1,198	1,731
MISSOURI 559 agencies; population 5,683,974	19,048	12,119	1,256	2,150	3,523
MONTANA 105 agencies; population 916,711	2,750	1,490	97	525	638
NEBRASKA 157 agencies; population 1,686,860	4,654	3,022	352	319	961
NEVADA 36 agencies; population 2,241,154	7,856	4,220	469	1,099	2,068
NEW HAMPSHIRE 134 agencies; population 980,388	2,670	1,906	130	181	453
NEW JERSEY 533 agencies; population 8,358,119	39,901	28,918	2,377	3,049	5,557
NEW MEXICO 86 agencies; population 1,571,837	4,869	3,265	324	363	917
NEW YORK 368 agencies; population 17,576,779	71,492	46,505	6,349	5,867	12,771
NORTH CAROLINA 507 agencies; population 8,310,332	28,458	17,969	2,221	3,444	4,824
NORTH DAKOTA 97 agencies; population 625,680	1,569	1,067	82	145	275
OHIO 540 agencies; population 10,734,993	31,580	20,339	2,524	3,160	5,557
OKLAHOMA 299 agencies; population 3,511,532	10,487	6,534	525	1,409	2,019
OREGON 162 agencies; population 3,529,899	7,503	4,946	528	407	1,622
PENNSYLVANIA 727 agencies; population 8,054,446	27,237	20,308	2,652	1,601	2,676
RHODE ISLAND 43 agencies; population 1,069,852	3,140	2,337	169	291	343
SOUTH CAROLINA 275 agencies; population 3,634,757	12,175	7,876	998	1,209	2,092
SOUTH DAKOTA 141 agencies; population 761,048	2,041	1,218	76	352	395
TENNESSEE 445 agencies; population 5,840,183	23,706	13,845	1,564	3,356	4,941
TEXAS 968 agencies; population 21,886,408	76,146	42,682	4,916	12,482	16,066
UTAH 124 agencies; population 2,321,175	7,048	4,249	380	1,024	1,395
VERMONT 57 agencies; population 364,662	1,322	908	72	104	238
VIRGINIA 274 agencies; population 7,381,636	21,806	14,893	1,868	1,403	3,642
WASHINGTON 250 agencies; population 6,125,732	14,080	8,954	947	1,378	2,801
WEST VIRGINIA 347 agencies; population 1,803,483	4,080	3,071	103	358	548
WISCONSIN 348 agencies; population 5,268,938	17,395	10,735	1,766	1,675	3,219
WYOMING 64 agencies; population 497,319	2,104	1,212	104	259	529

Table 78

Full-time Law Enforcement Employees as of October 31, 2003
by City by State

City by state	Total law enforcement employees	Total officers	Total civilians	City by state	Total law enforcement employees	Total officers	Total civilians
ALABAMA				**ALABAMA—Continued**			
Abbeville	17	10	7	Eutaw	13	7	6
Adamsville	31	18	13	Evergreen	22	16	6
Addison	3	3	0	Fairfield	51	35	16
Alabaster	59	51	8	Fairhope	38	24	14
Albertville	57	38	19	Falkville	4	4	0
Alexander City	64	47	17	Fayette	12	12	0
Aliceville	12	8	4	Flomaton	9	4	5
Andalusia	37	29	8	Florala	6	6	0
Anniston	122	91	31	Florence	115	91	24
Arab	34	24	10	Foley	58	35	23
Ardmore	11	7	4	Fort Payne	38	36	2
Argo	4	4	0	Frisco City	1	1	0
Ashford	10	6	4	Fultondale	24	18	6
Ashville	5	5	0	Gadsden	131	101	30
Athens	51	40	11	Gardendale	34	26	8
Atmore	32	25	7	Geneva	17	11	6
Attalla	25	20	5	Goodwater	7	4	3
Auburn	77	71	6	Gordo	4	4	0
Bay Minette	27	20	7	Graysville	11	7	4
Bayou La Batre	23	18	5	Greensboro	10	10	0
Bear Creek	2	2	0	Greenville	39	30	9
Berry	3	3	0	Grove Hill	6	6	0
Bessemer	130	110	20	Guin	5	5	0
Birmingham	1,115	810	305	Gulf Shores	38	28	10
Blountsville	7	7	0	Guntersville	37	28	9
Boaz	33	22	11	Hackleburg	4	4	0
Brantley	5	4	1	Haleyville	19	14	5
Brent	5	5	0	Hamilton	13	12	1
Brewton	27	19	8	Hanceville	12	9	3
Bridgeport	11	7	4	Hartford	15	8	7
Brundidge	11	6	5	Hartselle	37	28	9
Butler	9	6	3	Hayneville	4	4	0
Calera	29	23	6	Helena	20	15	5
Camden	9	8	1	Hillsboro	2	2	0
Camp Hill	3	3	0	Hobson City	6	3	3
Carbon Hill	4	4	0	Hokes Bluff	9	6	3
Cedar Bluff	5	5	0	Homewood	107	70	37
Centre	10	9	1	Hoover	189	139	50
Centreville	5	5	0	Hueytown	31	26	5
Chatom	6	6	0	Huntsville	461	349	112
Cherokee	3	3	0	Irondale	38	31	7
Chickasaw	22	17	5	Jackson	21	16	5
Childersburg	18	13	5	Jacksonville	28	24	4
Citronelle	12	8	4	Jasper	67	43	24
Clanton	21	20	1	Jemison	6	6	0
Clayhatchee	1	1	0	Killen	5	5	0
Coffeeville	1	1	0	Kimberly	4	4	0
Collinsville	9	5	4	Kinsey	4	3	1
Columbiana	15	11	4	Lafayette	16	15	1
Cottonwood	3	3	0	Lanett	22	20	2
Courtland	4	4	0	Leeds	33	26	7
Creola	11	7	4	Leighton	2	2	0
Cullman	70	48	22	Level Plains	8	4	4
Dadeville	11	11	0	Lexington	2	2	0
Daleville	24	17	7	Lincoln	21	15	6
Daphne	66	39	27	Linden	7	7	0
Dauphin Island	11	7	4	Lineville	12	8	4
Decatur	144	125	19	Littleville	6	4	2
Demopolis	23	19	4	Livingston	13	9	4
Dora	8	4	4	Louisville	4	4	0
Dothan	228	157	71	Loxley	14	8	6
Dozier	1	1	0	Luverne	14	10	4
East Brewton	6	4	2	Madison	75	54	21
Eclectic	10	5	5	Maplesville	5	5	0
Elba	29	19	10	Marion	12	7	5
Elberta	5	5	0	McIntosh	6	6	0
Enterprise	71	54	17	McKenzie	3	2	1
Eufaula	50	39	11	Midfield	17	13	4

Table 78

Full-time Law Enforcement Employees as of October 31, 2003
by City by State—Continued

City by state	Total law enforcement employees	Total officers	Total civilians	City by state	Total law enforcement employees	Total officers	Total civilians
ALABAMA—Continued				**ALABAMA—Continued**			
Millbrook	27	21	6	Talladega	54	42	12
Millport	2	2	0	Tallassee	23	17	6
Mobile	706	525	181	Tarrant City	26	20	6
Monroeville	25	20	5	Thomasville	23	18	5
Montevallo	17	12	5	Thorsby	4	4	0
Montgomery	674	472	202	Town Creek	3	3	0
Moody	16	16	0	Triana	3	2	1
Morris	9	7	2	Trinity	5	5	0
Moulton	11	11	0	Troy	63	47	16
Moundville	6	5	1	Trussville	49	39	10
Mountain Brook	58	48	10	Tuscaloosa	308	237	71
Mount Vernon	9	8	1	Tuscumbia	28	22	6
Muscle Shoals	42	33	9	Tuskegee	36	24	12
Napier Field	2	1	1	Valley	34	26	8
New Brockton	2	2	0	Valley Head	3	2	1
New Hope	5	5	0	Vernon	8	8	0
Newville	2	1	1	Vestavia Hills	69	67	2
Northport	75	57	18	Wadley	6	2	4
Notasulga	9	5	4	Warrior	19	14	5
Oneonta	19	18	1	Weaver	10	7	3
Opelika	105	80	25	Wedowee	8	8	0
Opp	26	20	6	Wetumpka	32	24	8
Orange Beach	50	32	18	Wilton	1	1	0
Oxford	56	45	11	Winfield	10	9	1
Ozark	43	37	6				
Pelham	76	61	15	**ALASKA**			
Pell City	33	31	2				
Pennington	1	1	0	Anchorage	465	309	156
Phenix City	87	68	19	Bethel	26	17	9
Phil Campbell	3	3	0	Bristol Bay Borough	9	3	6
Pickensville	2	2	0	Cordova	10	5	5
Piedmont	16	13	3	Craig	10	5	5
Pinckard	2	2	0	Dillingham	18	8	10
Pine Hill	5	5	0	Fairbanks	58	43	15
Pleasant Grove	23	17	6	Haines	10	5	5
Prattville	89	83	6	Homer	26	12	14
Priceville	4	4	0	Hoonah	5	4	1
Prichard	81	56	25	Juneau	87	47	40
Rainbow City	33	22	11	Kake	4	2	2
Rainsville	15	11	4	Kenai	27	16	11
Ranburne	2	2	0	Ketchikan	33	24	9
Red Level	1	1	0	Klawock	2	2	0
Reform	4	4	0	Kodiak	33	16	17
Riverside	5	5	0	Kotzebue	15	7	8
Roanoke	27	22	5	Nenana	2	2	0
Robertsdale	16	9	7	Nome	15	10	5
Rogersville	5	5	0	North Pole	14	10	4
Russellville	27	22	5	North Slope Borough	65	40	25
Samson	2	2	0	Palmer	24	11	13
Saraland	44	33	11	Petersburg	15	8	7
Sardis City	4	4	0	Sand Point	5	3	2
Satsuma	18	14	4	Seldovia	1	1	0
Scottsboro	65	44	21	Seward	23	10	13
Section	1	1	0	Sitka	32	17	15
Selma	89	59	30	Skagway	7	4	3
Sheffield	37	32	5	Soldotna	14	13	1
Shorter	12	5	7	St. Paul	8	4	4
Silverhill	3	3	0	Togiak	9	3	6
Sipsey	3	2	1	Unalaska	28	13	15
Slocomb	10	6	4	Valdez	21	11	10
Somerville	4	3	1	Wasilla	20	19	1
Southside	14	8	6	Whittier	4	3	1
Spanish Fort	7	7	0	Wrangell	12	6	6
Springville	7	7	0				
Stevenson	8	5	3	**ARIZONA**			
Sumiton	14	9	5				
Summerdale	4	4	0	Apache Junction	76	50	26
Sylacauga	49	38	11	Benson	18	12	6

Table 78

Full-time Law Enforcement Employees as of October 31, 2003
by City by State—Continued

City by state	Total law enforcement employees	Total officers	Total civilians	City by state	Total law enforcement employees	Total officers	Total civilians
ARIZONA—Continued				**ARIZONA—Continued**			
Bisbee	21	14	7	Williams	19	11	8
Buckeye	42	33	9	Winslow	35	26	9
Bullhead City	122	77	45	Youngtown	14	12	2
Casa Grande	82	58	24	Yuma	208	131	77
Chandler	434	294	140				
Chino Valley	31	20	11	**ARKANSAS**			
Clarkdale	11	9	2				
Clifton	9	5	4	Alma	15	8	7
Colorado City	6	5	1	Arkadelphia	29	24	5
Coolidge	35	27	8	Ashdown	12	11	1
Cottonwood	35	24	11	Atkins	7	6	1
Douglas	44	30	14	Bald Knob	10	5	5
Eagar	12	9	3	Barling	8	8	0
El Mirage	54	45	9	Beebe	14	9	5
Eloy	46	31	15	Benton	59	50	9
Flagstaff	138	90	48	Bentonville	65	44	21
Florence	22	14	8	Berryville	10	9	1
Fredonia	5	5	0	Blytheville	65	49	16
Gilbert	207	140	67	Booneville	11	7	4
Glendale	449	323	126	Brinkley	16	12	4
Globe	33	24	9	Bryant	36	28	8
Goodyear	65	47	18	Bull Shoals	3	3	0
Hayden	7	6	1	Cabot	40	29	11
Holbrook	26	18	8	Caddo Valley	5	4	1
Huachuca City	8	3	5	Camden	36	23	13
Jerome	4	4	0	Carlisle	10	6	4
Kearny	9	5	4	Cherokee Village	7	6	1
Kingman	73	51	22	Clarksville	22	18	4
Lake Havasu City	103	77	26	Clinton	8	7	1
Mammoth	9	6	3	Conway	128	97	31
Marana	75	57	18	Corning	10	6	4
Mesa	1,264	815	449	Crossett	27	16	11
Miami	9	6	3	Danville	6	5	1
Nogales	83	64	19	Dardanelle	12	8	4
Oro Valley	102	75	27	De Queen	16	13	3
Page	29	16	13	Dermott	14	8	6
Paradise Valley	44	32	12	Des Arc	4	4	0
Parker	12	10	2	De Witt	15	10	5
Patagonia	3	3	0	Dumas	29	13	16
Payson	39	28	11	Earle	11	8	3
Peoria	199	138	61	El Dorado	65	49	16
Phoenix	3,624	2,750	874	England	11	5	6
Pima	4	4	0	Etowah	1	1	0
Pinetop-Lakeside	24	15	9	Eudora	12	6	6
Prescott	99	62	37	Eureka Springs	16	10	6
Prescott Valley	57	47	10	Fairfield Bay	12	7	5
Quartzsite	12	10	2	Farmington	9	9	0
Safford	21	18	3	Fayetteville	168	104	64
Sahuarita	15	13	2	Flippin	6	6	0
Scottsdale	604	368	236	Fordyce	11	8	3
Sedona	33	24	9	Forrest City	45	34	11
Show Low	35	23	12	Fort Smith	191	148	43
Sierra Vista	85	56	29	Greenbrier	13	8	5
Snowflake-Taylor	15	9	6	Green Forest	8	7	1
Somerton	21	14	7	Greenland	4	4	0
South Tucson	34	25	9	Greenwood	19	17	2
Springerville	9	7	2	Gurdon	4	3	1
St. Johns	11	8	3	Hamburg	7	6	1
Superior	12	8	4	Harrisburg	4	3	1
Surprise	93	66	27	Harrison	46	29	17
Tempe	497	330	167	Hazen	8	5	3
Thatcher	11	10	1	Heber Springs	21	13	8
Tolleson	29	20	9	Helena	16	11	5
Tombstone	11	9	2	Hermitage	3	3	0
Tucson	1,285	941	344	Hope	34	24	10
Wellton	4	4	0	Horseshoe Bend	8	2	6
Wickenburg	17	11	6	Hot Springs	125	94	31
Willcox	19	11	8	Hoxie	5	4	1

Table 78

Full-time Law Enforcement Employees as of October 31, 2003
by City by State—Continued

City by state	Total law enforcement employees	Total officers	Total civilians	City by state	Total law enforcement employees	Total officers	Total civilians
ARKANSAS—Continued				**CALIFORNIA—Continued**			
Jacksonville	79	68	11	Anderson	26	16	10
Jonesboro	135	123	12	Antioch	151	104	47
Keiser	1	1	0	Arcadia	109	69	40
Lake Village	15	9	6	Arcata	36	24	12
Lincoln	4	4	0	Arroyo Grande	36	26	10
Little Rock	620	508	112	Arvin	16	10	6
Lonoke	18	13	5	Atascadero	38	29	9
Lowell	11	10	1	Atherton	27	21	6
Magnolia	25	19	6	Atwater	39	30	9
Malvern	25	21	4	Auburn	35	24	11
Marianna	16	12	4	Azusa	85	61	24
Marion	18	16	2	Bakersfield	437	315	122
Marked Tree	12	8	4	Baldwin Park	111	78	33
Maumelle	28	19	9	Banning	42	32	10
Mayflower	6	4	2	Barstow	52	33	19
McGehee	16	8	8	Bear Valley	12	7	5
Mena	15	13	2	Beaumont	33	25	8
Monticello	30	21	9	Bell	50	38	12
Morrilton	30	19	11	Bell Gardens	80	54	26
Mountain Home	38	29	9	Belmont	45	33	12
Mountain View	9	8	1	Belvedere	8	7	1
Mulberry	3	3	0	Benicia	50	36	14
Nashville	14	13	1	Berkeley	291	187	104
Newport	23	16	7	Beverly Hills	202	137	65
North Little Rock	240	194	46	Bishop	20	14	6
Osceola	38	22	16	Blue Lake	11	5	6
Ozark	10	8	2	Blythe	36	23	13
Paragould	48	42	6	Brawley	45	32	13
Paris	14	9	5	Brea	126	101	25
Piggott	9	9	0	Brentwood	57	44	13
Pine Bluff	165	143	22	Brisbane	20	17	3
Pocahontas	14	13	1	Broadmoor	10	10	0
Pottsville	4	4	0	Buena Park	136	86	50
Prairie Grove	8	7	1	Burbank	249	159	90
Prescott	10	9	1	Burlingame	62	44	18
Rogers	104	75	29	Calexico	63	43	20
Rose Bud	4	2	2	California City	18	13	5
Russellville	63	54	9	Calipatria	7	6	1
Searcy	57	42	15	Calistoga	16	11	5
Sheridan	27	11	16	Campbell	66	45	21
Sherwood	83	57	26	Capitola	33	21	12
Siloam Springs	40	25	15	Carlsbad	145	104	41
Smackover	5	4	1	Carmel	17	12	5
Springdale	134	93	41	Cathedral City	73	48	25
Star City	5	4	1	Ceres	55	37	18
Stuttgart	24	14	10	Chico	138	85	53
Texarkana	88	77	11	Chino	123	92	31
Trumann	30	15	15	Chowchilla	24	17	7
Tuckerman	5	4	1	Chula Vista	314	221	93
Van Buren	57	43	14	City of Angels	9	8	1
Vilonia	6	6	0	Claremont	63	41	22
Waldron	12	7	5	Clayton	14	11	3
Walnut Ridge	11	8	3	Clearlake	32	22	10
Ward	5	4	1	Cloverdale	19	12	7
Warren	22	13	9	Clovis	128	86	42
West Fork	6	5	1	Coalinga	23	17	6
West Helena	29	22	7	Colma	22	17	5
West Memphis	101	82	19	Colton	90	65	25
White Hall	13	11	2	Colusa	9	8	1
Wynne	20	17	3	Concord	220	161	59
				Corcoran	24	16	8
CALIFORNIA				Corning	23	14	9
				Corona	255	165	90
Alameda	161	102	59	Coronado	58	43	15
Albany	35	28	7	Costa Mesa	232	158	74
Alhambra	132	84	48	Cotati	19	12	7
Alturas	10	9	1	Covina	86	56	30
Anaheim	557	389	168	Crescent City	14	13	1

Table 78

Full-time Law Enforcement Employees as of October 31, 2003
by City by State—Continued

City by state	Total law enforcement employees	Total officers	Total civilians	City by state	Total law enforcement employees	Total officers	Total civilians
CALIFORNIA—Continued				**CALIFORNIA—Continued**			
Culver City	169	119	50	Inglewood	289	200	89
Cypress	74	55	19	Ione	7	6	1
Daly City	156	115	41	Irvine	218	152	66
Davis	90	56	34	Irwindale	33	25	8
Delano	57	40	17	Isleton	2	2	0
Del Rey Oaks	6	6	0	Jackson	12	9	3
Desert Hot Springs	27	20	7	Kensington	11	10	1
Dinuba	35	27	8	Kerman	19	16	3
Dixon	27	23	4	King City	16	13	3
Dos Palos	9	7	2	Kingsburg	21	15	6
Downey	157	109	48	Laguna Beach	82	47	35
East Palo Alto	46	36	10	La Habra	105	68	37
El Cajon	214	142	72	Lakeport	16	14	2
El Centro	67	48	19	Lake Shastina	5	4	1
El Cerrito	43	36	7	La Mesa	88	63	25
El Monte	208	149	59	La Palma	33	25	8
El Segundo	101	66	35	La Verne	62	45	17
Emeryville	50	35	15	Lemoore	35	28	7
Escalon	12	9	3	Lincoln	28	23	5
Escondido	224	158	66	Lindsay	22	15	7
Etna	3	2	1	Livermore	145	93	52
Eureka	75	47	28	Livingston	24	18	6
Exeter	18	16	2	Lodi	117	78	39
Fairfax	17	12	5	Lompoc	68	47	21
Fairfield	164	110	54	Long Beach	1,438	916	522
Farmersville	15	14	1	Los Alamitos	29	25	4
Ferndale	5	5	0	Los Altos	46	30	16
Firebaugh	16	11	5	Los Angeles	12,394	9,265	3,129
Folsom	87	62	25	Los Banos	57	34	23
Fontana	206	145	61	Los Gatos	65	46	19
Fort Bragg	19	15	4	Madera	69	50	19
Fortuna	21	14	7	Mammoth Lakes	23	18	5
Foster City	57	40	17	Manhattan Beach	93	58	35
Fountain Valley	87	61	26	Manteca	86	61	25
Fowler	7	6	1	Marina	41	32	9
Fremont	292	186	106	Martinez	55	39	16
Fresno	1,069	707	362	Marysville	31	21	10
Fullerton	216	147	69	Maywood	41	31	10
Galt	35	24	11	Menlo Park	65	48	17
Gardena	104	83	21	Merced	116	81	35
Garden Grove	233	162	71	Millbrae	36	25	11
Gilroy	105	60	45	Mill Valley	26	21	5
Glendale	348	245	103	Milpitas	122	92	30
Glendora	87	56	31	Modesto	351	247	104
Gonzales	13	12	1	Monrovia	82	56	26
Grass Valley	36	26	10	Montclair	81	56	25
Greenfield	18	16	2	Montebello	124	83	41
Gridley	21	15	6	Monterey	75	53	22
Grover Beach	29	19	10	Monterey Park	108	74	34
Guadalupe	15	12	3	Moraga	14	13	1
Gustine	10	9	1	Morgan Hill	50	33	17
Half Moon Bay	20	15	5	Morro Bay	27	20	7
Hanford	63	45	18	Mountain View	144	96	48
Hawthorne	161	101	60	Mount Shasta	17	9	8
Hayward	327	202	125	Murrieta	74	48	26
Healdsburg	28	18	10	Napa	118	74	44
Hemet	99	70	29	National City	120	87	33
Hercules	23	20	3	Nevada City	9	8	1
Hermosa Beach	61	37	24	Newark	83	57	26
Hillsborough	33	24	9	Newman	15	12	3
Hollister	41	34	7	Newport Beach	237	148	89
Holtville	9	7	2	Novato	79	58	21
Hughson	5	4	1	Oakdale	34	25	9
Huntington Beach	344	216	128	Oakland	1,212	792	420
Huntington Park	108	73	35	Oceanside	263	178	85
Huron	13	9	4	Ontario	320	220	100
Imperial	16	14	2	Orange	221	152	69
Indio	89	61	28	Orland	11	10	1

Table 78

Full-time Law Enforcement Employees as of October 31, 2003

by City by State—Continued

City by state	Total law enforcement employees	Total officers	Total civilians	City by state	Total law enforcement employees	Total officers	Total civilians
CALIFORNIA—Continued				**CALIFORNIA—Continued**			
Oroville	35	25	10	Santa Paula	39	31	8
Oxnard	338	218	120	Santa Rosa	259	176	83
Pacifica	53	37	16	Sausalito	24	19	5
Pacific Grove	26	20	6	Scotts Valley	30	21	9
Palm Springs	142	83	59	Seal Beach	45	36	9
Palo Alto	169	90	79	Seaside	53	42	11
Palos Verdes Estates	34	24	10	Sebastopol	21	14	7
Paradise	40	25	15	Selma	40	26	14
Parlier	13	11	2	Shafter	26	19	7
Pasadena	381	241	140	Sierra Madre	23	17	6
Paso Robles	48	37	11	Signal Hill	41	29	12
Patterson	15	13	2	Simi Valley	193	122	71
Petaluma	95	69	26	Soledad	12	10	2
Piedmont	28	20	8	Sonoma	20	13	7
Pinole	40	27	13	Sonora	17	13	4
Pismo Beach	34	23	11	South Gate	117	79	38
Pittsburg	98	69	29	South Lake Tahoe	64	46	18
Placentia	70	53	17	South Pasadena	46	34	12
Placerville	30	17	13	South San Francisco	105	79	26
Pleasant Hill	68	47	21	Stallion Springs	3	3	0
Pleasanton	117	82	35	St. Helena	16	12	4
Pomona	315	175	140	Stockton	571	374	197
Porterville	64	43	21	Suisun City	34	23	11
Port Hueneme	29	22	7	Sunnyvale	297	229	68
Red Bluff	37	26	11	Susanville	22	19	3
Redding	158	109	49	Sutter Creek	7	7	0
Redlands	169	90	79	Taft	18	12	6
Redondo Beach	149	101	48	Tiburon	18	15	3
Redwood City	138	95	43	Torrance	335	237	98
Reedley	40	27	13	Tracy	114	73	41
Rialto	142	104	38	Trinidad	3	3	0
Richmond	275	184	91	Truckee	25	20	5
Ridgecrest	42	30	12	Tulare	75	52	23
Rio Dell	5	5	0	Tulelake	4	4	0
Rio Vista	14	12	2	Turlock	105	65	40
Ripon	29	19	10	Tustin	144	94	50
Riverbank	17	14	3	Twin Cities	44	34	10
Riverside	522	356	166	Ukiah	36	27	9
Rocklin	60	41	19	Union City	102	73	29
Rohnert Park	99	66	33	Upland	118	79	39
Roseville	160	99	61	Vacaville	159	103	56
Ross	8	7	1	Vallejo	228	156	72
Sacramento	1,045	660	385	Ventura	183	129	54
Salinas	202	151	51	Vernon	81	58	23
San Anselmo	26	19	7	Visalia	155	109	46
San Bernardino	465	295	170	Walnut Creek	113	80	33
San Bruno	72	51	21	Watsonville	86	62	24
San Carlos	46	34	12	Weed	17	10	7
Sand City	10	9	1	West Covina	164	120	44
San Diego	2,823	2,062	761	Westminster	150	103	47
San Fernando	53	37	16	Westmorland	5	5	0
San Francisco	2,585	2,209	376	West Sacramento	90	63	27
San Gabriel	67	53	14	Wheatland	8	8	0
Sanger	34	25	9	Whittier	199	129	70
San Jacinto	35	26	9	Williams	10	9	1
San Jose	1,792	1,400	392	Willits	20	12	8
San Leandro	137	95	42	Willows	14	11	3
San Luis Obispo	86	56	30	Winters	11	10	1
San Marino	34	28	6	Woodlake	14	12	2
San Mateo	143	103	40	Woodland	81	60	21
San Pablo	59	45	14	Yreka	23	15	8
San Rafael	107	79	28	Yuba City	71	47	24
Santa Ana	643	352	291				
Santa Barbara	215	142	73	**COLORADO**			
Santa Clara	195	147	48				
Santa Cruz	125	92	33	Alamosa	30	25	5
Santa Maria	139	102	37	Antonito	2	2	0
Santa Monica	384	205	179	Arvada	204	134	70

Table 78

Full-time Law Enforcement Employees as of October 31, 2003
by City by State—Continued

City by state	Total law enforcement employees	Total officers	Total civilians	City by state	Total law enforcement employees	Total officers	Total civilians
COLORADO—Continued				**COLORADO—Continued**			
Aspen	38	27	11	Hayden	4	4	0
Ault	6	6	0	Holyoke	4	4	0
Aurora	772	593	179	Hotchkiss	3	3	0
Avon	15	13	2	Hugo	3	3	0
Basalt	10	8	2	Idaho Springs	9	7	2
Bayfield	4	4	0	Ignacio	7	7	0
Berthoud	8	7	1	Johnstown	12	11	1
Black Hawk	38	25	13	Kersey	3	3	0
Boulder	253	167	86	Kiowa	1	1	0
Breckenridge	27	22	5	Kremmling	4	4	0
Brighton	61	49	12	Lafayette	45	36	9
Brush	16	13	3	La Jara	4	4	0
Buena Vista	9	7	2	La Junta	16	12	4
Burlington	10	9	1	Lakeside	5	5	0
Calhan	2	2	0	Lakewood	401	268	133
Canon City	51	34	17	Lamar	35	22	13
Carbondale	17	14	3	La Salle	6	6	0
Castle Rock	56	42	14	Las Animas	8	7	1
Cedaredge	7	5	2	La Veta	4	3	1
Center	7	6	1	Leadville	11	9	2
Central City	6	6	0	Limon	6	5	1
Cherry Hills Village	23	21	2	Littleton	98	71	27
Collbran	1	1	0	Lochbuie	6	5	1
Colorado Springs	942	651	291	Log Lane Village	4	3	1
Columbine Valley	3	3	0	Longmont	156	106	50
Commerce City	105	75	30	Louisville	38	33	5
Cortez	48	26	22	Loveland	116	82	34
Craig	28	23	5	Mancos	2	2	0
Crested Butte	6	5	1	Manitou Springs	20	14	6
Cripple Creek	27	15	12	Manzanola	2	2	0
Dacono	9	8	1	Meeker	6	5	1
De Beque	2	2	0	Milliken	10	9	1
Del Norte	6	5	1	Minturn	3	3	0
Delta	20	15	5	Monte Vista	12	8	4
Denver	1,716	1,391	325	Montrose	43	28	15
Dillon	9	8	1	Monument	12	11	1
Dinosaur	1	1	0	Morrison	2	1	1
Durango	60	50	10	Mountain View	5	4	1
Eagle	8	7	1	Mount Crested Butte	7	6	1
Eaton	9	8	1	New Castle	7	7	0
Edgewater	20	17	3	Northglenn	82	63	19
Elizabeth	10	7	3	Olathe	4	4	0
Empire	1	1	0	Ouray	4	4	0
Erie	18	15	3	Pagosa Springs	7	7	0
Estes Park	29	17	12	Palmer Lake	4	4	0
Evans	29	25	4	Paonia	5	5	0
Federal Heights	37	25	12	Parachute	5	5	0
Firestone	17	13	4	Parker	58	47	11
Florence	12	7	5	Platteville	7	7	0
Fort Collins	234	155	79	Pueblo	248	190	58
Fort Lupton	19	15	4	Rangely	13	8	5
Fort Morgan	34	28	6	Ridgway	3	3	0
Fountain	48	35	13	Rifle	18	15	3
Fowler	2	2	0	Rocky Ford	10	9	1
Frederick	12	10	2	Salida	15	14	1
Frisco	13	11	2	Sheridan	28	21	7
Fruita	12	11	1	Silt	6	5	1
Georgetown	3	3	0	Silverthorne	21	17	4
Gilcrest	4	4	0	Simla	2	2	0
Glendale	36	24	12	Snowmass Village	12	9	3
Glenwood Springs	34	26	8	Springfield	3	3	0
Golden	57	40	17	Steamboat Springs	36	19	17
Grand Junction	144	85	59	Sterling	36	22	14
Greeley	214	119	95	Stratton	1	1	0
Green Mountain Falls	2	2	0	Telluride	14	10	4
Greenwood Village	87	64	23	Thornton	172	142	30
Gunnison	28	15	13	Trinidad	31	21	10
Haxtun	3	3	0	Vail	56	27	29

Table 78

Full-time Law Enforcement Employees as of October 31, 2003
by City by State—Continued

City by state	Total law enforcement employees	Total officers	Total civilians	City by state	Total law enforcement employees	Total officers	Total civilians
COLORADO—Continued				**CONNECTICUT—Continued**			
Victor	4	4	0	Plainville	39	33	6
Walsenburg	20	12	8	Plymouth	19	19	0
Westminster	221	153	68	Portland	11	10	1
Wheat Ridge	87	60	27	Putnam	17	13	4
Wiggins	2	2	0	Redding	17	13	4
Windsor	19	16	3	Ridgefield	46	39	7
Woodland Park	27	19	8	Rocky Hill	42	32	10
Wray	8	7	1	Seymour	38	36	2
Yuma	8	7	1	Shelton	62	54	8
				Simsbury	44	32	12
CONNECTICUT				Southington	74	59	15
				South Windsor	48	38	10
Ansonia	50	44	6	Stamford	355	292	63
Avon	38	31	7	Stonington	46	34	12
Berlin	48	39	9	Stratford	116	107	9
Bethel	44	33	11	Suffield	20	15	5
Bloomfield	55	47	8	Thomaston	16	13	3
Branford	61	48	13	Torrington	83	74	9
Bridgeport	555	447	108	Trumbull	74	66	8
Bristol	126	115	11	Vernon	64	51	13
Brookfield	40	30	10	Wallingford	93	71	22
Canton	20	15	5	Waterbury	376	324	52
Cheshire	55	47	8	Waterford	54	46	8
Clinton	27	24	3	Watertown	43	36	7
Coventry	18	13	5	West Hartford	146	128	18
Cromwell	32	24	8	West Haven	130	116	14
Danbury	154	148	6	Weston	15	14	1
Darien	55	49	6	Westport	85	68	17
Derby	28	27	1	Wethersfield	54	43	11
East Hampton	16	14	2	Willimantic	40	36	4
East Hartford	172	131	41	Wilton	47	43	4
East Haven	55	52	3	Winchester	27	22	5
Easton	22	15	7	Windsor	63	53	10
East Windsor	31	23	8	Windsor Locks	27	22	5
Enfield	110	92	18	Wolcott	33	25	8
Fairfield	112	106	6	Woodbridge	34	26	8
Farmington	58	42	16				
Glastonbury	73	57	16	**DELAWARE**			
Granby	19	14	5				
Greenwich	174	152	22	Bethany Beach	12	11	1
Groton	35	29	6	Blades	2	2	0
Groton Long Point	5	5	0	Bridgeville	5	5	0
Groton Town	70	66	4	Camden	10	9	1
Guilford	46	38	8	Cheswold	2	1	1
Hamden	119	97	22	Clayton	5	5	0
Hartford	472	408	64	Dagsboro	2	2	0
Madison	35	28	7	Delaware City	3	3	0
Manchester	146	115	31	Delmar	10	9	1
Meriden	143	132	11	Dewey Beach	8	8	0
Middlebury	18	12	6	Dover	113	84	29
Middletown	110	95	15	Ellendale	2	2	0
Milford	120	103	17	Elsmere	11	10	1
Monroe	50	39	11	Felton	4	4	0
Naugatuck	65	54	11	Fenwick Island	5	5	0
New Britain	163	152	11	Frederica	2	2	0
New Canaan	47	42	5	Georgetown	17	15	2
New Haven	517	421	96	Greenwood	5	4	1
Newington	56	45	11	Harrington	10	9	1
New London	99	83	16	Laurel	12	11	1
New Milford	60	45	15	Lewes	14	13	1
Newtown	49	42	7	Milford	34	26	8
North Branford	24	20	4	Millsboro	11	10	1
North Haven	55	46	9	Milton	7	7	0
Norwalk	193	168	25	Newark	76	59	17
Norwich	90	73	17	New Castle	19	17	2
Old Saybrook	29	21	8	Newport	7	7	0
Orange	47	37	10	Ocean View	9	8	1
Plainfield	22	18	4	Rehoboth Beach	29	19	10

Table 78

Full-time Law Enforcement Employees as of October 31, 2003

by City by State—Continued

City by state	Total law enforcement employees	Total officers	Total civilians	City by state	Total law enforcement employees	Total officers	Total civilians
DELAWARE—Continued				**FLORIDA—Continued**			
Seaford	33	24	9	Crystal River	18	16	2
Selbyville	7	6	1	Dade City	30	21	9
Smyrna	24	18	6	Davenport	7	6	1
South Bethany	6	6	0	Davie	224	168	56
Wilmington	357	285	72	Daytona Beach	326	245	81
Wyoming	3	3	0	Daytona Beach Shores	41	31	10
				De Funiak Springs	15	14	1
DISTRICT OF COLUMBIA				Deland	85	58	27
				Delray Beach	215	144	71
Washington	4,182	3,515	667	Dundee	15	10	5
				Dunedin	40	40	0
FLORIDA				Dunnellon	12	10	2
				Eagle Lake	6	6	0
Alachua	23	16	7	Eatonville	18	16	2
Altamonte Springs	131	98	33	Edgewater	40	35	5
Altha	1	1	0	Edgewood	11	10	1
Apalachicola	8	7	1	El Portal	8	8	0
Apopka	78	69	9	Eustis	54	40	14
Arcadia	24	20	4	Fellsmere	8	7	1
Astatula	4	4	0	Fernandina Beach	44	35	9
Atlantic Beach	35	24	11	Flagler Beach	15	13	2
Atlantis	18	13	5	Florida City	37	25	12
Auburndale	43	33	10	Fort Lauderdale	749	499	250
Aventura	100	73	27	Fort Meade	18	13	5
Avon Park	38	25	13	Fort Myers	226	158	68
Baldwin	13	8	5	Fort Pierce	133	100	33
Bal Harbour Village	31	24	7	Fort Walton Beach	70	56	14
Bartow	76	51	25	Frostproof	15	10	5
Bay Harbor Island	29	24	5	Fruitland Park	10	9	1
Belleair	16	11	5	Gainesville	337	267	70
Belleair Beach	6	6	0	Golden Beach	21	16	5
Belleair Bluffs	3	3	0	Graceville	10	8	2
Belle Glade	54	41	13	Greenacres City	66	44	22
Belleview	16	14	2	Green Cove Springs	24	18	6
Biscayne Park	10	9	1	Greensboro	1	1	0
Blountstown	15	10	5	Gretna	3	3	0
Boca Raton	245	158	87	Groveland	16	11	5
Bonifay	9	5	4	Gulf Breeze	25	18	7
Bowling Green	6	6	0	Gulfport	42	30	12
Boynton Beach	169	136	33	Gulf Stream	10	10	0
Bradenton	138	111	27	Haines City	57	41	16
Bradenton Beach	10	10	0	Hallandale	121	90	31
Brooksville	27	17	10	Hampton	1	1	0
Bunnell	10	9	1	Havana	13	9	4
Bushnell	10	9	1	Hialeah	401	333	68
Cape Coral	235	151	84	Hialeah Gardens	40	30	10
Carrabelle	4	4	0	Highland Beach	15	14	1
Casselberry	90	58	32	High Springs	15	10	5
Cedar Grove	6	5	1	Hillsboro Beach	16	14	2
Cedar Key	4	4	0	Holly Hill	32	24	8
Center Hill	2	2	0	Hollywood	498	323	175
Chattahoochee	11	10	1	Holmes Beach	20	13	7
Chiefland	12	9	3	Homestead	104	74	30
Chipley	10	9	1	Howey-in-the-Hills	5	5	0
Clearwater	398	254	144	Indialantic	18	12	6
Clermont	42	31	11	Indian Creek Village	14	10	4
Clewiston	26	17	9	Indian Harbour Beach	23	16	7
Cocoa	89	67	22	Indian River Shores	21	20	1
Cocoa Beach	54	36	18	Indian Rocks Beach	6	6	0
Coconut Creek	112	77	35	Indian Shores	11	10	1
Coleman	1	1	0	Inglis	6	5	1
Cooper City	78	56	22	Interlachen	4	4	0
Coral Gables	241	165	76	Inverness	15	14	1
Coral Springs	293	183	110	Jacksonville	2,662	1,607	1,055
Cottondale	2	2	0	Jacksonville Beach	80	58	22
Crescent City	10	9	1	Jasper	9	8	1
Crestview	41	32	9	Jennings	2	2	0
Cross City	5	5	0	Juno Beach	21	15	6

Table 78

Full-time Law Enforcement Employees as of October 31, 2003
by City by State—Continued

City by state	Total law enforcement employees	Total officers	Total civilians	City by state	Total law enforcement employees	Total officers	Total civilians
FLORIDA—Continued				**FLORIDA—Continued**			
Jupiter	139	99	40	Opa Locka	42	32	10
Jupiter Inlet Colony	5	5	0	Orange City	22	19	3
Jupiter Island	20	16	4	Orange Park	27	21	6
Kenneth City	15	13	2	Orlando	966	689	277
Key Biscayne	36	29	7	Ormond Beach	97	66	31
Key West	108	80	28	Oviedo	75	56	19
Kissimmee	172	115	57	Pahokee	17	15	2
Lady Lake	32	22	10	Palatka	39	32	7
Lake Alfred	14	10	4	Palm Bay	201	135	66
Lake City	50	37	13	Palm Beach	129	77	52
Lake Clarke Shores	11	11	0	Palm Beach Gardens	130	97	33
Lake Hamilton	7	6	1	Palm Beach Shores	15	10	5
Lake Helen	7	7	0	Palmetto	44	31	13
Lakeland	334	224	110	Palm Springs	48	33	15
Lake Mary	49	32	17	Panama City	139	97	42
Lake Placid	10	8	2	Panama City Beach	57	42	15
Lake Wales	57	40	17	Parker	10	9	1
Lake Worth	123	84	39	Parkland	33	30	3
Lantana	40	32	8	Pembroke Pines	293	228	65
Largo	179	123	56	Pensacola	219	156	63
Lauderhill	116	91	25	Perry	22	20	2
Lawtey	1	1	0	Pinellas Park	125	95	30
Leesburg	103	73	30	Plantation	287	185	102
Lighthouse Point	38	29	9	Plant City	93	68	25
Live Oak	20	16	4	Ponce Inlet	16	10	6
Longboat Key	28	20	8	Port Orange	87	73	14
Longwood	44	40	4	Port Richey	15	10	5
Lynn Haven	31	24	7	Port St. Joe	12	10	2
Madeira Beach	7	7	0	Port St. Lucie	198	154	44
Madison	15	14	1	Punta Gorda	48	33	15
Maitland	49	40	9	Quincy	43	31	12
Manalapan	13	9	4	Redington Beaches	3	3	0
Mangonia Park	16	15	1	Riviera Beach	150	102	48
Marco Island	31	29	2	Rockledge	63	46	17
Margate	172	110	62	Royal Palm Beach	56	41	15
Marianna	25	18	7	Safety Harbor	9	9	0
Mascotte	10	9	1	Sanford	130	108	22
Medley	36	29	7	Sanibel	32	21	11
Melbourne	216	158	58	Sarasota	266	197	69
Melbourne Beach	10	9	1	Satellite Beach	26	20	6
Melbourne Village	5	5	0	Sea Ranch Lakes	10	7	3
Mexico Beach	7	6	1	Sebastian	50	32	18
Miami	1,335	1,020	315	Sebring	49	37	12
Miami Beach	509	366	143	Seminole	12	12	0
Miami Shores	43	33	10	Sewall's Point	10	9	1
Miami Springs	51	39	12	Shalimar	3	3	0
Milton	27	19	8	Sneads	10	6	4
Miramar	208	158	50	South Bay	14	12	2
Monticello	14	10	4	South Daytona	35	26	9
Mount Dora	43	31	12	South Miami	59	51	8
Mulberry	17	12	5	South Palm Beach	9	9	0
Naples	114	73	41	South Pasadena	6	6	0
Neptune Beach	25	18	7	Springfield	19	15	4
New Port Richey	39	31	8	Starke	28	20	8
New Smyrna Beach	55	44	11	St. Augustine	61	48	13
Niceville	24	19	5	St. Augustine Beach	13	11	2
North Bay Village	31	25	6	St. Cloud	66	43	23
North Miami	151	115	36	St. Pete Beach	41	27	14
North Miami Beach	144	103	41	St. Petersburg	758	517	241
North Palm Beach	43	34	9	Stuart	59	42	17
North Port	56	49	7	Sunny Isles Beach	54	43	11
Oak Hill	8	8	0	Sunrise	233	166	67
Oakland	11	10	1	Surfside	34	21	13
Ocala	240	153	87	Sweetwater	30	23	7
Ocean Ridge	19	14	5	Tallahassee	474	334	140
Ocoee	70	63	7	Tampa	1,272	954	318
Okeechobee	26	20	6	Tarpon Springs	63	47	16
Oldsmar	9	9	0	Tavares	24	23	1

Table 78

Full-time Law Enforcement Employees as of October 31, 2003
by City by State—Continued

City by state	Total law enforcement employees	Total officers	Total civilians	City by state	Total law enforcement employees	Total officers	Total civilians
FLORIDA—Continued				**GEORGIA—Continued**			
Temple Terrace	66	45	21	Calhoun	48	42	6
Tequesta	25	19	6	Camilla	23	19	4
Titusville	113	80	33	Canon	1	1	0
Treasure Island	27	19	8	Canton	43	36	7
Trenton	2	2	0	Carrollton	76	64	12
Umatilla	9	8	1	Cave Spring	5	5	0
Valparaiso	12	8	4	Cedartown	25	22	3
Venice	72	54	18	Centerville	16	12	4
Vero Beach	88	61	27	Chamblee	45	31	14
Village of Pinecrest	75	53	22	Chatsworth	15	13	2
Virginia Gardens	8	7	1	Clarkesville	6	5	1
Waldo	8	7	1	Clarkston	20	16	4
Wauchula	16	13	3	Claxton	9	8	1
Webster	3	3	0	Clayton	12	11	1
Welaka	1	1	0	Cleveland	9	9	0
West Melbourne	31	27	4	Cochran	16	15	1
West Miami	19	14	5	College Park	129	102	27
West Palm Beach	376	272	104	Columbus	467	365	102
White Springs	4	4	0	Commerce	25	20	5
Wildwood	18	12	6	Conyers	61	46	15
Williston	18	12	6	Cordele	33	27	6
Wilton Manors	42	32	10	Cornelia	18	16	2
Windermere	13	12	1	Covington	58	51	7
Winter Garden	54	42	12	Crawfordville	2	2	0
Winter Haven	115	78	37	Cumming	21	14	7
Winter Park	115	86	29	Cuthbert	12	12	0
Winter Springs	80	60	20	Dallas	19	14	5
Zephyrhills	45	28	17	Dalton	102	86	16
Zolfo Springs	3	2	1	Damascus	1	1	0
				Danielsville	1	1	0
GEORGIA				Darien	5	5	0
				Dawson	21	17	4
Abbeville	3	3	0	Dillard	4	3	1
Adairsville	12	10	2	Doerun	4	3	1
Adel	22	18	4	Donalsonville	11	8	3
Albany	225	197	28	Doraville	70	39	31
Alma	14	11	3	Douglas	45	37	8
Alpharetta	101	74	27	Douglasville	100	82	18
Americus	58	41	17	Dublin	58	50	8
Aragon	5	4	1	Duluth	67	47	20
Arcade	5	4	1	Eastman	13	12	1
Arlington	3	3	0	East Point	159	118	41
Athens-Clarke County	269	217	52	Eatonton	21	15	6
Atlanta	2,049	1,562	487	Edison	3	3	0
Attapulgus	1	1	0	Elberton	22	21	1
Auburn	19	13	6	Ellaville	5	5	0
Austell	29	19	10	Ellijay	10	9	1
Avondale Estates	10	10	0	Emerson	7	5	2
Bainbridge	46	41	5	Enigma	1	1	0
Ball Ground	3	3	0	Eton	2	2	0
Barnesville	16	14	2	Euharlee	13	11	2
Baxley	16	14	2	Fairburn	33	23	10
Berlin	4	4	0	Fairmount	3	3	0
Blairsville	8	7	1	Fayetteville	44	40	4
Blakely	21	16	5	Fitzgerald	33	28	5
Bloomingdale	14	11	3	Folkston	8	5	3
Blue Ridge	9	8	1	Forest Park	92	69	23
Blythe	4	3	1	Fort Gaines	6	5	1
Bowdon	14	10	4	Fort Oglethorpe	31	25	6
Braswell	1	1	0	Fort Valley	34	30	4
Bremen	20	17	3	Franklin Springs	2	1	1
Brooklet	3	3	0	Gainesville	117	97	20
Brunswick	78	73	5	Georgetown	2	2	0
Buchanan	7	7	0	Glennville	15	10	5
Buena Vista	7	7	0	Gordon	11	6	5
Byromville	1	1	0	Grantville	6	6	0
Byron	19	15	4	Greensboro	14	13	1
Cairo	24	21	3	Griffin	103	90	13

Table 78

Full-time Law Enforcement Employees as of October 31, 2003

by City by State—Continued

City by state	Total law enforcement employees	Total officers	Total civilians	City by state	Total law enforcement employees	Total officers	Total civilians
GEORGIA—Continued				**GEORGIA—Continued**			
Grovetown	26	16	10	Nashville	20	15	5
Hagan	2	2	0	Nelson	3	2	1
Hahira	8	7	1	Newnan	80	70	10
Hamilton	1	1	0	Newton	2	2	0
Hampton	14	13	1	Nicholls	5	4	1
Hapeville	51	38	13	Norcross	35	27	8
Harlem	12	7	5	Oakwood	10	9	1
Hartwell	24	19	5	Ocilla	14	13	1
Hawkinsville	10	9	1	Oglethorpe	4	3	1
Hazlehurst	14	12	2	Palmetto	10	8	2
Helen	14	10	4	Patterson	2	2	0
Helena	2	2	0	Pavo	4	3	1
Hephzibah	4	4	0	Peachtree City	58	54	4
Hiawassee	5	4	1	Pearson	6	5	1
Hinesville	83	73	10	Pembroke	8	7	1
Hiram	9	8	1	Perry	45	37	8
Hoboken	2	1	1	Pine Mountain	8	7	1
Hogansville	13	10	3	Pooler	25	21	4
Holly Springs	14	13	1	Porterdale	10	9	1
Homerville	9	8	1	Port Wentworth	18	16	2
Hoschton	4	4	0	Powder Springs	34	30	4
Irwinton	2	2	0	Reidsville	9	8	1
Ivey	2	2	0	Remerton	10	9	1
Jackson	17	12	5	Richland	4	4	0
Jasper	12	11	1	Richmond Hill	25	19	6
Jefferson	26	23	3	Rincon	14	12	2
Jeffersonville	5	5	0	Riverdale	48	43	5
Jesup	32	28	4	Roberta	3	3	0
Jonesboro	19	17	2	Rochelle	7	4	3
Kennesaw	68	42	26	Rome	109	96	13
Kingsland	38	34	4	Rossville	9	8	1
Lafayette	22	19	3	Royston	18	15	3
LaGrange	100	86	14	Sandersville	26	21	5
Lake City	13	12	1	Savannah	534	425	109
Lake Park	3	3	0	Screven	3	3	0
Lavonia	14	13	1	Senoia	6	5	1
Lawrenceville	70	54	16	Sky Valley	7	7	0
Leesburg	10	9	1	Smithville	3	2	1
Lenox	2	1	1	Smyrna	118	92	26
Lilburn	32	24	8	Snellville	43	35	8
Lithonia	12	7	5	Soperton	9	5	4
Locust Grove	17	15	2	Sparks	1	1	0
Lookout Mountain	7	7	0	Springfield	7	6	1
Louisville	8	8	0	Stapleton	1	1	0
Ludowici	9	5	4	Statesboro	67	56	11
Lumber City	7	4	3	Stillmore	1	1	0
Lumpkin	5	4	1	St. Marys	36	33	3
Luthersville	3	3	0	Stone Mountain	23	19	4
Lyons	16	15	1	Summerville	20	19	1
Macon	387	292	95	Suwanee	36	28	8
Madison	12	11	1	Sycamore	1	1	0
Marietta	166	136	30	Sylvania	15	11	4
Maysville	4	4	0	Sylvester	25	20	5
McCaysville	4	4	0	Talbotton	4	4	0
McDonough	35	33	2	Tallulah Falls	2	2	0
McRae	11	7	4	Temple	8	8	0
Metter	12	11	1	Tennille	8	8	0
Milan	1	1	0	Thomaston	37	30	7
Milledgeville	58	40	18	Tifton	57	47	10
Millen	10	10	0	Tignall	3	2	1
Milner	1	1	0	Toccoa	36	25	11
Molena	1	1	0	Trenton	7	7	0
Montezuma	16	11	5	Trion	8	8	0
Morrow	34	31	3	Tunnel Hill	3	3	0
Moultrie	47	42	5	Tybee Island	27	18	9
Mount Airy	1	1	0	Tyrone	12	12	0
Mount Vernon	4	3	1	Union City	48	44	4
Nahunta	3	3	0	Union Point	11	10	1

Table 78

Full-time Law Enforcement Employees as of October 31, 2003
by City by State—Continued

City by state	Total law enforcement employees	Total officers	Total civilians	City by state	Total law enforcement employees	Total officers	Total civilians
GEORGIA—Continued				**IDAHO—Continued**			
Valdosta	139	119	20	Payette	13	11	2
Vidalia	41	33	8	Pinehurst	2	2	0
Vienna	8	7	1	Pocatello	123	88	35
Villa Rica	41	33	8	Ponderay	4	4	0
Warm Springs	1	1	0	Post Falls	49	28	21
Warner Robins	127	98	29	Preston	6	6	0
Warrenton	7	7	0	Rathdrum	13	10	3
Warwick	3	3	0	Rexburg	42	35	7
Washington	18	16	2	Rigby	7	7	0
Watkinsville	5	5	0	Rupert	16	15	1
Waverly Hall	4	4	0	Sandpoint	37	19	18
Waycross	59	43	16	Shelley	8	8	0
Waynesboro	29	19	10	Shoshone	11	4	7
West Point	19	14	5	Soda Springs	8	7	1
Whitesburg	5	5	0	Spirit Lake	6	5	1
Willacoochee	6	5	1	St. Anthony	7	7	0
Winder	41	34	7	St. Maries	6	5	1
Woodbury	13	8	5	Sun Valley	10	9	1
Woodstock	40	35	5	Twin Falls	79	55	24
Wrens	12	8	4	Weiser	11	10	1
Wrightsville	6	6	0	Wendell	5	5	0
Zebulon	7	7	0	Wilder	3	3	0
HAWAII				**ILLINOIS**			
Honolulu	2,454	1,976	478	Abingdon	5	5	0
				Addison	90	64	26
IDAHO				Albany	1	1	0
				Albers	1	1	0
Aberdeen	9	6	3	Albion	3	3	0
American Falls	10	8	2	Aledo	7	6	1
Bellevue	5	4	1	Algonquin	55	41	14
Blackfoot	27	24	3	Alorton	4	4	0
Boise	342	269	73	Alsip	52	41	11
Bonners Ferry	8	8	0	Altamont	5	5	0
Buhl	10	8	2	Alton	89	66	23
Caldwell	61	48	13	Amboy	3	3	0
Cascade	4	4	0	Andalusia	2	2	0
Challis	1	1	0	Anna	8	8	0
Chubbuck	26	16	10	Annawan	2	2	0
Coeur d'Alene	75	61	14	Antioch	37	24	13
Cottonwood	1	1	0	Arcola	5	5	0
Emmett	13	12	1	Arlington Heights	148	110	38
Filer	5	5	0	Arthur	5	5	0
Fruitland	9	8	1	Ashland	1	1	0
Garden City	32	27	5	Assumption	1	1	0
Gooding	6	6	0	Astoria	1	1	0
Grangeville	6	6	0	Athens	3	3	0
Hagerman	2	2	0	Atkinson	1	1	0
Hailey	14	13	1	Atlanta	2	2	0
Heyburn	7	6	1	Auburn	9	5	4
Homedale	5	5	0	Augusta	1	1	0
Idaho City	1	1	0	Aurora	356	274	82
Idaho Falls	118	86	32	Aviston	1	1	0
Jerome	19	17	2	Bannockburn	6	6	0
Kellogg	8	7	1	Barrington	43	34	9
Ketchum	26	12	14	Barrington Hills	26	18	8
Kimberly	7	6	1	Barry	1	1	0
Lewiston	64	45	19	Bartlett	64	47	17
McCall	12	10	2	Bartonville	14	9	5
Meridian	58	47	11	Batavia	49	42	7
Montpelier	6	6	0	Beardstown	12	8	4
Moscow	47	34	13	Beckemeyer	1	1	0
Mountain Home	25	21	4	Bedford Park	45	37	8
Nampa	114	84	30	Beecher	6	6	0
Orofino	7	6	1	Belleville	94	78	16
Osburn	2	2	0	Bellwood	62	51	11
Parma	4	4	0	Belvidere	36	33	3

Table 78

Full-time Law Enforcement Employees as of October 31, 2003
by City by State—Continued

City by state	Total law enforcement employees	Total officers	Total civilians	City by state	Total law enforcement employees	Total officers	Total civilians
ILLINOIS—Continued				**ILLINOIS—Continued**			
Benld	4	4	0	Clinton	14	13	1
Bensenville	45	34	11	Coal City	11	11	0
Benton	14	10	4	Coal Valley	7	6	1
Berkeley	20	16	4	Cobden	3	3	0
Berwyn	117	91	26	Collinsville	47	38	9
Bethalto	23	16	7	Colona	12	10	2
Bloomingdale	63	47	16	Columbia	18	13	5
Bloomington	132	112	20	Cordova	1	1	0
Blue Island	62	39	23	Cortland	3	3	0
Blue Mound	2	2	0	Coulterville	2	2	0
Bolingbrook	142	102	40	Country Club Hills	44	31	13
Bourbonnais	27	20	7	Countryside	31	25	6
Bradley	44	30	14	Crest Hill	26	23	3
Braidwood	23	15	8	Crestwood	3	2	1
Breese	7	6	1	Crete	15	14	1
Bridgeport	3	3	0	Creve Coeur	10	8	2
Bridgeview	47	44	3	Crystal Lake	84	63	21
Brighton	6	4	2	Cuba	2	2	0
Broadview	47	38	9	Dallas City	1	1	0
Brookfield	38	31	7	Danvers	1	1	0
Brooklyn	6	6	0	Danville	79	63	16
Buffalo Grove	83	71	12	Darien	51	37	14
Bull Valley	3	3	0	Decatur	192	162	30
Bunker Hill	6	4	2	Deerfield	53	38	15
Burbank	66	49	17	De Kalb	70	55	15
Burnham	15	10	5	De Pue	2	2	0
Burr Ridge	30	26	4	De Soto	3	3	0
Byron	7	6	1	Des Plaines	128	103	25
Cahokia	44	33	11	Divernon	1	1	0
Cairo	15	10	5	Dixmoor	17	10	7
Calumet City	108	79	29	Dixon	29	25	4
Calumet Park	27	19	8	Dolton	66	51	15
Cambridge	1	1	0	Downers Grove	116	82	34
Camp Point	2	2	0	Dupo	7	7	0
Canton	31	22	9	Du Quoin	14	10	4
Carbon Cliff	3	3	0	Durand	1	1	0
Carbondale	78	60	18	Dwight	9	8	1
Carlinville	20	14	6	Earlville	3	3	0
Carlyle	8	7	1	East Alton	16	11	5
Carmi	9	9	0	East Carondelet	1	1	0
Carol Stream	86	60	26	East Dubuque	7	7	0
Carpentersville	72	60	12	East Dundee	15	14	1
Carrier Mills	2	2	0	East Galesburg	1	1	0
Carrollton	6	6	0	East Hazel Crest	12	10	2
Carterville	6	6	0	East Moline	50	39	11
Carthage	3	3	0	East Peoria	50	39	11
Cary	35	26	9	East St. Louis	94	66	28
Casey	9	8	1	Edwardsville	50	36	14
Caseyville	14	10	4	Effingham	34	21	13
Catlin	1	1	0	Elburn	8	7	1
Central City	4	4	0	Eldorado	12	7	5
Centralia	39	26	13	Elgin	218	165	53
Centreville	22	16	6	Elizabeth	1	1	0
Chadwick	1	1	0	Elk Grove Village	108	95	13
Champaign	137	107	30	Elmhurst	89	68	21
Channahon	18	16	2	Elmwood	1	1	0
Charleston	36	33	3	Elmwood Park	46	35	11
Chatham	18	13	5	El Paso	5	5	0
Chenoa	4	4	0	Energy	4	4	0
Cherry Valley	15	15	0	Enfield	1	1	0
Chester	13	10	3	Erie	3	3	0
Chicago	14,777	13,553	1,224	Essex	2	2	0
Chicago Heights	112	81	31	Eureka	6	6	0
Chicago Ridge	33	29	4	Evanston	211	159	52
Chillicothe	13	9	4	Evergreen Park	68	56	12
Christopher	2	2	0	Fairbury	7	7	0
Cicero	155	137	18	Fairfield	16	12	4
Clarendon Hills	15	15	0	Fairmont City	8	5	3

Table 78

Full-time Law Enforcement Employees as of October 31, 2003
by City by State—Continued

City by state	Total law enforcement employees	Total officers	Total civilians	City by state	Total law enforcement employees	Total officers	Total civilians
ILLINOIS—Continued				**ILLINOIS—Continued**			
Fairview	1	1	0	Hickory Hills	37	29	8
Fairview Heights	48	38	10	Highland	27	19	8
Farmer City	6	3	3	Highland Park	75	54	21
Farmington	4	4	0	Highwood	13	12	1
Fisher	2	2	0	Hillsboro	8	8	0
Flora	16	11	5	Hillside	39	30	9
Flossmoor	24	18	6	Hinckley	3	3	0
Ford Heights	12	11	1	Hinsdale	39	28	11
Forest Park	53	38	15	Hodgkins	19	17	2
Forest View	11	8	3	Hoffman Estates	114	95	19
Fox Lake	23	21	2	Homer	1	1	0
Fox River Grove	11	11	0	Hometown	5	1	4
Frankfort	31	28	3	Homewood	47	36	11
Franklin Park	63	47	16	Hoopeston	17	11	6
Freeburg	9	8	1	Hopedale	1	1	0
Freeport	73	55	18	Hopkins Park	1	1	0
Fulton	7	6	1	Huntley	25	21	4
Galena	12	9	3	Indian Head Park	13	10	3
Galesburg	75	50	25	Island Lake	17	12	5
Galva	4	4	0	Itasca	38	28	10
Geneseo	21	14	7	Jacksonville	47	39	8
Geneva	48	36	12	Jerome	7	7	0
Genoa	9	9	0	Jerseyville	19	13	6
Georgetown	4	4	0	Johnsburg	9	8	1
Germantown	1	1	0	Johnston City	4	4	0
Gibson City	11	6	5	Joliet	347	269	78
Gifford	1	1	0	Jonesboro	2	2	0
Gilberts	7	6	1	Justice	32	27	5
Gillespie	11	7	4	Kankakee	91	71	20
Gilman	2	2	0	Kenilworth	14	10	4
Girard	5	5	0	Kewanee	28	22	6
Glasford	5	5	0	Kildeer	19	18	1
Glen Carbon	24	17	7	Kirkland	2	2	0
Glencoe	45	35	10	Knoxville	4	4	0
Glendale Heights	80	54	26	Lacon	3	3	0
Glen Ellyn	44	36	8	La Grange	37	29	8
Glenview	102	76	26	La Grange Park	29	24	5
Glenwood	26	20	6	Lake Bluff	22	16	6
Golf	4	4	0	Lake Forest	63	45	18
Grafton	2	2	0	Lake in the Hills	52	39	13
Granite City	61	51	10	Lakemoor	9	8	1
Grant Park	5	5	0	Lake Villa	17	15	2
Granville	3	3	0	Lakewood	9	8	1
Grayslake	46	32	14	Lake Zurich	56	37	19
Grayville	7	3	4	La Moille	1	1	0
Greenfield	2	2	0	Lanark	3	3	0
Greenup	4	4	0	Lansing	82	63	19
Green Valley	1	1	0	La Salle	22	17	5
Greenville	14	10	4	Lebanon	11	11	0
Gridley	1	1	0	Leland	1	1	0
Gurnee	86	61	25	Leland Grove	6	6	0
Hamilton	4	4	0	Lemont	32	29	3
Hampshire	9	9	0	Lenzburg	1	1	0
Hampton	3	3	0	Le Roy	6	6	0
Hanover	1	1	0	Lewistown	3	3	0
Hanover Park	68	48	20	Lexington	3	3	0
Harrisburg	14	13	1	Libertyville	59	42	17
Hartford	5	4	1	Lincoln	30	26	4
Harvard	23	17	6	Lincolnshire	32	21	11
Harvey	93	56	37	Lincolnwood	45	34	11
Harwood Heights	37	28	9	Lindenhurst	16	14	2
Havana	13	9	4	Lisle	58	43	15
Hawthorn Woods	11	10	1	Litchfield	24	16	8
Hazel Crest	38	30	8	Livingston	1	1	0
Hebron	4	4	0	Lockport	36	32	4
Henry	4	4	0	Lombard	88	71	17
Herrin	21	15	6	Loves Park	40	30	10
Herscher	2	2	0	Ludlow	3	3	0

Table 78

Full-time Law Enforcement Employees as of October 31, 2003

by City by State—Continued

City by state	Total law enforcement employees	Total officers	Total civilians	City by state	Total law enforcement employees	Total officers	Total civilians
ILLINOIS—Continued				**ILLINOIS—Continued**			
Lynwood	22	17	5	Nauvoo	1	1	0
Lyons	35	28	7	Neoga	2	2	0
Mackinaw	2	2	0	New Athens	5	5	0
Macomb	28	25	3	New Baden	4	4	0
Madison	16	12	4	New Lenox	35	32	3
Mahomet	7	6	1	Newman	1	1	0
Manhattan	7	7	0	Newton	7	6	1
Manito	3	3	0	Niles	76	62	14
Manteno	15	14	1	Nokomis	8	5	3
Maple Park	1	1	0	Normal	82	72	10
Marengo	22	16	6	Norridge	54	38	16
Marion	33	23	10	North Aurora	25	23	2
Marissa	5	5	0	Northbrook	88	61	27
Markham	39	32	7	North Chicago	68	50	18
Maroa	4	4	0	Northfield	30	21	9
Marquette Heights	5	5	0	Northlake	50	33	17
Marseilles	14	10	4	North Pekin	2	2	0
Marshall	10	9	1	North Riverside	42	33	9
Martinsville	2	2	0	Oak Brook	52	44	8
Maryville	15	10	5	Oakbrook Terrace	22	20	2
Mascoutah	15	13	2	Oak Forest	52	39	13
Mason City	5	5	0	Oak Lawn	155	106	49
Matteson	47	37	10	Oak Park	130	115	15
Mattoon	53	41	12	Oblong	3	3	0
Maywood	72	52	20	O'Fallon	58	43	15
McCook	20	15	5	Oglesby	13	9	4
McCullom Lake	1	1	0	Okawville	3	3	0
McHenry	63	47	16	Olney	18	12	6
McLean	1	1	0	Olympia Fields	20	19	1
McLeansboro	5	5	0	Oregon	9	8	1
Melrose Park	88	71	17	Orion	3	3	0
Mendota	20	15	5	Orland Hills	16	14	2
Meredosia	3	3	0	Orland Park	118	91	27
Metamora	6	6	0	Oswego	42	39	3
Metropolis	20	15	5	Ottawa	40	31	9
Midlothian	31	24	7	Palatine	136	107	29
Milan	17	12	5	Palestine	3	3	0
Milledgeville	2	2	0	Palos Heights	28	27	1
Millstadt	5	5	0	Palos Hills	38	35	3
Minier	2	2	0	Palos Park	9	9	0
Minonk	2	2	0	Pana	13	9	4
Minooka	15	13	2	Paris	22	17	5
Mokena	29	27	2	Park City	9	6	3
Moline	108	82	26	Park Forest	53	37	16
Momence	8	8	0	Park Ridge	70	56	14
Monee	11	10	1	Pawnee	10	6	4
Monmouth	26	17	9	Paxton	7	7	0
Montgomery	26	18	8	Pecatonica	2	2	0
Monticello	6	5	1	Pekin	60	54	6
Morris	33	26	7	Peoria	268	226	42
Morrison	6	6	0	Peoria Heights	13	9	4
Morton	29	22	7	Peotone	10	9	1
Morton Grove	58	46	12	Peru	28	21	7
Mound City	2	2	0	Petersburg	6	6	0
Mount Carmel	15	11	4	Phoenix	4	3	1
Mount Carroll	3	3	0	Pinckneyville	8	7	1
Mount Morris	5	4	1	Piper City	1	1	0
Mount Olive	6	4	2	Pittsfield	5	5	0
Mount Prospect	104	82	22	Plainfield	47	40	7
Mount Pulaski	4	4	0	Plano	16	14	2
Mount Sterling	11	6	5	Polo	4	4	0
Mount Vernon	57	43	14	Pontiac	24	22	2
Mount Zion	10	8	2	Pontoon Beach	17	11	6
Moweaqua	2	2	0	Port Barrington	1	1	0
Mundelein	65	47	18	Port Byron	3	3	0
Murphysboro	24	16	8	Posen	12	11	1
Naperville	280	179	101	Princeton	16	15	1
Nashville	8	7	1	Prophetstown	4	3	1

Table 78

Full-time Law Enforcement Employees as of October 31, 2003
by City by State—Continued

City by state	Total law enforcement employees	Total officers	Total civilians	City by state	Total law enforcement employees	Total officers	Total civilians
ILLINOIS—Continued				**ILLINOIS—Continued**			
Prospect Heights	34	26	8	Spring Valley	14	10	4
Quincy	87	74	13	St. Anne	3	3	0
Rantoul	40	31	9	Staunton	10	7	3
Raymond	1	1	0	St. Charles	63	53	10
Red Bud	5	5	0	Steger	22	15	7
Richmond	6	5	1	Sterling	43	30	13
Richton Park	32	27	5	Stickney	21	16	5
Ridge Farm	2	2	0	Stockton	4	4	0
Ridgway	3	3	0	Stone Park	26	19	7
Riverdale	45	31	14	Stonington	1	1	0
River Forest	32	29	3	Streamwood	70	59	11
River Grove	30	23	7	Streator	31	24	7
Riverside	24	19	5	Sugar Grove	11	10	1
Robbins	12	5	7	Sullivan	10	8	2
Robinson	15	13	2	Summit	40	34	6
Rochelle	25	19	6	Sumner	2	2	0
Rochester	6	6	0	Swansea	23	17	6
Rockdale	4	4	0	Sycamore	25	23	2
Rock Falls	28	20	8	Taylorville	29	23	6
Rockford	327	293	34	Thomasboro	2	2	0
Rock Island	112	85	27	Thomson	1	1	0
Rockton	14	13	1	Thornton	11	10	1
Rolling Meadows	82	56	26	Tilton	3	3	0
Romeoville	66	51	15	Tinley Park	93	70	23
Roodhouse	5	5	0	Tolono	4	4	0
Roscoe	12	11	1	Tremont	3	3	0
Roselle	50	36	14	Trenton	3	3	0
Rosemont	86	73	13	Troy	21	16	5
Rossville	2	2	0	Tuscola	8	7	1
Round Lake	20	15	5	University Park	20	16	4
Round Lake Beach	46	39	7	Urbana	63	50	13
Round Lake Heights	3	3	0	Valmeyer	2	2	0
Round Lake Park	14	12	2	Vandalia	18	13	5
Roxana	6	5	1	Venice	9	6	3
Royalton	1	1	0	Vernon Hills	70	47	23
Rushville	5	5	0	Vienna	3	3	0
Salem	21	14	7	Villa Grove	5	4	1
Sandwich	18	12	6	Villa Park	53	38	15
Sauget	16	15	1	Virden	10	6	4
Sauk Village	31	23	8	Virginia	1	1	0
Savanna	8	8	0	Wamac	4	4	0
Schaumburg	203	133	70	Warren	4	3	1
Schiller Park	40	33	7	Warrensburg	1	1	0
Seneca	9	4	5	Warrenville	29	22	7
Sesser	5	5	0	Washburn	2	2	0
Shawneetown	5	5	0	Washington	25	16	9
Shelbyville	8	7	1	Washington Park	11	8	3
Sheridan	2	2	0	Waterloo	16	14	2
Sherman	6	6	0	Waterman	2	2	0
Shiloh	12	12	0	Watseka	11	10	1
Shorewood	24	21	3	Wauconda	33	20	13
Silvis	20	13	7	Waukegan	215	167	48
Skokie	140	106	34	Wayne	5	5	0
Sleepy Hollow	7	6	1	Wayne City	1	1	0
Smithton	4	3	1	Westchester	53	38	15
Somonauk	2	2	0	West Chicago	59	47	12
South Barrington	19	15	4	West City	9	5	4
South Beloit	12	10	2	West Dundee	25	22	3
South Chicago Heights	13	10	3	Western Springs	27	21	6
South Elgin	35	28	7	West Frankfort	21	15	6
Southern View	4	4	0	Westmont	58	42	16
South Holland	54	43	11	West Salem	1	1	0
South Jacksonville	6	5	1	Westville	3	3	0
South Pekin	2	2	0	Wheaton	94	70	24
South Roxana	5	5	0	Wheeling	91	64	27
Sparta	16	11	5	White Hall	10	6	4
Springfield	317	270	47	Williamsville	2	2	0
Spring Grove	9	8	1	Willowbrook	29	25	4

Table 78

Full-time Law Enforcement Employees as of October 31, 2003
by City by State—Continued

City by state	Total law enforcement employees	Total officers	Total civilians	City by state	Total law enforcement employees	Total officers	Total civilians
ILLINOIS—Continued				**INDIANA—Continued**			
Willow Springs	19	14	5	Fishers	72	65	7
Wilmette	64	45	19	Fort Wayne	459	417	42
Wilmington	18	13	5	Frankfort	39	28	11
Winchester	4	4	0	Franklin	47	35	12
Winfield	22	20	2	Gary	378	292	86
Winnebago	5	5	0	Gas City	15	11	4
Winnetka	37	28	9	Georgetown	4	4	0
Winthrop Harbor	16	9	7	Goshen	59	53	6
Witt	1	1	0	Greencastle	18	15	3
Wood Dale	51	33	18	Greendale	15	11	4
Woodhull	1	1	0	Greenfield	38	29	9
Woodridge	73	52	21	Greensburg	27	18	9
Wood River	25	18	7	Greenwood	74	51	23
Woodstock	45	32	13	Griffith	39	31	8
Worden	1	1	0	Hagerstown	5	5	0
Worth	29	27	2	Hammond	259	210	49
Yates City	1	1	0	Hartford City	15	13	2
Yorkville	21	19	2	Hebron	7	6	1
Zeigler	4	4	0	Highland	50	42	8
Zion	56	41	15	Hobart	70	55	15
				Huntingburg	10	9	1
INDIANA				Huntington	44	35	9
				Indianapolis	2,648	1,581	1,067
Alexandria	17	13	4	Jasonville	5	5	0
Anderson	150	129	21	Jasper	27	20	7
Angola	20	16	4	Jeffersonville	64	55	9
Attica	6	6	0	Kendallville	25	18	7
Auburn	28	21	7	Kingsford Heights	2	2	0
Aurora	13	9	4	Knox	7	7	0
Austin	6	6	0	Kokomo	139	101	38
Batesville	15	10	5	Kouts	7	7	0
Bedford	40	32	8	Lafayette	139	110	29
Beech Grove	41	30	11	Lake Station	27	22	5
Berne	6	6	0	La Porte	51	45	6
Bicknell	10	7	3	Lawrence	59	53	6
Bloomington	117	80	37	Lawrenceburg	20	17	3
Bluffton	29	20	9	Lebanon	30	29	1
Boonville	14	13	1	Ligonier	10	9	1
Brazil	16	12	4	Linton	13	8	5
Bremen	16	12	4	Logansport	53	43	10
Brownsburg	45	30	15	Long Beach	7	5	2
Burns Harbor	2	2	0	Loogootee	6	4	2
Cambridge City	5	5	0	Lowell	19	14	5
Carmel	96	82	14	Madison	32	25	7
Cedar Lake	20	15	5	Marion	88	72	16
Charlestown	17	12	5	Martinsville	26	19	7
Chesterfield	6	6	0	Merrillville	67	52	15
Chesterton	24	19	5	Michigan City	105	87	18
Clarksville	43	35	8	Mishawaka	134	100	34
Clinton	13	7	6	Mitchell	14	9	5
Columbia City	20	18	2	Monticello	16	12	4
Columbus	80	74	6	Mooresville	25	19	6
Connersville	37	35	2	Mount Vernon	16	14	2
Corydon	7	7	0	Muncie	121	113	8
Covington	6	6	0	Munster	50	38	12
Crawfordsville	43	29	14	Nappanee	21	15	6
Crown Point	43	32	11	New Albany	83	65	18
Culver	4	4	0	New Castle	39	36	3
Decatur	21	17	4	New Chicago	8	4	4
Delphi	11	7	4	New Haven	25	18	7
Dunkirk	10	6	4	New Whiteland	11	7	4
Dyer	35	28	7	Noblesville	75	65	10
East Chicago	146	116	30	North Liberty	4	4	0
Edinburgh	14	9	5	North Manchester	14	10	4
Elkhart	148	117	31	North Vernon	20	17	3
Elwood	22	18	4	Oakland City	5	5	0
Evansville	317	278	39	Peru	32	30	2
Fairmount	9	5	4	Petersburg	5	5	0

Table 78

Full-time Law Enforcement Employees as of October 31, 2003
by City by State—Continued

City by state	Total law enforcement employees	Total officers	Total civilians	City by state	Total law enforcement employees	Total officers	Total civilians
INDIANA—Continued				**IOWA—Continued**			
Plainfield	44	39	5	Clarinda	15	11	4
Plymouth	27	21	6	Clarion	7	6	1
Portage	69	52	17	Clear Lake	19	14	5
Portland	17	13	4	Clinton	51	43	8
Princeton	17	16	1	Clive	23	20	3
Rensselaer	14	9	5	Coralville	31	28	3
Richmond	95	80	15	Council Bluffs	130	112	18
Rochester	20	14	6	Cresco	7	7	0
Roseland	3	3	0	Creston	15	10	5
Rushville	18	13	5	Davenport	202	159	43
Salem	18	12	6	Decorah	19	13	6
Schererville	60	47	13	Denison	17	12	5
Scottsburg	14	13	1	Des Moines	480	355	125
Sellersburg	17	12	5	De Witt	9	9	0
Seymour	53	39	14	Dubuque	91	86	5
Shelbyville	54	41	13	Dyersville	10	6	4
South Bend	329	255	74	Eagle Grove	6	6	0
South Whitley	3	3	0	Eldora	6	6	0
Speedway	39	30	9	Eldridge	7	7	0
St. John	19	14	5	Emmetsburg	7	6	1
Sullivan	8	8	0	Estherville	12	12	0
Tell City	17	12	5	Evansdale	8	7	1
Terre Haute	153	132	21	Fairfield	19	13	6
Tipton	17	12	5	Forest City	8	8	0
Trail Creek	4	4	0	Fort Dodge	44	39	5
Union City	11	7	4	Fort Madison	24	19	5
Valparaiso	63	45	18	Garner	5	5	0
Vincennes	42	37	5	Glenwood	11	10	1
Wabash	32	26	6	Grinnell	18	16	2
Walkerton	12	7	5	Grundy Center	4	4	0
Warsaw	41	35	6	Hampton	13	8	5
Washington	24	18	6	Harlan	9	8	1
Waterloo	5	5	0	Hawarden	4	4	0
Westfield	31	27	4	Hiawatha	8	8	0
West Lafayette	58	44	14	Humboldt	7	7	0
West Terre Haute	12	7	5	Independence	14	11	3
Westville	4	4	0	Indianola	20	18	2
Whiting	26	20	6	Iowa City	101	72	29
Winchester	16	12	4	Iowa Falls	16	11	5
Winona Lake	5	5	0	Jefferson	8	8	0
				Johnston	14	13	1
IOWA				Keokuk	36	26	10
				Knoxville	15	12	3
Adel	9	8	1	Le Claire	8	7	1
Albia	7	6	1	Le Mars	15	14	1
Algona	15	10	5	Manchester	14	9	5
Altoona	21	19	2	Maquoketa	18	12	6
Ames	69	47	22	Marion	46	37	9
Anamosa	7	6	1	Marshalltown	60	42	18
Ankeny	44	37	7	Mason City	63	49	14
Atlantic	13	11	2	Missouri Valley	6	6	0
Audubon	3	3	0	Monticello	7	6	1
Belle Plaine	5	4	1	Mount Pleasant	14	13	1
Belmond	5	5	0	Mount Vernon	6	6	0
Bettendorf	56	42	14	Muscatine	50	38	12
Bloomfield	4	4	0	Nevada	7	7	0
Boone	22	17	5	New Hampton	7	7	0
Burlington	56	42	14	Newton	31	27	4
Camanche	7	7	0	North Liberty	4	4	0
Carlisle	5	5	0	Norwalk	12	10	2
Carroll	16	15	1	Oelwein	15	10	5
Carter Lake	7	7	0	Ogden	3	3	0
Cedar Falls	44	41	3	Onawa	6	6	0
Cedar Rapids	221	182	39	Orange City	7	7	0
Centerville	17	13	4	Osage	5	5	0
Chariton	8	7	1	Osceola	10	9	1
Charles City	18	12	6	Oskaloosa	18	16	2
Cherokee	9	8	1	Ottumwa	43	35	8

Table 78

Full-time Law Enforcement Employees as of October 31, 2003
by City by State—Continued

City by state	Total law enforcement employees	Total officers	Total civilians	City by state	Total law enforcement employees	Total officers	Total civilians
IOWA—Continued				**KANSAS—Continued**			
Pella	17	14	3	Caldwell	4	4	0
Perry	19	12	7	Caney	9	5	4
Pleasant Hill	13	12	1	Canton	2	2	0
Polk City	5	5	0	Carbondale	4	3	1
Red Oak	12	11	1	Cawker City	1	1	0
Rock Rapids	3	3	0	Cedar Vale	1	1	0
Rock Valley	3	3	0	Chanute	24	20	4
Sac City	4	4	0	Chapman	3	3	0
Sergeant Bluff	9	8	1	Cheney	4	4	0
Sheldon	11	7	4	Cherokee	2	2	0
Shenandoah	11	7	4	Cherryvale	7	6	1
Sioux Center	7	7	0	Chetopa	4	4	0
Sioux City	156	125	31	Cimarron	2	2	0
Spencer	27	20	7	Claflin	2	2	0
Spirit Lake	9	8	1	Clay Center	7	6	1
St. Ansgar	1	1	0	Clearwater	6	6	0
State Center	1	1	0	Coffeyville	29	23	6
Storm Lake	22	18	4	Colby	23	18	5
Story City	5	5	0	Columbus	9	9	0
Tama	6	6	0	Colwich	3	3	0
Tipton	5	5	0	Concordia	15	9	6
Urbandale	46	42	4	Conway Springs	4	4	0
Vinton	7	7	0	Council Grove	8	7	1
Washington	11	11	0	Derby	47	34	13
Waterloo	128	117	11	Dodge City	62	43	19
Waukee	11	9	2	Eastborough	7	7	0
Waukon	7	7	0	Edwardsville	16	15	1
Waverly	16	15	1	El Dorado	29	27	2
Webster City	19	13	6	Elkhart	3	3	0
West Burlington	11	10	1	Ellinwood	5	5	0
West Des Moines	76	61	15	Ellis	5	5	0
West Liberty	7	6	1	Ellsworth	7	6	1
West Union	5	5	0	Elwood	3	3	0
Williamsburg	5	5	0	Emporia	70	46	24
Wilton	5	5	0	Enterprise	1	1	0
Windsor Heights	13	12	1	Erie	3	3	0
Winterset	8	7	1	Eskridge	2	2	0
				Eudora	8	8	0
KANSAS				Fairway	10	9	1
				Florence	1	1	0
Abilene	17	14	3	Fort Scott	27	20	7
Alma	1	1	0	Fredonia	6	5	1
Altamont	4	4	0	Frontenac	9	6	3
Americus	1	1	0	Galena	12	7	5
Andale	1	1	0	Galva	1	1	0
Andover	20	14	6	Garden City	86	57	29
Anthony	5	5	0	Garden Plain	2	2	0
Arkansas City	33	25	8	Gardner	24	23	1
Arma	4	4	0	Garnett	13	9	4
Atchison	24	23	1	Girard	7	7	0
Attica	1	1	0	Goddard	5	5	0
Atwood	3	3	0	Goodland	11	10	1
Augusta	32	24	8	Grandview Plaza	3	3	0
Baldwin City	8	7	1	Great Bend	37	32	5
Basehor	6	5	1	Halstead	6	5	1
Baxter Springs	14	10	4	Harper	3	3	0
Bel Aire	11	10	1	Haven	3	3	0
Belle Plaine	4	4	0	Hays	43	27	16
Belleville	5	5	0	Haysville	30	23	7
Beloit	14	10	4	Herington	11	6	5
Blue Rapids	2	2	0	Hesston	7	6	1
Bonner Springs	26	24	2	Hiawatha	7	6	1
Buhler	3	3	0	Highland	3	3	0
Burden	1	1	0	Hill City	4	4	0
Burlingame	2	2	0	Hillsboro	5	5	0
Burlington	8	6	2	Hoisington	9	7	2
Burrton	1	1	0	Holcomb	4	3	1
Bushton	1	1	0	Holton	11	7	4

Table 78

Full-time Law Enforcement Employees as of October 31, 2003
by City by State—Continued

City by state	Total law enforcement employees	Total officers	Total civilians	City by state	Total law enforcement employees	Total officers	Total civilians
KANSAS—Continued				**KANSAS—Continued**			
Holyrood	1	1	0	Paola	22	16	6
Hope	1	1	0	Park City	19	17	2
Horton	10	10	0	Parsons	27	21	6
Hoxie	2	2	0	Peabody	3	3	0
Hugoton	6	5	1	Perry	1	1	0
Humboldt	5	5	0	Pittsburg	52	38	14
Hutchinson	89	68	21	Plainville	5	5	0
Independence	30	21	9	Pleasanton	1	1	0
Inman	2	2	0	Prairie Village	53	41	12
Iola	30	18	12	Pratt	21	14	7
Junction City	60	43	17	Protection	1	1	0
Kansas City	463	339	124	Quinter	1	1	0
Kechi	2	2	0	Roeland Park	17	15	2
Kingman	7	7	0	Rolla	1	1	0
Kinsley	3	3	0	Rose Hill	9	8	1
Kiowa	2	2	0	Rossville	3	3	0
La Crosse	3	3	0	Russell	19	8	11
La Cygne	2	2	0	Sabetha	5	5	0
Lake Quivira	2	2	0	Salina	109	79	30
Lansing	14	12	2	Scott City	13	7	6
Larned	14	9	5	Scranton	1	1	0
Lawrence	167	135	32	Sedan	3	3	0
Leavenworth	83	60	23	Sedgwick	2	2	0
Leawood	78	56	22	Seneca	5	5	0
Lebo	1	1	0	Shawnee	109	88	21
Lenexa	114	71	43	Silver Lake	2	2	0
Le Roy	1	1	0	Smith Center	3	3	0
Liberal	46	34	12	South Hutchinson	9	7	2
Lindsborg	7	6	1	Spearville	1	1	0
Linn Valley	1	1	0	Spring Hill	8	7	1
Little River	1	1	0	Stafford	4	4	0
Louisburg	9	9	0	Sterling	5	5	0
Lyndon	3	3	0	St. Francis	4	3	1
Lyons	8	7	1	St. George	1	1	0
Macksville	1	1	0	St. John	4	4	0
Maize	8	6	2	St. Marys	5	5	0
Marion	5	5	0	Stockton	4	4	0
Marquette	1	1	0	Tonganoxie	8	7	1
Marysville	7	6	1	Topeka	325	277	48
McLouth	1	1	0	Towanda	3	3	0
McPherson	31	26	5	Troy	1	1	0
Meade	3	3	0	Udall	2	2	0
Medicine Lodge	6	5	1	Ulysses	11	10	1
Merriam	30	26	4	Valley Center	11	8	3
Minneapolis	5	5	0	Valley Falls	2	2	0
Mission	28	27	1	Victoria	2	2	0
Moran	1	1	0	Wa Keeney	5	5	0
Moundridge	3	3	0	Wakefield	1	1	0
Mount Hope	2	2	0	Wamego	11	6	5
Mulberry	1	1	0	Waterville	1	1	0
Mulvane	18	12	6	Wathena	2	2	0
Neodesha	8	7	1	Waverly	1	1	0
Newton	33	29	4	Weir	2	2	0
Nickerson	5	5	0	Wellington	20	16	4
North Newton	2	2	0	Wellsville	3	3	0
Norton	5	5	0	Westwood	8	7	1
Norwich	1	1	0	Wichita	811	631	180
Oakley	11	6	5	Wilson	1	1	0
Oberlin	3	3	0	Winfield	29	19	10
Olathe	186	146	40	Yates Center	3	3	0
Osage City	6	6	0				
Osawatomie	11	6	5	**KENTUCKY**			
Osborne	4	4	0				
Oswego	6	5	1	Adairville	1	1	0
Ottawa	30	26	4	Albany	10	9	1
Overbrook	2	2	0	Alexandria	13	12	1
Overland Park	257	210	47	Allen	1	1	0
Oxford	2	2	0	Anchorage	14	10	4

Table 78

Full-time Law Enforcement Employees as of October 31, 2003
by City by State—Continued

City by state	Total law enforcement employees	Total officers	Total civilians	City by state	Total law enforcement employees	Total officers	Total civilians
KENTUCKY—Continued				**KENTUCKY—Continued**			
Ashland	53	45	8	Fleming-Neon	3	2	1
Auburn	3	3	0	Flemingsburg	6	6	0
Audubon Park	8	7	1	Florence	53	49	4
Augusta	3	3	0	Fort Mitchell	13	12	1
Barbourville	17	14	3	Fort Thomas	24	23	1
Bardstown	25	20	5	Fort Wright	12	11	1
Bardwell	1	1	0	Frankfort	69	64	5
Barlow	1	1	0	Franklin	22	19	3
Beattyville	8	6	2	Fulton	13	9	4
Beaver Dam	6	6	0	Gamaliel	1	1	0
Bellefonte	2	2	0	Georgetown	51	44	7
Bellevue	11	10	1	Glasgow	51	36	15
Benham	6	4	2	Graymoor-Devondale	3	3	0
Benton	9	7	2	Grayson	8	8	0
Berea	31	25	6	Greensburg	12	6	6
Bloomfield	1	1	0	Greenup	3	3	0
Booneville	4	4	0	Greenville	9	9	0
Bowling Green	123	93	30	Guthrie	6	5	1
Brandenburg	4	4	0	Hardinsburg	5	5	0
Brodhead	2	2	0	Harlan	15	11	4
Brooksville	2	2	0	Harrodsburg	29	19	10
Brownsville	2	2	0	Hartford	5	5	0
Burkesville	9	5	4	Hazard	25	19	6
Burnside	4	4	0	Henderson	64	57	7
Butler	1	1	0	Hickman	4	4	0
Cadiz	10	9	1	Highland Heights	10	10	0
Calhoun	2	2	0	Hillview	9	9	0
Calvert City	6	5	1	Hindman	2	2	0
Campbellsburg	1	1	0	Hodgenville	6	6	0
Campbellsville	29	18	11	Hopkinsville	77	69	8
Campton	1	1	0	Horse Cave	5	5	0
Caneyville	1	1	0	Hustonville	1	1	0
Carlisle	9	6	3	Independence	27	25	2
Carrollton	12	11	1	Indian Hills	8	8	0
Catlettsburg	8	8	0	Inez	3	2	1
Cave City	6	6	0	Irvine	6	6	0
Central City	13	12	1	Irvington	4	4	0
Clarkson	1	1	0	Jackson	11	10	1
Clay	1	1	0	Jamestown	5	5	0
Clay City	3	3	0	Jeffersontown	59	50	9
Clinton	5	5	0	Jenkins	6	5	1
Cloverport	2	2	0	Junction City	4	4	0
Cold Spring	10	10	0	La Center	2	2	0
Columbia	10	10	0	La Grange	10	10	0
Corbin	29	21	8	Lakeside Park-Crestview Hills	8	7	1
Covington	123	113	10	Lancaster	9	9	0
Crab Orchard	1	1	0	Lawrenceburg	23	15	8
Crescent Springs	9	9	0	Lebanon	23	16	7
Crofton	1	1	0	Lebanon Junction	5	5	0
Cumberland	9	7	2	Leitchfield	17	16	1
Cynthiana	18	17	1	Lewisburg	1	1	0
Danville	32	30	2	Lewisport	3	3	0
Dawson Springs	10	6	4	Lexington	629	478	151
Dayton	8	8	0	Liberty	5	5	0
Earlington	2	2	0	Livermore	1	1	0
Eddyville	5	5	0	Livingston	1	1	0
Edgewood	12	12	0	London	34	31	3
Edmonton	7	7	0	Lone Oak	2	2	0
Elizabethtown	55	42	13	Louisa	6	5	1
Elkhorn City	5	5	0	Louisville Metro	1,579	1,192	387
Elkton	8	8	0	Loyall	1	1	0
Elsmere	12	11	1	Ludlow	11	9	2
Eminence	6	6	0	Lynch	1	1	0
Erlanger	39	32	7	Lynnview	2	2	0
Eubank	1	1	0	Madisonville	49	39	10
Evarts	3	3	0	Manchester	17	15	2
Falmouth	8	7	1	Marion	7	7	0
Flatwoods	14	10	4	Martin	4	4	0

Table 78

Full-time Law Enforcement Employees as of October 31, 2003
by City by State—Continued

City by state	Total law enforcement employees	Total officers	Total civilians	City by state	Total law enforcement employees	Total officers	Total civilians
KENTUCKY—Continued				**KENTUCKY—Continued**			
Mayfield	32	24	8	Trenton	1	1	0
Maysville	30	24	6	Uniontown	2	2	0
McKee	2	2	0	Vanceburg	6	6	0
Middlesboro	28	24	4	Versailles	30	21	9
Millersburg	1	1	0	Villa Hills	9	8	1
Monticello	8	8	0	Vine Grove	8	8	0
Morehead	29	20	9	Warsaw	5	5	0
Morganfield	13	8	5	West Buechel	11	11	0
Morgantown	5	5	0	West Liberty	11	6	5
Mortons Gap	1	1	0	West Point	4	4	0
Mount Sterling	29	21	8	Wheelwright	1	1	0
Mount Vernon	8	8	0	Whitesburg	8	8	0
Mount Washington	14	13	1	Wilder	7	7	0
Muldraugh	3	3	0	Williamsburg	12	11	1
Munfordville	4	4	0	Williamstown	6	6	0
Murray	36	30	6	Wilmore	8	7	1
New Castle	1	1	0	Winchester	48	33	15
New Haven	1	1	0	Worthington	4	4	0
Newport	62	51	11	Wurtland	1	1	0
Nicholasville	58	54	4				
Nortonville	1	1	0	**LOUISIANA**			
Oak Grove	18	13	5				
Olive Hill	7	6	1	Abbeville	48	46	2
Owensboro	132	98	34	Abita Springs	6	5	1
Owenton	3	3	0	Addis	7	6	1
Owingsville	5	5	0	Alexandria	177	142	35
Paducah	90	77	13	Amite	20	20	0
Paintsville	12	12	0	Arnaudville	10	5	5
Paris	29	21	8	Baker	33	32	1
Park City	1	1	0	Baldwin	9	8	1
Park Hills	6	6	0	Ball	6	5	1
Pembroke	1	1	0	Basile	12	7	5
Perryville	1	1	0	Bastrop	53	48	5
Pikeville	27	19	8	Baton Rouge	764	608	156
Pineville	8	8	0	Bernice	5	5	0
Pioneer Village	4	4	0	Berwick	12	11	1
Pippa Passes	1	1	0	Blanchard	5	4	1
Powderly	2	2	0	Bogalusa	58	37	21
Prestonsburg	17	17	0	Bossier City	208	169	39
Princeton	17	15	2	Breaux Bridge	25	25	0
Prospect	10	9	1	Broussard	17	14	3
Providence	8	8	0	Brusly	8	7	1
Raceland	5	5	0	Cheneyville	7	6	1
Radcliff	50	35	15	Church Point	21	17	4
Ravenna	1	1	0	Clinton	7	7	0
Richmond	69	54	15	Coushatta	6	6	0
Russell	13	13	0	Covington	41	30	11
Russell Springs	9	8	1	Crowley	35	34	1
Russellville	25	23	2	Cullen	5	5	0
Sadieville	2	2	0	Delhi	12	8	4
Salyersville	4	4	0	Denham Springs	41	27	14
Scottsville	19	14	5	De Quincy	13	13	0
Sebree	2	2	0	De Ridder	28	22	6
Shelbyville	19	18	1	Dixie Inn	4	3	1
Shepherdsville	17	16	1	Dubach	2	2	0
Shively	25	20	5	Duson	5	5	0
Silver Grove	1	1	0	Elton	5	5	0
Somerset	37	34	3	Erath	9	5	4
Southgate	6	6	0	Eunice	45	36	9
Springfield	13	8	5	Farmerville	9	9	0
Stamping Ground	1	1	0	Ferriday	18	12	6
Stanford	9	9	0	Folsom	4	3	1
Stanton	10	10	0	Franklin	23	21	2
St. Matthews	38	32	6	Franklinton	19	14	5
Sturgis	4	4	0	French Settlement	2	2	0
Taylor Mill	10	9	1	Golden Meadow	5	5	0
Taylorsville	5	5	0	Gonzales	30	30	0
Tompkinsville	9	6	3	Grambling	18	12	6

Table 78

Full-time Law Enforcement Employees as of October 31, 2003

by City by State—Continued

City by state	Total law enforcement employees	Total officers	Total civilians	City by state	Total law enforcement employees	Total officers	Total civilians
LOUISIANA—Continued				**LOUISIANA—Continued**			
Gramercy	7	7	0	Springhill	14	14	0
Gretna	99	79	20	Sterlington	6	5	1
Hammond	99	76	23	St. Francisville	8	7	1
Harahan	29	28	1	St. Gabriel	13	7	6
Haughton	8	6	2	St. Joseph	3	3	0
Haynesville	7	7	0	St. Martinville	20	14	6
Homer	11	11	0	Stonewall	1	1	0
Houma	88	71	17	Sulphur	65	46	19
Independence	7	7	0	Sunset	10	5	5
Iota	4	4	0	Tallulah	15	15	0
Iowa	14	12	2	Thibodaux	74	62	12
Jackson	8	7	1	Tickfaw	5	5	0
Jeanerette	17	17	0	Vidalia	21	21	0
Jena	7	6	1	Ville Platte	25	25	0
Jennings	38	32	6	Vinton	13	13	0
Jonesboro	18	14	4	Vivian	15	9	6
Kaplan	20	20	0	Washington	5	5	0
Kenner	268	179	89	Waterproof	2	2	0
Kentwood	10	10	0	Welsh	12	10	2
Kinder	17	12	5	Westlake	21	20	1
Lafayette	297	233	64	West Monroe	75	70	5
Lake Arthur	10	10	0	Westwego	37	36	1
Lake Charles	195	154	41	White Castle	13	9	4
Lake Providence	12	12	0	Winnfield	22	15	7
Leesville	28	28	0	Woodworth	6	4	2
Lockport	5	5	0	Youngsville	10	10	0
Mandeville	51	37	14	Zachary	36	34	2
Mansfield	17	13	4				
Many	14	13	1	**MAINE**			
Marksville	22	16	6				
McNary	2	1	1	Ashland	3	3	0
Minden	33	32	1	Auburn	58	51	7
Monroe	224	182	42	Augusta	57	42	15
Moreauville	1	1	0	Baileyville	7	7	0
Morgan City	56	46	10	Bangor	93	76	17
Napoleonville	2	2	0	Bar Harbor	13	9	4
Natchitoches	76	58	18	Bath	25	20	5
Newellton	2	2	0	Belfast	15	13	2
New Iberia	83	67	16	Berwick	10	10	0
Newllano	8	8	0	Bethel	4	4	0
New Orleans	1,995	1,612	383	Biddeford	66	48	18
New Roads	18	16	2	Boothbay Harbor	8	7	1
Norwood	2	1	1	Brewer	21	19	2
Oakdale	25	25	0	Bridgton	12	8	4
Oberlin	12	6	6	Brownville	2	2	0
Olla	4	4	0	Brunswick	51	37	14
Opelousas	66	50	16	Bucksport	11	7	4
Parks	2	2	0	Buxton	13	8	5
Patterson	17	17	0	Calais	12	8	4
Pearl River	11	6	5	Camden	16	11	5
Pineville	53	46	7	Cape Elizabeth	18	13	5
Plaquemine	32	24	8	Caribou	16	14	2
Pollock	2	2	0	Carrabassett Valley	10	1	9
Ponchatoula	22	17	5	Clinton	2	2	0
Port Allen	22	18	4	Cumberland	16	11	5
Port Barre	15	10	5	Damariscotta	6	5	1
Port Vincent	4	4	0	Dexter	6	5	1
Rayne	23	22	1	Dixfield	4	4	0
Rayville	7	7	0	Dover-Foxcroft	5	5	0
Richwood	15	10	5	East Millinocket	4	4	0
Rosedale	1	1	0	Eastport	5	5	0
Ruston	48	39	9	Eddington	1	1	0
Scott	19	18	1	Eliot	8	7	1
Shreveport	642	487	155	Ellsworth	17	13	4
Sicily Island	3	2	1	Fairfield	13	12	1
Simmesport	4	3	1	Falmouth	23	16	7
Slidell	114	82	32	Farmington	15	14	1
Sorrento	5	4	1	Fort Fairfield	4	4	0

Table 78

Full-time Law Enforcement Employees as of October 31, 2003
by City by State—Continued

City by state	Total law enforcement employees	Total officers	Total civilians	City by state	Total law enforcement employees	Total officers	Total civilians
MAINE—Continued				**MAINE—Continued**			
Fort Kent	9	5	4	Wilton	5	5	0
Freeport	17	12	5	Windham	32	23	9
Fryeburg	5	5	0	Winslow	10	9	1
Gardiner	16	11	5	Winter Harbor	1	1	0
Gorham	26	20	6	Winthrop	14	10	4
Gouldsboro	1	1	0	Wiscasset	6	5	1
Greenville	5	3	2	Yarmouth	17	12	5
Hallowell	5	5	0	York	39	28	11
Hampden	12	11	1				
Holden	2	2	0	**MARYLAND**			
Houlton	18	13	5				
Jay	11	7	4	Aberdeen	46	37	9
Kennebunk	27	20	7	Annapolis	157	116	41
Kennebunkport	16	11	5	Baltimore	3,789	3,275	514
Kittery	28	21	7	Baltimore City Sheriff	113	87	26
Lewiston	95	81	14	Bel Air	42	30	12
Limestone	4	4	0	Berlin	18	13	5
Lincoln	6	5	1	Berwyn Heights	7	6	1
Lisbon	22	16	6	Bladensburg	25	16	9
Livermore Falls	10	6	4	Brunswick	13	11	2
Machias	4	4	0	Cambridge	53	42	11
Madawaska	7	6	1	Capitol Heights	10	8	2
Madison	6	5	1	Centreville	9	8	1
Mechanic Falls	5	5	0	Chestertown	11	10	1
Mexico	4	4	0	Cheverly	12	10	2
Milbridge	2	2	0	Cottage City	4	4	0
Millinocket	8	8	0	Crisfield	14	11	3
Milo	3	3	0	Cumberland	55	48	7
Monmouth	5	5	0	Delmar	10	9	1
Mount Desert	10	6	4	Denton	11	10	1
Newport	5	5	0	District Heights	9	6	3
North Berwick	9	8	1	Easton	59	45	14
Norway	8	7	1	Edmonston	6	6	0
Oakland	10	9	1	Elkton	38	28	10
Ogunquit	10	9	1	Fairmount Heights	4	3	1
Old Orchard Beach	25	17	8	Federalsburg	11	10	1
Old Town	18	15	3	Forest Heights	5	4	1
Orono	14	14	0	Frederick	159	120	39
Oxford	5	4	1	Frostburg	17	14	3
Paris	8	7	1	Fruitland	14	13	1
Phippsburg	1	1	0	Glenarden	6	4	2
Pittsfield	6	6	0	Greenbelt	66	53	13
Portland	222	158	64	Greensboro	2	2	0
Presque Isle	23	19	4	Hagerstown	116	97	19
Rangeley	3	3	0	Hampstead	8	7	1
Richmond	5	5	0	Hancock	5	4	1
Rockland	21	18	3	Havre de Grace	37	28	9
Rockport	8	7	1	Hurlock	8	6	2
Rumford	16	16	0	Hyattsville	41	31	10
Sabattus	7	6	1	Landover Hills	4	3	1
Saco	45	33	12	La Plata	11	10	1
Sanford	51	37	14	Laurel	60	45	15
Scarborough	47	32	15	Luke	1	1	0
Searsport	3	3	0	Manchester	5	5	0
Skowhegan	19	13	6	Morningside	10	9	1
South Berwick	11	7	4	Mount Rainier	19	13	6
South Portland	68	51	17	North East	8	7	1
Southwest Harbor	9	5	4	Oakland	7	6	1
Swan's Island	1	1	0	Ocean City	113	93	20
Thomaston	5	5	0	Ocean Pines	19	14	5
Topsham	18	14	4	Oxford	4	4	0
Van Buren	3	3	0	Pocomoke City	19	14	5
Veazie	7	6	1	Port Deposit	3	3	0
Waldoboro	7	6	1	Preston	2	2	0
Washburn	2	2	0	Princess Anne	12	11	1
Waterville	38	30	8	Ridgely	5	5	0
Wells	27	22	5	Rising Sun	6	4	2
Westbrook	37	33	4	Riverdale Park	25	19	6

Table 78

Full-time Law Enforcement Employees as of October 31, 2003
by City by State—Continued

City by state	Total law enforcement employees	Total officers	Total civilians	City by state	Total law enforcement employees	Total officers	Total civilians
MARYLAND—Continued				**MASSACHUSETTS—Continued**			
Rock Hall	4	4	0	Chelmsford	71	56	15
Salisbury	106	80	26	Chelsea	97	80	17
Seat Pleasant	14	10	4	Chicopee	118	114	4
Smithsburg	4	3	1	Clinton	32	29	3
Snow Hill	8	7	1	Cohasset	25	19	6
St. Michaels	8	7	1	Concord	40	34	6
Sykesville	7	6	1	Dalton	14	12	2
Takoma Park	49	36	13	Danvers	57	44	13
Taneytown	9	8	1	Dartmouth	71	57	14
Thurmont	9	8	1	Dedham	67	60	7
University Park	8	8	0	Deerfield	7	6	1
Upper Marlboro	2	2	0	Dennis	50	41	9
Westernport	1	1	0	Dighton	10	9	1
Westminster	54	41	13	Douglas	15	11	4
				Dover	17	16	1
MASSACHUSETTS				Dracut	46	41	5
				Dudley	20	16	4
Abington	27	25	2	Dunstable	7	7	0
Acton	39	33	6	Duxbury	37	29	8
Acushnet	18	16	2	East Bridgewater	26	23	3
Adams	23	16	7	East Brookfield	3	3	0
Agawam	59	50	9	Eastham	19	14	5
Amesbury	42	33	9	Easthampton	31	25	6
Amherst	65	50	15	East Longmeadow	24	21	3
Andover	70	52	18	Easton	34	30	4
Aquinnah	4	4	0	Edgartown	16	15	1
Arlington	74	62	12	Egremont	3	3	0
Ashburnham	9	9	0	Erving	4	4	0
Ashby	5	5	0	Essex	9	8	1
Ashfield	2	2	0	Everett	95	87	8
Ashland	29	23	6	Fairhaven	36	31	5
Athol	23	17	6	Fall River	271	215	56
Attleboro	85	72	13	Falmouth	73	63	10
Auburn	39	29	10	Fitchburg	101	84	17
Avon	18	14	4	Foxborough	32	28	4
Ayer	22	17	5	Framingham	125	114	11
Barnstable	131	111	20	Franklin	54	43	11
Barre	11	7	4	Freetown	20	15	5
Becket	2	2	0	Gardner	36	28	8
Bedford	40	27	13	Georgetown	13	10	3
Belchertown	22	17	5	Gill	3	3	0
Bellingham	38	31	7	Gloucester	67	61	6
Belmont	51	47	4	Grafton	22	18	4
Berkley	5	5	0	Granby	12	10	2
Berlin	11	7	4	Great Barrington	14	14	0
Beverly	76	71	5	Greenfield	48	36	12
Billerica	77	65	12	Groton	22	17	5
Blackstone	19	16	3	Groveland	13	9	4
Bolton	13	8	5	Hadley	14	10	4
Boston	2,645	2,053	592	Halifax	14	10	4
Bourne	41	34	7	Hamilton	21	15	6
Boxborough	10	9	1	Hampden	13	10	3
Boxford	13	13	0	Hanover	32	29	3
Boylston	12	9	3	Hanson	28	23	5
Braintree	76	68	8	Hardwick	3	3	0
Brewster	24	18	6	Harvard	13	8	5
Bridgewater	39	35	4	Harwich	44	41	3
Brockton	218	189	29	Hatfield	2	2	0
Brookfield	3	3	0	Haverhill	88	80	8
Brookline	160	136	24	Hingham	57	48	9
Buckland	2	2	0	Hinsdale	1	1	0
Burlington	69	61	8	Holbrook	20	19	1
Cambridge	301	273	28	Holden	24	23	1
Canton	44	43	1	Holliston	24	23	1
Carlisle	14	11	3	Holyoke	142	124	18
Carver	20	15	5	Hopedale	16	12	4
Charlton	22	18	4	Hopkinton	25	20	5
Chatham	29	23	6	Hubbardston	9	5	4

Table 78

Full-time Law Enforcement Employees as of October 31, 2003
by City by State—Continued

City by state	Total law enforcement employees	Total officers	Total civilians	City by state	Total law enforcement employees	Total officers	Total civilians
MASSACHUSETTS—Continued				**MASSACHUSETTS—Continued**			
Hudson	37	31	6	Norwell	26	24	2
Hull	30	28	2	Norwood	71	61	10
Ipswich	30	25	5	Oak Bluffs	16	14	2
Kingston	31	23	8	Orleans	28	21	7
Lakeville	21	16	5	Oxford	22	18	4
Lancaster	10	10	0	Palmer	27	21	6
Lanesboro	6	6	0	Paxton	8	7	1
Lawrence	178	153	25	Peabody	108	92	16
Lee	12	11	1	Pembroke	27	25	2
Leicester	21	16	5	Pepperell	18	17	1
Lenox	10	10	0	Petersham	2	2	0
Leominster	79	62	17	Phillipston	1	1	0
Leverett	1	1	0	Pittsfield	103	84	19
Lexington	44	39	5	Plainville	17	14	3
Lincoln	17	13	4	Plymouth	117	102	15
Littleton	23	17	6	Plympton	6	6	0
Longmeadow	32	28	4	Princeton	8	5	3
Lowell	318	239	79	Provincetown	24	16	8
Ludlow	34	30	4	Quincy	241	212	29
Lunenburg	12	12	0	Randolph	58	57	1
Lynn	204	186	18	Raynham	31	23	8
Lynnfield	23	18	5	Reading	48	38	10
Malden	101	92	9	Rehoboth	25	21	4
Manchester-by-the-Sea	16	14	2	Revere	102	87	15
Mansfield	43	31	12	Rochester	10	10	0
Marblehead	50	34	16	Rockland	40	32	8
Marion	14	14	0	Rockport	17	16	1
Marlborough	71	60	11	Rowley	17	14	3
Marshfield	38	35	3	Rutland	7	6	1
Mashpee	41	33	8	Salem	99	92	7
Mattapoisett	18	18	0	Salisbury	13	12	1
Maynard	24	22	2	Sandwich	35	34	1
Medfield	21	16	5	Saugus	66	50	16
Medford	123	118	5	Scituate	34	29	5
Medway	21	20	1	Seekonk	40	34	6
Melrose	50	48	2	Sharon	28	24	4
Mendon	17	13	4	Sheffield	6	6	0
Merrimac	9	6	3	Shelburne	2	2	0
Methuen	94	83	11	Sherborn	14	14	0
Middleboro	52	42	10	Shirley	15	10	5
Middleton	12	11	1	Shrewsbury	52	40	12
Milford	48	44	4	Somerset	40	32	8
Millbury	24	19	5	Somerville	141	121	20
Millis	18	14	4	Southampton	7	7	0
Millville	6	4	2	Southborough	20	15	5
Milton	61	52	9	Southbridge	41	38	3
Monson	18	12	6	South Hadley	34	30	4
Montague	19	14	5	Southwick	19	14	5
Monterey	2	2	0	Spencer	20	16	4
Nahant	12	12	0	Springfield	529	464	65
Nantucket	36	33	3	Sterling	11	10	1
Natick	63	50	13	Stockbridge	6	6	0
Needham	57	49	8	Stoneham	49	37	12
New Bedford	320	268	52	Stoughton	62	55	7
Newbury	14	9	5	Stow	16	11	5
Newburyport	41	34	7	Sturbridge	23	18	5
Newton	190	159	31	Sudbury	33	27	6
Norfolk	19	17	2	Sunderland	5	5	0
North Adams	35	28	7	Sutton	19	15	4
Northampton	62	57	5	Swampscott	38	36	2
North Andover	62	50	12	Swansea	32	27	5
North Attleboro	59	49	10	Taunton	111	107	4
Northborough	26	20	6	Templeton	10	7	3
Northbridge	25	20	5	Tewksbury	67	51	16
North Brookfield	5	5	0	Tisbury	14	13	1
Northfield	5	4	1	Topsfield	14	10	4
North Reading	31	30	1	Townsend	22	16	6
Norton	29	27	2	Truro	16	11	5

Table 78

Full-time Law Enforcement Employees as of October 31, 2003
by City by State—Continued

City by state	Total law enforcement employees	Total officers	Total civilians	City by state	Total law enforcement employees	Total officers	Total civilians
MASSACHUSETTS—Continued				**MICHIGAN—Continued**			
Tyngsboro	31	25	6	Belleville	13	11	2
Upton	16	12	4	Bellevue	3	3	0
Uxbridge	18	15	3	Benton Harbor	31	24	7
Wakefield	45	44	1	Benton Township	34	25	9
Walpole	43	38	5	Berkley	34	28	6
Waltham	161	150	11	Berrien Springs-Oronoko Township	8	7	1
Ware	17	17	0	Beverly Hills	30	25	5
Wareham	55	45	10	Big Rapids	20	19	1
Warren	11	6	5	Birch Run	7	6	1
Watertown	82	70	12	Birmingham	53	35	18
Wayland	24	23	1	Blackman Township	31	29	2
Webster	31	28	3	Blissfield	7	6	1
Wellesley	50	44	6	Bloomfield Hills	29	25	4
Wellfleet	18	13	5	Bloomfield Township	97	73	24
Wenham	11	10	1	Bloomingdale	1	1	0
Westborough	35	28	7	Boyne City	8	7	1
West Boylston	18	13	5	Breckenridge	3	3	0
West Bridgewater	21	20	1	Bridgeport Township	10	9	1
West Brookfield	5	5	0	Bridgman	4	4	0
Westfield	81	73	8	Brighton	18	16	2
Westford	50	40	10	Bronson	5	5	0
Westminster	16	11	5	Brooklyn/Columbia	4	3	1
West Newbury	14	7	7	Brown City	1	1	0
Weston	30	25	5	Brownstown Township	53	39	14
Westport	34	29	5	Buchanan	10	9	1
West Springfield	90	81	9	Buena Vista Township	14	13	1
Westwood	34	27	7	Burr Oak	1	1	0
Weymouth	117	98	19	Burton	48	42	6
Whitman	26	25	1	Cadillac	18	15	3
Wilbraham	27	26	1	Calumet	2	2	0
Williamsburg	1	1	0	Cambridge Township	4	3	1
Williamstown	16	12	4	Canton Township	105	77	28
Wilmington	48	46	2	Capac	5	4	1
Winchendon	19	13	6	Carleton	4	3	1
Winchester	46	38	8	Caro	9	8	1
Winthrop	37	35	2	Carrollton Township	8	7	1
Woburn	80	73	7	Carson City	2	2	0
Worcester	483	436	47	Carsonville	2	1	1
Wrentham	21	19	2	Caseville	3	3	0
Yarmouth	64	54	10	Caspian	1	1	0
				Cass City	4	4	0
MICHIGAN				Cassopolis	5	5	0
				Cedar Springs	7	7	0
Adrian	36	33	3	Center Line	34	29	5
Akron-Fairgrove	1	1	0	Central Lake	1	1	0
Albion	33	27	6	Charlevoix	7	7	0
Algonac	9	8	1	Charlotte	20	19	1
Allegan	13	12	1	Cheboygan	11	10	1
Allen Park	59	53	6	Chelsea	12	8	4
Alma	14	13	1	Chesterfield Township	61	46	15
Almont	9	9	0	Chikaming Township	3	3	0
Alpena	19	17	2	Chocolay Township	5	4	1
Ann Arbor	229	165	64	Clare	9	8	1
Argentine Township	5	5	0	Clarkston	10	10	0
Armada	3	3	0	Clawson	21	18	3
Auburn	3	2	1	Clay Township	20	15	5
Auburn Hills	69	54	15	Clinton	4	4	0
Augusta	5	4	1	Clinton Township	148	112	36
Bad Axe	9	9	0	Clio	8	8	0
Bancroft	1	1	0	Coldwater	20	18	2
Bangor	6	6	0	Coleman	2	2	0
Baraga	3	3	0	Coloma Township	7	6	1
Barry Township	2	2	0	Colon	3	3	0
Bath Township	11	10	1	Concord	3	3	0
Battle Creek	141	117	24	Constantine	6	5	1
Bay City	78	70	8	Corunna	5	5	0
Belding	11	9	2	Covert Township	6	6	0
Bellaire	3	3	0	Croswell	8	7	1

Table 78

Full-time Law Enforcement Employees as of October 31, 2003
by City by State—Continued

City by state	Total law enforcement employees	Total officers	Total civilians	City by state	Total law enforcement employees	Total officers	Total civilians
MICHIGAN—Continued				**MICHIGAN—Continued**			
Crystal Falls	5	5	0	Grosse Ile Township	24	17	7
Davison	12	11	1	Grosse Pointe	27	25	2
Davison Township	20	18	2	Grosse Pointe Farms	45	35	10
Dearborn	219	193	26	Grosse Pointe Park	52	43	9
Dearborn Heights	112	90	22	Grosse Pointe Shores	23	20	3
Decatur	4	4	0	Grosse Pointe Woods	53	40	13
Deckerville	1	1	0	Hamburg Township	14	13	1
Denmark Township	1	1	0	Hampton Township	11	10	1
Denton Township	4	4	0	Hamtramck	42	42	0
Detroit	4,387	3,837	550	Hancock	7	7	0
Dewitt	6	5	1	Harbor Beach	4	4	0
Dewitt Township	16	15	1	Harbor Springs	6	5	1
Douglas	9	8	1	Harper Woods	39	34	5
Dowagiac	15	14	1	Hart	4	4	0
Dryden Township	3	3	0	Hartford	7	7	0
Durand	6	6	0	Hastings	17	15	2
East Grand Rapids	34	31	3	Hazel Park	44	37	7
East Jordan	6	5	1	Hesperia	2	2	0
East Lansing	124	64	60	Highland Park	29	20	9
Eastpointe	57	52	5	Hillsdale	18	16	2
East Tawas	7	6	1	Holland	74	62	12
Eaton Rapids	10	9	1	Holly	17	12	5
Ecorse	30	27	3	Homer	2	2	0
Edmore-Home	1	1	0	Hopkins	3	3	0
Elk Rapids	4	4	0	Houghton	8	8	0
Elkton	2	2	0	Howard City	3	3	0
Elsie	2	2	0	Howell	22	20	2
Emmett Township	17	15	2	Hudson	3	3	0
Erie Township	6	5	1	Hudsonville	9	8	1
Escanaba	48	35	13	Huntington Woods	18	17	1
Essexville	8	8	0	Huron Township	30	24	6
Evart	4	3	1	Imlay City	9	8	1
Farmington	28	22	6	Inkster	73	60	13
Farmington Hills	165	114	51	Ionia	19	17	2
Fenton	21	15	6	Iron Mountain	14	14	0
Ferndale	56	47	9	Iron River	8	7	1
Flat Rock	30	25	5	Ironwood	15	13	2
Flint	282	247	35	Ishpeming	14	13	1
Flint Township	51	43	8	Ishpeming Township	1	1	0
Flushing	14	13	1	Ithaca	4	4	0
Flushing Township	11	10	1	Jackson	94	69	25
Forsyth Township	7	6	1	Jonesville	5	5	0
Fowlerville	7	6	1	Kalamazoo	297	241	56
Frankenmuth	8	8	0	Kalamazoo Township	40	32	8
Frankfort	3	3	0	Kalkaska	6	5	1
Franklin	10	10	0	Keego Harbor	7	6	1
Fraser	60	46	14	Kentwood	86	70	16
Fremont	9	8	1	Kingsford	19	19	0
Frost Township	2	1	1	Kingston	1	1	0
Galesburg	3	2	1	Kinross Township	3	3	0
Garden City	51	40	11	Laingsburg	2	2	0
Gaylord	14	12	2	Lake Angelus	2	2	0
Genesee Township	30	26	4	Lake Linden	3	3	0
Gerrish Township	7	7	0	Lake Odessa	4	4	0
Gibraltar	12	11	1	Lake Orion	8	4	4
Gladstone	13	12	1	Lakeview	3	3	0
Gladwin	6	6	0	L'anse	5	5	0
Grand Beach	4	4	0	Lansing	353	251	102
Grand Blanc	23	19	4	Lansing Township	17	16	1
Grand Blanc Township	51	45	6	Lapeer	22	19	3
Grand Haven	37	32	5	Lathrup Village	10	9	1
Grand Ledge	15	14	1	Laurium	4	4	0
Grand Rapids	446	355	91	Lawton	6	6	0
Grandville	34	28	6	Lennon	1	1	0
Grant	1	1	0	Leoni Township	6	5	1
Grayling	6	6	0	Leslie	3	3	0
Green Oak Township	14	13	1	Lexington	3	3	0
Greenville	23	17	6	Lincoln Park	66	56	10

Table 78

Full-time Law Enforcement Employees as of October 31, 2003

by City by State—Continued

City by state	Total law enforcement employees	Total officers	Total civilians	City by state	Total law enforcement employees	Total officers	Total civilians
MICHIGAN—Continued				**MICHIGAN—Continued**			
Lincoln Township	13	11	2	Novi	96	63	33
Linden	5	5	0	Oak Park	76	65	11
Litchfield	5	5	0	Olivet	3	3	0
Livonia	188	164	24	Onaway	1	1	0
Lowell	9	7	2	Ontwa Township-Edwardsburg	9	7	2
Ludington	17	15	2	Orchard Lake	9	8	1
Luna Pier	4	4	0	Oscoda Township	13	12	1
Mackinac Island	11	10	1	Otisville	1	1	0
Mackinaw City	7	7	0	Otsego	8	7	1
Madison Heights	77	61	16	Ovid	3	3	0
Madison Township	2	2	0	Owosso	24	22	2
Mancelona	3	3	0	Oxford	7	4	3
Manistee	15	13	2	Parchment	3	3	0
Manistique	10	9	1	Parma-Sandstone	2	2	0
Manton	1	1	0	Paw Paw	10	8	2
Marenisco Township	2	2	0	Pentwater	3	3	0
Marine City	8	7	1	Perry	7	7	0
Marion	1	1	0	Petoskey	19	17	2
Marlette	5	5	0	Pigeon	2	2	0
Marquette	42	36	6	Pinckney	4	4	0
Marshall	19	14	5	Pinconning	3	3	0
Marysville	19	16	3	Pittsfield Township	48	36	12
Mason	14	13	1	Plainwell	10	9	1
Mattawan	6	6	0	Pleasant Ridge	7	7	0
Mayville	2	2	0	Plymouth	17	16	1
Melvindale	30	27	3	Plymouth Township	46	30	16
Memphis	3	3	0	Pontiac	219	170	49
Mendon	2	2	0	Portage	82	58	24
Menominee	19	17	2	Port Austin	1	1	0
Meridian Township	49	43	6	Port Huron	72	51	21
Metamora Township	6	6	0	Portland	6	5	1
Michiana	3	3	0	Port Sanilac	1	1	0
Midland	52	49	3	Potterville	3	3	0
Milan	16	12	4	Prairieville Township	2	2	0
Milford	23	18	5	Raisin Township	2	2	0
Millington	1	1	0	Reading	2	2	0
Monroe	52	45	7	Redford Township	86	68	18
Montague	5	5	0	Reed City	4	4	0
Montrose Township	13	12	1	Reese	2	2	0
Morenci	5	5	0	Richfield Township (Genesee County)	11	9	2
Morrice	2	2	0	Richfield Township (Roscommon County)	5	5	0
Mount Clemens	37	32	5	Richland	2	2	0
Mount Morris	9	8	1	Richland Township	4	4	0
Mount Morris Township	38	34	4	Richmond	12	9	3
Mount Pleasant	41	34	7	River Rouge	30	27	3
Mundy Township	21	18	3	Riverview	33	29	4
Munising	6	6	0	Rochester	28	20	8
Muskegon	89	79	10	Rockford	13	10	3
Muskegon Heights	29	27	2	Rockwood	14	8	6
Muskegon Township	16	15	1	Rogers City	8	8	0
Napoleon Township	3	3	0	Romeo	12	8	4
Nashville	2	2	0	Romulus	77	61	16
Negaunee	11	10	1	Roosevelt Park	11	10	1
Newaygo	5	4	1	Rose City	3	3	0
New Baltimore	17	16	1	Roseville	101	89	12
Newberry	3	3	0	Royal Oak	114	95	19
New Buffalo	7	6	1	Saginaw	122	110	12
New Haven	7	6	1	Saginaw Township	45	41	4
Niles	31	21	10	Saline	19	14	5
Niles Township	11	10	1	Sand Lake	1	1	0
North Branch	4	4	0	Sandusky	6	6	0
Northfield Township	14	12	2	Sault Ste. Marie	32	27	5
North Muskegon	12	11	1	Schoolcraft	3	3	0
Northville	19	16	3	Scottville	3	3	0
Northville Township	40	29	11	Sebewaing	3	3	0
Norton Shores	31	29	2	Shelby	3	3	0
Norvell Township	2	2	0	Shelby Township	83	63	20
Norway	6	6	0	Shepherd	1	1	0

Table 78

Full-time Law Enforcement Employees as of October 31, 2003
by City by State—Continued

City by state	Total law enforcement employees	Total officers	Total civilians	City by state	Total law enforcement employees	Total officers	Total civilians
MICHIGAN—Continued				**MICHIGAN—Continued**			
Somerset Township	2	2	0	Wyoming	136	101	35
Southfield	177	157	20	Yale	5	5	0
Southgate	49	39	10	Ypsilanti	52	40	12
South Haven	26	19	7	Zeeland	10	9	1
South Lyon	19	17	2	Zilwaukee	2	2	0
South Rockwood	3	3	0				
Sparta	8	7	1	**MINNESOTA**			
Spaulding Township	1	1	0				
Spring Arbor Township	2	2	0	Albany	4	4	0
Springfield	17	16	1	Albert Lea	40	30	10
Spring Lake-Ferrysburg	10	9	1	Alexandria	20	16	4
Springport Township	2	2	0	Annandale	5	5	0
Stanton	1	1	0	Anoka	35	28	7
St. Charles	3	3	0	Appleton	4	4	0
St. Clair	12	10	2	Apple Valley	67	47	20
St. Clair Shores	101	85	16	Austin	33	30	3
Sterling Heights	222	167	55	Avon	2	2	0
St. Ignace	6	6	0	Babbitt	4	4	0
St. Johns	13	11	2	Baxter	12	11	1
St. Joseph	25	18	7	Bayport	9	9	0
St. Joseph Township	13	12	1	Becker	6	5	1
St. Louis	6	5	1	Belle Plaine	7	6	1
Sturgis	24	17	7	Bemidji	29	26	3
Summit Township	6	6	0	Benson	8	7	1
Sumpter Township	16	13	3	Big Lake	12	10	2
Suttons Bay	1	1	0	Biwabik	7	7	0
Swartz Creek	9	8	1	Blaine	61	47	14
Sylvan Lake	5	5	0	Blooming Prairie	3	3	0
Taylor	130	99	31	Bloomington	141	109	32
Tecumseh	17	15	2	Blue Earth	6	6	0
Thomas Township	9	8	1	Brainerd	30	24	6
Three Oaks	3	3	0	Breckenridge	10	7	3
Three Rivers	20	16	4	Brooklyn Center	55	42	13
Tittabawassee Township	4	4	0	Brooklyn Park	105	81	24
Traverse City	36	33	3	Browns Valley	2	2	0
Trenton	43	41	2	Brownton	2	2	0
Troy	193	135	58	Buffalo	18	15	3
Tuscarora Township	8	7	1	Burnsville	86	70	16
Ubly	2	2	0	Caledonia	5	4	1
Unadilla Township	2	2	0	Cambridge	10	10	0
Union City	4	4	0	Cannon Falls	7	6	1
Utica	21	16	5	Centennial Lakes	19	15	4
Van Buren Township	45	33	12	Champlin	26	22	4
Vassar	7	7	0	Chaska	27	21	6
Vernon	2	2	0	Chisago City	6	5	1
Vicksburg	4	4	0	Chisholm	12	11	1
Walker	47	38	9	Cloquet	21	19	2
Walled Lake	20	14	6	Cold Spring	7	6	1
Warren	291	247	44	Columbia Heights	29	22	7
Waterford Township	111	85	26	Coon Rapids	71	61	10
Waterloo Township	2	2	0	Corcoran	4	4	0
Watertown Township	1	1	0	Cottage Grove	48	36	12
Watervliet	3	3	0	Crookston	16	14	2
Wayland	6	5	1	Crosby	8	6	2
Wayne	55	43	12	Crystal	34	25	9
West Bloomfield Township	101	75	26	Dawson	3	3	0
West Branch	7	6	1	Dayton	5	5	0
Westland	120	94	26	Deephaven-Woodland	9	7	2
White Cloud	3	2	1	Detroit Lakes	15	13	2
Whitehall	9	8	1	Dilworth	6	5	1
White Lake Township	35	25	10	Duluth	171	143	28
White Pigeon	4	4	0	Eagan	87	67	20
Williamston	5	5	0	Eagle Lake	3	3	0
Wixom	27	23	4	East Grand Forks	22	20	2
Wolverine Lake	9	8	1	Eden Prairie	86	62	24
Woodhaven	38	33	5	Edina	65	49	16
Woodstock Township	1	1	0	Elk River	34	27	7
Wyandotte	58	43	15	Elmore	1	1	0

Table 78

Full-time Law Enforcement Employees as of October 31, 2003
by City by State—Continued

City by state	Total law enforcement employees	Total officers	Total civilians	City by state	Total law enforcement employees	Total officers	Total civilians
MINNESOTA—Continued				**MINNESOTA—Continued**			
Ely	12	7	5	North Branch	12	10	2
Eveleth	11	10	1	Northfield	25	19	6
Fairmont	20	17	3	North Mankato	13	12	1
Faribault	36	28	8	North St. Paul	18	16	2
Farmington	18	16	2	Oakdale	36	28	8
Fergus Falls	24	20	4	Oak Park Heights	10	9	1
Floodwood	3	3	0	Olivia	5	5	0
Forest Lake	21	19	2	Orono	20	18	2
Fridley	43	37	6	Ortonville	5	4	1
Gilbert	6	6	0	Osseo	6	5	1
Glencoe	12	11	1	Owatonna	28	26	2
Glenwood	4	4	0	Park Rapids	8	7	1
Golden Valley	39	30	9	Paynesville	4	4	0
Goodview	4	4	0	Plainview	5	5	0
Grand Rapids	18	14	4	Plymouth	74	59	15
Granite Falls	5	4	1	Princeton	10	9	1
Hallock	1	1	0	Prior Lake	25	21	4
Hastings	28	25	3	Proctor	8	7	1
Hermantown	12	10	2	Ramsey	21	17	4
Hibbing	33	29	4	Red Wing	30	24	6
Hopkins	38	25	13	Redwood Falls	10	9	1
Hoyt Lakes	9	9	0	Richfield	56	43	13
Hutchinson	35	23	12	Richmond	2	2	0
International Falls	13	12	1	Robbinsdale	25	20	5
Inver Grove Heights	36	29	7	Rochester	163	120	43
Jackson	7	6	1	Roseau	6	5	1
Janesville	6	5	1	Rosemount	21	18	3
Jordan	10	8	2	Roseville	53	46	7
Kasson	8	8	0	Sartell	14	12	2
Kimball	2	2	0	Sauk Centre	6	5	1
La Crescent	8	7	1	Sauk Rapids	13	12	1
Lake City	10	9	1	Savage	32	26	6
Lake Crystal	2	2	0	Shakopee	38	33	5
Lakefield	3	3	0	Silver Lake	2	2	0
Lakeville	63	46	17	Sleepy Eye	6	6	0
Lester Prairie	3	3	0	South Lake Minnetonka	16	14	2
Le Sueur	7	7	0	South St. Paul	27	25	2
Lindstrom	7	6	1	Springfield	5	5	0
Lino Lakes	25	22	3	Spring Lake Park	13	11	2
Litchfield	10	9	1	St. Anthony	22	20	2
Little Falls	13	11	2	Staples	5	5	0
Long Prairie	6	6	0	St. Cloud	106	86	20
Madison	8	8	0	Stewart	2	2	0
Mankato	55	45	10	St. Francis	10	9	1
Maple Grove	66	56	10	Stillwater	23	20	3
Maplewood	65	47	18	St. James	8	7	1
Marshall	23	21	2	St. Joseph	6	6	0
Medina	9	7	2	St. Louis Park	65	49	16
Melrose	6	5	1	St. Paul	758	552	206
Mendota Heights	17	15	2	St. Paul Park	8	8	0
Milaca	4	4	0	St. Peter	19	14	5
Minneapolis	1,035	800	235	Thief River Falls	17	16	1
Minnetonka	74	55	19	Tracy	4	4	0
Minnetrista	12	10	2	Two Harbors	8	7	1
Montevideo	10	9	1	Virginia	21	20	1
Montgomery	6	5	1	Wabasha	7	6	1
Moorhead	57	45	12	Wadena	7	6	1
Moose Lake	4	4	0	Waite Park	15	12	3
Mora	9	8	1	Warroad	6	5	1
Morris	9	8	1	Waseca	15	13	2
Mound	15	12	3	Wayzata	8	8	0
Mounds View	19	17	2	Wells	4	4	0
Mountain Lake	4	4	0	West Hennepin	10	8	2
New Brighton	30	27	3	West St. Paul	33	24	9
New Hope	33	27	6	Wheaton	4	3	1
Newport	8	8	0	White Bear Lake	34	27	7
New Prague	11	9	2	Willmar	36	32	4
New Ulm	22	19	3	Windom	9	8	1

Table 78

Full-time Law Enforcement Employees as of October 31, 2003

by City by State—Continued

City by state	Total law enforcement employees	Total officers	Total civilians	City by state	Total law enforcement employees	Total officers	Total civilians
MINNESOTA—Continued				**MISSISSIPPI—Continued**			
Winnebago	2	2	0	Mound Bayou	4	2	2
Winona	43	38	5	Natchez	79	53	26
Woodbury	55	49	6	New Albany	21	19	2
Worthington	30	22	8	Newton	15	10	5
Wyoming	5	5	0	Ocean Springs	47	34	13
Zumbrota	6	6	0	Okolona	6	6	0
				Olive Branch	67	52	15
MISSISSIPPI				Oxford	59	50	9
				Pascagoula	90	59	31
Aberdeen	20	16	4	Pass Christian	25	19	6
Ackerman	5	5	0	Pearl	64	51	13
Amory	23	17	6	Pelahatchie	7	5	2
Baldwyn	12	11	1	Petal	28	21	7
Batesville	45	35	10	Picayune	56	36	20
Bay St. Louis	35	26	9	Pickens	2	2	0
Belzoni	16	10	6	Poplarville	11	10	1
Booneville	35	27	8	Port Gibson	13	10	3
Brandon	39	27	12	Purvis	10	7	3
Brookhaven	40	33	7	Quitman	11	11	0
Bruce	5	5	0	Raymond	6	6	0
Byhalia	13	9	4	Richland	38	27	11
Carthage	17	13	4	Ridgeland	78	51	27
Clarksdale	45	40	5	Ripley	12	11	1
Cleveland	49	40	9	Rolling Fork	7	7	0
Collins	14	10	4	Ruleville	12	8	4
Columbia	38	27	11	Sandersville	3	3	0
Como	5	4	1	Senatobia	19	15	4
Corinth	46	37	9	Shelby	10	6	4
Decatur	6	5	1	Southaven	91	75	16
De Kalb	6	5	1	Starkville	51	44	7
Drew	7	4	3	Summit	8	7	1
Durant	5	5	0	Sunflower	3	3	0
Edwards	3	3	0	Tchula	4	4	0
Eupora	9	7	2	Tupelo	120	106	14
Florence	16	11	5	Tylertown	4	3	1
Flowood	45	35	10	Utica	7	7	0
Fulton	10	10	0	Vaiden	2	2	0
Gloster	6	4	2	Verona	6	6	0
Greenville	125	87	38	Vicksburg	98	73	25
Greenwood	75	55	20	Water Valley	10	9	1
Grenada	47	42	5	Waveland	28	23	5
Gulfport	260	194	66	Waynesboro	21	15	6
Heidelberg	6	5	1	West Point	34	25	9
Hollandale	12	8	4	Wiggins	13	10	3
Holly Springs	22	17	5	Winona	15	13	2
Horn Lake	66	54	12	Yazoo City	39	25	14
Houston	9	9	0				
Indianola	26	19	7	**MISSOURI**			
Inverness	4	4	0				
Iuka	13	10	3	Adrian	2	2	0
Jackson	693	455	238	Advance	3	3	0
Laurel	78	52	26	Alton	2	2	0
Leakesville	3	2	1	Anderson	4	4	0
Leland	21	16	5	Appleton City	3	3	0
Lexington	11	10	1	Arbyrd	1	1	0
Long Beach	45	30	15	Archie	2	2	0
Lucedale	17	11	6	Arnold	57	45	12
Macon	11	10	1	Ash Grove	3	3	0
Madison	52	39	13	Ashland	5	5	0
Magee	16	16	0	Aurora	20	14	6
Magnolia	6	6	0	Auxvasse	1	1	0
Marks	5	4	1	Ava	10	8	2
McComb	51	31	20	Ballwin	65	50	15
McLain	2	1	1	Bates City	2	2	0
Mendenhall	10	7	3	Battlefield	4	4	0
Meridian	105	90	15	Belle	4	3	1
Moorhead	6	6	0	Bellefontaine Neighbors	26	25	1
Morton	14	10	4	Bel-Nor	10	9	1

Table 78

Full-time Law Enforcement Employees as of October 31, 2003

by City by State—Continued

City by state	Total law enforcement employees	Total officers	Total civilians	City by state	Total law enforcement employees	Total officers	Total civilians
MISSOURI—Continued				**MISSOURI—Continued**			
Bel-Ridge	16	15	1	Creve Coeur	61	50	11
Belton	59	39	20	Crocker	3	3	0
Berkeley	57	46	11	Crystal City	21	16	5
Bernie	9	5	4	Cuba	14	12	2
Bethany	6	6	0	Dellwood	19	17	2
Beverly Hills	4	4	0	Desloge	10	10	0
Billings	4	4	0	De Soto	20	15	5
Birch Tree	2	1	1	Des Peres	48	41	7
Bismarck	2	2	0	Dexter	24	18	6
Bloomfield	2	2	0	Diamond	2	2	0
Blue Springs	101	71	30	Dixon	7	4	3
Bolivar	21	16	5	Doniphan	13	10	3
Bonne Terre	10	10	0	Drexel	2	2	0
Boonville	28	21	7	Duenweg	4	4	0
Bourbon	6	6	0	Duquesne	9	6	3
Bowling Green	9	6	3	East Lynne	1	1	0
Branson	53	38	15	East Prairie	10	7	3
Branson West	7	6	1	Edina	4	3	1
Braymer	1	1	0	Edmundson	10	9	1
Breckenridge Hills	15	14	1	Eldon	15	9	6
Brentwood	34	25	9	El Dorado Springs	11	7	4
Bridgeton	68	56	12	Ellington	2	2	0
Brookfield	16	10	6	Ellisville	20	19	1
Bucklin	1	1	0	Elsberry	4	4	0
Buckner	1	1	0	Eureka	27	23	4
Buffalo	9	8	1	Excelsior Springs	29	20	9
Bunker	1	1	0	Exeter	1	1	0
Butler	17	10	7	Fair Grove	3	3	0
Byrnes Mill	5	5	0	Fair Play	1	1	0
Cabool	11	6	5	Farber	2	2	0
California	6	5	1	Farmington	34	26	8
Calverton Park	8	6	2	Fayette	9	9	0
Camdenton	14	11	3	Ferguson	62	52	10
Cameron	20	15	5	Festus	38	27	11
Campbell	8	4	4	Florissant	103	81	22
Canalou	1	1	0	Foley	1	1	0
Canton	5	4	1	Fordland	1	1	0
Cape Girardeau	97	70	27	Foristell	5	5	0
Cardwell	2	2	0	Forsyth	7	6	1
Carl Junction	14	10	4	Fredericktown	8	8	0
Carrollton	8	7	1	Freeman	1	1	0
Carterville	6	6	0	Frontenac	27	21	6
Carthage	35	27	8	Fulton	32	25	7
Caruthersville	21	20	1	Gainesville	2	2	0
Cassville	8	8	0	Galena	1	1	0
Center	2	2	0	Gallatin	3	3	0
Centralia	12	7	5	Garden City	3	3	0
Chaffee	9	5	4	Gerald	5	5	0
Charlack	8	8	0	Gideon	3	3	0
Charleston	21	15	6	Gladstone	54	42	12
Chesterfield	91	79	12	Glasgow	3	3	0
Chillicothe	23	17	6	Glendale	14	11	3
Clarence	1	1	0	Golden City	3	2	1
Clarkton	3	3	0	Goodman	1	1	0
Claycomo	16	11	5	Gower	4	4	0
Clayton	71	53	18	Grain Valley	17	15	2
Clever	2	2	0	Granby	6	5	1
Clinton	21	20	1	Grandin	1	1	0
Cole Camp	3	3	0	Grandview	62	49	13
Columbia	175	141	34	Greenwood	6	6	0
Concordia	6	6	0	Hallsville	2	2	0
Cool Valley	11	10	1	Hamilton	3	3	0
Cooter	1	1	0	Hannibal	44	32	12
Corder	2	1	1	Hardin	2	1	1
Cottleville	8	8	0	Harrisonville	29	21	8
Country Club Hills	9	9	0	Hartville	1	1	0
Crane	5	4	1	Hayti	9	8	1
Crestwood	45	35	10	Hayti Heights	4	4	0

Table 78

Full-time Law Enforcement Employees as of October 31, 2003
by City by State—Continued

City by state	Total law enforcement employees	Total officers	Total civilians	City by state	Total law enforcement employees	Total officers	Total civilians
MISSOURI—Continued				**MISSOURI—Continued**			
Hazelwood	75	58	17	Linn	3	3	0
Henrietta	1	1	0	Linn Creek	3	3	0
Herculaneum	11	10	1	Lockwood	2	2	0
Hermann	10	5	5	Lone Jack	2	2	0
Higbee	1	1	0	Louisiana	17	9	8
Higginsville	14	9	5	Lowry City	2	2	0
Highlandville	2	2	0	Macon	13	11	2
Hillsboro	6	6	0	Malden	14	12	2
Hillsdale	15	14	1	Manchester	41	38	3
Holcomb	2	2	0	Mansfield	5	5	0
Holden	8	7	1	Maplewood	24	22	2
Hollister	16	10	6	Marble Hill	5	5	0
Holt	2	2	0	Marceline	9	6	3
Holts Summit	10	9	1	Marionville	2	2	0
Hornersville	2	2	0	Marquand	1	1	0
Houston	5	5	0	Marshall	34	23	11
Houston Lake	5	5	0	Marshfield	8	8	0
Humansville	2	2	0	Marston	2	2	0
Huntsville	2	2	0	Marthasville	1	1	0
Iberia	2	2	0	Maryland Heights	94	78	16
Independence	293	206	87	Maryville	23	19	4
Irondale	1	1	0	Matthews	1	1	0
Ironton	5	5	0	Maysville	1	1	0
Jackson	29	23	6	Memphis	5	4	1
JASCO Metropolitian	6	4	2	Merriam Woods	1	1	0
Jasper	2	2	0	Mexico	36	33	3
Jefferson City	113	85	28	Milan	5	5	0
Jennings	51	46	5	Miner	9	5	4
Jonesburg	1	1	0	Moberly	47	35	12
Joplin	89	79	10	Moline Acres	10	9	1
Kahoka	3	3	0	Monett	30	21	9
Kansas City	1,947	1,263	684	Monroe City	7	6	1
Kearney	12	11	1	Montgomery City	6	6	0
Kennett	30	23	7	Montrose	1	1	0
Kimberling City	9	6	3	Morehouse	1	1	0
Kimmswick	1	1	0	Mosby	1	1	0
Kingsville	1	1	0	Moscow Mills	6	5	1
Kirksville	28	26	2	Mound City	2	2	0
Kirkwood	67	56	11	Mountain Grove	16	10	6
Knob Noster	11	6	5	Mountain View	7	7	0
La Belle	1	1	0	Mount Vernon	10	10	0
Ladue	31	24	7	Napoleon	3	3	0
La Grange	10	8	2	Neosho	28	26	2
Lake Lotawana	8	7	1	Nevada	31	22	9
Lake Ozark	15	10	5	New Florence	3	3	0
Lakeshire	4	4	0	New Franklin	3	2	1
Lake St. Louis	31	23	8	New Haven	7	7	0
Lake Tapawingo	1	1	0	New London	2	2	0
Lake Waukomis	3	1	2	New Madrid	8	7	1
Lake Winnebago	4	4	0	New Melle	2	2	0
Lamar	12	11	1	Nixa	26	19	7
La Monte	2	2	0	Noel	5	5	0
Lanagan	1	1	0	Norborne	1	1	0
La Plata	3	3	0	Normandy	23	22	1
Lathrop	5	5	0	North Kansas City	61	46	15
Laurie	6	6	0	Northmoor	2	2	0
Lawson	7	6	1	Northwoods	16	14	2
Leadington	6	5	1	Norwood	1	1	0
Leadwood	4	4	0	Oak Grove	12	11	1
Lebanon	35	26	9	Oakview Village	4	4	0
Lee's Summit	149	103	46	Odessa	10	10	0
Leeton	1	1	0	O'Fallon	123	95	28
Lexington	8	7	1	Olivette	37	22	15
Liberal	2	2	0	Olympian Village	1	1	0
Liberty	52	37	15	Oran	1	1	0
Licking	5	5	0	Osage Beach	35	22	13
Lilbourn	2	2	0	Otterville	1	1	0
Lincoln	3	3	0	Overland	56	45	11

Table 78

Full-time Law Enforcement Employees as of October 31, 2003

by City by State—Continued

City by state	Total law enforcement employees	Total officers	Total civilians	City by state	Total law enforcement employees	Total officers	Total civilians
MISSOURI—Continued				**MISSOURI—Continued**			
Owensville	8	7	1	St. Clair	16	13	3
Ozark	25	22	3	Steele	4	4	0
Pacific	25	18	7	Steelville	6	6	0
Pagedale	15	14	1	Ste. Genevieve	10	9	1
Palmyra	10	6	4	St. George	4	4	0
Park Hills	16	14	2	St. James	8	8	0
Parkville	12	11	1	St. John	26	24	2
Parma	2	2	0	St. Joseph	157	114	43
Peculiar	9	8	1	St. Louis	2,047	1,489	558
Perry	1	1	0	St. Marys	1	1	0
Perryville	25	24	1	Stover	3	3	0
Pevely	20	14	6	St. Peters	101	82	19
Piedmont	4	4	0	Strafford	5	5	0
Pierce City	3	3	0	St. Robert	22	16	6
Pilot Grove	1	1	0	Sturgeon	2	2	0
Pilot Knob	1	1	0	Sugar Creek	21	15	6
Pine Lawn	27	21	6	Sullivan	24	16	8
Pineville	4	4	0	Summersville	1	1	0
Platte City	9	9	0	Sunrise Beach	2	2	0
Platte Woods	2	2	0	Sunset Hills	30	23	7
Plattsburg	5	5	0	Sweet Springs	3	3	0
Pleasant Hill	16	11	5	Tarkio	3	3	0
Pleasant Hope	2	2	0	Thayer	9	6	3
Pleasant Valley	12	8	4	Theodosia	1	1	0
Polo	1	1	0	Tipton	3	3	0
Poplar Bluff	53	43	10	Town and Country	38	33	5
Portageville	14	10	4	Trenton	17	11	6
Potosi	13	9	4	Troy	15	14	1
Puxico	2	2	0	Truesdale	1	1	0
Randolph	3	3	0	Union	19	17	2
Raymore	32	22	10	Unionville	2	2	0
Raytown	73	54	19	University City	101	79	22
Reeds Spring	4	4	0	Van Buren	2	2	0
Republic	26	16	10	Vandalia	9	5	4
Rich Hill	7	3	4	Velda City	12	8	4
Richland	6	5	1	Verona	1	1	0
Richmond	19	12	7	Versailles	11	11	0
Richmond Heights	49	41	8	Viburnum	1	1	0
Risco	1	1	0	Vinita Park	13	12	1
Riverside	25	21	4	Walnut Grove	2	2	0
Riverview	11	10	1	Wardell	2	1	1
Rockaway Beach	2	2	0	Warrensburg	33	30	3
Rock Hill	12	11	1	Warrenton	17	15	2
Rock Port	3	3	0	Warsaw	7	7	0
Rogersville	6	6	0	Warson Woods	8	7	1
Rolla	47	28	19	Washburn	1	1	0
Salem	18	13	5	Washington	30	26	4
Salisbury	8	4	4	Waynesville	9	8	1
Sarcoxie	3	3	0	Weatherby Lake	4	4	0
Savannah	5	5	0	Webb City	27	21	6
Scott City	13	9	4	Webster Groves	50	41	9
Sedalia	55	45	10	Wellington	1	1	0
Seligman	2	2	0	Wellston	13	12	1
Senath	3	3	0	Wellsville	4	4	0
Seneca	7	7	0	Wentzville	59	42	17
Seymour	5	5	0	Weston	4	4	0
Shelbina	5	5	0	West Plains	27	22	5
Shrewsbury	21	18	3	Wheaton	1	1	0
Sikeston	66	57	9	Willard	10	9	1
Silex	1	1	0	Willow Springs	6	5	1
Slater	6	3	3	Windsor	6	6	0
Smithville	12	11	1	Winfield	2	2	0
Southwest City	4	4	0	Winona	2	2	0
Sparta	2	2	0	Wood Heights	2	2	0
Springfield	408	332	76	Woodson Terrace	19	17	2
Stanberry	1	1	0	Wright City	7	6	1
St. Ann	45	37	8				
St. Charles	146	110	36				

Table 78

Full-time Law Enforcement Employees as of October 31, 2003
by City by State—Continued

City by state	Total law enforcement employees	Total officers	Total civilians	City by state	Total law enforcement employees	Total officers	Total civilians
MONTANA				**NEBRASKA—Continued**			
Baker	3	3	0	Geneva	4	4	0
Belgrade	11	9	2	Gering	18	15	3
Billings	159	129	30	Gordon	6	5	1
Boulder	2	2	0	Gothenburg	10	6	4
Bozeman	49	40	9	Grand Island	83	75	8
Bridger	2	2	0	Hastings	50	35	15
Chinook	4	4	0	Holdrege	16	10	6
Columbia Falls	9	9	0	Imperial	4	4	0
Conrad	5	5	0	Kearney	63	51	12
Cut Bank	8	7	1	Kimball	6	5	1
Dillon	8	7	1	La Vista	30	26	4
East Helena	4	4	0	Lexington	16	14	2
Eureka	3	3	0	Lincoln	407	308	99
Fort Benton	3	3	0	Lyons	2	2	0
Glasgow	12	7	5	Madison	4	4	0
Glendive	12	9	3	McCook	20	16	4
Great Falls	117	80	37	Milford	5	5	0
Hamilton	15	14	1	Minden	6	5	1
Havre	25	19	6	Mitchell	5	5	0
Helena	69	48	21	Nebraska City	13	12	1
Hot Springs	2	2	0	Neligh	3	3	0
Joliet	2	2	0	Norfolk	64	42	22
Kalispell	40	31	9	North Platte	67	42	25
Laurel	16	12	4	Ogallala	11	10	1
Lewistown	18	13	5	Omaha	888	719	169
Libby	6	6	0	O'Neill	8	7	1
Livingston	13	13	0	Ord	7	4	3
Manhattan	3	3	0	Papillion	32	28	4
Miles City	20	16	4	Pierce	3	3	0
Missoula	102	84	18	Plainview	5	2	3
Plains	3	3	0	Plattsmouth	19	16	3
Plentywood	5	4	1	Ralston	14	13	1
Polson	12	11	1	Schuyler	9	7	2
Red Lodge	7	7	0	Scottsbluff	36	32	4
Ronan City	4	4	0	Seward	11	10	1
Sidney	10	9	1	Sidney	14	12	2
Stevensville	4	4	0	South Sioux City	28	27	1
St. Ignatius	2	2	0	Superior	4	4	0
Thompson Falls	3	3	0	Syracuse	3	3	0
Three Forks	4	3	1	Tecumseh	4	3	1
Troy	3	3	0	Tekamah	3	3	0
West Yellowstone	11	5	6	Valentine	5	4	1
Whitefish	18	13	5	Valley	5	5	0
Whitehall	2	1	1	Wahoo	6	6	0
Wolf Point	7	6	1	Wayne	14	9	5
				West Point	7	6	1
NEBRASKA				Wilber	4	4	0
				Wymore	3	3	0
Alliance	26	18	8	York	20	14	6
Ashland	4	4	0				
Auburn	5	5	0	**NEVADA**			
Aurora	7	7	0				
Bayard	3	3	0	Boulder City	38	29	9
Beatrice	31	21	10	Carlin	8	6	2
Bellevue	92	81	11	Elko	38	35	3
Blair	15	13	2	Fallon	31	20	11
Bridgeport	3	3	0	Henderson	387	291	96
Broken Bow	5	4	1	Las Vegas Metropolitan Police			
Central City	6	5	1	Department	4,055	1,981	2,074
Chadron	17	11	6	Lovelock	6	5	1
Columbus	46	31	15	Mesquite	36	24	12
Cozad	10	6	4	North Las Vegas	319	213	106
Crete	18	11	7	Reno	441	339	102
David City	7	6	1	Sparks	133	93	40
Elkhorn	15	14	1	West Wendover	21	14	7
Fairbury	9	8	1	Winnemucca	20	16	4
Falls City	13	9	4	Yerington	8	7	1
Fremont	43	36	7				

Table 78

Full-time Law Enforcement Employees as of October 31, 2003

by City by State—Continued

City by state	Total law enforcement employees	Total officers	Total civilians	City by state	Total law enforcement employees	Total officers	Total civilians
NEW HAMPSHIRE				**NEW HAMPSHIRE—Continued**			
Alstead	2	2	0	Lebanon	43	32	11
Alton	14	11	3	Lee	7	6	1
Amherst	18	16	2	Lincoln	11	6	5
Antrim	4	4	0	Lisbon	3	3	0
Ashland	6	6	0	Litchfield	11	9	2
Auburn	9	7	2	Littleton	14	11	3
Barnstead	4	4	0	Londonderry	59	43	16
Barrington	7	6	1	Loudon	7	6	1
Bartlett	5	4	1	Manchester	271	203	68
Bedford	42	29	13	Meredith	17	13	4
Belmont	17	14	3	Merrimack	48	37	11
Bennington	2	2	0	Middleton	2	2	0
Berlin	26	20	6	Milford	28	25	3
Bethlehem	6	5	1	Milton	7	6	1
Boscawen	6	5	1	Mont Vernon	3	3	0
Brentwood	4	4	0	Moultonboro	12	9	3
Bristol	9	7	2	New Boston	4	3	1
Campton	6	5	1	New Castle	3	3	0
Candia	6	5	1	New Durham	5	4	1
Canterbury	2	2	0	Newfields	2	2	0
Carroll	4	4	0	New Hampton	6	6	0
Charlestown	8	5	3	Newington	10	9	1
Chester	3	2	1	Newmarket	21	14	7
Chesterfield	6	5	1	Newport	18	13	5
Claremont	28	23	5	Newton	6	5	1
Colebrook	5	5	0	Northfield	10	9	1
Concord	95	80	15	North Hampton	11	10	1
Conway	30	21	9	Northwood	6	5	1
Danville	1	1	0	Nottingham	7	6	1
Deerfield	8	7	1	Ossipee	8	7	1
Deering	2	2	0	Pelham	24	18	6
Derry	71	57	14	Peterborough	12	10	2
Dover	65	53	12	Pittsfield	8	7	1
Dublin	3	3	0	Plymouth	16	10	6
Enfield	8	7	1	Portsmouth	86	65	21
Epping	12	11	1	Raymond	26	18	8
Epsom	5	4	1	Rindge	9	8	1
Exeter	34	24	10	Rochester	64	50	14
Farmington	13	11	2	Rollinsford	4	4	0
Fitzwilliam	4	3	1	Sanbornton	8	7	1
Franconia	3	3	0	Sandown	6	6	0
Franklin	23	16	7	Sandwich	2	2	0
Freedom	2	2	0	Somersworth	32	25	7
Fremont	3	3	0	Springfield	1	1	0
Gilford	23	17	6	Strafford	3	3	0
Gilmanton	5	4	1	Stratham	10	9	1
Goffstown	40	28	12	Sugar Hill	2	2	0
Gorham	11	8	3	Swanzey	14	11	3
Grantham	4	3	1	Thornton	5	4	1
Greenland	6	6	0	Tilton	15	13	2
Hampstead	6	6	0	Troy	3	3	0
Hampton	43	34	9	Tuftonboro	3	3	0
Hancock	2	2	0	Wakefield	9	8	1
Hanover	34	20	14	Walpole	4	3	1
Henniker	10	8	2	Warner	5	4	1
Hillsborough	17	11	6	Waterville Valley	6	5	1
Hinsdale	8	7	1	Weare	10	9	1
Holderness	4	4	0	Webster	2	2	0
Hooksett	32	21	11	Winchester	7	6	1
Hopkinton	7	6	1	Windham	24	18	6
Hudson	58	43	15	Wolfeboro	18	12	6
Jaffrey	12	11	1				
Keene	56	42	14	**NEW JERSEY**			
Kensington	3	3	0				
Kingston	9	8	1	Aberdeen Township	40	33	7
Laconia	44	34	10	Absecon	33	26	7
Lancaster	7	6	1	Allendale	19	14	5
Langdon	1	1	0	Allenhurst	13	9	4

Table 78

Full-time Law Enforcement Employees as of October 31, 2003
by City by State—Continued

City by state	Total law enforcement employees	Total officers	Total civilians	City by state	Total law enforcement employees	Total officers	Total civilians
NEW JERSEY—Continued				**NEW JERSEY—Continued**			
Allentown	6	6	0	Clark Township	53	41	12
Alpha	6	6	0	Clayton	19	17	2
Alpine	13	13	0	Clementon	15	14	1
Andover Township	16	11	5	Cliffside Park	48	42	6
Asbury Park	90	75	15	Clifton	186	155	31
Atlantic City	515	412	103	Clinton	10	10	0
Atlantic Highlands	20	15	5	Clinton Township	25	22	3
Audubon	20	18	2	Closter	28	22	6
Audubon Park	6	5	1	Collingswood	34	30	4
Avalon	32	20	12	Colts Neck Township	21	20	1
Avon-by-the-Sea	12	12	0	Cranbury Township	18	17	1
Barnegat Township	40	31	9	Cranford Township	69	49	20
Barrington	16	15	1	Cresskill	29	24	5
Bay Head	9	8	1	Deal	20	16	4
Bayonne	271	233	38	Delanco Township	9	8	1
Beach Haven	16	11	5	Delaware Township	8	7	1
Beachwood	20	18	2	Delran Township	34	29	5
Bedminster Township	18	17	1	Demarest	14	14	0
Belleville	117	110	7	Denville Township	40	32	8
Bellmawr	25	23	2	Deptford Township	68	62	6
Belmar	28	21	7	Dover	42	36	6
Belvidere	6	6	0	Dover Township	198	151	47
Bergenfield	52	45	7	Dumont	38	31	7
Berkeley Heights Township	33	26	7	Dunellen	20	16	4
Berkeley Township	92	71	21	Eastampton Township	15	14	1
Berlin	19	18	1	East Brunswick Township	123	93	30
Berlin Township	21	19	2	East Greenwich Township	18	16	2
Bernards Township	45	36	9	East Hanover Township	40	34	6
Bernardsville	24	18	6	East Newark	10	7	3
Beverly	9	8	1	East Orange	332	287	45
Blairstown Township	9	8	1	East Rutherford	40	36	4
Bloomfield	137	119	18	East Windsor Township	62	48	14
Bloomingdale	17	16	1	Eatontown	44	35	9
Bogota	20	15	5	Edgewater	31	30	1
Boonton	31	24	7	Edgewater Park Township	14	13	1
Boonton Township	12	12	0	Edison Township	264	212	52
Bordentown	12	10	2	Egg Harbor City	18	13	5
Bordentown Township	32	24	8	Egg Harbor Township	123	93	30
Bound Brook	27	22	5	Elizabeth	456	339	117
Bradley Beach	19	15	4	Elk Township	10	10	0
Branchburg Township	28	26	2	Elmer	1	1	0
Brick Township	159	125	34	Elmwood Park	37	36	1
Bridgeton	75	60	15	Emerson	21	18	3
Bridgewater Township	96	78	18	Englewood	92	77	15
Brielle	15	14	1	Englewood Cliffs	29	28	1
Brigantine	50	36	14	Englishtown	7	7	0
Brooklawn	7	7	0	Essex Fells	17	13	4
Buena	15	9	6	Evesham Township	80	72	8
Burlington	35	31	4	Ewing Township	95	83	12
Burlington Township	53	44	9	Fairfield Township	46	39	7
Butler	21	17	4	Fair Haven	17	13	4
Byram Township	16	15	1	Fair Lawn	68	57	11
Caldwell	21	20	1	Fairview	33	27	6
Califon	2	2	0	Fanwood	22	21	1
Camden	520	435	85	Far Hills	5	5	0
Cape May	28	22	6	Flemington	15	14	1
Carlstadt	33	31	2	Florence Township	31	25	6
Carney's Point Township	25	20	5	Florham Park	37	31	6
Carteret	64	53	11	Fort Lee	124	104	20
Cedar Grove Township	35	32	3	Franklin	14	13	1
Chatham	28	23	5	Franklin Lakes	27	22	5
Chatham Township	31	23	8	Franklin Township (Gloucester County)	29	26	3
Cherry Hill Township	166	132	34	Franklin Township (Hunterdon County)	6	6	0
Chesilhurst	11	10	1	Franklin Township (Somerset County)	116	99	17
Chester	9	8	1	Freehold	41	32	9
Chesterfield Township	7	7	0	Freehold Township	79	63	16
Chester Township	17	16	1	Frenchtown	2	2	0
Cinnaminson Township	36	31	5	Galloway Township	71	58	13

Table 78

Full-time Law Enforcement Employees as of October 31, 2003
by City by State—Continued

City by state	Total law enforcement employees	Total officers	Total civilians	City by state	Total law enforcement employees	Total officers	Total civilians
NEW JERSEY—Continued				**NEW JERSEY—Continued**			
Garfield	70	58	12	Lawnside	11	10	1
Garwood	19	16	3	Lawrence Township	85	70	15
Gibbsboro	6	6	0	Lebanon Township	10	9	1
Glassboro	55	49	6	Leonia	25	18	7
Glen Ridge	33	27	6	Lincoln Park	27	25	2
Glen Rock	24	21	3	Linden	139	129	10
Gloucester City	32	29	3	Lindenwold	44	41	3
Gloucester Township	125	104	21	Linwood	25	21	4
Green Brook Township	26	21	5	Little Egg Harbor Township	47	38	9
Greenwich Township (Gloucester County)	22	17	5	Little Falls Township	28	24	4
Greenwich Township (Warren County)	9	8	1	Little Ferry	32	26	6
Guttenberg	30	23	7	Little Silver	20	15	5
Hackensack	134	112	22	Livingston Township	82	72	10
Hackettstown	21	20	1	Lodi	54	41	13
Haddonfield	27	25	2	Logan Township	18	17	1
Haddon Heights	18	17	1	Long Beach Township	51	40	11
Haddon Township	32	30	2	Long Branch	115	95	20
Haledon	20	17	3	Long Hill Township	37	29	8
Hamburg	9	8	1	Longport	19	15	4
Hamilton Township (Atlantic County)	73	59	14	Lopatcong Township	15	14	1
Hamilton Township (Mercer County)	209	179	30	Lower Alloways Creek Township	21	16	5
Hammonton	39	31	8	Lower Township	60	45	15
Hanover Township	39	32	7	Lumberton Township	35	31	4
Harding Township	14	13	1	Lyndhurst Township	55	50	5
Hardyston Township	23	17	6	Madison	40	36	4
Harrington Park	10	10	0	Magnolia	11	11	0
Harrison	66	53	13	Mahwah Township	65	56	9
Harrison Township	18	15	3	Manalapan Township	76	62	14
Harvey Cedars	9	8	1	Manasquan	23	17	6
Hasbrouck Heights	34	32	2	Manchester Township	80	64	16
Haworth	13	12	1	Mansfield Township (Burlington County)	13	11	2
Hawthorne	37	32	5	Mansfield Township (Warren County)	15	14	1
Hazlet Township	55	48	7	Mantoloking	7	7	0
Helmetta	4	4	0	Mantua Township	28	26	2
High Bridge	6	6	0	Manville	28	22	6
Highland Park	35	29	6	Maple Shade Township	43	34	9
Highlands	16	12	4	Maplewood Township	74	60	14
Hightstown	19	14	5	Margate City	48	37	11
Hillsborough Township	69	58	11	Marlboro Township	95	76	19
Hillsdale	21	19	2	Matawan	27	22	5
Hillside Township	92	78	14	Maywood	28	24	4
Hi-Nella	1	1	0	Medford Lakes	10	9	1
Hoboken	194	167	27	Medford Township	53	42	11
Ho-Ho-Kus	17	15	2	Mendham	12	10	2
Holland Township	7	6	1	Mendham Township	15	13	2
Holmdel Township	53	42	11	Merchantville	16	14	2
Hopatcong	31	28	3	Metuchen	34	28	6
Hopewell Township	45	36	9	Middlesex	32	30	2
Howell Township	107	89	18	Middle Township	62	46	16
Independence Township	9	8	1	Middletown Township	130	103	27
Interlaken	5	5	0	Midland Park	14	13	1
Irvington	212	181	31	Millburn Township	60	50	10
Island Heights	4	4	0	Milltown	19	16	3
Jackson Township	101	83	18	Millville	82	69	13
Jamesburg	17	12	5	Monmouth Beach	11	10	1
Jefferson Township	46	39	7	Monroe Township (Gloucester County)	80	67	13
Jersey City	948	806	142	Monroe Township (Middlesex County)	56	42	14
Keansburg	33	26	7	Montclair	145	110	35
Kearny	131	123	8	Montgomery Township	40	29	11
Kenilworth	31	30	1	Montvale	22	20	2
Keyport	25	19	6	Montville Township	49	42	7
Kinnelon	17	16	1	Moonachie	20	17	3
Lacey Township	55	41	14	Moorestown Township	48	38	10
Lakehurst	9	8	1	Morris Plains	22	17	5
Lakewood Township	128	101	27	Morristown	68	60	8
Lambertville	12	10	2	Morris Township	49	41	8
Laurel Springs	7	7	0	Mountain Lakes	18	14	4
Lavallette	17	12	5	Mountainside	27	22	5

Table 78

Full-time Law Enforcement Employees as of October 31, 2003

by City by State—Continued

City by state	Total law enforcement employees	Total officers	Total civilians	City by state	Total law enforcement employees	Total officers	Total civilians
NEW JERSEY—Continued				**NEW JERSEY—Continued**			
Mount Arlington	12	11	1	Plumsted Township	9	8	1
Mount Ephraim	13	12	1	Pohatcong Township	11	10	1
Mount Holly Township	29	27	2	Point Pleasant	41	33	8
Mount Laurel Township	86	74	12	Point Pleasant Beach	34	26	8
Mount Olive Township	58	50	8	Pompton Lakes	29	25	4
Mullica Township	15	14	1	Princeton	45	34	11
National Park	8	8	0	Princeton Township	43	35	8
Neptune City	22	17	5	Prospect Park	15	14	1
Neptune Township	92	74	18	Rahway	94	80	14
Netcong	12	10	2	Ramsey	38	32	6
Newark	1,562	1,335	227	Randolph Township	47	39	8
New Brunswick	169	134	35	Raritan	23	18	5
Newfield	5	5	0	Raritan Township	37	35	2
New Hanover Township	4	3	1	Readington Township	26	24	2
New Milford	40	37	3	Red Bank	47	40	7
New Providence	32	26	6	Ridgefield	38	28	10
Newton	31	23	8	Ridgefield Park	38	29	9
North Arlington	44	35	9	Ridgewood	49	44	5
North Bergen Township	139	120	19	Ringwood	27	22	5
North Brunswick Township	100	84	16	Riverdale	19	15	4
North Caldwell	20	16	4	River Edge	26	22	4
Northfield	26	24	2	Riverside Township	13	13	0
North Haledon	25	17	8	Riverton	7	6	1
North Hanover Township	10	9	1	River Vale Township	23	21	2
North Plainfield	50	45	5	Rochelle Park Township	20	20	0
Northvale	13	12	1	Rockaway	15	14	1
North Wildwood	37	31	6	Rockaway Township	66	54	12
Norwood	15	14	1	Roseland	34	28	6
Nutley Township	78	66	12	Roselle	66	56	10
Oakland	34	29	5	Roselle Park	40	33	7
Oaklyn	16	14	2	Roxbury Township	53	46	7
Ocean City	80	64	16	Rumson	21	16	5
Ocean Gate	6	6	0	Runnemede	23	21	2
Oceanport	19	14	5	Rutherford	48	43	5
Ocean Township (Monmouth County)	78	62	16	Saddle Brook Township	33	32	1
Ocean Township (Ocean County)	24	17	7	Saddle River	21	17	4
Ogdensburg	7	7	0	Salem	29	23	6
Old Bridge Township	133	98	35	Sayreville	99	84	15
Old Tappan	14	13	1	Scotch Plains Township	53	46	7
Oradell	22	21	1	Sea Bright	11	11	0
Orange	137	115	22	Sea Girt	16	12	4
Oxford Township	5	4	1	Sea Isle City	27	20	7
Palisades Park	36	30	6	Seaside Heights	34	24	10
Palmyra	19	17	2	Seaside Park	20	15	5
Paramus	117	98	19	Secaucus	66	57	9
Park Ridge	20	18	2	Ship Bottom	12	11	1
Parsippany-Troy Hills Township	131	107	24	Shrewsbury	20	15	5
Passaic	217	179	38	Somerdale	14	13	1
Paterson	465	376	89	Somers Point	33	27	6
Paulsboro	22	20	2	Somerville	39	32	7
Peapack and Gladstone	8	7	1	South Amboy	27	22	5
Pemberton	4	4	0	South Belmar	11	11	0
Pemberton Township	65	57	8	South Bound Brook	13	12	1
Pennington	7	6	1	South Brunswick Township	106	78	28
Pennsauken Township	117	92	25	South Hackensack Township	20	19	1
Penns Grove	18	14	4	South Harrison Township	5	4	1
Pennsville Township	27	25	2	South Orange	63	57	6
Pequannock Township	31	26	5	South Plainfield	71	56	15
Perth Amboy	169	132	37	South River	36	29	7
Phillipsburg	41	32	9	South Toms River	12	11	1
Pine Beach	7	6	1	Sparta Township	42	34	8
Pine Hill	22	20	2	Spotswood	23	19	4
Pine Valley	4	4	0	Springfield	43	38	5
Piscataway Township	104	89	15	Springfield Township	10	9	1
Pitman	16	15	1	Spring Lake	18	14	4
Plainfield	197	165	32	Spring Lake Heights	15	12	3
Plainsboro Township	47	33	14	Stafford Township	71	50	21
Pleasantville	69	55	14	Stanhope	10	9	1

Table 78

Full-time Law Enforcement Employees as of October 31, 2003
by City by State—Continued

City by state	Total law enforcement employees	Total officers	Total civilians	City by state	Total law enforcement employees	Total officers	Total civilians
NEW JERSEY—Continued				**NEW MEXICO**			
Stillwater Township	3	3	0	Alamogordo	106	61	45
Stone Harbor	27	19	8	Albuquerque	1,190	879	311
Stratford	15	14	1	Angel Fire	3	2	1
Summit	55	47	8	Artesia	41	24	17
Surf City	9	9	0	Aztec	18	15	3
Swedesboro	10	9	1	Bayard	7	6	1
Teaneck Township	116	101	15	Belen	28	17	11
Tenafly	38	32	6	Bloomfield	19	15	4
Tewksbury Township	13	12	1	Bosque Farms	10	9	1
Tinton Falls	40	39	1	Capitan	3	3	0
Totowa	31	28	3	Carlsbad	74	53	21
Trenton	430	374	56	Cimarron	3	3	0
Tuckerton	9	9	0	Clovis	78	55	23
Union Beach	19	15	4	Corrales	22	19	3
Union City	219	179	40	Cuba	5	5	0
Union Township	186	133	53	Deming	41	36	5
Upper Saddle River	24	18	6	Dexter	4	4	0
Ventnor City	50	38	12	Espanola	57	33	24
Vernon Township	43	32	11	Estancia	4	3	1
Verona	34	30	4	Eunice	10	6	4
Vineland	160	139	21	Farmington	145	104	41
Voorhees Township	65	52	13	Gallup	90	55	35
Waldwick	24	20	4	Grants	28	19	9
Wallington	27	26	1	Hatch	8	5	3
Wall Township	82	71	11	Hobbs	106	69	37
Wanaque	26	22	4	Jal	8	4	4
Warren Township	34	27	7	Jemez Springs	2	2	0
Washington	13	12	1	Las Vegas	56	39	17
Washington Township (Bergen County)	26	24	2	Lordsburg	13	10	3
Washington Township (Gloucester County)	101	92	9	Los Alamos	50	29	21
Washington Township (Mercer County)	36	27	9	Los Lunas	37	28	9
Washington Township (Morris County)	46	33	13	Melrose	3	2	1
Washington Township (Warren County)	14	13	1	Milan	14	8	6
Watchung	33	26	7	Moriarty	10	9	1
Waterford Township	25	23	2	Portales	37	25	12
Wayne Township	147	118	29	Questa	4	3	1
Weehawken Township	67	62	5	Raton	24	17	7
Wenonah	6	6	0	Red River	9	4	5
Westampton Township	24	21	3	Roswell	106	79	27
West Amwell Township	6	5	1	Ruidoso	38	25	13
West Caldwell Township	32	28	4	Ruidoso Downs	20	11	9
West Deptford Township	41	37	4	Santa Clara	3	2	1
Westfield	74	60	14	Santa Fe	175	134	41
West Long Branch	23	19	4	Santa Rosa	11	7	4
West Milford Township	54	47	7	Silver City	31	26	5
West New York	129	120	9	Socorro	27	18	9
West Orange	126	109	17	Sunland Park	27	21	6
West Paterson	30	27	3	Tatum	10	5	5
Westville	11	10	1	Texico	3	3	0
West Wildwood	5	5	0	Truth or Consequences	16	12	4
West Windsor Township	55	44	11	Tucumcari	23	18	5
Westwood	35	28	7				
Wharton	22	21	1	**NEW YORK**			
Wildwood	59	47	12				
Wildwood Crest	28	22	6	Albany	403	330	73
Willingboro Township	82	68	14	Albion Village	13	12	1
Winfield Township	9	9	0	Alexandria Bay Village	3	3	0
Winslow Township	93	74	19	Alfred Village	6	6	0
Woodbine	3	3	0	Allegany Village	2	2	0
Woodbridge Township	242	197	45	Altamont Village	2	2	0
Woodbury	29	27	2	Amherst Town	184	151	33
Woodbury Heights	8	7	1	Amity Town and Belmont Village	1	1	0
Woodcliff Lake	19	18	1	Amityville Village	25	25	0
Woodlynne	9	8	1	Amsterdam	42	40	2
Wood-Ridge	26	22	4	Angola Village	3	3	0
Woodstown	10	9	1	Ardsley Village	19	19	0
Woolwich Township	17	15	2	Asharoken Village	3	3	0
Wyckoff Township	34	26	8	Auburn	77	69	8

Table 78

Full-time Law Enforcement Employees as of October 31, 2003
by City by State—Continued

City by state	Total law enforcement employees	Total officers	Total civilians	City by state	Total law enforcement employees	Total officers	Total civilians
NEW YORK—Continued				**NEW YORK—Continued**			
Avon Village	3	3	0	Elmira Heights Village	11	11	0
Baldwinsville Village	16	13	3	Elmira Town	4	4	0
Ballston Spa Village	11	7	4	Elmsford Village	18	18	0
Batavia	35	30	5	Endicott Village	40	36	4
Bedford Town	52	45	7	Evans Town	27	22	5
Bethlehem Town	59	41	18	Fairport Village	11	10	1
Binghamton	158	148	10	Fallsburg Town	23	19	4
Blooming Grove Town	18	16	2	Floral Park Village	47	36	11
Bolivar Village	1	1	0	Florida Village	1	1	0
Brant Town	1	1	0	Fort Edward Village	5	5	0
Briarcliff Manor Village	21	21	0	Fort Plain Village	4	4	0
Brighton Town	47	41	6	Frankfort Town	1	1	0
Brockport Village	13	12	1	Frankfort Village	4	4	0
Bronxville Village	29	22	7	Franklinville Village	3	3	0
Buchanan Village	7	7	0	Freeville Village	1	1	0
Buffalo	1,037	862	175	Friendship Town	1	1	0
Caledonia Village	3	3	0	Fulton City	37	34	3
Cambridge Village	2	2	0	Garden City Village	67	54	13
Camden Village	4	4	0	Gates Town	42	34	8
Camillus Town and Village	26	23	3	Geddes Town	18	16	2
Canastota Village	8	7	1	Geneseo Village	9	9	0
Canton Village	11	9	2	Geneva	41	36	5
Carmel Town	39	32	7	Glens Falls	35	29	6
Carthage Village	5	5	0	Gloversville	36	34	2
Catskill Village	16	16	0	Goshen Town	8	8	0
Cayuga Heights Village	7	6	1	Goshen Village	18	16	2
Chester Town	9	9	0	Gouverneur Village	11	8	3
Chester Village	13	12	1	Granville Village	6	6	0
Chittenango Village	7	6	1	Great Neck Estates Village	15	13	2
Cicero Town	6	5	1	Greece Town	98	91	7
Clarkstown Town	195	170	25	Greenburgh Town	128	113	15
Clayton Village	4	3	1	Greene Village	3	2	1
Clay Town	24	19	5	Greenwich Village	1	1	0
Clyde Village	6	5	1	Greenwood Lake Village	11	8	3
Cobleskill Village	11	11	0	Guilderland Town	50	35	15
Coeymans Town	15	11	4	Hamburg Village	17	15	2
Cohoes	47	34	13	Hamilton Village	4	4	0
Colchester Town	2	2	0	Harriman Village	7	7	0
Colonie Town	155	110	45	Harrison Town	82	74	8
Cooperstown Village	5	4	1	Hastings-on-Hudson Village	21	21	0
Corinth Village	10	5	5	Haverstraw Town	50	44	6
Corning	28	24	4	Hempstead Village	142	115	27
Cornwall-on-Hudson Village	5	5	0	Herkimer Village	22	21	1
Cornwall Town	18	14	4	Highland Falls Village	13	10	3
Cortland	43	41	2	Highlands Town	1	1	0
Coxsackie Village	1	1	0	Holley Village	2	2	0
Croton-on-Hudson Village	20	20	0	Hornell	23	22	1
Cuba Town	5	5	0	Horseheads Village	16	13	3
Dansville Village	12	9	3	Hudson Falls Village	14	10	4
Delhi Village	4	4	0	Hyde Park Town	18	15	3
Depew Village	36	29	7	Ilion Village	20	18	2
Deposit Village	1	1	0	Inlet Town	3	2	1
Dewitt Town	40	36	4	Irondequoit Town	68	56	12
Dobbs Ferry Village	30	28	2	Irvington Village	23	21	2
Dolgeville Village	5	5	0	Ithaca	86	72	14
Dryden Village	5	5	0	Jamestown	78	63	15
Dunkirk	35	34	1	Johnson City Village	51	42	9
East Aurora-Aurora Town	20	16	4	Kensington Village	6	6	0
Eastchester Town	57	50	7	Kent Town	26	21	5
East Fishkill Town	35	26	9	Kings Point Village	26	24	2
East Greenbush Town	31	23	8	Kingston	85	79	6
East Hampton Town	71	55	16	Lackawanna	70	51	19
East Hampton Village	27	24	3	Lake Placid Village	17	14	3
East Rochester Village	9	8	1	Lake Success Village	24	21	3
East Syracuse Village	12	10	2	Lakewood-Busti	10	9	1
Ellenville Village	15	13	2	Lancaster Town	60	46	14
Ellicott Town	13	12	1	Larchmont Village	31	28	3
Ellicottville	2	2	0	Lewiston Town and Village	11	10	1

Table 78

Full-time Law Enforcement Employees as of October 31, 2003
by City by State—Continued

City by state	Total law enforcement employees	Total officers	Total civilians	City by state	Total law enforcement employees	Total officers	Total civilians
NEW YORK—Continued				**NEW YORK—Continued**			
Liberty Village	20	17	3	Plattsburgh City	51	44	7
Liverpool Village	6	5	1	Pleasantville Village	17	16	1
Lloyd Harbor Village	13	12	1	Port Chester Village	67	64	3
Lloyd Town	9	8	1	Port Dickinson Village	5	4	1
Lockport	54	51	3	Port Jervis	33	32	1
Lowville Village	6	6	0	Port Washington	69	63	6
Lynbrook Village	55	46	9	Poughkeepsie	135	102	33
Lyons Village	11	9	2	Poughkeepsie Town	91	85	6
Macedon Town and Village	4	4	0	Pound Ridge Town	1	1	0
Malone Village	16	16	0	Pulaski Village	2	2	0
Mamaroneck Town	40	39	1	Quogue Village	15	15	0
Mamaroneck Village	57	51	6	Ramapo Town	136	114	22
Manlius Town	43	36	7	Ravena Village	2	1	1
Marcellus Village	1	1	0	Red Hook Village	2	2	0
Marlborough Town	7	6	1	Riverhead Town	93	74	19
Massena Village	27	22	5	Rochester	864	677	187
Maybrook Village	1	1	0	Rockville Centre Village	61	51	10
Mechanicville	12	11	1	Rosendale Town	5	4	1
Medina Village	12	11	1	Rotterdam Town	66	44	22
Menands Village	13	10	3	Rouses Point Village	2	2	0
Middleport Village	2	2	0	Rye	45	41	4
Middletown	77	65	12	Rye Brook Village	29	28	1
Monroe Village	23	18	5	Sag Harbor Village	13	12	1
Montgomery Town	7	6	1	Salamanca	16	16	0
Monticello Village	28	26	2	Saranac Lake Village	14	13	1
Moravia Village	2	2	0	Saratoga Springs	83	70	13
Moriah Town	2	2	0	Saugerties Town	20	15	5
Mount Morris Village	5	5	0	Scarsdale Village	44	39	5
Mount Pleasant Town	55	46	9	Schodack Town	11	10	1
Nassau Village	1	1	0	Schoharie Village	1	1	0
Newark Village	19	18	1	Scotia Village	14	13	1
New Berlin Town	1	1	0	Shawangunk Town	4	4	0
Newburgh	107	93	14	Shelter Island Town	10	8	2
Newburgh Town	65	52	13	Sherrill	4	4	0
New Hartford Town and Village	32	21	11	Sidney Village	9	9	0
New Rochelle	233	168	65	Silver Creek Village	6	5	1
New Windsor Town	49	37	12	Skaneateles Village	5	5	0
New York	42,128	28,614	13,514	Sleepy Hollow Village	25	25	0
Niagara Town	6	5	1	Sodus Village	1	1	0
Niskayuna Town	42	31	11	Solvay Village	15	14	1
Nissequogue Village	4	4	0	Southampton Town	127	100	27
North Castle Town	41	38	3	Southampton Village	41	30	11
North Greenbush Town	17	15	2	South Glens Falls Village	6	6	0
Northport Village	19	15	4	South Nyack Village	7	7	0
North Syracuse Village	16	14	2	Southport Town	1	1	0
North Tonawanda	58	49	9	Spring Valley Village	76	68	8
Norwich	20	19	1	St. Johnsville Village	1	1	0
Ogdensburg	33	28	5	Stony Point Town	30	29	1
Old Brookville Village	51	40	11	Suffern Village	33	28	5
Old Westbury Village	29	24	5	Syracuse	516	463	53
Olean	40	39	1	Tarrytown Village	42	35	7
Olive Town	1	1	0	Tonawanda	34	29	5
Oneida	26	23	3	Tonawanda Town	160	106	54
Oneonta City	30	26	4	Troy	129	113	16
Orangetown Town	98	89	9	Trumansburg Village	1	1	0
Orchard Park Town	37	32	5	Tuckahoe Village	28	25	3
Ossining Town	16	16	0	Tupper Lake Village	11	11	0
Ossining Village	64	55	9	Tuxedo Town	16	12	4
Oswego City	56	49	7	Ulster Town	27	23	4
Oxford Village	2	2	0	Utica	192	170	22
Oyster Bay Cove Village	11	11	0	Vernon Village	1	1	0
Painted Post Village	4	4	0	Wallkill Town	34	28	6
Palmyra Village	6	5	1	Walton Village	6	5	1
Peekskill	76	60	16	Wappingers Falls Village	5	4	1
Pelham Manor Village	29	28	1	Warsaw Village	6	6	0
Pelham Village	27	25	2	Washingtonville Village	17	14	3
Penn Yan Village	13	12	1	Waterford Town and Village	14	11	3
Perry Village	9	8	1	Waterloo Village	8	7	1

Table 78

Full-time Law Enforcement Employees as of October 31, 2003
by City by State—Continued

City by state	Total law enforcement employees	Total officers	Total civilians	City by state	Total law enforcement employees	Total officers	Total civilians
NEW YORK—Continued				**NORTH CAROLINA—Continued**			
Watertown	68	64	4	Cape Carteret	5	5	0
Watkins Glen Village	4	4	0	Carolina Beach	25	22	3
Waverly Village	11	10	1	Carrboro	35	32	3
Wayland Village	1	1	0	Carthage	9	9	0
Webster Town and Village	39	33	6	Cary	165	135	30
Wellsville Village	16	12	4	Caswell Beach	4	4	0
Westfield Village	6	5	1	Catawba	2	2	0
Westhampton Beach Village	17	15	2	Chadbourn	10	9	1
West Seneca Town	76	62	14	Chapel Hill	123	101	22
Whitehall Village	5	5	0	Charlotte-Mecklenburg[1]	1,966	1,510	456
White Plains	250	208	42	Cherryville	19	14	5
Whitesboro Village	7	7	0	China Grove	11	11	0
Whitestown Town	5	5	0	Chocowinity	2	2	0
Windham Town	2	2	0	Claremont	9	8	1
Wolcott Village	2	2	0	Clayton	42	36	6
Woodbury Town	26	22	4	Cleveland	4	4	0
Woodstock Town	15	10	5	Clinton	38	34	4
Yonkers	694	618	76	Clyde	4	4	0
Yorktown Town	60	53	7	Coats	5	5	0
				Columbus	5	5	0
NORTH CAROLINA				Concord	146	124	22
				Conover	25	24	1
Aberdeen	23	21	2	Conway	1	1	0
Ahoskie	17	12	5	Cooleemee	3	3	0
Albemarle	53	47	6	Cornelius	49	35	14
Andrews	7	6	1	Cramerton	10	10	0
Angier	11	10	1	Creedmoor	13	9	4
Apex	44	34	10	Dallas	17	13	4
Archdale	26	22	4	Davidson	19	18	1
Asheboro	72	67	5	Denton	7	7	0
Asheville	219	170	49	Dobson	3	3	0
Atlantic Beach	23	17	6	Drexel	5	5	0
Aulander	2	2	0	Dunn	49	37	12
Aurora	2	2	0	Durham	531	445	86
Ayden	20	16	4	East Bend	2	2	0
Badin	4	4	0	East Spencer	4	4	0
Bailey	3	3	0	Eden	55	46	9
Bakersville	2	1	1	Edenton	17	15	2
Bald Head Islands	12	11	1	Elizabeth City	59	49	10
Banner Elk	7	7	0	Elizabethtown	16	15	1
Beaufort	15	14	1	Elkin	21	17	4
Beech Mountain	14	10	4	Elon	14	13	1
Belhaven	10	7	3	Emerald Isle	20	15	5
Belmont	35	30	5	Enfield	12	11	1
Benson	14	13	1	Erwin	10	9	1
Bethel	7	7	0	Fair Bluff	3	3	0
Beulaville	5	5	0	Fairmont	17	13	4
Biltmore Forest	14	13	1	Faison	2	2	0
Biscoe	8	7	1	Farmville	19	15	4
Black Creek	1	1	0	Fayetteville	387	296	91
Black Mountain	22	18	4	Fletcher	13	12	1
Bladenboro	6	6	0	Forest City	37	31	6
Blowing Rock	15	11	4	Four Oaks	6	5	1
Boiling Spring Lakes	7	6	1	Foxfire Village	2	2	0
Boiling Springs	6	6	0	Franklin	17	16	1
Bolton	1	1	0	Franklinton	8	8	0
Boone	43	35	8	Fremont	3	3	0
Brevard	28	23	5	Fuquay-Varina	29	24	5
Broadway	4	4	0	Garland	2	2	0
Brookford	1	1	0	Garner	58	52	6
Bryson City	7	7	0	Garysburg	2	2	0
Bunn	2	2	0	Gaston	2	2	0
Burgaw	10	9	1	Gastonia	180	161	19
Burlington	145	109	36	Gibsonville	17	14	3
Butner	46	36	10	Glen Alpine	2	2	0
Cameron	1	1	0	Goldsboro	109	98	11
Candor	4	4	0	Graham	32	28	4
Canton	16	11	5	Granite Falls	14	12	2

Table 78

Full-time Law Enforcement Employees as of October 31, 2003

by City by State—Continued

City by state	Total law enforcement employees	Total officers	Total civilians	City by state	Total law enforcement employees	Total officers	Total civilians
NORTH CAROLINA—Continued				**NORTH CAROLINA—Continued**			
Granite Quarry	5	5	0	Matthews	64	53	11
Greensboro	669	500	169	Maxton	14	10	4
Greenville	191	150	41	Mayodan	15	12	3
Grifton	6	6	0	Maysville	4	4	0
Hamlet	21	17	4	McAdenville	2	2	0
Havelock	33	27	6	Mebane	20	17	3
Haw River	8	8	0	Middlesex	5	5	0
Henderson	58	51	7	Mocksville	15	14	1
Hendersonville	46	35	11	Monroe	84	73	11
Hertford	8	7	1	Montreat	5	5	0
Hickory	140	112	28	Mooresville	57	45	12
Highlands	11	11	0	Morehead City	42	34	8
High Point	238	199	39	Morganton	86	59	27
Hillsborough	27	25	2	Morrisville	27	26	1
Holden Beach	7	7	0	Mount Airy	51	38	13
Holly Ridge	4	4	0	Mount Gilead	5	5	0
Holly Springs	31	24	7	Mount Holly	41	33	8
Hope Mills	32	23	9	Mount Olive	16	15	1
Hudson	12	11	1	Murfreesboro	12	8	4
Huntersville	58	52	6	Murphy	13	9	4
Indian Beach	4	4	0	Nags Head	23	21	2
Jackson	2	1	1	Nashville	13	12	1
Jacksonville	120	96	24	Navassa	3	3	0
Jefferson	2	2	0	New Bern	117	84	33
Jonesville	11	10	1	Newland	5	5	0
Kannapolis	90	70	20	Newport	7	7	0
Kenansville	4	4	0	Newton	44	36	8
Kenly	9	9	0	Newton Grove	3	3	0
Kernersville	71	55	16	Norlina	5	5	0
Kill Devil Hills	27	22	5	North Topsail Beach	11	10	1
King	18	16	2	Northwest	3	3	0
Kings Mountain	38	31	7	North Wilkesboro	27	24	3
Kingstown	1	1	0	Norwood	7	6	1
Kinston	77	72	5	Oakboro	4	4	0
Kitty Hawk	17	15	2	Oak Island	28	24	4
Knightdale	14	13	1	Ocean Isle Beach	12	12	0
Kure Beach	11	10	1	Old Fort	8	7	1
La Grange	7	7	0	Oxford	36	29	7
Lake Lure	10	9	1	Parkton	3	3	0
Lake Royale	5	5	0	Pembroke	16	12	4
Lake Waccamaw	3	3	0	Pikeville	2	2	0
Landis	9	9	0	Pilot Mountain	9	8	1
Laurel Park	6	6	0	Pinebluff	3	3	0
Laurinburg	44	38	6	Pinehurst	28	23	5
Lawndale	1	1	0	Pine Knoll Shores	8	8	0
Leland	13	12	1	Pine Level	4	4	0
Lenoir	67	54	13	Pinetops	8	6	2
Lexington	75	64	11	Pineville	42	32	10
Liberty	9	9	0	Pink Hill	2	2	0
Lilesville	1	1	0	Pittsboro	11	10	1
Lillington	11	11	0	Plymouth	14	14	0
Lincolnton	37	32	5	Princeton	4	4	0
Littleton	3	3	0	Raeford	16	15	1
Locust	6	6	0	Raleigh	762	648	114
Longview	15	15	0	Ramseur	7	7	0
Louisburg	14	13	1	Randleman	12	12	0
Lowell	8	8	0	Ranlo	6	6	0
Lucama	2	2	0	Red Springs	22	17	5
Lumberton	90	78	12	Reidsville	51	42	9
Madison	16	15	1	Rhodhiss	1	1	0
Maggie Valley	6	5	1	Richlands	7	7	0
Magnolia	2	2	0	Rich Square	2	2	0
Maiden	16	15	1	River Bend	4	4	0
Manteo	9	8	1	Roanoke Rapids	44	41	3
Marion	25	20	5	Robbins	8	7	1
Marshall	3	3	0	Robersonville	6	6	0
Mars Hill	5	5	0	Rockingham	35	30	5
Marshville	8	8	0	Rockwell	3	3	0

Table 78

Full-time Law Enforcement Employees as of October 31, 2003
by City by State—Continued

City by state	Total law enforcement employees	Total officers	Total civilians	City by state	Total law enforcement employees	Total officers	Total civilians
NORTH CAROLINA—Continued				**NORTH CAROLINA—Continued**			
Rocky Mount	175	135	40	Whispering Pines	7	7	0
Rolesville	5	5	0	Whitakers	5	5	0
Roseboro	4	4	0	White Lake	5	5	0
Rose Hill	4	4	0	Whiteville	26	22	4
Rowland	7	6	1	Wilkesboro	24	22	2
Roxboro	36	32	4	Williamston	21	20	1
Rutherfordton	14	14	0	Wilmington	273	229	44
Salemburg	1	1	0	Wilson	133	111	22
Salisbury	98	78	20	Windsor	8	8	0
Saluda	4	4	0	Wingate	6	6	0
Sanford	96	77	19	Winston-Salem	607	460	147
Scotland Neck	7	6	1	Winterville	14	13	1
Selma	28	23	5	Winton	1	1	0
Seven Devils	5	5	0	Woodfin	8	8	0
Shallotte	11	10	1	Woodland	1	1	0
Sharpsburg	9	8	1	Wrightsville Beach	27	22	5
Shelby	80	67	13	Yadkinville	11	10	1
Siler City	23	18	5	Yanceyville	4	4	0
Smithfield	36	32	4	Youngsville	8	7	1
Southern Pines	36	28	8	Zebulon	21	20	1
Southern Shores	8	8	0				
Southport	10	9	1	**NORTH DAKOTA**			
Sparta	5	5	0				
Spencer	13	12	1	Beulah	7	6	1
Spindale	13	13	0	Bismarck	108	84	24
Spring Hope	6	6	0	Bowman	4	3	1
Spring Lake	24	18	6	Cando	3	3	0
Spruce Pine	10	10	0	Carrington	4	4	0
Stanfield	4	4	0	Cavalier	4	4	0
Stanley	14	10	4	Crosby	2	2	0
Stantonsburg	3	3	0	Devils Lake	17	15	2
Star	4	4	0	Dickinson	36	24	12
Statesville	85	68	17	Elgin	1	1	0
Stoneville	5	5	0	Emerado	1	1	0
St. Pauls	17	12	5	Fargo	135	119	16
Sugar Mountain	6	6	0	Fessenden	1	1	0
Sunset Beach	12	12	0	Grafton	11	10	1
Surf City	11	10	1	Grand Forks	92	77	15
Swansboro	6	6	0	Harvey	3	3	0
Sylva	12	11	1	Hatton	1	1	0
Tabor City	9	8	1	Hazen	4	4	0
Tarboro	33	25	8	Hillsboro	2	2	0
Taylorsville	11	11	0	Jamestown	32	28	4
Taylortown	1	1	0	Lamoure	2	2	0
Thomasville	82	74	8	Lincoln	2	2	0
Topsail Beach	7	6	1	Linton	1	1	0
Trent Woods	4	4	0	Lisbon	3	3	0
Troutman	7	7	0	Mandan	39	29	10
Troy	10	9	1	Mayville	3	3	0
Tryon	11	7	4	Minot	82	61	21
Valdese	13	12	1	Napoleon	1	1	0
Vanceboro	2	2	0	Northwood	2	2	0
Vass	3	3	0	Oakes	3	3	0
Wadesboro	33	28	5	Powers Lake	1	1	0
Wagram	2	2	0	Rugby	4	4	0
Wake Forest	37	31	6	South Heart	1	1	0
Wallace	16	13	3	Steele	1	1	0
Walnut Cove	6	6	0	Thompson	1	1	0
Walnut Creek	2	2	0	Valley City	18	12	6
Warrenton	3	2	1	Velva	2	2	0
Warsaw	14	11	3	Wahpeton	15	13	2
Washington	38	30	8	Watford City	4	4	0
Waxhaw	9	8	1	West Fargo	37	26	11
Waynesville	37	31	6	Williston	29	21	8
Weaverville	12	11	1	Wishek	2	2	0
Weldon	6	6	0				
Wendell	14	11	3				
West Jefferson	7	7	0				

Table 78

Full-time Law Enforcement Employees as of October 31, 2003
by City by State—Continued

City by state	Total law enforcement employees	Total officers	Total civilians	City by state	Total law enforcement employees	Total officers	Total civilians
OHIO				**OHIO—Continued**			
Ada	10	7	3	Carrollton	8	8	0
Addyston	1	1	0	Celina	22	16	6
Akron	530	486	44	Centerville	56	42	14
Alliance	56	43	13	Chagrin Falls	20	12	8
Amberley Village	19	15	4	Chardon	16	10	6
Amherst	26	20	6	Chester Township	18	13	5
Ansonia	2	2	0	Cheviot	10	10	0
Arcanum	4	4	0	Chillicothe	57	50	7
Archbold	9	8	1	Cincinnati	1,338	1,054	284
Arlington Heights	2	2	0	Circleville	38	26	12
Ashland	41	31	10	Clayton	15	15	0
Ashtabula	40	35	5	Clearcreek Township	12	11	1
Athens	37	26	11	Cleveland	2,319	1,825	494
Aurora	30	23	7	Cleveland Heights	127	109	18
Austintown	47	36	11	Cleves	3	3	0
Avon	28	22	6	Clinton Township	9	8	1
Avon Lake	34	29	5	Clyde	19	15	4
Bainbridge Township	28	20	8	Coitsville Township	3	3	0
Baltic	2	2	0	Columbiana	16	12	4
Barberton	57	43	14	Columbus	2,150	1,789	361
Barnesville	11	7	4	Conneaut	26	19	7
Bath Township	25	17	8	Cortland	10	10	0
Bay Village	26	24	2	Covington	6	5	1
Beachwood	56	43	13	Crestline	14	10	4
Beavercreek	63	47	16	Creston	3	3	0
Beaver Township	16	12	4	Crooksville	6	5	1
Bedford	39	30	9	Cuyahoga Falls	111	91	20
Bedford Heights	64	34	30	Dalton	2	2	0
Bellaire	10	10	0	Dayton	569	472	97
Bellbrook	18	12	6	Deer Park	15	11	4
Bellefontaine	32	24	8	Defiance	33	28	5
Bellevue	17	13	4	Delaware	52	37	15
Bellville	3	3	0	Delhi Township	36	32	4
Belpre	16	11	5	Delta	7	7	0
Berea	39	32	7	Deshler	3	3	0
Bethel	5	4	1	Donnelsville	1	1	0
Bethesda	1	1	0	Dover	22	21	1
Beverly	4	3	1	Dublin	81	62	19
Bexley	35	28	7	East Cleveland	75	60	15
Blanchester	8	8	0	Eastlake	49	36	13
Blendon Township	13	12	1	East Liverpool	26	22	4
Boardman	82	63	19	East Palestine	11	7	4
Bolivar	1	1	0	Eaton	22	15	7
Bowling Green	57	42	15	Elmwood Place	8	6	2
Bradford	3	3	0	Elyria	140	92	48
Brecksville	36	31	5	Englewood	27	18	9
Brewster	4	4	0	Euclid	157	95	62
Bridgeport	11	7	4	Evendale	22	20	2
Broadview Heights	45	32	13	Fairborn	56	42	14
Brookfield Township	9	8	1	Fairfax	9	9	0
Brooklyn	41	33	8	Fairfield	81	61	20
Brooklyn Heights	17	17	0	Fairfield Township	13	12	1
Brook Park	53	44	9	Fairlawn	32	22	10
Brookville	16	11	5	Fairport Harbor	8	7	1
Brunswick	53	39	14	Fairview Park	29	26	3
Bryan	28	20	8	Forest	2	2	0
Buckeye Lake	5	5	0	Forest Park	39	33	6
Bucyrus	30	22	8	Fort Recovery	1	1	0
Burton	3	3	0	Fort Shawnee	5	4	1
Butler Township	14	13	1	Franklin	28	23	5
Cadiz	5	5	0	Franklin Township	16	11	5
Cambridge	31	24	7	Fredericktown	4	4	0
Campbell	13	13	0	Fremont	38	33	5
Canal Fulton	8	7	1	Gahanna	63	53	10
Canfield	22	16	6	Gallipolis	15	14	1
Canton	202	173	29	Garfield Heights	80	62	18
Carey	11	7	4	Gates Mills	16	12	4
Carlisle	8	7	1	Geneva	17	13	4

Table 78

Full-time Law Enforcement Employees as of October 31, 2003
by City by State—Continued

City by state	Total law enforcement employees	Total officers	Total civilians	City by state	Total law enforcement employees	Total officers	Total civilians
OHIO—Continued				**OHIO—Continued**			
Genoa	5	5	0	Louisville	12	12	0
Genoa Township	25	23	2	Loveland	20	18	2
Germantown	14	10	4	Lyndhurst	39	30	9
German Township (Clark County)	3	3	0	Macedonia	27	21	6
German Township (Montgomery County)	5	5	0	Madeira	11	10	1
Gibsonburg	4	4	0	Madison Township	18	16	2
Girard	18	15	3	Magnolia	3	3	0
Glendale	8	7	1	Mansfield	125	90	35
Golf Manor	8	7	1	Maple Heights	63	46	17
Goshen Township (Clermont County)	11	10	1	Mariemont	11	10	1
Goshen Township (Mahoning County)	5	4	1	Marietta	38	31	7
Grandview Heights	25	20	5	Marion	85	66	19
Granville	13	10	3	Marlboro Township	3	3	0
Gratis	1	1	0	Martins Ferry	21	16	5
Greenfield	15	14	1	Marysville	36	29	7
Greenhills	8	8	0	Mason	40	36	4
Greenville	31	22	9	Massillon	52	49	3
Greenwich	4	4	0	Maumee	60	44	16
Grove City	70	50	20	Mayfield Village	24	16	8
Hamilton	157	130	27	McComb	5	4	1
Harrison	23	21	2	McConnelsville	7	5	2
Hartville	7	7	0	Mechanicsburg	3	3	0
Hebron	7	6	1	Medina	40	32	8
Hicksville	10	8	2	Medina Township	6	6	0
Highland Heights	29	22	7	Mentor	108	77	31
Highland Hills	11	10	1	Mentor-on-the-Lake	17	11	6
Hilliard	62	47	15	Miamisburg	50	39	11
Hillsboro	22	18	4	Miami Township	44	40	4
Hinckley Township	10	9	1	Middlefield	12	7	5
Holgate	1	1	0	Middleport	7	4	3
Holland	7	7	0	Middletown	135	90	45
Howland Township	21	20	1	Milford	17	15	2
Hubbard	17	13	4	Millersburg	9	7	2
Hubbard Township	8	7	1	Milton Township	1	1	0
Huber Heights	71	55	16	Minerva	13	9	4
Hudson	36	29	7	Minerva Park	5	5	0
Hunting Valley	13	12	1	Mingo Junction	11	10	1
Huron	20	15	5	Mogadore	9	9	0
Independence	50	34	16	Monroe	21	17	4
Indian Hill	25	20	5	Monroeville	8	8	0
Ironton	18	14	4	Montgomery	23	21	2
Jackson	23	17	6	Montpelier	9	8	1
Jefferson	6	5	1	Montville Township	8	8	0
Johnstown	13	9	4	Moraine	43	33	10
Kent	55	41	14	Mount Gilead	6	6	0
Kenton	16	16	0	Mount Healthy	12	11	1
Kettering	109	82	27	Mount Orab	6	6	0
Kirtland	14	9	5	Mount Sterling	11	7	4
Kirtland Hills	8	7	1	Mount Vernon	29	26	3
Lagrange	3	3	0	Munroe Falls	8	8	0
Lakemore	7	7	0	Napoleon	21	16	5
Lake Township	13	12	1	Navarre	5	5	0
Lakewood	110	87	23	Nelsonville	10	7	3
Lancaster	86	66	20	New Albany	23	15	8
Lawrence Township	6	6	0	Newark	98	78	20
Lebanon	34	25	9	New Boston	14	10	4
Leipsic	2	2	0	Newburgh Heights	7	4	3
Lexington	12	8	4	Newcomerstown	10	6	4
Liberty Township	23	22	1	New Lebanon	7	7	0
Lima	100	81	19	New Lexington	12	8	4
Lincoln Heights	10	9	1	New Madison	8	8	0
Lisbon	10	6	4	New Matamoras	1	1	0
Lockland	12	11	1	New Middletown	3	3	0
Logan	23	18	5	New Paris	4	4	0
London	20	15	5	New Philadelphia	26	22	4
Lorain	126	98	28	New Richmond	5	5	0
Lordstown	12	8	4	Newton Falls	11	7	4
Loudonville	9	5	4	Newtown	5	5	0

Table 78

Full-time Law Enforcement Employees as of October 31, 2003
by City by State—Continued

City by state	Total law enforcement employees	Total officers	Total civilians	City by state	Total law enforcement employees	Total officers	Total civilians
OHIO—Continued				**OHIO—Continued**			
Niles	42	36	6	Shawnee Township	16	10	6
North Baltimore	6	6	0	Sheffield Lake	16	12	4
North Canton	33	25	8	Shelby	18	14	4
North College Hill	15	14	1	Shreve	3	3	0
North Kingsville	5	5	0	Sidney	50	38	12
North Olmsted	74	57	17	Silverton	13	10	3
North Randall	21	17	4	Smith Township	5	4	1
North Ridgeville	42	34	8	Solon	75	46	29
North Royalton	61	40	21	South Charleston	4	4	0
Northwood	28	21	7	South Euclid	47	39	8
Norton	22	16	6	South Russell	9	9	0
Norwalk	32	24	8	South Zanesville	3	3	0
Norwood	53	51	2	Spencerville	5	4	1
Oak Harbor	6	4	2	Springboro	27	21	6
Oakwood	37	31	6	Springdale	43	34	9
Oakwood Village	16	12	4	Springfield	151	127	24
Oberlin	20	16	4	Springfield Township (Hamilton County)	52	44	8
Olmsted Falls	18	12	6	Springfield Township (Mahoning County)	6	6	0
Olmsted Township	20	17	3	St. Bernard	19	18	1
Ontario	26	20	6	Steubenville	57	47	10
Oregon	60	46	14	St. Henry	2	2	0
Orrville	19	14	5	St. Marys	19	15	4
Ottawa	7	7	0	Stow	45	36	9
Ottawa Hills	11	11	0	Strasburg	4	4	0
Oxford	28	26	2	Streetsboro	32	24	8
Painesville	44	40	4	Strongsville	95	73	22
Parma	131	96	35	Struthers	21	16	5
Parma Heights	40	34	6	Sunbury	10	10	0
Pataskala	18	17	1	Swanton	9	8	1
Paulding	5	4	1	Sylvania	39	32	7
Payne	1	1	0	Sylvania Township	65	48	17
Peninsula	6	5	1	Tallmadge	38	26	12
Pepper Pike	26	20	6	Terrace Park	7	6	1
Perrysburg	39	32	7	Tiffin	43	30	13
Perry Township (Franklin County)	14	9	5	Tipp City	21	18	3
Perry Township (Montgomery County)	7	7	0	Toledo	804	678	126
Perry Township (Stark County)	29	23	6	Toronto	10	10	0
Pierce Township	14	13	1	Trenton	19	14	5
Piqua	41	35	6	Trotwood	54	49	5
Plain City	9	9	0	Troy	49	43	6
Poland Township	15	13	2	Twinsburg	48	34	14
Poland Village	6	6	0	Uhrichsville	8	8	0
Port Clinton	18	13	5	Union	5	5	0
Portsmouth	47	43	4	Union City	4	4	0
Powell	17	16	1	Uniontown	10	8	2
Ravenna	32	24	8	Union Township (Clermont County)	60	45	15
Reading	23	18	5	Union Township (Licking County)	2	2	0
Reynoldsburg	64	51	13	University Heights	37	30	7
Richfield	23	17	6	Upper Arlington	60	49	11
Richmond Heights	30	22	8	Upper Sandusky	17	12	5
Richwood	6	6	0	Urbana	24	19	5
Rittman	12	9	3	Valley View	21	19	2
Riverside	32	31	1	Vandalia	37	29	8
Roseville	2	2	0	Van Wert	30	22	8
Rossford	18	17	1	Vermilion	24	19	5
Russell Township	9	8	1	Village of Leesburg	3	3	0
Sagamore Hills	12	9	3	Wadsworth	35	26	9
Salem	25	24	1	Waite Hill	6	6	0
Salineville	3	3	0	Walbridge	3	3	0
Sandusky	66	55	11	Walton Hills	18	13	5
Seaman	2	2	0	Wapakoneta	19	14	5
Sebring	10	6	4	Warren	96	78	18
Seven Hills	20	19	1	Warrensville Heights	52	39	13
Seville	7	6	1	Warren Township	8	8	0
Shadyside	10	6	4	Waterville Township	5	5	0
Shaker Heights	96	67	29	Waverly	15	11	4
Sharon Township	9	9	0				
Sharonville	49	40	9				

Table 78

Full-time Law Enforcement Employees as of October 31, 2003
by City by State—Continued

City by state	Total law enforcement employees	Total officers	Total civilians	City by state	Total law enforcement employees	Total officers	Total civilians
OHIO—Continued				**OKLAHOMA—Continued**			
Waynesville	5	4	1	Clayton	6	4	2
Wellington	9	6	3	Cleveland	6	6	0
Wellston	14	11	3	Clinton	26	18	8
Wellsville	6	6	0	Coalgate	7	7	0
West Carrollton	32	25	7	Colbert	3	3	0
West Chester Township	87	77	10	Collinsville	15	10	5
Westerville	79	69	10	Comanche	4	4	0
West Jefferson	15	11	4	Commerce	5	5	0
Westlake	71	50	21	Cordell	8	5	3
West Union	7	6	1	Coweta	21	15	6
Whitehall	54	45	9	Crescent	8	5	3
Wickliffe	41	31	10	Cushing	22	17	5
Willard	18	14	4	Davis	37	6	31
Willoughby	60	45	15	Del City	37	28	9
Willoughby Hills	25	18	7	Dewey	9	8	1
Willowick	33	25	8	Drumright	5	5	0
Wilmington	30	21	9	Duncan	56	42	14
Winchester	2	2	0	Durant	42	28	14
Windham	7	5	2	Edmond	119	97	22
Wintersville	9	8	1	Elk City	37	23	14
Woodlawn	18	17	1	El Reno	37	27	10
Woodsfield	6	6	0	Enid	111	92	19
Woodville	5	5	0	Erick	3	3	0
Wooster	43	38	5	Eufaula	15	10	5
Worthington	41	32	9	Fairfax	6	3	3
Wyoming	20	16	4	Fairview	8	5	3
Xenia	70	46	24	Fletcher	1	1	0
Yellow Springs	9	6	3	Fort Gibson	13	10	3
Youngstown	240	197	43	Frederick	12	10	2
Zanesville	95	55	40	Geary	9	5	4
				Glenpool	21	14	7
OKLAHOMA				Goodwell	3	3	0
				Granite	2	2	0
Ada	40	35	5	Grove	25	19	6
Agra	1	1	0	Guthrie	27	20	7
Altus	61	44	17	Guymon	29	17	12
Alva	13	8	5	Haileyville	3	1	2
Anadarko	25	18	7	Harrah	11	10	1
Antlers	10	6	4	Hartshorne	5	5	0
Apache	6	3	3	Haskell	5	5	0
Ardmore	73	55	18	Healdton	9	5	4
Arkoma	6	3	3	Heavener	12	8	4
Atoka	15	14	1	Henryetta	15	11	4
Barnsdall	6	4	2	Hinton	4	4	0
Bartlesville	80	52	28	Hobart	16	10	6
Beaver	3	3	0	Holdenville	13	8	5
Beggs	8	5	3	Hollis	12	8	4
Bethany	36	25	11	Hominy	11	6	5
Bixby	20	16	4	Hooker	4	4	0
Blackwell	22	15	7	Hugo	18	14	4
Blanchard	4	2	2	Hulbert	4	4	0
Boise City	2	2	0	Hydro	2	2	0
Bristow	13	9	4	Idabel	26	20	6
Broken Arrow	145	107	38	Inola	4	4	0
Broken Bow	17	12	5	Jay	12	7	5
Buffalo	3	3	0	Jenks	18	12	6
Caddo	3	2	1	Jones	4	4	0
Calera	7	5	2	Kingfisher	9	7	2
Carnegie	7	4	3	Kingston	7	7	0
Catoosa	15	14	1	Konawa	8	4	4
Chandler	12	8	4	Krebs	4	4	0
Checotah	15	11	4	Laverne	7	3	4
Chelsea	6	6	0	Lawton	180	155	25
Cherokee	4	3	1	Lexington	10	6	4
Chickasha	41	29	12	Lindsay	10	6	4
Choctaw	15	13	2	Locust Grove	11	6	5
Chouteau	7	6	1	Lone Grove	8	5	3
Claremore	49	36	13	Luther	3	3	0

Table 78

Full-time Law Enforcement Employees as of October 31, 2003
by City by State—Continued

City by state	Total law enforcement employees	Total officers	Total civilians	City by state	Total law enforcement employees	Total officers	Total civilians
OKLAHOMA—Continued				**OKLAHOMA—Continued**			
Madill	13	11	2	Talihina	10	6	4
Mangum	11	7	4	Tecumseh	15	10	5
Mannford	13	9	4	The Village	26	21	5
Marietta	6	5	1	Tishomingo	7	7	0
Marlow	14	12	2	Tonkawa	12	8	4
Maysville	4	3	1	Tulsa	904	764	140
McAlester	59	46	13	Tushka	3	3	0
McLoud	8	5	3	Tuttle	14	10	4
Meeker	6	6	0	Valliant	8	4	4
Miami	43	31	12	Vian	9	5	4
Midwest City	119	93	26	Vinita	23	18	5
Minco	4	4	0	Wagoner	19	13	6
Moore	76	60	16	Walters	4	4	0
Mooreland	2	2	0	Warner	3	3	0
Morris	5	5	0	Warr Acres	31	22	9
Mountain View	2	2	0	Watonga	11	8	3
Muldrow	12	7	5	Waukomis	3	3	0
Muskogee	106	84	22	Waurika	3	3	0
Mustang	26	19	7	Waynoka	3	3	0
Newcastle	19	13	6	Weatherford	29	19	10
Newkirk	7	6	1	Westville	9	5	4
Nichols Hills	19	14	5	Wetumka	5	5	0
Nicoma Park	7	7	0	Wewoka	17	11	6
Noble	16	12	4	Wilburton	6	5	1
Norman	184	130	54	Wilson	3	3	0
Nowata	8	6	2	Woodward	27	19	8
Oilton	4	4	0	Wright City	3	3	0
Okeene	3	3	0	Wynnewood	5	4	1
Okemah	15	11	4	Yale	5	2	3
Oklahoma City	1,268	1,031	237	Yukon	43	30	13
Okmulgee	35	28	7				
Oologah	4	3	1	**OREGON**			
Owasso	46	34	12				
Pauls Valley	19	13	6	Albany	72	52	20
Pawhuska	10	6	4	Amity	3	3	0
Pawnee	6	6	0	Ashland	32	26	6
Perkins	4	4	0	Astoria	24	15	9
Perry	18	13	5	Athena	2	2	0
Piedmont	8	6	2	Aumsville	5	4	1
Pocola	8	5	3	Aurora	3	2	1
Ponca City	67	55	12	Baker City	15	15	0
Porum	2	2	0	Bandon	7	6	1
Poteau	30	21	9	Beaverton	140	114	26
Prague	11	7	4	Bend	94	70	24
Pryor	29	21	8	Black Butte	7	6	1
Purcell	30	17	13	Boardman	9	8	1
Ringling	2	2	0	Brookings	19	13	6
Roland	14	9	5	Burns	9	5	4
Rush Springs	4	4	0	Butte Falls	4	2	2
Sallisaw	29	20	9	Canby	25	22	3
Sand Springs	43	34	9	Cannon Beach	8	7	1
Sapulpa	50	41	9	Carlton	4	3	1
Sayre	10	6	4	Central Point	26	22	4
Seiling	2	2	0	Clatskanie	5	4	1
Seminole	16	11	5	Coburg	8	7	1
Shawnee	74	53	21	Columbia City	1	1	0
Skiatook	17	12	5	Condon	2	1	1
Snyder	4	4	0	Coos Bay	32	23	9
Spencer	11	10	1	Coquille	7	6	1
Spiro	4	4	0	Cornelius	13	12	1
Stigler	12	8	4	Corvallis	78	52	26
Stillwater	105	70	35	Cottage Grove	22	15	7
Stilwell	21	14	7	Culver	1	1	0
Stratford	6	3	3	Dallas	19	18	1
Stringtown	8	7	1	Dundee	4	4	0
Stroud	12	7	5	Eagle Point	10	9	1
Sulphur	16	11	5	Elgin	3	3	0
Tahlequah	36	28	8	Enterprise	4	4	0

Table 78

Full-time Law Enforcement Employees as of October 31, 2003
by City by State—Continued

City by state	Total law enforcement employees	Total officers	Total civilians	City by state	Total law enforcement employees	Total officers	Total civilians
OREGON—Continued				**OREGON—Continued**			
Eugene	299	172	127	Stanfield	5	5	0
Fairview	11	10	1	Stayton	18	15	3
Florence	22	14	8	St. Helens	19	17	2
Forest Grove	29	26	3	Sutherlin	16	13	3
Gearhart	3	3	0	Sweet Home	18	11	7
Gervais	2	2	0	Talent	8	7	1
Gladstone	21	16	5	The Dalles	21	19	2
Gold Beach	7	5	2	Tigard	71	57	14
Grants Pass	62	39	23	Tillamook	10	9	1
Gresham	141	106	35	Toledo	13	8	5
Hermiston	30	21	9	Troutdale	23	19	4
Hillsboro	142	104	38	Tualatin	38	33	5
Hines	4	3	1	Turner	2	2	0
Hood River	17	14	3	Umatilla	10	9	1
Hubbard	6	5	1	Vernonia	4	4	0
Independence	15	13	2	Warrenton	9	8	1
Jacksonville	5	4	1	West Linn	32	27	5
John Day	9	4	5	Weston	1	1	0
Junction City	13	8	5	Winston	7	6	1
Keizer	44	37	7	Woodburn	31	23	8
King City	4	4	0	Yamhill	2	2	0
Klamath Falls	44	40	4				
La Grande	32	18	14	**PENNSYLVANIA**			
Lake Oswego	67	39	28				
Lakeview	5	5	0	Abington Township	112	89	23
Lebanon	31	23	8	Adams Township (Butler County)	4	4	0
Lincoln City	27	18	9	Adams Township (Cambria County)	4	4	0
Madras	10	9	1	Akron	4	4	0
Manzanita	3	3	0	Albion	2	2	0
McMinnville	39	31	8	Alburtis	4	4	0
Medford	150	96	54	Aldan	4	4	0
Milton-Freewater	17	11	6	Aleppo Township	10	5	5
Milwaukie	36	31	5	Aliquippa	19	19	0
Molalla	16	12	4	Allegheny Township (Blair County)	7	7	0
Monmouth	14	12	2	Allegheny Township (Westmoreland County)	9	8	1
Mount Angel	6	5	1	Allentown	262	240	22
Myrtle Creek	13	7	6	Altoona	86	76	10
Myrtle Point	6	6	0	Ambler	14	12	2
Newberg	33	22	11	Ambridge	13	13	0
Newport	28	23	5	Amity Township	12	11	1
North Bend	26	19	7	Apollo	1	1	0
North Plains	3	3	0	Arnold	12	11	1
Nyssa	7	7	0	Ashland	5	5	0
Oakridge	11	6	5	Ashley	2	2	0
Ontario	30	23	7	Aston Township	18	16	2
Oregon City	39	32	7	Athens	8	7	1
Pendleton	26	23	3	Avalon	6	6	0
Philomath	9	8	1	Baldwin Borough	35	29	6
Phoenix	9	8	1	Baldwin Township	5	5	0
Pilot Rock	3	3	0	Bally	1	1	0
Portland	1,267	1,005	262	Bangor	10	9	1
Powers	2	2	0	Barrett Township	7	7	0
Prairie City	2	2	0	Beaver	13	9	4
Prineville	24	15	9	Beaver Falls	19	18	1
Rainier	7	6	1	Bedford	7	6	1
Redmond	39	30	9	Bedminster Township	6	5	1
Reedsport	16	11	5	Bell Acres	4	4	0
Rockaway Beach	3	3	0	Bellefonte	11	9	2
Rogue River	6	5	1	Bellevue	16	13	3
Roseburg	36	32	4	Bellwood	2	2	0
Salem	284	166	118	Bensalem Township	103	84	19
Sandy	10	9	1	Berks-Lehigh Regional	21	21	0
Scappoose	9	8	1	Berlin	1	1	0
Seaside	26	18	8	Bern Township	11	11	0
Shady Cove	3	3	0	Berwick	14	13	1
Sherwood	19	16	3	Bethel Park	44	38	6
Silverton	16	15	1	Bethel Township (Berks County)	6	2	4
Springfield	101	66	35				

Table 78

Full-time Law Enforcement Employees as of October 31, 2003
by City by State—Continued

City by state	Total law enforcement employees	Total officers	Total civilians	City by state	Total law enforcement employees	Total officers	Total civilians
PENNSYLVANIA—Continued				**PENNSYLVANIA—Continued**			
Bethlehem	163	140	23	Colonial Regional	24	22	2
Bethlehem Township	30	28	2	Columbia	21	18	3
Birdsboro	8	7	1	Colwyn	2	2	0
Birmingham Township	3	3	0	Conemaugh Township (Cambria			
Blairsville	4	4	0	County)	2	2	0
Blair Township	4	4	0	Conemaugh Township (Somerset			
Blakely	4	4	0	County)	6	5	1
Blawnox	4	4	0	Conewago Township	7	6	1
Bloomsburg Town	19	15	4	Conewango Township	4	4	0
Brackenridge	5	5	0	Conneaut Lake Regional	3	3	0
Braddock Hills	2	2	0	Conshohocken	17	15	2
Bradford	21	21	0	Coopersburg	6	6	0
Bradford Township	5	5	0	Coplay	4	4	0
Brandywine Regional	14	13	1	Coraopolis	12	9	3
Brecknock Township	3	3	0	Cornwall	8	7	1
Briar Creek Township	3	3	0	Corry	16	12	4
Bridgeport	10	9	1	Covington Township	2	2	0
Bridgeville	10	9	1	Cranberry Township	27	24	3
Bridgewater	2	2	0	Cresson	1	1	0
Brighton Township	6	6	0	Cresson Township	3	3	0
Brockway	2	2	0	Croyle Township	1	1	0
Brookhaven	9	8	1	Cumberland Township (Adams County)	6	6	0
Brookville	6	5	1	Cumru Township	28	25	3
Brownsville	4	4	0	Curwensville	4	4	0
Bryn Athyn	5	5	0	Dale	2	2	0
Buckingham Township	23	21	2	Dallas Township	8	8	0
Bushkill Township	12	10	2	Darby	18	15	3
Butler	26	26	0	Delmont	4	4	0
Butler Township (Butler County)	25	21	4	Derry	2	2	0
Butler Township (Luzerne County)	9	8	1	Derry Township (Dauphin County)	42	36	6
Caernarvon Township	7	6	1	Dickson City	11	11	0
California	8	7	1	Donegal Township	2	2	0
Caln Township	19	17	2	Dormont	16	15	1
Cambria Township	4	4	0	Douglass Township (Berks County)	2	2	0
Cambridge Springs	3	3	0	Downingtown	17	15	2
Camp Hill	12	11	1	Doylestown	20	15	5
Canonsburg	16	16	0	Doylestown Township	23	20	3
Carbondale	15	15	0	Duboistown	2	2	0
Carlisle	37	32	5	Duncannon	3	3	0
Carnegie	14	13	1	Dunmore	9	8	1
Carrolltown	1	1	0	Duquesne	16	15	1
Carroll Township (Washington County)	3	3	0	Duryea	3	3	0
Carroll Township (York County)	7	7	0	East Bethlehem Township	2	2	0
Carroll Valley	4	3	1	East Cocalico Township	23	21	2
Castle Shannon	12	11	1	East Conemaugh	2	2	0
Center Township	26	26	0	East Coventry Township	5	5	0
Centerville	3	3	0	East Earl Township	5	5	0
Central Berks Regional	13	12	1	Eastern Adams Regional	7	7	0
Chalfont	7	6	1	East Fallowfield Township	5	5	0
Chambersburg	34	31	3	East Franklin Township	2	2	0
Chartiers Township	11	11	0	East Hempfield Township	35	29	6
Cheltenham Township	95	84	11	East Lampeter Township	41	37	4
Chester	110	102	8	East Lansdowne	4	2	2
Chester Hill	1	1	0	East Norriton Township	32	29	3
Cheswick	3	3	0	East Pennsboro Township	20	19	1
Chippewa Township	15	14	1	East Pikeland Township	9	8	1
Churchill	9	9	0	Easttown Township	15	14	1
Clairton	11	10	1	East Vincent Township	7	7	0
Clarion	9	8	1	East Washington	1	1	0
Claysville	2	2	0	East Whiteland Township	21	19	2
Clearfield	8	8	0	Ebensburg	4	4	0
Cleona	4	4	0	Economy	13	12	1
Clifton Heights	9	8	1	Edgewood	9	9	0
Cochranton	2	2	0	Edgeworth	6	4	2
Colebrookdale District	10	9	1	Edinboro	10	9	1
Collegeville	9	8	1	Edwardsville	6	6	0
Collier Township	12	11	1	Elizabeth Township	16	15	1
Collingdale	10	8	2	Elkland	2	2	0

Table 78

Full-time Law Enforcement Employees as of October 31, 2003
by City by State—Continued

City by state	Total law enforcement employees	Total officers	Total civilians	City by state	Total law enforcement employees	Total officers	Total civilians
PENNSYLVANIA—Continued				**PENNSYLVANIA—Continued**			
Ellwood City	13	11	2	Jeannette	18	17	1
Emmaus	17	16	1	Jefferson Hills Borough	17	16	1
Emporium	1	1	0	Jenkins Township	2	2	0
Ephrata	26	22	4	Jenkintown	8	8	0
Ephrata Township	10	9	1	Jermyn	1	1	0
Erie	259	209	50	Jersey Shore	7	6	1
Etna	7	6	1	Johnsonburg	4	4	0
Everett	3	3	0	Johnstown	53	46	7
Exeter Township (Berks County)	34	32	2	Kane	3	3	0
Fairview Township (Luzerne County)	5	5	0	Kennedy Township	15	11	4
Fairview Township (York County)	15	13	2	Kidder Township	9	9	0
Falls Township (Bucks County)	60	52	8	Kingston	26	21	5
Fawn Township	4	4	0	Kingston Township	12	11	1
Ferguson Township	18	16	2	Kittanning	9	8	1
Ferndale	1	1	0	Kline Township	2	2	0
Findlay Township	21	14	7	Koppel	1	1	0
Fleetwood	6	6	0	Kutztown	10	9	1
Ford City	4	4	0	Laflin Borough	3	3	0
Forest City	2	2	0	Lake City	3	3	0
Forest Hills	14	11	3	Lancaster	187	152	35
Forty Fort	6	5	1	Lancaster Township (Butler County)	2	2	0
Foster Township	5	5	0	Lansdale	29	23	6
Fountain Hill	8	8	0	Larksville	4	4	0
Frackville	6	6	0	Latrobe	14	13	1
Franconia Township	13	12	1	Lawrence Township	9	9	0
Franklin Park	10	9	1	Lebanon	50	47	3
Franklin Township (Carbon County)	4	4	0	Leechburg	2	2	0
Gallitzin	1	1	0	Leetsdale	4	4	0
Gettysburg	17	15	2	Leet Township	5	5	0
Girard	5	4	1	Lehighton	9	8	1
Glenolden	10	9	1	Lehigh Township (Northampton			
Granville Township	7	6	1	County)	11	10	1
Greencastle	4	4	0	Lehman Township	3	3	0
Greensburg	37	27	10	Lewisburg	8	8	0
Green Tree	12	11	1	Ligonier Township	4	4	0
Greenwood Township	1	1	0	Limerick Township	17	15	2
Grove City	8	7	1	Lincoln	2	2	0
Halifax	1	1	0	Linesville	1	1	0
Hamburg	7	6	1	Lititz	15	12	3
Hampden Township	22	21	1	Littlestown	6	6	0
Hanover Township (Luzerne County)	16	16	0	Locust Township	3	3	0
Harmar Township	7	7	0	Logan Township	17	15	2
Harmony Township	4	4	0	Lower Allen Township	21	18	3
Harrisburg	230	179	51	Lower Burrell	17	17	0
Harrison Township	16	12	4	Lower Gwynedd Township	18	17	1
Hatboro	18	14	4	Lower Heidelberg Township	7	6	1
Hatfield Township	28	22	6	Lower Makefield Township	35	31	4
Haverford Township	85	68	17	Lower Merion Township	161	135	26
Hazleton	31	28	3	Lower Moreland Township	26	21	5
Heidelberg	3	3	0	Lower Paxton Township	55	49	6
Hellam Township	10	10	0	Lower Pottsgrove Township	16	14	2
Hemlock Township	3	3	0	Lower Providence Township	34	27	7
Hermitage	56	28	28	Lower Salford Township	19	17	2
Highspire	6	5	1	Lower Southampton Township	32	29	3
Hilltown Township	20	17	3	Lower Swatara Township	11	10	1
Homestead	13	13	0	Luzerne Township	1	1	0
Honesdale	9	8	1	Macungie	3	3	0
Honey Brook Township	3	3	0	Mahoning Township (Carbon County)	5	5	0
Horsham Township	49	40	9	Mahoning Township (Montour County)	7	6	1
Hughesville	3	3	0	Malvern	6	5	1
Hummelstown	7	7	0	Manheim	8	7	1
Huntingdon	13	12	1	Manheim Township	64	50	14
Indiana	26	20	6	Manor Township	23	21	2
Indiana Township	10	10	0	Mansfield	5	5	0
Ingram	4	4	0	Marlborough Township	4	4	0
Irwin	5	5	0	Marple Township	38	32	6
Jackson Township (Butler County)	6	6	0	Martinsburg	2	2	0
Jackson Township (Luzerne County)	4	4	0	Mayfield	1	1	0

Table 78

Full-time Law Enforcement Employees as of October 31, 2003

by City by State—Continued

City by state	Total law enforcement employees	Total officers	Total civilians	City by state	Total law enforcement employees	Total officers	Total civilians
PENNSYLVANIA—Continued				**PENNSYLVANIA—Continued**			
McCandless	29	27	2	Northeastern Regional	11	10	1
McKeesport	63	60	3	Northern Berks Regional	15	14	1
McSherrystown	4	4	0	Northern York Regional	47	43	4
Meadville	27	21	6	North Fayette Township	23	19	4
Mechanicsburg	16	15	1	North Franklin Township	7	7	0
Mercer	4	4	0	North Huntingdon Township	36	29	7
Meyersdale	2	2	0	North Lebanon Township	10	9	1
Middlesex Township (Butler County)	6	6	0	North Londonderry Township	8	7	1
Middletown	16	15	1	North Middleton Township	9	8	1
Middletown Township	59	51	8	North Strabane Township	17	16	1
Midland	5	5	0	North Versailles Township	23	20	3
Mifflinburg	5	5	0	North Wales	7	6	1
Mifflin County Regional	25	24	1	Norwegian Township	1	1	0
Mifflin Township	3	3	0	Norwood	7	7	0
Millcreek Township	71	56	15	Oakmont	7	7	0
Millersburg	4	4	0	O'Hara Township	15	14	1
Millersville	15	13	2	Ohioville	2	2	0
Millvale	5	5	0	Oil City	24	19	5
Millville	1	1	0	Old Lycoming Township	10	9	1
Milton	11	10	1	Oley Township	4	4	0
Minersville	6	6	0	Olyphant	5	5	0
Mohnton	4	4	0	Oxford	9	8	1
Monaca	6	6	0	Paint Township	2	2	0
Monessen	12	12	0	Palmerton	9	8	1
Monongahela	11	10	1	Palmyra	10	9	1
Monroeville	56	51	5	Parkesburg	8	8	0
Montgomery Township	41	32	9	Parkside	3	3	0
Montoursville	7	7	0	Parks Township	1	1	0
Moon Township	36	30	6	Patterson Area	4	4	0
Moore Township	9	8	1	Patton Township	17	15	2
Moosic	7	7	0	Paxtang	3	3	0
Morton	4	4	0	Pen Argyl	5	5	0
Mount Holly Springs	3	3	0	Penbrook	6	6	0
Mount Joy	12	10	2	Penn Hills	65	56	9
Mount Lebanon	57	46	11	Pennridge Regional	23	15	8
Mount Pleasant	5	5	0	Penn Township (Butler County)	4	3	1
Mount Union	6	6	0	Penn Township (Lancaster County)	8	7	1
Muhlenberg Township	29	27	2	Penn Township (Westmoreland County)	22	20	2
Munhall	23	19	4	Penn Township (York County)	24	22	2
Murrysville	26	21	5	Perkasie	17	15	2
Nanticoke	13	12	1	Peters Township	23	21	2
Narberth	7	7	0	Philadelphia	7,844	6,932	912
Neshannock Township	7	7	0	Philipsburg	1	1	0
Nether Providence Township	17	15	2	Phoenixville	26	24	2
Neville Township	7	5	2	Pine-Marshall-Bradford Woods	19	18	1
Newberry Township	12	11	1	Pittsburgh	981	896	85
New Bethlehem	1	1	0	Plains Township	14	13	1
New Britain	4	3	1	Pleasant Hills	24	19	5
New Britain Township	13	11	2	Plumstead Township	15	13	2
New Cumberland	9	8	1	Plymouth Township (Luzerne County)	2	2	0
New Hanover Township	9	8	1	Plymouth Township (Montgomery County)	54	46	8
New Holland	12	11	1	Pocono Mountain Regional	39	35	4
New Hope	11	9	2	Point Township	5	5	0
Newport	2	2	0	Portage	2	2	0
New Sewickley Township	9	8	1	Port Allegany	3	3	0
Newtown	4	3	1	Pottstown	48	39	9
Newtown Township (Bucks County)	32	29	3	Pottsville	32	31	1
Newtown Township (Delaware County)	18	16	2	Prospect Park	9	9	0
Newville	1	1	0	Punxsutawney	11	7	4
New Wilmington	4	4	0	Pymatuning Township	3	3	0
Norristown	78	67	11	Quakertown	14	12	2
Northampton	13	12	1	Rankin	1	1	0
Northampton Township	47	41	6	Reading	241	212	29
North Apollo	1	1	0	Reynoldsville	2	2	0
North Catasauqua	5	5	0	Rice Township	4	4	0
North Cornwall Township	10	9	1	Richland Township (Allegheny County)	11	10	1
North Coventry Township	13	12	1	Richland Township (Bucks County)	9	8	1
North East	7	6	1				

Table 78

Full-time Law Enforcement Employees as of October 31, 2003
by City by State—Continued

City by state	Total law enforcement employees	Total officers	Total civilians	City by state	Total law enforcement employees	Total officers	Total civilians
PENNSYLVANIA—Continued				**PENNSYLVANIA—Continued**			
Ridgway	7	6	1	St. Marys City	14	13	1
Ridley Park	14	10	4	Stonycreek Township	2	2	0
Ridley Township	41	33	8	Strasburg	4	4	0
Rimersburg	1	1	0	Stroud Area Regional	59	55	4
Roaring Spring	2	2	0	Sugarcreek	6	6	0
Robesonia	2	2	0	Sugarloaf Township (Luzerne County)	3	3	0
Robeson Township	6	5	1	Sunbury	17	15	2
Robinson Township (Allegheny County)	20	15	5	Susquehanna Township (Dauphin			
Rochester	13	11	2	County)	39	37	2
Rochester Township	2	2	0	Swarthmore	9	9	0
Rosslyn Farms	2	2	0	Swissvale	11	11	0
Ross Township	43	41	2	Swoyersville	7	7	0
Rostraver Township	15	14	1	Sykesville	1	1	0
Salisbury Township	14	12	2	Tamaqua	10	9	1
Saltsburg	1	1	0	Tarentum	11	7	4
Sandy Township	7	7	0	Telford	8	7	1
Sayre	11	9	2	Terre Hill	5	5	0
Schuylkill Township	11	10	1	Tinicum Township (Bucks County)	5	5	0
Scottdale	7	7	0	Tinicum Township (Delaware County)	14	13	1
Scott Township (Columbia County)	5	5	0	Titusville	16	16	0
Scranton	170	150	20	Towamencin Township	33	25	8
Selinsgrove	6	5	1	Towanda	7	7	0
Sewickley	9	8	1	Trainer	7	7	0
Sewickley Heights	8	7	1	Troy	3	3	0
Shaler Township	28	27	1	Tullytown	7	6	1
Sharon Hill	8	7	1	Tunkhannock	5	5	0
Sharpsburg	7	7	0	Tunkhannock Township (Wyoming			
Sharpsville	7	6	1	County)	4	4	0
Shenandoah	8	7	1	Union City	1	1	0
Shenango Township (Lawrence County)	5	5	0	Uniontown	16	16	0
Shippingport	2	2	0	Upland	2	2	0
Shiremanstown	2	2	0	Upper Allen Township	16	15	1
Silver Spring Township	12	11	1	Upper Chichester Township	24	20	4
Sinking Spring	5	5	0	Upper Darby Township	135	125	10
Slatington	6	6	0	Upper Dublin Township	45	39	6
Slippery Rock	5	5	0	Upper Gwynedd Township	22	20	2
Smethport	2	2	0	Upper Leacock Township	41	37	4
Solebury Township	14	13	1	Upper Makefield Township	12	11	1
South Beaver Township	4	4	0	Upper Merion Township	89	62	27
South Buffalo Township	2	2	0	Upper Moreland Township	49	38	11
South Centre Township	3	3	0	Upper Perkiomen	8	7	1
Southern Regional (Lancaster County)	7	7	0	Upper Pottsgrove Township	7	7	0
South Fayette Township	16	15	1	Upper Providence Township			
South Greensburg	2	2	0	(Delaware County)	11	10	1
South Heidelberg Township	5	5	0	Upper Providence Township			
South Lebanon Township	8	7	1	(Montgomery County)	19	17	2
South Londonderry Township	6	6	0	Upper Saucon Township	18	17	1
South Park Township	17	16	1	Upper Southampton Township	25	22	3
South Pymatuning Township	2	2	0	Upper St. Clair Township	35	28	7
South Waverly	3	3	0	Upper Uwchlan Township	9	9	0
Southwest Greensburg	2	2	0	Uwchlan Township	26	24	2
Southwest Mercer County Regional	16	14	2	Vandergrift	8	8	0
South Whitehall Township	40	37	3	Vernon Township	3	3	0
South Williamsport	7	6	1	Walnutport	4	4	0
Spring City	4	3	1	Warminster Township	56	47	9
Springdale	1	1	0	Warren	20	15	5
Springettsbury Township	30	28	2	Warrington Township	32	29	3
Springfield Township (Bucks County)	5	5	0	Warwick Township (Bucks County)	21	19	2
Springfield Township (Delaware County)	43	36	7	Warwick Township (Lancaster County)	17	16	1
Springfield Township (Montgomery				Washington Township (Franklin			
County)	30	29	1	County)	13	12	1
Spring Garden Township	19	17	2	Washington Township (Westmoreland			
Spring Township (Berks County)	23	22	1	County)	6	6	0
Spring Township (Centre County)	6	5	1	Watsontown	4	4	0
State College	74	62	12	Waynesboro	17	15	2
St. Clair Township	2	2	0	Waynesburg	9	8	1
Steelton	9	8	1	Weatherly	4	4	0
Stewartstown	5	5	0	Wellsboro	5	5	0

Table 78

Full-time Law Enforcement Employees as of October 31, 2003

by City by State—Continued

City by state	Total law enforcement employees	Total officers	Total civilians	City by state	Total law enforcement employees	Total officers	Total civilians
PENNSYLVANIA—Continued				**RHODE ISLAND—Continued**			
Wernersville	2	2	0	Narragansett	50	38	12
West Alexander	2	2	0	Newport	109	87	22
West Brandywine Township	6	6	0	New Shoreham	9	4	5
West Carroll Township	1	1	0	North Kingstown	63	52	11
West Chester	49	39	10	North Providence	93	71	22
West Conshohocken	10	9	1	North Smithfield	26	22	4
West Deer Township	9	8	1	Pawtucket	185	153	32
West Donegal Township	8	8	0	Portsmouth	34	32	2
West Elizabeth	17	16	1	Providence	544	463	81
Westfall Township	5	5	0	Richmond	15	11	4
West Goshen Township	33	26	7	Scituate	26	18	8
West Hempfield Township	22	20	2	Smithfield	53	40	13
West Hills Regional	12	11	1	South Kingstown	73	55	18
West Homestead	5	4	1	Tiverton	34	26	8
West Lampeter Township	14	13	1	Warren	27	22	5
West Lebanon Township	10	9	1	Warwick	228	180	48
West Manchester Township	29	26	3	Westerly	60	48	12
West Manheim Township	7	7	0	West Greenwich	17	11	6
West Mifflin	42	36	6	West Warwick	69	57	12
West Norriton Township	32	27	5	Woonsocket	122	101	21
West Pikeland Township	3	3	0				
West Pittston	3	3	0	**SOUTH CAROLINA**			
West Pottsgrove Township	10	9	1				
West Reading	14	12	2	Abbeville	22	19	3
West Shore Regional	12	10	2	Aiken	103	83	20
Westtown-East Goshen Township	32	29	3	Allendale	8	7	1
West View	10	9	1	Anderson	119	90	29
West Whiteland Township	29	27	2	Andrews	13	12	1
West Wyoming	2	2	0	Aynor	8	6	2
Whitehall	25	20	5	Bamberg	11	10	1
Whitehall Township	55	47	8	Barnwell	15	13	2
White Haven Borough	2	2	0	Batesburg-Leesville	24	19	5
Whitpain Township	36	29	7	Beaufort	50	45	5
Wilkes-Barre	99	88	11	Belton	16	11	5
Wilkes-Barre Township	14	12	2	Bethune	1	1	0
Wilkinsburg	37	30	7	Bishopville	17	15	2
Wilkins Township	12	12	0	Blacksburg	15	14	1
Williamsport	59	55	4	Blackville	4	3	1
Willistown Township	17	15	2	Bluffton	10	10	0
Windber	3	2	1	Bonneau	3	3	0
Wright Township	6	6	0	Bowman	3	3	0
Wyomissing	27	22	5	Branchville	1	1	0
Yardley	3	3	0	Calhoun Falls	11	10	1
Yeadon	14	12	2	Camden	30	26	4
York Area Regional	50	45	5	Campobello	5	5	0
York Springs-Latimore Township	2	2	0	Cayce	68	55	13
Youngsville	2	2	0	Central	11	10	1
				Chapin	7	6	1
RHODE ISLAND				Charleston	487	356	131
				Cheraw	25	25	0
Barrington	30	23	7	Chester	29	24	5
Bristol	47	36	11	Chesterfield	5	4	1
Burrillville	35	25	10	Clemson	33	25	8
Central Falls	46	37	9	Clinton	32	26	6
Charlestown	26	21	5	Clio	5	4	1
Coventry	69	56	13	Clover	16	12	4
Cranston	188	149	39	Columbia	377	302	75
Cumberland	54	46	8	Conway	65	50	15
East Greenwich	40	31	9	Cottageville	5	5	0
East Providence	124	98	26	Coward	1	1	0
Foster	12	7	5	Darlington	27	24	3
Glocester	19	14	5	Denmark	13	11	2
Hopkinton	21	16	5	Dillon	28	23	5
Jamestown	17	13	4	Due West	5	5	0
Johnston	92	75	17	Easley	45	34	11
Lincoln	42	34	8	Eastover	4	4	0
Little Compton	13	9	4	Edgefield	9	9	0
Middletown	41	38	3	Edisto Beach	5	5	0

Table 78

Full-time Law Enforcement Employees as of October 31, 2003
by City by State—Continued

City by state	Total law enforcement employees	Total officers	Total civilians	City by state	Total law enforcement employees	Total officers	Total civilians
SOUTH CAROLINA—Continued				**SOUTH CAROLINA—Continued**			
Elgin	4	4	0	Perry	1	1	0
Elloree	3	3	0	Pickens	12	12	0
Estill	10	7	3	Pine Ridge	2	1	1
Eutawville	3	3	0	Port Royal	19	17	2
Fairfax	8	7	1	Prosperity	4	4	0
Florence	111	88	23	Ridgeland	11	10	1
Folly Beach	17	11	6	Ridge Spring	2	2	0
Forest Acres	34	26	8	Ridgeville	2	2	0
Fort Lawn	2	2	0	Ridgeway	2	2	0
Fort Mill	27	21	6	Rock Hill	145	107	38
Fountain Inn	29	22	7	Salem	3	3	0
Gaffney	44	40	4	Salley	2	2	0
Georgetown	46	38	8	Saluda	12	11	1
Goose Creek	69	53	16	Santee	12	8	4
Great Falls	6	5	1	Scranton	3	2	1
Greeleyville	3	2	1	Seneca	44	33	11
Greenville	230	185	45	Simpsonville	46	36	10
Greenwood	62	53	9	Society Hill	16	5	11
Hampton	9	8	1	South Congaree	7	6	1
Hanahan	31	23	8	Spartanburg	147	125	22
Hartsville	38	35	3	Springdale	8	8	0
Hemingway	7	3	4	St. George	10	9	1
Holly Hill	10	9	1	St. Matthews	7	7	0
Honea Path	15	11	4	St. Stephen	7	7	0
Irmo	20	18	2	Sullivans Island	9	8	1
Isle of Palms	24	16	8	Summerton	10	9	1
Iva	6	5	1	Summerville	84	64	20
Jackson	4	4	0	Sumter	157	108	49
Johnsonville	5	4	1	Surfside Beach	21	15	6
Johnston	8	8	0	Swansea	5	4	1
Jonesville	6	6	0	Timmonsville	7	6	1
Kingstree	20	18	2	Travelers Rest	22	15	7
Lake View	3	3	0	Turbeville	3	3	0
Lamar	5	5	0	Union	33	31	2
Lancaster	47	38	9	Vance	2	2	0
Landrum	9	8	1	Wagener	4	4	0
Lane	1	1	0	Walhalla	15	14	1
Latta	10	10	0	Walterboro	28	19	9
Laurens	36	30	6	Ware Shoals	10	9	1
Lexington	34	29	5	Wellford	6	5	1
Liberty	14	13	1	West Columbia	52	41	11
Loris	13	9	4	Westminster	10	9	1
Lyman	8	7	1	West Union	2	2	0
Lynchburg	3	3	0	Whitmire	4	4	0
Manning	21	19	2	Williamston	19	13	6
Marion	31	28	3	Williston	9	8	1
McBee	3	3	0	Winnsboro	26	24	2
McColl	4	3	1	Yemassee	5	4	1
McCormick	5	5	0	York	34	28	6
Moncks Corner	24	22	2				
Mount Pleasant	167	127	40	**SOUTH DAKOTA**			
Mullins	21	18	3				
Myrtle Beach	235	176	59	Aberdeen	50	41	9
Newberry	29	25	4	Alcester	1	1	0
New Ellenton	6	6	0	Armour	1	1	0
Nichols	3	3	0	Avon	1	1	0
Ninety Six	8	7	1	Belle Fourche	10	9	1
North	4	3	1	Beresford	8	4	4
North Augusta	63	47	16	Box Elder	8	7	1
North Charleston	344	270	74	Brandon	9	8	1
North Myrtle Beach	101	74	27	Brookings	33	25	8
Norway	8	3	5	Burke	1	1	0
Olar	1	1	0	Canistota	1	1	0
Orangeburg	94	80	14	Canton	5	5	0
Pacolet	5	5	0	Castlewood	1	1	0
Pageland	16	11	5	Centerville	1	1	0
Pawleys Island	5	4	1	Chamberlain	5	5	0
Pendleton	11	10	1	Chancellor-Davis	1	1	0

Table 78

Full-time Law Enforcement Employees as of October 31, 2003
by City by State—Continued

City by state	Total law enforcement employees	Total officers	Total civilians	City by state	Total law enforcement employees	Total officers	Total civilians
SOUTH DAKOTA—Continued				**TENNESSEE—Continued**			
Clark	2	2	0	Atoka	8	8	0
Colman	1	1	0	Baileyton	1	1	0
Corsica	1	1	0	Bartlett	115	84	31
Deadwood	12	9	3	Baxter	6	5	1
Eagle Butte	3	3	0	Bean Station	8	7	1
Elk Point	5	4	1	Belle Meade	20	16	4
Estelline	1	1	0	Bells	5	5	0
Eureka	3	3	0	Benton	8	7	1
Faith	4	1	3	Berry Hill	17	13	4
Garretson	2	2	0	Bethel Springs	2	1	1
Gettysburg	1	1	0	Big Sandy	2	2	0
Gregory	3	3	0	Blaine	5	3	2
Groton	3	3	0	Bluff City	9	9	0
Harrisburg	2	2	0	Bolivar	28	22	6
Highmore	1	1	0	Bradford	4	3	1
Hot Springs	8	7	1	Brentwood	65	52	13
Huron	29	23	6	Brighton	5	5	0
Jefferson	1	1	0	Bristol	86	66	20
Kadoka	1	1	0	Brownsville	31	26	5
Kimball	1	1	0	Bruceton	4	4	0
Lake Andes	4	4	0	Burns	4	4	0
Lead	6	5	1	Calhoun	4	3	1
Lemmon	3	3	0	Camden	17	12	5
Lennox	4	4	0	Carthage	12	7	5
Madison	11	10	1	Caryville	5	5	0
McIntosh	1	1	0	Celina	5	4	1
McLaughlin	2	1	1	Centerville	18	13	5
Milbank	5	5	0	Chapel Hill	5	5	0
Miller	4	4	0	Charleston	4	3	1
Mitchell	35	27	8	Chattanooga	600	432	168
Mobridge	12	7	5	Church Hill	9	8	1
Montrose	1	1	0	Clarksville	243	213	30
Murdo	1	1	0	Cleveland	98	87	11
New Effington	1	1	0	Clifton	7	7	0
North Sioux City	6	5	1	Clinton	32	30	2
Parkston	2	2	0	Collegedale	16	15	1
Philip	2	2	0	Collierville	114	78	36
Pierre	34	23	11	Collinwood	3	3	0
Platte	2	2	0	Columbia	93	84	9
Rapid City	134	106	28	Cookeville	88	68	20
Salem	2	2	0	Coopertown	2	2	0
Selby	1	1	0	Copperhill	3	2	1
Sioux Falls	233	205	28	Cornersville	6	4	2
Sisseton	7	7	0	Covington	31	30	1
Spearfish	23	17	6	Cowan	5	5	0
Sturgis	20	15	5	Cross Plains	3	3	0
Tea	3	3	0	Crossville	38	33	5
Tripp	1	1	0	Crump	2	2	0
Tyndall	2	2	0	Cumberland City	2	2	0
Vermillion	18	16	2	Cumberland Gap	1	1	0
Viborg	1	1	0	Dandridge	10	9	1
Watertown	42	31	11	Dayton	15	13	2
Webster	4	4	0	Decatur	5	5	0
Whitewood	2	2	0	Decaturville	2	2	0
Winner	20	8	12	Decherd	14	13	1
Worthing	1	1	0	Dickson	48	43	5
Yankton	45	26	19	Dover	6	6	0
				Dresden	9	8	1
TENNESSEE				Dunlap	10	9	1
				Dyer	6	6	0
Adamsville	9	6	3	Dyersburg	82	60	22
Alamo	3	3	0	Eagleville	2	2	0
Alcoa	42	36	6	East Ridge	41	34	7
Alexandria	4	4	0	Elizabethton	40	37	3
Algood	9	8	1	Elkton	1	1	0
Ardmore	11	7	4	Englewood	6	6	0
Ashland City	14	13	1	Erin	6	6	0
Athens	29	27	2	Erwin	10	10	0

Table 78

Full-time Law Enforcement Employees as of October 31, 2003

by City by State—Continued

City by state	Total law enforcement employees	Total officers	Total civilians	City by state	Total law enforcement employees	Total officers	Total civilians
TENNESSEE—Continued				**TENNESSEE—Continued**			
Estill Springs	6	6	0	Mason	9	8	1
Ethridge	1	1	0	Maynardville	4	4	0
Etowah	13	9	4	McEwen	5	4	1
Fairview	16	15	1	McKenzie	19	15	4
Fayetteville	25	23	2	McMinnville	36	32	4
Franklin	126	102	24	Medina	6	6	0
Friendship	1	1	0	Memphis	2,668	1,931	737
Gainesboro	5	5	0	Middleton	3	3	0
Gallatin	64	47	17	Milan	29	24	5
Gallaway	6	6	0	Millersville	17	13	4
Gates	2	2	0	Millington	33	26	7
Gatlinburg	51	42	9	Minor Hill	3	2	1
Germantown	100	79	21	Monteagle	10	6	4
Gibson	2	2	0	Monterey	8	8	0
Gleason	5	5	0	Morristown	80	74	6
Goodlettsville	49	36	13	Moscow	5	5	0
Gordonsville	5	5	0	Mountain City	9	9	0
Grand Junction	3	3	0	Mount Carmel	8	8	0
Graysville	3	3	0	Mount Juliet	35	27	8
Greenbrier	11	10	1	Mount Pleasant	13	12	1
Greeneville	46	44	2	Munford	13	12	1
Greenfield	9	8	1	Murfreesboro	188	149	39
Halls	7	7	0	Nashville	1,712	1,294	418
Harriman	25	24	1	Newbern	19	13	6
Henderson	14	13	1	New Hope	1	1	0
Hendersonville	82	63	19	New Johnsonville	4	4	0
Henning	3	3	0	New Market	2	2	0
Henry	2	2	0	Newport	32	25	7
Hohenwald	14	13	1	New Tazewell	9	9	0
Hollow Rock	3	2	1	Niota	4	3	1
Hornbeak	2	1	1	Nolensville	1	1	0
Humboldt	32	26	6	Norris	7	7	0
Huntingdon	16	12	4	Oakland	13	11	2
Huntland	4	4	0	Oak Ridge	67	55	12
Jacksboro	6	6	0	Obion	4	4	0
Jackson	239	185	54	Oliver Springs	14	10	4
Jamestown	8	7	1	Oneida	19	14	5
Jasper	8	8	0	Paris	36	26	10
Jefferson City	21	19	2	Parsons	7	7	0
Jellico	10	10	0	Petersburg	3	3	0
Johnson City	180	152	28	Pigeon Forge	66	54	12
Jonesborough	20	15	5	Pikeville	4	4	0
Kenton	5	5	0	Pittman Center	2	2	0
Kimball	7	7	0	Pleasant View	3	3	0
Kingsport	136	95	41	Portland	27	21	6
Kingston	12	11	1	Powells Crossroads	2	2	0
Kingston Springs	6	5	1	Pulaski	28	25	3
Knoxville	493	397	96	Puryear	1	1	0
Lafayette	25	16	9	Red Bank	22	20	2
La Follette	23	16	7	Red Boiling Springs	5	5	0
La Grange	1	1	0	Ridgely	6	5	1
Lake City	10	7	3	Ridgetop	6	6	0
Lakewood	7	7	0	Ripley	31	25	6
La Vergne	49	34	15	Rockwood	17	16	1
Lawrenceburg	44	38	6	Rogersville	13	13	0
Lebanon	83	67	16	Rossville	4	4	0
Lenoir City	21	20	1	Rutherford	5	5	0
Lewisburg	38	30	8	Rutledge	6	4	2
Lexington	30	25	5	Savannah	27	16	11
Livingston	22	17	5	Scotts Hill	4	4	0
Lookout Mountain	21	16	5	Selmer	18	17	1
Loretto	4	4	0	Sevierville	62	48	14
Loudon	15	14	1	Sewanee	13	9	4
Lynnville	1	1	0	Sharon	1	1	0
Madisonville	16	14	2	Shelbyville	50	39	11
Manchester	35	30	5	Signal Mountain	16	14	2
Martin	35	28	7	Smithville	14	9	5
Maryville	53	43	10	Smyrna	79	57	22

Table 78

Full-time Law Enforcement Employees as of October 31, 2003
by City by State—Continued

City by state	Total law enforcement employees	Total officers	Total civilians	City by state	Total law enforcement employees	Total officers	Total civilians
TENNESSEE—Continued				**TEXAS—Continued**			
Sneedville	1	1	0	Athens	35	27	8
Soddy-Daisy	26	21	5	Atlanta	20	15	5
Somerville	17	14	3	Austin	1,744	1,314	430
South Carthage	4	4	0	Azle	30	21	9
South Fulton	8	7	1	Baird	2	2	0
South Pittsburg	12	8	4	Balch Springs	43	30	13
Sparta	16	15	1	Balcones Heights	20	15	5
Spencer	2	2	0	Ballinger	7	5	2
Spring City	10	9	1	Bangs	3	3	0
Springfield	50	38	12	Bartlett	4	4	0
Spring Hill	21	20	1	Bastrop	18	16	2
St. Joseph	1	1	0	Bay City	49	35	14
Surgoinsville	3	3	0	Bayou Vista	5	5	0
Sweetwater	19	17	2	Baytown	169	116	53
Tazewell	6	6	0	Beaumont	310	250	60
Tellico Plains	4	4	0	Bedford	116	70	46
Tiptonville	6	6	0	Beeville	24	19	5
Toone	1	1	0	Bellaire	52	39	13
Townsend	3	3	0	Bellmead	22	16	6
Tracy City	5	4	1	Bellville	11	10	1
Trenton	25	19	6	Belton	33	24	9
Trezevant	1	1	0	Benbrook	47	35	12
Trimble	3	3	0	Beverly Hills	12	8	4
Troy	4	4	0	Big Sandy	6	5	1
Tullahoma	39	34	5	Big Spring	61	40	21
Tusculum	2	2	0	Bishop	8	4	4
Union City	45	38	7	Blanco	4	4	0
Vonore	7	7	0	Bloomburg	1	1	0
Wartburg	3	3	0	Blue Mound	10	6	4
Wartrace	1	1	0	Boerne	36	22	14
Watauga	1	1	0	Bogata	3	3	0
Watertown	5	4	1	Bonham	29	22	7
Waverly	12	11	1	Borger	35	25	10
Waynesboro	9	8	1	Bovina	2	2	0
Westmoreland	9	5	4	Bowie	18	13	5
White Bluff	4	4	0	Brady	15	8	7
White House	27	19	8	Brazoria	12	8	4
White Pine	8	7	1	Breckenridge	17	11	6
Whiteville	8	8	0	Brenham	33	28	5
Whitwell	7	5	2	Bridge City	19	13	6
Winchester	23	22	1	Bridgeport	19	12	7
Winfield	3	3	0	Brookshire	11	7	4
Woodbury	9	8	1	Brookside Village	5	5	0
				Brownfield	24	17	7
TEXAS				Brownsville	295	218	77
				Brownwood	53	33	20
Abernathy	4	4	0	Bruceville-Eddy	3	3	0
Abilene	216	162	54	Bryan	141	106	35
Addison	80	60	20	Bullard	5	4	1
Alamo	32	23	9	Burkburnett	23	18	5
Alamo Heights	29	21	8	Burleson	56	41	15
Alice	49	36	13	Burnet	14	13	1
Allen	112	85	27	Caddo Mills	2	2	0
Alpine	13	8	5	Caldwell	11	10	1
Alto	4	3	1	Cameron	14	9	5
Alton	12	7	5	Caney City	2	2	0
Alvarado	17	12	5	Canton	21	15	6
Alvin	69	43	26	Canyon	23	20	3
Amarillo	369	283	86	Carrollton	198	136	62
Andrews	22	16	6	Carthage	21	14	7
Angleton	44	33	11	Castle Hills	27	21	6
Anson	6	5	1	Cedar Hill	62	51	11
Anthony	11	9	2	Cedar Park	70	51	19
Aransas Pass	24	17	7	Celina	6	6	0
Arcola	7	6	1	Center	21	14	7
Argyle	7	7	0	Childress	12	8	4
Arlington	707	540	167	Chillicothe	2	2	0
Arp	4	4	0	Cisco	7	6	1

Table 78

Full-time Law Enforcement Employees as of October 31, 2003
by City by State—Continued

City by state	Total law enforcement employees	Total officers	Total civilians	City by state	Total law enforcement employees	Total officers	Total civilians
TEXAS—Continued				**TEXAS—Continued**			
Clarksville	9	9	0	Edna	11	9	2
Cleburne	63	46	17	El Campo	33	23	10
Cleveland	28	20	8	Electra	12	6	6
Clifton	6	5	1	Elgin	21	14	7
Clint	2	2	0	El Paso	1,449	1,126	323
Clute	37	23	14	Elsa	19	11	8
Clyde	4	4	0	Ennis	39	33	6
Cockrell Hill	16	11	5	Euless	115	80	35
Coffee City	2	2	0	Everman	16	11	5
Coleman	15	9	6	Fairfield	7	7	0
College Station	141	96	45	Fair Oaks Ranch	12	12	0
Colleyville	41	31	10	Falfurrias	11	10	1
Collinsville	2	2	0	Farmers Branch	112	71	41
Colorado City	14	7	7	Farmersville	7	7	0
Columbus	10	9	1	Farwell	1	1	0
Comanche	8	7	1	Ferris	15	11	4
Combes	6	6	0	Flatonia	4	4	0
Commerce	21	15	6	Florence	2	2	0
Conroe	105	80	25	Floresville	14	13	1
Converse	26	23	3	Flower Mound	95	64	31
Coppell	68	55	13	Floydada	5	5	0
Copperas Cove	65	51	14	Forest Hill	30	23	7
Corinth	23	22	1	Forney	20	13	7
Corpus Christi	615	444	171	Fort Stockton	22	16	6
Corrigan	9	6	3	Fort Worth	1,600	1,263	337
Corsicana	60	45	15	Frankston	3	3	0
Cottonwood Shores	2	2	0	Fredericksburg	28	25	3
Crane	11	7	4	Freeport	35	26	9
Crockett	19	16	3	Freer	10	5	5
Crowell	1	1	0	Friendswood	63	47	16
Crowley	24	18	6	Friona	10	6	4
Crystal City	14	10	4	Frisco	95	71	24
Cuero	14	12	2	Gainesville	55	38	17
Daingerfield	7	6	1	Galena Park	24	18	6
Dalhart	18	15	3	Galveston	204	160	44
Dallas	3,510	2,973	537	Ganado	4	3	1
Dalworthington Gardens	18	12	6	Garland	453	298	155
Danbury	3	3	0	Gatesville	21	15	6
Dayton	19	14	5	Georgetown	70	49	21
Decatur	19	13	6	Giddings	16	10	6
Deer Park	65	48	17	Gilmer	18	15	3
De Kalb	9	6	3	Gladewater	21	15	6
De Leon	5	5	0	Glenn Heights	20	14	6
Del Rio	86	65	21	Godley	3	3	0
Denison	56	44	12	Gonzales	20	15	5
Denton	174	137	37	Gorman	5	4	1
Denver City	13	8	5	Graham	19	18	1
DeSoto	72	60	12	Granbury	27	23	4
Devine	11	9	2	Grand Prairie	296	200	96
Diboll	18	12	6	Grand Saline	7	7	0
Dickinson	37	28	9	Granger	3	3	0
Dilley	7	6	1	Granite Shoals	7	7	0
Dimmitt	9	7	2	Grapeland	3	2	1
Donna	33	22	11	Grapevine	130	94	36
Double Oak	3	3	0	Greenville	73	46	27
Dublin	11	9	2	Gregory	4	4	0
Dumas	28	24	4	Groesbeck	7	7	0
Duncanville	74	62	12	Groves	19	17	2
Eagle Lake	10	9	1	Gruver	2	2	0
Eagle Pass	86	68	18	Gun Barrel City	20	15	5
Early	7	6	1	Hale Center	3	3	0
Earth	2	2	0	Hallettsville	7	6	1
Eastland	11	9	2	Haltom City	84	62	22
East Mountain	1	1	0	Hamlin	9	5	4
Edcouch	14	9	5	Harker Heights	43	36	7
Eden	4	4	0	Harlingen	136	104	32
Edgewood	4	4	0	Hart	1	1	0
Edinburg	109	76	33	Haskell	4	4	0

Table 78

Full-time Law Enforcement Employees as of October 31, 2003

by City by State—Continued

City by state	Total law enforcement employees	Total officers	Total civilians	City by state	Total law enforcement employees	Total officers	Total civilians
TEXAS—Continued				**TEXAS—Continued**			
Hawk Cove	1	1	0	Kingsville	59	46	13
Hawkins	5	5	0	Kirby	16	12	4
Hearne	16	9	7	Kirbyville	5	5	0
Heath	12	11	1	Knox City	2	2	0
Hedwig Village	22	15	7	Kountze	5	5	0
Helotes	14	13	1	Kress	1	1	0
Hemphill	3	3	0	Kyle	14	13	1
Hempstead	14	12	2	Lacy-Lakeview	22	14	8
Henderson	47	40	7	La Feria	15	11	4
Hereford	27	21	6	Lago Vista	21	14	7
Hewitt	29	21	8	La Grange	8	8	0
Hickory Creek	11	11	0	Laguna Vista	3	3	0
Hico	4	4	0	La Joya	18	13	5
Hidalgo	44	32	12	Lake Dallas	17	10	7
Highland Park	68	55	13	Lake Jackson	57	42	15
Highland Village	31	23	8	Lakeside	4	4	0
Hill Country Village	10	10	0	Lakeview	16	12	4
Hillsboro	27	18	9	Lakeway	32	26	6
Hitchcock	18	13	5	Lake Worth	26	19	7
Holland	1	1	0	La Marque	31	24	7
Holliday	2	2	0	Lamesa	22	16	6
Hollywood Park	9	9	0	Lampasas	26	17	9
Hondo	19	16	3	Lancaster	58	42	16
Hooks	5	5	0	La Porte	96	70	26
Horizon City	10	9	1	Laredo	472	387	85
Horseshoe Bay	11	10	1	La Vernia	4	4	0
Houston	6,804	5,372	1,432	La Villa	1	1	0
Howe	6	6	0	Lavon	5	4	1
Hubbard	4	4	0	League City	102	66	36
Hudson	4	4	0	Leander	34	22	12
Hudson Oaks	10	9	1	Leon Valley	26	18	8
Humble	75	58	17	Levelland	27	19	8
Huntsville	53	47	6	Lewisville	176	125	51
Hurst	108	69	39	Lexington	4	4	0
Hutchins	16	11	5	Liberty	22	13	9
Hutto	10	9	1	Lindale	15	11	4
Idalou	3	3	0	Linden	4	4	0
Ingleside	21	15	6	Littlefield	20	13	7
Ingram	7	6	1	Live Oak	40	27	13
Iowa Park	17	11	6	Livingston	21	14	7
Irving	450	313	137	Llano	9	7	2
Italy	5	5	0	Lockhart	36	27	9
Itasca	3	3	0	Lockney	3	3	0
Jacinto City	24	18	6	Lone Star	5	4	1
Jacksboro	16	10	6	Longview	158	137	21
Jacksonville	34	25	9	Lorena	5	5	0
Jamaica Beach	6	5	1	Lorenzo	2	2	0
Jasper	26	18	8	Los Fresnos	10	6	4
Jefferson	7	6	1	Lubbock	407	308	99
Jersey Village	31	22	9	Lufkin	98	75	23
Johnson City	4	4	0	Luling	24	15	9
Jones Creek	3	3	0	Lumberton	18	14	4
Joshua	15	13	2	Lytle	5	5	0
Jourdanton	6	6	0	Madisonville	11	10	1
Junction	5	5	0	Magnolia	14	11	3
Karnes City	7	6	1	Malakoff	7	6	1
Katy	57	42	15	Manor	7	6	1
Kaufman	23	16	7	Mansfield	69	49	20
Keene	14	10	4	Manvel	8	8	0
Keller	64	46	18	Marble Falls	31	21	10
Kemah	24	19	5	Marfa	4	3	1
Kemp	6	6	0	Marlin	21	17	4
Kenedy	10	7	3	Marshall	61	49	12
Kennedale	24	17	7	Mart	4	4	0
Kermit	15	9	6	Martindale	5	5	0
Kerrville	64	48	16	Mathis	12	7	5
Kilgore	39	31	8	McAllen	369	240	129
Killeen	188	149	39	McGregor	17	12	5

Table 78

Full-time Law Enforcement Employees as of October 31, 2003
by City by State—Continued

City by state	Total law enforcement employees	Total officers	Total civilians	City by state	Total law enforcement employees	Total officers	Total civilians
TEXAS—Continued				**TEXAS—Continued**			
McKinney	117	94	23	Pharr	116	84	32
Meadows Place	16	16	0	Pilot Point	5	5	0
Melissa	6	5	1	Pinehurst	10	6	4
Memorial Villages	38	32	6	Pittsburg	14	12	2
Memphis	4	4	0	Plainview	39	32	7
Mercedes	29	22	7	Plano	459	325	134
Meridian	3	2	1	Pleasanton	22	16	6
Merkel	5	4	1	Point Comfort	1	1	0
Mesquite	265	200	65	Port Aransas	21	13	8
Mexia	23	18	5	Port Arthur	140	108	32
Midland	208	160	48	Port Isabel	23	18	5
Midlothian	32	25	7	Portland	28	20	8
Mineola	14	12	2	Port Lavaca	25	19	6
Mineral Wells	35	26	9	Port Neches	21	18	3
Mission	149	111	38	Poteet	6	5	1
Missouri City	79	59	20	Pottsboro	6	6	0
Monahans	17	10	7	Premont	4	4	0
Mont Belvieu	15	10	5	Presidio	3	3	0
Montgomery	7	7	0	Primera	5	5	0
Morgans Point Resort	7	7	0	Princeton	6	5	1
Mount Pleasant	37	27	10	Progreso	4	4	0
Muleshoe	12	7	5	Quanah	4	4	0
Munday	2	2	0	Queen City	5	5	0
Mustang Ridge	5	3	2	Quinlan	6	6	0
Nacogdoches	73	58	15	Quitman	6	6	0
Naples	2	2	0	Ranger	6	5	1
Nash	9	8	1	Ransom Canyon	2	2	0
Nassau Bay	16	12	4	Raymondville	22	15	7
Navasota	26	17	9	Red Oak	19	12	7
Nederland	32	21	11	Refugio	11	8	3
Needville	7	7	0	Reno	5	4	1
New Boston	12	9	3	Richardson	219	132	87
New Braunfels	88	69	19	Richland Hills	23	17	6
New Deal	3	2	1	Richmond	36	26	10
Nocona	12	6	6	Richwood	6	5	1
Nolanville	6	6	0	Riesel	3	2	1
Northlake	6	6	0	Rio Grande City	30	22	8
North Richland Hills	152	105	47	Rising Star	1	1	0
Oak Ridge	1	1	0	River Oaks	23	17	6
Oak Ridge North	15	14	1	Roanoke	26	18	8
Odessa	208	159	49	Robinson	21	14	7
O'Donnell	1	1	0	Robstown	32	24	8
Olmos Park	12	12	0	Rockdale	14	10	4
Olney	9	5	4	Rockport	25	19	6
Olton	5	5	0	Rockwall	68	50	18
Onalaska	7	7	0	Rollingwood	7	7	0
Orange	53	41	12	Roma	33	26	7
Orange Grove	7	7	0	Roman Forest	6	6	0
Overton	9	6	3	Ropesville	1	1	0
Ovilla	8	8	0	Roscoe	1	1	0
Oyster Creek	9	5	4	Rosebud	3	3	0
Paducah	7	2	5	Rose City	2	1	1
Palacios	12	8	4	Round Rock	158	114	44
Palestine	43	35	8	Rowlett	88	62	26
Palmer	8	7	1	Royse City	11	10	1
Pampa	33	23	10	Runaway Bay	5	5	0
Panhandle	3	3	0	Rusk	11	9	2
Pantego	17	12	5	Sabinal	4	3	1
Paris	87	64	23	Sachse	33	24	9
Parker	6	6	0	Saginaw	30	25	5
Pasadena	345	253	92	Salado	3	3	0
Pearland	113	85	28	San Angelo	172	142	30
Pearsall	11	10	1	San Antonio	2,504	2,009	495
Pecos	42	22	20	San Augustine	7	6	1
Pelican Bay	4	4	0	San Benito	51	43	8
Penitas	5	4	1	San Diego	9	8	1
Perryton	15	8	7	Sanger	11	11	0
Pflugerville	56	42	14	San Marcos	103	80	23

Table 78

Full-time Law Enforcement Employees as of October 31, 2003

by City by State—Continued

City by state	Total law enforcement employees	Total officers	Total civilians	City by state	Total law enforcement employees	Total officers	Total civilians
TEXAS—Continued				**TEXAS—Continued**			
San Saba	4	3	1	Trophy Club	15	14	1
Sansom Park Village	14	10	4	Troup	5	5	0
Santa Anna	3	2	1	Tulia	11	7	4
Santa Fe	24	18	6	Tye	4	4	0
Santa Rosa	5	5	0	Tyler	237	182	55
Schertz	46	33	13	Universal City	35	26	9
Seabrook	35	29	6	University Park	47	34	13
Seadrift	1	1	0	Van	6	6	0
Seagoville	23	18	5	Van Alstyne	10	8	2
Seagraves	3	3	0	Vernon	29	22	7
Sealy	15	13	2	Victoria	135	91	44
Seguin	58	44	14	Vidor	27	20	7
Selma	20	18	2	Waco	307	215	92
Seminole	13	11	2	Waelder	2	2	0
Seven Points	11	7	4	Wake Village	7	6	1
Seymour	10	7	3	Waller	7	6	1
Shallowater	5	5	0	Wallis	4	4	0
Shamrock	7	2	5	Watauga	49	39	10
Shavano Park	14	13	1	Waxahachie	55	42	13
Shenandoah	19	18	1	Weatherford	69	52	17
Sherman	83	60	23	Webster	58	41	17
Silsbee	21	16	5	Weimar	8	7	1
Sinton	12	11	1	Wells	1	1	0
Slaton	16	10	6	Weslaco	97	65	32
Smithville	17	10	7	West	6	6	0
Snyder	21	17	4	West Lake Hills	21	15	6
Socorro	22	18	4	West Orange	10	9	1
Somerset	4	4	0	Westover Hills	14	11	3
Somerville	4	4	0	West Tawakoni	6	5	1
Sonora	7	5	2	West University Place	31	22	9
Sour Lake	6	5	1	Westworth	13	9	4
South Houston	42	32	10	Wharton	30	21	9
Southlake	61	58	3	Whitehouse	22	16	6
South Padre Island	30	22	8	White Oak	17	13	4
Southside Place	9	5	4	Whitesboro	13	8	5
Spearman	5	4	1	White Settlement	46	30	16
Springtown	13	9	4	Whitney	7	6	1
Spring Valley	21	16	5	Wichita Falls	262	174	88
Spur	2	2	0	Willow Park	9	8	1
Stafford	51	37	14	Wills Point	11	9	2
Stamford	11	7	4	Wilmer	18	13	5
Stanton	4	4	0	Windcrest	22	16	6
Stephenville	41	31	10	Wink	2	2	0
Stratford	3	3	0	Winnsboro	13	8	5
Sugar Land	137	107	30	Winters	4	4	0
Sulphur Springs	37	29	8	Wolfforth	5	5	0
Sunrise Beach Village	2	2	0	Woodville	8	7	1
Sunset Valley	10	10	0	Woodway	35	24	11
Surfside Beach	5	4	1	Wortham	4	3	1
Sweeny	7	7	0	Wylie	29	26	3
Sweetwater	26	21	5	Yoakum	17	10	7
Taft	7	7	0	Yorktown	3	3	0
Tahoka	4	4	0				
Tatum	3	3	0	**UTAH**			
Taylor	40	29	11				
Teague	6	6	0	Alpine/Highland	15	15	0
Temple	146	122	24	Alta	8	4	4
Terrell	45	33	12	American Fork	38	33	5
Terrell Hills	13	13	0	Big Water	2	2	0
Texarkana	93	81	12	Blanding	7	6	1
Texas City	94	77	17	Bountiful	46	33	13
The Colony	57	41	16	Brian Head	5	5	0
Thorndale	2	2	0	Brigham City	29	24	5
Thrall	4	4	0	Cedar City	33	28	5
Three Rivers	7	6	1	Centerville	19	16	3
Tioga	3	2	1	Clearfield	53	32	21
Tool	7	7	0	Clinton	12	11	1
Trinity	10	6	4	East Carbon	2	2	0

Table 78

Full-time Law Enforcement Employees as of October 31, 2003
by City by State—Continued

City by state	Total law enforcement employees	Total officers	Total civilians	City by state	Total law enforcement employees	Total officers	Total civilians
UTAH—Continued				**UTAH—Continued**			
Ephraim	5	5	0	Willard	2	2	0
Fairview	1	1	0	Woods Cross	13	11	2
Farmington	14	11	3				
Garland	4	4	0	**VERMONT**			
Grantsville	10	8	2				
Gunnison	2	2	0	Barre	26	20	6
Harrisville	7	6	1	Barre Town	9	8	1
Heber	13	12	1	Bellows Falls	12	8	4
Helper	6	5	1	Bennington	30	25	5
Hildale	5	5	0	Berlin	7	6	1
Hurricane	16	12	4	Brandon	2	2	0
Kamas	2	2	0	Brattleboro	39	25	14
Kanab	8	6	2	Bristol	3	3	0
Kaysville	20	18	2	Burlington	131	94	37
Layton	99	74	25	Castleton	3	3	0
Lehi	26	24	2	Chester	5	5	0
Logan	85	61	24	Colchester	33	26	7
Mantua	1	1	0	Dover	6	5	1
Mapleton	9	7	2	Essex	32	26	6
Midvale	47	43	4	Fair Haven	3	3	0
Minersville	1	1	0	Hardwick	8	7	1
Moab	16	12	4	Hartford	28	21	7
Monticello	5	4	1	Hinesburg	2	2	0
Moroni	1	1	0	Ludlow	9	5	4
Mount Pleasant	5	5	0	Manchester	12	8	4
Murray	88	69	19	Middlebury	15	14	1
Naples	4	3	1	Milton	14	13	1
Nephi	10	9	1	Montpelier	23	16	7
North Ogden	18	15	3	Morristown	10	9	1
North Park	9	8	1	Newport	13	11	2
North Salt Lake	13	11	2	Northfield	8	7	1
Ogden	151	126	25	Norwich	6	5	1
Orem	117	82	35	Randolph	5	5	0
Park City	33	25	8	Richmond	5	5	0
Parowan	2	2	0	Rutland	52	41	11
Payson	19	17	2	Shelburne	16	10	6
Perry	5	5	0	South Burlington	43	36	7
Pleasant Grove/Lindon	37	31	6	Springfield	17	12	5
Pleasant View	7	6	1	St. Albans	22	14	8
Price	18	16	2	St. Johnsbury	16	11	5
Provo	147	92	55	Stowe	15	13	2
Richfield	16	14	2	Swanton	5	4	1
Riverdale	23	19	4	Thetford	2	2	0
Roosevelt	11	10	1	Vergennes	5	5	0
Roy	42	37	5	Vernon	4	3	1
Salem/Woodland Hills	7	7	0	Waterbury	4	4	0
Salina	7	6	1	Weathersfield	1	1	0
Salt Lake City	559	403	156	Williston	12	10	2
Sandy	150	117	33	Wilmington	6	5	1
Santaquin/Genola	6	6	0	Windsor	11	6	5
Smithfield	8	7	1	Winhall	5	5	0
South Jordan	44	37	7	Winooski	19	14	5
South Ogden	27	23	4	Woodstock	6	5	1
South Salt Lake	70	59	11				
Spanish Fork	23	21	2	**VIRGINIA**			
Springville	32	24	8				
St. George	108	80	28	Abingdon	23	21	2
Stockton	2	2	0	Alexandria	427	296	131
Sunset	9	8	1	Altavista	11	11	0
Syracuse	13	11	2	Amherst	5	5	0
Tooele	28	25	3	Appalachia	5	5	0
Tremonton	11	9	2	Ashland	24	21	3
Vernal	19	16	3	Bedford	24	22	2
Wellington	4	4	0	Berryville	8	7	1
Wendover	5	4	1	Big Stone Gap	18	16	2
West Bountiful	8	7	1	Blacksburg	68	53	15
West Jordan	118	92	26	Blackstone	16	11	5
West Valley	227	184	43	Bluefield	18	14	4

Table 78

Full-time Law Enforcement Employees as of October 31, 2003
by City by State—Continued

City by state	Total law enforcement employees	Total officers	Total civilians	City by state	Total law enforcement employees	Total officers	Total civilians
VIRGINIA—Continued				**VIRGINIA—Continued**			
Boykins	4	1	3	Louisa	5	5	0
Bridgewater	8	8	0	Luray	17	15	2
Bristol	77	56	21	Lynchburg	217	141	76
Broadway	4	4	0	Manassas	104	83	21
Brookneal	4	4	0	Manassas Park	32	23	9
Buena Vista	15	13	2	Marion	21	19	2
Cape Charles	5	5	0	Martinsville	60	54	6
Cedar Bluff	3	3	0	McKenney	1	1	0
Charlottesville	137	111	26	Middleburg	4	4	0
Chase City	8	7	1	Middletown	2	2	0
Chatham	4	4	0	Mount Jackson	4	4	0
Chesapeake	489	358	131	Narrows	5	5	0
Chilhowie	6	6	0	New Market	7	7	0
Chincoteague	13	10	3	Newport News	548	407	141
Christiansburg	59	44	15	Norfolk	909	769	140
Clarksville	9	8	1	Norton	21	16	5
Clifton Forge	15	9	6	Occoquan	1	1	0
Clintwood	3	3	0	Onancock	4	4	0
Coeburn	8	7	1	Onley	3	3	0
Colonial Beach	13	8	5	Orange	15	14	1
Colonial Heights	49	45	4	Parksley	3	3	0
Courtland	3	1	2	Pearisburg	8	7	1
Covington	27	14	13	Pembroke	2	2	0
Crewe	5	5	0	Pennington Gap	6	5	1
Culpeper	38	32	6	Petersburg	150	108	42
Damascus	4	4	0	Pocahontas	3	3	0
Danville	134	127	7	Poquoson	24	20	4
Dayton	5	5	0	Portsmouth	312	220	92
Dublin	9	8	1	Pound	5	5	0
Dumfries	12	10	2	Pulaski	34	25	9
Edinburg	3	3	0	Purcellville	10	9	1
Elkton	7	6	1	Quantico	3	2	1
Emporia	34	25	9	Radford	48	36	12
Exmore	5	5	0	Richlands	19	14	5
Fairfax City	75	61	14	Richmond	765	632	133
Falls Church	43	31	12	Roanoke	292	235	57
Farmville	36	24	12	Rocky Mount	18	17	1
Franklin	41	30	11	Rural Retreat	1	1	0
Fredericksburg	90	64	26	Salem	89	63	26
Fries	1	1	0	Saltville	8	7	1
Front Royal	44	34	10	Shenandoah	4	4	0
Galax	40	24	16	Smithfield	21	18	3
Glade Spring	5	5	0	South Boston	32	27	5
Glasgow	1	1	0	South Hill	25	20	5
Glen Lyn	1	1	0	Stanley	3	3	0
Gordonsville	5	5	0	Staunton	62	47	15
Gretna	4	4	0	Stephens City	3	3	0
Grottoes	5	5	0	St. Paul	5	5	0
Grundy	5	4	1	Strasburg	14	12	2
Halifax	5	5	0	Suffolk	177	134	43
Hampton	368	266	102	Tappahannock	10	9	1
Harrisonburg	101	80	21	Tazewell	11	10	1
Haymarket	5	4	1	Timberville	3	3	0
Haysi	2	2	0	Victoria	6	5	1
Herndon	71	56	15	Vienna	48	39	9
Hillsville	12	11	1	Vinton	28	20	8
Honaker	5	4	1	Virginia Beach	946	783	163
Hopewell	64	50	14	Warrenton	23	20	3
Hurt	3	3	0	Warsaw	3	3	0
Independence	2	2	0	Waverly	14	8	6
Jonesville	3	2	1	Waynesboro	59	51	8
Kenbridge	8	8	0	Weber City	6	6	0
Kilmarnock	4	4	0	West Point	10	9	1
La Crosse	3	3	0	Williamsburg	47	34	13
Lawrenceville	5	5	0	Winchester	77	65	12
Lebanon	13	12	1	Wise	12	11	1
Leesburg	70	58	12	Woodstock	15	14	1
Lexington	17	15	2	Wytheville	38	24	14

Table 78

Full-time Law Enforcement Employees as of October 31, 2003

by City by State—Continued

City by state	Total law enforcement employees	Total officers	Total civilians	City by state	Total law enforcement employees	Total officers	Total civilians
WASHINGTON				**WASHINGTON—Continued**			
Aberdeen	48	36	12	Kalama	4	4	0
Airway Heights	10	9	1	Kelso	33	29	4
Algona	8	6	2	Kenmore	11	11	0
Anacortes	32	24	8	Kennewick	101	82	19
Arlington	26	22	4	Kent	171	119	52
Auburn	115	83	32	Kettle Falls	6	5	1
Bainbridge Island	25	20	5	Kirkland	98	65	33
Battle Ground	20	17	3	Kittitas	2	2	0
Bellevue	267	175	92	La Center	7	6	1
Bellingham	161	107	54	Lacey	53	45	8
Black Diamond	12	12	0	Lake Forest Park	26	22	4
Blaine	16	14	2	Lake Stevens	11	9	2
Bonney Lake	25	21	4	Lakewood	98	87	11
Bothell	76	53	23	Langley	2	2	0
Bremerton	76	62	14	Long Beach	7	6	1
Brewster	8	6	2	Longview	65	54	11
Brier	8	7	1	Lynden	17	13	4
Buckley	18	8	10	Lynnwood	95	67	28
Burien	31	30	1	Mabton	3	3	0
Burlington	27	21	6	Maple Valley	11	11	0
Camas	27	23	4	Marysville	68	39	29
Carnation	3	3	0	Mattawa	3	3	0
Castle Rock	5	5	0	McCleary	5	5	0
Centralia	32	27	5	Medical Lake	8	7	1
Chehalis	20	16	4	Medina	12	10	2
Chelan	14	8	6	Mercer Island	40	30	10
Cheney	15	11	4	Mill Creek	23	19	4
Chewelah	6	5	1	Milton	12	11	1
Clarkston	14	13	1	Monroe	41	30	11
Cle Elum	7	6	1	Montesano	10	8	2
Clyde Hill	8	7	1	Morton	3	2	1
Colfax	5	5	0	Moses Lake	32	25	7
College Place	14	11	3	Mossyrock	1	1	0
Colton	1	1	0	Mountlake Terrace	39	31	8
Colville	13	11	2	Mount Vernon	54	43	11
Connell	7	7	0	Moxee	2	2	0
Cosmopolis	6	5	1	Mukilteo	27	24	3
Coulee Dam	8	8	0	Napavine	4	3	1
Coupeville	5	5	0	Newcastle	7	7	0
Covington	10	10	0	Newport	4	3	1
Des Moines	55	43	12	Normandy Park	15	13	2
Dupont	6	6	0	North Bend	5	5	0
Duvall	11	10	1	Oak Harbor	38	26	12
East Wenatchee	17	15	2	Oakville	2	2	0
Eatonville	7	6	1	Ocean Shores	16	13	3
Edgewood	8	8	0	Odessa	2	2	0
Edmonds	68	53	15	Olympia	101	68	33
Ellensburg	31	23	8	Omak	14	12	2
Elma	7	6	1	Oroville	6	5	1
Elmer City	2	2	0	Orting	8	8	0
Enumclaw	28	17	11	Othello	20	13	7
Ephrata	16	13	3	Pacific	11	7	4
Everett	222	181	41	Palouse	2	2	0
Everson	5	5	0	Pasco	61	51	10
Federal Way	147	113	34	Pe Ell	2	2	0
Ferndale	18	15	3	Port Angeles	53	29	24
Fife	41	22	19	Port Orchard	21	19	2
Fircrest	10	9	1	Port Townsend	17	14	3
Forks	16	9	7	Poulsbo	20	17	3
Garfield	1	1	0	Prosser	19	12	7
Gig Harbor	14	12	2	Pullman	38	28	10
Goldendale	10	9	1	Puyallup	87	51	36
Grand Coulee	7	7	0	Quincy	12	10	2
Grandview	21	16	5	Rainier	5	4	1
Granger	10	8	2	Raymond	6	5	1
Granite Falls	9	8	1	Reardan	1	1	0
Hoquiam	23	20	3	Redmond	102	70	32
Issaquah	54	28	26	Renton	128	88	40

Table 78

Full-time Law Enforcement Employees as of October 31, 2003
by City by State—Continued

City by state	Total law enforcement employees	Total officers	Total civilians	City by state	Total law enforcement employees	Total officers	Total civilians
WASHINGTON—Continued				**WEST VIRGINIA—Continued**			
Republic	3	3	0	Barrackville	1	1	0
Richland	63	56	7	Beckley	68	47	21
Ridgefield	6	6	0	Belington	2	2	0
Ritzville	4	4	0	Belle	4	4	0
Rosalia	1	1	0	Benwood	8	5	3
Roy	3	3	0	Berkeley Springs	3	2	1
Royal City	3	3	0	Bethlehem	4	4	0
Ruston	2	2	0	Bluefield	28	22	6
Sammamish	22	21	1	Bradshaw	1	1	0
SeaTac	36	34	2	Bramwell	2	2	0
Seattle	1,719	1,231	488	Bridgeport	22	20	2
Sedro Woolley	17	13	4	Buckhannon	8	7	1
Selah	13	12	1	Burnsville	2	1	1
Sequim	16	13	3	Cameron	4	4	0
Shelton	36	19	17	Capon Bridge	2	2	0
Shoreline	45	43	2	Cedar Grove	1	1	0
Snohomish	24	20	4	Ceredo	10	7	3
Snoqualmie	17	14	3	Chapmanville	5	5	0
Soap Lake	4	4	0	Charleston	189	161	28
South Bend	4	3	1	Charles Town	19	16	3
Spokane	410	303	107	Chesapeake	4	4	0
Spokane Valley	100	99	1	Chester	5	5	0
Springdale	1	1	0	Clarksburg	45	38	7
Stanwood	12	10	2	Clendenin	3	3	0
Steilacoom	11	10	1	Danville	3	3	0
Sultan	10	9	1	Delbarton	2	2	0
Sumas	6	6	0	Dunbar	19	15	4
Sumner	28	19	9	East Bank	4	4	0
Sunnyside	37	31	6	Eleanor	1	1	0
Tacoma	388	355	33	Elkins	15	9	6
Tekoa	2	2	0	Fairmont	42	33	9
Tenino	4	4	0	Fairview	1	1	0
Tieton	1	1	0	Farmington	1	1	0
Toledo	2	2	0	Fayetteville	8	7	1
Tonasket	6	5	1	Follansbee	7	7	0
Toppenish	22	15	7	Fort Gay	2	2	0
Tukwila	81	66	15	Gary	1	1	0
Tumwater	29	25	4	Gassaway	1	1	0
Twisp	4	3	1	Gauley Bridge	7	5	2
Union Gap	23	18	5	Gilbert	4	4	0
Uniontown	1	1	0	Glasgow	2	2	0
University Place	25	24	1	Glen Dale	6	5	1
Vader	2	2	0	Glenville	4	3	1
Vancouver	211	179	32	Grafton	7	6	1
Walla Walla	69	43	26	Grantsville	1	1	0
Wapato	21	13	8	Granville	1	1	0
Warden	5	4	1	Hamlin	3	3	0
Washougal	16	14	2	Handley	2	2	0
Wenatchee	61	40	21	Harpers Ferry/Bolivar	5	4	1
Westport	9	7	2	Harrisville	1	1	0
West Richland	16	14	2	Henderson	1	1	0
White Salmon	9	9	0	Hinton	7	7	0
Wilbur	2	2	0	Hundred	1	1	0
Winlock	2	2	0	Huntington	90	85	5
Winthrop	2	2	0	Hurricane	16	14	2
Woodinville	7	7	0	Iaeger	1	1	0
Woodland	9	7	2	Kenova	13	9	4
Yakima	160	112	48	Kermit	2	2	0
Yelm	12	10	2	Keyser	14	9	5
Zillah	6	5	1	Keystone	3	3	0
				Kimball	1	1	0
WEST VIRGINIA				Kingwood	4	4	0
				Lewisburg	12	10	2
Alderson	2	2	0	Logan	9	7	2
Anmoore	2	2	0	Lumberport	2	2	0
Ansted	1	1	0	Mabscott	2	2	0
Athens	1	1	0	Madison	5	4	1
Barboursville	19	17	2	Man	5	5	0

Table 78

Full-time Law Enforcement Employees as of October 31, 2003
by City by State—Continued

City by state	Total law enforcement employees	Total officers	Total civilians	City by state	Total law enforcement employees	Total officers	Total civilians
WEST VIRGINIA—Continued				**WEST VIRGINIA—Continued**			
Mannington	4	4	0	War	2	2	0
Marlinton	1	1	0	Wardensville	1	1	0
Marmet	5	5	0	Wayne	5	2	3
Martinsburg	49	41	8	Webster Springs	1	1	0
Mason	4	4	0	Weirton	47	38	9
Masontown	1	1	0	Welch	9	8	1
Matewan	2	2	0	Wellsburg	7	6	1
Matoaka	5	5	0	West Logan	1	1	0
McMechen	4	4	0	West Milford	2	2	0
Milton	6	5	1	Weston	9	8	1
Mitchell Heights	1	1	0	Westover	7	7	0
Monongah	1	1	0	West Union	1	1	0
Montgomery	9	7	2	Wheeling	78	76	2
Moorefield	6	6	0	White Sulphur Springs	8	7	1
Morgantown	55	51	4	Whitesville	2	2	0
Moundsville	21	17	4	Williamson	11	9	2
Mount Hope	4	3	1	Williamstown	6	5	1
Mullens	5	5	0	Winfield	4	4	0
New Cumberland	3	3	0				
New Haven	4	4	0	**WISCONSIN**			
New Martinsville	14	10	4				
Nitro	18	17	1	Algoma	5	5	0
Northfork	2	2	0	Altoona	12	11	1
Nutter Fort	6	6	0	Amery	7	6	1
Oak Hill	16	14	2	Antigo	17	14	3
Oceana	4	4	0	Appleton	136	107	29
Paden City	5	4	1	Arcadia	5	5	0
Parkersburg	76	64	12	Ashland	22	20	2
Parsons	1	1	0	Ashwaubenon	55	44	11
Paw Paw	1	1	0	Augusta	4	4	0
Pennsboro	1	1	0	Bangor	3	3	0
Petersburg	1	1	0	Baraboo	31	25	6
Peterstown	3	3	0	Barron	7	7	0
Philippi	6	6	0	Bayfield	4	4	0
Piedmont	1	1	0	Beaver Dam	40	30	10
Pineville	3	3	0	Belleville	4	4	0
Point Pleasant	9	8	1	Beloit	91	78	13
Pratt	2	2	0	Beloit Town	10	9	1
Princeton	17	14	3	Berlin	13	12	1
Rainelle	2	2	0	Black River Falls	8	7	1
Ranson	10	9	1	Blair	3	3	0
Ravenswood	10	9	1	Blanchardville	1	1	0
Reedsville	1	1	0	Bloomer	7	6	1
Richwood	5	4	1	Bloomfield	8	7	1
Ridgeley	2	2	0	Boscobel	6	6	0
Ripley	9	8	1	Brillion	8	7	1
Rivesville	1	1	0	Brodhead	12	8	4
Romney	4	3	1	Brookfield	83	60	23
Ronceverte	4	4	0	Brown Deer	40	31	9
Rowlesburg	3	3	0	Burlington	26	20	6
Salem	3	3	0	Burlington Town	8	8	0
Shepherdstown	6	4	2	Butler	8	7	1
Shinnston	6	6	0	Caledonia	36	28	8
Sistersville	4	4	0	Campbellsport	2	2	0
Smithers	8	8	0	Cedarburg	29	20	9
Sophia	3	3	0	Chenequa	9	9	0
South Charleston	35	30	5	Chetek	6	5	1
Spencer	6	5	1	Chilton	7	7	0
St. Albans	26	20	6	Chippewa Falls	35	27	8
Star City	6	5	1	Cleveland	3	2	1
St. Marys	4	4	0	Colby-Abbotsford	7	6	1
Stonewood	3	3	0	Columbus	16	11	5
Summersville	16	16	0	Combined Locks	5	5	0
Sutton	3	2	1	Cornell	3	3	0
Sylvester	1	1	0	Cottage Grove	11	10	1
Terra Alta	2	2	0	Crandon	4	3	1
Triadelphia	2	1	1	Cuba City	5	4	1
Vienna	19	15	4	Cudahy	40	28	12

Table 78

Full-time Law Enforcement Employees as of October 31, 2003
by City by State—Continued

City by state	Total law enforcement employees	Total officers	Total civilians	City by state	Total law enforcement employees	Total officers	Total civilians
WISCONSIN—Continued				**WISCONSIN—Continued**			
Cumberland	5	5	0	Kewaunee	6	6	0
Darien	7	6	1	Kiel	9	7	2
Darlington	5	5	0	Kohler	8	7	1
Deerfield	3	3	0	Lac du Flambeau	12	10	2
DeForest	14	12	2	La Crosse	115	94	21
Delafield	15	14	1	Ladysmith	9	8	1
Delavan	22	17	5	Lake Delton	15	14	1
Delavan Town	11	10	1	Lake Geneva	28	20	8
Denmark	2	2	0	Lake Mills	13	11	2
De Pere	38	34	4	Lancaster	7	7	0
Dodgeville	11	10	1	Lodi	6	5	1
Durand	4	4	0	Luxemburg	2	2	0
Eagle River	6	6	0	Madison	465	382	83
Eagle Village	2	2	0	Manitowoc	75	65	10
East Troy	7	7	0	Maple Bluff	5	5	0
Eau Claire	129	99	30	Marinette	31	24	7
Edgerton	11	10	1	Marion	3	3	0
Eleva	1	1	0	Markesan	4	4	0
Elkhart Lake	3	3	0	Marshall Village	8	7	1
Elkhorn	19	16	3	Marshfield	54	38	16
Elk Mound	1	1	0	Mauston	8	7	1
Ellsworth	7	6	1	Mayville	13	11	2
Elm Grove	25	17	8	McFarland	12	11	1
Elroy	2	2	0	Medford	10	9	1
Evansville	9	8	1	Menasha	38	32	6
Everest	27	24	3	Menomonee Falls	70	59	11
Fall Creek	2	2	0	Menomonie	34	27	7
Fennimore	5	5	0	Mequon	45	37	8
Fitchburg	46	36	10	Merrill	25	21	4
Fond du Lac	80	69	11	Middleton	39	31	8
Fontana	7	6	1	Milton	10	9	1
Fort Atkinson	27	20	7	Milwaukee	2,433	1,962	471
Fox Lake	4	3	1	Mineral Point	6	6	0
Fox Point	18	16	2	Minocqua	16	11	5
Fox Valley	29	26	3	Mondovi	4	4	0
Franklin	78	59	19	Monona	23	19	4
Frederic	2	2	0	Monroe	35	26	9
Geneva Town	8	6	2	Mosinee	8	7	1
Genoa City	5	4	1	Mount Horeb	12	10	2
Germantown	43	31	12	Mount Pleasant	40	32	8
Glendale	48	47	1	Mukwonago	19	12	7
Grafton	28	21	7	Muskego	47	36	11
Grand Chute	29	25	4	Neenah	51	41	10
Grantsburg	2	2	0	Neillsville	7	6	1
Green Bay	226	187	39	New Berlin	93	74	19
Greendale	36	28	8	New Glarus	5	5	0
Greenfield	78	57	21	New Holstein	10	7	3
Hales Corners	17	17	0	New Lisbon	3	3	0
Hallie	7	6	1	New London	19	17	2
Hartford	27	22	5	New Richmond	13	12	1
Hartland	17	15	2	Niagara	5	5	0
Hayward	8	7	1	North Fond du Lac	13	10	3
Hazel Green	2	2	0	North Hudson	6	5	1
Hobart-Lawrence	3	2	1	Oak Creek	66	49	17
Holmen	9	8	1	Oconomowoc	30	23	7
Horicon	12	9	3	Oconto	8	8	0
Hortonville	4	4	0	Oconto Falls	5	5	0
Hudson	22	19	3	Omro	6	5	1
Hurley	6	5	1	Onalaska	31	28	3
Independence	2	2	0	Oregon	15	14	1
Iron Ridge	1	1	0	Osceola	5	5	0
Jackson	11	10	1	Oshkosh	115	98	17
Janesville	115	102	13	Osseo	4	4	0
Jefferson	18	14	4	Palmyra	5	5	0
Juneau	5	4	1	Park Falls	8	7	1
Kaukauna	25	24	1	Pepin	1	1	0
Kenosha	263	186	77	Peshtigo	7	6	1
Kewaskum	7	7	0	Pewaukee	17	15	2

Table 78

Full-time Law Enforcement Employees as of October 31, 2003
by City by State—Continued

City by state	Total law enforcement employees	Total officers	Total civilians	City by state	Total law enforcement employees	Total officers	Total civilians
WISCONSIN—Continued				**WISCONSIN—Continued**			
Pewaukee Township	25	23	2	Watertown	52	38	14
Phillips	7	6	1	Waukesha	148	110	38
Platteville	28	21	7	Waunakee	16	14	2
Pleasant Prairie	27	26	1	Waupun	19	17	2
Plover	19	16	3	Wausau	67	60	7
Plymouth	16	16	0	Wautoma	5	5	0
Portage	30	22	8	Wauwatosa	117	88	29
Port Washington	24	19	5	West Allis	160	134	26
Poynette	6	5	1	West Bend	75	56	19
Prairie du Chien	19	14	5	West Milwaukee	23	18	5
Prescott	8	7	1	West Salem	6	5	1
Pulaski	4	4	0	Whitefish Bay	28	24	4
Reedsburg	23	16	7	Whitehall	4	4	0
Rhinelander	22	16	6	Whitewater	31	22	9
Rice Lake	26	23	3	Williams Bay	7	6	1
Richland Center	13	11	2	Winneconne	6	5	1
Ripon	19	14	5	Wisconsin Dells	16	11	5
River Falls	25	22	3	Wisconsin Rapids	48	37	11
River Hills	13	13	0	Woodruff	6	5	1
Rothschild	12	10	2				
Sauk Prairie	14	13	1	**WYOMING**			
Saukville	11	9	2				
Shawano	22	19	3	Afton	4	4	0
Sheboygan	112	84	28	Basin	4	4	0
Sheboygan Falls	15	13	2	Buffalo	16	9	7
Shorewood	34	26	8	Casper	94	80	14
Shorewood Hills	7	6	1	Cheyenne	117	89	28
Silver Lake	4	3	1	Cody	22	19	3
Siren	2	2	0	Diamondville	4	3	1
Slinger	10	9	1	Douglas	19	13	6
Somerset	6	5	1	Evanston	31	26	5
South Milwaukee	39	32	7	Evansville	13	8	5
Sparta	17	15	2	Gillette	66	44	22
Spencer	3	3	0	Glenrock	9	6	3
Spooner	7	6	1	Green River	36	27	9
Spring Green	4	3	1	Guernsey	4	4	0
Stanley	4	4	0	Hanna	9	4	5
St. Croix Falls	4	4	0	Jackson	32	21	11
Stevens Point	58	44	14	Kemmerer	9	7	2
St. Francis	25	20	5	La Barge	2	2	0
Stoughton	23	18	5	Lander	21	19	2
Sturgeon Bay	22	21	1	Laramie	71	44	27
Sturtevant	15	9	6	Lovell	9	6	3
Summit	8	8	0	Lusk	4	4	0
Sun Prairie	67	43	24	Lyman	7	5	2
Superior	64	57	7	Mills	10	9	1
Theresa	2	2	0	Moorcroft	4	3	1
Thiensville	8	7	1	Newcastle	16	9	7
Three Lakes	5	5	0	Pine Bluffs	6	2	4
Tomah	20	18	2	Powell	21	14	7
Tomahawk	8	7	1	Rawlins	30	19	11
Town of East Troy	7	6	1	Riverton	35	24	11
Town of Madison	19	17	2	Rock Springs	59	39	20
Twin Lakes	14	10	4	Saratoga	10	5	5
Two Rivers	29	25	4	Sheridan	46	28	18
Valders	1	1	0	Sundance	5	5	0
Verona	15	14	1	Thermopolis	13	8	5
Viroqua	9	8	1	Torrington	21	15	6
Walworth	7	6	1	Wheatland	12	11	1
Washburn	5	5	0	Worland	10	10	0
Waterloo	9	8	1				

[1] The data presented in this table for *Charlotte-Mecklenburg* represent only those law enforcement employees that work for the Charlotte-Mecklenburg Police Department and exclude Mecklenburg County Sheriff's Office employees.

Table 79

Full-time Law Enforcement Employees as of October 31, 2003
by University and College by State[1]

University/College by state	Total law enforcement employees	Total officers	Total civilians	University/College by state	Total law enforcement employees	Total officers	Total civilians
ALABAMA				**CALIFORNIA—Continued**			
				San Marcos	17	11	6
Auburn University:				Stanislaus	22	11	11
Main Campus	47	34	13	College of the Sequoias	6	5	1
Montgomery	26	13	13	Contra Costa Community College	30	19	11
Calhoun Community College	8	6	2	Cuesta College	8	6	2
Faulkner University	10	10	0	El Camino College	20	14	6
Jacksonville State University	17	13	4	Foothill-De Anza College	18	10	8
Talladega College	6	5	1	Fresno Community College	16	13	3
Troy State University	11	9	2	Humboldt State University	20	12	8
University of Alabama:				Marin Community College	8	5	3
Birmingham	136	57	79	Pasadena Community College	11	6	5
Huntsville	15	11	4	Riverside Community College	24	19	5
Tuscaloosa	48	39	9	San Bernardino Community College	11	8	3
University of Montevallo	15	9	6	San Diego State University	49	30	19
University of North Alabama	16	13	3	San Francisco State University	43	21	22
University of South Alabama	35	23	12	San Jose/Evergreen Community College	10	6	4
University of West Alabama	8	5	3	Santa Rosa Junior College	19	12	7
				Solano Community College	7	6	1
ALASKA				Sonoma State University	21	12	9
				University of California:			
University of Alaska:				Berkeley	124	64	60
Anchorage	18	12	6	Davis	85	41	44
Fairbanks	11	10	1	Hastings College of Law	12	12	0
				Irvine	33	24	9
ARIZONA				Lawrence-Livermore Laboratory	9	2	7
				Los Angeles	79	57	22
Arizona State University, Main Campus	88	58	30	Riverside	34	26	8
Arizona Western College	7	6	1	San Diego	49	28	21
Central Arizona College	6	5	1	San Francisco	48	34	14
Northern Arizona University	24	14	10	Santa Barbara	39	28	11
Pima Community College	37	29	8	Santa Cruz	44	19	25
University of Arizona	76	46	30	West Valley-Mission College	13	9	4
Yavapai College	7	6	1				
				COLORADO			
ARKANSAS							
				Adams State College	2	2	0
Arkansas State University	22	17	5	Arapahoe Community College	9	6	3
Henderson State University	8	7	1	Auraria Higher Education Center	28	18	10
Northwest Arkansas Community College	9	5	4	Colorado School of Mines	7	6	1
Southern Arkansas University	7	6	1	Colorado State University	26	20	6
University of Arkansas:				Fort Lewis College	8	6	2
Fayetteville	37	28	9	Pikes Peak Community College	16	15	1
Little Rock	31	25	6	Red Rocks Community College	1	1	0
Medical Sciences	43	37	6	University of Colorado:			
Monticello	8	7	1	Boulder	51	37	14
Pine Bluff	36	28	8	Colorado Springs	24	13	11
University of Central Arkansas	28	23	5	Health Sciences Center	65	31	34
				University of Northern Colorado	16	10	6
CALIFORNIA							
				CONNECTICUT			
Allan Hancock College	19	5	14				
California State Polytechnic University:				Central Connecticut State University	27	22	5
Pomona	26	15	11	Eastern Connecticut State University	19	14	5
San Luis Obispo	33	15	18	Southern Connecticut State University	37	27	10
California State University:				University of Connecticut:			
Bakersfield	14	10	4	Health Center	21	14	7
Channel Islands	16	12	4	Storrs, Avery Point, and Hartford	78	65	13
Chico	17	11	6	Western Connecticut State University	21	13	8
Dominguez Hills	20	15	5	Yale University	92	78	14
Fresno	26	16	10				
Fullerton	29	21	8	**DELAWARE**			
Hayward	27	14	13				
Long Beach	33	25	8	University of Delaware	82	47	35
Los Angeles	26	19	7				
Monterey Bay	15	13	2	**FLORIDA**			
Northridge	32	22	10				
Sacramento	20	14	6	Florida A&M University	38	27	11
San Bernardino	20	13	7	Florida Atlantic University	51	35	16
San Jose	70	34	36				

Table 79

Full-time Law Enforcement Employees as of October 31, 2003
by University and College by State[1]—Continued

University/College by state	Total law enforcement employees	Total officers	Total civilians
FLORIDA—Continued			
Florida Gulf Coast University	19	12	7
Florida International University	64	44	20
Florida State University:			
Panama City	4	3	1
Tallahassee	78	57	21
New College of Florida	15	11	4
Pensacola Junior College	19	15	4
Santa Fe Community College	23	17	6
Tallahassee Community College	28	14	14
University of Central Florida	70	43	27
University of Florida	142	88	54
University of North Florida	36	26	10
University of South Florida:			
St. Petersburg	16	12	4
Tampa	59	41	18
University of West Florida	33	23	10
GEORGIA			
Abraham Baldwin Agricultural College	12	11	1
Albany State University	25	12	13
Armstrong Atlantic State University	16	13	3
Augusta State University	18	14	4
Berry College	16	11	5
Clark Atlanta University	39	14	25
Clayton College and State University	19	13	6
Coastal Georgia Community College	7	6	1
Columbus State University	17	16	1
Dalton State College	7	7	0
Emory University	57	41	16
Fort Valley State University	21	13	8
Georgia College and State University	20	14	6
Georgia Institute of Technology	74	40	34
Georgia Perimeter College	44	13	31
Georgia Southern University	36	29	7
Georgia Southwestern State University	11	10	1
Georgia State University	122	84	38
Gordon College	8	7	1
Kennesaw State University	37	22	15
Medical College of Georgia	45	35	10
Mercer University	31	23	8
Middle Georgia College	8	7	1
Morehouse College	39	15	24
Morris-Brown College	5	5	0
North Georgia College	12	9	3
Piedmont College	2	2	0
Savannah State University	22	9	13
Southern Polytechnic State University	17	12	5
South Georgia College	6	6	0
University of Georgia	72	57	15
University of West Georgia	42	18	24
Valdosta State University	26	18	8
Wesleyan College	5	5	0
ILLINOIS			
Black Hawk College	9	8	1
Chicago State University	33	21	12
College of DuPage	20	14	6
College of Lake County	17	9	8
Eastern Illinois University	26	23	3
Governors State University	12	9	3
Illinois State University	25	22	3
John A. Logan College	8	6	2
Joliet Junior College	14	6	8
Loyola University of Chicago	37	20	17
Morton College	6	4	2
Northeastern Illinois University	21	14	7
ILLINOIS—Continued			
Northern Illinois University	55	38	17
Northwestern University:			
Chicago	17	13	4
Evanston	35	24	11
Oakton Community College	11	10	1
Parkland College	18	13	5
Rock Valley College	13	11	2
Southern Illinois University:			
Carbondale	47	37	10
Edwardsville	41	33	8
School of Medicine	11	2	9
South Suburban College	15	11	4
Triton College	14	9	5
University of Illinois:			
Chicago	105	61	44
Springfield	17	11	6
Urbana	69	55	14
Waubonsee College	2	2	0
Western Illinois University	30	25	5
William Rainey Harper College	16	10	6
INDIANA			
Ball State University	37	30	7
DePauw University	11	7	4
Indiana State University	33	24	9
Indiana University:			
Bloomington	52	42	10
Gary	12	10	2
Indianapolis	48	32	16
New Albany	10	8	2
Marian College	6	3	3
Purdue University	43	35	8
IOWA			
Iowa State University	31	28	3
University of Iowa	51	27	24
University of Northern Iowa	24	18	6
KANSAS			
Emporia State University	9	9	0
Fort Hays State University	11	10	1
Kansas State University	37	24	13
Pittsburg State University	15	13	2
University of Kansas:			
Main Campus	45	26	19
Medical Center	50	28	22
Wichita State University	29	21	8
KENTUCKY			
Eastern Kentucky University	27	16	11
Kentucky State University	15	8	7
Morehead State University	21	13	8
Murray State University	20	14	6
Northern Kentucky University	24	14	10
University of Kentucky	49	35	14
University of Louisville	32	24	8
Western Kentucky University	34	23	11
LOUISIANA			
Delgado Community College	36	26	10
Grambling State University	11	10	1
Louisiana State University:			
Baton Rouge	67	65	2

Table 79

Full-time Law Enforcement Employees as of October 31, 2003

by University and College by State[1]—Continued

University/College by state	Total law enforcement employees	Total officers	Total civilians	University/College by state	Total law enforcement employees	Total officers	Total civilians
LOUISIANA—Continued				**MASSACHUSETTS—Continued**			
Eunice	1	1	0	University of Massachusetts:			
Health Sciences Center, New Orleans	60	59	1	Amherst	66	55	11
Health Sciences Center, Shreveport	58	40	18	Dartmouth	35	23	12
Shreveport	11	10	1	Harbor Campus, Boston	35	26	9
Louisiana Tech University	20	18	2	Medical Center, Worcester	26	21	5
McNeese State University	18	11	7	Wellesley College	18	13	5
Nicholls State University	14	10	4	Western New England College	21	13	8
Northwestern State University	16	14	2	Westfield State College	25	13	12
Southeastern Louisiana University	34	25	9				
Southern University and A&M College:				**MICHIGAN**			
Baton Rouge	25	22	3	Central Michigan University	30	20	10
New Orleans	11	9	2	Delta College	7	5	2
Shreveport	10	9	1	Eastern Michigan University	31	25	6
Tulane University	50	37	13	Ferris State University	18	13	5
University of Louisiana:				Grand Rapids Community College	14	11	3
Lafayette	26	24	2	Grand Valley State University	17	13	4
Monroe	25	22	3	Lansing Community College	13	11	2
University of New Orleans	31	23	8	Macomb Community College	35	28	7
				Michigan State University	97	63	34
MAINE				Michigan Technological University	12	9	3
				Mott Community College	3	3	0
University of Maine:				Northern Michigan University	16	14	2
Farmington	4	4	0	Oakland Community College	21	20	1
Orono	30	19	11	Oakland University	24	18	6
University of Southern Maine	25	16	9	Saginaw Valley State University	10	8	2
				University of Michigan:			
MARYLAND				Ann Arbor	95	52	43
				Flint	20	7	13
Bowie State University	23	15	8	Western Michigan University	61	29	32
Coppin State College	18	14	4				
Frostburg State University	18	15	3	**MINNESOTA**			
Morgan State University	40	34	6				
Salisbury University	21	17	4	University of Minnesota:			
St. Mary's College	13	2	11	Duluth	10	9	1
Towson University	52	37	15	Twin Cities	65	43	22
University of Baltimore	45	11	34				
University of Maryland:				**MISSISSIPPI**			
Baltimore City	119	48	71				
Baltimore County	31	24	7	Coahoma Community College	7	6	1
College Park	105	76	29	Hinds Community College	26	25	1
Eastern Shore	15	10	5	Itawamba Community College	7	6	1
				Jackson State University	54	36	18
MASSACHUSETTS				Mississippi State University	35	26	9
				University of Mississippi:			
Assumption College	21	13	8	Medical Center	81	59	22
Boston College	60	43	17	Oxford	40	25	15
Boston University	54	49	5				
Brandeis University	17	14	3	**MISSOURI**			
Bristol Community College	13	7	6				
Emerson College	17	16	1	Central Missouri State University	23	18	5
Fitchburg State College	15	13	2	Lincoln University	11	7	4
Framingham State College	14	13	1	Mineral Area College	4	3	1
Harvard University	104	74	30	Missouri Western State College	11	9	2
Holyoke Community College	9	9	0	Northwest Missouri State University	16	9	7
Lasell College	11	11	0	Southeast Missouri State University	23	17	6
Massachusetts College of Art	8	8	0	St. Louis Community College, Meramec	11	8	3
Massachusetts College of Liberal Arts	10	7	3	Truman State University	11	10	1
Massachusetts Institute of Technology	61	57	4	University of Missouri:			
Massasoit Community College	11	9	2	Columbia	46	29	17
Mount Holyoke College	18	14	4	Kansas City	37	24	13
Northeastern University	72	50	22	Rolla	17	9	8
North Shore Community College	18	16	2	St. Louis	21	16	5
Quinsigamond Community College	10	10	0	Washington University	37	24	13
Salem State College	26	24	2				
Springfield College	32	17	15	**MONTANA**			
Tufts University:							
Medford	56	41	15	Montana State University	24	14	10
Worcester	27	13	14	University of Montana	18	13	5

Table 79

Full-time Law Enforcement Employees as of October 31, 2003

by University and College by State[1]—Continued

University/College by state	Total law enforcement employees	Total officers	Total civilians	University/College by state	Total law enforcement employees	Total officers	Total civilians
NEBRASKA				**NORTH CAROLINA—Continued**			
				Chapel Hill	80	46	34
University of Nebraska:				Charlotte	40	33	7
Kearney	6	5	1	Greensboro	41	27	14
Lincoln	47	28	19	Pembroke	16	12	4
				Wilmington	32	24	8
NEVADA				Wake Forest University	37	16	21
				Western Carolina University	18	13	5
Truckee Meadows Community College	7	6	1	Winston-Salem State University	19	13	6
University of Nevada:							
Las Vegas	45	31	14	**NORTH DAKOTA**			
Reno	28	20	8				
				North Dakota State College of Science	3	3	0
NEW JERSEY				North Dakota State University	12	10	2
				University of North Dakota	15	11	4
Brookdale Community College	15	12	3				
Essex County College	55	14	41	**OHIO**			
Kean University of New Jersey	32	22	10				
Middlesex County College	15	10	5	Bowling Green State University	30	24	6
Monmouth University	31	20	11	Cleveland State University	33	24	9
Montclair State University	39	26	13	Columbus State Community College	31	25	6
New Jersey Institute of Technology	62	27	35	Cuyahoga Community College	34	29	5
Richard Stockton College	22	17	5	Kent State University	32	25	7
Rowan University	44	6	38	Lakeland Community College	13	9	4
Rutgers University:				Marietta College	7	6	1
Camden	36	17	19	Miami University	37	28	9
Newark	39	29	10	Ohio State University	59	45	14
New Brunswick	113	56	57	Ohio University	31	25	6
The College of New Jersey	27	17	10	Sinclair Community College	25	21	4
University of Medicine and Dentistry:				University of Akron	38	31	7
Camden	17	15	2	University of Cincinnati	135	52	83
Newark	121	46	75	University of Toledo	42	33	9
Piscataway	35	30	5	Wright State University	27	17	10
William Paterson University	44	22	22	Youngstown State University	27	22	5
NEW MEXICO				**OKLAHOMA**			
Eastern New Mexico University	9	8	1	Cameron University	9	8	1
New Mexico Highlands University	9	1	8	East Central University	5	5	0
University of New Mexico	45	31	14	Murray State College	1	1	0
Western New Mexico University	3	3	0	Northeastern Oklahoma A&M College	9	7	2
				Northeastern State College	11	9	2
NEW YORK				Oklahoma State University:			
				Main Campus	39	29	10
Cornell University	57	45	·12	Okmulgee	6	6	0
Ithaca College	31	18	13	Tulsa	4	2	2
Rensselaer Polytechnic Institute	30	20	10	Rogers State University	4	4	0
Syracuse University	65	58	7	Seminole State College	3	3	0
United States Merchant Marine Academy	8	4	4	Southeastern Oklahoma State University	8	7	1
				Southwestern Oklahoma State University	8	7	1
NORTH CAROLINA				Tulsa Community College	17	10	7
				University of Central Oklahoma	23	16	7
Appalachian State University	32	21	11	University of Oklahoma:			
Beaufort County Community College	2	2	0	Health Sciences Center	56	36	20
Belmont Abbey College	7	7	0	Norman	46	28	18
Davidson College	9	8	1				
Duke University	129	53	76	**PENNSYLVANIA**			
East Carolina University	64	49	15				
Elizabeth City State University	16	10	6	Bloomsburg University	21	17	4
Elon University	9	8	1	California University	13	13	0
Fayetteville State University	20	12	8	Cheyney University	12	11	1
North Carolina Agricultural and				Clarion University	18	13	5
Technical State University	40	27	13	East Stroudsburg University	17	14	3
North Carolina Central University	36	22	14	Edinboro University	14	13	1
North Carolina School of the Arts	14	13	1	Elizabethtown College	14	9	5
North Carolina State University, Raleigh	61	50	11	Indiana University	26	21	5
Queens University	6	4	2	Kutztown University	18	12	6
Saint Augustine's College	13	8	5	Lehigh University	29	21	8
University of North Carolina:				Lock Haven University	10	9	1
Asheville	15	9	6				

Table 79

Full-time Law Enforcement Employees as of October 31, 2003
by University and College by State[1]—Continued

University/College by state	Total law enforcement employees	Total officers	Total civilians	University/College by state	Total law enforcement employees	Total officers	Total civilians
PENNSYLVANIA—Continued				**TEXAS**			
				Alamo Community College District	71	47	24
Mansfield University	11	11	0	Alvin Community College	11	9	2
Millersville University	17	14	3	Amarillo College	16	14	2
Moravian College	13	9	4	Angelo State University	12	9	3
Pennsylvania State University:				Austin College	8	7	1
Altoona	9	8	1	Baylor Health Care System	133	47	86
Beaver	4	4	0	Baylor University, Waco	32	20	12
Behrend	9	6	3	Central Texas College	8	7	1
Berks	8	7	1	College of the Mainland	7	6	1
Harrisburg	7	6	1	Eastfield College	11	10	1
McKeesport	3	3	0	El Paso Community College	39	32	7
Mont Alto	2	2	0	Grayson County College	3	2	1
University Park	63	47	16	Hardin-Simmons University	7	4	3
Shippensburg University	18	15	3	Houston Baptist University	9	9	0
Slippery Rock University	19	17	2	Lamar University, Beaumont	33	18	15
University of Pittsburgh:				Laredo Community College	13	12	1
Bradford	6	5	1	McLennan Community College	10	5	5
Pittsburgh	115	71	44	Midwestern State University	8	7	1
West Chester University	38	19	19	Mountain View College	9	9	0
				North Lake College	15	14	1
RHODE ISLAND				Paris Junior College	3	3	0
				Prairie View A&M University	38	22	16
Brown University	65	30	35	Rice University	43	28	15
University of Rhode Island	31	18	13	Richland College	13	12	1
				Southern Methodist University	30	21	9
SOUTH CAROLINA				South Plains College	6	6	0
				Southwestern University	7	6	1
Aiken Technical College	8	3	5	Stephen F. Austin State University	39	22	17
Benedict College	26	15	11	St. Mary's University	18	12	6
Bob Jones University	4	4	0	St. Thomas University	8	1	7
Clemson University	47	30	17	Sul Ross State University	8	6	2
Coastal Carolina University	34	14	20	Tarleton State University	13	11	2
College of Charleston	58	34	24	Texas A&M International University	15	9	6
Columbia College	11	9	2	Texas A&M University:			
Erskine College	2	2	0	College Station	123	50	73
Francis Marion University	12	12	0	Commerce	24	16	8
Lander University	10	9	1	Corpus Christi	22	11	11
Medical University of South Carolina	59	37	22	Galveston	8	7	1
Midlands Technical College	23	23	0	Kingsville	18	12	6
Presbyterian College	9	8	1	Texas Christian University	31	20	11
Trident Technical College	20	18	2	Texas Southern University	37	25	12
University of South Carolina:				Texas State Technical College:			
Aiken	7	7	0	Harlingen	12	9	3
Columbia	70	53	17	Waco	15	13	2
Spartanburg	9	9	0	Texas State University, San Marco	60	29	31
Winthrop University	20	14	6	Texas Technological University, Lubbock	53	35	18
				Texas Woman's University	29	14	15
SOUTH DAKOTA				Trinity University	27	14	13
				Tyler Junior College	12	5	7
South Dakota State University	17	12	5	University of Houston:			
				Central Campus	76	39	37
TENNESSEE				Clearlake	22	14	8
				Downtown Campus	20	14	6
Austin Peay State University	17	10	7	University of Mary Hardin-Baylor	8	8	0
Chattanooga State Technical				University of North Texas,			
Community College	12	8	4	Health Science Center	19	8	11
East Tennessee State University	25	19	6	University of Texas:			
Middle Tennessee State University	33	29	4	Arlington	64	33	31
Southwest Tennessee Community College	31	29	2	Austin	128	58	70
Tennessee State University	41	35	6	Brownsville	32	10	22
Tennessee Technological University	22	14	8	Dallas	39	18	21
University of Memphis	32	29	3	El Paso	54	20	34
University of Tennessee:				Health Science Center, San Antonio	82	34	48
Chattanooga	21	15	6	Health Science Center, Tyler	28	5	23
Knoxville	64	52	12	Houston	246	82	164
Martin	15	11	4	Medical Branch	100	36	64
Memphis	36	22	14	Pan American	31	16	15
Vanderbilt University	99	74	25	Permian Basin	11	5	6
Volunteer State Community College	6	5	1				
Walters State Community College	7	7	0				

Table 79

Full-time Law Enforcement Employees as of October 31, 2003
by University and College by State[1]—Continued

University/College by state	Total law enforcement employees	Total officers	Total civilians	University/College by state	Total law enforcement employees	Total officers	Total civilians
TEXAS—Continued				**WASHINGTON**			
San Antonio	72	36	36	Central Washington University	13	12	1
Southwestern Medical School	92	38	54	Eastern Washington University	10	10	0
Tyler	10	4	6	Evergreen State College	15	10	5
West Texas A&M University	11	8	3	University of Washington	56	44	12
				Washington State University:			
UTAH				Pullman	19	17	2
				Vancouver	4	3	1
Brigham Young University	37	25	12	Western Washington University	18	12	6
College of Eastern Utah	2	2	0				
Southern Utah University	5	4	1	**WEST VIRGINIA**			
University of Utah	95	30	65				
Utah State University	17	12	5	Bluefield State College	1	1	0
Utah Valley State College	8	6	2	Concord College	7	5	2
Weber State University	11	10	1	Fairmont State College	8	7	1
				Glenville State College	5	2	3
VIRGINIA				Marshall University	21	20	1
				Potomac State College	5	5	0
Christopher Newport University	18	13	5	Shepherd College	10	9	1
College of William and Mary	22	18	4	West Liberty State College	4	4	0
Emory and Henry College	4	1	3	West Virginia State College	10	10	0
Ferrum College	7	7	0	West Virginia Tech	5	5	0
George Mason University	56	43	13	West Virginia University	55	45	10
Hampton University	34	20	14				
James Madison University	26	21	5	**WISCONSIN**			
Longwood College	16	11	5				
Mary Washington College	17	9	8	University of Wisconsin:			
Norfolk State University	51	27	24	Eau Claire	12	11	1
Northern Virginia Community College	33	33	0	Green Bay	12	5	7
Old Dominion University	55	34	21	La Crosse	8	8	0
Radford University	24	19	5	Madison	103	58	45
Thomas Nelson Community College	9	7	2	Milwaukee	37	30	7
University of Richmond	32	16	16	Oshkosh	12	10	2
University of Virginia	112	50	62	Parkside	13	9	4
University of Virginia, College at Wise	8	7	1	Platteville	7	6	1
Virginia Commonwealth University	156	70	86	Stevens Point	6	2	4
Virginia Military Institute	6	6	0	Stout	9	8	1
Virginia Polytechnic Institute and				Superior	5	1	4
State University	56	38	18	Whitewater	11	10	1
Virginia State University	31	16	15				
Virginia Western Community College	6	6	0	**WYOMING**			
				Sheridan College	2	2	0
				University of Wyoming	23	13	10

[1] These agencies have no resident population associated with them.

Table 80

Full-time Law Enforcement Employees as of October 31, 2003
by Metropolitan County by State

County by state	Total law enforcement employees	Total officers	Total civilians	County by state	Total law enforcement employees	Total officers	Total civilians
ALABAMA				**CALIFORNIA—Continued**			
Autauga	47	19	28	Kings	193	74	119
Bibb	29	11	18	Los Angeles	14,461	8,581	5,880
Blount	64	38	26	Madera	110	78	32
Calhoun	38	32	6	Marin	306	207	99
Colbert	49	28	21	Merced	233	176	57
Elmore	73	29	44	Monterey	444	327	117
Etowah	70	56	14	Napa	115	86	29
Geneva	13	11	2	Orange	3,573	1,793	1,780
Greene	25	11	14	Placer	396	219	177
Hale	7	6	1	Riverside	2,944	1,517	1,427
Henry	15	10	5	Sacramento	2,258	1,507	751
Houston	73	46	27	San Benito	62	30	32
Jefferson	643	509	134	San Bernardino	2,748	1,534	1,214
Lauderdale	40	31	9	San Diego	3,166	1,980	1,186
Lee	117	52	65	San Francisco	994	827	167
Limestone	78	37	41	San Joaquin	718	298	420
Lowndes	37	11	26	San Luis Obispo	370	156	214
Madison	270	103	167	San Mateo	568	410	158
Mobile	494	145	349	Santa Barbara	623	447	176
Montgomery	266	123	143	Santa Clara	710	553	157
Morgan	127	47	80	Santa Cruz	319	176	143
Russell	83	29	54	Shasta	249	135	114
Shelby	155	94	61	Solano	472	110	362
St. Clair	37	32	5	Sonoma	663	269	394
Tuscaloosa	108	87	21	Stanislaus	571	228	343
Walker	75	33	42	Sutter	136	108	28
				Tulare	602	424	178
ARIZONA				Ventura	1,343	798	545
				Yolo	214	76	138
Coconino	212	58	154	Yuba	163	77	86
Maricopa	2,396	678	1,718				
Pima	1,188	472	716	**COLORADO**			
Pinal	319	138	181				
Yavapai	279	107	172	Adams	443	299	144
Yuma	283	69	214	Arapahoe	625	396	229
				Boulder	337	204	133
ARKANSAS				Broomfield	181	95	86
				Clear Creek	54	23	31
Benton	159	72	87	Douglas	406	248	158
Cleveland	11	6	5	Elbert	41	30	11
Craighead	38	26	12	El Paso	547	388	159
Crawford	54	22	32	Gilpin	33	23	10
Crittenden	145	36	109	Jefferson	658	459	199
Faulkner	104	39	65	Larimer	370	232	138
Franklin	16	10	6	Mesa	179	99	80
Garland	114	38	76	Park	58	26	32
Grant	11	9	2	Pueblo	252	145	107
Jefferson	50	44	6	Teller	73	38	35
Lincoln	20	7	13	Weld	243	105	138
Lonoke	34	17	17				
Madison	14	8	6	**DELAWARE**			
Miller	30	23	7				
Perry	21	7	14	New Castle County Police Department	538	330	208
Poinsett	46	12	34				
Pulaski	505	402	103	**FLORIDA**			
Saline	68	41	27				
Sebastian	129	31	98	Alachua	449	247	202
Washington	155	93	62	Baker	75	40	35
				Bay	282	195	87
CALIFORNIA				Brevard	703	467	236
				Broward	3,391	1,515	1,876
Alameda	1,506	936	570	Charlotte	351	238	113
Butte	256	106	150	Clay	513	262	251
Contra Costa	1,060	710	350	Collier	1,079	567	512
El Dorado	384	170	214	Escambia	1,097	709	388
Fresno	1,076	467	609	Gadsden	72	50	22
Imperial	259	173	86	Gilchrist	38	24	14
Kern	1,063	474	589	Hernando	362	221	141

Table 80

Full-time Law Enforcement Employees as of October 31, 2003
by Metropolitan County by State—Continued

County by state	Total law enforcement employees	Total officers	Total civilians	County by state	Total law enforcement employees	Total officers	Total civilians
FLORIDA—Continued				**GEORGIA—Continued**			
Hillsborough	3,076	1,118	1,958	Henry	161	86	75
Indian River	406	278	128	Henry County Police Department	176	155	21
Jefferson	47	16	31	Houston	282	108	174
Lake	309	203	106	Jones	70	37	33
Lee	830	526	304	Lamar	48	23	25
Leon	320	229	91	Lanier	12	7	5
Manatee	958	642	316	Lee	79	37	42
Marion	776	276	500	Liberty	86	58	28
Martin	559	248	311	Long	16	15	1
Miami-Dade	4,628	3,088	1,540	Lowndes	205	188	17
Nassau	202	131	71	Madison	47	26	21
Okaloosa	314	237	77	Meriwether	36	20	16
Orange	1,930	1,295	635	Murray	63	34	29
Osceola	449	305	144	Muscogee	328	270	58
Palm Beach	2,810	1,186	1,624	Newton	143	82	61
Pasco	607	347	260	Oconee	57	38	19
Pinellas	2,531	781	1,750	Oglethorpe	16	11	5
Polk	1,383	523	860	Paulding	131	106	25
Santa Rosa	257	170	87	Pike	30	23	7
Sarasota	950	413	537	Spalding	141	83	58
Seminole	889	348	541	Twiggs	29	11	18
St. Johns	415	250	165	Walker	114	71	43
St. Lucie	334	238	96	Walton	149	132	17
Volusia	657	443	214	Whitfield	175	90	85
Wakulla	80	53	27	Worth	32	21	11
GEORGIA				**IDAHO**			
Augusta-Richmond	703	494	209	Ada	263	119	144
Barrow	108	100	8	Bannock	73	38	35
Bartow	212	165	47	Boise	17	10	7
Bibb	283	244	39	Bonneville	78	53	25
Brantley	19	12	7	Canyon	146	63	83
Brooks	30	17	13	Gem	21	11	10
Burke	70	34	36	Jefferson	25	16	9
Carroll	173	89	84	Kootenai	108	79	29
Catoosa	118	58	60	Nez Perce	36	24	12
Chatham	328	252	76	Owyhee	21	12	9
Chatham County Police Department	191	132	59	Power	18	10	8
Chattahoochee	9	4	5				
Cherokee	328	287	41	**ILLINOIS**			
Clarke	158	109	49				
Clayton	350	137	213	Bond	17	9	8
Clayton County Police Department	278	256	22	Boone	84	34	50
Cobb	604	389	215	Calhoun	10	5	5
Cobb County Police Department	597	541	56	Champaign	59	53	6
Columbia	293	239	54	Clinton	36	15	21
Coweta	173	149	24	Cook	6,269	2,534	3,735
Dade	37	21	16	De Kalb	89	41	48
Dawson	72	54	18	Du Page	556	439	117
DeKalb	699	533	166	Ford	26	9	17
DeKalb County Police Department	1,272	940	332	Grundy	50	30	20
Dougherty County Police Department	52	49	3	Henry	73	23	50
Douglas	298	200	98	Jersey	28	13	15
Effingham	96	58	38	Kane	282	96	186
Fayette	207	123	84	Kankakee	115	60	55
Floyd	133	79	54	Kendall	87	79	8
Floyd County Police Department	77	71	6	Lake	421	168	253
Forsyth	249	165	84	Macon	142	40	102
Fulton	913	629	284	Macoupin	55	24	31
Fulton County Police Department	386	306	80	Madison	152	73	79
Glynn	115	39	76	Marshall	17	8	9
Glynn County Police Department	120	108	12	McHenry	274	92	182
Gwinnett County Police Department	803	521	282	McLean	63	51	12
Hall	348	242	106	Menard	14	7	7
Haralson	48	24	24	Mercer	23	11	12
Harris	58	41	17	Monroe	28	14	14
Heard	20	14	6	Peoria	187	62	125

Table 80

Full-time Law Enforcement Employees as of October 31, 2003
by Metropolitan County by State—Continued

County by state	Total law enforcement employees	Total officers	Total civilians	County by state	Total law enforcement employees	Total officers	Total civilians
ILLINOIS—Continued				**IOWA—Continued**			
Piatt	27	11	16	Johnson	83	55	28
Rock Island	145	61	84	Jones	23	10	13
Sangamon	225	75	150	Linn	177	117	60
Stark	11	4	7	Madison	15	6	9
St. Clair	171	164	7	Mills	28	11	17
Tazewell	94	41	53	Polk	349	181	168
Vermilion	87	34	53	Pottawattamie	147	46	101
Will	467	260	207	Scott	155	41	114
Winnebago	281	121	160	Story	78	33	45
Woodford	37	33	4	Warren	32	22	10
				Washington	24	13	11
INDIANA				Woodbury	116	35	81
Allen	288	124	164	**KANSAS**			
Bartholomew	72	38	34				
Benton	19	6	13	Butler	51	47	4
Boone	52	23	29	Doniphan	10	5	5
Brown	32	13	19	Douglas	120	73	47
Carroll	25	11	14	Franklin	47	22	25
Clark	97	35	62	Harvey	35	15	20
Clay	35	11	24	Jackson	41	18	23
Dearborn	67	24	43	Jefferson	41	24	17
Delaware	111	43	68	Johnson	557	435	122
Elkhart	163	67	96	Leavenworth	77	54	23
Floyd	75	26	49	Linn	23	12	11
Franklin	32	10	22	Miami	39	22	17
Gibson	40	16	24	Osage	36	18	18
Greene	39	13	26	Sedgwick	488	161	327
Hamilton	72	58	14	Shawnee	148	114	34
Hancock	72	35	37	Sumner	29	19	10
Harrison	68	21	47	Wabaunsee	12	6	6
Hendricks	106	40	66	Wyandotte	146	42	104
Howard	114	35	79				
Jasper	43	19	24	**KENTUCKY**			
Johnson	114	51	63				
Lake	508	170	338	Boone	137	126	11
La Porte	131	56	75	Bourbon	5	4	1
Madison	119	51	68	Boyd	22	17	5
Monroe	89	30	59	Boyd County Police Department	2	2	0
Morgan	67	23	44	Bracken	4	3	1
Newton	40	14	26	Bullitt	37	31	6
Ohio	9	9	0	Campbell	13	10	3
Owen	29	11	18	Campbell County Police Department	31	30	1
Porter	144	121	23	Christian	28	25	3
Posey	32	13	19	Christian County Police Department	8	7	1
Putnam	33	14	19	Clark	16	13	3
Shelby	81	29	52	Daviess	49	35	14
St. Joseph	288	131	157	Edmonson	6	4	2
Sullivan	33	11	22	Fayette	77	45	32
Tippecanoe	141	45	96	Gallatin	5	5	0
Vanderburgh	223	106	117	Grant	22	20	2
Vermillion	24	7	17	Greenup	12	11	1
Vigo	96	36	60	Hancock	6	6	0
Warrick	78	37	41	Hardin	32	30	2
Washington	29	11	18	Henderson	23	20	3
Wells	38	14	24	Henry	6	6	0
Whitley	45	14	31	Jefferson	265	217	48
				Jessamine	28	23	5
IOWA				Kenton	33	29	4
				Kenton County Police Department	51	45	6
Benton	25	10	15	Larue	4	4	0
Black Hawk	136	104	32	McLean	9	7	2
Bremer	24	12	12	Meade	11	9	2
Dallas	40	16	24	Nelson	28	24	4
Dubuque	65	55	10	Oldham	19	18	1
Grundy	16	12	4	Oldham County Police Department	32	29	3
Guthrie	9	4	5	Pendleton	7	6	1
Harrison	11	9	2	Scott	28	26	2

Table 80

Full-time Law Enforcement Employees as of October 31, 2003
by Metropolitan County by State—Continued

County by state	Total law enforcement employees	Total officers	Total civilians	County by state	Total law enforcement employees	Total officers	Total civilians
KENTUCKY—Continued				**MICHIGAN**			
Shelby	22	20	2	Barry	51	30	21
Spencer	5	4	1	Bay	85	39	46
Trigg	6	6	0	Berrien	172	62	110
Trimble	3	2	1	Calhoun	169	62	107
Warren	53	43	10	Cass	75	38	37
Webster	7	6	1	Clinton	60	26	34
Woodford	6	6	0	Eaton	134	68	66
Woodford County Police Department	17	16	1	Genesee	263	142	121
				Ingham	216	123	93
LOUISIANA				Ionia	52	21	31
				Jackson	139	54	85
Ascension	244	188	56	Kalamazoo	194	156	38
Bossier	206	183	23	Kent	592	151	441
Caddo	625	416	209	Lapeer	83	52	31
Calcasieu	676	665	11	Livingston	127	73	54
Cameron	76	76	0	Macomb	458	217	241
De Soto	82	74	8	Monroe	206	99	107
East Baton Rouge	830	710	120	Muskegon	117	49	68
East Feliciana	71	43	28	Newaygo	31	28	3
Grant	52	52	0	Oakland	973	821	152
Iberville	146	69	77	Ottawa	130	117	13
Jefferson	1,566	1,060	506	Saginaw	130	76	54
Lafayette	504	325	179	St. Clair	154	81	73
Lafourche	321	220	101	Van Buren	89	46	43
Livingston	187	187	0	Washtenaw	171	136	35
Ouachita	365	105	260	Wayne	1,391	901	490
Plaquemines	197	158	39				
Pointe Coupee	110	43	67	**MINNESOTA**			
Rapides	456	371	85				
St. Bernard	376	271	105	Anoka	201	99	102
St. Charles	350	252	98	Benton	66	24	42
St. Helena	46	17	29	Carlton	43	23	20
St. John the Baptist	210	209	1	Carver	135	72	63
St. Martin	215	174	41	Chisago	65	33	32
St. Tammany	598	497	101	Clay	58	29	29
Union	50	37	13	Dakota	165	76	89
West Feliciana	72	37	35	Dodge	29	21	8
				Hennepin	692	296	396
MAINE				Houston	23	11	12
				Isanti	51	16	35
Androscoggin	27	18	9	Olmsted	120	49	71
Cumberland	45	44	1	Polk	36	24	12
Penobscot	26	22	4	Ramsey	386	256	130
Sagadahoc	15	15	0	Scott	117	35	82
York	30	26	4	Sherburne	159	48	111
				Stearns	121	50	71
MARYLAND				St. Louis	190	97	93
				Wabasha	29	15	14
Allegany	24	19	5	Washington	213	79	134
Anne Arundel	100	74	26	Wright	166	103	63
Anne Arundel County Police Department	830	611	219				
Baltimore County Police Department	2,077	1,780	297	**MISSISSIPPI**			
Baltimore County Sheriff	78	61	17				
Calvert	95	80	15	Harrison	321	136	185
Carroll	63	49	14	Hinds	442	99	343
Cecil	81	65	16	Jackson	132	75	57
Charles	334	230	104	Lamar	30	26	4
Frederick	190	144	46	Madison	104	38	66
Harford	290	233	57	Marshall	41	21	20
Howard	58	34	24	Perry	15	9	6
Howard County Police Department	504	357	147	Rankin	138	67	71
Montgomery	167	138	29	Stone	14	12	2
Montgomery County Police Department	1,499	1,141	358	Tate	33	16	17
Prince George's	235	151	84	Tunica	131	52	79
Prince George's County Police Department	1,551	1,323	228				
Queen Anne's	51	48	3	**MISSOURI**			
Somerset	17	15	2				
Washington	196	79	117	Andrew	14	11	3
Wicomico	111	89	22	Bates	25	9	16

Table 80

Full-time Law Enforcement Employees as of October 31, 2003
by Metropolitan County by State—Continued

County by state	Total law enforcement employees	Total officers	Total civilians	County by state	Total law enforcement employees	Total officers	Total civilians
MISSOURI—Continued				**NEW JERSEY—Continued**			
Boone	73	56	17	Gloucester	73	63	10
Buchanan	67	52	15	Hudson	273	177	96
Caldwell	11	6	5	Hunterdon	34	29	5
Callaway	24	22	2	Mercer	152	119	33
Cass	59	47	12	Middlesex	235	196	39
Christian	61	40	21	Monmouth	691	463	228
Clay	181	116	65	Morris	315	235	80
Clinton	18	12	6	Ocean	195	98	97
Cole	46	34	12	Passaic	819	634	185
Dallas	17	13	4	Salem	156	136	20
De Kalb	9	4	5	Somerset	217	177	40
Franklin	132	110	22	Sussex	133	107	26
Greene	225	143	82	Union	185	160	25
Howard	12	7	5	Warren	22	18	4
Jackson	124	87	37				
Jasper	107	74	33	**NEW MEXICO**			
Jefferson	219	146	73				
Lafayette	32	24	8	Bernalillo	333	268	65
Lincoln	84	48	36	Sandoval	43	37	6
McDonald	18	11	7	San Juan	104	84	20
Moniteau	7	4	3	Santa Fe	90	74	16
Newton	67	36	31	Torrance	26	24	2
Osage	7	6	1	Valencia	47	38	9
Platte	119	84	35				
Polk	33	24	9	**NEW YORK**			
Ray	27	14	13				
St. Charles	200	140	60	Albany	137	102	35
St. Louis County Police Department	971	739	232	Broome	70	53	17
Warren	55	27	28	Chemung	48	42	6
Washington	32	17	15	Herkimer	10	5	5
Webster	30	14	16	Livingston	62	45	17
				Madison	36	29	7
MONTANA				Monroe	316	260	56
				Nassau	3,174	2,479	695
Carbon	12	7	5	Niagara	136	110	26
Cascade	131	32	99	Oneida	164	91	73
Missoula	188	50	138	Onondaga	280	239	41
Yellowstone	144	48	96	Ontario	91	61	30
				Orange	140	129	11
NEBRASKA				Orleans	41	27	14
				Oswego	75	65	10
Cass	63	31	32	Putnam	105	85	20
Dakota	25	11	14	Rensselaer	34	26	8
Dixon	12	7	5	Rockland	83	72	11
Douglas	193	127	66	Schenectady	16	9	7
Lancaster	88	70	18	Schoharie	26	15	11
Sarpy	181	124	57	Suffolk	362	243	119
Saunders	19	11	8	Suffolk County Police Department	3,397	2,808	589
Seward	21	11	10	Tioga	54	35	19
Washington	40	21	19	Ulster	76	71	5
				Warren	91	68	23
NEVADA				Washington	38	32	6
				Wayne	63	51	12
Carson City	134	88	46	Westchester Public Safety	309	252	57
Storey	23	20	3				
Washoe	672	403	269	**NORTH CAROLINA**			
				Alamance	145	94	51
NEW JERSEY				Alexander	34	27	7
				Anson	30	26	4
Atlantic	115	87	28	Brunswick	107	84	23
Bergen	488	412	76	Buncombe	291	199	92
Bergen County Police Department	144	83	61	Burke	103	82	21
Burlington	87	70	17	Cabarrus	153	143	10
Camden	212	184	28	Caldwell	96	57	39
Cape May	121	109	12	Catawba	111	103	8
Cumberland	59	51	8	Chatham	72	56	16
Essex	536	456	80	Cumberland	502	270	232
Essex County Police Department	42	41	1				

Table 80

Full-time Law Enforcement Employees as of October 31, 2003
by Metropolitan County by State—Continued

County by state	Total law enforcement employees	Total officers	Total civilians	County by state	Total law enforcement employees	Total officers	Total civilians
NORTH CAROLINA—Continued				**OHIO—Continued**			
Currituck	66	49	17	Richland	113	50	63
Davie	61	32	29	Stark	221	120	101
Durham	431	141	290	Summit	481	392	89
Edgecombe	109	47	62	Trumbull	130	45	85
Forsyth	459	192	267	Union	65	43	22
Franklin	75	38	37	Warren	161	84	77
Gaston[1]	192	100	92	Washington	45	30	15
Gaston County Police Department[1]	217	137	80	Wood	122	117	5
Greene	35	24	11				
Guilford	468	233	235	**OKLAHOMA**			
Haywood	69	47	22				
Henderson	153	117	36	Canadian	62	34	28
Hoke	59	37	22	Cleveland	103	49	54
Johnston	164	90	74	Comanche	35	27	8
Madison	28	20	8	Creek	57	33	24
Mecklenburg[2]	1,035	271	764	Grady	18	14	4
Nash	118	66	52	Le Flore	24	11	13
New Hanover	310	263	47	Lincoln	19	10	9
Onslow	146	97	49	Logan	21	10	11
Orange	132	101	31	McClain	24	12	12
Pender	74	42	32	Oklahoma	660	150	510
Person	64	38	26	Okmulgee	10	9	1
Pitt	228	102	126	Osage	55	36	19
Randolph	203	141	62	Pawnee	19	10	9
Rockingham	124	88	36	Rogers	25	21	4
Stokes	59	38	21	Sequoyah	23	9	14
Union	170	124	46	Tulsa	191	166	25
Wake	628	322	306	Wagoner	36	10	26
Wayne	141	77	64				
Yadkin	57	34	23	**OREGON**			
				Benton	35	30	5
NORTH DAKOTA				Clackamas	236	192	44
				Columbia	16	12	4
Burleigh	61	34	27	Deschutes	90	73	17
Cass	111	59	52	Jackson	66	47	19
Grand Forks	29	24	5	Lane	116	65	51
Morton	33	20	13	Marion	101	77	24
				Multnomah	123	93	30
OHIO				Polk	27	22	5
				Washington	254	185	69
Allen	148	68	80	Yamhill	35	31	4
Belmont	67	55	12				
Brown	55	35	20	**PENNSYLVANIA**			
Butler	313	169	144				
Carroll	18	17	1	Allegheny	184	153	31
Clark	150	126	24	Allegheny County Police Department	238	214	24
Clermont	209	86	123	Beaver	32	26	6
Delaware	151	81	70	Centre	13	11	2
Erie	71	34	37	Cumberland	30	25	5
Fairfield	145	109	36	Lancaster	48	39	9
Franklin	816	454	362	Washington	27	23	4
Fulton	33	22	11	York	69	58	11
Geauga	93	43	50				
Greene	160	138	22	**SOUTH CAROLINA**			
Jefferson	77	30	47				
Lake	181	52	129	Aiken	144	106	38
Lawrence	43	35	8	Anderson	165	132	33
Licking	185	130	55	Berkeley	167	107	60
Lorain	239	78	161	Calhoun	22	20	2
Lucas	517	300	217	Charleston	674	249	425
Madison	28	24	4	Darlington	114	61	53
Mahoning	219	208	11	Dorchester	164	77	87
Medina	169	73	96	Fairfield	52	44	8
Miami	139	50	89	Florence	219	110	109
Montgomery	422	209	213	Greenville	435	354	81
Ottawa	62	59	3	Horry County Police Department	215	195	20
Portage	131	54	77	Kershaw	65	52	13
Preble	63	19	44				

Table 80

Full-time Law Enforcement Employees as of October 31, 2003
by Metropolitan County by State—Continued

County by state	Total law enforcement employees	Total officers	Total civilians	County by state	Total law enforcement employees	Total officers	Total civilians
SOUTH CAROLINA—Continued				**TEXAS—Continued**			
Laurens	102	54	48	Bexar	1,684	447	1,237
Pickens	121	85	36	Bowie	43	38	5
Richland	565	434	131	Brazoria	301	116	185
Saluda	50	18	32	Brazos	176	73	103
Spartanburg	300	277	23	Burleson	25	14	11
York	284	125	159	Caldwell	68	22	46
				Calhoun	39	23	16
SOUTH DAKOTA				Callahan	11	5	6
				Cameron	333	96	237
Lincoln	10	9	1	Carson	13	6	7
McCook	4	3	1	Chambers	73	32	41
Meade	48	15	33	Clay	19	11	8
Minnehaha	190	77	113	Collin	439	112	327
Pennington	161	57	104	Comal	231	120	111
Turner	6	4	2	Coryell	53	19	34
Union	19	6	13	Crosby	16	6	10
				Delta	17	10	7
TENNESSEE				Denton	409	116	293
				Ector	189	81	108
Anderson	115	44	71	Ellis	165	61	104
Blount	278	239	39	El Paso	1,025	235	790
Bradley	140	129	11	Fort Bend	484	299	185
Cannon	38	14	24	Goliad	24	10	14
Carter	63	57	6	Grayson	122	56	66
Cheatham	66	31	35	Gregg	151	69	82
Chester	22	10	12	Guadalupe	162	52	110
Dickson	105	48	57	Hardin	64	37	27
Fayette	53	30	23	Harris	3,506	2,519	987
Grainger	24	19	5	Hays	234	98	136
Hamblen	60	57	3	Hidalgo	623	210	413
Hamilton	374	142	232	Hunt	82	36	46
Hartsville-Trousdale	30	16	14	Irion	8	4	4
Hawkins	56	53	3	Jefferson	387	94	293
Hickman	28	17	11	Johnson	202	77	125
Jefferson	52	37	15	Jones	15	5	10
Knox	981	466	515	Kaufman	106	44	62
Loudon	61	60	1	Kendall	47	34	13
Macon	54	21	33	Lampasas	35	21	14
Madison	202	197	5	Liberty	59	43	16
Marion	38	17	21	Lubbock	249	149	100
Montgomery	229	196	33	McLennan	293	108	185
Polk	34	17	17	Medina	60	25	35
Robertson	97	79	18	Midland	176	78	98
Rutherford	336	160	176	Montgomery	448	280	168
Sequatchie	19	11	8	Nueces	280	81	199
Shelby	2,059	494	1,565	Parker	112	58	54
Shelby County Police Department	39	30	9	Potter	201	104	97
Smith	40	21	19	Randall	145	64	81
Stewart	28	13	15	Robertson	23	10	13
Sullivan	218	176	42	Rockwall	90	34	56
Sumner	140	61	79	Rusk	57	46	11
Tipton	40	36	4	San Jacinto	31	16	15
Unicoi	36	21	15	San Patricio	84	40	44
Union	30	26	4	Smith	244	113	131
Washington	171	77	94	Tarrant	1,247	455	792
Williamson	90	80	10	Taylor	168	72	96
Wilson	148	129	19	Tom Green	148	37	111
				Travis	1,334	623	711
TEXAS				Upshur	59	27	32
				Victoria	156	98	58
Aransas	48	21	27	Waller	53	27	26
Archer	12	7	5	Webb	269	164	105
Armstrong	7	3	4	Wichita	157	40	117
Atascosa	70	27	43	Williamson	406	175	231
Austin	41	24	17	Wilson	68	24	44
Bandera	36	22	14	Wise	95	47	48
Bastrop	134	52	82				
Bell	242	92	150				

Table 80

Full-time Law Enforcement Employees as of October 31, 2003
by Metropolitan County by State—Continued

County by state	Total law enforcement employees	Total officers	Total civilians	County by state	Total law enforcement employees	Total officers	Total civilians
UTAH				**VIRGINIA—Continued**			
				Washington	86	74	12
Cache	101	60	41	York	93	88	5
Davis	243	181	62				
Juab	21	8	13	**WASHINGTON**			
Morgan	12	11	1				
Salt Lake	1,287	386	901	Asotin	13	11	2
Summit	76	38	38	Benton	84	56	28
Tooele	76	50	26	Chelan	68	50	18
Utah	263	184	79	Clark	197	123	74
Washington	153	128	25	Cowlitz	50	40	10
Weber	364	293	71	Douglas	42	28	14
				Franklin	25	22	3
VERMONT				King	834	514	320
				Kitsap	154	122	32
Chittenden	16	12	4	Pierce	308	253	55
Franklin	17	13	4	Skagit	106	57	49
Grand Isle	2	1	1	Skamania	24	20	4
				Snohomish	336	256	80
VIRGINIA				Spokane	185	129	56
				Thurston	112	86	26
Albemarle County Police Department	123	101	22	Whatcom	88	74	14
Amelia	19	12	7	Yakima	98	65	33
Amherst	68	63	5				
Appomattox	34	31	3	**WEST VIRGINIA**			
Arlington County Police Department	490	350	140				
Bedford	72	71	1	Berkeley	70	45	25
Botetourt	77	60	17	Berkeley-Martinsburg State Police	22	20	2
Campbell	55	52	3	Boone	23	21	2
Caroline	39	31	8	Boone State Police:			
Charles City	15	9	6	Danville	7	6	1
Chesterfield County Police Department	529	430	99	Whitesville	4	3	1
Clarke	24	14	10	Brooke	24	16	8
Craig	13	8	5	Brooke-Wellsburg State Police	4	3	1
Cumberland	16	11	5	Cabell	55	37	18
Dinwiddie	62	51	11	Cabell-Huntington State Police	17	11	6
Fairfax County Police Department	1,804	1,326	478	Clay	7	6	1
Fauquier	112	95	17	Clay-Clay State Police	4	4	0
Fluvanna	31	21	10	Hampshire	11	9	2
Franklin	90	73	17	Hampshire-Romney State Police	19	8	11
Frederick	99	85	14	Hancock	38	27	11
Giles	30	20	10	Hancock-New Cumberland State Police	4	3	1
Gloucester	95	79	16	Jefferson	18	16	2
Goochland	33	25	8	Jefferson-Kearneysville State Police	20	12	8
Greene	24	17	7	Kanawha	104	81	23
Hanover	188	169	19	Kanawha State Police:			
Henrico County Police Department	766	541	225	Parkway Authority	23	23	0
Isle of Wight	28	26	2	Quincy	11	10	1
James City County Police Department	76	72	4	South Charleston	30	21	9
King and Queen	16	9	7	Lincoln	8	8	0
King William	29	17	12	Lincoln-Hamlin State Police	12	11	1
Loudoun	383	323	60	Marshall	25	23	2
Louisa	44	32	12	Marshall-Moundsville State Police	16	7	9
Mathews	17	11	6	Mineral	11	9	2
Montgomery	111	94	17	Mineral-Keyser State Police	7	6	1
Nelson	20	14	6	Monongalia	52	31	21
New Kent	37	27	10	Monongalia-Morgantown State Police	26	17	9
Pittsylvania	122	66	56	Morgan	10	9	1
Powhatan	44	33	11	Morgan-Berkeley Springs State Police	5	4	1
Prince George County Police Department	65	51	14	Ohio	28	27	1
Prince William County Police Department	530	440	90	Ohio-Wheeling State Police	7	6	1
Pulaski	52	42	10	Pleasants	7	6	1
Roanoke County Police Department	155	113	42	Pleasants-St. Marys State Police	4	3	1
Rockingham	156	49	107	Preston	28	15	13
Scott	41	40	1	Preston-Kingwood State Police	7	6	1
Spotsylvania	105	98	7	Putnam	40	35	5
Stafford	162	123	39	Putnam State Police:			
Surry	18	13	5	Teays Valley	6	5	1
Sussex	41	37	4	Winfield	4	3	1
Warren	62	61	1				

Table 80

Full-time Law Enforcement Employees as of October 31, 2003
by Metropolitan County by State—Continued

County by state	Total law enforcement employees	Total officers	Total civilians	County by state	Total law enforcement employees	Total officers	Total civilians
WEST VIRGINIA—Continued				**WISCONSIN—Continued**			
Wayne	31	22	9	La Crosse	107	38	69
Wayne-Wayne State Police	10	9	1	Marathon	172	64	108
Wirt	2	2	0	Milwaukee	1,018	703	315
Wirt-Elizabeth State Police	4	3	1	Oconto	55	23	32
Wood	65	37	28	Outagamie	213	78	135
Wood-Parkersburg State Police	16	9	7	Ozaukee	104	78	26
				Pierce	49	45	4
WISCONSIN				Racine	265	195	70
				Rock	183	92	91
Brown	305	143	162	Sheboygan	170	76	94
Calumet	44	23	21	St. Croix	73	39	34
Chippewa	65	51	14	Washington	155	63	92
Columbia	84	40	44	Waukesha	317	152	165
Dane	501	412	89	Winnebago	198	135	63
Douglas	51	47	4				
Eau Claire	96	52	44	**WYOMING**			
Fond du Lac	119	51	68				
Iowa	37	35	2	Laramie	133	90	43
Kenosha	305	104	201	Natrona	52	43	9
Kewaunee	38	36	2				

[1] The data are listed separately for both Gaston County and Gaston County Police Department, North Carolina. However, Gaston County reports its crime figures combined with those of the Gaston County Police Department; they can be found in Table 10 under Gaston County Police Department.

[2] The data presented in this table for *Mecklenburg* represent only those law enforcement employees that work for the Mecklenburg County Sheriff's Office and exclude Charlotte-Mecklenburg Police Department employees.

Table 81

Full-time Law Enforcement Employees as of October 31, 2003
by Nonmetropolitan County by State

County by state	Total law enforcement employees	Total officers	Total civilians	County by state	Total law enforcement employees	Total officers	Total civilians
ALABAMA				**ARKANSAS—Continued**			
Baldwin	202	72	130	Fulton	12	6	6
Barbour	34	31	3	Greene	43	12	31
Bullock	12	6	6	Hempstead	15	12	3
Butler	21	7	14	Hot Spring	34	26	8
Chambers	51	18	33	Howard	20	9	11
Cherokee	18	16	2	Independence	76	49	27
Choctaw	16	7	9	Izard	22	9	13
Clarke	34	15	19	Jackson	20	10	10
Clay	24	11	13	Johnson	31	11	20
Cleburne	23	9	14	Lafayette	16	7	9
Coffee	18	15	3	Lawrence	20	11	9
Conecuh	8	8	0	Lee	7	5	2
Coosa	18	7	11	Little River	18	7	11
Covington	52	26	26	Logan	25	12	13
Crenshaw	11	10	1	Marion	22	12	10
Cullman	90	61	29	Mississippi	83	24	59
Dale	17	14	3	Monroe	16	6	10
Dallas	60	28	32	Montgomery	15	7	8
De Kalb	33	27	6	Nevada	17	6	11
Escambia	41	19	22	Newton	10	7	3
Fayette	15	10	5	Ouachita	34	19	15
Franklin	36	19	17	Phillips	15	9	6
Jackson	75	34	41	Pike	13	7	6
Lamar	17	6	11	Polk	23	11	12
Macon	36	20	16	Pope	34	29	5
Marengo	28	11	17	Prairie	14	7	7
Marion	30	15	15	Randolph	11	9	2
Marshall	73	36	37	Scott	13	6	7
Monroe	48	22	26	Searcy	12	6	6
Perry	13	6	7	Sevier	20	11	9
Pickens	20	7	13	Sharp	20	11	9
Pike	29	15	14	St. Francis	34	15	19
Randolph	12	12	0	Stone	19	8	11
Talladega	78	35	43	Union	56	27	29
Tallapoosa	54	21	33	Van Buren	28	15	13
Washington	14	7	7	White	84	37	47
Winston	22	9	13	Woodruff	12	6	6
				Yell	20	12	8
ARIZONA				**CALIFORNIA**			
Apache	74	31	43				
Cochise	182	71	111	Alpine	14	11	3
Gila	122	48	74	Amador	90	48	42
Graham	53	21	32	Calaveras	95	55	40
Greenlee	26	13	13	Colusa	60	32	28
Mohave	212	80	132	Del Norte	56	29	27
Navajo	113	47	66	Glenn	66	29	37
Santa Cruz	72	40	32	Humboldt	236	189	47
				Inyo	73	58	15
ARKANSAS				Lake	150	61	89
				Lassen	96	74	22
Arkansas	46	12	34	Mariposa	59	49	10
Ashley	25	13	12	Mendocino	173	134	39
Baxter	42	28	14	Modoc	27	22	5
Boone	36	21	15	Mono	43	26	17
Bradley	5	4	1	Nevada	197	71	126
Calhoun	12	6	6	Plumas	71	38	33
Carroll	34	17	17	Sierra	17	11	6
Chicot	7	6	1	Siskiyou	128	96	32
Clark	30	14	16	Tehama	114	87	27
Clay	23	8	15	Trinity	27	20	7
Cleburne	29	18	11	Tuolumne	139	71	68
Columbia	34	13	21				
Conway	30	13	17	**COLORADO**			
Cross	32	15	17				
Dallas	28	6	22	Alamosa	36	27	9
Desha	9	7	2	Baca	10	4	6
Drew	12	11	1	Bent	8	7	1

Table 81

Full-time Law Enforcement Employees as of October 31, 2003
by Nonmetropolitan County by State—Continued

County by state	Total law enforcement employees	Total officers	Total civilians
COLORADO—Continued			
Chaffee	41	23	18
Cheyenne	10	5	5
Conejos	12	6	6
Costilla	13	8	5
Crowley	12	8	4
Custer	20	9	11
Delta	41	20	21
Dolores	7	4	3
Eagle	77	64	13
Fremont	72	67	5
Garfield	95	27	68
Grand	58	32	26
Gunnison	27	12	15
Hinsdale	5	4	1
Huerfano	20	8	12
Jackson	8	4	4
Kiowa	4	3	1
Kit Carson	20	6	14
Lake	17	9	8
La Plata	101	78	23
Las Animas	39	14	25
Lincoln	17	5	12
Logan	46	21	25
Mineral	3	3	0
Moffat	36	33	3
Montezuma	57	23	34
Montrose	102	47	55
Morgan	53	28	25
Otero	24	22	2
Ouray	7	6	1
Phillips	4	3	1
Pitkin	38	22	16
Prowers	31	10	21
Rio Blanco	20	14	6
Rio Grande	24	8	16
Routt	43	28	15
Saguache	18	8	10
San Juan	5	4	1
San Miguel	35	16	19
Sedgwick	9	4	5
Summit	60	51	9
Washington	37	10	27
Yuma	16	8	8
FLORIDA			
Bradford	32	21	11
Calhoun	23	13	10
Citrus	286	179	107
Columbia	174	131	43
DeSoto	95	42	53
Dixie	59	22	37
Flagler	116	78	38
Franklin	82	65	17
Glades	52	26	26
Gulf	50	30	20
Hamilton	57	16	41
Hardee	84	37	47
Hendry	134	74	60
Highlands	246	163	83
Holmes	26	20	6
Jackson	68	49	19
Lafayette	11	9	2
Levy	136	75	61
Liberty	15	12	3
Madison	39	27	12
Monroe	539	332	207
Okeechobee	101	71	30

County by state	Total law enforcement employees	Total officers	Total civilians
FLORIDA—Continued			
Putnam	151	103	48
Sumter	156	114	42
Suwannee	94	50	44
Taylor	49	33	16
Union	15	11	4
Walton	193	146	47
Washington	65	29	36
GEORGIA			
Appling	36	14	22
Atkinson	17	6	11
Bacon	26	7	19
Baldwin	89	48	41
Banks	32	24	8
Ben Hill	39	20	19
Berrien	21	14	7
Bleckley	32	16	16
Bulloch	77	43	34
Camden	122	73	49
Candler	17	6	11
Charlton	28	14	14
Chattooga	42	26	16
Clay	7	3	4
Clinch	22	11	11
Coffee	69	36	33
Colquitt	90	45	45
Cook	42	16	26
Crisp	65	43	22
Decatur	38	33	5
Dooly	61	17	44
Emanuel	35	29	6
Evans	17	8	9
Fannin	22	21	1
Franklin	44	25	19
Glascock	4	3	1
Grady	36	13	23
Greene	50	32	18
Habersham	49	27	22
Hart	37	22	15
Jackson	72	47	25
Jeff Davis	29	12	17
Jefferson	26	24	2
Jenkins	7	3	4
Johnson	9	6	3
Laurens	94	53	41
Lincoln	26	21	5
Lumpkin	70	40	30
Macon	9	9	0
Miller	21	11	10
Mitchell	47	45	2
Peach	52	26	26
Pierce	29	12	17
Polk County Police Department	37	34	3
Pulaski	23	12	11
Putnam	60	25	35
Quitman	4	3	1
Rabun	26	17	9
Randolph	7	6	1
Schley	6	4	2
Screven	20	18	2
Stephens	47	30	17
Sumter	94	37	57
Talbot	16	8	8
Taliaferro	11	6	5
Tattnall	39	15	24
Taylor	19	10	9
Telfair	10	9	1

Table 81

Full-time Law Enforcement Employees as of October 31, 2003
by Nonmetropolitan County by State—Continued

County by state	Total law enforcement employees	Total officers	Total civilians	County by state	Total law enforcement employees	Total officers	Total civilians
GEORGIA—Continued				**ILLINOIS—Continued**			
Thomas	71	67	4	Cumberland	20	6	14
Tift	111	57	54	De Witt	44	16	28
Toombs	65	24	41	Douglas	24	9	15
Towns	32	14	18	Edgar	19	9	10
Troup	109	61	48	Edwards	8	3	5
Upson	62	34	28	Effingham	41	17	24
Ware	91	34	57	Fayette	24	10	14
Ware County Police Department	16	1	15	Franklin	41	17	24
Warren	4	4	0	Fulton	38	21	17
Washington	33	17	16	Gallatin	4	3	1
Wheeler	8	3	5	Greene	14	6	8
White	50	31	19	Hamilton	7	3	4
Wilkes	22	12	10	Hancock	21	10	11
Wilkinson	21	11	10	Hardin	6	3	3
				Henderson	9	8	1
HAWAII				Iroquois	30	17	13
				Jackson	65	23	42
Hawaii Police Department	518	383	135	Jasper	19	9	10
Kauai Police Department	172	130	42	Jefferson	43	23	20
Maui Police Department	429	327	102	Jo Daviess	37	19	18
				Johnson	11	6	5
IDAHO				Knox	57	53	4
				La Salle	102	55	47
Adams	14	9	5	Lawrence	13	6	7
Bear Lake	11	5	6	Lee	41	23	18
Benewah	8	8	0	Livingston	54	29	25
Bingham	46	28	18	Logan	36	20	16
Blaine	30	17	13	Marion	34	15	19
Bonner	82	45	37	Mason	20	9	11
Boundary	19	10	9	Massac	28	10	18
Butte	10	4	6	McDonough	24	13	11
Camas	4	2	2	Montgomery	26	13	13
Caribou	16	8	8	Morgan	41	17	24
Cassia	45	32	13	Moultrie	19	10	9
Clark	7	3	4	Ogle	62	46	16
Clearwater	24	18	6	Perry	34	12	22
Custer	13	7	6	Pike	23	9	14
Elmore	32	21	11	Pope	6	3	3
Fremont	20	14	6	Pulaski	18	12	6
Gooding	15	10	5	Putnam	10	5	5
Idaho	29	19	10	Randolph	21	11	10
Jerome	18	15	3	Richland	20	8	12
Latah	41	27	14	Saline	33	10	23
Lewis	15	10	5	Schuyler	10	4	6
Lincoln	6	5	1	Scott	11	3	8
Madison	28	18	10	Shelby	24	12	12
Minidoka	22	14	8	Stephenson	34	24	10
Oneida	13	8	5	Union	14	8	6
Payette	30	16	14	Wabash	9	4	5
Shoshone	26	17	9	Warren	19	12	7
Teton	17	9	8	Washington	17	7	10
Twin Falls	61	39	22	Wayne	15	8	7
Valley	25	13	12	White	7	6	1
Washington	14	9	5	Whiteside	54	24	30
				Williamson	67	63	4
ILLINOIS							
				INDIANA			
Adams	29	26	3				
Alexander	6	5	1	Adams	33	16	17
Brown	5	4	1	Blackford	30	9	21
Bureau	37	21	16	Cass	61	18	43
Carroll	22	8	14	Clinton	56	14	42
Cass	8	7	1	Crawford	12	8	4
Christian	29	16	13	Daviess	33	14	19
Clark	15	10	5	Decatur	26	8	18
Clay	13	7	6	De Kalb	52	18	34
Coles	46	26	20	Dubois	31	15	16
Crawford	20	9	11	Fayette	34	11	23

Table 81

Full-time Law Enforcement Employees as of October 31, 2003
by Nonmetropolitan County by State—Continued

County by state	Total law enforcement employees	Total officers	Total civilians	County by state	Total law enforcement employees	Total officers	Total civilians
INDIANA—Continued				**IOWA—Continued**			
Fountain	19	8	11	Hamilton	11	9	2
Fulton	21	10	11	Hancock	9	7	2
Grant	140	45	95	Hardin	28	10	18
Henry	62	29	33	Henry	25	11	14
Huntington	40	14	26	Howard	8	7	1
Jackson	50	14	36	Humboldt	9	9	0
Jay	32	11	21	Ida	13	8	5
Jefferson	29	13	16	Iowa	20	11	9
Jennings	39	14	25	Jackson	15	9	6
Knox	30	12	18	Jasper	33	13	20
Kosciusko	85	35	50	Jefferson	43	19	24
LaGrange	50	17	33	Keokuk	8	4	4
Lawrence	61	25	36	Kossuth	24	9	15
Marshall	51	20	31	Lee	29	15	14
Martin	16	8	8	Louisa	21	10	11
Miami	35	15	20	Lucas	12	5	7
Noble	72	19	53	Lyon	21	9	12
Orange	28	8	20	Mahaska	25	10	15
Perry	14	6	8	Marion	23	11	12
Pulaski	41	11	30	Marshall	63	18	45
Randolph	40	17	23	Mitchell	16	6	10
Ripley	10	10	0	Monona	19	8	11
Rush	23	17	6	Monroe	12	5	7
Scott	21	8	13	Montgomery	19	7	12
Spencer	45	13	32	Muscatine	24	22	2
Starke	25	14	11	O'Brien	28	10	18
Steuben	64	21	43	Osceola	17	10	7
Switzerland	17	10	7	Page	13	7	6
Union	11	11	0	Palo Alto	15	8	7
Wabash	33	18	15	Plymouth	24	9	15
Warren	21	7	14	Pocahontas	13	7	6
Wayne	91	30	61	Poweshiek	16	10	6
White	42	12	30	Ringgold	11	6	5
				Sac	13	7	6
IOWA				Shelby	14	8	6
				Sioux	37	15	22
Adair	8	6	2	Tama	20	12	8
Adams	10	5	5	Taylor	10	6	4
Allamakee	15	8	7	Union	11	5	6
Appanoose	16	9	7	Van Buren	11	5	6
Audubon	9	5	4	Wapello	41	10	31
Boone	12	10	2	Wayne	10	5	5
Buchanan	30	13	17	Webster	32	15	17
Buena Vista	16	10	6	Winnebago	12	5	7
Butler	19	11	8	Winneshiek	20	10	10
Calhoun	11	7	4	Worth	17	6	11
Carroll	14	10	4	Wright	18	7	11
Cass	10	7	3				
Cedar	34	9	25	**KANSAS**			
Cerro Gordo	52	18	34				
Cherokee	16	6	10	Allen	17	8	9
Chickasaw	13	8	5	Anderson	16	10	6
Clarke	21	6	15	Atchison	26	9	17
Clay	16	9	7	Barber	9	4	5
Clayton	22	11	11	Barton	37	19	18
Clinton	40	28	12	Bourbon	8	6	2
Crawford	13	11	2	Brown	18	13	5
Davis	6	5	1	Chase	10	5	5
Decatur	11	6	5	Chautauqua	8	3	5
Delaware	15	10	5	Cherokee	31	26	5
Des Moines	46	21	25	Cheyenne	3	2	1
Dickinson	19	9	10	Clark	9	4	5
Emmet	16	8	8	Clay	13	6	7
Fayette	33	10	23	Cloud	15	11	4
Floyd	15	9	6	Coffey	28	12	16
Franklin	10	7	3	Comanche	3	3	0
Fremont	18	7	11	Cowley	19	17	2
Greene	13	7	6	Crawford	66	30	36

Table 81

Full-time Law Enforcement Employees as of October 31, 2003
by Nonmetropolitan County by State—Continued

County by state	Total law enforcement employees	Total officers	Total civilians	County by state	Total law enforcement employees	Total officers	Total civilians
KANSAS—Continued				**KENTUCKY**			
Decatur	3	3	0	Adair	6	4	2
Dickinson	26	14	12	Allen	11	9	2
Edwards	8	4	4	Ballard	11	11	0
Elk	7	3	4	Barren	15	12	3
Ellis	24	12	12	Bell	10	7	3
Ellsworth	16	8	8	Boyle	9	8	1
Finney	100	45	55	Breathitt	5	4	1
Ford	51	22	29	Breckinridge ·	9	7	2
Geary	72	57	15	Butler	5	4	1
Gove	5	4	1	Caldwell	8	6	2
Graham	7	3	4	Calloway	24	19	5
Grant	15	6	9	Carlisle	3	3	0
Gray	10	5	5	Carroll	5	5	0
Greeley	6	3	3	Carter	7	5	2
Greenwood	22	13	9	Casey	6	5	1
Hamilton	14	7	7	Clay	8	5	3
Harper	16	5	11	Clinton	5	4	1
Haskell	16	11	5	Crittenden	4	3	1
Hodgeman	9	4	5	Cumberland	5	4	1
Jewell	8	4	4	Elliott	3	2	1
Kingman	16	7	9	Estill	4	3	1
Kiowa	14	14	0	Fleming	8	8	0
Labette	36	18	18	Floyd	20	11	9
Lane	7	4	3	Franklin	18	17	1
Lincoln	11	7	4	Fulton	4	4	0
Logan	4	3	1	Garrard	6	5	1
Lyon	68	15	53	Graves	15	11	4
Marion	9	8	1	Grayson	12	10	2
Marshall	15	7	8	Green	3	3	0
McPherson	32	15	17	Harlan	17	14	3
Meade	15	5	10	Harrison	9	9	0
Mitchell	11	11	0	Hart	7	7	0
Montgomery	26	18	8	Hickman	3	3	0
Morris	12	7	5	Hopkins	17	14	3
Morton	10	5	5	Jackson	9	7	2
Nemaha	16	10	6	Johnson	13	9	4
Neosho	27	12	15	Knott	7	4	3
Ness	12	6	6	Knox	24	12	12
Norton	10	5	5	Laurel	32	26	6
Osborne	13	9	4	Lawrence	7	5	2
Ottawa	19	5	14	Lee	3	2	1
Pawnee	15	7	8	Leslie	10	7	3
Phillips	15	10	5	Letcher	11	7	4
Pottawatomie	28	20	8	Lewis	7	5	2
Pratt	13	8	5	Lincoln	9	8	1
Rawlins	4	3	1	Livingston	7	7	0
Reno	76	50	26	Logan	15	15	0
Republic	12	7	5	Lyon	4	4	0
Rice	20	5	15	Madison	18	16	2
Riley County Police Department	157	89	68	Magoffin	5	3	2
Rooks	9	5	4	Marion	7	6	1
Rush	9	4	5	Marshall	19	16	3
Russell	17	9	8	Martin	7	5	2
Saline	94	41	53	Mason	13	11	2
Scott	5	4	1	McCracken	38	37	1
Seward	41	13	28	McCreary	4	4	0
Sheridan	6	3	3	Menifee	6	6	0
Sherman	11	5	6	Mercer	9	8	1
Smith	10	4	6	Metcalfe	5	4	1
Stafford	9	4	5	Monroe	5	4	1
Stanton	14	5	9	Montgomery	18	15	3
Stevens	17	9	8	Morgan	5	3	2
Thomas	17	11	6	Muhlenberg	11	11	0
Trego	3	3	0	Nicholas	3	2	1
Wallace	2	2	0	Ohio	22	18	4
Washington	6	6	0	Owen	6	4	2
Wichita	4	4	0	Owsley	4	4	0
Wilson	23	10	13	Perry	16	13	3
Woodson	9	5	4				

Table 81

Full-time Law Enforcement Employees as of October 31, 2003
by Nonmetropolitan County by State—Continued

County by state	Total law enforcement employees	Total officers	Total civilians	County by state	Total law enforcement employees	Total officers	Total civilians
KENTUCKY—Continued				**MARYLAND**			
Pike	23	13	10	Caroline	28	25	3
Powell	7	5	2	Dorchester	32	26	6
Pulaski	34	25	9	Garrett	43	21	22
Robertson	1	1	0	Kent	22	20	2
Rockcastle	8	7	1	St. Mary's	205	106	99
Rowan	12	9	3	Talbot	20	18	2
Russell	10	9	1	Worcester	56	50	6
Simpson	13	12	1				
Taylor	13	11	2	**MICHIGAN**			
Todd	4	3	1				
Union	9	8	1	Alcona	26	15	11
Washington	5	5	0	Alger	13	9	4
Wayne	10	7	3	Allegan	106	63	43
Whitley	13	11	2	Alpena	17	14	3
Wolfe	4	3	1	Antrim	38	21	17
				Arenac	21	11	10
LOUISIANA				Baraga	6	6	0
				Benzie	45	17	28
Acadia	122	81	41	Branch	47	25	22
Allen	46	30	16	Charlevoix	37	18	19
Assumption	78	44	34	Cheboygan	35	18	17
Beauregard	71	55	16	Chippewa	19	15	4
Bienville	40	24	16	Clare	23	18	5
Caldwell	32	32	0	Crawford	25	13	12
Catahoula	104	24	80	Delta	30	16	14
Claiborne	91	21	70	Dickinson	34	17	17
Concordia	218	217	1	Emmet	42	22	20
East Carroll	207	187	20	Gladwin	35	17	18
Evangeline	61	22	39	Gogebic	21	15	6
Franklin	73	73	0	Grand Traverse	116	63	53
Jackson	34	34	0	Gratiot	36	19	17
Jefferson Davis	45	32	13	Hillsdale	39	27	12
La Salle	48	43	5	Houghton	29	18	11
Lincoln	50	48	2	Huron	25	24	1
Madison	61	61	0	Iosco	23	5	18
Morehouse	131	131	0	Iron	23	8	15
Natchitoches	65	55	10	Isabella	54	27	27
Red River	45	37	8	Kalkaska	40	23	17
Richland	125	112	13	Keweenaw	7	6	1
Sabine	59	59	0	Lake	56	18	38
St. James	101	75	26	Leelanau	40	21	19
St. Landry	116	114	2	Lenawee	107	53	54
St. Mary	166	122	44	Luce	4	3	1
Tangipahoa	243	243	0	Mackinac	21	8	13
Tensas	131	35	96	Manistee	27	13	14
Vermilion	95	50	45	Marquette	57	29	28
Vernon	129	129	0	Mason	37	20	17
Webster	133	133	0	Mecosta	46	25	21
West Carroll	19	16	3	Menominee	13	12	1
Winn	28	28	0	Midland	65	42	23
				Missaukee	27	14	13
MAINE				Montcalm	71	26	45
				Montmorency	13	11	2
Aroostook	20	15	5	Oceana	35	21	14
Franklin	26	15	11	Ogemaw	36	17	19
Hancock	44	13	31	Ontonagon	12	9	3
Kennebec	29	20	9	Osceola	38	21	17
Knox	20	18	2	Oscoda	16	11	5
Lincoln	22	20	2	Otsego	25	13	12
Oxford	13	12	1	Presque Isle	26	12	14
Piscataquis	15	7	8	Roscommon	22	22	0
Somerset	17	15	2	Sanilac	62	29	33
Waldo	18	16	2	Schoolcraft	12	5	7
Washington	23	13	10	Shiawassee	46	32	14
				St. Joseph	52	25	27
				Tuscola	49	31	18
				Wexford	51	25	26

Table 81

Full-time Law Enforcement Employees as of October 31, 2003
by Nonmetropolitan County by State—Continued

County by state	Total law enforcement employees	Total officers	Total civilians	County by state	Total law enforcement employees	Total officers	Total civilians
MINNESOTA				**MISSISSIPPI**			
Aitkin	48	18	30	Adams	52	50	2
Becker	48	21	27	Attala	13	8	5
Beltrami	55	25	30	Benton	15	7	8
Big Stone	7	4	3	Bolivar	84	17	67
Blue Earth	51	22	29	Chickasaw	20	12	8
Brown	35	9	26	Choctaw	11	7	4
Cass	52	28	24	Claiborne	22	10	12
Chippewa	17	7	10	Clay	26	8	18
Clearwater	18	7	11	Coahoma	18	17	1
Cook	17	12	5	Covington	11	6	5
Cottonwood	16	7	9	Greene	13	6	7
Crow Wing	87	34	53	Grenada	15	12	3
Douglas	65	27	38	Holmes	51	10	41
Faribault	20	9	11	Humphreys	15	10	5
Fillmore	31	18	13	Issaquena	5	3	2
Freeborn	43	18	25	Jefferson	51	11	40
Goodhue	101	39	62	Jones	26	22	4
Grant	10	5	5	Lauderdale	135	47	88
Hubbard	30	15	15	Lawrence	21	10	11
Itasca	66	64	2	Leake	14	12	2
Jackson	18	7	11	Lee	122	42	80
Kanabec	25	11	14	Leflore	56	21	35
Kandiyohi	103	32	71	Lincoln	41	18	23
Kittson	10	5	5	Lowndes	49	41	8
Koochiching	17	9	8	Monroe	42	16	26
Lac Qui Parle	8	5	3	Montgomery	7	6	1
Lake	26	14	12	Newton	10	9	1
Lake of the Woods	8	5	3	Noxubee	10	4	6
Le Sueur	29	16	13	Oktibbeha	23	21	2
Lincoln	9	4	5	Panola	53	18	35
Lyon	36	12	24	Pearl River	66	31	35
Mahnomen	19	12	7	Pontotoc	29	17	12
Marshall	18	11	7	Prentiss	30	15	15
Martin	29	10	19	Scott	50	17	33
McLeod	55	21	34	Sharkey	9	5	4
Meeker	34	14	20	Smith	14	8	6
Mille Lacs	58	19	39	Tallahatchie	26	10	16
Morrison	47	16	31	Tippah	26	7	19
Mower	35	20	15	Union	40	30	10
Murray	10	5	5	Walthall	23	19	4
Nicollet	23	10	13	Warren	40	32	8
Nobles	31	9	22	Washington	47	31	16
Norman	8	5	3	Wayne	17	5	12
Otter Tail	71	28	43	Webster	9	6	3
Pennington	35	8	27	Winston	7	6	1
Pine	47	25	22	Yalobusha	15	11	4
Pipestone	21	11	10	Yazoo	14	10	4
Pope	12	5	7				
Red Lake	10	6	4	**MISSOURI**			
Redwood	21	9	12				
Renville	17	11	6	Adair	27	10	17
Rice	45	20	25	Atchison	8	5	3
Rock	16	11	5	Audrain	49	34	15
Roseau	18	10	8	Barry	32	21	11
Sibley	21	9	12	Barton	13	6	7
Steele	58	17	41	Benton	22	16	6
Stevens	10	5	5	Bollinger	11	7	4
Swift	14	6	8	Butler	36	22	14
Todd	28	14	14	Camden	95	43	52
Traverse	6	4	2	Cape Girardeau	64	41	23
Wadena	16	6	10	Carroll	15	7	8
Waseca	23	10	13	Carter	8	3	5
Watonwan	20	9	11	Cedar	22	14	8
Wilkin	8	6	2	Chariton	15	10	5
Winona	46	17	29	Clark	17	9	8
Yellow Medicine	20	7	13	Cooper	11	9	2
				Crawford	30	19	11
				Dade	12	6	6

Table 81

Full-time Law Enforcement Employees as of October 31, 2003

by Nonmetropolitan County by State—Continued

County by state	Total law enforcement employees	Total officers	Total civilians	County by state	Total law enforcement employees	Total officers	Total civilians
MISSOURI—Continued				**MONTANA—Continued**			
Daviess	5	4	1	Blaine	15	7	8
Dent	13	10	3	Broadwater	10	7	3
Douglas	12	8	4	Carter	2	2	0
Dunklin	26	9	17	Chouteau	15	9	6
Gasconade	10	9	1	Custer	12	6	6
Gentry	7	6	1	Daniels	8	3	5
Grundy	8	3	5	Dawson	52	6	46
Harrison	11	5	6	Deer Lodge	26	17	9
Henry	24	18	6	Fallon	8	2	6
Hickory	13	8	5	Fergus	20	8	12
Holt	8	5	3	Flathead	105	45	60
Howell	37	27	10	Gallatin	71	38	33
Iron	12	7	5	Garfield	4	3	1
Johnson	46	38	8	Glacier	18	9	9
Knox	4	1	3	Golden Valley	2	2	0
Laclede	15	15	0	Granite	9	5	4
Lawrence	25	18	7	Hill	25	12	13
Lewis	10	4	6	Jefferson	20	10	10
Linn	7	6	1	Judith Basin	5	4	1
Livingston	17	10	7	Lake	48	19	29
Macon	16	13	3	Lewis and Clark	65	40	25
Madison	10	8	2	Liberty	9	4	5
Maries	8	6	2	Lincoln	33	18	15
Marion	36	14	22	Madison	9	6	3
Mercer	7	3	4	McCone	7	3	4
Miller	19	15	4	Meagher	8	4	4
Mississippi	45	13	32	Mineral	18	7	11
Monroe	9	9	0	Musselshell	7	7	0
Montgomery	13	12	1	Park	20	12	8
Morgan	39	19	20	Petroleum	1	1	0
New Madrid	24	14	10	Phillips	16	7	9
Nodaway	20	9	11	Pondera	15	8	7
Oregon	10	6	4	Powder River	7	3	4
Ozark	19	8	11	Powell	19	11	8
Pemiscot	40	16	24	Prairie	3	3	0
Perry	27	16	11	Ravalli	76	30	46
Pettis	30	15	15	Richland	19	7	12
Phelps	35	27	8	Roosevelt	26	9	17
Pike	29	14	15	Rosebud	31	16	15
Pulaski	19	16	3	Sanders	16	7	9
Putnam	7	3	4	Sheridan	11	5	6
Ralls	7	6	1	Silver Bow	84	42	42
Randolph	33	22	11	Stillwater	11	7	4
Reynolds	12	7	5	Sweet Grass	14	7	7
Ripley	11	9	2	Teton	12	9	3
Saline	30	17	13	Toole	19	11	8
Schuyler	8	3	5	Treasure	2	2	0
Scotland	7	3	4	Valley	16	7	9
Scott	42	21	21	Wheatland	9	5	4
Shannon	6	2	4	Wibaux	2	2	0
Shelby	9	4	5				
St. Clair	62	18	44	**NEBRASKA**			
Ste. Genevieve	55	41	14				
St. Francois	63	51	12	Adams	19	17	2
Stoddard	22	9	13	Antelope	10	6	4
Stone	47	36	11	Arthur	1	1	0
Sullivan	11	5	6	Banner	1	1	0
Taney	62	30	32	Blaine	1	1	0
Texas	11	5	6	Boone	11	4	7
Vernon	21	12	9	Brown	10	5	5
Wayne	15	8	7	Burt	11	6	5
Worth	2	1	1	Butler	11	7	4
Wright	11	5	6	Cedar	9	4	5
				Cherry	11	5	6
MONTANA				Cheyenne	4	4	0
				Colfax	10	5	5
Beaverhead	17	8	9	Cuming	6	5	1
Big Horn	30	15	15	Custer	11	6	5

Table 81

Full-time Law Enforcement Employees as of October 31, 2003
by Nonmetropolitan County by State—Continued

County by state	Total law enforcement employees	Total officers	Total civilians	County by state	Total law enforcement employees	Total officers	Total civilians
NEBRASKA—Continued				**NEVADA—Continued**			
Dawes	4	3	1	Humboldt	44	32	12
Dawson	31	18	13	Lander	28	18	10
Deuel	5	4	1	Lincoln	21	19	2
Dodge	24	17	7	Lyon	93	66	27
Dundy	9	5	4	Mineral	23	17	6
Fillmore	11	5	6	Nye	133	99	34
Franklin	7	3	4	Pershing	19	12	7
Frontier	8	5	3	White Pine	28	23	5
Furnas	14	9	5				
Garden	9	4	5	**NEW HAMPSHIRE**			
Garfield	2	2	0				
Gosper	5	4	1	Carroll	26	11	15
Grant	1	1	0	Cheshire	16	8	8
Greeley	3	2	1	Merrimack	26	15	11
Hall	34	28	6				
Hamilton	8	8	0	**NEW MEXICO**			
Harlan	8	4	4				
Hayes	1	1	0	Catron	13	6	7
Hitchcock	7	4	3	Chaves	58	38	20
Holt	6	5	1	Cibola	21	12	9
Hooker	1	1	0	Colfax	11	9	2
Howard	13	6	7	Curry	18	14	4
Jefferson	12	6	6	De Baca	10	2	8
Johnson	7	3	4	Eddy	55	42	13
Kearney	11	6	5	Grant	29	27	2
Keith	14	8	6	Guadalupe	4	3	1
Keya Paha	2	1	1	Harding	3	2	1
Kimball	9	3	6	Lea	62	45	17
Knox	12	5	7	Lincoln	25	16	9
Lincoln	44	24	20	Luna	31	27	4
Logan	2	2	0	McKinley	39	31	8
Loup	1	1	0	Mora	8	6	2
Madison	49	24	25	Otero	39	30	9
McPherson	1	1	0	Roosevelt	17	12	5
Merrick	10	5	5	San Miguel	11	9	2
Morrill	8	3	5	Sierra	11	9	2
Nance	11	7	4	Taos	24	17	7
Nuckolls	7	4	3	Union	4	3	1
Otoe	20	11	9				
Pawnee	4	3	1	**NEW YORK**			
Perkins	8	4	4				
Phelps	16	7	9	Allegany	47	37	10
Pierce	8	4	4	Cattaraugus	70	50	20
Platte	53	19	34	Cayuga	58	34	24
Polk	11	7	4	Chautauqua	116	81	35
Red Willow	7	5	2	Clinton	34	21	13
Richardson	10	6	4	Columbia	53	44	9
Rock	8	3	5	Cortland	50	31	19
Saline	15	10	5	Delaware	21	15	6
Scotts Bluff	26	18	8	Essex	27	26	1
Sheridan	5	4	1	Fulton	52	35	17
Sherman	6	5	1	Greene	26	24	2
Stanton	8	7	1	Jefferson	44	35	9
Thayer	11	7	4	Lewis	24	14	10
Thomas	1	1	0	Montgomery	19	18	1
Thurston	11	6	5	Otsego	19	16	3
Valley	3	2	1	Schuyler	40	36	4
Wayne	4	3	1	Seneca	45	29	16
Webster	10	6	4	Steuben	28	24	4
Wheeler	2	2	0	St. Lawrence	40	36	4
York	21	9	12	Sullivan	70	42	28
				Wyoming	42	31	11
NEVADA				Yates	40	21	19
Churchill	45	38	7	**NORTH CAROLINA**			
Douglas	112	95	17				
Elko	62	51	11	Alleghany	26	10	16
Esmeralda	15	11	4	Ashe	25	17	8
Eureka	17	14	3	Avery	27	21	6

Table 81

Full-time Law Enforcement Employees as of October 31, 2003

by Nonmetropolitan County by State—Continued

County by state	Total law enforcement employees	Total officers	Total civilians	County by state	Total law enforcement employees	Total officers	Total civilians
NORTH CAROLINA—Continued				**NORTH DAKOTA—Continued**			
Beaufort	73	43	30	Dunn	4	3	1
Bertie	26	19	7	Eddy	5	5	0
Bladen	67	42	25	Emmons	3	3	0
Camden	14	12	2	Foster	3	2	1
Carteret	84	42	42	Golden Valley	5	4	1
Caswell	44	25	19	Grant	3	3	0
Cherokee	32	19	13	Griggs	4	4	0
Chowan	34	16	18	Hettinger	5	5	0
Clay	18	10	8	Kidder	2	2	0
Cleveland	122	81	41	Lamoure	5	4	1
Columbus	93	55	38	Logan	2	2	0
Craven	78	61	17	McHenry	7	6	1
Dare	140	59	81	McIntosh	3	3	0
Davidson	185	124	61	McKenzie	12	5	7
Duplin	61	50	11	McLean	27	21	6
Gates	19	9	10	Mercer	21	10	11
Graham	11	10	1	Mountrail	9	5	4
Granville	72	37	35	Nelson	5	4	1
Halifax	69	47	22	Oliver	2	2	0
Harnett	130	84	46	Pembina	15	9	6
Hertford	51	18	33	Pierce	7	4	3
Hyde	14	9	5	Ramsey	7	6	1
Jackson	56	53	3	Ransom	5	5	0
Jones	26	14	12	Renville	4	4	0
Lee	70	36	34	Richland	29	13	16
Lenoir	81	51	30	Rolette	10	9	1
Lincoln	125	71	54	Sargent	4	3	1
Macon	54	40	14	Slope	1	1	0
Martin	32	29	3	Stark	13	10	3
McDowell	55	37	18	Steele	3	3	0
Mitchell	14	13	1	Stutsman	10	8	2
Montgomery	49	29	20	Towner	3	2	1
Moore	104	62	42	Traill	9	4	5
Northampton	43	20	23	Walsh	18	12	6
Pamlico	27	14	13	Ward	43	20	23
Pasquotank	40	37	3	Wells	4	3	1
Perquimans	11	9	2	Williams	28	18	10
Polk	33	24	9				
Richmond	66	44	22	**OHIO**			
Robeson	209	95	114				
Rowan	150	136	14	Adams	33	25	8
Rutherford	101	67	34	Ashland	71	51	20
Sampson	79	50	29	Ashtabula	89	43	46
Scotland	56	34	22	Athens	30	25	5
Stanly	62	44	18	Auglaize	54	20	34
Surry	84	48	36	Champaign	36	29	7
Swain	27	14	13	Clinton	70	46	24
Transylvania	56	42	14	Columbiana	34	25	9
Tyrrell	12	6	6	Coshocton	63	52	11
Vance	82	37	45	Crawford	70	22	48
Warren	33	24	9	Darke	67	40	27
Washington	35	16	19	Defiance	33	20	13
Watauga	54	32	22	Fayette	40	28	12
Wilkes	106	67	39	Gallia	29	23	6
Wilson	104	65	39	Guernsey	48	21	27
Yancey	24	15	9	Hancock	87	36	51
				Hardin	26	19	7
NORTH DAKOTA				Henry	23	23	0
				Highland	55	55	0
Adams	3	3	0	Hocking	21	20	1
Barnes	7	6	1	Holmes	48	45	3
Benson	4	4	0	Huron	75	27	48
Billings	4	3	1	Jackson	38	15	23
Bottineau	13	9	4	Knox	73	54	19
Bowman	2	2	0	Logan	105	38	67
Burke	3	3	0	Marion	35	26	9
Cavalier	11	5	6	Meigs	15	13	2
Dickey	6	5	1	Mercer	42	30	12
Divide	3	3	0	Monroe	19	14	5

Table 81

Full-time Law Enforcement Employees as of October 31, 2003
by Nonmetropolitan County by State—Continued

County by state	Total law enforcement employees	Total officers	Total civilians	County by state	Total law enforcement employees	Total officers	Total civilians
OHIO—Continued				**OKLAHOMA—Continued**			
Morgan	14	10	4	Roger Mills	13	8	5
Muskingum	118	84	34	Seminole	24	16	8
Paulding	24	13	11	Stephens	20	10	10
Perry	18	12	6	Texas	33	11	22
Pike	22	19	3	Tillman	14	5	9
Putnam	47	30	17	Washington	17	15	2
Sandusky	64	45	19	Washita	14	8	6
Scioto	66	52	14	Woods	5	5	0
Seneca	60	16	44	Woodward	17	11	6
Shelby	73	33	40				
Tuscarawas	99	31	68	**OREGON**			
Van Wert	39	18	21				
Vinton	19	16	3	Baker	19	10	9
Wayne	83	67	16	Clatsop	29	25	4
Williams	25	22	3	Coos	52	30	22
Wyandot	21	10	11	Crook	17	12	5
				Curry	23	15	8
OKLAHOMA				Douglas	108	71	37
				Gilliam	6	5	1
Adair	30	13	17	Grant	6	5	1
Alfalfa	9	4	5	Harney	5	5	0
Atoka	11	6	5	Hood River	20	18	2
Beaver	13	7	6	Jefferson	25	16	9
Beckham	18	9	9	Josephine	61	37	24
Blaine	10	5	5	Klamath	38	31	7
Bryan	24	12	12	Lake	8	7	1
Caddo	29	16	13	Lincoln	28	26	2
Carter	55	17	38	Linn	96	64	32
Cherokee	32	20	12	Malheur	23	14	9
Choctaw	19	7	12	Morrow	26	15	11
Cimarron	10	4	6	Sherman	5	4	1
Coal	5	3	2	Tillamook	26	24	2
Cotton	12	6	6	Umatilla	30	12	18
Craig	20	10	10	Union	10	8	2
Custer	26	13	13	Wallowa	14	8	6
Delaware	34	17	17	Wasco	19	16	3
Dewey	11	4	7	Wheeler	4	3	1
Ellis	11	3	8				
Garfield	37	15	22	**PENNSYLVANIA**			
Garvin	23	11	12				
Grant	13	6	7	Bradford	11	9	2
Greer	5	3	2	Clarion	9	6	3
Harmon	3	3	0	Clearfield	11	8	3
Harper	11	4	7	Elk	6	5	1
Haskell	16	7	9	Jefferson	6	6	0
Hughes	15	9	6	Warren	50	21	29
Jackson	30	9	21				
Jefferson	9	4	5	**SOUTH CAROLINA**			
Johnston	13	7	6				
Kay	26	12	14	Abbeville	53	25	28
Kingfisher	13	6	7	Allendale	13	12	1
Kiowa	9	6	3	Bamberg	14	12	2
Latimer	11	6	5	Barnwell	35	24	11
Love	6	6	0	Beaufort	202	182	20
Major	10	4	6	Chester	56	52	4
Marshall	26	6	20	Chesterfield	54	36	18
Mayes	39	18	21	Clarendon	47	29	18
McCurtain	26	20	6	Dillon	67	30	37
McIntosh	20	13	7	Georgetown	135	70	65
Murray	10	5	5	Greenwood	109	61	48
Muskogee	25	23	2	Hampton	27	21	6
Noble	10	5	5	Jasper	35	29	6
Nowata	21	14	7	Lancaster	92	50	42
Okfuskee	14	6	8	Lee	29	26	3
Ottawa	33	18	15	Marion	39	33	6
Payne	51	25	26	Marlboro	56	23	33
Pittsburg	32	21	11	McCormick	27	14	13
Pontotoc	17	10	7	Newberry	82	39	43
Pottawatomie	24	16	8	Oconee	120	74	46
Pushmataha	13	8	5	Union	47	30	17

Table 81

Full-time Law Enforcement Employees as of October 31, 2003
by Nonmetropolitan County by State—Continued

County by state	Total law enforcement employees	Total officers	Total civilians
SOUTH DAKOTA			
Aurora	4	3	1
Beadle	22	6	16
Bennett	7	4	3
Bon Homme	7	3	4
Brookings	18	11	7
Brown	46	15	31
Brule	11	3	8
Buffalo	1	1	0
Butte	7	5	2
Campbell	2	2	0
Charles Mix	9	3	6
Clark	2	2	0
Clay	11	8	3
Codington	9	6	3
Corson	3	3	0
Custer	11	10	1
Davison	23	5	18
Day	6	3	3
Deuel	8	4	4
Dewey	3	2	1
Douglas	2	2	0
Edmunds	6	4	2
Fall River	14	5	9
Faulk	7	1	6
Grant	10	3	7
Gregory	3	2	1
Haakon	2	2	0
Hamlin	2	2	0
Hand	3	2	1
Hanson	2	2	0
Harding	3	2	1
Hughes	22	6	16
Hutchinson	3	3	0
Hyde	1	1	0
Jackson	1	1	0
Jerauld	2	2	0
Jones	2	1	1
Kingsbury	5	4	1
Lake	9	4	5
Lawrence	40	18	22
Lyman	4	3	1
Marshall	9	5	4
McPherson	1	1	0
Mellette	5	4	1
Miner	4	3	1
Moody	10	5	5
Perkins	4	3	1
Potter	6	2	4
Roberts	10	3	7
Sanborn	2	2	0
Shannon	1	1	0
Spink	13	8	5
Stanley	6	5	1
Sully	3	3	0
Todd	1	1	0
Tripp	3	2	1
Walworth	10	2	8
Yankton	10	9	1
Ziebach	2	2	0
TENNESSEE			
Bedford	78	27	51
Benton	37	15	22
Bledsoe	17	13	4
Campbell	47	41	6
Carroll	32	15	17
Claiborne	52	36	16
TENNESSEE—Continued			
Clay	18	11	7
Cocke	65	34	31
Coffee	59	59	0
Crockett	30	12	18
Cumberland	78	36	42
Decatur	14	9	5
DeKalb	39	17	22
Dyer	67	27	40
Fentress	26	17	9
Franklin	57	31	26
Gibson	59	32	27
Giles	53	20	33
Greene	147	59	88
Grundy	18	10	8
Hancock	41	17	24
Hardeman	44	24	20
Hardin	29	15	14
Haywood	35	14	21
Henderson	24	21	3
Henry	61	53	8
Houston	19	8	11
Humphreys	25	13	12
Jackson	23	14	9
Johnson	31	16	15
Lake	18	8	10
Lauderdale	44	18	26
Lawrence	48	34	14
Lewis	23	11	12
Lincoln	48	21	27
Marshall	45	21	24
Maury	113	61	52
McMinn	65	41	24
McNairy	27	14	13
Meigs	21	11	10
Monroe	45	41	4
Moore	23	12	11
Morgan	32	15	17
Obion	55	20	35
Overton	52	19	33
Perry	18	11	7
Pickett	12	12	0
Putnam	105	50	55
Rhea	49	49	0
Roane	55	29	26
Scott	45	30	15
Sevier	125	79	46
Van Buren	13	7	6
Warren	73	37	36
Wayne	20	10	10
Weakley	38	18	20
White	54	22	32
TEXAS			
Anderson	55	26	29
Andrews	32	12	20
Angelina	105	41	64
Bailey	9	4	5
Bee	34	17	17
Blanco	16	9	7
Borden	3	2	1
Bosque	20	11	9
Brewster	20	9	11
Briscoe	3	2	1
Brown	50	23	27
Burnet	72	37	35
Camp	17	6	11
Cass	36	14	22

Table 81

Full-time Law Enforcement Employees as of October 31, 2003

by Nonmetropolitan County by State—Continued

County by state	Total law enforcement employees	Total officers	Total civilians	County by state	Total law enforcement employees	Total officers	Total civilians
TEXAS—Continued				**TEXAS—Continued**			
Castro	20	8	12	Kimble	13	9	4
Cherokee	51	25	26	King	1	1	0
Childress	14	5	9	Kinney	13	6	7
Cochran	13	8	5	Knox	5	3	2
Coke	6	5	1	Lamar	74	23	51
Coleman	11	5	6	Lamb	29	12	17
Collingsworth	9	5	4	La Salle	20	14	6
Colorado	41	19	22	Lavaca	23	11	12
Comanche	29	7	22	Lee	15	9	6
Concho	12	4	8	Leon	33	16	17
Cooke	48	21	27	Limestone	51	19	32
Cottle	2	2	0	Lipscomb	11	11	0
Crane	12	7	5	Live Oak	26	12	14
Crockett	19	13	6	Llano	40	20	20
Dallam	13	3	10	Loving	3	2	1
Dawson	16	5	11	Lynn	20	6	14
Deaf Smith	30	11	19	Madison	22	7	15
Dewitt	24	10	14	Marion	17	12	5
Dickens	6	2	4	Martin	9	3	6
Dimmit	19	10	9	Mason	10	5	5
Donley	8	5	3	Matagorda	68	40	28
Duval	32	18	14	Maverick	114	50	64
Eastland	24	8	16	McCulloch	12	6	6
Edwards	10	4	6	McMullen	3	3	0
Erath	47	21	26	Menard	9	5	4
Falls	14	8	6	Milam	29	12	17
Fannin	38	15	23	Mills	8	5	3
Fayette	36	16	20	Mitchell	11	5	6
Fisher	9	5	4	Montague	24	8	16
Floyd	14	3	11	Moore	40	14	26
Foard	4	3	1	Morris	22	8	14
Franklin	18	8	10	Motley	2	2	0
Freestone	32	18	14	Nacogdoches	112	60	52
Frio	20	11	9	Navarro	99	54	45
Gaines	20	9	11	Newton	19	11	8
Garza	12	7	5	Nolan	24	11	13
Gillespie	33	18	15	Ochiltree	17	8	9
Glasscock	3	3	0	Oldham	10	5	5
Gonzales	45	16	29	Palo Pinto	50	21	29
Gray	38	14	24	Panola	36	24	12
Grimes	42	22	20	Parmer	13	5	8
Hall	4	3	1	Pecos	28	14	14
Hamilton	20	9	11	Polk	67	46	21
Hansford	9	4	5	Presidio	31	6	25
Hardeman	10	5	5	Rains	20	8	12
Harrison	87	38	49	Reagan	21	8	13
Hartley	4	4	0	Real	7	3	4
Haskell	8	2	6	Red River	31	13	18
Hemphill	14	8	6	Reeves	458	16	442
Henderson	97	57	40	Refugio	32	11	21
Hill	50	23	27	Roberts	5	4	1
Hockley	23	14	9	Runnels	30	7	23
Hood	86	31	55	Sabine	18	8	10
Hopkins	50	25	25	San Augustine	15	5	10
Houston	28	13	15	San Saba	8	4	4
Howard	30	14	16	Schleicher	10	5	5
Hudspeth	38	12	26	Scurry	23	7	16
Hutchinson	32	14	18	Shackelford	13	4	9
Jack	16	10	6	Shelby	28	11	17
Jackson	28	9	19	Sherman	9	4	5
Jasper	33	15	18	Somervell	40	19	21
Jeff Davis	4	3	1	Starr	88	27	61
Jim Hogg	38	22	16	Stephens	11	5	6
Jim Wells	51	30	21	Sterling	3	3	0
Karnes	18	8	10	Stonewall	7	3	4
Kenedy	11	10	1	Sutton	15	5	10
Kent	8	3	5	Swisher	11	5	6
Kerr	91	44	47	Terrell	5	3	2

Table 81

Full-time Law Enforcement Employees as of October 31, 2003
by Nonmetropolitan County by State—Continued

County by state	Total law enforcement employees	Total officers	Total civilians	County by state	Total law enforcement employees	Total officers	Total civilians
TEXAS—Continued				**VIRGINIA—Continued**			
Terry	41	7	34	Floyd	27	17	10
Throckmorton	7	2	5	Grayson	25	19	6
Titus	51	22	29	Greensville	30	21	9
Trinity	19	12	7	Halifax	48	36	12
Tyler	28	18	10	Henry	122	109	13
Upton	16	9	7	Highland	12	7	5
Uvalde	29	16	13	King George	38	25	13
Val Verde	48	39	9	Lancaster	32	26	6
Van Zandt	67	26	41	Lee	47	47	0
Walker	63	30	33	Lunenburg	21	14	7
Ward	29	14	15	Madison	16	10	6
Washington	57	30	27	Mecklenburg	43	41	2
Wharton	62	38	24	Middlesex	18	12	6
Wheeler	10	6	4	Northampton	48	39	9
Wilbarger	16	7	9	Northumberland	24	15	9
Willacy	35	16	19	Nottoway	20	13	7
Winkler	28	10	18	Orange	36	28	8
Wood	61	26	35	Page	44	41	3
Yoakum	20	10	10	Patrick	42	30	12
Young	34	19	15	Prince Edward	25	25	0
Zapata	97	32	65	Rappahannock	23	22	1
Zavala	28	26	2	Richmond	14	8	6
				Rockbridge	30	23	7
UTAH				Russell	49	41	8
				Shenandoah	64	55	9
Beaver	43	13	30	Smyth	53	53	0
Box Elder	77	28	49	Southampton	39	30	9
Carbon	37	17	20	Tazewell	87	76	11
Daggett	31	7	24	Westmoreland	30	21	9
Duchesne	50	17	33	Wise	85	71	14
Emery	41	27	14	Wythe	35	28	7
Garfield	27	7	20				
Grand	28	16	12	**WASHINGTON**			
Iron	65	30	35				
Kane	22	15	7	Adams	31	19	12
Millard	48	28	20	Clallam	53	36	17
Piute	3	3	0	Columbia	13	8	5
Rich	10	4	6	Ferry	28	8	20
San Juan	33	27	6	Garfield	13	7	6
Sanpete	24	19	5	Grant	58	43	15
Sevier	58	45	13	Grays Harbor	80	40	40
Uintah	42	34	8	Island	46	39	7
Wasatch	40	19	21	Jefferson	43	21	22
Wayne	5	4	1	Kittitas	31	27	4
				Klickitat	44	16	28
VERMONT				Lewis	58	41	17
				Lincoln	26	15	11
Bennington	23	17	6	Mason	57	42	15
Lamoille	17	7	10	Okanogan	36	31	5
Orleans	7	5	2	Pacific	20	16	4
Rutland	36	31	5	Pend Oreille	29	14	15
Washington	9	7	2	San Juan	29	19	10
				Stevens	32	28	4
VIRGINIA				Wahkiakum	10	8	2
				Walla Walla	48	22	26
Accomack	63	52	11	Whitman	18	16	2
Alleghany	57	41	16				
Augusta	121	59	62	**WEST VIRGINIA**			
Bath	16	16	0				
Bland	15	8	7	Barbour	7	4	3
Brunswick	46	34	12	Barbour-Philippi State Police	5	4	1
Buchanan	51	41	10	Braxton	12	11	1
Buckingham	22	16	6	Braxton-Sutton State Police	5	4	1
Carroll	32	27	5	Calhoun	5	3	2
Charlotte	32	29	3	Calhoun-Grantsville State Police	4	3	1
Culpeper	94	77	17	Doddridge	2	2	0
Dickenson	40	37	3	Doddridge-West Union State Police	5	4	1
Essex	13	13	0	Fayette	34	30	4

Table 81

Full-time Law Enforcement Employees as of October 31, 2003
by Nonmetropolitan County by State—Continued

County by state	Total law enforcement employees	Total officers	Total civilians	County by state	Total law enforcement employees	Total officers	Total civilians
WEST VIRGINIA—Continued				**WISCONSIN**			
Fayette State Police:				Adams	49	49	0
Gauley Bridge	4	3	1	Ashland	34	28	6
Oak Hill	11	10	1	Barron	7	7	0
Gilmer	4	4	0	Bayfield	37	21	16
Gilmer-Glenville State Police	4	3	1	Buffalo	21	20	1
Grant	8	7	1	Burnett	31	16	15
Grant-Petersburg State Police	1	1	0	Clark	52	47	5
Greenbrier	27	23	4	Crawford	27	26	1
Greenbrier State Police:				Dodge	159	48	111
Lewisburg	9	8	1	Door	46	42	4
Rainelle	4	3	1	Dunn	51	23	28
Hardy	8	7	1	Florence	19	11	8
Hardy-Moorefield State Police	4	3	1	Forest	37	35	2
Harrison	42	38	4	Grant	45	24	21
Harrison-Bridgeport State Police	16	15	1	Green	55	44	11
Jackson	19	14	5	Green Lake	42	18	24
Jackson-Ripley State Police	4	3	1	Iron	20	20	0
Lewis	13	11	2	Jefferson	120	95	25
Lewis-Weston State Police	5	4	1	Juneau	50	41	9
Logan	21	14	7	Lafayette	23	14	9
Logan-Logan State Police	24	16	8	Langlade	41	17	24
Marion	38	25	13	Lincoln	54	27	27
Marion-Fairmont State Police	7	7	0	Manitowoc	102	61	41
Mason	26	16	10	Marinette	76	30	46
Mason-Point Pleasant State Police	5	4	1	Marquette	37	37	0
McDowell	16	15	1	Menominee	7	6	1
McDowell-Welch State Police	9	8	1	Monroe	40	37	3
Mercer	32	24	8	Pepin	16	15	1
Mercer-Princeton State Police	17	14	3	Polk	72	26	46
Mingo	20	17	3	Portage	93	44	49
Mingo State Police:				Price	22	20	2
Gilbert	3	2	1	Sauk	147	112	35
Williamson	6	5	1	Sawyer	41	34	7
Monroe	6	6	0	Shawano	58	39	19
Monroe-Union State Police	4	3	1	Taylor	40	17	23
Nicholas	29	21	8	Trempealeau	44	22	22
Nicholas State Police:				Vernon	26	26	0
Richwood	4	3	1	Vilas	70	33	37
Summersville	4	3	1	Walworth	216	83	133
Pendleton	4	3	1	Washburn	29	13	16
Pendleton-Franklin State Police	5	4	1	Waupaca	78	33	45
Pocahontas	17	7	10	Waushara	61	25	36
Pocahontas-Buckeye State Police	5	4	1	Wood	78	43	35
Raleigh	60	45	15				
Raleigh-Beckley State Police	14	12	2	**WYOMING**			
Randolph	5	5	0				
Randolph-Elkins State Police	20	12	8	Albany	45	20	25
Ritchie	7	6	1	Big Horn	17	10	7
Ritchie-Harrisville State Police	6	5	1	Campbell	65	43	22
Roane	8	7	1	Carbon	38	17	21
Roane-Spencer State Police	6	5	1	Converse	16	9	7
Summers	7	6	1	Crook	18	6	12
Summers-Hinton State Police	5	4	1	Fremont	94	31	63
Taylor	23	6	17	Goshen	17	8	9
Taylor-Grafton State Police	3	2	1	Hot Springs	12	4	8
Tucker	5	4	1	Johnson	10	9	1
Tucker-Parsons State Police	4	3	1	Lincoln	35	16	19
Tyler	5	4	1	Niobrara	15	3	12
Tyler-Paden City State Police	4	3	1	Park	39	18	21
Upshur	12	10	2	Platte	10	8	2
Upshur-Buckhannon State Police	7	6	1	Sheridan	26	20	6
Webster	4	4	0	Sublette	52	23	29
Webster-Upperglade State Police	6	5	1	Sweetwater	50	31	19
Wetzel	8	8	0	Teton	49	27	22
Wetzel-Hundred State Police	4	3	1	Uinta	32	21	11
Wyoming	19	18	1	Washakie	10	8	2
Wyoming-Jesse State Police	4	3	1	Weston	8	6	2

Table 82

Full-time Law Enforcement Employees as of October 31, 2003
by Other Agencies by State

Other agency by state	Total law enforcement employees	Total officers	Total civilians	Other agency by state	Total law enforcement employees	Total officers	Total civilians
ALABAMA				**GEORGIA—Continued**			
				Gwinnett County Public Schools	22	18	4
22nd Judicial Circuit Drug Task Force	6	5	1	Hall County Marshal	15	13	2
24th Judicial Circuit Drug and Violent				Metropolitan Atlanta Rapid			
Crime Task Force	5	4	1	Transit Authority	317	269	48
City of Montgomery, Housing Authority,				Mitchell County Drug Unit	9	8	1
Investigative Unit	5	4	1	Muscogee City Marshal	14	13	1
Huntsville International Airport	23	18	5	Richmond County Marshal	38	33	5
Marshall County Drug Enforcement	6	5	1	Southeast Georgia Drug Task Force	4	4	0
				Washington County Board of			
ALASKA				Education	5	5	0
Anchorage International Airport	61	58	3	**ILLINOIS**			
Fairbanks International Airport	23	22	1				
				Capitol Airport Authority	5	5	0
CALIFORNIA				Chicago Fire Department, Arson			
				Investigations	9	1	8
East Bay Regional Parks, Alameda				Cook County Forest Preserve	82	77	5
County	73	51	22	Crystal Lake Park District	3	3	0
Fontana Unified School District	24	15	9	CSX Transportation	22	22	0
Grant Joint Union High School	23	19	4	Decatur Park District	6	6	0
Monterey Peninsula Airport	6	6	0	Du Page County Forest Preserve	29	25	4
Port of San Diego Harbor	156	127	29	Elgin, Joliet and Eastern Railway	6	6	0
San Bernardino Unified School District	77	26	51	Indiana Harbor Belt Railroad	15	14	1
San Francisco Bay Area Rapid				John H. Stroger Hospital	67	61	6
Transit, Contra Costa County	279	192	87	Lake County Forest Preserve	12	12	0
Stockton Unified School District	21	15	6	Norfolk Southern Railway	54	53	1
				Pekin Park District	1	1	0
DISTRICT OF COLUMBIA				Rockford Park District	18	17	1
				Springfield Park District	7	7	0
Metro Transit Police	491	365	126	Will County Forest Preserve	11	10	1
National Zoological Park	30	29	1				
				INDIANA			
DELAWARE							
				St. Joseph County Airport Authority	16	16	0
Wilmington Fire Department	173	169	4				
				KANSAS			
FLORIDA							
				Johnson County Park	14	13	1
Florida School for the Deaf and Blind	17	9	8	Metropolitan Topeka Airport			
Jacksonville Airport Authority	33	32	1	Authority	26	20	6
Lee County Port Authority	57	36	21	Shawnee Mission Public Schools	11	11	0
Melbourne International Airport	12	11	1	Topeka Fire Department, Arson			
Miami-Dade County Public Schools	262	203	59	Investigation	3	3	0
Miccosukee Tribal	57	41	16	Unified School District:			
Palm Beach County School District	209	140	69	Goddard	4	4	0
Sarasota-Bradenton International				Maize	4	3	1
Airport	17	16	1	Topeka	16	15	1
Seminole Tribal	94	70	24	Wyandotte County Parks and Recreation	10	10	0
St. Petersburg-Clearwater International							
Airport	8	8	0	**KENTUCKY**			
Tampa International Airport	130	57	73				
Volusia County Beach Management	68	64	4	Buffalo Trace-Gateway Narcotics			
				Task Force	4	4	0
GEORGIA				Cincinnati-Northern Kentucky			
				International Airport	69	54	15
Albany-Dougherty Metropolitan				Fayette County Schools	31	27	4
Drug Squad	23	19	4	FIVCO Area Drug Task Force	6	5	1
Augusta Board of Education	42	39	3	Jefferson County Board of Education	24	18	6
Bibb County Board of Education	28	23	5	Land Between The Lakes	12	11	1
Chatham County Board of Education	44	37	7	Lexington Bluegrass Airport	28	20	8
Chatham-Savannah Narcotics Team	42	37	5	Northern Kentucky Narcotics			
Cherokee County Board of Education	13	11	2	Enforcement	3	1	2
Cherokee County Marshal	13	6	7	Pennyrile Narcotics Task Force	8	7	1
Decatur County Schools	4	4	0				
Fayette County Marshal	9	8	1	**MARYLAND**			
Forsyth County Fire Investigation Unit	2	2	0				
Fulton County Marshal	64	57	7	Maryland-National Capital Park Police:			
Fulton County School System	52	50	2	Montgomery County	104	85	19
Gwinnett County Marshal	1	1	0	Prince George's County	111	88	23

Table 82

Full-time Law Enforcement Employees as of October 31, 2003
by Other Agencies by State—Continued

Other agency by state	Total law enforcement employees	Total officers	Total civilians	Other agency by state	Total law enforcement employees	Total officers	Total civilians
MICHIGAN				**NEW YORK—Continued**			
Bishop International Airport	6	6	0	Onondaga County Parks	1	1	0
Capitol Region Airport Authority	22	18	4	Staten Island Rapid Transit	25	24	1
Hudson Mills Metropark	7	7	0	Suffolk County Parks	45	41	4
Kensington Metropark	8	7	1				
Lower Huron Metropark	7	7	0	**NORTH CAROLINA**			
Metro Beach Metropark	6	6	0				
Stoney Creek Metropark	7	7	0	Asheville Regional Airport	14	14	0
Wayne County Airport	148	140	8	Caswell Center Hospital	4	4	0
				Cherokee Tribal	49	37	12
MINNESOTA				Piedmont Triad International Airport	29	17	12
				Raleigh-Durham International Airport	36	34	2
Minneapolis-St. Paul International Airport	101	71	30	Wilmington International Airport	16	12	4
Three Rivers Park District	33	18	15				
				OHIO			
MISSOURI							
				Cleveland Metropolitan Park District	77	70	7
Clay County Park Authority	7	6	1	Greater Cleveland Regional Transit Authority	112	98	14
Jackson County Park Rangers	21	19	2	Port Columbus International Airport	53	36	17
Lambert-St. Louis International Airport	108	92	16	Robinson Memorial Hospital	7	6	1
St. Charles County Park Rangers	8	8	0	Toledo-Lucas County Port Authority	14	14	0
St. Peters Ranger Division	10	9	1	Wood County Park District	6	6	0
NEVADA				**OKLAHOMA**			
Clark County School District	164	145	19	Jenks Public Schools	7	5	2
Washoe County School District	35	30	5	Norman Public Schools	5	4	1
				Putnam City Campus	12	8	4
NEW JERSEY							
				OREGON			
Park Police:							
Camden County	41	40	1	Port of Portland	63	50	13
Morris County	33	32	1				
Union County	365	317	48	**PENNSYLVANIA**			
Prosecutor:							
Atlantic County	171	73	98	Allegheny County Port Authority	65	44	21
Bergen County	255	172	83	County Detective:			
Burlington County	140	50	90	Butler County	4	4	0
Camden County	268	173	95	Cumberland County	8	6	2
Cape May County	53	19	34	Dauphin County	15	12	3
Cumberland County	69	19	50	Lebanon County	6	5	1
Essex County	428	291	137	Lehigh County	9	9	0
Gloucester County	98	52	46	Westmoreland County	61	16	45
Hudson County	222	98	124	York County	13	12	1
Hunterdon County	52	21	31	Delaware County District Attorney, Criminal Investigation Division	33	30	3
Mercer County	151	97	54	Delaware County Park	50	49	1
Middlesex County	204	129	75	Harrisburg International Airport	19	14	5
Monmouth County	296	82	214	Lehigh Valley International Airport	14	12	2
Morris County	154	72	82	Westmoreland County Park	23	23	0
Ocean County	151	104	47				
Passaic County	213	86	127	**RHODE ISLAND**			
Salem County	41	15	26				
Somerset County	114	50	64	Narragansett Tribal	7	6	1
Sussex County	53	32	21				
Union County	223	67	156	**SOUTH CAROLINA**			
Warren County	57	33	24				
				Charleston County Aviation Authority	36	28	8
NEW MEXICO				Columbia Metropolitan Airport	18	18	0
				Greenville-Spartanburg International Airport	19	18	1
Santa Clara Tribal	13	7	6	Whitten Center	3	3	0
Taos Pueblo Tribal	16	10	6				
Zuni Tribal	53	25	28	**TENNESSEE**			
NEW YORK				Chattanooga Metropolitan Airport	18	12	6
				Drug Task Force:			
Delaware and Hudson Railroad, Albany County	9	8	1	3rd Judicial District	5	4	1
Norfolk Southern Railway, Erie County	4	4	0	8th Judicial District	3	3	0
				9th Judicial District	2	1	1

Table 82

Full-time Law Enforcement Employees as of October 31, 2003
by Other Agencies by State—Continued

Other agency by state	Total law enforcement employees	Total officers	Total civilians	Other agency by state	Total law enforcement employees	Total officers	Total civilians
TENNESSEE—Continued				**TEXAS—Continued**			
10th Judicial District	6	5	1	Killeen	11	11	0
12th Judicial District	2	2	0	Klein	37	25	12
14th Judicial District	3	3	0	Mexia	2	2	0
15th Judicial District	3	2	1	Midland	22	7	15
17th Judicial District	6	5	1	North East	40	34	6
18th Judicial District	10	9	1	Pasadena	33	25	8
19th Judicial District	6	5	1	Raymondville	4	4	0
21st Judicial District	9	8	1	Socorro	25	20	5
22nd Judicial District	1	1	0	Spring	30	29	1
23rd Judicial District	3	3	0	Spring Branch	40	31	9
24th Judicial District	5	4	1	Taft	2	2	0
27th Judicial District	3	2	1	Tyler	8	7	1
31st Judicial District	1	1	0	United	90	23	67
Knoxville Metropolitan Airport	45	27	18	Weslaco	15	15	0
Memphis International Airport	55	45	10				
Metropolitan Board of Parks and Recreation (Nashville-Davidson)	20	19	1	**UTAH**			
Nashville International Airport	74	61	13	Granite School District	29	16	13
Tri-Cities Regional Airport	19	17	2				
West Tennessee Violent Crime Task Force	7	6	1	**VIRGINIA**			
				Norfolk Airport Authority	41	34	7
TEXAS				Reagan National Airport	250	188	62
				Richmond International Airport	31	31	0
Amarillo International Airport	15	15	0				
Cameron County Park Rangers	10	10	0	**WASHINGTON**			
Dallas-Fort Worth International Airport	390	292	98	Colville Tribal	46	34	12
Hospital District:				Lummi Tribal	21	19	2
Dallas County	95	64	31	Nisqually Tribal	14	13	1
Tarrant County	65	31	34	Nooksack Tribal	6	5	1
Houston Metropolitan Transit Authority	248	156	92	Port of Seattle	135	107	28
Independent School District:				Skokomish Tribal	11	10	1
Aldine	44	35	9	Swinomish Tribal	12	9	3
Alvin	15	13	2				
Angleton	5	4	1	**WEST VIRGINIA**			
Athens	2	2	0	Kanawha County Parks and Recreation	5	5	0
Austin	83	56	27				
Bay City	8	7	1	**WISCONSIN**			
Brownsville	89	17	72	Menominee Tribal	34	26	8
Conroe	63	44	19	Oneida Tribal	31	24	7
Corpus Christi	53	27	26				
East Central	12	11	1	**U.S. TERRITORIES**			
Ector County	23	21	2	Puerto Rico	21,497	19,540	1,957
El Paso	39	30	9				
Fort Bend	48	42	6	**FEDERAL AGENCIES**			
Hempstead	1	1	0	National Institutes of Health	83	74	9
Judson	20	18	2				
Katy	33	26	7				

SECTION VII

Agencies that contribute to the Uniform Crime Reporting (UCR) Program forward crime data through the state UCR Programs in 46 states and the District of Columbia. Local agencies in states that do not have a state Program submit statistics directly to the FBI, which provides continuing guidance and support to individual contributing agencies. The state UCR Programs are very effective liaisons between local contributors and the FBI. Many of the state Programs have mandatory reporting requirements and collect data beyond the national UCR Program's scope to address crime problems germane to their particular locales. In most cases, these state Programs also provide more direct and frequent service to participating law enforcement agencies, make information more readily available for statewide use, and streamline the national Program's operations.

The criteria established for state Programs ensure consistency and comparability in the data submitted to the national Program, as well as regular and timely reporting. These criteria are (1) The state Program must conform to national UCR Program standards, definitions, and information required. (2) The state criminal justice agency must have a proven, effective, statewide Program and have instituted acceptable quality control procedures. (3) The state crime reporting must cover a percentage of the population at least equal to that covered by the national UCR Program through direct reporting. (4) The state Program must have adequate field staff assigned to conduct audits and to assist contributing agencies in record-keeping practices and crime-reporting procedures. (5) The state Program must furnish the FBI with all of the detailed data regularly collected by the FBI from individual agencies that report to the State Program in the form of duplicate returns, computer printouts, and/or appropriate electronic media. (6) The state agency must have the proven capability (tested over a period of time) to supply all the statistical data required in time to meet publication deadlines of the national UCR Program.

To fulfill its responsibilities in connection with the UCR Program, the FBI continues to edit and review individual agency reports for both completeness and quality. The national UCR Program staff have direct contact with individual contributors within the state, as necessary, in connection with crime-reporting matters, coordinating such contact with the state agency. On request, staff members conduct training programs within the state on law enforcement record-keeping and crime-reporting procedures. Following audit standards established by the federal government, the FBI conducts an audit of each state's UCR data collection procedures once every 3 years. Should circumstances develop whereby the state agency does not comply with the aforementioned requirements, the national Program may reinstitute a direct collection of Uniform Crime Reports from law enforcement agencies within the state.

Reporting Procedures

Each month the UCR Program tabulates the number of Part I offenses brought to the attention of law enforcement agencies based on all reports of crime received from victims, officers who discover infractions, or other sources. Specifically, the Part I crimes reported to the FBI are murder and nonnegligent manslaughter, forcible rape, robbery, aggravated assault, burglary, larceny-theft, motor vehicle theft, and arson.

Law enforcement agencies report to the FBI the number of actual offenses known regardless of whether anyone is arrested for the crime, stolen property is recovered, or prosecution is undertaken. Complaints of crime that are determined through investigation to be unfounded or false are eliminated from an agency's count.

Another integral part of the monthly submission is the total number of actual Part I offenses cleared. Crimes are cleared in one of two ways: by arrest of at least one person, who is charged and turned over to the court for prosecution, or by exceptional means, when some element beyond law enforcement control precludes the arrest of a known offender. Law enforcement agencies also report the number of clearances that involve only offenders under the age of 18, the value of property stolen and recovered in connection with the offenses, and detailed information pertaining to criminal homicide and arson.

In addition to its primary collection of Part I offenses, the UCR Program solicits monthly data on persons arrested for all crimes except traffic violations. Agencies report the age, sex, and race of arrestees for both Part I and Part II offenses. Part II offenses include all crimes not classified as Part I.

The UCR Program also collects monthly data on law enforcement officers killed or assaulted, and, yearly, the number of full-time sworn and civilian law enforcement personnel employed on October 31.

At the end of each quarter, the Program collects summarized information on hate crimes, i.e., specific offenses that were motivated by an offender's bias against the perceived race, religion, ethnic origin, sexual orientation, or physical or mental disability of the victim. Those agencies participating in the National Incident-Based Reporting System (NIBRS) submit hate crime data monthly.

Editing Procedures

The UCR Program thoroughly examines each report it receives for arithmetical accuracy and for deviations that may indicate errors. To identify any unusual fluctuations in an agency's crime count, UCR staff compare monthly reports with previous submissions of the agency and with those for similar agencies. Large variations in crime levels may indicate modified records procedures, incomplete reporting, or changes in the jurisdiction's geopolitical structure.

Data reliability is a high priority of the Program, which brings to the attention of the state UCR Program or the submitting agency any deviations or arithmetical adjustments noted by the national staff. A standard FBI procedure is to study the monthly reports and to evaluate periodic trends

prepared for individual reporting units. Any significant increase or decrease becomes the subject of a special inquiry. Changes in crime reporting procedures or annexations can influence the level of reported crime. When this occurs, the UCR Program excludes the figures for specific crime categories or totals, if necessary, from trend tabulations.

To assist contributors in complying with UCR standards, the national Program provides training seminars and instructional materials on crime reporting procedures. Throughout the country, the national UCR Program maintains liaison with state Programs and law enforcement personnel and holds training sessions to explain the purpose of the Program, the rules of uniform classification and scoring, and the methods of assembling the information for reporting. When an individual agency has specific problems in compiling its crime statistics and its remedial efforts are unsuccessful, personnel from the FBI's Criminal Justice Information Services Division may visit the contributor to aid in resolving the difficulties.

The national UCR Program publishes a *Uniform Crime Reporting Handbook*, which details procedures for classifying and scoring offenses and serves as the contributing agencies' basic resource for preparing reports. The national staff produce letters to UCR contributors and UCR *State Program Bulletins* as needed. These provide policy updates and new information, as well as clarification of reporting issues.

The final responsibility for data submissions rests with the individual contributing law enforcement agency. Although the Program makes every effort through its editing procedures, training practices, and correspondence to assure the validity of the data it receives, the accuracy of the statistics depends primarily on the adherence of each contributor to the established standards of reporting. Deviations from these established standards, which cannot be resolved by the national UCR Program, may be brought to the attention of the Criminal Justice Information Systems Committees of the International Association of Chiefs of Police and the National Sheriffs' Association.

Arrest Data

Due to changes in reporting practices, arrest data for Arkansas and New Hampshire are not comparable to previous years' data. Twelve months of complete arrest data were not received for contributing Nevada law enforcement agencies by the established publication deadline. Limited arrest data were received from Illinois, Kentucky, and South Carolina. No 2003 arrest data were received from the District of Columbia Metropolitan Police Department; the two agencies (Zoological Police and Metro Transit Police) for which 12 months of arrest data were received have no attributable population. Twelve months of arrest figures for New York City Police Department, New York; law enforcement agencies in Florida; and the newly formed city-county law enforcement agency of Louisville Metro Police Department, Kentucky, were not available for inclusion in this book. However, arrest totals for these areas were estimated by the UCR Program for inclusion in Table 29, "Estimated Number of Arrests, United States, 2003."

Population

For the 2003 edition of *Crime in the United States*, the UCR Program obtained current population estimates from the Bureau of the Census to estimate 2003 population counts for all contributing law enforcement agencies. The Bureau of the Census provided revised 2002 state/national population estimates and 2003 state/national population estimates. Using these provisional census data, the national UCR Program updated the 2002 Bureau of the Census city and county estimates and calculated the 2003 state growth rates. Subsequently, the Program updated population figures for individual jurisdictions by applying the 2003 state growth rates to the updated 2002 Bureau of the Census data.

NIBRS Conversion

Several states provide their UCR data in the expanded NIBRS format. For presentation in this book, NIBRS data were converted to the historical Summary UCR formats. The NIBRS database was constructed to allow for such conversion so that UCR's long-running time series could continue.

Crime Trends

By showing fluctuations from year to year, trend statistics offer the data user an added perspective from which to study crime. Percent change tabulations in this publication are computed only for reporting agencies that provided comparable data for the periods under consideration. The Program excludes from the trend calculations all figures except those received for common months from common agencies. Also excluded are unusual fluctuations that the Program determines are due to variables such as improved records procedures, annexations, etc.

Data users should exercise care in making any direct comparison between data in this publication and those in prior issues of *Crime in the United States*. Due to differing levels of participation from year to year and transient reporting problems that require the Program to estimate crime counts for certain contributors, the data are not comparable from year to year.

Offense Estimation

Tables 1 through 5 and 7 of this publication contain statistics for the entire United States. Because not all law enforcement agencies provide data for complete reporting periods, the UCR Program includes estimated crime counts in these presentations. Offense estimation occurs within each of three areas: Metropolitan Statistical Areas (MSAs), cities outside MSAs, and nonmetropolitan counties. Using the known crime experiences of similar areas within a state, the national Program computes estimates by assigning the same proportional crime volumes to nonreporting agencies. The population size of agency; type of jurisdiction, e.g., police department versus sheriffs office; and geographic location are considered in the estimation process.

Various circumstances require the national Program to estimate certain state offense totals. For example, some states do not provide forcible rape figures in accordance with UCR guidelines; reporting problems at the state level have, at times, resulted in no usable data. Additionally, the conversion of Summary reporting to NIBRS has contributed to the need for unique estimation procedures. A summary of state-specific and offense-specific estimation procedures follows.

Year	State(s)	Reason for Estimation	Estimation Method
1985	Illinois	The state UCR Program was unable to provide forcible rape figures in accordance with UCR guidelines.	The rape totals were estimated using national rates per 100,000 inhabitants within the eight population groups and assigning the forcible rape volumes proportionally to the state.
1986	Illinois	The state UCR Program was unable to provide forcible rape figures in accordance with UCR guidelines.	The rape totals were estimated using national rates per 100,000 inhabitants within the eight population groups and assigning the forcible rape volumes proportionally to the state.
1987	Illinois	The state UCR Program was unable to provide forcible rape figures in accordance with UCR guidelines.	The rape totals were estimated using national rates per 100,000 inhabitants within the eight population groups and assigning the forcible rape volumes proportionally to the state.
1988	Illinois	The state UCR Program was unable to provide forcible rape figures in accordance with UCR guidelines.	The rape totals were estimated using national rates per 100,000 inhabitants within the eight population groups and assigning the forcible rape volumes proportionally to the state.
	Florida, Kentucky	Reporting problems at the state level resulted in no usable data.	State totals were estimated by updating previous valid annual totals for individual jurisdictions, subdivided by population group. Percent changes for each offense within each population group of the geographic divisions in which the states reside were applied to the previous valid annual totals. The state totals were compiled from the sums of the population group estimates.
1989	Illinois	The state UCR Program was unable to provide forcible rape figures in accordance with UCR guidelines.	The rape totals were estimated using national rates per 100,000 inhabitants within the eight population groups and assigning the forcible rape volumes proportionally to the state.
1990	Illinois	The state UCR Program was unable to provide forcible rape figures in accordance with UCR guidelines.	The rape totals were estimated using national rates per 100,000 inhabitants within the eight population groups and assigning the forcible rape volumes proportionally to the state.
1991	Illinois	The state UCR Program was unable to provide forcible rape figures in accordance with UCR guidelines.	The rape totals were estimated using national rates per 100,000 inhabitants within the eight population groups and assigning the forcible rape volumes proportionally to the state.
	Iowa	NIBRS conversion efforts resulted in estimation for Iowa.	State totals were estimated by updating previous valid annual totals for individual jurisdictions, subdivided by population group. Percent changes for each offense within each population group of the West North Central Division were applied to the previous valid annual totals. The state totals were compiled from the sums of the population group estimates.
1992	Illinois	The state UCR Program was unable to provide forcible rape figures in accordance with UCR guidelines.	The rape totals were estimated using national rates per 100,000 inhabitants within the eight population groups and assigning the forcible rape volumes proportionally to the state.

Year	State(s)	Reason for Estimation	Estimation Method
1993	Michigan, Minnesota	The state UCR Programs were unable to provide forcible rape figures in accordance with UCR guidelines.	The rape totals were estimated using national rates per 100,000 inhabitants within the eight population groups and assigning the forcible rape volumes proportionally to each state.
	Kansas	NIBRS conversion efforts resulted in estimation for Kansas.	State totals were estimated by updating previous valid annual totals for individual jurisdictions, subdivided by population group. Percent changes for each offense within each population group of the West North Central Division were applied to the previous valid annual totals. The state totals were compiled from the sums of the population group estimates.
	Illinois	NIBRS conversion efforts resulted in estimation for Illinois.	Since valid annual totals were available for approximately 60 Illinois agencies, those counts were maintained. The counts for the remaining jurisdictions were replaced with the most recent valid annual totals or were generated using standard estimation procedures. The results of all sources were then combined to arrive at the 1993 state total for Illinois.
		The state UCR Program was unable to provide forcible rape figures in accordance with UCR guidelines.	The rape totals were estimated using national rates per 100,000 inhabitants within the eight population groups and assigning the forcible rape volumes proportionally to the state.
1994	Illinois	NIBRS conversion efforts resulted in estimation for Illinois.	Illinois totals were generated using only the valid crime rates for the East North Central Division. Within each population group, the state's offense totals were estimated based on the rate per 100,000 inhabitants within the remainder of the division.
		The state UCR Program was unable to provide forcible rape figures in accordance with UCR guidelines.	The rape totals were estimated using national rates per 100,000 inhabitants within the eight population groups and assigning the forcible rape volumes proportionally to the state.
	Kansas	NIBRS conversion efforts resulted in estimation for Kansas.	State totals were generated using only the valid crime rates for the West North Central Division. Within each population group, the state's offense totals were estimated based on the rate per 100,000 inhabitants within the remainder of the division.
	Montana	The state UCR Program was unable to provide complete 1994 offense figures in accordance with UCR guidelines.	State totals were estimated by updating previous valid annual totals for individual jurisdictions, subdivided by population group. Percent changes for each offense within each population group of the Mountain Division were applied to the previous valid annual totals. The state totals were compiled from the sums of the population group estimates.
1995	Kansas	The state UCR Program was unable to provide complete 1995 offense figures in accordance with UCR guidelines.	The state UCR Program was able to provide valid 1994 state totals which were then updated using 1995 crime trends for the West North Central Division.

Year	State(s)	Reason for Estimation	Estimation Method
	Illinois	The state UCR Program was unable to provide complete 1995 offense figures in accordance with UCR guidelines.	Valid Crime Index (Part I) counts were available for most of the largest cities. For other agencies, the only available counts were generated without application of the UCR Hierarchy Rule. (The Hierarchy Rule requires that only the most serious offense in a multiple-offense criminal incident is counted.) To arrive at a comparable state estimate to be included in national compilations, the total supplied by the Illinois State Program (which was inflated because of the nonapplication of the Hierarchy Rule) was reduced by the proportion of multiple offenses reported within single incidents in the available NIBRS data. Valid totals for the large cities were excluded from the reduction process.
	Montana	The state UCR Program was unable to provide complete 1995 offense figures in accordance with UCR guidelines.	State estimates were computed by updating the previous valid annual totals using the 1994 versus 1995 percent changes for the Mountain Division.
1996	Florida	The state UCR Program was unable to provide complete 1996 offense figures in accordance with UCR guidelines.	The state UCR Program was able to provide an aggregated state total; data received from 94 individual Florida agencies are shown in the 1996 jurisdictional figures presented in Tables 8 through 11.
	Illinois	The state UCR Program was unable to provide complete 1996 offense figures in accordance with UCR guidelines.	Valid Crime Index (Part I) counts were available for most of the largest cities. For other agencies, the only available counts were generated without application of the UCR Hierarchy Rule. (The Hierarchy Rule requires that only the most serious offense in a multiple-offense criminal incident is counted.) To arrive at a comparable state estimate to be included in national compilations, the total supplied by the Illinois State Program (which was inflated because of the nonapplication of the Hierarchy Rule) was reduced by the proportion of multiple offenses reported within single incidents in the available NIBRS data. Valid totals for the large cities were excluded from the reduction process.
	Kansas	The state UCR Program was unable to provide complete 1996 offense figures in accordance with UCR guidelines.	The Kansas state estimate was extrapolated from 1996 January-June state totals provided by the Kansas State UCR Program.
	Kentucky, Montana	The state UCR Programs were unable to provide complete 1996 offense figures in accordance with UCR guidelines.	The 1995 and 1996 percent changes within each geographic division were applied to valid 1995 state totals to generate 1996 state totals.
1997	Illinois	The state UCR Program was unable to provide complete 1997 offense figures in accordance with UCR guidelines.	Valid Crime Index (Part I) counts were available for most of the largest cities. For other agencies, the only available counts were generated without application of the UCR Hierarchy Rule. (The Hierarchy Rule requires that only the most serious offense in a multiple-offense criminal incident is counted.) To arrive at a comparable state estimate to be included in national compilations, the total supplied by the Illinois State Program (which was inflated because of the nonapplication of the Hierarchy Rule) was reduced by the proportion of multiple offenses reported within single incidents in the available NIBRS data. Valid totals for the large cities were excluded from the reduction process.
	Kansas	The state UCR Program was unable to provide complete 1997 offense figures in accordance with UCR guidelines.	The Kansas state estimate was extrapolated from 1996 January-June state totals provided by the Kansas State UCR Program.

Year	State(s)	Reason for Estimation	Estimation Method
	Kentucky, Montana, New Hampshire, Vermont	The state UCR Programs were unable to provide complete 1997 offense figures in accordance with UCR guidelines.	The 1996 and 1997 percent changes registered for each geographic division in which the states of Kentucky, Montana, New Hampshire, and Vermont are categorized were applied to valid 1996 state totals to effect 1997 state totals.
1998	Delaware	The state UCR Program was unable to provide forcible rape figures in accordance with national UCR guidelines.	The 1998 forcible rape total for Delaware was estimated by reducing the number of reported offenses by the proportion of male forcible rape victims statewide.
	Kentucky, Montana, New Hampshire, Wisconsin	The state UCR Programs were unable to provide complete 1998 offense figures in accordance with UCR guidelines.	State totals were estimated by using the 1997 figures for the nonreporting areas and applying 1997 versus 1998 percentage changes for the division in which each state is located. The estimates for the nonreporting areas were then increased by any actual 1998 crime counts received.
	Kansas	The state UCR Program was unable to provide complete 1998 offense figures in accordance with UCR guidelines.	To arrive at 1998 estimates, 1997 state totals supplied by the Kansas State UCR Program were updated using 1998 crime trends for the West North Central Division.
	Illinois	The state UCR Program was unable to provide complete 1998 offense figures in accordance with UCR guidelines.	Valid Crime Index (Part I) counts were available for most of the largest cities. For other agencies, the only available counts were generated without application of the UCR Hierarchy Rule. (The Hierarchy Rule requires that only the most serious offense in a multiple-offense criminal incident is counted.) To arrive at a comparable state estimate to be included in national compilations, the total supplied by the Illinois State Program (which was inflated because of the nonapplication of the Hierarchy Rule) was reduced by the proportion of multiple offenses reported within single incidents in the available NIBRS data. Valid totals for the large cities were excluded from the reduction process.
1999	Illinois	The state UCR Program was unable to provide complete 1999 offense figures in accordance with UCR guidelines.	Valid Crime Index (Part I) counts were available for most of the largest cities. For other agencies, the only available counts were generated without application of the UCR Hierarchy Rule. (The Hierarchy Rule requires that only the most serious offense in a multiple-offense criminal incident is counted.) To arrive at a comparable state estimate to be included in national compilations, the total supplied by the Illinois State Program (which was inflated because of the nonapplication of the Hierarchy Rule) was reduced by the proportion of multiple offenses reported within single incidents in the available NIBRS data. Valid totals for the large cities were excluded from the reduction process.
	Maine	The state UCR Program was unable to provide complete 1999 offense figures in accordance with UCR guidelines.	The Maine Department of Public Safety forwarded monthly January through October crime counts for each law enforcement contributor; since 12 months of data were not received, the national Program estimated for the missing data following standard estimation procedures to arrive at a 1999 state total.
	Kansas, Kentucky, Montana	The state UCR Programs were unable to provide complete 1999 offense figures in accordance with UCR guidelines.	To arrive at 1999 estimates for Kansas, Kentucky, and Montana, 1998 state totals supplied by each state's UCR Program were updated using 1999 crime trends for the divisions in which each state is located.
	New Hampshire	The state UCR Program was unable to provide complete 1999 offense figures in accordance with UCR guidelines.	The state total for New Hampshire was estimated by using the 1998 figures for the 1999 nonreporting areas and applying the 2-year percent change for the New England Division.

Year	State(s)	Reason for Estimation	Estimation Method
2000	Kansas	The state UCR Program was unable to provide complete 2000 offense figures in accordance with UCR guidelines.	To arrive at 2000 estimates for Kansas, 1999 state estimates were updated using 2000 crime trends for the West North Central Division.
	Kentucky, Montana	The state UCR Programs were unable to provide complete 2000 offense figures in accordance with UCR guidelines.	To arrive at 2000 estimates for Kentucky and Montana, 1999 state totals supplied by each state's UCR Program were updated using 2000 crime trends for the divisions in which each state is located.
	Illinois	The state UCR Programs were unable to provide complete 2000 offense figures or forcible rape figures in accordance with UCR guidelines.	Valid Crime Index (Part I) counts were available for most of the largest cities. For other agencies, the only available counts were generated without application of the UCR Hierarchy Rule. (The Hierarchy Rule requires that only the most serious offense in a multiple-offense criminal incident be counted.) To arrive at a comparable state estimate to be included in national compilations, the total supplied by the Illinois State Program (which was inflated due to the nonapplication of the Hierarchy Rule) was reduced by the proportion of multiple offenses reported within single incidents in the available NIBRS data. Valid totals for the large cities were excluded from the reduction process.
2001	Kentucky	The state UCR Program was unable to provide complete 2000 offense figures in accordance with UCR guidelines.	To arrive at the 2001 estimate for Kentucky, the 2000 state estimates were updated using 2001 crime trends reported for the East South Central Division.
	Illinois	The state UCR Program submitted complete data for only seven agencies within the state. Additionally, the state UCR Program was unable to provide forcible rape figures in accordance with UCR guidelines.	Valid Crime Index (Part I) counts were available for most of the largest cities. For other agencies, the only available counts were generated without application of the UCR Hierarchy Rule. (The Hierarchy Rule requires that only the most serious offense in a multiple-offense criminal incident is counted.) To arrive at a comparable state estimate to be included in national compilations, the total supplied by the Illinois State Program (which was inflated because of the nonapplication of the Hierarchy Rule) was reduced by the proportion of multiple offenses reported within single incidents in the available NIBRS data. Valid totals for the large cities were excluded from the reduction process.
2002	Kentucky	The state UCR Program was unable to provide complete 2002 offense figures in accordance with UCR guidelines.	To obtain the 2002 state crime count, the FBI contacted the state UCR Program, and the state agency was able to provide their latest state total, 2000. Therefore, the 2001 state estimate was updated for inclusion in the 2002 edition of *Crime in the United States* by using the 2001 crime trends for the division in which the state is located. To derive the 2002 state estimate, the 2002 crime trends for the division were applied to the adjusted 2001 state estimate.
	Illinois	The state UCR Program was unable to provide complete 2002 offense figures in accordance with UCR guidelines.	Valid Crime Index (Part I) counts were only available for most of the largest cities. For other agencies, the only available counts were generated without application of the UCR Hierarchy Rule. (The Hierarchy Rule requires that only the most serious offense in a multiple-offense criminal incident is counted.) To arrive at a comparable state estimate to be included in national compilations, the total supplied by the Illinois State Program (which was inflated because of the nonapplication of the Hierarchy Rule) was reduced by the proportion of multiple offenses reported within single incidents in the available NIBRS data. Valid totals for the large cities were excluded from the reduction process.

Year	State(s)	Reason for Estimation	Estimation Method
2003	Kentucky	The state UCR Program was unable to provide complete 2003 offense figures in accordance with UCR guidelines.	To obtain the 2003 state estimate, the 2003 crime trend for the East South Central Division was applied to an adjusted 2002 state estimate. The 2002 state count was reestimated by applying the 2002 crime trend for the East South Central Division using a more current figure, 2001 state totals, provided by the state UCR Program. The adjusted 2002 estimate differs from the figure published in the 2002 edition of *Crime in the United States* which was originally estimated using 2000 state totals.
	Illinois	The state UCR Program was unable to provide complete 2003 offense figures in accordance with UCR guidelines.	Valid Part I counts were available only for most of the largest cities. For other agencies, the only available counts were generated by the Illinois State Program without application of the UCR Hierarchy Rule. (The Hierarchy Rule requires that only the most serious offense in a multiple-offense criminal incident is counted.) To arrive at a comparable state estimate to be included in national compilations, the NIBRS total (which was inflated because the Hierarchy Rule was not applied) supplied by the Illinois State Program was reduced by the proportion of multiple offenses reported within single incidents in NIBRS data nationwide.

Table Methodology

Although most law enforcement agencies submit crime reports to the UCR Program, not all agencies send 12 months of complete data for the reporting year. For example, to be included in this publication's Tables 8 through 11, which show specific jurisdictional statistics, the FBI must receive figures for all 12 months of the reporting year prior to established publication deadlines. Other tabular presentations are based on varied levels of submission. With the exception of the tables that consist of estimates for the total United States population, each table in this publication shows the number of agencies reporting and the extent of population coverage.

Designed to assist the reader, the following table explains the construction of many of this book's tabular presentations.

(1) Table	(2) Database	(3) Table Construction	(4) General Comments
1	All law enforcement agencies in the UCR Program. Crime statistics include estimated offense totals (except arson) for agencies submitting less than 12 months of offense reports for each year.	The 2003 statistics are consistent with Table 2. Pre-2003 crime statistics may have been updated and, therefore, may not be consistent with those published in prior publications. Population statistics represent July 1 provisional estimations for each year except 1990 and 2000, which are the Census Bureau's decennial census data. (See the Population section in this appendix.)	• Represents an estimation of reported crime for the Nation from 1984 to 2003. • Sufficient data are not available to provide arson estimates.
2	All law enforcement agencies in the UCR Program. Crime statistics include estimated offense totals (except arson) for agencies submitting less than 12 months of offense reports for 2003.	Statistics are aggregated from individual state statistics as shown in Table 5. Population statistics for 2003 represent estimates based on the percent change in state population from the Census Bureau's 2002 revised estimates and 2003 provisional estimates. (See the Population section in this appendix.)	• Represents an estimation of reported crime in 2003 for the: 1. Nation 2. MSAs 3. Cities outside metropolitan areas 4. Nonmetropolitan counties • Sufficient data are not available to provide arson estimates.
3	All law enforcement agencies in the UCR Program (including those submitting less than 12 months of offense reports for 2003). Arson is not included.	Regional offense distributions are computed from volume figures as shown in Table 4. Population distributions are based on the Census Bureau's provisional estimates for 2003.	• Represents the 2003 geographical distribution of estimated offenses and population. • Sufficient data are not available to provide arson estimates.
4	All law enforcement agencies in the UCR Program. Crime statistics include estimated offense totals (except arson) for agencies submitting less than 12 months of offense reports for 2002 and 2003.	The 2003 statistics are aggregated from individual state statistics as shown in Table 5. Population statistics represent the Census Bureau's 2002 revised estimates and 2003 provisional estimates.	• Represents an estimation of reported crime for the: 1. Nation 2. Regions 3. Divisions 4. States • Sufficient data are not available to provide arson estimates. • Any comparison of UCR statistics should take into consideration factors in addition to reported crime. More details concerning the proper use of UCR statistics are provided in Crime Factors in this report.
5	All law enforcement agencies in the UCR Program. Crime statistics include estimated offense totals (except arson) for agencies submitting less than 12 months of offense reports for 2003.	Population statistics for 2003 represent estimates based on the percent change in state population from the Census Bureau's 2002 revised estimates and 2003 provisional estimates. (See the Population section in this appendix.) Statistics under the heading Area Actually Reporting represent reported offense totals for agencies submitting 12 months of offense reports and estimated totals for agencies submitting less than 12 but more than 2 months of offense reports. The statistics under the heading Estimated Totals represent the above plus estimated offense totals for agencies submitting 2 months or less of offense reports.	• Represents an estimation of reported crime for states. • Sufficient data are not available to provide arson estimates. • Any comparison of UCR statistics should take into consideration factors in addition to reported crime. More details concerning the proper use of UCR statistics are provided in Crime Factors in this report.

(1) Table	(2) Database	(3) Table Construction	(4) General Comments
6	All law enforcement agencies in the UCR Program. Crime statistics include estimated offense totals (except arson) for agencies submitting less than 12 months of offense reports for 2003.	Statistics are published for all currently designated Metropolitan Statistical Areas (MSAs) having at least 75% of the area's agencies reporting and for which the principal city/cities submitted 12 months of complete data for 2003. Population statistics for 2003 represent estimates based on the percent change in state population from the Census Bureau's 2002 revised estimates and 2003 provisional estimates. (See the Population section in this appendix.) The statistics under the heading Area Actually Reporting represent offense totals for agencies submitting 12 months of complete data and estimated totals for agencies submitting less than 12 but more than 2 months of data. The statistics under the heading Estimated Total represent the above plus estimated totals for agencies submitting 2 months or less of data. The tabular breakdowns are according to UCR definitions. (See Appendix II.)	• Represents an estimation of reported crime for MSAs. • Sufficient data are not available to provide arson estimates. • Any comparison of UCR statistics should take into consideration factors in addition to reported crime. More details concerning the proper use of UCR statistics are provided in Crime Factors in this report.
7	All law enforcement agencies in the UCR Program. Crime statistics include estimated offense totals for agencies submitting less than 12 months of offense reports for 1999 through 2003.	Offense totals are for all Part I offenses other than aggravated assault and arson. (Appendix II of this report defines the UCR Program's Part I offenses.)	• Represents an estimation of reported crime for the Nation from 1999 to 2003. • Aggravated assault and arson are not included in the data source from which this table is derived.
8	All city and town law enforcement agencies (10,000 and over in population) submitting 12 months of complete data for 2003.	Cities and towns are agencies in Population Groups I through V. Population statistics for 2003 represent estimates based on the percent change in state population from the Census Bureau's 2002 revised estimates and 2003 provisional estimates. (See the Population section in this appendix.)	• Represents reported crime of individual agencies in cities and towns 10,000 and over in population. • Any comparison of UCR statistics should take into consideration factors in addition to reported crime. More details concerning the proper use of UCR statistics are provided in Crime Factors in this report.
9	All university/college law enforcement agencies submitting 12 months of complete data for 2003.	The 2001 student enrollment figures, which are provided by the U.S. Department of Education, are the most recent available. They include full- and part-time students. No adjustments to equate part-time enrollments into full-time equivalents have been made.	• Represents reported crime from those individual university/college law enforcement agencies (listed alphabetically by state) contributing data to the UCR Program. • Any comparison of these UCR statistics should take into consideration size of enrollment, number of on-campus residents, and other demographic factors.
10	All county law enforcement agencies submitting 12 months of complete data for 2003.	Metropolitan counties are the areas covered by non-city agencies within a currently designated MSA. Nonmetropolitan counties are those outside currently designated MSAs whose jurisdictions are not covered by city police agencies. (See Appendix III.) Population classifications for counties are based on 2003 UCR estimates for individual agencies. (See the Population section in this appendix.)	• Represents reported crime from individual law enforcement agencies in metropolitan counties and nonmetropolitan counties covering populations of 25,000 and over (i.e., the individual sheriff's office and/or county police department). • These figures do not represent the county totals because they exclude city crime counts. • Any comparison of UCR statistics should take into consideration factors in addition to reported crime. More details concerning the proper use of UCR statistics are provided in Crime Factors in this report.

(1) Table	(2) Database	(3) Table Construction	(4) General Comments
11	All state law enforcement agencies submitting 12 months of complete data for 2003.	State and federal agencies are those agencies, regardless of jurisdiction, that are managed by their respective state and federal governments.	• Represents reported crime from individual state law enforcement agencies (i.e., state police, highway patrol and/or other law enforcement agencies managed by the state) and any federally-managed law enforcement agency participating in the UCR Program. • Any comparison of UCR statistics should take into consideration factors in addition to reported crime. More details concerning the proper use of UCR statistics are provided in Crime Factors in this report.
12-15	All law enforcement agencies submitting at least 6 common months of complete offense reports for 2002 and 2003.	The 2003 crime trend statistics are 2-year comparisons based on 2003 reported crime. Only common reported months for individual agencies are included in 2003 trend calculations. Population statistics for 2003 represent estimates based on the percent change in state population from the Census Bureau's 2002 revised estimates and 2003 provisional estimates. (See the Population section in this appendix.) UCR population breakdowns are furnished in Appendix III. Note that suburban and nonsuburban cities are all municipal agencies other than central cities in MSAs.	Due to changes in reporting practices, agencies in Arkansas (which otherwise would meet the criteria for this table) were excluded.
16-19	All law enforcement agencies submitting 12 months of complete data (except arson) for 2003.	The 2003 crime rates are the ratios, per 100,000 inhabitants, of the aggregated 2003 crime volumes and the aggregated 2003 populations of the contributing agencies. Population statistics for 2003 represent estimates based on the percent change in state population from the Census Bureau's 2002 revised estimates and 2003 provisional estimates. (See the Population section in this appendix.) UCR population breakdowns are furnished in Appendix III. Note that suburban and nonsuburban cities are all municipal agencies other than central cities in MSAs.	• The forcible rape figures furnished by the Delaware and Illinois state UCR Programs were not in accordance with national guidelines. For inclusion in these tables, the Delaware and Illinois forcible rape figures were estimated by using the national rates for each population group applied to the population by group for Delaware and Illinois agencies supplying all 12 months of complete data. • Sufficient data are not available to provide arson estimates. • There is a slight decrease in national coverage for Table 19 due to FBI editing procedures and fewer submissions from reporting agencies. • Due to changes in reporting practices, agencies in Arkansas (which otherwise would meet the criteria for this table) were excluded.
20	All law enforcement agencies submitting Supplementary Homicide Report (SHR) data for 2003.	The weapon totals are the aggregate for each murder victim recorded on the SHRs for calendar year 2003.	The SHR is the monthly report form concerning homicides. It details victim and offender characteristics, circumstances, weapons used, etc.
21, 22	All law enforcement agencies submitting 12 months of complete offense reports for 2003.	The weapon totals are aggregated 2003 totals. Population statistics represent 2003 UCR estimates.	
23, 24	All law enforcement agencies submitting at least 6 months of complete offense reports for 2003.	Offense total and value lost total are computed for all Part I offenses other than aggravated assault and arson. Percent distribution is derived based on the offense total of each Part I offense. Trend statistics are derived based on agencies with at least 6 common months of complete data for 2002 and 2003. (Appendix II of this report defines the UCR Program's Part I offenses.)	• Aggravated assault and arson are excluded from Table 23. • For UCR Program purposes, the taking of money or property in connection with an assault is reported as robbery. • Arson is not included in the data source from which this table is derived.
25-28	All law enforcement agencies submitting at least 6 months of complete offense reports for 2003.	The 2003 clearance rates are based on offense and clearance volume totals of the contributing agencies for 2003. Population statistics for 2003 represent estimates based on the percent change in state population from the Census Bureau's 2002 revised estimates and 2003 provisional estimates. (See the Population section in this appendix.) UCR population breakdowns are furnished in Appendix III.	Due to changes in reporting practices, agencies in Arkansas (which otherwise would meet the criteria for this table) were excluded.

(1) Table	(2) Database	(3) Table Construction	(4) General Comments
29	All law enforcement agencies in the UCR Program (including those submitting less than 12 months of complete arrest data for 2003).	The arrest totals presented are national estimates based on the arrest statistics of all law enforcement agencies in the UCR Program (including those submitting less than 12 months). The estimated total number of arrests is the sum of estimated arrest volumes for each of 28 offenses, not including suspicion. Each individual arrest total is the sum of the estimated volumes within each of the eight population groups. (See Appendix III.) Each group's estimate is the reported volume (as shown in Table 31) divided by the percent of the total group population reporting, according to 2003 UCR estimates for individual agencies. (See the Population section in this appendix.)	
30, 31	All law enforcement agencies submitting 12 months of complete arrest data for 2003.	The 2003 arrest rates are the ratios, per 100,000 inhabitants, of the aggregated 2003 reported arrest statistics and population. The population statistics for 2003 represent estimates based on the percent change in state population from the Census Bureau's 2002 revised estimates and 2003 provisional estimates. (See the Population section in this appendix.) UCR population classifications and geographical configuration are provided in Appendix III.	
32, 33	All law enforcement agencies submitting 12 months of complete arrest data for 1994 and 2003.	The arrest trends are the percentage differences between 1994 and 2003 arrest volumes aggregated from all common agencies. The population statistics for 2003 represent estimates based on the percent change in state population from the Census Bureau's 2002 revised estimates and 2003 provisional estimates. (See the Population section in this appendix.) Population statistics for 1994 are based on the percent change in state population from the Census Bureau's 1993 and 1994 provisional estimates.	
34, 35	All law enforcement agencies submitting 12 months of complete arrest data for 1999 and 2003.	The arrest trends are the percentage differences between 1999 and 2003 arrest volumes aggregated from common agencies. The population statistics for 2003 represent estimates based on the percent change in state population from the Census Bureau's 2002 revised estimates and 2003 provisional estimates. (See the Population section in this appendix.) Population statistics for 1999 are based on the percent change in state population from the Census Bureau's 1998 and 1999 provisional estimates.	
36, 37	All law enforcement agencies submitting 12 months of complete arrest data for 2002 and 2003.	The arrest trends are 2-year comparisons between 2002 and 2003 arrest volumes aggregated from common agencies. Population statistics for 2002 represent estimates based on the percent change in state population from the Census Bureau's 2001 revised estimates and 2002 provisional estimates. Population statistics for 2003 represent estimates based on the percent change in state populations from the Census Bureau's 2002 revised estimates and 2003 provisional estimates. (See the Population section in this appendix.)	
38-43	All law enforcement agencies submitting 12 months of complete arrest data for 2003.	Population statistics for 2003 represent estimates based on the percent change in state population from the Census Bureau's 2002 revised estimates and 2003 provisional estimates. (See the Population section in this appendix.)	

(1) Table	(2) Database	(3) Table Construction	(4) General Comments
44, 45	All city law enforcement agencies submitting 12 months of complete arrest data for 2002 and 2003.	The 2003 city arrest trends represent the percentage differences between 2002 and 2003 arrest volumes aggregated from common city agencies. City agencies are all agencies within Population Groups I-VI. (See Appendix III.) Population statistics for 2002 represent estimates based on the percent change in state population from the Census Bureau's 2001 revised estimates and 2002 provisional estimates. Population statistics for 2003 represent estimates based on the percent change in state population from the Census Bureau's 2002 revised estimates and 2003 provisional estimates. (See the Population section in this appendix.)	
46-49	All city law enforcement agencies submitting 12 months of complete arrest data for 2003.	City agencies are all agencies within Population Groups I-VI. (See Appendix III.) Population statistics for 2003 represent estimates based on the percent change in state population from the Census Bureau's 2002 revised estimates and 2003 provisional estimates. (See the Population section in this appendix.)	There is a slight decrease in coverage for Table 49 due to FBI editing procedures and fewer submissions of race data from reporting agencies.
50, 51	All metropolitan county law enforcement agencies submitting 12 months of complete arrest data for 2002 and 2003.	The 2003 metropolitan county arrest trends represent percentage differences between 2002 and 2003 volumes aggregated from contributing agencies. Metropolitan counties are the areas covered by noncity agencies within a currently designated MSA. (See Appendix III.) Population statistics for 2002 represent estimates based on the percent change in state population from the Census Bureau's 2001 revised estimates and 2002 provisional estimates. Population statistics for 2003 represent estimates based on the percent change in state populations from the Census Bureau's 2002 revised estimates and 2003 provisional estimates. (See the Population section in this appendix.)	
52-55	All metropolitan county law enforcement agencies submitting 12 months of complete arrest data for 2003.	Metropolitan counties are the areas covered by noncity agencies within a currently designated MSA. (See Appendix III.) Population statistics for 2003 represent estimates based on the percent change in state population from the Census Bureau's 2002 revised estimates and 2003 provisional estimates. (See the Population section in this appendix.)	There is a slight decrease in coverage for Table 55 due to FBI editing procedures and fewer submissions of race data from reporting agencies.
56, 57	All nonmetropolitan county law enforcement agencies submitting 12 months of complete arrest data for 2002 and 2003.	The 2003 nonmetropolitan county arrest trends represent percentage differences between 2002 and 2003 volumes aggregated from contributing agencies. Nonmetropolitan counties are noncity agencies outside currently designated MSAs. (See Appendix III.) Population statistics for 2002 represent estimates based on the percent change in state population from the Census Bureau's 2001 revised estimates and 2002 provisional estimates. Population statistics for 2003 represent estimates based on the percent change in state populations from the Census Bureau's 2002 revised estimates and 2003 provisional estimates. (See the Population section in this appendix.)	
58-61	All nonmetropolitan county law enforcement agencies submitting 12 months of complete arrest data for 2003.	Nonmetropolitan counties are noncity agencies outside currently designated MSAs. (See Appendix III.) Population statistics for 2003 represent estimates based on the percent change in state population from the Census Bureau's 2002 revised estimates and 2003 provisional estimates. (See the Population section in this appendix.)	

(1) Table	(2) Database	(3) Table Construction	(4) General Comments
62, 63	All suburban area law enforcement agencies submitting 12 months of complete arrest data for 2002 and 2003.	The 2003 suburban area arrest trends represent percentage differences between 2002 and 2003 arrest volumes aggregated from contributing agencies. Suburban area includes agencies within a currently designated metropolitan area excluding those that cover principal cities as defined by the Office of Management and Budget. (See Appendix III.) Population statistics for 2002 represent estimates based on the percent change in state population from the Census Bureau's 2001 revised estimates and 2002 provisional estimates. Population statistics for 2003 represent estimates based on the percent change in state populations from the Census Bureau's 2002 revised estimates and 2003 provisional estimates. (See the Population section in this appendix.)	
64-67	All suburban area law enforcement agencies submitting 12 months of complete arrest data for 2003.	Suburban area includes agencies within a currently designated metropolitan area excluding those that cover principal cities as defined by the Office of Management and Budget. (See Appendix III.) Population statistics for 2003 represent estimates based on the percent change in state population from the Census Bureau's 2002 revised estimates and 2003 provisional estimates. (See the Population section in this appendix.)	
68	All law enforcement agencies submitting 12 months of complete arrest data for 2003.	Population statistics for 2003 represent estimates based on the percent change in state population from the Census Bureau's 2002 revised estimates and 2003 provisional estimates. (See the Population section in this appendix.)	Data furnished are based on individual states' age definitions for juveniles.
69	All law enforcement agencies submitting 12 months of complete arrest data for 2003.	Arrest totals are aggregated for individual agencies within each state. Population statistics represent the Census Bureau's provisional estimates for 2003. (See the Population section in this appendix.)	Any comparison of statistics should take into consideration variances in arrest practices, particularly for Part II crimes. (Appendix II of this report defines the UCR Program's Part II offenses.)

The Uniform Crime Reporting (UCR) Program divides offenses into two groups, Part I and Part II crimes. Each month, contributing agencies submit information on the number of Part I offenses known to law enforcement; those offenses cleared by arrest or exceptional means; and the age, sex, and race of persons arrested for each of the offenses. Contributors provide only arrest data for Part II offenses.

The UCR Program collects the **Part I** offenses in order to measure the level and scope of crime occurring throughout the Nation. The Program's founders chose these offenses, in particular, because they are serious crimes, they occur with regularity in all areas of the country, and they are likely to be reported to police. The **Part I** offenses are defined below:

Criminal homicide—a.) Murder and non-negligent manslaughter: the willful (nonnegligent) killing of one human being by another. Deaths caused by negligence, attempts to kill, assaults to kill, suicides, and accidental deaths are excluded. The Program classifies justifiable homicides separately and limits the definition to: (1) the killing of a felon by a law enforcement officer in the line of duty; or (2) the killing of a felon, during the commission of a felony, by a private citizen. b.) Manslaughter by negligence: the killing of another person through gross negligence. Traffic fatalities are excluded.

Forcible rape—The carnal knowledge of a female forcibly and against her will. Rapes by force and attempts or assaults to rape, regardless of the age of the victim, are included. Statutory offenses (no force used—victim under age of consent) are excluded.

Robbery—The taking or attempted taking of anything of value from the care, custody, or control of a person or persons by force or threat of force or violence and/or by putting the victim in fear.

Aggravated assault—An unlawful attack by one person upon another for the purpose of inflicting severe or aggravated bodily injury. This type of assault usually is accompanied by the use of a weapon or by means likely to produce death or great bodily harm. Simple assaults are excluded.

Burglary (breaking or entering)—The unlawful entry of a structure to commit a felony or a theft. Attempted forcible entry is included.

Larceny-theft (except motor vehicle theft)—The unlawful taking, carrying, leading, or riding away of property from the possession or constructive possession of another. Examples are thefts of bicycles or automobile accessories, shoplifting, pocket-picking, or the stealing of any property or article that is not taken by force and violence or by fraud. Attempted larcenies are included. Embezzlement, confidence games, forgery, worthless checks, etc., are excluded.

Motor vehicle theft—The theft or attempted theft of a motor vehicle. A motor vehicle is self-propelled and runs on land surface and not on rails. Motorboats, construction equipment, airplanes, and farming equipment are specifically excluded from this category.

Arson—Any willful or malicious burning or attempt to burn, with or without intent to defraud, a dwelling house, public building, motor vehicle or aircraft, personal property of another, etc.

The **Part II** offenses, for which only arrest data are collected, are defined below:

Other assaults (simple)—Assaults and attempted assaults which are not of an aggravated nature and do not result in serious injury to the victim.

Forgery and counterfeiting—The altering, copying, or imitating of something without authority or right, with the intent to deceive or defraud by passing the copy or thing altered or imitated as that which is original or genuine; or the selling, buying, or possession of an altered, copied, or imitated thing with the intent to deceive or defraud. Attempts are included.

Fraud—The intentional perversion of the truth for the purpose of inducing another person or other entity in reliance upon it to part with something of value or to surrender a legal right. Fraudulent conversion and obtaining of money or property by false pretenses. Confidence games and bad checks, except forgeries and counterfeiting, are included.

Embezzlement—The unlawful misappropriation or misapplication by an offender to his/her own use or purpose of money, property, or some other thing of value entrusted to his/her care, custody, or control.

Stolen property; buying, receiving, possessing—Buying, receiving, possessing, selling, concealing, or transporting any property with the knowledge that it has been unlawfully taken, as by burglary, embezzlement, fraud, larceny, robbery, etc. Attempts are included.

Vandalism—To willfully or maliciously destroy, injure, disfigure, or deface any public or private property, real or personal, without the consent of the owner or person having custody or control by cutting, tearing, breaking, marking, painting, drawing, covering with filth, or any other such means as may be specified by local law. Attempts are included.

Weapons; carrying, possessing, etc.—The violation of laws or ordinances prohibiting the manufacture, sale, purchase, transportation, possession, concealment, or use of firearms, cutting instruments, explosives, incendiary devices, or other deadly weapons. Attempts are included.

Prostitution and commercialized vice—The unlawful promotion of or participation in sexual activities for profit, including attempts. Sex offenses (except forcible rape, prostitution, and commercialized vice)—Statutory rape, offenses against chastity, common decency, morals, and the like. Attempts are included.

Drug abuse violations—The violation of laws prohibiting the production, distribution, and/or use of certain controlled substances and the equipment or devices utilized in their preparation and/or use. The unlawful cultivation, manufacture, distribution, sale, purchase, use, possession, transportation, or importation of any controlled drug or narcotic substance. Arrests for violations of state and local laws, specifically those relating to the unlawful possession, sale, use, growing, manufacturing, and making of narcotic drugs. The following drug categories are specified: opium or cocaine and their derivatives (morphine, heroin, codeine); marijuana; synthetic narcotics—manufactured narcotics that can cause true addiction (demerol, methadone); and dangerous nonnarcotic drugs (barbiturates, benzedrine).

Gambling—To unlawfully bet or wager money or something else of value; assist, promote, or operate a game of chance for money or some other stake; possess or transmit wagering information; manufacture, sell, purchase, possess, or transport gambling equipment, devices or goods; or tamper with the outcome of a sporting event or contest to gain a gambling advantage.

Offenses against the family and children—Unlawful nonviolent acts by a family member (or legal guardian) which threaten the physical, mental, or economic well-being or morals of another family member and which are not classifiable as other offenses, such as Assault or Sex Offenses. Attempts are included.

Driving under the influence—Driving or operating a motor vehicle or common carrier while mentally or physically impaired as the result of consuming an alcoholic beverage or using a drug or narcotic.

Liquor laws—The violation of state or local laws or ordinances prohibiting the manufacture, sale, purchase, transportation, possession, or use of alcoholic beverages, not including driving under the influence and drunkenness. Federal violations are excluded.

Drunkenness—To drink alcoholic beverages to the extent that one's mental faculties and physical coordination are substantially impaired. Exclude driving under the influence.

Disorderly conduct—Any behavior that tends to disturb the public peace or decorum, scandalize the community, or shock the public sense of morality.

Vagrancy—The violation of a court order, regulation, ordinance, or law requiring the withdrawal of persons from the streets or other specified areas; prohibiting persons from remaining in an area or place in an idle or aimless manner; or prohibiting persons from going from place to place without visible means of support.

All other offenses—All violations of state or local laws not specifically identified as Part I or Part II offenses, except traffic violations.

Suspicion—Arrested for no specific offense and released without formal charges being placed.

Curfew and loitering laws (persons under age 18)—Violations by juveniles of local curfew or loitering ordinances.

Runaways (persons under age 18)—Limited to juveniles taken into protective custody under the provisions of local statutes.

APPENDIX III – Uniform Crime Reporting Area Definitions

By presenting crime data by area, the Uniform Crime Reporting (UCR) Program provides its data users with the opportunity to analyze local crime statistics in relation to crime statistics reported in other areas of a like community type, population size, or geographic location. In determining community type, the UCR Program considers proximity to metropolitan areas, using U.S. Bureau of the Census designations. (Generally, sheriffs, county police, and state police report crimes within counties but outside cities; local police report crime within city limits.) A locale's population figures will determine the population group into which the Program places it. In its geographic breakdowns, the UCR Program divides the United States into regions, divisions, and states.

Community Types

Establishing reporting units representing major population centers assists data users in analyzing and presenting uniform statistical data on metropolitan areas. The UCR Program displays data aggregated by three types of communities:

1. Metropolitan Statistical Areas (MSAs)—Each MSA has a principal city or urbanized area with a population of at least 50,000 inhabitants. MSAs include the county that contains the principal city and other adjacent counties that have, as defined by the U.S. Census Bureau, a high degree of economic and social integration with the principal city and county as measured through commuting. In the UCR Program, counties in an MSA are considered metropolitan. Additionally, MSAs may cross state boundaries.

About 83 percent of the Nation's population inhabited MSAs in 2003. Integrated within MSAs and referenced in this publication are suburban areas. These include cities with less than 50,000 population as well as unincorporated areas within the MSA but exclude the principal cities. The suburban area concept is important because of the distinctive crime conditions in the communities around the Nation's largest cities. The Program discourages data users from making year-to-year

comparisons of MSA data because of changes in the geographic composition of MSAs.

2. Cities Outside MSAs—Cities outside MSAs are mostly incorporated areas and made up nearly 7 percent (6.7) of the Nation's population in 2003.

3. Nonmetropolitan Counties Outside MSAs—Most nonmetropolitan counties are composed of unincorporated areas. In 2003, over 10 percent (10.4) of the population resided in nonmetropolitan counties.

Community types are illustrated below:

Metropolitan	Nonmetropolitan
Principal Cities (50,000+)	Cities outside Metropolitan Areas
Suburban Cities	
Metropolitan Counties	Nonmetropolitan Counties

Population Groups

The UCR Program uses the following population group designations:

Population Group	Political Label	Population Range
I	City	250,000 and over
II	City	100,000 to 249,999
III	City	50,000 to 99,999
IV	City	25,000 to 49,999
V	City	10,000 to 24,999
VI	City[1]	Less than 10,000
VIII (Nonmetropolitan County)	County[2]	N/A
IX (Metropolitan County)	County[2]	N/A

[1] Includes universities and colleges to which no population is attributed.

[2] Includes state police to which no population is attributed.

Individual law enforcement agencies are the major source of UCR data. Annually, the number of agencies included in each population group varies because of population growth, geopolitical consolidation, municipal incorporation, etc. In noncensus years, the UCR Program estimates population figures for individual jurisdictions. A more comprehensive explanation of population estimations can be found in Appendix I of this publication.

The table below displays the number of agencies contributing to the UCR Program within each population group for 2003.

Population Group	Number of Agencies	Population Covered
I	71	53,436,860
II	176	26,238,733
III	431	29,641,812
IV	823	28,480,363
V	1,873	29,615,324
VI[1]	8,776	26,149,056
VIII (Nonmetropolitan County)[2]	3,070	30,282,628
IX (Metropolitan County)[2]	2,161	66,965,001
Total	**17,381**	**290,809,777**

[1] Includes universities and colleges to which no population is attributed.

[2] Includes state police to which no population is attributed.

Regions and Divisions

The accompanying map illustrates the four regions of the United States along with their nine subdivisions as established by the U.S. Census Bureau. The UCR Program uses this widely recognized geographic organization when compiling the Nation's crime data. The following table lists the 50 states arranged according to the regions and divisions of the United States.

NORTHEASTERN STATES

Middle Atlantic
    New Jersey
    New York
    Pennsylvania

New England
    Connecticut
    Maine
    Massachusetts
    New Hampshire
    Rhode Island
    Vermont

MIDWESTERN STATES

East North Central
    Illinois
    Indiana
    Michigan
    Ohio
    Wisconsin

West North Central
    Iowa
    Kansas
    Minnesota
    Missouri
    Nebraska
    North Dakota
    South Dakota

SOUTHERN STATES

South Atlantic
    Delaware
    District of Columbia
    Florida
    Georgia
    Maryland
    North Carolina
    South Carolina
    Virginia
    West Virginia

East South Central
    Alabama
    Kentucky
    Mississippi
    Tennessee

West South Central
    Arkansas
    Louisiana
    Oklahoma
    Texas

WESTERN STATES

Mountain
    Arizona
    Colorado
    Idaho
    Montana
    Nevada
    New Mexico
    Utah
    Wyoming

Pacific
    Alaska
    California
    Hawaii
    Oregon
    Washington

Regions and Divisions of the United States, 2003

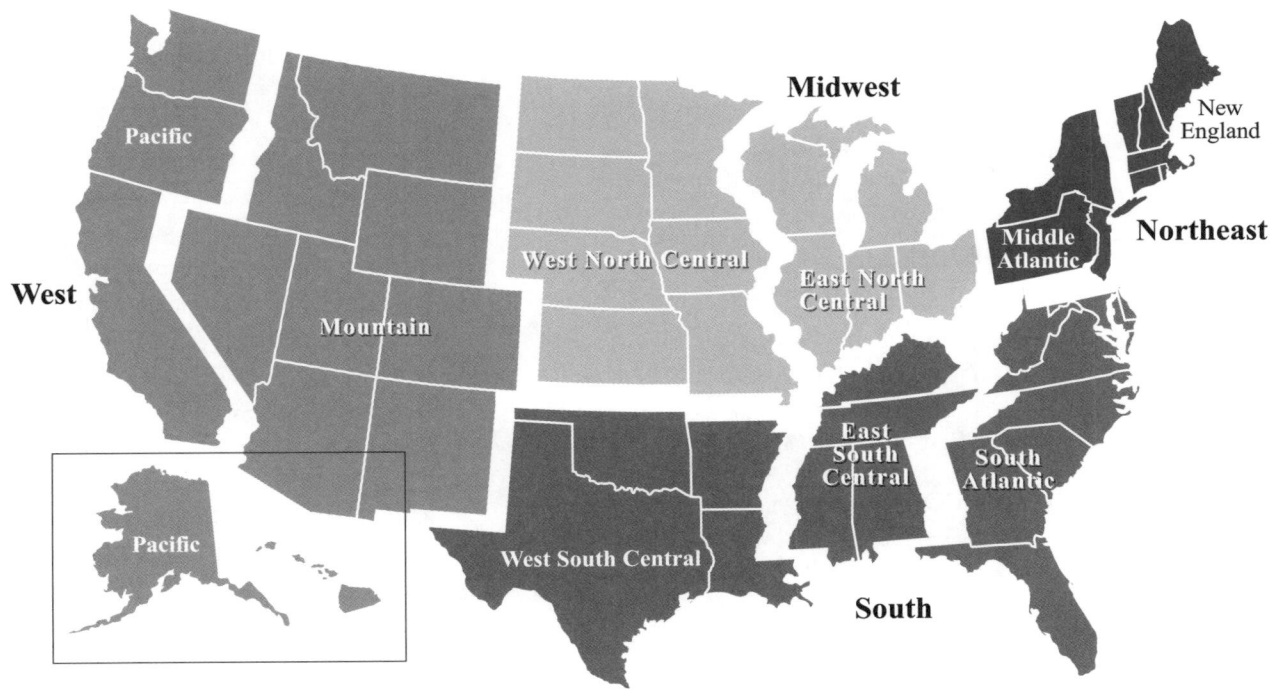

The U.S. Department of Justice administers two statistical programs to measure the magnitude, nature, and impact of crime in the Nation: the Uniform Crime Reporting (UCR) Program and the National Crime Victimization Survey (NCVS). Each of these programs produces valuable information about aspects of the Nation's crime problem. Because the UCR and NCVS programs are conducted for different purposes, use different methods, and focus on somewhat different aspects of crime, the information they produce together provides a more comprehensive panorama of the Nation's crime problem than either could produce alone.

Uniform Crime Reports

The FBI's UCR Program, which began in 1929, collects information on the following crimes reported to law enforcement authorities: homicide, forcible rape, robbery, aggravated assault, burglary, larceny-theft, motor vehicle theft, and arson. Law enforcement agencies report arrest data for 21 additional crime categories.

The UCR Program compiles data from monthly law enforcement reports or individual crime incident records transmitted directly to the FBI or to centralized state agencies that then report to the FBI. The Program thoroughly examines each report it receives for reasonableness, accuracy, and deviations that may indicate errors. Large variations in crime levels may indicate modified records procedures, incomplete reporting, or changes in a jurisdiction's boundaries. To identify any unusual fluctuations in an agency's crime counts, the Program compares monthly reports to previous submissions of the agency and with those for similar agencies.

In 2003, law enforcement agencies active in the UCR Program represented nearly 291 million United States inhabitants—93.0 percent of the total population.

The UCR Program provides crime counts for the Nation as a whole, as well as for regions, states, counties, cities, and towns. This permits studies among neighboring jurisdictions and among those with similar populations and other common characteristics.

The UCR Program annually publishes its findings in a preliminary release in the spring of the following calendar year, followed by a detailed annual report, *Crime in the United States*, issued in the fall. In addition to crime counts and trends, this report includes data on crimes cleared, persons arrested (age, sex, and race), law enforcement personnel (including the number of sworn officers killed or assaulted), and the characteristics of homicides (including age, sex, and race of victims and offenders; victim-offender relationships; weapons used; and circumstances surrounding the homicides). Other periodic reports are also available from the UCR Program.

The UCR Program is continually converting to the more comprehensive and detailed National Incident-Based Reporting System (NIBRS). NIBRS can provide detailed information about each criminal incident in 22 broad categories of offenses.

National Crime Victimization Survey

The Bureau of Justice Statistics' (BJS) NCVS, which began in 1973, provides a detailed picture of crime incidents, victims, and trends. After a substantial period of research, the BJS completed an intensive methodological redesign of the survey in 1993. The BJS conducted the redesign to improve the questions used to uncover crime, update the survey methods, and broaden the scope of crimes measured. The redesigned survey collects detailed information on the frequency and nature of the crimes of rape, sexual assault, personal robbery, aggravated and simple assault, household burglary, theft, and motor vehicle theft. It does not measure homicide or commercial crimes (such as burglaries of stores).

Two times a year, U.S. Bureau of the Census personnel interview household members in a nationally representative sample of approximately 43,000 households (about 76,000 people). Approximately 150,000 interviews of persons age 12 or older are conducted annually. Households stay in the sample for 3 years. New households rotate into the sample on an ongoing basis.

The NCVS collects information on crimes suffered by individuals and households, whether or not those crimes were reported to law enforcement. It estimates the proportion of each crime type reported to law enforcement, and it summarizes the reasons that victims give for reporting or not reporting.

The survey provides information about victims (age, sex, race, ethnicity, marital status, income, and educational level), offenders (sex, race, approximate age, and victim-offender relationship), and the crimes (time and place of occurrence, use of weapons, nature of injury, and economic consequences). Questions also cover the experiences of victims with the criminal justice system, self-protective measures used by victims, and possible substance abuse by offenders. Supplements are added periodically to the survey to obtain detailed information on topics like school crime.

The BJS published the first data from the redesigned NCVS in a BJS bulletin in June 1995. BJS publication of NCVS data includes *Criminal Victimization in the United States*, an annual report that covers the broad range of detailed information collected by the NCVS. The BJS publishes detailed reports on topics such as crime against women, urban crime, and gun use in crime. The National Archive of Criminal Justice Data at the University of Michigan archives the NCVS data files to enable researchers to perform independent analyses.

Comparing UCR and NCVS

Because the BJS designed the NCVS to complement the UCR Program, the two programs share many similarities. As much as their different collection methods permit, the two measure the same subset of serious crimes, defined alike. Both programs cover rape, robbery, aggravated assault, burglary, theft, and motor vehicle theft. Rape, robbery, theft, and motor vehicle theft are defined virtually identically by both the UCR and NCVS. (While rape is defined analogously, the UCR Program measures the crime against women only, and the NCVS measures it against both sexes.)

There are also significant differences between the two programs. First, the two programs were created to serve different purposes. The UCR Program's primary objective is to provide a reliable set of criminal justice statistics for law enforcement administration, operation, and management. The BJS established the NCVS to provide previously unavailable information about crime (including crime not reported to police), victims, and offenders.

Second, the two programs measure an overlapping but nonidentical set of crimes. The NCVS includes crimes both reported and not reported to law enforcement. The NCVS excludes, but the UCR includes, homicide, arson, commercial crimes, and crimes against children under age 12. The UCR captures crimes reported to law enforcement but collects only arrest data for simple assaults and sexual assaults other than forcible rape.

Third, because of methodology, the NCVS and UCR definitions of some crimes differ. For example, the UCR defines burglary as the unlawful entry or attempted entry of a structure to commit a felony or theft. The NCVS, not wanting to ask victims to ascertain offender motives, defines burglary as the entry or attempted entry of a residence by a person who had no right to be there.

Fourth, for property crimes (burglary, theft, and motor vehicle theft), the two programs calculate crime rates using different bases. The UCR rates for these crimes are per capita (number of crimes per 100,000 persons), whereas the NCVS rates for these crimes are per household (number of crimes per 1,000 households). Because the number of households may not grow at the same rate each year as the total population, trend data for rates of property crimes measured by the two programs may not be comparable.

In addition, some differences in the data from the two programs may result from sampling variation in the NCVS and from estimating for nonresponse in the UCR. The BJS derives the NCVS estimates from interviewing a sample and are, therefore, subject to a margin of error. The BJS uses rigorous statistical methods to calculate confidence intervals around all survey estimates. The BJS describes trend data in the NCVS reports as genuine only if there is at least a 90-percent certainty that the measured changes are not the result of sampling variation. The UCR Program bases its data on the actual counts of offenses reported by law enforcement agencies. In some circumstances, the UCR Program estimates its data for nonparticipating agencies or those reporting partial data.

Apparent discrepancies between statistics from the two programs can usually be accounted for by their definitional and procedural differences or resolved by comparing NCVS sampling variations (confidence intervals) of those crimes said to have been reported to police with UCR statistics.

For most types of crimes measured by both the UCR and NCVS, analysts familiar with the programs can exclude from analysis those aspects of crime not common to both. Resulting long-term trend lines can be brought into close concordance. The impact of such adjustments is most striking for robbery, burglary, and motor vehicle theft, whose definitions most closely coincide.

With robbery, the BJS bases the NCVS victimization rates only on robberies reported to the police. It is also possible to remove UCR robberies of commercial establishments such as gas stations, convenience stores, and banks from analysis. When users compare the resulting NCVS police-reported robbery rates and the UCR noncommercial robbery rates, the results reveal closely corresponding long-term trends.

Each program has unique strengths. The UCR provides a measure of the number of crimes reported to law enforcement agencies throughout the country. The UCR's Supplementary Homicide Reports provide the most reliable, timely data on the extent and nature of homicides in the Nation. The NCVS is the primary source of information on the characteristics of criminal victimization and on the number and types of crimes not reported to law enforcement authorities.

By understanding the strengths and limitations of each program, it is possible to use the UCR and NCVS to achieve a greater understanding of crime trends and the nature of crime in the United States. For example, changes in police procedures, shifting attitudes towards crime and police, and other societal changes can affect the extent to which people report and law enforcement agencies record crime. NCVS and UCR data can be used in concert to explore why trends in reported and police-recorded crime may differ.

APPENDIX V – Directory of State Uniform Crime Reporting Programs

Alabama
Alabama Criminal Justice Information Center
Suite 350
770 Washington Avenue
Montgomery, Alabama 36104
(334) 242-4900
www.acjic.state.al.us

Alaska
Alaska Department of Public Safety
Criminal Records and Identification Bureau
5700 East Tudor Road
Anchorage, Alaska 99507
(907) 269-5765

American Samoa
Department of Public Safety
Post Office Box 1086
Pago Pago
American Samoa 96799
(684) 633-1111

Arizona
Access Integrity Unit
Uniform Crime Reporting Program
Arizona Department of Public Safety
Mail Drop 1190
Post Office Box 6638
Phoenix, Arizona 85005-6638
(602) 223-2263
www.dps.state.az.us

Arkansas
Arkansas Crime Information Center
One Capitol Mall, 4D-200
Little Rock, Arkansas 72201
(501) 682-2222
www.acic.org

California
Criminal Justice Statistics Center
Department of Justice
Post Office Box 903427
Sacramento, California 94203-4270
(916) 227-3515

Colorado	Uniform Crime Reporting
	Colorado Bureau of Investigation
	Suite 3000
	690 Kipling Street
	Denver, Colorado 80215
	(303) 239-4222
	www.cbi.state.co.us

Colorado

Uniform Crime Reporting
Colorado Bureau of Investigation
Suite 3000
690 Kipling Street
Denver, Colorado 80215
(303) 239-4222
www.cbi.state.co.us

Connecticut

Uniform Crime Reporting Program
Post Office Box 2794
Middletown, Connecticut 06457-9294
(860) 685-8030
www.state.ct.us/dps/crime_analysis/crime_analysis.asp

Delaware

Delaware State Bureau of Identification
Post Office Box 430
Dover, Delaware 19903-0430
(302) 739-5901

District of Columbia

Research and Resource Development
Metropolitan Police Department
300 Indiana Avenue, N.W.
Washington, D.C. 20001
(202) 727-4174
www.mpdc.dc.gov

Florida

Criminal Justice Information Services
Uniform Crime Reports
Florida Department of Law Enforcement
Post Office Box 1489
Tallahassee, Florida 32302-1489
(850) 410-7121

Georgia

Georgia Crime Information Center
Georgia Bureau of Investigation
Post Office Box 370748
Decatur, Georgia 30037-0748
(404) 244-2840
www.ganet.org/gbi/

Guam

Guam Police Department
Planning, Research and Development
Building #233
Central Avenue
Tiyan, Guam 96913
(671) 475-8434

Hawaii	Crime Prevention and Justice Assistance Division Department of the Attorney General Suite 401 235 South Beretania Street Honolulu, Hawaii 96813 (808) 586-1420 www.cpja.ag.state.hi.us/rs/
Idaho	Bureau of Criminal Identification Idaho State Police Post Office Box 700 Meridian, Idaho 83680-0700 (208) 884-7155 www.isp.state.id.us/identification/ucr/
Illinois	Uniform Crime Reporting Program Division of Administration; Crime Statistics Illinois State Police 3rd Floor 400 Iles Park Place Springfield, Illinois 62703-2978 (217) 782-5794 www.isp.state.il.us
Iowa	Iowa Department of Public Safety Wallace State Office Building East Ninth and Grand Des Moines, Iowa 50319 (515) 281-8494 www.state.ia.us/government/dps/asd/stats.htm
Kansas	Kansas Bureau of Investigation Information Services Division Incident Based Reporting Section 1620 Southwest Tyler Street Topeka, Kansas 66612 (785) 296-8279 www.accesskansas.org/kbi/
Kentucky	Criminal Identification and Records Branch Kentucky State Police 1250 Louisville Road Frankfort, Kentucky 40601 (502) 227-8790 www.kentuckystatepolice.org

Louisiana	Louisiana Commission on Law Enforcement
	Uniform Crime Reporting
	12th Floor
	1885 Wooddale Boulevard
	Baton Rouge, Louisiana 70806
	(225) 925-7465
	www.cole.state.la.us/lucr.htm
Maine	Records Management Services
	Uniform Crime Reporting Division
	Maine Department of Public Safety
	Maine State Police
	36 Hospital Street, Station 42
	Augusta, Maine 04333
	(207) 624-7003
	www.maine.gov/dps/
Maryland	Central Records Division
	Maryland State Police
	1711 Belmont Avenue
	Baltimore, Maryland 21244
	(410) 298-3883
Massachusetts	Crime Reporting Unit
	Uniform Crime Reports
	Massachusetts State Police
	470 Worcester Road
	Framingham, Massachusetts 01702
	(508) 820-2111
Michigan	Uniform Crime Reporting Section
	Criminal Justice Information Center
	Michigan State Police
	7150 Harris Drive
	Lansing, Michigan 48913
	(517) 322-1424
	www.michigan.gov/msp
Minnesota	Criminal Justice Information Systems
	Bureau of Criminal Apprehension
	Minnesota Department of Public Safety
	1430 Maryland Avenue East
	St. Paul, Minnesota 55106
	(651) 793-2400
	www.dps.state.mn.us/bca/bca.html

Missouri	Missouri State Highway Patrol
	Criminal Records & Identification Division
	CJIS Section – UCR Program Office
	1510 East Elm Street
	Post Office Box 9500
	Jefferson City, Missouri 65102-9500
	(573) 526-6278
Montana	Montana Board of Crime Control
	Post Office Box 201408
	Helena, Montana 59620-1408
	(406) 444-4298
	www.mbcc.state.mt.us
Nebraska	Uniform Crime Reporting Section
	The Nebraska Commission on Law
	Enforcement and Criminal Justice
	Post Office Box 94946
	Lincoln, Nebraska 68509-4946
	(402) 471-3982
	www.nol.org/home/crimecom/
Nevada	Uniform Crime Reporting Program
	Records and Identification Bureau
	808 West Nye Lane
	Carson City, Nevada 89703
	(775) 687-1600 x235
	www.nvrepository.state.nv.us
New Hampshire	Uniform Crime Reporting Unit
	New Hampshire State Police
	New Hampshire Department
	of Public Safety
	33 Hazen Drive
	Concord, New Hampshire 03305
	(603) 271-2509
New Jersey	Uniform Crime Reporting Unit
	New Jersey State Police
	Post Office Box 7068
	West Trenton, New Jersey 08628-0068
	(609) 882-2000 x2392
	www.njsp.org

New York	Statistical Services
	New York State Division of Criminal
	Justice Services
	8th Floor, Mail Room
	4 Tower Place
	Albany, New York 12203
	(518) 457-8381

North Carolina	Crime Reporting and Criminal Statistics
	State Bureau of Investigation
	Post Office Box 29500
	Raleigh, North Carolina 27626-0500
	(919) 662-4509
	sbi2.jus.state.nc.us/crp/public/Default.htm

North Dakota	Information Services Section
	Bureau of Criminal Investigation
	Attorney General's Office
	Post Office Box 1054
	Bismarck, North Dakota 58502
	(701) 328-5500
	www.ag.state.nd.us

Ohio*	Office of Criminal Justice Services
	14th Floor
	140 East Town Street
	Columbus, Ohio 43215
	(614) 644-6797

Oklahoma	Uniform Crime Reporting Section
	Oklahoma State Bureau of Investigation
	6600 North Harvey
	Oklahoma City, Oklahoma 73116
	(405) 879-2533
	www.osbi.state.ok.us

Oregon	Law Enforcement Data System Division
	Oregon State Police
	Post Office Box 14360
	Salem, Oregon 97309
	(503) 378-3055 x55002

*National Incident-Based Reporting System Only

Pennsylvania	Bureau of Research and Development
	Pennsylvania State Police
	1800 Elmerton Avenue
	Harrisburg, Pennsylvania 17110
	(717) 783-5536
	ucr.psp.state.pa.us
Puerto Rico	Statistics Division
	Puerto Rico Police
	Post Office Box 70166
	San Juan, Puerto Rico 00936-8166
	(787) 793-1234 x3113
	www.policia.gobierno.pr
Rhode Island	Rhode Island State Police
	311 Danielson Pike
	North Scituate, Rhode Island 02857
	(401) 444-1156
	www.risp.ri.gov/
South Carolina	South Carolina Law Enforcement Division
	Post Office Box 21398
	Columbia, South Carolina 29221-1398
	(803) 896-7016
	www.sled.state.sc.us
South Dakota	South Dakota Statistical Analysis Center
	3444 East Highway 34
	Pierre, South Dakota 57501-5070
	(605) 773-6312
	www.sddci.com
Tennessee*	Tennessee Bureau of Investigation
	901 R.S. Gass Boulevard
	Nashville, Tennessee 37216-2639
	(615) 744-4014
	www.tbi.state.tn.us
Texas	Uniform Crime Reporting
	Crime Information Bureau
	Texas Department of Public Safety
	Post Office Box 4143
	Austin, Texas 78765-9968
	(512) 424-2091
	www.txdps.state.tx.us/crimereports/citindex.htm

*National Incident-Based Reporting System Only

Utah	Data Collection and Analysis
	Uniform Crime Reporting
	Bureau of Criminal Identification
	Utah Department of Public Safety
	Post Office Box 148280
	Salt Lake City, Utah 84114-8280
	(801) 965-4812
	www.bci.utah.gov

Utah

Data Collection and Analysis
Uniform Crime Reporting
Bureau of Criminal Identification
Utah Department of Public Safety
Post Office Box 148280
Salt Lake City, Utah 84114-8280
(801) 965-4812
www.bci.utah.gov

Vermont

Vermont Crime Information Center
103 South Main Street
Waterbury, Vermont 05671
(802) 244-8727
www.dps.state.vt.us/cjs/vcic.htm

Virginia

Criminal Justice Information Services
Division
Virginia State Police
Post Office Box 27472
Richmond, Virginia 23261-7472
(804) 674-2143
www.vsp.state.va.us/crimestatistics.htm

Virgin Islands

Virgin Islands Police Department
Criminal Justice Complex
Saint Thomas, Virgin Islands 00802
(340) 774-2211

Washington

Uniform Crime Reporting Program
Washington Association of Sheriffs and
  Police Chiefs
Suite 200
3060 Willamette Drive, Northeast
Lacey, Washington 98516
(360) 486-2380
www.waspc.org

West Virginia

Uniform Crime Reporting Program
West Virginia State Police
725 Jefferson Road
South Charleston, West Virginia 25309
(304) 746-2159
www.wvstatepolice.com

Wisconsin

Wisconsin Office of Justice Assistance
Suite 202
131 West Wilson Street
Madison, Wisconsin 53702-0001
(608) 266-7644
oja.state.wi.us

Wyoming

Uniform Crime Reporting
Criminal Records Section
Division of Criminal Investigation
316 West 22nd Street
Cheyenne, Wyoming 82002
(307) 777-7625
attorneygeneral.state.wy.us/dci/

Administration

Program administration; management; policy

Telephone: (304) 625-3691

Crime Analysis, Research and Development

Statistical models; special studies and analyses; crime forecasting

Telephone: (304) 625-3600
Facsimile: (304) 625-2868
E-mail: <sberhanu@leo.gov>

Information Dissemination

Requests for published and unpublished data; printouts, electronic media, and books

Telephone: (304) 625-4995
Facsimile: (304) 625-5394
E-mail: <cjis_comm@leo.gov>

National Incident-Based Reporting System (NIBRS)

Information for law enforcement agencies regarding the NIBRS certification process; federal funding for NIBRS-compliant records management systems; and data submission specifications

Telephone: (304) 625-2998
Facsimile: (304) 625-3458
E-mail: <gswanson@leo.gov>

Quality Assurance

Assistance in confirming statistical validity and ensuring agency reporting integrity

Telephone: (304) 625-2941
Facsimile: (304) 625-3457
E-mail: <acjis@leo.gov>

Statistical Processing

Processing of summary and incident-based reports from data contributors; reporting problems; requests for reporting forms; data processing; data quality

Telephone: (304) 625-4830
Facsimile: (304) 625-3455
E-mail: <ucrstat@leo.gov>

Training/Education

Requests for training of law enforcement personnel; information on police reporting systems; technical assistance

Telephone: 1 (888) UCR-NIBR
[827-6427]

Send correspondence to:
Federal Bureau of Investigation
Criminal Justice Information Services Division
Attention: Uniform Crime Reports
1000 Custer Hollow Road
Clarksburg, West Virginia 26306

APPENDIX VII – Uniform Crime Reporting Publications List

Crime in the United States (annual)*

Law Enforcement Officers Killed and Assaulted (annual)*

Hate Crime Statistics (annual)*

Killed in the Line of Duty: A Study of Selected Felonious Killings of Law Enforcement Officers (special report)

In the Line of Fire: Violence Against Law Enforcement—A Study of Felonious Assaults on Law Enforcement Officers (special report)

Uniform Crime Reports: Their Proper Use (brochure)

National Incident-Based Reporting System (brochure)

Preliminary Semiannual Uniform Crime Report, January–June

Preliminary Annual Uniform Crime Report

Uniform Crime Reporting Handbook:
   National Incident-Based Reporting System (NIBRS)
   Summary System

NIBRS:
   *Data Collection Guidelines**
   Data Submission Specifications (Web exclusive)*
   *Error Message Manual**
   *Addendum to the NIBRS Volumes**
   *Conversion of NIBRS Data to Summary Data**
   *NIBRS Addendum for Submitting LEOKA Data**
   Supplemental Guidelines for Federal Participation
   Developments in the NIBRS (Web exclusive)*

Manual of Law Enforcement Records

Hate Crime:
   *Hate Crime Data Collection Guidelines**
   Hate Crime Magnetic Media Specifications for Tapes & Diskettes
   Hate Crime Statistics, 1990: A Resource Book
   *Training Guide for Hate Crime Data Collection**

Age-Specific Arrest Rates and Race-Specific Arrest Rates for Selected Offenses, 1965-1992

*Age-Specific Arrest Rates and Race-Specific Arrest Rates for Selected Offenses, 1993-2001**

* These publications are available on the FBI's Internet site at <www.fbi.gov/ucr/ucr.htm>.

Evaluation Form For *Crime in the United States, 2003*

1. For what purpose did you use this edition of *Crime in the United States*?

   ☐ Research   ☐ Administrative/Operational

   ☐ Training   ☐ Tactical

   ☐ Informational   ☐ Other _____

2. How helpful did you find this publication?

   Very helpful   Not helpful at all

   5   4   3   2   1

3. Did you find the information you were seeking?

   ☐ Yes   ☐ No

   → Why didn't you find the information?

   ☐ The UCR Program does not collect this information.

   ☐ The information was available but not presented in a manner that answered my question.

   ☐ I found the presentation of the information difficult to understand.

   ☐ Other _____

4. Are there terms that could be explained more clearly?

   ☐ Yes   ☐ No

   → Which terms were unclear? _____

   _____

5. Is there information presented in the tables that could be clearer?

   ☐ Yes   ☐ No

   → What information in the tables was unclear? _____

   _____

6. What changes would you recommend for future editions of this publication?

7. Which of the following best describes you as a user of the information from *Crime in the United States*?

   ☐ Law enforcement/criminal justice employee (specify functional area)   ☐ Member of media

   ☐ Government employee   ☐ Employee of private company

   ☐ Academic   ☐ Private citizen

   ☐ Researcher   ☐ Other (specify)

8. Please provide additional comments.

Name _____   **Telephone**

( )

Number and Street _____

City _____   **State**   **Zip Code**

_____

— — — — — _Fold Here_ — — — — —

U.S. Department of Justice
Federal Bureau of Investigation
Washington, D.C. 20535

Uniform Crime Reports
Programs Support Section
Criminal Justice Information Services Division
Federal Bureau of Investigation
1000 Custer Hollow Road
Clarksburg, West Virginia 26306

— — — — — _Fold Here_ — — — — —